Lecture Notes in Computer Science 3189

Commenced Publication in 1973
Founding and Former Series Editors:
Gerhard Goos, Juris Hartmanis, and Jan van Leeuwen

T0181223

Pen-Chung Yew   Jingling Xue (Eds.)

Advances in Computer Systems Architecture

9th Asia-Pacific Conference, ACSAC 2004
Beijing, China, September 7-9, 2004
Proceedings

 Springer

Volume Editors

Pen-Chung Yew
University of Minnesota at Twin Cities
Department of Computer Science and Engineering
Twin Cities, MN, USA
E-mail: yew@cs.umn.edu

Jingling Xue
The University of New South Wales
School of Computer Science and Engineering
Sydney, NSW 2052, Australia
E-mail: jxue@cse.unsw.edu.au

Library of Congress Control Number: 2004111113

CR Subject Classification (1998): B.2, B.4, B.5, C.2, C.1, D.4

ISSN 0302-9743
ISBN 3-540-23003-3 Springer Berlin Heidelberg New York

Springer is a part of Springer Science+Business Media

springeronline.com

© Springer-Verlag Berlin Heidelberg 2004
Printed in Germany

Typesetting: Camera-ready by author, data conversion by PTP-Berlin, Protago-TeX-Production GmbH
Printed on acid-free paper   SPIN: 11318651   06/3142   5 4 3 2 1 0

Preface

On behalf of the program committee, we were pleased to present this year's program for *ACSAC: Asia-Pacific Computer Systems Architecture Conference.*

Now in its ninth year, ACSAC continues to provide an excellent forum for researchers, educators and practitioners to come to the Asia-Pacific region to exchange ideas on the latest developments in computer systems architecture. This year, the paper submission and review processes were semiautomated using the free version of CyberChair. We received 152 submissions, the largest number ever. Each paper was assigned at least three, mostly four, and in a few cases even five committee members for review. All of the papers were reviewed in a two-month period, during which the program chairs regularly monitored the progress of the review process. When reviewers claimed inadequate expertise, additional reviewers were solicited. In the end, we received a total of 594 reviews (3.9 per paper) from committee members as well as 248 coreviewers whose names are acknowledged in the proceedings. We would like to thank all of them for their time and effort in providing us with such timely and high-quality reviews, some of them on extremely short notice.

After all of the reviews were received, there was a one-week electronic program committee meeting during May 14 and May 21. All of the papers were reviewed and discussed by the program committee, and the final set of papers were selected. Program committee members were allowed to submit papers, but their papers were handled separately. Each of their papers was assigned to at least four committee members and reviewed under the same rigorous review process. The program committee accepted 7 out of 11 "PC" submissions. In the end, the program committee selected a total of 45 papers for this year's program with an acceptance rate close to 30%. Unfortunately, many fine papers could not be accommodated in this year's program because of our schedule.

In addition to the contributed papers, this year's program included invited presentations. We were very pleased that three distinguished experts accepted our invitation to share their views on various aspects of computer systems architecture design: James E. Smith (University of Winconsin-Madison, USA) on *Some Real Observations on Virtual Machines*, Jesse Z. Fang (Intel, USA) on *A Generation Ahead of Microprocessor: Where Software Can Drive uArchitecture to?*, and, finally, Guojie Li (Chinese Academy of Sciences, China) on *Make Computers Cheaper and Simpler.*

On behalf of the program committee, we thank all of the authors for their submissions, and the authors of the accepted papers for their cooperation in getting their final versions ready in time for the conference. We would also like to thank the Web Chair, Lian Li, for installing and maintaining CyberChair, and the Local Arrangements Chair, Wenguang Chen, for publicizing this conference.

Finally, we want to acknowledge the outstanding work of this year's program committee. We would like to thank them for their dedication and effort in providing timely and thorough reviews for the largest number of submissions ever in our conference history, and their contribution during the paper selection process. It was a great pleasure working with these esteemed members of our community. Without their extraordinary effort and commitment, it would have been impossible to put such an excellent program together in a timely fashion. We also want to thank all our sponsors for their support of this event. Last, but not least, we would like to thank the General Chair, Weimin Zheng for his advice and support to the program committee and his administrative support for all of the local arrangements.

June 2004   Pen-Chung Yew
                                                                 Jingling Xue

Conference Organization

General Chair

Weimin Zheng   Tsinghua University, China

Program Chairs

Pen-Chung Yew   University of Minnesota, USA
Jingling Xue   University of New South Wales, Australia

Local Arrangements Chair

Wenguang Chen   Tsinghua University, China

Local Arrangements Committee

Hongliang Yu   Tsinghua University, China
Jianian Yan   Tsinghua University, China
Jidong Zhai   Tsinghua University, China
Ruini Xue   Tsinghua University, China
Jiao Lin   Tsinghua University, China

Web Chair

Lian Li   University of New South Wales, Australia

Program Committee

Lars Bengtsson	Chalmers University of Technology, Sweden
Sangyeun Cho	Samsung Electronics, Co., Korea
Lynn Choi	Korea University, Korea
Rudolf Eigenmann	Purdue University, USA
Jean-Luc Gaudiot	University of California, Irvine, USA
Antonio Gonzalez	Universitat Politecnica de Catalunya & Intel Labs, Spain
Gernot Heiser	National ICT Australia, Australia
Wei-Chung Hsu	University of Minnesota, USA
Chris Jesshope	University of Hull, UK
Angkul Kongmunvattana	University of Nevada, Reno, USA
Feipei Lai	National Taiwan University
Zhiyong Liu	National Natural Science Foundation of China, China
Guei-Yuan Lueh	Intel, USA
John Morris	Chung-Ang University, Korea & University of Auckland, New Zealand
Tadao Nakamura	Tohoku University, Japan
Yukihiro Nakamura	Kyoto University, Japan
Amos Omondi	Flinders University, Australia
Lalit M. Patnaik	Indian Institute of Science, Bangalore, India
Jih-Kwon Peir	University of Florida, USA
Ronald Pose	Monash University, Australia
Depei Qian	Xian Jiaotong University, China
Stanislav G. Sedukhin	University of Aizu, Japan
Naofumi Takagi	Nagoya University, Japan
Zhimin Tang	Chinese Academy of Sciences, China
Rajeev Thakur	Argonne National Laboratory, USA
Theo Ungerer	University of Augsburg, Germany
Winfried W. Wilcke	IBM Research, USA
Weng Fai Wong	National University of Singapore, Singapore
Chengyong Wu	Chinese Academy of Sciences, China
Ming Xu	National University of Defense Technology, China
Yuanyuan Yang	State University of New York at Stony Brook, USA
Rumi Zahir	Intel, USA
Chuanqi Zhu	Fudan University, China

Co-reviewers

Tom Adelmeyer
Alex Aletà
Jalal Almhana
Madhusudhanan Anantha
Juan Luis Aragon
Brian Armstrong
Eduard Ayguade
Faruk Bagci
Nitin Bahadur
Vishwanath P. Baligar
Bin Bao
Ayon Basumallik
Jürgen Beckeer
Ramón Beivide
Bryan Black
Tatiana Bokareva
Uwe Brinkschulte
Ralph Butler
Luis M. Díaz de Cerio
Jason Chang
Yen-Jen Chang
Mei Chao
Cheng Chen
Dong-Yuan Chen
Gen-Huey Chen
Haibo Chen
Howard Chen
Ronghua Chen
Tien-Fu Chen
Wen-Hsien Chen
Wenguang Chen
Yinwen Chen
Yung-Chiao Chen
Avery Ching
Seng-Cho Chou
Yang Wai Chow
Peter Chubb
C.G. Chung
Chung-Ping Chung
Sung Woo Chung
Josep M. Codina
Tim Conrad
Nawal Copty
Julita Corbalan

Toni Cortes
Alfredo Cristobal-Salas
Abhinav Das
Xiaotie Deng
Qiang Ding
Yingfei Dong
Klaus Dorfmüller-Ulhaas
David Du
Colin Egan
Kevin Elphinstone
Dongrui Fan
Hao Feng
Konrad Froitzheim
Rao Fu
Antonia Gallardo
Boon-Ping Gan
Enric Gibert
Marc Gonzalez
Charles Gray
Yi Guo
Weili Han
Wessam Hassanein
Guojin He
Gerolf Hoflehner
Scott Hoyte
Pao-Ann Hsiung
Wen Hu
Dandan Huan
Ing-Jer Huang
Junwei Huang
Lei Huang
Yi-Ping Hung
Wei Huo
Tomonori Izumi
Muhammad Mahmudul Islam
Yaocang Jia
Hong Jiang
Weihua Jiang
Yi Jiang
Troy A. Johnson
Edward Sim Joon
Sourabh Joshi
Roy Ju
Marcelo E. Kaihara

Dongsoo Kang
Ryosuke Kato
Jörg Keller
Ihn Kim
JinPyo Kim
Sunil Kim
Chung-Ta King
Jon Krueger
Fumio Kumazawa
Ihor Kuz
Atul Kwatra
Hsiu-Hui Lee
Hung-Chang Lee
Sanghoon Lee
Yong-fong Lee
Jianping Li
Jie Li
Shengjun Li
Wei Li
Yingsheng Li
Yunchun Li
Weifa Liang
Shih-wei Liao
Wanjiun Liao
Björn Liljeqvist
Ching Lin
Fang-Chang Lin
Fang-Pang Lin
Hung-Yau Lin
Shian-Hua Lin
Xiaobin Lin
Bin Liu
Chen Liu
Jiangchuan Liu
Jyi-shane Liu
Michael Liu
Tao Liu
Zhanglin Liu
Jiwei Lu
Peng Lu
Zhongzhi Luan
Jesus Luna
Yuh-Dauh Lyuu
Takahiko Masuzaki
Ryusuke Miyamoto

Chi Ma
Xiaosong Ma
Erik Maehle
Mike Mesnier
Neill Miller
Do Quang Minh
Dave Minturn
Steven Molnar
Rafael Moreno-Vozmediano
Alberto J. Munoz
Hashem Hashemi Najaf-abadi
Gil Neiger
Anindya Neogi
Tin-Fook Ngai
Qizhi Ni
Rong Ni
Hiroyuki Ochi
Robert Olson
Ming Ouhyoung
Deng Pan
Zhelong Pan
Marina Papatriantafilou
Chan-Ik Park
Gi-Ho Park
Junho Park
Enric Pastor
Jan Petzold
Matthias Pfeffer
Andy D. Pimentel
Dhiraj Pradhan
Nol Premasathian
Rolf Rabenseifner
Ryan Rakvic
Rajiv Ranjan
Xiaojuan (Joanne) Ren
Won Woo Ro
Shanq-Jang Ruan
Hariharan Sandanagobalane
Kentaro Sano
Hartmut Schmeck
Ioannis T. Schoinas
Peter Schulthess
André Seznec
Hemal Shah
Shrikant Shah

Table of Contents

Session 2A: Processor Architecture and Design I

Session 2B: Power and Energy Management

Session 3A: Processor Architecture and Design II

Session 3B: Compiler and Operating System Issues

Keynote Address II

Session 4A: Application-Specific Systems

Session 4B: Interconnection Networks

Keynote Address III

Session 5A: Prediction Techniques

Session 5B: Parallel Architecture and Programming

Session 6A: Microarchitecture Design and Evaluations

Session 6B: Memory and I/O Systems

Session 7A: Potpourri

Author Index

Some Real Observations on Virtual Machines

James E. Smith

Department of Electrical and Computing Engineering
University of Wisconsin-Madison
jes@ece.wisc.edu

Abstract. Virtual machines can enhance computer systems in a number of ways, including improved security, flexibility, fault tolerance, power efficiency, and performance. Virtualization can be done at the system level and the process level. Virtual machines can support high level languages as in Java, or can be implemented using a low level co-designed paradigm as in the Transmeta Crusoe. This talk will survey the spectrum of virtual machines and discuss important design problems and research issues. Special attention will be given to co-designed VMs and their application to performance- and power-efficient microprocessor design.

Replica Victim Caching to Improve Reliability of In-Cache Replication

W. Zhang

Dept of ECE, SIUC, Carbondale, IL 62901, USA
zhang@engr.siu.edu

Abstract. Soft error conscious cache design is a necessity for reliable computing. ECC or parity-based integrity checking techniques in use today either compromise performance for reliability or vice versa. The recently-proposed ICR (In-Cache Replication) scheme can enhance data reliability with minimal impact on performance, however, it can only exploit a limited space for replication and thus cannot solve the conflicts between the replicas and the primary data without compromising either performance or reliability. This paper proposes to add a small cache, called replica victim cache, to solve this dilemma effectively. Our experimental results show that a replica victim cache of 4 entries can increase reliability of L1 data caches 21.7% more than ICR without impacting performance, and the area overhead is within 10%.

1 Introduction and Motivation

Soft errors are unintended transitions of logic states caused by external radiations such as alpha particle and cosmic ray strikes. Recent studies [4,6,5,9] indicate that soft errors are responsible for a large percentage of computation failures. In current microprocessors, over 60% of the on-chip estate is taken by caches, making them more susceptible to external radiations. The soft errors in cache memories can easily propagate into the processor registers and other memory elements, resulting in catastrophic consequences on the execution. Therefore, soft error tolerant cache design is becoming increasingly important for failure-free computation.

Information redundancy is the main technique to improve data integrity. Currently the popular information redundancy scheme for memories is either byte-parity (one bit parity per 8-bit data) [1], or single error correcting-double error detecting (SEC-DED) code (ECC)[2,3]. However, both of these two schemes have deficiencies. Briefly, parity check can only detect single-bit errors. While SEC-DEC based schemes can correct single-bit errors and detect two-bit errors, they can also increase the access latency of the L1 cache, and thus not suitable for high-end processors clocked over 1GHz [7]. Recently, an approach called ICR (In-Cache Replication) has been proposed to enhance reliability of the L1 data cache for high-performance processors [7]. The idea of ICR is to exploit "dead" blocks in the L1 data cache to store the replicas for "hot" blocks so that a large percentage of read hits in the L1 can find their replicas in the same cache, which

P.-C. Yew and J. Xue (Eds.): ACSAC 2004, LNCS 3189, pp. 2–15, 2004.

can be used to detect and correct single bit and/or multiple bit errors. While the ICR approach can achieve a better tradeoff between performance and reliability than parity-only or ECC-only protection, it can only exploit a limited space (namely the "dead" blocks in the data cache) for replication. In addition, since the replica and the primary data are stored in the same cache, they inevitably have conflicts with each other. The current policy adopted by ICR [7] is to give priority to the primary data for minimizing the impact on performance. In other words, the data reliability is compromised. As illustrated in [7], 10% to 35% of data in the L1 data cache is not protected (i.e. having no replicas) by ICR schemes, which may cause severe consequences in computation and thus are not useful for applications that require high reliability or operate under highly noisy environments.

This paper proposes a novel scheme to enhance the reliability of ICR further by adding a small fully-associative cache to store the replica victims, which is called the replica victim cache in this paper. Unlike the victim cache proposed by jouppi [10] for reducing the conflict misses for a direct-mapped cache without In-Cache Replication, the proposed replica victim cache is utilized to store the replica victims, which are conflicting with the primary data or other replicas in the primary data cache, for enhancing reliability of the ICR approaches significantly without compromising performance. Moreover, since the replica is used to improve data integrity, the replica victim cache does not need to swap the replica with the primary data when accessed. In contrast, the traditional victim cache stores different data (i.e., victim) from the primary cache, and the victims need to be swapped to the L1 cache in the case of a miss in the L1 data cache that hits in the victim cache[10]. The paper examines the following problems.

1. How does reliability, in terms of loads with replica (see the definition in 4), relate to the size of the replica victim cache, the size and associativity of the primary cache? How much loads with replica can be increased by the addition of a replica victim cache?
2. How to exploit the replicas in either the primary cache or the replica victim cache to provide different levels of reliability and performance?
3. What is the error detection and correction behavior of different replica-based schemes under different soft error rates?

We implemented the proposed replica victim caching schemes by modifying the Simplesclar 3.0 [14]. The error injection experiments are based on *random injection model* [5]. Our experimental results reveal that a replica victim cache of 4 entries can increase the reliability of ICR by 21.7% without impacting performance and its area overhead is less than 10%, compared to most L1 data caches.

The rest of the paper is organized as follows. Section 2 introduces the background information about In-Cache Replication and its limitation. Section 3 describes the architecture of replica victim caching and different schemes to exploit the replica victim lines for improving data reliability. The evaluation methodology is given in section 4. Section 5 presents the experimental results. Finally, section 6 summarizes the contributions of this paper and identifies directions for future research.

2   Background and Motivation

A recent paper [7] presents ICR (In-Cache Replication) for enhancing data cache reliability without significant impact on performance. The idea of ICR is to replicate hot cache lines in active use within the dead cache lines. The mapping between the primary data and the replica is controlled by a simple function. Two straightforward mapping functions are studies in [7], namely, the vertical mapping (replication across sets) and the horizontal mapping (replication within the ways of a set) [7] , as shown in figure 1. The dead cache lines are predicted by a time-based dead block predictor, which is shown to be highly accurate and has low hardware overhead [8]. The ICR approach can be used either with parity or ECC based schemes and there is a large design space to explore, including what, when and where to replicate the data, etc [7]. The design decisions adopted in this paper is presented in table 1.

The results in [7] demonstrate that the ICR schemes can achieve better performance and/or reliability than the schemes that use ECC or parity check alone, however, it can only achieve modest reliability improvement due to the limited space it can exploit. Since each L1 data cache has a fixed number of cache lines, and each cache line can be either used to store the primary data to benefit performance or to store the replicas for enhancing data reliability, ICR approaches

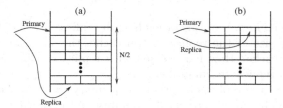

Fig. 1. Cache line replication (a) vertical replication (b) horizontal replication [7].

Table 1. Default implementation strategies regarding cache line replication.

Question	Answer
When do we replicate?	Only during writes
Where do we replicate?	N/2 sets away from the primary location
How many times do we attempt replication?	Once for each write
How many replicas do we create?	At most 1 per line
How do we protect unreplicated cache lines?	Using parity
How do we protect replicated cache lines?	Using parity or parallel comparison between the primary data and its replica, depending on the scheme we use (see section 3)
How do we place a replica in a set?	Candidates include both dead lines and replicas (we check the dead lines first)
What needs to be done upon a replacement?	We remove replica as well

give priority to performance by using several strategies. Firstly, the dead block predictor is designed to be very accurate so that the blocks predicted dead will most likely not be accessed in the near future. Otherwise, the primary data has to be loaded from the higher level memory hierarchy, resulting in performance penalty. Secondly, in case of a conflict between the primary data and the replica, ICR gives higher priority to the primary data and the replica is simply discarded. For instance, when a primary data is written to a cache block, which stores a replica for another primary data, the replica will be overwritten by the coming primary data. As a result, ICR approach can only the replicas that do not conflict with the primary data, resulting in moderate data reliability improvement. The experiments in [7] also reveal that 10% to 35% of load hits in L1 cannot find their replicas and ICR schemes have more than 20% unrecoverable loads under intense error injection. With the trend of increasing soft error rate, the reliability of ICR approaches need to be improved further, especially for applications that demand very high data reliability or operate under highly-noisy environments.

3   Replica Victim Cache

While one straightforward way to enhance data reliability of ICR further is to make more replicas in the L1 data cache by giving priority to replicas in case of their conflicts with the primary data. This approach, however, can inevitably degrade performance and thus is not acceptable. Another approach used in mission-critical applications is the NMR (N Modular Redundancy) scheme, which replicate the data cache for multiple times. However, the NMR scheme is too costly for microprocessors or embedded system with cost and area constraint.

This paper proposes an approach to enhance data reliability of ICR without performance degradation or significant area overheads. The idea is to add a small fully-associative replica victim cache to store the replica victim lines whenever they are conflicting with primary cache lines. Due to the fully associativity of the replica victim cache and data locality (replicas also exhibit temperal and spatial locality, since they are the "images" of the primary data), a very large percentage of load hits in the L1 can find their replicas available either in the L1 data cache or in the replica victim cache.

Victim cache is not a new idea in cache design. Jouppi proposed the victim cache to store the victim lines evicted from the L1 cache for reducing the conflict misses [10]. However, the victim cache proposed by Jouppi cannot be used to enhance data reliability, since there is no redundant copies in both the L1 cache and the victim cache (i.e., only the blocks evicted from the L1 are stored in the victim cache). While the original victim cache aims at performance enhancement, the objective of the replica victim cache is to improve data integrity of ICR approaches significantly without impacting performance. The replica victim cache is a small fully associative cache in parallel with the L1 data cache, as shown in figure 2. In addition to In-Cache Replication, the replica victim cache is used to store replicas for the primary data in the L1 in the following cases:

1. There is no dead block available in the L1 data cache to store the replica.

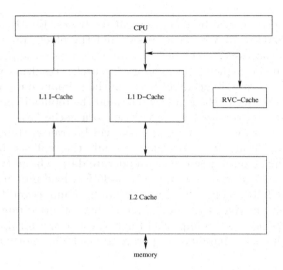

Fig. 2. The architecture of replica victim cache.

2. The replica is replaced by the primary data since ICR gives priority to the primary data.
3. The replica is replaced by another replica for another primary data (note that for a set-associative data cache, multiple replicas can be mapped to the same dead block with ICR approach [7]).

Since ECC computation has performance overhead, we assume all the cache blocks of the L1 and the replica victim cache are protected by parity check. The replicas (both in the replica victim cache and the L1 data cache due to ICR) can be read at each read hits in the L1 for parallel comparison with the primary data to detect multiple bit errors. Alternatively, the replicas can be read only when the parity bit of the primary data indicates an error. The former scheme can enhance data reliability greatly, but there is a performance penalty for the parallel comparison. We assume it takes 1 extra cycle to compare the primary data and the replica in our simulations. The latter scheme also improve the reliability by being able to recover from single bit errors.

The paper examines the following problems.

1. How does the reliability, in terms of loads with replica (see 4), relate to the size of the replica victim cache, the size and associativity of the primary cache? How much loads with replica can be increased by the addition of a replica victim cache?

2. How to exploit the replicas in either the primary cache or the replica victim cache to provide different levels of reliability and performance?

3. How does the error detection and correction behavior of different replica-based schemes under different soft error rates?

To answer the above questions, we propose and evaluate the following schemes:

- BaseP: This is a normal L1 data cache without the replica victim cache. All cache blocks are protected by parity. The load and store operations are modeled to take 1 cycle in our experiments.
- BaseECC: This scheme is similar to BaseP scheme except that all cache blocks are protected by ECC. Store operations still take 1 cycle (as the writes are buffered), but loads take 2 cycles to account for the ECC verification.
- RVC-P: This scheme implements the In-Cache Replication and the proposed replica victim caching. When there is a conflict between the primary data and the replica, the replica victim is stored to the replica victim cache. If the replica victim cache is full, the least-recently used replica is discarded. All cache blocks are protected by parity and the replica is only checked if the parity bit of the primary data indicates an error. Load and store operations are modeled to take 1 cycle in our experiments.
- RVC-C: This scheme is similar to RVC-P scheme except that the replica is compared with the primary data before the load returns. The search of replica can be executed simultaneously in both the L1 data cache and the replica victim cache. If the replica hits in the L1 data cache, that replica is used to compare with the primary data; otherwise, the replica in the replica victim cache is used for comparison if there is a hit in the replica victim cache. Note that we give priority to the replicas found in the L1 data cache, because the L1 contains the most updated replicas while the replica victim cache may not (because it only contains the most updated replica victims). However, for the given primary data, if its replica cannot be found in the L1 data cache, the replica found in the replica victim cache must contain the most updated value because every replica victim of the data must have been written to the replica victim cache. We conservatively assume that the load operations take 2 cycles, and store operations take 1 cycle as usual.

It should be noted that in addition to parity check and ECC, the write-through cache and speculative ECC loads are also widely employed for improving data reliability. For write-through caches, data redundancy is provided by propagating every write into the L2 cache. However, write-through caches increase the number of writes to the L2 dramatically, resulting in the increase of write stalls even with a write-buffer. Thus both performance and energy consumption can be impacted [7]. Another way to improve data reliability while circumventing the ECC time cost is the speculative ECC load scheme, which performs the ECC checks in the background while data is loaded and the computation is allowed to proceed speculatively. While speculative ECC loads can potentially hide the access latency, it is difficult to stop the error propagation in a timely manner and may result in high error recovery cost. Since ECC computation consumes more energy than parity check, it is also shown that speculative ECC load has worse energy behavior than the ICR approach that uses parity check only (i.e., ICR-P-PS) [7]. Due to these reasons, we focus on investigating approaches to improve reliability for write-back data caches, and we only compare our approach directly with the recently-proposed ICR approaches, which have exhibited better performance and/or energy behavior than the write-through L1 data cache and the speculative ECC load [7].

4   Evaluation Methodology

4.1   Evaluation Metrics

To compare performance and reliability of different schemes, we mainly use the following two metrics:

- *Execution Cycles* is the time taken to execute 200 million application instructions.
- *Loads with Replica* is the metric proposed in [7] to evaluate the reliability enhancement for data caches. A higher loads with replica indicates higher data reliability, as illustrated by error injection experiments [7]. Since we add a replica victim cache to the conventional L1 data cache architecture, we modify the definition of loads with replica proposed in [7] to be the fraction of read hits that also find their replicas either in the L1 data cache or in the replica victim cache. Note that the difference between our definition and the definition in [7] is that in our scheme, the replica of "dirty" data can be found either in the L1 data cache or in the replica victim cache; while in the ICR scheme [7], the replicas can be only found in the L1 data cache.

4.2   Configuration and Benchmarks

We have implemented the proposed replica victim caching schemes by modifying the Simplesclar 3.0 [14]. We conduct detailed cycle level simulations with sim-outorder to model a multiple issue superscalar processor with a small fully-associative replica victim cache. The default simulation values used in our experiments are listed in Table 2 (note that we do not list the configuration of the replica victim cache in Table 2, since we need to make experiments with different replica cache size).

We select ten applications from the SPEC 2000 suite [16] for this evaluation. Since the simulations of these applications are extremely time consuming, we fast forward the first half billion instructions and present results for the next 200 million instructions. Important performance characteristics of these applications in the base scheme are given in Table 3.

5   Results

5.1   The Size of the Replica Victim Cache and Data Integrity Improvement

Our first experiment is to investigate what is the appropriate size for the replica victim cache. On one hand, the replica victim cache must be small to minimize

Table 2. Configuration parameters in our base configuration for a superscalar architecture. All caches are write-back.

Configuration Parameter	Value
Processor	
Functional Units	4 IALUs, 4FPU
LSQ Size	8 Instructions
RUU Size	16 Instructions
Fetch Width	4 instructions/cycle
Decode Width	4 instructions/cycle
Issue Width	4 instructions/cycle
Commit Width	4 instructions/cycle
Fetch Queue Size	4 instructions
Cycle Time	1ns
Cache and Memory Hierarchy	
L1 Instruction Cache	16KB, 1-way, 32 byte blocks, 1 cycle latency
L1 Data Cache	16KB, 4-way, 32 byte blocks, 1 cycle latency
L2	256K, 4-way, 64 byte blocks, 6 cycle latency
Memory	100 cycle latency

Table 3. Benchmarks from SPEC2000. The last column give the execution cycles for Base scheme.

Benchmark Name	Description	Number of Data References	Number of Cache Misses	Execution Cycles of Base
164.gzip	Compression	58582206	1167237	129215053
175.vpr	FPGA circuit placement and routing	87602536	1968330	202606221
176.gcc	C programming language compiler	79860452	982483	220017658
181.mcf	Combinational optimization	112113406	10423182	240140816
255.vortex	Object-oriented database	110330626	1591461	231793925
256.bzip2	Compression	96251361	1550219	134186684
177.mesa	3D graphics library	98933099	224339	199721006
179.art	C Image recognition/neural networks	87569639	7144640	236659516
183.equake	Seismic wave propagation simulation	64742897	373522	118643743
188.ammp	C Computational chemistry	118184707	15826817	354806058

the hardware overheads. On the other hand, the replica victim cache should be large enough to accommodate the replica victims as many as possible. Due to data locality, it is possible to use a small replica victim cache to store the replica victims for the data, which is most likely accessed in the future. We use an empirical approach to find the best size for the replica victim cache. Specifically, we make experiments on two randomly selected benchmarks (i.e., bzip2 and equake) for replica victim caches with different sizes varying from 1 block to 16 blocks and the L1 data cache is fixed to be 16K-Byte, 4-way set associative, as given in table 2. The loads with replica results are presented in figure 3. As can be seen, the loads with replica increases dramatically when the size of the replica victim cache is increased from 1 block to 2 blocks, because the conflicts of replicas in the replica victim cache can be reduced by exploiting the associativity. For the replica victim cache of 4 or more blocks, the loads with replica is larger than 98.6%, which is tremendously larger than the loads with replica achieved by ICR schemes. We use cacti 3.2 model [15] to estimate the area overhead and the results are shown in table 4. As can be seen, the area overhead of the 4-entry replica victim cache is less than 10%, compared to a data cache of 16K, 32K or 64K bytes. Considering both reliability enhancement and hardware overhead, we fix the size of the replica victim cache to be 4 entries.

Table 4. The area of a 4-entry fully associative replica victim cache, compared with 4-way associative L1 data caches of 16K, 32K and 64K bytes respectively. The cache block size of both the replica victim cache and the data cache are 32 bytes.

	128B RVC	16KB D-cache	32KB D-cache	64KB D-cache
area(cm^2)	0.001183	0.011899	0.021325	0.038569
ratio	100%	9.94%	5.55%	3.07%

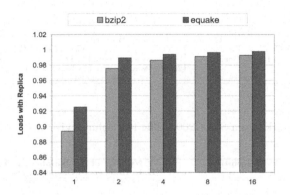

Fig. 3. Loads with replica for replica victim caches of 1, 2, 4, 8 and 16 blocks.

Figure 4 illustrates the loads with replica for a replica victim cache with 4 blocks for all the 10 benchmarks. The replicas can be found either from the L1 data cache (as the ICR approach) or from the replica victim cache. We find that for each benchmark, replica victim cache can store a large portion of the replica victims that are most likely accessed in the future, in addition to the replicas produced by the ICR approach, resulting in significant enhancement on data reliability. The average loads with replica with the replica victim cache is 94.4%, which is 21.7% larger than the ICR approach alone.

5.2   Performance Comparison

Using the above settings for the replica victim cache, we next study the performance of the replica victim caching. Since the replica victim cache is only used to store the replica victims from the L1 data cache, there is no performance degradation compared to the corresponding ICR approaches [7]. Therefore, we only compare the performance implications of the four schemes described in Section 3.

As shown in figure 5, the performance of the RVC-P scheme is comparable to the BaseP scheme and the performance of the RVC-C scheme is comparable to the BaseECC scheme. Specifically, the average performance degradation of RVC-P to BaseP and RVC-C to BaseECC is 1.8% and 1.7% respectively. It should be noted that this performance degradation comes from ICR, not from the replica victim caching. Since ICR relies on dead block prediction and there is no perfect dead block predictor, some cache blocks in the L1 may be predicted

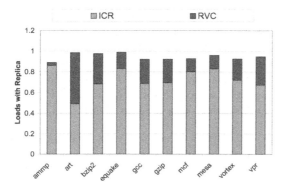

Fig. 4. Loads with replica for replica victim caches of 4 blocks.

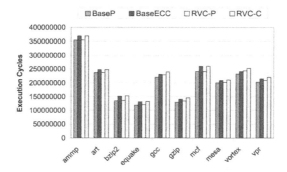

Fig. 5. Performance comparison of different schemes.

dead (and thus are utilized to store replicas) but are actually accessed later (i.e., not "dead" yet), which can result in performance degradation.

5.3   Error Injection Results

We conduct the error injection experiment based on *random injection model* [5]. In this model, an error is injected in a random bit of a random word in the L1 data cache. Such errors are injected at each clock cycle based on a constant probability (called error injection rate in this paper).

Figure 6 and figure 7 present the fraction of loads that could not be recovered from errors (including single-bit or mult-bit errors) for BaseP, BaseECC, ICR-P-PS, RVC-P and RVC-C for bzip2 and vpr respectively. In both experiments, the data is loaded as a function of the probability of an error occurring in each cycle and the error injection rate varies from 1/100 to 1/1000 and 1/10000. Note that the intention here is to study the data reliability under intense error behavior, thus very high error injection rates are used. As can be seen, BaseP always has the worst error resilient behavior, since the parity bit can only detect single-bit errors. When the error injection rate is relatively low (i.e., 1/10000), BaseECC has similar percentage of unrecoverable loads as RVC-C. However, as the error injection rate increases, the difference between BaseECC and RVC-C grows larger. Specifically, when the error injection rate is 1/1000, RVC-C can reduce the unrecoverable load by 9.1% and 4.5% for bzip2 and vpr respectively, compared to the BaseECC scheme. Similarly, the RVC-P scheme exhibits much better error resilient behavior compared to BaseP and ICR-P-PS at different error injection rate.

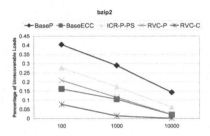
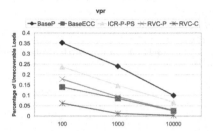

Fig. 6. Percentage of unrecoverable loads for bzip2.

Fig. 7. Percentage of unrecoverable loads for vpr.

5.4   Sensitivity Analysis

To verify the effectiveness of the replica victim cache of 4 blocks for L1 data caches with different configurations, we also make experiments to study the loads with replica by varying the L1 data cache size and the number of associativity. In both experiments, the replica victim cache is fixed to be a fully-associative cache of 4 blocks.

Figure 8 gives the loads with replica for L1 data caches of 8K, 16K, 32K, 64K and 128K bytes. The block size and the associativity of the L1 data cache are 32 bytes and 4 way respectively. The results are very interesting. As can be seen, bzip2 and equake exhibit different trends in loads with replica. As the data cache size increases, the loads with replica of bzip2 decreases slightly, while the loads with replica of equake increases slightly. The reason is that replicas can be found in two places: the L1 data cache and the replica victim cache. The number of replicas that can be stored in the L1 increases as the L1 data cache size increases, however, the relative number of replicas that can be stored in the replica victim cache decreases since the size of replica victim cache is fixed. Therefore, the effect of increasing the L1 data cache size on the loads with replica is dependent on these two factors. The breakdown of loads with replica from the L1 data cache and from the replica victim cache for bzip2 and equake are presented in figure 9 and figure 10 respectively. In figure 9, the decrease of loads with replica from the replica victim cache dominates, and thus the total loads with replica decreases as the L1 data cache size increases. In contrast, in figure 10, the increase of loads with replica from the L1 data cache dominates, and hence the total loads with replica increases with the increase of the L1 data cache size. However, for all the L1 data cache configurations, the replica victim cache of 4 entries can achieve the loads with replica more than 98.1% on average, which is substantially larger than what the ICR approach alone can achieve.

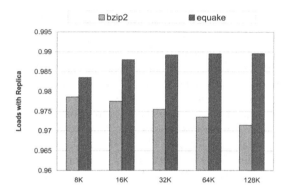

Fig. 8. Loads with replica for 4-way associative L1 data caches of 8K, 16K, 32K, 64K and 128K bytes. The replica victim cache is fully associative with 4 blocks. The block size of both the L1 data cache and the replica victim cache is 32 bytes. Insensitive to the L1 data cache size, the addition of the fully associative replica victim cache of 4 blocks can achieve the loads with replica more than 98.1% on average.

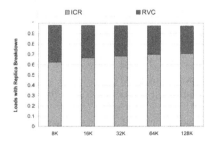

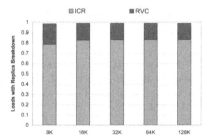

Fig. 9. Loads with replica breakdown for L1 data caches of 8K, 16K, 32K, 64K and 128K for bzip2.

Fig. 10. Loads with replica breakdown for L1 data caches of 8K, 16K, 32K, 64K and 128K for equake.

We also study the loads with replica for L1 data caches with different associativity and find similar results. Therefore, with the addition of a small fully-associative replica victim cache of 4 entries, a very high loads with replica can be achieved to enhance data reliability of ICR further for a variety of L1 data caches.

6 Conclusion

This paper studies the limitation of In-Cache Replication and proposes to add a small fully-associative replica victim cache to store the replica victim lines in case of their conflicts with the primary data. We find that with the addition of a small replica victim cache of 4 entries, the loads with replica of the ICR scheme can be increased by 21.7%. On average, 94.4% load hits in L1 can find replicas either in the L1 data cache or in the replica victim cache. We also propose and evaluate two different reliability enhancing schemes — RVC-P and RVC-C — that are proven to be quite useful.

RVC-P is a much better alternative for ICR-P-PS where one may want simple parity protection. It can enhance reliability significantly by providing additional replicas in the replica victim cache without compromising performance. RVC-P also has better performance than RVC-C or ECC based schemes (i.e., BaseECC).

RVC-C can increase the error detection/correction capability by comparing the primary data and the replica before the load returns. Our error injection experiments reveal that RVC-C has the best reliability and can be used for applications that demand very high reliability or operate under highly noisy environments. Compared with the BaseECC scheme, the performance degradation of RVC-C is only 1.7% on average.

In summary, this paper proposes the addition of a small fully-associative replica victim cache to enhance data reliability of ICR schemes significantly without compromising performance. Our future work will concentrate on studying the reliability and performance impact of replica victim cache for multiprogramming workloads. In addition, we plan to investigate how to use a unified victim cache efficiently to store both primary victims and replica victims and the possibility to make a better tradeoff between performance and reliability.

References

1. P. Sweazey. SRAM organization, control, and speed, and their effect on cache memory design. Midcon/87, pages 434-437, Septembe, 1987.
2. H. Imai. Essentials of error-control coding techniques. Academic Press, San Diego, CA, 1990.
3. C.L. Chen and M.Y Hsiao. Error-correcting codes for semiconductor memory applications: a state of the art review. In Reliable Computer Systems - Design and Evaluation, pages 771-786, Digital Press, 2nd edition, 1992.
4. J. Karlsson, P. Ledan, P. Dahlgren, and R. Johansson. Using heavy-ion radiation to validate fault handling mechanisms. IEEE Micro, 14(1):8–23, February 1994.
5. S. Kim and A. Somani. Area efficient architectures for information integrity checking in cache memories. ISCA, May 1999, pp. 246–256.
6. J. Sosnowski. Transient fault tolerance in digital systems. *IEEE Micro,* 14(1):24–35, February 1994.
7. W. Zhang, S. Gurumurthi, M. kandemir and A. Sivasubramaniam. ICR: in-cache replication for enhancing data cache reliability, DSN, 2003.
8. S. Kaxiras, Z. Hu, and M. Martonosi. Cache decay: exploiting generational behaviour to reduce cache leakage power, ISCA, June 2001.

9. P.Shivakumar, M. Kistler, S. Keckler, D. Burger and L. Alvisi. Modeling the effect of technology trends on soft error rate of combinational logic, DSN, June, 2002.
10. N.P. Jouppi. Improving direct-mapped cache performance by the audition of a small fully-associative cache and prefetch buffers, ISCA, 1990.
11. M. Hamada and E. Fujiwara. A class of error control codes for byte organized memory system-SbEC-(Sb+S)ED codes. IEEE Trans. on Computers, 46(1):105-110, January 1997.
12. S. Park and B. Bose. Burst asymmetric/unidirectional error correcting/detecting codes, FTC, June, 1990.
13. Understanding Soft and Firm Errors in Semiconductor Devices. Actel Whitepaper, 2002.
14. http://www.simplescalar.com.
15. S Wilton and N. Jouppi. CACTI: An enhanced cache access and cycle time model. IEEE Journal of Solid-State Circuits, Vol. 31(5):677-688, May 1996.
16. http://www.spec.org.

Efficient Victim Mechanism on Sector Cache Organization

Chunrong Lai [1] and Shih-Lien Lu [2]

[1] Intel China Research Center, 8F, Raycom Infotech Park A, No.2 Kexueyuan South Road
ZhongGuanCun, Haidian District, Beijing China, 100080
chunrong.lai@intel.com
[2] Microprocessor Research, Intel Labs
shih-lien.l.lu@intel.com

Abstract. In this paper we present an victim cache design for caches organized with line that contains multiple sectors (sector cache). Sector caches use less memory bits to store tags than non-sectored caches. Victim cache has been proposed to alleviate conflict misses in a lower associative cache design. This paper examines how victim cache can be implemented in a sector cache and proposes a further optimization of the victim buffer design in which only the tags of the victim lines are remembered to re-use data in the sector cache. This design is more efficient because only an additional "OR" operation is needed in the tag checking critical path. We use a full system simulator to generate traces and a cache simulator to compare the miss ratios of different victim cache designs in sector caches. Simulation results show that this proposed design has comparable miss ratios with designs having much more complexity.

1 Introduction

In a cache an address tag (or tag) is used to identify the memory unit stored in the cache. The size of this memory unit affects how well a cache functions. For a fixed size cache larger unit size needs less memory bits to store tags and helps programs that possess special locality. However, larger unit may cause fragmentation making the cache less efficient when spatial locally is not there. Moreover, transferring each unit from lower memory hierarchy takes higher bandwidth. Smaller unit size allows more units to be included and may help programs that spread memory usage.

Sector cache[1][2] has been proposed as an alternative to strike a balance of cache unit sizes. A sector cache's memory unit is divided into sub-sections. Each unit needs only one tag thus saves tag memory bits. These sub-sections of a sector cache need not to be simultaneously brought in the cache allowing lower transferring bandwidth. Another advantage of sector caches is observed for multiprocessors systems because they reduce false sharing[3][4]. Sector cache's advantage is evident in that many microprocessors employ sector caches in their designs. For example, Intel's Pen-

P.-C. Yew and J. Xue (Eds.): ACSAC 2004, LNCS 3189, pp. 16–29, 2004.
© Springer-Verlag Berlin Heidelberg 2004

tium® 4[5], SUN's SPARC™[6] and IBM's POWERPC™ G4™[7]/G5™[8] all employ sector cache in their cache organization.

This work intends to propose and evaluate further optimization techniques to improve performance of a sector cache. One of those designs is the victim cache[9]. A victim cache includes an additional victim buffer. When a line is replaced it is put into this small buffer which is full associative instead of just being discarded. The idea is to share the victim buffer entries among all sets since only a few of them are hotly contended usually. First, we discuss how victim buffer/cache idea can be applied in a sector cache. We evaluate two implementations of victim cache. One is called "line-victim" and the other is "sector-victim". We further propose a third victim mechanism design named "victim sector tag buffer"(VST buffer) for further utilize the sector cache lines. This design tries to address a sector cache's potential disadvantage of having larger unit size and could be under-utilized.

Since there are many different names[3][6][10][11][12][13][14][15] used to describe the units used in a sector cache, we first describe the terminology used in this paper. In our terminology a cache consist of lines which have tags associated with each of them. Each line consists of sub-units which are called sectors. This naming convention is the same as described in the manuals of Pentium® 4[5] and POWERPC™[7][8]. An example 4-way set-associative cache set is shown in figure 1. A valid bit is added to every sector to identify a partial valid cache line. We also use the terminology s-ratio which is defined as the ratio between the line size and the sector size. A sector cache with s-ratio equals to p is called p-sectored cache as [1]. The example in figure 1 it is a 4-sectored cache.

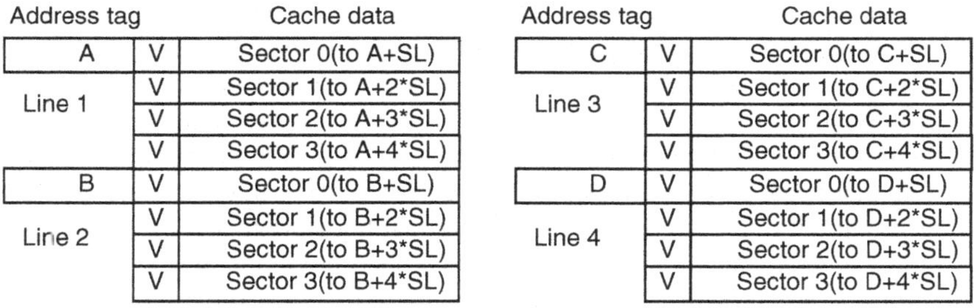

Address tag		Cache data	Address tag		Cache data
A	V	Sector 0(to A+SL)	C	V	Sector 0(to C+SL)
Line 1	V	Sector 1(to A+2*SL)	Line 3	V	Sector 1(to C+2*SL)
	V	Sector 2(to A+3*SL)		V	Sector 2(to C+3*SL)
	V	Sector 3(to A+4*SL)		V	Sector 3(to C+4*SL)
B	V	Sector 0(to B+SL)	D	V	Sector 0(to D+SL)
Line 2	V	Sector 1(to B+2*SL)	Line 4	V	Sector 1(to D+2*SL)
	V	Sector 2(to B+3*SL)		V	Sector 2(to D+3*SL)
	V	Sector 3(to B+4*SL)		V	Sector 3(to D+4*SL)

Fig. 1. Principles of sectored cache

This paper is organized as follows. In this section we introduce the concept of sector cache and victim mechanism. In the next section we first review other related works in this area. We then describe in more detail of our design. In section three we present the simulation methodology. In section four and five we introduce our simulation results on different cache levels. Finally we conclude with some observations.

---

[1] Pentium is a registered trademark of Intel Corp. or its subsidiaries in the United States and other countries.

2 Sector Cache with Victim Buffer

2.1 Related Work

Sector caches can be used to reduce bus traffic with only a small increase in miss ratio[15]. Sector cache can benefit in two-level cache systems in which tags of the second level cache are placed at the first level, thus permitting small tag storage to control a large cache. Sector cache also is able to improve single level cache system performance in some cases, particularly if the cache is small, the line size is small or the miss penalty is small. The main drawback, cache space underutilization is also shown in [13].

Rothman propose "sector pool" for cache space underutilization[13]. In the design, each set of set-associative cache compose of totally s-ratio sector lists. Each list has a fix number of sectors that the number is less than the associativity. S-ratio additional pointer bits, associate with a line tag, point to the actual sector as the index of the sector list. Thus a physical sector can be shared in different cache lines to make the cache space more efficient. Unlike our victim mechanism who tries to reduce the cache Miss ratio, this design more focus on cache space reduction. It depends on a high degree set associative cache. The additional pointer bits and the sector lists will make the control more complex. For example, the output of tag comparison need to be used to get the respond pointer bit first then can get the result sector. This lengthens the critical path. Another example is that different replacement algorithms for the cache lines and sector list need to be employed at the same time.

Seznec propose "decoupled sectored cache"[1][11]. A [N,P] decoupled sectored cache means that in this P-sectored cache there exists a number N such that for any cache sector, the address tag associated with it is dynamically chosen among N possible address tags. Thus a log2N bits tag, known as the selection tag, is associated with each cache sector in order to allow it to retrieve its address tag. This design increases the cache performance by allow N memory lines share a cache line if they use different sectors that some of the sectors have to be invalid at normal sector cache design. Our concern about this design is that the additional tag storage, say N-1 address tags and s-ratio * log2N selection tags for each line, need large amount of extra storage. Seznec himself use large(32 or 64) s-raio, which will make the validity check and coherence control very complex, to reduce tag storage before decoupling. We tried to implement this idea and saw the line-fill-in and line-replacement policy is important for the performance. If with a line-based-LRU-like fill-in/replacement policy proposed by ourselves, since Seznec did not give enough details of his policies, the decoupled sector cache will not perform better than our VST design, if with similar extra storage, given s-ratio range of 2~8. And, an additional compare need to be performed to the retrieved selection tag to ensure the sector data is right corresponded to the address tag which causes the tag matching. This also lengthens the tag checking critical path.

Victim caching was proposed by Jouppi[9] as an approach to reduce the cache Miss ratio in a low associative cache. This approach augments the main cache with a small fully-associate victim cache that stores cache blocks evicted from the main cache as a result of replacements. Victim cache is effective. Depending on the program, a four-entry victim cache might remove one quarter of the misses in a 4-KB direct-mapped data cache. Recently [16] shows that victim cache is the most power/energy efficient design among the general cache misses reduction mechanisms. Thus it becomes a more attractive design because of the increasing demand of low power micro-architecture.

2.2 Proposed Design

In order to make our description clearer, we define several terms here. We call a reference to a sector cache a *block-miss* if the reference finds no matching tag within the selected set. We call a reference a *data-miss* if the tag matches but the referenced word is in an invalid sector. Thus a *miss* can be either block-miss or data-miss. Similar to [1][11] describe, for a P-sectored cache we divide the address A of a memory block in four sub-strings (A3, A2, A1, A0) defined as: A0 is a log2SL bit string which SL is the sector length, A1 is a log2P bit string show which sector this block is in if it is in a cache line, A2 is a log2nS bit string which nS is the number of the cache sets, A3 consists of the remaining highest significant bits. The main cache line need store only the bits in A3. Figure 2 show tag checking of directed-mapped case. A2 identify the only position of the tag to be compared in the tag array. (A2, A1) identify the only position the data sector can be. The data can be fetched without any dependency on the tag comparison. The processor pipeline may even start consuming the data speculatively without waiting for the tag comparison result, only roll back and restart with the correct data in the case of cache miss which is rarely happened, as line prediction.

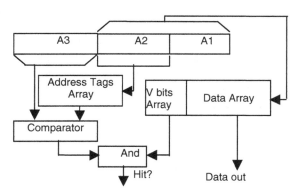

Fig. 2. Directed mapped sector cache tag checking

In the case of set-associative cache, (A2, A1) can only select the conceptual "sector set", then waiting for the comparison result of the address tags to get a line ID to deliver the correspond sector. Figure 3 is such an example of a 2-way associate sector cache. In a lower-associate cache the sector data and the valid bits being select can be got independently with the tag comparison.

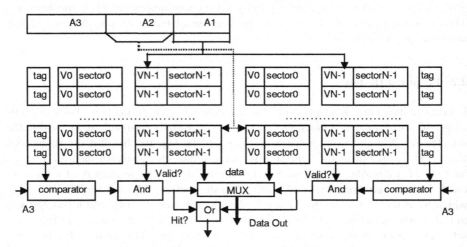

Fig. 3. 2-way associate sector cache tag checking

In figure 3 a line ID is needed, in critical path, as selection signal of the MUX. Line ID is founded after the tag comparison result. For a higher associate cache like a CAM, where a simple MUX may not be used, the data and valid bits could be not right at hand immediately. But Line ID retrieving still dominates in the critical path there[17].

As mentioned by many researchers victim cache can reduce cache Miss ratio. There are two straightforward victim designs for sector cache. One is line-victim cache(LVC), the other is sector-victim cache(SVC). Figure4 show their tag checking. Tag checking of the line victim cache is in the left and the other is in the right. The most difference between them is the data unit associate with the victim tag. In line-victim cache, the data unit is a cache line. And the data unit is a sector in the sector-victim cache. Thus the lengths of the victim tags of LVC and SVC are different. For same entries number LVC can be expected more cache misses saved due to more storage there, where SVC can be expected a little faster tag checking and data retrieve. Figure 4 do not connect the victim cache with main cache to avoid unnecessary complexity and allow architects to decide if swap the victim data with the main cache data when hit victim cache.

Both line-victim cache and sector-victim cache are paralleled accessed with the main sector cache. A cache line is evicted to the line- victim cache in case of cache replacement happens. As to the sector-victim cache, only the valid sectors in the whole line are evicted to the sector-victim-cache. Also when a new line is brought into cache, the sector-victim cache is checked to see if there are other sectors in the same line. If so the victim sectors are also brought into the main cache line to maintain a unique position of a cache line.

We know some of the requested data may still be in the data cache but it is just inaccessible because it has been invalidated. This paper describes another approach, called "VST buffer" to remember what is still in the data cache.

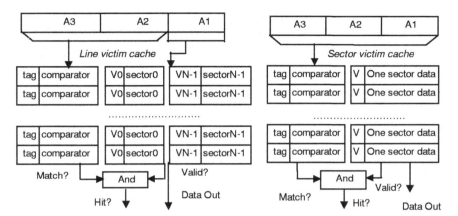

Fig. 4. Tag checking of line-victim cache and sector-victim cache

When a block miss happens and the set is full, a cache line must be replaced. Each sector of the replaced line will be mark as invalid. A new sector will be brought into the replaced line, and the cache tag will be updated. Thus some of the previously replaced line's sector data may still be in the data array since not all sector, of the newly brought in cache line, is brought in. Only their valid bits are marked invalid. VST buffer is used to keep track of these sectors whose data is still the data array. Thus a VST entry consists of the victim tag, the victim valid bits and the "real location" line ID in the cache set. For a directed mapped main cache the line ID field is needless. The left side of figure 5 shows the VST buffer tag checking with a directed-mapped main cache. As seen from the figure the VST buffer produce an additional "VST hit" signal to be perform "or" operation with the main cache hit signal in the critical path, without affecting the sector fetching and consuming. In either a VST hit or a main cache hit the data can be processed continuously.

The right side of figure 5 shows the VST buffer tag checking of a set-associate main cache. A VST hit not only leads to a hit result but also deliver a line ID to the main cache selector to get the result data. This line ID signal is performed "or" operation with the main cache line ID signal to select final line. One extra cost here is when a new sector is brought into the main cache, if a data miss happens, the VST needs to be checked if the position contains a sector being victimized. If so the victim entry is invalidated or thrashed. This does not increase cache-hit latency since it happens when cache miss. Since there is already cache miss penalty the additional cost seems to be acceptable.

When compare the cost of the three victim mechanism connected with a p-Sectored Cache all compose of N entries. We see beside the similar comparators and the control, the line- victim cache need N line tags, data of N * line size and N*P

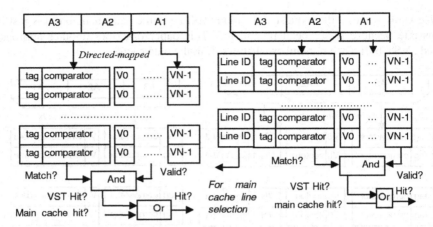

Fig. 5. Tag checking of Victim Sector Tag Buffer (VST buffer) with sector cache

valid bits; the sector-victim cache need N sector tags (each of it is log2P bits longer than a line tag), data of N * sector size and N valid bits; and the VST buffer need N line tags, N * P valid bits and N * log2Assoc bits of line IDs which Assoc is the cache associativity. So the line victim cache needs most resource among them as VST buffer need least resource.

In MP system, where the sector cache is proved efficient, there need additional cache coherence protocol, like MESI, to maintain the cache coherence. We think the victim mechanism will make the MP sector cache coherence protocol more complex. But we will not discuss the details here since it is beyond this paper's scope.

3   Simulation Methodology

Several SpecCPU2K[18] benchmarks (compiled with compiler option "–O3 –Qipo"), Java workload SpecJBB2K[19] with Java runtime environment JSEV1.4.1 which is an integer benchmark, and two commercial-like floating-point benchmarks, one is a speech recognition engine[20], the other is an echo cancellation algorithm[21] in audio signal processing, are used in our study.

In order to consider all the effects, including system calls, we use a full system simulator to generate memory reference traces. The simulator used is called SoftSDV[22]. The host system runs Windows 2000 and the simulated system is WindowsNT in batch mode using solid input captured in files. Then we run the traces through a trace-driven cache simulator.

We generate both L1 memory reference traces and L2 memory reference traces. After 20 billion instructions after system start up (the target application is configured auto-run in the simulation) we collect 200 million memory references as our L1 traces. We use 100 million references of them to warm up L1 cache and analysis the behavior of the latter 100 million. The L1 sector cache we simulated is mainly configured as below with small varieties: 16KBsize, 64B line size, 16B sector size, 4 way associate, LRU replacement algorithm and write-back approach. For L2 cache behavior we use a built-in first level cache together with trace generation. We warm up the built-in cache with 1 billion instructions. Then we collect L2 traces consist of 200 million read references. Also in our simulation we use 50 million L2 references to warm up the L2 cache. The hierarchy consist L2 sector cache we simulated is mainly configured as below with small varieties: L1: 16KBsize, 32B line size, 4-way associate, LRU replacement algorithm and write-back approach. L2: 1MB size, 128 byte line size, 32 byte sector size, 8-way associate, LRU replacement algorithm and write-back approach.

4   Level 1 Sector-Cache Simulation Results and Discussion

We present the L1 simulation data as the Miss Ratio Improvement Percentage (MRIP) of all benchmarks. The reason that we present L1 data first is that it is easier to correlate the observed L1 behavior back with the source code. Figure 6,7 are the MRIP trends with various parameters as the variable. All the numbers are computed as the geometric means of the different workload data also list in the paper. Figure 6 indicates that with larger number of the victim mechanism entries the miss ratio improvement increases. Since VST requires no data array we can implement a much larger victim buffer at the same cost of a smaller SVC/LVC and achieve the same (or even better) performance improvement. For example 128 entries VST performs comparably with 64 entries SVC or 32 entries LVC. Figure 6 also explores the improvement with several sector cache line sizes and sector sizes. We observed that VST performs better with larger s-ratios. This is because of higher underutilization cache space exist with higher s-ratio. On the other hand SVC and LVC performs better with larger line and sector sizes. Figure 7 compares how the victim mechanisms affect caches with different associativities or different cache sizes. It is not surprising to learn that all three forms of victim mechanisms help the lower associative cache better. This is because higher associativity already reduced much of the conflict misses victim cache is targeting. It is also seen smaller L1 cache benefits more from the victim mechanisms. As frequency of microprocessors continues to grow, smaller but faster (lower associativity gives faster cache too) cache will be more prevalent.

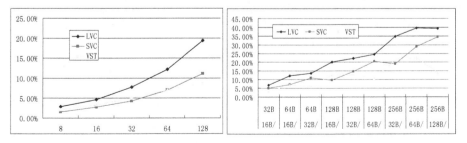

Fig. 6. MRIP with victim entries or line/sector sizes (higher is better)

We observe that LVC gives the best Miss ratio improvement at the highest hard-ware cost. While the SVC approach we used for this study needs the second highest hardware cost, it is not better than VST approach. The VST approach is a reasonable approach in terms of hardware design complexity and overhead.

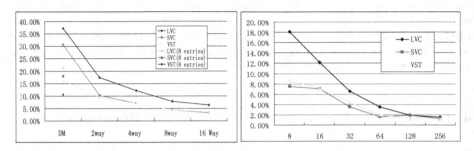

Fig. 7. MRIP with different associativities or L1 sizes

The cache miss ratios with different number of victim entries, correspond to the left figure of figure 6, are listed in table 1. The data of other figures are listed in appendix. Table 1 also list corresponding block misses ratios for further investigation.

Table 1. Miss Ratios and Block Miss Ratios with numbers of victim entries

L1 victim entries		Miss ratios						Block Miss ratios					
		8	16	32	64	128	origin	8	16	32	64	128	origin
LVCS	LVC	2.77	2.73	2.69	2.64	2.57	2.92	1.22	1.20	1.17	1.14	1.10	1.36
	SVC	2.79	2.76	2.73	2.69	2.64	2.92	1.25	1.23	1.20	1.18	1.15	1.36
	VST	2.81	2.78	2.76	2.73	2.71	2.92	1.25	1.23	1.20	1.18	1.16	1.36
AMMP	LVC	9.01	8.94	8.81	8.58	8.25	9.08	3.88	3.85	3.77	3.63	3.42	3.91
	SVC	9.04	9.00	8.93	8.77	8.50	9.08	3.90	3.88	3.85	3.77	3.65	3.91
	VST	9.02	8.96	8.86	8.71	8.56	9.08	3.87	3.83	3.76	3.67	3.57	3.91
MESA	LVC	0.63	0.57	0.56	0.54	0.51	1.67	0.27	0.21	0.20	0.19	0.18	0.95
	SVC	0.72	0.65	0.58	0.55	0.54	1.67	0.35	0.29	0.23	0.20	0.20	0.95
	VST	0.99	1.01	1.02	1.03	1.02	1.67	0.49	0.49	0.49	0.48	0.48	0.95
SAEC	LVC	3.29	3.26	3.19	3.07	2.84	3.35	0.93	0.92	0.90	0.86	0.80	0.95
	SVC	3.34	3.32	3.29	3.25	3.18	3.35	0.94	0.94	0.93	0.92	0.90	0.95
	VST	3.33	3.32	3.30	3.27	3.25	3.35	0.94	0.93	0.92	0.91	0.90	0.95
GZIP	LVC	10.67	10.56	10.37	10.04	9.45	10.81	7.44	7.33	7.13	6.76	6.13	7.58
	SVC	10.68	10.58	10.41	10.12	9.63	10.81	7.47	7.39	7.23	6.97	6.55	7.58
	VST	10.69	10.65	10.45	10.13	9.70	10.81	7.45	7.33	7.12	6.75	6.14	7.58
GCC	LVC	2.32	2.27	2.09	1.76	0.88	2.35	0.68	0.67	0.62	0.53	0.29	0.69
	SVC	2.34	2.33	2.31	2.23	2.02	2.35	0.69	0.68	0.68	0.66	0.60	0.69
	VST	2.30	2.24	2.14	2.07	2.06	2.35	0.67	0.66	0.62	0.60	0.59	0.69
SJBB	LVC	3.88	3.83	3.76	3.67	3.51	3.96	1.63	1.60	1.56	1.52	1.45	1.67
	SVC	3.90	3.88	3.84	3.77	3.69	3.96	1.65	1.63	1.61	1.57	1.53	1.67
	VST	3.91	3.88	3.84	3.78	3.71	3.96	1.65	1.62	1.59	1.55	1.50	1.67

As shown in table 1, the benchmark "mesa" got most of cache misses reduction with victim mechanism regardless LVC/SVC, or VST we used. "ammp" got least misses reduction with LVC and "saec" got least misses reduction with SVC and VST.

For the workload "mesa", we observed the block Miss ratio reduce much more significantly with victim mechanism compared to the cache Miss ratio. Thus with victim mechanism the workload basically keeps more cache lines to save cache misses in this level. Other issues, like quantitative spatial localities that make SVC performs differently, say reduces different percentage of miss ratio reduced by LVC with same entries, play minor role in this level.

In some cases (GCC with 8 victim entries), the VST buffer approach performs better than LVC even without any data array. After investigation we concluded that the VST buffer approach sometimes uses the victim buffer more efficiently and can avoid be thrashed. Victim cache contains data that may be used in future. But the data can also be kicked out of the victim cache before it is needed. For example, streaming accesses, if miss the main cache, will evict main cache lines to update the victim cache. Thus the victim cache gets thrashed and may lost useful information. It plays differently in VST approach. We see in non-sector cache, streaming accesses are mapping in different sets of cache which make it difficult to be detected. In a sector cache the next sector of a cache is inherently subsequence of the previous sector. Figure 8 shows the VST states with one by one streaming accesses (or sequential) going to the cache, only one VST entry is enough handling them since the entry can be re-used(disabled) after a whole main cache line fill-in. Thus the whole buffer will keep longer history. This is right the case VST performs better than LVC for GCC.

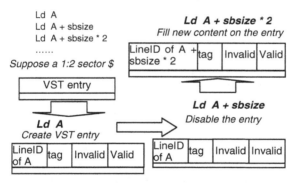

Fig. 8. Avoid be thrashed by streaming access

5   Level 2 Sector-Cache Simulation Results and Discussion

We also explore the possibility of applying our proposed methods on level-two cache design. This time only those references that missed the build-in level one cache are collected in the trace file. Table 2 illustrates the tabulated result in terms of miss ratio for various entries. Data with other parameters are also listed in appendix.

There are several observations made from the L2 data. First, LVC performs better than SVC with same entries but worse than SVC with s-ratios, here 4 times, of entries, same as be observed from L1 data. Second, in lower level set-associative cache, victim mechanism performs differently as L1. It does not save so many cache misses as

Table 2. L2 Miss Ratio with Victim Mechanism

Entries		16	32	64	128	256	Origin
Ammp	LVC	15.36	15.06	14.52	13.71	12.85	15.62
	SVC	15.49	15.34	15.06	14.58	13.89	15.62
	VST	14.82	14.24	13.71	13.30	12.91	15.62
LVCSR	LVC	36.57	36.53	36.46	36.33	36.06	36.60
	SVC	36.59	36.57	36.54	36.49	36.38	36.60
	VST	36.57	36.54	36.48	36.36	36.14	36.60
Mesa	LVC	9.64	9.64	9.63	9.63	9.63	9.64
	SVC	9.64	9.64	9.64	9.64	9.63	9.64
	VST	9.64	9.64	9.64	9.64	9.64	9.64
Gcc	LVC	8.52	8.51	8.50	8.48	8.44	8.52
	SVC	8.52	8.52	8.51	8.50	8.49	8.52
	VST	8.51	8.51	8.49	8.47	8.45	8.52
Gzip	LVC	0.33	0.33	0.33	0.33	0.33	0.33
	SVC	0.33	0.33	0.33	0.33	0.33	0.33
	VST	0.33	0.33	0.33	0.33	0.33	0.33
Mcf	LVC	50.47	50.43	50.36	50.23	49.98	50.50
	SVC	50.48	50.47	50.44	50.38	50.26	50.50
	VST	50.47	50.45	50.40	50.35	50.24	50.50
SAEC	LVC	0.40	0.38	0.37	0.37	0.37	0.41
	SVC	0.41	0.40	0.39	0.38	0.37	0.41
	VST	0.42	0.42	0.42	0.42	0.42	0.41

L1 cache. This is not surprising since a small L1 already catch a significant part of data locality and L2 reference patterns tend to be more irregular. Third, the VST buffer performs well among the three victim mechanisms in this memory hierarchy level. It can outperform LVC and SVC for the benchmark "ammp". Even it is more difficult to correlate the L2 references back with the source or binary, than L1 references. We still ascribe the better VST performance to its property of avoiding be thrashed. As to the workloads, "ammp" and "SAEC" get most significant cache misses reduction here. This behavior is opposite to the L1 behavior. Also the significant block miss reduction can not be observed in this level as the data in appendix shows. Thus we suggest that the extra storage of LVC and SVC benefit more from the general data locality; and VST benefit more from the cache underutilization whether the reference pattern is regular or not.

6 Conclusion

We have described three possible implementation of victim buffer design in a sector cache. They have different complexity and hardware overhead. Several up-to-date applications are used to evaluate their performance in terms of miss ratio. Overall three mechanisms have comparable cache misses reduction. For a directed-mapped Level 1 cache, the mechanisms can save significant amount of cache misses.

Among the three mechanisms LVC gives the best performance with highest overhead. Whether SVC is performance/cost effective or not rely on the quantitative spatial locality of the workload.

We also investigate several benefits of VST in this paper. Include the low-cost design, keeping longer victim history and be more able to capture irregular reference pattern in lower memory hierarchy.

Acknowledgement. We thank the AudioProcessing group and the OpenRuntimePlatform group of Intel China Research center for giving us their up-to-date workloads and providing helpful discussions on porting workloads to our simulator. We also thank Zhu Ning and Peter Liou for providing necessary computing infrastructure support.

References

[1]   Andre. Seznec. "Decoupled sectored caches". IEEE Trans. on Computers, February, 1997
[2]   D.A.Patterson, J.L.Hennessy, "Computer architecture: A quantitative approach", Morgan Kaufmann Publishers Inc., San Francisco,1996.
[3]   Kuang-Chih Liu, Chung-Ta King, "On the effectiveness of sectored caches in reducing false sharing misses" International Conference on Parallel and Distributed Systems, 1997
[4]   Won-Kee Hong, Tack-Don Han, Shin-Dug Kim and Sung-Bong Yang, "An Effective Full-Map Directory Scheme for the Sectored Caches", International Conference/Exhibition on High Performance Computing in Asia Pacific Region, 1997
[5]   Hinton, G; Sager, D.; Upton, M.; Boggs, D.; Carmean, D.; Kyker, A.; Roussel, P., "The Microarchitecture of the Pentium® 4 processor", Intel Technology Journal, 1st quarter, 2001, http://developer.intel.com/technology/itj/q12001/articles/art_2.htm
[6]   "UltraSPARC™ Iii User's Manual", Sun Microsystems, 1999
[7]   PowerPC™ , "MPC7400 RISC Microprocessor Technical Summary ", Mororola, Order Number: MPC7400TS/D, Rev. 0, 8/1999
[8]   Victor Kartunov, "IBM PowerPC G5: Another World", X-bit Labs, Jan. 2004 http://www.xbitlabs.com/articles/cpu/display/powerpc-g5_6.html
[9]   N. Jouppi, "Improving direct-mapped cache performance by the addition of a small fully associative cache and prefetch buffers", International Symposium on. Computer Architecture 1990
[10]   Jeffrey B. Rothman, Alan Jay Smith: "Sector Cache Design and Performance". International Symposium on Modeling, Analysis and Simulation of Computer and Telecommunication Systems, 2000
[11]   Andre. Seznec. "Decoupled sectored caches: conciliating low tag implementation cost". International Symposium on. Computer Architecture, 1994
[12]   J.S.Lipty. "Structural Aspects of the System/360 Model 85, Part II: The Cache. IBM Systems Journal, Vol. 7, 1968
[13]   Jeffrey B. Rothman and Alan Jay Smith. "The Pool of SubSectors Cache Design". International Conference on Supercomputing, 1999
[14]   Mark D. Hill and Alan Jay Smith. "Experimental Evaluation of On-Chip Microprocessor Cache Memories". International Symposium on Computer Architecture, June 1984
[15]   James R. Goodman. "Using Cache Memory to Reduce Processor Memory Traffic". International Symposium on. Computer Architecture 1983

28   C. Lai and S.-L. Lu

[16] G. Albera and R. Bahar, " Power/performance Advantages of Victim Buffer in High-Performance Processors", IEEE Alessandro Volta Memorial Workshop on Low-Power Design,1999
[17] Farhad Shafai, Kenneth J. Schultz, G..F. Randall Gibson, Armin G. Bluschke and David E. Somppi, "Fully Parallel 30-MHz, 2.5-Mb CAM", IEEE journal of solid-state circuits, Vol. 33, No. 11, November 1998
[18] SPEC CPU2000, http://www.specbench.org/osg/cpu2000
[19] SPEC JBB 2000, http://www.specbench.org/jbb2000
[20] C.Lai, S. Lu and Q. Zhao, "Performance Analysis of Speech Recognition Software", Workshop on Computer Architecture Evaluation using Commercial Workloads, International Symposium on High Performance Computer Architecture, 2002
[21] J. Song, J. Li, and Y.-K. Chen, "Quality-Delay and Computation Trade-Off Analysis of Acoustic Echo Cancellation On General-Purpose CPU," International Conference on Acoustics, Speech, and Signal Processing, 2003.
[22] R. Uhlig et. al., "SoftSDV: A Pre-silicon Software Development Environment for the IA-64 Architecture", Intel Technology Journal, 4th quarter, 1999. http://developer.intel.com/technology/itj/q41999/articles/art_2.htm

Appendix: More Simulation Data

Sector/ line size		16B/ 32B	16B/ 64B	32B/ 64B	16B/ 128B	32B/ 128B	64B/ 128B	32B/ 256B	64B/ 256B	128B/ 256B
LVCSR	LVC	2.52	2.64	1.68	2.70	1.72	1.17	1.74	1.18	0.87
	SVC	2.53	2.69	1.70	2.83	1.78	1.19	1.87	1.24	0.88
	VST	2.59	2.73	1.79	2.90	1.89	1.38	2.02	1.51	1.20
	ORI	2.65	2.92	1.92	3.23	2.15	1.55	2.86	2.19	1.69
AMMP	LVC	8.17	8.58	5.32	9.00	5.64	3.88	5.74	3.96	3.04
	SVC	8.23	8.77	5.37	9.36	5.76	3.90	6.12	4.12	3.06
	VST	8.27	8.71	5.46	9.09	5.72	4.02	5.90	4.16	3.40
	ORI	8.38	9.08	5.67	9.86	6.25	4.37	6.68	4.69	3.66
MESA	LVC	0.53	0.54	0.31	0.54	0.31	0.19	0.31	0.20	0.14
	SVC	0.54	0.55	0.32	0.63	0.33	0.20	0.53	0.25	0.15
	VST	0.95	1.03	0.75	1.08	0.78	0.69	0.86	0.75	1.39
	ORI	1.36	1.67	1.20	2.72	1.98	1.62	2.72	2.29	1.93
SAEC	LVC	3.11	3.07	1.60	2.95	1.54	0.83	1.45	0.78	0.45
	SVC	3.16	3.25	1.66	3.38	1.73	0.89	1.83	0.93	0.49
	VST	3.22	3.27	1.72	3.33	1.75	0.96	1.80	0.99	0.58
	ORI	3.25	3.35	1.75	3.50	1.83	0.99	1.98	1.08	0.62
GZIP	LVC	9.09	10.0	8.28	10.7	9.00	7.54	9.36	7.95	6.57
	SVC	9.10	10.1	8.29	11.0	9.16	7.59	10.0	8.38	6.76
	VST	9.18	10.13	8.46	10.86	9.26	8.02	9.83	8.66	7.97
	ORI	9.54	10.8	9.09	12.1	10.5	9.09	12.1	10.8	9.48
GCC	LVC	1.92	1.76	0.95	1.46	0.79	0.45	0.46	0.27	0.18
	SVC	2.05	2.23	1.09	2.49	1.19	0.57	1.36	0.63	0.31
	VST	2.04	2.07	1.15	2.08	1.16	0.69	1.17	0.69	0.45
	ORI	2.14	2.35	1.25	2.64	1.40	0.77	1.60	0.88	0.51
SJBB	LVC	3.55	3.67	2.31	3.72	2.34	1.54	2.36	1.55	1.08
	SVC	3.59	3.77	2.34	3.97	2.45	1.58	2.70	1.70	1.11
	VST	3.62	3.78	2.40	3.91	2.50	1.72	2.47	1.89	1.41
	ORI	3.70	3.96	2.52	4.33	2.79	1.89	3.34	2.83	1.68

L1 Data		DM	2way	4way	8way	16 Way	DM(8 Entries)	8KB	16KB	32KB	64KB	128KB	256KB
LVCSR	LVC	2.71	2.68	2.64	2.61	2.60	3.35	2.77	2.64	2.50	2.35	2.18	1.92
	SVC	2.75	2.71	2.69	2.64	2.63	3.70	2.90	2.69	2.52	2.36	2.18	1.93
	VST	4.16	3.10	2.73	2.63	2.62	4.33	3.01	2.73	2.52	2.35	2.18	1.92
	ORI	5.31	3.64	2.92	2.69	2.66	5.31	3.35	2.92	2.58	2.37	2.19	1.93
AMMP	LVC	9.11	8.76	8.58	8.51	8.49	9.76	9.47	8.58	7.92	7.64	7.44	6.20
	SVC	9.35	9.01	8.77	8.65	8.65	9.89	9.80	8.77	8.00	7.66	7.45	6.22
	VST	10.08	8.95	8.71	8.61	8.59	10.44	9.89	8.71	7.96	7.65	7.44	6.13
	ORI	11.36	9.38	9.08	8.94	8.94	11.36	10.27	9.08	8.10	7.68	7.45	6.23
MESA	LVC	0.56	0.54	0.54	0.54	0.55	4.10	0.63	0.54	0.41	0.30	0.16	0.10
	SVC	0.74	0.55	0.55	0.56	0.57	4.91	0.67	0.55	0.44	0.31	0.17	0.10
	VST	4.08	1.56	1.03	0.60	0.58	4.94	1.48	1.03	0.45	0.35	0.18	0.10
	ORI	6.68	3.02	1.67	0.66	0.60	6.68	3.22	1.67	0.47	0.32	0.17	0.11
SAEC	LVC	3.27	3.15	3.07	3.01	3.02	4.09	3.82	3.07	2.27	1.20	1.00	0.64
	SVC	3.76	3.37	3.25	3.23	3.23	4.26	4.19	3.25	2.39	1.31	1.01	0.65
	VST	4.22	3.43	3.27	3.24	3.23	4.38	4.38	3.27	2.31	1.29	1.00	0.64
	ORI	4.72	3.56	3.35	3.32	3.32	4.72	4.59	3.35	2.43	1.35	1.01	0.65
GZIP	LVC	10.30	10.13	10.04	10.00	9.97	11.53	11.27	10.04	8.08	5.05	1.81	0.37
	SVC	10.35	10.21	10.12	10.07	10.04	11.50	11.35	10.12	8.19	5.19	1.91	0.38
	VST	14.62	10.30	10.13	10.07	10.03	15.51	11.58	10.13	8.13	5.05	1.83	0.38
	ORI	16.32	11.17	10.81	10.68	10.62	16.32	12.90	10.81	8.65	5.47	2.02	0.39
GCC	LVC	1.55	1.69	1.76	1.82	1.82	1.98	3.82	1.76	0.32	0.21	0.17	0.15
	SVC	1.88	2.17	2.23	2.24	2.19	2.00	4.46	2.23	0.37	0.22	0.17	0.15
	VST	1.86	2.00	2.19	2.19	2.23	2.05	4.32	2.07	0.36	0.22	0.18	0.15
	ORI	2.30	2.26	2.35	2.43	2.47	2.30	4.47	2.35	0.49	0.23	0.19	0.15
SJBB	LVC	3.76	3.71	3.67	3.67	3.68	4.38	4.05	3.67	3.19	2.58	2.00	1.76
	SVC	4.07	3.89	3.77	3.75	3.75	4.56	4.42	3.77	3.26	2.63	2.03	1.76
	VST	4.56	3.98	3.78	3.73	3.71	4.86	4.42	3.78	3.25	2.63	2.06	1.78
	ORI	5.37	4.23	3.96	3.84	3.80	5.37	5.00	3.96	3.32	2.66	2.04	1.77

L2 Data		256KB	512KB	1MB	2MB	4MB	8MB	DM	2way	4way	8way	16way
Ammp	LVC	55.76	38.38	13.71	8.21	7.36	2.28	35.49	33.31	19.93	13.71	12.59
	SVC	56.64	39.05	14.58	8.27	7.41	2.31	36.26	34.04	20.67	14.58	13.00
	VST	54.37	36.69	13.30	8.24	7.39	2.27	36.13	33.16	18.76	13.30	12.59
	ORI	57.57	40.07	15.62	8.49	7.58	2.34	38.18	35.11	21.65	15.62	13.75
LVCS	LVC	52.63	46.03	36.33	26.49	20.72	14.66	40.69	37.79	36.65	36.33	36.08
	SVC	52.89	46.21	36.49	26.57	20.75	14.68	41.31	38.00	36.83	36.49	36.23
	VST	52.81	46.11	36.36	26.51	20.72	14.67	41.32	37.88	36.70	36.36	36.10
	ORI	53.28	46.40	36.60	26.63	20.76	14.69	42.29	38.19	36.96	36.60	36.35
SAEC	LVC	14.86	0.54	0.37	0.36	0.34	0.32	7.16	0.52	0.38	0.37	0.36
	SVC	15.63	0.82	0.38	0.36	0.34	0.32	7.64	0.64	0.45	0.38	0.36
	VST	14.70	0.87	0.42	0.36	0.34	0.32	7.45	0.76	0.45	0.42	0.36
	ORI	15.78	1.07	0.41	0.36	0.34	0.32	8.48	0.95	0.49	0.41	0.36

Cache Behavior Analysis of
a Compiler-Assisted Cache Replacement Policy[*]

Xingyan Tian[1], Kejia Zhao[1], Huowang Chen[1], and Hongyan Du[2]

[1] Department of Computer Science, National University of Defense Technology,
Changsha, Hunan, 410073, China
tianxingyan@nudt.edu.cn
[2] Department of Computer Science, Changsha University,
Changsha, Hunan, 410003, China
csduhongyan@sina.com

Abstract. Recent research results show that conventional hardware-only cache replacement policies result in unsatisfactory cache utilization because of cache pollution. To overcome this problem, cache hints are introduced to assist cache replacement. Cache hints are used to specify the cache level at which the data is stored after accessing it. This paper present a compiler-assisted cache replacement policy, Optimum Cache Partition (OCP), which can be carried out through cache hints and LRU replacement policy. Presburger arithmetic is used to exactly model the behavior of loop nests under OCP policy. The OCP replacement policy results in plain cache behaviors, and makes cache misses analyzing and optimizing easily and efficiently. OCP replacement policy has been implemented in our compiler test-bed and evaluated on a set of scientific computing benchmarks. Initial results show that our approach is effective on reducing the cache miss rate.

1 Introduction

Caches play a very important role in the performance of modern computer systems due to the gap between the memory and the processor speed, but they are only effective when programs exhibit data locality. In the past, many compiler optimizations have been proposed to enhance the data locality. However, a conventional cache is typically designed in a hardware-only fashion, where data management including cache line replacement is decided purely by hardware. Research results [1] reveal that considerable fraction of cache lines are held by data that will not be reused again before it is displaced from the cache. This phenomenon, called cache pollution, severely degrades cache performance. A consequence of this design approach is that cache can make poor decisions in choosing data to be replaced, which may lead to poor cache performance.

---

[*] This work was supported by 863 National High Technology Program, grant No. 2002AA1Z2105

P.-C. Yew and J. Xue (Eds.): ACSAC 2004, LNCS 3189, pp. 30–43, 2004.

There are a number of efforts in architecture designed to address this problem, the cache hint in EPIC [2,3] (Explicitly Parallel Instruction Computing) architectures is one of them. Cache hints are used to specify the cache level where the data is stored after accessing it. Intuitively, two kinds of memory instructions should be given cache hints [12]: i) whose referenced data doesn't exhibit reuse; ii) whose referenced data does exhibit reuse, but it cannot be realized under the particular cache configuration. It sounds as though the problem is pretty simple for regular applications, and existing techniques for analyzing data reuse [4] and estimating cache misses [5, 6] suffice to solve this problem. This plausible statement, however, is not true because a fundamental technique used in cache miss estimation — footprint analysis — is based on the assumption that all accessed data compete for cache space equally. However, in EPIC architectures, memory instructions are not homogeneous— those with cache hints have much less demand for cache space. This makes the approach derived from traditional footprint analysis very conservative. In summary, the following *cyclic dependence* [12] exists: Accurate cache miss estimation must be known to cache hint assignment, while accurate cache miss estimation is only possible when cache hint assignment is finalized.

In this paper, we present a novel cache replacement policy, Optimum Cache Partition (OCP), to address the above problem. The OCP cache replacement policy can be carried out through combining hardware cache replacement policy LRU (Least Recently Used) with compiler generating cache hints. Presburger [15] arithmetic is used to exactly model the behavior of loop nests under OCP policy. the OCP replacement policy makes cache miss estimation simpler through simplifying cache behaviors fundamentally.

We have evaluated the benefit of the OCP cache replacement policy on reducing the cache miss rate through executing a set of SPEC benchmarks on Trimaran[7] and DineroIV[8]. Trimaran is a compiler infrastructure for supporting state of the art research in EPIC architectures, and DineroIV is a trace-driven cache simulator. Initial experimental results show that our approach reduces data cache misses by 20.32%.

The rest of this paper is organized as follows. Section 2 briefly reviews the basic concept of cache hint. Section 3 illustrates, through an example, a compiler-assisted cache replacement policy, Cache Partition. Section 4 uses Presburger arithmetic to analyze the relationship between reuse vector and cache miss rate, to estimate cache hits and misses, and then an optimum cache replacement policy, Optimum Cache Partition, is derived. Our implementation and experimental results are then presented in Section 5. Section 6 discusses related work. Section 7 concludes this paper.

2   Cache Hints

One of the basic principles of the EPIC-philosophy is to let the compiler decide when to issue operations and which resources to use. The existing EPIC architectures (HPL-PD [2] and IA-64[3]) communicate the compiler decisions about the cache hierarchy management to the processor through cache hints. The semantics of cache hints on both architectures are similar. Cache hints are used to specify the cache level at which the data is likely to be found, as well as the cache level where the data is stored after accessing it.

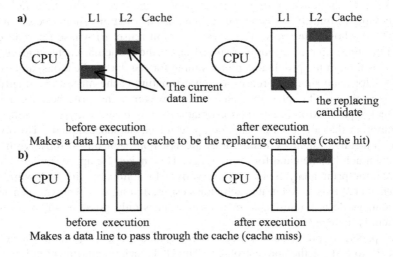

Fig. 1. Example of the effect of the cache hints in the load instruction *ld.nt1*

In the IA-64 architecture, the cache hints *t1*, *nt1*, *nt2* and *nta* are defined. *t1* means that the memory instruction has temporal locality in all the cache levels. *nt1* only has temporal locality in the L2 cache and below. Similarly, *nt2* respectively *nta* indicates that there's only temporal locality in L3 respectively no temporal locality at all. An example is given in figure 1 where the effect of the load instruction *ld.nt1* is shown.

Generating cache hints based on the data locality of the instruction, compiler can improve a program's cache behavior. As shown in figure 1, cache hints have two effects on cache behaviors: i) when cache hits, it make the current reference line, which is stayed in the cache, to be the replacing candidate, ii) when cache misses, it make the current reference line, which is not in the cache, to pass through the cache without being stored in the cache. Examples of these effects are given in figure 1a and 1b.

With cache hints, our compiler can carry out the OCP cache replacement policy through controlling cache staying time of accessed data, as a result, the cache pollution is reduced and cache miss rate is decreased availably.

3 A Compiler-Assisted Cache Replacement Policy: Cache Partition

Let's see a short memory access stream in Figure 2. For a 4-lines LRU cache, there are 10 cache misses for the memory access stream in Figure 2, $M_{LRU}=10$.

For the same cache, if the cache is partitioned into three parts logically: 3 lines, 0 lines, 1 line, and then the three parts has been assigned to the three references, A, B and C respectively. In that case, memory access stream of the reference A can hold 3 cache lines at most, the reference C can only hold 1 cache line, the reference B can not hold any cache line. Under this cache partition, the cache miss analysis of these 3 references is shown in Figure 3. It shows that the cache miss analysis of these 3 references can proceed independently, there are no influence mutually.

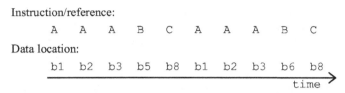

Instruction/reference:

    A   A   A   B   C   A   A   A   B   C

Data location:

    b1   b2   b3   b5   b8   b1   b2   b3   b6   b8

    time →

Fig. 2. The top row indicates 10 memory reference instructions. The bottom row shows the corresponding memory locations.

Making reasonable cache partition and limiting the appropriate number of cache lines hold by each reference, cache misses can decrease obviously. The "limiting" can be carried out by a compiler through appending cache hints to some memory instructions. For example, not to let reference B hold any cache line, a cache hint is appended to reference B instruction; To limit the number of cache lines hold by references A and C, a cache hint is appended to reference A and C instruction conditionally.

Cache lines	4		
Cache Partition	3	0	1
Reference	A	B	C
Access stream	b1,b2,b3,b1,b2,b3,	b5,b6	b8,b8
Cache misses	3	2	1

Cache miss analysis for Cache Partition (3,0,1)

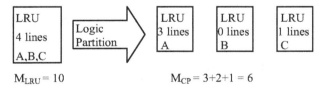

| LRU 4 lines A,B,C | Logic Partition ⇒ | LRU 3 lines A | LRU 0 lines B | LRU 1 lines C |

$M_{LRU} = 10$ $M_{CP} = 3+2+1 = 6$

Fig. 3. 4-lines LRU cache is divided logically into three LRU sub-caches, and cache misses decrease from 10 to 6.

With cache hints, as above example shows, a compiler can construct a novel cache replacement policy, where the cache has be partitioned logically into parts and each reference data in a loop nested program can be limited within one part, as if there is a *sub-cache* for each reference. Under this cache replacement policy, reference cache behaviors will not influence each other, and cache misses of a reference can be analyzed independently. The cache behaviors under the cache replacement policy are more plain and more independent than only-LRU replacement policy.

Definition 1. For a LRU cache with N lines, a *Cache Partition* $\mathcal{P}$ *of* a loop nest with m references is a m-tuple $(C_1, C_2, ..., C_m)$, where $\sum_{i=1}^{m} C_i \leq N$ and cache lines hold by i-th reference Ref_i at any moment can not exceeds C_i lines.

A Cache Partition (CP) is a cache replacement policy that achieves two aims for the reference Ref_i: (i) there are C_i lines in cache that can be hold by the reference Ref_i at any moment; (ii) the number of cache lines hold by the reference Ref_i cannot exceed C_i at any moment. The CP replacement policy, that can be carried out by a compiler through appending cache hints to some memory instructions, simplifies loop nest cache behaviors, however there is a crucial problem: can it minify cache misses? To address this problem, an analysis of cache misses under the CP policy is taken, and an optimum CP policy is derived in the next section.

4   Cache Misses Analysis and Optimum Cache Partition

In this section, the Optimum Cache Partition is derived after cache misses analysis under the CP replacement policy. A matrix-multiply loop nest program MXM(see Figure 4) is used as our primary example, and all arrays discussed here are assumed to be arranged in column-major order as in Fortran.

```
DO i = 1, U1
 DO k = 1, U2
  DO j = 1, U3
   Z(j,i)=Z(j,i)+X(k,i)*Y(j,k)
```

Fig. 4. Matrix-multiply loop nest, MXM

4.1   Terminology

Our research is based on analyzing references' cache behavior using iteration spaces and reuse vectors.

A *reference* is a static read or write in the program, while a particular execution of that read or write at runtime is a *memory access*.

Throughout this paper, we denote the cache size as C_s, line size as L_s, the number of cache lines as N_l, then $C_s = L_s * N_l$.

Iteration space. Every iteration of a loop nest is viewed as a single entity termed *an iteration point* in the set of all iteration points known as the *iteration space*. Formally, we represent a loop nest of depth n as a finite convex polyhedron of the n-dimensional iteration space $S = \prod_{i=1}^{n} [1, U_i] \subset Z^n$, bounded by the loop bounds U_i ($1 \leq i \leq n$). Each iteration in the loop corresponds to a node in the polyhedron and is called an *iteration point*. Every iteration point is identified by its index vector $\vec{i} = (i_1, i_2, ..., i_n) \in S$, where i_l is the loop index of the l-th loop in the nest with the outermost loop corresponding to the leftmost index. In this representation, if iteration $\vec{p}_2$ executes after iteration $\vec{p}_1$ we write $\vec{p}_2 \succ \vec{p}_1$ and say that $\vec{p}_2$ is lexicographically greater than $\vec{p}_1$.

Reuse Vector. Reuse vectors provide a mechanism for summarizing repeated memory access patterns in loop-oriented code[4]. If a reference accesses the same memory line in iterations $\vec{i}_1$ and $\vec{i}_2$, where $\vec{i}_2 \succ \vec{i}_1$, we say that there is reuse in direction $\vec{r} = \vec{i}_2 - \vec{i}_1$, and $\vec{r}$ is called a *reuse vector*. For example, the reference Z(j, i) in Figure 4 can access the same memory line at the iteration points (i, k, j) and (i, k+1, j), and hence one of its reuse vectors is (0, 1, 0). A reuse vector is repeated across the iteration space. Reuse vectors provide a concise mathematical representation of the reuse information of a loop nest.

A reuse vector is realized. If a reuse vector results in a cache hit we say that the *reuse vector is realized.*

Hence, if we have an infinitely large cache, every reuse vector would result in a cache hit. In practice, however, a reuse vector does not always result in cache hit. The central idea behind our model is to maximize realized reuse vectors.

4.2 Cache Misses Analysis Under Cache Partition Replacement Policy

Under a Cache Partition $\mathcal{P} = (C_1, C_2, ..., C_m)$ replacement policy, memory accesses of every reference Ref_i $(1 \le i \le m)$ in a loop nest can hold C_i cache lines at most, and cannot be influenced by other reference accesses, as if reference Ref_i engrosses a C_i-lines sub-cache, $Cache_i$, independently (see Figure 5). So, the cache behavior under Cache Partition $\mathcal{P} = (C_1, C_2, ..., C_m)$ replacement policy is same as the cache behavior of every reference Ref_i $(1 \le i \le m)$ in $Cache_i$ with C_i cache lines respectively.

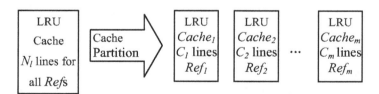

Cache misses for all *Refs* = sum($Cache_i$ misses for Ref_i) $(1 \le i \le m)$

Fig. 5. Cache Partition Replacement Policy $\mathcal{P} = (C_1, C_2, ..., C_m)$

Now, we use Presburger arithmetic[15] to exactly model the cache behavior of reference Ref_i $(1 \le i \le m)$ in $Cache_i$ with C_i cache lines. Mostly cache hits of a reference in a loop nest are produced by one or two reuse vectors of the reference, so we analyze primarily the cache behavior of a reference while only one or two reuse vectors of the reference are realized, but these conditions, that more than two reuse vectors are realized, are considered also. The cache behavior analyses have four steps:

1) When a reuse vector of a reference is realized in whole iteration space, the cache-hit iterations of the reference are formulated. For reuse vectors $\vec{r}$ of the reference Ref_i, a formula CHI($\vec{r}$) is generated. CHI($\vec{r}$) represents all cache-hit iterations when reuse vector $\vec{r}$ is realized in whole iteration space;

2) The number of cache lines, that $cache_i$ needed for to realize a reuse vector $\vec{r}$ of Ref_i in whole iteration space, is counted;

3) After steps 1 and 2, a *hits-cost pair*, <Hits, Cost>, for every reuse vector $\vec{r}$ of the reference Ref_i is constructed. This *hits-cost pair* <Hits, Cost> means that: if cache lines assigned to Ref_i is not less than the *cost*, namely $Cost \le C_i$, then Ref_i would produce cache hit *hits* times in whole iteration space by it's reuse vector $\vec{r}$. The set of hits-cost pairs of Ref_i is noted as $HCSet_i$.

4) According to $HCSet_i$ ($1 \le i \le m$), H_φ, the number of cache hits under the Cache Partition $\mathcal{P}$ replacement policy, is estimated, and then the Optimum Cache Partition, the Cache Partition that results in maximum cache hits, is derived.

The four steps are explained in further detail below.

1. Cache-Hit Iterations

When a reuse vector $\vec{r}$ of reference Ref_i is realized in whole iteration space S, the set of *cache-hit iterations* of reference Ref_i is formulated as CHI($\vec{r}$):

$$\text{CHI}(\vec{r}) = \left\{ \vec{p} \mid (\vec{p} \in S) \wedge (\exists \vec{p}' : (\vec{p}' \in S) \wedge (\vec{p} = \vec{p}' + \vec{r})) \right\} \quad (1)$$

The above formula means that reference Ref_i at iteration $\vec{p}$ can reuse through reuse vector $\vec{r}$ if and only if there is another iteration $\vec{p}'$ that can be hit by $\vec{p}$ through reuse vector $\vec{r}$, expressed as $\vec{p} = \vec{p}' + \vec{r}$.

The number of cache-hit iterations in CHI($\vec{r}$) can be calculated as following: (consider $\vec{r} = (r_1, r_2, ..., r_n)$)

$$|\text{CHI}(\vec{r})| = \prod_{i=1}^{n} (U_i - |r_i|) \quad (1.1)$$

For a spatial reuse vector $\vec{r}_s = (r_{s1}, r_{s2}, ..., r_{sn})$, formulas (1) and (1.1) is unsuitable. Cache behaviors of a loop nest with a spatial reuse vector are complicated. To get a concise formula for a spatial reuse vector, we modified formula (1.1) by appending a coefficient without a complicated model:

$$|\text{CHI}(\vec{r}_s)| = (\prod_{i=1}^{n} (U_i - |r_{si}|)) \times (\frac{b\vec{r}_s - 1}{b\vec{r}_s}) \quad (1.2)$$

In formula (1.2), $b\vec{r}_s$ stands for iteration times of the reference Ref_i in a single cache line along the spatial reuse vector $\vec{r}_s$. Among the $b\vec{r}_s$ times iterations in a single cache line, there are ($b\vec{r}_s - 1$) iterations to be reused, so the cache hits number of a spatial reuse vector has a coefficient ($b\vec{r}_s - 1$)/$b\vec{r}_s$.

When two reuse vectors $\vec{r}_1$ and $\vec{r}_2$ of reference Ref_i are realized in whole iteration space S, the set of *cache-hit iterations* of reference Ref_i is formulated as CHI($\vec{r}_1$, $\vec{r}_2$):

$$\text{CHI}(\vec{r}_1, \vec{r}_2) = \{\vec{p} \mid (\vec{p} \in S) \wedge (\exists \vec{p}': (\vec{p}' \in S) \wedge (\vec{p} = \vec{p}' + \vec{r}_1 \vee \vec{p} = \vec{p}' + \vec{r}_2))\} \quad (1')$$

When k reuse vectors $\vec{r}_1, \vec{r}_2, ..., \vec{r}_k$ of reference Ref_i are realized in whole iteration space S, the set of *cache-hit iterations* of reference Ref_i is formulated as CHI($\vec{r}_1$, $\vec{r}_2$, ..., $\vec{r}_k$):

$$\text{CHI}(\vec{r}_1, \vec{r}_2, ..., \vec{r}_k) =$$
$$\{\vec{p} \mid (\vec{p} \in S) \wedge (\exists \vec{p}': (\vec{p}' \in S) \wedge (\vec{p} = \vec{p}' + \vec{r}_1 \vee \vec{p} = \vec{p}' + \vec{r}_2 \vee ... \vee \vec{p} = \vec{p}' + \vec{r}_k))\}$$
$$(1'')$$

2. The Number of Cache Lines

This step is to count the number of cache lines NCL($\vec{r}$), that $cache_i$ needed for to realize a reuse vector $\vec{r}$ of Ref_i in whole iteration space. First, the iteration set ACI($\vec{r}$, $\vec{q}$) is defined. At any iteration $\vec{q} \in S$, if these data lines, accessed by Ref_i at these iterations in ACI($\vec{r}$, $\vec{q}$), is hold by $cache_i$, then the reuse vector $\vec{r}$ would be realized in whole iteration space. Furthermore, the number of cache lines NCL($\vec{r}$) in $cache_i$ is derived.

$$\forall \vec{q} \in S : \text{ACI}(\vec{r}, \vec{q}) = \{\vec{p} \mid (\vec{p} \in S) \wedge (\vec{p} + \vec{r} \in S) \wedge (\vec{p} \prec \vec{q}) \wedge (\vec{p} + \vec{r} \succ \vec{q})\}$$
$$(2)$$

ACI($\vec{r}$, $\vec{q}$) is similar as reference windows[14] which hold by a cache can result in the reuse vector $\vec{r}$ realized.

$$\text{NCL}(\vec{r}) = \max\{ |\text{ACI}(\vec{r}, \vec{q})| \mid \vec{q} \in S \} \quad (3)$$

When cache lines in $cache_i$ is not less than NCL($\vec{r}$), $cache_i$ can hold all data lines accessed at these iterations in ACI($\vec{r}$, $\vec{q}$), and then the reuse vector $\vec{r}$ would be realized in whole iteration space.

To avoid plentiful calculation for ACI($\vec{r}$, $\vec{q}$), we give a simple estimation formula (3.1). We observe that $|\text{ACI}(\vec{r}, \vec{q})|$ is not greater than $|\{\vec{p} \mid (\vec{p} \in S) \wedge (\vec{p} \prec \vec{q}) \wedge (\vec{p} + \vec{r} \succ \vec{q})\}|$ that is the number of the iteration points within a reuse vector $\vec{r}$ in the loop nest iteration space, so NCL($\vec{r}$) can be estimated as:

$$\text{NCL}(\vec{r}) \cong \sum_{i=1}^{n} (r_i * \prod_{j=i+1}^{n} U_j) \text{ where } \prod_{j=n+1}^{n} U_j = 1 \quad (3.1)$$

When two reuse vectors $\vec{r}_1$ and $\vec{r}_2$ of reference Ref_i are realized in whole iteration space S, the ACI($\vec{r}_1$, $\vec{r}_2$, $\vec{q}$) and NCL($\vec{r}_1$, $\vec{r}_2$) is formulated as following: (consider $\vec{r}_1 \prec \vec{r}_2$)

$\forall \vec{q} \in S : \text{ACI}(\vec{r}_1, \vec{r}_2, \vec{q}) = \text{ACI}(\vec{r}_1, \vec{q}) \cup$

$\{\vec{p} \mid (\vec{p} \in S) \wedge (\vec{p} + \vec{r}_2 \in S) \wedge (\vec{p} \prec \vec{q}) \wedge (\vec{p} + \vec{r}_2 \succ \vec{q}) \wedge (\vec{p} + \vec{r}_2 - \vec{r}_1 \notin S)\}$ (2')

$\text{NCL}(\vec{r}_1, \vec{r}_2) = \max\{ |\text{ACI}(\vec{r}_1, \vec{r}_2, \vec{q})| \mid \vec{q} \in S \}$ (3')

When two reuse vectors $\vec{r}_1, \vec{r}_2, \ldots, \vec{r}_k$ of reference Ref_i are realized in whole iteration space S, the $\text{ACI}(\vec{r}_1, \vec{r}_2, \ldots, \vec{r}_k, \vec{q})$ and $\text{NCL}(\vec{r}_1, \vec{r}_2, \ldots, \vec{r}_k)$ is formulated as following: (consider $\vec{r}_1 \prec \vec{r}_2 \prec \ldots \prec \vec{r}_k$)

$\forall \vec{q} \in S : \text{ACI}(\vec{r}_1, \vec{r}_2, \ldots, \vec{r}_k, \vec{q}) = \text{ACI}(\vec{r}_1, \vec{r}_2, \ldots, \vec{r}_{k-1}, \vec{q}) \cup$

$\{\vec{p} \mid (\vec{p} \in S) \wedge (\vec{p} + \vec{r}_k \in S) \wedge (\vec{p} \prec \vec{q}) \wedge (\vec{p} + \vec{r}_k \succ \vec{q}) \wedge$

$(\vec{p} + \vec{r}_k - \vec{r}_1 \notin S) \wedge \ldots \wedge (\vec{p} + \vec{r}_k - \vec{r}_{k-1} \notin S)\}$ (2'')

$\text{NCL}(\vec{r}_1, \vec{r}_2, \ldots, \vec{r}_k) = \max\{ |\text{ACI}(\vec{r}_1, \vec{r}_2, \ldots, \vec{r}_k, \vec{q})| \mid \vec{q} \in S \}$ (3'')

3. Hits-Cost Pairs Set

This *hits-cost pair*, *<Hits, Cost>*, means that: if cache lines C_i, assigned to Ref_i, is not less than the *Cost*, namely $Cost \leq C_i$, then Ref_i would produce cache hits *Hits* times in whole iteration space by it's reuse vectors. The set of hits-cost pairs of Ref_i is noted as $HCSet_i$.

$HCSet_i = \{ <0, 0>, < |\text{CHI}(\vec{r})|, \text{NCL}(\vec{r}) >, < |\text{CHI}(\vec{r}_1, \vec{r}_2)|, \text{NCL}(\vec{r}_1, \vec{r}_2) >, \ldots,$

$< |\text{CHI}(\vec{r}_1, \vec{r}_2, \ldots, \vec{r}_k)|, \text{NCL}(\vec{r}_1, \vec{r}_2, \ldots, \vec{r}_k) > \mid \vec{r}, \vec{r}_1, \vec{r}_2, \ldots, \vec{r}_k$

are reuse vectors of Ref_i \} (4)

The hits-cost pair $<0, 0>$ means that: no cache line assigned to Ref_i, no cache hit produced. $HCSet_i$ describes the relations of Ref_i between the number of cache lines and the number of cache hits. To calculate $HCSet_i$ in our experiments, these hits-cost pairs, $< |\text{CHI}(\vec{r}_1, \vec{r}_2, \ldots, \vec{r}_k)|, \text{NCL}(\vec{r}_1, \vec{r}_2, \ldots, \vec{r}_k) > (k > 2)$, were ignored, there are two reasons: i) the cache lines is not enough to realize more reuse vectors; ii) most cache hits of a reference is produced by one or two reuse vectors of the reference.

4. Optimum Cache Partition

To assign C_i cache lines to reference Ref_i under the Cache Partition $\mathcal{P}$ replacement policy, the number of cache hits of the reference Ref_i can be estimated as following:

$\text{Hit}_i(C_i) = \max \{ Hits \mid (<Hits, Cost> \in HCSet_i) \wedge (Cost \leq C_i) \}$ (5)

Under the Cache Partition $\mathcal{P} = (C_1, C_2, \ldots, C_m)$ replacement policy, cache hits of a loop nest can be estimated as follow:

$$H_{\mathcal{P}} = \sum_{i=1}^{m} [Hit_i(C_i)]$$ (6)

Formula (6) estimates cache hits number of a loop nest program under a Cache Partition. Different Cache Partitions can bring different cache hits number, a Cache

Partition, that brings the most cache hits, is called Optimum Cache Partition replacement policy.

Definition 2. Optimum Cache Partition of a loop nest. $\mathcal{P}$ is a Cache Partition of a loop nest, for any other Cache Partition $\mathcal{P}'$ if this inequation $H_{\mathcal{P}} \leq H_{\mathcal{P}'}$ is always true, then $\mathcal{P}$ is called *Optimum Cache Partition (OCP) for a loop nest.*

Figure 6 shows all hits-cost pairs for a MXM program while one temporal reuse vector or one spatial reuse vector is realized. The reference $X(k, i)$ has a temporal reuse vector $\vec{r}_t = (0,0,1)$, a spatial reuse vector $\vec{r}_s = (0,1,0)$. According to Formulas (1 ~ 6), when a temporal reuse vector $(0,0,1)$ is realized, there is a Hits-Cost pair < 990000, 1> that means if there is only 1 cache line assigned to reference $X(k, i)$, $X(k, i)$ would produce cache hit 990000 times by temporal reuse vector $(0,0,1)$; when a spatial reuse vector $(0,1,0)$ is realized, there is a Hits-Cost pair <742500, 100> that means if there is 100 cache line assigned to reference $X(k, i)$, $X(k, i)$ would produce cache hit 742500 times by spatial reuse vector $(0,1,0)$.

If there is 132 cache lines in a cache, $N_i = 132$, then Cache Partition $\mathcal{P} = (1, 1, 100)$ is a Optimum Cache Partition of the MXM loop nest, and under the OCP cache replacement policy the number of cache hits is estimated as following:

$H_{\mathcal{P}} = 990000+742500+990000 = 2722500$.

Ref_i	$\vec{r}_t$	$<Hits, Cost>$	$\vec{r}_s$	$< Hits, Cost >$
$X(k, i)$	$(0,0,1)$	$<990000, 1>$	$(0,1,0)$	$<742500,100>$
$Y(j, k)$	$(1,0,0)$	$<990000,10000>$	$(0,0,1)$	$<742500,1>$
$Z(j, i)$	$(0,1,0)$	$<990000,100>$	$(0,0,1)$	$<742500,1>$

Fig. 6. Hits-cost pairs for a MXM program where $U_1=U_2=U_3= 100$, cache line size $Ls = 16$ bytes, size of element in arrays is 4 bytes, then $b\,\vec{r}_s = 4$. If there is 132 cache lines in a cache, then Cache Partition $\mathcal{P} = (1, 1, 100)$ is a Optimum Cache Partition.

The Optimum Cache Partition(OCP) of a loop nest is a compiler-assisted cache replacement policy, that simplifies loop nest cache behavior, facilitates cache hits estimation, and decreases cache misses efficiently.

The OCP policy is carried out by the compiler according to following three primary steps: 1) Getting reuse vectors for loop nests. Reuse vectors can be calculated automatically according to some research works on loop optimization; 2) The Optimal Cache Partition is calculated automatically by the compiler; 3) Appending cache hints conditionally to realize the OCP policy.

Appending cache hints to a reference Ref_i to limit the number of cache lines hold by the reference is a difficult work if the limited cache lines number C_i is chosen discretionarily. But under the Optimum Cache Partition replacement policy, the limited cache lines number for a reference, C_i, is calculated based on it's reuse vector, and the condition for appending cache hints is straightforward.

Under OCP cache placement policy, if a reference Ref_i is limited to hold C_i cache lines, and is realized it's reuse vector $\vec{r}$, then at any loop iteration point $\vec{q}$, the condition of appending a cache hint to a reference Ref_i is that the reference Ref_i cannot produce a new reuse along the reuse vector $\vec{r}$ at the iteration point $\vec{q}$. Formally, when the point ($\vec{q} + \vec{r}$) is out of the loop iteration space, the reference Ref_i would be appended a cache hint on iteration point $\vec{q}$.

5   Experimental Results

5.1   Experimental Platform

We have implemented OCP cache replacement policy in the Trimaran compiler and evaluated its performance by running some SPEC benchmarks. Trimaran is a compiler infrastructure for supporting state of the art research in compiling for EPIC architectures. We have re-engineered the back-end of Trimaran. Implement of OCP cache replacement policy needed to update nothing but appending cache hints to some load/store instructions conditionally.

In the Trimaran compiler infrastructure, cache behavior is simulated in DineroIV that is a trace-driven cache simulator. We have extended DineroIV to support cache hints in memory instructions.

For a set associative cache, conflict misses may occur when too many data items map to the same set of cache locations. To eliminate or reduce conflict misses, we have implemented two data-layout transformations, inter- and intra-array padding[9].

5.2   Performance Results

We chosen 8 benchmarks from SPECint2000, and implemented OCP cache replacement policy on their loop kernels. We experimented our approach on 4K bytes caches with 64 bytes line size and varying associativity(4-way and full). Cache miss rates under LRU cache replacement policy and that under OCP cache replacement policy are compared in Table 1.

For a full associative cache, OCP policy is quite effective for all chosen benchmarks with average 24.04% cache misses reduction. For 4-way associative cache, OCP policy, reducing the number of cache misses by 16.59% averagely, is also quite effective except *vpr* and *vortex* benchmarks. The percentage reduction achieved on a 4-way cache is lower than that achieved by a full associative cache. This could be due to conflict misses produced by a set associative cache. The *vpr* and *vortex* benchmarks were likely to produce more conflict misses under OCP policy than under LRU replacement policy, so their cache miss rates under OCP is greater than under LRU in Table 1.

Table 1. Effective of OCP cache replacement policy in reducing cache misses. Row "LRU" reports cache miss rates under LRU replacement policy. Row "OCP" reports cache miss rates under OCP replacement policy. Row "Red." Gives the percentage reduction in cache miss rates due to our approach. There is average 20.32% cache misses reduction.

Cache		Benchmarks' cache miss rates (%)								
		gzip	vpr	gcc	mcf	parser	vortex	bzip2	twolf	average
4-way	LRU	2.56	5.72	1.96	11.2	2.24	1.71	1.18	3.66	
	OCP	2.13	5.75	1.61	6.51	1.87	1.77	0.98	2.68	
	Red.	**16.80%**	**-0.52%**	**17.86%**	**41.88%**	**16.52%**	**-3.51%**	**16.95%**	**26.78%**	**16.59%**
Full	LRU	2.53	4.57	1.86	10.9	1.94	1.36	1.04	3.35	
	OCP	1.81	3.91	1.44	6.32	1.58	1.18	0.83	2.25	
	Red.	**28.46%**	**14.44%**	**22.58%**	**42.02%**	**18.56%**	**13.24%**	**20.19%**	**32.84%**	**24.04%**

6 Related Work

Improving cache performance by cache hints has attracted a lot of attention from both the architecture and compiler perspective. In [10], keep and kill instructions are proposed by Jain et al. The keep instruction locks data into the cache, while the kill instruction indicates it as the first candidate to be replaced. Jain et al. also proof under which conditions the keep and kill instructions improve the cache hits rate. In [11], it is proposed to extend each cache line with an EM(Evict Me)-bit. The bit is set by software, based on a locality analysis. If the bit is set, that cache line is the first candidate to be evicted from the cache. These approaches all suggest interesting modifications to the cache hardware, which allow the compiler to improve the cache replacement policy.

Kristof Beyls et al proposed a framework to generate both source and target cache hints from the reuse distance metric in this paper [13]. Since the reuse distance indicates cache behavior irrespective of the cache size and associativity, it can be used to make caching decisions for all levels of cache simultaneously. Two methods were proposed to determine the reuse distances in the program, one based on profiling which statically assigns a cache hint to a memory instruction and one based on analytical calculation which allows to dynamically select the most appropriate hint. The advantage of the profiling-based method is that it works for all programs. The analytical calculation of reuse distances is applicable to loop-oriented code and has the advantage that the reuse distance is calculated independent of program input and for every single memory access. But their work, generating cache hints from the reuse distance, does have the cyclic dependency problem [12] mentioned in Section 1: Accurate reuse distance estimation must be known to cache hint assignment, while accurate reuse distance estimation is only possible when cache hint assignment is finalized. They ignored the impact of cache hints on the reuse distance.

Hongbo Yang et al [12] studied the relationship between cache miss rate and cache-residency of reference windows, known that in order for an array reference to realize its temporal reuse, its reference window must be fully accommodated in the cache. And then they formulated the problem as a 0/1 knapsack problem. The relationship between cache miss rate and cache-residency of reference windows is similar to the one considered in section 4.2, however our work has two major different aspects from their work:(i) we achieved cache hits analysis under the OCP cache replacement policy but they didn't in their 0/1 knapsack problem; (ii) we considered the impact of temporal and spatial reuse vectors on cache miss rate, while they have only considered the impact of reference windows that are decided by temporal reuse vectors.

7 Conclusions

EPIC architectures provide cache hints to allow the compiler to have more control on the data cache behavior. In this paper we constructed a compiler-assisted cache replacement policy, Optimum Cache Partition, which utilizes the cache more efficiently to achieve better performance. In particular, we presented a novel cache replacement policy, Cache Partition, which could be carried out through cache hints. Under the Cache Partition policy, we studied the relationship between cache hits rate and reuse vectors of a reference, and constructed hits-cost pairs of the reference. A hits-cost pair described a case: how many cache lines assigned to a reference could produce how many cache hits. After formulating cache hits number of a loop nest program under a Cache Partition, we could achieve Optimum Cache Partition replacement policy. To the best of our knowledge, the OCP cache replacement policy is the simplest effective cache optimization with cache hints, that results in plain cache behaviors and makes cache misses analyzing and optimizing easily and efficiently.

We evaluated our OCP cache replacement policy by implementing it in the Trimaran compiler and simulating cache behaviors in DineroIV. Our simulation results show that OCP policy exploited the architecture potential well. It reduced the number of data cache misses by 20.32% averagely.

References

1.   Kathryn S. McKinley and Olivier Temam.: Quantifying loop nest locality using spec'95 and the perfect benchmarks. ACM Transactions on Computer Systems (TOCS), 17(4) 288–336, 1999.
2.   V. Kathail, M. S. Schlansker, and B. R. Rau.: HPL-PD architecture specification: Version 1.1. Technical Report HPL-93-80 (R.1), Hewlett-Packard, February 2000.
3.   IA-64 Application Developer's Architecture Guide, May 1999.
4.   Michael E. Wolf and Monica S. Lam.: A data locality optimizing algorithm. In Proc. Of SIGPLAN PLDI '91, pages 30–44, Toronto, Ont., Jun. 1991.

5.   Guang R. Gao, Vivek Sarkar, and Shaohua Han.: Locality analysis for distributed sharedmemory multiprocesors. In Proc. of the 1996 International Workshop on Languages and Compilers for Parallel Computing(LCPC), San Jose, California, Aug 1996.
6.   Somnath Ghosh, Margaret Martonosi, and Sharad Malik.: Cache miss equations: An analytical representation of cache misses. In Conf. Proc., 1997 Intl. Conf. on Supercomputing,pages 317–324, Vienna, Austria, Jul. 1997.
7.   The Trimaran Compiler Research Infrastructure. www.trimaran.org
8.   Dinero IV Trace-Driven Uniprocessor Cache Simulator.
      http://www.cs.wisc.edu/~markhill/DineroIV
9.   G. Rivera and C.-W. Tseng.: Eliminating conflict misses for high performance architectures. In ACM Internacional Conference on Supercomputing (ICS'98),1998
10.   P.Jain, S.Devadas, D.Engels, and L.Rudolph.: Software-assisted replacement mecharisms for embedded systems. In International Conference on Computer Aided Design, pages 119-126, nov 2001.
11.   Z.Wang, K.McKinley, A.Rosenberg, and C.Weems.: Using the compiler to improve cache replacement decisions.In PACT'02, September 2002.
12.   Hongbo Yang, R. Govindarajan, Guang R. Gao, and Ziang Hu.: Compiler-assisted cache replacement: Problem formulation and performance evaluation. In Proceedings of the 16th International Workshop on Languages and Compilers for Parallel Compuing (LCPC' 03), College Station, Texas, Oct 2003.
13.   Kristof Beyls and Erik H.D'Hollander.: Compile-Time Cache Hint Generation for EPIC Architectures. In Proceedings of the 2nd International Workshop on Explicitly Parallel Instruction Computing (EPIC) Architectures and Compiler Techniques, Istanbul, Turkey, November 2002.
14.   Dennis Gannon, William Jalby, and Kyle Gallivan.: Strategies for cache and local memory management by global programming transformation. Journal of Parallel and Distributed Computing, 5(5):587–616, October 1988.
15.   W. Pugh.: Counting solutions to Presburger formulas: How and why. ACM SIGPLAN Notices, 29(6):121-134, jun 1994.

Modeling the Cache Behavior of Codes with Arbitrary Data-Dependent Conditional Structures*

Diego Andrade, Basilio B. Fraguela, and Ramón Doallo

Universidade da Coruña
Dept. de Electrónica e Sistemas
Facultade de Informática
Campus de Elviña, 15071 A Coruña, Spain
{dcanosa,basilio,doallo}@udc.es

Abstract. Analytical modeling is one of the most interesting approaches to evaluate the memory hierarchy behavior. Unfortunately, models have many limitations regarding the structure of the code they can be applied to, particularly when the path of execution depends on conditions calculated at run-time that depend on the input or intermediate data. In this paper we extend in this direction a modular analytical modeling technique that provides very accurate estimations of the number of misses produced by codes with regular access patterns and structures while having a low computing cost. Namely, we have extended this model in order to be able to analyze codes with data-dependent conditionals. In a previous work we studied how to analyze codes with a single and simple conditional sentence. In this work we introduce and validate a general and completely systematic strategy that enables the analysis of codes with any number of conditionals, possibly nested in any arbitrary way, while allowing the conditionals to depend on any number of items and atomic conditions.

1 Introduction

Memory hierarchies try to cushion the increasing gap between the processor and the memory speed. Fast and accurate methods to evaluate the performance of the memory hierarchies are needed in order to guide the compiler in choosing the best transformations and parameters for them when trying to make the optimal usage of this hierarchy. Trace-driven simulation [1] was the preferred approach to study the memory behavior for many years. This technique is very accurate, but its high computational cost makes it unsuitable for many applications. This way, analytical modeling, which requires much shorter computing times than previous approaches and provides more information about the reasons for the predicted

---

* This work has been supported in part by the Ministry of Science and Technology of Spain under contract TIC2001-3694-C02-02, and by the Xunta de Galicia under contract PGIDIT03-TIC10502PR.

P.-C. Yew and J. Xue (Eds.): ACSAC 2004, LNCS 3189, pp. 44–57, 2004.

behavior, has gained importance in recent years [2,3,4]. Still, it has important drawbacks like the lack of modularity in some models, and the limited set of codes that they can model.

In this work we present an extension to an existing analytical model that allows to analyze codes with any kind of conditional sentences. The model was already improved in [5] to enable it to analyze codes with a reference inside a simple and single conditional sentence. We now extend it to analyze codes with any kind and number of conditional sentences, even with references controlled by several nested conditionals, and nested in any arbitrary way. Like in previous works, we require the verification of the conditions in the IF statements to follow an uniform distribution.

This model is built around the idea of the Probabilistic Miss Equations (PMEs) [2]. These equations estimate analytically the number of misses generated by a given code in set-associative caches with LRU replacement policy. The PME model can be applied both to perfectly nested loops and imperfectly nested loops, with one loop per nesting level. It allows several references per data structure and loops controlled by other loops. Loop nests with several loops per level can also be analyzed by this model, although certain conditions need to be fulfilled in order to obtain accurate estimations. This work is part of an ongoing research line whose aim is to build a compiler framework [6,7], which extracts information from the analytical modeling, in order to optimize the execution of complete scientific codes.

The rest of the paper is organized as follows. The next section presents some important concepts to understand the PME model and our extension. Section 3 describes the process of formulation after adapting the previous existing model to the new structures it has to model. In Sect. 4 we describe the process of validation of our model, using codes with several conditional sentences. A brief review of the related work is presented in Sect. 5, followed by our conclusions and a discussion on the future work in Sect. 6.

2   Introduction to the PME Model

The Probabilistic Miss Equations (PME) model, described in [2], generates accurately and efficiently cache behavior predictions for codes with regular access patterns. The model classifies misses as either compulsory or interference misses. The former take place the first time that the lines are accessed, while the latter are associated to new accesses for which the corresponding cache line has been evicted since its previous access. The PME model builds an equation for each reference and nesting level that encloses the reference. This equation estimates the number of misses generated by the reference in that loop taking into account both kinds of misses. Its probabilistic nature comes from the fact that interference misses are estimated through the computation of a miss interference probability for every attempt of reuse of a line.

2.1 Area Vectors

The miss probability when attempting to reuse a line depends on the cache footprint of the regions accessed since the immediately preceding reference to the considered line. The PME model represents these footprints by means of what it calls *area vectors*. Given a data structure V and a k-way set-associative cache, $S_V = S_{V_0}, S_{V_1}, \ldots, S_{V_k}$ is the area vector associated with the access to V during a given period of the program execution. The i-th element, $i > 0$, of this vector represents the ratio of sets that have received $k - i$ lines from the structure; while S_{V_0} is the ratio of sets that have received k or more lines.

The PME model analyzes the access pattern of the references for each different data structure found in a program and derives the corresponding area vectors from the parameters that define those access patterns. The two most common access patterns found in the kind of codes we intend to model are the sequential access and the access to groups of elements separated by a constant stride. See [2] for more information about how the model estimates the area vectors from the access pattern parameters.

Due to the existence of references that take place with a given probability in codes with data-dependent conditionals, a new kind of access pattern arises in them that we had not previously analyzed. This pattern can ben described as an access to groups of consecutive elements separated by a constant stride, in which every access happens with a given fixed probability. The calculation of the area vector associated to this new access pattern is not included in this paper because of size limitations. This pattern will be denoted as $R_{rl}(M, N, P, p)$, which represents the access to M groups of N elements separated by a distance P where every access happens with a given probability p (see example in Sect. 4).

Very often, several data structures are referenced between two accesses to the same line of a data structure. As a result, a mechanism is needed to calculate the global area vector that represents as a whole the impact on the cache of the accesses to several structures. This is achieved by adding the area vectors associated to the different data structures. The mechanism to add two area vectors has also been described in [2], so although it is used in the following sections, we do not explain it here. The addition algorithm treats the different ratios in the area vectors as independent probabilities, thus disregarding the relative positions of the data structures in memory. This is in fact an advantage of the model, as in most situations these addresses are unknown at compile time (dynamically allocated data structures, physically indexed caches, etc.). This way, the PME model is still able to generate reasonable predictions in these cases, as opposed to most of those in the bibliography [3,4], which require the base addresses of the data structures in order to generate their estimations. Still, when such positions are known, the PME model can estimate the overlapping coefficients of the footprints associated with the accesses to each one of the structures involved, so they can be used to improve the accuracy of the addition.

```
DO I₀=1, N₀, L₀
   DO I₁=1, N₁, L₁
      ...
      IF cond(D(f_D1(I_D1), ..., f_DdD(I_DdD)))
         ...
         DO I_Z=1, N_Z, L_Z
            A(f_A1(I_A1), ..., f_AdA(I_AdA))
            ...
            IF cond(B(f_B1(I_B1), ..., f_BdB(I_BdB)))
               C(f_C1(I_C1), ..., f_CdC(I_CdC))
               ...
            END IF
            ...
         END DO
         ...
      END IF
      ...
   END DO
END DO
```

Fig. 1. Nested loops with several data-dependent conditions

2.2 Scope of Application

The original PME model in [2] did not support the modeling of codes with any kind of conditionals. Figure 1 shows the kind of codes that it can analyze after applying our extension. The figure shows several nested loops that have a constant number of iterations known at compile time. Several references, which need not be in the innermost nesting level, are found in the code. Some references are affected by one or more nested conditional sentences that depend on the data arrays. All the structures are indexed using affine functions of the loop indexes $f_{A1}(I_{A1}) = \alpha_{A1} I_{A1} + \delta_{A1}$. We assume also that the verification of the conditions in the IF statements follows an uniform distribution, although the different conditions may hold with different probabilities. Such probabilities are inputs to our model that are obtained either by means of profiling tools, or knowledge of the behavior of the application. We assume also the conditions are independent.

As for the hardware, the PME model is oriented to set-associative caches with LRU replacement policy. In what follows, we will refer to the total size of this cache as C_s, to the line size as L_s, and k will be the degree of associativity or number of lines per set.

3 Miss Equations

The PME model estimates the number of misses generated by a code using the concept of miss equation. Given a reference, the analysis of its behavior begins in the innermost loop containing it, and proceeds outwards. In this analysis, a probabilistic miss equation is generated for each reference and in each nesting level that encloses it following a series of rules.

We will refer as $F_i(R, \text{RegInput}, \vec{p})$ to the miss equation for reference R in nesting level i. Its expression depends on RegInput, the region accessed since the last access to a given line of the data structure. Since we now consider the existence of conditional sentences, the original PME parameters have been extended with a new one, $\vec{p}$. This vector contains in position j the probability p_j that the (possible) conditionals that guard the execution of the reference R in nesting level j are verified. If no conditionals are found in level j, then $p_j = 1$. When there are several nested IF statements in the same nesting level, p_j corresponds to the product of their respective probabilities of holding their respective conditions. This is a first improvement with respect to our previous approach [5], which used a scalar because only a single conditional was considered.

Depending on the situation, two different kinds of formulas can be applied:

- If the variable associated to the current loop i does not index any of the references found in the condition(s) of the conditional(s) sentence(s), then we apply a formula from the group of formulas called *Condition Independent Reference Formulas* (CIRF). This is the kind of PME described in [2].
- If the loop variable indexes any of such references, then we apply a formula from the group called *Condition Dependent Reference Formulas* (CDRF).

Another factor influencing the construction of a PME is the existence of other references to same data structure, as they may carry some kind of group reuse. For simplicity, in what follows we will restrict our explanation to references that carry no reuse with other references.

3.1   Condition Independent Reference Formulas

When the index variable for the current loop i is not among those used in the indexing of the variables referenced in the conditional statements that enclose the reference R, the PME for this reference and nesting level is given by

$$
\begin{aligned}
F_i(R, \text{RegInput}, \vec{p}) = & L_{Ri} F_{i+1}(R, \text{RegInput}, \vec{p}) \\
& + (N_i - L_{Ri}) F_{i+1}(R, \text{Reg}(A, i, 1), \vec{p}) ,
\end{aligned}
\tag{1}
$$

being N_i the number of iterations in the loop of the nesting level i, and L_{Ri} the number of iterations in which there is no possible reuse for the lines referenced by R. $\text{Reg}(A, i, j)$ stands for the memory region accessed during j iterations of the loop in the nesting level i that can interfere with data structure A.

The formula calculates the number of misses for a given reference R in nesting level i, as the sum of two values. The first one is the number of misses produced by the L_{Ri} iterations in which there can be no reuse in this loop. The miss probability for these iterations depends on the accesses and reference pattern in the outer loops. The second value corresponds to the iterations in which there can be reuse of cache lines accessed in the previous iteration, and so it depends on the memory regions accesses during one iteration of the loop.

The indexes of the reference R are affine functions of the variables of the loops that enclose it. As a result, R has a constant stride S_{Ri} along the iterations of loop i. This value is calculated as $S_{Ri} = \alpha_{A_j} d_{A_j}$, where j is the dimension whose index depends on I_i, the variable of the loop; α_{A_j} is the scalar that multiplies the loop variable in the affine function, and d_{A_j} is the size of the j-th dimension. If I_i does not index reference R, then $S_{Ri} = 0$. This way, L_{Ri} can be calculated as,

$$L_{Ri} = 1 + \left\lfloor \frac{N_i - 1}{max\{L_s/S_{Ri}, 1\}} \right\rfloor , \tag{2}$$

The formula calculates the number of accesses of R that cannot exploit either spatial or temporal locality, which is equivalent to estimating the number of different lines that are accessed during N_i iterations with stride S_{Ri}.

3.2   Condition Dependent Reference Formulas

If the index variable for the curret loop i is used in the indexes of the arrays used in the conditions that control the reference R, the behavior of R with respect to this loop is irregular. The reason is that different values of the index access different pieces of data to test in the conditions. This way, in some iterations the conditions hold and R is executed, thus affecting the cache, while in other iterations the associated conditions do not hold and no access of R takes place. As a result, the reuse distance for the accesses of R is no longer fixed: it depends on the probabilities $\vec{p}$ that the conditions that control the execution of R are verified. If the probabilities the different conditions hold are known, the number of misses associated to the different reuse distances can be weighted using the probability each reuse distante takes place.

As we have just seen, eq. (2) estimates the number L_{Ri} of iterations of the loop in level i in which reference R cannot explote reuse. Since the loop has N_i iterations, this means on average each different line can be reused in up to $G_{Ri} = N_i/L_{Ri}$ consecutive iterations. Besides, either directly reference R or the loop in level $i + 1$ that contains it can be inside a conditional in level i that holds with probability p_i. Thus, $p_i L_{Ri}$ different groups of lines will be accessed on average, and each one of them can be reused up to G_{Ri} times. Taking this into account, the general form of a condition-dependent PME is

$$F_i(R, \text{RegInput}, \vec{p}) = p_i L_{Ri} \sum_{j=1}^{G_{Ri}} \text{WMR}_i(R, \text{RegInput}, j, \vec{p}) . \tag{3}$$

where $\text{WMR}_i(\text{RegInput}, j, \vec{p})$ is the weighted number of misses generated by reference R in level i considering the j-th attempt of reuse of the G_{Ri} ones potentially possible. As in Sect. 3.1, RegInput is the region accessed since the last access to a given line of the considered data structure when the execution of the loop begins. Notice that if no condition encloses R or the loop around it in this level, simply $p_i = 1$.

The number of misses associated to reuse distance j weigthed with the probability an access with such reuse distante does take place, is calculated as

$$
\mathrm{WMR}_i(\mathrm{RegInput}, j, \vec{p}) = (1 - P_i(R, \vec{p}))^{j-1} F_{i+1}(R, \mathrm{RegInput} \cup \mathrm{Reg}(A, i, j-1), \vec{p}) +
$$
$$
\sum_{k=1}^{j-1} P_i(R, \vec{p})(1 - P_i(R, \vec{p}))^{k-1} F_{i+1}(R, \mathrm{Reg}(A, i, k-1), \vec{p}) ,
$$

$$(4)$$

where $P_i(R, \vec{p})$ yields the probability that R accesses each of the lines it can potentially reference during one iteration of the loop in nesting level i. This probability is a function of those conditionals in $\vec{p}$ in or below the nesting level analyzed. The first term in (4) considers the case that the line has not been accessed during any of the previous $j - 1$ iterations. In this case, the RegInput region that could generate interference with the new access to the line when the execution of the loop begins must be added to the regions accessed during these $j-1$ previous iterations of the loop in order to estimate the complete interference region. The second term weights the probability that the last access took place in each of the $k = 1, \ldots, j - 1$ previous iterations of the considered loop.

Line Access Probability. The probability $P_i(R, \vec{p})$ that the reference R whose behavior is being analyzed does access one of the lines that belong to the region that it can potentially access during one iteration of loop i is a basic parameter to derive $\mathrm{WMR}_i(\mathrm{RegInput}, j, \vec{p})$, as we have just seen. This probability depends not only on the access pattern of the reference in this nesting level, but also in the inner ones, so its calculation takes into account all the loops from the i-th down to the one containing the reference. If fact, this probability is calculated recursively in the following way:

$$
P_i(R, \vec{p}) = \begin{cases} p_i & \text{if } i \text{ is the innermost loop} \\ & \text{that contains } R \\ p_i P_{i+1}(R, \vec{p}) & \text{if the index of loop } i + 1 \text{ is} \\ & \text{not used in the references} \\ & \text{in conditions that control } R \\ p_i(1 - (1 - P_{i+1}(R, \vec{p}))^{G_{R_{i+1}}}) & \text{otherwise} \end{cases} \quad (5)
$$

where we must remember that p_i is the product of all the probabilities associated to the conditional sentences affecting R that are located in nesting level i.

This algorithm to estimate the probability of access per line at level i has been improved with respect to our previous work [5], as it is now able to integrate different conditions found in different nesting levels, while the previous one only considered a single condition.

```
posB=1
DO I=1,N
    offB(I)=posB
    DO J=1,M
        IF A(I,J).NEQ.0
            B(posB)=A(I,J)
            jB(posB)=J
            posB=posB+1
        ENDIF
    ENDDO
ENDDO
```

Fig. 2. CRS Storage Algorithm

```
DO I=1,M
  DO K=1,N
    IF A(I,K).NEQ.0
      DO J=1,P
        IF B(K,J).NEQ.0
          C(I,J)=C(I,J)+A(I,K)*B(K,J)
        ENDIF
      ENDDO
    ENDIF
  ENDDO
ENDDO
```

Fig. 3. Optimized product of matrices

3.3   Calculation of the Number of Misses

In the innermost level that contains the reference R, both in CIRFs and CDRFs, $F_{i+1}(R, \text{RegInput}, \vec{p})$, the number of misses caused by the reference in the immediately inner level is $AV_0(\text{RegInput})$, this is, the first element in the area vector associated to the region RegInput.

The number of misses generated by reference R in the analyzed nest is finally estimated as $F_0(R, \text{RegInput}_{\text{total}}, \vec{p})$ once the PME for the outermost loop is generated. In this expression, $\text{RegInput}_{\text{total}}$ is the total region, this is, the region that covers the whole cache. The miss probability associated with this region is one.

4   Model Validation

We have validated our model by applying it manually to the two quite simple but representative codes shown in Fig. 2 and Fig. 3. The first code implements the storage of a matrix in CRS format (Compressed Row Storage), which is widely used in the storage of sparse matrices. It has two nested loops and a conditional sentence that affects three of the references. The second code is an optimized product of matrices; that consists of a nest of loops that contain references inside several nested conditional sentences.

Results for both codes will be shown in Sect. 4.2, but we will first focus on the second code in order to provide a detailed idea about the modeling procedure.

4.1   Optimized Product Modeling

This code is shown in Fig. 3. It implements the product between two matrix, A and B, with a uniform distribution of nonzero entries. As a first optimization, when the element of A to be used in the current product is 0, then all its products with the corresponding elements of B are not performed. As a final optimization, if the element of B to be used in the current product is 0 then that operation is not performed. This avoids two floating point operations and the load and storage of C(I,J).

Without loss of generality, we assume a compiler that maps scalar variables to registers and which tries to reuse the memory values recently read in processor registers. Under these conditions, the code in Fig. 3 contains three references to memory. The model in [2] can estimate the behavior of the references A(I,K), which take place in every iteration of their enclosing loops.

Thus, we will focus our explanation on the modeling of the behavior of the references C(I,J) and B(K,J) which are not covered in previous publications.

C(I,J) **Modeling.** The analysis begins in the innermost loop, in level 2. In this level the loop variable indexes one of the reference of one of the conditions, so the CDRF formula must be applied.

As $S_{R2} = P$, $L_{R2} = 1 + N$, $G_{R2} \simeq 1$ and p_2 is the component in vector $\vec{p}$ associated to the probability that the condition inside the loop in nesting level 2 holds. This loop is in the innermost level. Thus, $F_3(R, \text{RegInput}, \vec{p}) = AV_0(\text{RegInput})$, then after the simplification the formulation is,

$$F_2(R, \text{RegInput}, \vec{p}) = p_2 P AV_0(\text{RegInput}) . \tag{6}$$

In the next upper level, level 1, the loop variable indexes one reference of one of the conditions, so the CDRF formula has to be applied. Let $S_{R1} = 0$, $L_{R1} = 1$ and $G_{R1} \simeq N$, then

$$F_1(R, \text{RegInput}, \vec{p}) = p_1 \sum_{j=1}^{N} \text{WMR}_1(R, \text{RegInput}, j, \vec{p}) . \tag{7}$$

In order to compute WMR_1 we need to calculate the value for two functions. One is $P_1(R, \vec{p})$, which for our reference takes the value $p_1 p_2$, where p_i is the i-th element in vector $\vec{p}$. The other one is $\text{Reg}(C, 1, i)$, the region accessed during i iterations of the loop 1 that can interfere with the accesses to C.

$$\text{Reg}(C, 1, i) = R_{rl_{\text{auto}}}(P, 1, M, 1 - (1 - p_1 p_2)^i)$$
$$\cup R_r(i, 1, M) \cup R_{rl}(P, i, N, p_1) . \tag{8}$$

The first term is associated to the autointerference of C, which is the access to P groups of one element separated by a difference M and every access takes places with a given probability. The second term represents the access to i groups of 1 element separated by a distance M. The last element represents the access to P groups of i elements separated by a distance N. Every access is going to happen with a given probability p_1.

In the outermost level, the loop variable indexes the reference of the condition. As a result, the CDRF formula is to be applied again. Being $S_{R0} = 1$, $L_{R0} = 1 + \lfloor (N - 1)/L_s \rfloor$ and $G_{R0} \simeq L_s$, so the formulation is

$$F_0(R, \text{RegInput}, \vec{p}) = (1 + \lfloor (N - 1)/L_s \rfloor) \sum_{j=1}^{L_s} \text{WMR}_0(R, \text{RegInput}, j, \vec{p}) . \tag{9}$$

As before, two functions must be evaluated to compute WMR_0. They are $P_0(R, \vec{p}) = 1 - (1 - p_1 p_2)^N$ and $\text{Reg}(C, 0, i)$, given by

$$\text{Reg}(C, 0, i) = R_{rl_{\text{auto}}}(P, 1, M, 1 - (1 - p_1 p_2)^N)$$
$$\cup R_r(N, i, M) \cup R_l(PN, 1 - (1 - p_1)^{L_s}) . \tag{10}$$

The first term is associated to the autointerference of C, which is the access to P groups of one element separated by a difference M and every access takes places with a given probability. The second term represents the access to N groups of i elements separated by a distance M. The last element represents the access to PN consecutive elements with a given probability.

B(K,J) **Modeling.** The innermost loop for this reference is also the one in level 2. The variable that controls this loop, J, is found in the indexes of a reference found in the condition of an IF statements (in this case, the innermost one), one conditional, so a CDRF is to be built. As this is the innermost loop, we get $F_3(R, \text{RegInput}, \vec{p}) = AV_0 RegInput$. Since $S_{R_i} = N$, $L_{R_i} = P$ and $G_{R_i} = 1$ the formulation for this nesting level is

$$F_2(R, S(\text{RegInput}), \vec{p}) = PAV_0(\text{RegInput}) . \tag{11}$$

The next level is level 1. In this level the variable of the loops indexes any of the reference of any of the conditional, so we have to use the CDRF formula. Being $S_{R1} = 1$, $L_{R1} = 1 + \lfloor (N - 1)/L_s \rfloor$ and $G_{R1} \simeq L_s$ the formulation is

$$F_1(R, \text{RegInput}, \vec{p}) = p_1 \left(1 + \left\lfloor \frac{N-1}{L_s} \right\rfloor\right) \sum_{j=1}^{L_s} \text{WMR}_1(R, \text{RegInput}, j, \vec{p}) . \tag{12}$$

We need to know $P_1(R, \vec{p}) = p_1$ and the value of the accessed regions $\text{Reg}(B, 1, i)$ in order to compute WMR_1:

$$\text{Reg}(B, 1, i) = Rrl_{\text{auto}}(P, i, N, p_1]) \cup R_r(i, 1, M) \cup R_{rl}(P, 1, M, p_1 p_2) . \tag{13}$$

Table 1. Validation data for the code in Fig. 2 for several cache configurations and different problem sizes and condition probabilities

M	N	p	C_s	L_s	K	Δ_{MR}	T_{sim}	T_{exe}	T_{mod}
6200	10150	0.4	32K	8	4	0.001	82	19	0.001
4200	17150	0.1	4K	4	2	0.401	107	18	0.001
16220	7200	0.2	16K	4	2	2.635	152	24	0.044
6200	14250	0.3	32K	8	4	0.005	146	22	0.001
9200	14250	0.1	4K	4	8	2.374	582	50	0.001
1100	15550	0.5	4K	4	8	0.027	2	1	0.001
2900	17250	0.3	32K	16	4	1.847	65	32	0.001
8900	9250	0.1	64K	8	4	3.055	118	46	0.010
4200	12150	0.1	4K	4	2	0.571	64	33	0.001
5000	15000	0.3	32K	8	4	0.183	125	54	0.001
7200	12250	0.1	4K	4	8	0.044	139	64	0.010

The first term is associated to the autointerference of B, which is the access to P groups of i elements separated by a difference N and every access takes places with a given probability. The second term represents the access to i groups of one element separated by a distance M. The last element represents the access to P groups of one element separated by a distance M, every access takes places with a given probability $p_1 p_2$.

In the outermost level, the level 0, the variable of the loop indexes a reference in one of the conditions, so we have to apply again the CDRF formula. Being $S_{R0} = 0$, $L_{R0} = 1$, $G_{R0} \simeq M$, so the formulation is

$$F_0(R, \text{RegInput}, \vec{p}) = \sum_{j=1}^{M} \text{WMR}_0(R, \text{RegInput}, j, \vec{p}) \ . \tag{14}$$

In this loop, WMR_0 is a function of $P_0(R, \vec{p} = 1 - (1 - p_1)^{L_s}$ and the value of the accessed regions $\text{Reg}(B, 0, i)$:

$$\text{Reg}(B, 0, i) = R_{l_{\text{auto}}}(PN, 1 - (1 - p_1)^{L_s}) \cup R_r(N, i, M)$$
$$\cup R_{rl}(P, i, M, 1 - (1 - p_1 p_2)^N) \ . \tag{15}$$

The first term is associated to the autointerference of B, which is the access to PN elements with a given probability. The second term represents the access to N groups of i elements separated by a distance M. The last element represents the access to P groups of i elements separated by a distance M, every access takes places with a given probability.

4.2   Validation Results

We have done the validation by comparing the results of the predictions given by the model with the results of a trace-driven simulation. We have tried several cache configurations, problem sizes and probabilities for the conditional sentences.

Table 2. Validation data for the code in Fig. 3 for several cache configurations and different problem sizes and condition probabilities

M	N	P	p_1	p_2	C_s	L_s	K	Δ_{MR}	T_{sim}	T_{exe}	T_{mod}
750	750	1000	0.2	0.1	16K	8	8	0.808	35	17	0.075
750	750	1000	0.8	0.3	8K	16	16	5.081	164	62	0.053
900	850	900	0.8	0.1	16K	32	2	0.224	78	54	0.795
900	850	900	0.9	0.1	64K	8	8	0.589	136	66	0.523
900	950	1500	0.8	0.3	16K	4	2	2.411	236	159	0.110
900	950	1500	0.1	0.4	32K	8	4	5.408	51	38	0.357
1000	850	900	0.7	0.5	4K	8	2	4.394	98	97	0.054
200	250	150	0.8	0.2	16K	4	2	0.604	1	0	0.690
200	250	150	0.1	0.3	32K	8	4	2.161	0	0	0.145
200	250	150	0.3	0.1	4K	4	8	1.208	0	0	0.008
100	350	90	0.8	0.5	4K	4	8	0.070	0	1	0.042
100	350	90	0.4	0.4	8K	8	4	0.417	0	0	0.324
100	350	90	0.2	0.3	4K	8	2	0.744	0	0	0.218

Tables 1 and 2 display the validation results for the codes in Fig. 2 and 3, respectively. In Table 1 the two first columns contain the problem size and the third column stands for the probability p that the condition in the code is fulfilled. In Table 2 the first three columns contain the problem size, while the next two columns contain the probabilities p_1 and p_2 that each of of the two conditions in Fig. 3 is fulfilled. Then the cache configuration is given in both tables by C_s, the cache size, L_s, the line size, and the degree of associativity of the cache, K. The sizes are measured in the number of elements of the arrays used in the codes. The accuracy of the model is used by the metric Δ_{MR}, which is based on the miss rate (MR); it stands for the absolute value of the difference between the predicted and the measured miss rate.

For every combination of cache configuration, problem size and probabilities of the conditions, 25 different simulations have been made using different base addresses for the data structures.

The results show that the model provides a good estimation of the cache behavior in the two example codes. The last three columns in both tables reflect the corresponding simulation times, source code execution time and modeling times expressed in seconds and measured in a 2,08 Ghz AMD K7 processor-based system. We can see that the modeling times are much smaller than the trace-driven simulation and even execution times. Furthermore, modeling times are several orders of magnitude shorter than trace-driven simulation and even execution times. The modeling time does not include the time required to build the formulas for the example codes. This will be made automatically by the tool we are currently developing. According to our experience in [2], the overhead of such tool is negligible.

5   Related Work

Over the years, several analytical models have been proposed to study the behavior of caches. Probably the most well-known model of this kind is [8], based on the Cache Miss Equations (CMEs), which are lineal systems of Diophantine equations. Its main drawbacks are its high computational cost and that it is restricted to analyzing regular access patterns that take place in isolated perfectly nested loops. In the past few years, some models that can overcome some of these limitations have arisen. This is the case of the accurate model based on Presburger formulas introduced in [3], which can analyze codes with non-perfectly nested loops and consider reuses between loops in different nesting levels. Still, it can only model small levels of associativity and it has a extremely high computational cost. More recently [4], which is based on [8], can also analyze these kinds of codes in competitive times thanks to the statistical techniques it applies in the resolution of the CMEs.

A more recent work [9], can model codes with conditional statements. Still, it does not consider conditions on the input or intermediate data computed by the programs. It is restricted to conditional sentences whose conditions refer to the variables that index the loops.

All these models and others in the bibliography have fundamental differences with ours. One of the most important ones is that all of them require a knowledge about the base address of the data structures. In practice this is not possible or useful in many situations because of a wide variety of reasons: data structures allocated at run-time, physically-indexed caches, etc. Also, thanks to the general strategy described in this paper, the PME model becomes the first one to be able to model codes with data-dependent conditionals.

6   Conclusions and Future Work

In this work we have presented an extension to the PME model described in [2]. The extension allows this model to be the first one that can analyze codes with data-dependent conditionals and considering, not only simple conditional sentences but also nested conditionals affecting a given reference. We are currently limited by the fact that the conditions must follow an uniform distribution, but we think our research is an important step in the direction of broadening the scope of applicability of analytical models. Our validation shows that this model provides accurate estimations of the number of misses generated by a given code while requiring quite short computing times. In fact the model is typically two orders of maginute faster than the native execution of the code.

The properties of this model turn it into an ideal tool to guide the optimization process in a production compiler. In fact, the original PME model has been used to guide the optimization process in a compiler framework [7]. We are now working in an automatic implementation of the extension of the model described in this paper in order to integrate it in that framework. As for the scope of the program structures that we wish to be amenable to analysis using the PME model, our next step will be to consider codes with irregular accesses due to the use of indirections or pointers.

References

1. Uhlig, R., Mudge, T.: Trace-Driven Memory Simulation: A Survey. ACM Computing Surveys **29** (1997) 128–170
2. Fraguela, B.B., Doallo, R., Zapata, E.L.: Probabilistic Miss Equations: Evaluating Memory Hierarchy Performance. IEEE Transactions on Computers **52** (2003) 321–336
3. Chatterjee, S., Parker, E., Hanlon, P., Lebeck, A.: Exact Analysis of the Cache Behavior of Nested Loops. In: Proc. of the ACM SIGPLAN'01 Conference on Programming Language Design and Implementation (PLDI'01). (2001) 286–297
4. Vera, X., Xue, J.: Let's Study Whole-Program Behaviour Analytically. In: Proc. of the 8th Int'l Symposium on High-Performance Computer Architecture (HPCA8). (2002) 175–186
5. Andrade, D., Fraguela, B., Doallo, R.: Cache behavior modeling of codes with data-dependent conditionals. In Springer-Verlag, ed.: 7th Intl. Workshop on Software and Compilers for Embedded Systems, SCOPES 2003. Volume 2826 of Lecture Note in Computer Science. (2003) 373–387
6. Blume, W., Doallo, R., Eigenmann, R., Grout, J., Hoeflinger, J., Lawrence, T., Lee, J., Padua, D., Paek, Y., Pottenger, B., Rauchwerger, L., Tu, P.: Parallel Programming with Polaris. IEEE Computer **29** (1996) 78–82
7. Fraguela, B.B., Touri o, J., Doallo, R., Zapata, E.L.: A compiler tool to predict memory hierarchy performance of scientific codes. Parallel Computing **30** (2004) 225–248
8. Ghosh, S., Martonosi, M., Malik, S.: Cache Miss Equations: A Compiler Framework for Analyzing and Tuning Memory Behavior. ACM Transactions on Programming Languages and Systems **21** (1999) 702–745
9. Vera, X., Xue, J.: Efficient Compile-Time Analysis of Cache Behaviour for Programs with IF Statements. In: 5th International Conference on Algorthms and Archiectures for Parallel Processing. (2002) 396–407

A Configurable System-on-Chip Architecture for Embedded Devices

Sebastian Wallner

Department of Distributed Systems, Technical University Hamburg-Harburg,
Schwarzenbergstrasse 95, D-21073 Hamburg, Germany
{wallner@tu-harburg.de}

Abstract. This paper describes a novel Configurable System-on-Chip
(CSoC) architecture for stream-based computations and real-time signal
processing. It offers high computational performance and a high degree of
flexibility and adaptability by employing a micro Task Controller (mTC)
unit in conjunction with programmable and configurable hardware. The
hierarchically organized architecture provides a programming model, allows an efficient mapping of applications and is shown to be easy scalable to future VLSI technologies where over a hundred processing cells
on a single chip will be feasible to deal with the inherent dynamics of
future application domains and system requirements. Several mappings
of commonly used digital signal processing algorithms and implementation results are given for a standard-cell ASIC design realization in 0.18
micron 6-layer UMC CMOS technology.

1 Introduction

We are currently experiencing an explosive growth in development and deployment of embedded devices such as multimedia set-top-boxes and personal mobile
computing systems which demands an increasing support of multiple standards
[1,2]. This flexibility requirement points to the need of various communication,
audio and video algorithms which differ in complexity. They have mostly a heterogenous nature and comprise several sub-tasks with real-time performance
requirements for data-parallel tasks [3]. A hardware which can cope with these
demands needs different processing architectures: some are parallel, some are
rather pipelined. In general, they need a combination. Moreover, various algorithms needs different levels of control over the functional units and different
memory access. For instance, multimedia applications (like different video de-
compression schemes) may include a data-parallel task, a bit-level task, irregular computations, high-precision word operations and a real-time component
[4]. The addressed requirements becomes even more relevant when Quality-of-
Service (QoS) requirements e.g. varying the communication bandwidth in wireless terminals, variable audio quality or a change from full color to black/white
picture quality becomes a more important factor. A way to solve the flexibility
and adaptability demands has been to use General Purpose Processors (GPP)
or Digital Signal Processors (DSP), i.e. trying to solve all kinds of applications

P.-C. Yew and J. Xue (Eds.): ACSAC 2004, LNCS 3189, pp. 58–71, 2004.

running on a very high speed processor. A major drawback of using these general-purpose devices is that they are extremely inefficient in terms of utilizing their resources to best take advantage of data-level parallelism in the algorithms. Todays demands motivate the use of hybrid architectures which integrate programmable logic together with different embedded resources and Configurable Systems-on-Chip which can be realized by integrating reconfigurable (re-usable) and programmable hardware components. In contrast to processors, they totally lack programming models that would allow for device independent compilation and forward compatibility to other architecture families.

The approach in this paper describes a Configurable System-on-Chip approach with configurable and programmable properties. The architecture combines a wide variety of macro-module resources including a MIPS-like scalar processor core, coarse-grained reconfigurable processing arrays, embedded memories and custom modules supervised by a micro Task Controller. In the architecture, functions can be dynamically assigned to physical hardware resources such that the most efficient computation can be obtained. It can be forward compatible to other CSoC families with variable numbers of reconfigurable processing cells for different performance features. A major key issue for the CSoC system integration includes the coupling of the macro-module resources for efficient mapping and transfer of data. The programming aspect is another important aspect in this paper.

This work is organized as follows. Section 2 presents related work. Section 3 the reconfigurable processing array which based on previous research activities. Section 4 introduces the CSoC architecture composition and the system control mechanism in detail. The next section (section 5) presents the programming paradigm. Algorithms mapping and performance analysis are present in Section 6. Finally, section 7 discusses the design- and physical implementation while conclusions and future work are drawn in Section 8.

2   Related Work

There have been several research efforts as well as commercial products that have tried to explore the use of reconfigurable- and System-on-Chip architectures. They integrate existing components (IP-cores) into a single chip or explore complete new architectures. In the Pleiades project at UC Berkeley [5], the goal is to create a low-power high-performance DSP system. Yet, the Pleiades architecture template differs from the proposed CSOC architecture. In the Pleiades architecture a general purpose microprocessor is surrounded by a heterogeneous array of autonomous special-purpose satellite processors communicated over a reconfigurable communication network. In contrast to the Pleiades system the proposed architecture offers reconfigurable hardware and data-paths supervised by a flexible controller unit with a simple instruction set which allows conditional reconfiguration and efficient hardware virtualization. The reconfigurable architecture CS2112 Reconfigurable Communication Processor [6] from Chameleon Systems couples a processor with a reconfigurable fabric composed of 32-bit processor tiles. The fabric holds a background plane with configuration data which can be loaded while the active plane is in use. A small state-machine controls every tile. The embedded processor manages the reconfiguration and streaming data. The chameleon chip has a fixed architecture targeting communication applications. The Configurable SoC architecture offers a micro Task Controller which allows variable handling of different processing resources and provides forward compatability with other CSoC architecture families for different performance demands. The scalar processor core is not involved in the configuration process. Furthermore, the configuration mechanism differs completely from the configuration approach used by Chameleon Systems. MorphoSys from the University of California Irvine [7] has a MIPS-like "TinyRISC" processor with extended instruction set, a mesh-connected 8 by 8 reconfigurable array of 28 bit ALUs. The "TiniRISC" controls system execution by initiating context memory and frame buffer loads using extra instructions via a DMA controller. MorphoSys offers dynamic reconfiguration with several local configuration memories. The suggested architecture model includes a micro Task Controller with a simple instruction set and a single local configuration memory in each cluster. It uses a pipelined configuration concept to configure multiple reconfigurable processing cells. The micro task program and the descriptor set can be reused in other CSoC families without a recompilation task.

3   Background

The Configurable System-on-Chip architecture approach build on previous research activities in identifying reconfigurable hardware structures and providing a new hardware virtualization concept for coarse-grained reconfigurable architectures. A reconfigurable processing cell array (RPCA) has been designed which targets applications with inherent data-parallelism, high regularity and high throughput requirements [8]. The architecture is based on a synchronous multifunctional pipeline flow model using reconfigurable processing cells and configurable data-paths. A configuration manager allows run-time- and partial reconfiguration. The RPCA consists of an array of configurable coarse-grained processing cells linked to each other via broadcast- and pipelined data buses. It is fragmented into four parallel stripes which can be configured in parallel. The configuration technique based of an pipelined configuration process via descriptors. Descriptors represent configuration templates abutted to instruction operation-codes in conventional Instruction Set Architectures (ISA). They can be sliced into fixed-size computation threads that, in analogy to virtual memory pages, are swapped onto available physical hardware within a few clock cycles. The architecture approach results in a flexible reconfigurable hardware component with performance and function flexibility. Figure 1 shows a cluster with overall 16 processing cells.

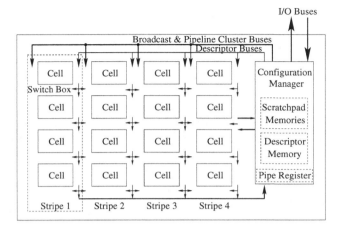

Fig. 1. The structure of a cluster with the configuration manager, the processing cells with the switch boxes for routing, the dual-port scratch pad memories and the descriptor memory. In order to adjust configuration cycles, three pipeline registers for every stripe are implemented.

Some important characteristics of the reconfigurable architecture are:

- Coarse-grained reconfigurable processing model: Each reconfigurable processing cell contains a multifunctional ALU that operates on 48-bit or $2 * 24$-bit data words (split ALU mode) on signed integer and signed fixed-point arithmetic.
- Computation concept via compute threads: An application is divided in several computation threads which are mapped and executed on the processing array.
- Hardware virtualization: Hardware on demand with a single context memory and unbounded configuration contexts (descriptors) with low overhead context switching for high computational density.
- Configuration data minimization: Reuse of a descriptor, to configure several processing cells, minimizes the configuration memory.
- Library-based design approach: Library contains application-specific kernel modules composed of several descriptors to reduce the developing-time and cost.
- Scalable architecture for future VLSI technologies: Configuration concept easy expandable to larger RPCA.

The RPCA is proposed to be the reconfigurable module of the Configurable System-on-Chip design. It executes the signal processing algorithms in the application domain to enhance the performance of critical loops and computation intensive functions.

4   Architecture Composition

The CSoC architecture model is hierarchically organized. It is composed of a micro Task Controller (mTC) unit which includes a set of heterogeneous processing resources and the reconfigurable processing cell array. Figure 2 gives a structure overview. To avoid that a global bus is becoming a bottleneck, a high-speed crossbar switch connects the heterogeneous processing resources and the RPCA. It allows multiple data transfers in parallel. Many algorithms in the applications domain contains abundant parallelism and are compute intensive. They are preferable spatially mapped onto the RPCA via a set of descriptors while the other parts can be computed with the heterogeneous processing resources [8]. An advantage of such a architecture partitioning is the more efficient mapping of algorithms as the Fast Fourier Transformation example in section 6 illustrates.

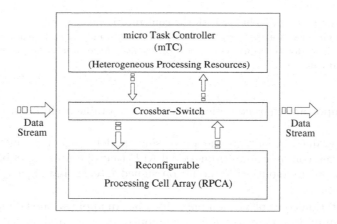

Fig. 2. The hierarchically organized CSoC structure with the heterogeneous processing resources and the reconfigurable processing cell arrays are connected via a crossbar switch. The RCPA is partitioned in several clusters.

4.1   Configurable System-on-Chip Overview

The CSoC architecture consists of the mTC and two clusters of reconfigurable processing cells. Every cluster comprises sixteen 48-bit coarse-grained reconfigurable processing cells. It offers variable parallelism and pipelining for different performance requirements. A two channel programmable DMA controller handles the data transfers between the external main memory banks and the processing cell array. Figure 3 outlines the architecture overview.

In high performance systems high memory bandwidth is mandatory. Thus the architecture uses a bandwidth hierarchy to bridge the gap between deliverable

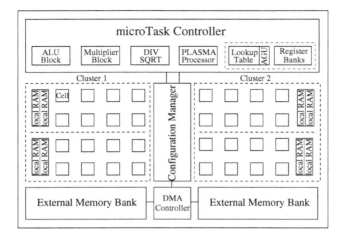

Fig. 3. The overall CSoC architecture with the mTC unit which includes the heterogeneous processing resources, two clusters of reconfigurable processing cells with the scratch-pad memories (local RAM) and the Plasma scalar processor.

off-chip memory bandwidth and the bandwidth necessary for the computation required by the application. The hierarchy has two levels: a main memory level (External Memory Bank) for large, infrequently accessed data realized as external memory block and a local level for temporary use during calculation realized as high-speed dual ported scratch-pad memories (local RAM).

4.2   Processing Resource Implementation

Due to the application field in digital signal, image and video processing applications the heterogeneous processing resources comprises

- two ALU (Arithmetic Logic Unit) blocks with four independent 48- or eight 24-bit adder units, saturation logic and boolean function,
- a multiplier block with two 24-bit signed/unsigned multipliers,
- a 24-bit division and square root unit,
- a MIPS-I compatible 32-bit Plasma scalar processor core,
- a $256 * 24$-bit lookup table with two independent Address Generation Units (AGU),
- two register banks of $4 * 48$-bit universal registers ($R0 - R3$; $R0' - R3'$).

The 32-bit Plasma scalar processor core can be used for general-purpose processing or for tasks which can not be very well accomplished on the other processing resources. It can directly address the local RAMs of the reconfigurable processing cells. Bit computation is achievable with the ALU block. The lookup-table and the address generation unit can be used to construct e.g. a Direct Digital Frequency Synthesis (DDFS) generator which is frequently used in telecommunication applications.

4.3   System Control Mechanism and Instruction Set

The micro Task Controller is a global micro-programmed control machine which offers a versatile degree of sharing the architecture resources. It manages the heterogeneous processing resources and controls the configuration manager without retarding the whole system. The mTC executes a sequence of micro-instructions which are located in a micro-program code memory. It has a micro-program address counter which can be simply increment by one on each clock cycle to select the address of the next micro-instruction. Additionally, the micro Task Controller provides an instruction to initiate the configuration and control-flow instructions for branching. The following four instructions are implemented:

- GOTO [Address]: Unconditional jump to a dedicated position in the micro-program code.
- FTEST [Flag, Address]: Test a flag and branch if equal; If the flag is set (e.g. saturation flag), jump to a dedicated position in the micro-program code otherwise continue.
- TEST [Value, Register, Address]: Test a 48/24-bit value and branch if equal; The instruction is equivalent to the FTEST instruction. It tests the content of an universal register.
- CONFIG [Function Address]: Start address of the configuration context in the descriptor memory; The configuration manager fetches the descriptors in addiction to the descriptor type. The configuration process must only be triggered. The configuration manager notifies the termination of the configuration process by a finish flag.

The instruction set allows to control the implemented heterogeneous processing resources, the configuration manager and the data-streams. It allows conditional reconfiguration and data dependent branching. $If-then-else$, $while$ and $select$ assignations can be easily modeled.

5   Programming Paradigm

An application is represented as a Control Data-Flow Graph (CDFG). In this graph, control (order of execution) and data are modeled in the same way. It conveys the potential concurrencies within an algorithm and facilitates the parallelization and mapping to arbitrary architectures. The graph nodes usually correspond to primitives, such as FFT, FIR-filter or complex multiplication (CMUL). For a given network architecture, the programmer starts with partitioning and mapping of the graph in micro-tasks (subtasks), by allocate the flow graph nodes to the reconfigurable and heterogeneous processing resources in the system. It specifies the program structure: the sequence of micro-tasks that comprises the application, the connection between them and the input and output ports for the data streams. A micro-task processes input data and produces output data. After a task finishes, its output is typically input to the next micro-task. Figure 4 shows an example composed of several micro-tasks with data feed-back.

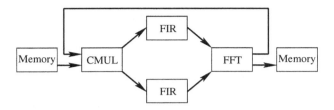

Fig. 4. An example of a cascade of computation tasks with data feedback. A task may consists of a configuration and a processing part.

After the partitioning and mapping, a scheduling process produces the schedule for the application which determines the order of the micro-task execution. The schedule for a computation flow is stored in a microprogram as a sequence of steps that directs the processing resources. It is represented as a mTC reservation table with a number of usable reservation time slots. The allocation of these time slots can be predefined by the scheduler process via a determined programming sequence. The sequence consists of micro-instructions which can be interpreted as a series of bit fields. A bit field is associated with exactly one particular micro operation. When a field is executed it's value is interpreted to provide the control for this function during that clock period. Descriptor specification: Descriptors can be used separately or application kernels can be chosen from a function library [8]. Plasma program: This is generated through the GNU-C language compiler. The compiler generates an MIPS-I instruction compatible code for the Plasma processor. The programming paradigm allows to find the maximum parallelism found in the application. Exploiting this parallelism allows the high computation rates which are necessary to achieve high performance.

6 Mapping Algorithms and Performance Analysis

This section discusses the mapping of some applications onto the Configurable System-on-Chip architecture. First, the Fast Fourier Transform (FFT) is mapped due to his high degree of important and tight real-time constraints for telecommunication and multimedia systems. Then other typical kernels are mapped and some results becomes introduced.

The Sande and Tukey Fast Fourier Transformation (FFT) algorithm with DIF (Decimation in Frequency) is chosen [9]. It can be more efficiently mapped on the CSoC hardware resources due to a better processing resource utilization. The butterfly calculation is the basic operation of the FFT. An implementation use a DIF-FFT radix-2 butterfly. It is shown in figure 5a). The radix-2 butterfly takes a pair of input data values "X" and "Y" and produces a pair of outputs "X'" and "Y'" where

$$X' = X + Y \ , \ Y' = X - Y\,W\frac{k}{N}. \tag{1}$$

In general the input samples as well as the twiddle factors are complex and can be expressed as

$$X = X_r + jX_i \ , \ \ Y = Y_r + jY_i, \tag{2}$$

$$W\frac{k}{N} = e^{-j2\pi k/N} = cos(2\pi k/N) - jsin(2\pi k/N) \tag{3}$$

where the suffix r indicates the real part and the i the imaginary part of the data. In order to execute a 24-bit radix-2 butterfly in parallel, a set of descriptors for the RPCA and the mTC microcode for controlling the heterogeneous processing resources and the configuration manager are necessary. The butterfly operation requires four real multiplications and six real additions/subtractions. To map the complex multiplication, two multiplier and two multiplier/add descriptors as configuration templates are needed. It can be mapped in parallel onto four processing cells of the RPCA. The complex- adder and subtracter are mapped onto the ALU block. The whole structure is shown in figure 5b). The pipelined execution of the radix-2 butterfly takes five clock cycles. The execution is best illustrated using the reservation table. It shows the hardware resource allocation in every clock cycle. Figure 6 shows the reservation table for the first stage of an n-point FFT fragmented into three phases. The *initialize* phase is comprised of static configurations of the processing resources. It initiates the configuration which maps four complex multiplier onto the RPCA by using the CONFIG instruction. In the *configuration* phase, the configuration of the reconfigurable array is accomplished. The *process* phase starts the computation of the n-points. It is controlled by the FTEST instruction. The twiddle-factors $W\frac{k}{N}$ are generated for each stage via the lookup-table and the address generation units.

The example in figure 7 shows the execution of the n-point radix-2 FFT. Each oval in the figure corresponds to the execution of a FFT compute stage (micro-task), while each arrow represents a data stream transfer. The example uses an in-place FFT implementation variant. It allows the results of each FFT butterfly to replace its input. This makes efficient use of the dual ported scratch-pad memories as the transformed data overwrites the input data. The re-order of the output data is simply arranged by reversing the address bits via the scratch-pad memory data sequencer unit (bit-reverse addressing). For demonstration, a 64- point FFT computation, a 16x16 Matrix-Vector-Multiplication (MVM), a 32-tap systolic FIR-filter and 32-tap symmetrical FIR-filter with 12-bit integer coefficients and data and a 32-tap real IIR filter implementation are mapped. Generally larger kernels can be calculated by time-division multiple access (TDMA).

One key to achieve high performance is keeping each functional unit as busy as possible. This goal can be quantified by efficiently mapping applications to the CSoC model including how to partition the kernel structure or large computations. An important aspect is the resource occupancy of the architecture; the percentage of used hardware resources which are involved to process a kernel or an application. The occupancy of the architecture resources for several kernels

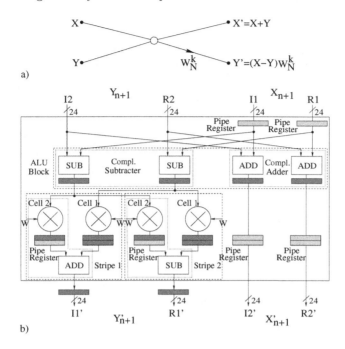

Fig. 5. The butterfly structure for the decimation in frequency radix-2 FFT in a). In b) the mapping of the complex adders onto the ALU block of the heterogeneous processing resources and the complex multiplier which are mapped onto the reconfigurable processing array. The implementation uses additional pipeline registers (Pipe Register) provided by the configuration manager (light hatched) for timing balance.

are shown in figure 8 a). The hierarchically architecture composition allows to map four complex radix-2 butterflies in parallel onto the CSoC with a single cluster. As shown, the complex butterfly can be efficiently implemented due to the mapping of the complex adders to the heterogeneous processing resources and the complex multipliers to the reconfigurable processing cells. The resource unit occupancy of the cluster (Reconfigurable Resources) is 75%. The expensive multipliers in the reconfigurable processing cells are completely used.

The 16x16 MVM kernel is mapped and calculated in parallel with 24-bit precision. The partial data accumulation is done via the adder resources in the ALU block. A 48-bit MVM calculation is not feasible due to limited broadcast bus resources in the cluster [8]. This results in a relative poor resource occupancy as a 24-bit multiplier in the reconfigurable processing cells can not be used. The FIR-filter structures can be mapped directly onto the RPCA. It can be calculated with 48-bit precision. As a result of insufficient adder resources in a reconfigurable processing cell, the 32-tap symmetrical FIR-filter can only be calculated with 24-bit precision. The resource occupancy in a reconfigurable processing cell is poor as a 24-bit multiplier can not be used [8]. The IIR-filter

Configurable Resources	Stage	0	Time Slots				
			1	2	3	4	5
Descriptor Wave Stripe 1	1		MUL/ADD	MUL	MUL/ADD	MUL	MUL
	2			MUL/ADD	MUL	MUL/ADD	MUL/ADD
	3				MUL/ADD	MUL	MUL
	4					MUL/ADD	MUL/ADD
Descriptor Wave Stripe 2	1		MUL/SUB	MUL	MUL/SUB	MUL	MUL
	2			MUL/SUB	MUL	MUL/SUB	MUL/SUB
	3				MUL/SUB	MUL	MUL
	4					MUL/SUB	MUL/SUB
Descriptor Wave Stripe 3	1		MUL/ADD	MUL	MUL/ADD	MUL	MUL
	2			MUL/ADD	MUL	MUL/ADD	MUL/ADD
	3				MUL/ADD	MUL	MUL
	4					MUL/ADD	MUL/ADD
Descriptor Wave Stripe 4	1		MUL/SUB	MUL	MUL/SUB	MUL	MUL
	2			MUL/SUB	MUL	MUL/SUB	MUL/SUB
	3				MUL/SUB	MUL	MUL
	4					MUL/SUB	MUL/SUB
Heterogeneous Processing Resources							
ALU Block		Complex Add/Sub					
Lookup Table		Sin/Cos					
LUT AGU		Twiddle F.					
XBar		Data Buses					
Memory DSUs		BitReverse Mode					
mTC Control–Instruction		CONFIG					FTEST
		<CMUL>					M–DSU
		Initialize	Configuration (mTC waits until the configuration is finished)				Process FFT Stage 1

Fig. 6. The simplified reservation table of the first FFT stage to process four complex butterflies in parallel. The hardware resources are listed on the left-hand side. First the time slots for the reconfigurable processing array (four parallel stripes) with the pipe stages (Stage), then the heterogeneous processing resources and the mTC control-instructions are illustrated. The hatched area marks the initialization phase. The reconfigurable processing array is configured after the fourth cycle. The Memory Data Sequencer Units (M-DSU) starts after the configuration process (time slot 5) to provide the input data. The heterogeneous and configurable processing resources are statically configured.

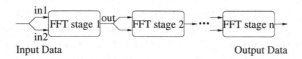

Input Data   Output Data

Fig. 7. A n-point FFT (n=max. 1024) is split onto several compute stages (microtasks) which are performed sequentially. The compute stages are separated into several parts in the reservation table.

is composed of two parallel 32-tap systolic FIR-filters and an adder from the ALU block. It can only be calculated with full 48-bit precision by using TDMA processing. The lack of wiring resources (broadcast buses in a cluster) limits the resource load in a cluster as the MVM and the 32-tap symmetrical FIR-filter mapping illustrates. The wiring problem cannot always be completely hidden but can be reduced as shown in the case of the mapping of the complex butterfly.

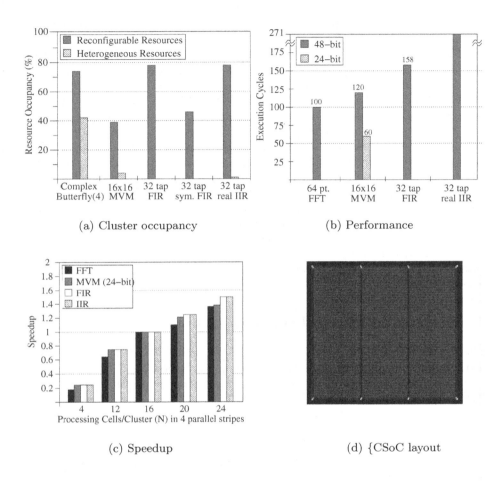

(a) Cluster occupancy

(b) Performance

(c) Speedup

(d) {CSoC layout

Fig. 8. (a) Resource unit occupancy of selected kernels on the CSoC architecture with a single cluster. The dark area shows the cluster utilization while the striped area shows the functional unit utilization of the heterogeneous processing resources. (b) Performance results for the applications using a single cluster. The results do not include the configuration cycles. (c) Speedup results relative to a single cluster with 16 reconfigurable processing cells for selected kernels. Plot (d) shows the CSoC ASIC prototype layout without the pad ring.

Achieved performance results for some of the kernels above are summarized in figure 8 b). It shows the 24- and 48-bit realization of the MVM kernel.

The 48-bit MVM computation needs twice as much clock cycles as the 24-bit realization due to the broadcast bus bottleneck. The other kernels can be calculated with 48-bit precision. The 32-tap FIR-filter can be executed onto the processing array by feeding back the partial data. The 64-point FFT uses four complex butterflies in parallel. The 32-tap IIR-filter needs more then twice as much clock cycles due to the need of TDMA processing to compute the 32-tap FIR-filters in parallel. Speedups with reconfigurable processing cell scaling in four parallel stripes is shown in figure 8 c). The filter kernels have linear speedups to $N = 24$ because they can be directly mapped onto the RPCA. The MVM computation has linear speedup until $N = 16$. The increased number of processing cells gives an performance decrease due to the broadcast bus bottleneck for a stripe. The FFT computation with the parallel implementation of the butterflies shows a resource bottleneck in the reconfigurable processing cells for $N = 4$ and $N = 12$. In this case, it is not possible to map complete complex multipliers in parallel onto the RPCA. In the case of $N = 20$, the broadcast bus bottleneck and a ALU adder bottleneck decrease the performance rapidly due to the absence of adder resources for the butterfly computation. The performance degradation in the $N = 24$ case results from the ALU adder resource bottleneck, the complex multipliers can be mapped perfectly onto four parallel stripes with 24 processing cells. Scaling the number of clusters results in a near-linear speedup for the most kernels unless a resource bottleneck in the heterogeneous resources occurs.

7   Design and Physical Implementation

The CSoC architecture has been implemented using a standard cell design methodology for an UMC 0.18 micron, six metal layer CMOS (1.8V) process available through the european joined academic/industry project *EUROPRAC-TICE*. The architecture was modeled using VHDL as hardware description language. The RPCA and the mTC with the heterogeneous processing resources are simulated separately with the *VHDL System-Simulator (VSS)*. They were then synthesized using appropriate timing constraints with the *Synopsys Design-Compiler (DC)* and mapped using *Cadence Silicon Ensemble*. The first implementation includes a single cluster with 16 processing cells and the mTC unit with the heterogeneous processing resources. The Plasma scalar processor includes a $1k * 32$ program cache. No further caches are implemented. The final layout, shown in figure 8 d), has a total area of $10\,mm^2$. A cluster with 16 processing cells needs $7.1\,mm^2$ silicon area, the Plasma processor core in 0.18 micron CMOS technology approximately $0.4\,mm^2$. It can be clocked up to 210 MHz. After a static timing analysis with *Cadence Pearl*, the CSoC design runs at clock frequencies up to 140MHz.

8   Conclusions and Future Work

A Configurable System-on-Chip for embedded devices has been described in this paper. The CSoC introduces an architecture for telecommunication-, audio-, and video algorithms in order to meet the high performance and flexibility demands. The architecture provides high computational density and flexibility of changing behaviors during run-time. The system consists of two clusters of reconfigurable processing cells, heterogeneous processing resources and a programmable micro Task Controller unit with a small instruction set. The reconfigurable processing array has been designed for data-parallel and computation-intensive tasks. However, the CSoC architecture proposed here is different from many CSoC architectures in an important and fundamental way. It is hierarchically organized and offers a programming model. The architecture allows an efficient mapping of application kernels as the FFT mapping have illustrated and is scalable by either adding more reconfigurable processing cells in a cluster, by increasing the number of clusters or by adding more processing units to the heterogeneous resources. A major advantage of the CSoC architecture approach is to provide forward compatability with other CSoC architecture families. They may offer a different number of clusters or reconfigurable processing cells to provide variable performance requirements. The micro-task program and the descriptor set can be reused. A prototype chip layout with a single cluster has been developed using a UMC 0.18 micron 6-layer CMOS process.

Apart from tuning and evaluating the CSoC architecture for additional applications, there are several directions for future work. One key challenge is to extended the mTC instruction in order to enlarge the flexibility. Another challenge is to create an automatic partitioning and mapping tool to assist the user. The programmable micro Task Controller and the reconfigurable processing array with the descriptors as configuration templates can be a solid base for such an intention.

References

1. R. Berezdivin, R. Breinig, R. Topp, "Next-generation wireless communication concepts and technologies", IEEE Communication Magazine, vol. 40, no. 3, pp. 108-117, Mar. 2002
2. K. Lewis, "Information Appliances, "Gadget Netopia", IEEE Computer., vol. 31, pp. 59-66, Jan. 1998
3. K. Diefendorff and P. Dubey, "How Multimedia Workloads Will Change Processor Design", IEEE Computer, 30(9) : 43-45, Sept. 1997
4. T. M. Conte, P. K. Dubey, M. D. Jennings, R. B. Lee, A. Peleg, S. Rathnam, M. S. Schlansker, P. Song, A. Wolfe, "Challenges to Combining General-Purpose and Multimedia Processors", IEEE Computer, pp. 33-37, Dec. 1997
5. M. Wan, H. Zhang, V. George , M. Benes, A. Abnous, V. Prabhu, J. Rabaey, "Design methodology of a low-energy reconfigurable single-chip DSP system", Journal of VLSI Signal Processing, vol.28, no.1-2, pp.47-61, May-Jun. 2001
6. B. Salefski, L. Caglar, "Re-Configurable Computing in Wireless", 38th Design Automation Conference, Las Vegas, Nevade, USA, Jun. 2001
7. H. Singh, M. H. Lee, G. Lu, F. J. Kurdahi, N. Bagherzadeh, E. M. C. Filho, "MorphoSys: An Integrated Reconfigurable System for Data-Parallel and Computation-Intensive Applications", IEEE Transactions on Computers 49(5): 465-481, May 2000
8. S. Wallner, "A Reconfigurable Multi-threaded Architecture Model", Eighth Asia-Pacific Computer Systems Architecture Conference (ACSAC 2003), Fukushima, Japan, Springer LNCS 2823, pp. 193-207, Sep. 23-26 2003
9. A. V. Oppenheim, R. W. Schafer, "Discrete-Time Signal Processing", Englewood Cliffs, Prentice-Hall, 1989

An Auto-adaptative Reconfigurable Architecture for the Control

Nicolas Ventroux, Stéphane Chevobbe, Fréderic Blanc, and Thierry Collette

CEA-List DRT/DTSI/SARC
Image and Embedded Computers Laboratory
F-91191 Gif-Sur-Yvette - FRANCE
phone: (33) 1-69-08-66-37
firstname.surname@cea.fr

Abstract. Previous works have shown that reconfigurable architectures are particularly well-adapted for implementing regular processing applications. Nevertheless, they are inefficient for designing complex control systems. In order to solve this drawback, microprocessors are jointly used with reconfigurable devices. However, only regular, modular and reconfigurable architectures can easily take into account constant technology improvements, since they are based on the repetition of small units. This paper focuses on the self-adaptative features of a new reconfigurable architecture dedicated to the control from the application to the computation level. This reconfigurable device can itself adapt its resources to the application at run-time, and can exploit a high level of parallelism into an architecture called *RAMPASS*.

Keywords: dynamic reconfiguration, adaptative reconfigurable architecture, control parallelism

1 Introduction

The silicon area of reconfigurable devices are filled with a large number of computing primitives, interconnected via a configurable network. The functionality of each element can be programmed as well as the interconnect pattern. These regular and modular structures are adapted to exploit future microelectronic technology improvements. In fact, semiconductor road maps [1] indicate that integration density of regular structures (like memories) increases faster than irregular ones (Tab. 1). In this introduction, existing reconfigurable architectures as well as solutions to control these structures, are first presented. This permits us to highlight the interests of our architecture dedicated to the control, which is then depicted in details.

A reconfigurable circuit can adapt its features, completely or partially, to applications during a process called reconfiguration. These reconfigurations are statically or dynamically managed by hardware mechanisms [2]. These architectures can efficiently perform hardware computations, while retaining much of

P.-C. Yew and J. Xue (Eds.): ACSAC 2004, LNCS 3189, pp. 72–87, 2004.

Table 1. Integration density for future VLSI devices

Year	1999	2001	2003	2005	2009	2012
Process (nm)	180	150	130	100	70	50
DRAM (bit/chip)	1,07 G	1,7 G	4,29 G	17,2 G	68,7 G	275 G
MPU (transistors/chip)	21 M	40 M	76 M	200 M	520 M	1,4 G

the flexibility of a software solution [3]. Their resources can be arranged to implement specific and heterogeneous applications. Three kinds of reconfiguration level can be distinguished :

– **gate level**: FPGA (Field Programmable Gate Array) are the most well-known and used gate-level reconfigurable architectures [4,5]. These devices merge three kinds of resources: the first one is an interconnection network, the second one is a set of processing blocks (LUT, registers, etc.) and the third one regroups I/O blocks. The reconfiguration process consists in using the interconnection network to connect different reconfigurable processing elements. Furthermore, each LUT is configured to perform any logical operations on its inputs. These devices can exploit bit-level parallelism.

– **operator level**: the reconfiguration takes place at the interconnection and the operator levels (PipeRench[6], DREAM [7], MorphoSys [8], REMARC [9], etc.). The main difference concerns the reconfiguration granularity, which is at the word level. The use of coarse-grain reconfigurable operators provides significant savings in time and area for word-based applications. They preserve a high level of flexibility in spite of the limitations imposed by the use of coarse-grain operators for better performances, which do not allow bit-level parallelism.

– **functional level**: these architectures have been developed in order to implement intensive arithmetic computing applications (RaPiD [10], DART [11], Systolic Ring [12], etc.). These reconfigurable architectures are reconfigured in modifying the way their functional units are interconnected. The low reconfiguration data volume of these architectures makes it easier to implement dynamic reconfigurations and allows the definition of simple execution models.

These architectures can own different levels of physical granularity, and whatever the reconfiguration grain is, partial reconfigurations are possible, allowing the virtualization of their resources. Thus for instance, to increase performances (area, consumption, speed, etc.), an application based on arithmetic operators is optimally implemented on word-level reconfigurable architectures.

Besides, according to Amdahl's law [13], an application is always composed of regular and irregular processings. It is always possible to reduce and optimize the regular parts of an application in increasing the parallelism, but irregular code is irreductible. Moreover, it is difficult to map these irregular parts on reconfigurable architectures. Therefore, most reconfigurable systems need to be coupled with an external controller especially for irregular processing or dynamic context switching. Performances are directly dependent on the position and the level of this coupling. Presently, four possibilities can be exploited by designers:

- **microprocessor**: this solution is often chosen when reconfigurable units are used as coprocessors in a SoC (System on Chip) framework. The microprocessor can both execute its own processes (and irregular codes) and configure its reconfigurable resources (PACT XPP-/Leon [14], PipeRench [15], MorphoSys [8], DREAM [7], etc.). These systems can execute critical processings on the microprocessor, while other concurrent processes can be executed on reconfigurable units. However, in order to only configure and execute irregular code, this solution may be considered as too expensive in terms of area and energy consumption, and would most likely be the bottelneck due to off-chip communication overheads in synchronization and instruction bandwidth.

- **processor core**: this approach is completely different since the processor is mainly used as a reconfigurable unit controller. A processor is inserted near reconfigurable resources to configure them and to execute irregular processes. Performances can also be increased by exploiting the control parallelism thanks to tight coupling (Matrix [16], Chimaera [17], NAPA [18], etc.). Marginal improvements are often noticed compared to a general-purpose microprocessor but these solutions give an adapted answer for controlling reconfigurable devices.

- **microsequencer**: these control elements are only used to process irregular processing or to configure resources. They can be found in the RaPiD architecture, for instance, [10] as a smaller programmed control with a short instruction set. Furthermore, the GARP architecture uses a processor in order to only load and execute array configurations [19]. A microsequencer is an optimal solution in terms of area and speed. Its features do not allow itself to be considered as a coprocessor like the other solutions, but this approach is however best fitted for specifically controlling reconfigurable units. Nevertheless, control parallelisms can be exploited with difficulty.

- **FPGA**: this last solution consists in converting the control into a set of state machines, which could then be mapped to an FPGA. This approach can take advantage of traditional synthesis techniques for optimizing control. However, FPGA are not optimized for implementing FSM (Finite State Machines) because whole graphs of the application must be implemented even if non-deterministic processes occur. Indeed, these devices can hardly manage dynamic reconfigurations at the state-level.

Reconfigurable devices are often used with a processor for non-deterministic processes. To minimize control and configuration overheads, the best solution consists in tightly coupling a processor core with the reconfigurable architecture [20]. However, designing for such systems is similar to a HW/SW co-design problem. In addition, the use of reconfigurable devices can be better adapted to deep sub-microelectronic technological improvements. Nonetheless, the controller needs other physical implementation features rather than operators, and FPGA can not always be an optimal solution for computation. Indeed, the control handles small data and requires global communications to control all the processing elements, whereas the computation processes large data and uses local communications between operators.

To deal with control for reconfigurable architectures, we have developed the *RAMPASS* architecture (Reconfigurable and Advanced Multi-Processing Architecture for future Silicon Systems) [21]. It is composed of two reconfigurable resources. The first one is suitable for computation purposes but is not a topic of interest for this paper. The second part of our architecture is dedicated to control processes. It is a self-reconfigurable and asynchronous architecture, which supports SIMD (Single Instruction Multiple Data), MIMD (Multiple Instruction Multiple Data) and multi-threading processes.

This paper presents the mechanisms used to auto-adapt resource allocations to the application in the control part of *RAMPASS*. The paper is structured as follows: section 2 outlines a functional description of *RAMPASS*. Section 3 presents a detailed functional description of the part of *RAMPASS* dedicated to the control. This presentation focuses on some concepts presented in [21]. Then, section 4 depicts auto-adaptative reconfiguration mechanisms of this control part. Finally, section 5 presents the development flow, some results and deals with the SystemC model of our architecture.

2   Functional Description of RAMPASS

In this section, the global functionality of *RAMPASS* is described. It is composed of two main reconfigurable parts (Fig. 1):

- One dedicated to the control of applications (*RAC*: Reconfigurable Adapted to the Control);
- One dedicated to the computation (*RAO*: Reconfigurable Adapted to Operators).

Even if the *RAC* is a part of *RAMPASS*, it can be dissociated to be integrated with other different architectures with any computational grain. Each computation block can be either a general-purpose processor or a functional unit. The *RAC* is a generic control architecture and is the main interest of this paper. In this article, the *RAO* can be considered as a computational device adapted to the application, with a specific interface in order to communicate with the *RAC*. This interface must support instructions from the *RAC* and return one-bit flags according to its processes.

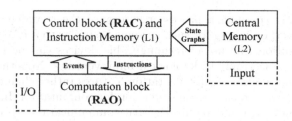

Fig. 1. Organization of RAMPASS

2.1 Overview

From a C description, any application can be translated as a *CDFG* (Control Data Flow Graph), which is a *CFG* (Control Flow Graph) with the instructions of the basic blocks expressed as a *DFG* (Data Flow Graph). Thus, their partition is easily conceivable [22,23].

A *CFG* or a *State Graph* (*SG*) represents the control relationships between the set of basic blocks. Each basic block contains a set of deterministic instructions, called *actions*. Thus, every state in a SG is linked to an action. Besides, every arc in a SG either connects a state to a transition, or a transition to a state. A SG executes by firing transitions. When a transition fires, one token is removed from each input state of the transition and one token is added to each output state of the transition. These transistions determine the appropriate control edge to follow. On the other hand, a *DFG* represents the overall corresponding method compiled onto hardware.

Consequently, whatever the application is, it can be composed of two different parts (Fig. 2). The first one computes operations (*DFG*) and the second one schedules these executions on a limited amount of processing resources (*CFG*).

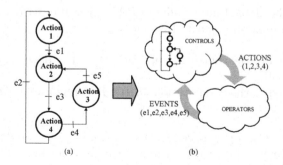

Fig. 2. Partitioning of an application (a) in Control/Computation (b)

The first block of our architecture can physically store any application described as a *CFG*. States drive the computation elements in the *RAO*, and events coming from the *RAO* validate transitions in the SG. Moreover, self-routing mechanisms have been introduced in the *RAC* block to simplify SG mapping. The *RAC* can auto-implement a SG according to its free resources. The *RAC* controls connections between cells and manages its resources. All these mechanisms will be discussed in future sections.

2.2   Mapping and Running an Application with RAMPASS

In this part, the configuration and the execution of an application in *RAMPASS* are described. Applications are stored in an external memory. As soon as the SG begins to be loaded in the *RAC*, its execution begins. In fact, the configuration and the execution are simultaneously performed. Contrary to microprocessor, this has the advantage of never blocking the execution of applications, since the following executed actions are always mapped in the *RAC*.

The reconfiguration of the *RAC* is self-managed and depends on the application progress. This concept is called auto-adaptative. The *RAC Net* has a limited number of cells, which must be dynamically used in order to map larger applications. Indeed, due to a lack of resources, whole SGs can not always be mapped in the *RAC*. Dynamic reconfiguration has been introduced to increase the virtual size of the architecture. In our approach, no pre-divided contexts are required. Sub-blocks implemented in the *RAC Net* are continuously updated without any user help. Figure 3 shows a sub-graph of a 7-state application implemented at run-time in a 3-cell *RAC* according to the position of the token.

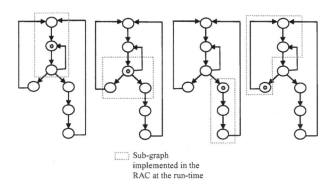

Sub-graph
implemented in the
RAC at the run-time

Fig. 3. Evolution of an implemented SG in the RAC Net

Each time a token is received in a cell of a SG implemented in the *RAC*, its associated instructions are sent to the *RAO*. When the *RAO* has finished its processes, it returns an event to the cell. This event corresponds to an edge in the SG mapped in the *RAC*. These transitions permit the propagation of tokens in SGs. Besides, each block has its synchronization mechanisms. In this globally asynchronous architecture, blocks are synchronized by 2-phase protocols [24].

It is possible to execute concurrently any parallel branches of a SG, or any independant SGs in the *RAC*. This ensures *SIMD*, *MIMD*, and multi-threading control parallelisms. Besides, semaphore and mutex can be directly mapped inside the *RAC* in order to manage shared resources or synchronization between SGs. Even if SGs are implemented cell by cell, their instantiations are concurrent.

3   Functional Description of the Control Block: The RAC

As previously mentioned, the *RAC* is a reconfigurable block dedicated to the control of an application. It is composed of five units (Fig. 4). The *CPL* (*Configuration Protocol Layer*), the *CAM* (*Content Addressable Memory*) and the *LeafFinder* are used to configure the *RAC Net* and to load the *Instruction Memory*.

3.1   Overview

The *RAC Net* can support physical implementation of SGs. When a cell is configured in the *RAC Net*, its associated instructions are stored in the *Instruction Memory* as well as the address of its description in the *CAM*. Descriptions of cells are placed in a central memory and each description contains the instruction of the associated cell and the configuration of cells, which must be connected (daughter cells). In order to extend SGs in the *RAC Net*, the last cells of SGs, which are called *leaf cells*, are identified in the *LeafFinder*. These cells allow the extension of SGs. When a leaf cell is detected, a signal is sent to the *CAM* and the description of this cell is read in the central memory. From this description,

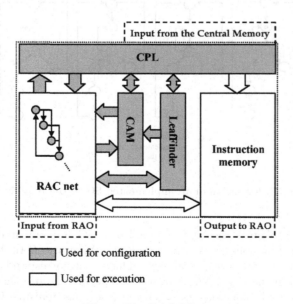

Fig. 4. The RAC block

the daughter cells of this leaf cell are configured and links are established between the cells in the *RAC Net*. The *CAM* can also find a cell mapped in the *RAC Net* thanks to its address. This is necessary if loop kernels try to connect already mapped cells. Finally, the propagation of tokens through SGs, thanks to events from the *RAO*, schedule the execution of instructions stored in the *Instruction Memory*. In the next section, the details of each block are given.

3.2   Blocks Description

RAC Net, this element is composed of cells and interconnect components. SGs are physically implemented thanks to these resources. One state of a SG is implemented by one cell. Each cell directly drives instructions, which are sent to the *RAO*. The *RAC Net* is dynamically reconfigurable. Its resources can be released or used at the run-time according to the execution of the application. Moreover, configuration and execution of SGs are fully concurrent. *RAC Net* owns primitives to ensure the auto-routing and the managing of its resources (cf §4.1). The *RAC Net* is composed of three one-hot asynchronous FSMs (5 ,8 and 2 states) to ensure the propagation of tokens, its dynamical destruction and the creation of connections. It represents about one thousand transistors in ST 0.18μm technology.

Instruction memory, the *Instruction Memory* contains the instructions, which are sent by the *RAC Net* to the *RAO* when tokens run through SGs. An instruction can eventually be either configurations or context addresses. As shown in figure 5, the split instruction bus allows the support of *EPIC* (Explicitly Parallel Instruction Computing) and the different kinds of parallelism introduced in the first section. Each column is reserved for a computation block in the *RAO*. For instance, the instructions A and B could be sent together to different computational blocks mapped in the *RAO* without creating conflicts, whereas the instruction C would be sent alone. A bit of selection is also used to minimize energy consumption by disabling unused blocks.

Furthermore, each line is separately driven by a state, e.g. each cell of the *RAC Net* is dedicated to the management of one line of this memory. This memory does not require address decoding since its access is directly done through its word lines. We call this kind of memory a *word-line memory*.

CPL, this unit manages SG implementation in the *RAC Net*. It sends all the useful information to connect cells, which can auto-route themselves. It drives either a new connection if the next state is not mapped in the *RAC net*, or a connection between two states already mapped. It also sends primitives to release resources when the *RAC Net* is full.

CAM, this memory links each cell of the *RAC Net* used to map a state of a SG, with its address in the external memory. Again, it can be driven directly

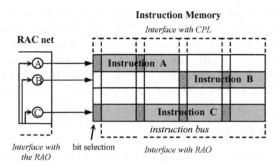

Fig. 5. Relation RAC Net/Instruction Memory

through its word lines. It is used by the *CPL* to check if a cell is already mapped in the *RAC Net*. The *CAM* can select a cell in the *RAC Net* when its address is presented by the *CPL* at its input. Besides, the *CAM* contains the size of cell descriptions to optimize the bandwidth with the central memory.

LeafFinder, this word-line memory identifies all the leaf cells. Leaf cells are in a semi-mapped state which does not yet have an associated instruction. The research is done by a logic ring, which runs each time a leaf cell appears.

4   Auto-adaptative Reconfiguration Control

The first part of this section deals with the creation of connections between cells and their configuration. A cell, which takes part in a SG, must be configured in a special state corresponding to its function in the SG. Finally, the second part focuses on the release of already used cells.

4.1   Graph Creation and Configuration

New connection. To realize a new connection e.g. a connection with a free cell, the *CPL* sends a primitive called *connection*. This carries out automatically a connection between an existing cell (the source cell), which is driven by the *LeafFinder*, and a new cell (the target cell), which is a free cell chosen in the neighborhood of the source cell. Thus, each daughter in the neighborhood of the source cell are successively tested until a free cell is found. The *RAC Net* and its network can self-manage these connections. In fact, carrying out a connection consists of validating existing physical connections between both cells. Finally, the path between the two cells can be considered as auto-routed in the *RAC Net*.

Connection between two existing cells. When the *RAC* finds the two cells, which must be connected, two primitives called *preparation* and *search* are successively sent by the *CPL* to the *RAC Net*. The first one initializes the research process and the second one executes it. The source cell is driven by the *LeafFinder* via the signal *start* and the target cell by the *CAM* via the signal *finish*. According to the application, the network of the RAC Net can be either fully or partially interconnected. Indeed, the interconnection network area is a function of the square of the number of cells in the RAC Net. Thus, a fully connected network should be used only in highly irregular computing application.

If the network is fully interconnected, the connection is simply done by the interconnect, which receives both the signals *start* and *finish*. On the other hand, if cells are partially interconnected, handshaking mechanisms allow the source cells to find the target. Two signals called *find* and *found* link each cells together (Fig. 6). On the reception of the signal *search*, the source cell sends a *find* signal to its daughters. The free cell receiving this signal sends it again to its daughters (this signal can be received only one time). So, the signal *find* spreads through free cells until it reaches the target cell. Then this cell sends back the signal *found* via the same path to the source cell. Finally, the path is validated and a hardware connection is established between the two cells. The intermediate and free cells, which take part in the connection, are in a special mode named *bypass*.

Configuration. The dynamic management of cells is done by a signal called *accessibility*. This signal links every cell of a SG when a connection is done. Each cell owns an *Up Accessibility* (*UA*) (from its mother cells) and a *Down Accessibility* (*DA*) (distributed to its daughter cells). At the time of a new connection, a cell receives the *UA* from its mother cells and stores its configuration coming from the *CPL*. In the case of multiple convergences (details on SG topologies have been presented in [21]), it receives the *UA* as soon as the first connection is established. Then, a configured cell is ready to receive and to give a token. After its configuration, the cell transmits its *accessibility* to its daughters.

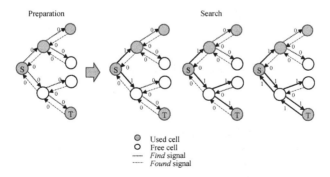

Fig. 6. Connection between the source cell (S) and its target cell (T)

When the connection has succeeded, the *RAC Net* notifies the *CPL*. Consequently, the *CPL* updates the *CAM* with the address of the new mapped state, the *LeafFinder* defines the new cell as a leaf cell, and the *Instruction Memory* stored the correct instructions.

When a connection fails, the *RAC Net* indicates an error to the *CPL*. The *CPL* deallocates resources in the *RAC Net* and searches the next leaf cell with the *LeafFinder*. These two operations are repeated until a connection succeeds. Release mechanisms are detailed in the next paragraph.

4.2   Graph Release

A cell stops to deliver its *accessibility* when it no more receives an *UA* and does not own a token. When a cell loses its accessibility, all the daughter cells are successively free and can be used for other SG implementations. In order to prevent the release of frequently used cells, which may happen in loop kernels, a configuration signal called *stop point* can be used.

Due to resource limitations, a connection attempt may fail. For this reason, a complete error management system has been developed. It is composed of three primitives, which can release more or less cells. The appearing frequency of connection errors is evaluated by the *CPL*. When predefined thresholds are reached, adapted primitives are sent to the *RAC Net* to free unused resources. The first one is called *test acces*. It can free a cell in a *stop point* mode (Fig. 7). Every cell between two *stop point* cells are free. Indeed, a *stop point* cell is free on a rising edge of the *test acces* signal when it receives the *accessibility* from its mothers.

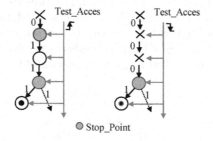

Fig. 7. Releasing of cells with test access

The second release primitive is named *reset stop point*. It can force the liberation of any *stop point* cells when they do not have any token. This mode keeps cells implied in the implementation of loop kernels and reduces the release. In some critical cases (when resources are very limited), it can become an idle state.

Finally, the last primitive called *reset idle state* guarantees no idle state in the *RAC*. This is done by freeing all the cells, which do not own a token. This solution is of course the more efficient but is very expensive in time and energy consumption. It must only be used in case of repeated desallocation errors.

No heuristics decide how many cells must be reclaimed or loaded. This is done automatically even if the desallocation is not optimal. That is why *stop point* cells must be adequately placed in SGs to limit releases.

Non-deterministic algorithms need to make decisions to follow their processes. This can be translated as OR divergences, e.g. events determine which branch will be followed by firing transitions. To prevent speculative construction and to configure too many unemployed cells, the construction of SGs is blocked until correct decisions are taken. This does not slow the execution of the application since the *RAC Net* contains always the next processes. Moreover, we consider that execution is slower than reconfiguration, and that an optimal computation time is about $3ns$. Indeed, we estimate the reconfiguration time of a cell equals to $7.5ns$ and the minimum time between two successive instructions for a fully interconnected network of $3ns + 1.5ns$, where $1.5ns$ is the interconnect propagation time for a 32-cell *RAC*.

5   Implementation and Performance Estimation

An architecture can not be exploited without a development flow. For this reason, a development flow is currently a major research concern of our laboratory (Fig. 8). From a description of the application in C-language, an intermediate representation can be obtained by a front-end like SUIF [22,23]. Then, a parallelism exploration from the *CDFG* must be done to assign tasks to the multiple computing resources of the *RAO*. This parallelism exploration under constraints increases performances and minimizes the energy consumption and the memory

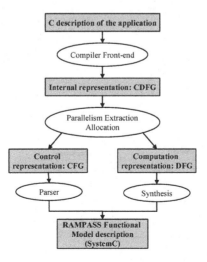

Fig. 8. RAMPASS Development Flow Graph

bandwidth. The allocation of multiple resources in the *RAO* can also increase the level of parallelism. From this optimized *CDFG*, *DFGs* must be extracted in order to be executed on *RAO* resources. Each *DFG* is then translated into *RAO* configurations, thanks to behavioral synthesis scheme. This function is currently under development through the *OSGAR* project, which consists in designing a general-purpose synthesizer for any reconfigurable architectures. This *RNTL* project under the ward of the French research ministry, associates TNI-Valiosys, the Occidental Brittany University and the R2D2 team of the IRISA. On the other hand, a parser used to translate a *CFG* into the *RAMPASS* description language, has been successfully developed.

Besides, a functional model of the *RAC* block has been designed with SystemC. Our functional-level description of the *RAC* is a CABA (Cycle Accurate and Bit Accurate) hardware model. It permits the change of the size and the features of the *RAC Net* and allows the evaluation of its energy consumption. The characteristics of this description language easily allows hardware descriptions, it has the flexibility of the C++ language and brings all the primitives for the modelization of hardware architectures [25,26].

A lot of different programming structures have been implemented in the *RAC* block, e.g. exclusion mechanisms, AND convergence and divergence, synchronizations between separated graphs, etc. Moreover, an application of video processing (spinal search algorithm for motion estimation [27]) has been mapped (Fig. 9). The latency overhead is insignificant without reconfiguration when the

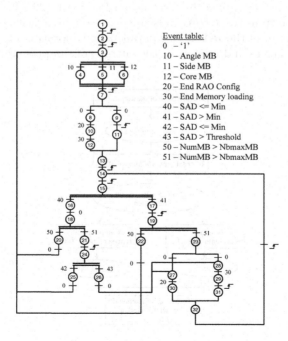

Fig. 9. Motion estimation graph

RAC owns 32 cells, or with a 15-cell RAC when the whole main loop kernel can be implemented (0.01%), even if we cannot predict reconfigurations. Finally with a 7-cell RAC (the minimal required for this application), the overhead raises only 10% in spite of multiple reconfigurations, since the implementation of the SG must be continuously updated.

Besides, hardware simulations have shown the benefits of release primitives. Indeed, the more cells are released, the more the energy consumption increases since they will have to be re-generated, especially in case of loops. Simulations have shown that these releases are done only when necessary.

Some SG structures implemented in the RAC Net need an imperative number of cells. This constraints the minimal number of cells to prevent dead-locks. For instance, a multiple AND divergence has to be entirely mapped before the token is transmitted. Consequently, an 8-state AND divergence needs at least nine cells to work. Dynamic reconfiguration ensures the progress of SGs but can not prevent dead-locks if complex structures need more cells than available inside the RAC Net. On the contrary, the user can map a linear SG of thousands of cells with only two free cells.

6   Conclusion and Future Work

New paradigm of dynamically self-reconfigurable architecture has been proposed in this paper. The part depicted is dedicated to the control and can physically implement control graphs of applications. This architecture brings a novel approach for controlling reconfigurable resources. It can answer future technology improvements, allow a high level of parallelism and keep a constant execution flow, even for non-predictible processing.

Our hardware simulation model has successfully validated static and dynamic reconfiguration paradigms. According to these results, further works will be performed. To evaluate performances of RAMPASS, a synthesized model and a prototype of the RAC block is currently designed in a ST 0.18μm technology.

Moreover, the coupling between the RAC and other reconfigurable architectures (DART, Systolic Ring, etc.) will be studied. The aim of these further collaborations consists in demonstrating the high aptitudes of the RAC to adapt itself to different computation architectures.

Acknowledgements. We thank Dominique Lavenier (IRISA, France), Laurent Letellier and Raphaël David (CEA, France) for helpful discussions and comments on this work.

References

1. Semiconductor Industry Association. International Technology Roadmap for Semiconductors. Technical report, 2003.
2. K. Compton and S. Hauck. Reconfigurable Computing: A Survey of Systems and Software. *ACM Computing Surveys*, 34(2):171–210, June 2002.

3. R. Hartenstein. A Decade of Reconfigurable Computing: a Visionary Retrospective. In *IEEE Design Automation and Test in Europe (DATE)*, Munich, Germany, March 2001.
4. Xilinx, http://www.xilinx.com.
5. Altera, http://www.altera.com.
6. S.C. Goldstein, H. Schmit, M. Budiu, S. Cadambi, M. Moe, and R.R. Taylor. PipeRench: A Reconfigurable Architecture and Compiler. *Computer: Innovative Technology for Computer Profesionals*, 33(4):70–77, April 2000.
7. J. Becker, M. Glesner, A. Alsolaim, and J. Starzyk. Fast Communication Mechanisms in Coarse-grained Dynamically Reconfigurable Array Architectures. In *Workshop on Engineering of Reconfigurable Hardware/Software Objects (ENRE-GLE)*, Las Vegas, USA, June 2000.
8. H. Singh, M.-H. Lee, G. Lu, F.J. Kurdahi, N. Bagherzadeh, and E.M. Chaves Filho. MorphoSys: An Integrated Reconfigurable System for Data-Parallel and Computation-Intensive Applications. *IEEE Trans. on Computers*, Vol.49, No.5:465–481, May 2000.
9. T. Miyamori and K. Olukotun. REMARC: Reconfigurable Multimedia Array Coprocessor. In *ACM/SIGDA Field Programmable Gate Array (FPGA)*, Monterey, USA, February 1998.
10. D. Cronquist. Architecture Design of Reconfigurable Pipelined Datapaths. In *Advanced Research in VLSI (ARVLSI)*, Atlanta, USA, March 1999.
11. R. David, S. Pillement, and O. Sentieys. *Low-Power Electronics Design*, chapter 20: Low-Power Reconfigurable Processors. CRC press edited by C. Piguet, April 2004.
12. G. Sassateli, L. Torres, P. Benoit, T. Gil, G. Cambon, and J. Galy. Highly Scalable Dynamically Reconfigurable Systolic Ring-Architecture for DSP applications. In *IEEE Design Automation and Test in Europe (DATE)*, Paris, France, March 2002.
13. G.M. Amdahl. Validity of the Single-Processor Approach to Achieving Large Scale Computing Capabilities. In *AFIPS Conference Proceedings vol.30*, Atlantic City, USA, April 1967.
14. J. Becker and M. Vorbach. Architecture, Memory and Interface Technology Integration of an Industrial/Academic Configurable System-on-Chip (CSoC). In *IEEE Computer Society Annual Workshop on VLSI (WVLSI)*, Florida, USA, February 2003.
15. Y. Chou, P. Pillai, H. Schmit, and J.P. Shen. PipeRench Implementation of the Instruction Path Coprocessor. In *Symposium on Microarchitecture (MICRO-33)*, Monterey, USA, December 2000.
16. B. Mei, S. Vernalde, D. Verkest, and R. Lauwereins. Design Methodology for a Tightly Coupled VLIW/Reconfigurable Matrix Architecture: A Case Study. In *Design Automation and Test in Europe (DATE)*, Paris, France, February 2004.
17. Z. Ye, P. Banerjee, S. Hauck, and A. Moshovos. CHIMAERA: A High-Performance Architecture with a Tightly-Coupled RFU. In the *27th Annual International Symposium on Computer Architecture (ISCA)*, Vancouver, Canada, June 2000.
18. C. Rupp, M. Landguth, T. Garverick, E. Gomersall, H. Holt, J. Arnold, and M. Gokhale. The NAPA Adaptive Processing Architecture. In *IEEE Symposium on Field-Programmable Custom Computing Machines (FCCM)*, Napa Valley, USA, April 1998.
19. J.R. Hauser and J. Wawrzynek. GARP: A MIPS Processor with a Reconfigurable Coprocessor. In *IEEE Symposium on Field-Programmable Custom Computing Machines (FCCM)*, Napa Valley, USA, April 1997.

20. D. Rizzo and O. Colavin. A Video Compression Case Study on a Reconfigurable VLIW Architecture. In *Design Automation and Test in Europe (DATE)*, Paris, France, March 2002.

21. S. Chevobbe, N. Ventroux, F. Blanc, and T. Collette. RAMPASS: Reconfigurable and Advanced Multi-Processing Architecture for future Silicon System. In *3rd International Workshop on Systems, Architectures, Modeling and Simulation (SAMOS)*, Samos, Greece, July 2003.

22. G. Aigner, A. Diwan, D.L. Heine, M.S. Lam, D.L. Moore, B.R. Murphy, and C. Sapuntzakis. The Basic SUIF Programming Guide. Technical report, Computer Systems Laboratory, Stanford University, USA, August 2000.

23. M.D. Smith and G. Holloway. An Introduction to Machine SUIF and its Portable Libraries for Analysis and Optimization. Technical report, Division of Engineering and Applied Sciences, Harvard University, USA, July 2002.

24. I.E. Sutherland. Micropipelines. *Communications of the ACM*, 32(6):720–738, 1989.

25. J. Gerlach and W. Rosenstiel. System level design using the SystemC modeling platform. In *the 3rd Workshop on System Design Automation (SDA)*, Rathen, Germany, 2000.

26. S. Swan. An Introduction to System Level Modeling in SystemC 2.0. Technical report, Cadence Design Systems, Inc., May 2001.

27. T. Zahariadis and D. Kalivas. A Spiral Search Algorithm for Fast Estimation of Block Motion Vectors. In *the 8th European Signal Processing Conference (EU-SIPCO)*, Trieste, Italy, September 1996.

Enhancing the Memory Performance of Embedded Systems with the Flexible Sequential and Random Access Memory

Ying Chen, Karthik Ranganathan, Vasudev V. Pai, David J. Lilja, and Kia Bazargan

Department of Electrical and Computer Engineering
University of Minnesota
200 Union St. S.E., Minneapolis, MN 55455, USA
{wildfire, kar, pvasudev, lilja, kia}@ece.umn.edu

Abstract. The on-chip memory performance of embedded systems directly affects the system designers' decision about how to allocate expensive silicon area. We investigate a novel memory architecture, *flexible sequential and random access memory* (FSRAM), for embedded systems. To realize sequential accesses, small "links" are added to each row in the RAM array to point to the next row to be prefetched. The potential cache pollution is ameliorated by a small *sequential access buffer* (SAB). To evaluate the architecture-level performance of FSRAM, we run the Mediabench benchmark programs [1] on a modified version of the Simplescalar simulator [2]. Our results show that the FSRAM improves the performance of a baseline processor with a 16KB data cache up to 55%, with an average of 9%. We also designed RTL and SPICE models of the FSRAM [3], which show that the FSRAM significantly improves memory access time, while reducing power consumption, with negligible area overhead.

1   Introduction

Rapid advances in high-performance computing architectures and semiconductor technologies have drawn considerable interest to high performance memories. Increases in hardware capabilities have led to performance bottlenecks due to the time required to access the memory. Furthermore, the on-chip memory performance in embedded systems directly affects designers' decisions about how to allocate expensive silicon area. Off-chip memory power consumption has become the energy consumption bottleneck as embedded applications become more data-centric.

Most of the recent research has tended to focus on improving performance and power consumption of on-chip memory structures [4, 5, 6] rather than off-chip memory. Moon *et al* [7] investigated a low-power sequential access on-chip memory designed to exploit the numerous sequential access patterns in digital signal processing (DSP) applications. Prefetching techniques from traditional computer architecture have also been used to enhance on-chip memory performance for embedded systems [8, 9, 10]. Other studies have investigated energy efficient off-chip memory for embedded systems, such as automatic data migration for multi-bank memory systems [11].

P.-C. Yew and J. Xue (Eds.): ACSAC 2004, LNCS 3189, pp. 88–101, 2004.
© Springer-Verlag Berlin Heidelberg 2004

None of these previous studies, however, have investigated using off-chip memory structures to improve on-chip memory performance. This study demonstrates the performance potential of a novel, low-power, off-chip memory structure, which we call the *flexible sequential and random access memory* (FSRAM), to support flexible memory access patterns. In addition to normal random access, the FSRAM uses an extra "link" structure, which bypasses the row decoder, for sequential accesses. The link structure reduces power consumption and decreases memory access times; moreover, it aggressively prefetches data into the on-chip memory. In order to eliminate the potential data cache pollution caused by prefetching, a small fully associative *sequential access buffer* (SAB) is used in parallel with the data cache. VHDL and HSPICE models of the FSRAM have been developed to evaluate its effectiveness at the circuit level. Embedded multimedia applications are simulated to demonstrate its performance potential at the architecture level. Our results show significant performance improvement with little extra area used by the link structures.

The remainder of this paper is organized as follows. Section 2 introduces and explains the FSRAM and the SAB. In Section 3, the experimental setup is described. The architecture level performance analysis and area, timing and power consumption evaluations of the FSRAM are presented in Section 4. Section 5 discusses related work. Finally, Section 6 summarizes and concludes.

2   Flexible Sequential Access Memory

Our flexible sequential and random access memory (FSRAM) architecture is an extension of the sequential memory architecture developed by Moon, *et al* [7]. They argued that since many DSP applications have static and highly predictable memory traces, row address decoders can be eliminated. As a result, memory access would be sequential with data accesses determined at compile time. They showed considerable power savings at the circuit level.

While preserving the power reduction property, our work extends their work in two ways: (1) in addition to circuit-level simulations, we perform architectural-level simulations to assess the performance benefits at the application level; and (2) we extend the sequential access mechanism using a novel enhancement that increases sequential access flexibility.

2.1   Structure of the FSRAM

Fig. 1 shows the basic structure of our proposed FSRAM. There are two address decoders to allow simultaneous read and write accesses[1]. The read address decoder is shared by both the memory and the "link" structure. However, the same structure is used as the write decoder for the link structure, while the read/write decoder is required only for the memory. As can be seen, each memory word is associated with a link structure, an OR gate, a multiplexer, and a sequencer.

---

[1] Throughout the paper, all experiments are performed assuming dual-port memories. It is important to note that our FSAM does not *require* the memory to have two ports. The reason we chose two ports is that most modern memory architectures have multiple ports to improve memory latency.

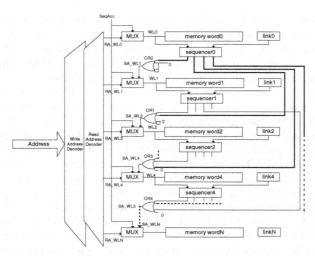

Fig. 1. The FSRAM adds a link, an OR gate, a multiplexer, and a sequencer to each memory word.

The link structure indicates which successor memory word to access when the memory is being used in the sequential access mode. With 2 bits, the link can point to four unique successor memory word lines (*e.g.*, N+1, N+2, N+4, and N+8). This link structure is similar to the "next" pointer in a linked-list data structure. Note that Moon *et al* [7] hardwired the sequencer cell of each row to the row below it. By allowing more flexibility, and the ability to dynamically modify the link destination, the row address decoder can be bypassed for many more memory accesses than previous mechanisms to provide greater potential speedup.

(a)   (b)

Fig. 2. (a) Block diagram of the OR block, (b) block diagram of the sequencer.

The OR block shown in Fig. 1 is used to generate the sequential address. If any of the four inputs to the OR block is high, the sequential access address (SA_WL) will be high (Fig. 2.a). Depending on the access mode signal (SeqAcc), the multiplexers choose between the row address decoder and the sequential cells. The role of the sequencer is to determine the next sequential address according to the value of the link (Fig. 2.b). If WL is high, then one of the four outputs is high. However if *reset* is high, then all four outputs go low irrespective of WL. The timing diagram of the signals in Fig. 2 is shown in our previous study [3].

The area overhead of the FSRAM consists of four parts - the link, OR gate, multiplexer, and sequencer. The overhead is in about the order of 3-7% of the total memory area for the word line size of 32 bytes and 64 bytes. More detailed area overhead results are shown in Table 2 in Section 4.2.

2.2   Update of the Link Structure

The link associated with each off-chip memory word line is dynamically updated using data cache miss trace information and run-time reconfiguration of the sequential access target. In this manner, the sequentially accessed data blocks are linked when compulsory misses occur. Since the read decoder for the memory is the same physical structure as the write decoder for the link structure, the link can be updated in parallel with a memory access. The default link value of the link is 0, which actually means the next line ($2^0 = 1$).

We note that the read and write operations to the memory data elements and the link RAM cells can be done independently. The word lines can be used to activate both the links and the data RAM cells for read or write (not all of the control signals are shown in Fig. 1).

There are a number of options for writing the link values:

1.   The links can be computed at compile-time and loaded into the data memory while instructions are being
        loaded into the instruction memory.
2.   The link of one row could be written while the data from another row is being read.
3.   The link can be updated while the data of the same row is being read or written.

Option 1 is the least flexible approach since it exploits only static information. However, it could eliminate some control circuitry that supports the runtime updating of the links. Options 2 and 3 update the link structure at run-time and so that both exploit dynamic run-time information. Option 2, however, needs more run-time data access information compared to Option 3 and thus requires more control logic. We decided to examine Option 3 in this paper since the dynamic configuration of the links can help in subsequent prefetches.

2.3   Accessing the FSRAM and the SAB

In order to eliminate potential cache pollution caused by the prefetching effect of the FSRAM, we use a small fully associative cache structure, which we call the *Sequential Access Buffer* (SAB). In our experiments, the on-chip data cache and the SAB are accessed in parallel, as shown in Fig. 3. The data access operation is summarized in Fig. 4. When a memory reference misses in both the data cache and the SAB, the required block is fetched into the data cache from the off-chip memory. Furthermore, a data block pointed to by the link of the data word being currently read is pushed into the SAB if it is not already in the on-chip memory. That is, the link is followed and the result is stored in the SAB. When a memory reference misses in the data cache but hits in the SAB, the required block and the victim block in the data cache are swapped. Additionally, the data block linked to the required data block, but not already in on-chip memory, is pushed into the SAB.

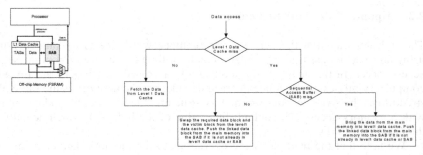

Fig. 3. The placement of the **Fig. 4.** Flowchart of a data access when using the SAB and
Sequential   Access   Buffer the FSRAM.
(SAB) in the memory hierar-
chy.

3   Experimental Methodology

To evaluate the system level performance of the FSRAM, we used SimpleScalar 3.0
[2] to run the Mediabench [1] benchmarks using this new memory structure. The
basic processor configurations are based on Intel Xscale [12], The Intel XScale
microarchitecture is a RISC core that can be combined with peripherals to provide
applications specific standard products (ASSP) targeted at selected market segments.
The basic processor configurations are as the following: 32 KB data and instruction
L1 caches with 32-byte data lines, 2-way associativity and 1 cycle latency, no L2
cache, and 50 cycle main memory access latency. The default SAB size is 8 entries.
The machine can issue two instructions per cycle. It has a 32-entry load/store queue
and one integer unit, one floating point unit, and one multiplication/division unit, all
with 1 cycle latency. The branch predictor is bimodal and has 128 entries. The
instruction and data TLBs are fully associative and have 32 entries. The link structure
in the off-chip memory was simulated by using a large enough table to hold both the
miss addresses and their link values. The link values are updated by monitoring the
L1 data cache miss trace. Whenever the gap between two continuous misses is 1x, 2x,
3x, 4x block line size, we update the link value correlated to the memory line that
causes the first miss in the two continuous misses.

3.1   Benchmark Programs

We used the Mediabench [13] benchmarks ported to the SimpleScalar simulator for
the architecture-level simulations of the FSRAM. We used four of the benchmark
programs, *adpcm, epic, g721* and *mesa*, for these simulations since they were the only
ones that worked with the Simplescalar PISA instruction set architecture.

Since the FSRAM link structure links successor memory word lines (Section 3.1),
we show the counts of the address gap distances between two consecutive data cache
misses in Table 1. We see from these results that the address gap distances of 32, 64,
128, 256 and 512 bytes are the most common, while the other address gap distances
occur more randomly. Therefore, the FSRAM evaluated in this study supports address

gap distances of 32, 64, 128 and 256 bytes for a 32-byte cache line, while distances of 64, 128, 256 and 512 bytes are supported for a 64-byte cache line.

For all of the benchmark programs tested, the dominant gap distances are between 32 and 128 bytes. Most of the tested benchmarks, except *g721*, have various gap distances distributed among 32 to 256 bytes. When the gap increases to 512 bytes, *epic* and *mesa* still exhibit similar access patterns while *adpcm* and *g721* have no repeating patterns at this gap distance.

Table 1. The frequencies (counts) of the various address distance gaps between two consecutive data cache misses for the tested benchmark programs

	adpcm encode	adpcm decode	epic encode	epic decode	g721 encode	g721 decode	mesa mipmap	mesa osdemo	Mesa texgen
32Bytes	121	121	167	82	609512	590181	78740	2212	229004
64 Bytes	7157	7157	3552	43	93	94	9	50896	22809
128 Bytes	979	979	1864	80	0	0	5	497	13441
256 Bytes	3237	3237	36	392	0	0	14	9	2
512 Bytes	0	0	5	896	0	0	3	1	16457

Another important issue for the evaluation of benchmark program performance is the overall memory footprint estimated from the cache miss rates. Table 2 shows the change in the L1 data cache miss rates for the baseline architecture as the size of the data cache is changed. In general, these benchmarks have small memory footprints, especially *adpcm* and *g721*. Therefore, we chose data cache sizes in these simulations to approximately match the performance that would be observed with larger caches in real systems. The default data cache configuration throughout this study is 16 KB with a 32-byte line and 2-way set associativity.

Table 2. The L1 data cache miss rates for the baseline architecture with various L1 cache sizes

	adpcm encode	adpam decode	epic encode	epic decode	g721 encode	g721 decode	mesa mipmap	mesa osdemo	Mesa Texge n
2KB	0.0214	0.0174	0.1424	0.1248	0.0010	0.0013	0.0894	0.0207	0.0735
4KB	0.001	0.0011	0.0703	0.0612	0.0003	0.0004	0.0444	0.0173	0.0337
8KB	0.0011	0.0011	0.0362	0.0591	0.0001	0.0001	0.0176	0.0142	0.0127
16KB	0.0010	0.0010	0.0162	0.0569	0.0000	0.0000	0.0086	0.0123	0.0068
32KB	0.0010	0.0010	0.0150	0.0535	0.0000	0.0000	0.0059	0.0112	0.0048

3.2   Processor Configurations

The following processor configurations are simulated to determine the performance impact of adding an FSRAM to the processor and the additional performance enhancement that can be attributed to the SAB.

orig: This is the baseline architecture with no link structure in the off-chip memory and no prefetching mechanism.

FSRAM: This configuration is described in detail in Section 3.1. To summarize, this configuration incorporates a link structure in the off-chip memory to exploit sequential data accesses.

FSRAM_SAB: This configuration uses the *FSRAM* with an additional small, fully associative SAB in parallel with the L1 data cache. The details of the SAB were given in Section 3.3.

tnlp: This configuration adds tagged next line prefetching [14] to the baseline architecture. With tagged next line prefetching, a prefetch operation is initiated on a miss and on the first hit to a previously prefetched block. Tagged next line prefetching has been shown to be more effective than prefetching only on a miss [15]. We use this configuration to compare against the prefetching ability of the *FSRAM*.

tnlp_PB: This configuration enhances the *tnlp* configuration with a small, fully associative Prefetch Buffer (PB) in parallel with the L1 data cache to eliminate the potential cache pollution caused by next line prefetching. We use this configuration to compare against the prefetching ability of the *FSRAM_SAB* configuration.

4   Performance Evaluation

In this section we evaluate the performance of an embedded processor with the FSRAM and the SAB by analyzing the sensitivity of the processor configuration *FSRAM_SAB* as the on-chip data cache parameters are varied. We also show the timing, area, and power consumption results based RTL and SPICE models of the FSRAM.

4.1   Architecture-Level Performance

We first examine the *FSRAM_SAB* performance compared to the other processor configurations to show the data prefetching effect provided by the FSRAM and the cache pollution elimination effect provided by the SAB. Since the FSRAM improves the overall performance by improving the performance of the on-chip data cache, we evaluate the *FSRAM_SAB* performance while varying the values for different data cache parameters including the cache size, associativity, block size, and the SAB size.

Throughout Section 4.1, the baseline cache structure configuration is a 16 KB L1 on-chip data cache with a 32-byte data block size, 2-way associativity, and an 8-entry SAB. The average speedups are calculated using the execution time weighted average of all of the benchmarks [16].

Performance Improvement due to FSRAM. To show the performance obtained from the FSRAM and the SAB, we compare the relative speedup obtained by all four processor configurations described in Section 3.2 (i.e., *tnlp*, *tnlp_PB*, *FSRAM*, *FSRAM_SAB*) against the baseline processor configuration (*orig*). All of the processor configurations use a 16 KB L1 data cache with a 32-byte data block size and 2-way set associativity.

As shown in Fig. 5, the *FSRAM* configuration produces an average speedup of slightly more than 4% over the baseline configuration compared to a speedup of less than 1% for *tnlp*. Adding a small prefetch buffer (PB) to the *tnlp* configuration (*tnlp_PB*) improves the performance by about 1% compared to the *tnlp* configuration without the prefetch buffer. Adding the same size SAB to the FSRAM configuration (*FSRAM_SAB*) improves the performance compared to the FSRAM without the SAB by an additional 8.5%. These speedups are due to the extra small cache structures that eliminate the potential cache pollution caused by prefetching directly into the L1 cache. Furthermore, we see that the FSRAM without the SAB outperforms tagged next-line prefetching both with and without the prefetch buffer. The speedup of the FSRAM with the SAB compared to the baseline configuration is 8.5% on average and can be as high as 54% (*mesa_mipmap*).

Benchmark programs *adpcm* and *g721* have very small performance improvements, because their memory footprints are so small that there are very few data cache misses to eliminate in a 16KB data cache (Table 2) Never the less, from the statistics shown in Fig. 5, we can still see *adpcm* and *g721* follow the similar performance trend described above.

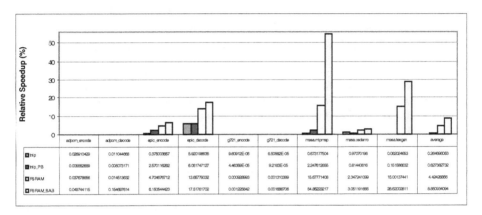

Fig. 5. Relative speedups obtained by the different processor configurations. The baseline is the original processor configuration. All of the processor configurations use a 16KB data L1 cache with 32-byte block and 2-way associativity.

Parameter Sensitivity Analysis. We are interested in the performance of FSRAM with different on-chip data cache to exam how the off-chip FSRAM main memory structure improves on-chip memory performance. So in this section we study the effects of various data cache sizes (i.e., 2KB, 4KB, 8KB, 16KB, 32KB), data cache associativities (i.e., 1way, 2way, 4way, 8way), cache block sizes (i.e., 32 bytes, 64 bytes) and the SAB sizes (i.e., 4 entries, 8entries, 16entreis) on the performance. The baseline processor configuration through this section is the original processor configuration with a 2KB data L1 cache with 32-byte block size and 2-way associativity.

The Effect of Data Cache Size. Fig. 6 shows the relative speedup distribution among orig, tnlp_PB and FSRAM_SAB for various L1 data cache sizes (i.e., 2KB, 4KB, 8KB, 16KB, 32KB). The total relative speedup is FSRAM_SAB with a L1 data cache sizes over orig with a 2KB L1 data, which is divided into three parts: the relative speedup of orig with a L1 data cache size over orig with a 2KB L1 data cache; the relative speedup of tnlp_PB with a L1 data cache size over orig with a L1 data cache size; the relative speedup of FSRAM_SAB with a L1 data cache size over tnlp_PB with a L1 data cache size.

As shown, with the increase of L1 data cache size the relative speedup of *tnlp_PB* over *orig* decreases. FSRAM_SAB, in contrast, constantly keeps speedup on top of *tnlp_PB* across the different L1 data cache sizes. Furthermore, *FSRAM_SAB* even outperforms *tnlp_PB* with a larger size L1 data cache for most of the cases and on average. For instance, *FSRAM* with a 8KB L1 data cache outperforms *tnlp_PB* with a 32KB L1 data cache. However, *tnlp_PB* only outperforms the baseline processor with a bigger size data cache for *epic_decode* and *mesa_osdemo*.

The improvement in the performance can be attributed to several factors. While the baseline processor does not perform any prefetching, the tagged next line prefetching prefetches only the next word line. The fact that our method can prefetch with strides is one contributing factor in the smaller memory access time. Furthermore, prefetching is realized using sequential access, which is faster than random access. Another benefit is that prefetching with different strides does not require an extra large table to store the next address to be accessed.

tnlp_PB and *FSRAM_SAB* improve performance in the case that the performance of *orig* increases with the increase of L1 data cache size. However, they have little effect in the case that the performance of *orig* increases with the increase of L1 data cache size, which means the benchmark program has small memory foot prints (i.e., *adpcm, g721*). For adpcm, *tnlp* and *FSRAM_SAB* still improve performance when the L1 data cache size is 2K. For g721, the performance almost keeps the same all the time due to the small memory footprint.

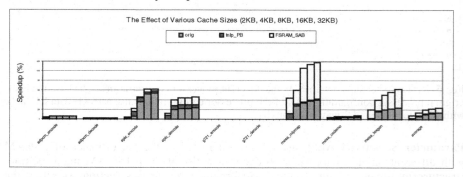

Fig. 6. Relative speedups distribution among the different processor configurations (i.e., *orig, tnlp_PB, FSRAM_SAB*) with various L1 data cache sizes (i.e., 2KB, 4KB, 8KB, 16KB, 32KB). The baseline is the original processor configuration with a 2KB data L1 cache with 32-byte block size and 2-way associativity.

The Effect of Data Cache Associativity. Fig. 7 shows the relative speedup distribution among orig, tnlp_PB and FSRAM_SAB for various L1 data cache associativity (i.e., 1way, 2way, 4way, 8way).

As known, increasing the L1 data cache associativity typically reduces the number of L1 data cache misses. The reduction in misses reduces the effect of prefetching from *tnlp_PB* and *FSRAM_SAB*. As can be seen, the performance speed up of *tnlp_PB* on top of *orig* decreases as the L1 data cache associativity increases. The speed up almost disappears when the associativity is increased to 8way for mesa_mipmap and mesa_texgen. However, FSRAM_SAB still provides significant speedups.

tnlp_PB and *FSRAM_SAB* still have little impact on the performance of adpcm and g721 because their small memory footprints.

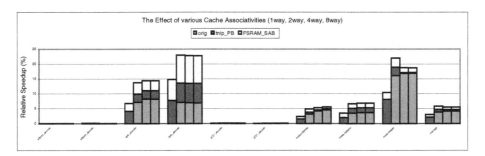

Fig. 7. Relative speedups distribution among the different processor configurations (i.e., *orig, tnlp_PB, FSRAM_SAB*) with various L1 data cache associativity (i.e., 1way, 2way, 4way, 8way). The baseline is the original processor configuration with a 2KB data L1 cache with 32-byte block size and 2-way associativity.

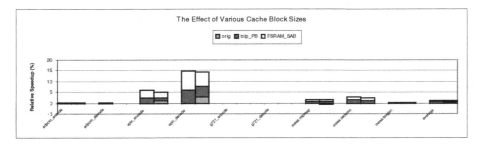

Fig. 8. Relative speedups distribution among the different processor configurations (i.e., *orig, tnlp_PB, FSRAM_SAB*) with various L1 data cache block sizes (i.e., 32B, 64B). The baseline is the original processor configuration with a 2KB data L1 cache with 32-byte block size and 2-way associativity.

The Effect of Data Cache Block Size. Fig. 8 shows the relative speedup distribution among *orig, tnlp_PB* and *FSRAM_SAB* for various L1 data cache block sizes (i.e., 32B, 64B).

As known increasing the L1 data cache block size typically reduces the number of L1 data cache misses. For all of the benchmarks the reduction in misses reduces the effect of prefetching from *tnlp_PB* and *FSRAM_SAB*. As can be seen, the performance speed up of *tnlp_PB* on top of *orig* decreases as the L1 data cache block size increases from 32-bytes to 64 bytes. However, the increasing of the L1 data cache block size can also cause potential pollutions as for *epic_encode* and *mesa_mipmap*. Tnlp with a small prefetching buffer reduces the pollution, and FSRAM_SAB further speeds up the performance.

The Effect of SAB Size. Fig. 9 shows the relative speedup distribution among orig, tnlp_PB and FSRAM_SAB for various SAB sizes (i.e., 4 entries, 8 entries, 16 entries).

Fig. 9 compares the FSRAM_SAB approach to a tagged next-line prefetching that uses the prefetch buffer that is the same size as SAB. As shown, FSRAM_SAB always add speedup on top of tnlp_PB. Further, *FSRAM_SAB* outperforms *tnlp* with a bigger size prefetch buffer. This result indicates that FSRAM_SAB is actually a more efficient prefetching mechanism than a traditional tagged next-line prefetching mechanism.

tnlp_PB and *FSRAM_SAB* still have little impact on the performance of adpcm and g721 because their small memory footprints.

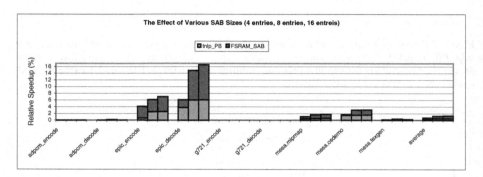

Fig. 9. Relative speedup distribution among the different processor configurations (i.e., *tnlp_PB, FSRAM_SAB*) with various SAB sizes (i.e., 4 entries, 8 entries, 16 entries). The baseline is the original processor configuration with a 2KB data L1 cache with 32-byte block size and 2-way associativity.

4.2   Timing, Area, and Power Consumption

We implemented the FSRAM architecture in VHDL to verify its functional correctness at the RTL level. We successfully tested various read/write combinations of row data *vs.* links. Depending on application requirements, one or two decoders can be provided so that the FSAM structure can be used as a dual-port or single-port memory structure. In all our experiments, we assumed dual-port memories since modern memory structures have multiple ports to decrease memory latency.

In addition to the RTL level design, we implemented a small 8x8 (8 rows, 8 bits per row) FSRAM in HSPICE using 0.18μm technology to test timing correctness and evaluate the delay of sequencer blocks. Note that unlike the decoder, the sequencer block's delay is independent of the size of the memory structure: it only depends on how many rows it links to (in our case: 4).

By adding sequencer cells, we will be adding to the area of the memory structure. However, in this section we show that the area overhead is not large, especially considering the fact that in today's RAMs, a large number of memory bits are arranged in a row. An estimate of the percentage increase in area was calculated using the formula $(\dfrac{A1}{A1-A2}-1)x100\%$ where A1 = Total Area and A2 = area occupied by the link, OR gate, MUX and the sequencer. Table 3 shows the results of the increases in area for different memory row sizes. The sequencer has two SRAM bits, which is not many compared to the number of bits packed in a row of the memory. We can see that the sequencer cell logic does not occupy a significant area either.

Table 3. Area overhead of FSRAM with various memory word line sizes

No. of bits per row of memory	Increase in area due to the MUX and the sequencer
8 (1 byte)	216%
16 (2 bytes)	119%
64 (8 bytes)	23.0%
256 (32 bytes)	7.12%
512 (64 bytes)	3.10%

As can be seen, the percentage increase in area drops substantially as the number of bits in each word line increases. Hence the area overhead is almost negligible for large memory blocks.

Using the HSPICE model, we compared the delay of the sequencer cell to the delay of a decoder. Furthermore, by scaling the capacity of the bit lines, we estimated the read/write delay and hence, calculated an overall speedup of 15% of sequential access compared to random access.

Furthermore, the power saving is 16% in sequential access at VDD = 3.3v in the 0.18 micron CMOS HSPICE model.

5   Related Work

The research related to this work can be classified into three categories: on-chip memory optimizations, off-chip memory optimizations, and hardware-supported prefetching techniques.

In their papers, Panda *et. al.* [4, 5] address data cache size and number of processor cycles as performance metrics for on-chip memory optimization. Shiue *et al.* [6] extend this work to include energy consumption and show that it is not enough to consider only memory size increase and miss rate reduction for performance optimization of on-chip memory because the power consumption actually increases. In order to reduce power consumption, Moon *et al.* [7] designed an on-chip sequential access only memory specifically for DSP applications that demonstrates the low-power potential of sequential access.

A few papers have addressed the issue of off-chip memory optimization, especially power optimization, in embedded systems. In a multi-bank memory system Dela Luz *et al.* [11] show promising power consumption reduction by using an automatic data migration strategy to co-locate the arrays with temporal affinity in a small set of memory banks. But their approach has major overhead due to extra time spent in data migration and extra power spent to copy data from bank to bank.

Zucker *et al.* [10] compared hardware prefeching techniques adopted from general-purpose applications to multimedia applications. They studied a stride prediction table associated with PC (program counter). A data-cache miss-address-based stride prefetching mechanism for multimedia applications is proposed by Dela Luz *et al.* [11]. Both studies show promising results at the cost of extra on-chip memory devoted to a table structure of non-negligible size. Although low-cost hybrid data prefetching slightly outperforms hardware prefetching, it limits the code that could benefit from prefetching [9]. Sbeyti *et. al.* [8] propose an adaptive prefetching mechanism which exploits both the miss stride and miss interval information of the memory access behavior of only MPEG4 in embedded systems.

Unlike previous approaches, we propose a novel off-chip memory with little area overhead (3-7% for 32 bytes and 64 bytes data block line) and significant performance improvements, compared to previous works that propose expensive on-chip memory structures. Our study investigated off-chip memory structure to improve on-chip memory performance, thus leaves flexibility for designer's to allocate expensive on-chip silicon area. Furthermore, we improved power consumption of off-chip memory.

6   Conclusions

In this study, we proposed the FSRAM mechanism that makes it possible to eliminate the use of address decoders during sequential accesses and also random accesses to a certain extent.

We find that FSRAM can efficiently prefetch the linked data block into on-chip data cache and improve performance by 4.42% on average for an embedded system using 16KB data cache. In order to eliminate the potential cache pollution caused by the prefetching, we used a small fully associative cache called SAB. The experiments show FSRAM can further improve the tested benchmark programs performances to 8.85% on average using the SAB. Compared to the tagged next-line prefetching, FSRAM_SAB constantly performs better and can still speedup performance when tnlp_PB cannot. This indicates that FSRM_SAB is more efficient prefetching mechanism.

FSRAM has both sequential accesses and random accesses. With the expense of negligible area overhead (3-7% for 32 bytes and 64 bytes data block line) from the link structure, we obtained a speedup of 15% of sequential access over random access from our designed RTL and SPICE models of FSRAM. Our design also shows that sequential access save 16% power consumption.

The link structure/configuration explored in this paper is not the only way; a multitude of other configurations can be used. Depending upon the requirement of an embedded application, a customized scheme can be adopted whose level of flexibility during accesses best suits the application. For this, prior knowledge of access patterns within the application is needed. In the future, it would be useful to explore power-speed trade-offs that may bring about a net optimization in the architecture.

References

[1]   C.Lee, M. Potkonjak, and W. H. Mangione-Smith. "Mediabench: A tool for evaluating and synthesizing multimedia and communications systems." In Proc. of the 30th Annual International Symposium on Microarchitecture (Micro 30), December 1997
[2]   Doug Burger and Todd M. Austin. "The simplescalar tool set version 2.0." Technical Report 1342, Computer Sciences Department, University of Wisconsin, June 1997.

[3]   Ying Chen, Karthik Ranganathan, Amit Puthenveetil, Kia Bazargan, and David J. Lilja, "FSRAM: Flexible Sequential and Random Access Memory for Embedded Systems." Laboratory for Advanced Research in Computing Technology and Compilers Technical Report No. ARCTiC 04-01, February, 2004.

[4]   P. R. Panda, N. D. Dutt, and A. Nicolau. "Data cache sizing for embedded processor applications." Technical Report TCS-TR-97-31, University of California, Irvine, June 1997.

[5]   P. R. Panda, N. D. Dutt, and A. Nicolau. "Architectural exploration and optimizatioin of local memory in embedded systems." International Symposium on System Synthesis (ISSS 97), Antwerp, Sept. 1997.

[6]   W. Shiue, C. Chakrabati, "Memory Exploration for Low Power Embedded Systems." IEEE/ACM Proc.of 36th. Design Automation Conference (DAC'99), June 1999.

[7]   J. Moon, W. C. Athas, P. A. Beerel, J. T. Draper, "Low-Power Sequential Access Memory Design.", IEEE 2002 Custom Integrated Circuits Conference, pp.741-744, Jun 2002.

[8]   H. Sbeyti, S. Niar, L. Eeckhout, "Adaptive Prefetching for Multimedia Applications in Embedded Systems." DATE'04, EDA IEEE, 16-18 february 2004,Paris, France

[9]   A. D. Pimentel, L. O. Hertzberger, P. Struik, P. Wolf, "Hardware versus Hybrid Data Prefetching in Multimedia Processors: A Case Study." in the Proc. of the IEEE Int. Performance, Computing and Communications Conference (IPCCC 2000), pp. 525-531, Phoenix, USA, Feb. 2000

[10]   D. F. Zucker, M. J. Flynn, R. B. Lee, "A Comparison of Hardware   Prefetching Techniques For Multimedia Benchfmarks." In Proceedings of the International Conferences on Multimedia Computing and Systems, Himshima, Japan, June 1996

[11]   V. De La Luz, M. Kandemir, I. Kolcu, "Automatic Data Migration for Reducing Energy Consumption in Multi-Bank Memory Systems." DAC, pp 213-218, 2002

[12]   Intel corparatin, "The intel XScale Microarchitecture technical summary", Technical report, 2001

[13]   http://www.cse.psu.edu/~mdl/mediabench.tar.gz

[14]   J. E. Smith, W. C. Hsu, "Prefetching in Supercomputer Instruction Caches." In proceedings of Supercomputing92, pp. 588-597, 1992

[15]   S. P. VanderWiel and D. J. Lilja, "Data Prefetch Mechanisms." ACM Computing Surveys, Vol. 32, Issue 2, June 2000, pp. 174-199

[16]   D. J. Lilja, "Measuring Computer Performance", Cambridge University Press, 2000

Heuristic Algorithm for Reducing Mapping Sets of Hardware-Software Partitioning in Reconfigurable System

Seong-Yong Ahn[1], Jun-Yong Kim[2], and Jeong-A Lee[1]

[1] Chosun University, School of Computer Engineering, South Korea
{dis, jalee}@chosun.ac.kr
[2] Seoul National University, Dept. of Computer Engineering, South Korea
itecmdr@hanafos.com

Abstract. One of many technical challenges facing the designers of reconfigurable systems is how to integrate hardware and software resources. The problem of allocating each application function to general purpose processors (GPPs) and Field Programmable Gate Array (FPGAs) considering the system resource restriction and application requirements becomes harder. We propose a solution employing Y-chart design space exploration approach to this problem and develop Y-Sim, a simulation tool employing the solution. Its procedure is as follows: First, generate the mapping set by matching each function in a given application with GPPs and FPGAs in the target reconfigurable system. Secondly, estimate throughput of each mapping case in the mapping set by simulation. With the simulation results, the most efficient configuration achieving the highest throughput among the mapping cases would be chosen. We also propose HARMS (Heuristic Algorithm for Reducing Mapping Sets), a heuristic algorithm minimizing the mapping set by eliminating unnecessary mapping cases according to their workload and parallelism to reduce the simulation time overhead. We show the experimental results of proposed solution using Y-Sim and efficiency of HARMS. The experiment results indicates that HARMS can minimize the mapping set by 87.5% and most likely pick out the mapping case with the highest throughput.

1 Introduction

When one considers implementing a certain computational task, obtaining the highest performance can be achieved by constructing a specialized machine, i.e., hardware. Indeed, this way of implementation exists in the form of Application-Specific Integrated Circuits (ASICs). As, however, many reconfigurable devices such as Field Programmable Gateway Array(FPGA) are developed and improved, many computational tasks can be implemented, or configured, on those devices almost at any point by the end user. Their computation performance has not exceeded ASIC performance but could surpass general purpose processors by factor of several hundreds depending on applications. In addition to the performance gain, reconfigurable devices have the advantage of flexibility, contrary to the fact the structure of ASIC cannot be modified

P.-C. Yew and J. Xue (Eds.): ACSAC 2004, LNCS 3189, pp. 102–114, 2004.
© Springer-Verlag Berlin Heidelberg 2004

after fabrication. Moreover, many independent computational units or circuits can be implemented on a single FPGA within its cell and connection limits and many FPGAs can be organized as a single system.

This novel technology brings about a primary distinction between programmable processors and configurable ones. The programmable paradigm involves a general-purpose processor, able to execute a limited set of operations, known as the instruction set. The programmer's task provids a description of the algorithm to be carried out, using only operations from this instruction set. This algorithm need not necessarily be written in the target machine language since compilation tools may be used; however, ultimately one must be in possession of an assembly language program, which can be directly executed on the processor in question. The prime advantage of programmability is the relatively short turnover time, as well as the low cost per application, resulting from the fact that one can reprogram the processor to carry out any other programmable task[1,3].

Reconfigurable Computing which promises performance and flexibility of systems has emerged as a significant area of research and development for both the academic and industrial communities. Still, there are many technical challenges facing the designers of reconfigurable systems. These systems are truly complex when we face how to integrate hardware and software resources[12]. Unfortunately, current design environments and computer aided design tools have not yet successfully integrated the technologies needed to design and analyze a complete reconfigurable system[11].

We propose a solution employing Y-chart design space exploration approach to this problem assuming pre-configuration policy and Y-Sim, a simulation tool for evaluating performance of the system. Its procedure is as follows: First, it generates the mapping set by matching each functions in given application with GPPs and FPGAs and estimates throughput of each mapping case in the mapping set by simulation. With the simulation results, the most efficient configuration achieving the highest throughput among the mapping cases would be chosen. During the simulation, Y-Sim resolves resource conflict problem arising when many subtasks try to occupy the same FPGA.

We also propose HARMS (Heuristic Algorithm for Reducing Mapping Sets), a heuristic algorithm reducing the huge size of a mapping set. Although each of mapping cases should be simulated to find an appropriate configuration, the elimination of unnecessary mapping cases according to the workload and parallelism helps to reduce the simulation time overhead significantly.

Section 2 summarizes previous related researches. Section 3 describes Y-Sim which employs Y-chart design space exploration approach. Section 4 explains HARMS and section 5 shows its efficiency with the minimization effect on simulation. Section 6 draws conclusions from the solution proposal and reduction algorithm.

2 Related Researches

Lee et al proposed reconfigurable system substructure targeting multi-application embedded system which executes various programs, such as PDA (Personal Digital

Assistant) and IMT2000 (International Mobile Telecommunication). They also proposed dynamic FPGA configuration model which interchanges several functional units on the same FPGA[5].

Keinhuis proposed Y-chart design space exploration[4]. This approach quantifies important performance metrics of system elements on which given applications will be executed. Keinhuis developed ORAS(Object Oriented Retargetable Architecture Simulator), a retargetable simulator, based on Y-chart approach[6]. ORAS calculates performance indicators of possible system configurations through simulation. However, simulation of reconfigurable system needs different simulation substructure other than ORAS since ORAS is limited to a specific calculation model of Stream-based Function.

Kalavade et al investigate the optimization problem in the design of multi-function embedded systems that run a pre-specified set of applications. They mapped given applications onto architecture template which contains one or more programmable processors, hardware accelerators and coprocessors. Their proposed model of hardware-software partitioning for multi-function system identifies sharable application functions and maps them onto same hardware resources. But, in this study, target applications is limited to a specific domain and FPGA is not considered[8].

Pruna et al. partitions huge applications into subtasks employing small size reconfigurable hardware and schedules data flows. Their study, however, is limited to one subtask - one FPGA configuration and multi-function FPGA is not considered[9].

3 Partitioning Tool

3.1 Design of Hardware Software Partitioning Tool

Y-Sim, a partitioning tool employing Y-chart approach, is designed to perform hardware-software partitioning for reconfigurable systems. This tool breaks down given application into subtasks and maps functions of each subtask and determines configuration of elements in the reconfigurable system. Performance indicators of each configuration is calculated to choose the best configuration. The same architecture model and application model in the Y-chart approach are employed and shown in Table 1.

The architecture model contains architecture elements(AEs) which indicate processing units such as general purpose processors and FPGAs. Each architecture element has its own AE_ID, and, in the case of FPGA, their maximum number of usable cells (Usable_Resource) and functional element (FE). Functional elements have resource request information which indicates the number of cells needed to configure the function. Functional elements also have execution time information which is needed for executing each data unit. In the case of FPGAs, those functions don't interfere others but do in the case of general purpose processors. Exclusion is considered in functional elements executed by general purpose processors. Fig. 1 shows an example of hardware model which has three architecture elements, each of which has two functional elements.

Table 1. Architecture Model and Application Model

Architecture Model	Application Model
Architecture := List_of_AE	Application := List_of_Pe
List_of_AE := AE | List_of_AE AE	List_of_PE := PE | List_of_PE PE
AE:=AE_ID Usable_Resources List_of_FE	PE:=PE_ID Next_PE_list FEQ_list
List_of_FE := FE | List_of_FE FE	Next_PE_list := PE_ID | Next_PE_list PE_ID
FE:=FE_ID Resource_Request	FEQ_list := FEQ | FEQ_list FEQ
Execution_Time Exclusion	

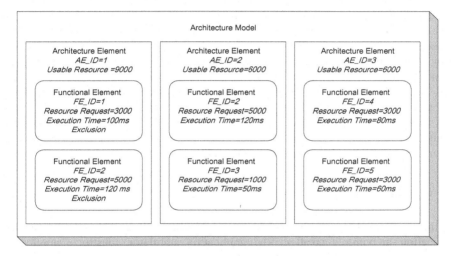

Fig. 1. An Example of Hardware Model

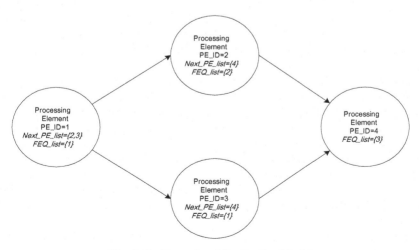

Fig. 2. An Example of Application Model

An application model is represented by processing elements(PE), subtasks of application and the direction of data flow indicated by Next_PE_list. The flow of data and the sequence of Processing Elements must have no feedback and no loop. Each process element has its own identifier, PE_ID and its function specified by FEQ_list. Fig. 2 shows an example of application model which has four process elements.

In Y-chart approach, mapping of Y-chart is done by generating mapping using architecture model and application model. A mapping set consists of mapping cases representing the configuration which directs Architecture elements to run identified functions of subtasks.

Y-Sim simulates each mapping cases in mapping set. Y-Sim handles resource conflict when many subtasks in given application simultaneously mapped on the same hardware element. The basic process of simulation is to let data units flow from the beginning of given application to the end of it. The measure of performance analysis, the timing information for each mapping is gathered when each Architecture Elements processes each data unit. Total elapsed time, one of the performance indicators, is calculated when all the given data units are processed. Other performance indicator includes throughput, the time taken to pass a data unit through the application, delay resulted from requested resource conflict, parallelism and usage of each architecture element. A system designer can choose the best mapping or the best system configuration from the performance indicators.

3.2 Structure of Y-Sim

Y-Sim consists of application simulator, architecture simulator and architecture-application mapping controller. The application simulator constructs application model from given application and simulates the flow of data units. The architecture simulator simulates each architecture element containing functional elements which executes requested function of data unit they received. The architecture-application mapping controller generates and maintains mapping information between subtasks and architecture elements and route of data unit from application subtasks to their mapped architecture elements. Fig. 3 shows the structure of Y-Sim constructed with an application shown before.

Application Simulator: The application simulator simulates the flow of data unit and controls the flow of data unit between processing elements which represent subtasks of given application. Each processing elements add their function request to data units received. The application simulator sends them to architecture-application mapping controller. Data units routed to and processed in architecture simulator are returned to the processing element and the processing element sends the data units to the next process. The application simulator generates data units and give them to the first processing element of generated application model and gathers processed data units to calculate the time taken to process a data unit with given application model and delay.

Architecture Simulator: The architecture simulator simulates the service of functional element requests from application simulator and calculates execution time taken to execute each data unit. When receiving a data unit, a processing element in application simulator invokes application-architecture mapping controller to ask that a functional element in an architecture element processes the data unit and other request should wait until the request is served. In addition, when the exclusion flag in some functional elements is set, the architecture element exclusively executes the functional elements. Because of the exclusion, hardware resource request conflicts are occurred under the many subtask-to-one architecture element configuration and many subtask-to-one functional element in an architecture element configurations. In fig 3, for example, resource conflict would occur in some mapping because of subtask 1 and 3 issuing the functional element request to the same functional element. Y-Sim takes into account the conflict and resolves it. After serving the request, the functional elements record execution time in the data unit and return it to the application simulator, which returns it to the processing element the data unit originated from. Each architecture element records its time for each mapping case.

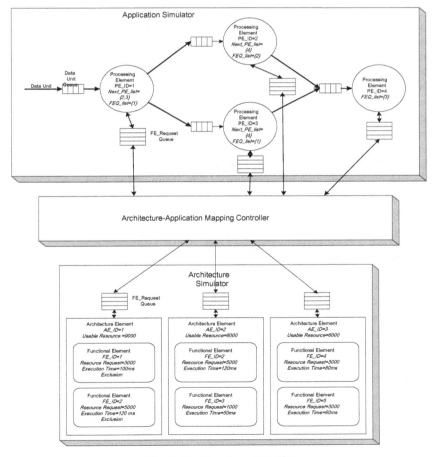

Fig. 3. The Structure of Y-Sim

Architecture-Application Mapping Controller: The architecture-application mapping controller generates all the possible mapping using information of subtask and functional elements of each architecture element and subtask information of given application. The size of mapping set is Πij where i is the number of functions which subtasks of given application executes and j is the number of possible functional elements which can execute functions of subtasks. The size of mapping set in Fig. 3 is 2 since function 2 requested by subtask 2 can be executed in architecture element 1 and architecture element 2. Y-Sim iterates each mapping case and during the simulation, the architecture-application mapping controller routes data units sent by processing elements in the application simulator to corresponding architecture elements in architectural simulator. Performance indicators of each iteration are gathered and used to choose the best mapping.

4 Simulation Time Reduction Heuristic

The architecture-application mapping controller generates Πij mapping. Therefore, as the number of subtasks of given application and the number of functional request of each subtask increases and as more architecture elements and functional elements in them are accommodated, the size of mapping set increases exponentially. The performance of simulator is directly influenced by the size of mapping set and can be improved if the size of mapping set is reduced before simulation. The simulation time reduction algorithm basically decreases the size of mapping set. The simulation time reduction algorithm, HARMS, decrease the size as follows: The algorithm first excludes impossible mapping cases by computing the available resources of FPGA (the number of FPGA cells) and requested number of FPGA cells in functional elements. Then it reduces mapping set by analyzing workload-time taken to process a data unit, parallelism and their relationship which can be identified when each mapping case is generated.

4.1 Mapping Set Reduction Based on Resource Restriction

Various functions can be configured and executed simultaneously on the same FPGA. However, because FPGAs have restricted number of programmable cells, these functions should be organized or synthesized to fit in the size of target FPGA. For example, XC5202 from Xilinx has 256 logic cells and the circuit size of below 3,000 gates can be configured. XC5210 has 1296 logic cells and logic circuit from the size of 10000 gates to 16000 gates can be configured. [10]

Because of this resource restriction, some mapping cases generated in architecture-application mapping controller are impossible to be configured. The reduction is done by comparing the number of cells in each FPGA of target system and the number of FPGAs cell required to configure each mapping case.

4.2 Mapping Set Reduction with Analysis of Workload Parallelism

Reconfigurable Systems improve system performance by configuring co-processors or hardware accelerators on reconfigurable devices such as FPGA. When a FPGA and a general purpose processor execute the same function, FPGA has better performance even though their shortcoming of low clock speed.[1,3]. In addition, reconfigurable systems have higher parallelism because functions executed on a FPGA also can be executed on a general purpose processors and simultaneously configured functions on the same FPGA without interfering each other. In a reconfigurable system using FPGA, Parallelism, *P1* and *P2*, Workload, *W1* and *W2* and throughput *T1* and *T2* of *m1* and *m2*, two mapping cases in a mapping set, *M* has following relationship.

$$IF\ W1{>}W2\ and\ P1{<}P2\ then\ T1{<}T2 \tag{1}$$

Throughput of a configuration accelerated with increased parallelism and decreased workload by FPGA is higher than a configuration without them. Heuristic Algorithm for Reducing Mapping Sets (HARMS) is based on this relationship. As shown later, HARMS exclude mapping cases which have more workload and less parallelism than any other mapping case. HARMS is a heuristic algorithm because some specific mapping cases have workload and parallelism which do not satisfy the equation 1 and HARMS exclude such mapping cases.

5 Experimental Results

Section 5 shows the effectiveness and efficiency of the proposed algorithm, HARMS. With simulation results, the efficiency of HARMS is presented showing the percentage of inefficient mapping cases that HARMS can eliminate. A specific case that HARMS excludes the best mapping cases is also represented and its reason is explained.

5.1 Simulation Environments

We assume that the architecture model is based on a reconfigurable system which has a general purpose processor and several FPGA and the application model is based on H.263 decoder algorithm shown in Fig. 4 and picture in picture algorithm shown in Fig. 5 used to display two images simultaneously on a television screen. A data flow of the H.263 decoder is modeled to encompass a feedback loop so as the application to be modeled as a streaming data processing model. The H.263 is a widely used for video signal processing algorithm and its data flow is easy to identify[13]. Some subtasks in picture in picture algorithm request the same functions and resource conflict usually arise when implemented on reconfigurable system. Therefore, these two algorithms are appropriate to evaluate the performance of Y-Sim and the efficiency of

HARMS. For each algorithm the reconfigurable system of architecture model was simulated and mapping cases was generated by Y-Sim.

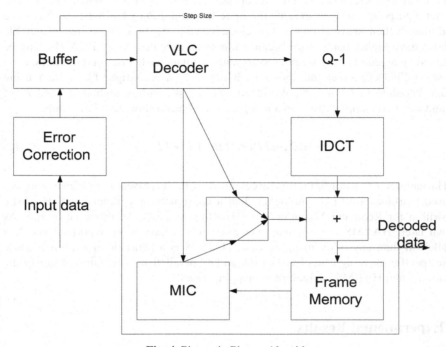

Fig. 4. Picture in Picture Algorithm

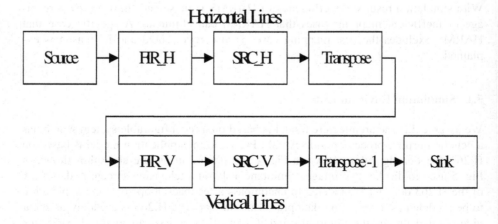

Fig. 5. Picture in Picture Algorithm

5.2   Efficiency and Accuracy of HARMS

In order to show the efficiency and accuracy of HARMS, simulation result illustrates that excluded mapping cases are not mostly the best mapping cases. The accuracy of HARMS is shown as follows: First, we assume that the generated mapping cases of H.263 decoder and picture in picture run on a reconfigurable system with one general purpose processor and three FPGA. Then, the accuracy of HARMS is proved by showing that reduced mapping set has the best mapping cases. Since HARMS doesn't analyze the structure of mapping cases, the best mapping case is excluded under some specific system configuration. For these cases, a solution resolving this problem is also presented.

5.2.1   Comparison of Before Running HARMS and After

Fig. 6 and Fig. 7 illustrate comparison of mapping set before and after applying HARMS. The initial size of the mapping set of picture in picture model is 16384 and the size is reduced to 1648 by resource restriction. HARMS reduce the size of the mapping set to 240 and the reduced mapping set contains the best mapping case. As the simulation results shows, HARMS reduces mapping set without excluding the best mapping case.

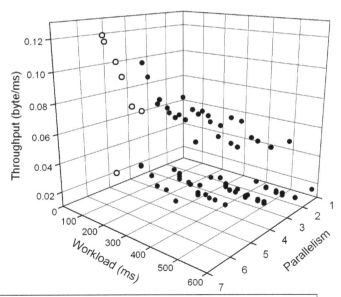

Fig. 6. Comparison of mapping set of H.263 before and after running HARMS

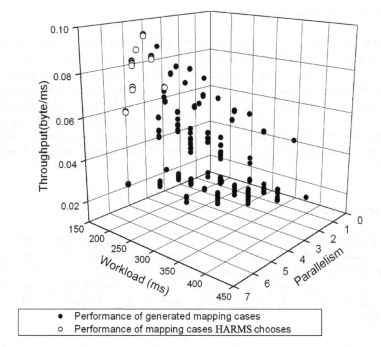

● Performance of generated mapping cases
○ Performance of mapping cases HARMS chooses

Fig. 7. Comparison of mapping set of Picture in Picture before and after running HARMS

Table 2. The Efficiency of HARMS

	Initial size of mapping set	Resource limitation is considered	HARMS is applied	
			size	efficiency(%)
H.263(1)	4096	4096	928	77.3
H.263(2)	729	624	186	70.2
H.263(3)	64	40	7	82.5
H.263(4)	64	64	8	87.5
H.263(5)	4096	4084	2175	46.7
Pip(1)	64	13	12	7.7
Pip(2)	16384	1648	240	85.4

5.3 Efficiency of HARMS

This section shows the reduction ratio of mapping set when HARMS is applied. Table 2 shows simulation and reduction results of five system configurations of H.263 decoder and two cases of picture in picture algorithm. Each system configuration is as follows:

H.263 (1) - two general purpose processors (GPPs) and two FPGAs.
H.263 (2) - one GPP and one FPGA.
H.263 (3) - one GPP and one FPGA.
H.263 (4) - Similar to H.263 (3) but smaller FPGA.
H.263 (5) - one GPP and three FPGAs.
Pip(1)-one GPP and one FPGAs,
Pip(2)-one GPP and three FPGAs,

The efficiency is the ratio of the size of mapping set HARMS applied on (Aft_size) to the size of mapping set resource limitation is considered(Bef_size). The following shows its equation

$$\textit{Efficiency of HARMS} = \textit{(Bef\_size - Aft\_size)/Befsize} \tag{2}$$

As shown in table 2, HARMS reduces the size of mapping set by about 80 percent. In the case of H.263(5), architecturally same mapping cases appeared on different mapping cases in the generated mapping set since the system has three same FPGAs of the same size on which the same functional element can be configured. As a result of redundant configuration, the efficiency of HARMS is comparatively low, 46.7%. In the case of Pip(1), the size of mapping set is minimized by resource restriction that the efficiency is very low, 7.7%.

6 Conclusion

This paper proposes Y-Sim, a hardware-software partitioning tool. With given application model and architecture model, representing configuration of reconfigurable system, Y-Sim explores possible mapping between architecture model and application model and generate mapping set which represents possible mapping set of given reconfigurable system. Then, Y-Sim simulates each mapping case in the mapping set and finds the best one. Y-Sim takes resource restriction of FPGA such as the number of usable cells into account and resolves resource conflicts arising when many subtasks of given application share the same resource.

As more FPGAs are installed in a reconfigurable system and more functions are configured on FPGAs, subtasks can be mapped on many FPGAs or general purpose processors. Consequently, the size of mapping set increases exponentially and the time taken to analyze performance of such system is heavily influenced by the size. Generally, throughput of reconfigurable system using FPGA has positive relationship to parallelism and negative relationship to workload. Based on this relationship, proposed heuristic algorithm, HARMS efficiently reduces mapping set. Experimental result shows that HARMS can reduce the size of the mapping set. For the various architecture and application model of reconfigurable system running H.263 decoder and picture in picture algorithm, HARMS reduces the size of mapping set by about 80% and up to 87.5%.

Acknowledgement. This work was supported by grant No. R04-2002-000-00081-0 from the research program of the KOSEF.

References

1.   O.T. Albahama, P. Cheung, and T.J. Clarke, "On the Viability of FPGA-Based Inte-grated Coprocessors," In Proceedings of IEEE Symposium of FPGAs for Custom Com-puting Machines, pp. 206-215, Apr. 1996

2.   J-L, Gaudiots. "Guest Editors' Introduction", IEEE Transactions on Computers, VOL.48, No.6, June 1999.

3.   E. Sanchez. M. Sipper, J.-O. Haenni, J.-L. Beuchat, A. Stauffer, and A. Perez-Uribe, "Static and Dynamic Configurable Systems", IEEE Transactions on Computers VOL.48, No.6, June 1999.

4.   B. Kienhuis, E. Deprettere, K.A. Vissers, and P. Wolf. An approach for quantitative analysis of application-specific dataflow architectures. In Proceedings of 11th Intl. Con-ference of Applications-specific Systems, Architectures and Processors (ASAP'97), pages 338-349, Zurich, Switzerland, 1997

5.   S. Lee ; K.Yun ; Choi, Kiyoung ; S. Hong ; S. Moon ; J. Lee, "Java-based programmable networked embedded system architecture with multiple application support.", *Interna-tional Conference on Chip Design Automation*, pp.448-451, Aug. 2000.

6.   A.C.J. Kienhuis, Design Space Exploration of Stream-based Dataflow Architectures, PhD thesis, Delft University of Technology, Netherlands, 1998.

7.   S. Bakshi, D. D. Gajaski, "Hardware/Software Partitioning and Pipelining", In Proceed-ings of the 34th annual conference on Design Automation Conference, 1997, pages 713-716

8.   A. Kalavade, P. A. Subrahmanyam, "Hardware/Software Partitioning for Multifunction Systems", In Proceedings of International Conference on Computer Aided Design, pages 516-521, 1997,

9.   K.M. Gajjala Purna and D. Bhatia "Temporal Partitioning and Scheduling Data Flow Graphs for Reconfigurable Computers" IEEE Transactions on Computers, VOL.48, No.6, June 1999.

10.   XC5200 Series Field Programmable Gate Arrays Databook, ver 5.2, Xilinx Inc, Nov 1998.

11.   S. Mohanty, V.K. Prasanna, S. Neema, J. Davis, "Rapid Design Space Exploration of Heterogeneous Embedded Systems using Symbolic Search and Multi-Granular Simula-tion", LCTES'02-SCOPES'02, Berlin, Germany, June 2002.

12.   Katherine Compton, Scott Hauck, "Reconfigurable Computing: A survey of Systems and Software" ACM Computing Surveys, Vol.34, No.2 June 2002, pp.171-210

13.   http://www.itut.int/itudoc/rec/h/h263.html

Architecture Design of a High-Performance 32-Bit Fixed-Point DSP

Jian Chen, Ruhao Xu, and Yuzhuo Fu

School of Microelectronics, Shanghai Jiao Tong University
1954 Huashan Road, Shanghai 200030, China
{chenjian, xuruhao, fuyuzhuo}@ic.sjtu.edu.cn

Abstract. In this paper, the architecture of a high-performance 32-bit fixed-point DSP called DSP3000 is proposed and implemented. The DSP3000 employs super-Harvard architecture and can issue three memory access operations in a single clock cycle. The processor has eight pipe stages with separated memory read and write stages, which alleviate the data dependency problems and improve the execution efficiency. The processor also possesses a modulo addressing unit with optimized structure to enhance the address generation speed. A fully pipelined MAC (Multiply Accumulate) unit is incorporated in the design, which enables $32 \times 32 + 72$ MAC operation in a single clock cycle. The processor is implemented with SMIC $0.18\mu m$ 1.8V 1P6M process and has a core size of 2.2mm by 2.4mm. Test result shows that it can operate at a maximum frequency of 300MHz with the average power consumption of $30mw/100MHz$.

1 Introduction

Digital signal processor finds its applications in a wide variety of areas, such as wireless communication, speech recognition and image processing, where high speed calculation capability is of primary concern. With the ever increasing applications in battery-powered electronics, such as cellular phones and digital cameras, the power dissipation of DSP is also becoming a critical issue. The trend of achieving high performance mean while preventing power consumption from surging is imposing a great challenge on modern DSP design.

Various approaches have been proposed to address the challenge by exploring different levels and aspects in the entire DSP design flow.[1][2] This paper, however, would focus its efforts on the architecture level design of a DSP to achieve both performance and power consumption requirements. It presents the overall architecture of DSP3000, a high-performance 32-bit fixed-point digital signal processor. It also proposes novel micro-architectures aiming at increasing the performance and reducing chip area. Techniques to reduce power consumption of the chip are described as well.

The rest of the paper is organized as follows. Section 2 gives a detailed description of the overall architecture of the processor as well as the micro-architectures

P.-C. Yew and J. Xue (Eds.): ACSAC 2004, LNCS 3189, pp. 115–125, 2004.

in pipeline organization, address generation unit and MAC unit. Section 3 describes the performance of the implemented processor. Section 4 presents the conclusion of the research.

2   Architecture of DSP3000

In order to enhance the performance, the design of the processor incorporates the ideas of deep pipelining, two-way superscalar and super-Harvard structure. Specifically speaking, the core of the DSP has eight pipe stages and two datapaths working in parallel. It is also capable of accessing data in two different data memory spaces simultaneously. Fig. 1 illustrates the major components of the processor, which is composed of the DSP core, on-chip memories, instruction cache and peripherals.

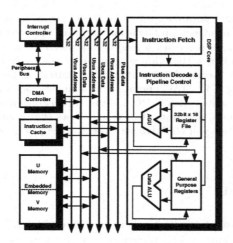

Fig. 1. The block diagram of DSP3000

The instructions are fetched from instruction cache by the instruction fetch unit and passed to the instruction decode unit, where the instructions are decoded into microcodes. This unit also has a hardware stack with a depth of sixteen to effectively support hardware loops. The decoded instructions are issued to AGU (Address Generation Unit) and DALU (Data Arithmetic Logic Unit) for corresponding operations. AGU is responsible for the calculation of the addresses of both U and V memories that the core is going to access. Various addressing modes, including register direct addressing mode and modulo addressing mode, are supported by this module. Among them, modulo addressing mode is particularly important to the performance of the DSP and will be examined in detail in section 2.2. DALU works in parallel with AGU and accomplishes the arithmetic and logic operations such as MAC (Multiply Accumulate), accumulation and shift. Besides, it also offers some powerful bit operations, such as bit set and bit clear, to enhance the control capability of the chip so that the chip can also be applied as an MCU (Micro Control Unit). The operation of MAC, critical to the performance of DSP algorithms, is implemented with a novel structure, which makes the chip finish MAC operation in one clock cycle and reduces the chip area and the power consumption at the same time. This structure will be highlighted in section 2.3.

2.1 Pipeline Organization and Write Back Strategy

The data-path of DSP3000 core is divided into eight pipe stages with their names P1-P8 respectively, as is shown in Fig. 2. In order to coordinate the operations between AGU and DALU, the execution actually occupies four pipe stages, i.e., P4-P7. Basically, P4 and P5 in DALU simply pipe the instructions down and do no extra operations except for some decode activities to prepare for the operations begin on P6.The pipeline organization features the separated memory read and write stages in AGU, which are introduced to deal with the data dependence problems aggravated by the wide span of execution pipe stages. This could be explained with the following instructions:

MAC R0, R1, R5 U: (AR0+), R0 V: (AR4+), R1
SUB R2, R4 U:(AR0+), R2 R5, V: (AR4+)

The first instruction accomplishes MAC operation with the data in register R0, R1 and R5 and stores the result into register R5. Meanwhile two parallel move operations load R0 and R1 with the data read from U and V memory respectively. The second instruction subtracts R4 from R2 and stores the result into R4. Also there are two parallel move operations in this instruction. The second one of them stores the value of register R5, which is the result of the first instruction, to V memory. If memory read and write are combined in a single stage, this operation must start on the beginning of P6 stage since arithmetic operation begins on this stage. Otherwise DALU may not get the desired data from memory for corresponding operations. Yet, the desired value of R5 is not available until the first instruction finishes the operation on P7. This would introduce a stall or a NOP between the two instructions to avoid the data hazard, reducing the instruction execution efficiency. With the separated memory read and write strategy, however, the memory write operation happens on P7 stage. The above data hazard can then be avoided by forwarding the accumulate result to the input of memory write function unit.

The new memory access strategy, however, would give rise to memory access contention problems if no other measures are taken. This problem can be illustrated by the following instructions:

MOVE R3,U:(AR6)
MOVE U:(AR7),R4

The first instruction writes the U memory indexed by AR6 with the value in R3, while the second instruction reads the data from U memory to R4. These two

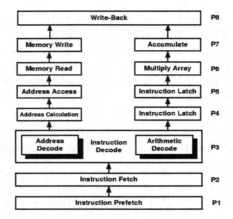

Fig. 2. The pipeline structure of DSP3000 core

instructions will cause the DSP core to access the U memory in different pipe stages simultaneously. In order to avoid this contention, the pipeline incorporates a buffer called write back queue in the write back stage P8, as is illustrated in Fig. 3. When the control unit detects memory access contentions, it holds the memory write operation and stores the corresponding data into the queue while continues the memory read operation. That is to say, the memory read instruction has a higher priority than the preceding memory write instruction. The memory write operation can be resumed as soon as the address bus is free.In order to prevent RAW(Read after Write) hazard during the execution of memory read operation, AGU first searches the write back queue for the desired data. If there is a hit, the data can be fetched directly from the write back queue. Otherwise, it goes to memory to continue the read operation.

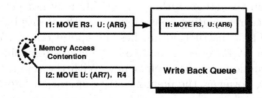

Fig. 3. The mechanism of write back queue

The depth of the write back queue is one, which could be proved by the following analysis. The contention problem could only happen in a read after write situation. If the following instruction is a read operation, the write operation can be still suspended in the write back queue and no new write instruction is pushed into this queue. On the other hand, if the following instruction is a write operation, then the memory bus would be free for one clock cycle, during which the suspended write operation can be finished. Consequently, the write back queue is only one level deep, which will not lead to the hardware overhead. Besides the benefit of increasing instruction execution efficiency, the proposed pipeline organization also contributes to the saving of the power that would otherwise be consumed on NOP instructions.

2.2 Modulo Addressing Unit in AGU

Modulo addressing is widely used in generating waveforms and creating circular buffers for delay lines.[6] The processor supports two kinds of modulo addressing, i.e., increment modulo addressing and decrement modulo addressing. Conventionally, they are realized by creating a circular buffer defined by the lower boundary (base address) and the upper boundary (base address + modulus - 1).When the calculated address surpasses the upper boundary, it wraps around through the lower boundary. On the other hand, if the address goes below the lower boundary, it wraps around through the upper boundary.[6] The modulo addressing unit of the processor adopts this basic idea, yet it employs a modified approach to improve the efficiency.

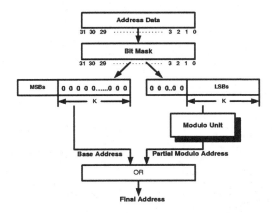

Fig. 4. The modified modulo addressing scheme

As is shown in Fig. 4, a bit mask generated according to value of modulus divides the pre-calculated address data into two sections, the MSBs(Most Significant Bit) and the LSBs(Least Significant Bit). The MSBs, together with the succeeding K-bit zeros, form the base address of the circular buffer, where $2K > modulus$ and $2K - 1 <= modulus$. The K-bit LSBs are zero extended to 32 bits before they are put into the Modulo Unit, where the modulo operation is performed. The base address and the partial modulo address generated in modulo unit are then ORed together to get the final address. With this scheme, the low boundary of the circular buffer becomes zero from the Modulo Unit's perspective. Consequently, the following algorithm can be applied in the Modulo Unit.

For increment modulo addressing:

```
Intermediate = LSBs + OffsetValue;
If (Intermediate > Modulus)
PartialModuloAddress=Intermediate-Modulus;
Else
PartialModuloAddress=Intermediate;
```

For decrement modulo addressing:

```
Intermediate = LSBs - OffsetValue;
If (Intermediate < 0)
PartialModuloAddress=Intermediate+Modulus;
Else
PartialModuloAddress=Intermediate;
```

It is required that OffsetValue should be no larger than Modulus, or the result is unpredictable.[6] The corresponding hardware implementation of increment modulo addressing is shown in Fig. 5(a). The longest path of this structure includes an adder, a subtracter and a multiplexer. Yet, further optimization on the unit can be carried out by dividing the timing critical path into two parallel data-paths to calculate the two possible addresses simultaneously, as is illustrated below:

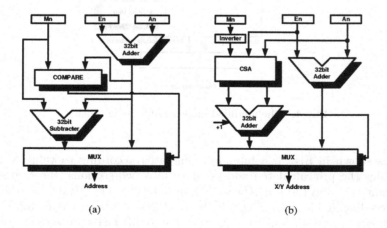

(a)   (b)

Fig. 5. The diagram of the modulo unit. An, En and Mn are the registers holding the LSBs , the offset value and the modulus respectively. (a).The diagram of the direct implementation of the unit. (b).The diagram of the proposed implementation of the unit, where CSA stands for Carry Save Adder.

Datapath 1: $LSBs + OffetValue$
Datapath 2: $LSBs + OffetValue - Modulus$
The operation of Data-path2 can also be written as:
Datapath 2: $LSBs + OffetValue+ \sim Modulus + 1$

The first three operands in Datapath 2 can be compressed into two data by one level CSA (Carry Save Adder)[3]. These two generated data can then be fed into a 32-bit adder. The carry in pin of this cascading adder, which is usually connected with 0, can be used to accept the remaining data 1. On the other hand, the carry out signal of the adder actually reflects the greatness of Intermediate and Modulus. That is, the signal is 1 if $Intermediate$ is less than $Modulus$, otherwise it is 0. Consequently, the carry out signal can be used as the select signal of the multiplexer so that the compare unit can be removed. The proposed modulo addressing unit structure is shown in Fig. 5(b). The critical path of this structure includes an inverter, a one level CSA, an adder and a multiplexer. Since one level CSA is actually an array of full adders, the delay of CSA equals that of a full adder. Further more, the delay on the inverter is negligible when calculating the entire delay of the timing path. Consequently, the delay on the critical path of this structure is significantly reduced compared with that of the former one. The implementation of the decrement modulo addressing follows the same idea as that of the increment modulo addressing. It can be achieved by adding control signals and multiplexers to the proposed structure so that both kinds of modulo addressing can be accomplished by sharing most of the components.

2.3   Fully Pipelined MAC Unit

In order to accelerate the operating speed of the DSP, MAC unit is divided into two pipe stages and takes a latency of two clock cycles to complete the operation. Instead of the conventional way to simply put multiplier and accumulator in different pipe stages[6], however, a different approach is employed in the division of the unit, as is shown in Fig. 6

In the first pipe stage, a radix-4 modified Booth encoder encodes the 32-bit multiplier and multiplicand into 17 partial products [4][5]. These partial products are compressed to two 64-bit data by Wallace Tree constructed with 4-2 compressors [4]. Traditionally these two results are put into an adder to produce the multiplication result. In this processor, however, the two results, together with the third operand which is sign-extended to 72 bits, are fed into a one level CSA, where they are compressed into another two intermediate results. In the second pipe stage, a multiplexer selects the signals piped down from the previous stage according to the SEL signal. If the SEL indicates a MAC or a multiplication operation, the multiplexer selects the signals from CSA. Otherwise, two 72-bit source operands are selected. A 72-bit adder then adds the selected signals to get the final result.

Since the adder inherent in a multiplier is substituted with a CSA, which has a delay of only one full adder, the proposed MAC structure achieves a more balanced pipeline than the traditional one. With the proposed structure, one MAC

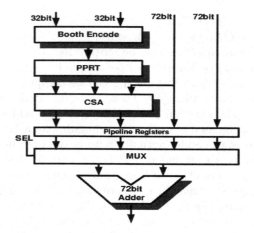

Fig. 6. The diagram of the proposed MAC unit, where PPRT stands for Partial Product Reduction Tree.

operation only needs one 72-bit adder. With the traditional style, however, two adders are involved in the MAC operation, one 64-bit adder for multiplication and one 72-bit adder for accumulation. Consequently, this structure can significantly reduce the area cost and the power consumption of the unit by the removal of 64-bit addition operation. Although the latency for a single multiply operation is increased, the fact that MAC is used more frequently than a single multiply operation in DSP algorithms justifies such kind of trade off.

2.4   Cache Strategy

The DSP3000 possesses a $2k \times 32$ bits instruction cache to enhance the performance and reduce power consumption by preventing the core from accessing external memory frequently. The cache is two-way set associative and adopts the write-through scheme. It also employs the LRU (Least Recently Used) algorithm to replace the data.

When cache miss occurs, the DSP core must enter wait state until the desired instructions are fetched from external program memory, which may take tens of clock cycles. In order to save power during that period of time, a clock gating approach is employed to hold the core state. Fig. 7 shows the clock gating circuit between the PLL and the DSP core. The *core_hold* signal is latched by a latch, which is used to prevent glitches[7], and ANDed with the clock signal from PLL to generate the core clock. In the real implementation, the latched signal of *core_hold* is ORed with scan_en before it is ANDed with the clock to meet the DFT(Design for Test) requirements. The scan_en signal is asserted only when the chip is in scan mode. When cache control module detects a cache miss, *core_hold* is pulled down before the end of the clock cycle and the core clock is stopped. In that case, no operation would happen within the DSP core until the *core_hold*

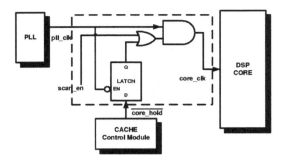

Fig. 7. Clock gating structure designed to stop the clock of the core when cache miss occurs

signal is released. With the proposed structure, the dynamic power consumption on the clock tree during cache miss is eliminated and thus the average power consumption on chip is further reduced.

3   Performance Analysis

The processor is modeled by Verilog-HDL and synthesized by Design Compiler with the SMIC (Semiconductor Manufacturing International Corporation) $0.18\mu m$ general standard cell libraries. The physical implementations of the processor, which include floorplanning, placement, clock tree synthesizing and routing, are carried out with Synopsys back end tools. Fig. 8 shows the final layout of DSP3000. The processor is fabricated with SMIC $0.18\mu m$ 1.8V 1P6M process and is tested on ADVANTEST T6672. The test result shows that processor can operate at a maximum speed of 300MHz with the average power consumption $30mw/100MHz$. Table 1 summarizes the main characteristics of the processor.

Table 1. DSP3000 Characteristics

Item	Characteristics
Process	SMIC 0.18um 1P6M
Core Voltage	1.8V
IO Voltage	3.3V
Core Size	$2.2mm \times 2.4mm$
Die Size	$4.8mm \times 4.8mm$
Operating frequency	$300MHz$
Average Power Consumption	$30mw/100MHz$

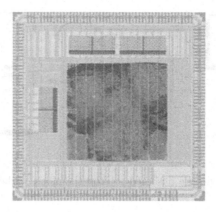

Fig. 8. The layout of DSP3000

Table 2. Comparison between DSP3000 and Other Commercialized DSPs

Item	DSP3000	TI C54X*	TI C55X*	Blackfin*
Category	32-bit fixed-point	16-bit fixed-point	16-bit fixed-point	dual MAC 16-bit fixed-point
Operating frequency	$300MHz$	$160MHz$	$300MHz$	$350MHz$
Benchmark:256-point FFT	2257 cycles	8542 cycles	4786 cycles	3176 cycles
Benchmark:Real FIR	$N/2 + 6$	$N/2 + 16$	$N/2 + 3$	$N/2 + 2$
Benchmark:Complex FIR	$4N + 12$	$8N + 13$	$2N + 4$	$2N + 2$
Benchmark:Delayed LMS	$2N + 10$	$2N + 14$	$2N + 5$	$1.5N + 4.5$

*Source: http://www.ti.com ; http://www.analog.com

Table 2 makes a comparison between DSP3000 and some other commercialized DSPs. Several benchmarks are listed in the table, which include 256-point complex radix-2 FFT with bit reversal, real coefficient FIR, complex FIR and Delayed LMS(Least Mean Square) filter.All the benchmarks take the unit of clock cycles per output sample unless otherwise noted. The data of the commercialized DSPs are based on the benchmarks provided by the cited websites. Due to the optimized MAC unit and enhanced AGU capability, DSP3000 exhibits competitively low clock cycle latency and short execution time in running such programs.

4   Conclusion

This paper presents the overall architecture as well as the novel microarchitectures of DSP3000, which is a 32-bit fixed-point digital signal processor. With the improvement in pipeline organization, address generation and MAC operation, the processor enjoys high efficiency in executing DSP programs mean while achieves a low average power consumption. Test result shows it can reach an operating frequency of $300MHz$ with average power consumption $30mw/100MHz$. This processor can be applied in fields where high performance and low power consumption are both required, such as mobile phones and digital cameras.

Acknowledgement. This work was supported by National High Technology 863 Program under the grant of $No.2002AA1Z$.

References

1. Sanjive Agarwala,etc.: A 600MHz VLIW DSP. IEEE Journal of Solid-State Circuits, Vol.**37**,No.**11** (2002)
2. Farooqui A.A., Oklobdzija V.G: General Data-path Organization of a MAC Unit for VLSI Implementation of DSP Processors. Proceedings of the 1998 IEEE International Symposium on Circuits and Systems, Vol. **2** (1998) 260–263.
3. Jan M. Rabeay: Digital Integrate Circuits-A Design Perspective. Second Edition. Prentice Hall.(2003) 591–592
4. Norio Ohkubo, Makoto Suzuki, Toshinobu Shinobo,Toshiaki Yamanaka: A 4.4ns CMOS 54×54-b Multiplier Using Pass-Transistor Multiplier. IEEE Journal of Solid-state Circuits,Vol.**30**,No.**3** (1995) 1013–1015
5. Wen-Chang Yeh and Chein-Wei Jen: High-Speed Booth Encoded Parallel Multiplier Design. IEEE Trans. Computer.Vol. **49**,No.**7** (2000) 28–55
6. DSP56300 Family Manual-24-Bit Digital Signal Processor, Revision 3.0.Motorola Inc. (2000) 4-1-4-10.
7. Darren Jose: How to successfully Use Gated Clocking in an ASIC Design. SNUG. **33** (2002) 609–633

TengYue-1[1]: A High Performance Embedded SoC[*]

Lei Wang, Hong-yi Lu, Kui Dai, and Zhi-ying Wang

National University of Defense Technology, School of Computer,
Changsha, Hunan 410073, P. R. of China
wanglei@chiplight.com.cn

Abstract. TengYue-1 is a microprocessor subsystem for embedded
applications. Its heart is a 32-bit RISC microprocessor based on an instruction
set architecture (ISA) designed by us. Through a WISHBONE compatible
on-chip bus, the microprocessor, a universal memory controller, a LCD
controller and other peripheral I/Os formed the SOC. TengYue-1 has been
implemented and verified in SMIC 0.18um CMOS technology, and the
maximum clock frequency is 300MHz@1.8V. This paper presents the design
and implementation of TengYue-1. We used 9 ARM benchmarks to evaluate
the performance of the microprocessor and the results showed that it met our
goal. We also found a simple solution to the memory access conflict problem
caused by the microprocessor core and the LCD controller.

1 Introduction

Currently, embedded system is hailed by major semiconductors and mobile device
manufacturers. They need simple, light, and low power micro-controller, not high
performance general purpose microprocessor. Obviously, current design goal is lower
power and higher performance within given constraints. And both on-chip and
off-chip configuration of peripheral device must be possible for various market
demands.

TengYue-1 is a design for embedded systems based on above characteristics.
TengYue-1 is an 'island' containing a 32-bit RISC microprocessor core (named CH)
and other macro modules, such as a universal memory controller, a LCD controller
and several peripherals I/O devices. Hardware debugging support and a production
test interface are also included. TengYue-1 was implemented in SMIC 0.18um CMOS
technology. Maximum clock frequencies can be 300MHz@1.8v. The design is
oriented for authentication and data encryption/decryption in information security
application. Coprocessor interface and abundant peripherals make it easy for system
integration.

The remainder of this paper organized as follows. Section 2 shows the architecture
of TengYue-1, and section 3 describes the design of each component of TengYue-1 in

---

[1] TengYue: In Chinese means jump over.

[*] This work was sponsored by High-Tech Research and Development Program of China 863
(No. 2002AA1Z1080); NSFC (No.60173040)

P.-C. Yew and J. Xue (Eds.): ACSAC 2004, LNCS 3189, pp. 126–136, 2004.
© Springer-Verlag Berlin Heidelberg 2004

detail. Implementation scheme is explained in section 4. Section 5 gives the result of performance evaluation. Finally, section 6 gives the conclusions.

2   Architecture of TengYue-1

As shown in Fig. 1, Tengyue-1 consists of a 32 bit RISC microprocessor core, a universal memory controller, a LCD controller, two UART serial ports, an I²C interface, 32-bit GPIO interface, programmable interrupt controller, power management unit and test interface.

The microprocessor core is the heart of TengYue-1. The instruction set architecture is a typical RISC architecture. The instruction set is summarized in Table 1. At the design of the instruction set, we emphasize design for pipelining efficiency and efficiency as a compiler target. In contrast to ARM architecture [2], CH architecture is simple and efficient for implementation. After detailed analyzing of the execution of ARM instructions [3], on the base of ARM instruction set, we add shift instructions and reduce the addressing modes of data manipulation instructions. Thus the length of execution path is reduced. We increase the number of GPRs, to help the compiler to exploit more parallelism.

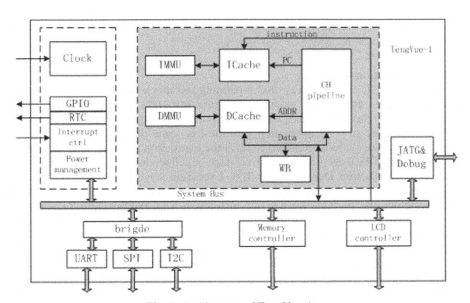

Fig. 1. Architecture of TengYue-1

CH has 32 32-bit general-purpose registers (GPRs), named R0, R1... R31. These GPRs can be mapped as two sets of 32-bit GPRs separately; each set contains 16 registers, for fast context switching in case of exception handling; or mapped as a single set of 32 32-bit GPRs. CH uses Harvard architecture, with separated instruction cache and data cache.

Table 1. Instruction set summary

Instruction Type	Number of this type
Branch	4 (16 conditions)
Data Manipulation	27
Load/Store	12 (6 addressing modes each)
Status Register Transfer	2
Exception generating Instructions	1
Coprocessor instructions	5 (2 for memory access, 6 addressing mode each)
JVM extension instructions	6
Total number	57

As shown in Fig. 1, the grey area is the RISC microprocessor core. To achieve high performance, we also have to pay attention to the clock frequency, execution efficiency (measured in terms of IPC or CPI), die size and power consumption in the design.

2.1   Microprocessor Core: CH

The 32-bit RISC microprocessor CH consists of two parts: the instruction pipeline and the memory subsystem. We will discuss these two parts in the following subsections.

2.1.1   Instruction Pipeline

In general, RISC architectures use pipelining as much as possible, in order to parallelize tasks and to use existing hardware resources efficiently. This usually results in a higher clock frequencies and therefore higher performance values. However the use of long instruction pipeline has some drawbacks. The longer the pipeline the more cycles is required to refill the instruction pipeline when executing a taken branch. CH used a classical five-stage pipeline, including Instruction Fetch stage (IF), Instruction Decode stage (ID), Execution stage (EXE), Memory Access stage (MEM) and Write Back stage (WB), as shown in Fig. 2. As CH has a single issue pipeline, the IF stage fetches one instruction from the instruction cache every cycle. The ID stage performs the instruction decoding and prepares the register operands. The instruction decoding can be done quickly because of the fixed instruction set encoding. Hazards (structure hazards and data hazards) detecting and resolving are also performed in ID stage. CH detects data hazards by Scoreboarding [1] and resolves them with bypassing and forwarding or simply stopping the successive instructions until the instruction that causes the hazards is completed. The EXE stage contains an ALU, a barrel shifter and a multiplier, executing arithmetic and logical instructions, shift instructions and multiplication instructions respectively. The EXE stage also generates the address for load/store instructions. Memory is accessed in MEM stage. In WB stage the results of the EXE stage or the data loaded from memory are written back to the register file.

Precise exception can be easily implemented since the hazards detecting and resolving algorithms are simple. When an interrupt or exception is detected, it only needs to flush the pipeline before handling the interrupt or exception.

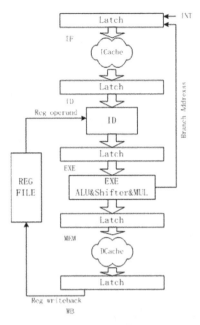

Fig. 2. Instruction Pipeline of CH

2.1.2 Memory Subsystem

The memory subsystem contains the instruction cache, data cache, write buffer and the memory management unit (MMU). The instruction cache and data cache are both 8KB, 4-way set-associative and both use LRU replacement algorithm. The write buffer has 32 16-byte entries. The instruction cache and data cache are both pipelined so that it is impossible to offer a instruction every cycle. All units in the memory subsystem can be enabled or disabled by user through configuring memory control register. Instruction TLB (Translation Look-aside Buffer) and data TLB are both full-associative.

The instruction cache uses virtual address as index and tag. A 7-bit identifier labels different processes. Thus the instruction cache does not need to be flushed on a context switch [1]. To avoid alias, the data cache uses physical address as index and tag. Using physical address has two advantages. Firstly, this resolves consistency problem of data cache; secondly, it is convenient for sharing data among processes (or threads). On a context switch, the data cache does not need to be flushed, so new processes can use the shared data without any costs [1].

Both the instruction cache and data cache use LRU replacement strategies. We implemented a simple systolic array that can keep track of LRU information for a set of cache lines. It can handle one cache access every cycle with less hardware cost [5]. The structure of a node of the array is shown in Fig.3 (b), where L is the LRU entry, M is the MRU entry, and index is the cache line access order kept by the array. The operation is illustrated in Fig.3 (a).

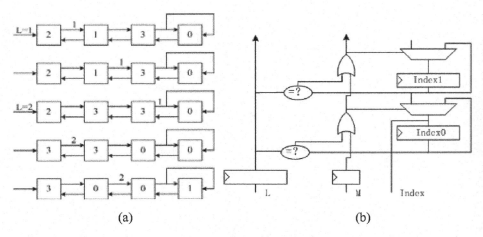

(a)   (b)

Fig. 3. (a) Operation of systolic array; (b) systolic array for implementing LRU algorithm

The write buffer works with the data cache. As the data cache uses write through policy. On write hit, the CPU write both the data cache and write buffer; On write miss, the CPU write into write buffer only. Whenever there is read miss, the write buffer is write back to the external memory before cache line refill begin. On read hit, the cache line in the data cache is the newest one, same as the external memory.

The virtual address is 32-bit and the physical address is 26-bit. Virtual memory is divided into pages. There are four kinds of page sizes: 1MB, 64KB, 4KB and 2KB. Memory protection information is kept with page table. The virtual-physical address translation is done by software. The TLB in the memory management unit acts as a cache to keep the historical conversion results, so a hit in TLB can accelerate the address translation.

2.2   Memory Controller

Interfaced with off-chip memory, the memory controller has 8 chip selects, each one is individually programmable. The memory types supported by TengYue-1's memory controller include SSRAM, SDRAM, FLASH and ROM etc. As a universal memory controller, the user can set the memory spaces mapped by the memory on each chip select and the timing sequences of the controller's interface by setting the chip select control registers and timing control registers to accommodate to different memory.

Fig. 4 shows the structure of the memory controller. The CPU bus interface and the memory interface are responsible for the communication with CPU and with memory individually. The configuration registers contain the information such as the types of memory, timing information, address mapping etc. All data paths and address paths are controlled by a FSM, which generates sequence of control signals according to the information stored in the configuration registers. The Power-on configuration block latches the value of the memory data bus during reset, which determines initial configuration of the memory controller and provides additional configuration bit for the system. The refresh counter and SDRAM control module are responsible for generating refresh cycles request and timing sequence for the attached SDRAM.

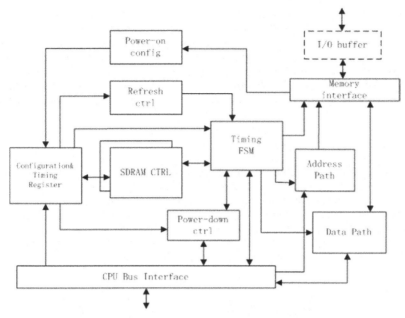

Fig. 4. Architecture of memory controller

The memory controller utilizes two clocks. One is the main clock of the system, the clock of microprocessor; the other is derived from main clock by dividing the main clock by two. The two clocks are required to be synchronized, but it's hard to keep strict synchronization in the actual physical circuits. We avoid the metastability problem caused by signals transfer across clock domains by two-level synchronization and this method works well in the implementation [4].

2.3   Peripherals

The peripherals of TengYue-1 include LCD controller, UART serial ports, SPI, I²C, GPIO interfaces, and programmable interrupt controller, power management unit, hardware debug and test interface. All peripherals are connected to the microprocessor by the on-chip bus. The peripherals are mapped into the addressing space of main memory and accessed by the microprocessor through load/store instructions.

The LCD controller can provide independent horizontal/vertical synchronization and combinational synchronization output signals. The size of screen and the polarities of each video timing signal can be programmed by user, thus providing compatibility with almost all available LCD displays. The LCD controller can support a number of color modes, including 32bpp (bit per pixel), 24bpp, 16bpp, 8bpp grayscale and 8bpp pseudo color. The color lookup table is inside the controller, to reduce memory bandwidth request. Video memory and color table are both double bank, which can be used to reduce flicker and cluttered images. This feature is good for application such as video game and video stream application.

TengYue-1 has power manager. It has three modes: run mode, idle mode and sleep mode. These modes are used to reduce power consumption at times when some functions are not needed. When the chip is under the latter two modes, it can be awoken by interrupts or software conditions. The interrupt controller can connect up to 32 external interrupts. The interrupt priority levels and response modes (level sensitive or edge sensitive) can be programmed by the user. The hardware debug and test interface help the test of the chip and accelerate the development of application.

2.4   On-Chip Bus

The WISHBONE compatible on-chip bus of TengYue-1 connects multiple master devices to multiple slave devices. The microprocessor acts as the master device, while the memory controller and the various peripherals are slave devices. The LCD controller can access the memory directly through its own DMA channel, but it also works as the microprocessor's slave device. So it is not only a master device, but also a slave device. When a slave device has multiple master devices, their access sequence is decided by priority bit in the bus configuration register.

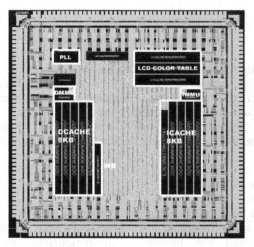

Fig. 5. TengYue-1 test chip's GDSII-based plot

3   Implementation

We use Synopsys Design Compiler for synthesis. The synthesis methodology is a combination of top-down and bottom-up synthesis. We use bottom-up synthesis for the critical modules by constraining their ports, paths, load and fan-outs; other modules are synthesized by top-down method. In the physical design, Physical Compiler is used to generate cell placement, freezing the data cache and instruction cache locations during the placement process and permitting the floorplanning to be data-driven. We generated the balanced clock tree with Cadence's CTGen. The maximum simulated skew across the core was 125ps under the worst case process and environmental conditions.

We fabricated the TengYue-1 in SMIC's 0.18um CMOS technology. Fig.5 shows GDSII-based plot of the test chip. Clock frequencies achieve 300MHz@1.8V; power dissipation is 0.47mW/MHz. Die size is 4.9mm*4.9mm in the total. For the microprocessor core, including instruction cache and data cache, die size is 4.73mm^2.

4   Performance Evaluation

4.1   Microprocessor Core Performance

Analysis of the results for 9 ARM benchmarks showed that the microprocessor core CH achieved an IPC count of about 0.64. All the benchmark programs are written in C language and compiled by gcc. Fig. 6 shows the CPI of each program.

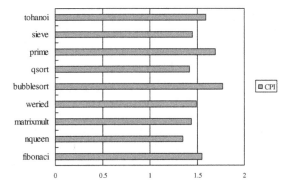

Fig. 6. IPC of benchmarks

4.2   Study of Memory Access Conflict Problem

Because the video memory of LCD is in the main memory, the memory controller has two master devices: the microprocessor and the LCD controller. Thus there exists conflict between memory access from the LCD controller and the microprocessor. If the LCD controller occupied most of the memory bus cycle, then the performance of CPU executing program or LCD driver maybe affected. For LCD driver, it can not write display information in time. One solution to this problem is to isolate the video memory of LCD from the main memory. The cost is adding another memory controller and the on-chip bus becomes more complex.

In our design, the microprocessor core and the LCD controller share the memory controller. To prove this method can satisfy the performance requirements of the system, we built a queue model to simulate this problem, as shown in Fig. 7.

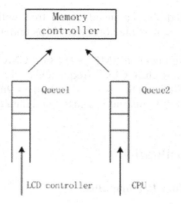

Fig. 7. Queue model

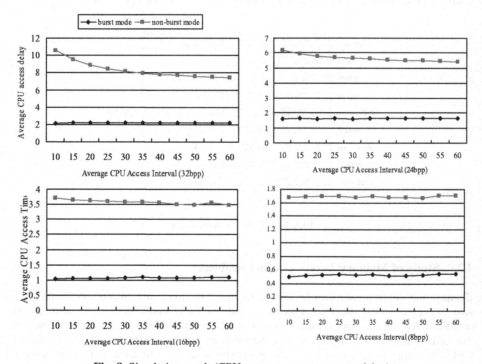

Fig. 8. Simulation result (CPU average memory access delay)

Queue 1 contains the memory access request from the LCD controller. As the LCD displays require pixel values being put on the screen in a fixed frequency, we suppose the arrival interval of video memory access request to be a fixed length distribution. Suppose the display period of the LCD selected is 156.25ns [7]. When the clock period of the microprocessor is 5ns(200MHz), to 32 bpp mode, a 32-bit word must be read out from memory every 31.25 cycles; to 16 bpp mode, a 32-bit word must be read out from memory every 62.5 cycles; 24 bpp and 8 bpp mode can be such deduced.

Queue 2 is for the microprocessor. We suppose that the arrival interval of memory access request from the microprocessor is an exponential distribution.

The memory controller acts as the server and the service time is a fixed value: 10 cycles without burst mode and 13 cycles with burst mode [6]. The burst mode returns four 32-bit words on one memory access while the non-burst mode returns just one. Suppose that the LCD controller has enough buffers to cache pixel data, the microprocessor doesn't use burst mode and the LCD has higher priority when conflict occurs.

We built a queue model by GPSS according to the previous assumptions and simulated the memory access behavior of the LCD controller and the microprocessor under different LCD display modes [8]. We studied the effect of memory access conflict to the performance of system. Fig.8 shows the simulation result.

From Fig.8 we can conclude that the LCD controller brings considerable impairment to the memory access of microprocessor when it doesn't use burst mode. In the worst case, about 33% load/store instructions of the microprocessor are delayed with an average of 11 cycles. However, when burst mode is enabled, the delay of memory access of the microprocessor is reduced to 1-2 cycles and the affected instructions are only 8% of all load/store instructions under the worst case. The cost is only three additional cycles to the memory access time of LCD controller.

Thus it can be seen that mapping the video memory to the main memory and sharing the memory controller between the LCD controller and the microprocessor can satisfy the performance requirement. The affection to the memory access of the microprocessor brought by the LCD controller can be reduced and even ignored when using the burst mode of the memory.

5   Conclusions

TengYue-1 is a high performance embedded SOC design. We studied the critical issues of the design and improved the overall performance by reducing the complexity of the hardware efficiently. This chip has been implemented and verified in SMIC 0.18um CMOS technology, and the frequency can achieve 300MHz@1.8V. TengYue-1 has a broad application prospect on RS encoding-decoding, information encryption/decryption and safety authentication.

References

1.   Patterson D A, Hennessy J L. Computer Architecture: A Quantitative Approach. 2nd ed. San Francisco: Morgan Kaufman Publish, 1996.
2.   S. B. Furber, *ARM System-on-chip Architecture*. Addison Wesley Longman(2000), ISBN: 0-201-67519-6.
3.   ARM Inc. ARM Architecture Reference Manual [Z]. ARM DDI 0100D, Write Paper, 2000

4.   Clifford E. Cummings, *Synthesis and Scripting Techniques for designing Multi-Asynchronous Clock Designs*, SNUG 2001 2.
5.   J. P. Grossman, *A Systolic Array for Implementing LRU Replacement*, Project Aries Technical Memo
6.   Micron Technology, *Synchronous DRAM Datasheet*
7.   NEC, *TFT COLOR LCD MODULE datasheet*
8.   Robert C. Crain, *SIMULATION WITH GPSS/H*, Proceedings of the 1998 Winter Simulation Conference

A Fault-Tolerant Single-Chip Multiprocessor

Wenbin Yao[1], Dongsheng Wang[2], and Weimin Zheng[1]

[1] Department of Computer Science and Technology, Tsinghua University, P. R. China
[2] Research Institute of Information Technology, Tsinghua University, P. R. China
{yao-wb, wds, zwm-cs}@tsinghua.edu.cn

Abstract. The microprocessor is a crucial component of a reliable system. With improvement in semiconductor manufacturing, more and more transistors may be integrated into a single chip with increased potential detriment to dependability. Fault-tolerant single-chip multiprocessors offer an ideal architecture for achieving high availability while maintaining high performance. The design of a fault-tolerant single-chip multiprocessor is described - from hardware redundancy to software support and firmware information strategies. The design aims at masking the influences of errors and automatically correcting system states, which differs from traditional approaches which mainly target errors in the memory and I/O subsystems. Dynamic recovery and reconfiguration are also described to provide adequate protection from catastrophic failure of the system.

1 Introduction

The growth of dependency on computer systems demands microprocessors which provide higher dependability whilst maintaining high computing performance. This is particularly true for mission-critical applications. With the development of deep-submicron technology, it is predicted that in the next 10 years a single chip can contain more than one billion transistors[1]. However, shrinking geometries, lower power voltages and high frequencies also have a negative impact on dependability.

Recently, as the trend toward thread-level parallelism matures, single-chip multiprocessors(CMP) present a promising solution to partly mitigate these influences[2-4]. CMPs integrating multiple processors into a single chip execute several threads concurrently to achieve high computing performance. The advantages of this technique include simplified design of critical paths and shrinking of development time and cost.

From an architectural viewpoint, CMPs combined with fault-tolerant techniques can further improve microprocessor dependability. Such designs follow two reliability principles. First, they observe the classical maxim: "simple is reliable". A design achieves this goal by incorporating simple control logic and replacing the traditional complex parallel structures with multiple simple processors. Second, CMPs, which may use multiple identical processors for error detection and recovery, have inherent features leading to flexible fault-tolerant architectures. Different fault-tolerant strategies can be implemented neatly by reasonably dispatching available redundant components.

P.-C. Yew and J. Xue (Eds.): ACSAC 2004, LNCS 3189, pp. 137–145, 2004.

In this paper, we propose an architecture for a fault-tolerant single-chip multiprocessor (F-CMP). Differing from the IBM pSeries 690[5] which pursues RAS and can tolerate duration of repair, F-CMP provides high levels of reliability and availability with strong automatic recovery capability. The architecture is configurable and supports the replacement of faulty components and the degeneration to lower reliability levels when uncorrectable errors occur. Users can also specify a fault-tolerant mode corresponding to the dependability requirements of ant applications. Fault-tolerant strategies have been designed with special characteristics to tradeoff among hardware and software.

The rest of the paper is organized as follows. Section 2 presents an overview of F-CMP architecture. Section 3 discusses the fault-tolerant design techniques used in F-CMP, including hardware redundancy, firmware and software support. Section 4 describes the recovery strategies of F-CMP and Section 5 concludes.

2 System Overview

The F-CMP architecture is based on Tsinghua University's Thump-107. The Thump-107 is a RISC-based microprocessor targetting embedded applications. Its instruction set is a superset of MIPS-4Kc and is compatible with MIPS 32-bit RISC architecture. It has a 4k-byte instruction cache, a 4k-byte data cache and a 7-stage pipeline structure able to execute up to seven instructions per clock cycle.

From an architectural point of view, F-CMP is a closely coupled multiprocessor that contains four identical Thump-107 processors, a shared cache and necessary control logic needed to realize the fault-tolerant strategies. A logical overview is shown in Fig. 1.

F-CMP has six kinds of functional units:

- Four identical Thump-107 processors
The Thump-107 processor is an independent 32-bit CPU core, which implements the MIPS 4Kc instruction set plus four instructions for multimedia applications. In F-CMP, the processors reuse the basic Thump-107 structure, adding two instructions specially for implementing synchronization primitives used by a standard CMP. These two instructions are the load locked(LL) and store conditional(SC) instruction, respectively. Each processor also includes an 8k-bytes instruction cache, an 8k-bytes data cache and corresponding control logic. The L1 cache is a write-through primary cache that allows all processors to snoop on all writes performed.

- Fault Handling Mechanism
A fault handling mechanism consisting of a crossbar and four sets of fault-tolerant selectable logic was designed to detect computing errors by comparing results from independent processors. Logically, the crossbar controlled by the centralized arbitration controller connects the outputs of four identical processors with select logic. Four fault-tolerant computing modes are provided: one-mode, dual-mode, triple-mode and quadruple-mode redundancy, named after the numbers of participating processors.

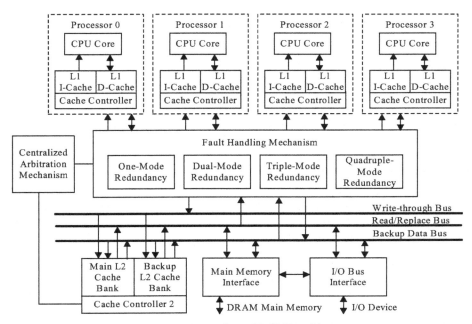

Fig. 1. Logical overview of F-CMP architecture

- A shared secondary cache

    Four processors share a unified L2 cache organized as two cache banks with separate controllers. The L2 cache can protect data with standard CRC words and its capacity is as large as 2M-bytes. In the non-fault-tolerant mode, the shared cache can be organized as a unified interleaved cache. In the fault-tolerant mode, the L2 cache consists of two independent sub-caches, each of which backs up the other. The main cache bank and the backup bank make up a fault-tolerant memory subsystem.

- A centralized arbitration controller

    Besides controlling the crossbar to provide fault-tolerance, the centralized arbitration controller manages access privileges on the shared bus. In F-CMP, three logic data buses including a write-through bus and a read/replace bus and a backup bus are used for data transmission. The backup bus is a standard data bus and may take over the tasks of the other buses if necessary.

- Main memory interface (MIU)

    The MIU handles all the interfacing transactions from and to F-CMP, including main memory accesses and external snoop processing.

- I/O interface unit

    The I/O interface unit handles all the input and output transactions of F-CMP.

3   Fault-Tolerant Design Techniques

F-CMP provides different levels of fault tolerance, including hardware redundancy, software support and firmware-based recovery. The architecture also allows system reconfiguration and dynamic graceful degeneration.

3.1   Fault-Tolerant Hardware Design

F-CMP provides some special structures to satisfy the requirements of different levels of fault tolerance. Here, three fault-tolerant strategies are presented:

- Fault-tolerant Computing
To achieve high reliability in the course of computing, three fault-tolerant strategies based on comparison techniques are provided in F-CMP. Fig. 2 shows the logic structure of different redundancy modes.

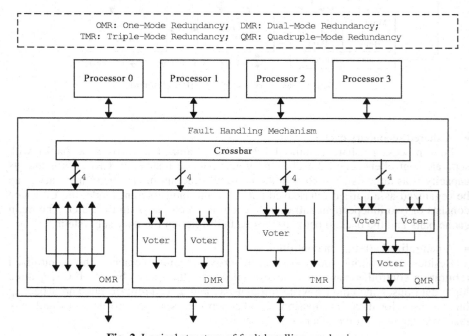

Fig. 2. Logical structure of fault handling mechanisms

In the fault handling mechanism, there are four sets of fault-tolerant logic. However, at any time, only one set of logic is activated.

One-mode redundancy represents a standard single-chip multiprocessor, in which every processor is an autonomous subsystem running applications independently. It is a non-fault-tolerant mode. In dual-mode redundancy, two processors form a simple comparison-based fault-tolerant subsystem while the others run as two independent single-processor subsystems. Similarly, triple-mode redundancy includes an autonomous single-processor subsystem and a voting fault-tolerant subsystem of three processors. The most complex form, quadruple-mode redundancy, uses all the four processors for fault-tolerant computing. In this mode, each pair of processors form a simple comparison-based fault-tolerant subsystem, and their outputs are compared once more to output a single result.

The fault-tolerant modes are controlled by an error-capture register (ECR). According to the different connection of the output of the processors, one-mode, dual-mode, triple-mode and quadruple-mode redundancy require 1 bit, 6 bits, 4 bits and 3 bits, respectively, in the ECR. As a result, the ECR has 14 controlling bits all together, each of which corresponds to a computing mode.

- Reliability Data Transmission

Connecting the processors, secondary cache and other control interfaces together are a read/replace bus, a write-through bus and a backup bus, along with address and control buses. While the read/replace and write-through buses are virtual buses, the physical wires are divided into multiple segments using repeaters and pipeline buffers. The backup bus is an independent physical bus, which implements standard reads and writes. Thus it can be used to replace the other two logical buses. As a result, the bus structure is actually a dual-bus system which protects transmitted information.

The read/replace bus acts as a general-purpose system bus for moving data between the processors, secondary cache and external interface to off-chip memory. The processors can fetch required data from secondary cache via the read bus simultaneously. Data from the external interface can be broadcast to both of the processors while it is sending to secondary cache.

The write-through bus permits F-CMP to use a write-update coherence protocol to maintain coherent primary caches. Data exchange among the processors is carried out via a write-through bus under the control of the centralized bus arbiter. When one processor modifies data shared by other processors, write broadcast over the bus updates all copies while the permanent machine state is written back to the secondary cache.

The backup bus design has two objectives. First, it can be used as an independent read and write bus to speed up communications between two levels of cache. Second, it can also be used as the single data bus when uncorrectable failures are detected on the other logical buses.

As in other high reliability microprocessor systems, data on the bus is augmented by a single-error-correct and double-error-detect Hamming ECC to further enhance fault-tolerance.

- Fault-tolerant Data Store

Both L1 and L2 caches have memory protection mechanisms designed to correct single event errors. Several bits are added to the banks to replace faulty bits. These techniques are analogous to the programmed steering logic in the structure of POWER4[6]. The controlling logic is activated by built-in self-test at power on.

As mentioned above, beside a normal unified cache, an L2 cache consisting of two banks can also implement a fault-tolerant memory subsystem by configuring one bank to back up the other. As a result, F-CMP may run in multiple different storage modes according the reliability states of caches. Possible storage configurations are shown in

Table 1, where '√' and '×' represent the availability and non-availability of the corresponding components, respectively.

Table 1. F-CMP Storage Configuration

Mode	L1 cache	L2 cache	
		Main Bank	Backup Bank
1	√	√	√
2	×	√	√
3	√	×	√
4	√	√	×
5	×	×	√
6	×	√	×
7	√	×	×
8	×	×	×

3.2   Firmware

Firmware was designed to record runtime error thresholds, indicating the number of corrected errors in the F-CMP microprocessor. The error information recorded in firmware becomes part of a system error log and is used for system reconfiguration. The replaceable components include the processors, cache banks and buses. When errors are detected in these components, error information is recorded in firmware.

Dynamic reconfiguration is implemented: firmware logs errors and is used to decide the current fault-tolerant mode. Hardware and firmware track periodically whether error numbers stay below a threshold. After exceeding this threshold, the system will initiate additional runtime availability actions, such as a controlled shutdown of processors and the replacement of a faulty cache line or a controlled shutdown of banks or even the whole L2 cache.

3.3   Software Support

Depending on hardware redundancy to achieve high reliability is not enough and software support plays a very important role on the design of F-CMP. Since each processor in F-CMP has its own program counter and register file, it is easy to execute multiple instruction streams in parallel. Actually, four independent instructions streams --- generally called threads --- can be simultaneously issued to the different processors to achieve software implemented fault tolerance (SIFT). The operations are scheduled under the control of the operating system.

As the mentioned above, the fault-tolerant modes of F-CMP are controlled by an error-capture register (ECR). This register is software-readable and can be reset by operating system. At bootstrap, the operating system may set the fault-tolerant mode of F-CMP according to application requirements and the current state of replaceable components in the microprocessor. Hardware and software may cooperate to implement runtime fault-tolerant handling, which is transparent to the users. F-CMP may also degenerate into a lower fault-tolerant mode if uncorrectable failures are encountered.

4   System Recovery Strategies

F-CMP implements concurrent error detection, dynamic fault isolation and error recovery while running. The most important principle of system recovery strategies is to guarantee the dependability of mission-critical applications even if system performance must be lowered. As a result, the replaceable components are considered first to take over from failed ones during the course of system reconfiguration. The error recovery flowchart of F-CMP is shown in Fig. 3.

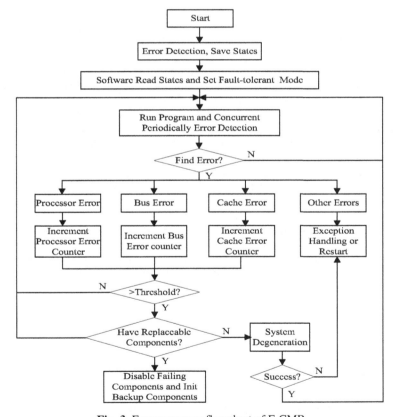

Fig. 3. Error recovery flowchart of F-CMP

While the numbers of errors are beyond the capability of the current fault-tolerant mode, F-CMP may commence system degeneration. Corresponding to the fault-tolerant levels, there are three kinds of system degenerations in the level of processors and the buses and the caches. Processor-level degeneration has four forms: from quadruple-mode to dual-mode or one-mode redundancy, and from triple-mode to one-mode redundancy, and from dual-mode to one-mode redundancy, respectively. Bus-level degeneration may go from dual-mode to one-mode redundancy. In the cache-level degeneration, each cache line and bank and even whole caches may be removed as uncorrectable errors increase.

Besides the system degeneration, F-CMP has dynamic reconfiguration capabilities, viz. the state conversion between different fault-tolerant modes. Actually, the dual-mode and triple-mode and quadruple-mode redundancy have different dependability characteristics and complement each other. For applications requiring more processor power, dual-mode is suitable because the two groups of processors may execute different threads individually. But for other critical applications, triple-mode or quadruple-mode may be much better. System reconfiguration controlled by software includes two forms: conversion between dual-mode and triple-mode redundancy, and conversion between quadruple-mode and triple-mode redundancy.

5   Conclusion

We have described a fault-tolerant single-chip multiprocessor aimed at providing adequate protection from system failure. The design has configurable levels of hardware redundancy, software support and firmware information techniques. The architecture provides multiple fault-tolerant modes and is thus adaptable to different mission-critical applications: it also allows smooth conversion between the different modes. Since all the redundancy components and corresponding controllers exploit the "simple design" principle, it is easy to validate the reliability of subsystems and this leads to a high dependability system.

To verify the properties of the architecture, two related software tools have been written. One is a behavior simulator written in C, which performs functional validation. The simulator can simulate the operational behavior of F-CMP cycle-by-cycle. The other tool is a dynamic runtime error injection system, which randomly injects permanent and intermittent and transient errors into the system. Initial validation tests showed that the F-CMP architecture improved system dependability effectively for some mission-critical applications and reached the design target of initial dependability.

References

1.   Cristian Constantinescu. Trends and Challenges in VLSI Circuit Reliability. IEEE Micro. Vol.23, No. 4(2003), 14-19
2.   Sang-Won Lee, Yun-Seob Song, et al. Raptor: A Single Chip Multiprocessor. The First IEEE Asia Pacific Conference on ASIC. (1999) 217-220
3.   Lucian Codrescu, D. Scott Wills, James Meindl. Architecture of Atlas Chip-Multiprocessor: Dynamically Parallelizing Irregular Applications. IEEE Transactions on Computers. Vol. 50, No. 1 (2001) 67-82
4.   John Nickolls, L. J. Madar III. Calisto: A Low-Power Single-Chip Multiporcessor Communications Platform. IEEE Micro. Vol. 23, No. 4 (2003) 29-43

5.   D. C. Bossen, A. Kitamorn, K. F. Reick, M. S. Floyd. Fault-tolerant Design of the IBM pSeries 690 System using POWER4 Processor Technology. IBM J. RES. & DEV. January Vol. 46, No. 1 (2002) 77-86
6.   D. C. Bossen, J. M. Tendler, Kevin Reick. POWER4 System Design for High Reliability. IEEE Micro. Vol. 22, No. 2 (2002) 16-24

Initial Experiences with Dreamy Memory and the RAMpage Memory Hierarchy

Philip Machanick

School of ITEE, University of Queensland
Brisbane, Qld 4072, Australia
philip@itee.uq.edu.au

Abstract. This paper is a first look at the value of the RAMpage memory hierarchy to low-energy design. The approach used, *dreamy memory*, is to put DRAM in a low-power mode, unless it is referenced. Simulation results show that RAMpage provides a better overall speed-energy compromise than the conventional architecture used for comparison. The most energy-efficient RAMpage configuration in dreamy mode ran 3% faster and used 71% of the energy for DRAM of the best dreamy run of the conventional model. As compared with the best non-dreamy run time, the best dreamy time was 9% slower, but used under 17% of the energy for DRAM. The lowest-energy dreamy simulation used less than 16% of the DRAM energy of the fastest non-dreamy version, a very useful gain, given that DRAM uses significantly more power than the processor in a low-energy design. The most energy-efficient variant ran 12% slower than the fastest, allowing several trade-offs between speed and energy.

1 Introduction

The RAMpage memory hierarchy moves main memory up a level to replace the lowest-level cache with an SRAM main memory, while DRAM becomes a paging device. Previous work has shown RAMpage to be a potentially viable design in terms of hardware-software trade-offs [16] and that it scales better as the CPU-DRAM speed gap grows, particularly when taking context switches on misses to DRAM [14]. In this paper, the value of RAMpage in hiding DRAM latency is further explored by introducing the idea of *dreamy memory.*

Dreamy memory is kept in a low-power mode unless it is referenced. While waking the memory up incurs significant overhead, RAMpage could hide this overhead as has previously been demonstrated.

In desktop and server designs, with processor power consumption on the order of tens of watts or even over 100W, reducing memory power usage is not a major issue. However, with a low-energy design, DRAM energy usage becomes significant. A 128Mbyte DRAM as simulated in this study uses about 0.5W, as compared with a 500MHz processor of the ARM11 family [1], which uses about 0.2W. A small mobile device with a relatively modest memory therefore has to allocate a significant fraction of its energy budget to DRAM.

P.-C. Yew and J. Xue (Eds.): ACSAC 2004, LNCS 3189, pp. 146–159, 2004.
© Springer-Verlag Berlin Heidelberg 2004

In this paper, the approach investigated is to use the self-refresh mode commonly available in double-data rate synchronous DRAM (DDR-SDRAM), which allows DRAM contents to be maintained with 1% of normal power [17], to implement dreamy memory. Simulations are based on parameters suited to a mobile device. The aim is to reduce DRAM energy usage to as close as possible to that of self-refresh mode, with performance as close as possible to that of full-power mode.

The remainder of this paper is structured as follows. Section 2 presents more detail of the RAMpage hierarchy and related research. Section 3 explains the experimental approach, while Section 4 presents experimental results. In conclusion, Section 5 summarizes the findings and outlines future work.

2   Background

2.1   Introduction

RAMpage was proposed [12] in response to the memory wall [21,9], which arises mainly with high-end systems, where processor improvements have not been matched by DRAM speed improvements. At the low end, energy use is a much more significant problem. RAMpage's ability to hide latency of (relatively) slow DRAM can potentially be used to hide the latency of waking a DRAM up from a low-power mode.

In this paper, low energy, rather than low power is the measure of interest, as we are concerned with total energy use over time, rather than an instantaneous measure.

The remainder of this section briefly surveys other approaches to low-energy memory design, followed by an outline of the RAMpage approach to the problem.

2.2   Low-Energy Memory Design

There have been several approaches to reducing the energy needs of memory.

IRAM (Intelligent RAM) was originally proposed to address the memory wall problem, by implementing a large DRAM on-chip with the processor, instead of the traditional trend of increasing on-chip cache size. While the on-chip DRAM is slower than an SRAM cache, it is faster than an off-chip DRAM [19]. More recently, IRAM has been shown to offer the potential for reduced energy usage, because of DRAM's lower energy requirement as compared to SRAM, and elimination of off-chip buses [6].

At the low end, work has been done on variations on memory organization like multiple banks (less commonly used banks can be put in low-power modes), finding optimum combinations of number of banks and bus width, and exploring compromises between performance-optimal and energy-optimal organization of caches and DRAM [2]. One specific proposal for a low-energy design for system-on-chip (SoC) applications is to organize static RAM into statically allocated banks, based on predicted data referencing behaviour [4]. The main problem with this approach is that it requires static allocation, and does not allow for changes in the relative sizes of the banks for different workloads.

The closest idea to that reported here are Power-Aware DRAM (PADRAM) [11] and Power-Aware Virtual Memory (PAVM) [8]: page placement is used in a memory in which different chips may be in different power modes. Frequently accessed pages are in a DRAM which is not in a low-power mode (or less often than other chips).

In a PADRAM study, it was shown that putting all DRAM into the lowest-power mode resulted in execution time of 2 to 60 times that of full-power mode, whereas a dynamic policy resulted in a relatively small speed loss, with significant energy saving. While various details of the PADRAM study differed from those reported in this paper (faster processor, smaller L2 cache, Rambus memory with higher wakeup latency), the most significant difference is that no operating system effects were modelled: single process execution times were reported, not a mix of workloads [11]. In addition, only a hardware-managed L2 cache was modelled, not a software-managed cache like the RAMpage SRAM main memory. RAMpage, especially with context switches on misses, relies on a multiprogramming workload to hide DRAM latency and is therfore able to get away with a simpler approach to managing DRAM.

PAVM has been investigated in more detail, but using an actual implementation on Linux and an otherwise-conventional memory hierarchy. Exploiting a combination of the different modes available in Rambus and dynamic page placement strategies, with DRAM energy savings of up to 59% with a heavy workload [8].

Since other low-energy techniques can apply to dreamy DRAM, approaches in areas such as reducing energy to drive a bus to DRAM [20] and reducing cache energy [10] have not been considered in detail as potential competing work.

2.3   The RAMpage Approach

RAMpage makes as few changes from a traditional hierarchy as possible. The lowest-level cache becomes the main memory (i.e., a paged virtually-addressed memory), with disk used as a secondary paging device. The RAMpage main memory page table is inverted, to minimize its size. Further, an inverted page table has another benefit: no TLB miss can result in a DRAM reference, unless the reference causing the TLB lookup is not in any of the SRAM layers [16].

RAMpage has in the past been shown to scale well in the face of the grown CPU-DRAM speed gap, particularly when context switches are taken on misses. The effect of taking context switches on misses is that, if other work is available for the CPU, waiting for DRAM can effectively be eliminated [14]. Performance characteristics of RAMpage have previously been reported [16, 13, 14]. For purposes of this paper, the key advantage of RAMpage is the ability to mask latency of DRAM references, with the aim of keeping DRAM in a low-power mode unless it is being referenced, without significant loss of speed.

Compared with most other approaches to low-energy memory systems, the RAMpage approach is very simple. No special hardware is needed, other than the RAMpage design itself. DRAM is put into a low-power mode, and turned on when it is referenced. As compared with the PADRAM approach, the architecture requires no complex dynamic placement strategy. Provided a process is ready to run on a miss to DRAM, the extra wake-up latency can be masked. PAVM is closer in philosophy, but RAMpage carries the idea further in managing the lowest-level cache in software, which has potential for other wins, as described in previous RAMpage work [16, 14].

The dynamic placement strategies of PADRAM and PAVM could be added to RAMpage, combining their benefits with a software-controlled SRAM main memory.

3   Experimental Approach

3.1   Introduction

This section outlines the approach to the reported experiments. Results are designed to be comparable to previously reported results as far as possible. The simulation strategy is explained, followed by some detail of simulation parameters; in conclusion, expected findings are discussed.

3.2   Simulation Strategy

The approach followed here is similar to that used in previously reported work. However, the processor speed characteristics are based on the ARM11 series [1] running at 500MHz. This processor consumes 0.2W at this speed; this power consumption makes the power needs of DRAM significant.

Simulations are trace-driven, and do not model the pipeline. It is assumed that pipeline timing is less significant than variations in DRAM referencing. Given that the ARM11 family only issues one instruction per clock and has accurate branch prediction, this approach to simulation is unlikely to introduce significant inaccuracies. For simplicity, the simulations do not use all features of the ARM11 series. The ARM11's two-level TLB is not simulated. Instead, a relatively small 1-level TLB is simulated. The RAMpage hierarchy is more disadvantaged by this approximation than a conventional hierarchy, since it relies on the TLB for mapping pages in the SRAM main memory, rather than in DRAM [15].

A standard 2-level hierarchy is compared to a similar version of a RAMpage hierarchy, with and without context switches on misses. RAMpage without context switches on misses is intended to convey the effects of adding associativity (with an operating system-style replacement strategy). Adding context switches on misses shows the value of having alternative work on a miss to DRAM. In all cases, the effect of running with DRAM permanently on is compared with the effect of running with DRAM in self-refresh mode, except when it is referenced.

In this study, given that energy and cost are more significant than for previous studies, L2 is reduced from 4 Mbytes to 1 Mbyte (the simulated 1MB SRAM consumes 0.8W [18]; 4 MB would use 3.2W, significant compared with a 0.2W processor). This reduction disadvantages RAMpage more than the standard hierarchy: part of the SRAM main memory is reserved for operating system data and code: in addition to a page table, RAMpage reserves 32 Kbytes for the operating system. The ARM11 series includes 64K bytes of SRAM (tightly coupled memory, TCM) which could be used for the operating system in RAMpage; the page table would also fit for SRAM page sizes of 256 bytes or more. This option was not explored in this study; using TCM, which operates at cache speed, in RAMpage simulations would likely result in significant speed gains.

3.3   Simulation Parameters

The processor modelled in this paper is slower than in recent RAMpage work, if comparable to one of the speeds in recent older work [16], to take into account the slower speeds of low-energy designs.

A major difference from previously reported results, which used Direct Rambus, is use of double-data-rate synchronous DRAM. The DDR-SDRAM modelled [17] has average power usage of 200mA, and self-refresh mode which uses 2mA, both at 2.6V. In self-refresh mode, the external clock is turned off, and contents of DRAM is maintained without external intervention. Actual DRAM power usage varies according to the reference pattern, but for this preliminary work, an average value is used, and the same value is used for entry to and exit from self-refresh mode. In previous work, detail of the DRAM was not considered important, as fixing DRAM speed while speeding up the CPU represented the increasing CPU-DRAM speed gap. In this paper, DRAM detail is more important because power usage is timing-dependent.

The following parameters are similar to previous simulations except as noted, and are common across RAMpage and the conventional hierarchy:

- L1 cache – 16 Kbytes each of data and instruction cache, physically tagged and indexed, direct-mapped, 32-byte blocks, 1-cycle read hit time, 12-cycle penalty for misses to L2 (or RAMpage SRAM main memory)
- TLB – 64 entries, fully associative, random replacement, 1-cycle hit time, misses modelled by interleaving a trace of page look-up software
- DRAM – DDR400 SDRAM: $40ns$ before first reference starts, 64-bit $5ns$ bus (data moves every $2.5ns$: transfer rate approximately $0.3ns$ per byte; DRAM time to exit self-refresh is $1\mu s$, and time to enter self-refresh mode is $20ns$)
- paging of DRAM – inverted page table: same organization as RAMpage main memory for simplicity, the workload is preloaded, so there are no page faults to disk; for energy calculations, a 128MB DRAM is assumed
- TLB and L1 data hits are fully pipelined: they do not add to execution time; only instruction fetch bits add to simulated run time; time for replacements or maintaining inclusion are costed as L1d or TLB "hits"

A context switch (modelled by interleaving a trace of text-book code) is generally taken every 500,000 references, though RAMpage with context switches on misses also switches processes on a miss to DRAM. TLB misses are handled by inserting a trace of page table lookup code, with variations on time for a lookup based on probable variations in probes into an inverted page table [16].

Specific to conventional hierarchy. L2 cache is 2-way associative, 1Mbyte. The bus connecting L2 to the CPU is 128 bits wide and runs at one third of the CPU issue rate ($6ns$ versus the CPU's 2 ns). The miss penalty from L1 to L2 overall is 12 CPU cycles. Inclusion between L1 and L2 is maintained [7], so L1 is always a subset of L2, except that some blocks in L1 may be dirty with respect to L2 (writebacks occur on replacement).

The TLB caches translations from virtual pages to DRAM physical frames.

Specific to RAMpage hierarchy. The TLB maps the SRAM main memory. Full associativity is implemented by a software miss handler. The operating system takes up 9 SRAM main memory pages when simulating a 4 Kbyte-SRAM page (36 Kbytes), up to 752 pages for a 128 byte block size (94 Kbytes).

The SRAM main memory uses an inverted page table. TLB misses do not reference DRAM, if the original reference can be found in an SRAM level.

Inputs and variations. Traces used are from the Tracebase trace archive at New Mexico State University[1]. Although these traces are from the obsolete SPEC92 benchmarks, they are sufficient to warm up the size of cache used here, because 1.1-billion references are used, with traces interleaved to create the effect of a multiprogramming workload.

To measure variations on energy use, the size of the SRAM main memory page (or L2 block size in the conventional model) was varied from 128 bytes to 4 Kbytes, and the simulation was instrumented to track energy use.

In dreamy mode, it was assumed that if a DRAM access started before the previous one had completed, DRAM would still be awake. Otherwise, once a DRAM reference completed, it was put into self-refresh mode. For comparison, simulations were run with DRAM permanently in full power mode. The simulator allows for a lag after references before entering self-refresh mode, but this option is still to be explored.

Total energy was calculated by multiplying time in each mode by the power of that mode.

3.4   Expected Findings

It was expected that speed differences would not be the most significant finding, given that early studies [16, 13] showed little difference between RAMpage and the conventional model at the clock speed being modelled in this paper. It was expected that the introduction of dreamy mode would have less of an effect on

---

[1] See `ftp://tracebase.nmsu.edu/pub/traces/uni/r2000/utilities/` and
`ftp://tracebase.nmsu.edu/pub/traces/uni/r2000/SPEC92/`.

RAMpage than on the conventional model, given that RAMpage has been shown to be more tolerant of an increased DRAM latency, especially when context switches are taken on misses [14].

With a significantly smaller SRAM main memory than in earlier experiments, it was expected that RAMpage, which pins parts of the operating system in the SRAM main memory, would be less competitive on speed than in earlier experiments even in dreamy mode, where the increased effective DRAM latency would make this experiment closer to earlier ones with faster processors.

RAMpage, however, has the potential to show a better overall combination of not only lower speed loss in dreamy mode and lower overall energy use in dreamy mode, than the conventional hierarchy. Since RAMpage in general (and more specifically when contect switches are taken on misses) spends a lower fraction of its time waiting for DRAM, it is likely that it will need DRAM to be in full-power mode less often than the standard hierarchy does.

4   Results

4.1   Introduction

This section presents results of simulations, with some discussion of their significance. The main focus here is on comparing the effects of varying the memory hierarchy on energy and power use.

Figure 1 shows an overall comparison of all the variations measured. Of most interest is the fact that it's hard to tell apart speed variations of the best cases for each configuration on the same scale, whereas energy variations for dreamy and non-dreamy cases are clearly separated. This observation illustrates that aiming to save energy while minimizing performance loss is achievable.

The remainder of this section presents more detail of results. Speed variations are followed by energy variations. Finally, design trade-offs are considered.

4.2   Speed Variations

Speed variations are shown in Table 1. Speedups are shown for the non-dreamy case of the best measured time versus each other time. For dreamy times, speedups are given both relative to the same parameters with and without dreamy mode (2nd-last column) and the best non-dreamy time (last column). The best dreamy and non-dreamy times are highlighted.

The best dreamy run time is for RAMpage with context switches on misses, with a 2KB SRAM page size. Execution time here is 9% slower than for the best non-dreamy case (conventional hierarchy, 512B L2 block size). More speed variation is accounted for by variations in the SRAM page or L2 block size than by using or not using dreamy mode. The slowest dreamy simulated execution time is 5.06s; the slowest non-dreamy time is 4.92s, a difference of under 3%.

The standard hierarchy's best dreamy time (1KB L2 block size) is 15% slower than the best non-dreamy time, while the best dreamy RAMpage time without context switches on misses is 12% slower than the best non-dreamy time.

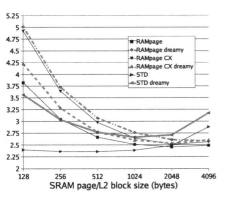

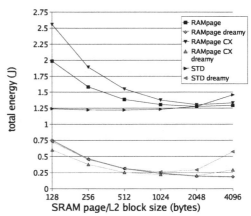

(a) Overall Speed Comparison

(b) Overall DRAM Energy Comparison

Fig. 1. Comparison of speed and energy usage. In all figures, "CX" means with context switches on misses.

Table 1. Speed variations. Each row shows standard hierarchy (top), RAMpage without (middle) and with context switches on misses (bottom).

L2 block/	Non-Dreamy		Dreamy Times (s)			Dreamy Speedups	
page size	time (s)	best speedup	asleep	awake	total	non-dreamy	best
128	2.395	1.015	2.224	1.378	3.602	1.504	1.526
	3.821	1.619	3.654	1.409	5.062	1.325	2.145
	4.919	2.085	3.127	1.124	4.251	0.864	1.802
256	2.362	1.001	2.220	0.845	3.065	1.298	1.299
	3.043	1.290	2.910	0.856	3.766	1.238	1.596
	3.638	1.542	2.602	0.698	3.301	0.907	1.399
512	2.359	1.000	2.220	0.584	2.804	1.188	1.188
	2.663	1.129	2.534	0.577	3.111	1.168	1.318
	2.977	1.262	2.328	0.466	2.794	0.938	1.184
1024	2.386	1.011	2.224	0.481	2.705	1.133	1.146
	2.510	1.064	2.368	0.439	2.807	1.118	1.190
	2.647	1.122	2.229	0.406	2.635	0.996	1.117
2048	2.483	1.052	2.237	0.540	2.777	1.119	1.177
	2.454	1.040	2.304	0.354	2.658	1.083	1.127
	2.506	1.062	2.201	0.371	2.572	1.026	1.090
4096	2.879	1.220	2.293	1.077	3.371	1.171	1.429
	2.487	1.054	2.304	0.334	2.638	1.061	1.118
	2.562	1.086	2.139	0.538	2.677	1.045	1.135

While RAMpage doesn't do well with small SRAM page sizes – as reported in earlier work [16] – time variations for cases with reasonable SRAM page sizes are low considering the relatively large energy saving of dreamy mode. RAMpage with and without context switches on misses does not differ as significantly as in earlier studies with a large CPU-DRAM speed gap and large L2 [14]. Dreamy mode does increase the effective CPU-DRAM speed gap: an extra miss penalty of 500 clock cycles similar to increasing the processor speed to the speeds previously modelled. However, as expected, the smaller SRAM main memory used in this study disadvantages RAMpage more than the conventional model.

More data is needed to understand why RAMpage with context switches on misses is faster in some cases in dreamy mode. A possible explanation is that dreamy mode, with its longer latency for DRAM accesses, loses less performance to context switches before a working set has loaded fully into SRAM.

4.3   Energy Variations

Table 2 shows the simulated DRAM energy usage for each variation.

The lowest-energy non-dreamy case is the standard hierarchy with a 512B L2 block size, which also has the quickest execution time. For dreamy runs, however, the lowest-energy case is RAMpage without context switches on misses for a 4KB SRAM page size, as compared with the fastest case: 2KB page size, *with* context switches on misses. The reason for this discrepancy results from the fact that in

Table 2. DRAM energy use. Each row shows standard hierarchy (top), RAMpage without (middle) and with context switches on misses (bottom).

L2 block/ page size	Non-Dreamy energy (J)	× best	Dreamy Energy asleep (J)	awake (J)	total (J)	% full	× best
128	1.241	6.7	0.0116	0.716	0.728	58.7	3.92
	1.987	10.7	0.0190	0.732	0.751	36.9	4.05
	2.558	13.8	0.0163	0.584	0.601	25.8	3.24
256	1.223	6.6	0.0115	0.440	0.451	22.9	2.43
	1.582	8.5	0.0151	0.445	0.460	39.2	2.48
	1.892	10.2	0.0135	0.363	0.377	21.3	2.03
512	1.220	6.6	0.0115	0.304	0.315	39.2	1.70
	1.385	7.5	0.0132	0.300	0.313	21.3	1.69
	1.548	8.3	0.0121	0.242	0.255	22.9	1.37
1024	1.232	6.6	0.0116	0.250	0.262	21.3	1.41
	1.305	7.0	0.0123	0.228	0.241	22.9	1.30
	1.376	7.4	0.0116	0.211	0.223	39.2	1.20
2048	1.276	6.9	0.0116	0.281	0.293	22.9	1.58
	1.276	6.9	0.0120	0.184	0.196	20.1	1.06
	1.303	7.0	0.0114	0.193	0.204	44.2	1.10
4096	1.458	7.9	0.0119	0.560	0.572	39.2	3.08
	1.293	7.0	0.0120	0.174	0.186	14.4	1.00
	1.332	7.2	0.0111	0.280	0.291	21.9	1.57

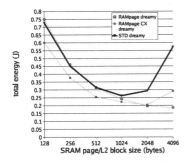
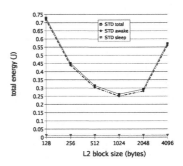

(a) Overall Dreamy Energy Comparison

(b) Standard Energy Breakdown

Fig. 2. All *vs.* Standard dreamy energy usage.

the 4KB case, DRAM is awake for a smaller total time (lower "awake" energy). The time DRAM is awake depends on time that transfers take. A larger page size may reduce the miss rate, but total transfer time may increase. Context switches on misses hides this effect by doing other work on a miss. However, increased energy is not disguised by overlapping transfers with other work.

Figure 2 compares energy use in dreamy mode for all variations with a breakdown of energy use by the standard architecture. Energy use increases significantly for large cache block sizes in the standard architecture, which is less true of RAMpage variations. The reason for this behaviour of the standard model can be seen in Figure 2. As L2 block size increases, energy use while asleep decreases, but awake energy increases, corresponding to a larger fraction of time being spent waiting for DRAM (as confirmed by the increase in execution time for the standard dreamy simulations for larger L2 block sizes, in Figure 1(a)).

Figure 3 compares RAMpage variations. The increase in energy use for context switches on misses with a 4KB page size needs further investigation. A likely cause is increased contention for SRAM pages resulting from the higher context switch rate. Large pages (or cache blocks) are likely to have the highest benefit if their prefetch effect can be put to good use.

4.4 Overall Trade-Offs

In summary, the fastest time does not necessarily correspond to lowest energy use, even if the system is not operating for as long overall. The quickest dreamy run time was 2.57s (context switches on misses, 2KB SRAM page size), while the lowest-energy variant took 2.64s (4KB SRAM page size, no context switches on misses). The lowest-energy variant ran about 3% slower than the fastest dreamy variant, or 12% slower than the fastest non-dreamy variant).

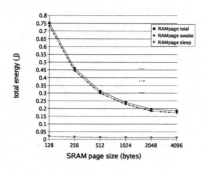
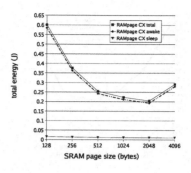

(a) No Context Switches on Misses   (b) Context Switches on Misses

Fig. 3. Comparison of RAMpage dreamy energy breakdown.

Electing to run RAMpage in its fastest dreamy mode would require 10% more energy for DRAM than its fastest variant. However, the overall fastest version (conventional, 512B L2 blocks) needs 6.6 times the energy of the most energy-efficient version, or 6 times the energy of the fastest dreamy variation.

A designer therefore can balance choices between maximum speed (no dreamy mode, standard two-level cache) and maximum energy saving (RAMpage without context switches on misses, SRAM page size chosen for lowest energy). As a compromise, it would be possible to use RAMpage with context switches on misses, with sub-optimal energy use, but better performance.

These speed-energy trade-offs only represent DRAM energy. The CPU and SRAM modelled use 1W (0.2W and 0.8W, respectively). For a run time of 2.57s, the pair uses 2.57J whereas over the best run time of 2.36s, the total goes to 2.36J. This difference is easily justified by saving over 1J in DRAM energy but, nonetheless, a more comprehensive energy analysis of the whole system is needed. For example, PADRAM runs uses *more* energy in its equivalent of a simply dreamy mode than without [11], probably because of its relatively small L2 cache. The relatively large L2 used here, on the other hand, uses more energy than one would like for a low-energy design.

5   Conclusion

5.1   Introduction

This paper has presented an initial study of use of the RAMpage memory hierarchy to reduce DRAM energy usage. The approach used was to simulate a *dreamy* memory, in which DRAM is turned off except when referenced. The motivation for this study is previous results which have showed RAMpage to be more tolerant of increased DRAM latency than a conventional hierarchy.

The remainder of this section summarizes results, outlines future work and presents overall conclusions.

5.2   Summary of Results

RAMpage, with the option of context switches on misses, presents some useful trade-offs in choosing an energy-speed design trade-off. Assuming a relatively low-energy processor design (as well as low-energy components for the remainder of the system), dreamy energy savings could be significant. The fastest configuration uses almost 7 times the energy of the most energy-efficient one, for a performance gain of only 12%. The performance cost of dreamy mode can be brought down to 9% by a relatively modest compromise on energy saving: this dreamy configuration still uses a sixth of the energy of the fastest version.

The best overall compromise is achieved by RAMpage with context switches on misses, though by a less significant margin than in earlier studies, which showed this variant to be most tolerant of high DRAM latencies [14]. A relatively small SRAM layer makes RAMpage less competitive than in these earlier studies.

5.3   Future Work

It is important that, while the savings were achieved with modest speed loss, overall energy usage should take into account other parts of the system, which would use more energy if left in full power mode for a longer time. If energy for the processor and L2 are added in, the fastest dreamy version also has the lowest overall energy by a small margin 2.78J versus 2.82J for the version with lowest DRAM energy). This should be compared against 3.58J for the best non-dreamy version, a saving of 29% which is useful but not as dramatic as a factor of 6.

Results should be extended to a more detailed analysis of overall system energy, including low-energy variations on caches, and low-energy versions of faster processors. The simulated SRAM has a relatively low latency for waking up from low-power mode (50% of the latency of an L2 hit). Since 1MB SRAM (0.8W) uses more power than DRAM in full-power mode (0.52W) – as simulated here – this would be a useful variation to explore.

A RAMpage implementation on the L4 Pistachio kernel [5] is planned. This kernel is small enough to permit implementation of its minimum memory-resident data and code in the 64KB static RAM memory in the ARM11 family. Using this extra SRAM would also make it viable to implement RAMpage with a smaller SRAM main memory, a significant factor in the overall energy budget of this kind of system. L4 has been ported to the M5 architecture simulator [3] by the NICTA group at University of New South Wales, creating the possibility of RAMpage on a full-system simulator, a goal of earlier work.

The existing simulator will be used to experiment with further variations on energy-efficient memories. For example, instead of an SRAM main memory, main memory could be implemented in a small fast permanently powered up DRAM, with the remaining DRAM operating as a dreamy paging device.

5.4   Overall Conclusion

In this latest study, investigating dreamy memory model has shown the potential for RAMpage in low-energy designs. While RAMpage did not run in the shortest time in full-power mode (expected with a relatively slow processor), it did have both the fastest and lowest-energy measurements in dreamy mode.

Results showed a fair fraction of the potential energy gain: full power mode needed 100 times that of self-refresh mode; the lowest-energy case used less than a sixth of full DRAM power. The aim of achieving close to an average of self-refresh power use with as close as possible to full speed has been partially met. More sophisticated approaches to minimizing power use (e.g., keeping power on for a period after a reference, exploiting a wider range of low-power modes, and dynamic page placement policies, as in PAVM) could further reduce energy use.

The design trade-offs discussed here represent a starting point: overall low-energy system design requires design of the whole system to minimise energy use. Just as Amdahl's Law shows that focus on one area of speed improvement has diminishing returns, we need to be careful not to interpret energy savings in isolation. Nonetheless RAMpage shows promise in the area of low-energy design, and this study will be followed up with others.

Acknowledgements. Financial support for this work has been received from the University of Queensland. I would like to thank Gernot Heiser for proposing that I investigate energy management using RAMpage.

References

1. ARM. *The ARM11 Microprocessor and ARM PrimeXsys Platform*. ARM, October 2002.
   http://www.arm.com/pdfs/ARM11%20Core%20&%20Platform%20Whitepaper.pdf.
2. Luca Benini, Alberto Macii, and Massimo Poncino. From Energy-aware design of embedded memories: A survey of technologies, architectures, and optimization techniques. From *ACM Trans. on Embedded Computing Sys.*, 2(1):5–32, 2003.
3. N. L. Binkert, E. G. Hallnor, and S. K. Reinhardt. From Network-oriented full-system simulation using M5. From In *Sixth Workshop on Computer Architecture Evaluation using Commercial Workloads (CAECW)*, pages 36–43, February 2003.
4. Yun Cao, Hiroyuki Tomiyama, Takanori Okuma, and Hiroto Yasuura. From Data memory design considering effective bitwidth for low-energy embedded systems. From In *Proc. 15th Int. Symp. on System Synthesis*, pages 201–206, Kyoto, Japan, 2002.
5. Uwe Dannowski, Kevin Elphinstone, Jochen Liedtke, Gerd Liefländer, Espen Skoglund, Volkmar Uhlig, Christian, Ceelen Andreas, and Haeberlen Marcus Völp. From The L4Ka vision. From Technical report, University of Karlsruhe, System Architecture Group, April 2001. From
   http://i30www.ira.uka.de/research/documents/l4ka/L4Ka.pdf.
6. Richard Fromm, Stylianos Perissakis, Neal Cardwell, Christoforos Kozyrakis, Bruce McGaughy, David Patterson, Tom Anderson, and Katherine Yelick. From The energy efficiency of IRAM architectures. From In *Proc. 24th Int. Symp. on Computer Architecture*, pages 327–337, Denver, CO, 1997.

7. J.L. Hennessy and D.A. Patterson. From *Computer Architecture: A Quantitative Approach*. From Morgan Kauffmann, San Francisco, CA, 3rd edition, 2003.

8. Hai Huang, Padmanabhan Pillai, and Kang G. Shin. From Design and implementation of power-aware virtual memory. From In *Proc. USENIX 2003 Annual Technical Conference*, pages 57–70, San Antonio, Tx, June 2003.

9. E.E. Johnson. From Graffiti on the memory wall. From *Computer Architecture News*, 23(4):7–8, September 1995.

10. Stefanos Kaxiras, Zhigang Hu, and Margaret Martonosi. From Cache decay: exploiting generational behavior to reduce cache leakage power. From In *Proc. 28th Ann. Int. Symp. on Computer architecture*, pages 240–251, G teborg, Sweden, 2001.

11. Alvin R. Lebeck, Xiaobo Fan, Heng Zeng, and Carla Ellis. From Power aware page allocation. From In *Proc. 9th Int. Conf. on Arch. Support for Programming Languages and Operating Systems (ASPLOS-9)*, pages 105–116, Cambridge, MA, November 2000.

12. P. Machanick. From The case for SRAM main memory. From *Computer Architecture News*, 24(5):23–30, December 1996.

13. P. Machanick. From Correction to RAMpage ASPLOS paper. From *Computer Architecture News*, 27(4):2–5, September 1999.

14. P. Machanick. From Scalability of the RAMpage memory hierarchy. From *South African Computer Journal*, (25):68–73, August 2000.

15. P. Machanick and Z. Patel. From L1 Cache and TLB Enhancements to the RAMpage Memory Hierarchy. From In *Proc. Eighth Asia-Pacific Computer Systems Architecture Conf.*, pages 305–319, Aizu-Wakamatsu City, Japan, September 2003.

16. P. Machanick, P. Salverda, and L. Pompe. From Hardware-software trade-offs in a Direct Rambus implementation of the RAMpage memory hierarchy. From In *Proc. 8th Int. Conf. on Architectural Support for Programming Languages and Operating Systems (ASPLOS-VIII)*, pages 105–114, San Jose, CA, October 1998.

17. Micron Technology. From 256Mb: x4, x8, x16 DDR SDRAM, December 2003. From Data Sheet,
    `http://download.micron.com/pdf/datasheets/dram/ddr/256Mx4x8x16DDR.pdf`.

18. NEC. From MOS integrated circuit μPD4482162, 4482182, 4482322, 4482362, December 2002. From Data Sheet No. M14522EJ3V0DS00,
    `http://www.necel.com/memory/pdfs/M14522EJ3V0DS00.pdf`.

19. Ashley Saulsbury, Fong Pong, and Andreas Nowatzyk. From Missing the memory wall: the case for processor/memory integration. From In *Proc. 23rd Ann. Int. Symp. on Computer architecture*, pages 90–101, 1996.

20. Hojun Shim, Yongsoo Joo, Yongseok Choi, Hyung Gyu Lee, and Naehyuck Chang. From Low-energy off-chip SDRAM memory systems for embedded applications. From *Trans. on Embedded Computing Sys.*, 2(1):98–130, 2003.

21. W.A. Wulf and S.A. McKee. From Hitting the memory wall: Implications of the obvious. From *Computer Architecture News*, 23(1):20–24, March 1995.

dDVS: An Efficient Dynamic Voltage Scaling Algorithm Based on the Differential of CPU Utilization*

Kui-Yon Mun, Dae-Woong Kim, Do-Hun Kim, and Chan-Ik Park

Department of Computer Science and Engineering/PIRL
Pohang University of Science and Technology
Pohang, Kyungbuk 790-784, Republic of Korea
{cipark}@postech.ac.kr

Abstract. Traditional dynamic voltage scaling algorithms periodically monitor CPU utilization and adapt its operating frequency to the upcoming performance requirement for CPU power management. Predicting CPU utilization is usually conducted by estimating upcoming performance requirement. In order for dynamic voltage scaling algorithms to be effective, the prediction accuracy of CPU utilization must be high. This paper proposes a power management algorithm that improves accuracy of predicting future CPU utilization using process state information. Experiments show that the proposed algorithm reduces power consumption by 11%–57% without any performance degradation.

1 Introduction

In mobile battery-powered systems, power is considered as a precious resource, and a CPU is known to consume more than 50 % of the whole system power [1]. Therefore, efficient CPU power management is required to reduce the power consumption of a system. In CPUs based on CMOS logic, the peak frequency is proportional to the supply voltage and power is proportional to the square of the supply voltage. Dynamic voltage scaling (DVS) has been implemented in most CPUs in order to control power consumption by dynamically changing its operating frequency.

Dynamic power management through DVS is classified into two approaches: an intra task approach and an inter task approach according to the location of the power management algorithm (*i.e.*, inside of a task or outside of a task). In intra-task approaches, compiler or software tool analyzes a task and determines when a CPU frequency has to be changed [2]. This approach can adjust the CPU frequency with considerable accuracy because the performance requirement of a

* The authors would like to thank the Ministry of Education of Korea for its support toward the Electrical and Computer Engineering Division at POSTECH through its BK21 program. This research was also supported in part by HY-SDR IT Research Center, and in part by grant No. R01-2003-000-10739-0 from the Basic Research Program of the Korea Science and Engineering Foundation.

P.-C. Yew and J. Xue (Eds.): ACSAC 2004, LNCS 3189, pp. 160–169, 2004.
© Springer-Verlag Berlin Heidelberg 2004

task is analyzed in advance. However, this approach is impractical because all applications have to be modified. Inter-task approach is divided into three approaches based on the type of information used for power management. The first approach uses the deadlines of tasks [3,4]. It achieves power reduction by considering the worst case execution time of a task and uses that information to exploit the slack time generated by the scheduler However, it requires the task deadline information, which reduces its applicability. The second approach uses the tasks' characteristics obtained from the analysis of events such as system calls and task creation/exit/switch [5]. This approach allows different power management algorithms to be applied to each task according to their characteristics. However, the overhead of event monitoring and analysis may be significant. For example, it would cost about 1% - 4% of the total CPU cycles, in order to monitor system calls and scheduler of the kernel on Transmeta Crusoe's CPU [5]. The third approach periodically monitors the CPU utilization, and uses that information to predict the expected CPU utilization [6,7]. The CPU frequency is changed adaptively to the predicted CPU utilization. Because this operation must be repeated periodically, it is called an interval-based approach. This approach provides higher applicability than other approaches while achieving simplicity. However, this approach could suffer from inefficiency due to its inaccurate prediction. We consider the interval-based approach promising because of its simplicity.

A careful investigation of existing interval-based approaches leads us to identify the reason for its inaccurate prediction. In Figure 1, we assume that there are only three processes P_1, P_2 and P_3 and their utilizations are 0.2, 0.3, and 0.3 respectively, on each run. At every interval, the CPU utilization for the next interval is computed as the exponential average (EXP) of the previous and current CPU utilizations [8]. As shown in Figure 1(a), there exists a large gap between the actual CPU utilization and the CPU utilization predicted by the EXP. We think this is mainly caused by the fact that we computed EXP over all processes regardless of their state. In Figure 1(b), after the fourth interval, P_1 and P_2 exist in the request queue (RQ). EXP predicts that P_1's utilization is 0.2 and P_2's utilization is 0.3, and computes the CPU utilization of the fifth interval as 0.5. Thus, considering the states of processes in the computation of EXP improves the prediction accuracy of the CPU utilization. Table 1 shows that there is a very low probability of a process to remain in the ready-to-run state for two consecutive intervals or more.

Table 1. Probability of a process to remain in ready-to-run state for two consecutive intervals or more: for example, the value 0.52 implies about half of the ready-to-run processes in current interval will remain in ready-to-run state until the next interval

Application type	Fraction
interactive (xpdf)	0.52
multimedia (mplayer)	0.34
I/O intensive (ubench/fsdisk)	0.93 (the fraction of cycles in which CPU is idle is 0.53)

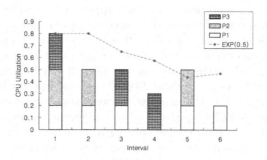

(a) Based on CPU utilization of all processes
executed in the past intervals

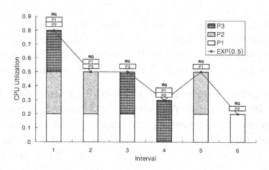

(b) Based on CPU utilization of processes in
the ready queue (RQ)

Fig. 1. Predicting CPU utilization

This paper proposes a dynamic power management algorithm that improves
the prediction accuracy of existing interval-based power management algorithms
using process information. The remainder of this paper is organized as follows.
Section 2 describes the proposed algorithm. Section 3 evaluates the amount
of power consumption of the proposed algorithm and existing interval-based
algorithms under various types of workloads. Finally, the conclusion is presented
in Section 4.

2   The Proposed Algorithm

In this section, we propose an algorithm that improves the efficiency of a dynamic power management by only considering the processes that are likely going

Table 2. Symbols and their meanings

Symbol	Meaning
Q	the length of time quantum
I	the length of an interval
PUP	per-Process Utilization Predictors such as PAST, EXP and PD
f_{min}	the minimum CPU frequency
e_i/e_i^*	the actual/estimated execution time of process i in the current interval
u_i/u_i^*	actual/estimated utilization of process i in the current interval
u_{i-}/u_{i-}^*	actual/estimated utilization of process i in the previous interval
f/f^*	CPU frequency in current/next interval
P	a set of processes executed in the current interval
P^*	a set of processes to be executed with a high probability in the next interval

---

Input : P, f **Output :** f^*

1. Update the execution time and utilization of all processes executed in the current interval

   $\forall p_i \in P$

   $e_i = e_i \times \frac{f}{f_{max}}$ // for normalizing utilization by f_{max} //

   $u_i = \frac{e_i}{I}$

2. Estimate CPU utilization in the next interval

   $U^* = \sum_{\forall p_i \in P^*} PUP(p_i)$,

   where $P^* = \{p_k | p_k$ is a process that is going to be executed in the next interval$\}$

   and $|P^*| \le \lceil \frac{I}{Q} \rceil$ //

3. Compute CPU frequency for next interval

   $f^* = U^* \times f_{max}$

Fig. 2. Description of the proposed algorithm

to be executed in the next interval. This algorithm periodically keeps track of utilizations of each process executed in previous intervals, finds the processes to be executed in the next interval, and predicts the future CPU utilization as the sum of their utilizations estimated by an existing interval-based approach. Thus, the proposed algorithm requires process information, such as the process's state, its scheduling priority and its past utilizations. Table 2 shows the description of the notations to be used in the subsequent section.

Figure 2 describes the proposed algorithm. First, it updates the utilization of all processes executed in the current interval. Utilization of process i is equal to $\frac{e_i}{I}$. The execution time of each process in this algorithm should be normalized by the maximum frequency f_{max} because it is dependent on CPU frequency when measured. For example, when the maximum frequency is 600 MHz and a process was executed at 300 MHz for 10 ms, the execution time of the process is 5 ms. Next, the proposed algorithm selects processes that are highly likely going to be executed. A process has three different states: READY to wait for run, WAIT to wait for I/O's completion or signals, and RUN to be executed on a CPU. The kernel's scheduler chooses a process with the highest scheduling priority from the set containing all processes with a ready state. Thus, the next process to be executed can be predicted by checking the priority of processes before its execution. Therefore, the proposed algorithm chooses $\lceil \frac{I}{Q} \rceil$ processes with high scheduling priority from the set of processes with READY state. The parameter $\lceil \frac{I}{Q} \rceil$ is chosen empirically. Next, it estimates the utilizations of each chosen processes. In order to predict them, it uses a per-Process Utilization Predictor (PUP). PUP predicts the utilization of a process on the next interval by using its past utilizations. Any interval-based approach can be used as PUP. Next, the proposed algorithm estimates the CPU utilization as the sum of the utilizations of each process estimated by PUP. Finally, it computes the CPU frequency in the next interval. Because the CPU utilization from the previous step is based on the minimum frequency, the CPU frequency in the next interval is equal to the multiplication of CPU utilization and the minimum frequency. The proposed algorithm applies existing interval-based approaches to each processes to be executed in the next interval instead of entire processes executed in the past intervals. Because it only considers processes with READY state, the creation/exit and state change of a process affects its prediction. Thus, in the cases where the state of a process often varies or its lifetime is short, this algorithm largely reduces the power consumption compared to existing interval-based approaches. By contrast, in the case of a process that seldom changes its state, both this algorithm and existing interval-based approaches show a similar performance.

3   Performance Evaluation

3.1   Experimental Environment

The proposed algorithm has been evaluated on a Sony VAIO-C1VJ notebook equipped with Transmeta's Crusoe CPU. The CPU provides four pairs of different frequency and voltage levels, which are (300 MHz, 1.3 V), (400 MHz, 1.35 V), (500 MHz, 1.4 V), and (600 MHz, 1.6 V). Thus, the maximum CPU frequency is 600 MHz ($f_{max} = 600$). To set the frequency and voltage, TM5600 stays in the sleep mode for 20 μsec and consumes 2 μJ–4 μJ energy. The experimental results in this paper includes the overheads such as time and power. PAST, EXP, and Proportional-Differential (PD) are used as PUPs of the proposed algorithm. PD is one of the traditional control theories and estimates the change concerning the direction of a slope [9]. PAST assumes that the future CPU utilization will be the same as the previous one. Table 3 shows the formulas of PUP when PAST, PD and EXP are used as the PUPs of the proposed algorithm.

The proposed algorithm is implemented within Linux kernel version 2.5.58 like Figure 3. The length of time quantum in Linux kernel is 10 ms ($Q = 10$). We added a new data structure, called the utilization history table, to keep track of the CPU utilization of each process. A process is allocated an entry in the table

I : length of an interval
Q: length of time quantum

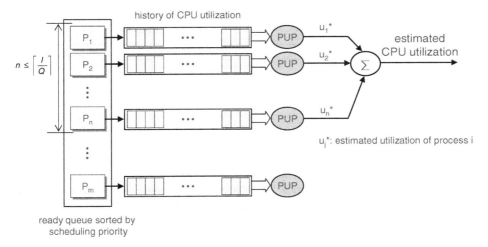

Fig. 3. Implementation of the proposed algorithm within Linux kernel

Table 3. Formulas of PD, PAST and EXP being used as a per-Process Utilization Predictors

	PD	$u_i^* = u_i + K_P(1 - u_i) + K_D((1 - u_i) - (1 - u_{i-}))$ $(K_P = -3$ and $K_D = -3)$
PUP	PAST	$u_i^* = u_i$
	EXP	$u_i^* = \alpha u_i + (1 - \alpha)u_{i-}^*$ $(\alpha = 0.5)$

right after its creation and releases the entry before its termination. Each entry of the table contains three fields: *valid_flag*, *curr_util* and *prev_util*. *valid_flag* indicates whether the corresponding information is valid or not, *curr_util* refers to the current utilization and *prev_util* holds the utilization of the previous periods. CPU utilization information is updated in the timer interrupt handler. The timer interrupt handler updates *curr_util* of the current process. This method has little computational overhead. More precise CPU utilization can be measured if it is updated every time processes change their states. A new kernel process is created to carry out the proposed power management. It not only periodically monitors the state of each process, but also adjusts the CPU frequency accordingly based on the predicted CPU utilization.

Table 4 shows the execution time of an application and the computing overhead when the proposed algorithm runs at different monitoring intervals. The computing overhead is calculated by taking a ratio of the execution time of the power management code to the total execution time. The interval length, denoted by I, is the interval at which the proposed power management code is

Table 4. The execution time of an application and the computing overhead when the proposed algorithm runs at different monitoring intervals

interval length (ms)	computing overhead (%)	execution time (sec)
10	0.67	89.9
50	0.12	90.1
100	0.06	90.0
200	0.02	124.1

executed. With an extremely short monitoring interval, the computing overhead of the algorithm increases, but the accuracy of prediction becomes high enough. For example, the 10 msec monitoring interval entails the 0.67% computing overhead shown in Table 4. By contrast, with an extremely long monitoring interval, the prediction accuracy becomes too low. For instance, Table 4 reveals that the 200 msec monitoring interval prolongs the execution time of the application by about 34 seconds, due to its inaccurate prediction. Because the number of processes on READY queue at any given moment is generally less than $\frac{I}{Q}$, so the estimated CPU utilization is prone to be less than the practical CPU utilization. The most desirable monitoring interval is observed to be 100 msec in Table 4. Note that the 100 msec monitoring interval will be used in subsequent experiments $(I = 100)$.

Three types of applications have been used to verify the efficiency of the proposed algorithm. The first type is a set of I/O intensive applications. They are Ubench4.0.1/fsdisk and fstime.[1] The second type is a set of interactive applications. In order to provide identical set of inputs to the applications we logged our desired set of input using "Interactive Linux application Benchmark"[2] before carrying on with the experiments involving XPDF and LLL-1.4.[3] The third stage of the experiment was conducted using the Mplayer (Linux's MPEG player[4]), and Xmms (Linux's MP3 player[5]). In order to make a fair comparison between the power management policies, a MPEG video clip and a MP3 file are deliberately chosen so that no frame drops will occur under any policies.

3.2   Experimental Results

In order to show the prediction accuracy improvement, the proposed algorithm was compared to PAST, EXP, and PD. In the remaining sections, we abbreviated the proposed algorithm by prefixing the name of its PUP with 'P', that is, PPAST, PEXP, and PPD. The experimental results of each application are appraised by considering the power saving gains, performance impact and the

---

[1] http://www.tux.org/pub/tux/benchmarks/System/unixbench, Unix Benchmark
[2] http://opensource.nus.edu.sg/~ctk/benchmark/bench.html, Benchmarking of interactive linux applications
[3] http://users.pandora.be/thomas.raes/LSS/lss.html, Linux Lunar Lander
[4] http://www.mplayerhq.hu/homepage/design6/info.html, Mplayer
[5] http://www.xmms.org, XMMS

Table 5. Consumed power, execution time and computing overhead of power management policies during the execution of an I/O application

policy	fsdisk			fstime		
	consumed power	execution time (second)	computing overhead (μsecond)	consumed power	execution time (second)	computing overhead (μsecond)
PD	0.59	130.6	41.67	0.64	131.1	33.34
PPD	0.50	131.0	63.82	0.54	130.1	52.76
EXP	0.77	131.2	18.49	0.84	129.8	15.26
PEXP	0.33	131.2	49.01	0.41	130.0	53.65
PAST	0.52	131.3	18.55	0.54	129.9	14.81
PPAST	0.33	132.7	45.51	0.38	130.0	52.31

Table 6. Consumed power, execution time and computing overhead of power management policies during the execution of an interactive application

policy	xpdf			LLL		
	consumed power	execution time (second)	computing overhead (μsecond)	consumed power	execution time (second)	computing overhead (μsecond)
PD	0.64	115.7	31.22	0.69	23.8	70.39
PPD	0.56	119.4	46.09	0.51	24.4	96.98
EXP	0.83	111.1	13.93	0.89	25.5	25.87
PEXP	0.38	123.0	37.88	0.49	29.5	75.99
PAST	0.42	143.9	15.06	0.61	25.6	26.41
PPAST	0.62	115.1	37.24	0.39	26.9	91.23

computing overhead. When an application runs without any power management policy (NPM), we assumed that the power consumption of NPM is 1. Thus, the consumed power is normalized by that of NPM. The computing overhead is calculated by taking the average of execution times of the power management code over all intervals.

As shown in Table 5, the performance of I/O applications can be assessed by their execution time. PPD, PEXP, and PPAST achieved a 15%–17%, 51%–57% and 30%–37% power reduction over PD, EXP, and PAST respectively. An I/O intensive process repeats the WAIT-READY-RUN cycle to handle I/O requests. By considering the current states of the processes, we can figure out when an I/O intensive process is going to take up a portion of the CPU time. This results in reduced power consumption of I/O applications by 15%–57% without delay in execution time.

Table 6 shows the experimental results when an interactive application, xpdf or LLL, generates workload. In general, the proposed algorithm reduces power consumption by 12.5%–54%. However, in the case of xpdf, PPAST consumes more power than PAST. Note that the PAST increases the execution time of the xpdf compared to other policies by 32.8 seconds in the worst case. This is

Table 7. Consumed power, execution time and computing overhead of power management policies during the execution of an multimedia application

policy	mplayer		xmms	
	consumed power	computing overhead (μsecond)	consumed power	computing overhead (μsecond)
PD	0.56	57.28	0.43	25.33
PPD	0.50	83.57	0.36	49.70
EXP	0.81	25.61	0.65	34.60
PEXP	0.42	69.53	0.35	46.83
PAST	0.64	25.68	0.47	38.70
PPAST	0.41	71.80	0.37	50.92

a severe performance degradation. It seems that PAST predicts a lower CPU utilization than the actual CPU utilization.

Table 7 shows the experimental results when the multimedia file chosen is played with any frame drops. The proposed algorithm diminished the power consumption by 11%–48% over PAST, EXP, and PD. However, the power reduction rate of the multimedia application is less than that of the other applications. Because the multimedia application process stays in READY and RUN state after its creation, a slight gap in the power reduction rate occurs.

As shown in the experimental results of Table 5–6, the proposed algorithm achieves a large power reductions over existing interval-based approaches, such as PAST, EXP and PD. Although the computing overhead increases to 3.5 times in the worst case, each application runs without any delay in its execution time and the power consumption also decreases as well.

4   Conclusion and Future Work

This paper proposed an efficient power management algorithm in order to improve prediction accuracy using processes' state information. The experiments with the proposed algorithm revealed that the power consumption of the proposed algorithm is reduced by 11%–57% when compared to the existing interval-based algorithms such as PD, EXP and PAST. However, the efficiency of the proposed algorithm is depended on the length of the monitoring interval. Choosing the optimal interval length for each type of applications still remains as our future work.

References

1. COMPAQ: Compaq presario based on amd mobile athlon 4 (2001)
2. Azevedo, A., Issenin, I.: Profile-based dynamic voltage scheduling using program checkpoints. In: Proceedings of design automation and test in Europe. (2002)

3. Krishna, C.M., Lee, Y.H.: Voltage-clock-scaling adaptive scheduling techniques for low power and real-time systems. In: Proceedings of the sixth IEEE real time technology and applications symposium. (2000)

4. Okuma, T., Ishihara, T., H.Yasuura: Real-time task scheduling for a variable voltage processor. In: Proceedings of the international symposium on system synthesis. (1999)

5. Flautner, K., Mudge, T.: Vertigo: automatic performance-setting for linux. In: Proceedings of operating systems design and implementation. (2002)

6. Govil, K., Chan, E., Wasserman, H.: Comparing algorithms for dynamic speed-setting of a low-power cpu. In: Proceedings of the first international conference on mobile computing and networking. (1995)

7. Pering, T., Burd, T., Brodersen, R.: The simulation and evaluation of dynamic voltage scaling algorithms. In: Proceedings of international symposium on electronics of lower power and design. (1998) 76–81

8. Lu, Y.H., Benini, L.: Power-aware operating systems for interactive systems. IEEE Trans. VLSI **10** (2002) 119–134

9. Kuo, B., Golnaraghi, F.: Automatic control systems. eighth edn. John Wiley & Sons, Inc. (2003)

High Performance Microprocessor Design Methods Exploiting Information Locality and Data Redundancy for Lower Area Cost and Power Consumption

Byung-Soo Choi[1], Jeong-A Lee[2], and Dong-Soo Har[3]

[1] Ultrafast Fiber-Optic Networks Research Center
K-JIST(Kwangju Institute of Science and Technology)
1 Oryong-dong Puk-gu Gwangju, 500-712, Republic of Korea
bschoi@kjist.ac.kr
[2] Department of Computer Engineering
Chosun University
375 Susuk-dong Dong-gu Gwangju, 501-759, Republic of Korea
jalee@chosun.ac.kr
[3] Department of Information and Communications
K-JIST(Kwangju Institute of Science and Technology)
1 Oryong-dong Puk-gu Gwangju, 500-712, Republic of Korea
hardon@kjist.ac.kr

Abstract. Value predictor predicting result of instruction before real execution to exceed the data flow limit, redundant operation table removing redundant computation dynamically, and asynchronous bus avoiding clock synchronization problem have been proposed as high performance microprocessor design methods. However, these methods increase area cost and power consumption problems because of the larger table for value predictor and redundant operation table, and the higher switching activity in asynchronous bus. To resolve the problems of data tables for value predictor and redundant operation table, we have investigated partial tag and narrow-width operand methods, which have been recently proposed separately and present an efficient update method for value predictor and a table organization method for redundant operation table, respectively. To reduce excessive switching activity of asynchronous bus, we also propose a bus encoding method using frequent value cache, which reduces the same data transmissions. The proposed three methods – an efficient update method for value predictor, a table organization method for redundant operation table, and a frequent value cache for asynchronous bus – exploit information locality such as instruction and data locality as well as data redundancy. Analysis with a conventional microprocessor model show that the proposed three methods reduce total area cost and power consumption by about 18.2% and 26.5%, respectively, with negligible performance variance.

P.-C. Yew and J. Xue (Eds.): ACSAC 2004, LNCS 3189, pp. 170–184, 2004.
© Springer-Verlag Berlin Heidelberg 2004

1   Introduction

Until a few years ago, performance improvement has been a key research issue in microprocessor design. Recently, however, the area cost and the power consumption of a microprocessor have been increased drastically as the number of transistors keeps increasing. As a result, research interest has been shifted to performance improvement while maintaining the efficiency of area cost and power consumption. In this paper, several design methods have been investigated for a high performance microprocessor with an emphasis on achieving efficient area cost and power consumption.

Among many design techniques for a high performance microprocessor, three methods are investigated such as value predictor, redundant operation table, and asynchronous dual-rail bus in this research. The value predictor predicts a result of an instruction before the instruction is actually executed. Hence dependent instructions can be executed at the same time when the instruction is executed. On the other hand, the redundant operation table stores recently executed instructions in a table and checks whether the current executable instruction is already stored in the table. In other words, the redundant operation table can skip the real execution of an instruction by a simple lookup procedure with the table, subsequently shortening the execution time of the instruction. Another alternative design technique, the asynchronous dual-rail bus is a reliable bus scheme for a complex system such as a futuristic high performance microprocessor. The asynchronous dual-rail bus can transmit data in a reliable fashion by making use of the dual-rail encoding, which combines the data and the control signals.

Analyzing the aforementioned three design methods from the area cost and power consumption points of view, several attempts are made especially to find some locality and redundancy of data used in each design method. Several information localities and data redundancies were found, which causes extra area cost and power consumption. More specifically, the value predictor and the redundant operation table store the same or a little different instructions (instruction locality), small operand values (operand data locality), and small result values (result data locality), whereas the asynchronous dual-rail bus transmits the same data items repeatedly (communication data locality). From what we observed about these localities, a conclusion was reached that each design method can be further enhanced for lower area cost and lower power consumption by exploiting such localities to reduce redundancy.

In this paper, we propose three enhanced methods as follows. First, for value predictors, we propose a method to combine the two previously proposed area cost reduction methods such as partial-tag and narrow-width methods. Second, we designed a partial resolution method to reduce the area cost of the tag fields in the redundant operation table. Third, we applied the previously proposed frequent value cache method into an asynchronous dual-rail bus to minimize the communication data redundancy.

As the last step, we investigated total area cost and power consumption reduction effects in a conventional microprocessor model. By using the proposed methods, the total area cost and power consumption in a microprocessor model would be reduced by about 18.2% and 26.5%, respectively.

This paper is organized as follows. Section 2 describes related work as three high performance design methods, information locality, and data redundancy. The proposed area and power reduction methods for value predictor and redundant operation table are described in Section 3 and 4, respectively. Also a designed power reduction method for asynchronous dual-rail bus is explained in Section 5. Meanwhile, total area cost and power consumption reduction effects in a microprocessor model are analyzed in Section 6. Section 7 concludes this research.

2   Related Work

2.1   High Performance Design Methods

Value Predictor: Value predictors have been proposed to overcome the data dependency problems in the instruction-level parallelism by predicting a result value of an instruction before its actual execution [1], [2].

Redundant Operation Table: When the instruction-level parallelism increases, there are many side effects. One of the side effects is the increased number of redundant executions because of speculative executions due to branch predictor or value predictor. Unfortunately, speculative or redundant operations limit the performance improvement and increase the power consumption as well [3]. To overcome such negative effects, many optimization methods have been proposed [4], [5]. One typical solution is eliminating redundant operations, where redundant executions of complex operations are replaced by simple table lookup operations [6].

Asynchronous Dual-Rail Bus: Because of the steady increase of the number of components in a chip, SOC design methods have been studied intensively and will be used for a futuristic high performance microprocessor. To succeed in the market, the time-to-market and the reliability of a SOC are very important. To help the design efforts for a short design time and reliability of SOCs, asynchronous design methods [7] have been studied recently. For a reliable asynchronous bus structure in SOC designs, the dual-rail data encoding method [8] has been intensively investigated.

2.2   Information Locality and Data Redundancy

Information Locality: Information localities in a microprocessor are defined, which are related to instructions, operands of instructions, results of instructions, and communication data over bus. First, *instruction locality* is defined as a small number of instructions is repeatedly or frequently executed, and usually the instructions are located closely to each other in a given time interval. Second, *operand locality* is defined as the data value of the operand is small in most instructions and can be represented with small number of bits. Third, *result locality* is defined as the results of most instructions are small which can be represented with small number of bits. Last, *communication data locality* is defined as a bus transmits the same or very similar data repeatedly or frequently in a given time interval.

Data Redundancy: Considering the above information localities, we can infer that there are data redundancy in instructions, operands of instructions, results of instructions, and communication data over bus, respectively. First, *data redundancy of instructions* is occurred when the instruction addresses in a given time interval are not so different, which can be inferred that the higher bits of instruction address are the same. Hence the higher bits of addresses of executed instructions in a given time interval are redundant. Second, *data redundancy of operands* is occurred when most operands of executed instructions in a given time interval require a small number of bits, and hence the higher bits of operands are considered as redundant bits. Third, *data redundancy of results* is occurred when the most results of executed instructions in a given time interval require a small number of bits, and hence the higher bits of results are redundant. Last, *data redundancy of communication data* is occurred when the most communication data in a given time interval are the same or similar, and hence most communications are redundant.

3   Value Predictor

3.1   Table Structure

In this research, we explain only the stride predictor for the simplicity. The stride predictor assumes that consecutive result values of an instruction have the same stride value [1]. Usually, a value predictor exploits a large data table to store required information and is referenced by the instruction address.

3.2   Combining Partial Tag and Narrow-Width Operand Method

Two Methods to Reduce Area and Power of Value Predictor: To reduce the area cost and power consumption of value predictor, two methods have been already proposed as follows.

Partial Tag Method: Instruction or data caches are usually based on a correct association between an instruction address and an indexed entry because the lookup data must be the same value as the previously stored value. In the value predictor, however, a lookup data is a prediction value so that it does not always require the correct association between a lookup address and an indexed data. Based on such a loose association between a lookup address and an indexed data, a value predictor does not necessarily use a full-tag, but can use a partial-tag, which reduces the area cost of the tag part [9]. Briefly, the full-tag method takes an address as a tag except for index bits, but the partial-tag method only uses some part of a full-tag.

Narrow-Width Operand Method: Analysis of the result values of a program shows that only a few result values require a full precision value supported by processor

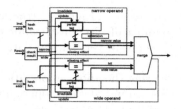

Fig. 1. Combining Method of Partial-Tag and Narrow-Width Methods

registers. Taking into account such locality, the narrow-width operand method classifies result values into two types as the narrow-width and the wide-width result values according to the required number of bits [10]. For the purpose of area cost reduction in data tables, the narrow-width operand method utilizes both the narrow-width and wide-width tables for storing the narrow-width and wide-width result values, respectively. If a result value of an instruction requires fewer bits than the predetermined number of bits, prediction information of the instruction is stored in the narrow-width table. Otherwise, prediction information is stored in the wide-width table. Because the narrow-width table stores fewer bits for each result value, it reduces the overall area cost of a data table. **Combining Partial Tag and Narrow-Width Operand Methods:** To date, two area cost reduction methods for value predictors have been proposed independently. In the present research, a combining method with an efficient table-update method is proposed to minimize the performance degradation. A simple method combining these two methods is conceivable. However, such a simple superposition method decreases the performance improvement ratio because two prediction values are generated from the two tables.

We propose a new table-update method as shown in Figure 1. When the result of an instruction is classified into a narrow-width result(wide-width result), the instruction is stored in the narrow-width table(wide-width table). At the same time, the wide-width table(narrow-width table) invalidates an indexed entry if the entry contains the same partial-tag with the instruction. In short, depending on the classification result of an instruction, only one of the two tables stores the instruction, and the other table must invalidate a corresponding entry if the tag is the same with the referenced address.

3.3   Analysis

To measure the effect of the proposed area reduction method, the die size and the power consumption of value predictor are measured by using CACTI 3.2 [11]. We also investigated IPC value when the proposed method is used with a SimpleScalar [12] model and SPEC 95 [13] benchmark programs. However, as we expected, the IPC value changes very little about 1%. Hence we skip the explanation of IPC variation when the proposed method is used.

Area Cost: Table 1 describes area cost reduction ratios over the conventional stride predictor. The reduction of area cost is higher with the narrow-width

Table 1. Area Cost and Power Consumption Reduction Ratios with Different Area Reduction Methods for Stride Predictor

Area Reduction Methods	Area Cost Number of Entries (K)				Power Consumption Number of Entries (K)			
	32	16	8	4	32	16	8	4
Narrow-Width	57%	55%	56%	47%	16%	17%	27%	24%
Partial-Tag	20%	19%	20%	20%	39%	31%	46%	49%
Proposed Combining Method	*72%*	*74%*	*72%*	*68%*	*58%*	*51%*	*63%*	*68%*

method than with the partial-tag method. The reason is as follows. The reduction ratio depends on the portion of the area cost reduced by the partial-tag and the narrow-width methods. The partial-tag method can decrease the area cost of the tag part only; however, the narrow-width method can decrease the area cost of all result values. Meanwhile, the proposed combining method decreases the area cost more than other area cost reduction methods. The proposed combining method decreases the area cost by about 71% for the stride predictor.

Power Consumption: Table 1 also describes power consumption reduction ratios over the conventional stride predictor. The reduction of power consumption is higher with the partial-tag method than with the narrow-width method. The reason is as follows. The power consumption of the tag part is larger than that of data part since each tag comparison requires more power consumption. Meanwhile, the proposed combining method decreases the power consumption more than other area cost reduction methods. The proposed combining method reduces the power consumption by about 61% for the stride predictor.

4   Redundant Operation Table

4.1   Table Structure

In a redundant operation table, operands are partitioned into two parts: an index and a tag parts. Meanwhile, all operations are classified into integer or floating-point operations. Hence redundant operation tables have different structures depending upon the operation type.

4.2   Narrow-Wide-Width Table

A preliminary analysis of operands for integer and floating-point operations in a SimpleScalar [12] microprocessor with SPEC [13] benchmarks reveals that most operands can be represented with a small number of bits. A partial resolution method is proposed to exploit this characteristics. The partial resolution method eliminates the area cost to store redundant bits for consecutive 0s in the higher bits for integer operands and the lower bits for floating-point operands in the conventional wide-width redundant operation table. A wide-narrow-width redundant operation table utilizing the partial resolution method is designed as shown in Figure 2. The wide-narrow-width redundant operation table dynamically classifies operations into wide-width and narrow-width operations depending on the

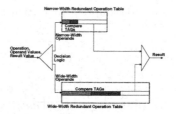

Fig. 2. Wide-Narrow-Width Redundant Operation Table

operand bit width. When the operation requires narrow-width operands, the instruction is stored in the narrow-width redundant operation table. Otherwise, the instruction is stored in the wide-width redundant operation table. Note that the concept of the partial resolution method is similar to the partial-tag method [9], which is proposed to apply for value predictors. The partial-tag method for value predictors stores imprecise tag information, but the partial resolution method for redundant operation table should store precise tag information. Hence, the partial-tag method for value predictor cannot be directly used for the redundant operation table.

4.3   Analysis

Note that we also investigated IPC value when the proposed method is used with a SimpleScalar [12] model and SPEC 95 [13] benchmark programs. However, since the IPC variance is very little, we skip the explanation of IPC variation when the proposed method is used.

Area Cost: The area cost of the conventional wide-width redundant operation table can be calculated easily. Meanwhile, the wide-narrow-width redundant operation table consists of two subsidiary predictors, hence the area cost of it is calculated by the summation of each area cost for narrow-width and wide-width tables. Based on the above considerations and methods, the relative area cost is measured as shown in Table 2. Note that the models containing above 512 entries are measured, since the redundant operation table usually requires many entries. As the table explains, the proposed partial resolution method reduces the area cost by 20%, for FP 2048-entry, at the maximum.

Power Consumption: Since the conventional wide-width redundant operation table is referred for all lookups, it can be easily calculated the dynamic power consumption of the wide-width table. On the other hand, since each subsidiary table in the wide-narrow-width redundant operation table is referred with different lookup ratios, the lookup ratio of each table should be considered. Hence the total dynamic power consumption of the proposed wide-narrow-width redundant operation table is calculated by the summation of each power consumption of narrow-width and wide-width tables considering each lookup ratios. Based on the above considerations and methods, the relative dynamic power consumption reduction ratio is measured as shown in Table 2. As the table explains, the

Table 2. Relative Area Cost and Power Consumption Reduction Ratio

Reduction Ratio over Wide-Width Table		Number of Entries	
		2048	512
Area Cost	INT	7%	9%
	FP	20%	10%
Power Consumption	INT	34%	24%
	FP	30%	31%

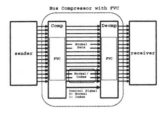

Fig. 3. Frequent Value Cache augmented Bus Scheme

proposed partial resolution method reduces the dynamic power consumption by about 34%, for INT 2048-entry, at the maximum.

5   Asynchronous Dual-Rail Bus

5.1   Frequent Value Cache

One-of-four data encoding method reduces the power consumption of the dual-rail encoding method by decreasing switching activities [14]. Meanwhile, the data pattern analysis illustrates that many data items are repeatedly transmitted in accordance with the result in [15]. Hence we can conclude that the conventional dual-rail and the previously proposed one-of-four data encoding methods waste the power when the data bus transmits the same data items repeatedly.

To reduce such waste of power, we proposed a different method, which utilizes a buffer to exploit the feature of repeatedly transmitted data item. The proposed buffer stores data items and sends an index for a data item when the data item to be sent is already stored in the buffer. Since the index requires fewer number of bits than the data itself, the wasted bandwidth or the switching activity can be decreased, resulting in low power consumption.

Figure 3 describes a frequent value cache(FVC) very briefly that stores data items of each communication. The normal *sender* and *receiver* deliver a data item with a normal fashion, while the *Comp* and *Decmp* deliver a data item by a data itself or an index of *FVC* depending on the hit of *FVC*. When a data itself is transferred, all bus lines are used; however, when an index of the data item is transferred, only the index lines are used. Thus, the index lines are used for both an index and a data item. To distinguish whether a transmitted information represents an index or a normal data item, a *control* signal is used.

5.2   Analysis

Three measures as hit ratio, switching activity reduction ratio, and power consumption reduction ratio are investigated. The hit ratio is the most important one since it decides the switching activity reduction ratio that finally determines the power consumption reduction ratio. To analyze, we investigated a memory bus in SimpleScalar model [12] and SPEC95 benchmark [13] programs.

Hit Ratio: We found the following conclusions through investigating data patterns over the above memory bus. First, even only one entry of FVC can detect 40% of the repeatedly transmitted data items. Second, over 256 entries can represent most data items.

Switching Activity: From the high hit ratio of the FVC, it is required to know how much switching activity can be reduced. In the research, only the change of signal levels between consecutive data items are measured to calculate the switching activity ratio of a bus. The normal dual-rail bus utilizes all 32-bit logical bits and each signal line causes two switchings, hence the switching activity is 32×2. Meanwhile, FVC delivers an index for a hit case and a normal data item for a miss case. In addition, the control signal changes for every communications, hence it changes two times for each communication. Therefore, the switching activity when FVC is used is calculated by Equation 1.

$$P_{hit} \times \{1 + \log(\#entry)\} \times 2 + (1 - P_{hit}) \times (1 + 32) \times 2 \qquad (1)$$

Based on the above analysis, the switching activity reduction ratio of FVC over the normal dual-rail bus model is calculated by Equation 2.

$$\frac{P_{hit} \times \{1 + \log(\#entry)\} \times 2 + (1 - P_{hit}) \times (1 + 32) \times 2}{32 \times 2} \qquad (2)$$

Analysis result illustrates that FVC reduces the switching activity of the conventional model by 75% at maximum. However, the switching activity reduction ratio is decreased after the maximum point because of the increased number of index bits.

Power Consumption: The total power consumption should include the power consumption of the FVC tables although the power consumption ratio of the table would be below 5% as explained in [16]. In addition, the power consumption of the bus itself should be considered as well. To measure the power consumption of FVC table and bus lines, it is assumed that 0.25 micron technology is used, and the length of the bus line is 10 mm, which follows the 2001 ITRS [17]. Power consumptions of the normal model and the FVC model are as follows:

Normal Model: The power consumption is only caused by the dual-rail bus for logical 32-bit bus lines. Based on the 0.25 micron technology, we assume that 10 mm bus lines consume about 0.4 nJ by using power measure tools.

FVC Model: The power consumption is caused by two parts as the FVC table and bus lines. To measure the power consumption of the FVC table, CACTI tool [11] is used. Since all entries should be checked at the same time, it is assumed that the table is a fully-associative content address memory. The power consumption of FVC model can be formulated as Equation 3. Specifically, the

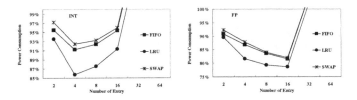

Fig. 4. Power Consumption Variation

power consumption of the FVC table is multiplied by two because FVC model requires two FVC tables for a sender and a receiver. Meanwhile, when the FVC miss, each FVC table must be updated and it consumes more power. To include this power consumption to update FVC, we include the $Miss\_Ratio$ in the equation.

$$Table\_Power \times 2 \times (1 + Miss\_Ratio)$$
$$+Bus\_Power \times Switching\_Activity\_Reduction\_Ratio \tag{3}$$

Finally, it can be derived a power consumption reduction ratio of the FVC model over the normal model as shown in Equation 4.

$$\frac{Table\_Power \times 2 \times (1 + Miss\_Ratio) + (0.4nJ) \times Switching\_Activity\_Reduction\_Ratio}{0.4nJ} \tag{4}$$

Figure 4 shows the power consumption reduction ratio when the FVC model is used. From the figure, it can be concluded that FVC reduces the total power consumption by about 14% and 22% at maximum for integer and floating-point benchmarks, respectively.

6   Analysis in a Microprocessor

Until previous sections, it have been analyzed independently the area cost and/or power consumption reduction ratios of the proposed methods for value predictor, redundant operation table, and asynchronous dual-rail bus. Meanwhile, because our main goal is to reduce the total area cost and power consumption of a high performance microprocessor, it is needed to know how much area cost and power consumption can be reduced when the proposed methods are used for each design method.

6.1   Area Cost and Power Consumption Breakdowns

Because no processor has been implemented with the value predictor, redundant operation table, and asynchronous dual-rail bus at the same time, it is required to model a futuristic microprocessor to investigate the portions of area cost and power consumption of each design method.

(a) Area Cost   (b)   Power   Con-
                                    sumption

Fig. 5. Area Cost and Power Consumption Breakdowns of Alpha 21264 Model

Conventional Model: The Alpha 21264 microprocessor [18], [19] is selected to find the breakdown of die size and power consumption of major blocks such as cache and core parts. Because value predictor and redundant operation table have similar structure with the cache, it can be assumed that the area cost and power consumption of tables for value predictor and redundant operation table are calculated by the relative area cost and power consumption over the cache. *Area Cost and Power Consumption Breakdown:* Alpha 21264 utilizes 128Kbyte Instruction and Data caches, which require about 30% of total area cost [18] and consumes about 15% of total power consumption [19]. Figure 5(a) and 5(b) show the breakdowns of area cost and power consumption of the Alpha 21264 model, respectively.

New Model: The new Alpha 21264 model consists of the old Alpha 21264 and other three design methods. Because of such modification of the old Alpha 21264 model, the area cost and power consumption breakdowns will be changed.

Area Cost Breakdown: The area cost of caches is about 30% and the others about 70% in the old Alpha 21264 processor. However, the value predictor and redundant operation tables add more area cost as 164Kbyte and 144Kbyte, respectively. In the old Alpha 21264 processor, 128Kbyte cache uses about 30% of total die size, hence it can be inferred that the value predictor increases the total area cost by about 38.4%, which is calculated by 30%*164/128. Also, the redundant operation table adds about 33.8% of total area cost, which is calculated by 30%*144/128. Finally, the total area cost is increased by about 72.2%, which is calculated by the summation of the extra area cost of value predictor and redundant operation table. From this total area cost increase, it should be rearranged the portion of area cost of each component as 17.4% for cache, 22.3% for value predictor, 19.6% for redundant operation table, and 40.7% for others as shown in Table 3. As shown in the table, it can be known that the portions of area cost for value predictor and redundant operation table are large, about 42%.

Power Consumption Breakdown: On the other hand, the portions of additional power consumption of value predictor and redundant operation table can be calculated by the relative power consumption over cache. It is inferred that the stride type value predictor consumes five times as much energy as cache from [4]. Hence, the value predictor consumes more energy by about 96.1%, which is calculated by 15%*(164/128)*5. Meanwhile, the redundant operation table also consumes more energy by about 16.9%, which is calculated by 15%*(144/128). From this increased total power consumption, it should be rearranged the portions of power consumption of each block as 7.1% for cache, 2.3% for bus, 45.1% for value

Table 3. Area Cost Breakdown, Reduction Ratios, Relative Reduction in the new Alpha 21264

Parts	Portion	Reduction Ratio	Relative Reduction
Cache	17.4%		
CPU Core	40.7%		
Value Predictor	**22.3%**	**64%**	**14.3%**
Redundant Operation Table	**19.6%**	**20%**	**3.9%**
Total	100%		**18.2%**

Table 4. Power Consumption Breakdown, Reduction Ratios, Relative Reduction in the new Alpha 21264

Parts	Portion	Reduction Ratio	Relative Reduction
Cache	7.1%		
CPU Core	37.6%		
Bus	**2.3%**	**14%**	**0.3%**
Value Predictor	**45.1%**	**52%**	**23.5%**
Redundant Operation Table	**7.9%**	**34%**	**2.7%**
Total	100%		**26.5%**

predictor, 7.9% for redundant operation table, and 37.6% for CPU Core as shown in Table 4. The extra power consumption caused by value predictor, redundant operation table, and asynchronous dual-rail bus is very large, about 55%.

6.2   Reduction of Total Area Cost and Power Consumption

Reduction of Total Area Cost and Power Consumption:
Area Cost Reduction: When the proposed area cost reduction methods for value predictor and redundant operation table are used, the total area cost can be reduced by about 18.2%, which is calculated by the summation of reduction ratios of area cost for value predictor (22.3% * 64% = 14.3%) and redundant operation table (19.6% * 20% = 3.9%), as shown in Table 3.
Power Consumption Reduction: Meanwhile, the proposed power consumption reduction methods can decrease the power consumption of each design method by about 52% for value predictor, 34% for redundant operation table, and 14% for asynchronous dual-rail bus, which are shown in Table 4. Therefore, the proposed area cost and power consumption reduction methods reduce the power consumption by about 23.45%(=45.1%*52%), 2.7%(=7.9%*34%), and 0.3%(=2.3%*14%), respectively, and finally the total power consumption by about 26.5% as shown in Table 4.

Area Cost and Power Consumption Breakdowns:
Area Cost Breakdown: The portions of area cost of value predictor and redundant operation table are changed as shown in Figure 6(a). As shown in the figure, the total portion of area cost for value predictor and redundant operation tables is reduced from 42% to 29%.

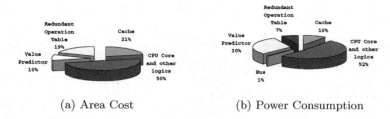

(a) Area Cost   (b) Power Consumption

Fig. 6. Area Cost and Power Consumption Breakdowns of Area Cost Reduced Alpha 21264 Model

Power Consumption Breakdown: The portions of power consumption of value predictor, redundant operation table, and asynchronous dual-rail bus are changed as shown in Figure 6(b). As shown in the figure, it can be known that the total portion of power consumption of value predictor, redundant operation table, and asynchronous dual-rail bus is reduced from 55% to 38%.

7   Conclusion

Throughout this research, we have pointed out that the low area and power design methods should be proposed for design techniques for a high performance microprocessor. Among many techniques, three high performance design techniques have been investigated.

Analysis of information locality and related data redundancy illustrates that the area and power are wasted by the data redundancy in each high performance design method. Therefore, the information locality was exploited and tried to minimize data redundancy in each method. Finally, three different approaches have been proposed for each method respectively.

First, to reduce the waste of area cost and power consumption in a value predictor, which is caused by data redundancy in tag and data part, we proposed a combining method of previously proposed partial tag and narrow-width method with an efficient table-update method. Structural and dynamic analysis show that the proposed method reduces the area cost by about 71% and the power consumption by about 61% over the conventional value predictor. Second, for the redundant operation table, we designed a partial tag method. Although the redundant operation table wastes area and power in both tag and data parts, a redundancy minimization method only for tag part has been discussed. The proposed method reduces the area cost by about 20% and the power consumption by about 34% over the ordinal redundant operation table structure. Third, to reduce the waste of power consumption of asynchronous dual-rail bus, we utilize the frequent value cache with several circuits. Analysis results show that the proposed method decreases the power consumption of a bus in a microprocessor by about 14% for integer and 22% for floating-point data communications over a memory bus in a microprocessor.

As well, we examined how much total area cost and power consumption can be reduced when the proposed area cost reduction methods are used for each design method. This analysis confirmed that the total area cost and power consumption would be reduced by about 18.2% and 26.5%, respectively.

Acknowledgments. This work was supported in part by the Korea Science and Engineering Foundation (KOSEF) through the Ultra-Fast Fiber-Optic Networks Research Center at Kwangju Institute of Science and Technology.

References

1. Mikko H. Lipasti and John P. Shen: Exceeding the Dataflow Limit via Value Prediction, Proc. of 29th Intl. Symp. on MICRO, (1996) 226-237
2. Sang-Jeong Lee, Yuan Wang, and Pen-Chung Yew: Decoupled Value Prediction on Trace Processors, Proc. of 6th IEEE Intl. Symp. on HPCA (2000) 231-240
3. Rafael Moreno, Luis Pinuel, Silvia del Pino, and Francisco Tirado: A Power Perspective of Value Speculation for Superscalar Microprocessors, Proc. of ICCD, (200) 147-154
4. Ravi Bhargava and Lizy K. John: Latency and Energy Aware Value Prediction for High-Frequency Processors, Proc. of the 16th ICS (2002) 45-56
5. Ravi Bhargava and Lizy K. John: Performance and Energy Impact of Instruction-Level Value Predictor Filtering, Proc. of the First Workshop of Value-Prediction (2003)
6. Daniel Citron and Dror G. Feitelson: Hardware Memoization of Mathematical and Trigonometric Functions, Technical Report-2000-5, Hebrew University of Jerusalem (2000)
7. Scott Hauck: Asynchronous Design Methodologies: An Overview, Proc. of the IEEE (1995) Vol.83, No.1, 69-93
8. Tom Verhoeff: Delay-Insensitive Codes: An Overview, Distributed Computing (1988) Vol.3, 1-8
9. Toshinori Sato and Itsujiro Arita: Partial Resolution in Data Value Predictors, Proc. of ICPP (2000) 69-76
10. Toshinori Sato and Itsujiro Arita: Table Size Reduction for Data Value Predictors by exploiting Narrow Width Values, Proc. of ICS (2000) 196-205
11. Premkishore Shivakumar and Norman P. Jouppi: CACTI 3.0: An Integrated Cache Timing, Power, and Area Model, WRL Research Report 2001/2, COMPAQ Western Research Laboratory (2001)
12. Doug Burger and Todd M. Austin: The SimpleScalar Tool Set, Version 2.0, Technical Report, CS-TR-97-1342, University of Wisconsin (1997)
13. SPEC CPU Benchmarks: Standard Performance Evaluation Cooperation http://www.specbench.org/osg/cpu95
14. John Bainbridge and Steve B. Furber: Delay Insensitive System-on-Chip Interconnect using 1-of-4 Data Encoding, Proc. of ASYNC. (2001) 118-126
15. Benjamin Bishop and Anil Bahuman: A Low-Energy Adaptive Bus Coding Scheme, Proc. of the IEEE Workshop of VLSI (2001) 118-122
16. Tiehan Lv, Jorg Henkel, Haris Lekatsas, and Wayne Wolf: An Adaptive Dictionary Encoding Scheme for SOC Data Buses, Proc. of DATE (2002) 1059-1064

17. The Semiconductor Industry Association: The International Technology Roadmap for Semiconductor (2001)
18. Srilatha Manne, Artur Klauser, and Dirk Grunwald: Pipeline Gating: Speculation Control for Energy Reduction, Proc. of ISCA (1998) 122-131
19. Michael K. Gowan, Larry L. Biro, and Daniel B. Jackson: Power Considerations in the Design of the Alpha 21264 Microprocessor, Proc. of DAC (1998) 726-731

Dynamic Reallocation of Functional Units in Superscalar Processors

Marc Epalza[1], Paolo Ienne[2], and Daniel Mlynek[1]

[1] Laboratoire de Traitement des Signaux 3,
[2] Laboratoire d'Architecture des Processeurs,
Swiss Institute of Technology Lausanne (EPFL), 1015 Ecublens, Switzerland
{marc.epalza, paolo.ienne, daniel.mlynek}@epfl.ch

Abstract. In the context of general-purpose processing, an increasing number of diverse functional units are added to cover a wide spectrum of applications. However, it is still possible to design custom logic adapted to a particular application that will perform far better than a processor. In an attempt to give it some adaptability, adding some reconfigurability can help improve performance. We propose to extend the possibilities of complex multifunction units by dynamically reallocating existing complex functional units as multiple simpler units. The fact that more than one simple unit is involved in the "reconfiguration" process implies that the decision is more global and needs to be taken for a longer period of time. We show that in typical superscalar architectures, there are no major impediments to implementing such a decision scheme, and that on a specific reallocation opportunity we can achieve speedups of up to 56% over a mainstream superscalar processor and practically no losses.

1 Introduction

In general purpose processors, the quest for ever higher performance leads to many trade-offs, since one aims to achieve the best average performance on a variety of tasks essentially unknown to the designer. Many methods to extract even more parallelism, such as speculative execution or *Very Long Instruction Word* (VLIW) compiler technologies are complex and achieve diminishing returns, since the resources available to the processor are fixed. Attempts to make the processor adaptable to the program it is currently executing, through the use of reconfigurable logic, have provided mixed results. We propose to introduce some adaptability without using slow reconfigurable logic. To this end, we focus on the large multi-function units present in a superscalar processor. As an example, we expose a modification of a superscalar processor's *floating point functional units* (FPU) to allow some adaptation to the current workload.

Section 2 will lay out the constraints of the field and existing methods to achieve high performance. Next, section 3 will present our proposal and its impact on processor design. Our test methodology and reference processors will be exposed in section 4, with simulation results shown in section 5. Section 6 will bring our conclusions, the limitations of our approach, and our future directions of study.

P.-C. Yew and J. Xue (Eds.): ACSAC 2004, LNCS 3189, pp. 185–198, 2004.

2 Background and Prior Art

2.1 Parallelism

The way to higher performance in general purpose processors is through forms of parallelism, especially by trying to execute as many instructions as possible at the same time. The theoretical limits in the parallelism offered by different programs are far higher than those achieved in reality by current processors, for a variety of reasons. In any case, the available hardware resources are fixed by the processor's designer, and cannot be tailored to a particular application. They are chosen to get the best average performance. Superscalar processors, executing many instructions out of order every cycle, extract as much parallelism as possible during the execution of a program. This leads to complex designs, but these optimizations don't require changes to the software. In an attempt to soften the restrictions of fixed hardware resources, configurable hardware has been examined.

2.2 Reconfigurable Functional Units

Given the limitations of a fixed set of hardware resources, much research has focused on adding some reconfigurability to a general-purpose system, usually based on FPGA technology. FPGAs are most efficient for code with simple control and large data parallelism (e.g., [2]).

One can distinguish three different approaches, each bringing closer integration with the processor, and thus more generality, at the expense of performance. The first and second couple an FPGA and a normal processor, and distribute the computing tasks according to what each can do best, the difference being whether to integrate the FPGA onto the processor chip or not. There is little automation possible, and selection and coding for the FPGA must be done by hand, including the needed communication and synchronization with the processor. With well chosen applications, the gains in performance can be of several orders of magnitude [15]. In a single-chip solution, some automation is possible, usually with a smaller increase in performance than if optimizations are performed by hand (e.g., [13]).

The last, most tightly coupled solution is to define the configurable logic as simply an extra *functional unit* (FU) of the processor. This reconfigurable functional unit can hold several instructions or sequences of instructions, that can be provided by a special compiler, and loaded by the processor when needed. Attempts to automate the process exist (e.g., [1], [16]), with gains similar to the second solution above (e.g., [5]). In each of these cases, the approach is to couple an existing FPGA-style block with a processor, in a more or less tightly coupled way.

We propose to consider configuration possibilities as an issue in the design of the processor's functional units, instead of adding a block of existing fully reconfigurable logic (such as FPGA technology) and trying to have the two cooperate. This implies a reduction in the configurability available, albeit with a significant gain in speed, which we hope to leverage.

2.3   Binary Compatibility

The issue of binary compatibility, ensuring that all code written for previous versions of a processor family will work on the newest model, is a complex one. However, it limits the innovation that can be implemented in the processor, since no completely novel approach may be used. As a solution to this problem, dynamic binary translation has been proposed. It aims to transform code for one architecture into another in real-time during the execution of the program. Several research projects exist [14], with one commercial implementation [8].

Our aim is to increase performance while avoiding code changes or having a major impact on timing. The lack of code changes allows our improvements to apply to all existing code and the re-use of all compiler achievements. Preserving the general timing will avoid breaking or severely limiting the performance of existing programs not suited to our modifications.

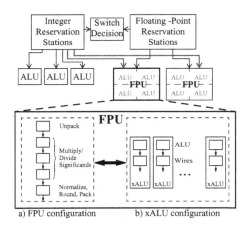

Fig. 1. Paths between reservation stations and functional units (top), and reallocation possibilities (bottom). Each FPU can be reallocated as a number of *extra ALUs (xALUs)*. FPU operations have 5 stages, thus the FPU must be idle for 5 cycles before reallocation is possible. Likewise, the *xALUs* have 2 stages, and must all be idle for 2 cycles at the same time to allow reallocation.

3   Proposed Modification

Studies on the ideal mix and functionality of functional units in a superscalar processor have been performed [7]. These studies show that good gains can be obtained by increasing the number of identical functional units, as well as the types of instructions these units can execute. We are interested in looking for ways to reconfigure expensive functional units to perform different operations. Given the

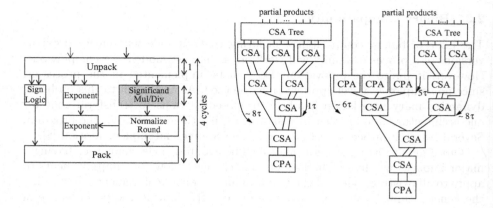

Fig. 2. Left: Structure of a floating point multiply/divide unit, with assumed cycle counts. Center and Right: Example of a 64 bit multiplier partial product reduction tree. Center: Original Wallace tree structure (total delay 14τ). Right: Proposed modification (total delay 15τ). CSAs have a delay of 1τ, CPAs have a delay of about 5τ. For clarity, the multiplexers from the Register file to the CPAs for the $xALU$ configuration are not shown.

speed disadvantage of fully programmable units, which are 5 to 10 times slower than a dedicated custom logic in the same technology, we restrict ourselves to very limited changes, while maintaining speeds close to non-configurable logic.

3.1 Basic Concept

Multifunction units, such as the FPUs in the Intel Itanium 2 processor, can execute one of many different instructions each cycle. As shown in figure 1, we propose to reallocate an FPU, with a latency of 5 (figure 1a) as several *extra ALUs (xALUs)* with a latency of 2 (figure 1b). These *extra ALUs* are assumed to perform all the operations normal Arithmetic Functional Units do. Our approach differs from multifunction units since, due to these latencies, the reconfiguration decision cannot be taken on a cycle-by-cycle basis, but with a view to the next several dozen cycles. This longer view is necessary to offset the idle time before reallocation, as we have to wait for the entire functional unit to be idle before reallocating it. We trade a small decrease in speed to obtain some configurability, with the hope that adapting to applications will offset the slightly slower configurable functional units to offer a net gain in performance. We focus on a processor's floating point unit, since it is fairly large, and can often be idle during a program's execution, if the current application uses mostly integer code. Simply adding extra ALUs would further increase power consumption and area, with little impact on the results (section 5).

3.2 Standard Arithmetic Units

Current fast multipliers for fixed point numbers can be built from a tree of *Carry-Save Adders* (CSA) that adds all the partial products into two words, with a final *Carry-Propagate Adder* (CPA) for the last addition [10]. The exact structure of the tree may vary to achieve better regularity, essential for good integration. A division unit can have a similar structure, if a convergence algorithm is used. This would lead to the common implementation of a Mul/Div unit [11], with the tree structure qualitatively as in figure 2 (center). Each CSA or CPA block might need an inverter to allow subtraction. The CSA tree has $\lceil \log_{3/2}(64) \rceil = 9$ levels.

A floating-point Mul/Div unit is essentially a fixed-point Mul/Div unit with some extra logic to unpack the operands, perform Booth recoding if it is used, normalize the result and re-pack it into floating-point notation, as shown in figure 2 (left). The presence of a full CPA adder allows the re-use of the unpack and pack logic to include all floating point operations in the unit. It is also possible to use the floating point unit for integer multiplication and division, as in the Intel Itanium 2 processor [9].

3.3 Dynamic Functional Units

We propose to use the adders in an FPU as a number of *xALUs*, with characteristics similar to normal ALUs. As a CSA cannot be used to perform a complete addition, several CSAs in the tree could be replaced by CPA adders as in figure 2 (right) with only a minimal impact on the overall critical path, area and power consumption. This figure shows the proposed modifications to the reduction tree, which affect only the steering of the data, not the logic performed on it. The CPAs directly receive some of the partial products while the other partial products go through the CSA tree to allow time for the far slower CPAs to finish execution, resulting in only a small extra delay due to the unbalancing of the tree. This requires some extra logic: to handle logic operations other than add/subtract, to bring the operands for the extra instructions that will be executed, to bypass the floating point logic, and to switch between the two different modes of execution.

3.4 Effects on Functional Unit Latencies

Our reference for instruction latencies is the Intel Itanium 2 processor, one of the fastest (and certainly the largest) existing processor [17]. This processor has a latency of 1 for all ALU operations, and a latency of 4 for all FP operations and Integer Mul/Div operations. These latencies are considered here representative of current 64-bit processors, and the functional units are fully pipelined.

In deep sub-micron technology, such as 0.13μm, wires account for about 2/3 of the delays, and the differences between 0.13μm and 0.09μm are not so important in this regard. The increase in wiring to reach the *xALUs* is estimated at about double that needed for normal ALUs. Thus, if a normal ALU has a latency of 1 cycle, split as 1/3 gates and 2/3 wires, doubling the wires gives a $xALU$ latency of 5/3. Taking the multiplexers to select the adders in the FPU into account, a conservative estimate for the latency of all *extra ALU* units is to double the latency of normal ALUs, for a latency of 2. As confirming this timing would require designing the entire functional core of a superscalar processor, a complex task beyond our means, simulations with a very conservative latency of 3, where about 89% of the delay is in the wires, have also been performed. Additionally, some of the bypass paths necessary to keep the pipeline as full as possible, and counted in the above calculations, are likely to already be present in the multiplier's tree linking the $xALUs$ together. This also means that the overhead is less than that of simply adding extra ALUs to the processor.

The latency of the entire FPU being 4, we consider that the unpack stage takes one cycle, the multiplier tree takes 2 cycles, and the normalization and pack take the last cycle (figure 2 left). The replacement of some of the CSA adders by CPA adders will increase the total delay of the multiplier tree. From [10], considering that a CSA has a delay of 1τ, a delay of 5τ for a 64-bit CPA can be derived. The total delay for a 64-bit CSA tree with 9 levels (see section 3.2) and the final CPA, is thus $9\tau + 5\tau = 14\tau$ (figure 2 center). We assume this delay represents 2 cycles (figure 2 left), as both real processor data [9] and arithmetic considerations [11] suggest. As shown in figure 2 (right), implementing our modifications on the FPU to embed 3 CPAs in the compressor tree would increase its delay to $8\tau + 2\tau + 5\tau = 15\tau$ plus the delay a multiplexer in front of each CPA (figure 2 right). To be on the conservative side, and since functional unit latencies must be integral, we have assumed the total delay of the modified tree to be 21τ, equivalent to 3 cycles, an increase of 50%, or one cycle, for a total delay of 5 cycles in the functional unit. This adds a margin of 6τ, almost 40%, that is, many layers of logic, to the timing of the FPUs CSA tree. In any case, the partial products reduction tree is a logarithmic tree which can be easily unbalanced as needed to hide the delay of the CPAs, and so the inaccuracy due to the delays of the multiplexors and the bypass paths should not be significant overall.

Since the reconfiguration is achieved by switching the inputs of a few multiplexers, it takes only a single cycle, in addition to having to wait for the functional units to be idle, with no changes to the pipeline except the activation of the forwarding paths discussed above. The routing of the processor core must be redone to take the new data paths into account, but this kind of work must be done for newer technologies in any case. These numbers are summarized in table 1.

3.5   Switch Decision Mechanism

Given the possibility of changing an FPU into a number of xALUs, the issue of deciding when to perform this change, and when to change back, is posed. Since this decision cannot be taken every cycle because it is a global decision affecting several functional units (figure 1), an algorithm to adapt the resources to the code running at a given moment is needed. The basis for the decision is the type of instructions in the reservation stations. This gives a measure of the type of instructions the processor can expect to be executing a few cycles later. In the simplest case, the number of instructions of each type are then compared to the number of available functional units of the same type to make a decision. A *switch* is decided when the difference between the proportion of instructions of a type in the reservation stations and the resources of that type becomes too large. In the relatively common case that an instruction type should appear very infrequently, such as an integer program with very few multiplications, the algorithm above will not trigger a *switch*, since the threshold is not reached by a single instruction. In this case, we must detect that an instruction cannot be executed due to the absence of the correct resource type, and force a *switch*, regardless of the contents of the reservation stations. In all cases, a *switch decision* must wait until the functional unit(s) it wants to reallocate are completely idle, in which case it takes only a single cycle. It would be possible to *switch* while the FPU is still finishing the last calculation, during the normalization/pack stage, but this would greatly increase the complexity of the control path without a great effect on performance, through the pipelining of the *switch* logic and extra complexity in the pipeline.

3.6   Additional Considerations

The act of *switching* one or more FPUs into a number of $xALUs$ increases the pressure on the memory system, as well as providing the need for extra issue, dispatch and commit width. Though the memory bandwidth remains the same, a higher number of Load/Store units are required to avoid stalling the processor due to many memory requests. In our simulations, 4 such units (as in the Itanium 2) were a good balance between performance and complexity. The widest issue rate in current processors is 8 instructions per cycle [17]. A larger issue rate increased the gains of dynamic reconfiguration, but only slightly. Thus, the issue and dispatch widths were kept at 8. The commit width need not be as large as the issue/dispatch width, since the average number of instructions committed per cycle is lower than the maximum. In our simulations, the highest average IPC was slightly below 4 (*vortex*), leading to a commit width of 8 to avoid limiting performance, as the simulator used requires it to be a power of 2, although a value of 4 could be considered.

4   Experimental Methodology

All the results presented in section 5 were obtained through the use of the Simplescalar tool set [3]. The models used for the hardware are detailed in section 4.2. On the software side, the SPEC CPU2000 [6] benchmarks were used for all tests.

Table 1. Processor model resources. The *baseline mainstream* and *baseline top* processors were compared to their *dynamic* counterparts in all simulations, with *original mainstream* and *original top* shown as references. *supertop* is equivalent to *dynamic top* with 4 additional ALUs and no reconfiguration.

Model	#ALUs (latency)	#FPUs (latency)	#Load/Store units	#xALUs per FPU (latency)	issue-dispatch-commit widths
original mainstream	3 (1)	2 (4)	2	-	4 - 4 - 4
original top	6 (1)	2 (4)	4	-	8 - 8 - 8
baseline mainstream	3 (1)	2 (4)	4	-	8 - 8 - 8
baseline top	6 (1)	2 (4)	5	-	12 - 12 - 8
dynamic mainstream	3 (1)	2 (5)	4	4 (2)	8 - 8 - 8
dynamic top	6 (1)	2 (5)	5	4 (2)	12 - 12 - 8
supertop	10(1)	2 (5)	5	-	12 - 12 - 8

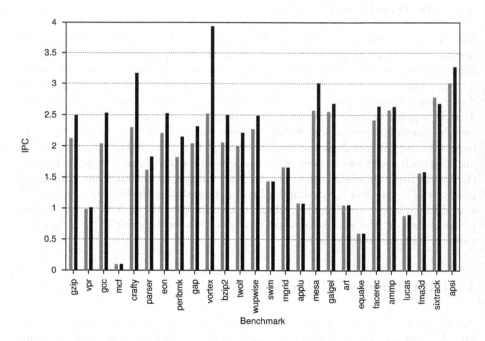

Fig. 3. Simulation results for the SPEC benchmarks for the *baseline mainstream* (light) and *dynamic mainstream* (dark) processors. There are large variations in the overall IPC, with some significant gains by the *dynamic* model.

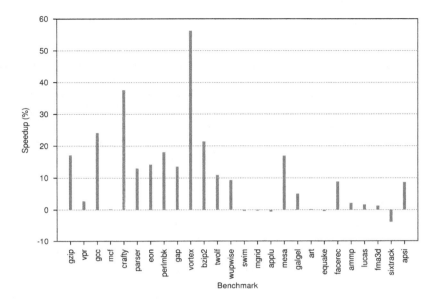

Fig. 4. Speedups between the *baseline mainstream* and the *dynamic mainstream* models. The integer benchmarks show universal gains, whereas the FP benchmark results are more varied. Except for *sixtrack*, all negative speedups are very small, less than 1% slower than the *baseline*.

4.1   Modifications to Simplescalar

The most accurate simulator in the Simplescalar tool set, `sim-outorder`, was modified so that a number of FPUs can be turned into several *xALUs*. The *switch decision algorithm* was also added to the simulator's main loop, to choose whether and how to change the allocation of resources during program execution.

4.2   Reference Processors and Models

Two different references, loosely inspired from mainstream and top server processors available today, and considered representative of the state of the art in general-purpose processors, were used:

Our *mainstream* reference is similar to the IBM Power4 processor (a single core), and is close to the average resource configuration of current processors. Each core is a 4-way superscalar processor, and has 2 ALUs, 2 load/store units, one branch unit and 2 FPUs.

Our *top* reference is loosely based on the Intel Itanium 2 processor, one of the fastest server processors available today, as measured by SPEC benchmarks. It has 2 ALUs, 4 load/store units that can also perform ALU operations, 3 branch units, and 2 floating point units that also take care of integer multiplication. Although it is a VLIW processor, its resources represent well the most aggressive configuration achievable nowadays.

For a fair comparison, both reference models are given the same memory access bandwidth and ports as our proposed model (4 or 5 load/store units and a 128-bit wide access to memory), as well as the same issue/dispatch/commit widths, giving us our *baseline mainstream* and *baseline top* models. Although these models are somewhat unbalanced, not increasing the number of load/store units would cripple the *dynamic* models, which are obtained by increasing the FPU latency as explained in section 3.4 and adding dynamic reallocation. *Supertop* is defined as a fully static top, with 4 additional ALUs and no reconfiguration, and is used to show the small difference in performance compared to the *dynamic top*. These characteristics are summarized in table 1.

4.3   SPEC CPU 2000 Benchmarks

All our tests considered the entire set of 26 benchmarks comprising the SPEC CPU2000 suite. The binaries are provided for the DEC Alpha [4] Instruction Set Architecture (ISA) on the Simplescalar WWW site [3], and have been compiled using the 'peak' configuration. The data sets chosen are the *reference* sets from the SPEC suite. given the length of the full simulations, early *Simpoints* [12] were used to provide statistically significant results for the *mainstream* model, detailed in figures 3 and 4. Due to time constraints, and since they are only intended to show the limits of reallocation, the *top* and *supertop* models were simulated skipping a smaller number of instructions than *Simpoint* suggests. Although the individual results may vary, the average over the 26 benchmarks is similar to that obtained using *early simpoints*, and sufficient to show a trend of diminishing returns.

5   Results

5.1   Performance Results

Figure 3 shows the results of our simulations for the *mainstream* model, using the configurations in table 1, lines 3 and 5. The speedups when using perfect memories, not shown, show little difference with those presented here, demonstrating that reasonable memory latencies have little effect on the gains made by dynamic reallocation. The best performing benchmark was *vortex*, with a gain of 56%, since it uses many independent ALU operations and very few FP instructions, thus being able to make good use of the *xALUs*, and the worst was *sixtrack*, with a loss of 3.8%, which is mostly composed of FP add and multiply, and is thus strongly affected by the increase in FPU latency. The average gain for the integer benchmarks was 19%, and 3.5% for the floating-point benchmarks. The overall average for the entire suite was a gain of a little more than 10%. For clarity, the corresponding speedups for the entire set of benchmarks are shown in figure 4. There is a systematic gain, only seldom insignificant, and the rare losses in heavily FP-oriented benchmarks are rather small, with the exception of *sixtrack*.

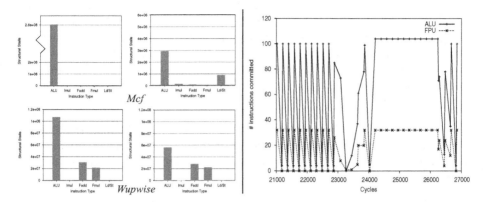

Fig. 5. Left: Structural stalls for *mcf* (top) and *wupwise* (bottom). The left side is the *mainstream baseline* case, the right side is with *dynamic reallocation*. *Mcf* is limited by ALU instructions, and shows a large reduction in ALU stalls. *Wupwise* sees little change in stalls, and thus cannot benefit from reallocation. Right: Instruction types for *galgel*. As there is no region with few FP instructions and many ALU requests, the allocation decision is to have no *xALUs*, resulting in lower performance.

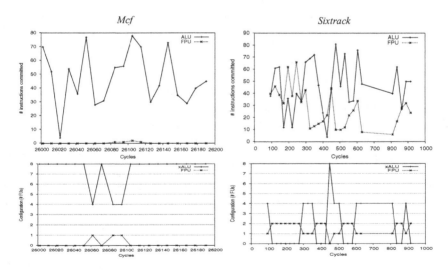

Fig. 6. Instruction types (top) and resource allocation (bottom) for *mcf* (left) and *sixtrack* (right). For *mcf*, as there are almost no FPU instructions, the configuration is always to use 8 *xALUs*. When an FPU instruction arrives, the FPU is switched to execute it, and then immediately switches back. In the case of *sixtrack*, the allocation of the FPU's resources adapts to the instruction types: when there are few FPU instructions, the units will be reallocated as *xALUs*.

The results for the *top* model, described by lines 4 and 6 in table 1, show a reduction in the gains obtained, due to far less usage of the *xALUs*, as there are already 6 ALUs in the processor. Again, memory latency did not significantly affect the speedups. The average gains were 3.7% for integer benchmarks, and 1.5% for floating-point, giving a total average gain of 2.5%. For comparison, the *Supertop* model gives an average gain of 3.1% versus the *baseline top*, at the cost of a larger set of functional units and resources on the die. If the *xALUs* latency is increased to 3, the results show a reduction in the average gain from 10% to 7%, and in the maximum gain from 56% to 35%. Thus, although this delay is somehow critical to our gain, the benefit of our system does not fully rely on these timing assumptions. Losses are not affected, since these benchmarks rarely use the *xALUs*, if ever.

5.2   Influence of Instruction Types

The large differences in speedups for the different benchmarks can be explained by looking at the instruction types used in these benchmarks. We shall use three benchmarks to illustrate this point: *mcf*, *wupwise* and *galgel*. The following graphs show good examples of the different behaviors reallocation produces. However, these are not necessarily representative of the overall benchmark results. Figure 5 (left) shows the number of structural stalls—i.e., the number of instructions of each type which had all operands ready, but couldn't execute due to a lack of functional unit, for the first two benchmarks with the *mainstream* model. The former, *mcf*, is limited here almost only by ALU instructions in addition to memory accesses, and thus benefits greatly from our proposal, since both FPUs get reallocated into many *xALUs*, switching back regularly to service the FP operations. This behavior is shown in figure 6 (left). The limitation by the Load/Store units appears because all ALU instructions that were previously waiting for a functional unit have been executed by one of the *xALUs*, and the memory accesses that had time to execute in the *baseline* case now stall the processor while waiting for the Load/Store units, which are now far less numerous than the ALUs. On the other hand, *wupwise* uses a fairly diverse mix of instruction types, with a heavy emphasis on floating-point add and multiply/divide instructions. The *switching mechanism* is constantly reallocating the functional units to try to match the instruction mix at each moment in time. In this case, the *extra ALUs* available at some moments cannot compensate for the slowdown of the FPUs' mul/div units and the delays in switching between the two. To illustrate this, a short trace of the instruction types for galgel is shown in figure 5 (right). The corresponding *switch decision*, not shown, is to never use the *xALUs*, leading to a loss in performance due to a longer latency in the FPU.

5.3   Switching Dynamics

For the resource reallocation to work, the *switch mechanism* must configure the hardware to make the best use of the configurable resources. Figure 6 (right) shows a short trace from the *sixtrack* benchmark, taken after approximately

10^9 instructions. Figure 6 (top right) displays the number of instructions committed from the ALUs and the FPUs, while figure 6 (bottom right) shows the configuration of the FPU over the same period of time.

The pattern shown is one of the startup loops in the application, and repeats regularly around the instruction count shown. At around 200 cycles, there are more FPU instructions than ALU ones, and the switching mechanism does not allocate any $xALUs$. However, at 300 cycles, the situation reverses, and one FPU is converted into 4 $xALUs$. A sharp spike in ALU instructions coupled with a sharp drop in FP instructions at 450 cycles will cause both FPUs to be reallocated as 8 $xALUs$ for a brief moment, before resuming FP functions. A long period of relative stability, between 650 and 850 cycles leads to a unchanging configuration.

6   Conclusions and Future Work

We have proposed a method to gain some hardware adaptability to the code running on a general-purpose processor that does not sacrifice the speed of the configurable unit or compromise binary compatibility. This technique is distinctive in requiring the logic of the superscalar processor to make more global decisions than it normally does. The conditions for the simulations have been derived from real data measured from 0.13μm technology. The results show the use of a dynamic FPU is quite interesting in the case of processors with a modest number of ALUs, and that naturally the interest declines with a large number of ALUs already in the processor. Our idea, based on giving the processor more possibilities for parallelism, should be seen as an example of the possibilities in superscalar processors that can be exploited by multi-cycle reallocation decisions. When superscalar processors will enter the embedded System-on-Chip world, the common use of domain-specific instructions or coprocessors for these applications will increase the opportunities for similar forms of reconfiguration.

We intend to apply control theory to the decision mechanism, in order to better tailor the resources to the application. Simulations on a SMT processor are expected to produce interesting results, due to the extra parallelism exposed by the multiple threads. We also envision to research the possibility of using software hints in the code to guide resource reallocation. While this would maintain backward binary compatibility, it will require a recompilation and some analysis of the code to produce better gains. In a similar vein, it might also be possible to apply this method to VLIW processors, in which case the resource allocation would simply be another information generated by the compiler.

Acknowledgment. We would like to thank the anonymous reviewers for their insightful comments.

References

1. K. Atasu, L. Pozzi, P. Ienne, *Automatic Application-Specific Instruction-Set Extensions under Microarchitectural Constraints*, Proc. of the 40th Design Automation Conference, June 2003.
2. M. Borgatti et al., *A Reconfigurable Signal Processing IC with embedded FPGA and Multi-Port Flash Memory*, Proc. of the 40th Design Automation Conference, June 2003.
3. D. Burger, T. M. Austin, *The Simplescalar Tool Set, Version 2.0*, www.simplescalar.com
4. J. H. Edmondson, et al., *Internal organization of the Alpha 21164, a 300-MHz 64-bit quad-issue CMOS RISC microprocessor*, Digital Technical Journal, 1995.
5. S. Hauck, T. W. Fry, M. M. Hosler, J. P. Kao, *The Chimaera Reconfigurable Functional Unit*, IEEE Symposium on Field-Programmable Custom Computing Machines, 1997.
6. J. L. Henning, *SPEC CPU2000: Measuring CPU Performance in the New Millennium*, IEEE COMPUTER, July 2000.
7. S. Jourdan, P. Sainrat, D. Litaize, *Exploring Configurations of Functional Units in Out-of-Order Superscalar Processors*, Proc. 22nd Annual Int'l Symposium on Computer Architecture, June 1995.
8. A. Klaiber, *The technology behind Crusoe processors*, Transmeta Corporation, Jan. 2000.
9. C. McNairy, D. Soltis, *Itanium 2 Processor Microarchitecture*, IEEE Micro, March 2003.
10. A. R. Omondi, *Computer Arithmetic Systems: Algorithms, Architecture and Implementations*, Prentice Hall, 1994.
11. B. Parhami, *Computer Arithmetic Algorithms and Hardware Designs*, Oxford University Press, 2000.
12. E. Perelman, G. Hamerly, B. Calder, *Picking Statistically Valid and Early Simulation Points*, International Conference on Parallel Architectures and Compilation Techniques, September 2003.
13. R. Razdan, M. D. Smith, *A High-Performance Microarchitecture with Hardware-Programmable Functional Units*, Proc. of MICRO-27, Nov. 1994.
14. G. T. Sullivan, D. L. Bruening, I. Baron, T. Garnett, S. Amarasinghe, *Dynamic Native Optimization of Interpreters*, IVME 03, June 2003.
15. R. D. Wittig, *OneChip: An FPGA Processor With Reconfigurable Logic*, IEEE Symposium on FPGAs for Custom Computing Machines, 1995.
16. Z. A. Ye, N. Shenoy, P. Banerjee, *A C Compiler for a Processor with a Reconfigurable Functional Unit*, ACM Int'l Symposium on Field Programmable Gate Arrays, 2000.
17. In-Stat/MDR Workstation and Server Processor Chart, http://www.mdronline.com/mpr/cw/cw_wks.html

Multiple-Dimension Scalable Adaptive Stream Architecture[1]

Mei Wen, Nan Wu, Haiyan Li, and Chunyuan Zhang

Computer School, National University of Defense Technology
Chang Sha, Hu Nan, P. R. of China, 410073
wxxwm@263.sina.com

Abstract. Intensive processing applications, such as scientific computation, signal processing, and graphics rendering, motivate new processor architectures that place new burdens on the designer. These applications named Stream Applications demand very high arithmetic rates and data bandwidth, but lack data reuse. At present modern VLSI technology makes arithmetic units relatively cheaper. MASA(Multiple-dimension scalable Adaptive Stream Architecture) presented in this paper is a prototype that operate on streams directly. It is different from DSP and special high performance single-chip architecture because it combines flexibility and high performance. It has basic features of all stream processing, provides bandwidth hierarchy, makes ALU array execute with full loads and decomposes application into a set of computation modules to execute space-multiplexing or time-multiplexing. The multiple dimensions scalability of MASA, includes task-level, loop-level, instruction-level and data-level, and enables it to meet the demand of stream applications. This paper describes MASA architecture and stream model in the first half, and explores the features and advantages of MASA through mapping stream applications to hardware in the second half.

1 Overview

Under the power of Moore's law, the number of transistors integrated on chips has been increasing rapidly and the performance of chips has been enhanced constantly. In a contemporary 0.15μm CMOS technology, a 32-bit integer adder requires less than $0.05mm^2$ of chip area. Integrating more ALUs on single chip is not a problem any more. On the other hand this situation brings some new problems to the computer designer. One is how to support so many ALUs with enough instruction and data. The long wire delay is becoming more and more unavoidable owing to the increase of the density on chip. The other is how to make full use of the ability of chips' integration, that is, how to make full use of chips' area to compute other than traditional general-purpose architecture, for example only 6.5% of the Itanium 2 die is devoted to arithmetic units[1], and large fraction of its die area is consumed by other processing such as data cache, branch prediction, out-of-order execution and communication

---

[1] This work was supported by the 973 Project(5131202) and the 863 Project(2001AA111050) of China.

P.-C. Yew and J. Xue (Eds.): ACSAC 2004, LNCS 3189, pp. 199–211, 2004.

schedule. In addition, low efficiency is worth attention as the demands of applications increase.

Under this condition, traditional microarchitecture has met the challenge. How is the performance of microprocessors kept on scaling at the rate of 50% or even more per year[2]? Many researches on new microarchitecture of billion or more transistor chips are going on very well. And some technologies have come to life, such as systolic arrays in 1970s, data flow in 1980s and vectors in 1990s.

Stream architecture operates on data streams. It is first applied in media processing because of intensive computation, high data parallelism, and little data reuse. Stream has various formats, fixed length or variable length, and supports for collections of complex or simple elements. But data stream is consistent with the colloquial sense. According to Webster, a stream is "an unbroken flow(as of gas or particles of matter)",a "steady succession (as of words or events)",a "constantly renewed supply," or "a continuous moving procession (a stream of traffic)"[3]. The difference between stream and data flow is that some architecture adopts instruction driven rather than data driven. Though there are several kinds of stream architectures, the common feature is to take stream as architectural primitives in hardware. Stream architecture is suitable for VLSI technology and supports enough functional units to achieve the needed arithmetic rates because it has scale register file architecture and so on. At the same time its organization is quite simple, so it will be a hotspot in the near future.

MASA (Multiple-dimension Scalable Adaptive Stream Architecture) is a kind of stream architecture. The definition of programming is expanded, meaning that almost all parts are programmable, including inter-ALU switch, inter-arithmetic pages communication and register organization. So it has perfect flexibility compared to special architecture. It shares common characteristics of all stream processing, provides multiple-level bandwidth hierarchy, make ALU arrays execute with full loads. According to the demands of various applications, MASA decomposes application into some modules to do space multiplexing or time multiplexing and can be scaled in multiple dimensions (including task-level, loop-level, instruction-level and data-level).

The remainder of this paper is organized as follows. Section 2("related work") cites prior work in streaming and architecture that has inspired MASA. Section 3("MASA microarchitecture") presents MASA. Section 4("the MASA's stream model") discusses executing model of stream in MASA. Section 5("stream application studies") analyses the computing process with mapping a typical application onto the stream executing model of MASA. Compared with processing model of scalar and vector, it explores the features and advantages of MASA. The last section (Section 6) summarizes the conclusions drawn in this paper.

2   Related Work

MASA draws heavily on the prior work of numerous parallel models and architectures. This section highlights only a few of those works.

Viram[4,5] adopts multiple-level vector pipeline and places large memory in the chip. It integrates typical vector with PIM technology. However, it has limited scalability.

Raw[6], as a typical representative of tiled architecture, implements thread-level parallelism and is reconfigurable. But the connection of inter-tile is complex and the cost of crossbar is very significant.

Score[7,8] exploits thread-level parallelism like Raw, and has good compatibility by hiding the size of hardware from programmer. Although computer pages are reconfigurable, the waste of logic is quite large and the implementation is hard.

Imagine[9,10,11], as a pioneer of stream architecture, expands vector technology. The structure is very simple. It provides bandwidth hierarchy and resolves the bottleneck very well. It performs time multiplexing for multiple kernels in single chip and implements instruction-level and data-level parallelism, but task-level parallelism is weak. On the basis of Imagine, a supercomputer called Merrimac[19] is developed. One Merrimac stream processor is very similar to Imagine. MASA is influenced by Imagine heavily.

VLIW[12] exploits instruction level parallelism well. A VLIW architecture is low power efficiency, because in this case, a compiler performs scheduling of operations rather than hardware in superscalar architecture. But the scalability is very poor. At present many improved VLIW have come out such as dynamic VLIW technology [13].

Trips[14,15] is a general-purpose chip facing 2010 which consists of one or more inconnected grid processors working in parallel. It is a Polymorphous system, meaning that hardware should adapt itself to a variety of runtime workloads. However, it is essentially a reconfigurable array, just that the task of compiler and OS is new. Anyhow, it is quite complex.

3 MASA Microarchitecture

The prototype microarchitecture of MASA is shown in Figure 1. MASA is a programmable stream processor, which works as a stream coprocessor. Scalar program is executed on the host processor. Actually, MASA implements logic stream model in a single chip. The whole architecture can be divided into three layers by different bandwidth levels, and each layer owns its special controller, communication style and storage unit.

In the outer layer, scalar processor executes scalar instructions like MIPS and transfers explicit stream instructions to instruction caches in each *compute engine* (CE), which is a set of units executing thread-level tasks partitioned ahead. *Compute engine* can complete a task independently, so that MASA may own only one *compute engine*, adding the engine only when more task level computing is required. Stream memory system transfers streams between *stream register file* (SRF) and off-chip SRAM or SDRAM. MMU and *compute engine* are connected with multiple buses that we call *Multi Stream-bus*. Engines get stream-bus ownership by asynchronous request-answer signal's competition. After request is granted, *stream records* are transferred to SRF in the form of group or burst sequentially. *Stream record* is the elementary particle of data block. *Arbiter* is responsible for the grant or other signals, and the Arbiter principle can be either time-multiplexing or dynamic priority. Use priority for each bus can be set dynamically, that means the priority may be modified by the host processor. For each bus, the Arbiter has a special register to indicate the priority. Because of continuity of stream data, the bus interface of each engine has a lot of buffers called *stream buffers* in order to hide the latency of memory access.

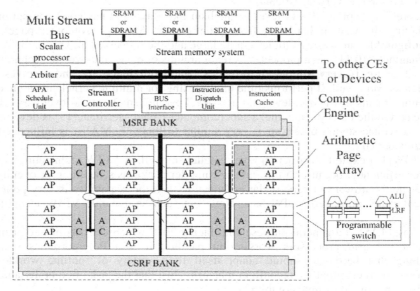

Fig. 1. Hypothetical, single-chip MASA system

The next layer is *compute engine*. Each engine consists of many *arithmetic page arrays* (APAs), SRF banks and a control unit. *Arithmetic page array*, which contains lots of arithmetic logic units, is the basic unit for executing kernel microcode program. APA schedule unit determines which APA executes a certain kernel, that means how to map the logic kernel to physical execute units. There is a scoreboard making records about the information of APA's status in the schedule unit. According to the information from schedule unit, *stream controller* dispatches stream instructions to one or more APAs. Scalar processor controls stream controller by stream instructions. These instructions determine kernels' process procedure and which APA is distributed to which kernel. Kernels are space-multiplexed or time-multiplexed that will be discussed in the next section. Instructions are combined as VLIW, and microcode consists of a series of 256~512 bit instruction words. When microcode is fetched from memory, it will be dynamically reorganized by an instruction issue unit to adapt to the scalability. Since instruction buffer of APA is limited and instruction will be regularly reused, an instruction cache is necessary, and the basic access unit is no longer an instruction but the whole microcode of a kernel. Instructions in the next execution that have been reorganized last time are fetched from instruction cache, so we needn't reorganize or distribute them again, otherwise it will be sent to off-chip memory instead. All transfers of data are passed through SRF. Stream data represents the principle of locality, so SRF is divided into several *banks*, whose size is tens Kilo-words. So that MASA can effectively increase the SRF's bandwidth. Data in a logic kernel is not allowed to store across banks. According to the destination of data, SRF may partition into main SRF (*MSRF*) banks and communication SRF (*CSRF*) banks. The former is responsible for the exchange of data between memory and engine, or dataflow between kernels. And the latter is responsible for the communication of global data among computer engines. MASA uses topology like tree to connect SRF to APA, which follows weak dependence and unilateral transformation of stream. At this layer, both instruction and data are transformed in the same data path, but in different time, so the execution of program is divided into two parts: configuration time and execution time. Partition of kernels and issue of instructions are completed in configuration time. After that, stream controller answers for transferring data and executing program according to kernels divided ahead. During this period, kernel program is kept unchangeable in APA and data streams are transformed from SRF to APA in sequence.

The most inner of MASA is kernel layer. Microcodes are executed in APA in the form of SIMD. Each APA consists of many *arithmetic pages* (APs) and one central *array controller*. And each AP contains eight to sixteen arithmetic logic units, including floating adder, floating multiplier, divider and some special function units. Each ALU owns its *local register file* (LRF) to keep its local data. A LRF is keeping a small suitable size that can be accessed fast enough. All ALUs in an AP are connected by programmable switch net, so ALUs in an AP are able to communicate each other fast and flexibly. But the communication between APs will take much more cycles; fortunately the stream application limits these communications in a negligible degree. VLIW codes of kernel program are buffered in array controller. AC has special instruction RAM to hold thousands of VLIW, and that is also responsible for decoding packed VLIW to control signals and transferring these signals to every AP in an APA.

The bandwidth hierarchy of stream processor insures kernel program not to access memory directly. The memory access latency can be effectively hidden by buffer and soft pipeline etc. All inputs and outputs of kernels have to transfer through SRF as the type of stream. Analogously, temporary results and local data that just exist or are used in a kernel are limited in the fast LRF, so the bandwidth requirement for SRF can be greatly reduced. By the way, operands' fetch time is explicitly determined so that no miss will happen. As a result, in kernel level all instructions' executing time are explicitly determined without any potential uncertain cycles, so in the control unit we can get an accurate static VLIW schedule time table. For this static structure, VLIW could be most efficient because it simplifies or cancels the hardware unit for some dynamic schedule such as extra register renaming, dependence detection, issue out of order and so on. Obviously, according to the features of stream algorithms, MASA emphatically solves the problem of high bandwidth and multi-kernel executing, so it can achieve very fast speed but simple structure which are of great benefit to reduce area and power efficiency.

According to bandwidth hierarchy, MASA defines different layers of architecture. In fact these layers correspond with different parallelisms that are task-level-parallelism (TLP), instruction-level- parallelism (ILP) and data-level-parallelism (DLP) strictly, which make us easily scale MASA in any dimension of these parallelisms. It means MASA can be emphatically scaled in the most needed dimension, so MASA's scalability is much more powerful and efficient. However, the most challenging work in scaling is how to partition basic APAs to different kernels in balance. MASA could solve this problem by the explicit definition in program or the cooperation of compiler and hardware (such as APA schedule unit). Therefore, MASA is well adaptive.

4 The MASA's Stream Model

The definition of stream in MASA is similar to that in other stream architectures. It consists of successive ordinal isomorphic elements. Stream has various formats, fixed or variable length, and complex or simple elements.

MASA works as a coprocessor for a scalar processor. It receives stream data and stream instructions from scalar processor, and transfers the results to the host. On the other hand, scalar processor performs scalar programs.

The application of stream on MASA is divided into three levels: stream-thread level, stream scheduling level and kernel execution level. The instance of the model is shown in Figure 2.

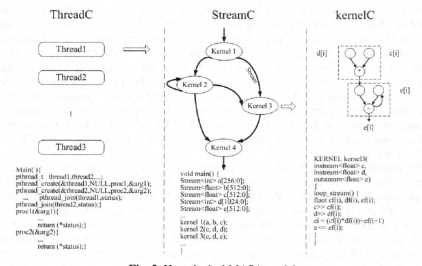

Fig. 2. Hypothetical MASA model

At the top level, the stream-thread level programming is done using thread C- like language. It is responsible for memory access scheduling in multi-buses and low-intensity communication among threads. Task is scheduled at the thread level. However, this level is not necessary, only used in large-scale computation. (For instance, there are 2 or more engines in MASA).

The second level programming is done using extended streamC[16] language. A *stream task* is decomposed to a series of computation kernels that deal with a great number of stream data. It permits determining executing order and size of kernel pattern by programmer. Program at stream scheduling level controls the whole flow of a stream task's execution, including communicating towards scalar processor, loading stream across the high-speed bus from off-chip, storing stream to off-chip memory, and starting kernel. The flow route of stream among kernels is similar to dataflow graph. The kernel operates successive data in the input stream, and produces the output stream as the input stream for other kernels. Similar to product line, each kernel just processes one record of input stream every time, and then appends result to the output stream. Kernels may be executed in two modes: time-multiplexing and space-multiplexing mode. In the former mode kernels are executed one by one at different time, and gain all the computing recourse exclusively. In the latter mode, several kernels share the whole computing recourse at the same time, we call the set of these kernels *synchronous kernels*. If adopting space-multiplexing mode, the output record will be sent to next kernel directly, as it may be transformed through buffer in time-multiplexing mode.

Computation kernels lie in the third level. It describes execution of single kernel in kernelC[16] -like language. The details of arithmetic operation and data executing mode are defined at this level. A kernel executed in AP is composed of VLIW instructions to exploit the great instruction parallelism. Moreover, by requiring programmers to explicitly use appropriate type of communication for each data element, this level expresses the application's inherent locality. All the temporary values just generate and exist within kernel. Thus the model does not use inter-kernel communication for temporary values.

Before the execution in chip, compiler and hardware decide how many APAs are available to execute several kernels simultaneously or time-sharing, and how many APAs each kernel occupies. Between APAs that implement different kernels, data is transferred in the form of stream. When forming logic kernels, programmer should consider the number of kernel's arithmetic operations and the size of intermediate results. An ideal kernel should have enough quantity of operation on local data but small set of intermediate results between kernels. At the same time, the balance between producer kernel and consumer kernel is important. We can introduce kernel fission and fusion technology into decomposing kernels.

5 Stream Application Studies - Fluid Compute

Stream applications are defined as the applications that can be mapped to stream programming model. Those focus on intensive computation domains, including scientific computation, graph rendering, media processing and so on. Features of stream application are obvious: First, computation is intensive and is limited within given time. Second, data has little reuse and weak dependence. Third, it is easy to divide program into some modules. Fluid compute is a typical scientific computation, which is applied in many important domains, such as aerospace, space flight, machine manufacture and so on. This paper takes numerical simulations of complex steady flow in hypersonic free stream as a stream application to map to MASA. We analyze kernel decomposing and intermediate result, and also compare MASA with some other architectures.

The whole computation has three steps in terms of LU-SGS: First, input the parameters and choose the format of space and time. Second, calculate the values of basic controlling equation group. Third, advance by time and iterate to solve the equations. Repeat the second and third steps till result is convergent[17]. Figure 3(a) diagrams part of LU-SGS algorithm.

The program has some characteristics shown in the following:

- Data represents locality and computation is advanced towards unilateral direction. The value of each point only needs information of two or three points around, so it can be paralleled on several points.

- The dependence distance of iteration is very small, because each iteration only needs the results of one to three latest iterations. It is convenient to exploit kernel-level parallelism by loop unrolling or software pipeline.
- There is no dependence between fluxes computation, so they can be executed in parallel as multiple tasks. The function in the program is easy to be divided into some blocks in accordance with loop. As a result, they can be mapped onto several kernels directly.
- Computationally intensive. The application requires many arithmetic operations per memory reference.
- There is few conditional branch which may be converted to conditional instruction. The characteristics of computation and data match MASA.

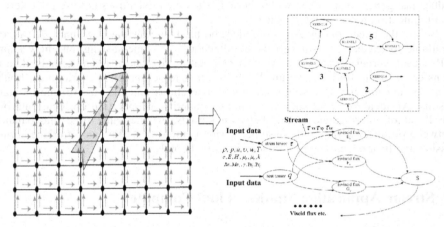

Fig. 3. (a) part of LU-SGS algorithm   (b) complex steady flow computing

The main part of the computation is to calculate partial differential equation to get six fluxes, that is $\dfrac{\partial U}{\partial t} + \dfrac{\partial E}{\partial x} + \dfrac{\partial F}{\partial y} + \dfrac{\partial G}{\partial z} = \dfrac{\partial E_v}{\partial x} + \dfrac{\partial F_v}{\partial y} + \dfrac{\partial G_v}{\partial z}$ where U is conservative variable, E, F, G, E_v, F_v, G_v are viscous or inviscid fluxes in the direction of x, y, and z. Computation of three inviscid fluxes is most intensive. Figure 3(b) shows how we map solving partial differential equation to the stream programming model in brief. Where τ and q mean stress tensor and heat tensor respectively. H is enthalpy of unit quality. ρ, p, u, v, w, T mean density, pressure, three components of the velocity and temperature respectively. e, E, H, μ_l, μ_t, k mean energy, enthalpy and coefficient of viscosity respectively. Re, Ma_∞, γ, Pr_l, Pr_t mean Reynolds Number, Mach Number, heat ratio and Prandtl Number respectively.

Take 300 thousands points as input data, the computation of three inviscid fluxes is 1.5 to 2 billion single precision floating operations for each iteration, which mainly contains addition and multiplication. The total computation for each iteration is about 2.5to 3.5 billion. The test program is small-scale, it needs 10000 steps to acquire constringent result at least. 15000 steps are assumed, and the total amount of arithmetic operations will be 4500 billion. It takes more than twenty hours, and the cost of memory is about 300MB, when the program is run on Pentium 4.

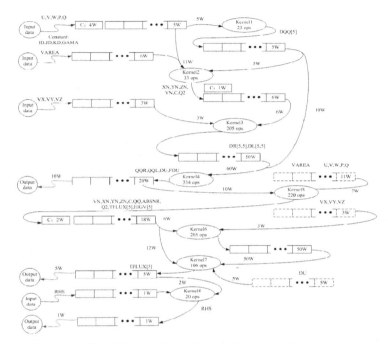

Fig. 4. Stream-Based inviscid flux computing

Figure 4 shows how we map computation of a inviscid flux to the stream programming model. The processing is composed of eight computation kernels that operate on data streams in succession. Where input data is fetched from memory and output data is stored to memory, rectangle represents stream in SRF, and a grid represents a stream element. Temporary data required by arithmetic operations is stored in LRF. For example, kernel3 receives 2 input streams and produces 1 output stream, performing 205 arithmetic Ops.

Table 1 compares the memory, global register, and local register bandwidth requirements of a stream architecture (MASA) with a vector processor and a scalar processor for the kernel3[2].

The content illuminated in the left-most column of Table 1 is the number of memory references, SRF references, and LRF references for the stream architecture. During the entire period of pipeline, the stream architecture performs 35 memory references as stated in Figure 4. Amortizing this across the eight kernels gives 4.375 memory references per kernel. The total SRF reference of the kernel3 is 59, that contains 9 words read from the SRF and 50 words written to the SRF. The 615 words of LRF bandwidth are used for each node to carry out the kernel that requires 205 arithmetic operations. The additional LRF accesses beyond the 615 come from

---

[2] This number is set by 8 ALUs in an AP of MASA.

register accesses to originally store data from the SRF into a local register file, and register transfers required for other kernels.

Table 1. 32-bit references per point for kernel3

	Stream	Vector	Scalar
Memory	4.375	59(13.5)	288(65.8)
Global RF	59	552(9.3)	1299(22.1)
Local RF	674	N/A	N/A

The next two columns present the number of references for the same kernel on a vector processor with an organization similar to the MASA processor. Considering vector operations are primitive arithmetic operations instead of compound stream operations, using global (vector) register file instead of local register files as a source and sink of data for the arithmetic units, and software pipeline, the vector processor requires respectively 13.5 times, 9.3 times as much memory bandwidth, global register file bandwidth as a stream processor.

The last two columns of Table 1 compare these numbers to a scalar processor by giving both the absolute number of references and the ratio to a stream processor (in parentheses). The scalar numbers were generated by compiling the kernel3 for MIPS using version 3.0.2 of the gcc compiler. The scalar processor requires respectively 65.8 times, 22.1 times as much memory bandwidth, global register file bandwidth as a stream processor. Considering that the number of memory references for the stream architecture is an average, and the kernel3 is run in the middle of pipeline, some data required would be in SRF, need not access memory, so the number of memory references for the scalar architecture is relatively magnified. However the difference is still great. Cache in the scalar processor is useful to shorten the gap, but there is little data reuse in stream application, so the benefit is limited.

MASA exploits the space parallelism that multi-kernels can run concurrently. The advantages of this feature can be appreciated by comparing it with other typical stream processors such as Imagine. Certainly, the advantage is at the cost of hardware complexity.

When SRF is full of intermediate results, the kernel which is running have to be changed to the other kernel to consume intermediate results. So each time the kernel runs, the number of records operated is limited. We call the number *kernel executing granularity* (KEG). Kernel executing granularity is limited by size of intermediate results and SRF. Table 2 compares the intermediate result size per node, maximum KEG and SRF requirement ratio of MASA with typical stream processor for inviscid flux computing. We analyze the intermediate result of each fluid node. These two processors are assumed to have the same computing ability and SRF size, though MASA's distributed SRF is different from Imagine's central SRF in bandwidth and utilization. In MASA, data between kernels running at the same time will be transferred and consumed immediately, so this procedure can generate smaller intermediate result. Therefore, smaller intermediate results could effectively increase Kernel executing granularity and utilization ratio, decrease the cost of exchanging kernels; and it also makes kernel operate on a longer stream that relieve the short stream problem.

For the same kernel executing granularity, MASA can decrease the SRF's size to a half of typical stream processor or even smaller. This advantage makes it much easier for larger scaling. Table 2 shows that kernel executing granularity is not linear with the number of synchronous kernels.

Table 2. SRF requirement for inviscid flux computing[3]

	Typical Stream architecture	MASA (2 synchronous kernels)	MASA (3 synchronous kernels)
Average intermediate result size per node	45	22.7	19
Maximum intermediate result size per node	94	52	26
Maximum KEG [4]	300s	600s	1200s
SRF size ratio at the same KEG	100%	55%	27%

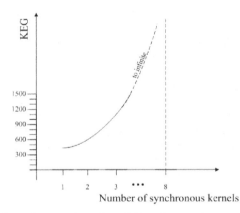

Fig. 5. The number of synchronous kernels and Kernel executing granularity for inviscid flux computing

According to different applications, as the number of synchronous kernels increases, consolidated intermediate results will decrease rapidly. For example, in table 2, typical stream processor's max intermediate result is 94W, that it is only 52W in column 2. As the number of synchronous kernels growing to 3, this value decreases to 26W. Support that when all of 8 kernels in figure 4 are running in MASA at the same time, intermediate result's size will become a constant which is irrelative with Kernel executing granularity. This means Kernel executing granularity may approach infinity in theory as figure 5 shows. However along with the number of synchronous kernels' increasing, decomposition and schedule will become more complex consequently. Also this complexity does not linearly increase and will go to

---

[3] Data of typical stream processor is estimated according to paper [18].
[4] 128KB SRF is assumed.

unacceptable at last. Furthermore, the load balance among kernels will be hard. In making a design trade-off, we think it better that the number of synchronous kernels should be fewer than 4 in middle-scale MASA.

6 Summary

MASA is a single-chip stream prototype architecture that supports the stream programming model by providing a data bandwidth hierarchy matched to the demands of typical computation-intensive applications. MASA supports multiple kernels running simultaneously or in sequence, dataflow among kernels organized around distributed SRF banks and all arithmetic operations are performed on streams transferred to and from the SRF.

Stream programming model exposes the parallelism and locality of stream applications in a manner that is well matched to the capabilities of modern VLSI technology. Through the analysis of above, it is known that stream application could be mapped to MASA model naturally, and a great number of ALUs on MASA will work fully. For complex steady flow in hypersonic free stream, a typical scientific computation, MASA infinitely reduces the demands for global register and memory bandwidth over a scalar processor and vector processor. This enables stream architecture to make efficient use of a large number of arithmetic units without global bandwidth becoming a bottleneck. About this, MASA is similar to other stream architectures.

Because MASA can do space multiplexing for multiple kernels, for some applications with computation-intensive in limited time, such as game system, set-top box, network switch and so on, they are easy to be mapped on MASA in order to achieve higher executing efficiency than other similar stream architectures. Another advantage is to reduce the demand of SRF size. As the number of kernels that run at the same time increases, the size of intermediate result decreases rapidly to a constant. So the runtime of the kernel each time trends to infinite ideally, kernel needs not to be changed, and it reduces the cost of kernel trembling.

MASA exposes concurrency at multiple levels: at AP level, DLP and ILP are exploited; at APA level, kernel level parallelism is exploited; at Engine level, TLP is exploited. In every dimension, MASA takes full advantage of function unit to do space multiplexing or time multiplexing for multiple kernels. The capability for adaptation is very good.

There are a lot of problems to solve remaining in the research of MASA architecture, such as the synchronous communication with scalar processor, the decomposition of multi-kernels, the dynamic scheduling algorithm, the appropriate size of register file at each level, the amount of ALUs in APA, the execution of conditional stream, the structure of communication network and the optimization of multiple-dimension scalability and so on.

Acknowledgements. The authors thank Tian Zhengyu for his knowledge of fluid compute. We also thank the reviewers for their valuable feedback.

References

1. U.J. Kapasi et al., programmable stream processor, IEEE computer, Aug 2003.
2. Bill Dally, Pat Hanrahan, and Ron Fedkiw, A Streaming Supercomputer, Whitepaper, Sep 2001.
3. H.Hoffmann et al., stream algorithms and architecture, MIT Laboratory for computer science, 2003.
4. C. E. Kozyrakis et al., Scalable Processors in the Billion-Transistors Era: IRAM, IEEE Computer, Vol 30 Issue 9, Sep 1997.
5. C. E. Kozyrakis, A Media-Enhanced Vector Architecture for Embedded Memory Systems Report No. UCB/CSD-99-1059, Jul 1999.
6. M. B. Taylor et al., The Raw Microprocessor: A Computational Fabric for Software Circuits and General Purpose Programs, IEEE Micro, 2002 ¾.
7. Score project, http://brass.cs.berkeley.edu/SCORE/
8. Eylon Caspi et al, A Streaming Multi-Threaded Model, the Third Workshop on Media and Stream Processors, in conjunction with MICRO34, Austin, Texas, Dec 2001.
9. B.khailany, W.J.Dally et al., Imagine: media processing with streams, IEEE micro, 2001.3/4
10. U.J. Kapasi,W.J.Dally et al., the Imagine stream processor, Proceedings of 2002 International Conference on Computer Design
11. Imagine project, http://cva.stanford.edu/Imagine/project/im_arch.html
12. Joseph A.Fisher, Very Long Instruction Word Architectures and the ELI-512, 25 Years ISCA: Retrospectives and Reprints 1998
13. Li Shen, The Research and Implementation on Key Issues of Dynamic VLIW Architecture, Ph.D. Thesis, Dept. of Computer Science , National University of Defense Technology, Dec 2003.
14. Trip project, http://www.cs.utexas.edu/users/cart/trips/
15. Karthikeyan Sankaralingam et al., Exploiting ILP, TLP, and DLP with the Polymorphous TRIPS architecture, 30th Annual International Symposium on Computer Architecture, May 2003.
16. Mattson, A Programming System for the Imagine Media Processor, Stanford Ph.D. Thesis, 2001
17. Zhengyu Tian, Numerical Simulations of Multiplex Unsteady Flow in Hypersonic Free Stream , Master Thesis, Dept. of Aerospace and Material Engineering, National University of Defense Technology, Dec 2003.
18. S. Rixner et al., A Bandwidth-Efficient Architecture for Media Processing, 31st Int'l Symp, Microarchitecture, IEEE Computer Society Press, 1998
19. W.J.Dally et al., Merrimac: Supercomputing with streams, SC'03, Nov 2003.

Impact of Register-Cache Bandwidth Variation on Processor Performance

Kentaro Hamayasu and Vasily G. Moshnyaga

Dept. of Electronics Engineering and Computer Science, Fukuoka University
8-19-1 Nanakuma, Jonan-ku, Fukuoka 814-0180, JAPAN
{hamayasu, vasily}@vlab.tl.fukuoka-u.ac.jp

Abstract. Modern general-purpose processors employ multi-port register files and multiple functional units to support instruction-level parallelism. Fixed (1 word per cycle) bandwidth between cache and register-file might limit processor's ability in spatial/temporal utilization. This paper presents an experimental study of conventional super-scalar processor architecture to determine benefits that we can expect to achieve by enabling variable data bandwidth between the L1 data cache and the register file. Our results demonstrate that by changing the bus width to 64, 128 and 256 bits we can reduce data traffic between the 32KB register-file and 32KB cache up to 29%, 45% and 53%, respectively, while lowering the program execution time by 8%, 13% and 17% on average in comparison to conventional single-word cache access. An adaptive bandwidth cache capable of adjusting the cache bandwidth to workload variation is also proposed.

1 Introduction

1.1 Motivation

With the higher levels of processor performance and widespread of memory latency tolerance techniques, memory bandwidth emerges as a major performance bottleneck. To avoid long delays associated with memory accesses, modern high-performance processors rely on caches. Conventional caches usually store multi-word data blocks per line while delivering only a single word per access. To select a target n-bit word among a number of candidate words, they employ a multiplexor, as shown in 1. When processor contains a single ALU and a 2-read 1-write port register file, such cache organization is reasonable, since no more than one data word is usually needed per cycle. The disparity between the size of data block stored within cache and the size of data delivered to register file is not only invisible but necessary in order to reduce the cost of bus and the I/O pins. However, when processors contain 8 functional units and an 8 read 4 write port register file (e.g. Alpha21264), the fixed (one word) cache bandwidth might lead to performance loss, especially in applications where large Instruction-Level Parallelism (ILP) is possible [1]. For example, Burger et al [2] report between 11% and 31% of the total memory stalls observed in several SPEC benchmarks

P.-C. Yew and J. Xue (Eds.): ACSAC 2004, LNCS 3189, pp. 212–225, 2004.
© Springer-Verlag Berlin Heidelberg 2004

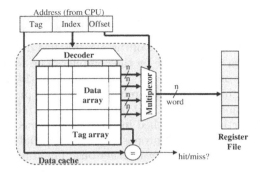

Fig. 1. Cache organization

are due to insufficient memory bandwidth. Rather than rely solely on wider and faster caches and register files, an alternative is to use existing memory bandwidth more efficiently. The main purpose of this paper is to investigate how the cache/register-file bandwidth affects the performance of conventional superscalar processor across SPEC95 benchmarks and to propose cache architecture capable to adapt the bandwidth to workload variation.

1.2   Related Research

A lot of work has been dedicated in the past to analysis of processor-memory interface. McCalpin [3] used the STREAM benchmark to demonstrate that processors had become increasingly unbalanced because of the limited memory bandwidth. Burger, et al [2] simulated on SPEC benchmarks the data traffic dependency on cache block size, associativity, replacement policy, write policy, etc. and proposed three policies (dual-size fetching, subblock prefetching and bus prioritization) to improve L1-L2 memory system interface. Huang and Shen [4] studied what they called intrinsic bandwidth requirement by directly measuring the reuse of values. Ding and Kennedy [5]evaluated the demand and supply of data bandwidth of several scientific kernels through a performance model called balance, and demonstrated the serious performance constraint due to the lack of memory bandwidth. To reduce the memory transfers they advocated compiler-based program transformation such as reuse-based computation fusion and write-back reduction. Johnson, et al, [6] presented a framework for automatic control of cache management techniques capable of determining data placement in run-time. The need to use super-words (i.e. data objects with the size larger than machine words) in order to improve the performance of media programs has been studied in [7].

Several MIPS processor [8] utilizes multiple cache line sizes which are configurable at boot time to minimize the cache miss rate. Virtual Cache Lines (VCL) [9] supports a fixed cache block size for normal references, and fetches multiple sequential cache blocks when the compiler detects high spatial reuse. The line size is sent to the processor at run time by special instructions. The stride prefetching cache [10] also utilizes specific hardware to change the line size based on profiling or other compiler transformations. In [11] is proposed to vary line size based on spatial locality of the miss fetched data, which is detected from the access pattern to the cache by the compiler. The selective sub-blocking technique relies either on hardware [12], [13] or software [14] predictors to track the portions of cache blocks that are referenced by the processor. On a cache miss, the predictors are consulted and only previously referenced (and possibly discontinuous) portions are fetched into the cache, thus conserving memory bandwidth. A sectored cache [15]is proposed to access variable-sized fine-grained data through the annotated memory instructions. The dual data cache [16] selects between two caches, also in hardware, tuned for either spatial locality or temporal locality. These techniques employ line-size selection algorithms that are designed for affine array references and are thus targeted to numeric codes. Run-time adaptive cache management scheme is presented in [6].

1.3   Contribution

This paper presents an experimental study of data cache accesses in conventional super-scalar architecture to determine benefits that we can expect to achieve by enabling variable data bandwidth between the L1 data cache and the register file. Similarly to [1], we analyze performance of modern super-scalar processor using a set of SPEC95 benchmarks. In contrast to previous studies which investigated bandwidth variation between cache and main-memory, we centralize here on bandwidth between data cache and register file. Moreover, unlike [14, 15], we neither employ specific compiler transformations nor restrict ourselves to specific multimedia applications. The study report on unexploited bandwidth potential, observed on SPEC95 benchmarks, and proposes new cache architecture capable of adapting the cache-register bandwidth to workload variation.

The paper is organized as follows. Section 2 presents our simulation methodology. Section 3 shows the results. Section 4 outlines the proposed adaptive bandwidth cache. Section 5 concludes the paper.

2   Methodology

2.1   Simulation Environment

We used SimpleScalarfs [10] sim-outorder to collect our results. SimpleScalar provides a simulation environment for modern out-of-order processors with speculative execution. The simulated processor contains a unified active instruction list, issue queue, and rename register file in one unit called the reservation update unit (RUU). The RUU is similar to the Metaflow DRIS (deferred-scheduling, register-renaming instruction shelf) [11] and the HP PA-8000 IRB (instruction reorder buffer). Separate banks of 32 integer and floating point registers make up the architected register file and are only written on commit. Table 1 summarizes the important features of the simulated processor. The baseline configuration parameters are roughly those of a modern out-of-order processor.

Table 1. Baseline configuration of simulated processor

Parameter	Value
RUU size	80 instructions
Load/store queue size	40
Fetch queue size	8 instructions
Fetch width	4 instructions/cycle
Decode width	4 instructions/cycle
Issue width	4 instructions/cycle (out-of-order)
Commit width	4 instructions/cycle (in-order)
Functional units	4 Integer ALUs (arithmetic, logical, shift, memory, branch ops), 1 integer multiply/divide
Branch Prediction	Combining: 4K 2-bit selector, 12-bit history; 1K 3-bit local predictor, 10-bit history, 4K 2-bit global predictor, 12-bit history
Register file (2 banks)	32 int. registers, 32 fp. registers
Status	6 registers
L1 data-cache	16K, s-way (LRU), 32B blocks, 1 cycle latency
L1 instruction-cache	16K, 2-way (LRU), 32B blocks, 1 cycle latency
L2 cache	Not available
Memory	18 cycles

In our simulation we assumed that:

1. The size of the register file is sufficient for processing the programs;
2. The number of accessing ports in RF is sufficient to run the program without port-sharing hazards;
3. Simultaneous register file accesses can be executed in parallel;
4. The data located in the same cache block can be loaded from the cache in parallel.

We experimented with four sizes of processor-cache bus (32 bit, 64 bit, 128bit, 256bit), and four values of data cache associativity (s), namely, $s=1$ (direct map cache), and $s=2$, 4, 8 (set-associative cache).

2.2 Benchmarks

A goal of this study is to investigate the impact of cache-RF bandwidth on processor performance even in applications outside the multimedia domain. We experimented with seven typical SPEC95 benchmark programs representative for both integer and floating point applications [13]. The training input sets (*train*) were selected for the benchmarks because they did not take too long to simulate to completion while maintaining behavior to simulating the reference

Table 2. Benchmarks and descriptions

Benchmark	Description	Symbol	Inst.($\times 10^6$)	%mem	%loads
Integer benchmarks (CINT95)					
129.compress	Compresses large text files (16MB) using adaptive Limpel-Ziv coding	comp95	35.7	37.4	64.9
130.li	Lisp interpreter	li	183.3	42.5	62.9
132.ijpeg	Performs jpeg image compression with various parameters.	ijpeg	1462.5	25.5	69.2
147.vortex	Builds and manipulates three interrelated databases.	vortex	2520.2	52.6	58.6
Floating point benchmarks (CFP95)					
102.swim	Solves shallow water equations using finite difference approximations.	swim	849,9	31.0	77.8
107.mgrid	Calculation of a 3D potential field in a 513x513 grid	mgrid	14292,3	36.9	96.2
110.applu	Solves matrix system with pivoting.	applu	531.9	25.5	81.5

data sets in full. Since our focus was on the processor-cache interface, we chose the workloads that sustain high miss rates. Table 2 characterizes the benchmarks in terms of the total amount of instructions executed, the percentage of memory instructions and the ratio of load operations among the total memory operations. Table 3 lists the average miss ratio obtained for 32KB cache (32B block size) by using the sim-cheetah simulator [2]. Each benchmark was run to completion.

2.3   Evaluation Approach

Our goal was to simulate the impact of cache-RF bandwidth on the processor performance. We modified the cache.c and sim-outorder programs of the Simple-Scalar simulator [12] to dynamically count the data-transfers between register-file and L1-data cache as well as bus utilization while varying the bit-sizes of bus, which connects the register file and cache. The data bandwidth was measured as the number of machine words which can be transferred in parallel between the register-file and cache due to both load and store operations. For the given bus limit of 256 bits, we used eight counters, which enumerated data transfers of 1, 2, 3c 8 machine words in size, respectively. We assumed that the data size of the first reference R[0] to cache block was always one word wide. Whenever the next cache reference R[j] was encountered, we checked whereas it was of the same type (e.g. load) and to the same cache block as the previous reference, R[i-1]. If all these conditions held, we computed the word-distance (d) between R[i] and the first reference R[0] to the block, and incremented the counter which counted words of size d, while decrementing the counter which counted words of size d-1. Thus, at the end of the program run, the counters indicated the data traffic distribution across the eight bus sizes. The final results displayed also the execution time (measured through the number of total clock cycles) taken by the benchmark; the number of data cache accesses and the bandwidth utilization

Table 3. Miss ratio of 32KB data cache (block size 32B)

Bench-	Miss ratio (%)			
mark	s=1	s=2	s=4	s=8
comp95	5.65	5.47	5.32	5.315
li	0.46	0.23	0.21	0.19
ijpeg	0.83	0.34	0.27	0.25
vortex	1.46	1.01	0.84	0.73
swim	6.65	3.98	3.39	3.29
mgrid	2.44	1.46	0.97	0.98
applu	1.57	1.23	1.22	1.21

ratio (Rj) computed for each benchmark as $R_j = N_i/N_{total} * 100\%$, where N_j is the number of data transfers of size j and N_{total} is the total number of transfers.

3   Results

Figures 2-3 list the simulation results in comparison to the results obtained for conventional 32 bit register-cache communication. We observe that enlarging the bit-width between the L1 data cache and the register file allows us to reduce both the number of cache accesses and, the number of total clock cycles required by the benchmarks. The reduction ratio strongly depends on the benchmarks and the allowable bit-width of cache accesses. The number of cache accesses which can be eliminated by adopting 64bit, 128bit and 256bit wide buses can vary from 31%, 47%, and 53%, respectively, for vortex, down to 8% for *mgrid*. Also, the reduction in clock cycles can be as much as 13%, 18%, 19% (see li benchmark) at 64bit, 128bit and 256bit bus size, respectively, and as low as 4%-6% (for

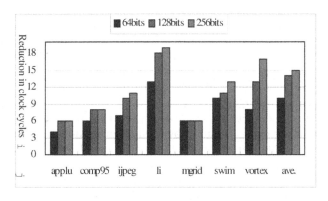

Fig. 2. Reduction in clock cycles in comparison to fixed 32 bit cache bandwidth (direct-map data cache)

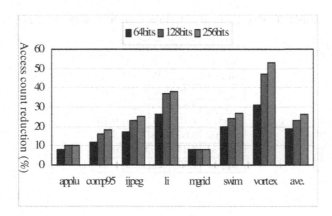

Fig. 3. Reduction in cache accesses (direct-map data cache)

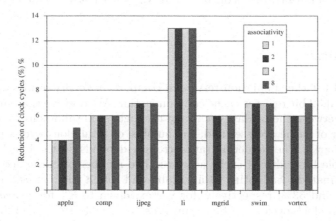

Fig. 4. Impact of cache associativity

applu). The right-most columns (*ave.*) in the figures show the average values across the benchmark. As these results indicate, restricting the cache-register file communication path to 32bits may slower the processor's performance by 10-15% on average, while increasing the cache access count by 17-26%.

To investigate the influence of cache configuration on the results, we repeated simulations by changing associativity of L1 data cache in the baseline processor from 1 to 8. Figure 4 depicts the results for the 64 bit wide bus. We see that the total number of clock cycles required by each program does not depend much on cache associativity. The same trend has been observed for the number of cache accesses as well.

Figure 5 shows the bus utilization statistics. The 32-bit wide cache accesses are the most frequent; they consume from 55% up to 91% of the total data traffic through the bus. When the bus becomes wider, the 64-bit data transfers are replaced by larger data bundles. However, we should note, that accesses

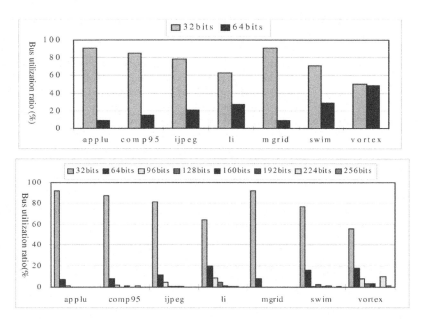

Fig. 5. Bit utilization for 64 bit wide bus (top) and 256bit wide bus (bottom)

wider than 8 bytes in size occur quite rarely (less than 10% of time) in all the benchmarks, but vortex.

To summarize, the results presented in this section have three notable implications:

1. The fixed 32-bit data width between the L1 data cache and register file increases the number of cache accesses by 20-26% on average, slowing the processor by 10-15% in comparison to multi-word transfers even for non-multimedia applications. The required data cache-register file bandwidth is thus significantly larger than that one provided by conventional caches.
2. The cache-register file bandwidth is application-dependent. Fixing the bus size at either extreme (32 or 256 bits) leads either to a poor performance or large area overhead, since multi-byte data transfer occur quite rarely.
3. For almost all the benchmarks, the dual-word data access per clock cycle is sufficient for more than 80% of total cache references. This feature presents an opportunity: if the cache and the register-file could support the dual word traffic, the number of accesses could be reduced by 1/5 on average, thus improving the performance.

These implications lead us to three requirements for on-chip L1-caches. (1) The cache-register file bandwidth should be larger than that of traditional caches, (2) the cache should be managed in such a way as to provide good performance across the entire range of applications, and (3) it should use intelligent (or adaptive) fetching, adjusting its bit-width to application workload without a large

Table 4. A table of instruction set extensions for manipulating AB-cache

Instruction	Explanation
ldw rt, off0(rs), off1	A dual-word load. Access mode, $M = 1$. Data from the cache block pointed to by the block offset bits of $rs + off0$, and by $off1$ is transferred to registers rt, dr, respectively.
sdw rt, off0(rs), off1	A dual word store. Access mode, $M = 1$. Contents of rt and dr are stored into the cache block at locations specified by the block offset bits of $rs + off0$, and by $off1$, respectively.

overhead in area or power. As a solution we propose an adaptive bandwidth cache, described in the next Section.

4 Adaptive Bandwidth Cache

4.1 Main Features

The key idea behind our adaptive bandwidth cache (or AB-cache) is to adjust the size of data transferred from (or to) the cache based on spatial locality of memory accesses. When programs have large spatial locality, the cache provides an extended bandwidth, enabling two adjacent words to be accessed in parallel. On the other hand, when spatial locality is small, it reduces the bandwidth down to a single word per access. The AB-cache is software-centric; it relies on the compiler to statically identify the spatial locality of adjacent memory references and replace the next reference to the same cache block by a register transfer operation. (The approach is similar to cache pre-fetching with the difference that it pre-fetches the register-file not cache. Our approach lets software tell the hardware when to perform dual-word fetch, so instead of accessing the same cache block again, the hardware fetches the data directly from the register-file. We augment the processor state with a special registers, $dr, off1$, which are set by software to temporally keep information about destination register and offset of the adjacent reference, respectively. Note, that software is only made aware of the length of the cache block, but not the total cache capacity or associativity. Table 4 outlines the instruction extensions for using the adaptive cache. (Only word accesses are shown, but half-word accesses are handled analogously). Software places values in the dr as an optional side effect of performing a load or store. A dual-word load or store specifies a full effective virtual address in addition to off1 number. Figure 6 shows an example code and its transformation. As we see the second and third memory references have been replaced by register transfer operation, mv. Note that no additional instructions where added and the performance is identical.

Old code	New code
```sub $sp(64)```	```sub $sp(64)```

```
            Old code                                      New code

sub $sp(64)                      sub $sp(64)
  lw $r1,56($sp)                   ldw $r1,56($sp),4  # 56($sp)→r1, 60($sp)→rd
  lw $r2,60($sp)                   mv  $r2,$rd        # rd →r1
  sw $r2, 4($sp)                   mv  $rd,$r2        # r2 →rd
  sw $r3,12($sp)                   sdw $r2,4($sp),8   # rd→4($sp), 12($sp):=$r3
```

Fig. 6. An example function entry code transformed for dual-word data transfers

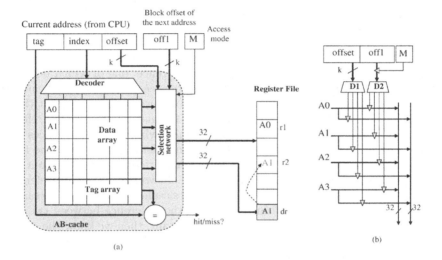

(a)

(b)

Fig. 7. (a) Block-diagram of AB-cache; (b) internal structure of selection network

4.2 Hardware Architecture

Figure 7(a) depicts a block-diagram of the proposed AB-cache. Additionally to the target address, it receives from CPU the block offset of the next reference $(off1)$ and the access mode indicator bit (M), both set by software. (Note that a conventional memory reference has $M=0$). The k-bit values of the offset and off1 determine which words among the 2K candidates in the cache block are accessed in parallel, while the access mode bit (M) indicates whether the cache operates in a conventional (single word) mode or in a dual-word mode. For example, if $offset=0$, $off1=1$, then the second instruction (ldw) of the transformed code in Fig.4,b will force the AB-cache to read two words $(A0, A1)$ in parallel and write them to registers $r1$ and rd, respectively. Figure 7 (b) shows in details the selection network structure, where triangles depict three-state buffers, $D1, D2$ denote decodes. In conventional access mode, the network disables unselective lines from the bus to save power.

4.3 Compiler Support

Determining whether a reference exhibits temporal or spatial locality, and whether this locality is worth being exploited is a well documented research topic [18]-[20]. Similarly to [19], we annotate the references as spatial, if the coefficient of the innermost loop in the reference subscript is smaller than 4 (the cache block size usually considered, i.e.16 bytes corresponding to 4 single precision data word). If the coefficient is parameter, the reference is not tagged spatial. Finding temporal dependences such as self-dependence (x[i],c,x[i]) or a uniformly generated temporal group-dependence (e.g. b(j,i), b(j,i+1)) amounts to simple subscript analysis. These two types of dependences account for a significant fraction of the dependences, as already mentioned in [20].

We use a two step approach to find adjacent cache references which can be performed in parallel. First, we look for two reference, one of which dominates the other, so all paths that cause the subordinate access to be executed cause the dominant to reference to be executed first. Second, we try to prove that the two references always point to the same cache line. In this case, the second reference can be read in parallel with the first. To determine whether two references are to the same cache block, we employ alignment and distance analysis. The former determines the address alignment of each memory reference relative to a cache boundary. The latter detects the byte distance of two static memory references. A load instruction is considered aligned when its cache alignment is the same for each dynamic execution of the instruction. If the difference between two static memory references (address calculations) is constant, then we know the distance between the references. In the initial compiler passes, when array indexes are represented at a high level, we tag them with their source array to aid in distance analysis. We use this tag once the array access has been decomposed into pointer manipulation. For accesses of the form x[i] and x[i+c], our tagging allows us to compute the distance as c. This pattern occurs very frequently in unrolled loops.

Once we know the distance, we can use the alignment to determine if two references are to the same cache line. We find the alignment of the dominant reference relative to the cache line boundary and then find the distance between the subordinate access and the dominant access. Simple arithmetic indicates if the references are on the same cache line. When the distance is 0, we can ignore the alignment information.

5 Estimation

We developed a prototype compiler to output instrumented C-code and then run the modified Simple-Scalar simulator to estimate benefits of the AB-cache. No extra code transformations have been applied to facilitate the spatial reuse and increase aligned memory operations. We simulated the baseline processor architecture (Tables 1, 2 $s=1$) and compared the results with the results reported in Section 3 for the direct-map cache. We assumed that dual-cache load and store instructions add 1 clock-cycle to the pipeline. Figure 6 outline the results. Though the proposed cache performs by 5-10% worst in comparison to ideal

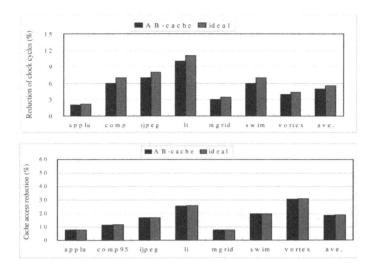

Fig. 8. Normalized execution time (top) and cache access reduction (bottom) in comparison to potential results for 64 bit-wide bus

execution time (i.e. the total number of cycles) presented in Section 2, the benefit of using it is high: in comparison to conventional cache it improves processor performance by 5-15%, lowering the total number of L1 data by a half.

6   Conclusion

This study indicated that fixed 32-bit data width between the L1 data cache and register file increases the number of cache accesses by 20-26% on average, slowing the processor by 10-15% in comparison to multi-word transfers even for non-multimedia applications. The results pointed out that the cache-register file bandwidth should be at least twice larger than currently used one in order to efficiently support even non-memory intensive applications. As a solution, we presented a dual-word cache capable of adaptively adjusting the bandwidth to workload variation. To use the AB-cache we need both the hardware and the compiler modifications. However, it is quite promising. Even our preliminary work had not incorporated program transformations (e.g. [5], [7], which proved to be effective in to facilitating spatial reuse of memory accesses, we could reduce the number of accesses to L1 data cache by half while improving the processor performance by 5-15%.

The mechanism we discussed could be extended to achieve cache bandwidth larger than dual-word. Large improvement is also expected from incorporating code transformations into the modified compiler. Furthermore, with a proper modification of the register-renaming algorithms, we can eliminate many register-transfer operations (currently added to the code) and reduce the number of data transfers at least twice. Moreover, the existing register files already support multi-word reads and writes so moving the data to and from dr register looks redundant. Future work also will be dedicated to studying effects of AB-cache on power consumption.

References

1. H.Liao, A.Wolfe, Available Parallelism in video applications, *Proc. Micro-97*, pp.321-329.
2. D.Burger, J.R.Goodman, and A.Kagi, Memory Bandwidth limitations of Future Microrocessors, *Proc. Annual 24th Int. Symp. On Computer Acrhitecture*, pp.78-89, 1996.
3. J.McCalpin, Sustainable memory bandwidth in current high-performance computers. http://reality.sgi.com/mccalpin_asd/papers/bandwidth.ps, 1995.
4. S.A.Huang and J.P.Chen, The intrinsic bandwidth requirements of ordinary programs. *Proc. 7th Int.Conf. on Arch.Support for Programming Languages and Operating Systems*, 1996
5. Ding and K.Kennedy, Memory Bandwidth Bottleneck and Its Amelioration by a Compiler, *Proc. Int.Parrallel and Distributed Process. Symp.*, 2000.
6. T.L.Johnson and W.W.Hwu, Run-time adaptive cache hierarchy management via reference analysis, *Proc. Annual 24th Int. Symp. On Computer Acrhitecture*, June 1997.
7. S.Larsen, S.Amarasinghe, Exploiting Superword Level Parallelism with Multimedia Instruction Sets, *Proc. ACM SIGPLAN Conf.on Progr.Language Design and Implementation*, 2000, pp.145-156.
8. MIPS Corporation, MIPS R3000 hardware manual, MIPS Corporation.
9. K.Inoue, K.Kai, and K.Murakami, High bandwidth, variable line-cache architecture for merged DRAM/logic LSIs, *IEICE Transactions on Electronics*, E81-C(9), pp.1438-1447, Sep.1999.
10. T.-F.Chen and J.-L.Baer, Reducing memory latency via non-blocking and prefetching caches, *Tech.Rep. 92-06-03, Dept. Computer Science and Engineering, Univ.Washington*, Seattle, WA, June 1992.
11. A.Veidenbaum, W.Tang, R.Gupta, A.Nicolau, and X.Ji, Adapting cache line size to application behavior, *Proc. Int. Conf. on Supercomputing*, pp.145-154, 1999.
12. D.Burger, Hardware Techniques to Improve the Performance of the Processor/Memory Interface, *Tech. Rep. Computer Science Dept., University of Wisconsin-Madison*, Dec. 1998.
13. S.Kumar and C.Wilkerson, Exploiting Spatial Locality in Data Caches using Spatial Footprints, *Proc. 25th Annual Int. Symp. On Computer Acrhitecture*, pp. 357-368, June 1998.
14. D.Agarwal, and D.Yeung, Exploiting Application-Level Information to reduce memory bandwidth consumption, *Technical Report UMIACS-TR-2002, Univ.of Maryland, Inst. For Advanced Computer Studies*, 2002.
15. A.R.Lebeck, D.Raymond, C-L.Yang, M.S.Thottethodi, *Annotated Memory References: A Mechanism for Informed Cache Management*, 1999
16. A.Gonzales, A.Aliagas, and M.Valero, A data cache with multiple caching strategies tuned to different types of locality, *Proc. 1995 Int.Conf. on Supercomputing*, pp.338-347, July 1995.
17. V. Popescu, M. Schultz, J. Spracklen, G. Gibson, B. Lightner, and D. Isaman. The Metaflow architecture. *IEEE Micro*, pp.10-13, 63-73, June 1991

18. J.Ferrante, V.Sarkar, W.Trash. On Estimating and Enhancing Cache Effectiveness, *Proc.4th Workshop on Languages and Compilers for Parallel Computing*, 1991.
19. O.Temmam and N.Drach, Software Assistance for Data Caches, *Proc. IEEE HPCA*, 1995.
20. M.S.Lam, et al., The SUIF compiler System, 1992-2001. http://www-suif.stanford.edu

Exploiting Free Execution Slots on EPIC Processors for Efficient and Accurate Runtime Profiling

Youfeng Wu and Yong-Fong Lee

Corporate Technology Group (CTG), Software and Solutions Group (SSG)
Intel Corporation
2200 Mission College Blvd
Santa Clara, CA 95054
{youfeng.wu, yong-fong.lee}@intel.com

Abstract. Dynamic optimization relies on runtime profile information to improve the performance of program execution. Traditional profiling techniques incur significant overhead and are not suitable for dynamic optimization. In this paper, we propose a new profiling technique that incorporates the strength of both software and hardware to achieve near-zero overhead profiling. The compiler passes profiling requests as a few bits of information in branch instructions to the hardware, and the hardware uses the free execution slots available in a user program to execute profiling operations. We have implemented the compiler instrumentation of this technique using an Itanium research compiler. Our result shows that the accurate block profiling incurs very little overhead to the user program in terms of the program scheduling cycles. For example, the average overhead is 0.6% for the SPECint95 benchmarks. The hardware support required for the new profiling is practical. We believe this will enable many profile-driven dynamic optimizations for EPIC processors such as the Itanium processors.

1 Introduction

For EPIC processors like the Itanium ([3][13][18]), the compiler needs a certain amount of knowledge about a user program to generate more efficient code. A static compiler obtains this information from profiling the program with its training data. A growing interest has been moving toward profiling and optimization at runtime with actual input data. This "runtime profiling and optimization" environment requires the collection of program profiles at runtime efficiently. The most commonly used profiles are block/edge and path profiles. The best-known edge and path profiling algorithms are from [4] and [5]. However, the instrumented code in the user program typically incurs about 30% overhead with block/edge profiling and 40% with path profiling. Our experience with Itanium processors shows that the overhead of block profiling ranges from 14% to 42% for SPECint95 benchmarks. In the context of dynamic optimization, this overhead is not acceptable during the execution of a deployed user program.

Recent researches have focused on sampling based profiling to reduce the profiling overhead ([1][19]). Sampling based profiling could potentially lose profile accuracy.

P.-C. Yew and J. Xue (Eds.): ACSAC 2004, LNCS 3189, pp. 226–240, 2004.
© Springer-Verlag Berlin Heidelberg 2004

It also requires operating system supports and incurs noticeable runtime overhead due to software interrupts. We are interested in a method such that accurate profiles can be obtained without OS support and without noticeable runtime overhead.

Here we present an approach that combines both hardware and software support to greatly reduce profiling overhead. We first focus on *block profiling*, namely to find the execution frequencies of the basic blocks in a user program, and later extend the technique to edge profiling. To collect block profile information, the traditional profiling technique inserts a load, an increment, and a store to each block that needs profiling. In our new profiling technique, the compiler passes profiling requests as a few bits in branch instructions to the hardware, and the hardware uses the free execution slots available during the execution of the user program to collect profile information. With this technique, the program execution with profiling can run almost as fast as without profiling. This will enable many profile-driven dynamic optimizations for EPIC processors such as the Itanium processors.

As an example, we look at the control flow graph (CFG) in Fig. 1. We only need to profile blocks b, c, d, f, and h, and the frequencies for other blocks can be derived from those of the profiled blocks. The traditional profiling technique would insert three instructions in each of the profiled blocks to load a counter from memory, increment the counter, and store the counter to memory. The inserted profiling code is listed in Fig. 1(a). For our new technique, we first assign ID's to the blocks that need to be profiled. The ID's are in the range of [1, ..., number of profiled blocks]. If a block already has a branch instruction and the profile ID fits into the ID field, we encode its ID in the field. The modified branch instructions are listed in Fig. 1(b). At runtime, the hardware derives the memory address of a profile counter from the ID field in a branch instruction and automatically generates load/increment/store instructions. These hardware-generated profile update operations are executed in free execution slots available in the user program.

Our proposed technique achieves "near zero" profiling overhead by combining two collaborative techniques: (1) powerful compiler analysis to insert minimal profiling instructions, and (2) hardware that asynchronously executes profile update operations in free execution slots available during the user program execution. The following are several interesting issues solved in our approach.

We need an algorithm to select a minimal number of blocks to profile so that the execution frequencies for other blocks can be derived from them. Furthermore, we require as many selected blocks to contain branch instructions as possible. In the following we will call a block selected for profiling a *profiled block*, which is further classified as a *branch block* or a *non-branch block* depending on whether it contains a branch instruction.

Although most profiled blocks have branch instructions in them, some may contain no branch instructions to encode the profile ID's. We provide an explicit instruction (prof_id) to pass profile ID's to the hardware for non-branch profiled blocks. Our experiment shows that we only need to use the prof_id instructions in very few blocks. We will use the term *profiling instructions* to refer to the instructions inserted by the compiler for passing profiling needs to the hardware. They include the *prof_id* instruction as well as the *initprof* and *setoffset* instructions that will be described later. The hardware will translate the information carried by profiling instructions into *profile update operations* to manipulate profile counters.

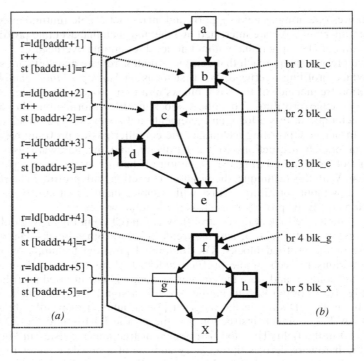

Fig. 1. An illustration example

A branch instruction may allow only for a few bits of profile ID. The number of profiled blocks in a function may be more than that the ID field can represent. We apply an algorithm to partition a CFG into regions such that the ID field can adequately represent the total number of ID's in each region. We also pass additional information in the region entry blocks to assist the hardware to derive profile counter addresses from these ID's.

The hardware intercepts profiling requests and generates instructions to update profile counters. Although the *profile update operations* are inserted into free execution slots available in a user program at runtime, they may have longer latencies than instructions from the user program. We do not want their execution to delay the user program. To achieve this, we devise a method for the hardware to arrange the update operations so that they do not stall the execution of the user program.

The rest of the paper is organized as follows. Section 2 describes relevant background material about Itanium. Section 3 discusses the architectural support. Section 4 presents the details of our new profiling technique, including the compiler algorithms for block selection and graph partitioning, and the hardware support. Section 5 gives our experimental results. Section 6 extends our technique to do edge frequency profiling. Section 7 describes related work. Section 8 gives concluding remarks and future work.

2   Relevant Itanium Features

Itanium [13] provides many features to aid the compiler in enhancing and exploiting instruction-level parallelism (ILP). These include an explicitly parallel instruction set (EPIC), large register files, and architectural support for predication, speculation, and software pipelining. An Itanium program must explicitly specify *instruction groups*, each of which is a sequence of instructions that have no register flow and output dependencies. Instruction groups are delimited by *architectural stops* in the code. Because an instruction group has no register flow and output dependencies, its instructions can be issued in parallel without hardware checks for register dependencies.

The compiler divides an instruction group into *bundles*. A bundle contains three instruction slots as shown below. Each instruction slot takes 41 bits. Most instructions take one instruction slot, while those taking a link-time symbol as an operand may take two slots. The template field specifies the mapping of instruction slots to execution unit types.

slot1	slot2	slot3	template

We have observed a significant number of free execution slots available in many machine cycles that can be utilized for profiling. The free execution slots arise from the following causes:

- Not all the possible mappings of instructions into functional units are permitted. For example, a bundle can contain at most two load operations. Thus an instruction group with three load instructions must be assigned into two bundles. This would leave three free execution slots in the two bundles if there were no other instructions in the group.
- When the number of instructions in an instruction group is not a multiple of the bundle size, the last bundle for the instruction group will have free execution slots due to fragmentation.
- The ILP available in applications may not be sufficient to fully utilize the machine width all the time. This is especially the case for control-intensive scalar code. Incidentally, an earlier study conducted by Diep et al. [9] reports an IPC of 1.05–1.25 for four integer benchmarks and 1.0–1.9 for three floating-point benchmarks on a 4-way PowerPC 620 processor. In [8] it is reported that on large commercial applications, average cycles-per-instruction (CPI) values may be as high as 2.5 or 3. With 4-way instruction issue, a CPI of 3 means that only one issue slot in every 12 is being put to good use.

To reduce code size, Itanium processors allow for in-bundle stops to pack dependent instructions into the same bundle to reduce explicit no-ops. The hardware dynamically inserts no-ops when the bundle is expanded before execution. We will modify the no-op insertion logic to insert profiling operations when no-ops are needed.

Another relevant Itanium architectural feature is the "multi-way branches", in which multiple branch instructions are placed in the same bundle and executed in the same cycle. Multi-way branches are helpful in reducing control dependence height and should be used as much as possible to increase ILP. Our partitioning algorithm will preserve multi-way branches.

3   Profiling Instructions and Registers

In this section, we outline extensions to the Itanium architecture required by our profiling technique. We assume that the processor has a special 64-bit status register dedicated for profiling. We call it the *profile information register (pir)*. This register contains the following fields with their respective widths in bit:

base_address 40	unused 3	offset 20	flag 1

In addition to an extension to the branch instruction to use the 8-bit branch hints in the current Itanium branch instructions for profile ID's, we also need several new instructions given in the following table.

Instructions	Descriptions
prof_id ID	Pass the profile ID to the hardware.
initprof baseAddr	Initialize pir.base_address as baseAddr.
setoffset offset	Set pir.offset as offset.
startprof	Set pir.flag as 1 to activate or resume profiling.
stopprof	Reset pir.flag as 0 to deactivate profiling.

By default, the value of the ID field in a branch instruction is zero. A non-zero ID is set for a profiled block. We assume that the ID field uses K bits, where K >=1 and is assumed to be K = 8 in this study. For a non-branch block, we use the instruction "prof_id ID" to explicitly pass a profile ID to the hardware.

The pir register is preserved on function calls. On entering a function, the value of pir except for its flag is initialized as zero. We require that each profiled function execute the "*initprof baseAddr*" instruction in its entry block to initialize pir.base_address. Normally, the "*startprof*" instruction is executed in the main function of a program to activate profiling. The dynamic optimizer can execute the "*stopprof*" and "*startprof*"instruction to stop and resume profiling.

We also need a few scratch profile registers, which will be described later. Note that none of the profiling instructions will affect the correctness of the user program. They can be safely ignored by a particular processor implementation if needed.

4   Details of Our Profiling Technique

With the new profiling instructions and registers, our technique performs compiler analysis and instrumentation to place profiling instructions in a user program. The compiler also allocates memory space for recording profile data. When the instrumented program runs, the hardware intercepts the profiling requests and translates them into profile update operations. The update operations are inserted into the free execution slots available during the execution of the user program.

4.1   Compiler Instrumentation

The compiler instrumentation performs the following tasks:

- Selecting profiled blocks
- Partitioning CFG into regions
- Inserting profiling instructions and adding profile ID's to branch instructions in profiled blocks

4.1.1   Selecting Profiled Blocks

The compiler first selects a set of profiled blocks. We extend the Knuth algorithm in [12] to find the minimal set of profiled blocks in a function. The original Knuth algorithm performs the following steps:

- Partition the CFG nodes into equivalence classes. Nodes b1 and b2 are equivalent, denoted by b1 ≡ b2, if there is another block b such that both b->b1 and b->b2 are CFG edges.
- Construct a graph with the equivalence classes as nodes and the original CFG blocks as edges. Select a maximal spanning tree from the graph. The original CFG blocks corresponding to the edges on the spanning tree do not need profiling, and all other blocks are profiled blocks.
- For each block that does not need profiling, find a set of profiled blocks from which the profile information for this block can be derived.

In general, it may be impossible to require that every profiled block contain a branch instruction. We thus extend Knuth's algorithm such that as many profiled blocks have branch instructions in them as possible. This is achieved by modifying the second step of the algorithm. Namely, during the maximal spanning tree computation, we treat blocks containing no branch instructions as having a very large weight. Consequently, it is more likely for these blocks to be included in the maximal spanning tree and thus excluded from profiling.

Assume n branch blocks and m non-branch blocks in a function are selected for profiling. Then the compiler allocates n + m memory locations to store profile information for these blocks.

4.1.2   Partitioning CFG into Regions

The input to the partitioning algorithm is a CFG, and each CFG block is marked as either a profiled block or not, and, for a profiled block, as either a branch or non-branch block. We want to partition the CFG into single-entry regions such that the number of regions is small and each region contains no more than $2^K - 1$ branch blocks.

Lee and Ryder have formulated the problem of partitioning an acyclic flow graph into single-entry regions subject to the size constraint [14]. They proposed two approximation algorithms for the problem, which was shown to be NP-hard. Here we are interested in partitioning a cyclic flow graph, and only branch blocks will be counted in the size constraint. Thus, we extend their algorithms by considering the following factors:

- Rather than limiting the number of blocks in a region, we limit the number of branch blocks.
- Cycles are allowed within a region as long as the region has only one single entry block.
- When two or three blocks are grouped together to allow for multi-way branches, we force them into the same region. This is to avoid using a block later in the sequence as a region entry block. Otherwise, the profiling instruction to be inserted in the region entry block will prevent it from being grouped with the earlier branch(es).

The extended algorithms partition the CFG into single-entry regions such that each region contains no more than 2^K-1 *branch blocks*. Note that a region may contain any number of non-branch blocks. Assume t regions are formed. We name the regions as R0, R1,…, Rt-1. For profiling efficiency, we name the region headed by the function entry block as R0. The number of branch blocks in Ri is denoted by NB(Ri) and the number of non-branch blocks in Ri is denoted by NN(Ri). Let size(Ri) = NB(Ri) + NN(Ri).

For each region Ri, the compiler assigns an ID number in the range of [1,.., NB(Ri)] to each of the branch blocks, and an ID number in the range [NB(Ri)+1, size(Ri)] to each of the non-branch blocks. Remember that ID=0 is assigned to branches that do not need profiling. Let ID(b, Ri) be the ID number of a profiled block b in Ri.

Assume the starting address of the profile storage is base_address. For the j'th block bij in region Ri, the starting address of its profile counters is "base_address + ID(bij, Ri) - 1 + $\sum_{v=0}^{i-1} size(R_v)$."

4.1.3 Inserting Profiling Instructions and Modifying Branch Instructions

The compiler inserts an "initprof baseAddr" instruction in the function entry block to load the base address of the profile counters storage into the profile information register.

For each region Ri, 0<i<t, the compiler inserts a "setoffset $\sum_{v=0}^{i-1} size(R_v)$" instruction

in its entry block. We do not need to perform this operation for R0 since its offset is zero.

For each profiled block bij in region Ri, if it is a branch block, the compiler modifies the branch instruction of the block from "br target" to "br ID(bij, Ri), target"; otherwise, the compiler inserts an instruction "prof_id ID(bij, Ri)" into the block bij.

A profiled block may have more than one profiling instruction inserted. For example, it is possible that an entry block with an "initprof" instruction also has a "prof_id" instruction inserted. We can combine the two instructions by extending the initprof and setoffet instructions to carry an ID field. In this case, the following peephole optimization can be applied.

- If an "initprof addr" and a "prof_id ID" are in the same block, replace them with "initprof addr, ID".

- If a "setoffset offset" and a "prof_id ID" are in the same block, replace them with "setoffset offset, ID".

With the peephole optimization, a profiled block will have at most one profiling instruction inserted. These peephole optimizations have not been implemented for this paper.

4.2 Profiling Hardware

At runtime, when a branch instruction "br ID, target" or "prof_id ID" retires, the profiling hardware first checks pir.flag. If the flag is set, it then checks the ID value. If the ID value is zero, the hardware does not need to profile the block. Otherwise, the hardware generates the address of the profile counter as

$$address = pir.base\_address + pir.offset + ID - 1$$

and performs the following update operation.

$$++(*address)$$

We want the hardware to perform the update operations asynchronously with the user program so as not to impact critical user program execution. One way is to utilize the free execution slots available in a EPIC processor. In this method, each update operation can be implemented by the following sequence of operations (assume the profiling hardware places the address of a profile counter into register raddr):

$$r = ld \ [raddr]$$
$$r = r + 1$$
$$st \ [raddr] = r$$

These operations are placed into a buffer, and the dispatch unit of the processor inserts the buffered operations into the user program execution stream whenever free execution slots become available. Notice that the update operations do not have to complete within a time limit if no free execution slots are available, as long as they eventually complete. However, the buffer is of a limited size and it may fill up when free execution slots are limited. When that happens, we can discard some of the buffered operations. This will reduce profiling accuracy but may still be acceptable if a majority of the profile update operations are performed. This approach is shown in Fig. 2.

Note that we will need to use an address register and an accumulator register during the three update operations (consisting of a load L, an increment I, and a store S) to temporarily store the address and the loaded value. If we are to interleave the operations from multiple updates, we will need multiple address and accumulator registers for simultaneously executing the update sequences.

To minimize the impact of the update operations on the user program execution, we mark the loads in the update operations to bypass the first level cache (L1) so they won't compete for cache resources with loads in user programs*. Therefore, we need to arrange the corresponding increment and store operations C and C + 1 cycles, respectively, later than the load instruction, where C is the L1 cache miss latency,

---

* Itanium processor allows a load to carry a hint to indicate no temporal locality at the L1 (nt1), L2 (nt2), or all cache levels (nta).

such as 5 cycles. The update operations can be arranged in a simple pipeline to hide the latencies.

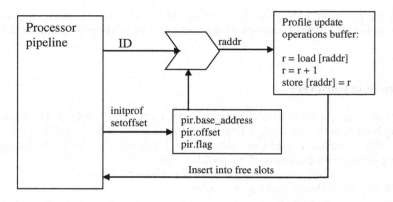

Fig. 2. Profiling hardware

Assume we have C address registers and C accumulator registers that are used in a round-robin fashion. Namely, if the update operations i (consisting of L_i, I_i, and S_i) use register j, then the update operations i+1 (consisting of L_{i+1}, I_{i+1}, and S_{i+1}) will use the register (j+1) modulo C. We will arrange the profile update operations buffer as a circular buffer. Each entry is a three-instruction tuple, consisting of "L_{i+C+1}, I_{i+1}, S_i", where L_{i+C+1} is the load for update i+C+1, I_{i+1} is the increment operation for update i+1, and S_i is the store operation for update i. As long as we insert instructions into free execution slots in the buffered instruction order, and we do not insert more than three instructions in a single execution cycle, the update operations will produce the correct profiling result. This pipelined execution is illustrated in Fig. 3 and it will hide the entire C-cycle latencies of the loads. If we use more address and accumulator registers we can insert more instructions in a single execution cycle.

Although we expect the current 6-wide issue Itanium processor to have enough free execution slots for the profiling update operations, for a narrower processor that do not have enough free execution slots available, we can use dedicated hardware to perform the update operations. The dedicated hardware only needs to perform the update efficiently so it can be easily built. With the dedicated hardware, little or none of the profile update operations will be discarded, and the resulting profile data can be more accurate.

```
L1  ..  ..
L2  ..  ..
L3  I1  ..
L4  I2  S1
..  I3  S2
..  I4  S3
....    S4
```

Fig. 3. Pipelined execution of profile update operations

This approach uses the hardware as shown in Fig. 4 to perform the update operations. After the profile counter ID is used to compute the profile data address addr, the update operation ++(*addr) is sent to the profile update operations buffer and performed by the dedicated hardware. The dedicated hardware performs the update directly without bringing data to the processor and then writing it back.

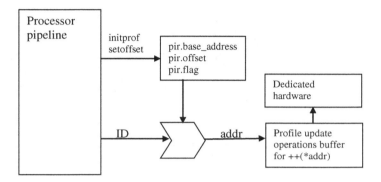

Fig. 4. Dedicated profiling hardware

5   Experimental Results

We have implemented the compiler instrumentation described earlier in an Itanium research compiler. Our experiment used the SPECint95 benchmarks as the test programs.

Table 1 shows the compile-time statistics for our profiling technique. With the extended Knuth algorithm, we need to statically select, on average, about 38% of the blocks for profiling, and only 2.3% of the profiled blocks do not contain branch instructions. The profiled blocks selected account for about 30% of the total *dynamic* block frequency.

By using an 8-bit ID field in branch instructions, each function can be partitioned into 1.15 regions on average. About 3.55% of the blocks are function entry blocks, and 0.11% of the blocks are region entry but not function entry blocks. Overall, about 5.8% of the blocks need to have profiling instructions inserted.

Since the new profiling technique requires hardware support and we don't have a cycle-accurate simulator to evaluate this new technique, we use "schedule length" increase as our metrics for the profiling overhead. For statically scheduled EPIC microprocessors, the schedule length represents the portion of the execution time spent in the CPU core, without considering such microarchitectural stalls as branch miss, cache miss, etc. We believe that the new profiling technique should not noticeably increase the stalls related to branch and cache misses, and therefore the overhead in term of "schedule length" should be a good estimate of the actual overhead in term of overall performance.

In Fig. 5, we compare the overhead of our new profiling technique with that of the traditional block profiling (with Knuth's optimization). Both are compared against the baseline with no profiling. The traditional block profiling incurs about 22%

Table 1. Static statistics for profiling instrumentation

SPECint95	%blk profiled	%blk w/ prof_id	%blk w/ initprof	%blk w/ setoffset
compress	41.4	3.3	4.07	0.00
gcc	39.5	2.2	2.32	0.71
go	44.8	4.4	2.46	0.02
ijpeg	36.4	4.6	5.71	0.00
li	32.0	0.8	6.16	0.00
m88ksim	38.4	1.3	3.79	0.36
perl	39.4	0.8	1.64	4.50
vortex	33.5	1.0	2.24	0.15
Average	38.2	2.3	3.55	0.11

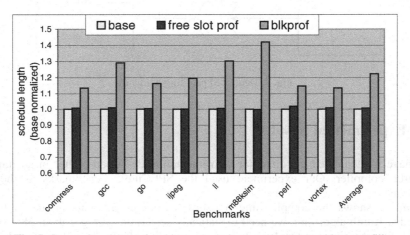

Fig. 5. Comparing the overhead in our technique and traditional block profiling

slowdown on average, ranging from 14% for compress to 42% for m88ksim. By contrast, our method has an average overhead of 0.6% because almost all the initprof, setoffset, and prof_id instructions can be scheduled into free execution slots at compile time, without increasing code size and execution cycles.

6   Extension to Edge Profiling

We may extend our technique for block profiling to do edge profiling. In this case, the profiled edges can be identified with an algorithm proposed in [4]. The CFG partitioning algorithm will be modified to use the number of profiled branch edges as the size constraints. The branch instruction will carry one of the following hints:

- "tk", for profiling the taken edge when the branch takes
- "nt", for profiling the not-taken edge when the branch fall-through
- "both", for profiling the taken edge when the branch takes and the not-taken edge when the branch fall-through

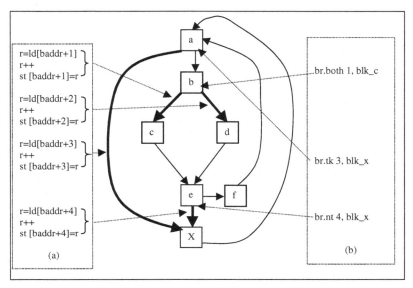

Fig. 6. An example of collaborative profiling

Notice that the "branch.both ID target" instruction may modify two profile counters, one for the taken edge and the other for the fall-through edge. We require that the two edges be assigned two consecutive IDs so the hardware can determine the counter addresses easily.

We use the control flow graph (CFG) in Fig. 6 to describe the edge profiling technique. In this CFG, we only need to profile the edges a•x, b•c, b•d, and e•x, and the frequencies for other edges can be derived from those of the profiled edges. The traditional edge profiling technique would insert three instructions in each of the profiled edges to load a counter from memory, increment the counter, and store the counter back to memory. The inserted profiling code is listed in Fig. 6 (a). Our new technique only needs to modify three branch instructions as shown in Fig. 6 (b). The processor derives the profile operations from the modified branch instructions and executes them without impacting the execution of the user program.

7   Related Work

Software only approaches to profiling can be found in [4][5]. They slow down user programs by about 30% so they may not suitable in the context of dynamic optimization. The main problem with software only approaches is that the inserted instructions compete with the user program for machine resources (e.g. the architectural registers), and they impose dependence that may lengthen the critical paths in the user program.

The sampling based profiling technique in [1][19] collects statistical block profiles by periodic timing interrupts. This technique requires operating system support, and the profile information collected may not be accurate enough for traditional profile-guided optimizations although it is shown to be useful for code layout optimization.

Bursy tracing [2] is a proposed technique to collect profile information via software controlled sampling. It generates two versions of code, one for profiling and one for optimized execution without profiling, and switch from the optimized code to the profiling code infrequently to collect sampling based profile information efficiently. The major drawback is the need to duplicate the code.

In [15][16], a hardware approach is proposed for identifying hot regions and collecting branch profiles for the hot regions. However, this approach requires significant hardware and also needs operating system support. In addition, the profiles collected by using this technique may not be complete and some edges in a hot region may be missed due to cache conflicts and the lack of backup storage. Heuristic patching of the profile may lead to inaccuracy.

Processors, such as Intel Pentium and Itanium, have software readable branch target buffers (BTB). In [6] a technique is described on how to cheaply estimate a program's edge execution frequencies by periodically reading the contents of BTB. In [7] a hardware called a profile buffer is proposed, which counts the number of times a branch is taken and not taken. These techniques require software interrupt to examine the hardware buffers to obtain sampled profiles.

In [10] a profiling technique is implemented for counting the number of times each region exit takes. The dynamic compiler instruments region exit and an 8K entry 8-way set associative hardware array caches counters indexed by the exit point identifiers. This method is specifically targeted for dynamic region formation and expansions.

In [11], the instrumented instructions are scheduled in a software pipelining fashion and that together with speculation and predication reduce the overhead of edge profiling to about 3.3% on an eight-wide machine, without considering cache and branch overhead. However, this technique may generate more memory traffic than necessary, as it may speculatively execute loads and stores for profiling. Furthermore, this technique may still have the instruction cache penalty due to code size expansion. In [17], it is reported that profiling instrumentation increases the text size of a program by a factor of 2-3. On an Itanium processor, since the in-bundle stops can be used to reduce explicit no-ops, the instrumentation code may still increase code size even when it does not increase cycle count.

Our approach goes beyond static scheduling of instrumented code. It attempts at minimal instrumentation in a user program and makes the hardware generate profile update operations and then execute them asynchronously with the user program. Its advantages include that the code size normally will not increase, and the update operations normally will not impact user code. Since the simple profile update operations are collected into a shared buffer, they can be easily pipelined to achieve the maximal execution efficiency.

8   Conclusion and Future Work

We have presented a technique that combines strengths from both the software and the hardware to efficiently collect accurate profiles. The compiler uses its powerful analysis capability to determine the profiling locations and minimize the profiling operations. The hardware uses runtime knowledge to discover free execution slots and performs profile update operations, with little impact on the user program performance. The program execution with profiling can run almost as fast as without profiling. We believe this is the first approach that attains accurate profile information with both hardware and software support. This will enable profile-driven dynamic optimizations on EPIC processors.

In the future, we would also like to simulate the profiling hardware to measure the buffer size and the memory traffic due to profile update operations. We have implemented the needed compiler support for cycle-accurate performance simulation, in which the new profiling instructions are emitted as special nops.

References

1. Anderson, J., L.M. Berc, J. Dean, S. Ghemawat, M.R. Henzinger, S.T. Leung, R.L. Sites, M.T. Vandevoorde, C.A. Waldspurger, and W.E. Weihl, "Continuous profiling: where have all the cycles gone?" In Proc. 16th Symposium on Operating System Principles, Oct. 1997.
2. Arnold, Matthew, Barbara G. Ryder, "A framework for reducing the cost of instrumented code", Proceedings of the ACM SIGPLAN'01 conference on Programming language design and implementation, p.168-179, June 2001, Snowbird, Utah, United States.
3. August, D.I.; Connors, D.A.; Mahlke, S.A.; Sias, J.W.; Crozier, K.M.; Ben-Chung Cheng; Eaton, P.R.; Olaniran, Q.B.; Hwu, W.-M. W. "Integrated predicated and speculative execution in the IMPACT EPIC architecture", , 1998. Proceedings of 25th Annual International Symposium on Computer Architecture, 1998, Page(s): 227 -237
4. Ball, Thomas and James Larus, "Optimally profiling and tracing programs," ACM Transactions on Programming Languages and Systems, 16(3): 1319-1360, July 1994.
5. Ball, Thomas and James Larus, "Efficient Path Profiling," MICRO-29, December 1996.
6. Conte, T.M., B.A. Petal, and J.S. Cox, "Using branch handling hardware to support profile-driven optimization," In Proc. 27th Annual Intl. Symposium on Microarchitecture, Dec. 1996, pp 36-45.
7. Conte, T.M., K.N.Menezes, and M.A. Hirsh, "Accurate and practical profile-driven compilation using the profile buffer," In Proc. 29th Annual Intl. Symposium on Microarchitecture, Nov. 1994, pp 12-21.
8. Dean, J., J.E. Hicks, C.A. Waldspurger, W.E. Weihl, and G. Chrysos, "ProfileMe: Hardware Support for Instruction-level Profiling on Out-of-Order Processors," Micro-30, Dec. 1997.
9. Diep, Trung A., Christopher Neslson, and John P. Shen, "Performance Evaluation of the PowerPC 620 Microarchitecture. In Proceeding of the 22nd Annual International Symposium on Computer Architecture, pp 163-174, June 1995.
10. Ebcioglu, K.; Altman, E.; Gschwind, M.; Sathaye, S. "Dynamic binary translation and optimization," IEEE Transactions on Computers, Volume: 50 Issue: 6, June 2001, Page(s): 529 -548
11. Eichenberger, A. and Sheldon M. Lobo, "Efficient Edge Profiling for ILP-Processor," PACT 98.
12. Knuth, D. E. and F. R. Stevenson, "Optimal measurement of points for program frequency counts," BIT 13 pp. 313-322 (1973).
13. Intel Corp, "Itanium Application Developers Architecture Guide," May 1999.
14. Lee, Yong-fong and Barbara G. Ryder, "A Comprehensive Approach to Parallel Data Flow Analysis", Proceedings of the ACM International Conference on Supercomputing, Pages 236-247, July 1992.

15. Merten, Matthew C., Andrew R. Trick, Christopher N. George, John C. Gyllenhaal, and Wen-mei W. Hwu, "A Hardware-Driven Profiling Scheme for Identifying Program Hot Spots to Support Runtime Optimization," Proceedings of the 26th International Symposium on Computer Architecture, May 1999

16. Merten, M.C.; Trick, A.R.; Nystrom, E.M.; Barnes, R.D.; Hwu, W.-M.W. "A hardware mechanism for dynamic extraction and relayout of program hot spots," 2000. Proceedings of the 27th International Symposium on Computer Architecture, 2000, Page(s): 59 -70

17. Schnarr, Eric and James Larus, "Instruction Scheduling and Executable Editing," Micro 29, Dec. 1996.

18. Schlansker, M.S., Rau, B.R. "EPIC: Explicitly Parallel Instruction Computing," Computer, Volume: 33 Issue: 2, Feb. 2000, pp 37-45

19. Zhang, Xiaolan, Zheng Wang, Nicholas Gloy, J. Bradley Chen, and Michael D. Smith. "System Support for Automated Profiling and Optimization," 16th ACM Symposium on Operating System Principles, Oct. 5-8, 1997.

Continuous Adaptive Object-Code Re-optimization Framework

Howard Chen, Jiwei Lu, Wei-Chung Hsu, and Pen-Chung Yew

University of Minnesota, Department of Computer Science
Minneapolis, MN 55414, USA
{chenh, jiwei, hsu, yew}@cs.umn.edu
http://www.cs.umn.edu/~hsu/dynopt

Abstract. Dynamic optimization presents opportunities for finding run-time bottlenecks and deploying optimizations in statically compiled programs. In this paper, we discuss our current implementation of our hardware sampling based dynamic optimization framework and applying our dynamic optimization system to various SPEC2000 benchmarks compiled with the ORC compiler at optimization level O2 and executed on an Itanium-2 machine. We use our optimization system to apply memory prefetching optimizations, improving the performance of multiple benchmark programs.

1 Introduction

Dynamic optimization presents an opportunity to perform many optimizations that are difficult to apply at compile time due to information that is unavailable during static compilation. For instance, dynamic link libraries limit the scope of procedure inlining and inter-procedural optimizations, two optimizations that are known to be very effective [2]. In addition, a typical shared library calling sequence includes expensive indirect loads and indirect branches. Such instruction sequences are good targets for dynamic optimizations once the shared libraries are loaded.

Dynamic optimization also provides an opportunity to perform micro-architectural optimizations. Recompiling a program to a new micro-architecture has been shown to greatly improve performance [9]. Dynamic optimization provides a way to re-optimize a program to new micro-architectures without requiring recompilation of the original source code.

Finally, dynamic optimization can specialize a program to a specific input set or user which has been applied successfully by Profile Based Optimization (PBO) [2],[5] in the past, but are difficult to apply for due to concerns over excessive compile time, instrumentation-based profiling overhead, complex build processes, and inadequate training input data set [14]. Dynamic optimization can be used to deploy more aggressive optimizations, such as predication [13], speculation [10], and even register allocation and instruction scheduling according to current program behavior and with less risk of degrading performance.

P.-C. Yew and J. Xue (Eds.): ACSAC 2004, LNCS 3189, pp. 241–255, 2004.

In short, dynamic object code re-optimization allows code to be generated specifically for a specific execution environment. It adapts optimizations to the actual execution profiles, micro-architectural behavior, and exploits the opportunity to optimize across shared libraries. However, a dynamic optimization system must detect and apply optimizations efficiently to be profitable. If the overhead of the system is greater than the time saved by optimizations, the runtime of the optimized program will increase.

We present our design and implementation of our adaptive object-code re-optimization framework to detect and deploy dynamic optimizations with a minimal amount of overhead on modern hardware. Our prototype system detects time-consuming execution paths and performance bottlenecks in several unmodified SPEC2000 benchmarks by *continuously* sampling Itanium performance monitoring registers throughout the program's execution [6]. We use the collected information to create executable traces at runtime, and deploy these optimizations by modifying branch instructions in existing code to execute our instructions in place of hot paths in the original code. We examine the overhead of our detection system, and show that this technique can be applied with less than 2% of overhead while speeding up various SPEC2000 benchmarks.

2 Background

Dynamic optimization has been presented in the past in frameworks such as Dynamo [3] and Continuous Profiling and Optimization (CPO)[12]. Dynamo uses a method similar to dynamic compilation used in virtual machines. Native binaries are interpreted to collect an execution profile and fragments of frequently executed code are emitted and executed in place of interpretation. Dynamo requires no additional information beyond the executable binary to operate, and this allows it to be applied on arbitrary binaries without needing access to the original code or IR. CPO presents a model closer to traditional PBO where the original code is instrumented, and the profile information is used to compile optimized versions of code. In CPO, profiled information is used to drive PBO while the program is running and the compiled result is hot-swapped into the program. The advantage of this scheme is that the IR information makes application of many optimizations easier.

However, since the applied optimizations compete with the dynamic optimization system's overhead, interpretation and instrumentation-based profiling dynamic optimizers often try to limit the time spent collecting profiled information, sometimes at the expense of optimizations. For example, Dynamo only interprets unique execution paths a small number of times before selecting traces to optimize to avoid interpretation overhead. Instrumentation incurs less overhead than interpretation, but even efficient implementations of instrumentation [4] generate measurable overheads. This may lead to profiling of initialization behaviors that do not represent dominant execution behavior. Even after attempting to reduce optimization system costs, the dynamic optimization systems still produce a relatively high amount of overhead, which works against the profitability of optimizations. In our system, we seek to limit the overhead of the techniques used to profile and deploy dynamic optimizations.

Existing dynamic optimization systems can generally be broken down into three stages: profiling/detection, optimization, and deployment. The detection stage deals with the collection of information necessary to select and guide optimizations. The optimization stage uses the collected information to select a set of optimizations to deploy in a target program. The deployment stage handles the application of the selected optimizations to a running program. Each of these stages requires runtime processing which leads to a slowdown of the original program. We try to reduce target profiling and deployment costs to improve the performance of the entire dynamic optimization system.

Our overall goal is to move towards a dynamic optimization framework that incurs minimal overhead while providing good potential for optimization speedups. Other techniques seek to perform similar goals [15], [16] using hardware. Like these schemes, our work uses specialized hardware to collect information useful for our planned optimizations. However, these schemes propose the implementation of new hardware to process data. In contrast, our work gathers data from existing performance monitoring hardware and analyzes it using a user program. Previous work in periodic sampling of hardware structures is presented in [1], [7], [8]. These schemes concentrate on applying this information to guide static PBO rather than dynamic optimizations.

3 Architecture

3.1 Overview

Our architecture performs three main tasks: detection, optimization, and deployment. Detection deals with the collection of raw performance event information that is useful for identifying and applying optimizations like D-cache misses, IPC, and branch paths commonly leading up to performance events. Optimization deals with generating optimized code to replace existing executable code. Deployment deals with the issues presented by redirecting execution from the original program to optimized code.

The code for our dynamic optimizer is first executed when a program executes the C run-time startup routines. We compile our own custom version of C run-time library to start a thread dedicated to dynamic optimization and initialize a shared memory area to place optimized code. The dynamic optimization thread begins monitoring the behavior of the original primary thread, and generates and deploys optimized code later in execution. After initialization of the dynamic optimization thread is complete, the C run-time library startup routines continue and begin executing the original program while the optimization thread begins detecting optimization opportunities.

3.2 Performance Event Detection

3.2.1 Performance Monitoring Hardware

We use the Performance Monitoring Unit (PMU) on Itanium processors to collect information and signal the operating system to collect and store profiled information. The primary PMU features we use for the detection work are the performance-event counters and the Branch Trace Buffer (BTB)[11]. The performance-event counters are a set of registers that track the number of times performance events like cache misses and branch mispredictions occur. These counters are used to throw interrupts periodically after a number of events occur. For instance, we can choose to throw a system interrupt once every million clock cycles, once every ten thousand D-cache misses, or once every one-hundred branch mispredictions. During each interrupt, we can save information about the type of interrupt and BTB information in memory for later processing.

The BTB, not to be confused with a branch target buffer used in branch prediction, is a set of eight registers that store the last four branches and branch targets. When the performance monitor throws an interrupt, we use the BTB to find the last four taken branch instructions and branch targets that lead up to the performance event interrupt. By monitoring only taken branches, we can form longer traces than if we had monitored all branches since not-taken branch information can easily be reconstructed by scanning the instructions between the last branch target and the next taken branch instruction. The BTB also allows us to generate an edge profile without scanning and decoding the original source code.

A detailed discussion of PMU hardware on Itanium processors can be found in [11].

3.2.2 Perfmon

Our hardware information is collected using perflib, a library from the Perfmon toolset. The Perfmon toolset configures and collects raw performance information from Itanium programs running on 64-bit Linux. Perfmon sends system calls to a Linux kernel driver to configure the PMU and automatically collects samples of the PMU registers for later processing.

Once the PMU stores raw register information to memory, it can be consumed independently from the monitored program. All information collected by Perfmon is done without modifying the original program binary. Perfmon is described in greater detail in [20].

3.2.3 Hot Trace Selection

The goal of our hot trace detector is to find a small number of traces that lead up to performance critical blocks. To collect these hot traces, we sample sets of four taken branches and branch targets from the BTB at regular intervals and sort the results into a hash table, while keeping track of the frequency of the different sample paths. The most frequently sampled paths are marked for optimization in the table under the assumption that they dominate execution time, and traces are selected to include these hot spots.

Since the optimization and deployment of traces requires processing time, we limit the traces we select to those we believe we can optimize profitably. The best traces to optimize are the traces that contribute the most execution time for the remainder of the program, and contain a performance event that we can optimize. The performance monitoring hardware provides the information we need to see if a performance event commonly occurs on any path we select. However, to predict which traces will continue to dominate execution time in the future and prevent optimizing traces with performance events that only occur for very short periods of time, we perform additional work to estimate when program behavior is most stable.

3.2.4 Phase Change Detection

We assume that programs generally enter different "phases" of execution, periods of time when characteristics like IPC, D-cache hit rate, and the current working set of hot code follow similar patterns throughout a phase [17],[18]. Since our current optimizations focus on optimizing D-cache misses and improving IPC, we use the number of D-cache misses per cycle and IPC over time as metrics to guess when the behaviors we wish to optimize are most stable.

Our goal is to select hot traces to optimize the first time we encounter a new phase and to keep it in our working set for the remainder of program execution. As long as the execution of the program remains in a stable phase, no further changes are made to the optimized traces. Changes in execution phases will be detected, and such changes will trigger further optimizations.

Every second of execution time, we measure the number of D-cache misses and IPC over the past second and compare it to previously measured values. If the D-cache and IPC values are stable for several seconds (deviating less than a set percentage), we assume that the D-cache and general program behavior is stable enough to select a set of hot traces that may execute for some time into the future, and select a set of traces from the samples in the current stable phase.

Conversely, when D-cache and IPC values fluctuate, it indicates that program behavior has changed and that new hot traces may need to be selected or existing selected traces may no longer be hot. When D-cache miss rate and IPC values deviate from the previous few seconds, we recheck our collected sampled data to look for new hot traces to add to our working set.

The weakness of this metric is that D-cache miss and IPC values are composite values for all the code that is executing in a program over an interval. This can lead to a false measurement of a stable phase since it is possible that program behavior has completely changed but averages out to similar values. In practice, we found that a stable D-cache miss rate and IPC values indicated a stable phase. We did not observe this behavior in any of our measurements of SPEC benchmarks, but it remains a possibility for other programs.

A more likely problem with this metric is that program behavior patterns commonly have sub-patterns. For instance, an outer loop may contain two inner loops: one with stable exploitable behavior, and one with unstable behavior. The stable subphase, or repeated stable behavior contained within the larger phase, can be optimized despite instability in the D-cache and IPC metrics. However, this behavior was also uncommon in the SPEC benchmarks we measured.

However, these problems indicate the potential need for deeper phase change detection to fully exploit all the stable behavior in a program that may be further supported in future work studying phase detection of programs outside of the SPEC benchmark suite.

3.3 Optimization

3.3.1 Trace Generation

Every time a set of traces is selected, executable code corresponding to each trace is assigned a type name according to its behavior. For instance, a loop is a type assigned to any trace that is completely enclosed in a trace. A subroutine is a type assigned to traces that are targeted by "br.call" instructions and end with a "br.ret" instruction, both indicators of a subroutine. Traces of different types are optimized in different ways. Data prefetching loop optimizations are particularly applied only to loop-typed traces, while inter-trace optimizations are more likely to be applied in subroutines. Code is then generated in our trace buffer for our selected traces, a shared memory area that contains our optimized executable code. The selected traces are then "cross-patched" or set to return to original code if execution leaves the path of the trace.

3.3.2 Trace Cross-Patching

Cross-patching refers to patching optimized traces to branch to other optimized traces. Ideally, once a good set of optimized traces is selected, control should rarely return to the original program. To perform cross-patching, a graph is generated with one node for each selected trace and edges to connected traces. When the code for the trace is generated, the branch instructions in optimized traces are then modified to branch to other optimized traces instead of returning to the original code.

3.3.3 Architecture Safe Optimization

Code scheduling/motion and other aggressive transformations may cause problems for preserving the original order of architecture state changes. This may create problems if a user trap handler expects to have the precise architecture state at the exception. To avoid these problems, we first attempt optimizations that do not change architecture states such as trace layout and data cache prefetching. Although data cache prefetch transformations require some temporary registers to hold prefetch addresses, we have the compiler (ORC compiler) reserve four general purpose and two predicate registers for such a purpose. Due to the large register file in the Itanium architecture, reserving a small number of registers has essentially no performance impact on the compiled code. We have verified this by comparing the performance of compiled code at various optimization levels with/without the reserved registers.

3.3.4 Data Prefetching

In our dynamic optimization system, we target D-cache misses for optimization because they are well known to be a common dominant performance problem in programs, but are difficult to detect statically [19]. Using our ability to detect instructions that cause D-cache misses, our dynamic optimization system can take advantage of information that is only available at run-time.

To detect which memory operation generates data cache misses during runtime, D-cache miss events are sampled by the performance monitoring unit and associated with the corresponding load/store instructions in the selected traces. Once a memory operation is found with a miss latency that contributes greater than 5% of execution time based on performance monitoring counters, the trace where this instruction resides will be scheduled for optimization.

The optimizer then determines if any of the implemented prefetch optimizations are appropriate. We implement three types of data prefetching for loops: array reference, indirect array reference, and pointer chasing.

Here is an example of the code generated in an indirect array reference before prefetching:

```
loop:

ld4 r17=[r43] // cache miss from loading the address stored in the array

sxt4 r17=r17

add r43=4,r43   // the array pointer is incremented

add r17=r39,r17

add r17=-1,r17

ld1 [r17]       // cache miss from loading the data value from the address

...

br loop
```

A frequent D-cache missed indirect array reference will trigger two-level data cache prefetching. The first level is a direct array reference prefetch to prefetch for the array containing the addresses of the data. The second level prefetches the value at the address from the array. Note that the first level runs a few iterations ahead of the second level of prefetching. Here is an example of the prefetch code generated to optimize the previous indirect array-reference code:

```
add  r30=128,r43 // this initializes the direct reference prefetch

add  r28=64,r43 // this initializes the indirect prefetch

loop:

lfetch [r30],4    // this prefetches the address from the array

...
```

```
ld4.sa r29=[r28],4 // this loads the prefetched address

          // (prefetched in a previous iteration)

sxt4   r29=r29

add   r29=r39,r29

add   r29=-1,r29

lfetch [r29]    // this prefetches the indirect value from the array address

...

br loop
```

This is an example of pointer chasing code before optimization:

```
loop:

add r22=24,r11 // calculate offset of pointer to next list element

ld8 r11=[r22] // cache miss from loading address of next list element

br loop
```

For pointer-chasing prefetching, the key memory address which controls the memory references (i.e.the possible "->next" pointer for linked lists) is found and prefetched by assuming a constant stride:

```
loop: (assume r28 is reserved unused by static compiler)

add   r28=0,r11     // remember the old value of r11

add   r22=24,r11

ld8   r11=[r22]

sub   r28=r11,r28   // calculate the difference of old and new value

shladd r28=r28,2,r11 // use the difference as stride to prefetch

lfetch [r28]     // prefetch ahead in the linked lists.
```

3.4 Deploying Optimizations

3.4.1 Patching Branch Targets

We redirect execution from the original code to traces in our trace buffer by modifying frequently executed branch instructions to branch to the corresponding optimized code in the trace buffer. However, modifying executable instructions in a running program creates a number of issues ranging from memory protection to updating the I-cache line with the modified instruction.

3.4.2 Memory Protection

The memory protection on the original code pages is read-only by default. When we wish to modify branch instructions in the address space of existing code, we make a system call to allow writing to memory pages of the original code. We then replace all branches at once, then restore write-protection to the original code to protect the original code from accidental changes.

3.4.3 Branch Patching Distance

Most programs compiled for the Itanium architecture use a short branch, which allows a relative branch distance of 20-bits or about a million bundles (i.e. 16 megabytes). There are cases when the original code size is larger than 16 megabytes and a branch cannot be easily patched by simply changing the address field of a branch instruction. In some cases, the entire bundle containing the branch instruction must be replaced with a long branch instruction to reach the memory space of the trace buffer. The long branch instruction in the Itanium architecture allows the branch to reach anywhere in the 64-bit virtual address space. One alternative to using a long branch is to use an indirect branch instruction sequence, but this is more expensive, more likely to be mispredicted, and is more difficult to patch atomically.

Since the Itanium uses an explicitly parallel instruction computing (EPIC) architecture, instructions are combined into 128-bit "bundles" which usually contain three instructions. Bundles with long-branch instructions can only contain two instructions. If the second instruction in a bundle that was replaced contains a "nop" in the middle slot, a common case, the entire bundle can be replaced at once. However, if the bundle you wish to replace with a long branch uses all three slots, the trace patcher cannot replace the instruction with a single instruction and we patch the target of the short branch instruction with an unconditional long branch to our optimized traces.

3.4.4 Atomic Write Issues

Another issue with replacing instruction bundles is that bundles are 128 bits long while the processor only supports 64-bit atomic write instructions. That means that we need to take steps to prevent partially modified bundles from being executed. To deal with this case, we first patch the first half of the bundle with an illegal bundle type and handle the exception if the bundle is executed before we finish patching it. We then modify the second half of the bundle with the replacement bundle, and complete the process by modifying the first half of the long-branch instruction bundle.

It is also possible that a context switch occurs while a bundle is only partially executed. This can happen if a cache miss occurs in a bundle. As long as the memory operation occurs in the first slot, this bundle can still be replaced with a long branch instruction. If the partially executed bundle is replaced with a bundle with a long branch, the bundle resumes execution at the second slot in the bundle, the long branch instruction.

3.4.5 Repatching Issues

When a phase changes, some previously optimized traces may not be "hot". In general we do not undo or remove existing patched traces for two reasons. First, when we optimize a trace, it often requires less execution time and therefore appears less "hot". However, removing the optimization would lead to the code taking more execution time, so we are better off keeping the trace patched into the program. There are cases when we attempt to optimize a trace, and it requires more execution time than before due to additional cache misses. In the future, we plan to further explore the benefits of tracking the performance of our optimization at run-time and removing optimizations that appear to degrade performance.

Second, we found that phase behavior tends to repeat over time and previously generated traces are often used again in the future. If existing traces are no longer hot, the patched traces generally have very little performance impact. This can save some processing work to regenerate the trace if the behavior becomes hot again. For long running programs that exercise many different execution paths, this may lead to fragmentation of generated traces that may affect I-cache performance. We plan to explore the benefits of optimized trace layout management in memory in the future.

4   Experiments and Discussion

Our results are collected using ORC version 2.0 compiled SPEC2000 benchmarks with -O2 and software pipelined loops disabled on a dual processor Itanium-2 machine. We compile using O2 because that is the typical optimization level used by software vendors. Our current optimizer does not support register renaming in software-pipelined loops, so we disable software pipelining at compile time. For SPECint benchmarks, we found that disabling pipelining results in a slightly higher runtime performance when measuring results using ORC.

4.1 Speedup and Coverage

Execution time is collected using the unix "time" command and averaged over several runs. The reported execution time includes all detection, profiling, optimization and deployment overhead. Relative speedup is calculated as ((baseline time)/(optimized time) - 1) * 100%.

Figures 1 and 2 show the speedup of applying our system to various spec programs. We apply different sampling rates to collect data and select new traces every second of execution time. Data that is "continuous" selects new phases upon a suspected phase change while "single" data selects the first stable phase identified in a program.

As Figure 3 shows, art, bzip, equake, fma, galgel, lucas, mcf, and swim benefit from regular and indirect array reference prefetching. Mcf benefits primarily from pointer reference prefetching. In Figure 2, at one hundred thousand cycles per sample facerec speeds up by 10%. Although the D-cache miss rate of facerec appears to increase in Figure 5, the actual execution time of the program decreases. The D-cache miss rate increases but these misses overlap with each other more effectively than in the original program leading to improved program performance. In contrast, equake's D-cache performance is noticeably improved in Figure 4. Lower sampling rates for

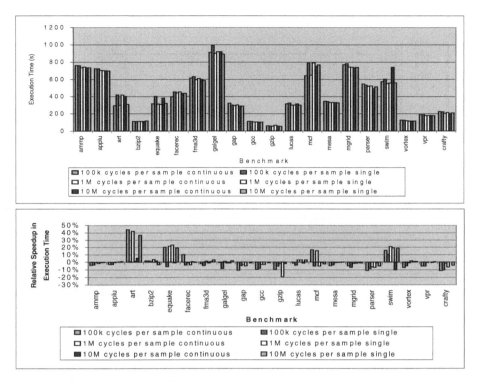

Figs. 1 (top) and 2 (bottom). Figure 1 shows the execution time of dynamically optimized programs with data collected at different sampling rates. Figure 2 shows the relative speedup at different sampling rates

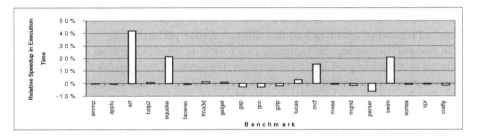

Fig. 3. Relative speedup at one million cycles per sample

facerec do not improve performance because at slower sampling rates the primary execution path is not optimized properly on the first pass and since we do not currently monitor the performance of generated traces, the problem is not corrected in future intervals. Although this problem is most dramatic in facerec, this trend can be seen in all the programs at a slower sampling rate. It may be valuable to study tracking and removal of sub-optimal traces in the future to deal with this problem.

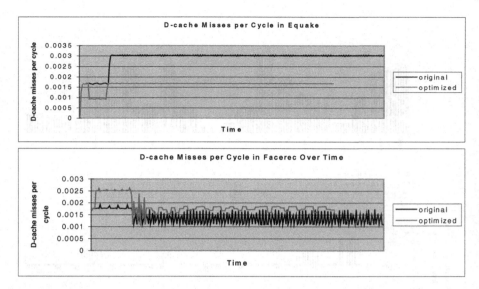

Figs. 4 and 5. Figure 4 shows the D-cache misses per cycle in Equake before and after optimization at one sample every 100k cycles. Figure 5 shows the D-cache misses per cycle in Facerec before and after optimization at one sample every 100k cycles.

Other benchmarks do not benefit from the implemented prefetching optimizations and are primarily slowed down by the overhead of sampling, additional I-cache misses from branching to our generated traces, and increased D-cache misses due to ineffectual prefetches. The overhead of our optimization and patching is generally very small, less than 1% of the original program's execution time, so the majority of the slowdown in programs can be attributed to these factors. The largest reported slowdown is from gzip due to failed prefetching increasing D-cache misses. This demonstrates the need for additional work in tracking the effectiveness of optimizations and removing optimizations that fail to improve performance.

In general, increasing the sampling rate results in higher overhead due to the time required to store sampled PMU information. However, it also detects a set of hotspots faster than slower sampling rates, which means hot traces may be applied earlier to a program than at slower sampling rates. Mcf and art both have small loops that noticeably speed up after being optimized and therefore benefit from higher sampling rates. In contrast, equake and swim perform better at one sample taken every one million cycles. At one sample every one million and hundred thousand cycles, these two programs generally found similar hotspots, but at one-hundred thousand cycles per sample, the overhead of sampling is about 5% higher than at one sample every 1 million cycles.

Using a rate of ten million cycles per sample, continuously selecting traces yields worse performance than selecting a single set of traces once. At a rate of ten million cycles per sample, the system starts with correctly selected paths and later selects suboptimal paths that degrade performance. Because traces occur after a fixed interval, one second, the sampling error from the small pool of samples falsely detects traces as hot. Since the sampling error of a program is related to the size of the footprint we need to detect, this indicates that it might be worthwhile to estimate the size of the working set and adjust the number of samples required to select hot-spots accordingly. However, performance is improved for continuously selected traces due to the ability to select new hot traces that do not occur earlier in execution.

The largest slowdown in figure 3 is parser at 5%. This is mainly due to generated trace overhead from the selection of a large number of traces, and the lack of any effective D-cache prefetching. However, other programs like gap, gcc, and gzip generate less than 2% overhead.

Finally, in some cases selecting a set of traces after the first detected hot phase performed better than continuous selection. Continuous selection is sensitive to short term behavior changes leading the optimizer to generate more traces and more overhead than making a single selection.

4.2 Run-Time Overhead

The overhead for our run-time system is fairly stable, with the profiling thread generating a consistent 0.3%-0.6% overhead over no profiling. Optimization overhead is proportional to the number of traces selected to optimize and consistently less than 1%. Turning off patching has a negligible effect on overhead indicating that the cost of patching traces is much smaller than the cost of profiling and optimization.

Sampling overhead averaged approximately 4% at one sample every hundred thousand cycles, about 1% at one sample every million cycles, and much less than 1% at lower sampling rates. The overhead is not directly proportional to the sampling rate because this includes the overhead of inserting branch information into the trace selection table. Slowdowns of greater than 1% are primarily due to optimizations resulting in larger loops.

5 Summary and Future Work

Dynamic optimization promises to provide a useful mechanism for deploying aggressive optimizations targeting run-time behavior. We present our system as a prototype for finding and deploying optimizations, and support this claim by using our prototype to speedup various SPEC2000 benchmarks compiled by the ORC 2.0 compiler at O2. We are able to speed up several benchmarks dominated by D-cache misses, while maintaining a maximum slowdown of 5% in parser and crafty.

Future directions for this work include enhancements to our current system, monitoring current optimizations and tracking the performance of generated traces, improving phase detection, evaluating other optimization techniques, and exploring dynamic optimization opportunities in different environments.

References

1.   J.M. Anderson, L.M. Berc, J. Dean, S. Ghemawat, M.R. Henzinger, S.A. Leung, R.L. Sites, M.T. Vandevoorde, C.A. Waldspurger and W.E. Weihl. "Continuous profiling: where have all the cycles gone?" *ACM Transaction on Computer Systems*, vol. 15, no. 4, Nov. 1997

2.   A. Andrew, S. De Jong, J. Peyton, and R. Schooler "Scalable Cross-Module Optimization", In *Proceedings of the ACM SIGPLAN '98 conference on Programming language design and implementation*, PLDI'98, June 1998.

3.   V. Bala, E. Duesterwald, S. Banerjia. "Dynamo: A Transparent Dynamic Optimization System", In *Proceedings of the ACM SIGPLAN '2000 conference on Programming language design and implementation*, PLDI'2000, June 2000.

4.   Ball, T., and Larus, J. R. "Efficient Path Profiling," In *Proceedings of the 29th Annual International Symposium on Microarchitecture* (Micro-29), Paris, 1996.

5.   P. Chang, S. Mahlke and W. Hwu, "Using Profile Information to Assist Classic Compiler Code Optimizations," *Software Practice and Experience*, Dec. 1991.

6.   H. Chen, W. Hsu, J. Lu, P. -C. Yew and D. -Y. Chen, "Dynamic Trace Selection Using Performance Monitoring Hardware Sampling", International Symposium on Code Generation and Optimization, CGO 2003, March, 2003.

7.   R.S. Cohn, D.W. Goodwin, P.G. Lowney, "Optimizing Alpha Executables on Windows NT with Spike", *Digital Technical Journal*, Vol 9 No 4, June 1998.

8.   T. Conte, B. Patel, J Cox. "Using Branch Handling Hardware to Support Profile-Driven Optimization", *In Proceedings of the 27th Annual International Symposium on Microarchitecture* (Micro-27), 1994

9.   A. M. Holler, "Optimization for a Superscalar Out-of-Order Machine," *In Proceedings of the 29th Annual International Symposium on Microarchitecture* (Micro-29), December 1996.

10.   Intel, *Intel IA-64 Architecture Software Developer's Manual*, Vol. 1: IA-64 Application Architecture.

11.   Intel, *Intel IA-64 Architecture Software Developer's Manual*, Vol. 2: IA-64 System Architecture.

12.   T. Kistler, M. Franz. "Continuous Program Optimization: Design and Evaluation", *IEEE Transaction on Computers*, vol. 50, no. 6, June 2001.

13.   S. A. Mahlke, D. C. Lin, W. Y. Chen, R. E. Hank, and R. A. Bringmann, "Effective Compiler Support for Predicated Execution Using the Hyperblock", *In Proceedings of the 25th Annual International Symposium on Microarchitectures.* (Micro-25), 1992 .

14.   S. McFarling, "Reality-Based Optimizations", International Symposium on Code Generation and Optimization, CGO 2003, March, 2003.

15.   M. Merten, A. Trick, E. M. Nystrom, R. D. Barnes, W. Hwu, "A Hardware Mechanism for Dynamic Extraction and Relayout of Program Hot Spots", *In Proceedings, International Symposium on Computer Architecture*, ISCA-27, 2000

16.   S. Patel, S. S. Lumetta, "Replay: A Hardware Framework for Dynamic Optimization", *IEEE Transaction on Computers*, vol. 50, no. 6, June 2001.

17.   T. Sherwood, E. Perelman, G. Hamerly, B. Calder. "Automatically Characterizing Large Scale Program Behavior. *10th International Conference on Architectural Support for Programming Languages and Operating Systems*, October 2002.

18.   T. Sherwood, E. Perelman, and B. Calder. Basic block distribution analysis to find periodic behavior and simulation points in applications. *In International Conference on Parallel Architectures and Compilation Techniques*, September 2001.

19. Y. Wu. "Efficient Discovery of Regular Stride Patterns in Irregular Programs", PLDI 2002:210-221.
20. Hewlett Packard, "Perfmon Project Website", webpage, http://www.hpl.hp.com/research /linux/perfmon/index.php4.

Initial Evaluation of a User-Level Device Driver Framework

Kevin Elphinstone[1] and Stefan Götz[2]

[1] National ICT Australia***
and
School of Computer Science and Engineering
University of NSW, Sydney 2052, Australia
kevine@cse.unsw.edu.au
[2] System Architecture Group, Universität Karlsruhe, 76128 Karlsruhe, Germany
sgoetz@ira.uka.de

Abstract. Device drivers are a significant source of system instability. In this paper, we make the case for running device drivers at user-level to improve robustness and resource management. We present a framework for running drivers at user-level whose goal is to provide similar performance when compared to in-kernel drivers. We also present initial promising performance results for the framework.

1 Introduction

Most modern operating systems feature monolithic operating system kernels. Most modern architectures are designed to efficiently support this form of construction. A kernel provides its services by combining the software that implements potentially independent services into a single large amalgamation. However, once we scale the size and complexity of a monolithic system to the levels of current systems, extensibility becomes more difficult due to legacy structure, security becomes more difficult to maintain and impossible to prove, and stability and robustness also suffer.

One promising approach to tackling the expanding complexity of modern operating systems is the microkernel approach [1]. A microkernel-based OS consists of a very small kernel at its core. The kernel only contains a minimal set of services that are efficient and flexible enough to construct services for applications as servers running on the microkernel. Only the microkernel itself runs in privileged mode. Although these servers provide operating system functionality, they are regular applications from the microkernel's point of view. Such a system enables extensibility as servers can be added or removed, it provides security as the core of the system is small enough to analyse or maybe even prove [2], and

---

*** National ICT Australia is funded by the Australia Government's Department of Communications, Information and Technology and the Arts and the Australian Research Council through Backing Australia's Ability and the ICT Centre of Excellence program.

P.-C. Yew and J. Xue (Eds.): ACSAC 2004, LNCS 3189, pp. 256–269, 2004.

stability and robustness is improved as services can be isolated from each other. The modular structure that is encouraged, and even enforced by virtual memory protection boundaries, improves maintainability.

Most microkernel based systems still include device drivers in the kernel. Drivers are included for either security [3], performance reasons [4] , or because the system's focus was toward goals other than decomposition and minimisation, such as distribution [5,6,7]. It has been shown that device drivers exhibit much higher bug rates (three to seven time higher) than other kernel code [8]. Microsoft has also identified drivers as the major cause of system instability and has instigated their driver signing program to combat the problem [9]. It remains to be seen whether signing a driver as having passed a quality control scheme has an affect on driver correctness. Simply digitally signing a piece of software obviously has no effect on the software itself.

This paper tackles the problem of device driver instability by running drivers at user-level and hence subjecting them to the normal controls applied to applications. We also aim to provide a flexible driver framework for microkernel-based systems that enables trade-offs between driver performance and containment. Attempts thus far can be characterised as being too concerned with compatibility with existing driver collections [10] or having an alternative focus such as realtime systems [11]. The achieved performance has been insufficient to make the approach convincing.

Device drivers at user level could be treated almost like normal applications. Like normal applications, drivers could be isolated from unneeded resources using the processor's virtual memory hardware. Being able to apply the principle of *least privilege* would greatly minimise the potential damage a malfunctioning driver could inflict. This is very much in contrast to the current situation where drivers have access to all resources in the system. A single malfunction often results in catastrophic failure of the entire system.

Developers of user-level drivers can use facilities usually only available to normal applications. Standard debuggers can provide a much richer debugging environment than usually available to kernel-level drivers (e.g., source level debugging versus kernel dumps). Application tracing facilities can also be used to monitor driver behaviour. Application resource management, such as CPU time controls, can be used to control driver resource usage.

User-level drivers are not a completely new idea. Drivers in the past have been incorporated into applications such as networking software (e.g distributed shared memory applications) [8,12]. The inclusion in this case was to improve performance by giving the application direct access to the device, and thus avoiding kernel entry and exit. Such scenarios relied on near exclusive access to the device in order to avoid issues in multiplexing the device between competing clients. In most cases, specialised hardware was developed to provide concurrent access via specialised access channels, and to provide performance via a specialised interface that required no kernel intervention.

We propose an architecture where the system designer can choose the most appropriate configuration for drivers based on requirements of the targeted system. We envisage drivers incorporated into specialised applications where performance is paramount. However, we also envisage drivers running as individual servers to improve security and robustness, or drivers clustered into a single server to reduce resource requirements. Immature drivers could be run in isolation until mature enough to be combined with other components when required.

While we intend to take advantage of specialised hardware (such as myrinet network cards which have their own programmable processors [13]), we also do not intend to restrict ourselves to such hardware. For the results of this project to be truly useful we must be able to support commodity hardware that is not necessarily tailored to the environment we are developing. Commodity hardware may not provide all features necessary for complete security. For instance, nearly all hardware is unable to restrict what a driver can access via DMA. On such a hardware platform, a malicious driver can always corrupt a system. However, even limited success in supporting commodity hardware with little performance impact would make our results applicable to the widest variety of platforms possible. Limited success could persuade more manufacturers to include the hardware features required for complete security. Our group has begun exploring restricting DMA access using the limited hardware available in high-end servers [14]. However, we do not focus on this problem for the remainder of this paper.

Past approaches to drivers at user-level have usually taken a top-down approach. The system was designed with a specific target in mind, built, and analysed. The results have varied widely. Some projects, specifically the user-level networking with specialised hardware, have been successful [12,15]. Other projects have been less successful and have usually disappeared without a clear analysis of why success eluded them [10,16]. In this paper we identify the fundamental operations performed by device drivers, their relevance to performance, and present how they can be implemented safely and efficiently at user-level.

In the remainder of the paper, Section 2 provides the background to running user-level drivers by describing a simple model of device drivers in existing monolithic systems. We use it as a reference for the rest of the paper. Section 3 describes the experimental operating system platform upon which we developed our driver framework. Section 4 describes the framework itself. The experimental evaluation and results follow in Section 5, with conclusions afterwards in Section 6.

2   Simple Driver Model

To define common terminology, help convey the issues we have identified, and introduce our framework itself, we present a simple model of a device driver and highlight the issues within that model. This model initially assumes a traditional monolithic kernel whose kernel address space is shared between all process contexts.

A driver broadly consists of two active software components, the *Interrupt Service Routine* (ISR) and the *Deferred Processing Component* (DPC). We ignore initialisation code and so forth. The ISR is responsible for reacting quickly and efficiently to device events. It is invoked almost directly via a hardware defined exception mechanism that interrupts the current flow of execution and enables the potential return to that flow after completion of the ISR. In general, the length of the ISR should be minimised so as to maximise the burst rate of device events that can be achieved, and to reduce ISR invocation latency of all ISRs (assuming they are mutually exclusive).

The ISR usually arranges for a DPC to continue the processing required to handle the device event. For example, a DPC might be an IP stack for a network device. A DPC could also be extra processing required to manage the device itself, or processing required to complete execution of a blocked kernel activity. Another way to view a DPC is that it is the kernel activities made runnable as a result of the execution of the ISR. It may be a new activity, or a previously suspended activity. DPCs are usually activated via some kernel synchronisation primitive which makes the activity runnable and adds it to the scheduler's run queue.

2.1   Driver Interfaces and Structure

A driver consists of an interface in order for clients (other components in the kernel) to direct the driver to perform work. For instance, sending packets on a network device. Drivers also expect an interface provided by the surrounding kernel in order to allocate memory, activate DPCs, translate virtual addresses, access the device information on the PCI bus, etc. We believe the following interfaces are important to driver performance:

Providing work to the driver. Drivers provide an interface for clients to enqueue work to be performed by the device. This involves passing the driver
  a work descriptor that describes the work to be performed. The descriptor
  may be a data structure or arguments to a function call. The work descriptor
  identifies the operation and any data (buffers) required to perform the work.
  Drivers and clients share the kernel address space which enables fast transfer
  (by reference) and access to descriptors and buffers.
DPCs and offloading work. Drivers also produce work for clients. A common example is a network driver receiving packets and therefore generating
  work for an IP stack. Like enqueueing work for the driver itself, an efficient mechanism is required for the reverse direction to enqueue work for,
  and activate, a DPC such as an IP stack. Work descriptors and buffers can
  be handled in a similar manner to enqueueing work for the driver, i.e. descriptors and buffers can be transferred and accessed directly in the kernel's
  address space.
  Once work is enqueued for a DPC, the DPC requires activation via a synchronisation primitive. Again, the primitive can rely on the shared kernel
  address space to mark a DPC runnable and place it on the appropriate
  scheduler queue.
Buffer allocation. The buffers containing the data that is provided to the
  driver must be allocated prior to use and deallocated for reuse after processing. Buffers may be produced by a client and consumed by a driver (or vice

versa) and are managed via a memory allocator (e.g. a slab allocator) in the shared kernel address space.

Translation. Buffers specified by user-level applications are identified using virtual addresses. DMA-capable devices require these addresses to be translated into a physical representation. This translation can be done simply and quickly by the device driver by accessing the page tables stored within the kernel address space. Additionally, some driver clients deal only with the kernel address space and can use physical addresses directly (or some fixed offset).

Pinning. DMA-capable devices access physical memory directly without any mediation via a MMU (though some architectures do possess I/O MMUs). Coordination between the page replacement policy and the device driver is required to avoid the situation where a page is swapped out and the underlying frame is recycled for another purpose while an outstanding DMA is yet to complete. Preventing pages from being swapped out is generally termed *pinning* the page in memory. This can be implemented with a bit in the frame table indicating to the page replacement algorithm that the frame is pinned.

Validation. Validation is the process of determining whether a request to the driver is permitted based on knowledge of the identity of the requester and the parameters supplied. Validation is simple when a client issues a request to a driver in a shared address-space kernel. The driver can implicitly trust the client to issue sensible requests. It only needs to check the validity of a request for robustness reasons or debugging. If needed, the client module in the kernel is usually responsible for the validity of any user-level supplied buffers or data which needs to reside in memory accessible to the user-level application. Such a validation is simple and inexpensive to perform within a shared address-space kernel — all the data required to validate an application's request is readily available.

It is clear that the model envisaged by computer architects is a fast hardware-supported mechanism to allow privileged drivers to respond to device events, and that the drivers themselves have cheap access to all the information required to perform their function via the privileged address space they share with the kernel. The high degree of integration with the privileged kernel allows drivers to maximise performance by minimising overheads needed to interact with their surrounds. This high degree of integration is also the problem: drivers detrimentally affect security, robustness, and reliability of the entire system.

3 Experimental Platform

We chose the L4 microkernel as the experimental platform for developing and evaluating our driver framework[1]. L4 is a minimal kernel running in privileged mode. It has two major abstractions: threads and address spaces. Threads are the unit of execution and are associated with an address space. A group of threads within an address space forms a task. Threads interact via a very light weight synchronous interprocess communication mechanism (IPC) [17].

L4 itself only provides primitive mechanisms to manage address spaces. Higher-level abstractions are needed to create a programming environment for application developers. The environment we use is a re-implementation of a subset of the SawMill multi-server operating system developed for L4 at IBM [10], called *Prime*. The most relevant component to this paper is the virtual memory framework [18], which we will briefly introduce here.

Dataspaces are the fundamental abstraction within the VM framework. A dataspace is a container that abstracts memory objects such as files, shared memory regions, frame buffers, etc. Any memory that is mappable or can be made mappable can be contained by a dataspace. For a thread to access the data contained in a dataspace, the dataspace is *attached* to, i.e. mapped into, the address space. Address spaces are constructed by attaching dataspaces including application code and data, heap and stack memory.

Dataspaces themselves are implemented by *Dataspace Managers*. Any task within the VM framework can be a dataspace manager by implementing the dataspace protocol. For example, a file system dataspace manager provides files as attachable dataspaces by caching disk contents within its address space, and using the underlying L4 mechanisms to map the cached content to clients who have the dataspace attached. Dataspace managers map pages of dataspaces to clients in response to the page fault handling mechanism which forwards page faults on attached dataspaces to the appropriate dataspace manager that implements the dataspace.

The dataspace and dataspace manager paradigms provide a flexible framework of object containers and object container implementors. Few restrictions are placed on participants other than implementing the defined interaction protocol correctly. However, while clients with attached dataspaces see a logical container, device drivers interacting with such a container require more information about the current dataspace state for DMA purposes. In particular, they have to know the translation between dataspace addresses and physical memory which is only known by the dataspaces' manager. In a traditional system we have the kernel implemented page tables as a central authority for translation information. With our VM framework, translation information is distributed amongst dataspace managers which creates the problem of efficient information retrieval. We describe our solution to this problem in Section 4

4   Driver Framework

As described in Section 2, the high degree of hardware and software integration in classic system architectures creates an environment for efficient driver implementation. The challenge is to keep the high level of integration when transforming drivers into user-level applications while enforcing protection boundaries between them and the surrounding system. There are obviously trade-offs to be made between the strength of the protection boundary and the cost of interacting across it. A network driver interface that copies packets across protection boundaries provides greater packet integrity and poorer performance compared to an interface that passes packets by reference. In choosing trade-offs for this paper we focused on maximising performance while still improving robustness. Drivers and their clients may corrupt the data they produce and consume, but should not be able to corrupt the operation of each other. However, our framework is not restricted to the particular trade-offs we made for this paper. A system designer can increase or decrease the degree of isolation between clients and drivers by small changes in interfaces, their implementation, or the composition of drivers and clients.

For this paper we took the following approach:

- Minimise the cost of interaction between clients and drivers by interacting via shared memory instead of direct invocation where possible. This sharing is secure in that it is done such that clients cannot interfere with the operation of drivers and vice versa. However, data buffers can be modified by clients or drivers at any point in the interaction.
- Minimise the cost of any overhead we must insert between clients and drivers (or between drivers and the kernel) to support interaction across protection boundaries.
- For any overhead that we must insert to enable interaction, we attempt to amortise the cost by combining operations or event handling where possible.

We now describe how we applied our approach to constructing a driver framework with reference to the model introduced in Section 2.

4.1 Interrupts

Direct delivery of interrupts to applications is not possible on current hardware. A mechanism is required for an ISR within a driver application to be invoked. We use the existing model developed for L4 where interrupts are represented as IPCs from virtual *interrupt threads* which uniquely identify the interrupt source. The real ISR within the kernel masks the interrupt, transforms the interrupt event into an IPC message from the interrupt thread which is delivered to the application's ISR. The blocked ISR within the application receives the message, unblocks, and performs the normal ISR functionality. Upon completion, the driver ISR sends a reply message to the interrupt thread resulting in the interrupt source being unmasked. The ISR can then block waiting for the next interrupt IPC.

While L4 IPC is very light-weight, it is not "free". We add a small amount of direct overhead to implement this clean model of interrupt delivery. Indirect overhead is incurred by context switching from an existing application to the driver application upon interrupt delivery. We expect this overhead to be low compared to the high cost of going off-chip to manage devices, and plan to reduce the overall overhead by using interrupt hold-off techniques currently applied to limit the rate at which interrupts are generated.

4.2   Session-Based Interaction

Copying data across protection boundaries is expensive. Where possible, we use shared memory to pass data by reference, or to make control and metadata information readily available to clients and drivers. Establishing shared memory is also an expensive operation both in terms of managing the hardware (manipulating page tables and TLB entries), and in terms of performing the book-keeping required in software. To amortise the cost of setting up shared memory we use a session-based model of interaction with drivers.

A *session* is the surrounding concept within which a sequence of interactions between client and driver are performed. It is expected that a session is relatively long lived compared to the duration of the individual interactions of which we expect many within a session. To enable pass-by-reference data delivery, one or more dataspaces can be associated with a session for its duration. Dataspaces can contain a shared memory region used to allocate buffers, a client's entire address space, or a small page-sized object. There are obviously trade-offs that can be made between cost of establishing a session, and the size and number of dataspaces associated with a session. To avoid potential misunderstanding, there can be many underlying sessions within our concept of a *session*. For example, an IP stack has a *session* with the network device driver through which many TCP/IP sessions can be managed.

4.3   Lock-Free Data Structures

There are obvious concurrency issues in managing data structures in shared memory. We make heavy use of lock-free techniques to manage data structures shared between drivers and their clients. We use lock-free techniques for predominately two reasons: to avoid external interaction and to avoid time-outs and recovery on locks.

Enqueueing work (packet/command descriptors and similar metadata) for a driver by explicitly invoking it requires at least two context switches per enqueued item. This would cause the high level of integration achieved in normal systems to be lost. Lock-free queues (implemented with linked lists or circular buffers) allow work to be enqueued for a driver (or a client) without requiring explicit interaction with the driver on every operation. This encourages a batching effect where several local lock-free operations follow each other, and finally the recipient driver is notified via explicit interaction (a queued-work notify event).

Lock-free techniques allow us to avoid dealing with excessive lock holding times. It is much easier to validate potentially corrupt data in a lock-free queue that is caused by a misbehaving client (we have to validate client provided data anyway), than to determine if a client is misbehaving because a lock is found held.

4.4   Translation, Validation, and Pinning

Drivers process work descriptors which can contain references to the actual buffers to be processed. Buffers are specified as ranges of addresses within dataspaces. The dataspaces are associated with the surrounding driver-client session. The dataspaces themselves are implemented by other applications (dataspace managers). This creates an interesting problem. The knowledge of a dataspace's existence, who is accessing it, and what physical frames implement it at any instant in time is known by the dataspace manager implementing the dataspace, not the client using the dataspace, and not the driver accessing the dataspace to process the requests of the client. In a traditional system, this information (page tables and frame tables) is readily available to the driver within the kernel address space. Ideally, we would again like to safely replicate the high degree of integration between driver, clients, and information required to operate.

The validation of buffers specified by the client within the above framework is simple. Given buffers are ranges of addresses within dataspaces, validation is a matter of confirming the dataspace specified is associated with the session between the driver and client.

The translation of dataspace pages to physical frames is required by drivers of DMA-capable devices. This translation is only known by a dataspace manager. Our approach thus far has been to avoid external interaction by the driver as much as possible, however translation requires this interaction in some form. To enable translation, the dataspace manager provides a shared memory region between it and the device driver: the translation cache. The translation cache is established between the manager and driver when a dataspace is added to a session between the driver and client. Multiple dataspaces from the same manager can share the same translation cache. The translation cache contains entries that translate pages within dataspaces into frames[1]. The cache is consulted directly by the driver to translate buffer addresses it has within dataspaces to physical addresses for DMA. After the translation cache is set up, the driver only needs to interact with the object implementor in the case of a cache miss. At present we use a simple on-demand cache refill policy, but we plan to explore more complex policies if later warranted.

In addition to translating a buffer address to a physical address for DMA, the driver needs a guarantee for the duration of DMA that the translation remains valid, i.e. the page (and associated translation) must remain *pinned* in memory. In this paper we have not focused on the problem of pinning in depth. We see at least two approaches to managing pinning for DMA. The first method is to use time-based pinning where entries in the translation cache have expiry times. The second method is to share state between the driver and dataspace implementor to indicate the page is in use and should not be paged out.

Time-based pinning has the difficult problem of the driver needing to estimate how long a DMA transaction might take, or even worse, how long it will take for a descriptor in a buffer ring to be processed, e.g. on a network card. However, time-based pinning has the nice property of not requiring interaction between

---

[1] In our virtual memory framework, dataspaces can also be composed of other dataspaces. In this case, the translation consist of a sequence of dataspace to dataspace translations, and then a final dataspace to physical frame translation. However, we ignore this scenario for the sake of clarity in the paper.

driver and object implementor. Further discussion of time-based pinning can be found our previous work [19].

State sharing to indicate to the dataspace manager that pinning is required could be achieved with a pin-bit within translation cache entries. This requires read-write shared memory between driver and dataspace implementor that was not required up until this point. It should be clear that the pin-bit has direct parallels with similar flags in a traditional frame table and thus warrants little further discussion. Note that the pin-bit would only be advisory. The memory implementor can enforce quotas on pin time or the amount of pinned memory by disabling the driver and resetting the device (if permitted) to recover pinned pages.

4.5   Notification

Unlike traditional systems where thread state and scheduler queues are readily available in shared kernel space, in a system with drivers in separate protection domains, system calls must be performed to manipulate the scheduler queues, i.e. block and activate threads. System calls are significantly more expensive than state changes and queue manipulations. An efficient activation mechanism is required for ISRs to hand-off work to DPCs, and for both clients and drivers to deliver work and potentially block as the sender and while activating the recipient.

By using queues in shared memory for message delivery, we create the environment required for user-level IPC (as opposed to IPC involving the kernel). User-level IPC has been explored by others [20,21], mostly in the context of multiprocessors where there is an opportunity to communicate without kernel interaction via shared memory between individual processors. Our motivation is two-fold. We wish to avoid kernel interaction (not activate the destination) if we know the destination is active (or will become active), and we wish to enable batching of requests between drivers and clients by delaying notifications when possible and desirable.

Our notification mechanism is layered over L4 IPC. Blocking involves waiting for a message, activating involves sending a message. To avoid notifications when unnecessary, the recipient of notifications indicates its thread state via shared memory. If marked inactive, a notification is sent; if not it is assumed that the recipient is (or will be) active and the notification is suppressed.

The delay between setting the state and blocking waiting for IPC creates a race condition if preempted between the modification and blocking waiting for IPC. There is a potential for notification messages to be missed if sent to a thread that has not yet blocked. However, if the sender does not trust the recipient, it is not safe for the sender to block on or re-send notifications without being vulnerable to denial-of-service attacks. Thus, recipients have to be able to recover from missed notifications on their own. We resolve this race by using a general mechanism called *preemption control*, which can make threads aware of preemption. In the rare case that a preemption is detected, the recipient rolls back to a safe active state from where it tries to block again.

The notification bit creates opportunities for delaying notification (to increase batching) or avoiding notification altogether. An example of avoidance is where a network driver would eventually receive a "packet sent" or "transmit queue empty" interrupt from the device. If such events are known to occur within acceptable latency bounds, notifying such a device when enqueueing an outgoing packet is unnecessary as the driver will eventually wake via the interrupt to discover the newly enqueued packets. This allows a driver client to submit requests continuously to maximise the batching effect.

5   Evaluation and Results

We evaluate our framework for running device drivers at user level in a network context. Handling modern high-speed networks is challenging for traditionally structured systems due to the very high packet rate and throughput they achieve.

Our test system consists of a user-level ISR that is comprised of generic low-level interrupt handling in the L4 kernel and device-specific interrupt handler for a dp83820 Gigabit ethernet card driver. The DPC is the lwIP IP stack and a UDP echo service that simply copies incoming packets once and echoes them to the sender. The driver and lwIP execute in separate processes which interact as described in Section 4. Note that the echo service is compiled into the process containing lwIP. The machine is a Pentium Xeon 2.66 GHz, with a 64-bit PCI bus.

We chose this test scenario as we believe it to be the extreme case that will expose the overheads of our framework most readily. The test does very little work other than handle interrupts, and send/receive packets across a protection boundary between the driver and lwIP, and then onto (or from) the network. In a more realistic scenario, we would expect the "real" application to dominate CPU execution compared to the drivers and IP stack. By removing the application, the driver and lwIP stack (and our overheads) will feature more prominently.

We used the ipbench network benchmarking suite[22] on four P4-class machines to generate the request UDP load that we applied to the test system. ipbench can apply specific load levels to the target machine, the packet size used was 1024 bytes. We performed two experiments, (a) that uses random-interval program counter sampling to develop an execution profile at an offered load of 450Mb/s using 100us interrupt hold-off, and (b) which ramps up the offered load gradually and records throughput and CPU utilisation at each offered load level. The load generators record echoed packets to calculate achieved throughput, CPU utilisation is measured by using the cycle counter to record time spent in a low priority background loop. Utilisation results obtained via random sampling and the cycle counter agree within one percent. The second experiment was performed for both $0\mu s$ and $100\mu s$ interrupt hold-off for Prime, and to compare, Linux with our driver and Linux's IP stack in-kernel, and user-level echo server.

The results show that for the profile experiment 68% of time was spent in the idle thread. For the remaining 32% of samples, we divided the samples into the following categories: *IPC* kernel code associated with the microkernel IPC path; *Driver* code associated with the network driver that would be common to all drivers for this card independent of whether it runs in-kernel or at user-level; *IP* code associated with lwIP that is also independent of running at user-level or in kernel; *Kernel* code that is independent of system structuring, this code is mostly related to interrupt masking and acknowledgement; User-level *Notification* code that implements notification within our framework; User-level *Translation* code that performs translation from dataspace addresses to physical memory; User-level *Interrupt* code related to interrupt acknowledgement; User-level *Buffer* code for managing packet buffers, including (de-)allocation, within our framework.

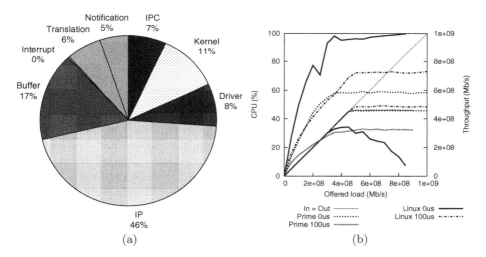

(a)   (b)

Fig. 1. (a) Execution profile. (b) CPU utilisation and throughput versus load level for Prime and Linux using $0\mu s$ and $100\mu s$ interrupt hold off.

The profile of execution within these categories is illustrated in Figure 1. The component of execution unrelated to our framework (Kernel + Driver + IP) forms 65% of non-idle execution time. Code related to our framework (Buffer + Interrupt + Translation + Notification + IPC) forms the remaining 35% of non-idle execution. Even when considering all framework related code as overhead introduced by running drivers at user-level, this is not a bad result. The test scenario we chose to analyse does so little work that we expect in a more realistic scenario our framework will consume a smaller fraction of execution time.

Considering all framework related code as overhead is not a fair comparison as two components of the framework (buffer management and translation) also have to be performed in a traditional system structure. If traditional buffer management and translation is comparable, then the overhead of running drivers at user-level (Notification + IPC + Interrupt) is only 12% of non-idle time.

Figure 1 also shows the result of the CPU utilisation and throughput experiment. The thin diagonal line represents where achieved throughput equals offered load. The lines beginning and rising above this reference represent CPU utilisation. The lines that track the reference and diverge to the right represent achieved throughput. We see that for 100μs interrupt hold off, both Prime and Linux achieve similar throughput of approximately 460Mb/s and 480Mb/s respectively. Prime uses much less CPU achieving the result (32% versus 72%). However, we make no claim of a fair comparison as Linux has a heavier weight IP stack, translation and pinning infrastructure, and uses a socket interface which results in an extra packet copy compared to Prime. We simply observe that we are currently competitive with a traditionally-structured existing system and are optimistic we can at least retain comparable performance in more similarly structured systems. For the 0μs hold-off results, we see Linux goes into live-lock near 100% CPU after which throughput tapers off as offered load increases. Prime achieves exactly the same throughput for 0μs and 100μs hold-off, though CPU utilisation differs markedly (58% versus 32%).

6   Conclusions

We have constructed a framework for running device drivers at user-level. Our goal was to preserve the high degree of system integration that enables high-performance driver construction while at the same time confining drivers safely to their own address space like normal applications. We analysed our framework's performance in the context of gigabit ethernet, and our initial results show modest overhead in an execution profile in a test scenario designed to exacerbate the overhead. In throughput oriented benchmarks, we demonstrated similar performance to Linux in terms of achieved throughput. We plan to further explore our framework's performance by constructing more realistic test scenarios (e.g. SPECweb), drivers and interfaces for other devices (e.g. disk). We also plan to explore system structures more comparable to existing systems (e.g. driver, IP stack, and web server all running as separate processes).

We eventually hope that our results will be encouraging enough to CPU and system architects to consider exploring efficient control of DMA for protection purposes in commodity hardware. Such hardware would ensure that device drivers are just normal applications under the complete control of the operating system.

References

1. Liedtke, J.: Toward real microkernels. Communications of the ACM **39** (1996)
2. Hohmuth, M., Tews, H., Stephens, S.G.: Applying source-code verification to a microkernel - the VFiasco project. In: Proc. 10th SIGOPS European Workshop. (2002)
3. Engler, D.R., Kaashoek, M.F., Jr., J.O.: Exokernel: An operating system architecture for application-level resource management. In: 15th Symp. on Operating Systems Principles, Copper Mountain Resort, CO, ACM (1995)

4. Accetta, M., Baron, R., Bolosky, W., Golub, D., Rashid, R., Tevanian, A., Young, M.: MACH: A new kernel foundation for UNIX development. In: Proc. Summer USENIX. (1986)
5. Cheriton, D.R.: The V kernel: A software based for distribution. IEEE Software **1** (1984) 19–42
6. Rozier, M., Abrossimov, V., Armand, F., Boule, I., Gien, M., Guillemont, M., Hermann, F., Kaiser, C., Langlois, S., Leonard, P., Neuhauser, W.: Chorus distributed operating system. Computer Systems **1** (1988)
7. Tanenbaum, A.S., van Renesse, R., van Staveren, H., Sharp, G.J., Mullender, S.J.: Experiences with the amoeba distributed operating system. Communications of the ACM **33** (1990) 46–63
8. Chou, A., Yang, J., Chelf, B., Hallem, S., Engler, D.: An empirical study of operating systems errors. (In: Proc. 18th Symp. on Operating Systems Principles)
9. Microsoft: Driver signing for windows. Available: http://www.microsoft.com/technet/prodtechnol/winxppro/proddocs/code_signing.asp (2002)
10. Gefflaut, A., Jaeger, T., Park, Y., Liedtke, J., Elphinstone, K., Uhlig, V., Tidswell, J., Deller, L., Reuther, L.: The SawMill multiserver approach. In: 9th SIGOPS European Workshop, Kolding, Denmark (2000)
11. Härtig, H., Baumgartl, R., Borriss, M., Hamann, C.J., Hohmuth, M., Mehnert, F., Reuther, L., Schönberg, S., Wolter, J.: DROPS - OS support for distributed multimedia applications. In: Proc. 8th SIGOPS European Workshop, Sintra, Portugal (1998)
12. von Eicken, T., Basu, A., Buch, V., Vogels, W.: U-net: a user-level network interface for parallel and distributed computing. In: Proc. 15th Symp. on Operating Systems Principles, Copper Mountain, Colorado, USA (1995) 40–53
13. Myrinet: Myrinet. Website: www.myrinet.com (2002)
14. Leslie, B., Heiser, G.: Towards untrusted device drivers. Technical Report UNSW-CSE-TR-0303, School Computer Science and Engineering, University of New South Wales, Sydney, 2052, Australia (2003)
15. Felten, E.W., Alpert, R.D., Bilas, A., Blumrich, M.A., Clark, D.W., Damianakis, S.N., Dubnicki, C., Iftode, L., Li, K.: Early experience with message-passing on the SHRIMP multicomputer. In: Proc. 23rd Symp. on Computer Architecture. (1996) 296–307
16. Rawson III, F.L.: An architecture for device drivers executing as user-level tasks. In: USENIX MACH III Symposium. (1993)
17. Liedtke, J., Elphinstone, K., Schönberg, S., Härtig, H., Heiser, G., Islam, N., Jaeger, T.: Achieved IPC performance. In: 6th Workshop on Hot Topics in Operating Systems (HotOS), Chatham, Massachusetts (1997)
18. Aron, M., Liedtke, J., Park, Y., Deller, L., Elphinstone, K., Jaeger, T.: The SawMill framework for virtual memory diversity. In: Australasian Computer Systems Architecture Conference, Gold Coast, Australia, IEEE Computer Society Press (2001)
19. Liedtke, J., Uhlig, V., Elphinstone, K., Jaeger, T., Park, Y.: How to schedule unlimited memory pinning of untrusted processes or provisional ideas about service-neutrality. In: 7th Workshop on Hot Topics in Operating Systems, Rio Rico, Arizona (1999)
20. Unrau, R., Krieger, O.: Efficient sleep/wake-up protocols for user-level IPC. In: International Conference on Parallel Processing. (1998)
21. Ritchie, D., Neufeld, G.: User level ipc and device management in the raven kernel. In: Proc. USENIX Microkernels and Other Kernel Architectures. (1993)
22. Wienand, I., Macpherson, L.: ipbench. Website: http://ipbench.sourceforge.net/ (2002)

A Generation Ahead of Microprocessor: Where Software Can Drive uArchitecture To?

Jesse Z. Fang

Intel

Abstract. The presentation will start with introduction of Microprocessor Technology Labs at Intel to show the Intel's efforts in the uArchitecture and system software research areas. As all of you know, Moore's law successfully leads Intel microprocessor business in decades. Transistor densities will continue to increase. However, device speed scaling will not follow historical trends and leakage power remains an issue. Meanwhile, new usage models and workloads will continue to demand greater performance. We can't run business as usual. We need to develop uArchitecture features more effectively with power constraints. Software in both applications and systems will play more and more important roles in uArchitecture research and microprocessor design. Emerging applications like mining, recognition and synthesis (MRS) will become the next generation dominated applications. Study of the characterizations of these applications is significant for the next generation of microprocessor design. System software has been changing its landscape as well. There are challenges and opportunities for microprocessor designers and researchers to explore new uArchitecture features to meet the needs of the new application and system software. The presentation will show the potential direction of uArchitecture for such emerging applications also. The talk will discuss the emerging paradigms of programming systems and its impact to uArchitecture design by giving couple examples of how compilation technologies enable HW design.

P.-C. Yew and J. Xue (Eds.): ACSAC 2004, LNCS 3189, p. 270, 2004.
© Springer-Verlag Berlin Heidelberg 2004

A Cost-Effective Supersampling for Full Scene AntiAliasing

Byung-Uck Kim[1], Woo-Chan Park[2], Sung-Bong Yang[1], and Tack-Don Han[1]

[1] Dept. of Computer Science, Yonsei University, Seoul, Korea,
kimbu@yonsei.ac.kr,
[2] Dept. of Internet Engineering, Sejong University, Seoul, Korea

Abstract. We present a graphics hardware system to implement supersampling cost-effectively. Supersampling is the well-known technique to produce high quality images. However, rendering the scene at a higher resolution requires a large amount of memory size and memory bandwidth. Such costs can be alleviated by grouping subpixels into a fragment with a coverage mask which indicates which part of the pixel is covered. However, this may cause color distortion when several objects either overlap or intersect with each other within a pixel. In order to minimize such errors, we introduce an extra buffer, called the *RuF(Recently used Fragment)-buffer*, for storing the footprint of a fragment most recently used in the color manipulation. In our experiments, the proposed system can produce high quality images as good as supersampling with a smaller amount of memory size and memory bandwidth, compared with the conventional supersampling.

Keywords: Antialiasing, Supersampling, Graphics Hardware, Rendering Algorithm

1 Introduction

With growth of user demand for high quality images, the hardware-supported full scene antialiasing (FSAA) has become commonplace in 3D graphics systems. Artifacts due to aliasing are mostly caused by insufficient sampling. To attenuate such aliasing problem, supersampling has been practiced in the high-end graphics system [2] and begins to be adopted by most pc-level graphics accelerator.

In supersampling, 3D objects are rendered at a higher resolution and then are averaged down to the screen resolution [8]. Hence it requires a large amount of memory size and memory bandwidth. For example, $n \times n$ supersampling requires n^2 times bigger both memory size and memory bandwidth than one-point sampling. Some reduced versions of it have been practiced; sparse supersampling [2] that populates sample points sparsely and adaptive supersampling [1] in which the only discontinuity edges are supersampled. In multi-pass approach, the accumulation buffer [4] has been proposed in which one scene is rendered several times and these images are then accumulated, one at a time, into the accumulation buffer. When the accumulation is done, the result is copied back into the

P.-C. Yew and J. Xue (Eds.): ACSAC 2004, LNCS 3189, pp. 271–281, 2004.

frame buffer for viewing. However, it is obvious that rendering the same scene n times takes n times longer than rendering it just once. Both supersampling and the accumulation buffer are well integrated into the Z-buffer (also called *depth buffer*) algorithm that is adopted by most rendering systems for the hidden surface removal. Moreover, Z-buffer algorithm handles correctly interpenetrating objects.

Rather than rendering each subpixel individually, A-buffer approach [3] groups subpixels into a fragment with a coverage mask that indicates which part of the pixel is covered. Such a representation is efficient in reduction of the memory and bandwidth requirements because it shares the common color value instead of having its own color value per subpixel. To apply Carpenter's blending formulation [3] for antialiasing of opaque objects, fragments should be sorted in the fragment list by their depth value. The fragment lists can be implemented by a pointer-based linked list [6] or a pointer-less approach [9]. For reducing noticeable artifacts, correct subpixel visibility calculations are more important that correct antialiasing of subpixels. Therefore, the more concise depth value representation has been practiced in [5].

This paper presents a cost-effective graphics hardware system that renders the supersampled graphics primitives with full scene antialiasing. In our approach, an area-weighted representation of a fragment using a coverage mask is adopted, as in A-buffer, to reduce the memory and bandwidth requirements. This may cause color distortion when several objects either overlap or intersect with each other within a pixel. In order to minimize such errors, we introduce an extra buffer, called the *RuF (Recently used Fragment)-buffer*, for storing the footprint of a fragment most recently used in the color manipulation. In addition, we introduce the new color blending formulation for minimizing color distortion by referencing the footprint of the RuF-buffer. In our simulation, we compared the amount of memory size and memory bandwidth of the proposed scheme with those of supersampling and investigated the per-pixel color difference of the images produced from both methods. For various 3D models with 8 sparse sample points, the proposed algorithm reduces the amount of memory size and memory bandwidth by 35.7% and 67.1%, respectively, with 1.3% per-pixel color difference as compared with supersampling.

The rest of this paper is organized as follows. In Section 2, we describe the proposed graphics architecture. Section 3 explains fragment processing algorithm for antialiasing. Section 4 provides the experimental results of image quality, memory and bandwidth requirement. Finally, the conclusions are given in Section 5.

2   The Proposed Graphics Architecture

In this section, we present the data structure and memory organization for processing a pixel with subpixels individually or a fragment. We also describe the proposed graphics hardware with the newly developed RuF-buffer.

2.1   Data Structure and Memory Organization for a Pixel

Figure 1 shows the data structure and memory organization for representing a pixel with subpixels individually and a fragment. Here we assumed that each pixel has 8 sparse sample points. In supersampling method, each subpixel is processed individually; the pair of color and depth value per subpixel is stored into color buffers and depth buffers in the frame buffer. Hence, the required memory size per pixel is $m \times (C + Z)$ bits where C and Z is color (32 bits) and depth value (24 bits), respectively and m is the number of sample points. In this example, $8 \times (32 + 24)$ bits $= 56$ bytes per pixel is required.

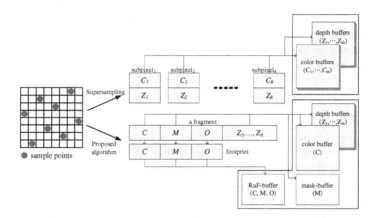

Fig. 1. Data structure and memory organization for a pixel.

In the proposed scheme, the data structure for a fragment is basically originated from the one of the A-buffer. Subpixels within a pixel are grouped into a fragment that shares the common color value (C) with a coverage mask (M). Moreover, we can easily compute the color contribution of a fragment within a pixel since a coverage mask represents an area-weighted value. For handling subpixel visibility correctly, depth value per subpixel $(Z_1, \cdots, Z_m)$ is kept individually. An object tag (O) is the unique identifier per object and can be generated sequentially by the rendering hardware incorporated with modelling software [6]. It is used for post-merging fragments; if two fragments in a pixel have the same object tag value then the footprint of both fragments can be merged into the RuF-buffer. The RuF-buffer holds the footprint of a fragment that is recently used in the color manipulation phase. The footprint of a fragment consists of color, coverage mask and object tag of a fragment and it will be used for correct handling the hidden surface removal. The required memory size per a pixel is $(2 \times (C + M) + m \times Z + O)$ bits where M is the coverage mask (m bits) and O is the object tag (16 bits). Here, 2^{16} objects are assumed to be enough for representing 3D model in a scene. Therefore, the memory size

Table 1. Memory requirement

m	Supersampling	Our approach	Reduction ratio
4	28 bytes	24 bytes	14.3%
8	56 bytes	36 bytes	35.7%
16	112 bytes	62 bytes	44.6%
64	448 bytes	218 bytes	51.3%

of $(2 \times (32 + 8) + 8 \times 24 + 16)$ bits $= 36$ bytes per pixel is required when 8 sparse sample points are used.

Table 1 shows the comparison of the memory requirement between supersampling and the proposed algorithm as the number of sample points increases. As shown in the results, the reduction ratio of the memory requirement begins to be larger as the number of sample points increases since our approach can save the memory requirement for representing individual color value per subpixel by sharing the common color value.

2.2   RuF-Buffer Graphics Architecture

Figure 2 shows the proposed graphics architecture with the conventional geometric-processing and rasterizer-processing. We add the mask-buffer and the RuF-buffer into the conventional architecture. Generally, 3D data are geometric-processed with rotating, scaling and translation. The processed results are fed into the rasterizer-processing. In rasterizer-processing, the fragments of each polygon are generated by scan-conversion and then passed through occlusion test such as Z-buffer algorithm and various image mapping such as texture mapping or bump mapping. Finally, the color value of each pixel is manipulated and stored into the color buffer in the frame buffer. When all the fragments are processed, the color values in the frame buffer are sent to a display device.

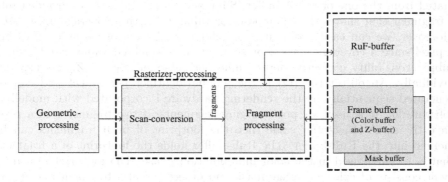

Fig. 2. The proposed graphics architecture.

3 Fragment Processing for Antialiasing

Figure 3 shows three phases of the newly introduced functional unit of fragment processing: the *occlusion test*, the *color manipulation*, and the *RuF-buffer recording*. Roughly speaking, the newly fragment incoming into the graphics pipeline is tested with Z-buffer algorithm per subpixel. If it is totally occluded by the one previously stored in the frame buffer, called a *prepixel*, then it will be discarded and the next fragment will be processing.

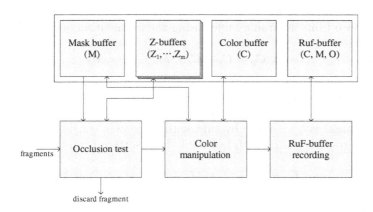

Fig. 3. Functional units for fragment processing.

Otherwise, we calculate the visible fraction of an incoming fragment, called a *survived surface*, and the hidden surface of the prepixel occluded by it. For calculating color value of a pixel, the survived surface will be added into and the hidden surface will be subtracted from the color buffer. In this phase, we look up the RuF-buffer for investigating the color value of the hidden surface. Finally, the survived fragment is merged into the RuF-buffer to allow more opportunity by covering the larger portion within a pixel. In describing each stage, the subscripts, 'i', 'p', and 'r' are used for denoting the attribute of an incoming fragment, the prepixel in the frame buffer, and the footprint in the RuF buffer. For instance, M_i is for the coverage mask of an incoming fragment. For simplicity, we assume that a coverage mask used in formulation returns the area-weighted value; for instance, if the number of sample points is eight and M_i covers three subpixels then M_i in formulation denotes the value of $3/8$.

Detail descriptions of each stage in the fragment processing are presented as follows:

The occlusion test : The depth comparison per subpixel between an incoming fragment and a prepixel are tested with the conventional Z-buffer algorithm. Then the mask composite for the survived surface (M_s) and the hidden surface

(M_h) are processed. Z-buffers are updated with new depth values of the survived surface.

The color manipulation : The survived surface is visible fraction of an incoming fragment. Hence, its area-weighted color value should be added into the color buffer. In addition, the hidden surface of a prepixel occluded by the survived surface should be subtracted from the color buffer. To look up the color value of the hidden surface, we investigate the match between the hidden surface and the footprint of the RuF-buffer through the mask comparison of $(M_k = M_h \cap M_r)$. If M_k is a subset of M_r then we can totally remove the color contribution of the hidden surface from the frame buffer using the formulation of Eq. 1.

$$\text{new } C_p = C_p + C_i \times M_s - C_r \times M_k \tag{1}$$

However, since the footprint of the RuF-buffer may not provide any information about some parts of the hidden surface we expand the formulation of Eq. 1 to compensate color value with a slight error. The fourth term of formation in Eq. 2 compensates color value by subtracting the area-weighted color value for the blind parts $(M_b = M_h - M_k)$ of the hidden surface from the frame buffer.

$$\text{new } C_p = C_p + C_i \times M_s - C_r \times M_k - C_p \times M_b \tag{2}$$

The RuF-buffer recording : Generally, the polygonal surfaces of an object exist in a coplanar space. Therefore, each neighbored surface generates fragments that share the same pixel on their boundary [3],[6]. So, they can be merged into one in the post-processing. Fragments that come from the same object will be merged into one since the same tagged object has same property. The merging process can be computed as follows:

$$\text{new } M_r = M_r \cup M_s; \text{new } C_r = C_r \times \frac{M_r}{\text{new } M_r} + C_r \times \frac{M_s}{\text{new } M_r} \tag{3}$$

However, if the survived fragment has the different object tag then the RuF-buffer is reset with the survived surface. The new object now begins to be drawn.

Figure 4 and Table 2 shows an example of fragment processing for each event and its associated color manipulation. In this example, subpixels are located on 3×3 grid sample points and three consecutive fragments (f_1, f_2, f_3) are incoming into the graphics pipeline. In Figure 4, we assume that a fragment f_1 was already processed in the previous phase; the frame buffer was initialized and then filled with f_1, where f_1 of object one (O_1) covers four subpixels with a color value C_0. Hence, the color value of a prepixel in the frame buffer (C_1) was computed as an area-weighted value of f_1, and then the footprint of f_1 was stored in the RuF-buffer. Now two fragments, f_2 and f_3, are newly fed into the graphics pipeline sequentially.

The left on the figure shows the processing of a fragment f_2 which of object 2 (O_2) has C_2 as a color value and covers four subpixels. The occlusion test is

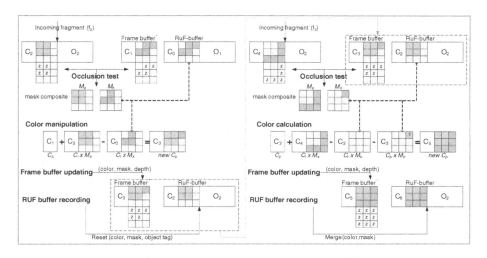

Fig. 4. Example of fragment processing

Table 2. The color manipulation process

Events	Color manipulation	Color buffer
Frame buffer initialize	—	$\emptyset$
f_1 incoming	$C_0 \times \frac{4}{9}$	C_1
f_2 incoming	$C_1 + C_2 \times \frac{4}{9} - C_0 \times \frac{3}{9}$	C_3
f_3 incoming	$C_3 + C_4 \times \frac{5}{9} - C_3 \times \frac{1}{9}$ (instead of $C_0 \times \frac{1}{9}$)	C_5

first processed, and then the survived and hidden masks are composited by Z-buffer algorithm per subpixel. In this example, four subpixels of f_2 are survived and three subpixels in a prepixel are occluded. Moreover, the information of the hidden surface can be referenced through the RuF-buffer. Thus the new color value (C_3) can be computed by Eq. 1 without any color distortion. Finally, the RuF-buffer is reset with the footprint of f_2 since the object tag of f_2 is different to the one of the RuF buffer stored in the previous phase.

The right on the figure shows the processing of a fragment f_3, which of object 2 (O_2) has C_4 as a color value and covers five subpixels. Similarly as in f_2 processing, the hidden and survived surfaces are computed in the occlusion test; in this example, five subpixels are survived and one subpixel is occluded. However, in the color manipulation, the footprint of the RuF-buffer cannot provide any information of the hidden surface (M_b). So, the color value is compensated by subtracting it from the prepixel; for instance, the color value of $C_3 \times \frac{1}{9}$ are used in formulation instead of $C_0 \times \frac{1}{9}$. This causes color distortion with the mere color difference of ($C_3 \times \frac{1}{9} - C_0 \times \frac{1}{9}$). In RuF-buffer recording, the footprint of two fragments f_2 and f_3 are merged into one since they have the same object tag, and then it covers the entire portion of a pixel.

4   Empirical Results

In our experiments, the 3D models described with OpenGL functions are geometric-processed and passed through scan-conversion in the Mesa library, which is the OpenGL-clone implementation and can be accessed in public domain [7]. We modified the Mesa library to output the tracefile of a fragment with a coverage mask. The resulted tracefile is fed into the simulator that implements the proposed architecture in C. Then the final image of 200×150 resolution is produced as shown in Figure 5.

Table 3 describes the characteristics of 3D models used in our experiments where the number of vertices (V), triangles (T), fragments (F), and objects (O) are provided. In our experiment, we decided to use eight-sparse sample point ($8\times RuF$) for the antialiasing architecture because it has been successfully practiced in high-end graphics systems [2]. To provide an indication of the performance in our approach, various supersampling methods are also simulated; one-point sampling ($1 \times S$, 1 subpixel per pixel), 8 sparse supersampling ($8 \times S$, 8 subpixels per pixel), 4 by 4 supersampling ($4 \times 4S$, 16 subpixels per pixel), and 8 by 8 supersampling ($8 \times 8S$, 64 subpixels per pixel).

Table 3. The characteristics of 3D models used in our experiments

Model Name	V	T	F	O
Al	3618	7124	11975	35
Castle	6620	13114	17444	16
Dolphins	885	1692	4570	3
Pig	3522	7040	7499	3
Rose+vase	4028	3360	5425	5
Teapot	3644	6320	6807	1
Venus	711	1418	5464	1

4.1   Image Quality

We present the image quality with respect to the number of sample points. To observe the quality of final scenes, the error metric of per-pixel color difference is used as shown in Eq. 4.

$$\text{Per-pixel color difference} = \sum_{\forall i,j} \sum_{c=r,g,b} (p_{ijc} - q_{ijc})^2, \qquad (4)$$

where p_{ij} and q_{ij} are the pixels from the same location of a reference image and a test image, respectively.

In order to make a small number of pixels with large difference more noticeable, the square of the difference is made [5]. We compute the per-pixel color difference for each 3D model where the reference image is produced by $8 \times 8S$,

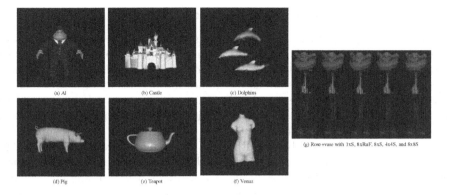

Fig. 5. The final images for each 3D model

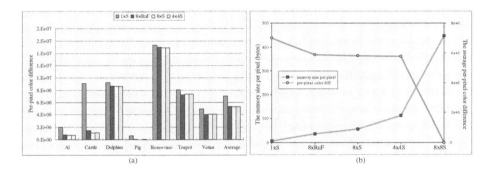

Fig. 6. Performance of color difference and memory size.

it is regarded as to be an ideal image, and each test image is produced by $1 \times S$, $8 \times S$, $8 \times RuF$ and $4 \times 4S$, respectively.

Figure 6(a) shows the results of the per-pixel color difference for each 3D dataset with various sample points. As can be seen from the results, the per-pixel color difference becomes to be smaller as the number of sampling points increase. Moreover, the final images of $8 \times RuF$ are almost as good quality as $8 \times S$; both of them have the same number of sample points.

4.2 Trade-Off Between Image Quality and Memory Requirement

In order to show the cost efficiency of the proposed architecture, two graphs for memory size per pixel and per-pixel color difference, respectively, are plotted together in Figure 6(b). The per-pixel color difference between $8 \times RuF$ and $8 \times S$ is 1.3% but the memory size per pixel is 35.7%. That is, our approach provides almost as good quality as supersampling with a less hardware cost.

4.3 Memory Bandwidth Requirement

Figure 7 shows the memory bandwidth requirements where two bar graphs for supersampling (left) and the proposed scheme (right) are plotted as a pair for each model. Arbitrary scenes for each 3D model are produced with both methods where 8 sparse sample points are used. As shown in the results, the proposed architecture can reduce the memory bandwidth requirement by 53.6% $\sim$ 75.5% for Castle and Rose+vase. The internal bandwidth is required for pixel processing between the graphics pipeline and the frame buffer (includes the RuF-buffer and mask-buffer). The external bandwidth is for swapping the front and back buffer or for average-down filtering. In supersampling, the external bandwidth dominates the memory bandwidth requirement. In other words, it implies that the screen-size color buffer is very efficient in reducing the bandwidth requirement since it does not require the overhead for average-down filtering process.

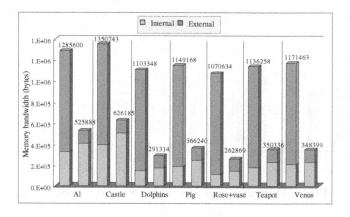

Fig. 7. The memory bandwidth requirement

5 Conclusion

In this paper, we present a graphics hardware system to implement supersampling in cost-effective manner. For hardware-implementation aspect, our graphics architecture uses same programming model as in Z-buffer algorithm for the hidden surface removal and adds only small additions to the conventional rendering process such as mask comparison and composite. In addition, mask comparison and composite can be simply processed with bitwise operations. In the color manipulation, computing the color contribution of a fragment can be processed through look-up tables, each entry of which holds the predefined floating point number divided by the number of sample points.

To provide an indication of the performance in terms of cost-effective full scene antialiasing, the results of memory requirement, bandwidth requirement,

Table 4. Summary of performance

	Memory size	Memory bandwidth	per-pixel color diff.
$8 \times S$	56 Bytes	1181030 Bytes	1338250
$8 \times RuF$	35 Bytes	395890 Bytes	1336154
Reduction ratio	35.7%	67.1%	1.3% (difference)

and per-pixel color difference are shown in Table 4 when 8 sparse sample points are used. It shows that the proposed architecture can reduce the memory size and the memory bandwidth size by 35.7% and by 67.1% with a slight color difference of 1.3%, compared with the conventional supersampling. As shown in the results, the proposed architecture can efficiently render the high quality scene with an economic hardware cost. Moreover, the simplicity of rendering process for our scheme allows us to have fast rendering through well-defined pipeline with a single pass.

Acknowledgment. The authors are grateful to the anonymous reviewers of the earlier version of this paper, whose incisive comments helped improve the presentation. This work is supported by the NRL-Fund from the Ministry of Science & Technology of Korea.

References

1. Aila, F., Miettine, V., Nord, P.: Delay Streams for Graphics Hardware. ACM Transactions on Graphics **22** (2003) 792–800
2. Akeley, K.: RealityEngine graphics. Computer Graphics (SIGGRAPH 93) **27** (1993) 109–116
3. Carpenter, L.: The A-buffer: an Antialiased Hidden Surface Method. Computer Graphics (SIGGRAPH 84) **18** (1984) 103–108
4. Haeberli, P.E., Akeley, K.: The Accumulation Buffer: Hardware Support for High-Quality Rendering. Computer Graphics (SIGGRAPH 90) **24** (1990) 309–318
5. Jouppi, N.P., Chang, C.F.: Z^3: an Economical Hardware Technique for High-quality Antialiasing and Transparency. In Proceeding of Graphics hardware (1993) 85–93
6. Lee, J.A., Kim, L.S.: Single-Pass Full-Screen Hardware Accelerated Antialiasing. In Proceeding of Graphics hardware (2000) 67–75
7. The Mesa 3D Graphics Library. http://www.mesa3d.org
8. Watt, A.: 3D Computer Graphics. Third Edition (2000) Addison-Wesley
9. Wittenbrink, C.M.: R-Buffer: A Pointless A-Buffer Hardware Architecture. In Proceeding of Graphics hardware (2001) 73–80

A Simple Architectural Enhancement for Fast and Flexible Elliptic Curve Cryptography over Binary Finite Fields GF(2^m)

Stefan Tillich and Johann Großschädl

Graz University of Technology
Institute for Applied Information Processing and Communications
Inffeldgasse 16a, A–8010 Graz, Austria
{Stefan.Tillich,Johann.Groszschaedl}@iaik.at

Abstract. Mobile and wireless devices like cell phones and network-enhanced PDAs have become increasingly popular in recent years. The security of data transmitted via these devices is a topic of growing importance and methods of public-key cryptography are able to satisfy this need. Elliptic curve cryptography (ECC) is especially attractive for devices which have restrictions in terms of computing power and energy supply. The efficiency of ECC implementations is highly dependent on the performance of arithmetic operations in the underlying finite field. This work presents a simple architectural enhancement to a general-purpose processor core which facilitates arithmetic operations in binary finite fields GF(2^m). A custom instruction for a multiply step for binary polynomials has been integrated into a SPARC V8 core, which subsequently served to compare the merits of the enhancement for two different ECC implementations. One was tailored to the use of GF(2^{191}) with a fixed reduction polynomial. The tailored implementation was sped up by 90% and its code size was reduced. The second implementation worked for arbitrary binary fields with a range of reduction polynomials. The flexible implementation was accelerated by a factor of nearly 10.

Keywords: Elliptic curve cryptography, application-specific instruction set extension, binary finite fields, SPARC V8, multiply step instruction.

1 Introduction

Security for mobile and wireless applications requires the involved devices to perform cryptographic operations. For open systems, the use of public-key cryptography is practically inevitable. There are likely to be two groups of devices which will participate in secure mobile and wireless environments [17]: end devices and servers. End devices are often constrained regarding computing power, memory for software code, RAM size and energy supply. Those devices require fast, memory- and energy-efficient implementations of public-key methods. Elliptic curve cryptography (ECC) reduces the size of the operands involved in computation (typically 160–250 bit) compared to the widely used RSA cryptosystem (typically 1024–3072 bit) and is therefore an attractive way to realize

P.-C. Yew and J. Xue (Eds.): ACSAC 2004, LNCS 3189, pp. 282–295, 2004.

security on constrained devices. With typical processor word-sizes of 8–64 bit, public-key cryptosystems call for efficient techniques to handle multiple-precision operands. Binary finite extension fields $GF(2^m)$ allow efficient representation and computation on a general-purpose processor which does not feature a hardware multiplier and are therefore well suited to be used as the underlying field of an elliptic curve cryptosystem.

ECC implementations require several choices of parameters regarding the underlying finite field (type of the field, representation of its elements, and the algorithms for the arithmetic operations) as well as the elliptic curve (representation of points, algorithms for point arithmetic). If some of these parameters are fixed, e.g. the field type, then implementations can be optimized yielding a considerable performance gain. Such an optimized ECC implementation will mainly be required by constrained end devices in order to cope with their limited computing power. The National Institute of Standards and Technology (NIST) has issued recommendations for specific sets of parameters [13]. As research in ECC advances, new sets of parameters with favorable properties are likely to become available and recommended. Therefore, not all end devices will use the same set of parameters. Server machines which must communicate with many different clients will therefore have a need for flexible and yet fast ECC implementations.

This paper introduces a simple extension to a general-purpose processor to accelerate the arithmetic operations in binary extension fields $GF(2^m)$. Our approach concentrates on a very important building block of these arithmetic operations; namely the multiplication of binary polynomials, i.e. polynomials with coefficients in $GF(2) = \{0, 1\}$. If this binary polynomial multiplication can be realized efficiently, then multiplication, squaring and inversion in $GF(2^m)$ and in turn the whole ECC operation is made significantly faster.

Two forms of a multiply step instruction are proposed, which can be implemented and used separately or in combination. These instructions perform an incremental multiplication of two binary polynomials by processing one or two bit(s) of one polynomial and accumulating the partial products. A modified ripple-carry adder is presented which facilitates the accumulation with little additional hardware cost. The proposed custom instructions have merits for implementations which are optimized for specific binary finite fields with a fixed reduction polynomial. Also, flexible implementations which can accommodate fields of arbitrary length with a range of reduction polynomials benefit from such instructions. Both types of implementations are general enough to support different elliptic curves and EC point operation algorithms.

The remainder of this paper is organized as follows. Some principles of elliptic curve cryptography in binary finite fields are given in the next Section. Section 3 outlines important aspects of modular multiplication in $GF(2^m)$. A modified ripple-carry adder which facilitates the implementation of our enhancement is presented in Section 4. Section 5 describes the proposed custom instructions in detail and Section 6 gives evaluation results from our implementation on an FPGA-board. Finally, conclusions are drawn in Section 7.

2   Elliptic Curve Cryptography

An elliptic curve over a field $\mathbb{K}$ can be formally defined as the set of all solutions $(x, y) \in \mathbb{K} \times \mathbb{K}$ to the general (affine) Weierstraß equation

$$y^2 + a_1 xy + a_3 y = x^3 + a_2 x^2 + a_4 x + a_6 \tag{1}$$

with the coefficients $a_i \in \mathbb{K}$. If $\mathbb{K}$ is a *finite field* GF(q), then the set of all pairs (x, y) satisfying Equation (1) is also finite. A finite field GF(q) is also called a *Galois field*. If the finite field is a binary extension field GF(2^m), then Equation (1) can be simplified to

$$y^2 + xy = x^3 + ax^2 + b \quad \text{with} \quad a, b \in \text{GF}(2^m) \tag{2}$$

The set of all solutions $(x, y) \in \text{GF}(2^m) \times \text{GF}(2^m)$, together with an additional special point $\mathcal{O}$, which is called the "point at infinity", forms an Abelian group whose identity element is $\mathcal{O}$. The group operation is the addition of points, which can be realized with addition, multiplication, squaring and inversion in GF(2^m). A variety of algorithms for point addition exists, where each requires a different number of those field operations. If, e.g. the points on the elliptic curve are represented in *projective coordinates* [2], then the number of field inversions is reduced at the expense of additional field multiplications.

All EC cryptosystems are based on an computation of the form $Q = k \cdot P$, with P and Q being points on the elliptic curve and $k \in \mathbb{N}$. This operation is called *point multiplication* (or *scalar multiplication*) and is defined as adding P exactly $k - 1$ times to itself: $k \cdot P = P + P + \cdots + P$. The execution time of the scalar multiplication is crucial to the overall performance of EC cryptosystems. Scalar multiplication in an additive group corresponds to exponentiation in a multiplicative group. The inverse operation, i.e. to recover k given P and $Q = k \cdot P$, is denoted as the elliptic curve discrete logarithm problem (ECDLP), for which no subexponential-time algorithm has been discovered yet. More information on EC cryptography is available from various sources, e.g. [2,8].

3   Arithmetic in Binary Extension Fields GF(2^m)

A common representation for the elements of a binary extension field GF(2^m) is the polynomial basis representation. Each element of GF(2^m) can be expressed as a binary polynomial of degree at most $m - 1$.

$$a(t) = \sum_{i=0}^{m-1} a_i \cdot t^i = a_{m-1} \cdot t^{m-1} + \cdots + a_1 \cdot t + a_0 \quad \text{with} \quad a_i \in \{0, 1\} \tag{3}$$

A very convenient property of binary extension fields is that the addition of two elements is done with a simple bitwise XOR, which means that the addition hardware does not need to deal with carry propagation in contrast to a conventional adder for integers. The instruction set of virtually any general-purpose processor includes an instruction for the bitwise XOR operation.

Algorithm 1. Multiple-precision multiplication of binary polynomials [5]

Input: Two binary polynomials, $a(t) = (\tilde{a}_{s-1}, \ldots, \tilde{a}_1, \tilde{a}_0)$ and $b(t) = (\tilde{b}_{s-1}, \ldots, \tilde{b}_1, \tilde{b}_0)$,
   each represented by an array of s single-precision (i.e. w-bit) words.
Output: Product $r(t) = a(t) \cdot b(t) = (\tilde{r}_{2s-1}, \ldots, \tilde{r}_1, \tilde{r}_0)$.

1:   $(\tilde{u}, \tilde{v}) \leftarrow 0$
2:   **for** i from 0 by 1 to $s - 1$ **do**
3:      **for** j from 0 by 1 to i **do**
4:         $(\tilde{u}, \tilde{v}) \leftarrow (\tilde{u}, \tilde{v}) \oplus (\tilde{a}_j \otimes \tilde{b}_{i-j})$
5:      **end for**
6:      $\tilde{r}_i \leftarrow \tilde{v}$
7:      $\tilde{v} \leftarrow \tilde{u}$, $\tilde{u} \leftarrow 0$
8:   **end for**
9:   **for** i from s by 1 to $2s - 2$ **do**
10:     **for** j from $i - s + 1$ by 1 to $s - 1$ **do**
11:        $(\tilde{u}, \tilde{v}) \leftarrow (\tilde{u}, \tilde{v}) \oplus (\tilde{a}_j \otimes \tilde{b}_{i-j})$
12:     **end for**
13:     $\tilde{r}_i \leftarrow \tilde{v}$
14:     $\tilde{v} \leftarrow \tilde{u}$, $\tilde{u} \leftarrow 0$
15: **end for**
16: $\tilde{r}_{2s-1} \leftarrow \tilde{v}$
17: **return** $r(t) = (\tilde{r}_{2s-1}, \ldots, \tilde{r}_1, \tilde{r}_0)$

When using a polynomial basis representation, the multiplication in $GF(2^m)$ is performed modulo an *irreducible polynomial* $p(t)$ of degree exactly m. In general, a multiplication in $GF(2^m)$ consists of multiplying two binary polynomials of degree up to $m - 1$, resulting in a product-polynomial of degree up to $2m - 2$, and then reducing this product modulo the irreducible polynomial $p(t)$ in order to get the final result. The simplest way to implement the multiplication of two binary polynomials $a(t), b(t) \in GF(2^m)$ in software is by means of the so-called *shift-and-xor method* [14]. In recent years, several improvements of the classical shift-and-xor method have been proposed [7]; the most efficient of these is the *left-to-right comb method* by López and Dahab [11], which employs a look-up table to reduce the number of both shift and XOR operations.

A completely different way to realize the multiplication of binary polynomials in software is based on the MULGF2 operation as proposed by Koç and Acar [9]. The MULGF2 operation performs a word-level multiplication of binary polynomials, similar to the $(w \times w)$-bit MUL operation for integers, whereby w denotes the word-size of the processor. More precisely, the MULGF2 operation takes two w-bit words as input, performs a multiplication over $GF(2)$ treating the words as binary polynomials, and returns a $2w$-bit word as result. All standard algorithms for multiple-precision arithmetic of integers can be applied to binary polynomials as well, using the MULGF2 operation as a subroutine [5]. Unfortunately, most general-purpose processors do not support the MULGF2 operation in hardware, although a dedicated instruction for this operation is simple to implement [12]. It was shown by the second author of this paper [6] that a conventional integer multiplier can be easily extended to support the MULGF2 operation, without significantly increasing the overall hardware cost. On the other hand, Koç and Acar [9] describe two efficient techniques to "emulate" the MULGF2 operation when it is not supported by the processor. For small word-sizes (e.g. $w = 8$), the MULGF2 operation can be accomplished with help of look-up tables. The second approach is to emulate MULGF2 using shift and XOR operations (see [9] for further details).

In the following, we briefly describe an efficient word-level algorithm for multiple-precision multiplication of binary polynomials with help of the MULGF2 operation. We write any binary polynomial $a(t) \in \mathrm{GF}(2^m)$ as a bit-string of its m coefficients, e.g. $a(t) = (a_{m-1}, \ldots, a_1, a_0)$. Then, we split the bit-string into $s = \lceil m/w \rceil$ words of w bits each, whereby w is the word-size of the target processor. These words are denoted as $\tilde{a}_i$ (for $0 \le i < s$), with $\tilde{a}_{s-1}$ and $\tilde{a}_0$ representing the most and least significant word of $a(t)$, respectively. In this way, we can conveniently store a binary polynomial $a(t)$ in an array of s single-precision words (unsigned integers), i.e. $a(t) = (\tilde{a}_{s-1}, \ldots, \tilde{a}_1, \tilde{a}_0)$. Based on the MULGF2 operation, a multiple-precision multiplication of binary polynomials can be performed according to Algorithm 1, which is taken from a previous paper of the second author [5]. The tuple $(\tilde{u}, \tilde{v})$ represents a double-precision quantity of the form $u(t) \cdot t^w + v(t)$, i.e. a polynomial of degree $2w - 1$. The characters $\otimes$ and $\oplus$ denote the MULGF2 and XOR operation, respectively. In summary, Algorithm 1 requires to carry out s^2 MULGF2 operations and $2s^2$ XOR operations in order to calculate the product of two s-word polynomials. We refer to the original paper [5] for a detailed treatment of this algorithm.

Once the product $a(t) \cdot b(t)$ has been formed, it must be reduced modulo the irreducible polynomial $p(t) = t^m + \sum_{i=0}^{m-1} p_i \cdot t^i$ to obtain the final result (i.e. a binary polynomial of degree up to $m - 1$). This reduction can be implemented very efficiently when $p(t)$ is a sparse polynomial, which means that $p(t)$ has few non-zero coefficients c_i. In such case, the modular reduction requires only a few shift and XOR operations and can be highly optimized for a given irreducible polynomial [14,7,8]. Most standards for ECC, such as from ANSI [1] and NIST [13], propose to use sparse irreducible polynomial like trinomials or pentanomials. On the other hand, an efficient word-level reduction method using the MULGF2 operation was introduced in the previously mentioned paper [5]. The word-level method also works with irreducible polynomials other than trinomials or pentanomials, but requires that all non-zero coefficients (except of p_m) are located within the least significant word of $p(t)$, i.e. $p_i = 0$ for $w \le i < m$. For example, we used the trinomial $t^{191} + t^9 + 1$ for our ECC implementations, which satisfies this condition for a word-size of $w = 32$.

4   Modified Ripple-Carry Adder

A previous paper of the second author [6] presents the design of a so-called unified multiply-accumulate unit that supports the MULGF2 operation. The efficiency of that design is based on integration of polynomial multiplication into the datapath of the integer multiplier. On the other hand, the datapath for our proposed multiply step instructions can be integrated into the ALU adder and does not require a multiplier. For SPARC V8 cores, the implementation of our extension is relatively easy, as those cores already feature a multiply step instruction for integer arithmetic. In comparison to the previous work [6], the multiply step instructions offer a tradeoff of hardware cost against speed.

The simplest way to implement adders in general-purpose processors is in the form of ripple-carry adders. For instance the SPARC V8 LEON-2 processor, which we have used for our evaluation, employs a such an adder. Principally, ripple-carry adders consist of a chain of full adder cells, where each cell takes three input bits (usually labeled a, b and c_{in}) and produces two output bits with different significance (sum and c_{out}). The cells are connected via their carry signals, with the c_{out} of one stage serving as c_{in} input for the next higher stage.

A conventional ripple-carry adder takes two n-bit values and a carry-in bit and produces a n-bit sum and a carry-out bit which can be seen as the $(n+1)$-th bit of the sum. To generate a bit of the sum vector, each full adder cell performs a logical XOR of its three inputs a, b and c_{in}. This property can be exploited to perform a bitwise logical XOR of three n-bit vectors with a slightly modified ripple-carry adder. As explained in Section 3, this XOR conforms to an addition of the three vectors if they are interpreted as binary polynomials.

The modification consists of the insertion of multiplexors into the carry-chain of the ripple-carry adder as illustrated in Figure 1. The $insert$ control signal selects the carry value which is used. If $insert$ is 0, the adder propagates the carry signal, selecting cp_i as c_{i+1}. In this mode the adder performs a conventional integer addition, setting s and c_{out} accordingly. If $insert$ is 1, the carry is not propagated, but the $cins$ vector is used to provide the c_i inputs for the full adder cells. The sum vector s is calculated as the bitwise logical XOR of the vectors a, b and $cins$. The value of c_{out} is not relevant in this mode. In Figure 1 the bits with the same significance of the three vectors are grouped together by braces. The carry input of the rightmost full adder cell acts as c_{in} for integer addition and as least significant bit of the $cins$ vector for addition of binary polynomials. The $insert$ signal of the modified adder therefore switches between the functionality of an integer adder and and a 3:1 compressor for binary polynomials.

Ripple-carry adders have the disadvantage that the delay of carry propagation can be rather high. Embedded processors normally feature other, longer combinational paths, so that the carry propagation delay is not the critical path delay. If however the carry propagation path of the adder constitutes the critical path and the proposed modifications increase its delay significantly, other approaches are possible to get the 3:1 compressor functionality for binary polynomials. One solution is to modify a faster adder, e.g. a carry-select adder [3]. Another possibility is the use of dedicated XOR-gates without any modification of the adder. Both of these options come with an increased hardware cost.

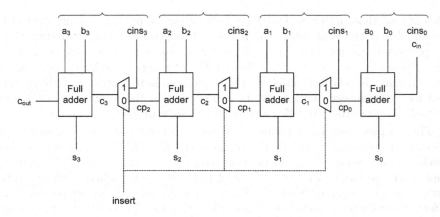

Fig. 1. A 4-bit modified ripple-carry adder

5 Multiply Step Instruction

Our enhancement is basically the addition of one or two custom instructions which can be realized with relatively little additional hardware. The basic idea is to provide a multiply step instruction for multiplication of binary polynomials. With a given word size w of the processor, a multiplication of two w-bit binary polynomials yielding a $2w$-bit result can be implemented efficiently with the proposed instructions. This word-size multiplication of binary polynomials corresponds to the MULGF2 operation mentioned in Section 3, which is an important building block for arithmetic operations in the field $GF(2^m)$.

The SPARC V8 Architecture Manual [16] defines a multiply step instruction for integer multiplication (MULSCC) and our proposed instructions are a modification thereof. MULSCC processes one bit of the multiplier and adds the resulting partial product to an 64-bit accumulator realized by two hardware registers. In the following, the register naming conventions of SPARC V8 will be used.

In order to perform a complete multiplication of two 32-bit binary polynomials, three registers have to be employed. Two of those registers form a 64-bit accumulator to hold the intermediate total during multiplication. These registers will be named %o0 and %y, with %o0 holding the 32 most significant and %y holding the 32 least significant bits. The register %o1 will be used as the third register. It contains the multiplicand during the whole course of the multiplication.

5.1 MULGFS Instruction

The first proposed instruction is named MULGFS and is only a slight variation of the MULSCC instruction. It can be used in the following fashion the perform a word-size polynomial multiplication (MULGF2 operation): At first, the multiplicand is loaded into %o1 and the multiplier is loaded into %y. Then the MULGFS instruction is executed 32 times to process each bit of the multiplier in %y. In each execution of the MULGFS instruction the value in the accumulator (%o0 and %y) is shifted right by one. The bit which is shifted out of the accumulator, i.e. the least significant unprocessed bit of the multiplier, is examined and a partial product is generated: If the bit is one, it is the value of the multiplicand, otherwise it is all zero. This partial product is added to the 32 highest bits of the accumulator, which reside in %o0. After 32 MULGFS instructions, the value in the accumulator must be shifted right by one to obtain the correct 64-bit result. Following the SPARC conventions, the MULGFS instruction is written in the following form in assembly code:

$$\text{MULGFS } \%o0, \%o1, \%o0$$

The first two registers are the source registers. The first one (%o0) contains the highest 32 bits of the accumulator while the second one (%o1) holds the multiplicand. The third register is the destination register (%o0) which is normally chosen to be the same as the first source register. The register for the 32 lowest bits of the accumulator (%y) is read and written implicitly for multiplication instructions in the SPARC architecture. In this case the 64-bit accumulator is formed by %o0 and %y. On other architectures, different approaches may be favorable, e.g. on a MIPS architecture the multiplication registers %hi and %lo could be implicitly used as accumulator. In detail, a single MULGFS instruction performs the following steps:

1. The value in the first source register (%o0) is shifted right by one. The shifted value is denoted as C.
2. The least significant unprocessed bit of the multiplier (last bit of %y) is examined. The partial product (denoted as A) is set to the value of the multiplicand (%o1), if the bit is one. Otherwise A is set to all zeros.
3. The contents of the %y register is shifted right by one with the least significant bit of %o0 shifted in from the left. The bit of the multiplier, which has been processed in the previous step, is therefore shifted out of %y.
4. A bitwise XOR of A and C is performed and the result is stored in the higher word of the accumulator (%o0).

The MULGFS instruction does not require the insertion of a carry vector for the adder. It is sufficient if the adder can suppress carry propagation whenever a specific control signal is set. The changes to the processor for the implementation of the MULGFS instruction are:

- Modifications to the decode logic to recognize the new opcode, and to generate an *insert* control signal for the ALU.
- Multiplexors to select the two operands for the adder and which allow shifting of the value in the two registers which form the accumulator.
- Gates which prevent carry propagation in the adder if *insert* is set.

5.2 MULGFS2 Instruction

The second proposed instruction (named MULGFS2) is a variation of the MULGFS instruction, which processes two bits of the multiplier simultaneously. In this fashion two partial products are generated and addition to the accumulated result can be done with a modified ripple-carry adder as specified as in Section 4.

A multiplication of two binary polynomials (MULGF2 operation) is done in the same way as described in the previous Section with the exception that the 32 subsequent MULGFS instructions are replaced by 16 MULGFS2 instructions. If only the MULGFS2 instruction is available, the final shift of the accumulator must be done with conventional bit-test and shift instructions. On the SPARC V8 this requires four instructions. If the MULGFS instruction is available, then the final shift can be done with a single instruction. The format for the MULGFS2 instruction remains the same as for the MULGFS instruction:

$$\text{MULGFS2 } \%\text{o0, } \%\text{o1, } \%\text{o0}$$

In detail, the MULGFS2 instruction works by executing these steps:

1. The value in the first source register (%o0) is shifted right by two. The shifted value is denoted as C.
2. The least significant unprocessed bit of the multiplier (last bit of %y) is examined. If the bit is one, a partial product (denoted as B) is set to the value of the multiplicand (%o1) shifted right by one. Otherwise B is all zeros.
3. The second lowest bit of the multiplier (penultimate bit of %y) is examined. If is is one, the second partial product (denoted as A) is set to the value of the multiplicand (%o1). Otherwise A is all zeros.
4. The contents of the %y register is shifted right by two with the following bits set as the new MSBs: The one but highest bit is set to the value of the least significant bit of %o0. The highest bit results from an XOR of the second lowest bit of %o0 and the logical and of the least significant bit of the multiplicand (%o1) and the second lowest bit of %y.
5. A bitwise XOR of A, B and C is performed and the result is stored in in the higher word of the accumulator (%o0).

The MULGFS2 instruction performs the XOR of the three 32-bit vectors with a modified ripple-carry adder. The required modifications to the processor are:

- Changed decode logic to recognize MULGFS2 instructions, and to generate an *insert* control signal for the modified ripple-carry adder.
- Multiplexors to select the three operands for the adder and which allow shifting by two of the values in the two registers which form the accumulator.
- A modified ripple-carry adder as described in Section 4 which is controlled by the *insert* signal.

The implementation of the MULGFS2 instruction for a SPARC V8 general-purpose processor can be seen in Figure 2.

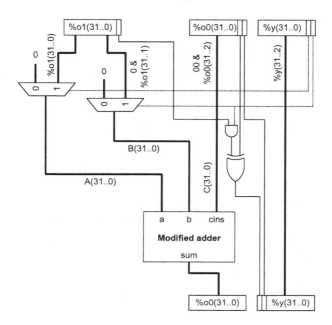

Fig. 2. MULGFS2 instruction implementation for a SPARC V8 processor

6   Experimental Results

Both MULGFS and MULGFS2 instructions have been implemented in the freely available SPARC V8-compliant LEON-2 processor [4]. The size for both instruction and data cache have been set to 4 kB. A tick counter register, whose content is incremented each clock cycle, has also been added to the LEON-2 to facilitate the measurement of the execution time of software routines. A XSV-800 Virtex FPGA prototyping board [18] has been used to implement the extended processor for verification of the design and for obtaining timing result for different realizations of ECC operations.

The ECC parameters given in Appendix J.2.1 of the ANSI standard X9.62 [1] have been used. The elliptic curve is defined over the binary finite field $GF(2^{191})$ with the reduction polynomial $t^{191} + t^9 + 1$. Most of the examined implementation variants use a multiplication of two binary polynomials (MULGF2 operation) as a building block for $GF(2^m)$ operations where the size of the binary polynomials equals the word-size w of the LEON-2 processor, namely 32 bit.

Two principal implementations of ECC operations have been employed for evaluation of the merits of the proposed multiply step instructions. One used the left-to-right comb method with a look-up table containing 16 entries, as mentioned in Section 3, for polynomial multiplication and shift and XOR instructions for reduction. This implementation was tailored to the use of $GF(2^{191})$ with the above reduction polynomial and therefore especially suited for constrained client devices. The different variants used for evaluation are denoted with the prefix

OPT in the rest of this text. The second implementation could work in a binary extension field of arbitrary length with any reduction polynomial, which fulfills the following requirement: It may only have non-zero coefficients for powers $< w$. Such an implementation is favorable for server machines in mobile and wireless environments. The variants are based on the MULGF2 operation as a building block for all $GF(2^m)$ multiplication, squaring and reduction. They vary only in the implementation of the MULGF2 operation and are denoted with the prefix FLEX. All OPT and FLEX implementations used the method described by López and Dahab to perform an elliptic scalar multiplication [10].

6.1 Running Times

Table 1 presents the running times of multiplication and squaring in $GF(2^{191})$ and of a complete elliptic scalar multiplication for the three variants of the flexible implementation. The running time is measured in clock cycles. The first column (FLEX1) gives the results for the pure software variant, where the MULGF2 operation has been implemented with shift and XOR instructions. The second and third column list the running times for adapted versions, where the word-size polynomial multiplication (MULGF2 operation) has been optimized. FLEX2 refers to the variant which made use of the MULGFS instruction as described in Section 5.1. The results for FLEX3 are for an implementation which utilizes both MULGFS and MULGFS2 instructions as outlined in Section 5.2. Both FLEX2 and FLEX3 necessitated only minor changes to the code of FLEX1.

Table 1. Execution times of important operations for ECC over $GF(2^{191})$ for the FLEX variants in clock cycles

	FLEX1	FLEX2	FLEX3
	Software	MULGFS instr.	MULGFS and MULGFS2 instr.
$GF(2^{191})$ multiplication	15,344	2,306	1,620
$GF(2^{191})$ squaring	5,335	691	476
EC scalar multiplication	22,485,650	3,260,478	2,319,558

The running times for the EC scalar multiplication from Table 1 are a representative measure to compare the overall speed of the three implementations. The use of the MULGFS instruction alone (FLEX2) yields a speedup factor of nearly 7 over the pure software version. If both multiply step instructions are available (FLEX3), the speedup factor is nearly 10. Note that squaring is a linear operation and therefore performs much faster than multiplication.

The optimized implementation in pure software (OPT1) can be enhanced with the proposed multiply step instructions. $GF(2^{191})$ multiplication which uses the MULGFS and MULGFS2 instructions is faster than the multiplication of the original software implementation. Table 2 lists the running times of the three versions, where OPT2 uses just the MULGFS instruction and OPT3 makes use of both MULGFS and MULGFS2 instructions to speed up $GF(2^{191})$ multiplication.

Table 2. Execution times of important operations for ECC over $GF(2^{191})$ for the OPT variants in clock cycles

	OPT1	OPT2	OPT3
	Software	MULGFS instr.	MULGFS and MULGFS2 instr.
$GF(2^{191})$ multiplication	3,182	2,076	1,500
$GF(2^{191})$ squaring	273	273	273
EC scalar multiplication	3,909,690	2,706,560	2,054,282

Table 3. Memory requirement of the OPT and FLEX variants of elliptic scalar multiplication in bytes

	OPT1	OPT3	FLEX1	FLEX3
Code section size	4,928	2,920	3,904	2,592
Data section size	1,024	1.024	264	264
Total size	5,952	3,944	4,168	2,856
Additional RAM usage	384	none	none	none

Note that the running time for the $GF(2^{191})$ multiplication for OPT2 and OPT3 are smaller than those of FLEX2 and FLEX3 because the former use a reduction step which is tailored to the reduction polynomial $t^{191} + t^9 + 1$. EC scalar multiplication is sped up by about 45% with the MULGFS instruction and by 90% through the use of both MULGFS and MULGFS2 instructions. Additionally, FLEX2 is about 15% faster than OPT1 and FLEX3 is about 40% faster.

6.2   Memory Requirements

Table 3 compares the size of the code and data sections of an SPARC executable which implements the full EC scalar multiplication for the OPT and FLEX variants. The executables have been obtained by linking the object files for each implementation without linking standard library routines. The size of the code and data sections have subsequently been dumped with the GNU *objdump* tool. As the values for OPT2 and OPT3 and those for FLEX2 and FLEX3 are nearly identical, only one implementation of each group has been listed exemplarily.

The executables of the FLEX2 and FLEX3 implementations are only half the size of OPT1. This is mainly because OPT1 uses a hard-coded look-up table for squaring and also features larger subroutines. OPT2 and OPT3 have 70% smaller code sections and a 50% smaller executable compared to OPT1. In addition, OPT1 uses an look-up table for $GF(2^{191})$ multiplication which is calculated on-the-fly and requires additional space in the RAM. This memory requirement is eliminated in OPT2, OPT3 and all FLEX variants.

The costs of additional hardware for implementation of both multiply step instructions have been evaluated by comparing the synthesis results for the different processor versions. The enhanced version had an increase in size of less than 1% and is therefore negligible.

The OPT variants are the most likely candidates for usage in devices which are constrained regarding their energy supply. To compare OPT1 with the enhanced versions OPT2 and OPT3, it is important to note that load and store instructions normally require more energy than other instructions on a common microprocessor; see e.g. the work of Sinha et al. [15]. Based on that fact it can be established that OPT2 and OPT3 have a better energy efficiency than OPT1 for two reasons: They have shorter running times and do not use as many load and store instructions, as they perform no table look-ups for field multiplication.

7 Conclusions

In this paper we presented an extension to general-purpose processors which speeds up ECC over $GF(2^m)$. The use of multiply step instructions accelerates multiplication of binary polynomials, i.e. the MULGF2 operation, which can be used to realize arithmetic operations in $GF(2^m)$ in an efficient manner. We have integrated both proposed versions of the multiply step instruction into a SPARC V8-compliant processor core. Two different ECC implementations have been accelerated through the use of our instructions. The implementation optimized for $GF(2^{191})$ and a fixed reduction polynomial has been sped up by 90% while reducing the size of its executable and its RAM usage. The flexible implementation, which could cater for different fields lengths m and an important set of reduction polynomials, was accelerated by an factor of over 10. Additionally, the enhanced flexible version could outperform the original optimized implementation by 40%. All enhancements required only minor changes to the software code of the ECC implementations.

We have discussed the merits of our enhancements for both constrained devices and server machines in a security-enhanced mobile and wireless environment. The benefits for devices constrained in available die size and memory seem especially significant, as our multiply step instructions require little additional hardware and reduce memory demand regarding both code size and runtime RAM requirements. Additionally, the implementations which use our instructions are likely to be more energy efficient on common general-purpose processors.

Acknowledgements. The research described in this paper was supported by the Austrian Science Fund (FWF) under grant number P16952-N04 ("Instruction Set Extensions for Public-Key Cryptography").

References

1. American National Standards Institute (ANSI). X9.62-1998, Public key cryptography for the financial services industry: The elliptic curve digital signature algorithm (ECDSA), Jan. 1999.
2. I. F. Blake, G. Seroussi, and N. P. Smart. *Elliptic Curves in Cryptography*. Cambridge University Press, 1999.

3. A. Chandrakasan, W. Bowhill, and F. Fox. *Design of High-Performance Microprocessor Circuits.* IEEE Press, 2001.
4. J. Gaisler. The LEON-2 Processor User's Manual (Version 1.0.10). Available for download at http://www.gaisler.com/doc/leon2-1.0.10.pdf, Jan. 2003.
5. J. Großschädl and G.-A. Kamendje. Instruction set extension for fast elliptic curve cryptography over binary finite fields GF(2^m). In *Proceedings of the 14th IEEE International Conference on Application-specific Systems, Architectures and Processors (ASAP 2003)*, pp. 455–468. IEEE Computer Society Press, 2003.
6. J. Großschädl and G.-A. Kamendje. Low-power design of a functional unit for arithmetic in finite fields GF(p) and GF(2^m). In *Information Security Applications*, vol. 2908 of *Lecture Notes in Computer Science*, pp. 227–243. Springer Verlag, 2003.
7. D. Hankerson, J. López Hernandez, and A. J. Menezes. Software implementation of elliptic curve cryptography over binary fields. In *Cryptographic Hardware and Embedded Systems — CHES 2000*, vol. 1965 of *Lecture Notes in Computer Science*, pp. 1–24. Springer Verlag, 2000.
8. D. Hankerson, A. Menezes, and S. Vanstone. *Guide to Elliptic Curve Cryptography.* Springer Verlag, 2004.
9. Ç. K. Koç and T. Acar. Montgomery multiplication in GF(2^k). *Designs, Codes and Cryptography*, 14(1):57–69, Apr. 1998.
10. J. López and R. Dahab. Fast multiplication on elliptic curves over $GF(2^m)$ without precomputation. In *Cryptographic Hardware and Embedded Systems*, vol. 1717 of *Lecture Notes in Computer Science*, pp. 316–327. Springer Verlag, 1999.
11. J. López and R. Dahab. High-speed software multiplication in $\mathbb{F}_{2^m}$. In *Progress in Cryptology — INDOCRYPT 2000*, vol. 1977 of *Lecture Notes in Computer Science*, pp. 203–212. Springer Verlag, 2000.
12. E. Nahum, S. O'Malley, H. Orman, and R. Schroeppel. Towards high performance cryptographic software. In *Proceedings of the 3rd IEEE Workshop on the Architecture and Implementation of High Performance Communication Subsystems (HPCS '95)*, pp. 69–72. IEEE, 1995.
13. National Institute of Standards and Technology (NIST). Digital Signature Standard (DSS). Federal Information Processing Standards Publication 186-2, 2000.
14. R. Schroeppel, H. Orman, S. O'Malley, and O. Spatscheck. Fast key exchange with elliptic curve systems. In *Advances in Cryptology — CRYPTO '95*, vol. 963 of *Lecture Notes in Computer Science*, pp. 43–56. Springer Verlag, 1995.
15. A. Sinha and A. Chandrakasan. Jouletrack – A web based tool for software energy profiling. In *Proceedings of the 38th Design Automation Conference (DAC 2001)*, pp. 220–225. ACM Press, 2001.
16. SPARC International, Inc. The SPARC Architecture Manual Version 8. Available for download at http://www.sparc.org/standards/V8.pdf, Aug. 1993.
17. A. Weimerskirch, D. Stebila, and S. Chang Shantz. Generic GF(2^m) arithmetic in software and its application to ECC. In *Information Security and Privacy — ACISP 2003*, vol. 2727 of *Lecture Notes in Computer Science*, pp. 79–92. Springer Verlag, 2003.
18. XESS Corporation. XSV-800 Virtex Prototyping Board with 2.5V, 800,000-gate FPGA. Product brief, available online at http://www.xess.com/prod014_4.php3, 2001.

Scalable Design Framework for JPEG2000 System Architecture

Hiroshi Tsutsui[1], Takahiko Masuzaki[1], Yoshiteru Hayashi[1], Yoshitaka Taki[1],
Tomonori Izumi[1], Takao Onoye[2], and Yukihiro Nakamura[1]

[1] Department of Communications and Computer Engineering, Kyoto University
Yoshida-hon-machi, Sakyo, Kyoto, 606-8501 Japan
{tsutsui, masuz, teru, taki}@easter.kuee.kyoto-u.ac.jp,
{izumi, nakamura}@kuee.kyoto-u.ac.jp
[2] Department of Information Systems Engineering, Osaka University
2-1 Yamada-Oka, Suita, Osaka, 565-0871 Japan
onoye@ist.osaka-u.ac.jp

Abstract. For the exploration of system architecture dedicated to
JPEG2000 coding, decoding and codec, a novel design framework is constructed. In order to utilize the scalability of JPEG2000 algorithm aggressively in system implementation, three types of modules are prepared
for JPEG2000 coding/decoding/codec procedures, i.e. software, software accelerated with user-defined instructions, and dedicated hardware.
Specifically, dedicated hardware modules for forward and inverse discrete
wavelet transformation (shortly DWT), entropy coder, entropy decoder,
and entropy codec as well as software acceleration of DWT procedure
are devised to be used in the framework. Furthermore, a JPEG2000 encoder LSI, which consists of a configurable processor Xtensa, the DWT
module, and the entropy coder, is fabricated to exemplify the system
implementation designed through the use of proposed framework.

1 Introduction

The increasing use of multimedia information requires image coding system to
compress different types of still images with different characteristics by a single
processing flow besides attaining high coding efficiency. To fulfill this requirement, JPEG2000 is currently being developed by ISO/ IEC JTC1/SC29 WG1
(commonly known as the JPEG), and JPEG2000 Part I[1] was standardized
in January, 2001. Distinctively, in JPEG2000, discrete wavelet transformation
(shortly DWT) is adopted to decorrelate images spatially to improve compression efficiency. With the use of this transformation, so-called *embedded stream*
can be generated, in which code for low quality/bitrate image is included in that
for high quality/bitrate image. Therefore, JPEG2000 can be regarded as the
viable image coding scheme in the coming network era to be used in a variety
of terminals for different application fields. However, this fact also implies that
performance requirement for terminals and applications varies widely. Thus any
of single software or hardware implementation can hardly fulfill performance

P.-C. Yew and J. Xue (Eds.): ACSAC 2004, LNCS 3189, pp. 296–308, 2004.

requirements for all range of terminals and applications. On the other hand, it is also impossible to arrange a full set of customized implementations for all of terminals or applications in terms of man-power resources.

Motivated by this tendency, we propose a novel framework of JPEG2000 system architecture, providing the distinctive ability of architectural exploration in accordance with the specification of each terminal. Through the use of this framework, an efficient JPEG2000 system organization is obtained by referring to performance requirements and limitations for implementation. The proposed framework is based on Tensilica's configurable processor Xtensa[2], which has an ability to be customized for a specific application by equipping user-defined instructions described in Tensilica Instruction Extension (TIE) language[3]. Enhancing this distinctive feature to such an extent to equip specific hardware modules prepared for procedures in JPEG2000, our framework provides scalable solution for JPEG2000 system architecture.

For each procedure of JPEG2000 coding and/or decoding, either of software implementation, software implementation accelerated by user-defined instructions, or hardware implementation is selectively employed. The implementation scheme for all procedures are decided by referring to performance requirements and/or limitations to design. In case extremely high processing performance is needed far more than that of hardware implementation, it is possible to equip two or more modules at the same time.

2   JPEG2000 Processing Flow

Fig. 1 depicts the procedures of JPEG2000 encoding scheme. First, a target image is divided into square regions, called *tiles*. Tiles of each color component are called *tile components*. Then 2-D forward DWT decomposes a tile component into LL, HL, LH, and HH subbands by applying 1-D forward DWT to a tile component vertically and horizontally. The low resolution version of the original tile component, i.e. LL subband, is to be decomposed into four subbands recursively. A subband is divided into *code-blocks*, each of which is coded individually by entropy coder. The entropy coder adopted in JPEG2000 is context-based adaptive binary arithmetic coder which consists of coefficient bit modeling process to generate contexts and arithmetic coding process, known as MQ-coder, to compress a binary sequence based on the context of each bit.

Decoding scheme of JPEG2000 is the reverse process of the encoding. During this process, 2-D backward DWT is realized by applying a series of 1-D backward DWTs (horizontal 1-D DWT and vertical 1-D DWT) to a tile component also in the reverse order of 2-D forward DWT. The set of filter coefficients used in 1-D backward DWT is the same as that in the forward DWT. Fig. 2 depicts the entropy coding and decoding procedure. Coefficient bit modeling is a common process to encoding and decoding. MQ-decoder extracts binary sequences from compressed data referring to contexts generated by the coefficient bit modeling process, while MQ-coder generates compressed data from contexts and binary sequences.

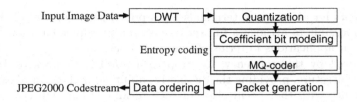

Fig. 1. Block diagram of JPEG2000 encoding

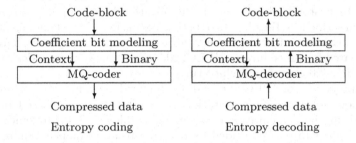

Fig. 2. Entropy coding and decoding

3   JPEG2000 System Framework

Our proposed framework is distinctive in that an efficient JPEG2000 encoding and decoding system architecture can be explored by selecting implementation scheme for each procedure considering performance requirements such as image resolution or processing throughput and limitations to design such as power consumption, process technology rule, or chip size. Three types of implementation schemes are prepared in our framework; software implementation, software implementation accelerated by user-defined instructions added to Xtensa, and dedicated hardware implementation. As for hardware implementation, multiple modules can be used at the same time if necessary. To embody such a Plug-and-Play like feature, each hardware module is designed to have a generic SRAM-based interface which can support various bus architectures by only designing interface converters. Therefore, our framework makes it much easier to design a JPEG2000 encoding and decoding system than conventional tedious manual design tasks of each procedure, which would be implemented as software or hardware. For forward/backward DWT and entropy coding/decoding, common hardware components are prepared. These procedures handle relatively large square regions of an image, called tile and code-block, respectively. Such a procedure is inherently suitable as a component, and the overhead of data transfer between the hardware component and memory can be concealed when direct memory access (DMA) is applied effectively. In addition to these common hardware components, an software module accelerated by user-defined instructions is prepared for DWT. Since the dominant operation in DWT procedure is filter operation, a set of instructions for filter operation is added to the Xtensa's

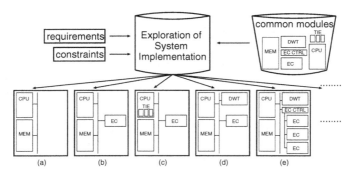

Fig. 3. Basic structure of the proposed framework

original instruction set so that considerable performance improvement can be achieved without any additional hardware component.

Moreover, to organize JPEG2000 codecs, an entropy codec hardware component is prepared. This component is smaller than the simple combination of the entropy coder and decoder in terms of the number of gates. As for DWT, the differences between encoding and decoding are ordering of two 1-D DWTs applied in series, ordering of filter coefficients, and signs of several filter coefficients. The first one seems to affect largely the DWT architecture. However, in the case of lossy compression, the error introduced by employing same DWT ordering for both forward and backward DWTs is quite slight. Therefore we employ the same ordering of DWTs to make it easy to design forward and/or backward 2-D DWT. As for other differences, we simply introduce multiplexers to select the signs of filter coefficients, etc.

Fig. 3 illustrates the basic structure of the proposed framework. Each system implementation exemplified in Fig. 3 is briefed below. Though only the case for JPEG2000 encoders is explained, JPEG2000 decoders and codecs can be implemented by the same way of the encoders.

Fig. 3(a) is a system implementation example where all modules are implemented as software so that the system is composed only of a CPU and a main memory. This solution is used when it is impossible to employ hardware modules to the system due to die size limitation, the processing speed is not the key point aimed at, or the CPU provides sufficient performance for application.

Fig. 3(b) is a system implementation example where only the entropy coding (shortly EC in the figure) procedure is implemented by a hardware module. The hardware implementation of the entropy coding makes a large contribution to improvement of the speed, since this procedure is the most computationally intensive one among all the procedures as its detailed discussion is given in the next section.

Fig. 3(c) is a system implementation example where the entropy coder is implemented by hardware module, and instructions for DWT's filter operations are added to Xtensa. Since DWT procedure handles a whole tile, the number of cycles needed to execute the procedure in DWT, except for filter operations, such as address calculation, memory accessing, and so forth, is still large. Performance improvement in comparison with Fig. 3(b), however, can be achieved without any additional hardware module.

Fig. 3(d) is a system implementation example where both the entropy coder and DWT are implemented as hardware modules. In addition to the performance improvement as the benefit of these modules, memory accessing bandwidth is reduced.

Fig. 3(e) is a system implementation example where DWT is implemented by hardware module, and the entropy coding procedure is implemented by multiple hardware modules. This solution is the fastest among Fig. 3(a) through (e), and attains very high throughput. In this case, an additional controller is needed to manage these modules.

In this manner, our framework successfully provides scalable solution for JPEG2000 system architecture with the use of common modules.

4   Analysis of JPEG2000 Encoding

To construct the framework, first we implemented software JPEG2000 encoder and decoder, and analyzed computational costs of all procedures. Since DWT is to be executed in fixed point arithmetic in our software, even embedded CPUs which has no floating-point unit (FPU) can execute this software without any additional cycles needed for floating arithmetic emulation. The main specifications of our software are summarized in Table 1, and the result of profiling encoding process by the instruction set simulator (shortly ISS) of the target CPU Xtensa using a test image LENA is summarized in Table 2. The function `encode` is to encode whole image and does not include the routines for input/output from/to a file. In the function `entropy_coding`, the entropy coding including coefficient bit modeling and arithmetic coding by MQ-coder is executed. The function `FDWT_97`

Table 1. Main specification of the JPEG2000 software

tile size	128×128
DWT	9/7 irreversible filter
DWT decomposition level	3
code-block size	32×32

Table 2. Result of profiling encoding process

%	function name	self cycle	child cycle	total cycle	call
99.5	main	0.13	1371191.89	1371192.02	1
96.3	encode	540.26	1326074.65	1326614.91	1
64.4	entropy_coding	84.50	887680.17	887764.67	304
20.2	FDWT_97	29298.20	249056.71	278354.91	16
14.0	FILTD_97	191668.46	771.41	192439.87	7168

unit of number of cycles is Kcycle

is to execute DWT on a tile component and includes `FILTD_97` for 1-D DWT on an array.

According to this table, it can be said that the coefficient bit modeling and arithmetic coding procedures occupy 64.4% of total encoding cycles, DWT procedure occupies 20.2% of total encoding cycles, and `FILTD_97` function occupies 69.1% of DWT processing cycles.

5 JPEG2000 Processing Modules

5.1 DWT Module

DWT hardware. When implementing DWT as dedicated hardware, the essential factor to be considered is memory organization for storing intermediate data during recursive filter processing. There are two methods to store intermediate data for DWT. One is to store the data to the main memory or a tile buffer which is placed in a DWT hardware module. In this case, whenever vertical and horizontal DWT is attempted, the data is read from the memory/buffer and the transformed coefficients are written back to it. The other is the so-called line-based method[4] which is to store the data to a line buffer containing several lines in a tile. In this case, vertical and horizontal DWT can be done at the same time by utilizing the line buffer, so that this method requests less amount of data transfer over a bus than that using the main memory. Thus, we adopted line-based method to implement DWT hardware module.

To implement DWT filters, we adopted straightforward finite impulse response (FIR) filter, where, for calculating each transformed coefficient, weighted addition of a coefficient sequence with the filter length is executed. Assuming that the depth of input image is 8-bit, this module can implement one level 2-D DWT over a tile whose width is 128 or less. The tile size of 128×128 is reasonable since it is adopted in JPEG2000 Profile 0[5], which is intended mainly for hardware implementation.

The architecture of our DWT hardware module is shown in Fig. 4, which consists of a core module, a line buffer, and an IO controller. This core module comprises the following sub-modules; an extension module which extends a sequence of coefficients at the edges by the so-called periodic symmetric extension procedure, low-pass FIR filters whose filter length is 9, high-pass FIR filters whose filter length is 7, and a pair of shift registers which receive output data from vertical DWT and store vertically low-passed and high-passed 9 coefficients to be fed to horizontal DWT.

The line buffer consists of 13 line memories each of which is a 15-bit 128-word memory. The number of the additional 7 bits for the input bit depth, 8 bits, is large enough to realize as high precision as floating point operations. Totally 9 coefficients, all of which belong to the identical column of an image, are loaded to the core module from 9 lines of the line buffer every clock. Other 2 lines of the line buffer are used for receiving transformed coefficients from the core modules every clock. The other 2 lines of the line buffer are used for IO access between the DWT and CPU.

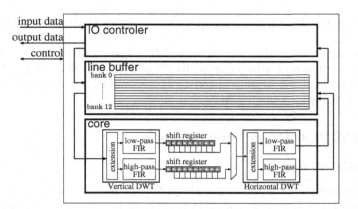

Fig. 4. Architecture of our DWT module

This core module works as follows. The 9 coefficients from the line buffer are transformed by the vertical DWT module and the results, i.e. low-passed and high-passed coefficients, are stored into the shift registers. At the same time, horizontal DWTs of vertically high-passed and low-passed sequences stored in shift registers are executed alternately, so that LL, HL, HH, and HH coefficients are output from the core module every 2 cycles.

As mentioned before, we employ the same 1-D DWT ordering for both forward and backward 2-D DWT, so as to make the architecture of forward and backward DWT almost identical. The proposed architecture of forward DWT module is designed through the use of Verilog-HDL. When this hardware module is used, the number of cycles needed for DWT with a test image LENA is 0.215 Mcycles, which is only 0.077 % of 278 Mcycles needed for software DWT. The DWT module is synthesized into 17,650 gates by using Synopsys's Design Compiler with 0.18 μm CMOS technology, with its critical path delay of 12 nsec.

Accelerated DWT software. According to the result of profiling, multiplications of fixed point variables and filter coefficients of Table 3; α, β, γ, δ, K, and $1/K$; need 6961.86 Kcycles, 7787.56 Kcycles, 7502.93 Kcycles, 6930.11 Kcycles, 6775.10 Kcycles, and 6971.17 Kcycles, respectively through entire image. Total of these values occupy 22.3% of execution cycles needed for function FILTD_97. Thus we implement these multiplications by user-defined instructions described in TIE. The circuits of the instructions consist of shifters and adders.

Custom instructions MUL_A, MUL_B, MUL_C, MUL_D, MUL_K, and MUL_R are to multiply positive input by lifting constants; α, β, γ, δ, K, and $1/K$, respectively. SMUL_A, SMUL_B, SMUL_C and SMUL_D are extended version of MUL_A, MUL_B, MUL_C and MUL_D, which can multiply negative input as well as positive input by lifting constants. At the final stage of lifting, target values must be shifted in right and rounded. These operations are also implemented as custom instructions. SMUL_K and SMUL_R are extended version of MUL_K and MUL_R. Same as SMUL_[A-D], these

Table 3. Filter coefficiets

α	-1.586 134 342 059 924
β	-0.052 980 118 572 961
γ	0.882 911 075 530 934
δ	0.443 506 852 043 971
K	1.230 174 104 914 001

Table 4. The number of gates of user-defined instructions

instruction	#gate
MUL_A	551.75
MUL_B	401.00
MUL_C	510.25
MUL_D	489.50
MUL_K	570.50
MUL_R	367.00
other	254.25
total	3144.25

Table 5. The number of gates of user-defined instructions

instruction	#gate
SMUL_A	1085.25
SMUL_B	739.25
SMUL_C	947.00
SMUL_D	1009.25
SMUL_K	1698.25
SMUL_R	1039.00
other	439.75
total	6957.75

instructions can handle negative values with equipping a right shifter and a rounding circuit.

The result of simulation by ISS using a test image LENA shows that when MUL_A, MUL_B, MUL_C, MUL_D, MUL_K, and MUL_R are equipped, the number of cycles to call FILTD_97 function is reduced to 175.564 Mcycles (88.6%) from 192.440 Mcycles, and that when SMUL_A, SMUL_B, SMUL_C, SMUL_D, SMUL_K, and SMUL_R are implemented, the number of cycles to call FILTD_97 function can be reduced to 133.461 Mcycles (69.4%) from 192.440 Mcycles.

According to the synthesis results attained by the same manner as the hardware DWT module, the critical path delay of MUL_A, MUL_B, MUL_C, MUL_D, MUL_K and MUL_R is 6.2 nsec, ant that of SMUL_A, SMUL_B, SMUL_C, SMUL_D, SMUL_K and SMUL_R is 9.5 nsec, The numbers of gates of custom instructions are summarized in Table 4 and 5.

5.2   Entropy Coder, Decoder, and Codec

There are two reasons why the entropy coding of JPEG2000 incurs such a high computational cost. One is that a context of a coefficient on a bit plane depends on sign bits, significant states, and some reference states of the eight nearest-neighbor coefficients. Therefore, there are many conditional branches and many operations which crop variables into a bit. The other is that MQ-coder updates its internal state after compression of every one binary symbol. When JPEG2000 entropy coder is implemented as hardware, MQ-coder may become the performance bottle-neck of the total system since the MQ-coder requires at least 1 cycle to process 1 binary symbol. Needless to say, considering hardware utilization efficiency coefficient bit modeling must be implemented with the same throughput as the MQ-coder. In our hardware entropy coder, pixel skipping scheme[6] is used to attain almost ideal performance.

Entropy Coder. Fig. 5 depicts the block diagram of our entropy coder, which consists of a coefficient bit modeling module, an MQ-coder, an IO controller, a plane controller, an FIFO, and a set of buffer memories. As buffer memories, the entropy coder has a code-block buffer to store code-block data, plane buffers to store bit plane as well as reference data needed to generate contexts, and stream buffer to store encoded data called *stream*. The FIFO is used to suppress the difference of the throughputs of the modeling module and the MQ-coder.

The above mentioned entropy coder is designed by Verilog-HDL. The result of logic simulation using sample image LENA indicates that when this hardware entropy coder is employed, the number of cycles needed for entropy coding of whole image is about 3.20 Mcycles, i.e. only 0.360 % of 887.76 Mcycles needed for software entropy coding.

The critical path delay is 7.0 nsec which is concluded by synthesis the entropy coder with 0.18 μm CMOS technology. The gate counts for this module is 7,901.

Next, let us discuss the size of memory for the entropy coder. The coder requests 12 bit $\times$ (32 $\times$ 32) = 12,288 bit as the code-block buffer, 4 $\times$ (32 $\times$ 32) = 4,096 bit as 4 plane buffers, and 2 $\times$ (32 $\times$ 32) = 2,048 bit as the double-buffered bit plane buffer. Here, the code-block buffer must have 12 bit depth in the case that the bit depth of input image is 8, and the number of guard bits is 2, which is enough to avoid the overflow of the result of DWT. As for the stream buffer for output, 8,192 bit is large enough when quantizer's step size equals 1, according to the software simulation. Consequently, 26,624 bit of memory elements are needed in total. It must be noticed that the size of stream buffer can be reduced when implementing it as an FIFO.

Entropy Decoder. Fig. 6 depicts the block diagram of our entropy decoder, which is similarly organized as the entropy coder. The differences are that the decoder does not equip FIFO, whereas controllers, MQ-decoder, and coefficient bit modeling module of the decoder are customized for decoding. Our MQ-decoder returns a binary to coefficient bit modeling module in 1cycle.

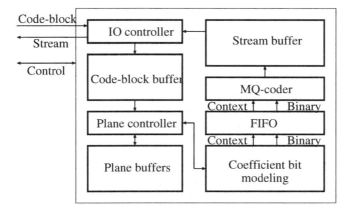

Fig. 5. Architecture of our entropy coder

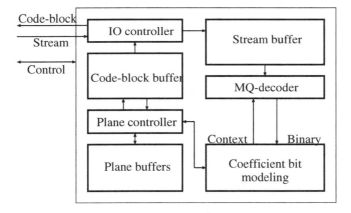

Fig. 6. Architecture of our entropy decoder

The entropy decoder is designed through the use of Verilog-HDL. The result of logic simulation using sample image LENA indicates that when this hardware entropy decoder is employed, the number of cycles needed for entropy coding of whole image is about 5.03 Mcycles, i.e. only 0.283 % of 1776 Mcycles needed for software entropy decoding.

The critical path delay is 7.0 nsec which is concluded by synthesis the entropy decoder with 0.18 μm CMOS technology. The gate counts for this module is 7,901.

Entropy Codec. In our framework, an entropy codec is also prepared in addition of the above mentioned entropy coder and decoder. By sharing some part of circuits between MQ-coder and MQ-decoder and the circuits to generate contexts of coefficient bit modeling for coding and decoding, we can successfully reduce

Table 6. Comparison of the number of gates between entropy coder, decoder and codec

	Submodule	#gate	total
Entropy	MQ-coder	2,983	
coder	Coefficient bit modeling	2,675	5,658
Entropy	MQ-decoder	3,881	
decoder	Coefficient bit modeling	2,645	6,454
Entropy	MQ-codec	6,048	
codec	Coefficient bit modeling	3,665	9,713

Table 7. Main features of the LSI

Technology	Hitachi 0.18μm CMOS
Interconnect	5 metal layers, PolySi
Power supply	1.8V
Chip area	5.9×5.9 mm^2
Design method	Standard-cell-based
Package	256pin BGA

Table 8. The numbers of gates and memory bits

#gate of Xtensa	44,000
#gate of DWT	17,650
#gate of Entropy coder	10,207
#bit of FF in DWT module	24,960
#bit of FF in Entropy coder	6,144
#bit of RAM of Entropy coder	65,536

#gate dose not include the gates of FF used as memory.

Table 9. The number of cycles

function name	total cycle by software	total cycle by using this LSI
encode	1326.6 (100%)	163.8 (12%)
entropy_coding	887.8 (67%)	3.20 (0.36%)
FDWT_97	278.4 (21%)	0.215 (0.08%)

Unit of number of cycles is Mcycle.
% of total cycle by software means the ratio to cycle of encode.
% of total cycle by using this LSI means the ratio to cycle by software.

the number of gates of the entropy codec with maintaining its performance. The comparison of the numbers of gates required for the dominant parts, which are MQ-coder/decoder and coefficient bit modeling, among entropy coder, decoder and codec is summarized in Table 6. The number of gates for MQ-codec is 88% of that for the combination of MQ-coder and MQ-decoder, and the number of gates of coefficient bit modeling for codec is 69% of that for the combination of those for encoding and decoding.

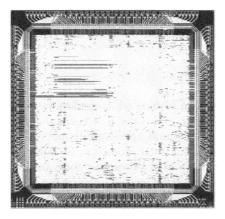

Fig. 7. Layout patterns for the LSI

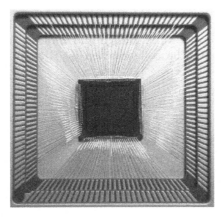

Fig. 8. Photograph of the LSI

6   LSI Implementation Result

In order to demonstrate the practicability of the proposed framework, we fabricated an JPEG2000 encoder LSI, which consists of our DWT hardware module, hardware entropy coder module, and Xtensa. A photograph of the LSI and layout patterns attained for the LSI are shown in Figs. 8 and 7, respectively.

Table 7 summarizes the specifications of the fabricated LSI. The LSI is with 1-Kword × 32-bit single port RAM as the code-block buffer and stream buffer of the entropy coder. The line buffer of DWT module and the plane buffers of entropy coding module are implemented by flip-flop (FF) arrays. The numbers of gates and memory bits are summarized in Table 8. The critical path delay of this LSI is 18 nsec, which assures 55.5 MHz operation.

The comparison between the number of cycles needed to encode the test image LENA by software and that by using this LSI is summarized in Table 9.

7 Conclusion

In this paper, a novel design framework to realize an efficient implementation of JPEG2000 encoder, decoder, and codec in accordance with the requirements and constraints of each terminals and applications has been proposed. This framework is distinctive in that for each procedure of JPEG2000 coding system, implementation scheme can be selected among software implementation, software implementation accelerated with user-defined instructions, and dedicated hardware implementation, so as to optimize the system organization. To demonstrate the practicability of the framework, we fabricated an LSI to exemplify a generated system implementation, in which our DWT hardware module and hardware entropy coder module were implemented with configurable processor Xtensa.

Acknowledgement. The VLSI chip in this study has been fabricated in the chip fabrication program of VLSI Design and Education Center (VDEC), the University of Tokyo with the collaboration by Hitachi Ltd. and Dai Nippon Printing Corporation.

References

1. ISO/IEC JTC1/SC29/WG1, "Information technology – JPEG2000 image coding system: Core coding system," Oct. 2002.
2. Tensilica, Inc., *Xtensa Application Specific Microprocessor Solutions — Overview Handbook*, Sept. 2000.
3. Tensilica, Inc., *Tensilica Instruction Extension (TIE) Language — User's Guide*, Sept. 2000.
4. ISO/IEC JTC1/SC29/WG1, "JPEG2000 verification model 9.1 (technical description)," June 2001.
5. ISO/IEC JTC1/SC29/WG1, "Draft of FPDRAM-1 to 15444-1," Dec. 2000.
6. Kuan-Fu Chen, Chung-Jr Lian, Hong-Hui Chen, and Liang-Gee Chen, "Analysis and architecture design of EBCOT for JPEG-2000," in *Proc. of the 2001 IEEE International Symposium on Circuits and Systems (ISCAS 2001)*, Vol. 2, pp. 765–768, Mar. 2001.

Real-Time Three Dimensional Vision

JongSu Yi[1], JunSeong Kim[1], LiPing Li[2], John Morris[1,3], Gareth Lee[4] and
Philippe Leclercq[5]

[1] School of Electrical and Electronics Engineering,
Chung-Ang University, Seoul 156-756, Korea
[2] Department of Computer Science, Harbin Normal University, Harbin, China 150080
[3] Department of Electrical and Electronic Engineering,
The University of Auckland, New Zealand
[4] Department of Computer Science and Software Engineering,
University of Western Australia, Nedlands, WA 6009, Australia
[5] Department of Electrical and Computer Engineering,
University of Western Australia, Nedlands, WA 6009, Australia

Abstract. Active systems for collision avoidance in 'noisy' environments such as traffic which contain large numbers of moving objects will be subject to considerable interference when the majority of the moving objects are equipped with common avoidance systems. Thus passive systems, which require only input from the environment, are the best candidates for this task. In this paper, we investigate the feasibility of real-time stereo vision for collision avoidance systems. Software simulations have determined that sum-of-absolute-difference correlation techniques match well but hardware accelerators are necessary to generate depth maps at camera frame rates. Regular structures, linear data flow and abundant parallelism make correlation algorithms good candidates for reconfigurable hardware. The SAD cost function requires only adders and comparators for which modern FPGAs provide good support. However accurate depth maps require large disparity ranges and high resolution images and fitting a full correlator on a single FPGA becomes a challenge. We implemented SAD algorithms in VHDL and synthesized them to determine resource requirements and performance. Altering the shape of the correlation window to reduce its height compared to its width reduces storage requirements with negligible effects on matching accuracy. Models which used the internal block memory provided by modern FPGAs to store the 'inactive' portions of scan lines were compared with simpler models which used the logic cell flip-flops. From these results, we have developed a simple predictor which enables one to rapidly determine whether a target appliction is feasible.

1 Introduction

A collision avoidance system for any mobile device - from a robot to a large vehicle - requires the ability to build a three-dimensional 'map' of its environment. Traditionally this has been accomplished by active sensors which send a pulse - either electromagnetic or sonar - and detect the reflected return. Such active

P.-C. Yew and J. Xue (Eds.): ACSAC 2004, LNCS 3189, pp. 309–320, 2004.

systems work well in low density environments where the number of moving vehicles is small and the probability that active sensors will interfere is small, so that simple techniques prevent a sensor from being confused by sensing pulses from other vehicles. For example, radar systems which detect impending aircraft collisions appear to be effective as do ultrasonic systems in small groups of robots. However, when the density of autonomous - and potentially colliding - objects becomes large, active systems create 'noisy' environments. Heavy traffic brings large numbers of vehicles with a wide range of speeds and directions into close proximity. If all vehicles were equipped with active sensors, distinguishing between extremely weak reflections and primary pulses from distant vehicles will present a daunting - and potentially insurmountable - problem for intelligent sensors. Passive systems, on the other hand, are much less sensitive to environmental interference. Stereo vision - or the use of pairs of images taken from different viewpoints - is able to provide detailed three-dimensional maps of the environment. Typical cameras can provide 30 or more images per second and each pair of images can provide an almost complete map of the environment[1]. However, processsing even small low resolution (200×200 pixel) images in software takes more than a second in software - ignoring any post-processing needed to determine the velocity of an approaching object and the optimum strategy for avoiding it. This is well below the frame rates obtainable with commodity cameras and may be far too slow to enable even relatively slow moving objects to avoid each other. Thus hardware accelerators are required in order to obtain real-time 3D environment maps. Software simulations have determined that correlation techniques using a simple sum of absolute differences (SAD) cost function perform well[1,2]. Higher quality matching can be obtained with graph cut algorithms[3], but the processing time is two orders of magnitude longer and the algorithm lacks the regularity needed for efficient hardware implementation[4].

Area-based correlation algorithms attempt to find the best match between a window of pixels in one image and a window in the other. Matching is simplified if the system is aligned so as to meet the epipolar constraint - implying that matching pixels must be found in the same scan line in both images. The matching process is illustrated in Figure 1 which shows how a right image window is shifted by an amount known as the disparity until the best match is found with the reference window in the left image. In the SAD algorithm, the criterion for the best match is minimization of the sum of the absolute differences of corresponding pixels in a window, w:

$$C(x,y,\delta) = \sum_{x,y \subset w} |I_L(x,y) - I_R(x - \delta, y)|$$

$C(x,y,\delta)$ is evaluated for all possible values of the disparity, δ, and the minimum chosen. For parallel camera axes, δ ranges from 0 for objects at infinity to Δ, corresponding to the closest possible approach to the camera. In collision avoid-

---

[1] Whilst complete maps are, in general, not attainable because some parts of the environment are not visible to both cameras simultaneously, this does not present a significant problem for the collision avoidance application.

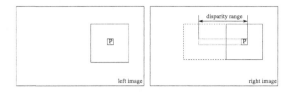

Fig. 1. Correlation based matching: the window centred on pixel, P, in the right image is moved through the disparity range until the best match (correlation) is found with a window centred at P in the left image. Aligning the cameras to meet the epipolar constraint ensures that P must lie on the same scan line in each image.

ance applications, Δ is readily set by considering the closest safe approach of the vehicle to an object. Correlation algorithms have regular structures and simple data flow making them excellent candidates for implementation in reconfigurable hardware. They also have abundant parallelism: $C(x, y, \delta)$ can evaluated in parallel for each $\delta \in [0, \Delta]$. The cost function requires only adders and comparators for which modern FPGAs provide good support. However accurate depth maps require large disparity ranges and high resolution images - both of which provide challenges to fitting a full correlator on a single FPGA. The aim of the study presented in this paper was to provide a simple predictor which would determine whether any given application, with its associated accuracy, speed, field of view, *etc.*, requirements could be fitted onto a single commercially available FPGA.

1.1   Stereo Hardware

Woodfill and von Herzen claimed that the Census algorithm implemented on an FPGA could compute depth maps for 320×240 pixel images at 42 frames per second for $\Delta = 24$[5]. The Census transform simply orders corresponding pixels in the left and right images and uses a single bit to indicate either '$<$' or '$\geq$', producing a simple, fast circuit. However, its performance falls far below that of SAD (or other correlation algorithms) and it is not very robust to noise[6]. Modifying the original ordering relation improves performance slightly, but not enough to match SAD[7]. Recently it has been used by Plakas[8] for real-time videoconferencing, but this is not a critical application and low performance may be tolerable. In related videoconferencing work, Schreer *et al.* could produce 'acceptable' depth maps in real time on an 800MHz Pentium[9], but the only statistics they provide are 'accepted' disparities, so it is unclear how their pyramidal approach (which has error propagation problems) affects resolution accuracy. In contrast, collision avoidance is a critical application: even if a system is used merely to assist a human operator, accuracy and the absence of false alarms become important.

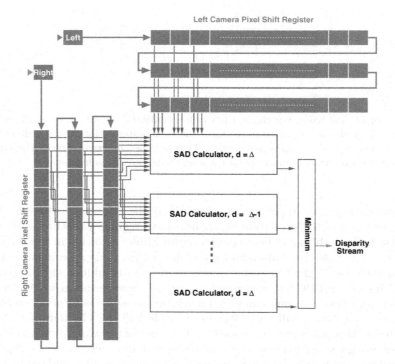

Fig. 2. Block diagram for SAD correlator: Note that the disparity calculator blocks are the source of parallelism in this circuit: each one is independent and operates in parallel.

2 Experiments

We have implemented SAD correlation algorithms in VHDL and synthesized them to determine their resource requirements and performance. Several approaches to handling high resolution images (with long scan lines which must be stored) have been investigated - storing scan lines in on-chip memory and altering the window shape to reduce the number of scan lines which must be stored.

2.1 SAD Correlator

A block diagram of the SAD circuit is shown in Figure 2. Pixels stream in from both cameras into the long left and right shift registers which store sufficient pixels so that all the pixels in a correlation window are available to the disparity calculators at the same time. The key parameters determing the size and performance of an SAD correlator are:

- sl - the scan line length,
- wh - the window height,

Table 1. SAD Correlator Resource requirements

Resource	Number required	Comments
SAD Correlator		
shift registers	2	Left and right registers are internally identical, but right register must provide more output connections
disparity calculators	$\Delta + 1$	Possible disparities range from $0..\Delta$
minimum detector	1	determine the minimum of $\Delta + 1$ sums
shift register size		
pixel registers	$(wh - 1)sl + ww\Delta$	
disparity calculator		
subtractors	$wh \times ww$	one subtractor for each pixel in a window
adders	$wh \times ww - 1$	correlator sum
minimum detector		
comparators	Δ	minimum of 2 (8-bit) pixels

- ww - the window width *and*
- Δ - the maximum disparity.

The basic resources have the following sizes:
Basic resource requirements are indicated in Table 1. To a first approximation, the resource requirements for an SAD correlator are given by:

$$
\begin{aligned}
cost_{SAD} \approx & (\Delta + 1)(c_{AD}wp + (wp - 1)c_{sum}) && \text{(disparity calculators)} \\
& + \Delta \cdot c_{comp} && \text{(minimum)} \\
& + (2(wh - 1)sl + ww(\Delta + 2) + 1)c_{reg} && \text{(shift registers)} \\
& + c_{overheads} && \text{(control, } etc.\text{)} \quad (1)
\end{aligned}
$$

where

$$
\begin{aligned}
wp &= wh \cdot ww = \text{number of pixels in matching window} \\
c_{AD} &= \text{cost of absolute difference circuit} \\
c_{sum} &= \text{cost of an adder} \\
c_{comp} &= \text{cost of a comparator} \\
c_{reg} &= \text{cost of a pixel register} \\
c_{overheads} &= \text{cost of control and steering logic}
\end{aligned}
$$

This relation should be a good predictor for low values of all the application parameters, where all overheads can be lumped effectively into the single overheads term. However, as packing density increases, poor placement would be expected to induce non-linear effects and to cause the overall cost to exceed that predicted by this model.

Key contributors to the delay of the correlator are the $wh \times ww - 1$ adders in each disparity calculator. A simple VHDL model which performs the additions in a loop adds a delay of $\mathcal{O}(wh \times ww)$ to the circuit. This sequential adder has two advantages:

1. the code in the VHDL model is trivial and
2. the sequential circuit generated[2] is very regular.

However, it is well known that a tree adder takes exactly the same number of circuit elements but improves the performance to $\mathcal{O}(\log ww \times wh)$[4]. The tree adder can be modelled in VHDL[10] and simulated. However, synthesizers tend to require 'statically determinable' numbers of circuit elements and are not prepared to run recursive code to build the tree. Whilst hand-coding adders for any particular window size is possible, stereo applications can have quite variable requirements and hand-coding models for many window sizes is not an attractive option. We overcame this problem by writing small programs in Python and Java[3] which generated the necessary VHDL code from a handful of input parameters[4]. The data in Table 2 shows the benefits of using the various adders. Two values for the tree adder are shown: one in which the model uses an 8-bit ripple-carry adder generated from full-adder blocks and the other in which the '+' operator is used. The latter model allows the synthesizer to produce more efficient packing of individual 1-bit adders (*cf.* the $\delta s/\delta p$ column) and uses the fast-carry logic to produce faster adders ($\delta t/\delta p$ column). Note that the synthesizer was able to produce a more compact circuit with the tree adder using the '+' operator, despite the triangular shape of the tree. Forcing the pixel adders to use small blocks of columns (so that they can use the fast carry logic) seems to have a good effect on overall routing, presumably because the placement module is constrained - with fewer degrees of freedom, it has less opportunity to produce a bad allocation of functions to logic blocks.

These results also show that a 'useful' circuit fits easily into a modern FPGA: commonly available small CMOS cameras have scan lines of the order of 200 or so pixels, $\Delta = 27$ implies that depths in the critical region may be measured to $\sim 4\%$ and a delay of $100ns$ allows a pixel clock of $10MHz$ - A 270×270 image at $30fps$ requires a $2.2MHz$ clock. Simulation shows that 9×9 windows produce good quality matching over a range of test images[2].

The last line in Table 2 shows an attempt to determine the largest value of Δ that the target chip could handle for the larger (9×9) window. At $\Delta = 33$, the model will fit, using 95% of the slices in a Xilinx XC2V8000 (8×10^6 'gates'). At

---

[2] This assumes that synthesizers are not yet able to recognize the potential to improve on the simple circuit as we have done by the procedure described next. We are optimistic that this will change soon!

[3] A consequence of the global distribution of the authors of this paper!

[4] Both versions were designed for re-use, so require the operator and operand type (*e.g.* bit width) as well as the circuit order.

Table 2. Effect of different adder styles

Adder type	Δ	Window size	Slices (Vertex2)	$\delta s/\delta p$	Progation delay (ns)	$\delta t/\delta p$
Sequential	27	3×3	8873	486	93.5	0.488
		9×9	43864		128.6	
Tree						
RC adder	27	3×3	9051	494	100.6	0.085
	27	9×9	44670		106.7	
+ operator	27	3×3	7363	421	100.3	0.066
	27	9×9	37695		105.1	
	33	9×9	46103^{a}		105.1	

Pixel size: 8 bits; Scan line length: 270 pixels
[a] 95% of a Xilinx XC2V8000.

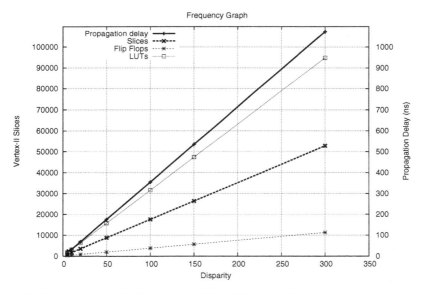

Fig. 3. Performance *vs* Δ. Pixel size: 8 bits; Window: 3×3; Scan line length: 270 pixels

this point, routing constraints start to dominate and although a simple linear model predicts that $\Delta = 34$ would also fit, there are insufficient routing resources and the router fails.

Accuracy depends on the disparity range that can be used, so we ran trials to determine the effect of increasing Δ on resource usage and performance. Figure 3 shows the regular structure of an SAD correlator leads to close to the expected linear relationship between Δ and logic cells needed.

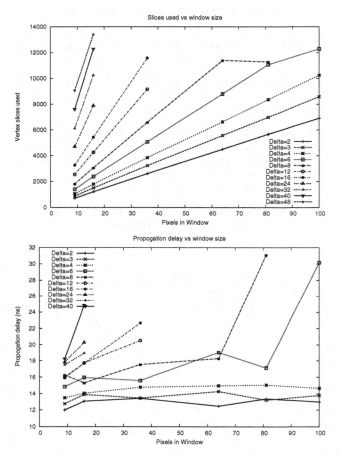

Fig. 4. Resource Usage *vs* window size for various Δ values

2.2   Using Block Memory

Typical FPGA logic cells contain look-up tables to implement the logic and a small number of flip-flops. Generally, these flip-flops provide adequate memory for the implementation of state machines, but the overall bit density is far too low for them to be used efficiently as 'plain' memory. To address this problem, modern FPGAs provide block memory - which can be configured in various ways, including as shift registers. The next set of trials sought to determine whether a practical circuit would fit onto a much smaller FPGA using the block memory to store scan lines. The family of curves in Figure 4 were obtained using the block memory on a Xilinx Vertex device to store the 'idle' (*i.e.* not involved in current matching) portions of scan lines. Results are presented for a much smaller (~ 10000 slices) suitable for an environment with cost or power constraints. A practical device is still feasible, but the disparity range (which

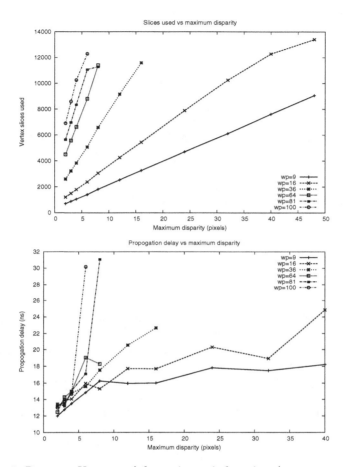

Fig. 5. Resource Usage *vs* Δ for various window sizes ($wp = ww \times wh$)

affects distance accuracy) and the window size (which affects matching quality) must be limited: but an 8×5 window (*cf.* Section 2.3) with $\Delta = 15$ is feasible. Real-time performance is easily achieved - see Figure 5(b) - without the need for pipelining. Accuracy and matching quality can be improved by using time series images[11,12] so it may be more important to achieve real-time performance than good initial matching.

2.3   Rectangular Windows

It is customary to use square matching windows in correlation-style stereo algorithms, probably because this is the simplest approach in a software system and there is little performance or other penalty. The matching process is generally only using a small part of each scan line at any time - specifically ww from the left image and $\Delta + 1 + ww$ from the right image. The remaining pixels are stored

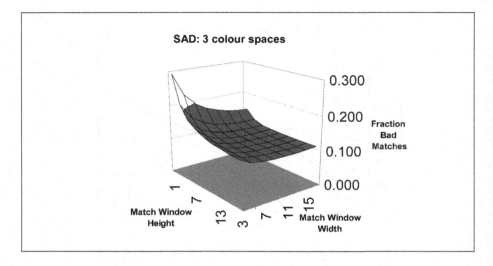

Fig. 6. Matching with rectangular windows: 'Corridor' data set[13]

in shift registers for use in subsequent cycles. In a simple model, these shift registers are trivially implemented in VHDL and synthesized to use the flip-flops in logic cells. Once the epipolar constraint has been satisfied, matches for each pixel should be found in the same scan line. Pixels in surrounding scan lines are only used to support matching by reducing noise effects. We ran a set of experiments to determine the effect of using different shaped matching windows: Figure 6 shows a large flat region with ~ 10% bad matches. Detailed examination of the actual numbers shows that a 'short' (low wh) wide window produces similar matching quality to a taller square one, *i.e.* the total number of pixels in the matching window is the critical factor. This implies that a considerable amount of space can be saved in an FPGA by using rectangular ($wh < ww$) windows without sacrificing matching quality.

3   Estimating Resource Needs

It is common for papers demonstrating the 'success' of some application to simply state a claim for that particular application, with little attention to extensions and variations. For stereo applications, this is particularly frustrating because every application presents its own criteria for accuracy, reliability, resources required, *etc.*Hence this work focussed on using the data gathered to enable feasibility of a proposed application to be quickly estimated. Whilst this can, in principle, be done by simply counting circuit elements needed to implement a module and using those counts in Equation 1, a place and route tool has to work from high level models and may have problems allocating and laying out circuits that a human engineer may not. FPGA implementations are also constrained by availability of routing resources and this factor is much harder to estimate than

Table 3. Cost factors

Cost	Range	Notes
Disparity calculator		
$c_{AD} + c_{sum}$	16-20	Essentially 2 8-bit adders
		The additional data needed to distinguish between c_{AD} and c_{sum} doesn't justify the small benefit - *cf.* Equation 1.
Minimum		
c_{comp}	14	8-bit comparator + steering logic
Shift Registers		
Using logic cells	7.3	1 eight bit pixel
Overheads		
$c_{overheads}$	0	Small - current data is insufficient to provide a reliable estimate

logic cell needs, thus practical trials of the type we carried out here are needed to determine real cost factors.

4 Conclusion

Accurate real-time 3D depth maps are feasible with modern FPGA technology. Simulations of the effect of changing the window shape show that altering the shape of the correlation window can be used to reduce the number of cells needed for 'inactive' parts of scan lines. Since even a 200 pixel scan line uses space similar to that required for a disparity calculator (working on a window large enough to produce good matching quality), it is clearly better to use the space to increase accuracy with more disparity calculators. Transferring the 'inactive' parts of scan lines to on chip memory enables small real-time systems to be implemented in quite small (*i.e.* 20% of current state-of-the-art) and thus economic systems.

The simple (unpipelined) circuits described here will provide real-time performance at pixel clock rates up to $\sim 10MHz$. For higher resolution images (and thus higher pixel clock frequencies if the same frame rate is to be maintained), an SAD correlator is easily pipelined. Three modules (SAD calculation, adder and minimum detector) of are readily identified in the data path suggesting that pixel clock rates of $\sim 2 - 3$ times greater (*i.e.* $\sim 20 - 30MHz$) are easily attained. The tree adder is the slowest of these and additional pipeline stages may be easily inserted within it. For large Δ circuits, the minimum detector will become the slowest element, but it is easily pipelined in the same way as the adder. In fact, since the major calculation elements are mainly 8-bit adders, the propagation delay for an 8-bit adder (plus pipeline overheads!) represents the lower limit for pixel clock time.

Acknowledgements. John Morris was supported by the Foreign Professors Invitation Program of The Korean IT Industry Promotion Agency at Chung Ang University in 2003-4.

References

1. Scharstein, D., Szeliski, R.: A taxonomy and evaluation of dense two-frame stereo correspondence algorithms. International Journal of Computer Vision **47** (2002) 7–42
2. Leclercq, P., Morris, J.: Assessing stereo algorithm accuracy. In Kenwright, D., ed.: Proceedings of Image and Vision Computing'02. (2002) 89–93
3. Boykov, Y., Veksler, O., Zabih, R.: Fast approximate energy minimization via graph cuts. In: ICCV 1999. (1999)
4. Morris, J.: Reconfigurable computing. In Oklobdzija, V.G., ed.: Computer Engineering Handbook, CRC Press, CRC Press (2001) 37–1 – 37–16
5. Woodfill, J., Herzen, B.V.: Real-time stereo vision on the PARTS reconfigurable computer. In Arnold, J., Pocek, K.L., eds.: Proceedings of IEEE Workshop on FPGAs for Custom Computing Machines, Napa, CA (1997) 201–210
6. Leclercq, P., Morris, J.: Robustness to noise of stereo matching. In: Proceedings of International Conference on Image Analysis and Processing'02. (2003) 89–93
7. Leclercq, P.: Evaluation of Stereo Matching Algorithm for Hardware Implementation. PhD thesis, University of Western Australia (2004)
8. Plakas, C., Trucco, E., Brandenburg, N., Kauff, P., Karl, M., Schreer, O.: Real-time disparity maps for immersive 3-d teleconferencing by hybrid recursive matching and census transform. In: VideoRegister01. (2001) xx–yy
9. Oliver Schreer, N.B., Kauff, P.: Real-time disparity analysis for applications in immersive tele-conference scenarios - a comparative study. In: ICIAP2001. (2001) x–x+5
10. Ashenden, P.J.: Recursive and repetitive hardware models in VHDL. Technical Report TR160/12/93/ECE, Electrical and Computer Engineering, University of Cincinatti, Cincinatti, Ohio 45221-0030 (1993)
11. Torreao, J.R.A.: Estimating 3D shape from the optical flow of photometric stereo images. Lecture Notes in Computer Science **1484** (1998) 253–??
12. Barniv, Y.: Error analysis of combined stereo/optical-flow passive ranging. In: SPIE Proceedings. Volume 1479., NASA/Ames Research Ctr., Moffett Field, CA, USA (1991) 259–267
13. Gerdes, V.: Modular Rendering Tools. www-student.informatik.uni-bonn.de/~gerdes/MRTStereo/index.html (2001)

A Router Architecture for QoS Capable Clusters*

Madhusudhanan Anantha and Bose Bella

School of Electrical Engineering and Computer Science, Oregon State University,
Corvallis, Oregon 97331
madhusan@cs.orst.edu, bose@eecs.orst.edu

Abstract. Many web servers and database servers make efficient use of clustering from cost, scalability and availability standpoints. Existing cluster interconnects use switching schemes which minimize transmission latency but do not provide any guarantee on the delay (e.g., Wormhole switching). The variety of applications which are run on clusters mandate that the cluster interconnect be capable of handling both best effort and delay bound traffic. A new router architecture capable of providing **soft guaranteed** service using wormhole switching was proposed. An improved router model with preemption capabilities has also been proposed in literature. In this paper a detailed analysis of the hardware complexity of the preemptive router is presented and some architectural modifications to reduce the hardware complexity of the preemptive router are proposed. An interconnection network simulator has been developed to compare and analyze the performance characteristics of the proposed router architecture.

1 Introduction

Commodity clusters have a high performance to cost ratio over commercial parallel computers. This has lead to their use in a lot of applications which require high processing power. These include applications which they were not intended for e.g., web-servers. The increase in multi-media applications has meant that web-servers should be capable of handling time sensisitive traffic. Since existing switching schemes do not provide a guaranteed delay and since the cost of providing different switching schemes for different traffic types using the network is high we try to use one switching scheme with some modifications to handle all traffic types. A new router architecture capable of providing such service using wormhole switching with a rate-based scheduler was proposed in the MediaWorm router design [8] . A preemptive router architecture, which can dynamically allocate a Virtual Channel(VC) to any traffic class, was proposed by Das et.al. [1]. In this paper the hardware complexity of the premptive router is analyzed and some architectural modifications to reduce the hardware complexity of the router without sacrificing performance are proposed. An interconnection network

---

* This work is supported by National Science Foundation Grant CCR-0105204

simulator has also been developed to compare the performance characteristics of the proposed router with the preemptive router.

In Sect.2 some background work in this area is presented. In Sect.3 we analyze the hardware complexity of the router presented in Sect.2. Section 4 describes the modifications to the router architecture. In Sect.5 we present an analytical model to estimate the performance of the proposed router. Then, in Sect.6, we describe the simulation frame work and compare the performance characteristics of the modified router with the existing router. The conclusions and future work are summarized in Sect.7.

2   Background

2.1   Baseline Router Model

The most intuitive way to support QoS provisioning, in wormhole switched networks, is to attach a notion of priority to the traffic flows and add a rate based scheduling scheme like Virtual Clock [4]. This allows us to provide soft guaranteed service to time bound data streams with minimal changes to the wormhole router hardware.

Non-preemptive routers statically divide the VCs among the traffic classes. This restricts the flexibility of the router to handle changes in the distibution of traffic priority classes. The proposed solution to this problem is to use a preemptive router model which allows several priority classes of traffic to share the same VC, with the provision that higher priority message can preempt a lower priority message. The preemptive model can dynamically handle changes in traffic better than the non-preemptive model and hence is well suited for this application. A pipelined router model with the aforesaid capabilites was proposed in [8].

The modifications to this router model suggested in [1] are:

1. **Preemption in the input buffer**: Preemption in the input buffer occurs when the header flit of a high priority message arrives at the input VC buffer, which is being held by a lower priority message. When this happens the router lets the higher priority flow use the buffer and resumes transmission of the lower priority message after the higher priority message releases the buffer.

2. **flit acceleration mechanism**: The next modification they proposed was the use of a flit accelerate mechanism to reduce the probability of a higher priority message getting struck at the later pipeline stages due to the presence of lower priority flows. Flit acceleration mechanism solved this problem by boosting the priority of the lower priority flow holding the resource which is needed by the high priority flow so that the blocking delay of the high priority flow is minimized.

3   Hardware Complexity Analysis

The architectural modifications proposed in Sect.2 incur a cost in implementation. In this section the harware complexity analysis of the *flit preemption logic* and the *flit acceleration logic* is presented. This analysis is used to investigate the possibility of modifications to the architecture to reduce the hardware complexity without sacrificing performance. Throughout the analysis n is the number of dimensions in the interconnect and s is the number of prioritized flow classes. The complexity is expressed in terms of number of gates used for a typical implementation.

3.1   Cost Analysis of the Flit Preemption Unit

Figure 1 shows a schematic of the flit preemption unit. The flit preemption unit has to do the following tasks in a clock cycle.

1. check the extra buffer to see if there is a header flit.
2. if there is a header flit, check whether this flit can preempt a flow in the virtual channel buffer.
3. if the tail flit of the preempted flow has already been received in which case a dummy tail flit is not created.
4. it is clear that at any given clock cyle there is only one buffer with a header flit in the extra buffer that needs to be processed.

It can be seen from Fig.1 the hardware complexity of the extra buffer and history stack scale in the order of number of prioritized flow classes at each input port. The hardware complexity of the flit preemption logic scales in the order number of VCs per physical channel because it has to maintain status information of all the VCs in the input buffer. However, this is fixed and its hardware complexity is constant. The effective hardware complexity of the flit preemption unit is:

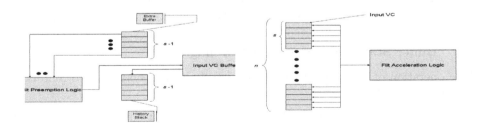

(a)Flit Preemption Unit   (b) Flit Acceleration Unit

Fig. 1. Modifications to Pipelined Router Model

- *flit preemption logic* $= c$
- *extra buffer complexity* $= (n \times s) + c$
- *history stack complexity* $= (n \times s) + c$
- *flit preemption unit complexity* $= 2(n \times s) + 3.c = O(s)$ (because $s \geq n$)

where c is a constant.

3.2 Cost Analysis of the Flit Acceleration Unit

Figure 1 shows a schematic of the flit acceleration unit. The flit acceleration unit has to do the following.

1. Check to see if any lower priority flow is occupying an output buffer. There are $(n \times s) - 1$ possible channels that have to be checked for a given channel.
2. if there exists such a buffer then the accelerate flag is set in the buffer.

The effective complexity in the flit acceleration unit is in the *flit acceleration logic*. Therefore it will suffice to compute the hardware complexity of the flit acceleration logic. This unit must check $(n \times s)$- 1 other flows to check if any of those flows is holding a resouce required by a given flow. This has to to done for all the $(n \times s)$ flows. Thus the hardware complexity of this unit is:

flit unit complexity $= (n \times s)(n \times s) = O(s^2)$ (because $s \geq n$)

Therefore it can seen that the effective complexity of the flit acceleration unit is higher than that of the flit preemption unit. In Sect.4 some modifications to the router to reduce the hardware complexity are proposed.

4 Proposed Modifications

From Sect.3 it can be seen that hardware complexity of the flit preemption unit is *linear* in the number of prioritized flow classes but the hardware complexity of the flit acceleration unit is *quadratic* in the number of prioritized flow classes. In this section we will propose modifications to the router architecture to replace the flit acceleration logic with lesser complexity functional units which perform the same function. These modifications are at the final stage in the router which multiplexes flits from various output VCs onto the phyiscal channel.

4.1 Buffer Status Aware Link Scheduling

The operation of an asynchronous flow control protocol between two routers is as follows:

1. Router 1 makes the request(RQ) line high to request permission to transmit a flit.
2. Router 2 sets the acknowledge(ACK) line to represent buffer availability and hence permission to transmit.
3. Router 1 begins transmission if the ACK line has been set to allow transmission of a flit. In which case the flit is transmitted as a series of *phits*.

A priority based link scheduler always tries to pick flits from the highest priority flow without considering the buffer occupancy status in the next router's input buffer. The disadvantage of this approach is that the router might keep picking a flit from a high priority flow for which there is no buffer space in the subsequent router repeatedly thereby wasting bandwidth and increasing the delay for other flows. The availability of buffer space for a flow in the subsequent router can be predicted from the value of acknowledgement received for the last sent flit. Therefore, it would be useful to include this information to decide which flow's flits must be picked for transmission. A single bit called ACK status(1 = buffer space available, 0 = no space) is associated with each VC in the output buffer. The scheduler picks a flit using both this bit and the priority of the flow in the buffer. Link scheduling algorithms which use both of these pieces of information are proposed.

Highest Non N-Ack Flow.

1. Get the list of channels ready for transmission at a given clock cycle. Let $\{S\}$ be the set of all channels which can be scheduled and $\{R\}$ be the set of ready channels. Assign $\{S\} \leftarrow \{R\}$
2. Pick a channel from $\{R\}$ which has the
   (1) *Highest* Flow class.
   (2) Does not have an *N-Ack* (Negative Acknowledgement).
   (3) Choose the *first such channel* in case of a tie.
3. Read the flit from this channel and record the ACK status for the next iteration.

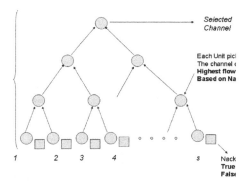

Fig. 2. Hardware implementing Highest Non N-ACK Scheduling

Discussion: Figure 2 shows a hardware implementation of the link scheduling algorithm.The algorithm uses a tree shaped circuit to pick the "winner" channel at a given clock when its starts flit transmission. At each clock cycle a flit from the selected channel is transmitted and the ACK status of the transmission is stored for use in a subsequent transmission.

Note that only one bit is added to the lowest level processing units because this level "filters" all channels that are ready and the subsequent levels work by picking a flow to *highest priority* among the ready channels. Thus the only addition in hardware complexity is the $O(s)$ bits.

The **disadvantage** of this algorithm is that a high priority flow class which received an N-ACK might not be picked for a long time if there are enough flits from other flows. In essence, a high priority flow might "starve". This disadvantage becomes crucial in heavily loaded networks.

A simple fix to this problem lies in the introduction of new variables.

1. *cycle_wait* which keeps track of the number of cycles after receiving a N-ACK and is updated each clock cycle.
2. *max_count*, maximum value after which *cycle_wait* update should stop.
3. *cycle_wait* is *initialized/reset* after receiving a N-ACK after *max_count* was reached and a re-transmission was tried.

Modified Highest Non N-Ack Flow.

1. Get the list of channels ready for transmission at a given clock cycle. Let $\{S\}$ be the set of all channels which can be scheduled and $\{R\}$ be the set of ready channels; Assign $\{S\} \leftarrow \{R\}$
2. Pick the channel of the *Highest Flow class*, among $\{R\}$, that does not have a N-ACK or whose counter has reached *max_count*.
3. Choose the *first such channel* in case of a tie.
4. Read the flit from this channel and record the ACK status for the next iteration.

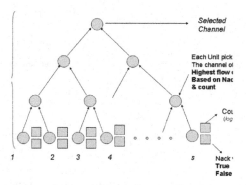

Fig. 3. Hardware implementing the Modified Highest Non N-ACK Scheduling

Discussion: Figure 3 shows the hardware implementation of the modified version of the algorithm. At each clock cycle a flit from the selected channel is transmitted and the ACK status of the transmission is stored for use in a subsequent transmission.

Note that one counter and a register of size $log(s)$ are added to the lowest level processing units because this level "filters" all channels that are ready and have the required counter constraints. The subsequent levels work by picking a flow of the *highest priority* among the channels selected at level 1. Thus, the only addition in hardware complexity is the $O(s.log(s))$ bits.

4.2   Flexible Output Virtual Channel Allocation

In this section we discuss the next modification to the router. The main disadvantage of using the link scheduling algorithms we presented is that even though they guarantee the presence of a free channel at the output VC buffer the fixed connection scheme between the crossbar ports and the VCs could lead to performance losses. This is because certain combinations of connections are not possible and header still incurs a blocking delay. To remedy this situation a dynamic mapping scheme between a crossbar port to a VC buffer is proposed.

Figure 4 shows a schematic of the proposed modification. The hardware addition to the router is a *channel identifier* at each crossbar output port which contains the address of the channel allocated to this port. Each output port is allocated a specific set of channels it can choose from and the size of this identifier is $\log(\log s)$ and there are multiplexer circuits of complexity $\log s$ giving an overall gate complexity of $s. \log s$.

4.3   Analysis

Figure 4 shows the router architecture with both of the modifications in place. These changes are valid in the context of replacing the *flit acceleration unit* because the main reason for introducing acceleration is to avoid the *blocking of high priority flows* due to other lower priority flows. Since the link scheduling algorithms work by maximizing the number of flits transmitted in a time frame and since the probability of servicing high priority flows is high, the probability

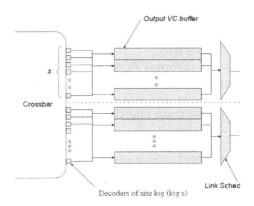

Fig. 4. Modified Router Architecture

of availability of a virtual channel is high. With a flexible channel allocation scheme to take advantage of the high availability of free channels the probability of blocking of a high priority flit is minimized. Therefore, we can see that this combination of modifications replaces the flit acceleration unit functionally.

The effective hardware complexity of the modifications is the total of the hardware complexities of the proposed modifications.

Total Complexity $= O(s.\log(s)) + O(s.\log(s)) \implies O(s.\log(s))$ This hardware complexity bound is therefore better than that of the flit acceleration unit ($O(s^2)$) that has been replaced.

5   An Analytical Model

In this section a mathematical model for deadline missing probability in a single router is proposed. It is extended to calculate the deadline missing probability of a message which traverses r routers to its destination. A router model with a pipelined architecture with 5 stages and augmented with the modifications proposed in Sect.4 is assumed. Stage 1 of the router performs flit de-multiplexing. Stages 2 and 3 are the routing and arbitration units. Stage 4 contains the crossbar and stage 5 contains multiplexes VCs over the physical channel. The model is described for S classes consisting of $(S-1)$ classes of real time traffic and one class of best-effort traffic.

Note that a message entering the pipelined router can experience delay at stages 1, 3 and 5. If the input VC buffer is full in stage 1, the message must wait outside the router until adequate space is available. In stage 3, the message again might be delayed because the destination crossbar ports are full. Crossbar output port arbitration is performed at a message level granularity. So the message has to wait until the required port is released by the message already holding it. Finally in stage 5, multiple virtual channels compete for the physical channel bandwidth. This is the delay experienced due to the link scheduler. The model is based on the following assumptions:

1. The arrival pattern of each class s follows a poisson process with an average arrival rate λ_s^g .
2. Message length is M flits long.
3. Message destination is uniformly distributed.
4. The input and output virtual channel buffers in stages 1 and 5 can hold b_s flits.
5. Each class is assigned separate injection/ejection queues outside the router, and these have infinite capacity.

The average message latency of a message of class s $(1 \leq s \leq S)$ is composed of the average network latency, $\overline{L_s}$, which is the time to traverse the router (network), and the average waiting time, $\overline{W_s}$, at the injection channel. Thus,

$$\overline{Latency_s} = \overline{L_s} + \overline{W_s} \tag{1}$$

Network latency can be calculated as follows

$$\overline{L}_s = P - 1 + (M + \overline{B}_s)\overline{S}_s \tag{2}$$

where $\overline{L}_s$ is the network latency of a class s message, $\overline{B}_s$ is the blocking length and $\overline{S}_s$ is the effect of the bandwidth sharing mechanism.

Blocking occurs in stages 1,3 and 5 and the average blocking length can be separated into three parts as

$$Input = P[\text{input buffer is occupied}].\{M/2\} \tag{3}$$
$$Arbiter = P[\text{Arbiter is busy}].\{M/2\} \tag{4}$$
$$LC = P[\text{ouput buffer is full}].\{M/2\} \tag{5}$$

where $Input$, $Arbiter$ and LC represent the corresponding blocking lengths at stages 1,3 and 5. In (3), (4) and (5), the first term represents the probability that the corresponding buffer is not empty, and the second term is the average message length that will be affected due to blocking. For example, if the input buffer is not empty, the header flit will face an average delay of $M/2$ flits.

In order to calculate the average blocking length the probability that the input buffer is full, the probability that the output buffer is full, and the delay due to bandwidth sharing have to be calculated. These terms can be calculated as follows:

5.1   Average Blocking Length in Stage 1

The router uses a *preemptive model* of virtual channel allocation. The preemptive model can dynamically allocate any virtual channel to any traffic class. Assuming a buffer size of b_s, a flit is blocked if the input virtual channel buffer is full and there are no flows whose priority is lower than this flit. In this case the flit will have to wait for channel to be released and hence a delay is incurred. Therefore the blocking delay is

$$delay1_s = P[\text{buffer is full with no flows priority} < s].\{M/2\} \tag{6}$$
$$P_s[\text{full}] = P[\text{each channel has a flow} \geq s] \tag{7}$$
$$= \prod_{i=0}^{S-1} \sum_{j=s}^{S-1} P[X_j] \tag{8}$$

where,
$P_s[\text{full}] = \text{P[buffer is full with no flows priority} < s]$
and $P[X_j] = \text{probability that a message is of flow class } j$.

5.2   Average Blocking Length in Stage 3

The header flit is blocked waiting at stage 3 if the arbiter has higher priority flows in the arbitration slots which reserve all crossbar ports that this flow might require or if all the crossbar ports are occupied. The blocking delay is:

$$delay2_s = P[\text{Arbiter Busy}].\{M/2\} \tag{9}$$

$$P[\text{arbiter busy}] = \prod_{i=0}^{k} \sum_{j=s}^{S-1} P[X_j] + \left(1 - \sum_{i=1}^{l} {}^l C_i . p^i . q^{l-i}\right) \tag{10}$$

where M is the message length in flits, k is the number of arbitration slots, l is the number of crossbar ports that could be assigned, p is the probability that a given output VC is full and $q = 1 - p$.

5.3   Average Blocking Length in Stage 5

Since a flexible virtual channel allocation scheme is used a flit is blocked waiting at the last stage only if no virtual channels are empty in the output virtual channel buffer.

$$delay3_s = P[\text{Ouput Buffer full}].\{M/2\} \tag{11}$$

$$P[\text{no VCs}] = 1 - P[\text{at least 1 free channel}] \tag{12}$$

$$P[\text{no VCs}] = 1 - \sum_{i=1}^{S-1} {}^{(S-1)} C_i . p^i . q^{n-i} \tag{13}$$

where M is the message length in flits and n is the number of virtual channels in the VC buffer.

5.4   Deadline Missing Probability

Using the average blocking lengths at stages 1, 3 and 5 of the router pipeline the probability of a packet of class s missing a deadline D_s can be calculated. The average blocking length ($delay$) for a message in a router is:

$$delay_s = delay1_s + delay2_s + delay3_s \tag{14}$$

Given a delay ($delay_s$) the actual time for transfer (β_s) of the message is given by:

$$\beta_s = delay_s . S_s \tag{15}$$

where S_s is the average number of cycles to transmit a flit of class s.

Equation (14) gives the average delay for a message of class s through a *single* router. The probability that the message misses its deadline is given by:

$$P_{m,s}(D_s, \beta_s) = P\{\beta_s > D_s\} = 1 - P\{\beta_s \le D_s\} = \sum_{i=0}^{i=B_l} P_s(i) \tag{16}$$

where $P_{m,s}$ is the probability of missing the deadline D_s for a class s message and β_s is the actual delay and $P\{\beta_s \le D_s\}$ is the probability that a class s message traverses the router within the deadline D_s and B_l is the highest blocking length such that $\beta_s \leq D_s$.

If a message were to traverse r routers to its destination, the probability that it misses its deadline can be calculated as the sum of the probabilities of all combinations of delays at these routers such that the total delay is less than B_m (B_m is the maximum total length such that the message reaches on or before its deadline(D_s)).

$$P\{\beta_s > D_s\} = 1 - P\{\beta_s \leq D_s\} = \sum P_s(D_0).P_s(D_1) \cdots P_s(D_{r-1}) \qquad (17)$$

where

$$\forall D_0, D_1, \cdots, D_{r-1} \in \mathbb{Z}^+ \qquad (18)$$

$$D_0 + D_1 + \cdots + D_{r-1} \leq B_m \qquad (19)$$

Equation (17) represents all possible combinations of delays at the routers. We need a solution to $P_s(B)$ to calculate the deadline missing probability. Since it is tough to exactly calculate this parameter, we approximate this probability using operational behaviour of a router. Under the uniform distribution assumption this probability can be calculated as follows.

$$P_s(B) \approx \begin{cases} 1 - \sum\limits_{i=1}^{B^u} P_{b,s}/B^u, & B = 0 \\ P_{b,s}/B^u, & 1 \leq B \leq B^u \\ 0, & \text{otherwise} \end{cases} \qquad (20)$$

where, B^u represents the worst case blocking length at a router and $P_{b,s}$ is the blocking probability of a class s message.

The probability of blocking of a class s message can be calculated as follows.

$$P_{b,s} = \prod_{i=0}^{S-1} \sum_{j=s}^{S-1} P[X_j] + (1 - \sum_{i=1}^{S-1} {}^{(S-1)}C_i.p^i.q^{n-i}) + \prod_{i=0}^{k} \sum_{j=s}^{S-1} P[X_j] + (1 - \sum_{i=1}^{l} {}^{l}C_i.p^i.q^{l-i}) \qquad (21)$$

and worst case blocking length is given by

$$B^u = M + M + M \Rightarrow 3.M \qquad (22)$$

Therefore we can roughly estimate the deadline missing probability of a class s message through a series of routers using (17), (20), (21) and (22).

6 Performance Analysis

6.1 Simulation Framework

An interconnection network simulator has been developed to compare the performance characteristics of the modified router with the QoS enabled architecture discussed in Sect.2 and a router with the modifications we have proposed. For our experiments we simulated a 8-port router and a 2×2 mesh network with 8-port routers. We have used 16 VCs per physical channel. The flit size is 128-bits and all the messages are 36 flits long. Physical link bandwidth is 1.6 Gbps and the flit buffers are 36 flits deep.

6.2 Workload

The workload includes messages from real time variable bit rate (VBR) traffic and best-effort traffic. The real time traffic streams are generated as synthetic MPEG streams at 30 frames/sec with different bandwidth requirements. Each stream generates a frame of data which is fragmented into flits. Best effort traffic is generated with a given injection rate λ and follows a poisson distribution. The message destination is assumed to be uniformly distributed.

An important parameter that is varied is the input load which is expressed as a fraction of the physical link bandwidth. For a specific input load, we vary the ratio of the two classes ($x : y$, where $x/(x + y)$ is the fraction of load for VBR traffic and $y/(x + y)$ is the fraction of load for best effort component) to generate mixed-mode traffic.

We vary the traffic ratio in 5 stages during the simulation to simulate dynamic workload. The important output parameters we measured were the *deadline missing probability* and *deadline missing time*. Deadline missing probability is the ratio between the number of frames which missed their deadline out of the total delivered frames. Deadline missing time is the average time by which the packets miss their deadline. The deadline was set to 33.3 msec after receiving a frame from the flow. We have assumed a core clock frequency of 100 MHz and set the respective number of clock cycles for the deadline and the results are also expressed in terms of clock cycles.

6.3 Single Router Results

The simulation test bed was used to study the performance of the proposed router model with that of the existing router model. We ran the simulations at 80% and 85% network load. Figure 5.a shows the deadline missing probabilities of the proposed router model to the existing preemptive router model and Fig.5.b shows the deadline missing times of the two router models.

Figure 5.a shows that for both the routers the deadline missing probability increases as the proportion of real time traffic increases. It also shows that at 80% load the deadline missing probabilities of the models are close and the proposed router starts to perform better as the proportion of real time traffic increases.

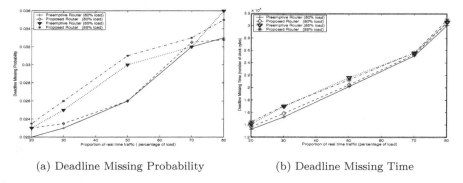

(a) Deadline Missing Probability   (b) Deadline Missing Time

Fig. 5. Single Router Results

This is the phase where the advantages of the modified link scheduler start showing up as the scheduler tries to maximize the amount of data transmitted. At 85% network loading the deadline missing probabilities of the proposed router architecture and the existing router architecture are very close but the difference in performance starts increasing because of the modified link scheduler.

Figure 5.b shows the deadline missing times of the two router models at 80% and 85% loads are comparable. It also shows that the average deadline missing time increases as the proportion of real time traffic increases. It is also seen that the average deadline missing time increases as the ratio of real time traffic increases.

6.4   A (2 × 2) Mesh Network Results

Figure 6 shows that at 80% load and at 85% network loading the deadline missing probabilities of the proposed router architecture and the existing router architecture are very close. Like the single router results it is seen that the number of frames missing the deadline increases as the ratio of real time traffic increases.

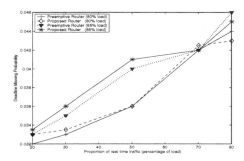

Fig. 6. Deadline Missing Probability (2×2 mesh)

From the results of the simulation it can be seen that the proposed router architecture achieves a slightly better performance than the existing model but at a reduced hardware complexity.

7   Conclusions and Future Work

This paper addresses the issue of hardware complexity in QoS capable routers to enable faster switching. The existing QoS capable router architecture was analyzed to identify sources of hardware complexity. Techniques like Buffer Status Aware Link Scheduling and Dynamic Output VC allocation were used to reduce the hardware complexity without sacrificing performance. Simulation was used to analyze the performance characteristics of the proposed router architecture. An analytical model for analyzing QoS capable clusters has been developed.

We are currently working on the verification of the proposed analytical model. It will be instructive to analyze the possibility of using adaptive routing and the preemptive router model in order to improve the QoS capabilities of the cluster interconnect.

References

[1] Das, C. R., Kim, E. J., and Yum, K. H.: QoS provisioning in clusters: An investigation of Router and NIC design. Proceedings of the 28th International Symposium on Computer Architecture, ISCA 01, Sweden, 2001

[2] Duato, J., Yalamanchili, S., and Ni, L.: Interconnection Networks: An Engineering Approach. Morgan Kaufmann Publishers, second edition, 2002.

[3] Das, C. R., Kim, E. J., and Yum, K. H.: Calculation of Deadline Missing Probability in a QoS Capable Cluster Interconnect. Proceedings of IEEE International Symposium on Network Computing and Applications (NCA '01), pp.34-43, February 2002, Cambridge, MA.

[4] Zhang, L.: VirtualClock: A New Traffic Control Algorithm for Packet-Switched Networks. ACM Transactions on Computer Systems, 9(2):101-124, May 1991.

[6] Chien, A. A.: A cost and speed model for k-ary n-cube wormhole routers. Proceedings of Hot Interconnects'93, August 1993.

[7] Duato, J., Yalamanchilli, S., Caminero, M. B., Love, D. and Quiles, F. J.: MMR: A High Performance Multimedia Router-Architecture and Design Tradeoffs. Proceedings of International Symposium on High Performance Computer Architecture. Pages 300-309, January 1999.

[8] Yum, K. H., Vaidya, A. S., Das, C. R. and Sivasubramaniam, A.: Investigation of QoS support for traffic mixes with the MediaWorm Router. Proceedings of International Symposium on High Performance Computer Architecture, pages 97-106, January 2000.

Optimal Scheduling Algorithms in WDM Optical Interconnects with Limited Range Wavelength Conversion Capability*

Zhenghao Zhang and Yuanyuan Yang

Department of Electrical & Computer Engineering, State University of New York, Stony Brook, NY 11794, USA

Abstract. In this paper we study optimal scheduling algorithms to resolve output contentions in time slotted WDM optical interconnects with wavelength conversion ability. We consider the general case of limited range wavelength conversion with arbitrary conversion capability, as it is easier to implement and more cost effective than full range wavelength conversion, and also includes full range wavelength conversion as a special case. We consider the conversion scheme in which each wavelength can be converted to multiple wavelengths belongs to an interval and the intervals for different wavelengths are "ordered". To be specific, the conversion range of λ_i can be written as $[begin(i), end(i)]$, where $begin(i)$ and $end(i)$ are positive integers and if $i < j$ then $begin(i) \leq begin(j)$ and $end(i) \leq end(j)$. We will present linear time optimal scheduling algorithms for both buffered and unbuffered WDM switches. We will also give performance studies of these switches when scheduled by these algorithms.

Keywords: Wavelength-division-multiplexing (WDM), optical interconnects, scheduling, wavelength conversion, limited range wavelength conversion, bipartite graphs, bipartite matching, matroid.

1 Introduction and Background

All-optical networking with *wavelength-division-multiplexing (WDM)* is emerging as the candidate for future high-bandwidth communication networks. In this paper, we will study time slotted WDM packet switching networks as it may offer better flexibility and better exploitations of the bandwidth [9]. As in [9] [17], we assume that the duration of an optical packet is one time slot and the traffic pattern is unicast, i.e., each packet is destined to only one output fiber.

In a WDM switch, output contention occurs when more than packets on the same wavelength are destined to the same output fiber. To resolve output contention we can translate the wavelength of a packet to some other idle wavelength by *wavelength converters*. We consider *limited range* wavelength converter which is capable of converting a wavelength to a limited number of wavelengths, since it is more realistic and cost-effective to provide wavelength conversion ability than *full range* wavelength converter

---

* The research work was supported in part by the U.S. National Science Foundation under grant numbers CCR-0073085 and CCR-0207999.

which is capable of converting a wavelength to any other wavelengths [10,8]. Also, full range wavelength converters can be regarded as a special case of limited range wavelength converters.

Another way to resolve output contention is to temporarily store the contending packets into the buffers, as practiced in all electronic switches. However, it is difficult to directly apply it to WDM switches, since optical buffers are made of fiber delay lines and quite costly and bulky [2]. Therefore we will consider unbuffered WDM switches first. Later on we will also consider buffered WDM switches.

In these switches, scheduling algorithms are needed to smartly allocate the resources (the wavelength channels) to the requests (the arrived packets) to optimize network performance, such as network throughput. This problem was first realized by [17], in which a simple algorithm, "storing the packet in the least occupied buffer", was suggested. However the authors didn't show that the algorithm is optimal, in the sense that the network throughput achieves maximum and total delay achieves minimum. In this paper we will present algorithms that are optimal, for both buffered and unbuffered switches.

2   Wavelength Conversion

We make two assumptions about limited range wavelength conversion:

Assumption 1. *The wavelengths that can be converted to by λ_i for $i \in [1, k]$, where k is the number of wavelengths on a fiber, can be represented by interval $[begin(i), end(i)]$, where $begin(i)$ and $end(i)$ are positive integers in $[1, k]$. The wavelengths belong to this interval is called the* adjacency set *of λ_i.*

Assumption 2. *For two wavelengths λ_i and λ_j, if $i < j$, then $begin(i) \leq begin(j)$ and $end(i) \leq end(j)$.*

We call this type of wavelength conversion "ordered interval" because the adjacency set of an wavelength can be represented by an interval of integers, and the intervals for different wavelengths are "ordered". The cardinality of the adjacency set is called the *conversion degree* of the wavelength. Different wavelengths may have different conversion degrees. The conversion degree of the interconnect, denoted by D, is defined as the largest conversion degree of all wavelengths. The *conversion distance* of a wavelength is defined as the largest difference between a wavelength and a wavelength that can be converted from it.

We can use a bipartite graph to visualize the wavelength conversion. Let the left side vertices represent input wavelengths and the right side vertices represent output wavelengths. λ_i on the left and λ_j on the right are connected if λ_i can be converted to λ_j. Figure 1 shows such a conversion graph for $k = 8$. The adjacency set of λ_3, for example, can be represented as $[1, 5]$, and the conversion degree of λ_3 is 5.

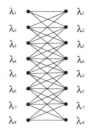

Fig. 1. Wavelength conversion in a 8-wavelength system with conversion distance 2.

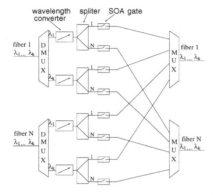

Fig. 2. A wavelength convertible WDM optical interconnect.

3   Optimal Scheduling in Unbuffered WDM Switching Networks

3.1   Network Model

An unbuffered WDM switch with wavelength conversion is shown in Fig.2. It has input N fibers and N output fibers. On each fiber there are k wavelengths that carry independent data. Thus, there are a total of Nk input wavelength channels and Nk output wavelength channels. It can be seen from the figure that an input fiber is first fed into a demultiplexer, where different wavelength channels are separated from one another. An input wavelength is then fed into a wavelength converter to be converted to a proper wavelength. The output of a wavelength converter is then split into N signals, which are connected to each of the output fibers under the control of N SOA gates. The signal can reach the output fiber if the SOA gate is on, otherwise it is blocked. Since the request has only one destination, only one of the SOA gates is in on at a time. In the front of each output fiber there is an optical combiner which multiplexes the signals on different wavelengths into one composite signal and send to the output fiber. Apparently, it is required that all signals to the optical combiner must be on different wavelengths.

To understand the problem that needs to be solved by the scheduling algorithm, we can use the following example. Consider a simple interconnect with 2 input/output fibers and 4 wavelengths per fiber shown in Fig.3. Suppose under limited range conversion, wavelength λ_i, $1 \leq i \leq 4$, can be converted to λ_j where $j \in [\max(i - 1, 1), \min(i + 1, 4)]$, as shown in the left part of the figure. At the beginning of a time slot, there are 4 packets on λ_1, λ_2, λ_3, λ_4 arrived at input fiber 1, destined for output fiber 2, 2, 1, 1, respectively. In the figure destination of a request is the number shown in the parenthesis. There are 2 packets on λ_1 and λ_2 arrived at input fiber 2, and all destined for output fiber 2. We first notice that there is no contention at output fiber 1, since there are only two requests destined to it, and they are on different wavelengths. These two requests can both be granted and no wavelength conversion is needed. However, there are contention at output fiber 2, since there are 4 requests, 2 on λ_1 and 2 on λ_2, destined for this output fiber. Without wavelength conversion, one request on each of the wavelengths must be dropped. With limited range wavelength conversion, 3 wavelengths, λ_1 to λ_3, can be converted from λ_1 and λ_2 and therefore 3 of the 4 requests destined for output fiber 2 can be granted. We can assign channel λ_1 to the request arrived at input fiber 1 on λ_1, assign channel λ_2 to the request arrived at input fiber 2 on λ_1, assign channel λ_3 to the request arrived at input fiber 1 on λ_2, and reject the request arrived at input fiber 2 on λ_2. Based on these decisions, the wavelength converters are configured to convert input wavelengths to proper output wavelengths, as shown in the figure. A SOA gate is set to on if the request is granted and is destined to the output fiber connected to the gate. We can see in the example that when contention arises at an output fiber, to maximize network throughput, we attempt to find the largest group of requests that are contention free.

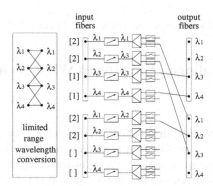

Fig. 3. Requests and wavelength channel assignments of an example interconnect with 2 input/output fibers and 4 wavelength per fiber. The number in the parenthesis are the destination of a request.

3.2   The First Available Algorithm

First, notice that if only to maximize network throughput, the packets destined to different output fibers can be scheduled independently, since a wavelength channel on output fiber p will not be assigned to a request destined to output fiber q if $p \neq q$. Therefore from now on we consider only one output fiber. The input to our scheduling algorithm will

Table 1. First Available Algorithm

```
current:=1;
for i := 1 to k do
        Find a packet on a lowest wavelength
        convertible to λ_i that has not been
        assigned to any wavelength channel yet.
        if there is such a packet
                assign λ_i to this packet;
        end if
end for
```

be the packets destined to this fiber. The output of the algorithm will be the decisions about whether a packet is granted or not, and if granted, which wavelength channel it is assigned to. To maximize network throughput, the algorithm should be able to find the maximum number of packets that can be granted without causing contention for any possible input pattern. The algorithm can be run independently and in a distributed manner to speed up the scheduling process.

[13] showed that due to the properties of limited wavelength conversion, the optimal scheduling can be found by a simple algorithm called the First Available Algorithm shown in Table 1. This algorithm scans the wavelength channels on the output fiber from λ_1 to λ_k. At step i, λ_i, can be assigned to packet a if (1) a has not been assigned to any wavelength channel yet, (2) the wavelength of a can be converted to λ_i. Moreover, the key part of the algorithm is that, it will find such a packet on the lowest wavelength, or the "first available" one.

The complexity of the algorithm is $O(k)$ where k is the number of wavelengths on a fiber, since the loop is executed exactly k times and the work within the loop can be done in constant time. However, the scheduling time is not completely independent of network size N, since to generate the input to the algorithm one might have to scan all the input channels.

4   Simulations

We implemented the proposed algorithm in software and tested it by simulations. We tested the interconnects of two typical sizes, one with 8 input fibers and 8 output fibers and with 8 wavelengths on each fiber, and the other with 16 input fibers and 16 output fibers and with 16 wavelengths on each fiber.

In the simulations, we assume that the arrivals of the packets at the input channels are bursty: an input channel alternates between two states, the "busy" state and the "idle" state. When in the "busy" state, it continuously receives packets and all the packets go to the same destination. When in the "idle" state, it does not receive any packets. The length of the busy and idle periods follows geometric distribution. The network performance is measured by the *blocking probability* which is defined as the ratio of the number of rejected packets over the number of arrived packets. The durations of the connections are one time slot and for each experiment the simulation program is run for 100,000 time slots. As a comparison, the results for an other type of wavelength conversion, the "circular symmetrical" wavelength conversion which is slightly stronger than the ordered interval wavelength conversion is also shown.

In Figure 4 we plot the packet loss probability of the interconnect as a function of conversion distance. We tested under two traffic loads, $\rho = 0.6$ where average busy period 15 time slots and average idle period 10 time slots, and $\rho = 0.8$ where average busy period 40 time slots and average idle period 10 time slots. We can see that the blocking probability decreases as the conversion distance increases. But when the conversion distance is larger than a certain value, the decease of blocking probability is marginal. In this case there is little benefit for further increasing the conversion degree, which is exactly the reason for using limited range wavelength converters other than full range wavelength converters.

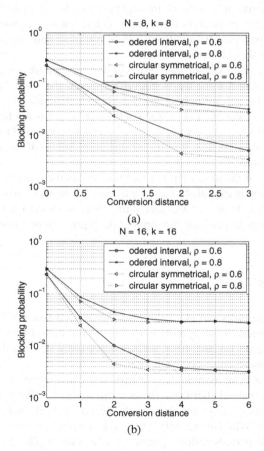

Fig. 4. Packet loss probability of WDM switch under bursty traffic where the packets have no priority. (a) 8×8 interconnect with 8 wavelengths per fiber. (b) 16×16 interconnect with 16 wavelengths per fiber.

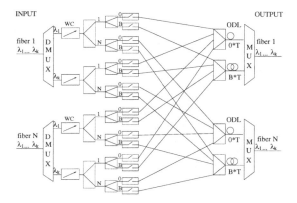

Fig. 5. A buffered wavelength convertible WDM optical switch.

5   Optimal Scheduling in Buffered WDM Switch

5.1   Network Model

A buffered WDM switch is shown in Fig.5. We can see that the only difference between Fig.5 and Fig.2 is the optical delay lines (ODL) placed in front of the output fibers. There are $B + 1$ optical delay lines, capable of delaying a packet for 0 to B time slots. The switching fabric is capable of connecting any input wavelength channel to any of the $B + 1$ ODLs for any output fiber. So if a packet that cannot be sent to the output fiber directly, it can be sent to one of the delay lines. A packet sent to delay line b will come out of the delay line after b time slots. The outputs of these $B + 1$ delay lines are directly combined together and sent to the output fiber.

Note that all the signals come out of the delay lines at the same time slot should be on different wavelengths. As a result, not all wavelength channels on the $B + 1$ ODLs are available to the new coming packets. Some of them, if assigned to the new packets, might cause collision later. Given the buffer occupancy state, we can find the set of available wavelength channels for newly arrived packets by scanning through the ODLs in linear time. To be specific, wavelength channel λ_i on ODL b denoted by λ_i^b is not available if we find that there is a packet that will come out of an ODL on wavelength λ_i after b time slots, for example, a packet on λ_i directed to ODL $b + 1$ at the previous time slot.

After getting the available wavelength channels, if only to maximize network throughput, we can simply run the First Available Algorithm described in the previous section. However, here we have another concern, since we also want to minimize the total delay, or, to send as many packets to shorter delays as possible. We can check the ODLs one by one, shorter ODLs first. By doing so we guarantee that the wavelength channels on shorter ODLs are given higher priorities. When checking ODL b, we should use as many wavelength channels on this ODL as possible, while making sure that all the wavelength channels checked previously on shorter delay lines that were assigned to some packets are still used, though not necessarily being assigned to the same packets.

To do so we can use the Scan and Swap Algorithm shown in Table 2. In the algorithm, the wavelength channels that were checked and assigned to packets prior to ODL b are

Table 2. Scan and Swap Algorithm

```
Set all packets as unmarked.
Π ← ∅.
for i=1 to n
        Find the first adjacent packet
        of aᵢ that has not been marked.
        if there is such a packet
                Π ← Π ∪ {aᵢ}
                Mark this packet.
        else
                if aᵢ is a compulsory channel
                        Π ← Π ∪ {aᵢ}
                        Let aₛ be the non-compulsory
                        channel in Π with the largest index
                        Π ← Π \ {aₛ}
                end if
        end if
end for
```

called the *compulsory channels*, and the available channels on ODL b are called the *non-compulsory channels*. For simplicity we use the a_i, $i \in [1, n]$ to denote the wavelength channels where n is the total number of compulsory channels and non-compulsory channels. Lower wavelengths are scanned first. That is to say, for two channels denoted by a_i and a_j, if a_i is on a lower wavelength then $i < j$. For channels on the same wavelength, the compulsory channels are checked prior to the non-compulsory channel. Compulsory channels on the same wavelength are checked in a arbitrary order. If the wavelength of a packet can be converted to a_i, we say this packet is *adjacent* to a_i. The *first* adjacent packet is the one on the lowest wavelength.

The algorithm outputs set Π initially set to be empty. Also, at the beginning all the packets is set to be unmarked. Then the algorithm starts scanning the channels from first to the last. When scanning to a_i, it checks if there is an unmarked packet adjacent to it a_i. If yes, it adds a_i to Π and mark the first such packet. Else it proceeds to the next channel if a_i is non-compulsory. Otherwise a_i is a compulsory channel, it adds a_i to Π and swap out a non-compulsory channel in Π with the largest index. When the algorithm terminates, Π will store the channels that can be assigned to the incoming packets. All the compulsory channels will be in Π, and the number of non-compulsory channels in Π is maximum.

This algorithm needs to be executed $B + 1$ times. The output of the b_{th} execution will be the compulsory channels of the $(b+1)_{th}$ execution. The output of the $(B+1)_t h$ execution stores the wavelength channels that can be assigned to the incoming packets. Then an assignment can be found by running the First Available Algorithm on these channels and the incoming packets.

5.2 Complexity Analysis

We now show that the running time of the Scan and Swap Algorithm is $O(k)$ where k is the number of wavelengths.

The input to this algorithm are the set of compulsory channels, the set of non-compulsory channels and the set of packets. We can use a $1 \times k$ vector to represent each of these set, with element i in the vector being the number of channels or packets on wavelength λ_i. We will refer to them as the "compulsory vector", the "non-compulsory vector" and the "packet vector" and denote them as C, N and R, respectively.

When running the Scan and Swap Algorithm, the channels will be added to set Π if they can be covered along with all the vertices previously in Π. Since algorithm makes sure that all the compulsory channels are in Π, only the status of the non-compulsory channels needs to be recorded. For this, a stack can be used. When a non-compulsory channel is added to Π, its wavelength index will be pushed into this stack. In some later steps we may decide to swap out some of the non-compulsory channels. By the algorithm, they will be the ones that were most recently added to Π, i.e., will be on the top of the stack. Therefore to swap them out is simply to perform several pop operations. When the algorithm terminates the content in the stack will be the desired output.

In the algorithm the packets that were chosen to match to some wavelength channels need to be "marked". We can use a $1 \times k$ vector called the "marked vector", denoted as D, to represent the set of marked packets, with each element being the number of marked packets on the corresponding wavelength.

We can also use pointer p which is the wavelength index of a packet immediately following the packet that was just marked. That is to say, if the Scan and Swap Algorithm just marked a packet on λ_j, then $p = j$ if there are still unmarked packets on λ_j, otherwise $p = j + 1$. Initially $p = q$ where q is the smallest wavelength with $r_q > 0$.

A more detailed Scan and Swap Algorithm, with implementation issues considered, is shown in Table 3. The algorithm scans the wavelengths from λ_1 to λ_k. When scan to λ_i, first it checks whether the packet pointed by p is in the conversion range of λ_i by comparing p with $begin(i)$ and $end(i)$. If $p > end(i)$, all the packets convertible to λ_i must have all been marked or be used by the wavelength channels on lower wavelengths, since we always try to mark the first available packets for any channel. Therefore, if there are compulsory channels on λ_i or $c_i > 0$, they cannot mark any new packet. By the algorithm, we should swap out exactly c_i non-compulsory channels, which is to perform c_i pop operations on the stack. If $p < begin(i)$, the packet is also out of the conversion range of λ_i, however, in this case all the packets convertible to λ_i are not marked, and we set $p = begin(i)$.

Now the algorithm will try to find the first c_i packets that are in the conversion set of λ_i, which is done by the *while* loop. The loop exits if enough packets are found, or the last wavelength adjacent to λ_i has been reached.

In the second case, not enough packets were found, and we should *pop* the stack several times accordingly. Then we should update pointer p, by moving it to the first wavelength that has some packets.

In the first case, all the compulsory channels can find some packets to mark, and we go on to check the non-compulsory channel on λ_i, if there is such a channel ($n_i == 1$). If the packet pointed by p is within the conversion range of λ_i ($p \leq end(i)$) and there

Table 3. Scan and Swap Algorithm in Implementation

```
p ← q where q is the smallest wavelength with r_q > 0;
Set D to be all zero vector;
for i=1 to k
      if end(i) < p
            pop stack c_i times
      else
            if begin(i) > p
                  p ← begin(i);
            end if

            Δ ← r_p − d_p ;
            while Δ < c_i
                  d_p ← r_p (mark all the packets on λ_p);
                  p ← p + 1;
                  if p > end(i)
                        break;
                  end if
                  Δ ← Δ + r_p;
            end while

            if p == end(i) + 1
                  pop stack c_i − Δ times
                  set p to the first q where p ≤ q and r_q > d_q
            else
                  d_p ← r_p − Δ + c_i (mark the needed packets on λ_p);
                  set p to the first q where p ≤ q and r_q > d_q
                  if n_i == 1 and p ≤ end(i) and r_p − d_p > 0
                        push i into the stack
                        d_p ← d_p + 1 (mark a packet on λ_p)
                        set p to the first q where p ≤ q and r_q > d_q
                  end if
            end if
      end if
end for
```

is still an unmarked packet $d_p < r_p$, this non-compulsory channel can be added in and we *push i* into the stack. Then we update the mark vector and p accordingly.

Now we analyze the complexity of the *Scan and Swap* algorithm, when implemented in this way. First, the *push* and *pop* operations takes $O(k)$ time, since there are up to k non-compulsory channels, and a channel can be pushed in at most once because a channel that was *popped* out will never be *pushed* in again. For other operations within the *for* loop, except for the *while* loop, also need no more than $O(k)$ time. One execution of the *while* loop takes constant time. And, because each execution moves the pointer p down by one, the *while* loop is executed at most k times. Combining these we conclude that the running time of the *Scan and Swap* algorithm is $O(k)$.

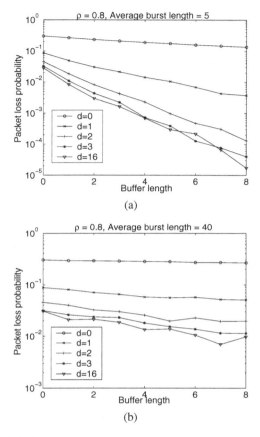

(a)

(b)

Fig. 6. Packet loss probability of the WDM switching network under bursty traffic. The load is $\rho = 0.8$. (a) Average burst length is 5 time slots. (b) Average burst length is 40 time slots.

In our applications the Scan and Swap Algorithm needs to run $B + 1$ times. Thus, when using this algorithm for optimal scheduling, we need $O(kB)$ time, where B is the length of the longest delay line and k is the number of wavelengths per fiber,

5.3   Simulation Results

We implemented Scan and Swap Algorithm in software and conducted simulations. The network in simulations has 16 input fibers and 16 output fibers with 16 wavelengths on each fiber. The arrivals of connection requests at input channels are bursty: an input channel alternates between two states, the "busy" state and the "idle" state. When it is in the "busy" state it continuously receives packets and all the packets go to the same destination; otherwise the input channel is in "idle" state and does not receive any packets. The length of the busy and idle periods follows geometric distribution. The network performance is measured by the *packet loss probability* which is defined as the

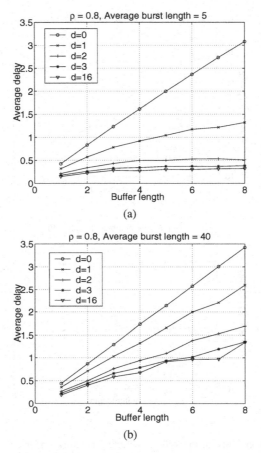

Fig. 7. Average delay of the WDM switching network under bursty traffic. The load is $\rho = 0.8$. (a) Average burst length is 5 time slots. (b) Average burst length is 40 time slots.

ratio of the total number of successfully transmitted packets over the total number of arrived packets. The durations of the packets are all one time slot and for each experiment the simulation program was run for 100,000 time slots.

In Fig. 6 we show the packet loss probability of the network as a function of the number of fiber delay lines. In Fig. 6(a) the average burst length is 5 time slots and the average idle period is 1.25 time slots. In Fig. 6(b) the average burst length is 40 time slots and the average idle period is 10 time slots. In both cases the traffic load is $\rho = 0.8$. As expected, packet loss probability decreases as the number of delay lines increases. For example, in Fig. 6(a), when the conversion distance $d = 2$, when $B = 0$ (no buffer), the packet loss probability is about $10^{-1.3}$. However, when $B = 4$, it is reduced to about 10^{-3}. As the traffic becomes more bursty, i.e., as the average burst length increases, the packet loss probability decreases much more slowly with the buffer depth, as can be observed in Fig. 6(b) where the curves are almost flat. This is because when the burst is too long it will always exceed the buffer capacity.

We can also notice that with the same buffer length, a larger conversion distance always results in a smaller packet loss probability. Also, when the burst is too long, increasing buffer length does not yield too much benefit, but increasing conversion distance always does. For example, in Fig. 6(b), when $d = 1$, increasing buffer length does not decrease much of the packet loss probability, but when we increase d to 2, the packet loss probability almost drops by $10^{-0.4}$. This suggests that wavelength conversion ability is more important than buffering in a WDM switching network. However, we can observe that only a relatively small conversion distance is needed to achieve good performance. As can be seen in Fig. 6, the packet loss probability for $d = 3$ is already very close to that for $d = 16$ (full range conversion). This is exactly the reason to use limited range wavelength converters instead of full range wavelength converters.

In Fig. 7 we show the average delay of a packet as a function of the number of fiber delay lines. The traffic is the same as in Fig. 6. We can see that as the buffer length increases the average packet delay also increases, since fewer packets are dropped and thus more are directed to a buffer before being actually transmitted. For the same buffer size, a larger conversion distance results in a shorter average delay. As in Fig. 7(a), when $B = 4$, the average delay for $d = 1$ is about 0.9 time slots and the average delay for $d = 3$ is only about 0.3 time slots.

6   Conclusions

In this paper we have presented optimal scheduling algorithms to resolve output contentions in time slotted WDM optical interconnects with limited range wavelength conversion ability. We gave the First Available Algorithm that runs in $O(k)$ time for finding an optimal scheduling in unbuffered interconnects where k is the number of wavelengths per fiber. We also gave the Scan and Swap Algorithm that runs in $O(Bk)$ time for finding an optimal scheduling in buffered interconnects where B is the buffer depth.

References

1. B. Mukherjee, "WDM optical communication networks: progress and challenges," *IEEE Journal on Selected Areas in Communications*, vol. 18, no. 10, pp. 1810-1824, Oct. 2000.
2. D. K. Hunter, M. C. Chia and I. Andonovic "Buffering in optical packet switches," *Journal of Lightwave Technology*, vol. 16 no. 12, pp. 2081-2094, 1998.
3. M. Kovacevic and A. Acampora, "Benefits of wavelength translation in all-optical clear-channel networks," *IEEE Journal on Selected Areas in Communications*, vol. 14, no. 5, pp. 868 -880, June 1996.
4. S.L. Danielsen, C. Joergensen, B. Mikkelsen and K.E. Stubkjaer, "Analysis of a WDM packet switch with improved performance under bursty traffic conditions due to tuneable wavelength converters," *Journal of Lightwave Technology*, vol. 16, no. 5, pp. 729-735, May 1998.
5. N. McKeown, "The iSLIP scheduling algorithm input-queued switch," *IEEE/ACM Trans. Networking*, vol. 7, pp. 188-201, Apr. 1999.
6. W.J. Goralski, *Optical Networking and WDM*, 1st Edition, McGraw-Hill, 2001.

7. R. Ramaswami and K. N. Sivarajan, *Optical Networks: A Practical Perspective*, 1st Edition, Academic Press, 2001.
8. T. Tripathi and K. N. Sivarajan, "Computing approximate blocking probabilities in wavelength routed all-optical networks with limited-range wavelength conversion," *IEEE Journal on Selected Areas in Communications*, vol. 18, pp. 2123–2129, Oct. 2000.
9. L. Xu, H.G. Perros and G. Rouskas, "Techniques for optical packet switching and optical burst switching," *IEEE communications Magazine*, pp. 136 - 142, Jan. 2001.
10. R. Ramaswami and G. Sasaki, "Multiwavelength optical networks with limited wavelength conversion," *IEEE/ACM Trans. Networking*, vol. 6, pp. 744–754, Dec. 1998.
11. Y. Yang and J. Wang, "WDM optical interconnect architecture under two connection models," *Proc. of IEEE Hot Interconnects 10*, pp. 146-151, Palo Alto, CA, August 2002.
12. Y. Yang, J. Wang and C. Qiao "Nonblocking WDM multicast switching networks," *IEEE Trans. Parallel and Distributed Systems*, vol. 11, no. 12, pp. 1274-1287, 2000.
13. Z. Zhang and Y. Yang, "Distributed scheduling algorithms for wavelength convertible WDM optical interconnects," *Proc. of the 17th IEEE International Parallel and Distributed Processing Symposium*, Nice, France, April, 2003.
14. E.L. Lawler, "Combinatorial Optimization:Networks and Matroids," *Holt, Rinehart and Winston*, 1976.
15. F. Glover "Maximum matching in convex bipartite graph," *Naval Res. Logist. Quart.*,14, pp. 313-316, 1967.
16. W. Lipski Jr and F.P. Preparata "Algorithms for maximum matchings in bipartite graphs," *Naval Res. Logist. Quart.*,14, pp. 313-316, 1981.
17. G. Shen, et. al, "Performance study on a WDM packet switch with limited-range wavelength converters," *IEEE Communications Letters* , vol. 5, no. 10, pp. 432-434, Oct. 2001.

Comparative Evaluation of Adaptive and Deterministic Routing in the OTIS-Hypercube

Hashem Hashemi Najaf-abadi[1] and Hamid Sarbazi-Azad[1,2]

[1] School of Computer Science, IPM, Tehran, Iran.
{h_hashemi, azad}@ipm.ir
[2] Computer Eng. Department, Sharif Univ. of Tech., Tehran, Iran.
azad@sharif.edu

Abstract. The OTIS-hypercube is an interesting class of the optoelectronic OTIS architecture for interconnection networks. In the OTIS architecture, optical connections are used to connect distant processors while closer processors are connected electronically. In this paper, we propose an adaptive routing algorithm for the wormhole switched OTIS-hypercube. We then present an empirical performance evaluation of adaptive wormhole routing in these networks for different structural conditions and traffic loads. The effect of maximum wire length and router delay on performance measures, such as average message latency and bandwidth of the interconnection network, are also briefly brought into consideration and compared with those of equivalent hypercubes. In addition, the performance merits of adaptive wormhole routing in the OTIS-hypercube are compared with those of deterministic routing using extensive simulation experiments.

1 Introduction

The conveyance of data between processing elements, in an interconnection network, is usually made through electrical conductance. But where communication distance exceeds a few millimeters, optical interconnect provides speed and power advantages over electronic interconnect [2, 3]. Therefore, in the design of very large multiprocessor systems, to interconnect physically close processors using electronic interconnect and to use optical interconnect for pairs of processors that are distant, seems a reasonable option. Marsden et al. [4], Hendrick et al. [5] and Zane et al. [6] have proposed such an architecture named the OTIS (Optical Transpose Interconnect System) in which the processors are partitioned into groups. Within each group electronic interconnect is used to connect the processors, and optical interconnect is used to bring about connection between processors in different groups.

The significance of an architecture depends on whether that architecture can be used to effectively solve problems that are of interest. The development of algorithms for OTIS-based computers has been the focus of much attention. Algorithms for OTIS-hypercubes have been developed by Sahni and Wang [10]. Algorithms for OTIS-mesh computers (in this type of OTIS each group is a mesh instead of a hypercube) have been studied more extensively by Zane *et al* [6], Sahni and Wang [11, 12, 13, 14], Rajasekeran and Sahni [15] and Osterloh [16]. Sahni and Wang [11]

P.-C. Yew and J. Xue (Eds.): ACSAC 2004, LNCS 3189, pp. 349–362, 2004.

have also developed a routing algorithm for the OTIS-mesh network. However, no work has, to our best knowledge, investigated the appropriateness of these systems for general purpose applications using realistic implementation assumptions, i.e. these studies have considered topological and algorithmic issues in OTIS computers and no study has been conducted to evaluate the performance of these systems in sight of parameters such as bandwidth and message latency.

The layout of the paper is as follows. OTIS parallel computers and specifically the OTIS-hypercube network are first described in detail. A deadlock-free adaptive routing algorithm is then suggested for this network. Simulation results of different cases of the network with different traffic loads are compared and a number of observations, based on these results, are made. Finally, an overview of the experimental results is provided and some concluding remarks are given.

2 Preliminaries

The reader is referred to [8] for an in-depth account of basic concepts such as topology, routing algorithms, flow control, wormhole switching and virtual channels. In this section, more specific concepts are described.

2.1 The OTIS-Hypercube Interconnection Network

In order to interconnect physically close processors using electronic interconnect and distant processors with optical interconnect, various combinations of interconnection networks have been proposed. In OTIS computers, optical interconnects are realized via a free space optical interconnect system proposed by Marsden et al. [4]. In this system, processors are partitioned into groups of the same size. Krishnamoorthy et al. [17] have shown that when the number of groups equals the number of processors within a group, the bandwidth and power efficiency are maximized, and system area and volume are minimized.

In the OTIS-hypercube parallel computer, there are 2^{2N} processors organized as 2^N groups of 2^N nodes each. The processors in each group form an N dimensional hypercube that employs electrical interconnect. The inter-group interconnections are realized by optics. In the OTIS interconnect system, processor (i, j), i.e. processor j of group i, is connected via optics to processor (j, i). A partial 3-dimensional OTIS-hypercube is illustrated in Fig. 1. In this figure, the optical interconnections corresponding to group 0 are shown by dashed lines. Electronic interconnections in each group are shown by solid lines. The address of each group is placed in parentheses above the group. The address of each node in group (001) is displayed near the node, and the nodes in other groups are assigned addresses in the same order.

2.2 Node Structure in the OTIS Architecture

A node, in the n-dimensional OTIS-hypercube, or OTIS-H_n for short, consists of a processing element (PE) and a switching element (SE), as illustrated in Fig. 2. The PE

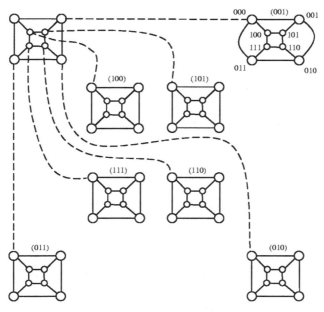

Fig. 1. A 3-dimensional OTIS-hypercube with the optical connections exiting one of the sub-graphs (numbers inside parenthesis are sub-graph addresses)

contains a processor and some local memory. A node is connected, through its SE, to its intra-group neighboring nodes using n input and n output electronic channels. Two electronic channels are used by the PE to inject/eject messages to/from the network. Messages generated by the PE are transferred to the router through the injection channel. At the destination node, messages are transferred to the local PE through the ejection channel. The optical channel is used to connect a node to its transpose node in another group for inter-group communication. The router contains flit buffers for each incoming channel. A number of flit buffers are associated with each physical input channel. The flit buffers associated with each channel may be organized into several lanes (or virtual channels), and the buffers in each virtual channel can be allocated independently of the buffers in any other virtual channel [8]. The concept of virtual channels has been first introduced in the context of the design of deadlock free routing algorithms, where the physical bandwidth of each channel is multiplexed between a number of messages [7, 8]. However, virtual channels can also reduce network contention. This is while it has been shown that virtual channels are expensive, increasing node delay considerably [1]. So, the number of virtual channels per physical channel should be reasonable. The input and output virtual channels are connected by a crossbar switch that can simultaneously connect multiple input channels to multiple output channels given that there is no contention over the output channels.

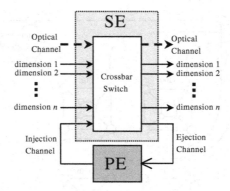

Fig. 2. The node structure in the OTIS-hypercube

3 Deadlock-Free Wormhole Routing in the OTIS-Hypercube

3.1 Deadlock-Free Adaptive Routing

With fully adaptive routing, the header of a message can be routed through any dimension that takes the message closer to its destination. But the actual dimension that the message is routed through depends on which dimension has a free virtual channel at the time. This is contrary to deterministic routing in which dimensions are traversed strictly in a predetermined order.

In the case of OTIS interconnection networks, two basic adaptive routing algorithms can be suggested. In the first algorithm, a message is routed adaptively in the local sub-graph (group) in which it starts until it reaches the node that has the same node address as the destination node. From that node, the optical channel is taken into another sub-graph. In this sub-graph, the message is routed (once again adaptively) until it reaches a node that has the same node address as the sub-graph address of the destination node. Once there, the message takes its final optical hop to the destination node. In the second algorithm, a message is first adaptively routed to a node that has a node address equal to the sub-graph address of the destination. Once there, the optical channel takes the message to the sub-graph of the destination node. The message is then adaptively routed to the destination node within this sub-graph. It is obvious that, although labeled adaptive, both algorithms make use of the optical channels deterministically. The reason for this is that utilization of the optical channels in any other manner will cause the routing algorithm to become non-minimal.

Of the former algorithms, the one that takes a shorter path depends on the full address (consisting of the sub-graph and node addresses) of the source and destination nodes. When considering the OTIS-hypercube, this can be determined effortlessly. If the number of differing bits of the full address of the source and destination nodes is less than the number of differing bits of the full address of the source node and the transpose of the address of the destination node, then the first routing algorithm will result in a shorter path. Otherwise, the second algorithm will. However, it should be obvious that in the first routing algorithm, once the first optical channel has been taken, the rest of the routing is identical to that of the second algorithm. Therefore, if in each node, a message is routed according to the algorithm that takes a shorter path to the destination of the message (without considering the source node), a more global optimal routing algorithm is obtained.

In order for a routing algorithm to be deadlock-free, cyclic buffer dependencies between messages and the virtual channels they allocate, must not occur. Duato [18] has suggested a virtual channel allocation scheme for fully-adaptive deadlock-free routing in the hypercube. In that scheme, all virtual channels except one are used for adaptive routing, and the leftover virtual channel is used only by messages that are traversing the lowest dimension they must traverse (just as they would have, if routed deterministically). But in an OTIS-hypercube, the optic channels between the sub-graphs (hypercubes) may also cause cyclic dependencies if no further restriction is enforced on the virtual channels a message may traverse. To prevent the occurrence of such cyclic dependencies, the virtual channels of each electronic physical channel must be divided into two sets, i.e. each sub-graph must be split into two virtual networks. A message, after being injected into the network, traverses the source sub-graph through its first virtual network. But once an optical channel has been traversed and the message has entered another sub-graph, that sub-graph is traversed through its second virtual network.

According to the minimal routing algorithm described above, each message traverses either one or two optical channels. Cyclic dependencies between messages that traverse one optical channel can obviously not occur. But, for messages that traverse two optical channels, that would not have been the case, had there been no restriction on the usage of the virtual optical channels. Since a message that has traversed its second optical channel has definitely entered its destination node, it can not be part of a cyclic buffer dependency. Therefore, reserving one of the virtual channels of each optical channel, specifically for such messages, eliminates the possibility of the occurrence of cyclic buffer dependencies.

In each virtual network of each sub-graph, virtual channel allocation is performed according to Duato's scheme. Thus, since the minimum number of virtual channels needed to implement Duato's scheme is equal to two (with one virtual channel, routing becomes fully deterministic) and there are two virtual networks per sub-graph, the minimum number of virtual channels needed for adaptive routing in the OTIS-hypercube is equal to four.

Fig. 3 displays the pseudo code of the minimal adaptive routing algorithm. In this code, all messages are considered to be inserted into the 0th virtual network (*InNet*=0). The | Offset | operator returns the number of one's in the binary representation of Offset, and the SelectOne( ) function adaptively selects a dimension, that has a free virtual channel, corresponding to a one in the binary representation of the input parameter. The ChannelsOfNet() function is considered to return the set of virtual channels of the virtual network determined by the parameter passed to it. The SelectVirtualChannel() function selects one of the free virtual channels passed to it. The names of the other functions are descriptive of their operation.

Algorithm: Adaptive deadlock-free routing in an n-D OTIS-hypercube
Inputs: Coordinates of current node ($Current_{Sub}$, $Current_{Node}$) and
destination node ($Dest_{sub}$, $Dest_{node}$) and input virtual network *InNet*.
Output: Selected output physical and virtual channel, $[p_c, v_c]$.
Procedure:
$Offset_{sub-sub} = Current_{Sub} \oplus Dest_{Sub}$
$Offset_{Node-Node} = Current_{Node} \oplus Dest_{Node}$
$Offset_{Node-Sub} = Current_{Node} \oplus Dest_{Sub}$
$Offset_{Sub-Node} = Current_{Sub} \oplus Dest_{Node}$

If *InFromOptic* **then**
  OutNet := 1;
Else
  OutNet := *InNet*;
Endif

If $\| Offset_{Sub-Sub} \| + \| Offset_{Node-Node} \| \leq \| Offset_{Sub-Node} \| + \| Offset_{Node-Sub} \|$ **then**
  If $Offset_{Node-Node} \neq 0$ **then**
    P_c := SelectOne ($Offset_{Node-Node}$);
    If P_c = LeastSignificantOne ($Offset_{Node-Node}$) **then**
      V_c := SelectVirtualChannel (ChannelsOfNet (*OutNet*));
    Else
      V_c := SelectVirtualChannel (ChannelsOfNet (*OutNet*) – {0});
    Endif
  Else
    If $Offset_{Sub-Sub} \neq 0$ **then**
      If *OutNet* = 1 **then**
        P_c := Optical; V_c := SelectVirtualChannel (*Any*);
      Else
        P_c:= Optical;
        V_c := SelectVirtualChannel(*Any* – {$Channel_{reserved}$});
      Endif
    Else
      P_c := Internal; V_c := SelectVirtualChannel(*Any*);
    Endif
  Endif
Else
  If $Offset_{Node-Sub} \neq 0$ **then**
  P_c := SelectOne($Offset_{Node-Sub}$);
    If P_c = LeastSignificantOne($Offset_{Node-Sub}$) **then**
      V_c := SelectVirtualChannel(ChannelsOfNet(*OutNet*));
    Else
      V_c := SelectVirtualChannel(ChannelsOfNet(*OutNet*) – {0});
    Endif
  Else
    If *OutNet* = 1 **then**
      P_c := Optical; V_c := SelectVirtualChannel(*Any*);
    Else
      P_c := Optical;
      V_c := SelectVirtualChannel (*Any* -{$Channel_{reserved}$});
    Endif
  Endif
Endif

Fig. 3. Adaptive deadlock-free wormhole routing algorithm for the OTIS-hypercube

3.2 Deadlock-Free Deterministic Routing

With deterministic routing, the routing within each sub-graph is performed according to a deterministic algorithm such as e-cube routing. However, for deadlock-free deterministic routing, the minimum number of virtual channels per physical channel in a hypercube is equal to one. Thus the minimum number of necessary virtual channels for deadlock-free deterministic routing in an OTIS-hypercube is equal to two.

3.3 Deadlock-Free Partially Adaptive Routing

A class of deadlock-free routing algorithms for the hypercube (that are not based on adding virtual channels to the structure of the network) are the partially adaptive routing algorithms, such as west-first and p-cube routing, presented by Glass and Ni [19]. A partially adaptive routing algorithm in the OTIS-hypercube is such that routing within each sub-graph is performed according to one of these partially-adaptive routing algorithms. One virtual channel is sufficient for the implementation of these algorithms in a hypercube. Thus, two virtual channels are sufficient to implement such partially adaptive routing algorithms in the OTIS-hypercube. But, as pointed out in [19], these partially-adaptive routing algorithms do not perform better than deterministic routing for random uniform traffic. Therefore, in what follows, we consider only the performance merits of adaptive and deterministic routing.

4 Empirical Performance Evaluation

To evaluate the functionality of the OTIS-hypercube network under different conditions, a discrete-event simulator has been developed that mimics the behavior of the described adaptive routing algorithm at the flit level in the OTIS-hypercube network. The simulator has been coded in C++ and consists of a number of different classes which are, at the highest hierarchical level, used to define the *network* class. Specifically, in the constructor of the *network* class, objects of the *node* and *channel* classes are defined. Each *node* has a number of pointers to its input and output channels, and each *channel* has a pointer to the *node* it is an input channel to. The way these pointers are initialized determines the topology of the network to be simulated. Once the *network* has been constructed, messages are injected into the network by *injection* events.

Four different types of *event* classes have been defined, namely, *injection*, *header-routing*, *handshaking* and *channel-switching* events. An event is specified to occur at a particular time and location. At each instance of time, all the events that must be executed at that time are completed. Only then is the time counter incremented and the events of the next time instance executed. This is while the execution of an event may generate another event to be executed at a future time. For instance, the execution of an injection event generates a header-routing event. That event, when executed, causes a channel-switching and a handshaking event.

When a flit is transferred from one buffer to the next, a counter at the corresponding virtual channel is decremented and a handshaking event, to be executed at the next time unit, is produced. This event notifies the preceding buffer allocated by the message that there is an empty space ahead into which it can transfer a new flit. A header-routing event, to be executed at a time determined by the channel cycle time of the network, is also produced. Once routed to a specific channel, a message waits until that channel is switched by a channel-switching event. If there is a free virtual channel available at the time of switching, it is allocated to that message and a counter corresponding to the virtual channel is initialized to the length of the message. The virtual channel on a physical channel is switched in a round-robin manner and every time a virtual channel is switched onto the physical channel, the corresponding counter is decremented if the buffer of that channel has a new flit and that of the next allocated virtual channel is empty. The execution of all these events put together, results in the simulation of the functionality of the entire interconnection network.

In each simulation experiment, a minimum of 120,000 messages have been delivered and the average message latency calculated. Statistics gathering was inhibited for the first 10,000 messages to avoid distortions due to startup transience. The mean message latency is defined as the average amount of time from the generation of a message until the last data flit of that message is consumed at the local PE at the destination node. The network cycle time is defined as the transmission time of a single flit from one router to the next, through an electric channel. The transmission time of a flit, through an optical channel is however a fraction of the network cycle time. In what follows, the ratio of optical channel transmission time to the network cycle time is referred to as the *channel cycle ratio*. Messages are generated at each node according to a Poisson process with a mean inter-arrival rate of λ_g messages per cycle. All messages have a fixed length of M flits. The destination node of each message has been determined through a uniform random number generator to simulate a uniform traffic pattern.

Numerous experiments have been performed for several combinations of network size, message length and number of virtual channels. The results of which are studied in the following subsections.

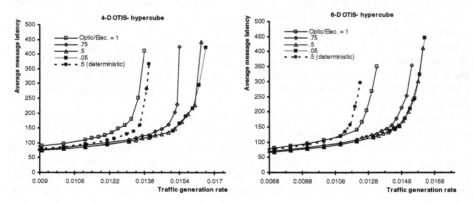

Fig. 4. Average message latency in OTIS-hypercubes with 4 virtual channels per physical channel, message length of 32 flits, and different channel cycle ratios; (a) 4-dimensional OTIS-hypercube, and (b) 6-dimensional OTIS-hypercube

4.1 The Effect of Channel Cycle Ratio

Fig. 4 depicts message latency results for the 4-dimensional and 6-dimensional OTIS-hypercubes for different cases of the *channel cycle ratio* with the number of virtual channels per physical channel equal to 4. It is evident from these figures that decreasing the channel cycle ratio results in an increase in the generation rate for which saturation occurs. But the effect gradually diminishes and from a point onwards, reducing the ratio any further has no effect on the saturation point.

In these figures, results obtained from deterministic routing when the effect of decreasing the channel cycle ratio is maximum, are also displayed to illustrate the fact that the effect of adaptivity is generally greater than the maximum effect of decreasing the channel cycle ratio.

4.2 The Effect of the Number of Virtual Channels

Fig. 5 shows the average message latency of 4-dimensional and 6-dimensional OTIS-hypercubes, with a channel cycle ratio of 0.1, for different numbers of virtual channels per physical channel and a message length of 32 flits. It is observed that, increasing the number of virtual channels initially causes a considerable increase in the generation rate for which saturation occurs, but gradually looses its effect. Eventually, the saturation point reaches the bandwidth of the system. At this point, increasing the number of virtual channels, no longer has any effect on the saturation point.

It is evident from Fig. 5 that the generation rate of the saturation point becomes equal to the bandwidth of the corresponding network when the number of virtual channels per physical channel is equal to 10. With this number of virtual channels, the network saturates with a generation rate of 0.022 messages per node per cycle. It can therefore be concluded that the bandwidth of a 4-D OTIS-hypercube (with messages 32 flits long) is approximately equal to 0.022. In the same figure the message latency of deterministic routing in an OTIS-hypercube with a small number of virtual channels is also depicted. This shows that, although two virtual channels are sufficient to implement deterministic routing in the OTIS-hypercube, deterministic routing performs considerably worse than adaptive routing even with four virtual channels.

The average message latency of a number of different sized OTIS-hypercubes (with a large number of virtual channels and a *channel cycle ratio* of 0.1), are depicted in Fig. 6. From this figure, it is evident that the bandwidth of the OTIS-hypercube is almost independent of its size. Therefore, in regard to performance, the OTIS-hypercube can be considered to be a scalable architecture.

Another network that possesses a very high degree of performance scalability is the hypercube. This can also be observed in the results of Fig. 6 where the average message latency of 6-D and 8-D hypercubes are depicted. These results show that when not considering implementation constraints (considering the channel cycle time of the fully-electronic hypercube and OTIS-hypercube to be the same), the OTIS-hypercube possesses less bandwidth than a hypercube with the same number of nodes. This may be due to the smaller number of channels in an OTIS-hypercube compared to an equivalent hypercube (with the same number of nodes). But the interesting point is that *when the channel cycle ratio is reduced, the maximum bandwidth of the OTIS*

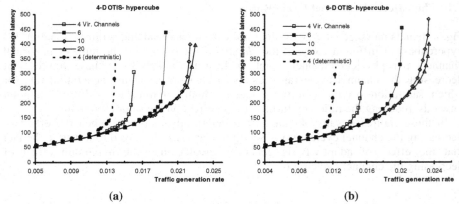

Fig. 5. Average message latency of OTIS-hypercubes with a channel cycle ratio of 0.1 and a message length of 32 flits, for different numbers of virtual channels per physical channel; (a) 4-dimesnional OTIS-hypercube, and; (b) 6-dimesnional OTIS-hypercube

hypercube becomes almost equal to the bandwidth of an equivalent hypercube. This is while, in a similar comparison of deterministic routing in hypercube and OTIS-hypercube networks, the maximum bandwidth of the OTIS-hypercube is found to be considerably less than that of the equivalent hypercube.

4.3 The Effect of Implementation Constraints

When implementation constraints are brought into account, considerable degradation in the performance of the hypercube becomes apparent as a result of the lengthy transmission time of long wires. But in the OTIS-hypercube, long electronic interconnections do not exist. The maximum channel transmission time of the OTIS-hypercube is therefore a fraction of that of a same sized hypercube. In Fig. 6, the average message latency of the 3-D OTIS-hypercube (with a channel cycle ratio of 1.0) is once again compared with that of an equivalent hypercube. This time however, the network cycle time of the OTIS-hypercube has been scaled to different fractions of the cycle time of the hypercube. Considering the performance scalability of the hypercube and OTIS-hypercube, and the fact that similar results to that of Fig. 7 have been obtained for different message lengths, it can be concluded that for the bandwidth of an OTIS-hypercube (with channel cycle ratio equal to 1.0) to be comparable to that of an equivalent hypercube, it is sufficient that the network cycle time of the OTIS-hypercube be roughly half that of the hypercube.

The network cycle time of a network consists of two important attributes, namely, intra-node and inter-node latency. The inter-node delay time depends primarily on topology and packaging. Specifically, the inter-node delay is proportional to the maximum wire length in the layout of the network. It is shown in [20] that the maximum wire length of the most compact layout, for the hypercube network, is equal to $N/3 + o(N)$. Therefore, inter-node delay in the hypercube is linearly proportional to the number of dimensions of the network. In an OTIS-hypercube, the

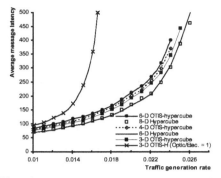 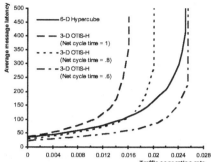

Fig. 6. The average message latency of equivalent hypercubes and OTIS-hypercubes with 30 virtual channels per physical channel (the default channel cycle ratio is 0.1).

Fig. 7. The average message latency of a 6-dimensional hypercube and its equivalent 3-dimensional OTIS-hypercube (with 30 virtual channels) for different values of the network cycle

number of dimensions of each sub-graph is equal to half that of an equivalent hypercube. Thus, the maximum wire length (electronic) in an OTIS-hypercube is approximately half that of an equivalent hypercube. On the other hand, according to [1], the intra-node delay of a network (which is dominated by the crossbar and router delays) is logarithmically proportional to the number of input and output channels to a node in the network.

Therefore, in an OTIS-hypercube network, a channel cycle time equal to half that of an equivalent hypercube may easily be achievable when the inter-node delay is the dominant delay factor. Even then, decreasing the channel cycle ratio will result in further superior performance by the OTIS-hypercube.

4.4 Performance-Cost Analysis

When the performance to cost ratio of the OTIS-hypercube is compared to that of an equivalent hypercube, it is observed that, for low generation rates, the OTIS-hypercube is superior to the hypercube, when the channel cycle ratio is equal to 1.0 (assuming the use of electronic channels for transpose communication). This is shown in Fig. 8, where the inverse of average message latency is considered to be representative of performance, and the number of physical channels entering (or exiting) the nodes of a network is considered to be representative of cost. From these results, it can be concluded that compared to a hypercube, the OTIS-hypercube topologically performs better at a lower cost for low generation rates.

4.5 An Adaptive-Deterministic Comparison

As a rule, the bandwidth of a network is independent of the routing algorithm used in the network. In other words, with a large number of virtual channels, the generation

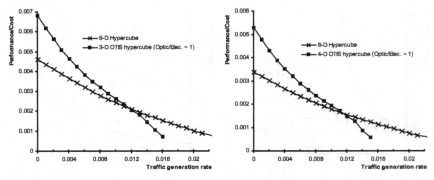

Fig. 8. Performance to cost ratio of adaptive routing in the hypercube compared to that of the OTIS-hypercube with a large number of virtual channels and the channel cycle ratio equal to 1.0

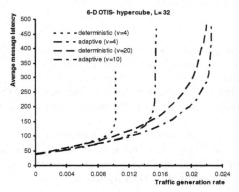

Fig. 9. OTIS-hypercube average message latency with different numbers of virtual channels per physical channel for adaptive and deterministic routing (the default channel cycle ratio is 0.1).

average message latency of deterministic and adaptive routing in the OTIS-hypercube are compared. The difference between adaptive and deterministic routing is more noticeable when there are a small number of virtual channels per physical channel. It is evident from the results of Fig. 9 that the network saturates at a higher generation rate with adaptive routing. But since the routing algorithm has no influence on the bandwidth of the network, a straightforward conclusion is that with adaptive routing fewer virtual channels are needed for the saturation point of the network to reach its maximum (the bandwidth of the network).

5   Conclusions

Unlike previous studies which have considered the topological and algorithmic issues in OTIS computers, in this study, we have investigated these systems in view of more realistic assumptions. An adaptive deadlock-free wormhole routing algorithm for the OTIS-hypercube is presented and the performance of this algorithm under uniform traffic is studied and compared to that of a deterministic routing algorithm.

Results reveal that decreasing the ratio of the optic to electronic channel transmission time is only of significance when the ratio is approximately less than half. In view of performance, the OTIS-hypercube is observed to be a scalable network. It has been shown that, for the bandwidth of an OTIS-hypercube to be comparable to that of a same sized hypercube, it is sufficient that the network cycle time of the OTIS-hypercube be half that of the hypercube. When implementation factors are accounted for, we find this condition to be easily attainable. It has also been shown that, even when the network cycle time of the OTIS-hypercube and the optical channel transmission time are equal to that of an equivalent fully-electronic hypercube, the performance-to-cost ratio of the OTIS-hypercube is higher than that of the hypercube for low generation rates. Finally, the bandwidth of the network is found to be independent of the routing algorithm used. Therefore, with adaptive routing fewer virtual channels are needed for the maximum saturation point to be attained.

Our next objective is to conduct an analysis of the OTIS-hypercube under different traffic patterns with different routing algorithms in order to evaluate the effect of adaptivity and minimality of routing, on performance.

References

1. A. A. Chien, "A cost and speed model for k-ary n-cube wormhole routers", *In Proceedings of Hot Interconnects'98*, August 1993.
2. M. Feldman, S. Esener, C. Guest and S. Lee, "comparison between electrical and free space optical interconnects based on power and speed considerations", *applied optics*, 27(9): 1742-1751, May 1988.
3. F. Kiamilev, P. Marchand, A. Krishnamoorthy, S. Esener, and S. Lee, "performance comparison between optoelectronic and VLSI multistage interconnection networks", *journal of lightwave technology*, 9(12): 1674-1692, Dec. 1991.
4. G. C. Marsden, P. J. Marchand, P. Harvey, and S. C. Esener, "Optical transpose interconnect system architectures", *Optical Letters*, 18(13): 1083-1085, July 1993.
5. W. Hendrick, O. Kibar, P. Marchand, C. Fan, D. V. Blerkom, F. McCormick, I. Cokgor, M. Hansen, and Esener, "modeling and optimization of the optical transpose interconnection system", *In optoelectronic technology Center*, Program Review, Cornel University, Sept. 1995.
6. F. Zane, P. Marchand, R. Paturi, and S. Esener, "Scalable network architectures using the optical transpose interconnection system (OTIS)", *In proceedings of the second International Conference on Massively Parallel Processing using Optical Interconnections* (MPPOI'96), pages 114-121, San Antonio, Texas, 1996.
7. W.J. Dally and C. Seitz, "Deadlock-free message routing in multiprocessor interconnection networks", *IEEE Trans. Computers*, 36 (5) (1987), 547-553.
8. W.J. Dally, "Virtual channel flow control", *IEEE Trans. Parallel and Distributed Systems*, 3 (2) (1992), 194-205.
9. J. Duato, "Why commercial multicomputers do not use adaptive routing", *IEEE Technical Committee on Computer Architecture Newsletter*, (1994), 20-22.
10. S. Sahni, C.-F. Wang, "BPC permutations on the OTIS-hypercube optoelectronic computer", *Informatica*, 22: 263-269, 1998.
11. S. Sahni and C.-F. Wang, "BPC permutations on the OTIS-mesh optoelectronic computer", In proceedings of the fourth international conference on massively parallel processing using *optical interconnections* (MPPOI'97), pages 130-135, 1997.

12.   C.-F. Wang and S. Sahni, "Matrix multiplication on the OTIS-mesh optoelectronic computer", *In Proceedings of the sixth international conference on Massively Parallel Processing using Optical Interconnections* (MPPOI'99), pages 131-138, 1999.
13.   C.–F. Wang and S. Sahni, "Image processing on the OTIS-mesh optoelectronic computer", *IEEE transaction on parallel and distributed systems*, 11(2): 97-107, 2000.
14.   C.–F. Wang and S. Sahni "Basic operations on the OTIS-mesh optoelectronic computer", *IEEE transaction on parallel and distributed systems*, 9(12): 1226-1236, 1998.
15.   S. Rajasekeran and S. Sahni "Randomized routing, selection and sorting on the OTIS-mesh", *IEEE transaction on parallel and distributed systems*, 9(9): 833-840, 1998.
16.   A. Osterloh, "Sorting on the OTIS-mesh", *In Proceedings of the 14th International Parallel and Distributed Processing Symposium* (IPDPS'2000), pp. 269-274, 2000.
17.   Krishnamoorthy, P. Marchand, F. Kiamilev, and S. Esener, "Grain–size considerations for optoelectronic multistage interconnection networks", *Applied Optics*, 31(26): 5480-5507, Sept. 1992.
18.   J. Duato, T. Pinkston, "A general theory for deadlock-free adaptive routing using a mixed set of resources", IEEE Transaction on Parallel and Distributed Systems, Vol. 12, 2001, pp. 1219-1235.
19.   L. Ni and C. Glass, "The Turn Model for Adaptive Routing", In Proc. of the 19th International Symposium on Computer Architecture, IEEE Computer Society, pp. 278-287, May 1992.
20.   Yeh, C.-H., E.A. Varvarigos, and B. Parhami, "Efficient VLSI layouts of hypercubic networks," *Proc. Symp. Frontiers of Massively Parallel Computation*, Feb. 1999, pp. 98-105.

A Two-Level On-Chip Bus System Based on Multiplexers

Kyoung-Sun Jhang[1], Kang Yi[2], and Soo Yun Hwang[1]

[1] Dept. of Computer Eng., ChungNam National University
sun@cnu.ac.kr, charisma@ce.cnu.ac.kr
[2] School of Computer Sci. and Electronic Eng., Handong Global University
yk@handong.edu

Abstract. The SoC (System on a Chip) design paradigm becomes a promising way of system integration as the level of design complexity is getting higher. There may be many IP modules to be integrated on a single chip in the modern SoC design. On-chip buses are usually used to interconnect the modules on a chip. Many bus architectures have been proposed for the interconnection of modules on a chip. We propose a two-level on-chip bus system that provides inter-bus transactions with multiplexers rather than with tri-state buffers or MOS switches such as in the segmented bus approaches. Our bus system can maximize the system throughput with concurrent inter-bus transactions as well as intra-bus transactions while preserving the already developed on-chip bus protocols for IP reuse. We present the performance simulation results of our approach with several different configurations compared with the existing segmented bus structures in terms of the total number of bus transactions executed in a given time.

1 Introduction

Today's deep submicron fabrication technologies enable design engineers to place billions of transistors on a single chip. These high-integrated circuit technologies make it possible for designers to integrate a number of function blocks like processors, memories, interfaces, and custom logic on a single chip. As the number of IP blocks increases, the communication among function blocks becomes the new system performance bottleneck [1].

The simplest way of connecting the multiple function blocks on a single chip is to use a traditional system bus. But, the existing buses may not be the solution to the communication traffic problem because only one pair of master and slave blocks can send and receive data at a particular time. There are several types of on-chip bus proposals like AMBA [2] from ARM, CoreConnect [3] from IBM, WISHBONE [4] and etc. to resolve this problem. However, they are also limited in the sense that they do not deal with communications among multiple buses on a single chip.

Bus segmentation that was proposed to reduce the average power to drive the long bus lines may contribute to the performance improvement with concurrent bus transactions [5]. However, the approach has limited concurrency due to the inherent nature of the segmented bus. To improve system throughput further, we propose a new two-level bus interconnection scheme. Our approach allows concurrent bus transactions

P.-C. Yew and J. Xue (Eds.): ACSAC 2004, LNCS 3189, pp. 363–372, 2004.

for a multiple bus clusters. We assume that the modules on a chip are clustered according to their traffic patterns. Our bus system is constructed in a two-level manner to separate local traffic from inter-bus traffic that is dealt with inter-bus connection paths. Our inter-bus connection scheme employs multiplexers rather than tri-state buffers or switches for reliable bus system operations and higher testability. With performance simulations, we observed that our MUX-based two-level on-chip bus architecture improves bus throughput by about 1.5 times compared with the existing segmented bus architecture. We also noticed from our preliminary implementations that our approach is more effective in reducing clock period than the segmented bus approach.

In the next section, previous works on the segmented bus were described and analyzed. In section 3, we describe our two-level bus architecture with several configurations. In section 4, we compare our bus structure with the existing segmented on-chip bus structure based on performance simulation. Finally, we summarize this paper and suggest future works.

2   Segmented On-Chip Bus System and Its Limitations

Several works on bus segmentation were proposed to reduce the average power consumption to drive long bus lines [6, 7]. In addition, the approach achieves throughput enhancement through parallelism [5]. The core idea of the existing segmented on-chip bus approach is to partition a bus system into several bus segments considering traffic localization. Each segment is a normal bus consisting of masters and slaves. Fig. 1 shows the segmented bus organization with four segments. Adjacent segments are connected via switches or tri-state buffers. The internal bus transactions of different segments can be performed concurrently while the switches connecting the segments are turned off. For example, four concurrent intra-segment transactions can be performed in the bus organization shown in Fig. 1 while all the switches connecting the segments are off. In addition, an inter-segment transaction between two different segments can also be performed through the switches connecting the corresponding segments. Multiple inter-segment transactions may be performed concurrently if the data paths of the transactions do not overlap. For example, we may perform the transaction between segments #1 and #2 and the transaction between segments #3 and #4 concurrently in the bus structure shown in Fig. 1.

The switches are controlled by a central arbiter that receives request signals and target segment identifiers from local arbiters. To implement the segmented bus structure, only arbiters need to be modified and the inter-segment transaction is transparent to all the function blocks in the system. Function blocks need not to be modified to allow inter-segment transactions on the segmented bus. In Fig. 1, CA represents central arbiter and LA local arbiter. LA selects one of transaction requests based on its own arbitration policy. If the transaction is an inter-segment, LA sends request to CA and CA sends acknowledge to LA when the inter-segment transaction is ready to start. CA has its own arbitration algorithm to select one transaction if several local arbiters ask more than one inter-segment transactions at a time.

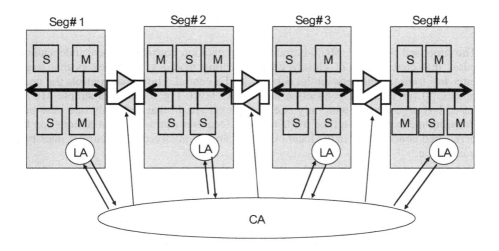

Fig. 1. Segmented Bus Organization

Though the segmented bus is beneficial in many aspects, it has several limitations as follows.

1. If several adjacent segments are occupied with an inter-segment bus transaction, other transactions (including inter- or intra- segment transactions) cannot be performed at the moment. It is because the related segments form a single bus that allows only one transaction at a time. For example, in Fig. 1, while segment #1 (master) sends data to segment #3 (slave), segment#2 cannot start any bus transaction until the inter-segment transaction between segments #1 and #2 finishes.

2. The effect of energy saving by the capacitive load reduction in the segmented bus may be alleviated by unnecessary power consumption due to tri-state buffers. Note that the undefined value (tri-state may result in an undefined value) of an input signal for CMOS logic makes a short circuit path between VDD and GND [9]. Such an undefined value also makes the logic testing difficult since undefined signal values prohibit the exact probing of logic values.

3. The clock period of the segmented bus system increases linearly as the number of segments increases, since all the bus segments need to be driven together in the worst case.

Thus, we proposed a new on-chip bus scheme that further improves parallelism while guaranteeing no undefined state and reducing clock period. Our approach is a two-level bus system using multiplexers instead of tri-state buffers in order to avoid adverse effects.

3   Proposed MUX-Based Two-Level Bus System

The proposed two-level MUX-based bus organization consists of local independent buses that contain sets of closely communicating modules, multiplexers that route inter-bus transactions between local buses, and a central arbiter that controls the multiplexer(s) for inter-bus connection at a higher level. Fig. 2 shows a simple MUX-based bus organization with only one multiplexer set. In that case only one inter-bus transaction can occur at a time while multiple local bus (intra-bus) transactions can be performed concurrently in the local buses that are not involved in the current inter-bus transaction.

Such a bus configuration has higher concurrency than the segmented bus because the local buses that are not involved in an inter-bus transaction need not suspend as in the case of the segmented bus organization. In addition, we can avoid unnecessary power consumption by employing multiplexers rather than tri-state buffers. If more than two inter-bus transactions are requested simultaneously the arbiter selects one of them by an arbitration algorithm and controls the local arbiters and the multiplexers accordingly.

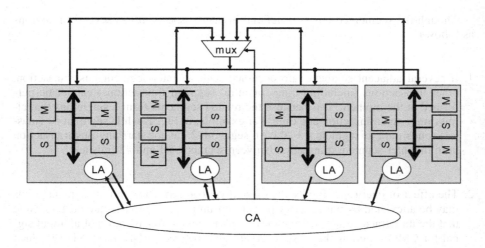

Fig. 2. A simple MUX-based bus organization

We can try another bus configuration and obtain more concurrency if we add more multiplexers as shown in Fig. 3 and Fig. 4. The bus configuration shown in Fig. 3 uses two 4-to-1 multiplexers and four 2-to-1 multiplexers to allow two concurrent inter-bus transactions. Since up to two inter-bus transactions may occur simultaneously in this configuration, we may expect more inter-bus transaction concurrency than in the bus configuration with one multiplexer. If more than two buses request for the same target local bus simultaneously, central arbiter selects one of them according to an arbitration policy.

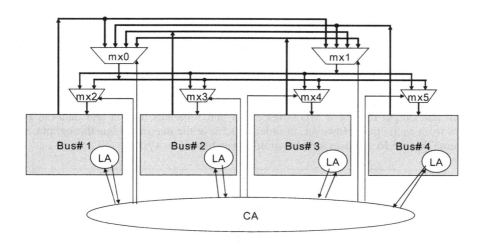

Fig. 3. MUX-based bus organization with two concurrent inter-bus transactions

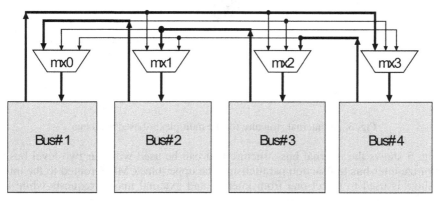

Bus#1 → Bus #4; Bus#4 → Bus#3; Bus#3 → Bus#2; Bus#2 → Bus#1

Fig. 4. Four concurrent inter-bus transactions in a structure with four 3-to-1 multiplexers

We can maximize inter-bus concurrency with four 3-to-1 multiplexers as shown in Fig. 4. It is possible for such a bus configuration to have up to four concurrent inter-bus transactions because the master part and the slave part in a local bus may be involved in different inter-bus transactions. For example, the master part of Bus#1 sends the data to the slave part of Bus#2 while the master part of Bus#2 sends data to the slave part of Bus#1 simultaneously. Fig. 4 shows an example of four concurrent inter-bus transactions.

Our approach is similar to the segmented bus approach with a central arbiter and local arbiters. But, our approach is different in that the master part and the slave part in a local bus can be involved in different inter-bus transactions resulting in maximal inter-bus transaction concurrency.

Note that we can use the existing modules without modification as is the case with segmented bus because the inter-bus transaction is transparent to each modules involved. In addition, our bus architecture has higher possibility to achieve more concurrency than the segmented bus especially when the local buses are also MUX-based. The local on-chip bus may be a bi-directional bus that use one bus line for both input and output data or a MUX-based bus that separates data-in and data-out bus lines from each other. However, in order to achieve the maximum bus throughput, we assume that the local buses are also multiplexer-based bus system.

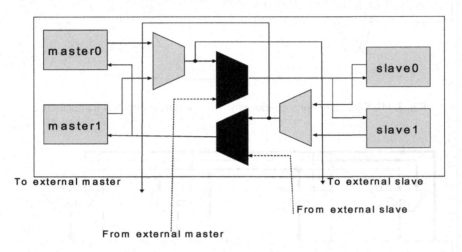

Fig. 5. An internal structure for the multiplexer-based local bus

Fig. 5 shows the internal bus structure that can be used with our two-level bus to maximize inter-bus transaction parallelism. The upper black MUX routed to the internal slave is used to select one from internal and external master requests while the lower black MUX routed to the internal master is to choose one from internal and external slave responses. The most important benefit of this structure is that the master part and the slave part in a bus can be involved in different inter-bus transactions, resulting in maximum inter-bus transaction concurrency.

4   Experiments and Analysis

We did the performance simulations for each bus configuration shown in the previous sections. The bus systems were modeled with VHDL in the behavioral level and simulated by ModelSim II simulator to measure the bus system performance. In the models we assumed that each bus transaction has the same length and target addresses are generated based on uniform distribution random number function. Each local arbiter selects one master if there is any intra-bus request. Or, the local arbiter selects one of masters requesting inter-bus transactions and forwards the request to the central arbiter. Central arbiter selects and grants one request for the same target bus based on a round-robin policy. In experiments, we have two adjustable parameters for each local bus: (1) idle time ratio (*idle_ratio*) that indicates how much portion of the time the local bus is idle (2) inter-bus or inter-segment transaction ratio (*inter_bus_ratio*) over the whole active bus transactions. So, the time spent for the inter-segment or inter-bus traffic can be calculated by the formula, (1- *idle_ratio*) * *inter_bus_ratio* * simulation_time. Our simulation assumes the number of segments or local buses is four and we deal with the following four types of bus configurations. The number of local buses can be larger than four to include more components in a system.

- The existing segmented bus of Fig. 1 (*segmented*)

- The MUX-based two-level bus with one multiplexer of Fig. 2 (*mux1*)

- The MUX-based two-level bus with two multiplexer of Fig. 3 (*mux2*)

- The MUX-based two-level bus with four multiplexer of Fig. 4 (*mux4*)

Fig. 6, Fig. 7 and Fig. 8 are graphical representations of the performance simulation results for the varying idle ratio (10%, 30% and 50% respectively) and inter-bus transaction ratio (X-axis). Y-axis indicates throughput, i.e. the time spent for transactions (inter-bus transactions + intra-bus transactions) divided by the total simulation time. We can see from the figures that the maximum throughput decreases as *idle_ratio* increases (Note the scales of Y-axis from Figure 6 to Figure 8). In addition, throughput goes down with the increase of *inter_bus_ratio* regardless of *idle_ratio*. This implies that when *inter_bus_ratio* is high, throughput is limited largely by the number of MUXes dedicated to inter-bus connections.

From the simulation results, we can confirm that *mux4* is better than any other bus configurations. The simulation graphs indicate that the structures, *segmented*, *mux1*, *mux2* and *mux4* can be ordered by the system throughput as follows.

$$mux\,4 \;>\; mux2 \;>\; mux1 \;>\; segmented$$

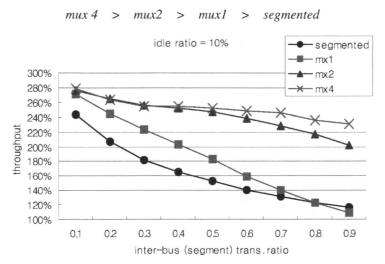

Fig. 6. Graphical Representation of Simulation Results for Idle Ratio=10%

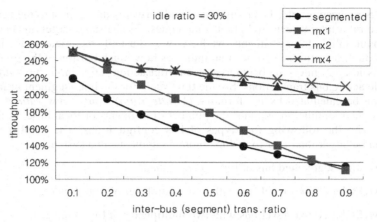

Fig. 7. Graphical Representation of Simulation Results for Idle Ratio=30%

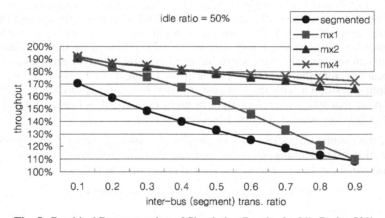

Fig. 8. Graphical Representation of Simulation Results for Idle Ratio=50%

Especially, *mux4* shows higher performance than *segmented* by 1.2 to 1.5 times. In addition, we observe that the slope of *mux4* configuration less steep than *mux1* and *segmented*. That means *mux4* configuration is less sensitive to the variation of the inter-bus transaction ratio than others. We can state that *mux4* bus configuration provides relatively stable bus traffic quality compared with other on-chip bus configurations for the fluctuating inter-bus transaction ratio.

For high inter-bus transaction ratio (0.9 or 0.8), *segmented* is slightly better for *mux1*. This is because *mux1* allow only one inter-bus transaction at a time, while *segmented* permits two concurrent inter-bus transactions at a time. Note that higher inter-bus (segment) ratio means most bus transactions are of inter-bus or inter-segment traffic. Remember that since clustering is made reflecting the traffic locality, the likelihood of high inter-bus transaction ratio is so small. Therefore, we can consider that *mux1* is better choice than *segmented* in a normal situation.

During the simulation, we assumed that the arbitration decision of each local arbiter and that of the central arbiter are independent. Thus, the selection of a master in each local bus is determined based on just the local information of the bus. Such a policy is so simple that it is easy to implement, but the policy has limited efficiency for the maximal throughput of the whole system. We suppose that *mux4* is just slightly better than *mux2* (especially for low inter-bus transaction ratio) due to this simple arbitration policy.

Clock period is another factor to determine the system performance in a synchronous system. We analyzed the circuit components affecting clock periods of the aforementioned configurations. Our analysis is summarized in Table 1. The configuration *segmented* seems to have more delay components than others since four separate buses must act like a single bus in the worst case. In that case, the bus system should drive four internal bus wires and three switches in a clock cycle. On the other hand, MUX-based bus configurations have similar delay factors to determine clock period regardless of the number of MUXes employed.

Table 1. Major components that affect clock period of each configuration.

Segmented	*mux1*	*mux2*	*mux4*
4 bus wires + 3 switches	1 bus wire + 1 int. MUX + 1 ext. MUX + ext. bus wire	1 bus wire + 1 int. MUX + 2 ext. MUX + ext. bus wire	1 bus wire + 1 int. MUX + 1 ext. MUX + ext. bus wire

We implemented partially our proposed architecture (*mux2*) and the segmented bus structure with synthesizable RTL VHDL targeting XILINX FPGA (XCV3000). Synthesis results with XILINX design tool (ISE 6.2) show that *segmented* configuration has about 2.5 times longer clock period than *mux2* configuration. On area and power consumption, two configurations exhibit similar results. This indicates that our approach is feasible and viable.

5   Summary and Future Works

As the system integration level gets higher, on-chip bus interconnection between many IP modules is required for higher performance through exploiting the bus transaction parallelism. In this paper, we propose a new on-chip bus interconnection architecture that could maximize parallelism among buses or segments. We compare the performance of our proposal with the existing segmented on chip bus proposal. Our idea is based on the two-level bus system with multiplexers rather than tri-state buffers or switches that cause some power consumption and testability problems. Our onchip bus system has more stability and testability as well as higher parallelism than the segmented bus system. The performance simulation results show that our interconnect method has higher system performance by 1.5 times than that of existing segmented bus approach. We can summarize the performance simulation results as follows.

1. Generally, the system performance relation is *mux4* > *mux2* > *mux1* > *segmented*

2. The bus configurations *mux4* and *mux2* show more stable traffic quality than *mux1* and *segmented* bus configuration for varying inter-bus transaction ratio.

The simulation result of our MUX-based bus (*mux4*) that allows four concurrent inter-bus transactions was slightly better than our MUX-based bus (*mux2*) that allows two concurrent inter-bus transactions due to the trivial arbitration policy. This implies a further study on the arbitration algorithm is necessary to maximally exploit the topological benefits of MUX-based bus system.

Our preliminary implementation on *segmented* and *mux2* shows that the clock period of *segmented* configuration is about 2.5 times longer than that of our proposed configuration *mux2* while both approaches exhibit similar area and power consumption. This indicates that our approach is feasible and viable.

We feel the necessity to adapt the idea to the popular existing MUX-based on chip bus architectures like AMBA. Currently, we are working towards to hardware implementation of the proposed MUX-based two-level bus system. Finally, we hope to apply our bus system to the real world examples such as multimedia processing application.

Acknowledgements. This work was supported in part by IT SoC Promotion Group of Korean IT Industry Promotion Agency and partly by ETRI (Electronics and Communications Research Institute) in Korea.

References

1.   D. Langen, A. Brinkmann, and U. Ruckert, "High Level Estimation of the Area and Power Consumption of On-Chip Interconnects", Proc. of the 13th Annual IEEE International ASIC/SOC Conference, Sep. 2000. pp. 297-301.
2.   "AMBA 2.0 Specification," http://www.arm.com/products/solutions/AMBA_Spec.html
3.   "The CoreConnect Bus Architecture," http://www-3.ibm.com/chips/products/coreconnect/
4.   "Wishbone," http://www.opencores.org
5.   T. Seceleanu, J. Plosila, and P. Liljeberg, "On-Chip Segmented Bus: A Self-timed approach",IEEE ASIC SoC Conference 2002.
6.   C.-T. Hsieh and M. Pedram, "Architectural energy optimization by bus splitting," IEEE Tran. CAD, vol. 21, no.4, APR. 2002.
7.   J.Y. Chen, W. B. Jone, J. S. Wang, H.-I. Lu, and T. F. Chen, "Segmented bus design for low-power systems" IEEE Tran. VLSI Systems, vol. 7, no.1, Mar. 1999.
8.   K. S. Jhang, K. Yi, and Y. S. Han, "An Efficient Switch Structure for Segmented On-Chip Bus", Proc. of Asia-Pacific International Symposium on Information Technology, Jan. 2004.
9.   Gary Yeap, Practical Low Power Digital VLSI Design, Kluwer Academic Publisher, 1998.

Make Computers Cheaper and Simpler

GuoJie Li

Institute of Computing Technology
Chinese Academy of Sciences

Abstract. It is expected that 700-800 millions of Chinese people will be connected to Internet in the next 15 years. What is really needed is reducing the cost of computers so that information services will be available for low income people rather than high performance only. In this talk, we briefly examine the research and development of computer architecture during the past decades and rethink the Moore's Law from the user's point of view. To explain the design principle of low cost and simplicity, we discuss the prospects of the new research direction by using examples from our own work, such as low cost CPU design, massive cluster computer (MCC) and reconfigurable computer system. Our research shows that it is possible to design and implement the deskside Teraflops-level supercomputer, which is less than $100K, and PC of $150 in the next 3-5 years.

P.-C. Yew and J. Xue (Eds.): ACSAC 2004, LNCS 3189, p. 373, 2004.
© Springer-Verlag Berlin Heidelberg 2004

A Low Power Branch Predictor to Selectively Access the BTB

Sung Woo Chung and Sung Bae Park

Processor Architecture Lab., Samsung Electronics,
Giheung-Eup, Yongin-Si, Gyeonggi-Do, 449-711 Korea
{s.w.chung, sung.park}@samsung.com

Abstract. As the pipeline length increases, the accuracy in a branch prediction gets critical to overall performance. In designing a branch predictor, in addition to accuracy, microarchitects should consider power consumption, especially in embedded processors. In this paper, we propose a low power branch predictor, which is based on the gshare predictor, by accessing the BTB (Branch Target Buffer) only when the prediction from the PHT (Prediction History Table) is taken. To enable this, the PHT is accessed one cycle earlier to prevent the additional delay. As a side effect, two predictions from the PHT are obtained at one access to the PHT, which leads to more power reduction. The proposed branch predictor reduces the power consumption, not requiring any additional storage arrays, not incurring additional delay (except just one MUX delay) and never harming accuracy. The simulation results show that the proposed predictor reduces the power consumption by 43-52%.

1 Introduction

As the pipeline length of today's embedded processors increases, the accuracy of a branch prediction affects the performance more significantly. In addition to accuracy, processor architects should consider the power consumption in a branch predictor, which is reported to account for more than 10% of the total processor's power consumption [1]. (In this paper, we define that a branch predictor is composed of a PHT (Prediction History Table) and a BTB (Branch Target Buffer)) Especially, in the embedded processor where the power consumption is crucial, it is important to reduce the power consumption of the branch predictor while maintaining the accuracy.

Some general purpose processors exploit the predecoding to detect whether the instruction is a branch or not, resulting in the selective access to the branch predictor(PHT and BTB) only when the instruction is a branch. In this case, the access to the branch predictor should be preceded by the access to the instruction cache. However, if the fetch stage is timing critical, the sequential access incurs additional delay. In embedded processors such as ARM 1136 [8] and ARM 1156 [9], the fetch stage is timing critical, leading to the simultaneous accesses to the branch predictor and the instruction cache. Accordingly the branch predictor

P.-C. Yew and J. Xue (Eds.): ACSAC 2004, LNCS 3189, pp. 374–384, 2004.
© Springer-Verlag Berlin Heidelberg 2004

should be accessed whenever instructions are fetched, resulting in significant power consumption.

Note that all the predictions from the branch predictor are not used to fetch the next instructions. In some processors that have timing margin in the fetch stage, instructions are predecoded after instructions are fetched. If the instruction is predecoded as a branch, the prediction is used to fetch the next instruction. Otherwise, the prediction is not used and the instruction of subsequent address is fetched. In other processors that have no timing margin in the fetch stage, the predictions are used to fetch the next instruction only when there is a hit in the BTB. In other words, a BTB hit is considered to indicate that the instruction is a branch.

Banking could be considered to reduce the power consumption in the branch predictor. However, the power reduction by banking is not more than 4% [1] and banking requires additional chip area. The PPD(Prediction Probe Detector), which is accessed earlier than the instruction cache, was proposed for a low power branch predictor [1]. It detects whether the instruction is a branch instruction in the fetch (branch prediction) stage to eliminate unnecessary accesses to the branch predictor. However, the PPD itself consumes extra power. Moreover, it may increase the pipeline latency, which may lead to the decrease the processor frequency [2][3].

In this paper, we propose a low power branch predictor. In the proposed branch predictor, the BTB is accessed only when the branch prediction is taken. To enable this without additional delay, the PHT is accessed one cycle earlier, resulting in selective access to the BTB.

2   Branch Predictors for Embedded Processors

Static branch predictors have been used for embedded processors. In some embedded processors, bimodal branch predictors, which are known as moderately accurate, are adopted. Recently, however, the increased pipeline length of embedded processors causes more performance penalty from branch mispredictions. Accordingly, a more accurate branch prediction is necessary to reduce the CPI loss that arises from the longer pipeline. Considering only accuracy, the tournament branch predictor [4], which was used for Alpha 21264, would be one of the best choices. However, it requires too large chip area to be adopted in embedded processors. The accurate branch predictor, which consumes reasonable area and power, such as gshare [4], is being considered for embedded processors [9].

Fig. 1 depicts the PHT of the traditional branch predictor, called gshare [4]. The PHT is an array of 2-bit saturating counters. It is indexed by the exclusive OR of the PC with the global history. Each counter of the PHT is increased/decreased when the branch is taken/untaken. The MSB (Most Significant Bit) of each entry determines the prediction (branch taken/untaken).

The branch predictor inevitably consumes unnecessary power. As shown in Fig. 2, whenever there is an instruction in the fetch stage, the PHT and the BTB should be accessed simultaneously. The reason is that there is no way to detect

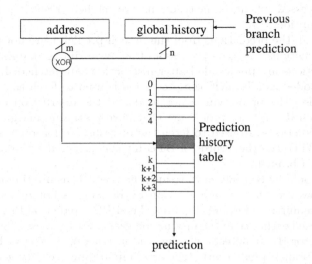

Fig. 1. The PHT of the Traditional Branch Predictor (Gshare Branch Predictor)

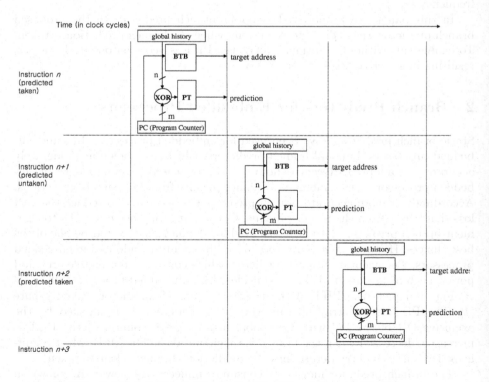

Fig. 2. Branch Prediction in the Traditional Branch Predictor

whether the instruction is a branch or not, in the early part of the fetch (branch prediction) stage. If the instruction is a branch, the PHT will be reaccessed later for training (update of the prediction information). Otherwise, there is no need to update the PHT for training.

3   Low Power Branch Predictor

In the proposed predictor, the BTB is accessed only when the prediction from the PHT is taken. To avoid the additional delay, the PHT should be accessed one cycle earlier.

3.1   Early Access to the PHT

In the traditional predictor, the PHT is accessed every cycle when there is a fetched instruction. To reduce the power consumption in the PHT, the proposed predictor looks up two predictions at every access to the PHT, which is described in Fig. 3. We double the width of the PHT but reduce the depth of the PHT by half for a fair comparison. The dynamic power consumption of the 4096 X 2 PHT is more than that of the 2048 X 4 PHT, though the difference is just 4.2 % - This data is obtained using Samsung Memory Compiler [5].

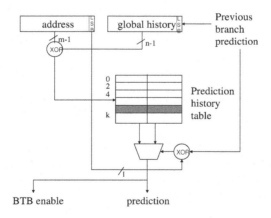

Fig. 3. Branch The PHT of the Proposed Branch Predictor

Different from the traditional predictor, the PHT in the proposed predictor is indexed by exclusive ORing of the PC excluding the LSB with the global history excluding the LSB. Note that if the global history is not changed and only the LSB of the PC is changed, two predictions can be acquired by accessing the PHT only once. The proposed predictor assumes that the previous instruction is not a predicted taken branch which changes global history. In other words, the propose predictor assumes that there is always sequential access to the PHT. If the previous instruction is a predicted taken branch, the PHT is reaccessed with new PC and new global history.

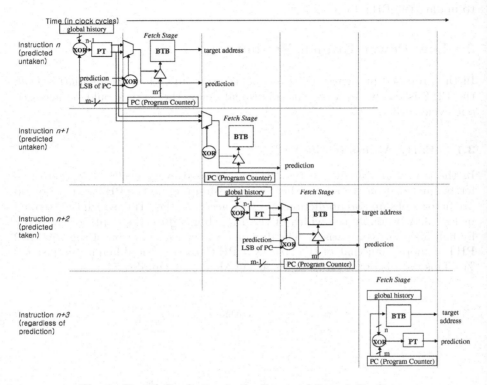

Fig. 4. Branch Prediction in the Proposed Branch Predictor

As shown in Fig. 4, the PHT lookup is done one cycle earlier compared to the traditional predictor. After the PHT lookup, the prediction is selected between the two predictors in the fetch (branch prediction) stage. Thus, the prediction can be obtained just after the MUX delay, which is early in the fetch stage compared to the traditional predictor (ex. in case of instruction n and instruction $n + 1$ in Fig. 4). If the previous instruction (instruction $n + 2$ in Fig. 4) is predicted as taken, the PHT should be reaccessed with a new PC in the fetch stage for the current instruction (instruction $n + 3$ in Fig.4). Note that two predictions can be used only when they are correctly aligned. For example, predictions for instruction n and instruction $n + 1$ can be looked up by accessing the PHT just once, whereas predictions for instruction $n + 3$ and instruction $n + 4$ can not since they are misaligned in PHT as shown in Fig. 3.

If the PHT were sequentially accessed, the number of accesses to the PHT would be decreased by 50% in the proposed predictor. Practically, however, the PHT is not always sequentially accessed because branch instructions, regardless of taken/untaken, change the global history (If the branch is predicted taken, the PC is also changed). Accordingly, the number of accesses to the PHT is decreased to ((total number of instructions)/2 + number of branch instructions). Generally, branch instructions occupies only 0-30% of total instructions in most applications [6][7], resulting in substantial power reduction.

As explained above, the power consumption is reduced. How much is the accuracy of the proposed predictor affected? If the previous instruction is predicted untaken, the prediction for the current instruction is also sequentially accessed, which does not make any difference. Thus, the prediction from the proposed predictor is same as that from the traditional predictor. If the previous instruction is predicted taken, the PHT is reaccessed in the fetch stage for the predicted address from the BTB. Though the prediction from the first access to the PHT is different, the prediction from the second access to the PHT of the proposed predictor is same as that of the traditional predictor. Therefore, the proposed predictor never affects the accuracy of the branch prediction.

3.2   Selective Access to the BTB

In the traditional predictor, the BTB as well as the PHT should be accessed every cycle. As mentioned in Sect. 3.1, the prediction is known early in the fetch stage of the proposed branch predictor, which enables the proposed predictor to selectively access to the BTB, as shown in Fig. 4. If the prediction is taken, the access to the BTB is enabled. Otherwise, the access to the BTB is disabled because the target address, which is obtained from the BTB, is useless. Though the number of predicted takens is generally more than that of predicted untakens, the predicted untakens still occupy 10-60% of total instructions, depending on the applications [6][7]. In other words, 10-60% of the BTB accesses can be decreased, resulting in the power reduction of the BTB.

4   Analysis Methodology

We presented analytical model and ran the simulations to evaluate the power consumption. Simulations were performed on a modified version of Simplescalar toolset [10]. The power parameters were obtained from the Samsung Memory Compiler [5] with Samsung 0.13 um generic process in a typical condition (25°C, VDD=1.20V). The configuration of the simulated processor is based on the specification of ARM 1136 [8]. We selected four applications (gcc, mcf, perl_bmk and vortex) from the Spec2000 benchmark suite [6]. Table 1 shows the sizes of the PHT and the BTB, which are expected for embedded processors in the near future. The power consumptions in Table 1 are normalized to the power consumption in the case of the power consumption of the read operation for 4096 X 2 PHT (We normalized the value since it is not permitted to officially present the absolute value by Samsung internal regulation).

Table 1. Size and normalized power consumption of components

Component	Type	Size	READ	WRITE
PHT	Traditional Predictor	4096 X 2	1.00	0.91
PHT	Proposed Predictor	2048 X 4	1.04	0.99
BTB	Traditional/Proposed Predictor	256 entry	1.88	2.14

Table 2. Notations for the analytical model

Notation	Meaning
P(trad.)	Total power consumption in the traditional predictor
P(prop.)	Total power consumption in the proposed predictor
$P_{pht\_traditional\_read}$	Power consumption of a read operation in the traditional PHT
$P_{pht\_traditional\_write}$	Power consumption of a write operation in the traditional PHT
$P_{pht\_proposed\_read}$	Power consumption of a read operation in the proposed PHT
$P_{pht\_proposed\_write}$	Power consumption of a write operation in the proposed PHT
P_{btb_read}	Power consumption of a read operation in the BTB
P_{btb_write}	Power consumption of a write operation in the BTB
N_{inst}	Number of total instructions
N_{branch}	Number of branch instructions
$N_{btb\_miss\_predictions}$	Number of BTB miss predictions for branch instructions
$N_{untaken\_predictions}$	Number of predicted untakens

5   Analysis Results

5.1   Analytical Models

We present the notations in Table 2 for analytical models.

The total power consumption in the traditional branch predictor is

$$P(\text{trad.}) = P_{pht\_traditional\_read} \text{ X } N_{inst} + P_{pht\_traditional\_write} \text{ X } N_{branch} + P_{btb\_read} \text{ X } N_{inst} + P_{btb\_write} \text{ X } N_{btb\_miss\_predictions}$$

In the traditional branch predictor, the PHT and the BTB are read at every instruction. The PHT is written (updated) for training when the instruction is a branch and the BTB is written when a BTB miss prediction occurs.

The total power consumption in the proposed branch predictor is

$$P(\text{prop.}) = P_{pht\_proposed\_read} \text{ X } (N_{inst}/2 + N_{branch}) + P_{pht\_proposed\_write} \text{ X } N_{branch} + P_{btb\_read} \text{ X } (N_{inst} - N_{untaken\_predictions}) + P_{btb\_write} \text{ X } N_{btb\_miss\_predictions}$$

In the proposed branch predictor, the number of read accesses to the PHT is decreased. In addition, the number of read accesses to the BTB is decreased from total number of instructions to the number of predicted takens, since the BTB

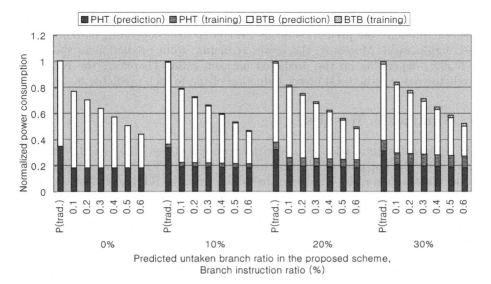

Fig. 5. Results from Analytical Models

is accesses only when the prediction from the PHT is taken. Thus the power consumption in the proposed branch predictor is expected to be reduced.

In Fig. 5, we vary the branch instruction ratio and the predicted untaken ratio to analyze the power consumption with analytical models. Each set of bars is classified, according to the branch instruction ratio in a program. In each set, all bars are normalized to the leftmost bar, which is the power consumption in the traditional predictor. As shown in above formula, as the traditional predictor is not related to the number of predicted untakens, leftmost one bar in a set is responsible for the traditional predictor with various predicted untaken ratios. Since the branch instruction ratio is 0-30% and the predicted untaken ratio is 0.1-0.6 in most applications [6][7], we showed the results in the range. In most applications, the BTB miss prediction ratio is between 0-20% but it does not affect the analysis result directly. Thus, the BTB miss prediction ratio is fixed to 10%.

The decrease of the branch instruction ratio reduces the number of accesses to the PHT and the increase of the predicted untaken ratio reduces the number of accesses to the BTB. Thus, as the branch instruction ratio decreases and the predicted untaken ratio from the branch predictor increases, the power consumption in the proposed predictor is more reduced.

The power consumption for training is same in the traditional predictor and in the proposed predictor, since the PHT training is necessary whenever there is a branch instruction and the BTB training is necessary whenever a BTB miss prediction occurs. As shown in Fig. 5, the power consumption for prediction (not training) in the PHT and in the BTB occupies 29-35% and 55-65% of the total power consumption in the branch predictor, respectively. The proposed predictor reduces the power consumption not for training but for prediction. The power reduction from prediction in the PHT is 11-16%, depending on the branch instruction ratio. Moreover, the power reduction from prediction in the BTB is 5-39%, depending on the predicted untaken ratio. Therefore, the proposed predictor reduces the total power reduction of the branch predictor by 16-55%.

6   Simulation Results

Fig. 6 shows the simulation results with four applications from Spec2000 benchmark suite [6]. The power reduction from the PHT is 13-16%, depending on the branch instruction ratio. The power reduction from the BTB is 30-36%, depending on predicted untaken ratio. The power reduction from the overall proposed branch predictor is 43-52%. On average, the power reduction from the PHT, from the BTB and from the overall proposed branch predictor is 14%, 32%, and 46%, respectively.

Table 3 shows the branch instruction ratio and the predicted   untaken ratio to compare the results from analytical models and results from simulations. If the parameters in Table 3 are put in the analytical models, the results from analytical models in Fig. 5 are similar to those from simulations in Fig. 6.

7   Conclusions

In this paper, we proposed a low power branch predictor for embedded processors by reducing the accesses to the PHT and the BTB without harming any

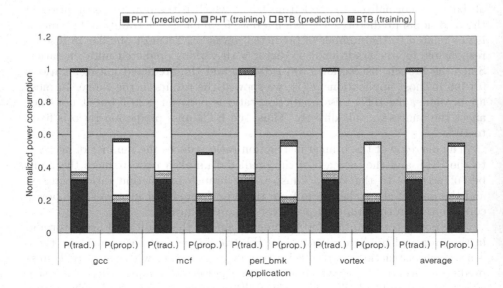

Fig. 6. Simulation Results

Table 3. Branch instruction ratio and predicted untaken ratio

Applications	Branch instruction ratio	Predicted untaken ratio
gcc	15.1 %	48.5 %
mcp	16.9 %	61.7 %
perl_bmk	14.9 %	50.0 %
vortex	13.0 %	51.5 %

accuracy: 1) Two predictions are looked up by accessing the PHT once. 2) The BTB is only accessed when the prediction from the PHT is taken, which does not incur any additional delay, since the prediction is obtained one cycle earlier compared to the traditional branch predictor.

We presented analytical models and analyzed the power consumption with the models. We also ran the simulation to investigate the power consumption in the real applications. Simulation results showed that the proposed predictor reduces the power consumption by 43-52%. Considering that the branch predictor accounts for more than 10% of overall processor power, it is expected to reduce overall processor power by about 5-7%. The proposed predictor is being considered as a next-generation embedded processor.

Acknowledgments. We would like to thank Gi Ho Park for his helpful comments; Woo Hyong Lee and for his survey of various branch predictors; Young Min Shin for his helpful comments on the 0.13 um process; Young Chul Rhee, Dong Wook Lee and Sang-Suk Kim for their assistances in setting up Samsung Memory Compiler System.

References

1. Parikh, K. Skadron, Y. Zhang, M. Barcella and M. Stan : Power issues related to branch prediction, Proc. Int. Conf. on High-Performance Computer Architecture, (2002) 233-242
2. Daniel A. Jimenez : Reconsidering complex branch predictors, Proc. Int. Conf. on High-Performance Computer Architecture (2003) 43-52
3. Daniel A. Jimenez, Stephen W. Keckler, and Calvin Lin : The impact of delay on the design of branch predictors, Proc. Int. Symp. on Microarchitecture (2000) 67-76
4. S. McFarling : Combining branch predictors, WRL Technical note TN-36, Digital (1993)
5. Samsung Electronics : Samsung Memory Compiler (2002)
6. Standard Performance Evaluation Corporation : SPEC CPU2000 Benchmarks, available at http://www.specbench.org/osg/cpu2000
7. C. Lee, M. Potkonjak, W Mangione-Smith. : MediaBench : A Tool for Evaluating Synthesizing Multimedia and Communication Systems, Proc. Int. Symp. On Microarchitecture (1997)
8. ARM Corp., ARM1136J(F)-S, available at http://www.arm.com/products/CPUs/ARM1136JF-S.html

9. ARM Corp., ARM1156T2(F)-S, available at
   http://www.arm.com/products/CPUs/ ARM1156T2-S.html
10. Simpelscalar LLC, The Simplescalar Tool Set 3.0 available at
    http://www.simplescalar.com

Static Techniques to Improve Power Efficiency of Branch Predictors

Weidong Shi, Tao Zhang, and Santosh Pande

College of computing
Georgia Institute of Technology, USA
{shiw, zhangtao, santosh}@cc.gatech.edu

Abstract. Current power-efficient designs focus on reducing the dynamic (activity-based) power consumption in a processor through different techniques. In this paper, we illustrate the application of two static techniques to reduce the activities of the branch predictor in a processor leading to its significant power reduction. We introduce the use of a static branch target buffer (BTB) that achieves the similar performance to the traditional branch target buffer but eliminates most of the state updates thus reducing the power consumption of the BTB significantly. We also introduce a correlation-based static prediction scheme into a dynamic branch predictor so that those branches that can be predicted statically or can be correlated to the previous ones will not go through normal prediction algorithm. This reduces the activities and conflicts in the branch history table (BHT). With these optimizations, the activities and conflicts of the BTB and BHT are reduced significantly and we are able to achieve a significant reduction (43.9% on average) in power consumption of the BPU without degradation in the performance.

1 Introduction

Branch prediction has a huge impact on the performance of high end processors which normally have a very deep pipeline, e.g. Pentium 4 which has 20 pipeline stages. Branch mis-prediction penalty for such a deep pipeline is very high, so it is critical to achieve accurate prediction. Many studies have been done to improve branch prediction rate by complicated designs, for example, combining several types of predictors together. Those designs often demand a significant silicon and power budget. As claimed in [5], branch predictor can potentially take up to 10% of the total processor power/energy consumption. With a new metric dimension of power, the focus becomes how to maintain the same prediction rate as a complex branch predictor but with significantly less power consumption and area.

In this paper, we propose two optimizations to reduce power consumption of the branch predictor with no degradation in the IPC or prediction accuracy but significant reduction in the branch predictor power consumption. The power consumption of a branch predictor is dominated by the large branch target buffer (BTB) and branch history table (BHT), both of which are introduced to achieve high prediction accuracy in a high-performance processor. To optimize the power consumption of branch target buffer, we introduce static branch target buffer that does not need state updates during runtime except when the program phase changes; thus activities in it are reduced

P.-C. Yew and J. Xue (Eds.): ACSAC 2004, LNCS 3189, pp. 385–398, 2004.

significantly. We use profiling to identify the branches that should reside in the branch target buffer in each program phase and preload those branches into branch target buffer when the program phase changes. The content of branch target buffer never changes during one program phase. Using static branch target buffer, we are able to maintain the performance of traditional branch target buffer at the same time eliminate most of the power consumption due to the updates to traditional branch target buffer.

To reduce power consumption of branch history table, we combine static branch prediction with hardware dynamic branch prediction. With a hybrid static and dynamic branch prediction, only branches that are hard to predict statically turn to hardware prediction, reducing branch history table activities and collisions. Such a hybrid predictor can often attain the same prediction rate as a pure hardware predictor with a much smaller branch history table and much less predictor lookups and updates, therefore consumes less power. Beyond traditional single direction static branch prediction [6, 12], we propose a hardware-assisted correlation-based static prediction scheme. This design can further improve static prediction rate and reduce hardware branch predictor overhead and power consumption. Our correlation-based static prediction encodes a branch correlation pattern into a branch instruction. Hardware assists the static prediction by providing a short 2-bit global branch history and uses it to reach a prediction according to the static correlation pattern.

The rest of the paper is organized as follows. In section 2, we present our study on power-optimized branch target buffer design and our solution, i.e., static branch target buffer. In section 3, we elaborate our correlation-based static prediction scheme. Those branches that cannot be predicted statically will turn to hardware dynamic predictor. So our predictor is a hybrid one. We describe the simulation environment and the benchmarks in section 4, then present results on the effectiveness of the two optimizations described earlier. Section 5 compares our work with previous work on static branch prediction and other recent approaches on low power branch predictors. Finally, in section 6, we conclude the paper.

2   Static Branch Target Buffer

To achieve a good address hit rate in branch target buffer, modern superscalar processors normally have a very large multi-way branch target buffer. This large buffer leads to high power consumption. Normally the power consumption of the branch target buffer takes at least 50% of the total power consumption of the branch predictor[1]. Thus, to design a power-efficient branch predictor, it is critical to reduce the power consumption of branch target buffer.

An intuitive approach to reduce the power consumption of BTB is to reduce the size of it. BTB is kept large because of two possible reasons. First, a large buffer helps reduce conflict misses. Second, a large buffer helps reduce capacity misses. If the main reason for a large BTB is the conflict misses, we can increase the associativity of the BTB. However, according to our experiments, capacity misses are major problems. Some programs have large working sets. To ensure a good address

---

[1] In this paper, when we talk about branch predictor, we mean both branch direction predictor and branch target buffer.

hit rate for those applications, a large BTB must be deployed. Figure 1 shows the address hit rate for six SPEC2000 benchmarks. In this paper, we will mainly study these six benchmarks because they exhibit relatively worse branch prediction performance in our experiments. The configurations are 128-entry fully-associative BTB, 256-entry fully-associative BTB, 512-set 1-way BTB, 512-set 2-way BTB and 512-set 4-way BTB. From Figure 1, for benchmarks like perl, vortex and gcc, even a 256-entry fully-associative BTB cannot achieve a comparable address hit rate to the other configurations that have much less ways but a larger number of entries. Since a fully-associative BTB does not have conflict misses, the above finding shows that some benchmarks have large working sets and complex branch behaviors, requiring a large BTB.

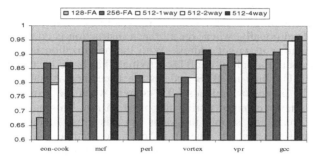

Fig. 1. Address hit rate of different BTBs

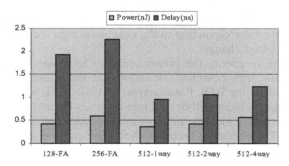

Fig. 2. Per-access Power Consumption and Delay of Different BTB Configurations

The address hit rate of fully-associative BTBs is very good for some benchmarks like mcf. For those benchmarks, we can achieve a comparable address hit rate using a fully-associative BTB with much less entries. However, Figure 2 shows per-access latency (in ns) and per-access power consumption (in nJ) of different BTBs got using CACTI timing and power model (version 3.0). From Figure 2, we can see fully-associative BTBs are not power efficient comparing to multi-way BTBs and the per-access delay of them are several times larger. Such kind of delay is intolerable to high-end processors. So the conclusion here is that we have to maintain a large enough BTB at the same time avoid introducing high associativity into the BTB.

Another way to reduce the power consumption of the BTB is to reduce its activities. With clock gating used extensively in modern processors, the power consumption of a particular function unit is significantly impacted by the activities it undertakes. Unfortunately, to reduce activities of the BTB is also a hard problem. To minimize pipeline stalls, the processor needs to know the target address of a branch as soon as possible if the branch is predicted as taken. The target address is provided by the BTB. In a traditional superscalar processor design, the processor will access BTB during the instruction fetch stage, so that the predicted target address can be fed into next fetch stage without stall. In [5], the authors proposed to reduce the activities due to BTB lookups by only accessing it when necessary. Our work is built upon the optimization proposed in [5]. We assume non-branch instructions have been filtered using a mechanism similar to the one in [5] and they will not lead to BTB lookups. Thus, our scheme can only deal with branch instructions. Except the work in [5], we are not aware of other optimizations to reduce the activities of the BTB.

In this paper, we propose static branch target buffer to reduce the activities due to BTB updates. Traditionally, whenever a branch instruction is completed, the BTB is updated to remember its target address. With the optimization in [5] enabled, BTB updates may account for half of the BTB activities. The basic idea is that if we fix the content of the BTB, then no BTB updates are necessary. A naïve implementation could be that the processor preloads BTB content when the program starts and the BTB content is never changed during the program run. This naïve implementation may work for small and simple programs but has great limitation for large and complicated programs, which may run for a long time and change behavior significantly. On the other hand, as shown in [13], although a complicated program does not exhibit a globally stable behavior, its execution can be divided into phases, in each phase the behavior is quite stable. In our static branch target buffer design, program phases are dynamically identified and program phase changes are dynamically detected in the processor. Upon a program phase change, the processor loads the BTB content corresponding to the new phase then the BTB content is fixed until next program phase change.

We use profiling to choose the proper branches to reside in the BTB for each phase. We first categorize branches encountered in the phase according to the set location it will reside in the BTB. For example, a 512-set BTB will have 512 different set locations. Normally, there will be multiple branches belonging to one set location due to collision. Next, we identify the most frequent ones belonging to a set location through profiling. The number of branches chosen are equal to the number of ways in the BTB. In that way, we choose a subset of branches which just fit into the BTB.

This idea works because program phase changes are infrequent events, otherwise, the power consumed by preloading BTB may eliminate the savings from eliminated BTB updates. We adopted the phase identification scheme from [13], which is very cost effective. Our experiment shows that GCC has the most unstable phase behavior, but on average the phases of GCC still have a length of about 1 million instructions. As pointed out by [13], integer programs tend to have much shorter program phases and much more program phase changes. For floating point programs, the length of program phases is normally tens of million instructions. All of our examined benchmarks are tough integer programs to stress test our scheme. Our static branch target buffer design will achieve even better results with floating point benchmarks.

There are several pitfalls regarding to static branch target buffer idea. Since we fix the BTB content for each phase now and it is possible that we cannot put all the branches seen in the phase into the BTB, static BTB may degrade address hit rate and runtime performance. However, sacrificing performance means the program will run for a longer time thus the other components in the processor will consume more power! Thus, although static BTB can reduce branch predictor power significantly, if the performance is degraded a lot, we may end up consume more power in the whole processor scale. Fortunately, we see near zero performance degradation under our static branch target buffer design. The major reason is that the phase identification scheme works well and captures program phases accurately. Another reason is that lots of BTB misses are actually due to some branches continuously kicking each other out of the BTB, reducing BTB effectiveness. That means fixing the content of BTB may instead help in some cases.

Static branch target buffer also introduces additional overhead to context switches. BTB content now becomes a part of process state. When a process is switched out, the current BTB of the process has to be saved. After a process is switched back, the corresponding BTB needs to be restored. However, context switches can be regarded as rare events in a processor. For example, the default time slice in Linux is 100ms, during which tens of million instructions could have been executed.

In our experiments, the power consumption of BTB preloading and phase identification has been modeled and counted in the total power consumption of the processor.

3   Correlation-Based Static Prediction

The power consumption of branch history table is another major source of branch predictor power consumption. Branch history table and branch target buffer normally take more than 95% of total branch predictor power. To reduce the power of BHT, we propose static branch prediction. The basic idea is that those branches that can be statically predicted will not go through the normal BHT lookup algorithm thus will not access BHT. So the accesses to the BHT are reduced, leading to less BHT activities thus reduced power consumption. The reduction of BHT accesses also leads to reduction of conflicts in BHT. Thus, a small history table can always achieve the same prediction rate as the traditional predictor with a much larger table. With the same BHT table, static branch prediction may help achieve a better prediction rate due to less conflicts in BHT.

The possible strategies of static branch prediction could be always predicting a branch is taken, or always not-taken, or branches with certain op code always taken, or branches with certain op code always not-taken, or always predict backward conditional branches as taken. Another approach for static branch prediction is to rely on compiler program analysis or profiling to come up with a direction hint to a conditional branch. The hint can be encoded with a single bit in the branch instruction. For example, when the bit is set, the corresponding branch is always considered as taken, otherwise not taken. Through profiling, [11] shows that a large percentage of branches are highly biased towards either taken or not-taken. In particular, 26% of conditional branches have a taken-rate of over 95% and another 36% of branches have a taken-rate below 5%. Together, over 62% of conditional branches are highly biased toward one direction. For such conditional branches, their predictions can be hard encoded and this will reduce (1) accesses to the BHT; (2) branch history table entries required for dynamic branch prediction; (3) potential conflicts and aliasing effects in BHT [4, 6]. In our approach, we further extend previous either taken or not-taken static prediction to correlation-based static prediction.

if
(x>2)
x =
0;
if
(y<10)

x>2	y<10	x<y
false	false	true
false	true	?
true	false	true
true	true	false

Fig. 3. Example of branch correlation

[12] shows that many conditional branches can be predicted by using only a short global history. This is the manifestation of branch correlation and gives the insight that many conditional branches may have fixed prediction patterns under a short global branch history. Figure 3 gives an example of branch correlation and prediction pattern.

This leads to the design of correlation-based static branch prediction. Correlation-based static branch prediction requires hardware assistance to record the recent global branch history. In many branch predictors, e.g., gshare predictors, such information is already there for dynamic branch prediction. The hardware chooses a prediction based on the current global branch history and the correlation pattern provided by the branch instruction. By using correlation-based static prediction, we can predict more conditional branches statically, which could further reduce area and power consumption of a dynamic branch predictor. The sources of power savings are listed below.

− Since many branches are predicted statically, the dynamic branch predictor can maintain the same prediction rate using a BHT with less number of entries.
− Static prediction can reduce destructive aliasing thus further alleviating the pressure on the BHT size.
− With static prediction, hardware only needs to look up BHT when a branch is not statically predicted. This reduces the number of BHT lookups. For statically predicted branches, the updates to the counters (or other finite state machines) are also eliminated, but the updates to histories are still necessary.

Static correlation pattern is conveyed to the hardware using encoding space in the displacement field of a conditional branch instruction, which is done by the compiler (binary translator). Other instructions are not affected. Conditional branch instructions in most RISC processors have a format such as [op code][disp]. For Alpha 21264 processor, the displacement field has 21 bits. However, most conditional branches are short-range branches. This leaves several bits in the displacement field that can be used for encoding correlation pattern for most conditional branches. In our correlation-based static prediction scheme, we use four bits in the displacement field (bit 4 to bit 1) to encode the prediction pattern based on two most recent branches. There are four possible histories for two branches: 1) [not-taken, not-taken], 2) [not-taken, taken], 3) [taken, not-taken], 4) [taken-taken]. Each bit of the four bits corresponds to the static prediction result for one possibility. Bit 1 corresponds to case 1, and so on. If we statically predict the branch taken, the corresponding bit is set to 1, otherwise, it is set to 0. Using the same example in Figure 3, the encoded correlation pattern for the third branch could be 0101, assume through profiling, we found if the branch history is [not-taken, taken], the third branch has a better chance to be not-taken.

Compiler has the freedom to choose whether correlation-based static prediction should be used. When it becomes unwise to use static prediction, e.g., hard to predict branches, or the displacement value is too large, compiler can always turn back to original branch prediction scheme. In our scheme, we take another bit (bit 0) of displacement field to distinguish extended branches with correlation information from original branches. Thus, besides the four bits of correlation information, we take five encoding bits in total from displacement field for extended branches. Since bit 0 of displacement field of original branches is used in our scheme, the compiler may have to transform an original branch to chained branches due to reduced displacement range, which is really rare.

First, we have to decide which conditional branches should use static branch prediction and which should use dynamic branch prediction. A conditional branch is classified as using static prediction if it satisfies the following criteria:

- highly biased towards one direction (taken or not-taken) under at least one correlation path (branch history). We maintain a history of two most recent branches in our scheme.
- branch target address's displacement within the range permitted by the shortened conditional branch displacement field. For alpha, the remaining width of displacement fields is 16 bits (21-5). The displacement permitted is [-32768, 32767]. According to our experiments, most of conditional branches (above 99.9%) are satisfied.

To evaluate the potential gains offered by correlation-based static prediction, we divide statically predictable conditional branches into three types:

- Non-correlation based type. This corresponds to conditional branches that can be statically predicted using a single-bit direction prediction. A conditional branch is classified into this type if all the program paths (histories) yield the same biased prediction, taken or not-taken.
- Correlation-based type. For this type of branches, prediction is biased towards different direction depending on the correlation path. For example, under one path (history), the branch may be biased towards taken, while under another path (history), it is biased towards not-taken.
- Others. This type corresponds to the branches that cannot be categorized to type I or type II. These branches are hard to be predicted statically.

Table 1 lists the total number of conditional branches for each type, and the total number of dynamic executions made by the branches in each type for six SPEC2000 benchmarks running for 200 million instructions with fast-forwarding 1 billion instructions. As shown in the table, many branches can be predicted statically.

One pitfall of encoding correlation information into the branch instruction is access timing. As discussed earlier, to achieve best throughput, the processor has to know the next PC address for instruction fetch at the end of current instruction fetch stage. Traditionally, during instruction fetch stage, the processor has no access to specific bits of the fetched instruction. To enable correlation-based static prediction, we use a separate extended branch information table (EBIT) with a number of entries exactly corresponding to the level-1 I-cache cache lines. Under our processor model, cache

Table 1. Conditional Branch Categorization

	# static branch	# dynamic branch	type 1 static (%)	type 1 dyna. (%)	type 2 static (%)	type 1 + 2 dyna. (%)
eon	4006	14381689	34.95	52.32	37.09	62.18
mcf	678	27299410	60.18	79.92	64.45	80.37
perl	4920	29600039	86.63	68.92	89.59	70.51
vortex	7830	32691578	91.74	84.14	93.74	85.52
vpr	1917	38016432	81.27	54.71	86.18	66.32
gcc	18166	34023907	79.58	49.28	86.03	53.56

line size is 32B and contains 8 instructions. We impose a limitation that in each cache line, there is at most one extended branch instruction with correlation information, which means that there is at most one extended branch instruction in every 8 instructions. The limitation has minor impact in our scheme. As shown in [5], about 40% of conditional branches have distance greater than 10 instructions. Moreover, only a part of conditional branches will be converted into extended branches. Each entry of EBIT is 8-bit information. Bit 7 indicates whether the cache line has an extended branch instruction. Bit 6 to 4 encodes the position of the extended branch in the cache line. Bit 3 to 0 records the correlation information for the extended branch if there is one. The size of EBIT is 4K bits.

The EBIT is updated with new pre-decoded bits while an I-cache line is refilled after a miss. During each instruction fetch stage, the EBIT is accessed to detect an extended branch instruction and obtain the corresponding correlation information. If the current instruction is an extended branch, further BHT look-up is not necessary. Otherwise, BHT is accessed. Thus, the EBIT access is done before any necessary BHT access. Since the EBIT is small, we assume EBIT access and BHT access together can be done in instruction fetch stage. Note if the current instruction is an original branch, we end up consuming more power since we have to access EBIT too. The validity of correlation-based static prediction relies on the fact that a large percentage of conditional branches can be predicted statically, as shown in Table 1. The power consumption of EBIT is modeled and counted in our experiments.

After we identify all the statically predictable branches and their correlation patterns, we use a compiler (binary-to-binary translator) to convert original branches into extended branches with correlation information properly and get a new transformed program binary. Then, performance results are collected using a modified Simplescalar simulator supporting static branch target buffer and correlation-based static prediction.

4   Experiments and Results

We use Simplescalar 3.0 plus wattch version 1.02 for performance simulation and power analysis. Simplescalar is a cycle-accurate superscalar processor simulator and Wattch is a power analysis model that can be integrated into Simplescalar simulator to track cycle-by-cycle power usage. In Wattch power model, branch predictor power consumption is modeled as three main components, branch direction predictor power, BTB power, and RAS (return address stack) power. BTB and BHT dominate the overall branch predictor power consumption (over 95%). We simulated a typical 8-wide superscalar processor. We choose BTB and BHT configurations comparable to the ones in [5].

We chose six SPEC2000 integer benchmarks that exhibit relatively worse branch prediction performance. They are, eon-cook, mcf, perl, vortex, vpr, gcc. Each benchmark was fast-forwarded 1 billion instructions then simulated for 200 million instructions. The profile information for each benchmark is gathered using standard test inputs. Then standard reference inputs are used to measure performance. Unless explicitly stated, all the branch predictor power consumption results reported are obtained under Wattch non-ideal aggressive clock-gating model (cc3). In this clock-gating model, power is scaled linearly with the number of ports or unit usage. When a unit is inactive, it will dissipate 10% of the maximum power. The power consumption of BTB preloading, phase identification and EBIT is measured using Wattch array structure power model.

Our scheme is built upon the scheme in [5]. We assume only branch instructions will lookup BTB. Thus, BTB updates account for almost half of the BTB activities.

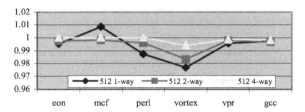

Fig. 4. Normalized Address Hit Rate for Static BTB

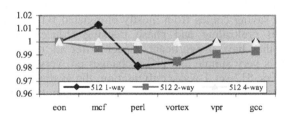

Fig. 5. Normalized IPC for Static BTB

First, we present the results for static branch target buffer. In our study, we assume a 16K PAg direction predictor without static prediction. Three common BTB configurations are examined: 512-set 1-way, 512-set 2-way and 512-set 4-way. Figure 4 shows the normalized address hit rate of static branch target buffer scheme. The address hit rate is normalized to original branch target buffer design. From Figure 4, the impact of our static branch target buffer to address hit rate is minor. For 512-set 1-way configuration, the average degradation in hit rate is 0.66%. For 512-set 2-way configuration, the average degradation is 0.51%. For 512-set 4-way configuration, the average degradation is 0.15%. From the results, we also observe that the degradation on address hit rate becomes even smaller with the increase of the number of entries in

BTB, since now more branches could be preloaded into BTB upon a phase change. *Mcf* benchmark under 512-set 1-way configuration is a corner case in which the address hit rate under static BTB is better than original BTB design. The reason may be destructive aliasing effect. Now that we seldom update BTB, we have much less chance to improperly kick out some branches from BTB.

Figure 5 shows the normalized IPC for static branch target buffer scheme. Note any optimization of power consumption to one component of the processor should not sacrifice the processor performance significantly. Otherwise, the program will run for a longer time and the power savings from the optimized component may be easily killed by more power consumption in other components. For 512-set 1-way BTB configuration, the average IPC degradation of static BTB is 0.34%. For 512-set 2-way configuration, the average IPC degradation is 0.69%. The IPC degradation should become smaller with a larger BTB. 512-set 1-way configuration is better because of the corner case benchmark *mcf*, which achieves better IPC under 512-set 1-way static BTB. The reason is explained earlier. For 512-set 4-way configuration, the degradation is very small thus is not visible in the graph.

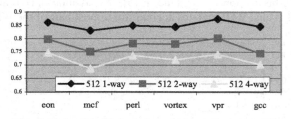

Fig. 6. Normalized Power Consumption for Static BTB

Figure 6 shows the normalized power consumption for the whole branch predictor (BTB + direction predictor) with static BTB design against one with original BTB design. The power saving comes from mostly eliminated BTB updates. The power consumed by BTB preloading and phase tracking reduces the saving but our experiments show they have insignificant impact. After all, our implemented phase tracking hardware is very simple and phase changes are very low-frequency events during execution. For 512-set 1-way configuration, the average power reduction for the branch predictor is 14.89%. For 512-set 2-way configuration, the average power reduction is 22.41%. For 512-set 4-way configuration, the average power reduction is 27.88%. For each configuration, static BTB is able to reduce the BTB activities (dynamic power) by almost half. A larger BTB leads to larger power reduction in percentage because the percentage of BTB power is larger in the whole branch predictor power.

Next, we present the results for correlation-based static prediction. Static prediction works along with a dynamic hardware predictor, which handles branches not predicted by static prediction. A large number of hardware branch prediction schemes have been proposed in the literature. Each one may have its own trade-off in terms of prediction rate, hardware overhead and power consumption. It is impossible for us to examine all of them. In this paper, we limited our scope to two types of predictors, i.e., gshare [9] and PAg [1, 2, 10]. We studied these two types of predictors rather than the default tournament predictor in Alpha 21264 because they are the most basic ones and they can represent two large categories of predictors, i.e. global history based predictors and local history based predictors. We studied them separately to get a deep understanding of the impacts of correlation-based static prediction to different types of predictors. Further, we can derive the impact of our proposed technique to more complicated predictors like the tournament predictor in Alpha, which is basically composed of two global predictors and one local predictor.

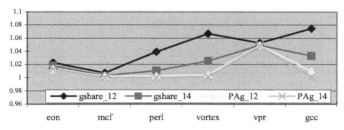

Fig. 7. Normalized Direction Prediction Rate

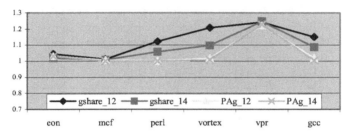

Fig. 8. Normalized IPC

Figure 7 shows branch direction prediction rate under our correlation-based static prediction and dynamic prediction hybrid scheme. The prediction rate is normalized to original pure dynamic direction predictor. In the study of direction predictor, we assume a 512-set 4-way BTB configuration. For gshare-based predictors, we experimented two sizes, 4K and 16K. For PAg based predictors, we also explored two configurations, 4K first level entries −11 bit local history and 16K first level entries − 13 bit local history. From the results, correlation-based static prediction helps prediction rate for gshare-based predictor significantly. For a 4K size gshare predictor, the average improvement in prediction rate is 4.39%. For a 16K size gshare predictor, the average improvement is 2.32%. With the increase of predictor size, the improvement on prediction rate due to correlation-based static prediction becomes smaller. Correlation-based static prediction cannot achieve significant improvement for PAg based predictors, since collision has much smaller impact to the performance of PAg based predictors. For a 4K size PAg predictor, the average improvement is 1.37%. For a 16K size PAg predictor, the average improvement is 1.05%.

Figure 8 shows normalized IPC for the same configurations. Improved direction prediction rate normally leads to improved IPC. For 4K gshare predictor, the average improvement is 13.02%. For 16K gshare predictor, the average improvement is 8.61%. For 4K PAg predictor, the average improvement is 4.97%. For 16K PAg predictor, the average improvement is 4.52%. The improvement on PAg predictors normally is small since the prediction rate improvement is small. Benchmark vpr is a corner case, in which correlation-based static prediction helps improve IPC over 20% in all configurations. Destructive collision effect in *vpr* benchmark must be severe.

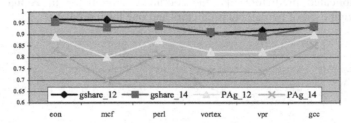

Fig. 9. Normalized Predictor Power Consumption

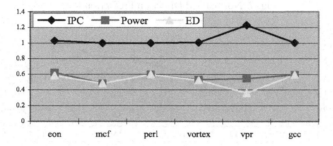

Fig. 10. Results for Combined Architecture

Figure 9 shows the normalized whole branch predictor power consumption under correlation-based static prediction and dynamic prediction hybrid scheme. Our static prediction helps reduce branch predictor power consumption significantly. First, those branches that can be statically predicted will not look up the large BHT, so a large part of BHT lookups are eliminated. Moreover, for a statically predicted branch, only global or local history is updated for the branch, no update is performed to the corresponding 2-bit counter or other finite state machines. For a two-level predictor such as gshare or PAg, this means only the first level of the branch predictor needs state updates. For 4K gshare predictor, the average power reduction is 6.2%. For 16K gshare predictor, the average power reduction is 7.2%. For 4K PAg predictor, the average reduction is 14.8%. For 16K PAg predictor, the average reduction is 22.2%. The reduction for gshare predictors is much smaller since there is no local history table and the power consumed by the EBIT is relatively large.

Our static BTB and correlation-based static prediction could be integrated together into the processor, so that we can achieve significant branch predictor power reduction at the same time with at least no performance degradation in branch predictor. For some benchmarks, the performance of branch predictor is actually improved. Figure 10 shows the results after integration. All the results are normalized against original branch predictor design. We assume a 512-set 4-way BTB configuration and a 16K PAg direction predictor. From the results, for all benchmarks, our optimizations never degrade IPC, i.e., the processor performance. For benchmark *vpr*, the performance is improved significantly instead. The average power consumption reduction is 43.86%. We also show the energy-delay product results, which is a metric to show the trade off between power consumption and performance. The average reduction in energy-delay (ED) product is even better, which is 47.73%.

5 Related Work

In [5], the authors use two major techniques to reduce branch predictor power consumption, banking and PPD (prediction probe detector). PPD is a specialized hardware that records whether lookups to the BTB or the direction-predictor is necessary, therefore saving power by reducing lookups to BTB and BHT when combined with clock gating. Our approach uses two static techniques to reduce the activities of branch predictor further. We propose static BTB to eliminate most of the BTB updates. We propose correlation-based static prediction to eliminate a large part of BHT lookups and updates. Correlation-based static prediction also helps alleviate pressure on the size of BHT, since collisions are reduced significantly. Our results show that we can reduce branch predictor power consumption further upon the optimizations in [5] by around 50% . Hybrid static and dynamic branch prediction has been proposed before for reducing destructive aliasing [6, 22]. Using a profile-based approach similar to ours in this paper, researchers are able to improve branch prediction rate significantly by combining static prediction with some well-known dynamic predictors. However, nobody has proposed using such a hybrid predictor for reducing branch predictor power consumption. In our study, we characterize the power behavior for static and dynamic hybrid branch predictor and claim that such a hybrid predictor is beneficial for both reducing collision and power consumption. We also extend the conventional static prediction by introducing a correlation-based static prediction approach. Smith and Young [3,7,8] have studied branch correlation from a compiler perspective. They have proposed a number of compiler techniques to identify correlated branches using program analysis. Their study is different from ours because their approach is to transform correlated branches in a manner so that they can be correctly predicted under a dynamic hardware predictor rather than directly encoding a correlation pattern into a branch instruction.

6 Conclusion

In this paper, we proposed two optimizations to reduce the power consumption of the branch predictor in a high-performance superscalar processor. We raised the idea of static branch target buffer to eliminate most of the update power of BTB. We also pointed out that a hybrid branch predictor combining static prediction and dynamic prediction not only can reduce branch predictor size and destructive aliasing but branch prediction power consumption as well. We extended the conventional static prediction by putting branch correlation pattern into spare bits in the conditional branches when they are not used. Such correlation-based static prediction can further improve static branch prediction rate comparing to single direction static prediction. We explored the effects of the two proposed optimizations on the trade off between performance and power consumption. Our simulation results show that the integration of the proposed optimizations can reduce the branch predictor power consumption by 44% and branch predictor energy-delay product by 48% while never degrading overall processor performance.

References

[1]   T. Y. Yeh, and Y. N. Patt. "Two Level Adaptive Branch prediction". 24th ACM/IEEE International Symposium on Microarchitecture, Nov. 1991.
[2]   T. Y. Yeh, and Y. N. Patt. "A Comparison of Dynamic Branch Predictors that Use Two levels of Branch History". 20th Annual International Symposium on Computer Architecture, May 1996.
[3]   Cliff Young, Nicolas Gloy, and Michael D. Smith. "A Comparative Analysis of Schemes For Correlated Branch Prediction". ACM SIGARCH Computer Architecture News, Proceedings of the 22nd annual International Symposium on Computer Architecture May 1995, Volume 23 Issue 2.
[4]   S. Sechrest, C. C. Lee, and Trevor Mudge. "Correlation and Aliasing in Dynamic Branch Predictors". ACM SIGARCH Computer Architecture News, Proceedings of the 23rd annual international symposium on Computer architecture May 1996, Volume 24 Issue 2.
[5]   D. Parikh, K. Skadron, Y. Zhang, M. Barcella, and M. Stan. "Power Issues Related to Branch Prediction". In Proc. of the 2002 International Symposium on High-Performance Computer Architecture, February, 2002, Cambridge, MA.
[6]   Harish Patil and Joel Emer. "Combining static and dynamic branch prediction to reduce destructive aliasing". Proceedings of the 6th Intl. Conference on High Performance Computer Architecture, pages 251-262, January 2000.
[7]   Cliff Young, Michael D. Smith. "Improving the Accuracy of Static Branch Prediction Using Branch Correlation". ASPLOS 1994: 232-241.
[8]   Cliff Young, Michael D. Smith. "Static correlated branch prediction". TOPLAS 21(5): 1028-1075. 1999.
[9]   S. McFarling. "Combining branch predictors". Tech. Note TN-36, DEC WRL, June 1993.
[10] Shien-Tai Pan, Kimming So, Joseph T. Rahmeh, "Improving the Accuracy of Dynamic Branch Prediction Using Branch Correlation", ASPLOS 1992: 76-84.
[11] Michael Haungs, Phil Sallee, Matthew K. Farrens. "Branch Transition Rate: A New Metric for Improved Branch Classification Analysis". HPCA 2000: 241-250.
[12] D. Grunwald, D. Lindsay, and B. Zorn. "Static methods in hybrid branch prediction". In Proc. Of the International Conference on Parallel Architectures and Compilation Techniques (PACT), Oct. 1998. Pages:222 – 229.
[13] A. S. Dhodapkar and J. E. Smith, "Managing Multi-Configuration Hardware via Dynamic Working Set Analysis," Proc. of the 29 Intl. Sym. on Computer Architecture, May 2002, pp. 233 –244.

Choice Predictor for Free

Mongkol Ekpanyapong, Pinar Korkmaz, and Hsien-Hsin S. Lee

School of Electrical and Computer Engineering
Georgia Institute of Technology
Atlanta, Georgia 30332
{pop, korkmazp, leehs}@ece.gatech.edu

Abstract. Reducing energy consumption has become the first priority in designing microprocessors for all market segments including embedded, mobile, and high performance processors. The trend of state-of-the-art branch predictor designs such as a hybrid predictor continues to feature more and larger prediction tables, thereby exacerbating the energy consumption. In this paper, we present two novel profile-guided static prediction techniques— Static Correlation Choice (SCC) prediction and Static Choice (SC) prediction for alleviating the energy consumption without compromising performance. Using our techniques, the hardware choice predictor of a hybrid predictor can be completely eliminated from the processor and replaced with our off-line profiling schemes. Our simulation results show an average 40% power reduction compared to several hybrid predictors. In addition, an average 27% die area can be saved in the branch predictor hardware for other performance features.

1 Introduction

Advances in microelectronics technology and design tools for the past decade enable microprocessor designers to incorporate more complex features to achieve high speed computing. Many architectural techniques have been proposed and implemented to enhance the instruction level parallelism (ILP). However, there are many bottlenecks that obstruct a processor from achieving a high degree of ILP. Branch misprediction disrupting instruction supply poses one of the major ILP limitations. Whenever a branch misprediction occurs in superscalar and/or superpipelined machines, it results in pipeline flushing and refilling and a large number of instructions is discarded, thereby reducing effective ILP dramatically. As a result, microprocessor architects and researchers continue to contrive more complicated branch predictors aiming at reducing branch misprediction rates.

Branch prediction mechanisms can be classified into two categories: static branch prediction and dynamic branch prediction. Static branch prediction techniques [1,6,17] predict branch directions at compile-time. Such prediction schemes, mainly based on instruction types or profiling information, work well for easy-to-predict branches such as while or for-loop branches. Since the static branch prediction completely relies on information available at compile-time, it does not take runtime dynamic branch behavior into account. Conversely,

P.-C. Yew and J. Xue (Eds.): ACSAC 2004, LNCS 3189, pp. 399–413, 2004.
© Springer-Verlag Berlin Heidelberg 2004

dynamic branch prediction techniques [12,14,16] employ dedicated hardware to track dynamic branch behavior during execution. The hybrid branch predictor [12], one flavor of the dynamic branch predictors, improves the prediction rate by combining the advantages demonstrated by different branch predictors. In the implementation of a hybrid branch predictor, a *choice predictor* is used to determine which branch predictor's results to use for each branch instruction fetched. Introducing a choice predictor, however, results in larger die area and additional power dissipation. Furthermore, updating other branch predictors that are not involved in a prediction draws unnecessary power consumption if the prediction can be done at compile-time. Given the program profiling information, a static choice prediction could be made by identifying the suitable branch predictor for each branch instruction. For example, for a steady branch history pattern such as 000000 or 10101010, the compiler will favor the local branch predictor. On the other hand, for a local branch history pattern of 01011011101 and global branch history pattern of 0011100111000111001 (**boldface** numbers correspond to the branch history of this target branch) it will bias toward the global predictor over the local predictor, because the global pattern history shows a repetition of the sequence 001 where 1 corresponds to the target branch.

The organization of this paper is as follows. Section 2 describes related work. Section 3 is devoted to our schemes. Section 4 presents our experimental framework. Results of power, areas and performance are presented in Section 5. Finally the last section concludes this work.

2   Related Work

Most of the branch prediction techniques focus on exploiting the local behavior of each individual branch as well as the global branch correlation to improve prediction accuracy, either at static compile-time or dynamic runtime. Static techniques include two major schemes— profile-guided and program-based schemes. Profile-guided schemes collect branch statistics by executing and profiling the application in advance. The compiler then analyzes the application using these statistics as a guide and regenerates an optimized binary code. Program-based schemes tackle branch prediction problems at source code, assembly, or executable file level without any advanced profiling. One early study on using profile-guided branch prediction was done by Fisher and Freundenberger [6] , in which they showed that profile-guided methods can be very effective for conditional branches as most of the branch paths are highly biased to one direction and this direction almost remains the same across different runs of the program. Ball and Larus [1] later studied a program-based branch prediction method by applying simple heuristics to program analysis at static compilation time for generating static branch predictions.

One important characteristics of branch prediction is that a branch can either exhibit self-correlation or can be correlated with other branches. Yang and Smith [17] proposed a static correlated branch prediction scheme using *path profiling* to find the correlated paths. After identifying all the correlated paths, the technique either duplicates or discriminates the paths depending on the type of correlation. Due to path duplication, their technique increases the code size while reducing misprediction rate.

In spite of the hardware savings, static branch prediction is infeasible for all the branches in a program since a branch can demonstrate very dynamic behavior due to various correlations and will not be strongly biased to one direction or another in their lifetime. Therefore, most of the sophisticated branch prediction mechanisms focus on dynamic prediction mechanisms. Dynamic branch predictors make predictions based on runtime branch direction history. Yeh and Patt [16] introduced the concept of two-level adaptive prediction that maintains a first level N-bit branch history register (BHR) and its corresponding 2^N entry pattern history table (PHT) as a second level for making predictions. The BHR stores the outcomes of the N most recently committed branches used to index into the PHT in which each entry contains a 2-bit saturating up-down counter. They studied both local and global prediction schemes. Local prediction schemes keep the local history of individual branches while global prediction schemes store the global direction history of a number of branches equal to the history register size.

McFarling [12] pioneered the idea of hybrid branch prediction that uses a meta-predictor (or choice predictor) to select a prediction from two different branch predictors. The two branch predictors studied in his paper were bimodal and gshare branch predictors. The bimodal branch predictor consists of a 2-bit counters array indexed by the low order address bits of the program counter (PC). The gshare predictor, which was also christened by McFarling in the same paper is a two-level predictor that exclusive-ORs the global branch history and the branch PC address as the PHT index to reduce destructive aliasing among different branches sharing the same global history pattern. The choice predictor, also a 2-bit counters, is updated to reward the predictor generating correct prediction. Chang et al. [3] studied branch classification. Their classification model groups branches based on profiling data. They also proposed a hybrid branch predictor which takes the advantages of both static and dynamic predictors. Using the profiling data, they perform static prediction for those branches that strongly bias to one direction in their lifetime. Their work is analogous to ours in the sense that we both employ static and dynamic branch prediction method. Comparison and simulation data will be presented and discussed in Section 5. Another work presented by Grunwald et al. in [7] also adopts static prediction for a hybrid predictor. Despite a large experimental data were presented, it remains unclear about their algorithms with respect to how they derive the choice prediction directions at static compile-time. In addition, they compared their static prediction scheme with only McFarling hybrid prediction scheme, while we compare our technique against several other hybrid branch predictors and evaluate the impact to both power and die area. Recently, Huang et al. [4] proposed an energy efficient methodology for branch prediction. Their baseline case is a **2Bc-gskew-pskew** hybrid branch predictor. They used profiling to find out the branch predictor usage of different modules in a program and used clock

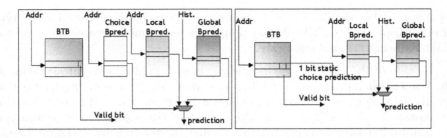

Fig. 1. Branch prediction lookup schemes.

gating to shut down the unused predictors of the above hybrid branch predictor. Different from them, we considered many hybrid branch prediction schemes and we collected profile data for each branch instead of for each module.

3   Static Prediction Generation

Profiling feedback is now a widely accepted technology for code optimization, in particular for static architectures such as Intel/HP's EPIC, we propose a new methodology that utilizes profiling data from prior executions, classifies branches according to the types of correlation exhibited (e.g. local or global), and then decides which prediction result to use. During profile-guided recompilation, these decisions are embedded in the corresponding branch instructions as static choice predictions. For example, the branch hint completer provided in the Itanium ISA [5] can be encoded with such information.

The basic branch prediction lookup scheme for a hybrid branch predictor with a hardware choice predictor and our scheme with static choice prediction are illustrated in Figure 1. In our scheme, the static choice prediction is inserted as an extra bit in the modified branch target buffer (BTB) entry. For each branch predicted, both the local and global predictors are accessed and the prediction implied by the static choice prediction bit in the indexed BTB entry is chosen. The critical path for this branch predictor is not lengthened with such a mechanism, hence no impact to clock speed. Furthermore, using this bit to clock gate the branch predictor might lead to further power reduction, however, it is not explored in this paper.

Most of the hybrid branch predictors with a dynamic choice predictor [9, 12] update all the branch prediction components for each branch access. This is because that, in a dynamic choice predictor, the choice predictor is updated dynamically depending on the prediction results of both branch predictors and for the further accesses to the same branch address there is uncertainty about which branch predictor will be used, hence updating both of them will result in more accuracy. In our model, we update only the branch predictor whose prediction is used, since every branch is already assigned to one of the predictors and updating only the assigned branch predictor is necessary. In our case, updating both branch predictors would not only consume more power but also increase the likelihood of aliasing.

In the following sections, we propose and evaluate two enabling techniques — *Static Correlation Choice (SCC)* prediction and *Static Choice (SC)* prediction from power and performance standpoints.

3.1   SCC Model

In the SCC model, we profile and collect branch history information for each branch. We apply this technique to a hybrid branch predictor that consists of a local bimodal branch predictor [15] and a global two-level branch predictor [16]. The algorithm for the SCC model with the hybrid branch predictor is described in the following steps:

1. If a branch is biased to one direction either *taken* or *not taken* during its lifetime in execution, we favor its prediction made by the bimodal branch predictor. The bias metric is based on a default *threshold* value that represents the execution frequency of the direction of a branch (e.g. 90% in this study, this is based on our intuition that higher than 90% hit rate is acceptable).

2. To model the bimodal branch predictor, we count the total number of consecutive *taken*'s and consecutive *not taken*'s for each branch collected from profile execution. This count based on the local bimodal branch predictor is denoted by C_{LP}. For example, if the branch history of a particular branch is 111100000101010: the number of consecutive ones is 4-1 = 3 and number of consecutive zeros is 4, therefore, $C_{LP} = 3+4 = 7$.

3. To model the global branch predictor, we collect global history information for each branch on-the-fly during profile execution and compare it against all prior global histories collected for the same branch. If the last k bits of the new global history match the last k bits of any prior global history, then the new prediction is called to be within the same history group. There are 2^k possible groups in total. For each branch that is included in a group, we count the total number of consecutive *taken*'s and consecutive *not taken*'s. At the end of the profile run, we sum up the consecutive counts including *taken* and *not taken* for each history group and denote the value by C_{GP}. For example, assume we have four history groups ($k=2$) — 00, 01, 10 and 11 for a profile run. For a particular target branch after the profile execution, we have a branch history 101000001111 for the 00 group, 11111111110 for the 01 group, 1110 for the 10 group, and 1000000 for the 11 group. Then the summation for this global branch predictor, for this particular branch would be $C_{GP} = 7+9+2+5 = 22$. Note that the history does not include the direction of the current reference.

4. C_{LP} and C_{GP} values are collected after the profiling execution. The static choice prediction is made off-line by comparing the values of C_{LP} and C_{GP}. The final choice, provided as a branch hint, as to which predictor to use for each branch is determined by favoring the larger value. In other words, if

C_{LP} is greater than C_{GP}, the choice prediction uses the prediction made by the bimodal predictor otherwise the prediction of the global branch predictor is used.

The SCC model basically targets McFarling's hybrid branch predictor yet collects these information at static compile-time. As aforementioned, McFarling's hybrid branch predictor consists of a bimodal local predictor and a gshare global predictor. The justification behind the calculation of C_{LP} (a metric for bimodal branch prediction) is that, for a bimodal predictor the more the branch result stays in state 00 (strongly not-taken) or 11 (strongly taken), the more stable the prediction will be. On the other hand, C_{GP} of a branch is the metric for the global branch prediction and its calculation is based on counting the number of occurrences of consecutive takens and not-takens (0's and 1's) for this branch for the possible number of different branch histories depending on the length of history. This is similar to the two-bit saturating counters which are chosen by the global history register in the gshare scheme.

3.2   SC Model

In the SC model, static choice predictions completely rely on the results collected from the software-based choice predictor of an architecture simulator. During profiling simulation, we collect the information with respect to how many times the choice predictor is biased to the bimodal predictor versus the global branch predictor for each branch. The final static choice prediction then relies on the majority reported from the profiling simulation.

4   Simulation Framework

Our experimental framework is based on sim-outorder from SimpleScalar toolkit version 3.0 [11]. We modified the simulator to (1) model a variety of hybrid branch predictors , (2) collect the profiling information for the SCC and SC models, and (3) perform static choice branch prediction. Table 1 shows the parameters of our processor model. The SPEC CPU2000 integer benchmark suite [8] was used for our evaluation. All of the benchmark programs were compiled into Alpha AXP binaries with optimization level -O3. All the data presented in Section 5 were obtained through runs of one billion instructions. Since profiling is involved, the experiments were performed among *test*, *train* and *reference* profiling input sets while all the performance evaluation results come from *reference* input set. In other words, we collected different profiling results in order to analyze the impact of our proposed mechanisms with different profiling input sets.

As our proposed technique provides an opportunity to eliminate the choice predictor hardware, we evaluate and quantify the overall power improvement using Wattch [2] toolkit due to the absence of a hardware choice predictor. We modified Wattch to enable clock-gating in different functional blocks of a branch predictor including the BTB, the local, global, and choice predictors, and return address stack.

Table 1. Parameters of the processor model.

Execution Engine	Out-of-order
Fetch Width	8 instruction
Issue Width	8 instruction
ALU Units	4 units
Branch Target Buffer	4-way, 4096 sets
Register Update Unit	128 entries
Cache organization	4-way split I- and D-L1: 64 KB each 2 cycle hit latency 32 bytes line
	4-way L2(unified): 512 KB 16 cycle hit latency 64 bytes line
Memory latency	120 core cycles

5   Experimental Results

This section presents our performance and power analysis. In the first experiment, we study the impact of our static models for choice prediction on performance, including branch prediction rate and speedup. The *train* input set in SPECint2000 benchmarks was used for collecting profile information, while the *reference* input set was used for performance evaluation. Results show that our prediction model performs on par or sometimes better than a hardware choice predictor. It is reported in [10] that energy-delay product is sometimes misleading, hence we report the performance and energy separately.

Figure 2 summarizes the branch prediction miss rates from different branch predictors for SPECint2000 benchmarks. For each benchmark program, experiments are conducted with a variety of branch prediction schemes. Among them are **gshare10**, **gshare11**, **gshare12**, **hybrid_g10**, **hybrid_g10+scc**, **hybrid_g10+sc**, **hybrid_g11+scc**, and **hybrid_g11+sc**. The **gshare10**, same as McFarling's gshare scheme [12], indexes a 1024-entry 2-bit counter array by exclusive-ORing the branch address and its corresponding 10-bit global history. Similarly, **gshare11** and **gshare12** perform the same algorithm by simply extending the sizes of their global history to 11 and 12 bits, thereby increasing their corresponding 2-bit counter arrays to 2048 and 4096 entries, respectively. The predictor, **hybrid_g10** uses a hybrid branch predictor approach similar to McFarling's combining branch predictor [12]. It consists of a bimodal predictor, a two-level predictor, and a choice predictor each of them with a size of 1024x2 bits. The **hybrid_g10+sc** is the same as **hybrid_g10** except replaces the hardware choice predictor with a profiling-based choice prediction mechanism using the SC model described in Section 3. Likewise, **hybrid_g10+scc** uses the SCC model for choice predictions. Predictors **hybrid_g11+scc** and **hybrid_g11+sc**

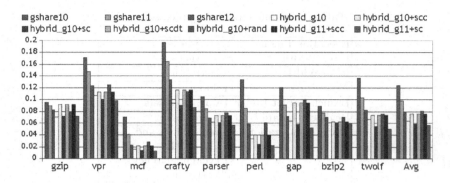

Fig. 2. Miss prediction rates with different branch predictors.

are extended versions of the **hybrid_g10+scc** and **hybrid_g10+sc** models, respectively, as they increase the size of the two-level branch predictor to 2048x2 bits.

Moreover, we also implement the prediction model proposed by Chang et al. [3] which we call SCDT model. In SCDT, profiling is used to classify branches into different groups based on dynamic taken rates and for each group the same branch predictor is used. If the dynamic taken rate of a branch is 0-5% or 95-100% then this branch is predicted using the bimodal predictor, otherwise it is predicted using gshare predictor. If there are a lot of branches that change their behavior dynamically, then SCC captures such behavior better than SCDT. For example, if the behavior of a branch has k consecutive 0's and k consecutive 1's, a bimodal prediction will be better off since it might reduce aliasing in gshare. By contrast SCDT will always use gshare. We also perform experiments using a random choice model which we call RAND model and it randomly selects a branch predictor statically. The **hybrid_g10+scdt** and **hybrid_g10+rand** results are based on the SCDT and RAND models respectively.

As shown in Figure 2, increasing the size of the global branch predictor alone does not perform as well as using a hybrid branch predictor. For example, the **gshare12** predictor consists of more prediction entries than the **hybrid_g10** branch predictor provides (area comparison is shown in Table 2), but none of the benchmarks shows the **gshare12** branch predictor outperforming the **hybrid_g10** branch predictor.

Also shown in Figure 2, instead of having a hardware choice predictor, we can achieve comparable prediction rates using a static off-line choice predictor. Our simulation results show that SCC does not perform as well as SC. This is because the SC model can account for aliasing in its model and hence is more accurate. The difference of these two models is less than 2% in branch miss prediction rates.

Comparing between SCC and SCDT, both schemes provide comparable results. This suggests that branches with varying behavior, as explained earlier,

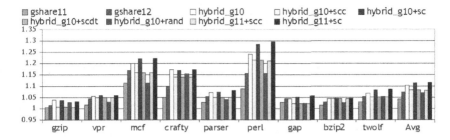

Fig. 3. Normalized speedup with different branch predictors.

rarely occur in SPEC2000. Selecting branch predictors at random does not provide as good an average result as our SCC and SC.

We also show that instead of having a hardware hybrid choice predictor, we can employ a static choice prediction and increase the size of the global branch predictor. The **hybrid_g11+sc** model demonstrates the best prediction rate among others for most of the benchmarks.

Figure 3 shows the normalized performance speedups of various prediction schemes; the baseline in this figure is **gshare10**. The results show that the speedup's improve as the prediction rates increase. We expect the increase will be more significant with deeper, and wider machine.

Previously, we explained that the motivation of our work is to reduce the area and power consumption of a branch predictor while retaining the performance. To this end, we use Wattch to collect the power statistics of the branch predictor and other functional units of the processor. Both dynamic and static power consumption were considered in our evaluation. For each functional block (such as BTB, branch predictor, i-cache, and d-cache), the switching power consumed per access is calculated along with the total number of accesses to that block. Additionally, when a block is not in use, we assume an amount of static power equal to 10% of its switching power is consumed. Note that this amount will increase significantly when migrating to the future process technology. Thus, the elimination of the choice predictor will gain more advantage in overall power dissipation. We also want to mention that we examined the effect of our branch prediction schemes on the power consumption of the branch direction predictor, and we claim improvements on the power consumption of the branch direction predictor.

Figure 4 shows the normalized power consumption values for different branch predictors, relative to the power consumption of **gshare10**. From this Figure and Figure 3, we can tell that for nearly all the benchmarks, **hybrid_g10+sc** yields the best processor performance for little branch prediction power. We can use Figures 3 and 4 as guides in a design space exploration framework, where the power budget of the branch predictor is limited, and a specific performance constraint has to be satisfied. For example, the results in Figure 4 show that the removal of the choice predictor in **hybrid_g10** can reduce the power consump-

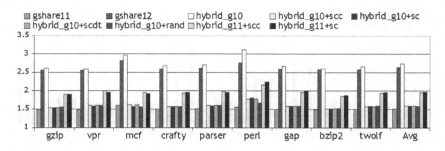

Fig. 4. Normalized power consumption of different branch predictors.

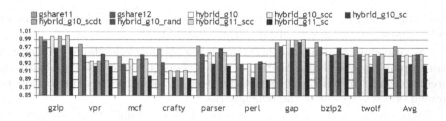

Fig. 5. Normalized processor energy with different branch predictors.

tion to a level comparable to that of **gshare11**. Similarly Figure 3 shows that **hybrid_g10+sc** outperforms **gshare11**, for all the benchmarks. Hence we can deduce that using **hybrid_g10+sc** is more advantageous in terms of both the power dissipation and performance. We present the total energy consumption of the processor in Figure 5. Despite the fact that **gshare10** has lowest power consumption, all other branch predictors outperform **gshare10** in terms of total energy consumption. When we compare the power consumption with static and dynamic methods for the same type of branch predictor, static choice predictor consumes less power. However the total energy consumption depends not only the power consumption but also execution time. Hence **hybrid_g10** model which has better the performance on average than **hybrid_g10+scc** has smaller energy consumption. **Hybrid_g10+sc** instead has the smaller energy consumption than most of branch predictors including **hybrid_g10** since it is faster and consumes less power. Moreover **hybrid_g11+sc** which has higher branch prediction's power dissipation than **hybrid_g10+sc** outperforms all branch predictors in terms of total energy consumption.

Next, we study the impact of profiling on the training input set of our SC and SCC training. We aim to show how our models SCC and SC are affected as a result of various training data. We use three different input sets for profiling: *test*, *train*, and *reference*. The results show little impact on the branch prediction outcomes. The results are detailed in Figure 6 where the baseline is again **gshare10**. Figure 6 shows that SCC is less sensitive to profile information than SC. This is because SC incorporates aliasing information in its model. Let us

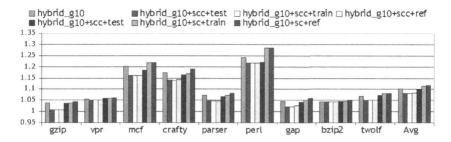

Fig. 6. Normalized speedup on different profiling input sets.

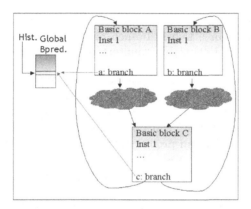

Fig. 7. CFG example showing aliasing impact.

consider the Control Flow Graph (CFG), which is shown in Figure 7. Assume that branches a and c point to the same location in global branch predictor and also are predicted accurately by a global branch predictor if there is no destructive aliasing. If branches a and c destructively interfere with each other, this results in profiling say that loop A-C is called more frequently than loop B-C hence static choice predictor will assign both branches a and c to local branch predictor. However on the running input set, if loop C-A runs more often than loop B-A then assigning both a and c to local branch predictor can reduce branch prediction accuracy. Figure 6 also shows that if profile information has the same behavior as the real input set, static choice predictor can outperform hardware choice predictor in most benchmarks.

We then perform experiments using different hybrid branch predictors to show that SC and SCC are equally compatible with different kinds of hybrid branch predictors. In this set of experiments, **gshare10** is our chosen baseline. The results are shown in Figure 8. Note that **hybrid_PAg** is a hybrid branch predictor similar to the one used in Alpha 21264 processor. It consists of a two-level local predictor with a local history table size of 1024x10 bits, local predictor

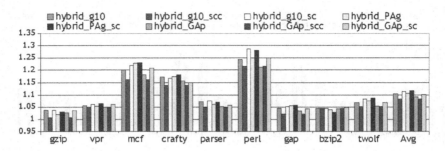

Fig. 8. Normalized speedup on different hybrid branch predictors.

size of 1024x2 bit and with global and choice predictors of size 1024x2 bit. **hybrid_GAp** stands for a hybrid branch predictor with a 1024x2 bit bimodal predictor and four of 1024x2 bit counters instead of one such counter as in **hybrid_g10**.

Since SCC is not intended to target **hybrid_PAg**, i.e it cannot exploit full advantages from local branch predictor in **hybrid_PAg**, we exclude the result of the SCC on **hybrid_PAg**. For example, if we have local history pattern of 1010101010, C_{LP} is 0 and SC will not choose local branch predictor but local predictor in **hybrid_PAg** can predict this pattern accurately.

Results shown in Figure 8 also indicate that SC works well with **hybrid_PAg**.

We now report the power consumption of different branch predictors and total energy consumption of the processor using these branch predictors. Figure 9 shows the normalized power consumption for different hybrid predictors relative to **gshare10**. In this figure, we observe that for **hybrid_g10**, and **hybrid_GAp**, using SC and SCC methods bring an improvement of 42% on average. The average improvement for **hybrid_PAg** is around 37%. The power consumption in **hybrid_GAp** is not too high compared with **hybrid_g10** since clock gating is applied to unused predictors. Figure 10 shows the total energy consumption of the processor using these hybrid predictors. Using SC method with **hybrid_PAg** branch predictor gives the best result in terms of the energy consumption of the processor and this is due to the high speedup obtained using **hybrid_PAg_sc** which is observed on Figure 8.

These results allow the possibility of replacing the hardware choice predictor with our schemes, and reclaim in its corresponding die area. Assuming a static memory array area model, as described in [13], for the branch predictor, the area can be quantified as followings:

$$area_{static\_memory} = 0.6 \ (size_w + 6) \ (line_b + 6) \ rbe \tag{1}$$

where $size_w$ is the number of words, $line_b$ is the number of bits and rbe is an area unit of a register cell. The two +6 terms approximate the overhead for the decoder logic and sense amplifiers. Based on equation 1, we derived the normalized areas of different branch predictors relative to **gshare10** in Table 2. Note that the branch predictor area saved by using our profile-guided SCC and SC

Table 2. Normalized area of hybrid branch predictors.

Branch predictor	Normalized area
gshare11	1.9822
gshare12	4.806
hybrid_g10	2.973
hybrid_g10+scc/sc	1.986
hybrid_g11	3.955
hybrid_g11+scc/sc	2.968
hybrid_PAg	4.946
hybrid_PAg+sc	3.959
hybrid_GAp	3.713
hybrid_GAp+sc/scc	2.726

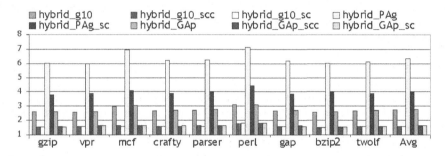

Fig. 9. Normalized power consumption of different hybrid branch predictors.

schemes for **hybrid_g10** predictor is 33.18%. The saving is less for other predictors because these predictors are comprised of more complicated local and global predictors which consume a lot of area. One interesting result in the table shows that the area of **hybrid_GAp+sc/scc** is smaller than the area of **hybrid_g10**. This is due to the fact that fewer decoders are needed for **hybrid_GAp+sc/scc** compared to **hybrid_g10**. The four 1024x2 bit tables in **hybrid_GAp** share the same decoder, hence we need only one 10x1024 decoder and one 2x4 decoder for **hybrid_GAp**, while **hybrid_g10** needs three separate 10x1024 decoders (one for each predictor).

6   Conclusions

In this paper, we study two profile-guided techniques: *Static Correlation Choice* and *Static Choice*, for performing off-line static choice predictions. Our work offers the possibility of eliminating the hardware choice predictor while achieving comparable performance results. In other words, the branch prediction rates attained by dynamic choice predictors can also be achieved using the two proposed

412   M. Ekpanyapong, P. Korkmaz, and H.-H.S. Lee

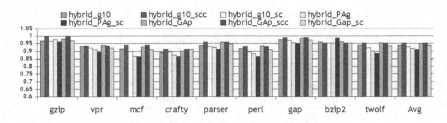

Fig. 10. Normalized processor energy with different hybrid branch predictors.

models, thus resulting in similar performance. The studies we carried out using different input data further indicate that the SC and SCC techniques are largely insensitive to profiling data. By using our techniques, we can reduct the power dissipation of the branch predictor by 40% on average. Moreover, an average saving of 27% in branch predictor area can be saved.

References

1. T. Ball and J. R. Larus. Branch Prediction for Free. In *PLDI-6*, 1993.
2. D. Brooks, V. Tiwari, and M. Martonosi. Wattch: A Framework for Architectural-Level Power Analysis and Optimizations. *ISCA-27*, June 2000.
3. P.-Y. Chang, E. Hao, T.-Y. Yeh, and Y. N. Patt. Branch Classification: a New Mechanism for Improving Branch Predictor Performance. *International Journal of Parallel Programming*, Vol. 24, No. 2:133–158, 1999.
4. Daniel Chaver, Luis Pinuel, Manuel Prieto, Francisco Tirado, and Michael C. Huang. Branch Prediction on Demand: an Energy-Efficient Solution . In *Proceedings of the 2003 International Symposium on Low Power Electronics and Design*, 2003.
5. Intel Corporation. IA-64 Application Developer's Architecture Guide. Intel Literature Centers, 1999.
6. J. A. Fisher and S. M. Freudenberger. Predicting Conditional Branch Directions From Previous Runs of a Program. In *ASPLOS-5*, pages 85–95, 1992.
7. D. Grunwald, D. Lindsay, and B. Zorn. Static Methods in Hybrid Branch Prediction. In *PACT'98*, 1998.
8. John L. Henning. SPEC CPU2000: Measuring CPU Performance in the New Millennium. *IEEE Micro*, July 2000.
9. R. E. Kessler. The ALPHA 21264 Microprocessor. *IEEE Micro*, March/April 1999.
10. H.-H. S. Lee, J. B. Fryman, A. U. Diril, and Y. S. Dhillon. The Elusive Metric for Low-Power Architecture Research. In *Workshop on Complexity-Effective Design*, 2003.
11. SimpleScalar LLC. SimpleScalar Toolkit version 3.0. http://www.simplescalar.com.
12. S. McFarling. Combining Branch Predictors. Technical Report TN-36, Compaq Western Research Lab, 1993.
13. J. M. Mulder, N. T. Quach, and M. J. Flynn. An Area Model for On-Chip Memories and its Application. *IEEE JSSC*, Vol. 26 No. 2, February 1991.

14. Shien-Tai Pan, Kimming So, and Joseph T. Rahmeh. Improving the Accuracy of Dynamic Branch Prediction Using Branch Correlation. *Proceedings of the 5th International Conference on Architectural Support for Programming Languages and Operating Systems*, 1992.
15. J. E. Smith. A Study of Branch Prediction Strategies. In *ISCA-8*, 1981.
16. T.-Y. Yeh and Y. N. Patt. Two-Level Adaptive Training Branch Prediction. In *MICRO-24*, 1991.
17. C. Young and M. D. Smith. Static Correlated Branch Prediction. *ACM TOPLAS*, 1999.

Performance Impact of Different Data Value Predictors

Yong Xiao, Kun Deng, and Xingming Zhou

National Laboratory for Parallel & Distributed Processing
Changsha, P.R. China, 410073
yxiao1977@hotmail.com

Abstract. Data value prediction has been widely accepted as an effective mechanism to exceed the dataflow limit in processor parallelism race. Several works have reported promising performance potential. However, there is hardly enough information that is presented in a clear way about performance comparison of these prediction mechanisms. This paper investigates the performance impact of four previously proposed value predictors, namely last value predictor, stride value predictor, two-level value predictor and hybrid (stride+two-level) predictor. The impact of misprediction penalty, which has been frequently ignored, is discussed in detail. Several other implementation issues, including instruction window size, issue width and branch predictor are also addressed and simulated. Simulation results indicate that data value predictors act differently under different configurations. In some cases, simpler schemes may be more beneficial than complicated ones. In some particular cases, value prediction may have negative impact on performance.

1 Introduction

The inevitably increasing density of transistors on one silicon die allows chip designers to put more and more execution resources into single chip to improve performance. However, the presence of data dependences in programs greatly impairs their effort. Value prediction is a speculative technique that uses the previous results of a static instruction to predict the value of the instruction's next output value. Recent studies have shown bright future of using data value prediction to exceed the dataflow limit [2, 3, 6, 10, 12, 13].

Previous studies have introduced many data value predictors. Performance impact of each predictor has been thoroughly investigated respectively. Yet no works have reported the performance comparison of these predictors in a clear way. Such study is helpful in better understanding the effects of value prediction mechanisms and is of great importance when designing an appropriate value predictor. In this paper, we integrate value prediction mechanism in a pipeline implementation and investigate the performance impact of different value predictors. Four previously proposed value predictors, namely last value predictor [1, 2, 3, 4], stride value predictor, two-level value predictor and hybrid (stride+two-level) predictor [4] are used as candidates. Different implementation configurations are also discussed.

P.-C. Yew and J. Xue (Eds.): ACSAC 2004, LNCS 3189, pp. 414–425, 2004.
© Springer-Verlag Berlin Heidelberg 2004

Simulation analysis indicates that we may need to re-evaluate the impact of data value prediction on performance. With different misprediction penalties and implementation issues, these predictors showed different characteristics. Some predictors may even cause performance degradation. To our surprise, complicated predictors may obtain lower IPC (instructions per cycle) than simpler schemes in some experiments. At last, many factors of value prediction implementation are still ambiguous by now. Further research must be done to fully evaluate data value prediction.

The remainder of the paper is organized as follows: Section 2 discusses recent relevant work in value prediction. Section 3 introduces the microarchitecture implementation. Section 4 summarizes our experimental methodology and presents performance results. Section 5 presents a summary of this work, and proposes some suggestions for future research.

2   Related Works

Value prediction is possible because of value locality - the property of recent values to recur in computer system storage locations [1]. [1] indicates that a large fraction of values computed by the same static load instruction are a repetition set within the 16 most recent values produced by the instruction. Follow-up studies [2, 3] extend value prediction to all register writing instructions. Rychlik et al [5] present a value-predicting wide superscalar machine with a speculative execution core. Their work indicates that many predictions may be useless in enhancing performance.

Wang Kai et al investigate a variety of techniques to carry out highly accurate value prediction [4]. Their simulation analysis shows that the four predictors used in our paper have different static prediction rate and prediction accuracy. Yet the simulation is made without pipeline involved. The limits of performance potential of data value speculation to boost ILP are addressed in [6]. The impact on stride value predictor of some features, such as instruction window size and branch prediction accuracy are discussed and simulated within an idealized experiment environment.

However, there exists no formalized method that defines the effects of value speculation on microarchitecture. Y. Sazeides thus proposes a methodical model for dynamically scheduled microarchitectures with value speculation [7]. The model isolates the parts of a microarchitecture that may be influenced by value speculation in terms of various variables and latency events. Simulation results obtained with a context-based predictor show that value speculation has non-uniform sensitivity to changes in the latency of such events.

3   Microarchitecture

This section first describes a base-microarchitecture and then introduces the value speculation microarchitecture used in the paper. Different data value predictors and misprediction penalty considerations are also introduced respectively.

3.1 Base Microarchitecture

For base microarchitecture we consider an out-of-order superscalar processor model used in SimpleScalar2.0 [15], where the Register Update Unit (RUU) structure unifies issue resources and retirement resources. Memory instructions consist of two operations: address generation and memory access. Fast forward is implemented, thus data dependent instructions can get executed in the same cycle when an instruction writes back its result to physical registers. The pipeline is six-stage implemented: Fetch (F), Dispatch (D), Issue (I), Execution (E), Write back (W) and Commit (C). The pipelined execution of three data dependent instructions *i*, *j* and *k* is shown in Figure 1. One-cycle execution latency is assumed for all instructions, which means the results are available just after I-stage, so E-stage is not shown.

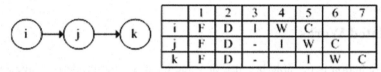

	1	2	3	4	5	6	7
i	F	D	I	W	C		
j	F	D	-	I	W	C	
k	F	D	-	-	I	W	C

Fig. 1. Execution Example of Base Architecture

3.2 Data Value Predictors

Four previously proposed predictors, namely last value predictor (LVP), stride value predictor (SVP), 2-level predictor (2LP), stride+2level hybrid predictor (S2P) are used here as candidates.

Last value prediction predicts the result of an instruction based on its most recently generated value. While stride value prediction predicts the value by adding the most recent value to the stride, namely the difference of the two most recently produced results.

The 2-level value predictor predicts the value based on the repeated pattern of the last several values observed. It consists of two tables: a value history table (VHT) and a pattern history table (PHT). The VHT stores up to four distinct values generated by an instruction and keeps track of the order in which they are generated. Several saturating counters maintained in PHT are used to decide whether a prediction should be made or not.

The hybrid value predictor is a combination of SVP and 2LP. Compared to the VHT in 2LP, the VHT of the hybrid predictor has two additional fields: state and stride, for the stride prediction. 2LP is always accessed first, but its prediction is used only if the maximum counter value is greater than or equal to the threshold value. Otherwise, SVP is used.

The work done by Sang [16], where schemes in [1, 4] are realized without pipeline involved, is referenced here for comparison. Configurations for these predictors used in the paper are summarized in Table 1. A maximum capacity of about 128K (1K=1024) bytes is considered for each predictor. All predictors are directly mapped.

Table 1. Configuration of Predictors

Predictor	Threshold	Saturate At	Update Method	Entry
LVP	2	3	Correct:+1, else:-1	16K
SVP	steady	state=steady	state transition diagram	8K
2LP	3	12	Correct:+3, else:-1	4K
S2P	SVP: steady	steady	state transition diagram	4K
	2LP: 6	12	Correct:+3, else:-1	

3.3 Microarchitecture with Value Prediction

The base machine model is modified to support result value prediction. In addition to adding the value predictor, each RUU is expanded to hold the predicted value and other information for speculative execution.

At fetch stage, instruction address is used to access the value predictor. And in our experiments, the number of value predictions made in a cycle is unlimited. Once a prediction is made, the predicted value will be available at dispatch stage. Later dependent instructions will be able to get issued with the predicted value. The data value predictor is updated when an instruction gets committed, namely the predictor can not be updated speculatively. Speculative update will be studied in the future.

Instructions can be speculative or non-speculative, predicted or un-predicted. Speculative instructions have at least one predicted source operand when they get executed; predicted instructions have a predicted result. In our implementation, data value prediction is performed only for load and simple ALU instructions. Branch instructions, store instructions, nops and double-precision instructions are not considered for data value prediction. For the complexity brought by speculative memory access, only simple ALU instructions and address generations can execute speculatively. Moreover, for configuration Conf4 (will be mentioned in section 4.2), when none-zero misprediction penalty is used, address generation is not permitted to execute speculatively. Even if address generation is allowed to do speculative execution, memory access can only be issued when all its operands are final.

A speculatively issued instruction is prevented from completing architecturally and is forced to retain possession of its issue resources until its inputs are no longer speculative. After execution, the speculative results are not broadcast on the result bus. Instead, they are locally written back to the same RUU. Once a prediction is verified, all dependent instructions can either release their issue resources and proceed into the commit stage (in the case of a correct prediction) or restart execution with the correct register values (if the prediction was incorrect). In our work, a predicted instruction can only verify its direct successors. The verified instructions can do the activation successively.

3.4 Misprediction Penalty Considerations

For misprediction penalty, two time parameters - T_{verify} and $T_{reissue}$ are considered. T_{verify} stands for the latency between a predicted instruction finishes execution and dependent speculatively executed instructions get verified. $T_{reissue}$ stands for the latency after a speculatively executed instruction using an incorrectly predicted value gets verified before it can reissue. T_{verify} and $T_{reissue}$ can be either 0 or 1 in our work. Latency that is bigger than 1 will be too pessimistic for our processor model. Figure 2 illustrates the pipelined execution of the three instructions used in figure 1 under all four combinations of T_{verify} and $T_{reissue}$. R and V stand for reissue and verify respectively. For each combination, two scenarios are considered: (1) both the outputs of i and j are correctly predicted, (2) both the outputs of i and j are mispredicted.

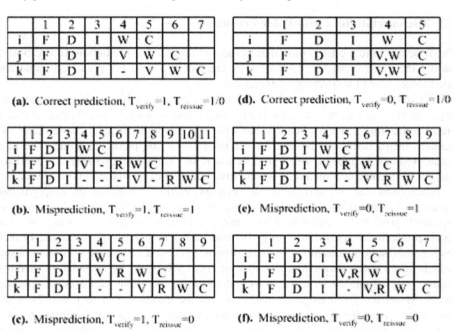

	1	2	3	4	5	6	7
i	F	D	I	W	C		
j	F	D	I	V	W	C	
k	F	D	I	-	V	W	C

(a). Correct prediction, $T_{verify}=1$, $T_{reissue}=1/0$

	1	2	3	4	5
i	F	D	I	W	C
j	F	D	I	V,W	C
k	F	D	I	V,W	C

(d). Correct prediction, $T_{verify}=0$, $T_{reissue}=1/0$

	1	2	3	4	5	6	7	8	9	10	11
i	F	D	I	W	C						
j	F	D	I	V	-	R	W	C			
k	F	D	I	-	-	-	V	-	R	W	C

(b). Misprediction, $T_{verify}=1$, $T_{reissue}=1$

	1	2	3	4	5	6	7	8	9
i	F	D	I	W	C				
j	F	D	I	V	R	W	C		
k	F	D	I	-	-	V	R	W	C

(e). Misprediction, $T_{verify}=0$, $T_{reissue}=1$

	1	2	3	4	5	6	7	8	9
i	F	D	I	W	C				
j	F	D	I	V	R	W	C		
k	F	D	I	-	-	V	R	W	C

(c). Misprediction, $T_{verify}=1$, $T_{reissue}=0$

	1	2	3	4	5	6	7
i	F	D	I	W	C		
j	F	D	I	V,R	W	C	
k	F	D	I	-	V,R	W	C

(f). Misprediction, $T_{verify}=0$, $T_{reissue}=0$

Fig. 2. Execution Example with Different T_{verify} and $T_{reissue}$ Configurations

Figure 2 indicates that when T_{verify} equals to 1, value prediction will not improve performance and sometimes will cause performance degradation. Under such situations, value speculation is not beneficial. In our work, only $T_{verify} = 0$ is analyzed.

There can also be structural hazard penalties due to value speculation implementation, especially when the execution resources are limited. Such structural hazard is also well simulated in the experiments.

4   Performance Evaluations

In this section we will introduce our experiment environments and present results obtained from the simulation experiments.

4.1 Benchmarks

The precompiled SPEC CINT95 benchmark suite supplied by SimpleScalar [15] is used in our simulation. Table 2 shows the benchmarks and the specific input sets used. The last column gives the percentage of dynamic instructions that are eligible for data value prediction. All benchmarks were run to completion.

Table 2. Benchmarks and Percentage of Instructions Eligible for Value Prediction

Benchmark	Input Set	VP-Eligible Instructions
099.go	9 9 go-null.in	77.69%
124.m88ksim	m88ksim-ctl.raw	66.38%
126.gcc(cc1)	-O cc1-cccp.i –o cc1-cccp.s	65.78%
129.compress	compress-test.in	35.23%
130.li	li-test.lsp	58.78%
132.ijpeg	-image_file ijpeg-specmun.ppm	74.48%
134.perl	jumble.pl < jumble.in	62.53%
147.vortex	vortex.raw	61.65%

4.2 Architecture Parameters

Our implementation has a 16K bytes directly mapped instruction cache. The first level data cache is 4-way associative, 16K bytes for Con4, 64K bytes for other configurations. Both caches have block sizes of 32 bytes and hit latency of 1 cycle. There is a unified second level 256K bytes 4-way associative cache with 64 byte blocks and a 6-cycle cache hit latency. The first 8 bytes of a data access request to memory will need 18 cycles and the rest of the access will take 2 cycles for each 8 bytes. There is a 16 entry 4-way associative instruction TLB and a 32 entry 4-way associative data TLB, each with a 30 cycle miss penalty. The branch target buffer (BTB) has 512 entries and is 4–way associatively organized. Moreover, an 8-entry return address stack is used.

The latencies of functional units are set as below: Integer ALU 1 cycle, Integer MULT 3 cycles, Integer DIV 20 cycles, FP Adder 2 cycles, FP MULT 4 cycles and FP DIV 12 cycles. All functional units, except the divide units, are pipelined to allow a new instruction to initiate execution each cycle.

Other architecture parameters are summarized in Table 3. Four configurations will be simulated. Conf4, which is very conservative, only allows small window size and issue width. While the next three configurations – Conf8, Conf8_bP and Conf8_bPvP are much closer to those of modern processors. Here "bP" means perfect branch prediction and "vP" means perfect value prediction. With perfect branch prediction, the fetch engine will always get instructions from the correct path and no instructions from the wrong path will be used. With perfect value prediction, value prediction will be used only if the predicted value equals to the final result. Meanwhile the value predictor will be updated immediately with the correct results along with the predictor lookup process, and needs not wait until the instruction gets committed.

Table 3. Processor Configurations

parameter	Conf4	Conf8	Conf8_bP(vP)
instruction window (entries)	16	128	256
load-store queue (entries)	8	128	256
fetch/decode/issue/commit width (instructions/cycle)	4	8	8
functional units (numbers) INT ALU INT MULT/DIV FP Adder FP MULT/DIV Memory Port	4 1 4 1 2	8 2 4 2 2	8 2 4 2 4
branch predictor	bimodal, 2K entries, 3 cycles miss penalty		perfect

4.3 Experimental Results

Two kinds of configurations: (1) $T_{verify}=0$, $T_{reissue} = 0$, (2) $T_{verify}=0$, $T_{reissue} = 1$ are simulated. To better understand the value speculation performance, we define two metrics: speculation rate (SR) and reissue rate (RR). Speculation rate is defined as the percentage of speculatively executed instructions over all executed instructions including those that are on the wrong path. Reissue rate is the percentage of speculative instructions that get reissued at least one time over all executed instructions.

4.3.1 Prediction Performance Using Conf4

Figure 3 shows the simulation results when $T_{reissue} = 0$. Figure 4 shows the performance when $T_{reissue} = 1$. In figure 3(b) and figure 4(b), for each benchmark, 4 groups of results are given; from left to right, these correspond to predictor LVP, SVP, 2LP and S2P respectively. Each group of results consists of 3 parts. The uppermost part (SR) indicates the speculation rate. The next part (RR) indicates the reissue rate, and the next part (delta) indicates the difference of speculation rate and reissue rate, namely the percentage of speculative instructions that are executed correctly over all executed instructions including those that are on the wrong path.

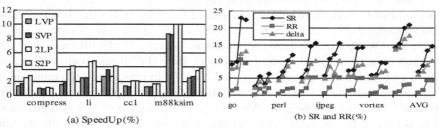

(a) SpeedUp(%)   (b) SR and RR(%)

Fig. 3. Prediction Performance of Four Predictors Using Conf4, $T_{verify}=0$, $T_{reissue}=0$

Figure 3(a) indicates that S2P performs the best among all predictors, while LVP performs the worst. When $T_{reissue}$ = 0, there is no misprediction penalty except the penalty brought by structural hazards. So the more correct speculations/predictions (delta in figure 3(b)) a scheme performs the more benefits it can obtain. Reissue rate or incorrect prediction rate is not a decisive factor in such a situation.

Figure 4(b) shows similar trend as figure 3(b), except that both the value of SR and RR are decreased a little. When $T_{reissue}$ equals to 1, address generation operations are not allowed to execute speculatively, which is mainly responsible for the difference. The impact of such factor needs further research.

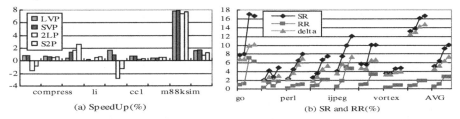

(a) SpeedUp(%)   (b) SR and RR(%)

Fig. 4. Prediction Performance of Four Predictors Using Conf4, $T_{verify}=0$, $T_{reissue}=1$

Figure 4(a) indicates that SVP obtains the highest average speedup among all four predictors. This is mainly due to the fact that when misprediction penalty is not negligible, prediction accuracy is more crucial than the amount. Although S2P still performs the most correct speculations, the higher reissue rate (figure 4(b)) impairs its benefit. A more noticeable fact is that value speculation may sometimes cause performance degradation. For benchmark *go* and *ijpeg*, negative impact on the performance is performed by both 2LP and S2P. This can be explained by the high reissue rate showed in figure 4(b). Especially for *ijpeg* by 2LP where RR is higher than delta, it's not surprising to obtain the worst performance.

4.3.2 Prediction Performance Using Conf8

In this subsection, Conf8 is used in our experiments. Figure 5 and Figure 6 show the simulation results for $T_{reissue}$ = 0 and $T_{reissue}$ = 1 respectively. As more instructions are allowed to be fetched and issued in one cycle, more instructions get executed speculatively. Meanwhile more wrong predictions are made. As a consequence, both SR and RR are higher in figure 5 and 6 than those in figure 3 and 4.

From figure 5(a), we find again that S2P performs the best among all predictors, while LVP performs the worst. Two other facts are worth mentioning here. First is that the speedup obtained with Conf8 is lower than that with Conf4. One reason is that with larger window size and issue width, the scheduling hardware has more opportunities rearranging instructions. Thus the effect of value prediction is weakened. The relative higher reissue rate is also responsible for performance decline. The other noticeable fact is the negative impact on benchmark *perl* by LVP and SVP. It is because that the number of instructions on the wrong path is greatly increased under LVP and SVP, which in turn result in performance degradation.

Due to the lowest reissue rate and stable behavior among all benchmark programs, LVP performs the best in figure 6(a). Meanwhile, SVP, for its bad performance with *compress* and *perl*, takes the second place. For the relative higher reissue rate, more programs perform worse with value speculation than in figure 4(a).

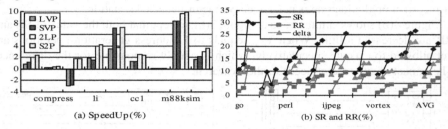

(a) SpeedUp(%)

(b) SR and RR(%)

Fig. 5. Prediction Performance of Four Predictors Using Conf8, $T_{verify}=0$, $T_{reissue}=0$

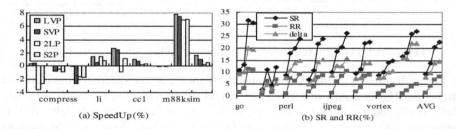

(a) SpeedUp(%)

(b) SR and RR(%)

Fig. 6. Prediction Performance of Four Predictors Using Conf8, $T_{verify}=0$, $T_{reissue}=1$

4.3.3   Prediction Performance Using Conf8_bP

Figure 7 and Figure 8 demonstrate the simulation results of using Conf8_bP for $T_{reissue}$ = 0 and $T_{reissue}$ = 1 respectively. It is disappointing to find that all value predictors can hardly obtain performance benefits in both cases. One possible explanation may be obtained from figure 7(b) and 8(b). For many programs, the reissue rate is greatly higher than delta, which means most speculatively executed instructions get incorrectly performed. To manage reissue rate under an acceptable level is of great importance in value prediction design.

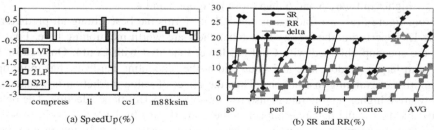

(a) SpeedUp(%)

(b) SR and RR(%)

Fig. 7. Prediction Performance of Four Predictors Using Conf8_bP, $T_{verify}=0$, $T_{reissue}=0$

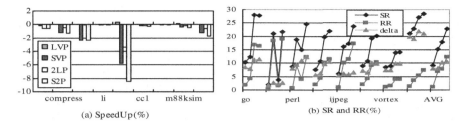

Fig. 8. Prediction Performance of Four Predictors Using Conf8_bP, $T_{verify}=0$, $T_{reissue}=1$

4.3.4 Prediction Performance Using Conf8_bPvP

In this subsection, we will check the performance impact of perfect value predictors. All predictors are configured to make predictions only if the predicted value equals to the final result. Thus all speculatively executed instructions need not be reissued. Results are presented in Figure 9.

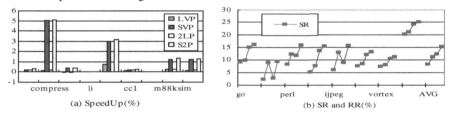

Fig. 9. Prediction Performance of Four Predictors Using Conf8_bPvP, $T_{verify}=0$, $T_{reissue}=1/0$

We can see that the performances of programs are improved mostly, especially for *compress*, *ijpeg* and *m88ksim*. However, for *li* and *vortex*, negligible benefits are obtained. And for *perl*, negative effect is taken. One possible explanation is that under such ideal simulation environments where branch prediction is perfect and instruction window is very large, the original hardware itself is enough to obtain the best performance through instruction rearranging. Also the speculatively executed instructions are useful only if they are on the critical path. Thus the high speculation rate does not mean high performance gains.

5 Summary and Future Works

In this paper, we have discussed the pipelined execution of value speculation with different misprediction penalties and different architecture configurations. And the performance impacts of different data value predictors are studied in detail. We find that with different misprediction penalties and implementation issues, these predictors showed different characteristics. Some value predictors may even cause performance degradation under some configurations. And to our surprise, complicated hybrid value predictor, due to its high reissue rates, obtains lower IPC than simpler schemes in some of the experiments. These observations are of great importance in future value prediction research.

In the experiments, the speedup obtained with value predictor is moderate; benefits are even negligible under ideal environments with large window size, high issue width and perfect branch predictions. Reasons include: 1) unlike branch prediction, in our six-stage pipeline implementation, the benefit of correct value prediction is moderate; 2) the high reissue rate impairs the effect of value prediction; 3) many correct speculative executions may not be useful, because they are not on the critical path; 4) the relative low fetch bandwidth may also impairs the performance [9].

There are several directions for future work. One important work is to study the impact of value prediction in future designs. As deeper pipeline will be widely used, the benefit of correct value prediction may be larger. How to combine value prediction with architectures that exploit higher level parallelism [10, 11, 13], such as trace processor, to achieve higher speedups is still not clearly studied. Another direction would be to design better confidence and filtering mechanisms [8, 14] to limit unnecessary value predictions. Moreover, exploiting new type of value predictions, such as global stride locality [12], may improve the performance ulteriorly.

Acknowledgements. Thanks to the reviewers for their insight and helpful suggestions. This research is supported by the National Natural Science Foundation of China, NO. 90307001.

References

1.   M. H. Lipasti, C. B. Wilkerson, and J. P. Shen. Value Locality and Load Value Prediction. Proceedings of VIIth International Conference on Architectural Support for Programming Languages and Operating Systems (ASPLOS- VII), 1996
2.   M. H. Lipasti and J. P. Shen. Exceeding the Dataflow Limit via Value Prediction. Proceedings of 29th International Symposium on Microarchitecture (MICRO-29), 1996: 226-237
3.   M. H. Lipasti and J. Shen. Exploiting Value Locality to Exceed the Dataflow Limit. International Journal of Parallel Programming, Vol. 28, No. 4, August 1998: 505-538
4.   K. Wang and M. Franklin. Highly Accurate Data Value Prediction using Hybrid Predictors. Proc. of the 30th Annual International Symp. on Microarchitecture, Dec. 1997: 281-290
5.   B. Rychlik, J. Faitl, B. Krug, J. P. Shen. Efficacy and Performance Impact of Value Prediction. Proceedings of International Conference on Parallel Architectures and Compilation Techniques, 1998
6.   J. Gonzalez and A. Gonzalez. The Potential of Data Value Speculation to Boost ILP. 12th International Conference on Supercomputing, 1998
7.   Y. Sazeides. Modeling value prediction. 8th International Symposium on High Performance Computer Architecture (HPCA-8), 2002
8.   B. Calder, G. Reinman, and D. Tullsen. Selective Value Prediction. Proceedings of the 26th Annual International Symposium on Computer Architecture, June 1999

9.   F. Gabbay and A. Mendelson. The Effect of Instruction Fetch Bandwidth on Value Prediction. 25th International Symposium on Computer Architecture (ISCA), 1998: 272-281

10. Y. F. Wu, D. Y. Chen, and J. Fang. Better Exploration of Region-Level Value Locality with Integrated Computation Reuse and Value Prediction. ISCA-28, July 2001

11. S. J. Lee, Y. Wang, and P. C. Yew. Decoupled value prediction on trace processors. In 6th International Symposium on High Performance Computer Architecture, Jan. 2000: 231-240

12. H. Zhou, J. Flanagan, and T. M. Conte. Detecting Global Stride Locality in Value Streams. The 30th ACM/IEEE International Symposium of Computer Architecture (ISCA-30), June 2003

13. S. J. Lee, P. C. Yew. On Some Implementation Issues for Value Prediction on Wide-Issue ILP Processors. IEEE PACT 2000: 145-156

14. R. Bhargava, L. K. John. Performance and Energy Impact of Instruction-Level Value Predictor Filtering. First Value-Prediction Workshop (VPW1) [held with ISCA'03], June 2003: 71-78

15. D. C. Burger, T. M. Austin. The SimpleScalar Tool Set, Version 2.0. Technical Report CSTR-97-1342, University of Wisconsin, Madison, June 1997.

16. S. J. Lee. Data Value Predictors. http://www.simplescalar.com/

Heterogeneous Networks of Workstations

SunHo Baek[1], KyuHo Lee[1], JunSeong Kim[1], and John Morris[1,2]

[1] School of Electrical and Electronics Engineering,
Chung-Ang University, Seoul 156-756, Korea
[2] Department of Electrical and Electronic Engineering,
The University of Auckland, New Zealand

Abstract. Parallel systems built from commodity CPUs and networking devices (Networks of Workstations or NoW) are easily and economically constructed. Rapid technological change means that as elements are added to or replaced in such a system, it will inevitably become heterogeneous.

This paper examines issues in effectively using all the processing power of a heterogeneous NoW system. In particular, it examines the use of two different parallel programming models: MPI, a popular message passing system and Cilk, an extension to C with dataflow semantics. We consider both the performance of the two systems for a set of simple benchmarks representative of real problems and the ease of programming these systems. We show that, in many cases, Cilk both performs better than MPI and, additionally, that it requires less programming effort to write programs that exploit the full power of a heterogeneous system.

1   Introduction

Demand for personal computers has led to production volumes that have meant that the most cost-effective way to obtain raw processing power is to buy commodity personal computers. The de facto requirement that most personal computers are connected to networks of some type has also meant that networking hardware (interfaces, routers, switches, *etc.*) is also readily available and economic. Thus potentially powerful, but economic, parallel processors or Networks of Workstations (NoWs) can be built from commodity PCs. In this paper, we focus on systems built from commodity components containing only very small numbers (say 1-2) processors on each system bus. Thus we assume either no or very limited shared memory.

Rapid and continual technological advances also mean that more powerful processors are almost continually available as manufacturers release new, faster processor chips. Volume production of personal computers allows manufacturers to rapidly incorporate the faster chips into systems - in fact, for many manufacturers the ability to release a system incorporating a faster processor as soon as the new CPU chip is available is vital for survival. Thus, unless a system has been put together from identical processors over a very short period of time, it will inevitably be a heterogeneous one: as processors are added or replaced,

P.-C. Yew and J. Xue (Eds.): ACSAC 2004, LNCS 3189, pp. 426–439, 2004.
© Springer-Verlag Berlin Heidelberg 2004

the downward pressure on prices means that more cost-effective processors are available. After quite a short period of time, it may even become impossible to locate processors matching the original components of a NoW: in today's market, processors that lag behind the state-of-art quickly become 'obsolete' - despite having considerable processing capability.

If the parallel processing run-time system (which could be a message passing one such as MPI[1], one which creates an illusion of shared memory[2] or the RTS supporting Cilk's dataflow mode of operation[3]) naively distributes equal amounts of work to each processor in a heterogeneous NoW, then the presence of a final barrier at which results from all sub-calculations are gathered together to generate the ultimate result leads to an n-processor system equivalent, at best, to n of the slowest processors. Parallel processing overheads will inevitably reduce the NoW system's power to considerably less than this. This obviously represents a considerable waste of resources in a system where the power of individual processors may vary by a factor of 10 or more. Thus, the ability to effectively exploit the more powerful processors in a heterogeneous system is important: it allows efficient systems to be built, maintained and augmented. Heterogeneity may come from sources other than raw CPU clock speed. Cache sizes and speeds, the mix of processing units in a superscalar, bus speeds, peripheral interface efficiency (particularly network cards) and memory speed and capacity may all change the 'power' of one element of a NoW relative to another. Relative powers are also problem dependent, so that simple load balancing schemes that rely on knowledge of relative processing powers are unlikely to be effective over a wide range of problems - as well as requiring significant set up or calibration effort.

1.1   Message Passing Run-Time Systems

A message passing run-time system provides one basic capability - the ability to send a message from one process to another. Thus the RTS needs to provide **send** and **receive** primitives. Generally, these will provide synchronization also: a process will block on a **receive** until the sending process has executed the **send**, synchronizing two threads of computation as well as transferring data. Providing very low level semantic support, message passing systems require more programmer effort to manage data, threads of computation and synchronization. This is usually reflected in higher program complexity - confirmed by our measurements in Section 3.6.

1.2   Cilk's Dataflow Model

Although Cilk is an extension of a weakly typed programming language, it has a strong semantic model. Only when all their data is available, do threads 'fire' (become ready for execution) Thus Cilk programs are data-driven as far as the main computational units - the threads - are concerned and control-driven within each thread. A quite small extension to C, Cilk is easy to learn but its safety (based on the strict dataflow model) is compromised by the ability to use C pointers (particularly global ones). On the other hand, it is able to leverage extensive experience in optimizing C compilers. A safer version of Cilk - Dataflow Java - has been implemented and has been demonstrated to run in fully heterogeneous environments consisting of processors running different operating systems[4], but its performance could not match that of C-based Cilk.

2 Experiments

Programs for several simple problems were written in both C using an MPI library[5] and Cilk. Some of the problems had parameters other than the basic problem size which could be used to change the characteristics (numbers and sizes of messages needed to transfer data between processors) and thus fully explore the relative efficiencies of various strategies.

The essential characteristics of the problems used are described in the following sections. The major basis for comparison was the speedup attainable for a suitably large (and therefore interesting!) problem.

In addition to measuring performance, we assessed program complexities by counting lines of code (separated into 'core' algorithm code and support code, *e.g.* code to manage work queues) and variables used. We also examined the effort needed to change a basic problem solution to better use the heterogeneous environment and report the gains resulting from these changes.

MPI lends itself to simple work distribution schemes in which fixed blocks of compuation are sent to individual processing engines (PEs). Prediction of the optimum block size in a heterogeneous NoW environment is not a simple task: we measured the relative performance of the PEs in our testbed when solving the test problems and observed a range of relative 'powers' (*cf.* Table 1). Thus any assumption of fixed powers is treacherous. We partly overcame this problem by probing: each PE was asked to solve the problem individually and the performance factors used to determine load balancing factors. Using these factors produced, as expected, much better speedups: without them (*i.e.* with equal work loads) the system was essentially constrained to be n copies of the slowest processor. However, conflicts for the communications network, queuing of large packets, *etc.*, mean that simple pre-determined loading factors are not ideal: better results can be obtained with dynamic load balancing schemes. The Cilk RTS's 'work-stealing' mode of operation is well suited to this and can lead to near-optimum use of the system (*cf.* Figure 3). It's ability to create work on slave processors further helps load balancing. To achieve a similar effect with MPI, we built a small work packet management suite of routines, which were sufficiently generic that they could be used with many problems. They provided a simple queue to which work descriptors could be added by the work generator (usually the master PE) and extracted for despatch to slaves as needed. Because this suite could have been transferred to a library and used without further alteration for many problems, its code was tallied separately in the code volume comparisons (see Table 2).

2.1   Fibonacci

We used the naive recursive algorithm taught in every course on recursive programming and then dumped by courses on algorithms and complexity! It is simple, provides a simple demonstration of the difficulties of MPI *vs* Cilk programming and can be parameterized to generate a wide range of loads on the underlying communications system by adjusting the depth at which new parallel computation threads are spawned.

2.2   Travelling Salesman Problem (TSP)

A classic 'hard' problem, TSP requires a search through $n!$ permutations of a list. As with Fibonacci, a simple recursive program solves the problem. In parallel, good speed-ups are trivially obtained with little communication overhead by despatching sub-tours to be evaluated to individual PEs. The cost matrix is moderately large ($\mathcal{O}(n^2)$), but it only needs to be distributed to each PE once. Sub-tour descriptors are short integer lists requiring short messages. An optimization distributes the cost of the best tour obtained so far to all PEs, enabling unprofitable searches (a sub-tour is already longer than the best tour found so far) to be abandoned. This optimization dramatically speeds up execution although it generates more messages to stress the RTS/communication system.

2.3   N-Queens Problem

Another 'hard' problem, $N - Queens$ requires an exhaustive search to find all the possible placements of non-threatening queens on an $N \times N$ chess-board. It has no set-up costs (*e.g.* distribution of a cost matrix for TSP) and spawns $\mathcal{O}(N)$ threads recursively at every stage: thus it has a 'pure' recursive code solution. It seeks to find all the possible placements, so does not have a cut-off optimization like TSP. Parallel overhead can be reduced in the Cilk version by introducing a sequential depth - or point at which no more threads are spawned (as with Fibonacci).

2.4   Matrix Multiplication

A simple, but important problem, matrix multiplication (MM) is trivially parallelized by dividing one of the operand matrices into bands and computing sub-products on each PE. The other operand matrix is distributed to all PEs in the initialization phase. It has $\mathcal{O}(n^2)$ communication cost and $\mathcal{O}(n^3)$ computation cost: with modern fast CPUs and relatively slow networks, this implies that speedup will only be observed with matrices large enough to overcome fixed overheads. Large blocks of data are also transmitted: in our test problem, a 6Mbyte block of data must be transferred to each PE at startup. Note that the algorithm tested here starts with the two operand matrices on a 'master' PE and finishes with the product on the same PE. Other work assumes distributed operand and product matrices: for example, Beaumont *et al.*'s study showed how to find an effective allocation in a heterogenous environment[6].

2.5   Finite Differencing

This problem solves Laplace's equation in a discrete form by updating a cell with the average of the four nearest-neighbour cells. One application is determination of heat flow through a conducting plate. The plate is represented by a rectangular matrix of cells. Each PE is assigned a band of cells (a set of rows of the matrix) to solve. The problem is solved iteratively: it converges when the cell values in successive iterations change by less than some accuracy criterion. Rows of boundary cells are shared between nearest neighbours: in each iteration each PE only needs to update its two neighbours with new cell values. This allows several synchronization schemes. The simplest one uses a 'master' PE. Each PE sends a signal to the master when its neighbours' boundaries have been updated[1]. It also sends a signal to the master which advises whether the band has converged or not. When the master has received all the synchronization signals, if any of the bands is yet to converge, the master signals each PE to calculate one more iteration. An alternative scheme synchronizes between nearest neighbours only, allowing a degree of asynchronous processing - processors may overlap computation and boundary value communication more efficiently. A further scheme allows the individual processors to run completely asynchronously: each PE will commence a new iteration whether boundary updates have arrived from neighbours or not. Boundary updates are despatched to neighbours when they are available.

Table 1. Characteristics of our NoW testbed

Name	Clock MHz	Memory Mbytes	Relative Power	OS Linux
ant1-6	400(P-II)	128	1.00	v7.3
ant7-8	450(P-III)	128	1.07-1.10	v7.3
ant9-10	800(P-III)	128	1.94-2.45	v9.0
ant11-16	800(P-III)	128	1.74-2.44	v7.3

2.6   Test Bed

Following usual practice when building NoW systems, we begged and borrowed a collection of PCs of varying ages and capabilities. Components were replaced as necessary to build working systems, not to produce a homogeneous system. The memory of each system was increased to at least 128Mbytes. Again, no attempt was made to ensure equality or fairness - except with respect to the minimum amount of memory. None of the programs had working sets large enough to cause significant amounts of paging. None of the benchmark programs used the disc system for anything except initial program loading (which was not included in

---

[1] An error in Cilk's specification was discovered when this program was written: see Appendix A.

the timed results) and trivial amounts of result logging. Thus the performance (or lack of it) of individual discs did not affect the results. Note that the Cilk program distribution system adds PEs to the system in the order in which they responded to the initial broadcast. No attempt was made to control this order as it mimics a real heterogeneous system in which PEs have been upgraded as old components were replaced. One of the slower processors was always used as the master and speedups are always referred to it. This arrangement is the optimal one for MPI where the simplest programming solution often uses a master PE for synchronization and data distribution but not for any significant amounts of computation.

3   Results

With a heterogeneous NoW, there are two possible bases for measuring speedup:

- simply counting PEs (*i.e.* making them all equal) so that for 16 PEs, a speedup of 16 is ideal, and
- weighting them by their 'raw' powers, *cf.* Table 1.

Thus two target speedup lines have been placed on speedup graphs - 'Basic speedup' assumes that all PEs are equal and 'Possible speedup' considers individual PE powers. In our system, the potential speedup for 16 PEs relative to the slowest PE was ~ 25: it is slightly problem dependent due mainly to differing cache utilization.

3.1   Fibonacci

This problem has the finest grain parallelism of all those tested: thus parallel overheads are quite high. To contain these overheads, the level at which new threads are spawned was controlled in both cases. For Cilk, this involved four additional lines of code. In the MPI version, the generation of sub-tasks for distribution has to stop at some level - otherwise most of the work goes into generating them! Thus no speedup can be observed at all without controlling this level, and so it is built into the general programming overhead. Figure 1 shows the results for the optimum spawning level for each system size (*i.e.* number of PEs). Cilk generally shows a slight performance edge: the speedup difference is very small for small numbers of PEs (with MPI occasionally being slightly faster), but for larger systems, Cilk consistently produces measurably better results.

Noting that the spawning level essentially controls the computational cost of a thread: a lower spawning level generates fewer, more expensive threads, we examined the effect of the spawning level on performance. Figure 2 shows that although the returns are diminishing, a large number of smaller cost threads increases performance. For $fib(43)$, $sp_{level} = 13 \rightarrow 8192$ threads - or considerably more than would be expected to be needed to keep 16 PEs busy. A simple model which ensured that the slowest processor received, say 10, packets and the faster

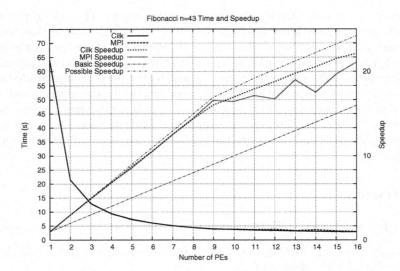

Fig. 1. Times and speedup for Fibonacci

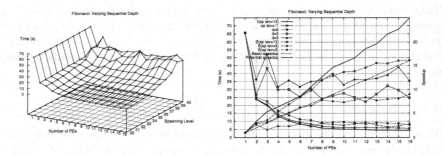

Fig. 2. Fibonacci: Effect of varying the spawning level

ones proportionately more - so that a time within 10% of the optimum was obtained requires only 250 packets for our system. However, going from $sp_{level} = 11 \rightarrow sp_{level} = 13$ (or 2048 $\rightarrow$ 8192 threads) produces a 20% improvement in time for 16 PEs (*cf.* Figure 2(b)).

With large numbers of threads (representing small work quanta) spawned, idle-initiated work-stealing in the Cilk RTS ensures that the heterogeneous system is efficiently used. Small work quanta are always available to a PE which becomes idle. However, if every PE is busy, they are executed locally with no communication overhead.

3.2   Travelling Salesman Problem

The unoptimized version of TSP shows excellent speedups because each spawned thread at the top level represents a large amount of work for a small communication effort. The results are shown in Figure 3(a). For Cilk, speedups approached the potential speedup. Note again the importance of creating sufficient threads, as Figure 3(a) shows, significant improvement is obtained by increasing the sequential depth from 3 to 4, which increases the number of threads generated from 990 to 7920. The unoptimized Cilk program is particularly simple: the core has only two parallel statements, one to spawn the initial thread and the other to spawn threads to work on sub-tours. Two `sync` statements are also needed[2]. The MPI version did not distribute the generated sub-computations in as efficient a way as the Cilk program and its speedup suffered.

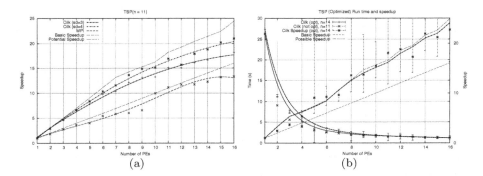

Fig. 3. TSP (a) unoptimized, $n = 11$ (b) $n = 14$(optimized) compared with $n = 11$(unoptimized)
Speedup - maximum speedup obtainable for n equal machines
Possible speedup - maximum speedup considering individual PE capabilities
Note the large variation in times for the optimized algorithm - reflecting the number of asynchronous processes present! Results from this optimization are very sensitive to the the order in which sub-tours are evaluated leading to the occasional 'super-linear' speedups seen here.

An optimization to the simple TSP program broadcasts the best tour found so far to all other processors. PEs use this value to cut off unprofitable searches in which a sub-tour cost is already greater than the best tour seen already. Whilst not altering the fundamental hard nature of the problem, it dramatically increases the rate at which the search is carried out by cutting off large portions of the search space: we observed speedups of nearly three orders of magnitude using it - enabling a 14-city problem to be solved in about the same time as the unoptimized version solves a 11-city one. However, it does generate a large number of additional messages which affects the speedups shown in Figure 3(b).

---

[2] The Cilk compiler could infer the need for these from a simple dataflow analysis of the code (detecting definition-use pairs), but its authors presumably considered that a programmer could do a better job of deciding the optimum placement of the minimum number of `sync`'s.

Adding this optimization to the Cilk programs was simple: a global variable was created which stores the cost of the best tour found on any processor. When a PE finds a better tour, it spawns a thread to update this value on each other PE. Several PEs might be doing this at any time, but Cilk's run-time model ensures that once a thread is started, it runs to completion, so that all these update threads are run in some order on each PE. The thread simply checks to ensure that it does not replace a better minimum cost that some other PE may have found. Two spawn statements (one ensures that the global best cost is initialized correctly on each PE, the other updates the best cost) and 6 lines of additional code suffice to produce a dramatic speedup.

3.3   N-Queens Problem

Cilk's ability to generate large numbers of threads ensures good utilization of all the PEs and speedups which are close to optimal and slightly better than MPI's. As with the other MPI implementations, a fixed number of computations were allocated to each PE. Using relative PE powers to determine how many computations are assigned to each PE is complicated by the fact that spawned computations represent different amounts of work - some positions are declared impossible at a high level in the tree and generate no further computation. In Cilk, this does not affect efficient load balancing because if a large amount of work is stolen by a slow PE, it will spawn several threads, some of which may be stolen by faster PEs. Again, larger numbers of work packets benefited the MPI implementation and brought its performance close to that of the Cilk version.

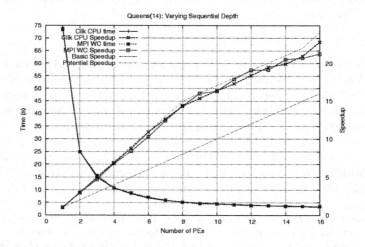

Fig. 4. Times and speedup for N-Queens $n = 14$

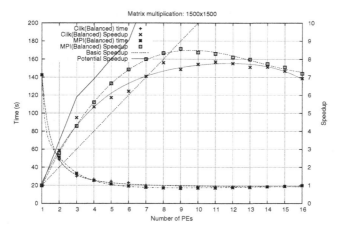

Fig. 5. Times and speedup for Matrix Multiplication

3.4 Matrix Multiplication

Since matrix multiplication is very regular with simple, predictable load patterns, it might be expected that MPI's direct message passing would have lower overheads and produce better results. However, in a previous study[7], Cilk performed better: this was attributed to Cilk's synchronize-in-any-order dataflow model resulting in cheaper synchronization for the final result. We repeated these experiments for the current heterogeneous system with several different approaches to load balancing: equal loads and balanced (or power-weighted) loads (with no work stealing). As expected, for this problem, the equal loads approach performs poorly when individual PE powers vary by a factor of ~ 2.44 and so we present only balanced load results.

Cilk programs exhibited slightly higher speedups with small numbers of PEs ($n \leq 3$). With a small number of large messages, out of order completion has relatively more effect and Cilk performs slightly better. However as the individual slice computation time and message size drops, delays introduced by the strict read order imposed by our MPI program become less significant and MPI's simple direct message-passing model produces higher speedups. Speedups reached peaked at 11 PEs with Cilk (vs 9 PEs with MPI): reflecting the increased competition for the common network in the initialization and completion stages of the algorithm. Thus for small systems, Cilk was able to perform better, but MPI's best performance was significantly better than Cilk's.

3.5 Finite Differencing

The simple, regular communication patterns required for this problem match MPI's capabilities well and this is reflected in the superior performance of MPI using the simplest master synchronization scheme. Even an elaborate distributed

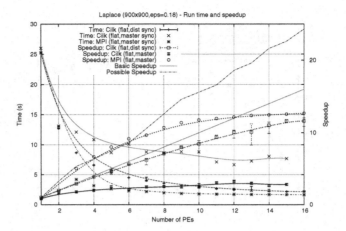

Fig. 6. Time and speedup for several variants of finite differencing program

synchronization scheme in which each PE only synchronized with its two neighbours did not allow Cilk to match the MPI results. Comparing the Cilk results for the two synchronization styles is a textbook example of the cost of synchronization in parallel systems! We did not implement the same scheme in MPI[3].
Although there is a simple dataflow solution to this problem, it is usually avoided as it requires unnecessary data copying. Our Cilk implementation used Cilk's ability to provide Active Messages[8] for the boundary updates and global pointers to the data arrays on each PE. This is a significant departure from Cilk's underlying dataflow model, so it is not surprising that its performance suffers.

3.6   Program Complexity

Whilst they are far from perfect metrics, we used counts of lines of code (LOC) and variables to provide some estimate of relative programming difficulty. The counts in Table 2 are for the 'core' code that solves the problem. Code that generated the test data set and code used for instrumentation (timing or measuring other aspects of performance, *e.g.* counting iterations in Laplace) was not included. The tallies were divided into two groups: basic code needed to solve the problem (code that would be present in a sequential version of the same problem) and parallel overhead - code to initialize and configure the system, create threads, transmit data, synchronize, *etc. Disclaimer: software metrics is not an exact science!*[4] The figures provided here are very basic and simply provide an

---

[3] Our time was consumed by the absence of a 'kill' instruction (to invalidate all spawned waiting threads when convergence has been reached) to support the Cilk RTS' requirement for all threads to fire and complete!

[4] Our counts were generated by hand: we considered that the additional effort required to remove instrumentation and diagnostic code in order to use a tool to obtain more sophisticated counts was unwarranted.

Table 2. Code complexities

Problem	Cilk Algorithm LOC	var	Cilk Overhead LOC	var	MPI Algorithm LOC	var	MPI Overhead LOC	var	Lib LOC
Fibonacci	6	2	1	0					a
+seq depth	10	2	3	1	7	3	12	5	52
TSP	20	13	9	0					a
+seq depth	23	13	9	1	18	10	14	6	59
+opt	30	14	9	1					b
MM	9	6	27	21	9	6	11	6	51
N-Queens	19	13	2	1					a
+seq depth	26	12	2	2	19	10	11	4	55
Laplace									
master synch	17	10	42	44	15	6	18	2	
dist synch	30	5	20	10					b

Notes: (a) Sequential depth optimization is fundamental to MPI version.
(b) Not implemented.

indication of programming effort. A small amount of 'noise' - in the form of individual programming style - was also added by the several authors of the programs used. However, the lower parallel programming overhead of Cilk is clear: by providing a simple semantic model, it provides considerably more support for a programmer than MPI. It is also notable that some of the optimizations are trivially added to Cilk programs.

With MPI, in order to obtain good speedups, it was necessary to build simple lists of 'work packets' which were distributed to each PE. The code to manage these queues has been included in the column marked 'Library' in Table 2 because generic code for this could be placed in a library so that each program could only see **create, add** and **get** methods: effectively these methods would become part of the MPI library.

4 Conclusion

With the exception of the finite differencing program, Cilk versions of the programs were considerably easier to write. Implicit synchronization using a dataflow model means fewer statements directing parallel execution are needed. Most Cilk programs (fib, TSP and N-queens in the set used here) will run on any number of processors (including a single PE) without any explicit consideration of the current size of the NoW system. The program that we used for distributing Cilk programs to individual PEs simply counts the number of PEs responding to a broadcast request and the RTS uses this number when making work stealing requests: thus Cilk programs work well in 'flexible' environments - where the number of PEs may change from day to day. The implicit generation of large numbers of threads by Cilk programs also leads to superior speedup numbers in heterogeneous environments. In cases where explicit distribution of work to

PEs is appropriate because obvious simple distribution policies are readily coded (MM, Laplace), both Cilk and MPI require similar numbers of statements, *i.e.* MPI has no significant advantage when it might be expected to have one.

When a strict dataflow model requires excessive data copying (Laplace), MPI both allows (slightly) simpler implementations and provides better performance. We note that both systems are C-based, so that hybrid programs which, for example, used Cilk's dataflow model when it was effective and MPI's 'direct' transfer of data from source to destination when it provided better performance, could readily be put together.

We speculate that the best way to improve the performance of MPI programs - particularly in heterogeneous environments - is to simulate Cilk's idle-initiated work stealing mode of operation: generating large numbers of relatively fine-grained work packets which are distributed to PEs on demand, *i.e.* as they become idle. However to fully emulate Cilk's flexibility - threads can be spawned and stolen from any PE - would require duplicating a large part of the Cilk RTS. It would seem more efficient to simply use the Cilk RTS!

Acknowledgements. John Morris was supported by the Foreign Professors Invitation Program of the Korean IT Industry Promotion Agency at Chung Ang University in 2003-4.

References

1. Snir, M.: MPI: The complete reference. MIT Press, MA: Cambridge, USA (1996)
2. Amza, C., Cox, A.L., Dwarkadas, S., Keleher, P., Lu, H., Rajamony, R., Yu, W., Zwaenepoel, W.: TreadMarks: Shared Memory Computing on Networks of Workstations. IEEE Computer **29** (1996) 18–28
3. Blumofe, R.D., Joerg, C.F., Kuszmaul, B.C., Leiserson, C.E., Randall, K.H., Zhou, Y.: Cilk: an efficient multithreaded runtime system. In: PPoPP'95, Santa Barbara (1995)
4. Lee, G., Morris, J.: Dataflow Java: Implicitly parallel Java. In: Proceedings of the Australasian Computer Systems Architecture Conference. (1998) 42–50
5. Gropp, W., Lusk, E., Doss, N., Skjellum, A.: A high-performance, portable implementation of the MPI message passing interface standard. Parallel Computing **22** (1996) 789–828
6. Beaumont, O., Boudet, V., Rastello, F., Robert, Y.: Matrix multiplication on heterogeneous platforms. IEEE Transactions on Parallel and Distributed Systems **12** (2001) 1033–1051
7. Tham, C.K.: Achilles: A high bandwidth, low latency, low overhead network interconnect for high performance parallel processing using a network of workstations. PhD thesis, The University of Western Australia (2003)
8. von Eicken, T., Culler, D.E., Goldstein, S.C., Schauser, K.E.: Active Messages: a Mechanism for Integrated Communication and Computation. In: Proceedings of the 19th Annual International Symposium on Computer Architecture, Gold Coast, Australia. (1992) 256–266

A   Cilk Signals

When writing the master synchronous version of the Laplace program, an error was discovered in the implementation of Cilk. The language specifies a `signal` which can be used to fire threads without transferring a data value. The syntax adopted allows the number of signals needed to fire a thread to be specified when it is spawned, *e.g.*

```
cont signal s;
spawn SynchThread( ?s{n}, ... );
```

The thread `SynchThread` will be fired after n signals have been sent to it. The continuation s may be sent as an argument to several threads:

```
cont signal s;
for(pe=0;pe<m;pe++)
spawn CompThread( s, ... )@pe;
```

Note that the cardinality of the signal is not passed to `CompThread`: each instance of it may send as many signals as it likes to `SynchThread`. As long as `SynchThread` receives n signals, it will eventually fire. This presents no problem unless `CompThread` passes the continuation to a thread which is executed (by stealing or explicit allocation) on another processor. When threads with continuations migrate, Cilk versions from 2.0 on, have created a **stub** on the executing processor and altered the continuation to address this stub. However, the stub does not know how many signals it will be expected to pass to the original thread, so it destroys itself after sending one signal. In the Laplace program, each iteration sends *two* signals back to the master's synchronization thread when the boundaries of the two neighbouring PEs are updated.

We solved this problem by

- defining a new `ArgCont` type which was used to transfer a continuation to another thread and
- creating a simple `SendSignal` thread which was used to transfer the signal back to the master processor.

Use of the `ArgCont` type prevented the Cilk pre-processor from recognizing the parameter as a continuation and creating a stub. The `SendSignal` thread was executed on the master - where the original continuation had been created and was valid.

Finding High Performance Solution in Reconfigurable Mesh-Connected VLSI Arrays

Jigang Wu and Thambipillai Srikanthan

Centre for High Performance Embedded Systems,
School of Computer Engineering,
Nanyang Technological University, Singapore, 639798
{asjgwu, astsrikan}@ntu.edu.sg

Abstract. Given an $m \times n$ mesh-connected VLSI array with some faulty elements, the reconfiguration problem is to find a maximum-sized fault-free sub-array under the row and column rerouting scheme. This problem has already been shown to be NP-complete. The power awareness problem of the reconfigurable array is first proposed in this paper. A heuristic algorithm has been presented for the same. The algorithm is simple but efficient. The performance of the proposed algorithm is more powerful than that of the older algorithm, without loss of harvest.

Keywords: Degradable VLSI array, reconfiguration, heuristic algorithm, fault-tolerance, NP-completeness.

1 Introduction

Area-time efficiency is one of the major considerations in VLSI designs. In recent years, the growth of personal computing devices (portable computers and real time audio and video-based multimedia products) and wireless communication systems (personal digital assistants and mobile phones) has forced designers to make high performance systems that consume less power. This necessitates the need to minimize the number of switches employed to implement the interconnection between two processing nodes during rerouting. Hence, degradable arrays that involve minimal number of switches will provide for higher performance while improving the overall reliability.

Mesh is one of the most thoroughly investigated network topologies for multiprocessors systems. It is of importance due to its simple structure and its good performance in practice and is becoming popular for reliable and high-speed communication switching. It has a regular and modular structure and allows fast implementation of many signal and image processing algorithms. With the advancement in VLSI technologies, integrated systems for mesh-connected processors can now be built on a single chip or wafer. As the density of VLSI arrays increases, probability of the occurrence of defects in the arrays during fabrication also increases. These defects obviously affect the reliability of the whole system. Thus, fault-tolerant technologies must be employed to enhance the yield and reliability of this mesh systems.

P.-C. Yew and J. Xue (Eds.): ACSAC 2004, LNCS 3189, pp. 440–448, 2004.
© Springer-Verlag Berlin Heidelberg 2004

Reconfiguration in a mesh structure has been investigated extensively, *e.g.*, [1-8] for redundancy approach and [9-12] for degradation approach. However, no previous work has been carried out in order to provide high performance sub-mesh for degradable VLSI arrays with faults. This paper proposes the problem of finding a fault-free sub-array which demonstrate higher performance in a two-dimensional mesh-connected VLSI arrays. A simple but efficient heuristic algorithm is proposed, which has higher performance requirements, while maintaining the same harvest.

2   Preliminaries

Let *host array H* be the original array obtained after manufacturing. Some of the elements in this array may be defective. A *target array T* is a fault-free sub-array of *H* after reconfiguration. The rows (columns) in the host array and target array are called the *physical row (columns)* and *logical rows (columns)*, respectively.

In this paper all the assumptions in architecture are the same as that in [9-12]. Neighboring elements are connected to each other by a four-port switch. A target array *T* is said to *contain* $\{R_1, R_2, \cdots, R_k\}$ if each logical column in *T* contains exactly one fault-free element from each of the rows. The previous problem and the related algorithms are as follows.

Problem $\mathcal{R}P$: *Given an $m \times n$ mesh-connected host array, find a maximal sized target array under the row and column rerouting scheme that contains the selected rows.*

The problem $\mathcal{R}P$ is optimally solved in linear time. Low proposed an algorithm, called *Greedy Column Rerouting (GCR)*, to solve $\mathcal{R}P$[10, 11]. Let $col(u)$ and $col(v)$ denote the physical column index of the element u and v, respectively. All operations in *GCR* are carried out on the adjacent sets of each fault-free element u in the row R_i, defined as

$Adj(u) = \{v : v \in R_{i+1}, v \text{ is fault-free and } |col(u) - col(v)| \leq 1\}$.

The elements in $Adj(u)$ are ordered in increasing column numbers for each $u \in R_i$ and for each $i \in \{1, 2, \cdots, k - 1\}$.

GCR constructs the target array in a left-to-right manner. It begins by selecting the leftmost fault-free element, say u, of the row R_1 for inclusion into a logical column. Next, the leftmost element in $Adj(u)$, say v, is connected to u. This process is repeated until a logical column is fully constructed. In each iteration, *GCR* produces the current leftmost logical column. A detailed description of *GCR* can be found in [11]. Theorem 1 describes the properties of the *GCR* algorithm.

Theorem 1.   *GCR solves the problem $\mathcal{R}P$ in linear time and produces the maximal sized target array*[11].

As shown in Fig. 1, there are 6 possible types of link-ways for a target array. They can be categorized into two classes based on the number of the switches used. In this paper, a link-way that uses only one switch to connect neighboring elements in a target array is called a *regular link-way*, while a link-way using two switches is called an *irregular link-way*. In Fig. 1, (a) and (d) are regular link-ways, but the others are irregular. (a), (b) and (c) are used for row rerouting, while (d), (e) and (f) are used for column rerouting. Obviously, the smaller the number of irregular link-ways the target array has, the lesser is the system delay, and therefore, the higher the performance.

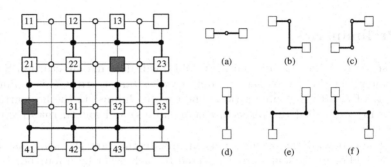

Fig. 1. A target array and its possible link-ways.

In this paper, the maximal sized target array with the minimal number of irregular link-ways is called the high performance target array or high performance solution. The problem that we proposed is described as follows.

Problem $\mathcal{HP}$: *Given an $m \times n$ mesh-connected host array, find a high performance solution under the row and column rerouting scheme that contains the selected rows.*

We aim to propose a heuristic algorithm to solve this optimization problem in this paper.

Given a host array H of size $m \times n$, let U be the set of logical columns that pass through each of the rows. Thus, each logical column in U contains exactly one fault-free element from each of the rows. Furthermore, the ith element in each logical column resides in row R_i, for each $i = 1, 2, \cdots, m$. We define a partial order on the logical columns in U as follows.

Definition 1. *For any two logical columns, C_p and C_q in U, and $p \neq q$,*

1. *we say that $C_p < C_q$ if the ith element in C_p lies to the left of the ith element in C_q, for $1 \leq i \leq m$.*
2. *We say that $C_p \leq C_q$ if the ith element in C_p lies to the left of, or is identical to, the ith element in C_q, for $1 \leq i \leq m$.*
3. *We say that C_p and C_q are independent, if $C_p < C_q$ or $C_p > C_q$.*

Assume $\mathcal{B}_l, \mathcal{B}_r \in U$ and $\mathcal{B}_l \leq \mathcal{B}_r$. We use $\mathcal{A}[\mathcal{B}_l, \mathcal{B}_r]$ to indicate the area consisted of the fault-free elements bounded by $\mathcal{B}_l$ and $\mathcal{B}_r$ (including $\mathcal{B}_l$ and $\mathcal{B}_r$).

$A[\mathcal{B}_l, \mathcal{B}_r)$ indicates the same area as above including $\mathcal{B}_l$ but not including $\mathcal{B}_r$. $\mathcal{B}_l$ and $\mathcal{B}_r$ are called the left boundary of $A[\mathcal{B}_l, \mathcal{B}_r)$ and the right boundary of $A[\mathcal{B}_l, \mathcal{B}_r)$, respectively.

3 Algorithms

Assume the solution of GCR is the target array T with k logical columns: $C_1, C_2, \cdots, C_k$. We revise each C_i, for $i = 1, 2, \cdots, k$. The proposed algorithm, denoted as $RGCR$ revises the solution of GCR to obtain an approximate high performance solution. It starts from the logical column C_k, revises it and then revises $C_{k-1}, \cdots, C_1$ one by one. In each iteration, $RGCR$ works in $A[\mathcal{B}_l, \mathcal{B}_r)$. In the first iteration, $\mathcal{B}_l$ is set to be C_k, and $\mathcal{B}_r$ is set to be a virtual column that lies to the right of the nth physical column of the host array.

In $RGCR$, a priority to each element $v \in Adj(u)$ is assigned according to the following function for each $u \in R_i$, and for each $i \in \{1, 2, 3, \cdots, m\}$.

$$Pri(v) = \begin{cases} 1, & \text{if } col(v) - col(u) = -1, \\ 3, & \text{if } col(v) - col(u) = 0. \\ 2, & \text{if } col(v) - col(u) = 1, \end{cases}$$

Suppose, the element $u \in C_k$ and it has the largest physical column index (it is the rightmost element) in the logical column C_k. In each iteration, the algorithm $RGCR$ calls a procedure $REROUT$ to revise the current logical column. $RGCR$ starts off with $(0, col(u))$ as the start element for rerouting. The highest priority element in $Adj(u)$, say v, is connected to u. This process is repeated such that in each step, $REROUT$ attempts to connect the current element v to the highest priority element of $Adj(v)$ that has not been previously examined. If $REROUT$ fails in doing so, we cannot form a logical column containing the current element v. In that case, $REROUT$ backtracks to the previous element, say w, that was connected to v and attempts to connect w to the highest priority element of $Adj(w) - v$, that has not been previously examined. This process is repeated until an element w in a row R_i is connected to an element in the next row R_{i+1}. Suppose $REROUT$ backtracks to u and u is an element of the first row, then the next element to be chosen as the starting element for rerouting is the element in $(0, (col(u) + 1)$. And if $REROUT$ fails for this case also, then the element in $(0, (col(u) - 1)$ is chosen to be the starting element for rerouting. Thus the starting element alternates between left and right of $(0, col(u))$. This process is repeated until a logical column is formed. $REROUT$ will stop at the row R_m as at least the left boundary C_k is a feasible logical column. When $REROUT$ terminate in this iteration, a new logical column based on C_k, denoted as C'_k, is obtained. We call C'_k the revised column of C_k.

In the next iteration, $REROUT$ attempts to obtain the revised logical column for C_{k-1}. The left boundary $\mathcal{B}_l$ and the right boundary $\mathcal{B}_r$ are updated to C_{k-1} and the just revised column C'_k, respectively. The revision process terminates when all logical columns $C_1, C_2, \cdots, C_k$ have been revised. The resultant target

```
Boolean REROUT(H, S, curt, Bₗ, Bᵣ, C ');
/* revise the logical column Bₗ from the element curt down to the last row Rₘ */
begin
    repeat
        if there are unmarked elements in Adj(curt) then
        begin
            q := the first priority unmarked element in Adj(curt)
                    and bounded by Bᵣ;
            pred(q) := curt; /* q is connected to curt */
            curt := q;
            mark q;
        end
        else curt := pred(curt); /* backtracking */
    until ((curt ∈ Rₘ)) or (curt ∈ R₁));
    if (curt ∈ Rₘ) then return true;
                else return false;
end.

Algorithm RGCR(H, S, T, T ');
/* revise the target array T to T '. T={C₁, C₂, ..., Cₖ}, T ' ={C'₁, C'₂, ..., C'ₖ}. */
begin
    Bₗ :=Cₖ,  Bᵣ := nil;
    for i := k down to 1 do
    begin
        temp := the column number of the rightmost element in Bₗ;
        curt := the element of column temp and row one;
        C ' := nil;
        While (C ' == nil) do
        begin
            if (REROUT(H, S, curt, Bₗ, Bᵣ, C'))
            then Store the revised column into C ';
            else curt := the closest element to curt (either on right
                        or left) which has not been examined;
        end
        Bₗ := Cᵢ₋₁,  Bᵣ := C'ᵢ;
    end;
end.
```

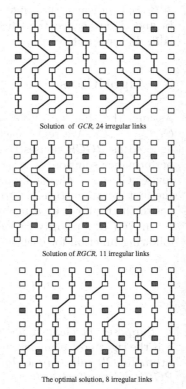

Solution of *GCR*, 24 irregular links

Solution of *RGCR*, 11 irregular links

The optimal solution, 8 irregular links

Fig. 2. The formal descriptions of *REROUT* and *RGCR*. The examples for the solutions of *GCR* and *RGCR* and the corresponding optimal solution for a 8×10 host array with 12 faults.

array, denoted as T', is called the revised target array of T. Fig. 2 shows the detailed description of the algorithm *RGCR*.

It is easy to see that, in rerouting, the selection of the highest priority element for inclusion into a logical column at each step is a greedy choice. Intuitively, it uses as many vertical links (low power interconnects) as possible to form the logical columns. Like *GCR*, it obviously runs in linear time, $i.e.$, the running time of the revision procedure is $O(N)$, $i.e.$ the number of valid interconnections in the host array with N fault-free elements. In addition, there are also k independent logical columns in T' as each revised column C'_i is produced in the area bounded by C_i and C'_{i+1}, $i = 1, 2, \cdots, k$. In other words, the revised algorithm does not decrease the size of the target array constructed by *GCR*. Hence, the harvest remains the same.

To summarize, Fig 2 shows the running results of the algorithms described in this section for a random instance of an 8×10 host array. The slant lines represent the irregular link-ways. The shaded boxes stand for faulty elements and the white ones stand for the fault-free elements. There are 8 irregular link-ways in the optimal solution for this instance. *GCR* produces a solution with 24 irregular link-ways while the proposed algorithm *RGCR* produces a nearly optimal solution with only 11 irregular link-ways.

4   Experimental Results

The proposed algorithms and *GCR* are implemented in C and run on a Pentium IV computer with one GB RAM. Both random fault model and clustered fault model are considered. These are acceptable because the random faults often occur during the system usage in real time configuration, while the clustered faults are typically caused during fabrication process.

The whole experiment is divided into two parts - one is for uniform fault distribution in the whole mesh, which is corresponding to random fault model. In this, the algorithms are run for different sized mesh. And, the other is for the uniform fault distribution in different localized portions of the mesh, which is corresponding to the clustered fault model. In this, the algorithms are run in 256×256 sized array for different fault density. Data are collected for different sized host arrays for three faulty density 0.1%, 1% and 10% of the size of the host array (same as in [11,12]), averaged over 10 random instances with the decimal being rounded off to the lower side in all cases.

Table 1. The performance comparison of the algorithms *GCR* and *RGCR* for uniform fault distribution, average of 10 random instances of different size

Host array		Target array	Performance		
Size	Fault	Size	*GCR*	*RGCR*	
$m \times n$	(%)	$m \times k$	*No.ir*	*No.ir*	*imp*
32×32	0.1	32×31	33	0	100%
32×32	1	32×30	265	76	71%
32×32	10	32×23	452	185	59%
64×64	0.1	64×63	292	59	80%
64×64	1	64×60	1471	403	73%
64×64	10	64×47	1992	885	56%
128×128	0.1	128×126	2012	499	75%
128×128	1	128×122	8168	3038	63%
128×128	10	128×95	8294	4138	50%
256×256	0.1	256×253	13827	3981	71%
256×256	1	256×246	38155	16947	56%
256×256	10	256×193	34167	18510	46%

In Table 1 and Table 2, the attribute *No.ir* denotes the number of the irregular link-ways. *imp* stands for the improvement in *No.ir* over *GCR*. It is calculated by

$$(1 - \frac{No.ir\_of\_RGCR}{No.ir\_of\_GCR}) \times 100\%.$$

In Table 1, data are collected for host arrays of different sizes from 32×32 to 256×256. For each algorithm, for smaller or medium host arrays, $No.ir$ increases with the increase in the number of faulty elements in the host array. This is because that there will be a percentage faulty density beyond which $No.ir$ will fall, as $No.ir$ is equal to 0 both for 0% fault and for 100% fault. While for larger host arrays, $No.ir$ first increases and then decreases due to heavy decrease in target size as the fault density increases beyond a certain point. For example, for GCR, $No.ir$ is 33, 265 and 452 for size 32×32 and fault densities 0.1%, 1% and 10%, respectively. But for size 256×256 and fault densities 0.1%, 1% and 10%, $No.ir$ increase to 13827, 38155 and 34167, respectively.

The improvement of $RGCR$ over GCR is significant, especially for the host arrays of small size or small fault density, which is occurred more frequently in applications. For example, the improvements are 100% and 80% for the size 32×32 with 0.1% faulty elements and for the size 64×64 with the same faulty density, respectively.

Table 2. The performance comparison of the algorithms GCR and $RGCR$ for clustered faulty distribution, average of 10 random instances of different size

Host array		Target array	Performance		
Size	Fault	Size	GCR	$RGCR$	
$m \times n$	(%)	$m \times k$	$No.ir$	$No.ir$	imp
	0.1	256×249	3290	153	95%
1/8	1	256×224	8446	0	100%
	10	NA	NA	NA	NA
	0.1	256×251	5911	542	91%
1/4	1	256×231	10179	842	92%
	10	NA	NA	NA	NA
	0.1	256×252	10175	1620	84%
1/2	1	256×241	16918	4553	73%
	10	256×145	15430	1016	93%
	0.1	256×253	12553	2941	77%
3/4	1	256×244	27090	10338	62%
	10	256×176	26208	8035	69%
	0.1	256×253	13827	3981	71%
whole	1	256×246	38155	16947	56%
	10	256×193	34167	18510	46%

In Table 2, data are collected for 256×256 sized host array, averaged over 10 random instances, each for a localized fault in the center 1/8, 1/4, 1/2, 3/4 and full portion of the host array. Here, center 1/8, 1/4, 1/2, 3/4 and *whole* in Table 2, is the situation when faulty elements are located in center area consisting of $32 * 32$ elements, $64 * 64$ elements, $128 * 128$ elements, $192 * 192$ elements and the full host array, respectively. For center 1/8 and 1/4, considering 10% fault density was not possible as 10% of 256×256 comes out to be 6554 elements, while center 1/8 comes out to be a $32 * 32$ mesh, *i.e.*, 1024 elements, and center

1/4 comes out to be 64×64 mesh, *i.e.*, 4096 elements. So it is clear that these two cannot accommodate 10% faulty elements. Hence, the row for these cases is marked as NA (Not Applicable).

From table 2, we observe that, for 1% faulty density and localized fault in center 1/8 portion of the host array, *No.ir* comes out to be 0. This is because the center gets so much concentrated with the faulty elements that no logical column passes through that portion in which the faulty elements are located. *GCR* is not better for performance because it uses the leftmost strategy. The improvement over *GCR* is more significant for localized fault distribution than for random fault distribution. For example, for 1% fault density, the improvements of *RGCR* for center 1/8 and 1/4 fault distribution are 100% and 92%, respectively. While for the fault distribution in center 3/4 and whole host array, the improvements are 62% and 56%, respectively. In other words, the improvement increases as the spread of faulty elements in the host array decreases.

As can be seen from above tables, for a given percentage of faulty processors in the host array, as the size of the array increases, the number of irregular links in the target array increases. In all the cases, the revised algorithm gives much better results than the older *GCR* algorithm. Even for arrays of a specific size, as the percentage of faulty elements in the array increases, our new algorithm performs much better than the old algorithm. We can therefore say that for all cases our algorithms gives us a high performance solution that consumes much low power than the solutions of the older algorithms like *GCR*.

5   Conclusions

High performance VLSI design has emerged as a major theme in the electronics industry today. It can be achieved at all levels of the VLSI system. In this paper, we have proposed a new problem based on a high performance solution for reconfigurable VLSI arrays and have presented an algorithm for the same. The proposed algorithm is based on a heuristic strategy that is easy to implement. Its performance is very high and the harvest remains unchanged. Experimental results reflect the underlying characteristics of the proposed algorithm.

References

1. T. Leighton and A. E. Gamal. "Wafer-scal Integration of Systoric Arrays", *IEEE Trans. on Computer*, vol. 34, no. 5, pp. 448-461, May 1985.
2. C. W. H Lam, H. F. Li and R. Jakakumar, "A Study of Two Approaches for Reconfiguring Fault-tolerant Systoric Array", *IEEE Trans. on Computers*, vol. 38, no. 6, pp. 833-844, June 1989.
3. I. Koren and A. D. Singh, "Fault Tolerance in VLSI Circuits", *Computer*, vol. 23, no. 7, pp. 73-83, July 1990.
4. Y. Y. Chen, S. J. Upadhyaya and C. H. Cheng, "A Comprehensive Reconfiguration Scheme for Fault-tolerant VLSI/WSI Array Processors", *IEEE Trans. on Computers*, vol. 46, no. 12, pp. 1363-1371, Dec. 1997.

5. T. Horita and I. Takanami, "Fault-tolerant Processor Arrays Based on the 1.5-track Switches with Flexible Spare Distributions", *IEEE Trans. on Computers*, vol. 49, no. 6, pp. 542-552, June 2000.
6. S. Y. Kuo and W. K. Fuchs, "Efficient Spare Allocation for Reconfigurable Arrays", *IEEE Design and Test*, vol. 4, no. 7, pp. 24-31, Feb. 1987.
7. C. L. Wey and F. Lombardi, "On the Repair of Redundant RAM's", *IEEE Trans. on CAD of Integrated Circuits and Systems*, vol. 6, no. 2, pp. 222-231, Mar. 1987.
8. Li Zhang, "Fault-Tolerant meshes with small degree", *IEEE Trans. on Computers*, col. 51, No.5, pp.553-560, May, 2002.
9. S. Y. Kuo and I. Y. Chen, "Efficient reconfiguration algorithms for degradable VLSI/WSI arrays," *IEEE Trans. Computer-Aided Design*, vol. 11, no. 10, pp. 1289-1300, Oct. 1992.
10. C. P. Low and H. W. Leong, "On the reconfiguration of degradable VLSI/WSI arrays," *IEEE Trans. Computer-Aided Design of integrated circuits and systems*, vol. 16, no. 10, pp. 1213-1221, Oct. 1997.
11. C. P. Low, "An efficient reconfiguration algorithm for degradable VLSI/WSI arrays," *IEEE Trans. on Computers*, vol. 49, no. 6, pp.553-559, June 2000.
12. Wu Jigang, Schroder Heiko & Srikanthan Thambipillai, "New architecture and algorithms for degradable VLSI/WSI arrays", in Proc. Of 8th International Computing and Combinatorics Conference, 2002, Singapore (COCOON'02), *Lecture Notes in Computer Science*, vol. 2387, pp.181-190, Aug, 2002.
13. A. V. Aho, J. E. Hopcroft, and J. D. Ullman, "The design and analysis of computer algorithms", Addison-Wesley, Reading, Mass., 1974.

Order Independent Transparency for Image Composition Parallel Rendering Machines

Woo-Chan Park[1], Tack-Don Han[2], and Sung-Bong Yang[2]

[1] Department of Internet Engineering,
Sejong University, Seoul 143-747, Korea,
pwchan@sejong.ac.kr
[2] Department of Computer Science,
Yonsei University, Seoul 120-749 Korea,
{hantack}@kurene.yonsei.ac.kr
{yang}@cs.yonsei.ac.kr

Abstract. In this paper, a hybrid architecture composed of both the object-order and the image-order rendering engines is proposed to achieve the order independent transparency on the image composition architecture. The proposed architecture utilizes the features of the object-order which may provide high performance and the image-order which can obtain the depth order of all primitives from a viewpoint for a given pixel. We will discuss a scalable architecture for image order rendering engines to improve the processing capability of the transparent primitives, a load distribution technique for hardware efficiency, and a preliminary timing analysis.

1 Introduction

3D computer graphics is a core field of study in developing multi media computing environment. In order to support realistic scene using 3D computer graphics, a special purpose high performance 3D accelerator is required. Recently, low cost and high performance 3D graphics accelerators are adopted rapidly in PCs and game machines[1,2,3].

To generate high-quality images, solid models composed of more than several millions polygons are often used. To display such a model at a rate of 30 frames per second, more than one hundred million polygons must be processed in one second. To achieve this goal in current technology, several tens of the graphic processors are required. Thus, parallel rendering using many graphics processors is an essential research issue.

According to [4], graphics machine architectures can be categorized into the three types: *sort-first architecture*, *sort-middle architecture*, *sort-last architecture*. Among them, sort-last architecture is a scalable architecture because the required bandwidth of its communication network is almost constant against the number of polygons. Thus, sort-last architecture is quite suitable for a large-scale rendering system.

P.-C. Yew and J. Xue (Eds.): ACSAC 2004, LNCS 3189, pp. 449–460, 2004.
© Springer-Verlag Berlin Heidelberg 2004

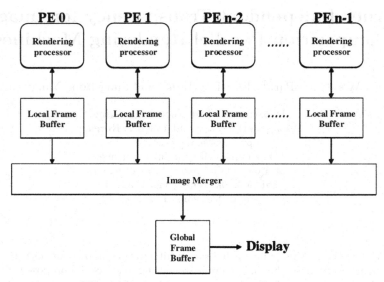

Fig. 1. An image composition architecture

One of the typical sort-last architectures is an image composition architecture [5,6,7,8,9]. Figure 1 shows the overall structure of image composition architecture. All polygonal model data are distributed into each rendering processor which generates a subimage with its own frame buffer, called a local frame buffer. The contents of all the local frame buffers are merged periodically by the image merger. During image merging, the depth comparisons with the contents of the same screen address for each local frame buffer should be performed to accomplish hidden surface removal. The final merged image is then transmitted into the global frame buffer.

In a realistic 3D scene, both opaque and transparent primitives are mixed each other. To generate a rendered final image properly with the transparent primitives, the order dependent transparency problem must be solved. That is, the processing order depends on the depth order by a viewpoint, not on the input order. Order dependent transparency problem may cause the serious performance degradation as the number of transparent primitives increases rapidly. Therefore, the order independent transparency, the opposite concept of the order dependent transparency, is a major for providing high performance rendering systems. But up until now we have not found any parallel 3D rendering machine supporting hardware accelerated order independent transparency.

In this paper, we propose a new method of the hardware accelerated order independent transparency for image composition in the parallel rendering architecture. To achieve this goal, we suggest a hybrid architecture composed of both the object order and the image order rendering engines. The proposed mechanism utilizes the features of the object order which may provide high performance and the image order which can obtain the depth order of all primitives from a viewpoint for a given pixel.

The proposed architecture has n object order rendering engines, from PE 0 to PE n-1 as in Figure 1 and one image order rendering engine, PE n, where n is the number of PEs. All the opaque primitives are allocated with each object order rendering engine. All the transparent primitives are sent to the image order rendering engine. Thus subimages generated from PE 0 to PE n-1 are merged into a single image during image merging. This merged image is fed into the image order rendering engine, PE n. With this single merged image and the information of the transparent primitives, PE n calculates the final image with order independent transparency. We also provide a scalable architecture for the image order rendering engines to improve the processing capability of transparent primitives and load distribution technique for hardware efficiency.

In the next section, we present a brief overview of the object order rendering, the image order rendering, the order independent transparency. Section 3 illustrates the proposed image composition architecture and its pipeline flow. We describe how the proposed architecture handles the order independent transparency. The timing analyses of the image merger and the image order rendering engine, and the scalability are also discussed. Section 4 concludes this paper with future research.

2   Background

In this section, we present a brief overview of the object order rendering and the image order rendering methods. We also discuss the order independent transparency.

2.1   Object Order and Image Order Rendering Methods

Polygonal rendering algorithms can be classified into the object order rendering and the image order rendering according to the rendering processing order for the input primitives [10]. In the object order rendering the processing at the rasterization step is performed primitive by primitive, while in the image order it is done pixel by pixel. According to their features, an object order rendering system is suitable for high performance systems and current design approaches [1,2,3,5,9], while the image order is low cost systems and later approaches [11,12, 13,14]. In most of parallel rendering machines, an object order rendering engine is adopted for each rendering processor for high performance computation.

The rendering process consists of geometry processing, rasterization, and display refresh steps. In an object order rendering system, the processing order at the rasterization step is performed primitive by primitive. Thus the geometry processing and the rasterization steps are pipelined between primitives and the object order rendering and the display refresh steps are pipelined between frames. An object order rendering system must have a full-screen sized frame buffer, consisted of a depth buffer and a color buffer, for hidden surface removal operations. To overlap the executions of the rendering and the screen refresh steps, double buffering for the frame buffer are used. The front frame buffer denotes the frame buffer used in the rendering step and the back frame buffer is used by the screen refresh step. Figure 2 shows the pipeline flow of the object order rendering system between two frames.

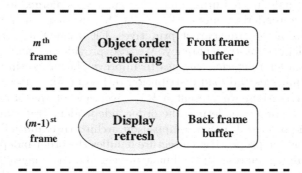

Fig. 2. The pipeline flow of the object order rendering method between two frames

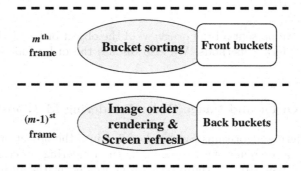

Fig. 3. The pipeline flow of the image order rendering method between two frames

In an image order rendering system, the processing order at the rasterization step is performed pixel by pixel. For example, if the screen address begins from $(0, 0)$ and ends with (v, w), the rasterization step is accomplished from $(0, 0)$ to (v, w). In rendering pixel by pixel, the lists of the all primitives, after geometry transformation, overlaying with a dedicated pixel must be kept for each pixel. These lists are called the *buckets* and bucket sorting denotes this listing. Thus the bucket sorting step including geometry processing and the image order rendering step including screen refresh are pipelined between frames. Figure 3 shows the pipeline flow of the image order rendering system between two frames.

The scan-line algorithm is a typical method of the image order rendering [10]. All primitives transformed into the screen space are assigned into buckets provided per scan-line. To avoid considering primitives that do not contribute to the current scan-line, the scan-line algorithm requires primitives to be transformed into the screen space and to sort the buckets according to the first scan-line in which they appear. After bucket sorting, rendering is performed with respect to each scan-line. Because the finally rendered data are generated by scan-line order, screen refresh can be performed immediately after scan-line rendering. Thus no frame buffer is needed and only a small amount of buffering is required. In this paper, the scan-line algorithm is used in the image order rendering engine.

2.2   Order Independent Transparency

In a realistic 3D scene, both opaque and transparent primitives are mixed each other. To generate a final rendered image properly, the order dependent transparency problem should be solved. Figure 4 shows an example of order dependent transparency with three fragments for a given pixel.

In Figure 4, A is a yellow transparent fragment, B is a blue opaque fragment, and C is a red opaque fragment. We assume that A is followed by B and B is followed by C in the point of depth value for the current view point. Then the final color results in green which is generated by blending the yellow color of A and the blue color of B. However, if the processing order of these three fragments are C, A, and B, then a wrong color will be generated. That is, when C comes first, the current color is red. When A comes next, the current color becomes orange and the depth value of the current color is that of A. When B comes last, B is ignored because the current depth value is smaller then depth value of B. Therefore, the calculated final color is orange, which is wrong. Therefore, the processing orders should be the same as the depth order to achieve the correct final color.

The order dependent transparency problem may cause serious performance degradation as the number of transparent primitives increases rapidly. Therefore, the order independent transparency is a crucial issue for high performance rendering systems. But, up until now we have not found any high performance 3D rendering machine supporting hardware accelerated.

Several order independent transparency techniques for object order rendering based on the A-buffer algorithm have been proposed [15,16,17,18,19]. But, these algorithms require either, for each pixel, the infinite number of lists of all the primitives overlaying with the dedicated pixel or multiple passes which are not suitable for high performance. On the other hand, image order rendering

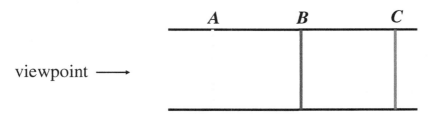

Fig. 4. An example of order independent transparency

techniques to support order independent transparency based on the A-buffer algorithm have been proposed in [13,14]. However, high performance rendering cannot be achieved with image order rendering technique.

3   Proposed Image Composition Architecture

In this section, an image composition architecture supporting hardware accelerated order independent transparency is proposed. We discuss its execution flow, preliminary timing analysis, and scalability.

3.1   Proposed Image Composition Architecture

Figure 5 shows the block diagram of the proposed image composition architecture, which can be divided into rendering accelerator, frame buffer, and display subsystems. The proposed architecture is capable of supporting hardware accelerated order independent transparency. To achieve this goal, hybrid architecture made up of the object order and the image order rendering engines are provided. The proposed mechanism utilizes the advantages of both the object order rendering and the image order rendering methods.

The proposed architecture has n object order rendering engine(ORE)s from PE 0 to PE n-1, and PE n with an image order rendering engine(IRE). Each PE consists of geometry engine(GE), either ORE or IRE, and a local memory which

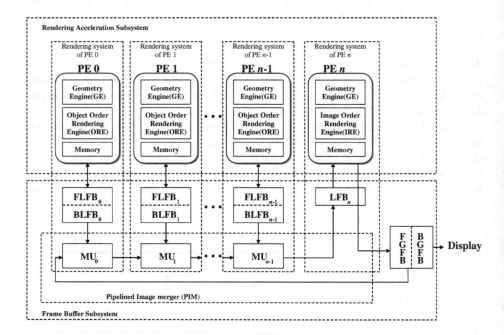

Fig. 5. Block diagram of the proposed image composition architecture

is not a frame memory but a working memory for the PE. The rendering system from PE 0 to PE n-1 is identical to that of the conventional sort-last architecture, while PE n is provided to achieve OIT. The local frame buffer(LFB) of each ORE is double-buffered so that the OREs can generate the image of the next frame in parallel with the image composition of the previous frame. One buffer is called the front local frame buffer(FLFB) and the other is called the back local frame buffer(BLFB). This double buffering scheme is also used in the buckets of IRE and in global frame buffer(GFB).

In the proposed architecture, the rendering systems from PE 0 to PE n-1 perform rendering all opaque primitives with an object order base and PE n performs rendering all transparent primitives with an image order base. Subimages generated from PE 0 to PE n-1 are merged into a single image which is transmitted into LFB_n. With this single merged image and the information of the transparent primitives, IRE calculates the final image with order independent transparency.

Pipelined image merger(PIM), provided in [6], is made up of a linearly connected array of n merging unit(MU)s. It performs image merging with n BLFBs and transmits the final merged image into GFB in a pipelined fashion. Each MU receives two pixel values and outputs the one with the smaller screen depth. We let the screen address begins from $(0, 0)$ and ends with (v, w). $BLFB_0$ denotes the BLFB of PE 0, $BLFB_1$ is the BLFB of PE 1, and so on. MU_0 denotes the MU connected with PE 0, MU_1 is the MU connected with PE 1, and so on.

The execution behavior of PIM can be described as follows. In the first cycle, MU_0 performs depth comparison with $(0, 0)$'s color and the depth data of $BLFB_0$ and $(0, 0)$'s color and depth data of FGFB, respectively, and transmits the results of color and depth data into MU_1. In the next cycle, MU_0 performs depth comparison with $(0, 1)$'s color and depth data of $BLFB_0$ and $(0, 1)$'s color and depth data of FGFB, and transmits the results of color and depth data into MU_1. Simultaneously, MU_1 performs depth comparison with $(0, 0)$'s color and depth data of $BLFB_1$ and the result values fed into the previous cycle, and transmits the results of color and depth data into MU_2. As PIM executes in this pipelined fashion, the final color data can be transmitted into FGFB.

3.2 Execution Flow of the Proposed Image Composition Architecture

All opaque primitives are allocated to each ORE and all transparent primitives are sent to IRE. A primitive allocation technique for load balance on the opaque primitives has been provided in [6]. In the first stage, from PE 0 to PE n-1, object order rendering is performed for the dedicated opaque primitives with geometry processing and rasterization steps. Simultaneously, PE n executes the bucket sorting for image order rendering through geometry processing with the transparent primitives. As a processing result, the rendered subimages for the opaque primitives are stored from $FLFB_0$ to $FLFB_{n-1}$ and the bucket sorted result for the transparent primitives are stored in buckets, which reside in the local memory of PE n.

In the next step, the subimages stored from $BLFB_0$ to $BLFB_{n-1}$ are merged by PIM according to the raster scan order, from $(0, 0)$ to (v, w), and the final merged image is transmitted into LFB_n with a pipelined fashion. Simultaneously, IRE performs image order rendering with LFB_n, which hold the rendered result of all opaque primitives and the bucket sorted results of all transparent primitives. To perform simultaneously both the write operation from MU_{n-1} and the read operation from IRE for two different memory addresses, a two-port memory should be used in LFB_n.

Using the scan-line algorithm for image order rendering, IRE should check all the color and depth values of the current scan-line of LFB_n. Therefore, they should be transmitted completely from MU_{n-1} before performing rendering operation for the current scan-line. Thus, IRE cannot perform rendering operation until all color and depth values of the 0th scan-line in LFB_n are transmitted completely from MU_{n-1}. But the transfer time between MU_{n-1} and LFB_n is too short to affect overall performance, as shown in Section 3.5. The final rendering results of IRE are generated and transmitted into GFB scan-line by scan-line order. Finally, GFB performs the screen refresh operation.

3.3   Pipeline Flow of the Proposed Image Composition Architecture

Figure 6 shows a pipelined execution of the proposed image composition architecture with respect to three frames. If the current processing frame is m, object order rendering is performed from PE 0 to PE n-1 with all the opaque primitives and PE n executes the bucket sorting for image order rendering with all the transparent primitives. The rendering results for the opaque primitives are stored from $FLFB_0$ to $FLFB_{n-1}$ and the bucket sorted results for the transparent primitives are stored in front buckets. Simultaneously, for the $(m-1)^{st}$ frame, image merging from $BLFB_0$ to $BLFB_{n-1}$ is performed by PIM according to the raster scan order, and the final merged image is transmitted into LFB_n with a pipelined fashion. Simultaneously, IRE of PE n performs image order rendering with LFB_n and the back bucket. The rendering results of IRE are generated and transmitted into GFB scan-line by scan-line. For the $(m-2)^{nd}$ frame, screen refresh is performed with a final merged image in FGFB.

3.4   Example of the Order Independent Transparency

Figure 7 shows an example of the order independent transparency for the proposed image composition architecture and illustrates the input and output values of OREs and IRE for a given pixel. For the current viewpoint, the depth values of A, B, C, D, E, F, and G are in increasing order, i.e., A is the nearest primitive and G is the farthest primitive. We assume that A is yellow and transparent, B is blue and opaque, C is red and transparent, D is blue and opaque, E is yellow and opaque, F is black and opaque, and G is green and transparent.

Among the opaque primitives (B, D, E, and F) generated in OREs, B is the final depth result of depth comparison. With the transparent primitives (A, C,

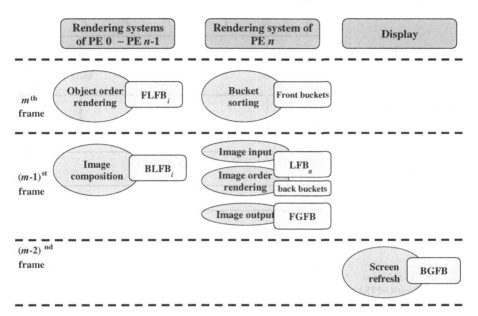

Fig. 6. Pipelined execution of the proposed architecture

and G) and B, image order rendering is performed in IRE. Therefore, green is generated as the final color with order independent transparency.

3.5   Timing Analysis of PIM and Image Order Renderer

In [6] each MU performs depth comparison and data selection through a 4-stage pipeline. Therefore, PIM, as a whole, constructs a $4n$-stage pipeline, where n represents the number of PEs. The time, T_m, needed for merging one full-screen image is equal to $(v + \beta) \cdot w \cdot t + 4 \cdot n \cdot t$, where v and w are horizontal and vertical screen sizes, respectively, t is the PIM clock period, and β is the number of PIM clocks required for overhead processing per scan-line in the GFB unit. The first term represents the time for scanning the entire screen and the second term represents the pipeline delay time. In [6] those parameters are $v = 640$, $w = 480$, $n = 16$, $\beta = 20$, and $t = 80$ nsec. Therefore, $T_m = 25.3$ msec, which is shorter than the target frame interval(33.3 msec).

Because the current screen resolution exceeds several times the resolution considered in [6] and the clock period of PIM can be shortened due to the advances in the semiconductor and network technologies, those parameters are not realistic for the current graphics environment and semiconductor technology. These parameters will be fixed after developing a prototype by the future work. However, considering the current technology, the parameters can be estimated reasonably as $v = 1280$, $w = 1024$, and $t = 20$ nsec, where n and β are not considered because the effect of those parameters is ignorable. Therefore, $T_m = 26.7$ msec, which is still sufficient time to support 30 frames per second.

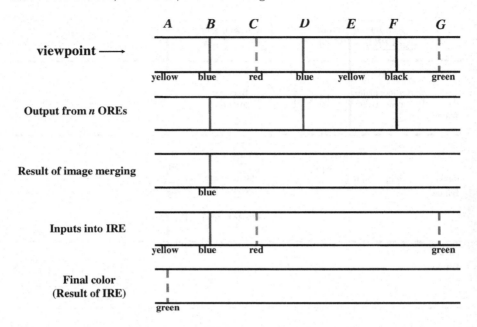

Fig. 7. An example of the order independent transparency on the proposed architecture

IRE cannot perform rendering operation until all color and depth values of the 0th scan-line in LFB_n are transmitted completely from MU_{n-1}. T_{in} denotes the time taken for the transmission. T_{out} denote the time needed to transmit the rendered results of the final scan-line into GFB. T_{in} and T_{out} can be estimated as $(v + \beta) \cdot w \cdot t + 4 \cdot n \cdot t$ and $(v + \beta) \cdot w \cdot t$, respectively. Then, the actual time to perform the image order rendering at IRE is $33.3\text{msec}-(T_{in} + T_{out})$. With $n = 16$, $T_{in} = 0.058\text{msec}$ and $T_{out} = 0.053\text{msec}$ in the case of [6] and $T_{in} = 0.038\text{msec}$ and $T_{out} = 0.026\text{msec}$ in the case of the estimated parameters for the current technology. Therefore, the performance degradation due to T_{in} and T_{out} with $n = 16$ is about $0.4 \sim 0.2\%$, which is negligible. Moreover, with $n=1024$, $T_{in}=0.38\text{msec}$ and $T_{out} = 0.053\text{msec}$ in the case of [6] and $T_{in} = 0.083\text{msec}$ and $T_{out} = 0.026\text{msec}$ in the case of the estimated parameters. Therefore, performance degradation due to T_{in} and T_{out} with $n = 1024$ is about $1.3 \sim 0.4\%$, which is also negligible.

3.6   Scalability on the IRE

In Figure 5 only one IRE is used. Thus, when the number of the transparent primitives is so large that all transparent primitives cannot be processed within the target frame interval, the bottleneck point is the performance of IRE. Figure 8 shows the proposed image composition architecture with r IREs. To achieve scalable parallel processing for IRE, the per-scan-line parallelism is used for the scan-line algorithm.

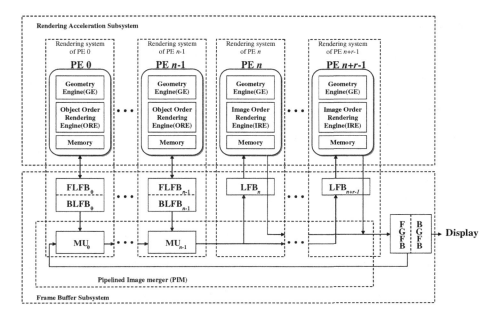

Fig. 8. Block diagram of proposed architecture with scalability on the IRE

In case that the full-screen consists of $r \cdot k$ scan-lines, each IRE has a copy of all transparent primitives and performs bucket sorting for all transparent primitives with dedicated k buckets instead of $r \cdot k$ buckets. Then, each IRE executes the image order rendering with an interleaving fashion. That is, IRE of PE n performs scan-line rendering with the 0th scan-line, the rth scan-line, and so on. IRE of PE $n+1$ performs scan-line rendering with the 1st scan-line, the $(r+1)^{st}$ scan-line, and so on. By this sequence, all scan-lines can be allocated to r IREs. Simultaneously, subimages stored in $BLFB_0$ to $BLFB_{n-1}$ are merged by PIM according to the raster scan order. Then, the merged image is transmitted into each LFB of IRE with an interleaving fashion. Therefore, overall performance of the image order rendering can be achieved with scalability. Finally, the rendered result of r IREs are also transmitted into GFB with an interleaving fashion.

4 Conclusion

In this paper, the order independent transparency problem for image composition in parallel rendering machines has been resolved by using hybrid architecture composed of both the object order rendering and the image order rendering engines. The proposed architecture is a scalable one with respect to both the object order rendering and the image order rendering engines.

References

1. M. Oka and M. Suzuoki. Designing and programming the emotion engine. IEEE Micro, 19(6):20–28, Nov. 1999.
2. A. K. Khan et al. A 150-MHz graphics rendering processor with 256-Mb embedded DRAM. IEEE Journal of Solid-State Circuits, 36(11):1775–1783, Nov. 2001.
3. Timo Aila, Ville Miettinen, and Petri Nordlund. Delay streams for graphics hardware. In Proceedings of SIGGRAPH, pages 792–800, 2003.
4. S. Molnar, M. Cox, M. Ellsworth, and H. Fuchs. A sorting classification of parallel rendering. IEEE Computer Graphics and Applications, 14(4):23–32, July 1994.
5. T. Ikedo and J. Ma. The Truga001: A scalable rendering processor. IEEE computer and graphics and applications, 18(2):59–79, March 1998.
6. S. Nishimura and T. Kunii. VC-1: A scalable graphics computer with virtual local frame buffers. In Proceedings of SIGGRAPH, pages 365–372, Aug. 1996.
7. S. Molnar, J. Eyles, and J. Poulton. PixelFlow: High-speed rendering using image composition. In Proceedings of SIGGRAPH, pages 231–240, July 1992.
8. J. Eyles, S. Molnar, J. Poulton, T. Greer, A. Lastra, N. England, and L. Westover. PixelFlow: The realization. In Proceedings of SIGGRAPH/Eurographics Workshop on graphics hardware, pp. 57–68, Aug. 1997.
9. M. Deering and D. Naegle. The SAGE Architecture. In Proceeddings of SIGGRAPH 2002, pages 683–692, July 2002.
10. J. D. Foley, A. Dam, S. K. Feiner, and J. F. Hughes. Computer Graphics, Principles and Practice. Second Edition, Addison-Wesley, Massachusetts, 1990.
11. J. Torborg and J. T. Kajiya. Talisman: Commodity Realtime 3D graphics for the PC. In Proceedings of SIGGRAPH, pages 353–363, 1996
12. M. Deering, S. Winner, B. Schediwy, C. Duffy, and N. Hunt. The triangle processor and normal vector shader: A VLSI system for high performance graphics. In Proceedings of SIGGRAPH, pages 21–30, 1988.
13. M. Kelley, S. Winner, and K. Gould. A scalable hardware render accelerator using a modified scanline algorithm. In Proceedings of SIGGRAPH, pages 241–248, 1992.
14. M. Kelley, K. Gould, B. Pease, S. Winner, and A. Yen. Hardware accelerated rendering of CSG and transparency. In proceedings of SIGGRAPH, pages 177–184, 1994.
15. L. Carpenter. The A-buffer, and antialiased hidden surface method. In Proceedings of SIGGRAPH, pages 103–108, 1984.
16. S. Winner, M. Kelly, B. Pease, B. Rivard, and A. Yen. Hardware accelerated rendering of antialiasing using a modified A-buffer algorithm. In Proceedings of SIGGRAPH, pages 307–316, 1997.
17. A. Mammeb. Transparency and antialiasing algorithms implemented with virtual pixel maps technique. IEEE computer and graphics and applications, 9(4):43–55, July 1989.
18. C. M. Wittenbrink. R-Buffer: A pointerless A-buffer hardware architecture. In Proceedings of SIGGRAPH/Eurographics Workshop on graphics hardware, pages 73–80, 2001.
19. J. A. Lee and L. S. Kim. Single-pass full-screen hardware accelerated anti-aliasing. In Proceedings of SIGGRAPH/Eurographics Workshop on graphics hardware, pages 67–75, 2000.

An Authorization Architecture Oriented to Engineering and Scientific Computation in Grid Environments

Changqin Huang [1,2], Guanghua Song[1,2], Yao Zheng[1,2], and Deren Chen[1]

[1] College of Computer Science, Zhejiang University, Hangzhou, 310027, P. R. China
[2] Center for Engineering and Scientific Computation, Zhejiang University, Hangzhou, 310027, P. R. China
{cqhuang, ghsong, yao.zheng, drchen}@zju.edu.cn

Abstract. Large-scale scientific and engineering computation is normally accomplished through the interaction of collaborating groups and diverse heterogeneous resources. Grid computing is emerging as an applicable paradigm, whilst, there is a critical challenge of authorization in the grid infrastructure. This paper proposes a Parallelized Subtask-level Authorization Service architecture (PSAS) based on the least privilege principle, and presents a context-aware authorization approach and a flexible task management mechanism. The minimization of the privileges is conducted by decomposing the parallelizable task and re-allotting the privileges required for each subtask. The dynamic authorization is carried out by constructing a multi-value community policy and adaptively transiting the mapping. Besides applying a relevant management policy, a delegation mechanism collaboratively performs the authorization delegation for task management. In the enforcement mechanisms involved, the authors have extended the RSL specification and the proxy certificate, and have modified the Globus gatekeeper, jobmanager and the GASS library to allow authorization callouts. Therefore the authorization requirement of an application is effectively met in the presented architecture.

1 Introduction

Grid Computing [1] emerges as a promising paradigm for coordinating the sharing of computational and data resource and wide-area distributed computing across organizational boundaries. The sharing of code and data on the grid gives rise to many great challenges. Grid infrastructure software such as Legion [2] and Globus [3] enables a user to identify and use the best available resource(s) irrespective of resource location and ownership. However, realizing such a pervasive grid infrastructure presents many challenges due to its inherent heterogeneity, multi-domain characteristic, and highly dynamic nature. One critical challenge is providing authentication, authorization and access control guarantees.

Among relevant grid applications, due to the capability of full utilization of many valuable resources, engineering and scientific computing is suited for being solved in grid environments. This type of task is commonly either computation-intensive or

P.-C. Yew and J. Xue (Eds.): ACSAC 2004, LNCS 3189, pp. 461–472, 2004.

data-intensive, the problem granularity is widely large and computational tasks are often long-lived. It needs be divided into many subtasks, and then be distributed to many relevant nodes and run in parallel, and the management of subtasks is dynamic. The issue needs not only fine-grained authorization for resource usage and management but also fine-grained authorization for task management to meet the needs of this type of application.

In this paper, we focus on the security requirements posed by engineering and scientific computation applications in grid. We present the Parallelized Subtask-Level Service Authorization (PSAS) architecture for fine-grained authorization policies and enforcement mechanism for both resource usage/management and task management. The context-aware authorization is exercised by mapping a community member to a multi-value community policy and adaptive transition, and a delegation mechanism collaboratively performs task management together with a relevant management policy. It enforces these mechanisms to enable fine-grained authorization based on Globus Toolkit version 2.2.

This paper is organized as follows: Section 2 reviews background and related work in the arena of grid security. In section 3, the proposed authorization architecture and overall policy are described. Context-aware authorization is presented in Section 4. Section 5 describes the current implementation of the architecture within Globus. Finally, conclusions and future work are addressed in Section 6.

2 Backgrounds and Related Work

2.1 Authorization in Grid Middleware

As the rapid advancement of the grid researches and applications, diverse grid middlewares are widely developed and deployed. At present, there are three main pieces of grid middlewares, Globus [3], Legion [2], and UNICORE [17]. The Globus toolkit is the most popular grid environment and the de facto grid standard. However its current security services are yet poor, for example: use of static user accounts, coarse granularity, and application dependent enforcement mechanisms. Globus has adopted the Grid Security Infrastructure (GSI) [5] as the primary authentication mechanism. GSI defines single sign-on algorithms and protocols, cross-domain authentication protocols, and temporary credentials called proxy credentials to support hierarchical delegation [6]. Main weaknesses of the Globus security services are described as follows:

1. Globus deals with all privileges of subtask irrespective of the privilege difference among its subtasks. That is, after the simple authentication is exercised, the resource allows the task to use all privileges of the user; similarly, so do subtasks run in parallel. It violates commonly the least privilege principle [7].
2. The issues of the context-aware community policy are not concentrated on, so the authorization of resource usage and task management is not flexibly characterized by the community. The scenario is not suited for large-scale wide-area collaboratively scientific computation in Virtual organization.

3. In Globus, normally, task management is only the responsibility of the users who have submitted the job. Due to the dynamic environment and the long-lived feature of engineering and scientific computation, this coarse-grain authorization for task management cannot meet the need of agile job management in VO.

2.2 Related Work

In recent years, many grid security issues (architectures, policies and enforcement mechanisms, etc) have been researched. And the related researches are making great progress. Among many related works, main researches are presented in the following:

I. Foster et al. [5] provide the basis of current grid security: "grid-map" mechanism, mapping grid entities to local user accounts at the grid resources, is a common approach to authorization. A grid request is allowed if such a mapping exists and the request will be served with all the privileges configured for the local user account. Obviously, these authorization and access control mechanisms are not suitable for flexible authorization decision.

L. Pearlman et al. [8] propose the Community Authorization Service (CAS) architecture. Based on CAS, resource providers grant access to a community accounts as a whole, and community administrators then decide what subset of a community's rights an individual member will have. Drawbacks of this approach include that enforcement mechanism does not support the use of legacy application, that the approach of limiting the group's privileges violates the least-privilege principle and that it does not consider authorization issue of task management.

W. Johnston et al. [9] provide grid resources and resource administrators with distributed mechanisms to define resource usage policy by multiple stakeholders and make dynamic authorization decisions based on supplied credentials and applicable usage policy statements. This system binds user attributes and privileges through attribute certificates (ACs) and thus separates authentication from authorization. Fine-grained access decisions are enforced via such policies and user attributes. However, It does not provide convenience for the use of legacy applications, and does not consider authorization issue of task management.

R. Alfieri et al. [10] present a system conceptually similar to CAS: the Virtual Organization Membership Service (VOMS), which also has a community centric attribute server that issues authorization attributes to members of the community. M. Lorch et al. [11] give the same architecture, called PRIMA. Except that in PRIMA the attributes are not issued by a community server but rather come directly from the individual attribute authorities, PRIMA and VOMS have similar security mechanisms. They utilize expressive enforcement mechanisms and/or dynamic account to facilitate highly dynamic authorization policies and least privilege access to resources. However, they do not consider authorization issue of task management, and in their study, the overhead of authorization management is larger. They only support the creation of small, transient and ad hoc communities.

Besides the typical paradigms mentioned above, M. Lorch et al. [12] enable the high-level management of such fine grained privileges based on PKIX attribute certificates and enforce resulting access policies through readily available POSIX operating system extensions. Although it enables partly the secure execution of legacy applications, it is mainly oriented to collaborating computing scenarios for small, ad hoc working groups. G. Zhang et al. [13] present the SESAME dynamic context-aware access control mechanism for pervasive Grid applications by extending the classic role based access control (RBAC) [14]. SESAME complements current authorization mechanisms to dynamically grant and adapt permissions to users based on their current context. But, monitoring grid context in time is high-cost. K. Keahey et al. [15] describe the design and implementation of an authorization system allowing for enforcement of fine-grained policies and VO-wide management of remote jobs. However, it does not specify and enforce community policies for resource usage and management currently. S. Kim et al. [16] give a WAS architecture to support a restricted proxy credential and rights management by using workflow. It does not consider the actual conditions of large-scale task running at many nodes in parallel, the large overhead of fine-grained division of task and associated authorization confine its application to a limited area.

3 PSAS Architecture

3.1 PSAS Architecture Overview

PSAS architecture is concerned with the different privilege requirements of subtasks, user privilege of resource usage and resource policy in virtual community, task management policy and task management delegation. So PSAS architecture includes three functional modules and a shared enforcement mechanism as shown in Figure 1.

To minimize privileges of a task, the parallelizable task is decomposed and the least privileges required for each subtask is re-allotted after analyzing the source codes of the task. This contribution is described in the part of Subtask-level authorization module in the next sub-section. To apply a flexible task management, a delegation mechanism collaboratively performs the authorization delegation for task management together with a relevant management policy. Its details exist in the part of Task management authorization module in the next sub-section. A context-aware authorization approach is another contribution based on PSAS architecture, and it is presented in Section 4.

3.2 Privilege Management and Overall Authorization Policy

Besides the shared enforcement mechanism, in PSAS, there exist three modules to implement Privilege management and overall authorization policy: Subtask-level authorization module, Community authorization module, and Task management authorization module.

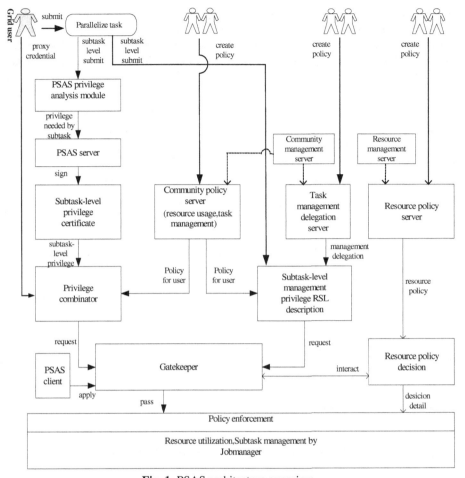

Fig. 1. PSAS architecture overview.

Subtask-level authorization module concentrates on minimizing privileges of tasks by decomposing the parallel task and analyzing the access requirement. To further conform to the least-privilege principle, a few traditional methods restrict the privileges via the delegation of users themselves rather than the architecture, more-over, they only restrict privileges of a whole specific task, not for its constituents (such as subtask). In engineering and scientific computation application, a task is commonly large-scale. It need be divided into many subtasks, and then be distributed to many relevant nodes and run in parallel. Whilst, even though the task is the same, privileges required for distinct subtasks may differ according to operations of these subtasks. By the parallelization and analysis of the task, PSAS can obtain the task's subtasks and relevant required privileges: subtask-level privilege pair. The privileges indicate the information about associated subtask required access to resources at cer-tain nodes. Each task has a subtask-level privilege certificate for recording subtask and privilege pair. An example of this certificate is shown in Figure 2. To prevent malicious third party from tampering with a subtask-level privilege certificate, a trusted third party (PSAS server) signs the certificate. To control a subtask's process and verify the subtask-level privilege certificate, PSAS client will run during resource utilization.

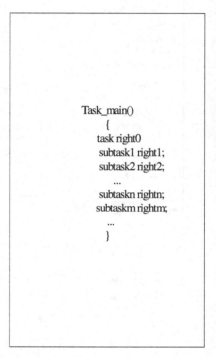

Fig. 2. An example of task and subtask-level privilege certificate.

Subtask-level authorization module contains PSAS privilege analysis module, PSAS server, privilege combinator (shared by community authorization mechanism) and PSAS client.

Community authorization module addresses community authorization mechanism for community member. In Globus, "grid-map" mechanism is conducted, but it is neglected that grid collaboration brings out common rules about privilege for resource usage, resource permission, and so forth, which makes grid security fall into shortage of adequate availability. PSAS architecture imposes similar CAS [8] mechanism with a combination of traditional grid user proxy credential and CAS, as well as the task management policy is added into the community policy server. Two trusted third parties (a community management server and a resource management server) and two policy servers (a community policy server and a resource policy server) are exercised. A community management server is responsible for managing the policies that govern access to a community's resources, and a resource management server is responsible for managing the policies that govern resource permission to grid users.

Two policy servers store the policy for community policy and resource policy respectively. The ultimate privileges of a grid user are formed by the relevant proxy credential and the policy for this user, and the actual rights need accord with resource policy by resource policy decision module during policy enforcement. The policy servers are built or modified by the community administrators or certain specific users.

Community authorization module is composed of a community management server, a resource management server, a community policy server, a resource policy server, privilege combinator, and resource policy decision module.

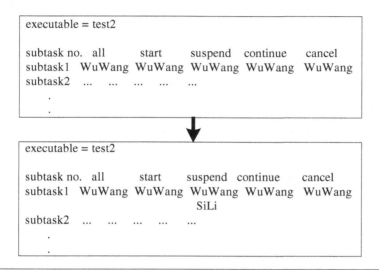

executable = test2

subtask no.	all	start	suspend	continue	cancel
subtask1	WuWang	WuWang	WuWang	WuWang	WuWang
subtask2	...	...	...	...	...

.
.

executable = test2

subtask no.	all	start	suspend	continue	cancel
subtask1	WuWang	WuWang	WuWang	WuWang	WuWang
			SiLi		
subtask2	...	...	...	...	...

.
.

/from:/O=Grid/O=Globus/OU=OU=zju.edu.cn/CN=WuWang/CNType= user
/to:/O=Grid/O=Globus/OU=OU=zju.edu.cn/CN=SiLi/CNType= user
&(action = suspend)(executable = test2)(subtask = subtask1)(directory = /tmp/test2)

Fig. 3. A task management delegation and the relevant change of the subject list.

/O=Grid/O=Globus/OU=OU=zju.edu.cn/CN=WuWang/CNType= user:
&(action = start)(executable = test1)(subtask = subtask1)(directory = /tmp/test1)(count<2)
&(action = start,suspend,cancel)(executable = test2)(subtask = subtask1)(directory = /tmp/test2)(count<4)

/O=Grid/O=Globus/OU=OU=zju.edu.cn/CN=Grid administrator/CNType= group:
&(action = all)(executable = all)(subtask = all)(directory = /tmp)

Fig. 4. An example of task management description.

Task management authorization module is responsible for managing privilege of task management, authorization to task management and related works. In dynamic grid environments, there are many long-lived tasks, for which static methods of policy management are not effective. Users may also start jobs that shouldn't be under the domain of the VO. Since going through the user who has submitted the original job may not always be an option, the VO wants to give a group of its members the ability to manage any tasks using VO resources. This module imposes a community task management policy and task management delegation to describe rules of task management, and both of the two mechanisms are beneficial to flexible task management in an expressive way. A community task management policy denotes the rules of task management in the whole community, and it is combined into the community policy server. Task management delegation server records a variety of management delegation relations among community users. Once the delegation relation is formed, this task will be able to be managed by the delegate user at its runtime. A community management server is responsible for authenticating task management delegation. To keep compatibility with special task management, the subject list only consists of the owner of the task by default. Figure 3 shows a task management delegation and the change of the subject list for task management privilege to this delegation. Subtask-level privilege management RSL description server produces the task management description, which is expressed by extending the RSL set of attributes. An example of task management description is shown in Figure 4.

Task management authorization module includes a community task management policy, task management delegation server and Subtask-level privilege management RSL description server.

4   Context-Aware Authorization

Based on the PSAS Architecture, the dynamic authorization is able to complement with a low overload; meantime, little impact is enforced on grid computation oriented to scientific and engineering. The main idea is that actual privileges of grid users are able to dynamically adapt to their current context. This work is similar to the study in the literature [13]; however, our context-aware authorization is exercised by constructing a multi-value community policy. The approach is completed according to the following steps:

1. Rank the privileges belonging to each item in a traditional community policy. We divide the privileges of a community member into three sets of privileges: Fat Set, medium Set and thin Set. Fat Set is rich set with the full privileges of this community member, and is suited for the best context at runtime; for example, at some time, the context is fully authorized nodes with least resources utilized, then the node will be able to provide its user most privileges. Medium Set is a set of privileges decreased, and Thin Set is the least privilege set for the community member. When Thin Set is enforced, the subtask belonging to this community member will use the less resources (i.e. less memory, less CPU cycles, etc) or be canceled.
2. Construct a multi-value community policy. After finishing the above, we must rebuild the community policy. To keep compatible with the traditional policy, we

only add two sub-items below each item, and the two sub-items are inserted for medium Set and thin Set, respectively. We apply the policy language defined by the literature [15], and introduce two new tags "$1" and "$2" as the respective beginning statement. An example of a policy of resource usage and task management is shown in Figure 5. The statement in the policy refers to a specific user, Wu Wang, and in the first item, it states that he can "start" and "cancel" jobs using the "test1" executables; The rules also place constraints on the directory "/usr/test1" and on the count "<4". In its multi-value community policy, corresponding Fat Set maps to the first item without the change of privileges, its Medium Set and Thin Set respectively map to the next two sub-items below the first item, and their authorizations are changed. For instance, in its corresponding Thin Set, the empty statement prevents him from doing any control using the "test1" executables, the statement "memory<20" places a constraint of used memory <20M, and the statement "directory=/tmp/test1" places a constraint of resource usage.

/O=Grid/O=Globus/OU=OU=zju.edu.cn/CN=WuWang/CNType= user:
&(action = start,cancel)(executable = test1)(subtask = subtask1)(directory = /usr/test1)(count<4)
&(action = start,suspend,cancel)(executable = test2)(subtask = subtask2)(directory = /usr/test2)(count<6)

/O=Grid/O=Globus/OU=OU=zju.edu.cn/CN=WuWang/CNType= user:
&(action = start,cancel)(executable = test1)(subtask = subtask1)(directory = /usr/test1)(count<4)
$1(action = cancel)(executable = test1)(subtask = subtask1)(directory = /usr/test1)(count<2)(memory<100)
$2(action =)(executable = test1)(subtask = subtask1)(directory = /tmp/test1)(count<2)(memory<20)
&(action = start,suspend,cancel)(executable = test2)(subtask = subtask2)(directory = /usr/test2)(count<6)
$1(action = start,cancel)(executable = test2)(subtask = subtask2)(directory = /usr/test2)(count<4)
$2(action = cancel)(executable = test2)(subtask = subtask2)(directory = /tmp/test2)(count<2)(memory<20)

Fig. 5. A traditional policy and its corresponding multi-value community policy.

3. The context-aware authorization is conducted via the above multi-value community policy at runtime. As shown in Figure 6, the model uses a Context Agent as an entity to sense the context information. The Transition Controller accepts the trigger from associated Context Agent and makes a decision of transition of privilege set. In addition to these common policies, the Community Policy Server contains transition policy, as a rule of state transition, and event policy, as a rule of sense event. For example, when the memory of hosting node becomes exhausted, the event notifies Context Agent and let it sense and trigger the Transition Controller.

5   Enforcement Mechanisms

Enforcement of fine-grained access rights is defined as the limitation of operations performed on resources or tasks/subtasks by a user to those permitted by an authoritative entity. Based on the Globus Toolkit 2.2, PSAS architecture implements the subtask-level authorization, flexible task management, and context-aware authorization.

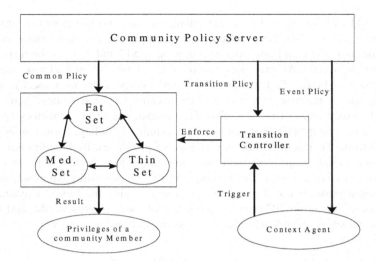

Fig. 6. The context-aware authorization model.

To implement task management authorization module, PSAS creates a job management controller- a component by extending jobmanager in GRAM. When the jobmanager parses users' job descriptions, the job management controller parses and evaluates subtask-level privilege certificate, and makes a decision of certain task management permission. The job management controller integrates with the jobmanager by an authorization callout API. The callout passes the relevant information to the job management controller, such as the credential of the user requesting a remote job, the action to be performed (such as start or cancel a job), a unique job identifier, and the job description expressed in RSL. The job management controller responds by the callout API with either success or an appropriate authorization error. This call is made whenever an action needs to be authorized; that is, it happens before creating a job manager request, and before calls to cancel, query, and signal a running job. PSAS extends the GRAM protocol to return authorization errors with reasons of authorization denial as well as authorization system failures. All of task management delegations and community policies are described in complex task management cases, and they are translated into a RSL regular description by Subtask-level privilege management RSL description server.

To enforce subtask-level authorization module, PSAS employs the proxy certificate with an extension field in the form of standardized X.509 v2 attribute certificates, and makes signed subtask-level privilege certificate embedded into the proxy certificate's extension field. At the same time, PSAS architecture modifies the Globus gatekeeper and jobmanager to put subtask-level authorization into practice. For PSAS client needs to manage a subtask's process and checks whether the subtask is running according to the subtask-level privilege certificate, the GASS library is modified to communicate with PSAS client, and the relevant callout APIs are created. After mutual authentication between a user and a resource, the resource obtains subtask-level privilege certificate located in the proxy certificate's extension field. Then the subtask-level privilege certificate is verified and finds out job identifier. Finally, PSAS client guarantees a subtask's process according to the subtask-level privilege certificate by interacting with GASS.

Community authorization module in PSAS is executed as in CAS [8]. The GSI delegation feature is extended to support rich restriction policies in order to allow grantors to place specific limits on rights that they grant. PSAS employs extensions to X.509 Certificates to carry out restriction policies. However, there exist some differences between CAS and PSAS in the community authorization module. That is, the CAS uses restricted proxy credentials to delegate to each user only those rights granted by the community policy; but the latter regards the ultimate privileges as a privilege combination of the "restricted proxy credentials" and the subtask-level privilege certificate. Proxy credentials are separated from identity credentials. The identity credentials are used for authentication, while the proxy credentials are used for authorization. That makes the PSAS architecture more flexible. Similar to the previous cases, the GASS library is modified to implement a policy evaluation, and the relevant callout functions are designed for call in the Globus gatekeeper. To implement the dynamic context awareness, Context Agent applies a context toolkit described in the literature [18].

6 Conclusions and Future Work

In this paper, we propose a Parallelized Subtask-level Authorization Service (PSAS) architecture to fully secure applications oriented to engineering and scientific computing. This type of task is generally large-scale and long-lived. It needs to be divided into many subtasks run in parallel, and these subtasks may require different privileges. The minimization of the privileges is conducted by decomposing the task and re-allotting the privileges required for each subtask with a subtask-level privilege certificate. With the aid of Context Agent, a multi-value community policy for resource usage and task management enables the context-aware authorization in addition to separating proxy credentials from identity credentials. The delegation mechanism collaboratively performs the authorization delegation for task management together with a relevant management policy. To enforce the architecture, the authors have extended the RSL specification and the proxy certificate and have modified the Globus gatekeeper, jobmanager and the GASS library to allow authorization callouts. The authorization requirement of an application is effectively met in the presented architecture.

At present, the PSAS architecture is only a prototype, and many issues need to be solved. So we plan, firstly, to improve the PSAS architecture in practice via complex applications, and secondly, to further study the policy based context-aware authorization of resource usage and task management based on performance metrics.

Acknowledgements. The authors wish to thank the National Natural Science Foundation of China for the National Science Fund for Distinguished Young Scholars under grant Number 60225009. We would like to thank the Center for Engineering and

Scientific Compu-tation, Zhejiang University, for its computational resources, with which the research project has been carried out.

References

1. I. Foster, C. Kesselman, and S. Tuecke, The Anatomy of the Grid: Enabling Scalable Virtual Organizations, *International Journal of Supercomputer Applications*, 15(3): pp.200-222, 2001.
2. A. Grimshaw, W. A. Wulf, et al., The Legion Vision of a Worldwide Virtual Machine, *Communications of the ACM*, 40(1): 39-45, January 1997.
3. I. Foster and C. Kesselman. Globus: a metacomputing infrastructure toolkit, *International Journal of Supercomputer Applications*, 11(2): 115-128, 1997.
4. S. Tuecke, et al., Internet X.509 Public Key Infrastructure Proxy Certificate Profile. 2002.
5. I. Foster, C. Kesselman, G. Tsudik, S. Tuecke, A Security Architecture for Computational Grids, *Proc. of 5th ACM Conference on Computer and Communications Security Conference*, 1998.
6. L. Kagal, T. Finin, and Y. Peng, A Delegation Based Model For Distributed Trust, *IJCAI-01 Workshop on Autonomy*, Delegation, and Control, 2001.
7. J. R. Salzer and M. D. Schroeder, The Protection of Information in Computer Systems, *Proc. of the IEEE*, 1975
8. L. Pearlman, V. Welch, et al., A Community Authorization Service for Group Collaboration, *Proc. of the 3rd IEEE International Workshop on Policies for Distributed Systems and Networks*, 2002.
9. W. Johnston, S. Mudumbai, et al., Authorization and Attribute Certificates for Widely Distributed Access Control, *Proc. of IEEE 7th International Workshops on Enabling Technologies: Infrastructures for Collaborative Enterprises*, 1998.
10. R. Alfieri, et al., VOMS: an Authorization System for Virtual Organizations, *Proc. of the 1st European Across Grids Conference*, 2003.
11. M. Lorch, D. B. Adams, et al., The PRIMA System for Privilege Management, Authorization and Enforcement in Grid Environments, *Proc. of the 4th International Workshop on Grid Computing*, 2003
12. M. Lorch and D. Kafura, Supporting Secure Ad-hoc User Collaboration in Grid Environments, *Proc. of the 3rd IEEE/ACM International Workshop on Grid Computing*, 2002.
13. G. Zhang and M. Parashar, Dynamic Context-aware Access Control for Grid Applications, *Proc. of the 4th International Workshop on Grid Computing*, 2003.
14. R. Sandhu, E. Coyne, et al., Role-based Access Control Models, *Proc. of the 5th ACM Workshop on Role-Based Access Control*, 2000
15. K. Keahey, V. Welch, et al., Fine-Grain Authorization Policies in the Grid: Design and Implementation, *Proc. of the1st International Workshop on Middleware for Grid Computing*, 2003.
16. S. Kim, J, Kim, S. Hong, et al., Workflow-based Authorization Service in Grid, *Proc. of the 4th International Workshop on Grid Computing*, 2003.
17. M. Romberg, The UNICORE Architecture: Seamless Access to Distributed Resources, *Proc. of the 8th IEEE International Symposium on High Performance Distributed Computing*, 1999.
18. A. K. Dey, G. D. Abowd, The Context Toolkit: Aiding the Development of Context-Aware Applications, *Proc. of Human Factors in Computing Systems: CHI 99*, 1999.

Validating Word-Oriented Processors for Bit and Multi-word Operations

Ruby B. Lee, Xiao Yang, and Zhijie Jerry Shi

Princeton Architecture Laboratory for Multimedia and Security (PALMS)
Princeton University
{rblee, xiaoyang, zshi}@princeton.edu

Abstract. We examine secure computing paradigms to identify any new architectural challenges for future general-purpose processors. Some essential security functions can be provided by different classes of cryptography algorithms. We identify two categories of operations in these algorithms that are not common in previous general-purpose workloads: bit operations within a word and multi-word operations. Both challenge the basic word orientation of processors. We show how very complex bit-level operations, namely arbitrary bit permutations within a word, can be achieved in $O(1)$ cycles, rather than $O(n)$ cycles as in existing RISC processors. We describe two solutions: one using only microarchitecture changes, and another with Instruction Set Architecture (ISA) support. We generalize our solutions to define *datarich execution* with MOMR (Multi-word Operands Multi-word Result) functional units. This can address both challenges, leveraging available resources in typical processors with minimal additional cost. Thus we validate the basic word-orientation of processor architectures, since they can also provide superior performance for both bit and multi-word operations needed by cryptographic processing.

1 Introduction

The dependence on the public Internet and wireless networks in modern society poses a growing need for secure communications, computations and storage. To provide basic security functions like data confidentiality, data integrity, and user authentication, different classes of cryptographic algorithms can be used with security protocols at network, system or application levels. Not only network transactions need to be protected, all data and programs may also need these security functions. As secure computing paradigms become more pervasive, it is likely that such cryptographic computations will become a major component of every processor's workload. Understanding the new requirements of secure information processing is critical for the design of all future processors, whether general-purpose, application-specific or embedded. In this paper, we especially target the needs of high performance microprocessors.

Basic security functions include confidentiality, integrity and authentication. Confidentiality of messages transmitted over the public networks, and of data stored in disks, can be achieved by encrypting the data, using symmetric-key cryptography algorithms such as DES [1], and AES [2]. Data integrity, where data is not changed in

P.-C. Yew and J. Xue (Eds.): ACSAC 2004, LNCS 3189, pp. 473–488, 2004.
© Springer-Verlag Berlin Heidelberg 2004

transit or in storage, can be accomplished with one-way hash functions such as SHA and MD-5 [1]. Authenticating users and devices remotely across the Internet can be accomplished with public-key cryptographic algorithms such as Diffie-Hellman and RSA [1]. They also allow digital signatures and the exchange of a shared secret key across the Internet.

We observe two categories of new requirements imposed by these three classes of cryptographic algorithms: bit-oriented operations and multi-word operations. Both challenge the basic word-orientation of modern processors. Symmetric-key cryptography introduces a new requirement: bit-level permutations. Previously, the bit-oriented operations in general-purpose workloads were SHIFT instructions and logical operations like AND, OR, XOR and NOT. These are supported efficiently by simple single-cycle instructions. Public-key cryptography introduces the other new requirement: multi-word arithmetic. While multiword integer arithmetic has been a requirement in previous high-precision integer computations, its need remained relatively low since the basic word size in general-purpose processors has increased from 16 to 32 to 64 bits. Frequent use of public-key cryptography algorithms may significantly increase the need for multi-word arithmetic. For example, multiplication of two 1024-bit operands in RSA involves two 16-word operands, if each word is 64 bits. If a hardwired multiply instruction operates on two words, many such 64-bit multiply instructions are needed, as well as add operations to accumulate the result. Public-key algorithms based on Elliptic Curve Cryptography (ECC) often perform polynomial operations requiring both bit-oriented and multi-word operations.

A key contribution of this paper is the observation that fast cryptographic processing depends on a processor's ability to support both complex bit-level manipulations as well as multiword operations. These requirements have more impact on performance than defining a new instruction or special-purpose functional unit for accelerating a particular cryptographic primitive. They also challenge the atomic word-orientation of processors, since they emphasize bit operations within a word, and operations requiring operands much larger than a word.

A second contribution is showing how arbitrary bit-level permutations can be accomplished very efficiently in only 1 or 2 cycles.

A third contribution is a generalized architectural solution that allows high-performance processors to support *datarich* operations with flexible, multi-word operands and multi-word result (MOMR) functional units. Our generalized solution supports both high performance bit permutations and multi-word operations. Hence, the basic word-orientation of processors is still a good design choice, since both bit-oriented and multi-word oriented operations can also be supported very efficiently.

In Section 2, we describe past work on permutation instructions, including how our recent past work has reduced the time taken to achieve any n-bit permutation down from $O(n)$ to $O(\log(n))$ instructions and cycles. In Section 3, we propose two new architectural methods for further bringing this down to $O(1)$ cycles. One method is purely micro-architectural, and the other involves new ISA. In Section 4, we describe the changes in the datapath and control path needed to implement our two methods. In Section 5, we generalize these two methods to solve the second challenge of achieving multi-word operations efficiently in word-oriented processors. In Section 6, we discuss performance, and conclude in Section 7.

2   Past Work

Past work in accelerating cryptographic processing included many hardware ASIC (Application Specific Integrated Circuit) implementations of specific ciphers. For programmable solutions, new instructions were proposed to accelerate symmetric-key ciphers in general-purpose processors [3], and in cryptographic coprocessors like Cryptomaniac [4] for ciphers used in secure networking protocols. In contrast, we do not propose any specific new instructions in this paper, but rather new methodologies for bringing more data to the functional units. This *datarich* computation is done with very low overhead, utilizing the datapaths and control already provided for superscalar execution found in most microprocessors, including out-of-order superscalar machines.

The datarich methodology allows us to accelerate both bit permutations used for symmetric-key ciphers, and multi-word operations used in public-key ciphers. It allows us to achieve one of our major contributions: performing arbitrary bit permutations in 1 or 2 cycles – a significant improvement over our recent past work achieving $O(\log(n))$ instructions and cycles [5], which we describe further below.

Performing bit-level permutation has been a hard problem for word-oriented general-purpose processors. Previously, processors only supported a very restricted subset of bit permutations known as rotations. Here, every bit in the n-bit word is moved by the same shift amount, with wrap-around. While some n-bit permutations can be achieved with fewer instructions, allowing arbitrary, data-dependent n-bit permutations is very slow. Conventional logical and shift instructions take $O(n)$ cycles to achieve any one of $n!$ permutations [5]. Alternatively, table lookup methods can be used, but this is limited to a few fixed permutations due to the high memory space requirement, and cache misses cause performance degradation.

More recently, permutation instructions have been introduced into certain microprocessors as multimedia ISA extensions to handle the re-arrangement of subwords packed in registers. Examples are MIX and PERMUTE in HP's MAX-2 [6], VPERM in Motorola's AltiVec [7], and MIX and MUX in IA-64 [8]. However, these instructions can only handle subword sizes down to 8 bits. They do not provide a general solution for performing arbitrary bit-level permutations efficiently.

Very recently, researchers have tackled the general bit permutation problem, and defined new permutation instructions that can achieve any n-bit permutation with only $\log(n)$ instructions. Several approaches were proposed. The CROSS [9] and OMFLIP [10] permutation instructions each performs the equivalent function of two stages of a "virtual" interconnection network. A sequence of $\log(n)$ CROSS or OMFLIP instructions can build a $2\log(n)$-stage virtual network that can achieve any one of the $n!$ permutations. Another approach was the GRP instruction [11], which partitions the data bits into two groups. At most $\log(n)$ GRP instructions are sufficient to achieve any one of $n!$ permutations [11]. A third approach involves specifying the order of the indices of the source bits in the permuted result. Examples are PPERM[11], and SWPERM and SIEVE [12]. The XBOX instruction [3] is similar to PPERM.

A comparison of CROSS, OMFLIP, GRP, and PPERM is presented in [5]. CROSS, OMFLIP and GRP all achieve arbitrary 64-bit permutations in 6 instructions. PPERM and SWPERM with SIEVE require more than $\log(n)$ instructions, but can be executed in as few as 4 cycles on a 4-way superscalar machine. Unfortunately, CROSS, OMFLIP and GRP cannot achieve speedup with superscalar machines, due to the strict data dependency between the sequence of log(n) permutation instructions. Below, we show how this data dependency can be overcome, so that arbitrary 64-bit permutations can be achieved in 1 or 2 cycles, rather than log(n) = 6 cycles.

This paper extends the concepts we presented in [13] with new work on the detailed ISA or microarchitectural changes required, and the detailed implementation in an out-of-order processor.

3   Achieving Arbitrary 64-Bit Permutations in 1 or 2 Cycles

The reason log(n) instructions are needed to achieve any permutation of n bits is because $n$log(n) configuration bits are needed to specify an arbitrary n-bit permutation [5][11]. Since a typical instruction reads up to 2 source operands and produces 1 result, a permutation instruction uses one source operand for the data and the other for n bits of configuration. The intermediate result produced by one permutation instruction is used as the data for the next. Hence, a sequence of log(n) instructions are needed to supply the $n$log(n) configuration bits and the data to be permuted, to achieve any n-bit permutation [5]. If all $n$log(n) configuration bits and the n data bits to be permuted can be specified by a single instruction, then it may be possible to execute any arbitrary n-bit permutation in 1 instruction. Hence, the main performance limiter is the ISA instruction format and the datapaths that support only two n-bit operands per instruction, and a design goal of not having to save states between permutation instructions. This is a reasonable goal since it reduces context-switch and operating system overhead.

Suppose that the latency through the permutation functional unit is not a cycle-time limiter. Then, the problem reduces to the following: how can $n(\log(n)+1)$ bits be sent from general registers to a permutation functional unit (PU) in a single instruction? If each register is n bits, this means sending $(\log(n)+1)$ register values, or operands, to a functional unit. We propose two methods to solve this problem. Method 1 identifies instruction groups dynamically with microarchitecture techniques; method 2 employs ISA techniques to identify instruction groups statically.

3.1   Datapath, MOMR, and Instruction Groups

We first define some new architectural terms: An *(s,t) functional unit* in a word-oriented processor is a functional unit that takes s word-sized operands and produces t word-sized results. A *standard functional unit* is a (2,1) functional unit.

An *(s,t) datapath* in a word-oriented processor is a datapath where s source buses and t destination buses are connected to functional units. If the datapath contains a register file, it has s read ports and at least t write ports for the results coming from the functional units in one cycle. In general, a k-way multi-issue processor has a $(2k,k)$ datapath, supporting the simultaneous execution of k standard (2,1) functional units each cycle.

A *datarich or MOMR (Multi-word Operands Multi-word Result) functional unit* in a word-oriented processor is a functional unit that requires more than the standard two word-sized operands and one word-sized result.

A sequence of consecutive instructions is called an *instruction group* if the instructions can be executed simultaneously by a datarich (or MOMR) functional unit.

Emerging secure computing paradigms may require extensive execution of algorithms where performance can be improved by the use of datarich functional units. Sometimes datarich functional units improve the performance, other times they improve the cost-performance. Our thesis is that a k-way multi-issue processor with a $(2k,k)$ datapath can accommodate different types of datarich functional units, with relatively minor changes to the pipeline control logic. In the rest of Section 3 and Section 4, we illustrate two methods for datarich MOMR execution, using bit permutation as the example. In Section 5, we generalize datarich MOMR execution to operations with multi-word operands.

3.2 Method 1: Microarchitecture Group Detection

A permutation instruction is defined as follows:

```
PERM rs,rc,rd
```

where rs contains data source, rc contains configuration bits and rd is the result. For example, PERM can be either a CROSS or OMFLIP instruction. Fig. 1(a) shows a 64-bit permutation specified with a sequence of 6 PERM instructions in 2 groups of 3 instructions each. Each group provides the data source and 3 configuration words for a $(4,1)$ permutation unit, PU. The group is dynamically detected, and then its 3 instructions are transformed into 2 "internal" instructions. The first one supplies the data source and one configuration word, and the second one provides the other 2 configuration words. When all the operands are ready, the two "internal" instructions are issued for execution simultaneously on one $(4,1)$ PU. Hence, the 6 instructions can be transformed into 4 internal instructions in 2 groups and executed over 2 cycles. If there are two or more $(4,1)$ PUs, we can pipeline the executions of the 2 groups and achieve a throughput of one permutation per cycle.

3.3 Method 2: New ISA for Group Identification

In the second method, we enhance the conventional RISC instruction encoding with 2 new subop bits, gs and gc, for identifying instructions which start a group (gs=1) or continue a group (gc=1). The meanings of these 2 bits are shown in . The permutation instruction is defined as:

```
PERM,subop  rs1,rs2,rd
```

where subop contains the gs and gc bits. If gs is set, the instruction is the first in a 2-instruction group, supplying the data word and one configuration word to the $(4,1)$ PU. If gc is set, it is the second instruction in a group, supplying 2 configuration words for the $(4,1)$ PU. We specify this 2-instruction group as follows:

```
PERM,gs  rs,rc1,rd
PERM,gc  rc2,rc3,rd
```

Unlike method 1, method 2 does not need the dynamic group detection and instruction transformation. It also helps reduce static code size, since only 4 permutation instructions (rather than 6) are required in the program. Similar to method 1, when all the source operands for the 2 grouped instructions are ready, they are issued for execution together on one (4,1) PU.

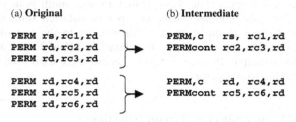

(a) **Original**   (b) **Intermediate**

```
PERM rs,rc1,rd  ⎤        PERM,c    rs, rc1,rd
PERM rd,rc2,rd  ⎬ →      PERMcont  rc2,rc3,rd
PERM rd,rc3,rd  ⎦

PERM rd,rc4,rd  ⎤        PERM,c    rd, rc4,rd
PERM rd,rc5,rd  ⎬ →      PERMcont  rc5,rc6,rd
PERM rd,rc6,rd  ⎦
```

Fig. 1. Instruction transformation for method 1

Table 1. Meanings of gs and gc bits

gs=0, gc=0	Normal instruction, not part of a group
gs=1, gc=0	First instruction in a group
gs=0, gc=1	Continuation instruction in a group
gs=1, gc=1	Reserved

4 Microarchitectural Changes

In this section, we show how either of the two above methods can leverage the resources already present in a superscalar processor, with minimal additional cost. We first describe a typical superscalar processor in Section 4.1, then detail changes that must be made to its datapath and control path in Sections 4.2 and 4.3, respectively.

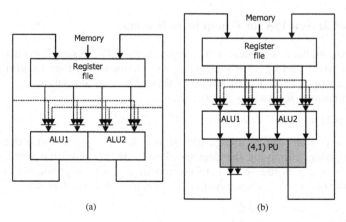

Fig. 2. (a) Standard 2-way superscalar processor datapath; (b) with a (4,1) PU added

4.1 Baseline Microarchitecture

Fig. 2(a) shows a standard 2-way superscalar RISC processor with a (4,2) datapath, i.e., 4 register read ports, 2 write ports and associated data buses and bypass paths.

Fig. 3 shows the pipeline frontend of a generic out-of-order superscalar processor [14]. A block of instructions is fetched from the instruction cache. These instructions are then decoded and their operands renamed (to physical registers to eliminate register-name dependencies) before entering the issue window. They will be issued for execution when all their source operands and required functional units become available (wakeup and select stage). Certain stages of the pipeline may take multiple cycles. For an in-order issue processor, there are no rename or select stages.

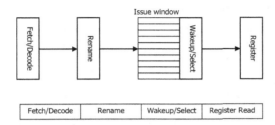

Fig. 3. Generic out-of-order superscalar processor pipeline frontend

4.2 Changes to the Datapath

Fig. 2(b) shows a (4,1) permutation unit (PU) added to a standard (4,2) datapath of a 2-way superscalar processor. Fig. 4 shows an implementation of the PU based on the butterfly network. There are 2 separate PUs, one contains a 6-stage butterfly network and the other contains an inverse butterfly network. In a 2-way processor, we have both of them in the datapath, but only one PU is used at a time, resulting in a 2-cycle latency and a throughput of one permutation per 2 cycles. In a 4-way or wider processor, we can use both of them in parallel. Then we can pipeline the permutation operation and achieve one permutation per cycle throughput (Fig. 5).

Inclusion of a datarich (4,1) MOMR functional unit in a 2-way superscalar processor causes minimal datapath overhead of one additional result multiplexer. All the expensive register ports, data buses and bypasses required have already been provided by the (4,2) datapath of the 2-way superscalar machine. Similarly, for the inclusion of two (4,1) MOMR units in a 4-way superscalar processor. Two (4,1) PUs leveraging the (8,4) datapath of a 4-way superscalar machine are sufficient to achieve the ultimate performance of a different 64-bit permutation every cycle. A key benefit of our solution is leveraging the existing resources of today's microprocessors, essentially all of which are at least 2-way superscalar.

4.3 Changes to the Control Path

We now show that even the required control path changes are minimal. Method 1, which uses the microarchitecture to detect a sequence of dependent instructions that

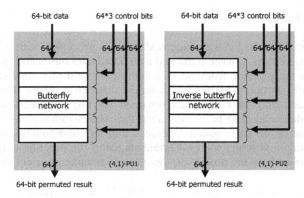

Fig. 4. One implementation of (4,1) permutation FU

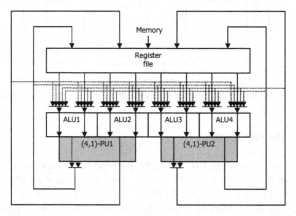

Fig. 5. Two (4,1) permutation FUs in 4-way superscalar processor

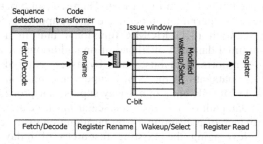

Fig. 6. Modified superscalar processor pipeline frontend

can be executed together, requires some modifications to the pipeline control front-end as shown in Fig. 6. The sequence detection unit detects sequences of 3 permutation instructions. These sequences are then transformed to groups of 2 instructions by the code transformer. The muxes pick the correct inputs to the issue window between the original instructions and the transformed instructions. A 1-bit field reserved for a C-bit is added to each entry in the instruction window to denote whether the corresponding instruction and the following one are in a group. The wakeup/select logic is also modified so that the 2 grouped instructions can be woken up and executed together. For method 2, since instruction groups are explicitly identified by instruction subop bits, the sequence detection unit, code transformer and muxes are not needed. The rest of the control path is the same as for method 1.

Group sequence detection. Dynamic instruction group detection is needed only by method 1. The group sequence detection unit (Fig. 7) recognizes 3 consecutive permutation instructions in a fetch block that satisfy the following two criteria: they have the same opcodes and the data source operand in a permutation instruction is the result of the previous permutation instruction. It then sets C-bits for the first instruction of the detected group sequence. For simplicity, sequences residing in two fetch blocks are not recognized to avoid keeping additional states.

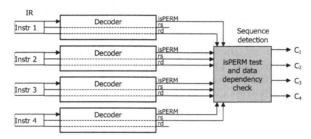

Fig. 7. Functions of sequence detection unit

Instruction transformation. The code transformer is also needed only by method 1. It transforms the group of 3-instruction sequences into 2-instruction sequences (see Fig. 1). The 2 new instructions are generated according to the C-bits produced by the sequence detection unit and the renamed operands of the original 3 instructions. The code transformer replaces the data operand in the second instruction with the configuration operand from the third instruction before discarding the third instruction. Then, it updates the C-bits in the newly generated instructions. An instruction that has its C-bit set starts a group. Grouped instructions are adjacent in the issue window. Fig. 8 shows the functions of the code transformer.

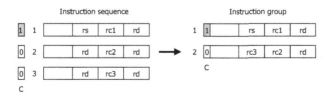

Fig. 8. Code transformer transforms 3-instruction sequence to 2-instruction group

Instruction wakeup. Fig. 9 shows the modified wakeup logic needed by both methods to wake up the 2 grouped instructions together. This is necessary because otherwise the 2 instructions might be issued separately, producing the wrong result.

Previously, an instruction is ready to issue when both of its source operands are ready. The modified wakeup logic ensures that grouped instructions become ready only when all the source operands in the group are ready.

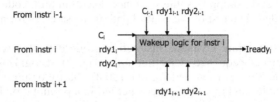

Fig. 9. Modified instruction wakeup logic

Instruction select. We can modify the select logic for ALU1 and ALU2 to handle the permutation unit as well. This is achieved by adding C-bit propagation to the original select logic for ALU1 and ALU2 and 2 small control units, as shown in Fig. 10(a). Assume the select logic for ALU1 selects instruction i. The control unit 1 tests the C-bit of i. If i's C-bit is set, then grant both instruction i and i+1 and bypass the select logic for ALU2. Otherwise grant i and proceed to select logic for ALU2. Suppose instruction j is selected for ALU2. The control unit 2 then tests the C-bit of j. We grant instruction j only if j's C-bit is not set.

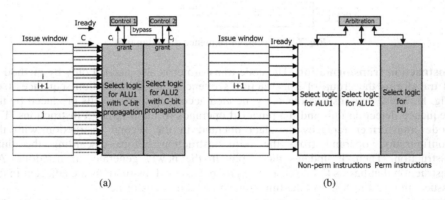

Fig. 10. (a) Select logic with modifications on the original select logic for ALU1 and ALU2; (b) Select logic with new set of logic for PU

Alternatively, we can add a new set of select logic for the PU, which deals only with instructions with C-bits set, while the select logic for ALU1 and ALU2 deals with normal instructions. The arbitration unit picks the result of either the select logic for ALU1 and ALU2 or the new select logic. (see Fig. 10(b)).

If there are multiple issue queues, such as proposed in [14], we can devise an instruction steering method so that the 2 permutation instructions in a group are dispatched to the same queue. This is easy to achieve because the 2 grouped instructions are adjacent. If the C-bit of the instruction at the head of a queue is set, we grant this instruction together with the following one.

4.4 Complexity and Delay of Control Path Modifications

The modifications to the control path consist of a small amount of combinatorial logic, estimated at a few thousand gates for a 4-way superscalar processor. As comparison, the issue logic of the Compaq Alpha 21264 processor, a 4-way superscalar RISC processor, contains about 141000 transistors [15], making the complexity of our modifications negligible.

In terms of delay, the sequence detection unit and the code transformer run in parallel with the decode and rename logic. Due to their simple functions, they should have no impact on the processor cycle time. Since the wakeup and select logic are already in the critical path for back-to-back executions of dependent instructions, our modifications may increase the cycle time. However, many methods have been proposed to reduce the latency of issue logic by either simplifying the instruction issue logic [14][16][17][18], or breaking wakeup/select to multiple stages [19][20] in order to achieve fast instruction scheduling. By incorporating these methods, we can integrate our modifications without affecting the processor cycle time.

5   Generalization to Multi-word Operations

We define *multi-word operations* as operations that use more than 2 word-sized operands and produce more than 1 word-sized result, i.e., they are operations that could use datarich MOMR functional units. Arbitrary bit permutation is one example of multi-word operations since the configuration bits span multiple words. Other multi-word operations include the multiplication of two 16-word operands in a 64-bit processor, for a public key algorithm like RSA using 1024-bit keys. If larger hardware multipliers can be accommodated within a high performance microprocessor, we can speed up the multiword multiplication by producing longer (and fewer) partial products with each instruction, resulting in fewer instructions needed to accumulate the partial products to get the final result. In particular, if the implementation can afford larger multipliers, we want to eliminate the ISA restriction of only performing the multiplication of two word-sized operands per instruction.

5.1 Multiplication of Multi-word Operands

The use of MOMR methods for speeding up n-bit permutations was described in Sections 3 and 4. We now describe how MOMR methods may be used to accelerate the multiplication of multi-word operands. Let the original multiply instructions be:

```
MUL,L ra,rb,rc
MUL,H ra,rb,rd
```

Two 64-bit registers ra and rb are multiplied together to generate the low and high 64 bits of the result in rc and rd, in successive instructions. Actually, both halves of the product are generated by the same hardware multiplier at the same time, and it is only because of the ISA restriction of one word-sized result per instruction that two separate instructions have to be used to generate the double-word result. If a (2,2) instruction were available, then these two instructions can be executed together on one multiplier simultaneously. Method 1 can recognize this case at run-time. Method 2 can specify this at compile time with the gs and gc bits:

```
MUL,L,gs ra,rb,rc
MUL,H,gc ra,rb,rd
```

A 2-way supercsalar processor with two (2,1) multipliers can achieve the same performance as a single (2,2) MOMR multiplier, but with twice the area for two multipliers. Hence, MOMR execution is more cost-effective.

Alternatively, an even higher performance microprocessor may be able to afford a 128-bit multiplier. Implemented as a (4,2) MOMR multiplier, we can execute 128-bit versions of the Multiply Low and High instructions, in method 2 as follows:

```
MUL,L,gs ra1,rb1,rc1
MUL,L,gc ra2,rb2,rc2
MUL,H,gs ra1,rb1,rd1
MUL,H,gc ra2,rb2,rd2
```

The first two MUL,L instructions would be executed together as a group on a 128-bit multiplier to generate the low 128 bits of the result. The next two MUL,H instructions generate the high 128 bits of the result. To get the equivalent 256-bit product using only 64-bit multipliers and conventional (2,1) instructions, we need to do 8 multiply's and 5 add's. A 128-bit multiplier can also be used for (4,4) MOMR execution, where all 4 instructions above belong to the same group and are executed together. Larger multipliers can also be used, for even further speedup.

5.2 Datarich MOMR Execution

We now define generalized MOMR or datarich execution. In Table 2 and Table 3, method 1 achieves a microarchitecture solution for MOMR execution, while method 2 yields an ISA solution, where the MOMR operations are explicitly specified with new gs and gc bits in the instruction encoding. The steps in these 2 methods are listed in Table 2. Method 1 requires a more complex group detection unit to recognize all the supported multi-word operations. For method 2, a similar unit is also necessary, but to check the correctness of groups. Examples of the criteria for recognizing or checking instruction groups are given in Table 3. The first 3 columns specify the instructions in the instruction stream, and the last 2 specify the data dependencies they must satisfy.

In order to simplify the architectural solution, we require that instructions to be executed together as a group be consecutive in sequential program order. That is, we are not trying to look through the whole program to find instructions that may be far apart which can be executed together in the same cycle. Rather, we target programs which can be re-compiled, or new programs, so that instructions that can be "grouped" for simultaneous execution are next to each other.

The ISA cost of method 2 is that we must define the gs bit for every instruction that can serve as the start of a multi-word operation and the gc bit for all instructions that can act as continuation instructions in a group. Encoding space may be tight in existing ISAs and one or two unused bits per instruction may not be available.

When there are different instruction groups, the microarchitecture needed to support method 2 is not significantly simpler than in method 1. However, method 2 can specify MOMR execution opportunities that are too difficult for method 1 to recognize dynamically. For example, it takes a long sequence of 64-bit multiply and add instructions to get the result equivalent to the multiplication of two 128-bit operands. With the gs and gc bits, method 2 only needs 4 instructions to specify this operation (last 2 rows in Table 3). Therefore, method 2 can support a broader scope of multi-word operations.

Table 2. Architectual methods for MOMR execution

Steps	Method 1: microarchitecture detected groups	Method 2: ISA specified groups
Group detection: Recognize a small set of pre-defined groups of instructions that can be executed together on a MOMR functional unit in the same cycle.	Need to consult a table like Table 3 to check multiple combinations of opcodes and data dependencies so as to recognize all the supported multi-word operations.	Although groups are already defined in the ISA, still need to consult a table similar to that for method 1 to determine whether gs and gc define legitimate (and complete) groups.
Instruction transformation: Transform the instructions in a group to fewer instructions with some operand register re-packaging, if necessary.	For different multi-word operations, different transformations are needed.	Set C-bits in microarchitecture according to gs and gc bits in instructions.
Wakeup and select: Wake up and select the instructions to be executed on one MOMR functional unit together	Similar to permutation-only case. The logic shown in Section 4 deals with simultaneous executions of up to 2 instructions. It can be extended if 3 or more instructions are to be issued together. This may result in increased latency and more stages for wakeup and select.	

Table 3. Examples of Group Definitions

	Instr i	i+1	i+2	Dependency criteria	Remarks
Method 1	PERM	PERM	PERM	$rd_i=rs1_{i+1}$ & $rd_{i+1}=rs1_{i+2}$ & $rd_i!=rs2_{i+1}$ & $rd_i!=rs2_{i+2}$ & $rd_{i+1}!=rs2_{i+2}$	Serial dependency No RAW hazard*
	MUL,L	MUL,H		$rs1_i=rs1_{i+1}$ & $rs2_i=rs2_{i+1}$ & $rd_i!=rd_{i+1}$ &	Same sources Diff dest for H, L
	PMIN	PMAX		$rd_i!=rs1_{i+1}$ & $rd_i!=rs2_{i+1}$	No RAW hazard
Method 2	PERM,gs	PERM,gc		$rd_i!=rs1_{i+1}$ & $rd_i!=rs2_{i+1}$	No RAW hazard
	MUL,L,gs	MUL,H,gc		$rs1_i=rs1_{i+1}$ & $rs2_i=rs2_{i+1}$ & $rd_i!=rd_{i+1}$ &	Same source Diff dest for H, L
	PMIN,gs	PMAX,gc		$rd_i!=rs1_{i+1}$ & $rd_i!=rs2_{i+1}$	No RAW hazard

* Since a PERM group is composed of 3 serially dependent instructions, there must be data dependencies (RAW hazards) between adjacent PERM instructions. No RAW hazard here means no additional data dependencies other than those required for a serial chain. For multi-word operations (all the rest), no RAW hazard means no RAW data dependencies.

6   Performance

We test two distinct aspects of our new architecture: support for fast bit permutations and for multi-word operations. Table 4 illustrates the performance of our architecture.

For bit permutation, we test DES encryption (DES enc) and round key generation (DES key) with the fastest software program on existing processors which uses table lookup to perform bit permutations (columns a and b). We then test DES using an enhanced ISA that has an OMFLIP permutation instruction [10] added to it (columns c and d). For multi-word operations, we test integer Diffie-Hellman (column e).

We implement these programs using a generic 64-bit RISC processor. First, we obtain the execution time, in cycles, of the programs running on a single-issue processor with one set of (2,1) functional units, including a 64-bit ALU, a 64-bit shifter, a 64-bit permutation unit (for columns c and d), and a 64-bit integer multiplier (for column e). Second, the same programs are executed on a standard 2-way superscalar processor with two sets of (2,1) functional units. The speedup is shown in the first row of Table 4.

Then, we simulate the programs on an enhanced 2-way superscalar processor with one MOMR functional unit. For DES, the MOMR unit is a (4,1) Butterfly permutation unit as detailed in Sections 3 and 4. For DH (columns e), the MOMR unit is a (4,2) multiplier as described in Section 5. This is a 128-bit multiplier, which we are now able to utilize, but could not previously because of ISA limitations in a standard 64-bit superscalar processor. We assume a latency of 3 cycles for a 64-bit multiplier, and 5 cycles for the 128-bit multiplier. Either method 1 or 2 can be used in the DES programs (columns a-d). Method 2 is used for the DH program which is re-coded using the new ISA features to specify grouped instructions with the gs and gc bits. The cache parameters used in the DES simulations are 16 kilobytes L1 data cache and 256 kilobytes L2 unified cache with 10-cycle and 50-cycle miss penalties, respectively.

Table 4. Speedup of execution time

	a. DES enc	b. DES key	c. DES enc	d. DES key	e. Integer DH	f. Binary ecDH
2-way vs. 1-way	1.49	1.04	1.50	1.19	1.81	1.97
2-way MOMR vs. 1-way	1.89	17.64	1.70	1.42	3.63	2.96
2-way MOMR vs. 2-way	1.27	17.04	1.13	1.19	2.00	1.50

The second row of Table 4 shows the speedup of our enhanced 2-way processor with a MOMR functional unit over a single-issue machine. In all cases, our new architecture achieves greater speedup over single-issue execution than the standard 2-way superscalar processor (first row). The third row illustrates the additional speedup provided by our 2-way MOMR architecture over standard 2-way superscalar processors. For DES, the performance gain is very pronounced for key generation (17X speedup in column b), where permutation operations are more frequent than for encryption. The MOMR speedup is less when compared to the enhanced ISAs (columns c and d) than when compared to existing ISAs (columns a and b). This is because the introduction of new permutation instructions (CROSS or OMFLIP) in columns c and d already yields huge speedup over the table lookup method (in columns a and b). The number of instructions for a 64-bit permutation is reduced from over 20 to at most 6, and most of the memory accesses are also eliminated, resulting in much fewer cache misses. Even then, our MOMR execution achieves an additional speedup of 13% to 19% by further reducing the cycles needed for a 64-bit permutation from 6 to 2 cycles.

For the integer DH, there is significant additional speedup of 2X over the standard 2-way superscalar processors. This is because our MOMR architecture allows the inclusion of wider functional units such as 128-bit multipliers. This reduces the overall number of instructions and cycles needed to complete a 1024 by 1024-bit multiplication, which is a primitive operation in the exponentiation function needed by public-key cryptography algorithms.

7   Conclusions

This paper makes several new contributions. First, we identify two categories of bit and multi-word operations as new challenges for word-oriented processor architecture for high-performance cryptographic processing. This insight is more useful from a broad architectural perspective than just picking out special-purpose operations to accelerate.

Second, we present two architectural solutions for achieving arbitrary 64-bit permutations in $O(1)$ cycles. This is a significant result since previously arbitrary n-bit bit permutations took $O(n)$ cycles. Even with our recent proposals of permutation instructions [5][9][10][11][12], this took at least $O(\log(n))$ cycles. We show how a different 64-bit dynamically–specified permutation can be achieved *every cycle* by a 4-way superscalar processor with datarich MOMR execution. Our software solution for achieving permutations is much more powerful than a hardware solution – the latter can only achieve a few statically-defined permutations, while our solution can achieve all possible dynamically-defined permutations. Furthermore, the incremental cost is minimal, since we leverage common microarchitecture trends like superscalar processors. Our result is also significant because it implies that word-oriented processors have no problem supplying very high performance (1 or 2 cycles) for even extremely challenging bit-oriented processing like arbitrary bit permutations. Cryptographers can use bit permutations freely in their new algorithms if microprocessor architectures include these bit permutation instructions.

Third, we define the concepts of datarich MOMR (Multi Operands Multi Result) execution and instruction groups. MOMR functional units can achieve extremely high performance for bit-level permutations as well as multi-word operations, with a single coherent architectural solution. The MOMR feature enables a very flexible extension of standard ISAs to support datarich operations of many flavors. We do not have to decide whether instruction formats of future processors should support (3,1), (4,1), (2,2), (3,2), or (4,2) functional units, all of which are useful for different operations. They can all be supported on a 2-way superscalar machine with minimal changes. Our proposal to base MOMR implementations on the $(2k,k)$ datapath of a k-way superscalar processor gives us the flexibility of supporting all MOMR functional unit sizes covered by these existing datapath resources. We have also shown the control path modifications needed to support MOMR; these are minimal when compared to the complex pipeline control in typical superscalar, out-of-order machines.

Finally, a fourth contribution is the validation of the word as the atomic unit upon which a processor is optimized, since we show how both bit and multi-word operations can be achieved with MOMR execution for either superior performance or enhanced cost-performance.

References

[1]   B. Schneier, *Applied Cryptography*, 2nd Ed., John Wiley & Sons, Inc.,1996.

[2]   NIST (National Institute of Standards and Technology), "Advanced Encryption Standard (AES) - FIPS Pub. 197", November 2001.

[3]   J. Burke, J. McDonald and T. Austin, "Architectural support for fast symmetric-key cryptography", *Proceedings of ASPLOS 2000*, pp. 178-189. November 2000.

[4]   L. Wu, C. Weaver, and T. Austin, "CryptoManiac: a fast flexible architecture for secure communication", *Proceedings of the 28th International Symposium on Computer Architecture*, pp. 110-119, June 2001.

[5]   R. B. Lee, Z. Shi, and X. Yang, "Efficient permutation instructions for fast software cryptography", *IEEE Micro*, vol. 21, no. 6, pp. 56-69, December 2001.

[6]   R. B. Lee, "Subword parallelism with MAX-2", *IEEE Micro*, Vol. 16, No. 4, pp. 51-59, August 1996.

[7]   K. Diefendorff et al, "AltiVec extension to PowerPC accelerates media processing", *IEEE Micro*, Vol. 20, No. 2, pp. 85-95, March/April 2000.

[8]   "IA-64 application developer's architecture guide", Intel Corp., May 1999.

[9]   X. Yang, M. Vachharajani, and R. B. Lee, "Fast subword permutation instructions based on butterfly networks", *Proceedings of SPIE 2000*, pp. 80-86, January 2000.

[10] X. Yang and R. B. Lee, "Fast subword permutation instructions using omega and flip network stages", *Proceedings of the International Conference on Computer Design*, pp. 15-22, September 2000.

[11] Z. Shi and R. B. Lee, "Bit permutation instructions for accelerating software cryptography", *Proceedings of the IEEE International Conference on Application-Specific Systems, Architectures and Processors*, pp. 138-148, July 2000.

[12] J. P. McGregor and R. B. Lee, "Architectural enhancements for fast subword permutations with repetitions in cryptographic applications", *Proceedings of the International Conference on Computer Design*, pp. 453-461, September 2001.

[13] R. B. Lee, Z. Shi, and X. Yang, "How a processor can permute n bits in O(1) cycles", *Proceedings of Hot Chips 14 - A Symposium on High Performance Chips*, August 2002.

[14] S. Palacharla, N. P. Jouppi, and J. E. Smith, "Complexity-effective superscalar processors", *Proceedings of the 24th Annual International Symposium on Computer Architecture*, pp. 206-218, 1997.

[15] J. A. Farell and T. C. Fischer, "Issue logic for a 600-mhz out-of-order execution microprocessor", *IEEE Journal of Solid-State Circuits*, Vol. 33, Issue 5, pp. 707-712, May 1998.

[16] S. Onder and R. Gupta, "Superscalar execution with direct data forwarding", *Proceedings of the 1998 ACM/IEEE Conference on Parallel Architectures and Compilation Techniques*, pp. 130--135, 1998.

[17] D. S. Henry, B. C. Kuszmaul, G. H. Loh, and R. Sami, "Circuits for wide-window superscalar processors", *Proceedings of the 27th Annual International Symposium on Computer Architecture*, pp. 236-247, 2000.

[18] R. Canal, A. Gonzalez, "A Low-complexity issue logic", *Proceedings of the 14th international conference on Supercomputing*, pp. 327-335, 2000

[19] J. Stark, M. D. Brown, and Y. N. Patt, "On pipelining dynamic instruction scheduling logic", *Proceedings of the 33th Annual ACM/IEEE International Symposium on Microarchitecture*, pp. 57-66, 2000.

[20] M. D. Brown, J. Stark, and Y. N. Patt, "Select-free instruction scheduling logic", *Proceedings of the 34th ACM/IEEE International Symposium on Microarchitecture*, pp. 204-213, December 2001.

Dynamic Fetch Engine for Simultaneous Multithreaded Processors

Tzung-Rei Yang and Jong-Jiann Shieh

Department of Computer Science and Engineering, Tatung University

Taipei, Taiwan

Abstract. While the fetch unit has been identified as one of the major bottle-necks of Simultaneous Multithreading architecture, several fetch schemes were proposed by prior works to enhance the fetching efficiency. Among these schemes, ICOUNT, proposed by Tullsen et al. were considered to be a great scheme. The ICOUNT scheme works mainly because it favors the thread which fast moving through the pipeline, thus use the resource effectively. We think it is better letting the thread which tends to have more long latency instructions to get the priority at adequate time since long latency instructions are very likely on program's critical path. We proposed a dynamic fetch scheme which gives the long latency bound thread higher priority while the RUU or LSQ is under low usage. Our motivation is to gain further performance by not only use the resource effectively but also by the urgency of the instructions.

1 Introduction

Simultaneous Multithreading [2, 4, 6, 10, 12] is a processor design that attempts to combine both the hardware features of superscalar and multithreaded processors, and allows instruction-level and thread-level parallelism to be used interchangeably.

Simultaneous multithreaded processor can be roughly divided into two parts. The fetch engine at the front end of the pipeline is composed of the fetch unit, the instruction cache, the decode unit, the register renaming unit and the branch predictor. This part of the processor is responsible for fetching more instructions from multiple threads as much as it can and feeding them to the execution engine which comprises the instruction issue logic, the functional units and the memory hierarchy at the later pipe-stages.

Take a look at the fetch engine, the fetch unit acts a more important role as it used to be. The instructions fetched for delivering to execution engine are now from multiple threads, thus there are likely more independent instructions capable of being issued each cycle. While issuing becomes more efficient, it means that the fetch unit now has to make more effort on fetching more instructions quickly to utilize the shared processor resources. Besides, since the instructions are from different threads

P.-C. Yew and J. Xue (Eds.): ACSAC 2004, LNCS 3189, pp. 489–502, 2004.

now, the fetch unit needs to be smart enough to know which thread to fetch from. In fact, the fetch unit becomes one of the major bottlenecks of the simultaneous multithreading architecture.

Prior works have shown that using intelligent fetch heuristics would do great helps on increasing performance of simultaneous multithreading. It is meant to define a scheme of designating priorities on threads to be fetched, letting fetch unit know which thread the next to fetch from. Through the proposed schemes, ICOUNT [10] proposed by Tullsen et al. has been identified as one of the best schemes of not only the improvement it gained but also the efficiency of implementation.

ICOUNT scheme gives the highest priority to thread which has the fewest instructions in the decode stage, the rename stage, and the instruction queues. It works mainly because the policy favors the threads fast moving through the pipeline. However, we think that favoring the fast moving through pipeline threads might degrade the utilization of shared resources. Further, take the ready queue implementation heuristics into consideration, long latency instructions, such as load instructions and floating point instructions, are very likely on program's critical path. If they do not get their chance to be fetched into pipeline early, they may prevent more other instructions from the thread to be executed.

In order to further utilize the processor resources and gain more improvements, we proposed a fetch scheme based on ICOUNT which aggressively attacks the resource usage by letting more long latency instructions being fetched while the register update unit (RUU) or load/store queue (LSQ) is under low usage. Otherwise, we let the thread with fewest instructions in the decode stage, the rename stage, and the instruction queues has the highest priority as ICOUNT does.

This paper is organized as follows: Section 2 reviews the related works. Section 3 introduces more detailed simultaneous multithreading architecture. Section 4 discusses the fetch scheme of simultaneous multithreaded processor. Section 5 shows the simulation methodology and results. Section 6 presents the conclusion.

2   Related Works

Hirata [4] presented the architecture which considered as predecessors of simultaneous multithreading with thread slots containing an instruction queue, decode unit and program counter. Branch instructions were executed inside the decoding unit and data dependencies were handled using scoreboarding that dispatched ready instructions to standby stations in this architecture. A large register file organized in a bank per thread is used to keep thread contexts.

Tullsen et al. [2, 6, 10, 12] proposed the simultaneous multithreading architecture and firstly implemented it on MIPS R1000 and DEC Alpha platform. They also studied fetch policies for SMT processors and investigated several fetch policies, such as ICOUNT, BRCOUNT, IQPOSN, MISSCOUNT which attempt to improve on the simple round-robin priority policy by using feedback from the processor pipeline. In particular, the ICOUNT fetch policy has been chosen by many researches as their base fetch policy. They further identified the impact of long-latency loads in a simultaneous multithreading processor in [11], and find that it is better to free the resources associated with a stalled thread rather than keep the thread ready to immediately begin execution upon return of the loaded data.

Luo et al. [7] proposed a fetch scheme that uses both fetch prioritizing and fetch gating for simultaneous multithreading processors. Fetch prioritizing sets up fetch priority for each thread based on the number of unresolved low-confidence branches from the thread to find threads that are most likely in their correct paths, while fetch gating prevents fetching from a thread once it has a stipulated number of outstanding low-confidence branches.

Knijnenburg et al. [5] proposed a fetch policy based on a dynamic branch classification mechanism that avoids issuing instructions to the pipeline if the instruction may not belong to the correct execution path. In this way, the resources, such as instruction queues, may be freed from useless wrong path instructions.

El-Moursy et al. [3] proposed a front-end policy that reduces the required integer and floating point issue queue size in simultaneous multithreaded processors. The structure focus on both speed-enhancing and power-saving of the issue queue, that is, they try to reduce the occupancy of the instruction issue queue by trying to limit the unready instructions and data missing instructions in the queue for the same level of performance.

Madon et al. [8] proposed an implementation of the simultaneous multithreaded processor called SSMT (SimpleScacar Multithreaded) using SimpleScalar tool set. The simulator is further enhanced by the Vortex Project [1] at the University of Maryland.

Marr et al. [9] proposed a technique called Hyper-Threading which implements the simultaneous multithreading architecture on modern x86 processors.

3   Simultaneous Multithreaded Processor Architecture

Before breaking into further discussions, we briefly describe the simultaneous multithreading architecture in this chapter.

3.1 Simultaneous Multithreading Architecture

The simultaneous multithreading architecture proposed by Tullsen et al. [6] can be roughly divided into two major parts. The fetch engine at the front end of the pipeline including the fetch unit, the instruction cache, the decode unit, the register renaming unit and the branch predictor is responsible for filling the later pipeline stages with instructions. On each cycle, the fetch unit fetches instructions from multiple threads and fills the instruction cache with them. After decoding, the register renaming logic removes false register dependences by mapping the architectural registers to physical renaming registers.

Instructions are then fed to the execution engine which consists of the instruction issue logic, the functional units, the memory hierarchy, the result forward mechanism, and the reorder buffer. This part of the processor executes the instructions as quickly as their inputs are ready. Processor resources are shared by multiple threads dynamically. Instructions stay in either the integer or floating point instruction queues until their operands become available, and are then issued from these queues to the corresponding functional units.

Conventional superscalar architecture suffers from low instruction level parallelism due to only fetch from one thread at a cycle. Simultaneous multithreading fetches from several multiple threads and shares all major resources to the active threads. In this architecture, instructions from all threads competing for the shared resources each cycle.

3.2 Simplescalar Multithreaded Architecture

While Tullsen et al. construct simultaneous multithreading architecture we discussed last section base on DEC Alpha platform, Madon et al. implement the architecture called SSMT (SimpleScalar Multithreaded) [8] using SimpleScalar tool set which simulates a superscalar architecture on a x86 machine.

The SSMT has been chosen as our base architecture since the hardware requirement of the simulator is quite easy to obtain. The important characteristics of the previous discussed architecture were maintained, such as fetching from multiple threads and issue multiple threads per cycle and dynamic resource sharing, etc. However, there are some differences of the two implementations. For example: the instruction queues of SSMT were divided in different manner: load and store instruction are fed into an independent Load/Store Queue (LSQ), while other instructions are delivered to normal instruction queue. The pipeline stages are different, too.

We will have the simulator discussed more detail in chapter 5.

3.3 Bottlenecks of Simultaneous Multithreading Architecture

Although the simultaneous multithreading architecture dynamically sharing the processor resources to exploit both the thread-level parallelism came from multiple threads and instruction-level parallelism from single thread and better utilizing the resources, there are several bottlenecks identified.

Simultaneous multithreading improves performance in the benefits of dynamic sharing of resources, but it does appear to have some potential drawbacks due to inter-thread contention. Instructions competed for resources now coming from multiple threads instead of a single one puts greater stress to the shared structures such as caches, translation look-aside buffers and branch target buffers than traditional processors do. For example, sharing the cache with multiple threads, that is, partitioning the cache into pieces for threads will eventually reducing the cache space used by each thread, hence decrease the degree of locality and cause cache misses to arise.

Instruction fetching unit is one of the major performance bottlenecks which also widely studied. On one hand, the simultaneous multithreading fetch unit benefits from inter-thread competition for instruction bandwidth by partitioning the bandwidth among threads and finding more useful instructions to fill the issue slot, which is often difficult to fill if there is only one thread to be accessed at a time. On the other hand, dynamic scheduler of simultaneous multithreaded processors which issuing more instructions (from multiple threads) than traditional processors (from a single thread) does put more stress on fetch unit. It must now fetch more quickly to keep pace with the speed that consumed by later pipe-stages.

In order to improve fetch efficiency, the fetch unit must smart enough to determine which thread to fetch from since there may be several threads running at any given time. Several fetch schemes have been proposed to improve the simultaneous multi-threading performance.

Another problem is the impact of the long-latency instructions. This happens when the memory-bond threads or threads with high concentration of long-latency instructions fills the instruction scheduling window with instructions that cannot be issued quickly hence prevent other threads to be fetched and even worse, stall the processor. This problem can be solved by either increasing the size of instruction queue or good fetch scheme design.

We are interested in thread priorities while fetching and proposed our fetch scheme which will discuss further in the later chapter.

4 Dynamic Fetch Scheme

Since instructions from different threads are fed into the same shared instruction queues in a simultaneous multithreaded processor, how the instruction fetch unit fills these instruction queues affect the performance of a simultaneous multithreaded processor seriously.

The fetch unit of a simultaneous multithreaded processor generally works as follows: fetch unit selects instructions from multiple threads each cycle. It will try to take instruction from the first thread to fill the fetch bandwidth until it encounters a branch instruction or the end of a cache line. As long as there is still available fetch bandwidth, it will then take instructions from next thread, if any, yielding more issued instructions per cycle and better utilization of the processor's resources.

A priority based fetch scheme is to determine the priorities among threads to let the fetch unit know which the next thread to fetch from.

Previous studies show that the fetch unit becomes one of the major bottlenecks of simultaneous multithreading architecture. We believe a good fetch policy will eventually improves the performance of simultaneous multithreaded processor, and better utilize the resource.

ICOUNT, with which highest priority is given to those threads that have the fewest instructions in the decode stage, the rename stage, and the instruction queues, has been widely used in researches not only because its efficiency but also the simplicity on implementation. It is fast because it gives fast moving through pipeline threads the highest priority.

To our knowledge, there exists some point to argue with. First, long latency instructions, such as load instructions and floating point instructions, are very likely on program's critical path. Actually, ready instruction queues are often designed to give these instructions higher priorities to improve the overall processor performance. Second, an instruction will never get it chance to execute if it is not even being fetched. That is, if a long latency instruction loses its opportunity to be fetched into the pipeline, it will potentially block further instructions. This might decrease the overall performance of execution of multiple threads.

But, if we just give the highest priority to the thread which is likely to have the most long latency instructions, it will eventually clog the queue and degrade the performance as [11] already specified. Thus we decide to monitor not only the numbers but also the characteristics of the instructions in the decode stage, the rename stage, and the instruction queues, that is, to keep track of the types of the instructions in stages mentioned above as well.

Appending our considerations to ICOUNT, the dynamic priority rules becomes as the following:

1. While LSQ under low usage, we let the thread which tends to have more load higher priority. This is done by monitoring the number of load instructions coming from each thread in the LSQ. Thread with more load instructions in the LSQ is considered to have more load instructions by the principle of locality.

2. If RUU usage is low, we let the thread which tends to have more floating point instructions higher priority. Similarly, we set a counter to monitor the number of floating point instructions coming from each thread in the RUU. Thread with more floating point instructions in the RUU is considered to have more floating instructions.

3. A thread that tends to have many branch instructions gets higher priority since branches pass through machine quicker and its help to reduce branch miss prediction latencies. The concept has already embedded in the ICOUNT.

4. We maintain ICOUNT rules if none of the above conditions is taken into consideration.

None of the implementation on each of these rules is more complex than ICOUNT does. As a matter of fact, they monitor the instructions in the same pipe-stages but to keep track of the instruction type.

We expect the policy above will further utilized the shared resource in simultaneous multithreaded processor and achieve higher performance.

5   Simulation and Results

In order to give a more clear view of how the parameters in our proposed policy affect the overall performance, we construct two schemes step by step according to the rules of proposed scheme.

Table 1. Simulated processor configuration

Parameter	Parameter	Value	Value
Base Fetch Policy	ICOUNT	Branch Predictor	2 level adaptive
Issue Width	8	L1 Cache Block Size	32B
Fetch Queue Size	32	ICache	32K, 2 way
Load/Store Queue Size	64	DCache	32K, 2 way
Register Update Unit Size	128	L2Cache Block Size	64B
Integer Functional Units	8	L2 Cache	512K, 4 way
Floating Point Functional Units	8		

Table 2. Latency table

Latency Type	Value (cycles)
Integer	1
FP Add	2
FP Mult	4
FP Div	12
Branch Mis-prediction Recovery	3
L1 Hit	1
L2 Hit	10
Memory Access	122

Table 3. Selected Application

Selected Applications	
Integer Based	mcf, gcc, gzip, crafty, bzip2, gap, vpr, twolf
Floating Point Based	ammp, art, mesa

In this chapter, we will first introduce our simulation framework with the simulator configurations and workloads in the first section. The two schemes we constructed will be described in the next section along with the ICOUNT, which has been chosen as our baseline scheme. The simulated results of the two schemes compared to the baseline scheme will be shown in the last section.

Table 4. Workloads of 2 threads

No	Applications	No	Applications
	All Integer Based		**Mix of Integer and Floating Point Based**
0	mcf, gcc	8	mcf, mesa
1	gzip, crafty	9	gzip, ammp
2	bzip2, gap	10	gcc, art
3	twolf, bzip2	11	gap, mesa
4	vpr, gap	12	vpr, ammp
	All Floating Point Based	13	twolf, art
5	ammp, art		
6	mesa, art		
7	ammp, mesa		

Table 5. Workloads of 4 threads

No	Applications	No	Applications
	All Integer Based		**Mix of Integer and Floating Point Based**
0	mcf, gzip, crafty, twolf	3	mcf, bzip2, mesa, art
1	gcc, crafty, gzip, bzip2	4	twolf, vpr, mesa, art
2	gap, bzip2, mcf, vpr	5	gcc-crafty-gzip-mesa
		6	mcf-vpr-bzip2-art

Table 6. Workloads of 6 threads

No	Applications
	All Integer Based
0	mcf, vpr, twolf, crafty, gzip, gap
1	gap, mcf, twolf, gcc, vpr, bzip2
	Mix of Integer and Floating Point Based
2	mcf, gzip, twolf, mesa, ammp, art
3	gcc, crafty, gzip, mesa, art, ammp
4	gcc, crafty, gzip, twolf, mesa, art

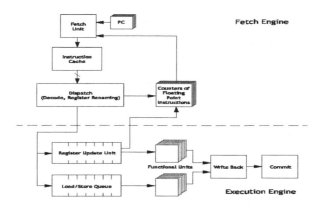

Fig. 1. The Floating Point First + ICOUNT scheme

5.1 Simulation Framework

Our simulator is derived from the SSMT simulator which originally developed by Madon [8] and further enhanced by the Vortex Project [1] at the University of Maryland. The simulator implements simultaneous multithreaded processor pipeline based on the out-of-order processor model from SimpleScalar tool set. It duplicated the SimpleScalar architecture's physical context according to the number of execution contexts to execute simultaneously. The characteristics of the simulated processor we used are given in Table 1. Table 2 shows the configurations of latencies.

We have picked up 11 applications from the SPEC CPU2000 suite to construct our workloads where 8 of them were integer based from CINT2000 suite and others were floating point based from CFP2000 suite. The applications selected are listed in Table 3. All the benchmarks were running on a GNU/Linux x86 box using reference data sets.

The workloads in our simulation are shown in Table 4 ~ 6. Table 4 lists 14 combinations of two benchmarks. Among these combinations, five of them were formed by two integer based applications; and three of them contained floating point based applications only; others were composed of an equal mix of integer and floating point based applications. Table 5 lists seven combinations of four benchmarks. Three of them were constructed by all integer applications, while others maintained an equal mix of applications from integer and floating point based. Table 6 shows five combinations of six benchmarks. Again, we had two combinations of all integer based applications and others were mixed with both kinds of applications.

5.2 Simulated Fetch Schemes

We formed two schemes from the policies proposed in section 4 and have them simulated along with the ICOUNT scheme and a random scheme to give a more clear view

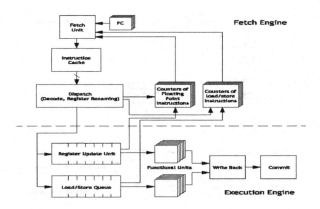

Fig. 2. The Long Latency First + ICOUNT scheme

about the impact of the parameters in the policies we proposed. The four simulated schemes are described as following:

1. Random Scheme: Random priorities are assigned to multiple threads each cycle. To avoid instructions from a single thread clog the RUU, a thread will loss its opportunity if instructions from a single thread fill 70% of the RUU. Intuitively, instructions fetched may have a fair distribution among different threads in this scheme.

2. ICOUNT Scheme: We will simulate the ICOUNT.x.8 scheme specified in [10] since we use it as our baseline scheme. It fetches up to 8 instructions from x threads each cycle, and the highest priority is given to the thread with the least instructions in the decode stage, the rename stage, and the instruction queues.

3. Floating Point First + ICOUNT Scheme: We then modify the processor and run the simulation with the following rules: while the RUU usage is lower than 50%, highest priority is given to thread tends to have more floating point instructions to execute, otherwise, we assign the priority as ICOUNT formally does. We expect the scheme to gain performance by further utilizing the RUU and floating functional units. The scheme is shown in Figure 1.

4. Long Latency First + ICOUNT Scheme: At last, we apply all the rules proposed in section 4.3 which benefits by not only utilizing the RUU but also the LSQ. It will first assign the highest priority to the threads which tens to have more loads if the usage of LSQ is lower than 60%; else it will check the usage of RUU. If the usage of RUU is lower than 50%, the highest priority is given to thread which most likely to have floating point instructions to execute. Otherwise, the ICOUNT rules are applied. The final scheme is shown in Figure 2.

5.3   Simulation Results

In this section we represent the results of simulation through Figure 3 to 7.

The weighted speedup is defined as:

$$\text{IPC of proposed scheme / IPC of the base scheme}$$

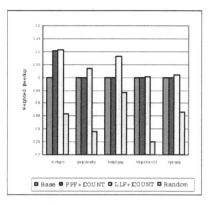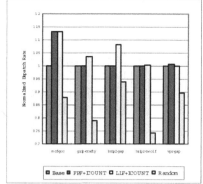

Fig. 3. Speedups and instruction dispatch rates of the workloads with two integer based threads

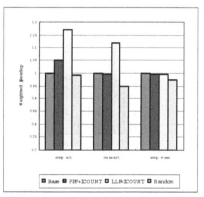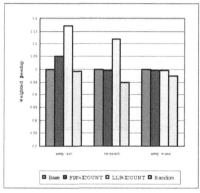

Fig. 4. Speedups and instruction dispatch rates of the workloads with two floating point based threads

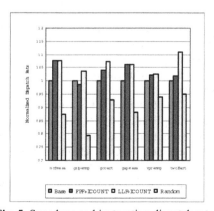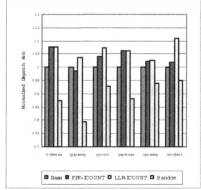

Fig. 5. Speedups and instruction dispatch rates of the workloads with equal mixed threads

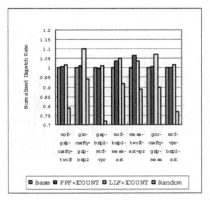
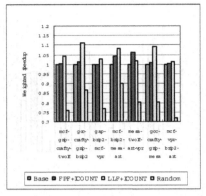

Fig. 6. Speedups and instruction dispatch rates of the four threads workloads

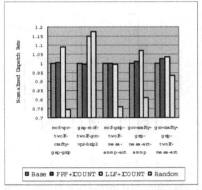
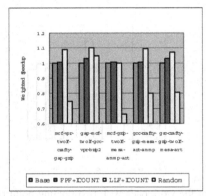

Fig. 7. Speedups and instruction dispatch rates of the six threads workloads

Figure 3 gives the speedups of our schemes relative to baseline scheme in two threads workload. All the workloads listed in this figure were integer based. Floating Point First + ICOUNT scheme didn't work in most combinations of thread, since there are either none or very few floating pointing instructions in these workloads. However, the Long Latency First + ICOUNT scheme which add the load instructions into consideration gained the overall performance.

We think the combination mcf-gcc boost the IPC because mcf is a memory- intensive application where as gcc is ILP-intensive application. ICOUNT scheme might give the higher priority to gcc in most of the execution time thus block the instructions of the mcf thread from fetching into the pipeline. Our scheme provides the ICOUNT scheme a reasonable feedback to balance the two threads.

Figure 4 gives the speedups of workloads which are all composed by floating point based threads. Floating Point First + ICOUNT scheme didn't work well in most combinations of thread. This may be because of lacking floating point functional units. Increase the floating point units may help.

The results of workloads which contain an equal mix of integer and floating point based threads are shown in Figure 5. Both the Floating Point First + ICOUNT scheme and Long Latency First + ICOUNT scheme gain improvements.

Our scheme works for four threads workload, too. Figure 5.6 gives the speedups of our schemes relative to baseline scheme in four threads workload. Most of the performances of the four configurations are increased.

Figure 7 gives the speedups of our schemes relative to baseline scheme in six threads workload.

Through all the figures also gives the improvements of overall resource usage of RUU/LSQ corresponding to the way workloads formed by representing the dispatch rate. As we can see, the shared processor resources are further utilized in most cases.

6   Conclusion

While the simultaneous multithreaded processors gain performance by sharing the processor resources dynamically to exploit thread-level parallelism along with instruction-level parallelism, it still has some potential drawbacks.

The fetch unit has been identified as one of the major bottlenecks of this architecture. Several fetch schemes were proposed by prior works to enhance the fetching efficiency. Among these schemes, ICOUNT, proposed by Tullsen et al. in which priority is assigned to a thread according to the number of instructions it has in the decode unit, register renaming unit and instruction queues were considered to be a great scheme not only the performance but also the efficiency of implementation.

The ICOUNT scheme works mainly because it favors the thread which fast moving through the pipeline, thus use the resource effectively, but this may degrade the usage of shared processor resource. We think it is better letting the thread which tends to have more long latency instructions get the priority at adequate time since long latency instructions are very likely on program's critical path.

We proposed a dynamic fetch scheme which gives the long latency bound thread higher priority while the RUU or LSQ is under low usage. Our motivation is to gain further performance by not only use the resource effectively but also by the urgency of the instructions. The proposed scheme aggressively attacks the LSQ and RUU usage which does further utilize the shared processor resources and achieve overall performance improvements. Further more, it maintains the characteristic of easy to implement.

Experiments shows that our scheme achieves an average speedup of 6% and 17% speedup in maximum with two threads workload; average speedup of 5% and 11% speedup in maximum with four threads workload; average speedup of 4% and 9% speedup in maximum with six threads workload. The resource usage is further utilized in most cases, too.

References

[1] G.. Dorai, and D. Yeung. Transparent threads: resource sharing in SMT processors for high single-thread performance. In *2002 International Conference on Parallel Architectures and Compilation Techniques (PACT'02)*, September 22 - 25, 2002

[2] S. Eggers, J. Emer, H. Levy, J. Lo, and R. Stamm, and D. Tullsen. Simultaneous multi-threading: A platform for next-generation processors. *Technical Report TR-97-04-02, University of Washington, Department of Computer Science and Engineering*, April 1997.

[3] A. El-Moursy, and D. Albonesi. Front-end policies for improved issue efficiency in SMT processors. *9th International Symposium on High-Performance Computer Architecture*, pages 31-40, February 2003.

[4] H. Hirata, K. Kimura, S. Nagamine, Y. Mochizuki, A. Nishimura, Y. Nakase, and T. Nishizawa. An elementary processor architecture with simultaneous instruction issuing from multiple threads. In *19th Annual International Symposium on Computer Architecture*, pages 136-145, May 1992.

[5] P.M.W. Knijnenburg, A. Ramirez, F. Latorre, J. Larriba, and M. Valero. Branch classification to control instruction fetch in simultaneous multithreaded architectures. In *International Workshop on Innovative Architecture for Future Generation High-Performance Processors and Systems (IWIA'02)*, January 10 - 11, 2002

[6] J. Lo, S. Eggers, J. Emer, H. Levy, R. Stamm, and D. Tullsen. Converting thread-level parallelism into instruction-Level parallelism via simultaneous multithreading. In *ACM Transactions on Computer Systems*, pages 322-354, August 1997.

[7] K. Luo, M. Franklin, S. Mukherjee, and A. Sezne. Boosting SMT performance by speculation control. In *15th Proceedings of International Parallel and Distributed Processing Symposium (IPDPS)*, 2001.

[8] D. Madon, E. Sanchez, and S. Monnier, A Study of a Simultaneous Multithreaded Architecture. In *Proceedings of EuroPar'99, Toulouse, Lectures Notes in Computer Science, Volume 1685, Springer-Verlag*, pages 716-726, August 31 - September 3 1999.

[9] D. Marr, F. Binns, D. Hill, G.. Hinton, D. Koufaty, J. Miller, and M. Upton. Hyper-threading technology architecture and microarchitecture. *Intel Technology Journal*, pages 4-15, February 2002.

[10]   D. Tullsen, S. Eggers, J. Emer, H. Levy, J. Lo, and R. Stamm. Exploiting choice: Instruction fetch and issue on an implementable simultaneous multithreading processor. In *23rd Annul International Symposium on Computer Architecture*, May 1996.

[11]   D. Tullsen, and J. Brown. Handling long-latency loads in a simultaneous multithreading processor. In *34th Annual International Symposium on Microarchitecture*, December, 2001

[12]   D. Tullsen, S. Eggers, and H. Levy. Simultaneous multithreading: Maximizing on-chip parallelism. In *22nd Annul International Symposium on Computer Architecture*, June 1995.

A Novel Rename Register Architecture and Performance Analysis

Zhenyu Liu and Jiayue Qi

Institute of Microelectronics of Tsinghua University, Beijing 100084, P. R. China
{liuzhenyu, qijy}@tsinghua.edu.cn

Abstract. In today's superscalar processors, the register renaming scheme is widely used to resolve data dependence constraints. The drawback of the conventional design is that the bit-line load of the storage cell is so heavy that the access time to these storage elements is more than one cycle, impacting the IPC adversely. Moreover, in order to implement precise exception handling, the conventional allocation and recovery strategy is very complex. A novel Rename Register architecture is presented in this paper to overcome these problems. This Rename Register has such features: 1) each storage cell has just one write port, which reduces the bit line load and simplifies the circuit design, so the access time of this Rename Register could be greatly improved; 2) the allocation and recovery strategy of this Rename Register is low-complex. This feature not only simplifies the Rename Register control circuit, but also improves the exception handling speed.

1 Introduction

Contemporary superscalar microprocessors rely on aggressive execution reordering mechanisms to achieve high performance. In superscalar architecture, crucial problems include accommodating results of in-flight instructions and resolving the data dependence between instructions in program. The register renaming implementations can be divided into two categories: In the first category, such as Pentium III and AMD K5 [1] [2], the physical registers are integrated into the reorder buffer (ROB) to support register renaming; the second scheme, such as SPARC and DEC 21264 [3][4], applies one dedicated Rename Register. In these designs, because multiple function units may write their results to the same physical register entry, the physical register bitcell must have several write ports. In order to bypass the in-flight instructions' results, multiple read ports are also needed. For example [3], the storage cell of SPARC Rename Register with 4 write-ports and 10 read-ports is illustrated in figure 1. In some aggressive designs, the port number of physical register is even more [5].

The large number of ports, aside from increasing the device count linearly with the number of ports, increases the layout area for the bitcell array almost quadratically with the number of port [6], as additional ports increase each lateral dimension of a bitcell linearly. What is more, the multiple write port structure makes it impossible to

P.-C. Yew and J. Xue (Eds.): ACSAC 2004, LNCS 3189, pp. 503–514, 2004.
© Springer-Verlag Berlin Heidelberg 2004

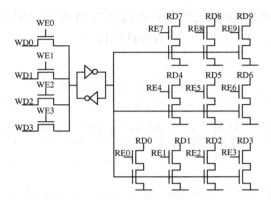

Fig. 1. 14-port data storage bit cell

reduce the bitcell load through duplicating the bitcell. Compared with ROB integrated renaming scheme, Rename Register scheme has fewer ports, but its allocation and free strategy is more complex. Two auxiliary lists, free-list and recovery-list, must be applied to maintain the precise state in case of exceptions and mispredictions. In some processors, function units (FUs) have different word width. For example, in MIPS32 architecture, the results of the arithmetic and logic unit (ALU) and the load and store unit (LSU) are 32-bit width, otherwise, the result width of the multiplication and division unit (MDU) is 64-bit. This makes the circuit design even more difficult.

A simplified Rename Register structure is proposed in this paper to overcome these draw-backs. This renaming scheme exploits the fact that the results produced by every FU are committed in program order. We divide the Rename Register into several partitions and each FU has its own private Rename Register partition. So every partition has just one write port, this character even makes it feasible to reduce the bit line load through duplicating bitcells.

Each partition is implemented as a circular FIFO queue with head and tail pointers. One entry is made at the tail of RR partition for each dispatched instruction. Instruction results are committed from the head of the RR partition to the Architecture Register File (ARF). This scheme is similar to conventional ROB. The entry width of each partition is equal to the execution unit result and depth of each partition could be optimized to save area and improve access time.

This paper is arranged as follows: In section 2, the system microarchitecture and structure of the Rename Register are presented. Dependency data bypass mechanism is explained in this section. In section 3, precise exception handling is described in details; the performance analysis in several conditions, such as level-1 D-Cache miss and level-2 D-Cache miss, is discussed in section 4 and section 5 provides conclusions.

2   Microarchitecture

In this section, the overview of the processor architecture is presented at first. Then the detailed structure and the allocation scheme of this RR are described.

2.1 Overview of the Processor Architecture

In order to analyze the function and performance of the RR, We build a RISC processor with the following features:

- MIPS32Kc instruction set compliance,
- Four function units: Jump_Branch_Unit (JBU), Arithmetic_Logic_Unit (ALU), Multiply_Divide_Unit (MDU) and Load_Store_Unit (LSU),
- MDU is non-pipelined,
- Fix map mode applied in address mapping,
- Out-of-order instruction execution.

The system block diagram is shown in figure 2. The dash line block is the Rename Register designed in this paper. The function and performance of execution units are listed in table 1 and the architecture configuration of this processor is shown in table 2.

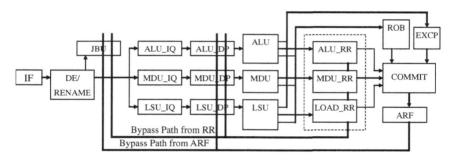

Fig. 2. The processor block diagram

Architecture registers are mapped to the Rename Register through Rename Table (RT). When an instruction enters DE/RENAME stage, it changes its destination architecture register's rename record and gets its operands' rename information from RT.

The dispatch component (ALU_DP, MDU_DP and LSU_DP) fetches the ready instruction from the head of the relative instruction queue (ALU_IQ, MDU_IQ and LSU_IQ). The operands of the dispatched instructions could be fetched from two places. If the operand is a result of an in-flight instruction and it is valid, this operand is bypassed from the RR partition. Otherwise, this operand is obtained from ARF. In the following sub-sections, we will describe how the dispatch components fetch the correct operands.

Compared with the traditional designs, we divide the Rename Register into three partitions: ALU Rename Register (ALU_RR), MDU Rename Register (MDU_RR) and LOAD Rename Register (LOAD_RR). So each partition has just one write port, which is the merit of this scheme. This architecture resolves the multiple write port problem of the traditional design. For example, if one bitcell has 12 read ports, the bit line load could be reduced through duplicating the storage cell (Fig 3). Because the bitcell area increases quadratically with port number, duplication scheme reduces the port number of every bitcell, total area of the storage array is still reduced.

Table 1. Function and operation latency of execution units

Execution Unit	Function/Latency
JBU	jump branch instructions/1 cycle
ALU	arithmetic logic instruction/1 cycle
MDU	multiply/2 cycles;
	multiply&add/2 cycles;
	divide/4 cycles
LSU	Store/1cycle
	Load(L1 D-Cache hit)/1 cycle
	Load(L1 D-Cache miss, L2 D-Cache hit)/5 cycles
	Load(L1-L2 D-Cache miss, L3 D-Cache hit)/10 cycles

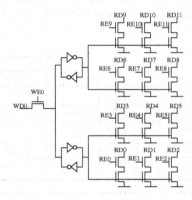

Fig. 3. Single write-port storage bit cell with duplicated storage cells

Because instructions dispatched to the same FU are committed in program order, each partition is implemented as a circular FIFO queue. The commitment component is in charge of retiring valid instructions from the heads of RR partitions. ROB just stores the crucial tags of in-flight instructions. The results of committed instructions could be obtained from the heads of RR partitions. In the following subsections, we will illustrate the structure of IQ, RR and ROB and explain the principle of how to implement the dependence data bypass.

Table 2. Architectural configuration of the processor

parameter	configuration
Machine wide	1-wide issue, 2-wide commit
ALU_RR	32 entry
MDU_RR	16 entry
LOAD_RR	32 entry
ROB	80 entry
ALU_IQ	32 entry
MDU_IQ	16 entry
LS_IQ	32 entry

2.2 Details of the Components

In order to implement this Rename Register design, other components, such as IQ, RT, ROB and EXCP, must be devised deliberately. We also show the structure of these components and explain how they work.

Rename Register Partition. Each RR partition is a circular FIFO. It has two pointers: head pointer indicates the first entry to be committed and tail pointer indicates the first empty entry to be allocated. Two flags, "empty" and "full", are used to present the status of the RR partition.

Every entry includes two fields, data field and valid field. The word width of the data field is equal to the result of the execution unit. For ALU and LSU, their RR partitions are 32-bit width. For MDU, because its result is 64 bits, MDU_RR is designed to 64-bit width. The depth of each partition can be optimized through usage statistic.

Once one instruction enters DE/RENAME stage, it is assigned one entry of RR partitions depending on its execution unit. For example, ALU instructions get entries from ALU_RR and MDU_RR is dedicated to MDU instructions. If the required partition is in "full" status, this instruction must be stalled.

The valid field is 1bit width. The valid bit of one allocated entry is set when the owner instruction writes its in-flight result to this entry. Now this entry's data can be bypassed to other consumer instructions in pipeline. So, each RR partition must have multiple read ports for data forwarding. When one instruction is committed, its RR partition entry is freed and the valid bit is reset.

The advantages of this scheme include: 1) the word width changeable feature simplifies circuit complexity; 2) the depth optimization can efficiently reduce the scale of RR partitions.

Rename Table Structure. In MIPS32Kc architecture, ARF includes Register File, Hi Register, Lo Register and CP0. Because CP0 is seldom written, scoreboard strategy is applied to it. So RT has thirty-four entries, where thirty-two entries for ARF (R0-R31), one for Hi and one for Lo. Each entry includes three fields: (1) a valid bit to indicate if the data in ARF is valid; (2) a map field (7 bits) to map this logic register to a physical register in RR, the most significant two bits are used to address the three partitions (00 indicates ALU_RR; 01 indicates LOAD_RR; 10 indicates MDU_RR); (3) a tag field (7 bits) to record the ROB tag of the last instruction that modifies this register.

When one instruction enters DE stage, it gets its operands map information from RT and modifies the RT entry of its destination register. At the same cycle, this instruction is assigned one available entry from the tail of ROB and one available entry from the tail of the RR partition. The ROB tag of this instruction is stored in the ROB tag field and the physical address of the RR entry is stored in the map field.

An example in figure 4 illustrates the procedure of physical register renaming. The logical architect registers are denoted with lower case letters and the physical registers use upper case. In the before side of the figure, the mapping table shows that register r1 maps to physical register LOAD_RR_R1 and its valid flag is reset. So r1 is mapped to LOAD_RR_R1. Because the other operand r2 is valid, this operand is still mapped

add r3, r1, r2

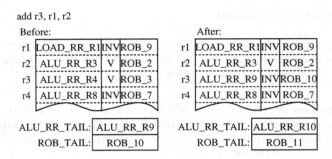

Fig. 4. Example of register renaming. Logical registers are shown in lowercase and physical registers are in upper case

to r2. During renaming, the 'add' instruction's source register r1 is replaced with LOAD_RR_R1, the physical register where a value will be placed by a preceding instruction. The destination register r3 is renamed to the first free physical register ALU_RR_R9, and this renaming is recorded in the mapping table. Before this 'add' instruction is committed, any subsequent instruction that reads the value produced by this 'add' will have its source register mapped to ALU_RR_R9, so that it gets the correct value.

Instruction Queue Structure. Each FU has its own instruction queue and instructions are steered to the proper instruction queue depend on their execution units. In order to reduce power dissipation and circuit complexity, the issue strategy is circular FIFO queue, which means that the dispatch logic fetches the ready instruction from the head of each instruction queue and entries are allocated from the tail.

Every IQ entry must store the operand information, which is used during instruction dispatch stage. The information includes: 1) operation code; 2) ARF addresses of source operands; 3) RR addresses of source operands; 4) valid bits of source operands 5) ROB tags of the operands; 6) the destination ARF address; 7) the destination RR address; 8) the ROB tag of the instruction; 9) ALU and LSU can cause exception, so ALU_IQ and LSU_IQ should store the instruction PC for exception handling. The formation of ALU_IQ entry is shown in figure 5.

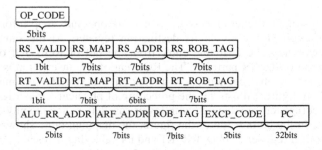

Fig. 5. ALU_IQ entry formation

IQ is also responsible for updating source dependence of instructions in the IQ waiting for their source operands to become available. Every time an instruction is committed, the ROB tag associated with this instruction is broadcast to all instructions in IQs. Each instruction then compares the tag with the tags of its source operands. If there is a match, the operand is marked available by setting its valid flag (RS_VALID or RT_VALID). This means that this source operand is available and should be fetch from ARF other than from RR partitions. Figure 6 illustrates the dynamic update logic. TAG1 and TAG2 represent the ROB tags of the two committed instructions. Reference [7] provides some methods to reduce the energy consumption of issue logic, such as disabling the wake-up for empty and ready entries and dynamic resizing of IQ. After applying these approaches, the IQ power consumption could be greatly reduced.

Dependency Data Bypass Mechanism. There exits two status of one source operand. First, the producer instruction of this source has been committed. In this case, the valid flag in IQ of this operand must have been set and this data should be fetched from ARF. Second, the producer instruction is still in-flight. Now, the consumer should check the RR partition entry allocated for the producer, if this producer has generated the result, it can be bypassed from RR, otherwise the consumer must wait until this source is generated. When all source operands of one instruction in the head entry of one IQ are available, this instruction is ready to be dispatched.

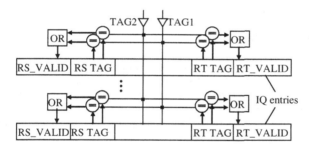

Fig. 6. IQ dynamic update logic

ROB Structure. The entry in the conventional ROB [6] includes at least following fields: (1) a result field to hold the value generated by the instruction that targets a register (32bits); (2) a bit to indicate if the result field is valid (1bit); (3) the address of the instruction ("PC value" 32bit); (4) exception codes (5 bits) and (5) architectural register id (7 bits, used for updating the architectural register within the ARF at the time of committing the instruction). If the depth of the ROB is D, the whole scale of the ROB is $(32+1+32+5+7) \times D$ bits, which consumes a non-trivial fraction of the total chip area and power. In the architecture presented in this paper, ROB scale is greatly reduced. At first, the in-flight instruction results are stored in the Rename Register; second, a dedicated exception component is applied to storage the exception message of the first exception instruction. So ROB has just these fields: (a) the destination architectural register ID (7 bits); (b) Rename Register partition ID (2 bits); (c) one bit to indicate the validity of the entry. The ROB scale is reduced to $(7+2+1) \times D$ bits. The depth of ROB is much deeper than other storage component. For example, in our design, the depth of ROB is 80. The area reduction of ROB causes the shortage of the bit line and word line of storage array. This optimization not only speeds up the access time of ROB but also lowers the power dissipation.

Commitment fetch the valid instruction from the head of ROB and the result of this instruction is fetched from the head of the RR partition denoted by the RR partition ID. The destination address is denoted by the destination address field of this ROB entry, where [0, 31] indicates architecture register file, [32, 63] indicates CP0 register, [64] indicates HI, [65] indicates LO, [66] indicates HILO and [67] indicates memory.

It is obviously that the ROB and all Rename Register partitions are circular FIFOs. This feature simplifies the management of RR and ROB, especially when the exception occurs.

3   Precise Exception Handling Mechanism

In this design, a dedicated exception component is applied to implement precise exception processing. As described in the following sub sections, this approach greatly reduces the scale and complexity of ROB. In section 4, the synthesized result shows that 80 entries ROB is reduced to 9% of total area, which dose not include caches. Compared with our design, traditional design ROB occupies no trivial area. For example, HP8000 ROB consumes 20% of whole die area [6].

3.1 Exception Component

In this microarchitecture, a dedicated exception component is applied to store the first exception instruction according to the program order. In fact, just the information of first exception is useful, because once this instruction is committed, it cancels the following instructions in pipeline. Exception component has four fields:1) a valid bit to indicate if the recorded exception information is valid; 2)a ROB tag (7bits) to store the ROB tag of the exception instruction; 3)a code field(5bit) to indicate the exception cause; 4) a PC field(32bits) to store the program counter of the exception instruction. ALU and LSU can both generate exception, so exception component has two groups of write ports. Figure 7 summarizes the port requirement.

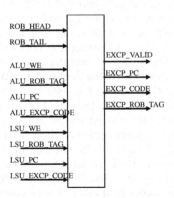

Fig. 7. Port requirement of exception component

Through comparing the ROB tags of the being written exception instructions and the stored exception instruction based upon the head and tail pointer of ROB, the exception component decides which is the first exception instruction and stores its information, such as PC, ROB tag and exception code.

3.2 Precise Exception Handling

For precise exception processing [10], Rename Register strategy is more complex than ROB strategy. Conventional Rename Register applies RAM scheme [8][9] or CAM scheme [3][4][8]. In RAM scheme, the map table is a RAM where each entry contains the physical register address that is mapped to the logical register. A shift register, present in every entry, is used for checkpointing old mappings. The width of individual entries is a function of the number of checkpoints because this number determines the length of the shift register in each entry. The CAM scheme uses two lists, free list and recovery list, to implement precise exception. When one exception instruction enters the commitment, the old mapping is recovered from the recovery list, this operation always takes more than one clock cycle.

In our design, the recovery operation is similar to ROB: When the valid of the exception component is set and the ROB tag stored in the exception component is equal to ROB head pointer, which means one exception instruction is being in commitment stage. Such operations should be taken to keep the precise status: 1) all entries in RT are set valid, that means all data stored in ARF are valid; 2) All RR Partitions and ROB are set empty, which is done by setting all entries invalid and equalizing the head and tail pointer; 3) The precise information, such as PC and exception code, are stored in CP0. In this way, the interrupted process could be resumed after the exception processing. These operations can be completed in one clock cycle. What is more, there is no auxiliary complex logic to realize this strategy.

4   Experimental Results

The performance of a microarchitecture depends on two aspects:1) instructions issued per-cycle (IPC); 2)critical path delay [8]. In this paper, we first compare the ordinary in-order architecture with this design. Next, we use TMSC0.18 standard library to synthesis this design with Synopsys DC and give the critical path delay and area overhead. The synthesized result is a useful guide for the circuit design.

We choose some benchmarks to test the performance of our design and compare them with the in-order architecture in different circumstances. During these simulations, we also can get the usage statistic of the RR partitions. Five benchmarks are applied, which include FFT, Taxis, Vector Multiplication, Matrix Multiplication and Matrix Absolute Subtraction. These algorithms are widely used in digital signal processing. Table 3 shows the percentage of instructions requiring different function units in these test vectors.

The IPC of the design applying the novel Rename Register and the conventional in-order with bypass architecture is compared in three cache statuses: (1) L1 cache hit; (2) L1 cache miss, L2 cache hit; (3) L1 and L2 cache miss, L3 cache hit. The

Table 3. Function unit utilization

Programs	ALU Inst.	MDU Inst.	LSU Inst.
FFT	48.3%	15.9%	35.8%
Taxis	77.7%	0%	22.3%
VM	72.6%	9.1%	18.3%
MM	61.4	16%	22.6%
MABS	80.6%	0%	19.4%

effect generated by cache miss is the problem that we are interested, because cache miss not only reduces the performance but also affects the RR partition usage. The performance comparison between these two architectures is shown in table 4.

Table 4. Performance comparison of this architecture and in-order architecture

Programs	this architecture(IPC)			in-order architecture(IPC)		
	L1-hit	L2-hit	L3-hit	L1-hit	L2-hit	L3-hit
FFT	1.000	1.000	1.000	0.863	0.801	0.701
Taxis	1.000	1.000	1.000	1.000	0.979	0.955
VM	1.000	1.000	0.997	0.913	0.777	0.655
MM	1.000	1.000	0.998	0.862	0.813	0.759
MABS	1.000	0.929	0.795	0.933	0.789	0.642

Applying the Rename Register, the performance is improved 10%-20%, especially when multi-cycle instructions are included, such as MDU instructions or L1-L2 cache miss occurs. Diagrams of RR partition usage under these test vectors are illustrated in figure 8.

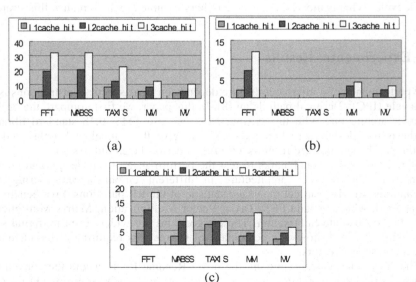

(a)   (b)

(c)

Fig. 8. Rename Register partition usage diagrams. (a) IU_RR usage diagram (b) MDU_RR usage diagram (c) LOAD_RR usage diagram

It is obviously that in different system configuration the partition usage status changes greatly. For example, in FFT benchmark, when L1-cahche hit, the maxim ALU_RR usage is 5 entries, otherwise, when L1-L2 cache miss and L3-cache hit, the maxim usage is 32 entries. This feature provides a useful way to optimize the design. In today's processor, because IO speed is much lower than internal logic, when cache-miss occurs, it must take tens of internal clock cycle to fill the missed cache line. The stall generated in this condition can not be avoided with reasonable RR hardware overhead. In these designs, the duty of RR is resolve the stall cause by data dependence and multi-cycle components, such as MDU operation, FPU operation or L1-L2 cache miss. In many embedded processors, there are no L2 and L3 caches. In these processors, the scale of the Rename Register can be greatly reduced and IPC will not be affected.

In order to provide useful data for hardware design, this design is synthesized with TMSC 0.18um standard cell library to analyze the design area and work clock speed. Besides cache (I-Cache and D-Cache), the total design area is 267926 gates. The area percentage of components in this processor is shown in table 5.

Table 5. Components size

components	area (gates)	area percentage
Rename Register & Rename Table	78607	29%
Register File	30680	11%
ROB	24631	9%
ALU_RSVST	36799	13%
LSU_RSVST	36014	13%
MDU_RSVST	15677	6%
ALU	6641	2.5%
MDU	16050	6%
LSU	9197	3.4
others	92237	7%

In our design, we combine the Architecture Register with Rename Register into one cluster, which is donated Regset. Function units get their operands from Regset, so the access time of Regset is very important. After synthesized with TMSC 0.18um standard cell library, in typical condition, the critical access time of the Rename Register is 1.61ns.

5   Conclusion

Through the optimized partition scheme, the storage cell in Rename Register partitions has just one write port. This architecture will bring following merits in the Rename Register circuit design: 1) Without multiple write ports, the circuit is simplified and the die area is greatly reduced; 2) the bit line load of the storage cell can be reduced, so the read access time is improved; 3) the scale of every Rename Register partition can be optimized flexibly depending on the usage; 4) the control logic of this Rename Register is as simple as ROB scheme. A synthesized result of this processor presented in this paper also provides some useful guidance for the circuit design.

Acknowledgement. Authors would like to thank Intel Corporation for its significant contribution to this research.

References

1. Case, B.: Intel Reveals Pentium Implementation Details. Microprocessor Report, Vol. 5, No. 23 (1993) 9-17
2. Slater, M.: AMD's K5 Designed to Outrun Pentium. Microprocessor Report, Vol. 8, No. 4 (1994) 1-7
3. Asato C.: A 14-Port 3.8ns 116-Word 64b Read-Renaming Register File. IEEE Journal of Solid-State Circuits, Vol. 30, No. 11 (1995) 1254-1258
4. Kessler, R.E.: The Alpha 21264 microprocessor. IEEE Journal of Micro, Vol. 19, No.2 (1999) 24-36
5. Jolly, R.D.: A 9-ns 1.4-Gigabyte/s 17-ported CMOS register file. IEEE Journal of Solid-State Circuits, Vol. 26, No. 10 (1991) 1407-1412
6. Kucuk, G., Ponomarev, D., Ghose, K.: Low-Complexity Reorder Buffer Architecture. Proceedings of the 16th International Conference on Supercomputing (2002) 57-66
7. Folegnani, D., Gonzalez, A.: Energy-effective issue logic. Proceedings of 28th Annual International Symposium on Computer Architecture (2001) 230-239
8. Palacharla, S.: Complexity effective superscalar processor. PhD Thesis, University of Winsconsin, Madison (1998)
9. Yeager, K.C.: The MIPS R10000 superscalar microprocessor. IEEE Journal of Micro, Vol. 16, No. 2 (1996) 28-41
10. Wang, C.-J., Emnett, F.: Implementing precise interruptions in pipelined RISC Processors. IEEE Journal of Micro, Vol. 13, No. 4 (1993) 36-41

A New Hierarchy Cache Scheme
Using RAM and Pagefile

Rui-fang Liu[1], Change-sheng Xie[1], Zhi-hu Tan[1], and Qing Yang[2]

[1] National Storage System Lab.,
Huazhong University of Science and Technology, Wuhan, Hubei, China
{relyfang, csxie, stan}@hust.edu.cn
[2] High Performance Computing Lab.,
University of Rhode Island, Kingston, RI 02881, U.S.A.
qyang@ele.uri.edu

Abstract. One newly designed hierarchical cache scheme is presented in this article. It is a two-level cache architecture using a RAM of a few megabytes and a large pagefile. Majority of cached data is in the pagefile that is nonvolatile and has better IO performance than that of normal data disks because of different data sizes and different access methods used. The RAM cache collects small writes first and then transfers them to the pagefile sequentially in large sizes. When the system is idle, data will be destaged from the pagefile to data disks. We have implemented the hierarchical cache as a filter driver that can be loaded onto the current Windows 2000/Windows XP operating system transparently. Benchmark test results show that the cache system can improve IO performance dramatically for small writes.

1 Introduction

Rapid advances in semiconductor technology have dramatically increased the speed gap between RAM and disks because of the mechanical nature of magnetic disks [1]. Magnetic disks must rotate the spindle and seek for the right track for every access [2]. As a result, disks have become the major performance bottleneck of a computer system. Extensive research has been reported in the literature. Existing studies on improving disk performance can be classified into two categories: improving the disk subsystem architecture and improving the software that control and manage the disk system [3].

RAID (Redundant Array of Independent Disks) is the most important architectural advance in disks in recent two decades [4]. The wide use of RAID in the computer industry has shown that RAID is a cost-effective way to obtain high performance and high reliability. The most popular RAID configuration is RAID5 in practical applications. However, RAID5 performance suffers from "small write" penalty because for every small write, 4 disk operations are required to read old data/parity and write new data/parity [5]. To mitigate the penalty, Stodolsky et al proposed a very interesting solution to the small write problem by means of adding a log buffer in controller's memory for parity logging [6]. They have shown that the solution can

P.-C. Yew and J. Xue (Eds.): ACSAC 2004, LNCS 3189, pp. 515–526, 2004.
© Springer-Verlag Berlin Heidelberg 2004

eliminate performance penalty caused by the RAID architectures for small writes with minimum overhead. Another interesting study was done by K.H. Yueng and T.S. Yum who presented a dynamic parity disk array for engineering database systems [7].

Besides high reliability, the primary objective of the RAID architecture is to improve throughput by means of parallelism rather than reducing access latency. In office/ engineering environment, workloads are usually random and scattered with moderate average throughput. For such workloads, performance enhancement due to RAID is limited. In addition, in today's commercial computing environment, write traffic has dominated disk traffic and may potentially become a system bottleneck. There has been a great amount of efforts to improve such write performance in file systems that control and manage disks. Log-structured file systems (LFS) can provide efficient writing even for small files [8]. LFS file systems have been implemented in prevalent operation systems. NTFS improves write performance by using a write-back caching strategy [9] that writes modifications to the cache and flushes the cache to disk as a background thread. It also logs every transaction as a log record in a log file and the file system check is based on the log record. In LINUX, ext3 and reiser file systems are all supported [10]. Ext3 and reiser are used as default file system for RedHat and SuSE LINUX distribution respectively. They all provide metadata journaling. With metadata journaling, the file system metadata is going to be rock solid, and exhaustive fsck is not needed. According to the logged metadata, fsck can finish in a few seconds without scanning the entire file system.

Caching is the main mechanism for reducing response time [1] and large RAM caches are generally used to speed up disk accesses. Such caches more effectively improve read performance than write performance, since write requests must be frequently written into disks to protect them from data loss or damage due to system failures. NVRAM (Non-Volatile RAM) caches can be used to improve write performance, but large NVRAM caches are prohibitively expensive for many applications. EMC Symmetrix 8000 has caches of 2GB to 32GB and claims to have 90% to 95% read hit rates for the largest cache size [11]. The large caches exploit spatial and temporal locality to reduce accesses to the disks, but they increase the cost of system.

This paper presents a design and implementation of an efficient and inexpensive hierarchical cache for improving disk IO performance on Windows 2000/Windows XP. The design involves a new hierarchy cache using a RAM and one pagefile. While our design is based on the DCD (Disk Caching Disk) architecture [12] proposed by Hu and Yang, we proposed a new way of implementing the cache disk using pagefile instead of physical disk or logical partition giving rise to greater flexibility and ease to install and use. Users can install our hierarchical cache at any time without the need of a new physical disk or doing a disk partition. The new cache structure can potentially improve disk write performance by 2 orders of magnitudes in the office/engineering environment. The new hierarchy cache converts multiple small writes into a large write thereby reducing the total access times. Measured performance results show that the server that loads the hierarchy cache driver runs significantly faster than the traditional system. For small and bursting writes, the hierarchy cache driver can improve synchronous writes by a factor of 6.5 in terms of response time seen by users. It can reduce the mail server response time by a factor of 3.6 in heavy workload cases. The filter driver is a WDM (Windows Driver Model) filter driver. It can be inserted into the disk driver stack transparently without requiring any changes to the current operation systems.

The paper is organized as follows. The next section presents the overview of the hierarchy cache and the system architecture, followed by the detailed descriptions of the design and implementation of the hierarchy cache driver in Section 3. Section 4 discusses the benchmark programs and the measured results. We conclude the paper in Section 5.

2   Theoretical Background

For disk accesses, there are 4 components that contribute to the total access time: controller overhead, seek time, rotational latency and data read/write time. The read/write time is a very small fraction even page-sized transfers often take less than 5% of the total access time. Disks spend most of their time waiting for seek and rotation. Therefore, amount of data accessed for each disk operation affects greatly the disk performance. The larger the data size, the better the I/O performance will be since more data are transferred for each time consuming seek and rotation.

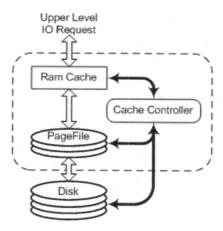

Fig. 1. Hierarchy cache architecture

The fundamental idea of the hierarchy cache is to use a pagefile, as an extension of a small faster RAM buffer on top of data disks where a normal file system exists. The RAM buffer and the pagefile together form a two-level cache to buffer write data. Small writes are first collected in the small RAM buffer. When the RAM buffer becomes full or the destaging is triggered, the hierarchy cache writes data in the RAM buffer, in multiple large and sequential data transfer, into the pagefile. These large writes finish quickly since they require only one seek instead of tens of seeks. As a result, the RAM buffer is very quickly made available again to buffer new incoming IO request packets. The hierarchy cache exploits the performance differences in different ways of disk accesses. The two-level hierarchy cache appears to the host as a large virtual NVRAM cache with a size close to the size of the pagefile. When data disks are idle or less busy, the hierarchy cache will destage from the pagefile to data disks. The destaging overhead is quite low because most data in the pagefile are short-lived and are quickly overwritten therefore requiring no destaging at all. The pagefile is much larger than the RAM cache. So the hierarchy cache can filter many IO requests, and take full advantage of spatial and temporal locality of disk accesses. The pagefile is non-volatile and hence highly reliable, too.

The hierarchical cache presented here extends the concept of DCD by using a pagefile as the cache disk as opposed to using a physical or logical partition as the cache disk. The advantage of using the page file instead of a partition is its flexibility and ease of use. Users can install the hierarchical cache any time without using a new physical disk or doing disk partitions that may destroy the current data in the disks. A pagefile has been employed to implement virtual memories in the past. Windows utilizes a pagefile to expand the physical memory and LINUX uses it for a swap partition where paging and swapping take place. In our implementation, we use the pagefile to expand the RAM cache. When we allocate space for the pagefile, we make sure that its space is physically continuous. After we intercept an IRP (IO request packet) from a user, we can keep the data in the pagefile, and we can exploit the speed difference between large sequential access and small random access of disks. By placing the pagefile in the current data partition, we do not need change the partition layout of the current system. The hierarchy cache filter driver will automatically manage the two levels of the hierarchy cache represented by the pagefile and RAM cache.

3   Design and Implementation

This section describes the key data structures and algorithms used to implement our hierarchical cache driver. As described above, we use a pagefile as the equivalent of cache disk in DCD to avoid modifying the current system partition layout. The filter driver can be inserted into the disk driver stack. It is a high level filter driver that typically provides added-value features for disks. The filter driver is a kernel-mode WDM driver and is source-code compatible with all Microsoft Windows operating systems. The filter driver can filter all the IRP targeted to data disks and reroute the IRP to the RAM cache or the pagefile according to the cache algorithm. There are many layered device drivers to finish a read/write operation. These drivers form a driver stack, and the IO manager of Windows will pass the IRP in the stacked drivers. With the help of the stack driver architecture, we can easily intercept the IRP. In order to develop the hierarchy cache driver, we use the Win2000 DDK (Device Driver Kit) and Numega Driver Suite. Numega Driver Suite is an object-oriented development tool for windows device drivers which can simplify the development of filter drivers so that the developers can concentrate on the key functionalities.

3.1 KHcDataDevice

KHcDataDevice is the son class of KFilterdevice that represents the virtual device class of the filter driver. In the driver initialization, we create an instance of the class and specify the target device when we initialize the instance. After that, we insert our driver into the target device driver stack. Our filter driver handles all the target device's standard dispatch routines, such as read, write, close, and create. After updating the new driver stack for the target device, the IRP is dispatched through the hierarchical cache driver by IO manager automatically. The main definitions of the class are as follows:

```
class DcdDataDevice : public KFilterDevice
{
public:
        DcdDataDevice(PCWSTR pwsTargetDevice);
        virtual NTSTATUS OnIrpComplete(KIrp I, PVOID Context);
        virtual NTSTATUS Write(KIrp I);
        ......
        PageFile *m_pPageFile;
        KList<HC_RAM_SECTOR> m_RamSector[HC_SECTOR_HASHSIZE];
        KList<HC_HISTORY_SLOT> m_HistorySector;
        ULONG m_WriteInLastPos;
        ULONG m_ReadInLastPos;
        NTSTATUS R2pfDestaging();
        NTSTATUS Pf2dDestaging();
        .....
};
```

We can use m_pPageFile to access the pagefile and m_RamSector to access the RAM. The member m_WriteInLastPos and m_ReadInLastPos record the read and write times in last statistical interval. With the help of them, we can judge if the system is idle or less busy. We can call the member function R2pfDestaging to destage data from the RAM cache to the pagefile. In the idle time, we should execute Pf2dDestaging to transfer data from the pagefile to data disks. m_HistorySecotro is used to record all the sectors in the pagefile. We can search all the sectors in the pagefile through the list, when we handle the read/write operations.

3.2 RAM Image

The RAM image plays the role of the RAM cache in our hierarchical cache. It is a set of contiguous memory locations reserved and allocated from the system nonpaged pool by using ExAllocatePool upon initialization of the hierarchical cache driver. m_RamSector is the hash table for the RAM. The disk is block device that is accessed in unit of sectors (512 bytes). Therefore, we divide the RAM image into sectors with the size of 512 bytes. After the filter driver intercepts a small write, it will allocate proper sectors according to the request size. Then every sector should be inserted into the proper hash table according to the sector offset. The hash table length is dynamic and there is no need to worry about collisions and replacements. We keep the hash table in sorted order when we insert a node into the list. In the mean time, we add two pointers to the other lists for every sector node to keep the continuity of sectors. Then every node is in the "+" lists. We introduce dynamic hash lists and serial sequential list, so we can position the first sector of the IO request packet with the help of the dynamic hash lists quickly, and we can get the continuous sectors according to the serial sequential list.

3.3 PageFile

In our implementation, the pagefile plays the role of cache disk in the DCD architecture [2] [3]. One pagefile can serve multiple data disks. We record the index information in the superblock, and we divide the pagefile into zones. Every zone is responsible for a partition. When data are destaged from the RAM cache to the pagefile, we write the pagefile in large writes (one segment: 64K). So we organize the pagefile using segments. Every segment has two parts. The first 1K keeps the index of the metadata of 126 sectors, and the other keeps the metadata contents. The detailed organization of the pagefile is shown in Figure 2.

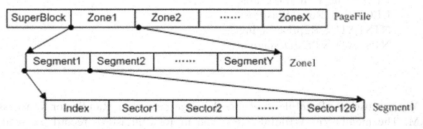

Fig. 2. Organization of pagefile

3.4 Basic Operations

3.4.1 Write Operations

When the driver filters a write request, it will retrieve the request size first. If it's a large write, the filter will pass through the request to the target disk and register a completion routine. When the request comes back, the completion routine will be executed. In the routine, we scan the RAM cache for every sector first, and we scan the pagefile later. If we find one sector, we must mark the sector stale. If the request is a small write, the filter driver will judge if it has enough spare sectors in the RAM cache. When the RAM cache is not large enough to hold the small write, it will start the destaging process to move data from RAM cache to the pagefile in large write. For every sector in the small write, we must record it in the hash tables. If the sector is already in the RAM cache, we need only update the metadata. In the process of insertion, we must keep the table in sorted order. After inserting the sector in the hash tables, the history list is also searched for the sector and marked stale if found.

3.4.2 Read Operations

When we intercept a read operation, the requested data may reside in one of multiple of three different places: the RAM cache, the pagefile and the data disk. For every sector in the read request packet, we search it in the RAM cache first. If we cannot find, we continue to search it in the pagefile according to the history list. If failed in the pagefile, the data will be read from the data disk. If the requested data is in the pagefile, we must read the entire segment where the sector is located, copy the needed sector from the segment, and update the hash tables to indicate that the segment is now in the RAM cache. The segment will stay in the RAM for future accesses.

3.4.3 Destage

The hierarchical cache consists of a RAM cache and the pagefile of top of data disks. There are two different destaging operations: destaging data from the RAM cache to the pagefile and destaging data from the pagefile to the data disk. The RAM cache is a few megabytes in size, and it is used to collect random small writes. When the RAM cache is full, we replace the sectors according to the LRU algorithm. The sectors to be destaged are combined to form a large chunk of data to be written into the page file sequentially. At the same time, we record every sector that is destaged in the history list. If the system is idle, the destaging thread will start after every 50 seconds to update the data in the RAM cache. The process is same as the forced destaging process. Destaging from the pagefile to data disks will happen in the system thread context. The thread priority is lower. When the system is idle and the filter driver finds the pagefile usage is higher than a predefined high water mark, the thread will start the destaging process. The process will read the segments from the pagefile according to the FIFO algorithm in large writes. In the previous destaging, we have combined the continuous sectors. We will build new IRP for every continuous block in the segments. And then we dispatch the IRP to the lower target device. When the pagefile usage is lower than the specified low water mark, the thread will stop destaging. We must update the history list whenever we do the destaging.

4 Performance Evaluation

4.1 Experimental Setup

To evaluate the performance of the hierarchical cache, and to give a realistic performance evaluation and comparison, we use different real world benchmarks to evaluate the effects of the hierarchical cache on an IO subsystem. We measure the performance results on a same server with or without the hierarchical cache filter driver for comparison purpose. All the tests are performed on a Tiger 7200 PC server with Pentium4 1.4G processor running Windows 2000 advanced server with service pack 1. The server is configured with 256M-SDRAM and high-performance disk with capacity of 60G. The disk is divided into three partitions. The first is the system partition, and we deploy the Exchange 2000 mail server in the second partition. And we place the data and the pagefile in the third partition. Two megabytes of system RAM is allocated to play the role of the RAM cache. Because of the limitation of the operating system, the maximum IO request packet size is 64K bytes, and the minimum IRP size is 512 bytes. In the following tests, the block size varies between 512 bytes and 64K bytes.

4.2 Benchmarks and Results

4.2.1 NTIOGEN

NTIOGEN is ported from a popular benchmark of UNIX. The input parameters of NTIOGEN are read/write percentage, IO block size, number of processes and random/sequential percentage. The output parameters are average response time, IOs per second, throughput. In the tests, we vary the block size while keeping other input parameters unchanged to observe the relationship between the average response time and the block size.

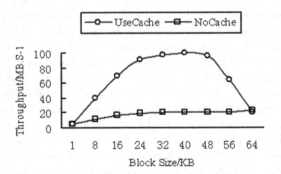

Fig. 3. Throughput comparison with different block size

NTIOGEN test results are shown in Figure 3 where the through is plotted against block size. The workload in the tests is close to the realistic workload of a working server. When there is a request, it is usually accompanied by a cluster of requests in a short time frame. In addition, there is usually a relatively long period of idle time between two consecutive request bursts. In the tests, the read/write ratio is 0/100, and the random/sequential ratio is 50/50. We can see from Fig.3 that the speed-up varies from 1 to 6 depending on the block size. The throughput increases as we use larger block sizes. But when the block size is 64K bytes, the performance is almost identical. This is because the hierarchy cache driver bypasses all IO request packets that are greater than 64K.

4.2.2 ZDESTT

ZDESTT is Ziff Davis email server test tool. It is based on the client/server architecture. The test platform includes the mail server, the controller and five clients. They are connected through 100Mbps Ethernet switch. During the tests, the clients send POP, SMTP or IMAP requests to the mail server and record the response time. All the results are reported to the controller that analyzes the results.

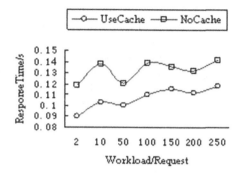

Fig. 4. Departmental POP Test Result

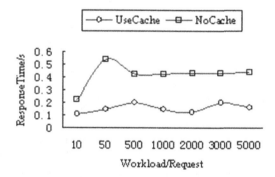

Fig. 5. Enterprise POP Test Result

We use the standard test suites: departmental POP and enterprise POP. The latter is a heavier workload. But the characteristic of both test suites is same. The test clients will spend 70% of time on logging on the email server, and retrieving the emails from randomly selected accounts using POP3 protocol. In this phase, all the requests are read operations. And the test clients will spend 30% of time on sending emails to the test accounts using SMTP protocol. In this phase, almost all requests are write requests. In these tests, the IO requests are bursty.

We can see from Fig. 4 and Fig. 5 that the hierarchical cache driver can improve the email server performance dramatically. On one hand, in the test using Departmental POP suite, the response time is reduced by approximately 30%. On the other hand, the prototype hierarchical cache driver achieves a performance improvement as high as a factor of 3.6 over the traditional device driver in the test using the enterprise POP suite. In the latter test suite, the workload is heavier, and the small writes is more intensive. The experimental results show that the more intensive the small write requests are, the more effective the hierarchical cache driver is.

4.2.3 IOMETER

IOMETER is an IO performance analysis tool that was first developed and maintained by the enterprise server group of Intel Corporation. IOMETER is both a workload generator and a performance measurement tool. IOMETER simulates workloads to stress the IO subsystem in specific ways. Under a simulated workload, IOMETER gathers data such as throughput, latency, and CPU utilization. By running the same workload on multiple system configurations, users can determine the optimum configuration. IOMETER can generate and measure loads on single or multiple (networked) systems.

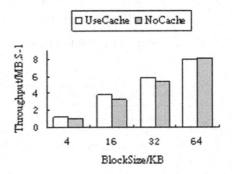

Fig. 6. IOMETER Test Results Comparison

In the tests, IOMETER worker of dynamo generates sustained IO requests to evaluate the sustained IO performance. The results reflect the extreme capability of the IO subsystem. The workload settings are 100% random, 100% write, and one hour of test duration. We performed tests with different block size on the two configurations: one with the hierarchical cache filter driver and the other without. Fig. 6 shows slight performance improvement for the hierarchy cache. It improves the sustained IO performance by about 15% when the block size is 4K. Compared with the previous tests, the performance gain is limited. This is because that IOMETER sends IO requests continuously in the tests so that the system keeps busy all the time. There is no idle time for the idle destaging but forced to destage. The performance improvement results mainly from the reduced rotation and seeks time. The performance is identical when the block size is 64K, because the filter driver will not buffer the IO request that is equal to or larger than 64K.

5 Conclusion

We have presented in this paper a design, implementation, and performance measurements of a new disk cache architecture. A pagefile and a small RAM cache are organized into a two-level hierarchical cache for disk accesses. Small writes are first collected in the RAM cache. When the system is idle, the data will be destaged from the RAM cache to the pagefile in large writes. The hierarchical cache exploits the performance difference between difference data sizes and different ways of accessing disks. One specific implementation has been carried out as a filter driver on the Windows 2000/Windows XP. Experimental results show that the hierarchical cache can improve the small write performance by a factor up to 6 for traffic intensive small write requests. It can increase the mail server performance dramatically when there are intensive random small writes. Moreover, the hierarchical cache driver is completely transparent to the file system and physical device. It does not require any modifications to the original OS nor the existing partition layout. It therefore can be inserted into the existing disk driver stack to obtain immediate performance gain.

Acknowledgements. The authors would like to thank the anonymous referees for their valuable comments on the original manuscript. Their detailed suggestions improve the quality of this paper greatly. This research is mainly sponsored by National Natural Science Foundation of China (No.60273073 and No. 60173043). Dr. Qing Yang's research is supported in part by National Science Foundation of USA under grants CCR-0073377 and CCR-0312613 and Elake Data Storage System Corporation.

References

1. Richard Stacpoole and Tariq Jamil, Cache memories – Bridging the Performance Gap, IEEE POTENTIALS, April/May 2000.
2. Y. Hu and Q. Yang, A New Hierarchical Disk Architecture, IEEE Micro, Vol. 18, No. 6, November/December 1998.
3. Y. Hu and Q. Yang, DCD-Disk Caching Disk: A New Approach for Boosting I/O Performance, 23rd Annual International Symposium on Computer Architecture, Philadelphia PA May, 1996, pp.169-178
4. P. Chen, E. Lee, G. Gibson, R. Katz, and D. Patterson, RAID: High-Performance, Reliable Secondary Storage, ACM Computing Surveys 26(2), 1994, pp.145-185
5. K. Treiber and J. Menon, Simulation Study of Cached RAID5 Designs, Proceedings of International Symposium on High Performance Computer Architectures, Jan. 1995, pp. 186-197
6. D. Stodolsky, M. Holland, W. V. Courtright II, and G. A. Gibson, Parity Logging Disk Arrays, ACM Transaction of Computer Systems, pp. 206-235, Aug. 1994.
7. K.H. Yueng and T.S. Yum, Dynamic Parity Logging Disk Arrays for Engineering Database, IEE Proc.-Comput. Digit. Tech., Vol. 144, No. 5, September 1997
8. J. Ousterhout and F. Douglas, Beating the I/O Bottleneck: A Case for Log-structured File Systems, Technical Report, Computer Science Division, Electrical Engineering and Computer Sciences, University of California at Berkeley, Oct. 1988.

9. Rajeev Nagar, Windows NT File System Internals: a Developer's Guide, ISBN: 1-56592-249-2, O'Reilly & Associates, 1997.
10. Daniel Robbins, Advanced File System Implementor's Guide, URL: http://www-106.ibm.com/ developerworks/linux/library/l-fs7, April 2001.
11. John L. Hennessy and David A. Patterson, Computer Architecture-A Quantitative Approach (Third Edition), ISBN: 1-55860-596-7, Elsevier Science Pte Ltd., 2003
12. T. Nightingale, Y. Hu and Q. Yang, The Design and Implementation of a DCD Device Driver for Unix, 1999 USENIX Technical Conference, Monterey, CA, June, 1999
13. Q. Yang and Y. Hu, Disk Caching Disk: A New Device for High Performance I/O System, U.S. Patent and Trademark Office, No. 5,754,888, Approved September 24th, 1997.

An Object-Oriented Data Storage System on Network-Attached Object Devices*

Youhui Zhang and Weimin Zheng

Institute of High Performance Computing Technology
Dept. of Computer Science, Tsinghua Univ.
100084, Beijing, P.R.C
zyh02@mail.tsinghua.edu.cn

Abstract. This paper presents a cluster-based storage platform--OStorage that employs Network-Attached Object Storage Device (NAOSD) as the low-level storage device. Owing to some features of NAOSD, including object-like access interface, simple computing abilities and self-management, OStorage supports structured-data directly to eliminate the data-model-mismatch problem of conventional storage systems. In addition, the OStorage prototype implements distributed data access, distributed transaction, some query functions and can simplify the building of scalable Internet services. The performance analysis shows that its access time increases with the system scale logarithmically, which is better than the conventional systems. And experiments show that its scalability is fairly satisfying.

1   Introduction

Today's Internet services demand the storage platform to posses many features including the ability to scale to large, high availability in the face of partial failure and operational manageability. It is challenging for a storage platform to achieve all of these properties. Many projects propose using software platforms on clusters to address these challenges.

Lore[1] is a database management system (DBMS) for XML from Stanford. The project focuses on defining a declarative query language for XML and developing new technology for interactive searches over XML data. Porcupine [2] provides one transactional record store, which combines the simplicity and manage -ability of the file system interface with a select few features for managing record-oriented data. Ninja [3] project implements DDS (distributed data structure) that presents a conventional single- site data structure interface to service authors, but partitions and replicates data across a cluster. Now a distributed hash table DDS is implemented.

However they use traditional block-based disks as low-level storage devices to construct new storage systems, which will cause a data-model-mismatch problem between applications and the storage systems. Because applications access storage through server bottlenecks[4], that a single "server" computer copies and converts data between the storage (peripheral) network and the client (local area) network.

---

* Supported by High Technology and Development Program of China (No. 2002AA1Z2103).

P.-C. Yew and J. Xue (Eds.): ACSAC 2004, LNCS 3189, pp. 527–538, 2004.

As processor performance increases and memory cost decreases, system intelligence continues to move away from the CPU and into peripherals. Storage system designers use this trend toward excess computing power to perform more complex processing and optimizations inside storage devices. Some research projects, including NASD[5], Attribute based Storage[6], Active Disks[7], bring forward the idea of Object-based Storage Device (OSD), which means that some overloads owned by traditional file servers are offloaded to peripheral storage devices.

Enlightened by this idea, we design a new network-attached object-based storage device (NAOSD). Compared with the previous projects, NAOSD supports structured-data storage directly to eliminate the data-model-mismatch problem. It can move portions of a server's processing to a storage device to improve the system scalability.

Then the usage of the prototype of NAOSD in cluster storage environments, OStorage, is proposed. It owns the following features,

- OStorage is an object-oriented data management layer as a cluster infrastructure software with transaction support, specifically for the construction of Internet services.
- Peer-Client and modular design are adapted. Many storage properties, including the storage capacity, network bandwidth and throughput, are highly scalable.
- OStorage supports transparent persistence in the Java programming language. The client interface is compatible with Java Data Objects API [8], an emerging standard for transparent data access in Java.
- Data & Meta-data uniform storage and query location mechanisms are introduced to improve the system scalability. The performance is analyzed in Part 3.4.

Now, OStorage has been achieved based on NAOSD prototypes. The usage shows that its scalability of throughput is nearly linear. The rest of this paper is organized as follows: Section 2 describes the features of NAOSD and system architecture of OStorage. The detailed design and implementation are introduced in section 3 that also presents the performance analyses. Section 4 gives the performance data and the last part summarizes this paper.

2   Cluster-Based Object Storage

2.1   Features of NAOSD

NAOSD owns the following basic features,
- Object-like access interface: Object data, the variable-length data unit and its different attributes, is supported by NASOD directly. Moreover, NAOSD has the ability to parse the object data to get one or more field values of its structure.
- Simple Computing abilities: Query and sorting are both supported by NAOSD, which act as a filter to data as it moves from the disk to upper-level services. This reduces the amount of data on the interconnect and offloads the host processor. The simplest example of this is a set select operation.
- Data and meta-data uniform storage: Object field values can also been used to define different attributes of the object, which contain the access mode, its priority of I/O and so on. That is, meta-data is a part of the object data.

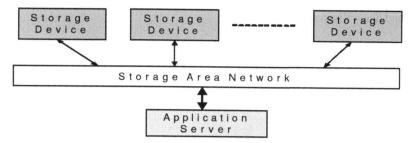

Fig. 1. IO-dense data access model

2.2 Potential Benefits of NAOSD

Three advantages are introduced when using NAOSD as the storage device:
- Direct storage-device-to-service transfers are supported to eliminate the traditional server bottleneck.
- Some server functions are ported to the storage devices to leverage the parallelism available in systems with large numbers of disks.
- The amount of data on the interconnection is reduced. It is specially useful for those data-intensive Internet services.

In the following IO-dense data access model, the performance of a server system with a number of "dumb" block-level devices is compared with the same system with the traditional devices replaced by NAOSD to determine the potential benefits.

As showed in Figure 1 the IO-dense service is running on the server. The service receives requests, processes the data from storage devices and returns the last result to requesters. Some parameters in Figure 2 are introduced to describe the whole model. We assume that d is so small that data can been processed distributedly by devices.

Application parameters:	System parameters:
number of bytes processed: D_{in}	CPU speed of the server: P
number of bytes produced: D_{out}	CPU speed of the device: P_i
cycles per byte: d	device read rate: R
run time for NAOSD system: T_i	device interconnect rate: N
throughput of NAOSD system: THROUGHPUT$_i$	device num: I
	Others:
run time for traditional system: T	$a = D_{in} / D_{out} > 1$
throughput of traditional system: THROUGHPUT	$b = P / P_i > 1$

Fig. 2. Parameters of distributed data access model for IO-dense applications

T_i and T are illustrated as follows.

$$T_i = \max\left(\frac{D_{in} / I}{R}, \frac{D_{out}}{N}, \frac{(D_{in} / I) * d}{P_i} \right)$$

$$T = \max\left(\frac{D_{in} / I}{R}, \frac{D_{in}}{N}, \frac{D_{in} * d}{P} \right)$$

That is, run time is determined by the minimum among device read rate, device interconnection rate and the CPU speed of the device if the data process is parallelized ideally.

Then the system throughput can been computed.

$$THROUGHPUT_i = \frac{D_{in}}{T_i} = \min\left(R*I, a*N, \frac{P*I}{d*b} \right)$$

$$THROUGHPUT = \frac{D_{in}}{T} = \min\left(R*I, N, \frac{P}{d} \right)$$

Therefore, some conclusions can been drew based on different assumptions.

1) Device read rate (R*I) is the minimum.

$$\frac{THROUGHPUT_i}{THROUGHPUT} = I / b$$

It means that the performance benefit will be introduced if the amount of processing capacities of all NASODs exceeds that of the server.

2) CPU speed of the device (P/d) is the minimum.

$$\frac{THROUGHPUT_i}{THROUGHPUT} = I / b$$

The conclusion is as same as 1).

3) Data transfer rate (N) is the minimum.

$$\frac{THROUGHPUT_i}{THROUGHPUT} = \min\left(\frac{R*I}{N}, a, \frac{P*I}{d*b*N} \right)$$

We know,

$$\frac{R*I}{N} > 1, a > 1 \text{ and } \frac{P*I}{d*b*N} > I/b.$$

So, it is still determined by the comparison between the amount of processing capacities of all NASODs and that of the server. Now many large scale storage systems, including Compaq TPC-C, Microsoft Terra- Server, Digital TPC-C and Digital TPC-D 300, satisfy this condition.

2.3   Overview of OStorage

OStorage system is defined as a self-contained object-oriented data management layer running on a server cluster to handle storage requests of Internet services running on the same cluster. The clients in Figure 3 connect to service instances through Internet by Internet application protocols such as HTTP, IMAP, etc.

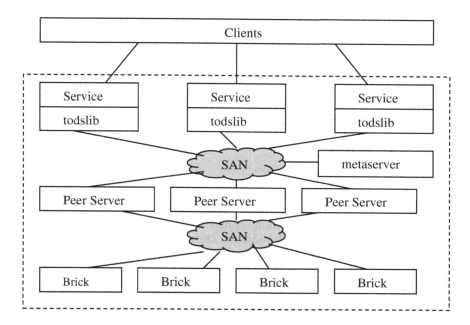

Fig. 3. OStorage overview

Services are multiple instances of the same Internet service. They connect to OStorage components known as Peer Servers to access data. They are inherently identical to each other from users' view, each presenting a single image of the whole system and they communicate with each other in a peer-to-peer style.

There are also other components (the lower blocks, named Brick), which the services do not connect to directly. Brick is the instance of NAOSD that provides storage and query interfaces for structured-data employing the power of embedded processors.

Within the service process, a library named TODSLib maps user API calls to messages sent to Peer Servers and parse results from them. Currently a Java version of TODSLib is implemented. As mentioned before, it implements transparent persistence and is compliant with the Java Data Objects API.

The Meta-Server maintains system configuration and meta-data. It is replicated and thus assumed fault-tolerant, providing a safe place for critical global information. System configuration includes location (IP, port) and parameters of all components such as Peer Servers and Bricks. This ensures centralized management of the whole system.

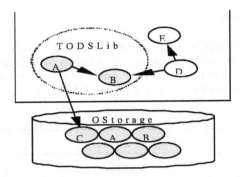

Fig. 4. Object references

3   Design and Implementation

3.1   Data Model

Objects managed by OStorage are put into name spaces known as Object Spaces. Each object space has its own set of class hierarchy and objects. An Object Space is analogous to a database or a table space in RDBMS, or a directory in file systems. The list of all Object Spaces, class meta-data and permission rules of each Object Space are all maintained by the Meta-Server. Data of an Object Space are stored on a subset of all the Bricks, whose list is managed by the Meta-Server. Object (or persistent object) is the granularity of most operations in OStorage. Every persistent object is associated with a OID. An object has a number of value fields and can reference other objects. Figure 4 illustrates an example of object references. A and B are active persistent objects, with A referring to an inactive one, C. D and E are transient objects not currently managed by TODSLib. However, they will become persistent by a make persistent call to TODSLib.

When a transient object is made persistent, all objects reachable from it are also made persistent (persistence by reachability). Persistent objects are long-lived and independent of life-cycles of the service instances or TODS runtime. Any modification to the object will be written to the store implicitly at some time (e.g., when transaction is committed). Persistent objects are loaded into memory automatically when needed.

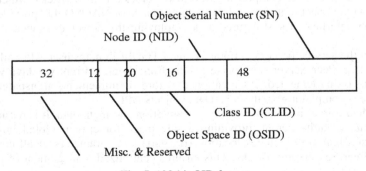

Fig. 5. 128-bit OID format

3.2   Object Identification

An Object ID is a 128bit integer, whose structure is shown in figure 5. Object Space ID (OSID) indicates which Object Space this object belongs to. Class ID (CLID) references to class definition in the Meta-Server, it is assigned when first object of its class is inserted into the system. Node ID (NID) denotes the location of the object, while Serial Number is the local ID of the object.

One thing to notice is that the OID is a physical ID, in the sense that it indicates on which node the object is located. The system can directly find the object just by the OID. This contrasts to the alternative approach of using a logical object ID or "path" and thus needs to look up the real location of objects before accessing them, which introduces more overhead and the problem of effectively and coherently caching the lookups. Logical ID or text path are often introduced for user friendliness and location transparency. The former is not a problem in OStorage because TODSLib completely hides from users the details of fetching and storing persistence objects. OIDs are not even seen by them. The latter reason is most justified for wide-area distributed systems, where nodes and network failures and changes are common. As OStorage is designed for well managed cluster environment, it is found that an OID with more information greatly simplifies system design and improves performance.

3.3   Access Interface

Moreover OStorage supports non-transactional and transactional modes of access. It is determined by whether data accesses are enclosed in a transaction.

For non-transactional accesses, data caching on Peer Servers are enabled, which results in much better performance. However there is no guarantee about data consistency under concurrent access. Different Peer Servers may report different value for the same object at some moment due to asynchronous cache invalidation. Consistency level of non-transactional access is PRAM Consistency [9], using parallel computing terminology, i.e., writes made by each specific client are seen by others in the original order, but the global order is not guaranteed.

Both Peer Servers and Bricks are designed to be transactional. Distributed transactions on multiple Bricks are managed using the two-phase commit protocol. In current prototype NAOSD is simulated on Berkeley DB[10], which is a embedded database with commit/abort functions. When distributed transaction must be done, the corresponding Peer Server acts as the transaction manager, and participating Bricks act as resource managers. All status information of ongoing distributed transactions is stored persistently in a simple database managed by the Peer Server, in order to make both Peer Server and Brick failures recoverable.

Bricks provide upper-level services with the following interfaces:

```
BeginTransaction, prepareTransaction, commitTransaction,
rollbackTransaction
```

In addition to the location mechanism through OID, distributed query is achieved to fetch objects from Bricks. It looks like a cursor operation in DBMS, which is managed by one Peer Server to command Bricks to filter objects according to some field condition. Then, services can browse all objects returned.

One important feature of OStorage is that some common functions of services are implemented in the storage layer, and NAOSD plays an important hole to simplify this achievement.

3.4 Performance Model

Data & meta-data uniform storage and query location mechanisms are introduced in previous sections and we give a performance model for them to argue OStorage owns higher scalability as compared with conventional systems.

Our model contains N Peer Servers and n Bricks connected with a high performance network. The CPU speed ratio of Peer Server and Brick is m (m>1) and a fixed amount of objects is stored in every Brick. In addition, the meta-data used to locate objects can be stored in two ways. First, they are stored as the fields of data on Bricks in uniform storage mode. Second, they are separated from the data and placed distributedly on every Peer Server in the conventional mode

Then, performance models of these two modes are computed respectively. At first the data location flow of the conventional mode is described in Fig 6 and the flow of uniform storage in Fig 7.

Some parameters are introduced to describe models.

T_{lookup} : time for Brick to browse the local meta-data, which is in direct ratio to the number of objects and in inverse ratio to the CPU speed. Then time used by Peer Server to query the local meta-data is $T_{lookup} * \dfrac{n}{N*m}$.

T_{access} : time used to access the local data and meta-data.

T_{remote} : the point-to-point communication speed between nodes.

$T_{p-broadcast}$: the broadcast speed among Peer Servers.

$T_{b-broadcast}$: the broadcast speed between one Peer Server and all Bricks.

Time to locate one object in the conventional mode, $T_{traditional}$, can be presented as the following equation.

$$T_{traditional} = T_{lookup} * \frac{n}{N*m} + T_{access} * \frac{1}{N} + (T_{p-broadcast} + T_{lookup} * \frac{n}{N*m} + T_{remote} + T_{remote})* \frac{N-1}{N} + (T_{remote} + T_{access})$$

The first term is the time spent by the Peer Server on looking for the local meta-data. Its hit probability is 1/N, so the next term is the time to access the hit meta-data. The third is the overhead of transmitting the location request to other Peer Servers if the meta-data is missed locally. The last is the time spent by the target Brick on reception and accessing the located object.

$$T_{traditional} = (\frac{2nN-n}{m*N^2})* T_{lookup} + 2* T_{access} + \frac{N-1}{N}* T_{p-broadcast} + \frac{2N-1}{N} * T_{remote}$$

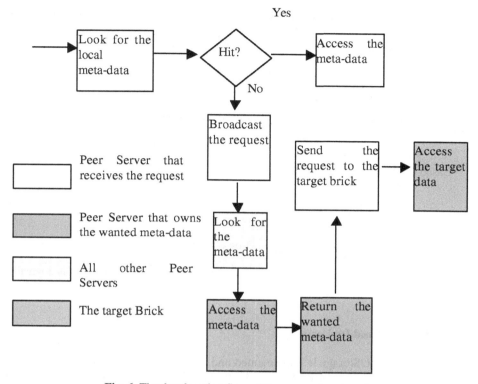

Fig. 6. The data location flow of the conventional mode

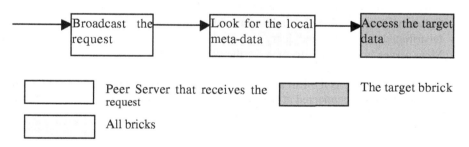

Fig. 7. The data location flow of uniform storage and query location mechanisms

In the uniform storage mode time to locate one object, T_{naosd}, is computed by the next equation.

$$T_{naosd} = T_{b-broadcast} + T_{lookup} + T_{access}$$

The first term is the overhead for one Brick to broadcast the location request to all others. The next two correspond to time consumed by every Brick to look for and access the local data respectively.

To simplify the analysis, T_{remote} is assumed a constant and binomial tree algorithm [11] is adopted for the broadcast communication. So broadcast overhead can be described as following equations.

$$T_{p-broadcast} = (\lfloor Log_2(N-1) \rfloor + 1) * T_{remote}$$
$$T_{b-broadcast} = (\lfloor Log_2(n-1) \rfloor + 1) * T_{remote}$$

Some other assumptions are also introduced as follows.

$$T_{remote} = 5, \ T_{lookup} = 1, \ T_{access} = 10, N = 5, m = 5.$$

Based on these hypotheses, $T_{traditional}$ and T_{naosd} can be computed.

$$T_{traditional} = \frac{9n}{125} + 20 + 0.8 * 5 * 3 + 9 = \frac{9n}{125} + 41$$

$$T_{naosd} = (\lfloor Log_2(n-1) \rfloor * 5) + 16$$

So, $T_{traditional}$ increases with the system scale linearly while T_{naosd} is logarithmical.

3.5   Prototype and Its Usage

The prototype of OStorage is implemented and its hardware platform contains a cluster of PC servers connected with 100M Ethernet. The whole system is coded with JDK 1.4 other than Bricks that are implemented in C language based on Berkeley DB. The following features are achieved.
- Structured-data storage functions, including object read/write/create/delete.
- Soft consistency replication and linearizability are both implemented.
- Distributed transaction and query.
- Meta server is employed to manage the whole system to provide a global consistent storage view of Bricks for Peer Servers.
- Requests between TODSLib and Peer Servers can been sent in a burst mode, that is, one session is connected at first and several requests can been transferred in one time if possible to decrease the overload.

4   Results

Performance experiment results are presented in this section. Our test environment is a 36-node server cluster and each node is equipped with 4 Intel Pentium III Xeon processors at 750 MHz, 1 GB of RAM and a 36 GB 10000 RPM SCSI disk. The network is 100M fast Ethernet. All nodes run Redhat Linux 7.2. The system and test programs were run with Sun JDK 1.4.0-b92 for x86 Linux.

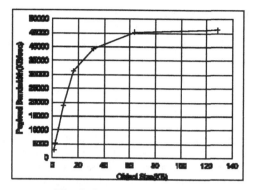

Fig. 8. On-disk Read Payload

4.1 On-Disk Reads

This test is closer to actual operational environment. To approximate real-world workload, we first populated each of the Bricks with 5000 objects of the object length being tested. Then we access these objects randomly by Object ID we gather when inserting them. Although random access is not a good "real-world" pattern, it effectively shows the bottom-line performance we should expect. The Object Caches in Peer Servers are turned off to show raw Brick read performance. It completes as many as 2740 reads of 1KB object in a second. As object size increases, payload bandwidth increases quickly, to 46MB/s when object size is 128KB. More detailed results are showed in Figure 8. This throughput result is satisfying. Since actual work-load usually has good locality, the efficiency of the Buffer Cache will be much better, thus overall throughput higher.

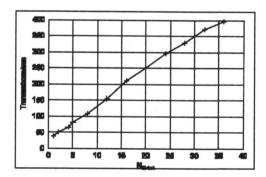

Fig. 9. Transactional Write

4.2 Transactional Writes

Transaction performance is directly tied to disk write performance because they include synchronous writes to the log file. Here we test inserting objects into Bricks by transactions. In each transaction, we insert four objects that are about 2K in size totally. From the results shown in Figure 9, we can see that the transaction performance grows linearly with Brick number, just as we expected. When all 36 Bricks participate in, 396 transactions can be done in a second.

5   Conclusion

In this paper, we present the design and implementation of OStorage, a cluster storage platform for Internet services. It is designed with the requirements of scalable services in mind and appeals to many advantageous properties of modern server clusters. One type of OSD, NAOSD is used as the low-level storage device, which supports structured-data directly to eliminates the data-model-mismatch problem. In addition, moving portions of an service's processing to a storage device significantly reduces data traffic and leverages the parallelism already present in large systems.

The user interface implements transparent persistence which relieves developers completely from writing I/O code. Different levels of availability are supported that make OStorage suits the requirements of different services.

References

1.   R. Goldman, J. McHugh, and J. Widom. From Semistructured Data to XML: Migrating the Lore Data Model and Query Language. Proceedings of the 2nd International Workshop on the Web and Databases, Philadelphia, Pennsylvania (1999).
2.   Robert Grimm, Michael M. Swift, and Henry M. Levy. Revisiting structured storage: A transactional record store. Technical Report UW-CSE-00-04-01, University of Washington, Department of Computer Science and Engineering (2000).
3.   Steven D. Gribble, Eric A. Brewer, Joseph M. Hellerstein, and David Culler. Scalable, Distributed Data Structures for Internet Service Construction. In Proceedings of OSDI 2000. San Diego, CA (2000).
4.   Garth A. Gibson, David F. Nagle, William Courtright II, etc. NASD Scalable Storage Systems. In the Proceedings of USENIX 1999, Linux Workshop, Monterey, CA (1999).
5.   G. A. Gibson, et al., A Case for Network Attached Secure Disks, Tech. Report CMU-CS-96-142, Carnegie Mellon University (1996).
6.   Elizabeth Shriver, A Formalization of the Attribute Mapping Problem. HP Labs Technical Reports, HPL-1999-127.
7.   Erik Riedel, Christos Faloutsos, Garth A. Gibson, etc. Active Disks for Large- Scale Data Processing. IEEE Computer, Vol.34, No.6 (2001). 68-74.
8.   C. Russell, Java Data Objects 1.0 Proposed Final Draft, JSR12, Sun Microsystems Inc., available from http://access1.sun.com/jdo (2001).
9.   M. Raynal and A. Shiper. A Suite of Formal Definitions for Consistency Criteria in Distributed Shared Memories. ISCA Proceedings of the International Conference PDCS, Dijon France (1996). 125-130.
10.   Sleepycat Software Inc., Berkeley DB Programmer's Tutorial and Reference Guide, available at www.sleepycat.com (2001).
11.   Thomas H. Cormen, Charles E. Leiserson, and Ronald L. Rivest. Introduction to Algorithms[M]. MIT Press (1990).

A Scalable and Adaptive Directory Scheme for Hardware Distributed Shared Memory

Kiyofumi Tanaka[1,2] and Toshihide Hagiwara[1]

[1] School of Information Science, Japan Advanced Institute of Science and Technology,
1–1 Asahidai, Tatsunokuchi, Ishikawa, 923–1292 Japan
[2] "Information and Systems", PRESTO, Japan Science and Technology Agency
{kiyofumi,t-hagiwa}@jaist.ac.jp

Abstract. In hardware distributed shared memory in the style of CC-NUMA, directory information that specifies locations of sharing processors is used for cache coherence. Structure of the directories affects the size of hardware, time required for coherence transaction, and network traffic. In this paper, we propose and evaluate a new scalable directory scheme, "*adaptive hierarchical coarse directory*", that exploits hierarchy in the system and exhibits appropriate values in terms of the above three items. The directory has tolerance to many copies of a memory block scattered in a large-scale parallel system. This characteristic makes it easy for operating systems to allocate parallel threads in multitasking/multiuser environment.

1 Introduction

In a distributed shared memory (DSM) system based on CC-NUMA (Cache Coherent Non-Uniform Memory Access) system, sharing information must be managed per block such as cache line, page, or object. Sharing information indicates whether or not the block is shared and whether it has been updated or not, and includes a directory that identifies the processors holding a copy of the block. A directory scheme in hardware DSM affects the amount of hardware, efficiency of coherence processing, and network traffic. For example, when the amount of memory required for storing directories increases in proportion to the number of processors in a system, the amount might get larger than that of general-purpose program data, which is unrealistic from the point of view of efficient use of memory. Therefore, it is difficult to apply the kind of directory to a large-scale system.

We proposed a small-size directory scheme and communication methods cooperating with the directory, and built a prototype parallel computer which implemented them [1]. The preliminary evaluation based on the information gained from the prototype showed that the directory with the communication methods had better scalability on the amount of memory required, efficiency of coherence processing, and network traffic in a large-scale system than other existing directories such as a full-map directory scheme [2]. However, the directory has a possibility of generating more traffic than other directory schemes when the

P.-C. Yew and J. Xue (Eds.): ACSAC 2004, LNCS 3189, pp. 539–553, 2004.
© Springer-Verlag Berlin Heidelberg 2004

number of processors sharing a block is not large and the copies of the block are scattered in the system. In this paper, we propose a new directory scheme which is adaptive to the situation where our previous scheme might increase redundant communications, and evaluate it quantitatively by using real programs.

In section 2, scalability issues of directory schemes in hardware DSM are discussed. Section 3 describes the outline of a lightweight hardware DSM we proposed. In section 4, we propose a new directory scheme. Section 5 compares our scheme with other schemes in terms of the size, time, and traffic required for coherence processing. Section 6 describes the related work and Section 7 concludes this paper.

2   Directory Schemes of Hardware DSM

The size of memory taken up by directories increases as the scale of the system is enlarged. Therefore, the structure and size of a directory will affect the hardware costs. Directory schemes are classified into two types: one type completely identifies the processors that hold a copy of a memory block, and the other incompletely. The former has a problem in that it requires a large amount of memory for directory storage when there are many processors in a system, or a problem in that an overhead of accessing a directory is large when the directory size is larger than the bit width of a memory component or when the structure of the directory is based on a linked list. On the other hand, there are two general schemes for the latter: one in which the number of processors that can share a block is limited and the other in which the processors that share a block are identified roughly, that is, a group that includes all the processors which share a block is indicated. Both take up relatively less memory than complete identification methods but there are still significant overheads caused by broadcasting or multicasting of coherence messages when many processors share a block.

Full-map directory [3], LimitLESS directory [4], chained directory [5,6] and hierarchical bit-map directory [7] hold complete information on sharing. The full-map directory assigns one bit to each processing node to indicate whether the processing node holds a copy of the relevant memory block. Since this scheme requires memory in proportion to the number of processing nodes, it is not suitable for large-scale systems. Multistage accesses to the directory memory are also required for getting one directory's information if the number of processing nodes exceeds the width of a single access, for example, 64 or 128 bits.

The LimitLESS directory places limitation on the number of processors that can share a block in order to reduce the memory requirement. The directory has the limited number of pointers to point to processors with the block copy. When the number of copies exceeds the limit, a protocol processor or processing element emulates the full-map scheme. Although this directory requires less memory than full-map when the system has many processors, execution of the software brings a large overhead.

Although the size of a chained directory is small because it is a pointer, the structure generates long access latencies caused by sequential accesses to the linked directories. Therefore, it is important to keep the number of sharing processors low by employing an invalidation protocol when this directory is used.

In the hierarchical bit-map directory, sharing information for a memory block is distributed, that is, full-map information is partitioned into sub-bitmaps among hierarchical levels in a tree network. The directory size, therefore, increases with the scale of the system. It requires about $\sum_{k=0}^{m-1}(n+1)n^k$ bits for each shared memory block in an n-ary tree with height m. More memory is thus required than for a full-map directory. The scheme inherently increases communication latency, since it requires access to a part of the directory at every level of the hierarchy. Accordingly, the directory should be stored in high speed memory to prevent the high network latency from degrading system performance.

Consequently, when directories which have complete information on the locations of block copies are used in a large-scale system, the problems are that the directory is large, that access latency is high, or that protocol processing by a protocol processor/processing element induces large overheads of software execution.

On the other hand, the limited directory [8] and pseudo-full-map directory [9,10] obtain a size that is not proportional to the number of processors by using incomplete information on sharing. The limited directory uses a limited number of pointers to processors with a cached copy, and the directory size, therefore, does not increase in proportion to the system scale. When the number of copies reaches the limit, the next generation of a copy forces cache replacement by victimizing an existing copy or broadcasting of a coherence message to all processors, which leads to a lot of extra communication[1]. It is thus inevitable to keep the sharing number low by using an invalidation protocol.

The pseudo-full-map directory reduces the required memory by holding a bitmap per each level of the hierarchy in a tree interconnection network. There are three schemes in the pseudo-full-map directory, LPRA (Local Precise Remote Approximate), SM (Single Map), and LARP (Local Approximate Remote Precise). LPRA scheme specifies near processors as precisely as possible and more distant processors roughly. LARP specifies distant processors as precisely as possible, and nearer processors roughly. In SM scheme, all network nodes at a level use a unique bitmap. Here, directories for memory blocks are accessed only at the respective home processors because each directory can be maintained at its home processor. This directory scheme takes up the amount of memory proportional to $\log n$ when the system has n processors, and the incompleteness of sharing information leads to redundant communications in cache coherence transactions.

3   Lightweight Hardware DSM

We proposed a directory scheme, *hierarchical coarse directory*, which is of incomplete sharing information [1]. The size is smaller than any other existing

---

[1] Although the limited directory with broadcasting is of incomplete information, that with replacement policy is regarded as of complete.

directory schemes except ones based on broadcasting. Dynamic combining and multicasting mechanisms of an interconnection network cuts down messages increased by the incompleteness of the directory.

3.1   Hierarchical Coarse Directory

We assume that a tree structure can be physically embedded in the interconnection network. A home processor is statically assigned to each memory block. A home processor records a "maximum shared distance" as directory information. Here, the "maximum shared distance" is half of the number of hops between the home processor and the most distant processor with a copy of the block. In other words, the distance is the height of the minimum subtree which includes all processors that have a copy of the block.

Figure 1 is an illustration of the hierarchical coarse directory structure. The gray leaves in the figure represent processors which have a copy of the block[2], and the mesh areas indicate the shared area which includes all processors with a copy. In figure 1(a), the home processor and one of its next-door neighbors in the network hierarchy hold a copy. Therefore, the maximum shared distance is one. On the other hand, the maximum shared distance in figure 1(b) is two since the shared area is the subtree the height of which is two[3].

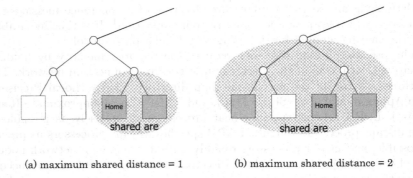

(a) maximum shared distance = 1   (b) maximum shared distance = 2

Fig. 1. Hierarchical coarse directory.

The shared area may include processors that don't have a copy (for example, in the figure, the white leaves in the shared area). To the home processor, these processors also seem to have a copy. The simplicity of the directory representation causes an inaccuracy, that is, an overestimation of the number of block

---

[2] To be exact, a home processor has an original block. Here, we don't distinguish between the original block and its copy.

[3] In the actual hardware implementation, the maximum shared distance is smaller by one than the height of the subtree tree in order to simplify the calculating hardware. Therefore, the distance in figure 1(a) is zero, and that in figure 1(b) is one.

holders. However, the overestimation does not influence cache coherence. When a processor that does not have a copy receives a coherence message from the home processor, it has only to return a dummy acknowledgment message. The procedure maintains coherence.

The hierarchical coarse directory is $\lceil \log_2 \log_k n \rceil$ wide where n is the number of processing elements and the network has a k-ary tree structure[4]. For example, a four-bit directory for each memory block is sufficient to cover directory information for a massively parallel system that contains more than 64,000 processors connected by a binary tree network. Moreover, this directory system accomplishes the reduction of required memory without limitations on the number of copies.

3.2   Hierarchical Multicasting and Combining

Identical messages must frequently be transported to many or all processing elements during coherence processing such as invalidation or update. The transport performance can be improved by utilizing hierarchical multicasting. For example, when an invalidation is processed for a shared memory block, the home processor assigned in advance to the memory block issues only a single invalidation message. Each switching node in the network that has received the message multicasts it in all the directions that lead to any node within the shared area. Figure 2 (a) shows the multicasting operation when the maximum shared distance is two.

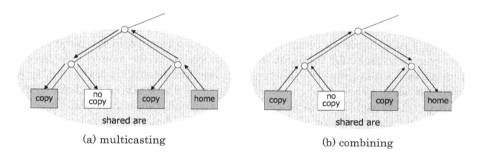

(a) multicasting   (b) combining

Fig. 2. Hierarchical multicasting and combining.

The directory scheme affects the multicasting method. In implementation of multicasting, a directory with complete information, such as a full-map directory, requires that a network packet for multicasting includes a group of destination processor numbers or the directory itself. The former approach makes the multicasting method impractical when the number of destination processors is large. For example, when the system has 1,024 processors that require 10 bits of a

---

[4] This is because the height of the tree can be decreased by one from the point of view of the actual hardware implementation, as mentioned before.

processor number to identify any processor, and 200 processors share a memory block, total 2,000 bits (250 bytes) must be included in the packet header, which is not small. The latter always requires the same number of bits as of all processors, which may be far from insignificant, and makes a switch perform an elaborate routing. On the other hand, the hierarchical coarse directory system is well-suited to multicasting. It is only necessary for network packets to include the directory information, that is, the maximum shared distance. The network switching nodes multicast by comparing the maximum shared distance with their own hierarchical level.

When two or more messages for an identical purpose are sent to a single processor, the messages can be combined into a single message at any level of the network hierarchy. This reduces the need for a series of processes at the destination processor. For example, every processor that has received an invalidation message returns an acknowledgment message which indicates the completion of invalidation processing within the processing node, even if it does not have a copy of the indicated block. All the acknowledgment messages are directed to the block's home processor. Each switching node forwards an acknowledgment message after it confirms the arrival of all acknowledgment messages from all branches along which it sent the invalidation message. The process is shown in Figure 2 (b).

The hierarchical coarse directory is also suited to the combining of messages. The number of messages to be combined at a switching node depends on whether the node is or is not a root of the shared subtree. When it is the root, the number is $k - 1$ where the network is k-ary. When it is not, the number is k. On the other hand, a switch must record the number of messages to be combined in some way for a full-map directory system.

The hierarchical multicasting and combining schemes require no serialized processing at a home processor. It takes only one round-trip latency between the home processor and the most distant processor in the shared area for the home processor to complete a coherence transaction, regardless of the number of processors with a copy. The combination of the reduced size of the hierarchical coarse directory and the hierarchical multicasting and combining make it possible actually to employ not only an invalidation protocol but also an update protocol even when there are a large number of sharing processors.

4   Adaptive Hierarchical Coarse Directory

The previous section indicated that the hierarchical coarse directory with multicasting and combining have quality of good scalability from the point of view of directory size and latency for a coherence transaction. However, more packets might be generated than other directory systems when copies are located irregularly or sparsely over the system, since the number of packets depends only on the hierarchical distance between a home and a most distant sharing processor, regardless of the number of sharing processors. This nature might influence other local processing in the system. In this section, we extend the hierarchical coarse

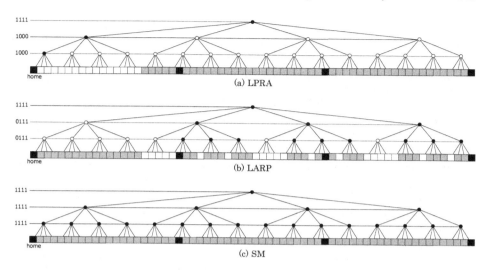

Fig. 3. Dummy sharing processors in the pseudo-full-map directory.

directory and propose a directory scheme which brings light traffic even if copies are scattered.

The hierarchical coarse directory makes use of hierarchy of a tree interconnection network as the pseudo-full-map directory does. The two directories bring almost the same processing time for a coherence transaction by using multicasting and combining. However, directory size of the hierarchical coarse directory is smaller than that of the pseudo-full-map. This is because sharing information of the former is more incomplete than that of the latter. On the number of packets generated, the pseudo-full-map directory gives better results since it has a bitmap corresponding to each hierarchy. However, accurate (or somewhat accurate) information from the bitmaps can be applied only to either a path from a home to the root of the shared area or the other paths. Therefore, the number of packets does not depend on the number of copies.

Traffic generated by both of the directories is influenced by the locations of copies. When the number of copies is two in the hierarchical coarse directory or when that is n in the pseudo-full-map with n-ary tree network, there is a possibility that traffic occurs all over the network. For example, Figure 3 illustrates sharing processors when there are three copies in the pseudo-full-map directory system. The black leaves represent a home and processors which have a copy. The gray leaves are dummy sharing processors which don't have a copy but receive a coherence request. A bitmap for each hierarchy is applied to the black internal nodes at the corresponding level. In all schemes of the pseudo-full-map, that is LPRA (Figure 3(a)), LARP (Figure 3(b)), and SM (Figure 3(c)), three copies cause a number of network communications. The locations of copies depend on the distribution of data in a running program, the algorithm of the computation, or scheduling by an operating system. Although applying optimization for spatial locality to the program and the scheduling is effective in the locations, a directory system in which traffic is affected by the number of copies, not by the location of copies, is desirable when the optimization is difficult to apply.

Agarwal et al. [8] indicated that, in an invalidation protocol, the number of copies which should be invalidated when a block is updated is lower than four in most cases. This knowledge is used in the limited directory which limits the number of copies. However, when the limited directory is used simultaneously with an update protocol, the number of copies tends to exceed the limit and broadcasting frequently occurs, which leads to heavy traffic. A directory scheme we propose in this section has a limited number of pointers. When the number of copies is not more than the limited number, the pointers indicate processors which have a copy directly. When the number exceeds the limit, as many shared areas as the limit can be formed. When a processor which does not belong to any shared area joins the sharing group, one of the shared areas is extended so that the processor is included in the share area.

Let N be a number which corresponds to the limit of the limited directory. A directory consists of N pointer fields and $N + 1$ maximum shared distances. It does not include a pointer field for indicating the home because the location is implicitly known. Therefore, the number of pointers is smaller than that of maximum shared distances by one. Each pointer plays a role as a "home agent", in other words, "base". A home agent and a maximum shared distance related to the home agent form a "partial shared area".

Initially, all pointers in a directory are invalidated. When a processor P starts to share a block and creates a copy of it, the home of the block reconstructs the directory according to the following algorithm.

if (One of partial shared areas includes P.)
- Perform nothing.

else if (There is an invalid pointer field.) {
- Set P to the pointer field.
- Set the maximum shared distance zero.
}

else {
- Calculate hierarchical distances between any two among home, all home agents and P.
- Select a pair (or a set of more than two) which generated a minimum distance. (If there is a pair or set which generated the distance and includes the home, select it.)
- Select one in the pair (or set) as the surviving home agent. (Select the home if it is in the pair or set.)
- Update the corresponding maximum shared distance.
    if (P is not in the pair (or set))
        - Set P to a vacated pointer field.
- Invalidate still vacated pointer fields.
}

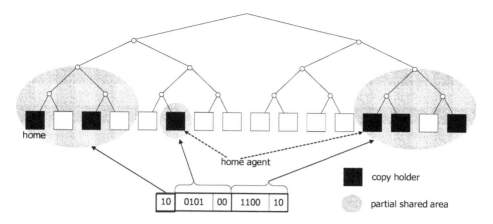

Fig. 4. Adaptive hierarchical coarse directory.

This scheme indicates the locations of copies accurately when the number of copies is not more than N. When more than N, the shared area consists of $N+1$ partial shared areas. From the point of view of adaptability to copy creation and utilization of maximum shared distances, we call the directory "*adaptive hierarchical coarse directory*". Figure 4 illustrates the directory when N is two. In the figure, a home and two home agents form three partial shared areas.

The size of the adaptive hierarchical coarse directory depends on the number of pointer fields. The size of the pseudo-full-map directory is $n \times m$ in a n-ary tree network the height of which is m. This size equals that of two pointers when n is two or four. From this point, the adaptive hierarchical coarse directory which has two pointer fields is almost equal to the pseudo-full-map in the size. Here, the directory includes the other three fields that hold each maximum shared distance. The minimum width of the field depends on n and N. For example, on a quad tree network which has 65,536 processors, the pseudo-full-map needs $4 \times \log_4 65536 = 32$ bits. On the other hand, the adaptive hierarchical coarse directory with $N = 2$ needs $2 \times \log_2 65536 + 3 \times \log_2 \log_4 65536 = 41$ bits.

When N is not large, it is really possible to perform multicasting and combining by adding the directory to a packet. Although it is desirable to give at least $N = n - 1$ pointer fields on a n-ary network system for preventing n copies from causing broadcasting over the system in the worst case, it is important to keep a balance between the amount of memory for directories and the performance improvement.

5   Evaluation of Scalability

In this section, we compare the adaptive hierarchical coarse directory with other directories in terms of the size, latency and traffic in coherence transactions.

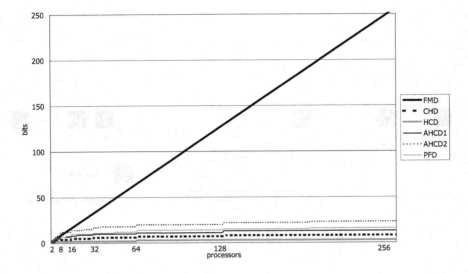

Fig. 5. Directory size.

5.1 Directory Size

The size of an adaptive hierarchical coarse directory is compared with those of other directories; a full-map directory, chained directory, hierarchical coarse directory and pseudo-full-map directory. Figure 5 shows the directory sizes per memory block when the network is a quad tree and the number of processors is from 2 to 256. In the figure, The horizontal axis indicates the number of processors, and the vertical axis indicates the bit width of the directories. "FMD", "CHD", "HCD" and "PFD" mean a full-map directory, chained directory, hierarchical coarse directory and pseudo-full-map directory, respectively. "AHCD1" and "AHCD2" means the adaptive hierarchical coarse directory with $N = 2$ and $N = 3$, respectively. Practically, the size of the chained directory per memory block depends on the number of existing copies. Here, the size with no copies, that is the size of a pointer, is given in CHD.

The figure indicates that the width of FMD is proportional to the number of processors and that of PFD is proportional to the logarithm of the number of processors, that is proportional to the height of the tree network. The width of HCD is proportional to the logarithm of the logarithm of the number of processors ($\log_2 \log_4 n$, n is the number of processors) and smaller than that of the other directories. The width of AHCD1 is a little smaller than that of PFD. Although AHCD2 is larger than PFD, the size is sufficiently small for large-scale systems.

5.2 Time Required for Coherence Transaction

From the actual implementation of the hardware DSM system on the prototype machine [1], various values were obtained, such as the time required for a message

Table 1. Parameters in each programs.

Program	Parameters
FFT	65,536 complex double
LU	256×256 matrix
	32 by 32 element blocks
OCEAN	Grid size; 130×130
	Grid resolution; 20,000
	Time between relaxations; 28,800
WATER-SPATIAL	Number of molecules; 4,096
WATER-NSQUARED	Number of molecules; 512

Table 2. The mean number of copies in coherence transaction.

Program	Mean number of copies	
	invalidate	update
FFT	3.14	25.94
LU	1.88	6.11
OCEAN	2.51	15.42
WATER-SPATIAL	2.04	6.03
WATER-NSQUARED	1.28	65.50

to pass through a switch. Using them, coherence processing (invalidation and update) in a larger scale system is considered, and the adaptive hierarchical coarse directory is compared with other directory schemes; full-map, hierarchical coarse directory and pseudo-full-map directory. The adaptive hierarchical coarse directory, hierarchical coarse directory and pseudo-full-map directory are used with multicasting and combining.

We employed ABSS [11] that is the augmentation-based SPARC simulator to generate traces of memory reference. In the simulation, the size of memory (cache) block is 32 bytes and the number of processors is 256. Then, the trace generated by ABSS is input to a directory simulator that computes the number of cycles taken to complete a coherent transaction for each write to shared blocks. In the directory simulator, the interconnection network is quad tree and the same values as those of the prototype machine are used for the times required by the system elements such as a memory controller, network interface and network switch.

We applied the simulation system to several programs from the SPLASH-2 benchmark suite [12]; FFT, LU, OCEAN, WATER-SPATIAL and WATER-NSQUARED. Table 1 shows values of parameters in the programs we selected. Table 2 shows the mean number of copies that should be invalidated or updated per coherence transaction in execution of these five programs.

Table 3 shows the mean number of cycles per transaction. "FMD", "HCD", "AHCD1" and "AHCD2" in the table are the same as section 5.1. "SM", "LARP" and "LPRA" are the tree methods in pseudo-full-map directory. In

Table 3. The mean number of cycles in coherence transaction.

Program	Protocol	Directory						
		FMD	HCD	AHCD1	AHCD2	SM	LARP	LPRA
FFT	Invalidate	119.0	171.0	163.6	154.1	157.1	154.6	167.9
	Update	423.4	263.9	219.4	176.4	192.6	183.1	249.4
LU	Invalidate	94.4	157.3	138.2	137.9	140.0	137.8	153.4
	Update	302.8	268.4	260.5	245.3	233.7	224.7	262.4
OCEAN	Invalidate	117.0	165.6	156.0	147.8	149.5	148.4	162.1
	Update	264.0	259.7	217.2	183.6	193.6	185.2	244.3
WATER-SPATIAL	Invalidate	103.9	159.2	141.2	139.9	143.2	139.8	155.3
	Update	207.9	266.6	218.5	189.7	228.6	216.3	252.3
WATER-NSQUARED	Invalidate	96.1	167.4	150.0	146.7	147.6	147.3	163.6
	Update	777.3	267.6	258.3	244.6	246.7	242.5	261.4

LU with an update protocol, AHCD2 is a little larger than SM and LARP. However, we confirmed that AHCD with three pointers generated smaller value, 137.9 cycles in the same program. In other cases, AHCD2 roughly generates the smallest or the secondly smallest value. From the results, AHCD with two or more pointers generates small number of cycles on average.

5.3   Network Traffic

We show network traffic during coherence processing generated by the same programs as in section 5.2. The same traces in section 5.2 are used. The directory simulator calculates the number of switch-to-switch packets on all branches in the quad tree interconnection network during a coherence transaction.

Table 4 shows the mean number of packets per transaction. Although AHCD2 is larger than the pseudo-full-map directory in LU with an update protocol, we confirmed that AHCD with three pointers generated 217.2 packets in LU. In other programs, AHCD2 is the smallest or the secondly smallest. From these results, AHCD with more than one pointer generates small number of packets on average.

6   Related Work

There are several directory schemes whose information dynamically changes from complete to incomplete, by reconstructing the directory structure[5].

In the superset scheme [8], pointers directly specify the location of sharing processors when the number of copies does not exceed that of pointers. When an overflow occurs, the directory is represented by a composite pointer that is made out of two pointers. Each field of the composite pointer is in one of three states: 0, 1, or X (both), and is thus composed of two bits. When a processor

---

[5] Pseudo-full-map directory is originally of this type, which switches from a full-bit vector to LPRA [9].

Table 4. The mean number of packets in coherence transaction.

Program	Protocol	Directory						
		FMD	HCD	AHCD1	AHCD2	SM	LARP	LPRA
FFT	Invalidate	45.4	654.5	379.2	76.6	137.6	199.0	255.3
	Update	381.4	643.9	366.5	100.6	163.3	232.6	279.5
LU	Invalidate	20.4	531.3	37.8	17.3	42.4	143.3	144.7
	Update	91.5	676.2	620.2	459.4	335.4	344.0	431.4
OCEAN	Invalidate	36.9	595.3	213.4	38.5	85.4	172.8	197.4
	Update	226.6	613.9	306.7	123.6	160.5	224.6	250.4
WATER-SPATIAL	Invalidate	25.5	531.1	120.3	22.9	68.9	142.3	154.7
	Update	84.3	638.8	321.2	153.2	189.0	214.5	240.9
WATER-NSQUARED	Invalidate	19.3	610.0	107.7	17.1	55.3	165.1	180.7
	Update	950.9	668.1	583.3	489.0	485.2	489.3	499.8

joins sharing members, the processor number is compared with the pointer, and bit fields which differ each other are set to X. This scheme makes a superset of the processors that have a copy, and can point to 2^k copies at maximum by using two pointers length of which is k. During a coherence transaction, a coherence message is sent to all processors that correspond to any bit pattern obtained by replacing each X field with 0 or 1. Hence, a processor which does not hold a copy might receive the coherence messages. This leads to redundant communications. This scheme generates traffic depending on the location of sharing processors, not on the number of copies. In the worst case, sharing by two processors can cause broadcasting for coherence processing. For example, when processors whose number is "0000" and "1111" share a block, this is the case.

In the coarse vector scheme [13], when an overflow of sharing occurs, processors are grouped and a bit is assigned to each group. Groups are then identified by the same way as a full-map scheme. The number of processors that the scheme can cover is k times as large as the bit width of the directory where k is the size of each group. All groups have the same fixed size. Here, redundant coherence messages might be sent as in the superset scheme since all processors in any group in which at least one processor has a copy are regarded as a copy holder. On the other hand, the adaptive hierarchical coarse directory can have groups (partial shared areas) whose size differs and is variable. The size changes according to the number of sharing processors in the neighborhood.

In the segment directory [14], after an overflow, a pointer field changes into the structure which consists of a segment vector and a segment pointer. A segment is a part of all processors and contains consecutive K processors. Therefore, when the number of processors is N, there are N/K segments. The segment vector is a bit vector within a segment and has K bits. The segment pointer indicates which segment the segment vector is applied to. The size of the segment pointer is $log_2 N/K$. In this scheme, the size of a group (segment) is fixed. When the size is large, it requires not a small number of bits for the segment vector. Since this directory makes complete sharing information for a memory block, the same number of directory elements as that of segments are needed to cover all processors. Each segment directory element is dynamically generated as the need arises. When sharing processors are scattered, many directory elements are generated and the total size of the directory for a memory block exceeds that of full-map directory, which means that this structure is not suitable for an update protocol.

Multilayer clustering [15] uses the level of the root of the minimum subtree that includes all the sharers as the sharing information. This technique is the same as the hierarchical coarse directory we proposed in [1]. Further, the multilayer clustering dynamically organizes several subtrees. In this scheme, only symmetric nodes of a home processor can become a home agent that forms a subtree. On the other hand, any node can be a home agent in the adaptive hierarchical coarse directory.

7 Conclusion

In this paper, we described scalability issues of directory schemes in DSM systems and showed that the hierarchical coarse directory provided good scalability in terms of directory size compared to other directories. However, there is a possibility that the directory generates more traffic than others when the number of sharing processors is not large and the copies are scattered.

We proposed a directory scheme, "*adaptive hierarchical coarse directory*" to alleviate the increase of network packets caused by scattered copies. When the number of copies is small, particularly in an invalidation protocol, the directory functions as a limited directory. On the other hand, when an update protocol increases copies, it adaptively makes up sharing information which consists of several partial shared areas.

The effectiveness of the adaptive hierarchical coarse directory was evaluated by using SPLASH-2 programs. This directory with two pointers exhibited the small number of cycles and packets required for processing an invalidation transaction. On the other hand, with an update protocol, it generated the small value for four programs. For LU, the organization of two pointers was not adequate to alleviate the time and traffic. However, three pointers well reduced them. The characteristics of the directory can decrease an obstacle to other local processing in a multitasking/multiuser environment when threads of a process are not locally allocated by an operating system or when false sharing occurs.

References

1. Tanaka, K., Matsumoto, T., Hiraki, K.: Lightweight Hardware Distributed Shared Memory Supported by Generalized Combining. *Proc. of 5th International Symposium on High-Performance Computer Architecture (HPCA)*, pp. 90–99, Jan 1999.
2. Tanaka, K., Matsumoto, T., Hiraki, K.: On Scalability Issue of Directory Schemes of Hardware Distributed Shared memory. *9th Workshop on Scalable Shared Memory Multiprocessors (SSMM)*, Jun 2000.
3. Censier, L.M., Feautrier, P.: A New Solution to Coherence Problems in Multicache Systems. *IEEE Transactions on Computers*, C-27(12), pp. 1112–1118, Dec 1978.

4. Chaiken, D., Kubiatowicz, J., Agarwal, A.: LimitLESS Directories: A Scalable Cache Coherence Scheme. *Proc. of 4th International Conference on Architectural Support for Programming Languages and Operating Systems (ASPLOS–IV).* pp. 224–234, Apr 1991.

5. James, D., Laundrie, A.T., Gjessing, S., Sohi, G.S.: Distibuted–Directory Scheme: Scalable Coherent Interface. *Computer*, 23(6), pp. 74–77, Jun 1990.

6. Thapar, M., Delagi, B.: Distributed–Directory Scheme: Stanford Distributed Directory Protocol. *Computer*, 23(6), pp. 78–80, Jun 1990.

7. Hagersten, E., Landin, A., Haridi, S.: DDM–A Cache-Only Memory Architecture. *Computer*, 25(9), pp. 44–54, Sep 1992.

8. Agarwal, A., Simoni, R., Hennessy, J., Horowitz, M.: An Evaluation of Directory Schemes for Cache Coherence. *Proc. of 15th International Symposium on Computer Architecture (ISCA)*, pp. 280–289, Jun 1988.

9. Matsumoto, T., Hiraki, K.: A Shared Memory Architecture for Massively Parallel Computer Systems. *IEICE Japan SIG Reports*, 92(173), pp. 47–55, Aug 1992. (In Japanese)

10. Matsumoto, T., Nishimura, K., Kudoh, T., Hiraki, K., Amano, H., Tanaka, H.: Distributed Shared Memory Architecture for JUMP-1: a General-Purpose MPP Prototype. *Proc. of International Symposium on Parallel Architectures, Algorithms and Networks (ISPAN)*, pp. 131–137, Jun 1996.

11. Sunada, D., Glasco, D., Flynn, M.: ABSS v2.0: a SPARC Simulator. *Proc. of the 8th Workshop on Synthesis And System Integration of Mixed Technologies (SASIMI '98)*, Oct 1998.

12. Woo, S.C., Ohara, M., Torrie, E., Singh, J.P., Gupta, A.: The SPLASH-2 Programs: Characterization and Methodological Considerations. *Proc. of 22th International Symposium on Computer Architecture (ISCA)*, pp. 24–36, Jun 1995.

13. Gupta, A., Weber, W., Mowry, T.: Reducing Memory and Traffic Requirements for Scalable Directory-Based Cache Coherence Schemes. *Proc. of International Conference on Parallel Processing (ICPP)*, pp. I-312–321, Aug 1990.

14. Choi, J.H., Park, K.H.: Segment Directory Enhancing the Limited Directory Cache Coherence Schemes. *Proc. of 13th International Parallel Processing Symposium and 10th Symposium on Parallel and Distributed Processing (IPPS/SPDP)*, pp. 258–267, Apr 1999.

15. Acacio, M.E., Gonzalez, J., Carcia, J.M., Duato, J.: A New Scalable Directory Architecture for Large-Scale Multiprocessors. *Proc. of 7th International Symposium on High-Performance Computer Architecture (HPCA)*, pp. 97–106, Jan 2001.

A Compiler-Assisted On-Chip Assigned-Signature Control Flow Checking[*]

Xiaobin Li and Jean-Luc Gaudiot

Department of Electrical Engineering and Computer Science
University of California, Irvine
{xiaobinl, gaudiot}@uci.edu
http://pascal.eng.uci.edu

Abstract. As device sizes continue shrinking, lower charges are needed to activate gates, and consequently ever smaller external events (such as single ionizing particles of naturally occurring radiation) will be able to upset the correct functioning of complex modern microprocessors. Therefore, designers of future processors must take this new fact into account and should incorporate in their design fault-tolerant features which will allow processors to continue operating correctly even when such faults have occurred. Many faulty conditions are control flow errors which cause processors to violate the correct sequencing of instructions. Indeed, they amount to between 33% and 77% of all run-time errors. We present here a new compile-time signature assignment algorithm (the signature checking technique is a well-known approach to detect control flow errors). We also present the theoretical proof as well as the fault detection coverage analysis of our algorithm. We then describe the required enhancement to the basic microarchitecture: an on-chip assigned-signature checker which is capable of executing three additional instructions (SIC, SIJ, SIJC). This allows the processor to efficiently check the run-time sequence and detect control flow errors.

1 Introduction

As computer systems have become irreplaceable tools of modern society, with the benefits these systems bring to us comes a great potential for harm when they fail to perform their functions or perform them incorrectly. This is further exacerbated by new technologies of integration as the number of transistors and the clock rate of processors have shown an exponential growth rate [1]. However, smaller device sizes, reduced voltage levels, and higher transistor counts correspondingly raise concerns of higher transient faults rates. For one thing, radiation-induced soft errors are predicted to become increasingly significant in the near future [2,3,4]. In order to handle these inevitable errors, we must integrate in our design fault-tolerant features so that the processor can continue to correctly perform its specified tasks despite the occurrence of logic errors [5]. Such designs as Itanium [6], IBM Power4 [7], Fujitsu SPARC64 [8], etc., already include transient fault detection and recovery mechanisms.

---

[*] This paper is based upon work supported in part by NSF grants CCR-0234444 and INT-0223647. Any opinions, findings, and conclusions or recommendations expressed in this material are those of the authors and do not necessarily reflect the views of the National Science Foundation.

We concentrate here on protecting against *control flow errors* (those which cause a processor to violate the correct sequencing of instructions). Indeed, abstractions of program execution behavior can be formed based on various considerations which include control flow, memory access, I/O, and object type or range [9]. The cause of control flow errors could be the failure of any one of a variety of microarchitectural components such as instruction cache, program counter operation, branch unit, etc. Indeed, it has been found that these control flow errors account for between 33% [10] and 77% [11] of all run-time errors.

Signature checking is a well-known technique used to detect control flow errors [9, 11,12,13,14,15,16,17,18,19]. It can be implemented as either assigned-signature control flow checking or derived-signature control flow checking. In this paper, we focus on the former because it could offer better fault detection coverage. At compile time, we assign to each basic block a signature, and then at run time, an on-chip checker executes three additional signature checking instructions in order to check run time-computed signatures against assigned signatures. Any discrepancy indicates that an error occurred.

The goal of this paper is to describe the algorithm which protects against run-time control flow errors and its simple implementation. In Section 2, we introduce the principles of signature checking. The compile time signature assignment algorithm is outlined in Section 3. An on-chip checker with the ability to execute three signature checking instructions and its possible implementation are described in Section 4. These three instructions are proposed additions to a conventional instruction set. Conclusions are presented in Section 5.

2   The Concept of Signature Checking

Signature control flow checking techniques are used to monitor the program execution sequence in order to determine if a legal control flow is being followed. Various signature checking techniques have been proposed in the past [9,11,12,13,14,15,16,17,18,19]. Basically, there are **two** phases of signature checking: compile-time signature generation and run-time signature validation.

In the back end stages, in order to express the program control flow, compilers usually build a control flow graph (CFG), in which a *node* or a basic block is a sequence of instructions with no branch-in except for the entry point and no branch-out except for the exit point and *directed edges* are used to represent jumps in the program control flow [20]. Fig. 1 illustrates this concept by a simple example. Thus, in the first phase of signature checking, which is based upon the CFG, the compiler pre-computes the signatures associated with each node of the CFG, and then either embeds signatures into the original codes [9,11,13,14,16,19] or provides that information directly to the watchdog [15,18]. At this point, we could have two techniques for pre-computing signatures: the first, assigned-signature control flow checking [15,16,19], associates with each node an arbitrary signature, for example, a prime number. Conversely, the second technique, derived-signature control flow checking [9,11,13,14,18], derives signatures from the nodes themselves, for example by deriving a checksum from the binary code of the instruction inside a node and then using that checksum as the signature.

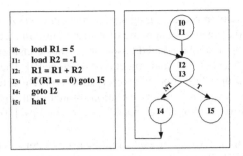

Fig. 1. An example program and its CFG

During the second phase, the checking engine, which can be either the watchdog or the host CPU, computes run time signatures and then check them against the compile time pre-computed signatures. If the signatures differ, it means that an error occurred.

Although the second phase of the assigned-signature checking algorithm and the derived-signature checking algorithm are essentially the same, assigned signature checking techniques have two major drawbacks: the need for registers to hold signatures and the performance overhead due to the need to execute extra instructions related to the assigned-signature checking [9,19]. For example, in [19], the overhead in terms of code size ranges from 26.6% to 61.9% while the overhead in terms of execution time ranges from 16.2% to 58.1%. Conversely, derived signature checking techniques require a signature generator/checker circuit to process the signature and might not guarantee that each node has a unique signature, which might consequently impact the fault coverage.

3   The Compiler-Assisted Signature Assignment Algorithm

The assigned-signature checking technique is based on a comparison between the compiler assigned signature with the one calculated at run time. Any difference between these two signatures indicates that a control flow error has occurred. To address the performance overhead associated with assigned-signature checking, we use additional hardware to trade this off, as will be explained in Section 4.

3.1   The Control Flow Checking Algorithm

Compiler time assigned reference signature (S). As discussed before, the program control flow can be expressed as a CFG. We start with a given node V_i of the CFG, and assign to it a **unique** number, which is called the *state code* of the node[1]. This code is denoted by $D(i)$. Then, we compute the reference signature $S(i)$ of this node by using the following formula:

$$S(i) = D(i) \oplus D(pred(V_i)) . \tag{1}$$

---

[1] A simple way to assign unique state codes to nodes may be to number each node of the CFG in sequence, as shown in Fig. 7.

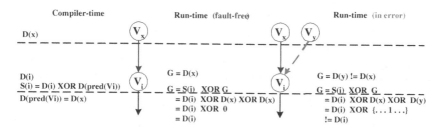

Fig. 2. Proof of the control flow checking algorithm

where $pred(V_i)$ is the immediate predecessor of node V_i in the CFG (note that $\oplus$ is an exclusive-OR function). Furthermore, we assume for the moment that each node has only one immediate predecessor. More complex cases will be discussed later.

Run time signature (G). A global register holds the *run time signature* G of the node currently executing. When the program execution changes the control flow to a new node, e.g., V_i, G is updated by the following formula:

$$G = G \oplus S(i) \ . \tag{2}$$

where $S(i)$ is the reference signature of the current new node V_i.

Then, the core of the control flow checking mechanism consists in checking the run time signature G against the static state code $D(i)$ (the one assigned by the compiler) as follows[2]:

```
Do   G ⊕ D(i)
BNEZ exception-handler
```

Note that this comparison would take place whenever the run time control flow enters a new node of the CFG.

Proof (of the control flow checking algorithm). Assume (Fig. 2) that, instead of transferring control from V_x to V_i (left side of Fig. 2), we had erroneously entered V_i from V_y (right side of Fig. 2). Further assume that the reference signature of V_i had been assigned by the compiler to be $S(i) = D(x) \oplus D(i)$. The run-time signature G when the control of program is at node V_y is: $G = D(y)$ which would be different from $D(x)$ since the state code is *unique* to each node. Then, after entering node V_i, the run time signature would be updated by the following formula:

$$G = G \oplus S(i)$$
$$= D(y) \oplus D(x) \oplus D(i)$$

Since $D(x) \neq D(y)$, some bits of the result from $D(x) \oplus D(y)$ are 1s, as shown by $\{\ldots 1 \ldots\}$ in Fig. 2. Because of these bits which have the value '1' instead of '0', when exclusive-ORed with $D(i)$, they will flip the corresponding bits of $D(i)$. As such, the final result is: $G \neq D(i)$ which means that a fault has been detected. $\square$

---

[2] BNEZ is equivalent to "branch to target if the result is not equal to zero." As such, if $G \oplus D(i) \neq 0$, the exception handler is triggered.

Justifying signature (J) — Handling multiple-branch-in nodes. Now, we need to consider the case when a node has multiple immediate predecessors. Indeed, in normally complex CFGs, a node may have multiple immediate predecessors. We would call such a node a *multiple-branch-in* (MBI) node: it is a node whose number of immediate predecessors is greater than one. To simplify the discussion, we denote the set of *pred(MBI)* as[3]:

$$\$ = \left\{ V_k \mid V_k \text{ is an immediate predecessor of MBI} \right\} . \tag{3}$$

When dealing with such MBI nodes, as required in (1), we must choose one of the immediate predecessors as the *primary immediate predecessor* (or primary node, for short). Also, since there is more than one path *up* from an MBI node, we associate with each immediate predecessor an additional parameter which we call the *justifying signature*. The justifying signature is used at run time to verify that all immediate predecessors to the MBI node are *legal* antecedents to that node.

The following outlines the *compile-time* MBI node handling algorithm:

1. Arbitrarily select a node from $\$$ as the MBI node primary node (assume V_j for the rest of this discussion). Note that we leave the discussion of primary node selection later.
2. The reference signature of the MBI node is governed by the selected primary node V_j as:
$$S(MBI) = D(MBI) \oplus D(j) . \tag{4}$$
3. For every node $V_k \in \$$, associate it with the justifying signature given by the following formula:
$$J(k) = D(k) \oplus D(j) . \tag{5}$$

Note that now each node $V_k \in \$$ has **two** signatures: the reference signature $S(k)$ and the justifying signature $J(k)$ as illustrated in Fig. 3 where V_7, V_8 and V_9 are the MBI nodes[4].

The *run-time* MBI node handling algorithm could be described as follows:

1. We denote control flow changes as: $V_k \to$ MBI. First, the run time signature is updated according to the following formula:
$$G = G \oplus S(MBI) \oplus J(k) . \tag{6}$$
2. Finally, the MBI node run-time control flow checking can be applied as discussed before:

```
Do    G ⊕ D(MBI)
BNEZ exception-handler
```

3.2   The Fault Detection Coverage of the MBI Node Handling Algorithm

Consider a general case of MBI node control flow change: $V_k \to$ MBI. According to the relationship between the node V_k and the node "MBI," there are three possible cases:

---

[3] Then the definition of an MBI node can be given as the cardinality of $\$$, i.e., the number of elements in the set $\$$, is greater than one: $|\$| > 1$.

[4] We use doubly circled nodes to represent primary nodes.

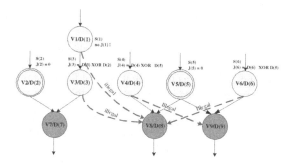

Fig. 3. Analysis of the MBI node handling algorithm

1. If $V_k \in \$$, which means that the control flow change is legal, as discussed before, we can easily prove that the updated run time signature is: $G = D(MBI)$.
2. If $V_k \notin \$$, which means that the control flow change is illegal, two cases must be separately considered:
   a) V_k is an immediate predecessor of *another* MBI node, which means that $J(K)$ has been defined;
   b) V_k is not an immediate predecessor of *any* MBI node. Then, $J(k)$ is null at compile-time and then without loss of generality, $J(k)$ will be a random number at run-time (whatever is left in the corresponding storage cell at that time).

Justifying signature has been defined. Consider the control flow change: $V_i \to V_j$ where V_j is an MBI node and its set of $pred(V_j)$ is $\$_j$. However, $V_i \notin \$_j$, i.e., the control flow change is illegal, V_i is instead an immediate predecessor of another MBI node, say V_m, hence $V_i \in \$_m$. Moreover, V_x has been selected as the primary node of V_j and V_y as the primary node of V_m. Then, when entering V_j, the run time signature is updated by using the following formula:

$$G = G \oplus S(j) \oplus J(i)$$
$$= D(i) \oplus D(j) \oplus D(x) \oplus D(i) \oplus D(y)$$
$$= D(j) \oplus D(x) \oplus D(y)$$

Therefore, two cases need to be considered:

1. As long as $D(x) \oplus D(y) = 0$, we end up with $G = D(j)$, which means that a control flow error has escaped detection. The faulty condition $D(x) \oplus D(y) = 0$ is satisfied only if $D(x) = D(y)$, i.e., node V_x is the same as node V_y (remember that the state code of each node is unique). Examples of illegal control flow changes such as $V_6 \to V_8$ and $V_4 \to V_9$, are shown in Fig. 3. In both cases, two MBI nodes V_8 and V_9 share node V_5 as their primary node.

Observation 1. *When two MBI nodes, V_j and V_m, share their primary node, V_x ($= V_y$), any illegal control flow change: $V_i(\in \$_m$ and $\notin \$_j) \to V_j$ and any illegal control flow change: $V_l(\in \$_j$ and $\notin \$_m) \to V_m$ cannot be detected.*

Further, we denote the probability of these illegal control flow changes as P_{ND1}.

2. On the other hand, if $V_x \neq V_y$, i.e., **no** primary node sharing, we have: $G \neq D(j)$ which means that the control flow error can be successfully detected. An example for this case is shown in Fig. 3 as the illegal control flow change: $V_3 \rightarrow V_8$.

To summary the above two cases, we can state the following:

Observation 2. *The fault detection coverage may decrease if two MBI nodes share the primary node. In another words, if a node V_x has multiple branch-outs, for example, the exit statement of the node is a conditional branch, and if more than two (including two) branch destination nodes are MBI nodes, the node V_x should not be selected as a primary node.*

Justifying signature is random. Consider the control flow change: $V_i \rightarrow V_j$ where V_j is an MBI node and its set of $pred(V_j) = \$_j$. Further assume that V_x has been selected as the primary node of V_j. However, $V_i \notin \$_j$, i.e., the control flow change $V_i \rightarrow V_j$ is illegal. Also, V_i is not an immediate predecessor of any MBI node such that $J(i)$ has not been defined and we deal with it as a random number. An example of an illegal control flow change: $V_1 \rightarrow V_8$ is shown in Fig. 3. In this case, when entering V_j, the run-time signature is updated by using the following formula:

$$G = G \oplus S(j) \oplus J(i)$$
$$= D(i) \oplus D(j) \oplus D(x) \oplus J(i)$$

Because of the randomness of $J(i)$, two cases must be considered:

1. If $D(i) \oplus D(x) \oplus J(i) = 0$, we have $G = D(j)$ which means that the control flow error escapes detection;
2. If $D(i) \oplus D(x) \oplus J(i) \neq 0$, we have $G \neq D(j)$ which means that the algorithm has successfully detected the control flow error.

Fortunately, the probability for $D(i) \oplus D(x) \oplus J(i)$ to be zero is very low: it can happen only if $J(i) = D(i) \oplus D(x)$. Given the n-bit size of state codes and signatures, the probability is:

$$P_{ND2} = P\{J(i) = D(i) \oplus D(x)\} = 2^{-n} . \tag{7}$$

In summary, the fault detection coverage of the MBI node handling algorithm is:

$$C \equiv P\{\text{fault detection}|\text{fault existence}\} \tag{8}$$
$$= P\{\text{control flow error detection}|V_k \rightarrow \text{MBI and } V_k \notin \$\} \tag{9}$$
$$= 1 - P_{ND1} - P_{ND2} . \tag{10}$$

3.3 The If-Then-Else Node Handling Algorithm

As mentioned by Oh et al. in [19], primary nodes are randomly selected which would contradict our Observation 2. Furthermore, randomly selecting the primary node may

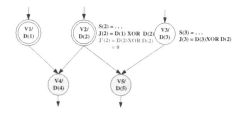

Fig. 4. An example of ITE node with two justifying signatures

result in conflicts as illustrated in Fig. 4. Indeed, if V_1 had been selected as the primary node for V_4 and V_2 for V_5, respectively, we would have to create two justifying signatures for node V_2: as far as MBI node V_4 is concerned, the justifying signature of V_2 is: $J(2) = D(1) \oplus D(2)$; whereas as far as MBI node V_5 is concerned, the justifying signature of V_2 is: $J'(2) = D(2) \oplus D(2) = 0$.

Hence, for the control flow change: $V_2 \to V_4$, $J(2)$ should be used to update the run-time signature whereas for the control flow change : $V_2 \to V_5$, only $J'(2)$ is the correct choice. Anything corrupted up to this level could result in faulty control flow error detection. Simply speaking, for the **legal** control flow change: $V_2 \to V_4$, if the justifying signature $J'(2)$ had been used to update the run time signature, we would end up with $G \neq D(4)$ such that a control flow error could be flagged, a false alarm. Unfortunately, such situations[5] have not been addressed in [19].

The necessary conditions for a node associated with two[6] justifying signatures are:

1. The exit of the node is a conditional branch, that is to say the node is an if-then-else (ITE) node;
2. Both branch destinations are MBI nodes.

In short, we need to distinguish the two justifying signatures: one for the then-branch flow (the resolved branch condition is not-taken), the other for the else-branch flow (the resolved branch condition is taken).

Figure 5 shows a hardware-based algorithm[7]: at **compile time**, when an MBI node traces back its immediate predecessors for the purpose of justifying signatures, the associated directed edges are checked (directed edges are given by the CFG): if the edge is a "taken" path, the associated justifying signature will be placed into the TJ register; whereas if it is a "not-taken" path, the NTJ register is used for the associated justifying

---

[5] These situations are not rare: conditional branches are extremely common in regular programs. From the following discussions, we will see that a node with a conditional branch could be associated with two justifying signatures.

[6] If switch statements are allowed, that more than two justifying signatures are associated with a node is possible. However, we assume that the compiler has converted all switch statements into the equivalent if-then-else constructs, as presented in [14].

[7] We have not, in this work, considered checking the flow of conditional branches. More specifically, refer to Fig. 5, the case when a transient fault causes the ITE node to branch to the else_node incorrectly whereas it should have branched to the then_node, has not been considered.

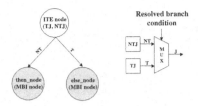

Fig. 5. An hardware approach for ITE node with two justifying signatures (T = taken; NT = not-taken; TJ = justifying signature for ITE_node → else_node; NTJ = justifying signature for ITE_node → then_node)

signature. At **run time**, the resolved branch condition is used to select the appropriate justifying signature for updating the run time signature. More details will be given in Section 4.

4   Hardware Enhancement for Control Flow Checking

As discussed before, the assigned-signature checking technique has an inherent performance overhead drawback. However, with advances in CMOS technology, we have an abundance of cheap hardware resources [1]. Moreover, our proposed mechanism can be simply implemented in any modern microprocessor at little additional cost. Hence, in this section, we first introduce three additional instructions dedicated to control flow checking, and then design a simple hardware implementation to execute these instructions. We will also provide a comprehensive control-flow checking algorithm based on these hardware enhancements. In the end, we will show the benefit from trading hardware off a reduction in performance overhead.

4.1   Additional Instructions

The three additional instructions dedicated to the assigned-signature control flow checking are succinctly described in Table 1. Instruction SIC is used to check for control flow errors in non-MBI nodes. Instruction SIJ is dedicated to signature justification. Instruction SIJC is used to check for control flow errors in MBI nodes. The compiler is responsible for the insertion of these additional instructions into the original program so as to achieve run-time control flow checking. The detailed algorithm will be presented in section 4.3.

4.2   Implementation of Additional Instructions — On-Chip Control Flow Checker

A simple on-chip control flow checker to execute the above three additional instructions can be easily designed. Assume a simple five-stage pipeline: Fetch → Decode → Execution → Memory access → Write back. Our on-chip control flow checker would be located in the "Decode" and "Execution" stages.

Table 1. Three additional instructions specification

No.	Mnemonic	Format	Function Description
1	SIC	`SIC imm1, imm2` where imm1 = S(i); imm2 = D(i)	**Signature checking :** 1 Update G as: G = G ⊕ imm1 2 **If** (G == imm2) fault free, **Else** control flow error;
2	SIJ	`SIJ imm1, imm2` where imm1 / imm2 = D(i) ⊕ D(j) and: **If** (ITE node) imm1 for NTJ, imm2 for TJ, **Else** imm1 for J	**Signature justifying:** Update J as: J = imm1/imm2 depended on resolved branch condition
3	SIJC	`SIJC imm1, imm2` where imm1 = S(i); imm2 = D(i)	**MBI node Signature checking:** 1 Update G as: G = G ⊕ imm1 ⊕ J 2 **If** (G == imm2) fault free, **Else** control flow error;

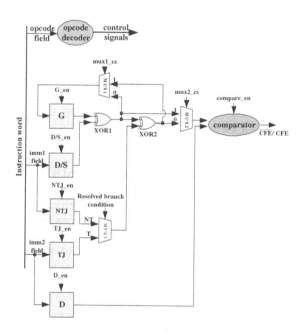

Fig. 6. On-chip control flow checker block diagram

As seen in Fig. 6, a total of five registers are needed to hold the necessary information: register **G** is used for the run time signature; registers **D/S** and **NTJ** receive immediate values from the `imm1` field of their instruction words and registers **D** and **TJ** receive immediate values from the `imm2` field of the instruction words. For each instruction, Table 2 shows the control signals generated by the opcode decoder (also shown in Fig. 6).

Table 2. On-chip control flow checker control signals (en = enable; $\overline{en}$ = disable; X = don't care; BRU = branch unit)

Instr.	G_en	D/S_en	D_en	NTJ_en	TJ_en	mux1_cs	mux2_cs	br. cond.	compare_en
SIC	en	en	en	$\overline{en}$	$\overline{en}$	0	1	$\overline{en}$	en
SIJ	$\overline{en}$	$\overline{en}$	$\overline{en}$	en	en	X	X	$\overline{en}$	$\overline{en}$
SIJC	en	en	en	$\overline{en}$	$\overline{en}$	1	0	from BRU	en

Operation of SIC *instructions.* When an instruction word SIC imm1, imm2 is decoded, its opcode field is fed into the opcode decoder. The decoder then generates the control signals specified in Table 2. The imm1 filed is received by the enabled register D/S (D/S_en = enable and NTJ_en = $\overline{enable}$) while the imm2 field is received by the enabled register D (D_en = enable and TJ_en = $\overline{enable}$).

The content of register D/S goes into XOR1 along with the content of register G (G_en = enable). The result is selected by mux2 (mux2_cs = 1). Now the enabled comparator compares the two inputs which are received from mux2 and register D. These have performed the run-time control flow checking. Also, we can see the result of XOR1 is sent to modify register G since we have mux1_cs = 0 and G_en = enable.

Operation of SIJ *instructions.* When an instruction word SIJ imm1, imm2 is decoded, its opcode field is fed into the opcode decoder. The decoder then generates the control signals specified in Table 2. The imm1 filed is received by the enabled register NTJ (NTJ_en = enable and D/S_en = $\overline{enable}$) while the imm2 field is received by the enabled register TJ (TJ_en = enable and D_en = $\overline{enable}$).

Operation of SIJC *instructions.* When an instruction word SIJC imm1, imm2 is decoded, its opcode field is fed into the opcode decoder. The decoder then generates the control signals specified in Table 2. The imm1 filed is received by the enabled register D/S (D/S_en = enable and NTJ_en = $\overline{enable}$) while the imm2 field is received by the enabled register D (D_en = enable and TJ_en = $\overline{enable}$).

The content of register D/S goes into XOR1 along with the content of register G (G_en = enable). Based on the resolved branch condition, either the content of register NTJ or that of register TJ XOR2 with the result of XOR1. Once again, if no conditional branch result from the branch unit, i.e., not an ITE node, the default "resolved branch condition = NT" such that the content of register NTJ is selected at this point. MUX2 selects the result of XOR2 (mux2_cs = 0). Now the enabled comparator compares the two inputs which are received from mux2 and register D. These have performed the run-time control flow checking. Furthermore, we can see that the result of XOR2 is sent to modify register G since we have mux1_cs = 1 and G_en = enable.

4.3   Using Additional Instructions

To summarize the above discussion, Algorithm 1 shows a comprehensive signature assignment algorithm based on our hardware enhancement instructions. Returning to the example of Fig. 1, our compiler algorithm would produce the modified diagram

---

Algorithm 1 Embedding three additional instructions into programs

---

Signature-Assignment(program)

Derive CFG of the given program

Assuming we have nodes: V_i ($i = 1,2,3,\ldots,N$) where N is the total number of nodes in the CFG

Assign a unique state code $D(i)$ to every node V_i

for every node V_i in the CFG **do**

  if V_i is not an MBI node **then**

    Compute its assigned reference signature as: $S(i) = D(i) \oplus D(pred(V_i))$;

    Place the instruction "SIC imm1, imm2"

    at the beginning of node V_i and before the SIJ instruction, if any

    Assign the values of imm1 and imm2 as: imm1 = S(i) and imm2 = D(i)

  else

    Select a primary node from: $\$$ = the set of pred(V_i) (assume V_j is selected)

    Assign the reference signature of V_i as: $S(i) = D(i) \oplus D(j)$

    Place the instruction "SIJC imm1, imm2"

    at the beginning of node V_i and before the SIJ instruction, if any

    Assign the values of imm1and imm2 as: imm1 = S(i), imm2 = D(i)

    for every node $V_k \in \$$ (including V_j) **do**

      Place instruction "SIJ imm1, imm2"

      into the node V_k and after the SIC and/or SIJC instructions

      Assign the values of imm1 and imm2 as follows:

      if $V_k \rightarrow V_i$ is a taken path **then**

        imm1 = X, imm2 = $D(k) \oplus D(j)$

      else if $V_k \rightarrow V_i$ is a not-taken path **then**

        imm1 = $D(k) \oplus D(j)$, imm2 = X

      else

        imm1 = $D(k) \oplus D(j)$, imm2 = X{$V_k \rightarrow V_i$ is not a conditional branch path}

      end if

    end for

  end if

end for

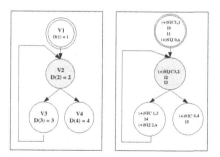

Fig. 7. State code and signature assignment example

shown in Fig. 7. The left-hand side illustrates the state code assignment results and the primary node selection of the MBI node V_2. The right-hand side shows the CFG after insertion of our control flow checking instructions.

Comparing code size overhead. To compare our algorithm with that of Oh et al. in [19], consider a *typical* node consisting of 7 to 8 instructions [1]. In order to check for control flow errors, [19] adds 2 to 4 instructions to each node. The overhead is between 27% and 53%. (As shown in [19], for a number of benchmarks, the code size overhead is between 26.6% and 61.9% whereas the execution time overhead is between 16.2% and 58.1%). Conversely, in our hardware-enhanced approach, the additional instructions are a maximum of 1 or 2 for each node. Therefore, the overhead is only 13% to 27%, which is a significant improvement over [19]. Furthermore, the execution time is given by the following formula [1]:

$$\text{Execution time} = \text{Instr count} \times \text{Clock cycle time} \times \text{Cycles per instr} . \quad (11)$$

With help from our on-chip control flow checker, we could expect a lower execution time than that obtained in [19] when executing the program with the signature checking. This is because we have a smaller instruction count given the same clock cycle time and cycles per instructions.

5   Conclusions

Control flow errors have a high error occurrence ratio relative to other kinds of errors. This is expected to continue increasing as design rules continue decreasing. Signature checking is a well-known and effective technique to detect such errors. We have used this approach to demonstrate our compiler-assisted assignment signature analysis. It includes a compile time algorithm based on a control flow graph which assigns signatures to nodes. We have also designed an on-chip checker for our dedicated instructions used for control flow checking. A comprehensive signature assignment algorithm has also been introduced, and a detailed performance overhead analysis has been presented.

References

1. Hennessy, J.L., Patterson, D.A.: Computer Architecture: A Quantitative Approach. Third edn. Morgan Kaufmann Publishers, Inc. (2002)
2. Borkar, S.: Design Challenges of Technology Scaling. IEEE Micro (1999)
3. Yang, P., Chern, J.H.: Design for Reliability: The Major Challenge for VLSI. Proceedings of the IEEE (1999)
4. Reinhardt, S.K., Mukherjee, S.S.: Transient Fault Detection via Simultaneous Multithreading. In: 27th International Symposium on Computer Architecture. (2000)
5. Hennessy, J.: The Future of Systems Research. IEEE Computer (1999)
6. Quach, N.: High Availability and Reliability in the Itanium Processor. IEEE Micro (2000)
7. Bossen, D.C., Tendler, J.M., Reick, K.: Power4 System Design for High Reliability. IEEE Micro (2002)
8. Ando, H., Yoshida, Y., Inoue, A., Sugiyama, I., Asakawa, T., Morita, K., Muta, T., Motokurumada, T., Okada, S., Yamashita, H., Satsukawa, Y., Konmoto, A., Yamashita, R., Sugiyama, H.: A 1.3-GHz Fifth-Generation SPARC64 Microprocessor. IEEE Journal of Solid-State Circuits (2003)
9. Wilken, K., Shen, J.P.: Continuous signature monitoring: Low-Cost Concurrent-Detection of Processor Control Errors. IEEE Transactions on Computer-Aided Design (1990)

10. Ohlsson, J., Rimen, M., Gunneflo, U.: A Study of the Effects of Transient Fault Injection Into a 32-bit RISC with Built-in Watchdog. In: 29th International Symposium on Fault-Tolerant Computing. (1991)
11. Schuette, M.A., Shen, J.P.: Processor Control Flow Monitoring Using Signatured Instruction Streams. IEEE Transactions on Computers (1987)
12. Mohmood, A., McCluskey, E.J.: Concurrent Error Detection Using Watchdog Processors – A Survey. IEEE Transactions on Computers (1988)
13. Schuette, M.A., Shen, J.P.: Exploiting Instruction-Level Parallelism for Integrated Control-Flow Checking. IEEE Transactions on Computers (1994)
14. Warter, N.J., Hwu, W.M.W.: A Software Based Approach to Achieving Optimal Performance for Signature Control Flow Checking. In: 20th International Symposium on Fault-Tolerant Computing. (1990)
15. Michel, T., Leveugle, R., Saucier, G.: A New Approach to Control Flow Checking without Program Modification. In: 21st International Symposium on Fault-Tolerant Computing. (1991)
16. Alkhalifa, Z., Nair, S., Krishnamurthy, N., Abraham, J.A.: Design and Evaluation of System-Level Checks for On-Line Control Flow Error Detection. IEEE Transactions on Parallel and Distributed Systems (1999)
17. Shirvani, P.P., McCluskey, E.J.: Fault-Tolerant Systems in a Space Environment: The CRC ARGOS Project. Technical Report CRC-TR 98-2, Stanford University (1998)
18. Bagchi, S., Srinivasan, B., Whisnant, K., Kalbarczyk, Z., Iyer, R.K.: Hierarchical Error Detection in a Software Implemented Fault Tolerance (SIFT) Environment. IEEE Transactions on Knowledge and Data Engineering (2000)
19. Oh, N., Shirvani, P.P., McCluskey, E.J.: Control-Flow Checking by Software Signatures. IEEE Transactions on Reliability (2002)
20. Aho, A.V., Sethi, R., Ullman, J.D.: Compilers: Principles, Techniques, and Tools. Addison-Wesley Publishing Company (1986)

A Floating Point Divider Performing IEEE Rounding and Quotient Conversion in Parallel

Woo-Chan Park[1], Tack-Don Han[2], and Sung-Bong Yang[2]

[1] Department of Internet Engineering,
Sejong University, Seoul 143-747, Korea,
pwchan@sejong.ac.kr
[2] Department of Computer Science,
Yonsei University, Seoul 120-749 Korea,
{hantack}@kurene.yonsei.ac.kr
{yang}@cs.yonsei.ac.kr

Abstract. Processing floating point division generally consists of SRT recurrence, quotient conversion, rounding, and normalization steps. In the rounding step, a high speed adder is required for increment operation, increasing the overall execution time. In this paper, a floating point divider performing quotient conversion and rounding in parallel is presented by analyzing the operational characteristics of floating point division. The proposed floating point divider does not require any additional execution time, nor does it need any high speed adder for the rounding step. The proposed divider can execute quotient conversion, rounding, and normalization within one cycle. To support design efficiency, the quotient conversion/rounding unit of the proposed divider can be shared efficiently with the addition/rounding hardware for floating point multiplier.

1 Introduction

An FPU (Floating Point Unit) is a principal component in graphics accelerators [1,2], digital signal processors, and high performance computer systems. As the chip integration density increases due to the advances in semiconductor technology, it has become possible for an FPU to be placed on a single chip together with the integer unit, allowing the FPU to exceed its original supplementary function and becoming a principal element in a CPU [2,3,4,5]. In recent microprocessors, a floating point division unit is built on a chip to speed up the floating point division operation.

In general, the processing flow of the floating point division operation consists of SRT recurrence, quotient conversion, rounding, and normalization steps [6,7,8]. SRT recurrence has been used to perform the division operation for the fraction part and to produce the final quotient and its remainder as in a redundant representation. In the quotient conversion step, the sign bit for the final remainder can be calculated from both the carry part and the sum part of the remainder in a redundant representation. Hence, a conventionally binary represented quotient is produced using the positive part and the negative part of the

P.-C. Yew and J. Xue (Eds.): ACSAC 2004, LNCS 3189, pp. 568–581, 2004.

redundantly represented quotient and the sign bit of the final remainder. After that, the rounding step can be performed using the results from the quotient conversion step. For the rounding step, a high speed adder for increment operation is usually required, increasing the overall execution time and occupying a large amount of chip area.

In some microprocessors, due to design efficiency, the rounding unit for a floating point divider is shared with a rounding hardware for a floating point multiplier or a floating point adder [7,9]. The reasons for this sharing are as follows. First, because the floating point division operation requires many cycles to complete its operation, it does not need to be implemented by a pipeline structure. Second, because the floating point division operation is not used more frequently than other floating point operations, additional hardware for the rounding unit in the floating point divider is not economical. Third, the hardware to support the rounding operation for floating point division can be developed simply by modifying the rounding unit for either a floating point multiplier or a floating point adder. However, this sharing must not affect any critical path of the shared one and should not complicate the control scheme. Therefore, an efficient sharing mechanism is required.

In this paper, a floating point divider performing quotient conversion and rounding in parallel is proposed by analyzing the operational characteristics of floating point division. The proposed floating point divider does not require any additional execution time, nor does it need any high speed adder for the rounding step. Also it can execute quotient conversion, rounding, and normalization within only one cycle, and can share the addition/rounding hardware logics for a floating point multiplier presented in [11] by adding several hardware logics. The additive hardware does not affect the execution time of the floating point multiplier and can be implemented with very simple hardware logics.

In [9], quotient conversion and rounding can be performed in parallel, and the addition/rounding hardware logics are shared with a floating point multiplier presented in [10]. However, it requires a more complex processing algorithm. This in turn requires additional hardware components which increase the length of the critical path on the pipeline. Such increase causes one more unit of pipeline delay in their approach and requires more hardware components than our approach.

The rest of this paper is organized as follows. Section 2 presents a brief overview of the IEEE rounding methods and the integer SRT division method. We also illustrate how the proposed floating point divider can share an addition/rounding unit of the floating point multiplier. Section 3 suggests a hardware model which can execute rounding and quotient conversion in parallel and its implementation with respect to IEEE four rounding modes. In Section 4, conclusion is given.

2   Backgrounds and Basic Equations

In this section, the IEEE rounding methods and the SRT division algorithm are discussed. An addition and rounding circuit for a floating point multiplier is also illustrated to be shared with the proposed floating point divider.

2.1   The IEEE Rounding Modes

The IEEE standard 754 stipulates four rounding modes; they are round-to-nearest, round-to-zero, round-to-positive-infinity, and round-to-negative-infinity. These four rounding modes can be classified mainly into round-to-nearest, round-to-zero, and round-to-infinity, because round-to-positive-infinity and round-to-negative-infinity can be divided into round-to-zero and round-to-infinity according to the sign of a number.

For the sake of the IEEE rounding, two additional bits, R and Sy, are required. R is the MSB among the less significant bits other than LSB. Sy is the ORed results of all the less significant bits except with R. The following three algorithms are the results of the rounding operation with LSB, R, and Sy when the MSB is zero, which is a normalized case. "return 0" means truncation, and "return 1" indicates increment as the result of any rounding operation.

Algorithm 1 : $Round_{nearest}(LSB, R, Sy)$

> if $(R{=}0)$ return 0
> else if $(Sy{=}1)$ return 1
> > else if $(LSB{=}0)$ return 0
> > > else return 1

Algorithm 2 : $Round_{zero}(LSB, R, Sy)$

> return 0

Algorithm 3 : $Round_{infinity}(LSB, R, Sy)$

> if $((R{=}1)$ or $(Sy{=}1))$ return 1
> else return 0

Assume that two input significands, *divisor* d and *dividend* x, have n bits each. To simplify the notation, the binary point is to be located between the LSB and the R bit positions. Then, the R and the Sy bit positions become the fraction portion. The significand bits above them, which are the most significant $(n + 1)$ bits, are the integer portion. The integer portion is represented with subscript I and the fractional portion with subscript T. Figure 1 shows that most significant $(n + 1)$ bits of H are the integer portion H_I, while R and Sy in H are the fractional portion H_T.

For the rest of this paper, '$\wedge$' denotes the boolean AND, '$\vee$' denotes the boolean OR, and '$\oplus$' denotes the boolean exclusive-OR. X denotes the "don't care" condition. If any overflow is generated from the result of Z operation then $overflow(Z)$ returns 1, otherwise it returns 0. C_k^{in} denotes the value of the carry signal from the $(k - 1)$-th bit position into the k-th bit position.

$$H = \overbrace{h_n h_{n-1} h_{n-2} \cdots h_1 h_0}^{H_I} . \overbrace{RSy}^{H_T}$$

Fig. 1. The definitions of H_I and H_T.

2.2   SRT Recurrence

Division operation can be defined by the following equation [6]:

$$x = q \times d + rem,$$

where $|rem| < |d| \times ulp$. The dividend x and the divisor d are the input operands. The quotient q and the remainder rem are the results of the division operation. The unit in the last position, denoted by ulp, defines the precision of the quotient, where $ulp = r^{-n}$ for n-digit and radix-r fractional results.

The following recurrence is used at each iteration:

$$rP_0 = x$$
$$P_{j+1} = rP_j - dq_{j+1},$$

where q_{j+1} is the $(j+1)$-th quotient digit, numbered from the highest to the lowest order, and P_j is the partial remainder at iteration j. In order for the next partial remainder P_{j+1} to be bounded, the value of the quotient-digit is chosen as follow:

$$|P_{j+1}| \le d.$$

The final quotient is the weighted sum of all of the quotient-digits selected through the iteration such that

$$Q_{final} = \sum_{j=1}^{n} q_j \times r^{-j}.$$

In general, to speed-up the recurrence, the partial remainder and the quotient are represented as in the redundant forms. That is, the partial remainder consists of the carry part and the sum part, and the quotient consists of the positive part and the negative part.

2.3   Calculating the Final Quotient, R, and Sy

Suppose that the quotient obtained after the l-th iteration is denoted by Q_l and the partial remainder is denoted by P_l. Then because P_l should be positive, the restoration step for P_l is required to produce the final quotient if P_l is negative. Therefore, considering the restoration step, Q_l and P_l can be converted as follows.

$$\tilde{Q}_l = Q_l - restore_l$$
$$\tilde{P}_l = P_l + restore_l \cdot d$$
$$restore_l = \begin{cases} 1 & \text{if } P_l < 0 \\ 0 & \text{otherwise.} \end{cases}$$

After the completion of SRT recurrence, the quotient and the remainder values are generated in the redundant binary representations. The quotient value from the result of SRT recurrence consists of the positive part Q^P and the negative part Q^N. Then Q^P and Q^N can be shown as follows.

$$Q^P = p_n \cdots p_0.p_{-1}$$
$$Q^N = n_n \cdots n_0.n_{-1},$$

where Q^N is represented in the one's complement form.

The remainder value generated after the completion of SRT recurrence consists of the carry part Rem_C and the sum part Rem_S. Both Rem_C and Rem_S are represented in the two's complement form and have length of $(n+1)$ bits each. Rem_C and Rem_S can be now represented as follows.

$$Rem_S = s_n \cdots s_1 s_0$$
$$Rem_C = c_n \cdots c_1 c_0.$$

The integer portions of Q^P and Q^N are denoted as Q_I^P and Q_I^N, respectively. Q_I^P and Q_I^N can be then defined as follows.

$$Q_I^P = p_n \cdots p_0$$
$$Q_I^N = n_n \cdots n_0.$$

Then, because Q^N is represented in the one's complement form, when the values in the redundant representation converted into the conventional binary representation, '1' should be added to the position of n_{-1}. Also, if the remainder is negative, '1' should be borrowed from the quotient to restore the final remainder. Therefore, H which is the conventional binary representation of the final quotient including R and Sy can be calculated as follows.

$$H = h_n h_{n-1} \cdots h_0.RSy$$
$$= (p_n \cdots p_0) + (n_n \cdots n_0) + 0.p_{-1} + 0.n_{-1} + \overline{restore_{-1}} + 0.0Sy, \quad (1)$$

where $restore_{-1}$ is the restoration signal to the (-1)-th position of the quotient and is identical to the sign value of the result of $(Rem_S + Rem_C)$. $Sy = 0$, if the result sum bits of $(Rem_S + Rem_C)$ are all zeros, otherwise $Sy = 1$.

Then, (1) can be converted as follows.

$$H = Q_I^P + Q_I^N + 0.p_{-1} + 0.n_{-1} + 0.\overline{restore_{-1}} + 0.0Sy$$
$$= Q_I^P + Q_I^N + C_0^{in} + 0.RSy$$
$$R = p_{-1} \oplus n_{-1} \oplus \overline{restore_{-1}}$$
$$C_0^{in} = overflow(p_{-1} + n_{-1} + \overline{restore_{-1}}),$$

where R is the round bit and C_0^{in} is the value of the carry signal from the (-1)-th bit position to the 0-th bit position. Hence, H_I, the integer portion of H, can be represented as follows.

$$H_I = Q_I^P + Q_I^N + C_0^{in}. \quad (2)$$

2.4   The Addition/Rounding Unit for a Floating-Point Multiplier

In general, processing floating point multiplication consists of multiplication, addition, rounding, and normalization steps. A floating point multiplier in [11, 12,13] can execute the addition/rounding operation within only one pipeline stage and hence simplify the hardware design. The hardware model presented in [11] is shown in Figure 2. The proposed floating point divider can share the addition/rounding unit for a floating point multiplier to process the quotient conversion, the rounding, and the normalization steps.

Sy which is calculated at the previous pipeline stage in parallel with a wallace tree is included in the input factors of the *predictor* logic in [11]. Because Sy can be generated after SRT recurrence in floating point division, Sy must not be included among the input elements for the *predictor* logic to perform addition and rounding in parallel. This is considered in the proposed floating point divider which is given in next section.

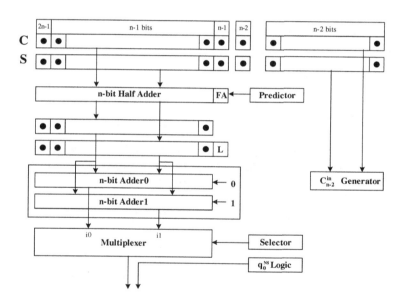

Fig. 2. The hardware model of the addition/rounding stage for a floating point multiplier.

3   The Proposed Floating-Point Divider

In this section, the operational characteristics in performing rounding and quotient conversion in parallel are illustrated. Based on these characteristics, a hardware model is presented. Finally, the proposed floating point divider is compared with respect to cycle time.

3.1   Analysis for the Quotient Conversion and Rounding Steps

Depending on the MSB of H, the shifting operation for normalization is performed. If $h_n = 1$ then no bit shifting for normalization is required, otherwise one bit shifting to the left should be performed in the normalization stage. The former case is denoted as NS (no shift) and the latter case is denoted as LS (left shift).

Normalization should be accounted for two different cases, i.e., the LS and the NS cases. In the LS case, the result value of H after normalization is denoted as O^{LS}. For the NS case, the result value of H after normalization is denoted as O^{NS}. Suppose that O_I^{LS}, O_R^{LS}, O_{Sy}^{LS} are the integer portion of O^{LS}, the R bit value, and the Sy bit value in the case of LS, respectively. Then they can be represented as follows.

$$O_I^{LS} = h_{n-1}h_{n-2}\cdots h_0$$
$$O_R^{LS} = R$$
$$O_{Sy}^{LS} = Sy. \tag{3}$$

O_I^{NS}, O_R^{NS}, and O_{Sy}^{NS} are defined similarly for the NS case as follows:

$$O_I^{NS} = h_n h_{n-1}\cdots h_1$$
$$O_R^{NS} = h_0$$
$$O_{Sy}^{NS} = R \vee Sy. \tag{4}$$

Suppose that Q is the result value after the rounding step which is performed prior to the normalization stage. Then in the LS case, Q is represented by Q^{LS}. Thus, Q^{LS} can be written as follows according to (2) and (3):

$$\begin{aligned}
Q^{LS} &= O_I^{LS} + Round_{mode}(h_0, R, Sy) \\
&= (h_{n-1}h_{n-2}\cdots h_0) + Round_{mode}(h_0, R, Sy) \\
&= Q_I^P + Q_I^N + C_0^{in} + Round_{mode}(h_0, R, Sy).
\end{aligned} \tag{5}$$

Also, for the NS case, Q is represented by Q^{NS}. Thus, Q^{NS} can be obtained as follows according to (2) and (4).

$$\begin{aligned}
Q^{NS} &= (O_I^{NS} + Round_{mode}(h_1, h_0, (R \vee Sy))) \times 2 \\
&= (h_n \cdots h_1 h_0) + 2 \times Round_{mode}(h_1, h_0, (R \vee Sy)) \\
&= Q_I^P + Q_I^N + C_0^{in} + 2 \times Round_{mode}(h_1, h_0, (R \vee Sy)).
\end{aligned} \tag{6}$$

3.2   The Proposed Hardware Model for Performing IEEE Rounding and Quotient Conversion in Parallel

A hardware model capable of performing rounding and quotient conversion in parallel is designed as shown in Figure 3. The proposed hardware model can be implemented by adding some hardware to the hardware model in Figure 2.

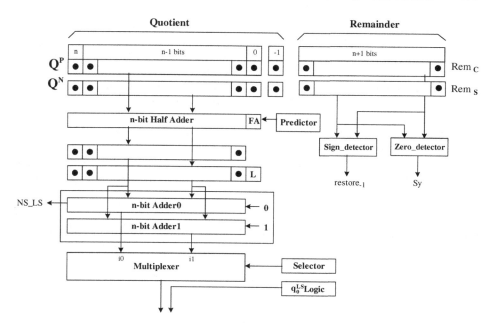

Fig. 3. The proposed hardware model for performing IEEE rounding and quotient conversion in parallel.

In *sign_detector*, the result value of *restore*$_{-1}$ in the (1) is calculated. The *zero_detector* logic determines whether the remainder is zero. If the result of *zero_detector* is zero, $Sy = 0$, otherwise $Sy = 1$. These logics can be implemented by adding additional logics to the C_{n-2}^{in} *generator* in Figure 2.

When Q_I^P and Q_I^N are added by the n bit HA and the one bit FA, the *predictor* bit is provided to the FA. Then the n bit carry and the $(n + 1)$ bit sum are generated. Here, the LSB of the sum is represented by L as shown in Figure 3. The n bit carry and the most significant n bit sum are added by a single carry select adder which is drawn as a dotted box in Figure 3. The *selector* selects one of the result values after executing addition and rounding from the two inputs $i0$ and $i1$. If *selector* $= 0$, then $i0$ is selected, otherwise $i1$ is selected as the output value of the multiplexer. The input values of $i0$ and $i1$ can be represented as follows.

$$i0 = Q_I^P + Q_I^N + predictor$$
$$i1 = Q_I^P + Q_I^N + 2 + predictor. \tag{7}$$

In Figure 3, the multiplexer output may be either $(Q_I^P + Q_I^N + predictor)$ or $(Q_I^P + Q_I^N + predictor + 2)$, depending on the value of *selector*. According to (5) and (6), one of four possible cases, i.e., $(Q_I^P + Q_I^N)$, $(Q_I^P + Q_I^N + 1)$, $(Q_I^P + Q_I^N + 2)$, and $(Q_I^P + Q_I^N + 3)$ needs to be generated to perform rounding and quotient conversion in parallel. Therefore, if *predictor* and *selector* are properly selected, then the result value Q after performing addition and rounding in parallel can be generated. Note that Q is defined in Section 3.1.

To configure *predictor*, the following two factors should be considered. First, the input signals of *predictor* must be generated before any addition operation performed by the carry select adder. Second, the delay of the *selector* logic which is finally configured after the determination of the *predictor* logic should be negligible. Thus, *predictor* must be selected very carefully.

The input value of $i0$ in the multiplexer is denoted by $E = e_n e_{n-1} \cdots e_1$. Because the LSB position of E corresponds to the first bit positions of Q^P and Q^N, the integer value of E is $E_I = E \times 2$. Thus, the $(n+1)$ bit integer field can be denoted as E_I^* and $E_I^* = E_I + L$. Hence, E_I^* can be represented as follows:

$$E_I^* = E_I + L = Q_I^P + Q_I^N + predictor = e_n \cdots e_1 L. \tag{8}$$

In the next subsections, the rounding position is analyzed, and *predictor* and *selector* are determined according to all the three rounding modes.

3.3   The Round-to-Nearest Mode

In the round-to-nearest mode and the LS case, one of three possible cases, i.e., $(Q_I^P + Q_I^N)$, $(Q_I^P + Q_I^N + 1)$, and $(Q_I^P + Q_I^N + 2)$ needs to be generated according to (5) to perform rounding and quotient conversion in parallel.

In the NS case, for increment as the result of $Round_{Nearest}(h_1, h_0, (R \vee Sy))$, h_0 should be '1' according to Algorithm 1. If the result of rounding is increment and the NS case, '1' should be added to the position of h_1. But because h_0 should be '1' for increment as a result of rounding in the NS case, adding '1' to the position of h_1 has the same most significant n bit result when '1' is added to the position of h_0. Therefore, one of the three possible cases, i.e., $(Q_I^P + Q_I^N)$, $(Q_I^P + Q_I^N + 1)$, and $(Q_I^P + Q_I^N + 2)$, is required to be generated also in the NS case.

According to (7), when *predictor* is selected to '0', $(Q_I^P + Q_I^N)$ and $(Q_I^P + Q_I^N + 2)$ are generated. Because the most significant n bits of either $(Q_I^P + Q_I^N)$ or $(Q_I^P + Q_I^N + 2)$ are identical to the most significant n bits of $(Q_I^P + Q_I^N + 1)$, $(Q_I^P + Q_I^N + 1)$ can be generated. However, *predictor* is selected as follows to simplify the *selector* logic.

$$predictor = p_{-1} \wedge n_{-1}. \tag{9}$$

Then, (2) can be converted as follows.

$$\begin{aligned} H &= Q_I^P + Q_I^N + 0.p_{-1} + 0.n_{-1} + 0.\overline{restore_{-1}} + 0.0Sy \\ &= Q_I^P + Q_I^N + overflow(p_{-1} + n_{-1}) + 0.(p_{-1} \oplus n_{-1}) + \\ &\quad 0.\overline{restore_{-1}} + 0.0Sy \\ &= Q_I^P + Q_I^N + predictor + 0.(p_{-1} \oplus n_{-1}) + 0.\overline{restore_{-1}} + 0.0Sy \\ &= E_I + L + C_0^{in} + 0.R + 0.0Sy \\ &= E_I + C_1^{in} \times 2 + h_0 + 0.R + 0.0Sy \end{aligned} \tag{10}$$

$$R = (p_{-1} \oplus n_{-1}) \oplus \overline{restore_{-1}}$$
$$C_0^{in} = (p_{-1} \oplus n_{-1}) \wedge \overline{restore_{-1}}$$
$$h_0 = L \oplus C_0^{in}$$
$$C_1^{in} = L \wedge C_0^{in}.$$

In the LS case, Q^{LS} can be expressed as follows according to (5) and (10).

$$Q^{LS} = E_I + C_1^{in} \times 2 + h_0 + Round_{nearest}(h_0, R, Sy). \tag{11}$$

Then, $selector$ and q_0^{LS} can be produced as follows.

$$selector = C_1^{in} \vee (h_0 \wedge Round_{nearest}(h_0, R, Sy))$$
$$q_0^{LS} = h_0 \oplus Round_{nearest}(h_0, R, Sy).$$

In the NS case, Q^{NS} is as follows according to (6) and (10).

$$Q^{NS} = E_I + 2 \times C_1^{in} + h_0 + 2 \times Round_{nearest}(h_1, h_0, R \vee Sy). \tag{12}$$

Then, $selector$ can be produced as follows.

$$selector = C_1^{in} \vee Round_{nearest}(h_1, h_0, R \vee Sy).$$

3.4 The Round-to-Zero Mode

It is considered that the $predictor$ of the round-to-zero mode is identical to that of the round-to-nearest mode. Because $Round_{Zero}(X, X, X) = 0$ for both the LS and the NS cases, both $selector$ and q_0^{LS} can be obtained by replacing both $Round_{Nearest}(h_0, R, Sy)$ and $Round_{Nearest}(h_1, h_0, R \vee Sy)$ of (11) and (12) with zeros. Therefore, $selector$ and q_0^{LS} can be written as follows:

$$selector = C_1^{in}$$
$$q_0^{LS} = h_0.$$

3.5 The Round-to-Infinity Mode

For a specific case such as $L = p_{-1} \oplus n_{-1} = C_0^{in} = Sy = 1$, if the $predictor$ of the round-to-nearest mode is used, then $C_1^{in} = 1$, $h_0 = 0$, $R = 0$, and $Sy = 1$. Thus the rounding result in the round-to-nearest mode can be obtained by truncation according to Algorithm 1. However, because the value of Sy is equal to '1', the rounding result in the round-to-infinity mode can be obtained by increment according to Algorithm 3. Therefore, in the NS case, the case of $C_1^{in} = 1$ and $Round_{infinity} = 1$ can be occurred. Eventually, in the round-to-infinity mode, the $predictor$ of the round-to-nearest mode cannot be used. Thus, the $predictor$ is given as follows.

$$predictor = p_{-1} \vee n_{-1}. \tag{13}$$

Table 1. The result values of C_0^{in}, R, *predictor* according to the values of the p_{-1}, n_{-1}, $\overline{restore_{-1}}$.

p_{-1}	n_{-1}	$\overline{restore_{-1}}$	$p_{-1} \oplus n_{-1}$	C_0^{in}	R	*predictor*
0	0	0	0	0	0	0
0	1	0	1	0	1	1
1	0	0	1	0	1	1
1	1	0	0	1	0	1
0	0	1	0	0	1	0
0	1	1	1	1	0	1
1	0	1	1	1	0	1
1	1	1	0	1	1	1

In Table 1, C_0^{in}, R, and *predictor* are illustrated as the values of p_{-1}, n_{-1}, and $\overline{restore_{-1}}$. The following two cases can be generated according to the values of $p_{-1} \oplus n_{-1}$ and $\overline{restore_{-1}}$. First, $\overline{restore_{-1}} = 0$ and $p_{-1} \oplus n_{-1} = 1$. In this case, C_0^{in} which represents the carry value to the position of h_0 is 0, both R and *predictor* are 1's. Second, the value of C_0^{in} has an identical value with *predictor* for all the cases except the first case.

In the first case, the result of rounding is increment because $R = 1$ according to Algorithm 3, *predictor* = 1 and $C_0^{in} = 0$. Then, Q^{LS} can be given as follows according to (5) and (8).

$$Q^{LS} = Q_I^P + Q_I^N + C_0^{in} + Round_{infinity}(h_0, R, Sy)$$
$$= Q_I^P + Q_I^N + 1 = Q_I^P + Q_I^N + predictor$$
$$= E_I + L.$$

Then, *selector* and q_0^{LS} can be produced as follows in this case.

$$selector = 0$$
$$q_0^{LS} = L. \tag{14}$$

In the NS case, Q^{NS} can be written as follows according to (6) and (8).

$$Q^{NS} = Q_I^P + Q_I^N + C_0^{in} + 2 \times Round_{infinity}(h_0, R, Sy)$$
$$= Q_I^P + Q_I^N + 2 = Q_I^P + Q_I^N + predictor + 1$$
$$= E_I + L + 1.$$

Hence, *selector* is as follows in this case.

$$selector = L.$$

In the second case, the value of C_0^{in} is identical to *predictor*. Then, Q^{LS} can be produced as follows.

$$Q^{LS} = Q_I^P + Q_I^N + C_0^{in} + Round_{infinity}(h_0, R, Sy)$$
$$= Q_I^P + Q_I^N + predictor + Round_{infinity}(h_0, R, Sy)$$
$$= E_I + L + Round_{infinity}(h_0, R, Sy).$$

Then, in this case, *selector* and q_0^{LS} can be determined as follows.

$$selector = L \wedge Round_{infinity}(h_0, R, Sy)$$
$$q_0^{LS} = L \oplus Round_{infinity}(h_0, R, Sy).$$

Thus, Q^{NS} is also obtained as follows.

$$Q^{NS} = Q_I^P + Q_I^N + C_0^{in} + 2 \times Round_{infinity}(h_1, h_0, R \vee Sy)$$
$$= Q_I^P + Q_I^N + predictor + 2 \times Round_{infinity}(h_1, h_0, R \vee Sy)$$
$$= E_I + L + 2 \times Round_{infinity}(h_1, h_0, R \vee Sy).$$

Hence, *selector* is represented as follows in this case.

$$selector = Round_{infinity}(h_1, h_0, R \vee Sy).$$

3.6 Critical Path Analysis

There are two dataflows in Figure 4. The critical path latency of the left hand side flow, denoted as L_{CP}^{div}, is (*predictor* + FA + carry select adder + *selector* + multiplexer). The right hand side flow, denoted as R_{CP}^{div}, is (*zero_detector* + *selector* + multiplexer). In L_{CP}^{div} and R_{CP}^{div}, q_0^{LS} is ignored because both *selector* and q_0^{LS} can be performed simultaneously and the delay characteristic of *selector* is more complex than that of q_0^{LS}. As aforementioned in Section 2.3, the result values of $restore_{-1}$ and Sy can be calculated with the result of $Rem_C + Rem_S$. Because the latency of *zero_detector* is either equal to or longer than that of *sign_detector*, *sign_detector* is not also included in R_{CP}^{div}.

If we compare L_{CP}^{div} with R_{CP}^{div}, it seems that the carry select adder and *zero_detector* reveal similar delay characteristic, because both can be implemented with a high speed adder. Thus, the critical path of the hardware model in Figure 4 will be L_{CP}^{div}.

L_{CP}^{div} is almost similar to the critical path L_{CP}^{mul} of the hardware model in Figure 2. Only the delay characteristics of *predictor* and *selector* are somewhat different. The logic delay of *predictor* on L_{CP}^{div} is one gate delay for each rounding mode, otherwise that of L_{CP}^{mul} is two gate delays in the case of the round-to-infinity mode. For the *selector* of L_{CP}^{div}, an additional exclusive-OR gate is required due to identify the two cases in Table 1, as shown in Section 3.5. The additive gate delay of L_{CP}^{div} amount to the gate delays of exclusive-OR minus one gate delay. This additive delay is so small that it may not affect the overall pipeline latency.

3.7 Comparison with On-the-Fly Rounding

In [14], on-the-fly rounding was suggested to avoid a carry-propagation addition in rounding operation, by combining the rounding process with the on-the-fly conversion of the quotient digits from redundant to conventional binary form. The on-the-fly rounding requires one cycle for the rounding operation because the

Table 2. The execution cycles for double precision according to radix-r.

Processor	cycles	radix
PowerPC604e [3]	31	4
PA-RISC 8000 [15]	31	4
Pentium [7]	33	4
UltraSPARC [4]	22	8
R10000 [5]	19	16
Proposed floating point divider	30	4
Proposed floating point divider	21	8
Proposed floating point divider	15	16

rounded quotient is selected after the sign bit detection. This one cycle latency is equal to the latency for the rounding operation of the proposed architecture. But, the on-the-fly rounding requires four shift registers with somewhat complex parallel load operations.

On the other hand, the proposed architecture can share the addition/rounding hardware logics for a floating point multiplier presented in [14]. Thus, the proposed architecture seems to require less hardware than the on-the-fly rounding. Moreover, the proposed architecture achieves low-power consumption over the on-the-fly rounding, because the parallel loading operations for four registers could be generated at each iteration in case of on-the-fly rounding, while only one rounding operation is required in the proposed architecture.

3.8 Comparison with Other Microprocessors

To complete double precision floating point division, the SRT recurrences on the radix-4 case, on the radix-8 case, and on the radix-16 case take 29 cycles, 20 cycles, and 14 cycles, respectively. Because the proposed floating point divider can perform quotient conversion and rounding within only one cycle, to complete the floating point division operation, 30 cycles should be taken in the radix-4 case, 21 cycles for the radix-8 case, and 15 cycles for the radix-16 case, respectively. As shown in Table 2 in the radix-4 case, PowerPC604e [3] takes 31 cycles, PA-RISC 8000 [15] takes 31 cycles, and Pentium [7] takes 33 cycles to complete the floating point division operation. In the radix-8 case, UltraSPARC [4] takes 22 cycles. Also, R10000 [5] takes 19 cycles in the radix-16 case.

4   Conclusion

In this paper, a floating point divider which is capable of performing the IEEE rounding and addition in parallel is proposed. Its hardware model is provided and evaluated with the proofs for correctness of the model. The performance improvement and cost effectiveness design for floating point division can be achieved by this approach.

References

1. M. Kameyama, Y. Kato, H. Fujimoto, H. Negishi, Y. Kodama, Y. Inoue, and H. Kawai. 3D graphics LSI core for mobile phone "Z3D". In Proceedings of the ACM SIGGRAPH/EUROGRAPHICS Conference on Graphics hardware, pages 60–67, 2003.
2. S. Oberman, G. Favor, and F. Weber. AMD 3DNow! technology: architecture and implementations. IEEE Micro, 19(2):37–48, April 1999.
3. S. P. Song, M. Denman, and J. Chang. The powerPC604 RISC microprocessor. IEEE Micro, 14(5):8–17, Oct. 1994.
4. M. Tremblay and J. M. O'Connor. Ultra SPARC I : A four-issue processor supporting multimedia. IEEE Micro, 16(2):42–50, April 1996.
5. K. C. Yeager. The MIPS R10000 superscalar microprocessor. IEEE Micro, 16(2):28–40, April 1996.
6. M. D. Ercegovac and T. Lang. Division and square root: digit recurrence algorithms and implementations. (Kluwer Academic Publishers, 1994).
7. D. Alpert and D. Avnon. Architecture of the Pentium microprocessor. IEEE Micro, 13(3):11–21, June 1993.
8. C. H. Jung, W. C. Park, T. D. Han, S. B. Yang, and M. K. Lee. An effective out-of-order execution control scheme for an embedded floating point coprocessor. Microprocessors and Microsystems, 27:171–180, April 2003.
9. J. A. Prabhu and G. B. Zyner. 167 MHz Radix-8 divide and square root using overlapped radix-2 stages. In Proceedings of the 12th IEEE Symposium on Computer Arithmetic, pages 155–162, July 1995.
10. J. Arjun Prabhu and Gregory B. Zyner. 167 MHZ radix–4 floating point multiplier. In Proceedings of the 12th IEEE Symposium on Computer Arithmetic, pages 149–154, July 1995.
11. W. C. Park, T. D. Han, and S. D. Kim. Floating point multiplier performing IEEE rounding and addition in parallel. Journal of Systems Architecture, 45:1195–1207, July 1999.
12. G. Even and P. M. Seidel. A comparison of three rounding algorithms for IEEE floating-point multiplication. IEEE Transactions on Computers, 49(7):638–650, July 2000.
13. M. R. Santoro, G. Bewick, and M. A. Horowitz. Rounding algorithms for IEEE multiplier. In Proceedings of the 9th IEEE Symposium on Computer Arithmetic, pages 176-183, 1989.
14. M. D. Ercegovac and T. Lang. On-the-fly Rounding. IEEE Transactions on Computers, 41(12):1497–1503, Dec. 1992.
15. P. Solderquist and M. Leeser. Division and square root: choosing the right implementation. IEEE Micro, 17(4):56–66, Aug. 1997.

Efficient Buffer Allocation for Asynchronous Linear Pipelines by Design Space Localization

Jeong-Gun Lee[1], Euiseok Kim[2], Jeong-A Lee[3], and Eunok Paek[4]

[1] Department of Information and Communications,
Gwangju Institute of Science and Technology, Republic of Korea
eulia@gist.ac.kr
[2] Samsung Advanced Institute of Technology, Republic of Korea
euiseok2003.kim@samsung.com
[3] Department of Computer Engineering, Chosun University, Republic of Korea
jalee@chosun.ac.kr
[4] Department of Mechanical and Information Engineering,
University of Seoul, Republic of Korea
paek@uos.ac.kr

Abstract. Asynchronous circuit design is very attractive as a high performance design method since it can achieve average-case delay. However, it is hard to make use of such an advantage in a pipelined architecture due to the blocking/starvation effects between stages. In most of current solutions, buffers are allocated to reduce the blocking/starvation effects but it is difficult to find a distribution of buffers over an asynchronous linear pipeline(ALP) that is optimal in terms of 'time*area' cost.
In this paper, we show that the design space of the buffer allocation on an ALP is non-convex by introducing a term, called additional cycle time reduction (ACTR) that can separate the effect of a simultaneous buffer insertion from an individual buffer insertion. Furthermore, we propose a hybrid algorithm such that hill-climbing search is first performed during the early stage of buffer allocation while more sophisticated simulated annealing is applied for the later stage. Such a hybrid approach makes use of the characteristics of buffer allocation design space. Experiments and comparison with conventional methods based on simulated annealing are presented to show the efficiency of the proposed algorithm.

1 Introduction

Recently, asynchronous designs have been reconsidered as a high performance and low power system design method by incorporating advanced circuit design techniques. In particular, the benefit of average case performance, characterized by data dependent operations, is very attractive in designing high-performance systems. In order to achieve the expected average case performance of asynchronous circuits, a lot of efforts have been made considering various aspects of the design problem [6,7,8]. Difficulties arise, however, when those circuits and blocks are combined in a pipeline, because the pipeline may not show the average case performance or may even show near worst-case performance due to

P.-C. Yew and J. Xue (Eds.): ACSAC 2004, LNCS 3189, pp. 582–595, 2004.
© Springer-Verlag Berlin Heidelberg 2004

blocking and starvation effects. Thus, it is strongly required to provide a way to achieve a near average case performance for asynchronous pipelines.

Asynchronous FIFO buffers have been considered as one of the best ways to achieve the average case performance in pipelines [5,6,9] as they help avoid blocking and starvation effects between pipeline stages. However it is difficult to answer the question, "How should the buffers be distributed in the circuit to ensure optimum time performance and time*area performance?" [9]. The difficulty comes from a non-convex characteristic and an enormous design space of the buffer allocation problem.

In this paper we propose an efficient 'performance*area' optimization method for an asynchronous linear pipeline (ALP) where the processing delay in each stage varies. In particular, we investigate the characteristics of buffer design space of ALPs and then suggest the localized space where the optima exist thus avoid exploring the entire buffer design space. Finally we propose an efficient buffer allocation algorithm exploring only a part of the design space based on the localization.

The paper is organized as follows. In Section 2, the previous work on performance analysis for an ALP is presented. An ALP model and its performance characteristics are described briefly in Section 3. In Section 4, we analyze optimums on the buffer design space of an ALP and present how to localize the search space. Section 5 proposes an efficient buffer allocation method based on the results presented in Section 4. Experimental results of the proposed algorithm are presented in Section 6. Finally, we conclude this paper in Section 7.

2   Related Work

Performance analysis and characterization have been done for asynchronous pipelined circuits in order to improve the speed of those pipelines through analytic approaches. In [2], the performance characterization of self-timed rings was performed and three types of performance region were classified as "data-limited", "bubble-limited", and "handshake-limited". For each classified performance region, the optimal number of tokens or stages was calculated in order to obtain best performance. However, only a fixed delay was used as a processing delay at each stage. In [3], asymptotic performance characteristics of an asynchronous pipeline were derived with probabilistic processing delay distributions. In [5], a coefficient variation for variable computation delay was used as an important factor affecting the system throughput. Using the coefficient variation, approximate performance formulas were derived through the empirical analysis. Then, the formulas were used to find the size of buffers required to achieve the specific rate of average case performance. In this work, it is assumed that all stages have identical and two-valued random delays only. Due to these restrictive and unrealistic assumptions, the formulas cannot be used effectively in real world designs with heterogeneous and complex logic stages.

Most recently, the limit for the average case performance was theoretically presented with diffusion equations [9] and percolation theory [11] independently.

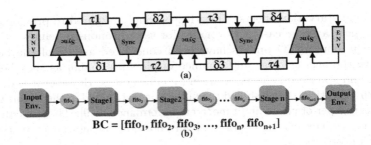

Fig. 1. (a) An ALP, (b) A conceptual model of the ALP and a buffer configuration

3   Target Model and Problem Description

3.1   An ALP Model and Its Performance

Fig.1(a) shows a four-stages ALP where τ_i is a forward latency and δ_i is a backward latency. The Sync module in the figure represents a synchronization mechanism between stages. The simplest implementation of Sync is a C-element, which is popular in asynchronous circuit design [4].

Each stage in the ALP has variable processing delays, that is, τ_i varies depending on the data being processed in each stage. Fig.1(b) illustrates an abstract model of an ALP. The first and the last stages communicate with input/output environments respectively. A buffer can be inserted to a channel to decouple operations of the two neighboring stages. To describe a buffer distribution over channels, a non-negative integer vector BC, a buffer configuration, is used. The dimension of BC is the same as the number of channels and BC[i] represents the number of buffers allocated to the channel 'i'.

Performance Characteristics of an ALP: Two special performance features of an ALP are shown in Figs.2. Parameters τ_i and δ_i in an ALP are assumed to be random variables with a uniform distribution in the interval [2, 12]. The delay of sf Sync is set to 0.5 unit delay, respectively. The environment is assumed to respond to an ALP immediately.

The dashed line in Fig.2(a) shows the performance of an ALP when the number of stages in an ALP increases. As the number of stages increase, the probability of blocking/starvation between stages becomes higher and therefore average cycle time becomes worse. Buffers can be used to reduce the blocking/starvation effects and improve the utilization of a functional logic in each stage by temporarily storing data between stages.

The solid line in Fig.2(b) illustrates the performance of an ALP, when buffers are sequentially inserted one by one to one channel in an ALP. The cycle time and reduction rate decrease monotonically and eventually converges to a certain point. The *exponential decrease of efficacy* with the number of buffers has also been observed in the simulation studies by [5]. When buffers are sufficiently allocated to *all the channels* in an ALP, the cycle time approaches to the average case.

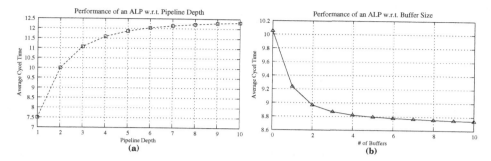

Fig. 2. Performance Impact of *Pipeline Depth* and *Buffer Size*

3.2   Terms and Problem Description

An ALP consisting of n stages has n+1 channels as shown in Fig.1(b). A buffer design space is composed of a set of possible buffer configurations. Assume that the number of available buffers is bn and the number of channels is cn. When i buffers are assigned to cn possible places, the number of i-combinations with repetition allowed from a set of cn channels is $_{i+|cn|-1}C_i$. Thus the size of a buffer design space is expressed by the following equation.

$$\Sigma_{i=0}^{bn} \,_{i+|cn|-1}C_i, \text{ where } C \text{ denotes a combination.}$$

The equation implies that the size of buffer design space can increase significantly fast as the number of channels or the number of available buffers increases. For example, suppose that an ALP has 20 channels and 20 available buffers, and that the simulation consumes 0.01 second for each buffer configuration. Then the overall processing time required to determine an optimal buffer configuration is $[1.37847 * 10^{11}] * 0.01 = 1.37847 * 10^9$ seconds (about 43 years).

As a cost function, 'performance×area' is used. For the performance metric, average cycle time of an ALP under a given buffer allocation is evaluated. The area is defined by the sum of functional logic and buffer area. The cost function for a given buffer configuration, BC, is expressed by the following equation.

$$cost(\text{BC}) = performance \times area$$

$$= cycle\_time(\text{BC}) \times (function\_area + \sum_{\forall \text{Channel}_i} \text{BC}[\text{Channel}_i] \times one\_buffer\_cell\_area)$$

With this cost definition, the optimal buffer allocation problem is described as "finding a buffer configuration BC with the lowest cost"

A buffer configuration in a buffer design space can be considered as a state in a search-space search [1]. From a state, a set of buffer configurations can be derived by inserting/eliminating a buffer to/from a certain channel. The action of the buffer insertion or elimination is called a move. A set of states that can be derived from a state S by a single move is called a neighbor set or neighborhood

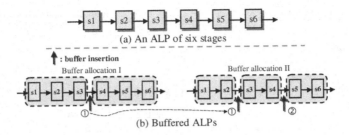

(a) An ALP of six stages

(b) Buffered ALPs

Fig. 3. Interaction between buffer allocations

of S. A gain of a move from BC to BC' is defined as the value of cost(BC) - cost(BC'). Thus, a positive gain of a move implies that cost is reduced by the move. The term, optimum is used to denote a local or a global optimum. When we need to distinguish between local and global optima, we use 'local' or 'global' explicitly. In this paper, a set of local optimums does not include global optimums. Finally, a convex design space is the space where only a single optimum exists. A non-convex space includes multiple optimums so a search can be trapped in a local optimum before reaching a global optimum in this space.

4 Buffer Allocation to an ALP

4.1 Local Optimums in a Buffer Design Space

Let us consider an ALP shown in Fig.3(a). Each stage is assumed to have a variable delay generation function that is identical across all the stages. It is easy to see that a local optimum can differ from a global optimum when we compare two simple cases of buffer allocation. One is allocating a single buffer and the other is simultaneously allocating two buffers. Let us assume that in the first case, "Buffer allocation I" shown in Fig.3(b) results in the biggest cost reduction. Also assume that in the second case, "Buffer allocation II" in Fig.3(b) generates the biggest cost reduction. Allocation of one buffer between stages s3 and s4, that enabled the biggest cost reduction in one-buffer allocation, prevents us from reaching the optimum in two-buffer allocation. However this phenomenon is unavoidable in a neighborhood-based search because it decides a search direction based only on neighbors reachable by a single move. Thus, this kind of a neighborhood-based search is easy to be trapped in a local optimum.

The best (optimum) position of one buffer changes when the other buffer is allocated additionally because *the cost reduction of one buffer allocation is affected by the other buffer allocation*. In order to quantify such an interaction between buffer allocations, we define a quantity called additional cycle time reduction (ACTR). Fig.4 shows a possible ACTR for the case of two-buffer allocation. ACTR shown in this figure is calculated by varying the channel positions of two buffers and is expressed in the following equation.

$$ACTR(\{i,j\}) = CTR(\{i,j\}) - \{CTR(\{i\}) + CTR(\{j\})\} - (1)$$

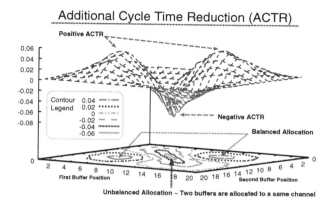

Fig. 4. Quantity of ACTR

The function CTR takes a multi-set[1] CP of channels as arguments and returns cycle time reduction achieved by allocating a buffer to each channel in CP (negative numbers can be used in the set CP to denote a buffer elimination). ACTR can be positive or negative depending on a buffer distribution over the channels, and it can be thought as an additional effect caused by an interaction between the two concurrent buffer insertions.

Particularly, a positive ACTR implies that *considering multiple moves simultaneously makes cycle time to be reduced further and results in a more cost reduction that is not foreseeable by any single move of a local search.* These kinds of interactions are the main causes of producing local optima in the buffer design space of an ALP since ACTR is the only way of generating local optima by invisible additional cost reduction. The following proposition addresses the relationship.

Proposition 1. *A buffer configuration* BC *is a local optimum iff the following two conditions are satisfied.*
1. The cost of BC *is lower than the costs of all of its neighbors.*
2. A positive ACTR is caused by a set of buffer insertions / eliminations that are simultaneously performed from BC *and such set of moves leads to another buffer configuration* BC' *whose cost is lower than that of* BC.

Notice that a local optimum is described in terms of ACTR. In the following, through observing the behavior of cycle time reductions and ACTR effects in buffer design space, the characteristic of buffer design space is investigated.

4.2 A Characteristic of a Buffer Design Space

When only a single channel is concerned, thanks to the monotonicity of cycle time change as shown in Fig.2(b), the cost also monotonically changes. Conse-

---

[1] A multi-set is a set that may have duplicates. For example, A = {1,1,2,2,2,3} is a multi-set and it is not the same as {1, 2, 3}.

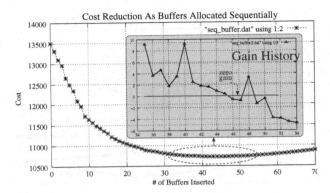

Fig. 5. A sequential buffer allocation and its corresponding cost reduction

quently, an optimal number of buffers at the channel can be found by checking the gradient on the cost surface.

When all the channels are concerned, however, finding a global optimum becomes computationally difficult due to the non-convexity of design space. Nevertheless, as shown in Fig.5, when the buffers are inserted sequentially to the channels from a zero buffer configuration (BC = **0**) while making the biggest cost reduction in each step, an initial part of the design space looks like a convex space. The cost decreases monotonically up to a certain value due to the high efficacy of initial buffer insertions.

As more buffers are inserted to each channel, the efficiency shrinks and the cost reduction becomes limited, and ACTR effects begin to generate local optima by satisfying the first condition of Proposition 1. In other words, initial insertions to each channel show relatively higher tendency of being on a way to a global optimum than later insertions. In an optimally buffered ALPs, latest insertions to each channel are prone to move away from a global optimum. Therefore, latest allocations to each channel need to be rearranged to find a global optimum. Since cycle time reduction achieved by these recent allocations is too small to reduce cost, the quantity of an ACTR becomes small too.

The graph drawn in Fig.6 shows an experimental evidence for the aforementioned claim. In this graph, the 'Max(Avg) Variation Effect' shows maximum (average) quantity of cycle time reduction achieved by a single buffer insertion at each sequential insertion step. Similarly, 'Max(Avg) ACTR Effect' is defined as maximum (average) quantity of cycle time reduction additionally achieved by simultaneous multiple buffer insertions.

As buffers are inserted to ALPs, the difference between a variation effect and an ACTR effect becomes smaller as well as their absolute values. There exists a point where cycle time reduction by single buffer insertions is not enough to reduce the overall cost. In the vicinity of this point, ACTR may shape like hills that correspond to local optima. Note that the quantity of ACTR at this point is so small that taking a small uphill move can lead to a global optimum.

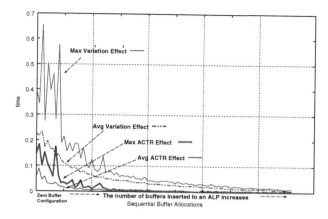

Fig. 6. A sequential buffer allocation and its corresponding ACTR

The equation (1) says that the cost reduction between two optima is determined by cycle time reduction CTR(CP), where CP is a set of moves that connects two optima. In the vicinity of the point where cycle time reduction saturated, the cycle time reduction of an individual move increases cost of the corresponding state and this causes uphill as a result. For CTR(CP) to be sufficient in order to reduce cost further, that is implying that a more optimized buffer configuration is obtained by accepting the set of moves, ACTR should be large enough to compensate the cost increases by the individual moves. Since the ACTR becomes small at the vicinity of the point, the cost increases by the individual moves is limited by the ACTR. In consequence, uphill height is also likely to be small. Finally, it implies that a search can escape from a local optimum with a small uphill potential barrier and this is substantiated by experiments in Section 6.

Fig.7 shows the simplified cost reduction graph where the part of non - monotonous cost surface is enlarged. In this figure, the horizontal axis represents the number of buffers inserted to a buffer configuration. The bowl shape of the cost line indicates an optimum since there is no move that can result in cost reduction. Since the cost reduction of moves can be described by a gain, the region in which optima appear can be detected by tracing the gain history presented as the shadowed graph embedded in Fig.5.

4.3   Localization of a Region

In the proposed buffer allocation algorithm, a buffer design space can be partitioned into two sorts of disjoint subspaces: (1) an Optimum Region (OPR) including optima and (2) a Non Optimum Region (NOPR) containing no optimum. OPR and NOPR are demarcated by a cost boundary as shown in Fig.8, where the horizontal axis represents the number of buffers inserted.

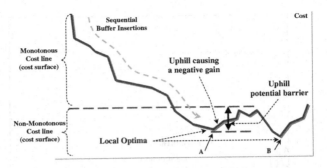

Fig. 7. Cost line and local optimums

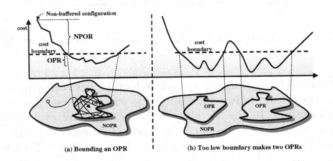

Fig. 8. Partitioning a design space

Definition 1. *OPR* *is a set of buffer configurations whose costs are lower than a given cost boundary. Between any two buffer configuration BC_i and BC_j of OPR, there exists at least one sequence of moves that passes through only buffer configurations in OPR*

Definition 2. *NOPR* *is a set of buffer configurations that are in a buffer design space but not in any OPR.*

As shown in Fig.8(a), the proposed search starts from a non-buffered configuration. In average-case optimized circuits, lots of buffers are allocated to each channel in order to reduce starvation/blocking effects caused by processing time variations. Thus, the non-buffered configuration is in NOPR in general. From the initial buffer configuration in NOPR, a search procedure based on single move decides the next buffer configuration simply by taking the biggest cost reduction till it reaches an optimum within an OPR. Once the search reaches OPR, a more refined search algorithm is executed within OPR.

The cost boundary between OPR and NOPR should be carefully selected since it plays a critical role in providing the optimality of search solutions as well as the efficiency of search. Selecting a very low cost boundary may result in a very small OPR. A small OPR means that only a small part of design space

Algorithm Buffer_Allocation
01: $BC = \mathbf{0}$;
02: *while* a negative gain does not appear in *stat* **begin**
03:      $BC' \leftarrow$ insert one buffer to the channel of BC that makes biggest cost reduction
04:      calculate the corresponding gain, $\text{cost}(BC) - \text{cost}(BC')$
05:      $BC = BC'$
06:      store the gain to *stat* & maintain only latest n gains
07: *end*
08: $LBC = BC'$
09: derive a *cost boundary* using *stat* and $\text{cost}(LBC)$
10: $OBC \leftarrow$ do simulated annealing with *cost bound* and LBC
11: *return OBC*;

Fig. 9. The proposed buffer allocation algorithm

is explored with a high complexity search and hence high efficiency is expected. However, the boundary can yield multiple OPRs and causes a search to be trapped in an OPR that does not include a global optimum or a near optimum. Fig.8(b) shows a case of multiple OPRs due to a cost boundary that is too low. Since there is a possibility that an optimum or a near optimum does not belong to OPR the search procedure is exploring within, the quality of solution may deteriorate.

There are two ways to solve this problem. One is making a cost boundary high enough so that it does not yield multiple OPRs. However, a higher boundary increases the size of OPR and the search becomes inefficient. The other is allowing a probabilistic transition from one OPR to another even though such a transition increases cost over the given boundary. In this case, some moves enabling an escape from OPR are allowed with a small probability while most of the time the search process works mainly within the OPR. The escaping probability should be determined carefully as well.

5   An Efficient Buffer Allocation Algorithm

Fig.9 shows a top-level flow of the proposed buffer allocation algorithm. In Line 1, the initial buffer configuration BC is set. From Line 2 to Line 7, the search inserts a buffer sequentially to a channel selected for maximum cost reduction in each loop. The while-loop is repeated until negative gain appears. In Line 8, after completing the loop, LBC, for instance, corresponds to buffer configuration A in Fig.7. As shown in Fig.7, the cost boundary can be derived by adding the uphill potential barrier to the cost of LBC in our algorithm. The uphill potential barrier should be decided as small as possible while making it possible to reach other optima below the boundary cost.

Within the while loop, the gain obtained by each allocation is stored to stat temporarily in Line 6. Gain information in stat is used at Line 2 to check whether BC reached an OPR or not. The gain history is also used to derive a cost boundary in Line 9. After completing the loop, a target OPR is decided as a set of buffer configurations that are reachable from LBC without making a move that goes over the derived cost boundary.

Begin with
     an initial configuration S & an initial temperature T
01: *Repeat*
02:    *Repeat*
03:        randomly select a similar configuration NewS
04:        ΔE = Energy(NewS) – Energy(S)
05:        probability of changing to NewS = (1 *if* $\Delta E \leq 0$) : ($e^{-\Delta E/T}$ *otherwise*)
06:        rnd = random number between 0 and 1
07:        *if* rnd < probability *then* change to NewS
08:    *Until* system is in a steady state
09:    update temperature T
10: *Until* freezing

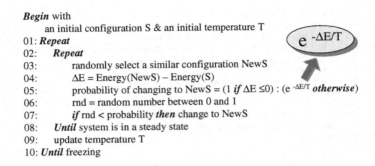

Fig. 10. An SA algorithm

Finally, in Line 10, a simulated annealing (SA) algorithm is executed so that the search is performed mainly within the target OPR with only a small escaping probability. LBC becomes an initial solution and the cost boundary is used for calculating an initial temperature for the SA. More detailed descriptions on the derivation of a cost boundary and initial temperature calculation for SA are as follows.

Cost Boundary Derivation : To make the algorithm efficient, a cost boundary should be chosen as small as possible. In this paper, we use a heuristic and experimentally validated cost boundary; cost(LBC) + D_{gain} where D_{gain} is the difference between the maximum and the minimum gain among the latest n gains in stat. The number n is set to the number of channels in an ALP.

D_{gain} can be seen as an approximation of the uphill potential barrier. A move is allowed only when a newly generated configuration by the move has a cost lower than cost(LBC) + D_{gain} once a high complexity search starts from LBC. Empirical results show that D_{gain} is a reasonable approximation of the maximum uphill potential barrier from LBC.

Applying Simulated Annealing : A traditional SA algorithm is presented in Fig.10. In simulated annealing, an energy function plays the same role as a cost function, hence in what we proposed, the energy function is implemented by the cost function defined in Section 3.2.

As mentioned earlier, LBC is used as an initial configuration for the SA. An initial temperature is derived using the cost boundary and the probability of escaping from an OPR. As shown in Line 5 - 7 of Fig.10, a decision on acceptance/rejection of a new configuration is made based on an energy function and a random number. If the new configuration decreases energy, then ΔE becomes negative and accepts the new configuration unconditionally. Otherwise, acceptance of an uphill move depends on the probability, $e^{-\Delta E/T}$. From the expression, $e^{-\Delta E/T}$, we can derive an initial temperature T using two parameters: the escaping probability from an OPR and an uphill potential barrier ΔE. ΔE is replaced by D_{gain} since the D_{gain} is considered as the maximum uphill potential that specifies the boundary of an OPR.

The escaping probability should be set to a small value in order to keep the boundary more or less strict. If escaping probability is set to 5%, an initial temperature is given as follows;

$$e^{-D_{gain}/\text{T}} = 0.05 \implies \text{T} = - D_{gain} / \log(0.05)$$

Generally, an initial temperature for simulated annealing is set to the higher value than a standard deviation, σ, of cost values in a design space or $\frac{-3*\sigma}{lnP}$ where P denotes the initial probability of accepting solutions. The conventional value of P is 0.9 and thus $\frac{-3}{lnP}$ is about 20 [10,12].

6   Experiments and Discussion

The proposed algorithm is implemented as a C++ program. Experiments are run on a 750MHz Sun Blade system. Since the previous work focused on mathematical analysis [5,9,11], there are no available benchmarks and comparable results. The test data in Table 1 are synthesized by varying "area of a buffer cell" and "range of variable processing delay in a stage" for an ALP consisting of ten stages. Each letter 'L', 'M', and 'H' in the name of test data corresponds to the delay range [10, 20], [5, 25], and [1, 29], respectively. The last single-digit in each test data name represents an area of a unit buffer cell. Three experiments are performed for each test data to eliminate a probabilistic variations of results by SA algorithm and the average over those three runs are presented in Table 1.

To show the effectiveness of the proposed method, we also show the results obtained by a conventional SA procedure in terms of solution quality and search time. As we mentioned in Section 4, ACTR is a proper metric for limiting the height of uphills to move from an OPR to another and was used to calculate an initial temperature for conventional SA. The initial temperature is calculated using a 'maximum ACTR' in a non-buffered configuration and '50% acceptance rate'. That is, $'Initial\_Temperature = \frac{Maximum\_ACTR}{log(0.5)}'$. Naturally, a non-buffered configuration is used as an initial configuration. When σ is evaluated on the test data, it is about two to four times higher than the ACTR-based initial temperature. When $\frac{-3*\sigma}{lnP}$ is used, temperature is over twenty times higher.

Except for the *initial temperature calculation* and the *initial configuration assignment*, the same cooling schedule is used for both conventional SA and the SA part of the proposed buffer allocation algorithm. Since there are many possible cooling schedules, overall execution times are variable. However, the initial temperatures are comparable between conventional and proposed SA. Consequently, the reduction rate of initial temperatures can be considered as a real contribution of this paper.

Over the synthesized test data, the proposed algorithm reduce the search time by 47% (1.98 speedup) in average while the optimality of solutions is kept when compared to the pure SA algorithm. Note that the reduction rate of the search time is not proportional to that of the temperature. This happens because that the number of iterations in the inner loop (Line 2 to Line 8 in Fig.10) of an SA algorithm tends to increase as temperature decreases.

Table 1. Experimental results

	Conventional SA			Proposed Algorithm			Speedup (times)
	Init. Temp	Search time	Solution Cost	Init. Temp	Search time	Solution Cost	
Bench1-L1	365.265	9416.26	18372.56	1.78	2745.68	18372.56	3.43
Bench2-L3	367.537	8548.25	19418.52	10.94	2463.81	19418.51	3.47
Bench3-L5	369.808	6073.57	20050.96	99.2204	716.31	20050.96	8.48
Bench4-M1	471.037	15454.90	19665.68	1.38	4575.24	19665.68	3.38
Bench5-M3	474.421	12061.05	21803.91	4.12	3807.39	21803.91	3.17
Bench6-M5	477.805	9801.49	23046.27	17.9	2566.41	23046.27	3.82
Bench7-H1	553.365	20696.76	20727.23	3.37	8574.89	20727.23	2.41
Bench8-H3	557.631	14921.70	23705.22	4.08	4936.35	23705.22	3.02
Bench9-H5	561.897	8481.02	25454.23	19.1414	3204.04	25454.23	2.65
<Average of 3 trials on the pipeline of 10 stages>							**3.76**

Proposed Algorithm with **5%** Accept. Probability without Strict Termination Rule	**1.98**
Proposed Algorithm with **1%** Accept. Probability with Strict Termination Rule	**4.34**

Thanks to "a low initial temperature at the beginning of the SA procedure" in the proposed algorithm and "a localized search space", the SA procedure shows the fast convergence to a solution, compared with the conventional SA. The fast convergence allows further optimization of SA procedure. When the temperature is high, search behavior is unpredictable and the behavior shows divergence during the initial search. When the temperature is low, however, the repetitive oscillating configuration transitions (moves) can be thought as in the way of search convergence. Consequently, the proposed algorithm can further reduce the search time by employing a more restrictive steady-state checking rule (at Line 8 in Fig.10) in the SA algorithm without loss of optimality.

The proposed algorithm is modified to have a strict equilibrium steady-state checking rule limit *the number of iterations that does not introduce more cost reduction.* In this case, the proposed algorithm runs **3.76 times faster without loss of optimality** as shown in Table 1 when compared with the conventional SA without the strict termination rule. When we apply the same steady-state checking rule to the conventional SA, it resulted in significantly worse solutions due to the diverging behavior of a high temperature search although the search time is reduced.

To see the effects of a boundary escaping probability, more experiments are performed with 1% probability of escaping a boundary instead of 5%. In this case, a speedup ratio of search time reaches up to **4.34 without loss of optimality** as shown in the last row of Table 1. Consequently, we guess that the uphill potential barrier between optima is very small. Further analysis is required to find the lowest escaping probability from OPR while keeping the quality of solutions.

7   Summary and Conclusions

In this paper, we have analyzed a buffer design space of an ALP and developed an effective way to reduce the search space. In the proposed approach, a buffer design space is partitioned into two subspaces, an OPR and an NOPR, according to the characteristics (monotonicity, convexity) of the cost surface. Then a hybrid search algorithm has been devised. It performs a hill climbing search in an NOPR and high-complexity search in an OPR. As a high-complexity search method, an SA algorithm is adopted. The proposed algorithm shows a speed up of up to 4.34 times without the loss of optimality, when tested with synthetic test data, compared to a conventional SA algorithm.

Future work is under way to develop a new heuristic search procedure to be applied to OPR instead of SA since SA still takes a long time to allocate buffers into a pipeline of only ten stages. Finally, it will be also interesting to do mathematical or theoretical analyses on a buffer design space of an ALP showing a dynamic average-case performance behavior.

References

1. N.J. Nilsson, "Principles of Artificial Intelligence," *Springer-Verlag*, 1980.
2. T.E. Williams, "Analyzing and improving the latency and throughput performance of self-timed pipelines and rings," *In Proc. of International Symposium on Circuits and Systems*, pp.665-668, vol. 2, May 1992.
3. M.R. Greenstreet, "STARI: A Technique for High-Bandwidth Communication," *PhD. Thesis, Princeton University*, Jan. 1993.
4. S. Hauck, "Asynchronous Design Methodologies: an Overview," *In Proceedings of the IEEE*, vol.83, no.1, pp. 69-93, 1995.
5. D. Kearney, "Performance Evaluation of Asynchronous Logic Pipelines with Data Dependant Processing Delays," *In Proc. of the Second Working Conference on Asynchronous Design Methodologies*, pp.4-13, London, May. 1995.
6. D. Kearney and N.W. Bergmann, "Bundled Data Asynchronous Multipliers with Data Dependent Computation Times," *In Proc. of International Symposium on Advanced Research in Asynchronous Circuits and Systems*, pp.186-197, Apr. 1997.
7. S.M. Nowick, K.Y. Yun et al., "Speculative completion for the design of high-performance asynchronous dynamic adders," *In Proc. of International Symposium on Advanced Research in Asynchronous Circuits and Systems*, pp.210-223, Apr. 1997.
8. W.C. Chou, P.A. Beerel, et al., "Average-case optimized technology mapping of one-hot domino circuits," *In Proc. of International Symposium on Advanced Research in Asynchronous Circuits and Systems*, pp.80-91, Apr. 1998.
9. D. Kearney, "Theoretical Limits on the Data Dependent Performance of Asynchronous Circuits," *In Proc. of International Symposium on Advanced Research in Asynchronous Circuits and Systems*, pp.201-207, Apr. 1999.
10. S.M. Sait, H. Youssef, "Iterative Computer Algorithms with Applications in Engineering," *IEEE Computer Society Press*, 1999.
11. M.R. Greenstreet and B. Alwis, "How to Achieve Worst-Case Performance," *In Proc. of International Symposium on Advanced Research in Asynchronous Circuits and Systems*, pp.206-216, Mar. 2001.
12. C.-C. Chang, J. Cong, Z. Pan and X. Yuan "Multilevel Global Placement With Congestion Control," *IEEE Tranc. on Computer-Aided Design of Integrated Circuits and Systems*, pp.395-409, Vol. 22, No. 4, Apr., 2003.

Author Index

Lecture Notes in Computer Science

For information about Vols. 1–3092

please contact your bookseller or Springer

Vol. 3143: W. Liu, Y. Shi, Q. Li (Eds.), Advances in Web-Based Learning – ICWL 2004. XIV, 459 pages. 2004.

Vol. 3142: J. Diaz, J. Karhumäki, A. Lepistö, D. Sannella (Eds.), Automata, Languages and Programming. XIX, 1253 pages. 2004.

Vol. 3140: N. Koch, P. Fraternali, M. Wirsing (Eds.), Web Engineering. XXI, 623 pages. 2004.

Vol. 3139: F. Iida, R. Pfeifer, L. Steels, Y. Kuniyoshi (Eds.), Embodied Artificial Intelligence. IX, 331 pages. 2004. (Subseries LNAI).

Vol. 3138: A. Fred, T. Caelli, R.P.W. Duin, A. Campilho, D.d. Ridder (Eds.), Structural, Syntactic, and Statistical Pattern Recognition. XXII, 1168 pages. 2004.

Vol. 3137: P. De Bra, W. Nejdl (Eds.), Adaptive Hypermedia and Adaptive Web-Based Systems. XIV, 442 pages. 2004.

Vol. 3136: F. Meziane, E. Métais (Eds.), Natural Language Processing and Information Systems. XII, 436 pages. 2004.

Vol. 3134: C. Zannier, H. Erdogmus, L. Lindstrom (Eds.), Extreme Programming and Agile Methods - XP/Agile Universe 2004. XIV, 233 pages. 2004.

Vol. 3133: A.D. Pimentel, S. Vassiliadis (Eds.), Computer Systems: Architectures, Modeling, and Simulation. XIII, 562 pages. 2004.

Vol. 3132: B. Demoen, V. Lifschitz (Eds.), Logic Programming. XII, 480 pages. 2004.

Vol. 3131: V. Torra, Y. Narukawa (Eds.), Modeling Decisions for Artificial Intelligence. XI, 327 pages. 2004. (Subseries LNAI).

Vol. 3130: A. Syropoulos, K. Berry, Y. Haralambous, B. Hughes, S. Peter, J. Plaice (Eds.), TeX, XML, and Digital Typography. VIII, 265 pages. 2004.

Vol. 3129: Q. Li, G. Wang, L. Feng (Eds.), Advances in Web-Age Information Management. XVII, 753 pages. 2004.

Vol. 3128: D. Asonov (Ed.), Querying Databases Privately. IX, 115 pages. 2004.

Vol. 3127: K.E. Wolff, H.D. Pfeiffer, H.S. Delugach (Eds.), Conceptual Structures at Work. XI, 403 pages. 2004. (Subseries LNAI).

Vol. 3126: P. Dini, P. Lorenz, J.N.d. Souza (Eds.), Service Assurance with Partial and Intermittent Resources. XI, 312 pages. 2004.

Vol. 3125: D. Kozen (Ed.), Mathematics of Program Construction. X, 401 pages. 2004.

Vol. 3124: J.N. de Souza, P. Dini, P. Lorenz (Eds.), Telecommunications and Networking - ICT 2004. XXVI, 1390 pages. 2004.

Vol. 3123: A. Belz, R. Evans, P. Piwek (Eds.), Natural Language Generation. X, 219 pages. 2004. (Subseries LNAI).

Vol. 3122: K. Jansen, S. Khanna, J.D.P. Rolim, D. Ron (Eds.), Approximation, Randomization, and Combinatorial Optimization. IX, 428 pages. 2004.

Vol. 3121: S. Nikoletseas, J.D.P. Rolim (Eds.), Algorithmic Aspects of Wireless Sensor Networks. X, 201 pages. 2004.

Vol. 3120: J. Shawe-Taylor, Y. Singer (Eds.), Learning Theory. X, 648 pages. 2004. (Subseries LNAI).

Vol. 3118: K. Miesenberger, J. Klaus, W. Zagler, D. Burger (Eds.), Computer Helping People with Special Needs. XXIII, 1191 pages. 2004.

Vol. 3116: C. Rattray, S. Maharaj, C. Shankland (Eds.), Algebraic Methodology and Software Technology. XI, 569 pages. 2004.

Vol. 3114: R. Alur, D.A. Peled (Eds.), Computer Aided Verification. XII, 536 pages. 2004.

Vol. 3113: J. Karhumäki, H. Maurer, G. Paun, G. Rozenberg (Eds.), Theory Is Forever. X, 283 pages. 2004.

Vol. 3112: H. Williams, L. MacKinnon (Eds.), Key Technologies for Data Management. XII, 265 pages. 2004.

Vol. 3111: T. Hagerup, J. Katajainen (Eds.), Algorithm Theory - SWAT 2004. XI, 506 pages. 2004.

Vol. 3110: A. Juels (Ed.), Financial Cryptography. XI, 281 pages. 2004.

Vol. 3109: S.C. Sahinalp, S. Muthukrishnan, U. Dogrusoz (Eds.), Combinatorial Pattern Matching. XII, 486 pages. 2004.

Vol. 3108: H. Wang, J. Pieprzyk, V. Varadharajan (Eds.), Information Security and Privacy. XII, 494 pages. 2004.

Vol. 3107: J. Bosch, C. Krueger (Eds.), Software Reuse: Methods, Techniques and Tools. XI, 339 pages. 2004.

Vol. 3106: K.-Y. Chwa, J.I. Munro (Eds.), Computing and Combinatorics. XIII, 474 pages. 2004.

Vol. 3105: S. Göbel, U. Spierling, A. Hoffmann, I. Iurgel, O. Schneider, J. Dechau, A. Feix (Eds.), Technologies for Interactive Digital Storytelling and Entertainment. XVI, 304 pages. 2004.

Vol. 3104: R. Kralovic, O. Sykora (Eds.), Structural Information and Communication Complexity. X, 303 pages. 2004.

Vol. 3103: K. Deb, e. al. (Eds.), Genetic and Evolutionary Computation – GECCO 2004. XLIX, 1439 pages. 2004.

Vol. 3102: K. Deb, e. al. (Eds.), Genetic and Evolutionary Computation – GECCO 2004. L, 1445 pages. 2004.

Vol. 3101: M. Masoodian, S. Jones, B. Rogers (Eds.), Computer Human Interaction. XIV, 694 pages. 2004.

Vol. 3100: J.F. Peters, A. Skowron, J.W. Grzymała-Busse, B. Kostek, R.W. Świniarski, M.S. Szczuka (Eds.), Transactions on Rough Sets I. X, 405 pages. 2004.

Vol. 3099: J. Cortadella, W. Reisig (Eds.), Applications and Theory of Petri Nets 2004. XI, 505 pages. 2004.

Vol. 3098: J. Desel, W. Reisig, G. Rozenberg (Eds.), Lectures on Concurrency and Petri Nets. VIII, 849 pages. 2004.

Vol. 3097: D. Basin, M. Rusinowitch (Eds.), Automated Reasoning. XII, 493 pages. 2004. (Subseries LNAI).

Vol. 3096: G. Melnik, H. Holz (Eds.), Advances in Learning Software Organizations. X, 173 pages. 2004.

Vol. 3095: C. Bussler, D. Fensel, M.E. Orlowska, J. Yang (Eds.), Web Services, E-Business, and the Semantic Web. X, 147 pages. 2004.

Vol. 3094: A. Nürnberger, M. Detyniecki (Eds.), Adaptive Multimedia Retrieval. VIII, 229 pages. 2004.

Vol. 3093: S. Katsikas, S. Gritzalis, J. Lopez (Eds.), Public Key Infrastructure. XIII, 380 pages. 2004.

IFIP Advances in Information and Communication Technology 456

Editor-in-Chief

Kai Rannenberg, Goethe University Frankfurt, Germany

Editorial Board

More information about this series at http://www.springer.com/series/6102

Abdelmalek Amine · Ladjel Bellatreche
Zakaria Elberrichi · Erich J. Neuhold
Robert Wrembel (Eds.)

Computer Science and Its Applications

5th IFIP TC 5 International Conference, CIIA 2015
Saida, Algeria, May 20–21, 2015
Proceedings

 Springer

Editors

Abdelmalek Amine
Tahar Moulay University
Saida
Algeria

Ladjel Bellatreche
LIAS/ISAE-ENSMA
Chasseneuil
France

Zakaria Elberrichi
Sidi Bel Abbès University
Sidi Bel Abbès
Algeria

Erich J. Neuhold
University of Vienna
Vienna
Austria

Robert Wrembel
Poznan University of Technology
Poznan
Poland

ISSN 1868-4238   ISSN 1868-422X   (electronic)
IFIP Advances in Information and Communication Technology
ISBN 978-3-319-38716-1   ISBN 978-3-319-19578-0   (eBook)
DOI 10.1007/978-3-319-19578-0

Springer Cham Heidelberg New York Dordrecht London
© IFIP International Federation for Information Processing 2015
Softcover reprint of the hardcover 1st edition 2015

Printed on acid-free paper

Springer International Publishing AG Switzerland is part of Springer Science+Business Media
(www.springer.com)

Preface

This volume contains research papers presented at the 5th IFIP International Conference on Computer Science and Its Applications (CIIA), held during May 20-21, 2015, in Saida, Algeria. CIIA 2015 continued the series of conferences whose main objective is to provide a forum for the dissemination of research accomplishments and to promote the interaction and collaboration between various research communities related to computer science and its applications. These conferences have been initiated by researchers from Algeria and extended to cover worldwide researchers focusing on promoting research, creating scientific networks, developing projects, as well as facilitating faculty and student exchanges, especially in Africa.

This year the CIIA conference attracted 225 submissions from 20 countries including: Algeria, Bangladesh, Belgium, Canada, China, Finland, France, India, Iran, Ireland, Italy, Jordan, Morocco, Norway, Poland, Qatar, Tunisia, United Arab Emirates, UK, and USA. In a rigorous reviewing process, the Program Committee (PC) selected 51 papers, which represents an acceptance rate of 22.6%. The PC included 200 researchers from 27 countries.

The accepted papers were organized into the four following research tracks: Computational Intelligence, co-chaired by: Sadok Ben Yahia (FST, Tunisia) and Nadjet Kamel (Setif University, Algeria); Security and Network Technologies, co-chaired by Nadjib Badache (CERIST, Algeria) and Alfredo Cuzzocrea (ICAR-CNR and University of Calabria, Italy); Information Technology, co-chaired by Jorge Bernardino (ISEC-Polytechnic Institute of Coimbra, Portugal) and Selma Khouri (ESI, Algiers, Algeria); as well as Software Engineering, co-chaired by Kamel Barkaoui (CNAM, Paris, France) and Abdelwahab Hamou-Lhadj (Concordia University, Montreal, Canada). Additionally, the conference hosted three keynote speakers, namely: Prof. Lynda Tamine-Lechani (IRIT Toukouse, France), Prof. Erich Neuhold (University of Vienna, Austria), and Prof. Mohamad Sawan (Polytechnique Montreal, Canada). This volume includes the abstracts of the keynote talks. We would like to express our warmest thanks to the keynote speakers.

We would also like to extend our gratitude to Prof. Erich Neuhold and the International Federation for Information Processing (IFIP) for accepting the CIIA papers to be published in the *IFIP Advances in Information and Communication Technology* (IFIP-AICT) by Springer.

We would also like to acknowledge the invaluable help of: the PC members for ensuring the quality of the scientific program, the Tahar Moulay University of Saida and the GeCoDe Laboratory, for hosting the conference and providing all the needed support, the track chairs, for managing the reviewing process, and Dr. Mickael Baron

(ISAE-ENSMA, Poitiers, France) and Dr. Mahieddine Djoudi (SIC/XLIM, University of Poitiers, France) for Webmaster efforts. Last but not least, we thank the EasyChair team for making available their conference management system to CIIA. Finally, we thank the authors who submitted papers to the conference.

April 2015

Abdelmalek Amine
Erich J. Neuhold
Ladjel Bellatreche
Zakaria Elberrichi
Robert Wrembel

Organization

CIIA 2015 was organized by the GeCoDe Laboratory and Tahar Moulay University of Saida (Algeria) in cooperation with the International Federation for Information Processing (IFIP).

Conference Committees

Honorary Chair

Prof. Fethallah Tebboune   Rector of the Tahar Moulay University of Saida, Algeria

General Chairs

Abdelmalek Amine   Tahar Moulay University of Saida, Algeria
Erich Neuhold   University of Vienna, Austria

PC Chairs

Ladjel Bellatreche   LIAS/ISAE-ENSMA, France
Zakaria Elberrichi   Sidi Bel Abbès University, Algeria
Robert Wrembel   Poznan University of Technology, Poland

Steering Committee

Abdelmalek Amine   Tahar Moulay University of Saida, Algeria
Otmane Ait Mohamed   Concordia University, Canada
Ladjel Bellatreche   ISAE-ENSMA, France
Mahieddine Djoudi   SIC/XLIM, University of Poitiers, France
Carlos Ordonez   University of Houston, USA

Track Chairs

Nadjib Badache   USTHB, CERIST, Algeria
Kamel Barkaoui   CNAM, France
Sadok Ben Yahia   FST Tunis, Tunisia
Jorge Bernardino   ISEC-Polytechnic Institute of Coimbra, Portugal
Alfredo Cuzzocrea   ICAR-CNR and University of Calabria, Italy
Abdelwahab Hamou-Lhadj   Concordia University, Montreal, Canada
Nadjet Kamel   University of Setif, Algeria
Selma Khouri   ESI, Algeria

Program Committee

Track 1: Computational Intelligence

Wiem Abdelbaki	University of Nizwa, Oman
Mustapha Kamel Abdi	University of Oran, Algeria
Reda Adjoudj	University of Sidi Bel Abbès, Algeria
Abbes Amira	Qatar University, Quatar and University of the West of Scotland, UK
Saliha Aouat	USTHB, Algeria
Sabeur Aridhi	University of Trento, Italy
Sarah Ayouni	ESIG Kairouan, Tunisia
Latifa Baba-Hamed	University of Oran, Algeria
Ghalem Belalem	University of Oran 1, Algeria
Sid Ahmed Ben Abderrahmane	University Paris 8, France
Mohamed Ben Mohamed	University of Constantine 2, Algeria
Mohamed Chaouki Babahenini	University of Biskra, Algeria
Nadia Baha Touzene	USTHB, Algeria
Mohamed Batouche	University of Constantine, Algeria
Leila Ben Othman	IPEI El Manar, Tunisia
Ismail Biskri	Université du Québec à Trois-Rivieres, Canada
Lydia Boudjeloud	University of Lorraine, France
Aoued Boukelif	University of Sidi Bel Abbès, Algeria
Belattar Brahim	University of Batna, Algeria
Imen Brahmi	FST, Tunisia
Hanen Brahmi	ESIG Kairouan, Tunisia
Laurence Capus	University Laval, Canada
Allaoua Chaoui	University of Constantine 2, Algeria
Salim Chikhi	University of Constantine 2, Algeria
Gayo Diallo	University of Bordeaux, France
Yassine Djouadi	USTHB University, Algeria
Narjes Doggaz	FST, Tunisia
Bourennane El-Bay	University of Bourgogne, France
Samir Elloumi	Qatar University, Qatar
Kamel Mohamed Faraoun	University of Sidi Bel Abbès, Algeria
Cherif Fodil	University of Biskra, Algeria
Ahmed Guessoum	USTHB, Algeria
Zahia Guessoum	University of Paris 6, France
Allel Hadj-Ali	LIAS/ISAE-ENSMA, France
Tarek Hamrouni	ISAM Manouba, Tunisia
Chihab Hanachi	IRIT, France
Salima Hassas	University of Lyon 1, France
Tutut Herawan	University of Malaya, Malaysia
Ali Mohamed Jaoua	Qatar University, Qatar
Warith Eddine Jeddi	Computer Science Institute of Kasserine, Tunisia

Nidhal Jelassi	FST, Tunisia
Marouen Kachroudi	Computer Science Institute of Kef, Tunisia
Samir Kechid	USTHB, Algeria
Hamamache Kheddouci	University of Lyon 1, France
Slimane Larabi	USTHB, Algeria
Phayung Meesad	KMUTNB, Thailand
Mohamed El Bachir Menai	King Saud University, Saudi Arabia
Hayet Merouani	University of Annaba, Algeria
Souhal Meshoul	University of Constantine, Algeria
Takao Miura	Hosei University, Japan
Abdelouahab Moussaoui	University of Setif, Algeria
Kazumi Nakamatsu	University of Hyogo, Japan
Binod Kumar Prasad	Maharashtra Academy of Engineering, India
Mohamed Quafafou	Aix-Marseille University, France
Abdellatif Rahmoun	University of Sidi Bel Abbès, Algeria
Sivaram Rajeyyagari	JNTUK, India
Olivier Raynaud	University of Blaise Pascal, France
Zaidi Sahnoun	University of Constantine, Algeria
Abdel-Badeeh Salem	Ain Shams University, Egypt
Ahmed Samet	Compiegne University, France
Minyar Sassi Hidri	Tunis El Manar University, Tunisia
Aymen Sellaouti	INSAT Tunis, Tunisia
Mohamed Senouci	University of Oran 1, Algeria
Hamid Seridi	University of Guelma, Algeria
Noria Taghezout	University of Oran, Algeria
Chiraz Trabelsi	ISAM Manouba
Taoufik Yeferny	ISLAIB of Béja, Tunisia
Bing Zhou	Sam Houston State University, USA

Track 2: Security and Network Technologies

Maurizio Atzori	University of Cagliari, Italy
Mohamed Aissani	EMP, Algeria
Makhlouf Aliouat	University of Setif 1, Algeria
Abderrahmane Amrouche	USTHB, Algeria
Nadjib Badache	USTHB, CERIST, Algeria
Mouloud Bagaa	CERIST, Algeria
Ghalem Belalem	University of Oran, Algeria
Yacine Belhoul	CERIST, Algeria
Mohamed Benmohamed	Constantine 2 University, Algeria
Chafika Benzaid	USTHB, Algeria
Abdelmadjid Bouabdallah	UTC, France
Yacine Challal	ESI, Algeria
Alfredo Cuzzocrea	ICAR-CNR and University of Calabria, Italy
Abdelouahid Derhab	CoEIA, Saudia Arabia

Djamel Djenouri	CERIST, Algeria
Josep Domingo-Ferrer	Universitat Rovira i Virgili, Spain
Nacira Ghoualmi-Zine	University of Annaba, Algeria
Mohamed Guerroumi	USTHB, Algeria
Abdelkrim Hamza	USTHB, Algeria
Michal Kalewski	Poznan University of Technology, Poland
Anna Kobusinska	Poznan University of Technology, Poland
Noureddine Lasla	CERIST, Algeria
Sekhri Larbi	University of Oran, Algeria
Giovanni Livraga	Università degli Studi di Milano, Italy
Sadegh Nobari	Skoltech Faculty, Russia
Mustapha Reda Senouci	EMP, Algeria
Anna Squicciarini	Pennsylvania State University, USA
Djamel Tandjaoui	CERIST, Algeria
Traian Marius Truta	Northern Kentucky University, USA
Dariusz Wawrzyniak	Poznan University of Technology, Poland
Ali Yachir	EMP, Algeria
Said Yahiaoui	CERIST, Algeria
Youcef Zafoune	USTHB, Algeria

Track 3: Information Technologies

Samir Aknine	University of Lyon 1, France
Ana Almeida	Polytechnic of Porto, Portugal
Karima Amrouche	Ecole Supérieure d'Informatique, Algeria
Witold Andrzejewski	Poznan University of Technology, Poland
Baghdad Atmani	University of Oran 1, Algeria
Bartosz Bebel	Poznan University of Technology, Poland
Orlando Belo	University of Minho, Portugal
Djamal Benslimane	Lyon 1 University, France
Sidi Mohamed Benslimane	University of Sidi Bel Abbès, Algeria
Karim Bouamrane	University of Oran 1, Algeria
Kamel Boukhalfa	USTHB University, Algeria
Nabila Bousbia	Ecole Supérieure d'Informatique, Algeria
Omar Boussaid	University of Lyon 2, France
Zouhaier Brahmia	Faculty of Economics and Management, Tunisia
Rachid Chalal	Ecole Supérieure d'Informatique, Algeria
Abderrahim El-Qadi	University of Moulay Ismail, Morocco
Marcin Gorawski	Silesian University, Poland
Reda Mohamed Hamou	Tahar Moulay University of Saida, Algeria
Saad Harous	UAE University, United Arab Emirates
Walaid Khaled Hidouci	Ecole Supérieure d'Informatique, Algeria
Abdessamad Imine	Loria Nancy, France
Stéphane Jean	LIAS/ISAE-ENSMA, France

Benatchba Karima	Ecole Supérieure d'Informatique, Algeria
Adel Kermi	Ecole Supérieure d'Informatique, Algeria
Ahmed Lehireche	University of Sidi Bel Abbès, Algeria
Moussa Lo	University of Gaston Berger, Senegal
Mimoun Malki	University of Sidi Bel Abbès, Algeria
Elio Masciari	Consiglio Nazionale delle Ricerche, Italy
Elsa Negre	University of Paris - Dauphine, France
Oscar Romero	Universitat Politecnica de Catalunya, Spain
Paolo Rosso	Universitat Politecnica de Valencia, Spain
Hala Skaf-Molli	University of Nantes, France
Rafael Tolosana	Universidad de Zaragoza, Spain
Satya Valluri	Oracle, USA
Leandro-Krug Wives	UFRGS, Brazil
Marek Wojciechowski	Poznan University, Poland
Leila Zemmouchi-Ghomari	USTHB University, Algeria

Track 4: Software Engineering

Mohamed Ahmed-Nacer	USTHB, Algiers, Algeria
Yamine Ait Ameur	ENSEEIHT, Toulouse, France
Hassane Alla	GIPSA, UJF Grenoble, France
Maria-Virginia Aponte	CEDRIC, CNAM, France
Mohamed Faouzi Atig	Uppsala University, Sweden
Abdelkrim Amirat	University of Souk Ahras, Algeria
Faiza Belala	University of Constantine 2, Algeria
Kamel Barkaoui	CNAM, France
Belgacem Ben Hedia	LIST-CEA, Saclay, France
Saddek Bensalem	VERIMAG, UJF Grenoble, France
Frederic Boniol	ONERA, Toulouse, France
Thouraya Bouabana Tebibel	ESI, Algiers, Algeria
Ahmed Bouajjani	LIAFA, University Paris 7, France
Hanifa Boucheneb	Polytechnique Montreal, Canada
Nacer Boudjlida	LORIA, University of Lorraine, France
Zizette Boufaida	LIRE, University Constantine 2, Algeria
Mohand Cherif Boukala	USTHB, Algiers, Algeria
Samia Bouzefrane	CEDRIC, CNAM, France
Manfred Broy	TU München, Germany
Christine Choppy	LIPN, University of Paris 13, France
Annie Choquet-Geniet	ISAE-ENSMA, France
Karim Djouani	F'SATI/TUT, Pretoria, South Africa
Amal El Fallah Seghrouchni	LIP6, UPMC, Paris, France
Mohamed Erradi	LAGI, ENSIAS Rabat, Morocco

Alessandro Fantechi	University of Florence, Italy
Mohamed Mohsen Gammoudi	University of Manouba, Tunisia
Faiez Gargouri	MIRACL, ISIM, Sfax, Tunisia
Stefan Haar	LSV- CNRS and ENS Cachan, France
Mohand Said Hacid	LIRIS, University of Lyon 1, France
Henda Hajjami Ben Ghezala	ENSI, Tunisia
Abdelwahab Hamou-Lhadj	Concordia University, Montreal, Canada
Rolf Hennicker	Ludwig-Maximilians-Universität München, Germany
Ali Mohamed Jaoua	Qatar University Qatar
Mohamed Jmaiel	ReDCAD, ENIS, Sfax, Tunisia
Okba Kazar	University of Biskra, Algeria
Anna-Lena Lamprecht	SSE, University of Potsdam, Germany
Zhiwu Li	Xidian University, China
Mourad Maouche	Philadelphia University Amman, Jordan
Tiziana Margaria	University of Limerick and Lero, Ireland
Mohamed Mezghiche	University of Boumerdes, Algeria
Ali Mili	NJIT, Newark, USA
Bruno Monsuez	UIIS, ENSTA ParisTech, France
Mohamed Mosbah	LaBRI, Bordeaux INP, France
Hassan Mountassir	LIFC, University of Franche-Comté, France
Mourad Chabane Oussalah	LINA, University of Nantes, France
Ahmed Rezine	Linköpings Universitet, Sweden
Riadh Robbana	LIP2, INSAT, Tunis, Tunisia
Samir Tata	Telecom SudParis, France
Farouk Toumani	LIMOS, University of Clermont-Ferrand, France
Nadia Zeghib	LIRE, University Constantine 2, Algeria

Local Organizing Committee

Chair: Reda Mohamed Hamou
Webmaster: Mahieddine Djoudi
Mohamed Derkaoui
Mahmoud Fahsi
Toufik Guendouzi
Abdelkader Khobzaoui
Ahmed Chaouki Lokbani
Kheireddine Mekkaoui
Abdelkader Mostefai
Mohamed Rahmani

Sponsoring Institutions

CIIA 2015 received the support of several sponsors, among them Tahar Moulay University of Saida, Algerie, GeCoDe Laboratory of Tahar Moulay University, Saida, IFIP, ISAE-ENSMA, LIAS Laboratory (Poitiers), XLIM/SIC (Poitiers), ARPT, DG-RSDT. Many thanks for their support.

Invited Talks

Interoperability: Models and Semantics - A Reoccurring Problem

Erich J. Neuhold

University of Vienna, Austria
erich.neuhold@univie.ac.at
http://cs.univie.ac.at/Erich.Neuhold

Abstract. Interoperability is a qualitative property of computing infrastructures that denotes the ability of the sending and receiving systems to exchange and properly interpret information objects across system boundaries.

Since this property is not given by default, the interoperability problem involves the representation of meaning and has been an active research topic for approximately four decades. Database models used schemas to express semantics and implicitly aimed at achieving interoperability by providing programming independence of data storage and access.

After a number of intermediate steps such as Hypertext and XML document models, the notions of semantics and interoperability became what they have been over the last ten years in the context of the World Wide Web and more recently the concept of Open Linked Data.

The talk will investigate the (reoccurring) problem of interoperability as it can be found in the massive data collections around the Big Data and Open Linked Data concepts. We investigate semantics and interoperability research from the point of view of information systems. It should give an overview of existing old and new interoperability techniques and point out future research directions, especially for concepts found in Open Linked Data, the Semantic WEB and Big Data.

Brain-Computer-Brain Interfaces for Sensing and Subsequent Treatment

Mohamad Sawan, Professor and Canada Research Chair

Polystim Neurotechnologies Laboratory, Polytechnique Montreal
mohamad.sawan@polymtl.ca

Abstract. Implantable Brain-Computer-Brain Interfaces (BCIs) for diagnostic and recovery of neural vital functions are promising alternative to study neural activities underlying cognitive functions and pathologies. This Keynote address covers the architecture of typical BCI intended for wireless neurorecording and neurostimulation. Massively parallel multichannel spike recording through large arrays of microelectrodes will be introduced. Attention will be paid to low-power mixed-signal circuit design optimization. Advanced signal processing implementation such as adaptive thresholding, spike detection, data compression, and transmission will be described. Also, the talk includes Lab-on-chip technologies intended to build biosensors, and wireless data links and harvesting power to implants. Tests and validation of devices : electrical, mechanical, package, heat, reliability will be summarized. Case studies will be covered and include research activities dedicated to vision recovery through implant used to apply direct electrical microstimulation, to present the environment as phosphenes in the visual field of the blind. And we will summarize latest activities on locating epileptic seizures using multi-modal fNIRS/EEG processing, and will show the onset detecting seizure and techniques to stop it, using bioelectronic implant.

Collaborative and Social Web Search

Lynda Tamine

Université Paul Sabatier, Institut de Recherche en Informatique de Toulouse
Toulouse, France
tamine@irit.fr

Abstract. Web search increasingly reflects problems grounded in the real-life world that requires the assistance of social resources. Social web search refers broadly to 1) the process of searching information over user-generated content (UGC) or 2) searching online with the help of users (such as friends, colleagues or experts) using large-scale social networking services. Examples of such services include Facebook, Twitter and MySpace and are considered as complementary to web search engines. Collaborative search is a kind of social search where small-scale groups of users are all together engaged in solving a shared information need. Collaborative and social search allow the gathering of users' complementary knowledge and skills that lead to the emergence of collective intelligence.

The aim of this talk is to 1) outline the paradigm of social search, 2) investigate the research issues that it gives rise to and then 3) point out the opportunities it brings to nowadays society.

I will look back over the past recent years highlighting some of the major changes in social-centred approaches of information search and related main research findings. I will also give an overview and share some experiences we gained through our previous research investigations in the area of collaborative and social search.

Contents

Computational Intelligence: BioInformatics

Information Technology: Text and Speech Processing

Information Technology: Requirement Engineering

Information Technology: OLAP and Web Services

Information Technology: Recommender Systems and Web Services

Information Technology: Ontologies

Security and Network Technologies: Security

Security and Network Technologies: Wireless Sensor Networks

Security and Network Technologies: Energy and Synchronisation

Security and Network Technologies: Potpourri

Software Engineering: Modeling and Meta Modeling

Software Engineering: Checking and Verification

Computational Intelligence: Meta-heuristics

Binary Bat Algorithm:
On The Efficiency of Mapping Functions When Handling Binary Problems Using Continuous-variable-based Metaheuristics

Zakaria Abd El Moiz Dahi[✉], Chaker Mezioud, and Amer Draa

Modeling and Implementation of Complex Systems laboratory
Dept. of New Technologies of Information and Communication
Constantine 2 university
Constantine City, Algeria
{zakaria.dahi,chaker.mezioud}@univ-constantine2.dz,
{draa_amer@yahoo.fr}

Abstract. Global optimisation plays a critical role in today's scientific and industrial fields. Optimisation problems are either continuous or combinatorial depending on the nature of the parameters to optimise. In the class of combinatorial problems, we find a sub-category which is the binary optimisation problems. Due to the complex nature of optimisation problems, exhaustive search-based methods are no longer a good choice. So, metaheuristics are more and more being opted in order to solve such problems. Some of them were designed originally to handle binary problems, whereas others need an adaptation to acquire this capacity. One of the principal adaptation schema is the use of a mapping function to decode real-valued solutions into binary-valued ones. The Antenna Positioning Problem (APP) is an NP-hard binary optimisation problem in cellular phone networks (2G, EDGE, GPRS, 3G, 3G$^+$, LTE, 4G). In this paper, the efficiency of the principal mapping functions existing in the literature is investigated through the proposition of five binary variants of one of the most recent metaheuristic called the Bat Algorithm (BA). The proposed binary variants are evaluated on the APP, and have been tested on a set of well-known benchmarks and given promising results.

1 Introduction

Combinatorial problems are problems whose parameters belong to a finit set of integers ($x_i \epsilon \mathbb{N}$). The latter includes a more specific type called *binary optimisation problems* : problems whose parameters can take values from a bi-valued search space called *genotype space* ($x_i \epsilon \{\,1\,,\,0\,\}$).

The design of cellular phone networks (2G, EDGE, GPRS, 3G, 3G$^+$, LTE, 4G) is one of the most critical tasks during the network implantation. Any design process that can not deal with this phase may alter the service quality

© IFIP International Federation for Information Processing 2015
A. Amine et al. (Eds.): CIIA 2015, IFIP AICT 456, pp. 3–14, 2015.
DOI: 10.1007/978-3-319-19578-0_1

of the network itself. The *Antenna Positioning Problem* (*APP*) is one of the most challenging optimisation issues in the design phase of cellular networks. The APP is formulated as a binary optimisation problem and was proven to be NP-hard.

Metaheuristics are efficient tools to use when tackling such optimisation problems. Regardless to the source of their inspiration, metaheuristics can be divided into algorithms who are originally designed to tackle continuous problems, and those who are designed to tackle combinatorial ones.

The *Bat Algorithm* (*BA*), is one of the recently proposed metaheuristics [14]. It was inspired by the natural phenomenon of echolocation used by bats. The BA was originally designed to tackle optimisation problems within continuous search space and it has shown encouraging performances.

Generally, when adapting a *continuous-variable-based metaheuristic* (i.e. *a metaheuristic that was designed originally to operate on variables within continuous search space*) to tackle binary problems, many schemas of adaptation exist. One of the most opted one, is the use of a mapping function to map the real-valued solutions into binary ones. Several sub-schemas of mapping exist as well in this last one : *one-to-one, many-to-one, one-to-many*.

Many questions still surround this schema of adaptation, such as the fact that the efficiency of these mapping functions is still fuzzy and unexplored. In addition, no clear statement exist on whether using *binary-variable-based metaheuristics* (i.e. *metaheuristics that were designed originally to operate on variables within binary-valued search space*) or continuous ones to tackle binary optimisation problems. Does the efficiency of these mapping functions depends on the algorithm used or the problem solved. Finally, no affined study shows if it is worth using this mapping functions and ultimately which kind of metaheuristics is more efficient when solving binary problems.

Through analysing the literature, the five principal mapping functions existing are used to propose new binary variants of the *Bat Algorithm*. The mapping functions used in this work were selected to illustrate different schemas of mapping. These functions are : The *Nearest Integer method* (*NI*), the *normalisation technique*, the *Angle Modulation method* (*AM*), the *Great Value Priority method* (*GVP*) and finally, the *Sigmoid Function* (*SF*). The proposed binary variants of the BA were tested on the APP using well-known benchmark instances, with different sizes and complexity as well. In addition, the last ones were compared to one of the most used binary-variable based algorithm : the *Genetic Algorithm*.

The remainder of this paper is structured as follows. In Section 2, we introduce basic concepts related to the antenna positioning problem, the bat algorithm, and the mapping functions used in this work. In Section 3, we introduce the proposed binary variants of the bat algorithm. Section 4 is dedicated to experimental results, their interpretation and disscussion. Finally, we present the conclusion of our work in Section 5.

2 Basic Concepts

In this Section, we introduce basic concepts related to the antenna positioning problem, the bat algorithm, and the used mapping functions.

2.1 Antenna Positioning Problem

In this section, we present a widely used formulation of the APP, that was given by Guidec et. al. [3]. This modeling of the antenna positioning problem consider two objectives : maximizing the covered area while minimizing the number of base station used.

The antenna positioning problem recalls NP-hard problems in graph theory such as the Minimum Dominating Set (MDS), the Maximum Independent Set (MIS), or the Unicast Set Covering Problem (USCP), see Sub-figures (a), (b), (c) of Figure 2.

Let L be the set of all potentially covered areas and M the set of all potential locations of base stations. Suppose G is a graph where E is the set of edges in the graph verifying that each transmitter is linked to the area that it covers. One seeks for the minimum subset of transmitters that covers the maximum surface of a given area. In other words, the objective is to find a subset M' such that $|M'|$ is minimised and $|\,Neighbours(M', E)\,|$ is maximised [4]; where $Neighbours$ represents the set of the covered area, and M' represents the set of transmitters used to cover this area.

$$|\,Neighbours(M', E)| \;=\; \{\, u \,\epsilon\, L \mid \exists\, v \,\epsilon\, M' , (u, v) \,\epsilon\, E \,\} \tag{1}$$

$$M' \;=\; \{\, t \,\epsilon\, B \mid x_t \,=\, 1 \,\} \tag{2}$$

A Base Tranceiver Station (BTS) is a radio transmitting device with a specific type of coverage (See Figure 1). In this work, we used three types of coverage introduced in [1]. A cell is a part of a geographical area that is covered by a base station.

Squared   Omnidirectional   Directive

Fig. 1. Antenna Coverage Models

The working area is discretized in a rectangular grid with Dim_x and Dim_y dimensions. Having $Sites = \{site_1, site_2, site_3, \dots, site_N\}$ is the set of potentially preselected sites, where the antennas can be placed. Each potential site location is identified by Cartesian coordinates $\{ site_1 = (x_1, y_1), site_2 = (x_2, y_2), site_3 = (x_3, y_3), \ldots, site_N = (x_N, y_N) \}$, see Sub-figures (d), (e), (f) of Figure 2.

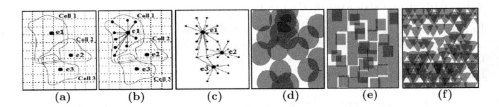

Fig. 2. Representation of The Discretized Area

A potential solution of the APP can be a binary vector described as follows. Each vector $\overrightarrow{X}$ represents a potential configuration of the mobile network. The number of elements of each vector represents the number of potential condidate sites. The rank of each dimsenion represents the rank of the corresponding base station $i = 1, 2, \ldots, Dimension_{\overrightarrow{x}}$. Each dimension of the vector is strictly binary valued : $x_i \in \overrightarrow{X} / x_i = 1 \vee x_i = 0$. If $x_i = 1$, the ith base station is selected, otherwise it is discarded. The objective function to optimize is defined by the formula 3.

$$Maximize: \quad f(x) = \frac{Cover\ ratio^{\alpha}}{Number\ of\ used\ base\ station} \tag{3}$$

with :

$$Number\ of\ used\ base\ station = \sum_{i=1}^{Dimension_{\overrightarrow{x}}} x_i\ , \tag{4}$$

with :

$$cover\ ratio = \left(\frac{Covered\ area}{Total\ area} \right) * 100 \tag{5}$$

And :

$$Covered\ area = \sum_{i=1}^{Dim_x} \sum_{j=1}^{Dim_y} cover(i,j)\ , \tag{6}$$

And :

$$Total\ area = Dim_x * Dim_y. \tag{7}$$

It is worth to mention that other mathematical models of the antenna positioning problem exist like the one proposed in [12]. Generally, these models differ by their mathematical formulations or modeling.

2.2   Bat Algorithm

The Bat Algorithm has been recently proposed. It is a swarm-based metaheuristic [14]. This algorithm is inspired by the natural echolocation behaviour of bats. Microbats use a type of sonar, called echolocation, to detect their preys, avoid obstacles, and locate their roosting crevices in the dark. These bats emit a very loud sound pulse and listen for the echo that bounces back from the surrounding objects. Their pulses vary in properties and can be correlated with their hunting strategies, depending on the species. The bats then adjust the pulse and rate of the sound as they get closer to the obstacles or the prey. This phenomenon has been translated into the newly proposed bat algorithm. The pseudo-code of Algorithm 1 describes the general framework of the bat algorithm.

Algorithm 1. The Bat Algorithm

1. Objective function $f(x), x = (x_1, ..., x_d)^T$
2. Initialize the bat population X_i (i = 1, 2, ..., n) and V_i
3. Define the pulse rate r_i and the loudness A_i
4. **Input :** Initial bat population
5. **while** ($t <$ Max number of iterations) **do**
6.   Generate new solutions by adjusting frequency, and updating velocities and locations/solutions (Equations 8 to 10)
7.   **if** ($rand > r_i$) **then**
8.   Select a solution among the best solutions
9.   Generate a local solution around the selected best solution
10.   **end if**
11.   Generate a new solution by flying randomly
12.   **if** ($rand < A_i \& f(X_i) < f(X_*)$) **then**
13.   Accept the new solutions
14.   Increase r_i and reduce A_i
15.   **end if**
16.   Rank the bats and find the current best X_*
17. **end while**
18. **Output :** Best bat found (i.e. best solution)

Equations 8, 9 and 10 define how the position X_i and velocity V_i in a d-dimensional search space are updated. The new solution X_i^t and velocity V_i^t at a time step t are given by :

$$f_i = f_{min} + (f_{max} - f_{min})\beta \qquad (8)$$

$$V_i^t = V_i^{t-1} + (X_i^t - X_*)f_i \qquad (9)$$

$$X_i^t = X_i^{t-1} + V_i^t \qquad (10)$$

Initially, each bat is randomly assigned a frequency which is drawn randomly from $[f_{min}, f_{max}]$. $\beta \, \epsilon \, [0, 1]$ is a random vector drawn from a uniform distribution. X_* is he current global best location (solution) which is located after comparing all the solutions.

When a local search is performed a solution is selected among the current best solutions. A new solution for each bat is generated using a random walk as described in Equation 11; Where ϵ is a random number from $[-1, 1]$, and $A^t = < A_i^t >$ is the average loudness of all bats at this time step.

$$X_{new} = X_{old} + \epsilon A^t \qquad (11)$$

Likewise, the loudness A_i and the rate ri of pulse are updated once the new solution is accepted. This is done using Formulas 12 and 13, where α and γ are constants. Initially, each bat is randomly assigned a loudness and a rate drawn respectively from the intervals $[A_{min}, A_{max}]$ and $[r_{min}, r_{max}]$.

$$A_i^{t+1} = \alpha A_i t \qquad (12)$$

$$r_i^{t+1} = r_i^0 [1 - exp(-\gamma t)] \qquad (13)$$

2.3   From Phenotype to Genotype Space

Several approaches exist for adapting a continuous-variable-based metaheuristic to work also in binary search space. The first schema of adaptation consists in replacing arithmetic operators of the metaheuristic by logical ones to operate directly on the binary solutions. The second aims to find the corresponding operators of the algorithms in the geometric space (*Hamming space*). Finally, the third approach consists in conserving the original operators, architecture and solution representation of the algorithm, and adding a complementary module that maps real-valued solutions into binary ones. The techniques used in this third category are generally known also as *mapping functions*. Several schemas of mapping exist. The pincipal ones are : *one-to-one*, *many-to-one*, and *one-to-many*.

The mapping functions used in this work have been chosen to illustrate several mapping schemas and several mathematical properties. In the following, the mapping functions used in this study are introduced.

Nearest Integer (NI):   This technique consists of assigning a real number to the nearest integer by rounding or truncating it up or down [2, 6].

Normalisation: This approach was proposed in [9, 10]. It consists of the normalisation of the solution by linearaly scaling it using the Formula 14. Then the condition 15 is applied to get the corresponding binary solution.

$$x'_{ij} = \frac{(x_{ij} + x_i^{min})}{(|x_i^{min}| + x_i^{max})} \tag{14}$$

$$x_{ij} = \begin{cases} 1, & If \ x'_{ij} \geqslant 0.5 \\ 0, & Otherwise \end{cases} \tag{15}$$

Assuming that $i = 1 \cdots N$ and $j = 1 \cdots D$. Where : N is the population size, D is the size of the solution vector. x_i^{min} and x_i^{max} are respectively the minimum and the maximum values in the ith vector at the iteration t.

Angle Modulation (AM): The idea is to use a trigonometric function to map real-valued solutions into binary ones. The generator function is used for signal processing in telecommunications and defined as follows [11, 13].

$$g(x_{ij}) = sin(2\Pi(x_{ij} - a) * b * cos(2\Pi(x_{ij} - a) * c)) + d \tag{16}$$

Where $i = 1 \cdots N$ and $j = 1 \cdots D$. N is the population size, D is the size of the solution vector. $g(x)$ is the generator function, and x_{ij} is a single element from a potential solution vector. Instead of optimizing a D-dimensional binary string solution, the search space is reduced to a 4-dimensional search space. Each vector of solution $\overrightarrow{G}$ represents potential values of the coefficients (a, b, c, d) in the generator function. At each iteration, every solution vector is applied to a sample vector $\overrightarrow{X}$ with the original D-dimensions of the problem. The sample vector is drawn from a uniform distribution and has equaly spaced intervals between each dimension and another. Finally, one has to apply the following formula on the resulting vector :

$$x_{ij} = \begin{cases} 1, & If \ g(x_{ij}) \geqslant 0 \\ 0, & Otherwise \end{cases} \tag{17}$$

Sigmoid Function (SF): In this technique, each real valued dimension of the solution vector is mapped into a strictly binary valued one [7,8]. The probability of each dimension to flip to one state or another is computed according to the real value of the dimension itself by applying Formula 18.

$$x_{ij} = \begin{cases} 1, & If \ Rand[0,1] \leq \frac{1}{1+e^{x_{ij}}} \\ 0, & Otherwise \end{cases} \tag{18}$$

Where $i = 1 \cdots N$ and $j = 1 \cdots D$. N is the population size, D is the size of the solution vector, and $Rand[0, 1]$ is a randomly generated positive number, drawn from a uniform distribution in the interval $[0, 1]$.

Great Value Priority (GVP):   Recently, authors in [5] have introduced this technique. Starting from a given real valued solution vector $\overrightarrow{X}$, a permutation vector $\overrightarrow{P}$ is created. The first element of the permutation vector p_1 will contain the position of the largest element in the original vector, the second element of the permutation vector p_2 will receive the position of the second largest element of the real valued vector, and so on. The procedure will be repeated until all the elements of the original vector are browsed. Finally, having the permutation vector $\overrightarrow{P}$, the following formula will be applied to recover back a binary valued vector.

$$x_{ij} = \begin{cases} 1\,, & If\ p_j\ >\ p_{j+1} \\ 0\,, & Otherwise \end{cases} \tag{19}$$

3   The proposed Binary Bat Algorithm

The inclusion of the discretisation step using one of the mapping functions after line code 10 in pseudo-code of Algorithm 1 results in giving birth to new variants of the bat algorithm. The first variant, using the nearest ineteger method as a discretising technique is called NI-BBA (for Nearest Integer based Binary Bat Algorithm). The second variant is called N-BBA (for Normalisation based Binary Bat Algorithm) is based on the normalisation method. The third variant uses the sigmoid function and is called SF-BBA (for Sigmoid Function based Binary Bat Algorithm). The fourth variant is the AM-BBA (for Angle Modulation based Binary Bat Algorithm) is based on the angle modulation method. Finally, GVP-BBA (for Great Value Priority based Binary Bat Algorithm) uses the great value priority technique.

4   Experimental Results and Discussion

The experiments where carried using an Intel I3 core with 2 GB Ram and a Windows 7 OS. The implementation was done using Matlab 7.12.0 (R2011a).

Two scenarios were randomly generated. Both are representing a working area of 20.25 Km^2. The first instance contains 549 available locations, whereas the second instance contains 749 available locations. Other instances of 149 and 349 preselected positions, are used here. They were provided by the university of Malaga, Spain. We used three types of coverage : squared, omnidirectional and directive [1]. It is worth to mention that directive antennas cover one sixth of the area of omnidirectionnal antennas having the same radius. Table 1 shows all the features of the used instances.

The proposed binary variants of the bat algorithm were also compared to one of the most used binary-variable-based metaheuristic and whose the efficiency is well established : the canonical Genetic Algorithm (GA). The GA uses a wheel selection and a two-point crossover with a probability equal to 0.7 and a bit-flip

Table 1. Instances : Size and Coverage

Instance Type	Grid Dimension	Instance	Coverage	Radius
Synthetic	287 x 287	149	Omnidirectional	22
			Squared	20
			Directive	22
		349	Omnidirectional	22
			Squared	20
			Directive	22
Random	300 x 300	549	Omnidirectional	26
			Squared	24
			Directive	26
		749	Omnidirectional	26
			Squared	24
			Directive	26

mutation with a probability of 0.05. The percentage of chromosomes used to create the matting pool is 50 %. The parameters of the bat algorithm used in this experiment are shown in Table 2.

Table 2. Bat Algorithm Parameters

Prameter	Value
f_{max}	10
f_{min}	-10
A_{max}	2
A_{min}	1
r_{max}	1
r_{min}	0
α	0.9
γ	0.9

The experiments were performed till reaching 20.000 evaluations, and each one is repeated for 20 runs. Several results are reported such as : the *best* and the *worst* fitness, and also the *mean* and *standard deviation* of fitness value over 20 runs.

Tables 3, 4, 5 and 6 show the results obtained when evaluating the five binary variants of the bat algorithm using the instances 149, 349, 549, 749 and this for each type of coverage : squared, omnidirectional and directive.

Based on the results shown in Tables 3, 4, 5 and 6 many observations can be made. The performances of the variants for small instances (149, 349) are close, but one can note that as the instance size increases (549, 749), the difference in the efficiency of the variants is more obvious. So, for some variants like the AM-BBA, N-BBA, GVP-BBA their efficiency depends highly on the size of the problem treated. Whereas for other variants such as the NI-BBA and the SF-BBA the efficiency is maintained even if the size of problem increases.

In general, NI-BBA and SF-BBA variants has shown better results than the other variants when solving the APP, especially the NI-BBA. The scalability of both variants is similar since both succeeded to solve the different sizes of

Table 3. Results of the Bat Algorithm Variants For Instance 149

Instance	Coverage	Algorithm	Best	Worst	Mean	Std
149	Squared	NI-BBA	120.582	120.582	**120.582**	1.458E-14
		N-BBA	106.361	95.006	100.501	2.70580121
		AM-BBA	111.120	97.564	104.250	4.63919122
		SF-BBA	103.012	102.112	102.157	0.20130794
		GVP-BBA	113.548	113.400	113.489	0.0745577
		GA	110.495	99.044	104.332	3.60183932
	Circle	NI-BBA	97.701	97.701	97.701	2.916E-14
		N-BBA	94.310	87.932	90.455	1.7646704
		AM-BBA	99.283	85.004	90.940	3.79249425
		SF-BBA	100.366	100.366	**100.366**	2.916E-14
		GVP-BBA	98.747	98.747	98.747	2.916E-14
		GA	97.282	85.472	90.832	2.99547967
	Directive	NI-BBA	41.473	41.473	41.473	1.458E-14
		N-BBA	40.354	37.315	38.905	0.81358109
		AM-BBA	42.560	40.963	41.594	0.44465264
		SF-BBA	42.388	41.859	**42.362**	0.11845141
		GVP-BBA	40.639	40.639	40.639	0
		GA	41.543	36.904	38.924	1.10100813

Table 4. Results of the Bat Algorithm Variants For Instance 349

Instance	Coverage	Algorithm	Best	Worst	Mean	Std
349	Squared	NI-BBA	95.371	95.371	95.371	2.916E-14
		N-BBA	61.664	58.335	59.981	1.03311284
		AM-BBA	188.758	89.671	**135.391**	30.2152069
		SF-BBA	102.880	98.142	102.643	1.05964286
		GVP-BBA	63.551	62.123	63.479	0.319142
		GA	63.643	57.858	61.196	1.60235842
	Circle	NI-BBA	95.081	95.081	**95.081**	2.916E-14
		N-BBA	60.350	56.624	58.753	0.98804881
		AM-BBA	127.577	75.920	88.332	13.1198896
		SF-BBA	90.144	88.803	88.911	0.3445047
		GVP-BBA	61.270	60.903	61.251	0.08199193
		GA	62.199	57.224	59.614	1.48976652
	Directive	NI-BBA	41.464	41.464	**41.464**	7.29E-15
		N-BBA	39.659	37.102	38.221	0.54525135
		AM-BBA	42.283	38.420	39.408	0.91636124
		SF-BBA	39.899	39.899	39.899	7.29E-15
		GVP-BBA	39.723	39.723	39.723	7.29E-15
		GA	39.450	37.199	38.304	0.66880293

the problem. No clear conclusion can be made about how the proposed variants behave when dealing with a specific type of coverage (squared, omnidirectional, directive), or a specific type of data (random, synthetic). One can note also that all the binary variants of the BA were able to outperform the results obtained by the canonical GA for all the instances and for all the sizes of the instances. But one can note also that the difference between the GA and the other variants decreases as the size of the instance decreases.

The conclusion that can be made concerning the impact of the mapping functions on the efficiency of an algorithm, is that the adequate use of a mapping function depends in some cases on the size of the problem engaged and in other cases on the type of the problem. Furthermore, one can note that in reality the bat algorithm do not need complex mapping functions since the basic *rounding function* has shown better results than the other complex mapping functions.

Table 5. Results of the Bat Algorithm Variants For Instance 549

Instance	Coverage	Algorithm	Best	Worst	Mean	Std
549	Squared	NI-BBA	139.973	139.973	139.973	2.916E-14
		N-BBA	40.668	38.939	40.063	0.46911297
		AM-BBA	134.322	96.348	112.442	8.45490438
		SF-BBA	147.445	147.445	**147.445**	2.916E-14
		GVP-BBA	40.529	40.365	40.521	0.03669093
		GA	42.777	38.927	41.070	1.19535659
	Circle	NI-BBA	127.289	126.025	**126.910**	0.59402311
		N-BBA	41.311	38.693	39.740	0.77547919
		AM-BBA	116.780	89.794	102.404	6.32663866
		SF-BBA	117.067	116.067	117.017	0.223514
		GVP-BBA	41.411	41.411	41.411	7.29E-15
		GA	42.640	39.027	40.620	1.06845162
	Directive	NI-BBA	49.046	49.046	**49.046**	1.458E-14
		N-BBA	36.371	34.536	35.468	0.4751343
		AM-BBA	52.156	45.135	48.721	1.83706437
		SF-BBA	51.874	51.808	51.870	0.01464278
		GVP-BBA	35.853	35.814	35.852	0.00873771
		GA	37.913	34.444	35.851	0.89470107

Table 6. Results of the Bat Algorithm Variants For Instance 749

Instance	Coverage	Algorithm	Best	Worst	Mean	Std
749	Squared	NI-BBA	135.888	135.888	**135.888**	2.92E-14
		N-BBA	29.847	28.486	29.175	0.40036354
		AM-BBA	126.827	90.586	109.403	11.4041269
		SF-BBA	130.915	130.915	130.915	0
		GVP-BBA	29.586	29.586	29.586	3.65E-15
		GA	30.788	28.477	29.437	0.52843974
	Circle	NI-BBA	101.870	101.870	101.870	1.46E-14
		N-BBA	29.917	28.275	29.018	0.45477513
		AM-BBA	110.941	87.658	97.607	6.66552368
		SF-BBA	114.077	114.077	**114.077**	0
		GVP-BBA	29.367	29.142	29.356	0.05020659
		GA	30.579	27.929	29.198	0.82131334
	Directive	NI-BBA	50.405	50.024	50.386	0.08519864
		N-BBA	28.674	27.113	27.730	0.4651209
		AM-BBA	50.920	45.767	48.605	1.36744246
		SF-BBA	51.189	49.877	**51.123**	0.29334724
		GVP-BBA	27.578	27.415	27.503	0.02651541
		GA	29.608	26.802	27.785	0.66481778

5   Conclusion

In this paper we conducted a comparative study on the impact of mapping functions on the efficiency of the continuous-variable-based metaheuristic. This was done by proposing five new variants of a recent metaheuristic which is the Bat Algorithm (BA). The proposed binary variants, were tested on an NP-hard optimisation problem in cellular phone networks which is the Antenna Positioning Problem (APP). The results showed that the impact of such mapping functions on the efficiency of an algorithm depends on two factors : the size of the problem, or the complexity of the problem. The best mapping functions found for the bat algorithm are the nearest integer and sigmoid function techniques.

This work illustrates a simple comparative study, and no deep and general conclusion can be made about the efficiency of the mapping functions, the controlling factor of these last ones or the usefulness of these mapping functions when solving binary problems. So, we seek to conduct a more deep statistical comparative study using several continuous-variable-based metaheuristics and compare them with more powerful binary-variable-based metaheuristics.

References

1. Alba, E., Molina, G., Chicano, J.F.: Optimal placement of antennae using metaheuristics. In: Boyanov, T., Dimova, S., Georgiev, K., Nikolov, G. (eds.) NMA 2006. LNCS, vol. 4310, pp. 214–222. Springer, Heidelberg (2007)
2. Burnwal, S., Deb, S.: Scheduling optimization of flexible manufacturing system using cuckoo search-based approach. The International Journal of Advanced Manufacturing Technology 64(5-8), 951–959 (2013)
3. Calegari, P., Guidec, F., Kuonen, P.: A parallel genetic approach to transceiver placement optimisation. In: Proceedings of the SIPAR Workshop: Parallel and Distributed Systems, pp. 21–24 (1996)
4. Calegari, P., Guidec, F., Kuonen, P., Kobler, D.: Parallel island-based genetic algorithm for radio network design. J. Parallel Distrib. Comput. 47(1), 86–90 (1997)
5. Congying, L., Huanping, Z., Xinfeng, Y.: Particle swarm optimization algorithm for quadratic assignment problem. In: Proceedings of the International Conference on Computer Science and Network Technology (ICCSNT), vol. 3, pp. 1728–1731 (2011)
6. Costa, M., Rocha, A.A.M., Francisco, B.R., Fernandes, M.E.: Heuristic-based firefly algorithm for bound constrained nonlinear binary optimization. Advances in Operations Research 1(215182), 12 (2014)
7. Liu, Q., Lu, W., Xu, W.: Spectrum allocation optimization for cognitive radio networks using binary firefly algorithm. In: Proceedings of the International Conference on Innovative Design and Manufacturing (ICIDM), pp. 257–262 (2014)
8. Palit, S., Sinha, S., Molla, M., Khanra, A.: A cryptanalytic attack on the knapsack cryptosystem using binary firefly algorithm. In: Proceedings of the 2nd International Conference on Computer and Communication Technology (ICCCT), pp. 428–432 (2011)
9. Pampara, G., Engelbrecht, A.: Binary artificial bee colony optimization. In: Proceedings of the IEEE Symposium on Swarm Intelligence (SIS), April 11-15, pp. 1–8 (2011)
10. Pampara, G., Engelbrecht, A., Franken, N.: Binary differential evolution. In: Proceedings of the IEEE Congress on Evolutionary Computation, CEC 2006, pp. 1873–1879 (2006)
11. Pampara, G., Franken, N., Engelbrecht, A.: Combining particle swarm optimisation with angle modulation to solve binary problems. In: Proceedings of the Congress on Evolutionary Computation, CEC 2005, pp. 89–96 (2005)
12. Segura, C., Segredo, E., González, Y., León, C.: Multiobjectivisation of the antenna positioning problem. In: International Symposium on Distributed Computing and Artificial Intelligence (DCAI), pp. 319–327 (2011)
13. Swagatam, D., Rohan, M., Rupam, K., Thanos, V.: Multi-user detection in multicarrier CDMA wireless broadband system using a binary adaptive differential evolution algorithm. In: Proceedings of the 15th Annual Conference on Genetic and Evolutionary Computation, GECCO 2013, pp. 1245–1252 (2013)
14. Yang, X.S.: A new metaheuristic bat-inspired algorithm. In: Nature Inspired Cooperative Strategies for Optimization (NICSO), vol. 284, pp. 65–74. Springer, Heidelberg (2010)

Relative Timed Model for Coordinated Multi Agent Systems

Said Layadi[1(✉)], Jean-Michel Ilié[2], Ilham Kitouni[1], and Djamel-Eddine Saidouni[1]

[1] MISC Laboratory, University of Abdelhamid Mehri – Constantine 2, 25000,
Constantine, Algeria
`{layadi,kitouni,saidouni}@misc-umc.org`
[2] Universities of Paris UPMC and Paris Descartes 4 place Jussieu, 75005, Paris, France
`jean-michel.ilie@upmc.fr`

Abstract. The MAS engineering is becoming very important, it is concerned with models, methods and tools. Therefore, verifying the correctness of MAS is the next challenge. We are interested by MAS where each participating agent has its own physical clock of varying frequency, while no global clock is available or desirable. Under such circumstances models must be adapted. In this paper we attempt a novel approach to model the MAS, with a respect of two characteristics, the concurrent aspect and heterogeneity of agents (perceived as a different time rates of agents plan execution). Timed automata with action durations are used; for the circumstance it's extended to deal with relative time rates. Its semantic is abstracted by a novel equivalence relation leading to a region automaton for decidability assessment and proof.

Keywords: Relative time rates · Timed automata with action durations · Region graph · Multi agent systems · Timed transport fleets

1 Introduction

Multi Agent Systems (MAS) are ever-present in computer science applications. This paradigm is used in different domains where reactivity, mobility, dynamicity and adaptation of the system to uncertain or unpredictable factors should be considered. The MAS engineering (i.e. specification, development, management, deployment…) is becoming very important. It is concerned with models, methods and tools. Therefore, verifying the correctness of MAS becomes a fantastic challenge.

We are interested by MAS where each participating agent has its own physical clock of varying frequency, while no global clock is available or desirable. Under such circumstances it's impossible to model system using discrete semantics of time without considering the clock frequencies of participating components. Hence it's natural to study these systems in terms of different time evolutions.

In this paper we attempt a novel approach to model the MAS, with a respect of two characteristics, the concurrent aspect of the MAS and the heterogeneous of components (agents) perceived as a different time rates of agents plan execution.

© IFIP International Federation for Information Processing 2015
A. Amine et al. (Eds.): CIIA 2015, IFIP AICT 456, pp. 15–27, 2015.
DOI: 10.1007/978-3-319-19578-0_2

Models. For this aim, timed models are suitable. The durational actions timed automata (daTA) [2] are a form of timed automata [1], that admits a more natural representation of action durations and advocates carrying true concurrency (which are realistic assumptions for specifying in natural way MAS). It's based on the Maximality semantics [4]. Maximality semantics has been proved necessary and sufficient for carrying both the refinement process and action durations. The daTA model has been defined and a nice characterization of the model was presented in [2] and [7]. So the concurrency aspect of MAS is modeled by the timed automata with action durations.

The daTA model assumes a "global clock" semantics, i.e., all clocks advance simultaneously and at the same rate (and there is a common initial instant). All possible executions of daTA are then represented by an infinite transition system where, for any given state, the system may evolve in two possible ways: either it executes an action or it delays with a given amount of time the potential execution. The decidability of the daTA has been proved using the so-called region graph construction [1]. In this paper we are concerned by the coordination problem in MAS. Mainly, this consists in maintaining the synchronization of the agent plans with respect to some objective in a consistent timed context. We consider real time application wherein the agent plans refers to timed actions whose durations are known. Agents are assumed to be able to communicate via reliable materials, in order to achieve some plan called coordinated plan.

The paper contribution. We propose to model plan in a more attractive way using the standard algebraic language based on LOTOS, seeing plans as the execution of concurrent processes [3]. In fact, LOTOS specifications supplies modular concepts useful to describe some plan over several agents. Moreover, LOTOS-basic specifications are translated in daTA relative time rates (daTA-RT). daTA-RT compactly represents the possibly infinite behaviors of the coordinated plans, this model is concerned by the timing constraints defined over the MAS plans, taking into account relative time rates that distinguish the speeds of the agents in coordination. In this paper, we show how to build a (finite) region graph structure from a daTA-RT specification, for decidability assessment and proof. We extend by this proposal the result of a precedent work [12] over timed automata with relative time rates to model heterogeneity property.

Related work. In the literature, the two aspects, verification and time management works are generally focused on how to consider clocks and time for example see [13]. In the main cases, clocks are synchronized and used by all processes (read and reset). Or clocks can drift by a certain amount of time Δ, particularly as long as the processes do not communicate (via synchronizing actions). In [14], distributed systems are modeled by means of network of timed automata evolving in different rates. However, checking emptiness or universality turns out to be undecidable in the majority of cases. In [12], we investigate the decidability for verification assessments of real time systems with relative speed of clocks (what we call heterogeneity property). More precisely, under same hypothesis we answer this question positively over the timed automata with relative time rates.

Regarding designing MAS, several recent papers focus on the framework based on refinement paradigm. In [6], the authors propose a formal modeling of critical MAS that aims to derive a secure system implementation. The approach is based on Event B language. They are interesting by modeling fault tolerant MAS. In the same context of Event B specification language, authors in [8] propose a formal approach for self-organizing MAS. [9] Addresses a top-down approach for MAS protocol description using Finite State Automata (FSA) and multi-Role Interaction (mRI) abstraction. We don't forget the work [11] in which MAS are specified by AgLOTOS. This latter language captures communication of processes (i.e. agents) by message passing, in addition to classical features of concurrent processes. In our case the basic LOTOS is sufficient for what we intend to present.

Paper outlines. In Section 2, the specification of coordinated MAS plans is presented, based on LOTOS concepts, the relative time rates are explained and our running example is built. In Section 3, the daTA model is recalled, its extension to relative time is defined and an informal meaner of generating daTA structure from LOTOS expression is shown. The main contribution of this paper is proposed in Section 4, where the semantic of daTA is presented and formally defined. In all the paper the same example is used to clarify concepts and applications. The end section concerns conclusion and some immediate perspectives.

2   Coordinated Mas Specification

In this paper, a multi agent system is a tuple $MAS = (Ag, Plan, Act, \tau, \gamma)$ where Ag is set of agents; Plan is a set of agent plans, called coordinated plans since some of them are realized by several agents, Act is the set of actions mentioned in these plans. $\tau = (\tau_p)_{p \in Ag}$ is a rate mapping associating a relative time rate with each agent characterizing the speed of the agent to execute their actions, γ is a duration mapping assigning a global duration value to each action of Act, evaluated in a number of execution cycles (called time units). In the following, we describe the specification of coordinated plans as an extension of the language Basic LOTOS, precising which parts of the plans are dedicated to each agent.

The relative time model. In the MAS systems, agents are assumed to have a notion of clocks to achieve their actions. Since agents can have different speeds, we assume that the speeds are relative according to a global time-scale (denoted absolute time), thus the duration performance of some action can be more or less important, depending on the agent considered to execute the action.

As example, Fig.1 shows an action a of duration 2, which requires 2 times more to be achieved by the agent p. According to any global time t, the time rate $\tau_q = 2t$ and $\tau_p = t$, in such a way that at any time $\frac{\tau_p}{\tau_q} \in Z$.

Coordinated plan specification. The plan of an agent p is specified by an agent expression E_p describing the actions to be executed for achieving the plan. The execution is assumed to be controlled by the agent p, however E_p can be composed of sub-expressions whose execution can be performed by other agents. An agent expression inherits from the syntax of (Basic) LOTOS [3] as follows: $P ::= E_p$ and $E_p ::= exit \quad | \quad stop \quad | \quad a; E_p \ (a \in Act) \quad | \quad E_q \sim E_r$.

Where $q, r \in Ag$ and $\sim \in \{|||, ||, |[L]|, [], \gg, [>\}$ is a LOTOS operator.

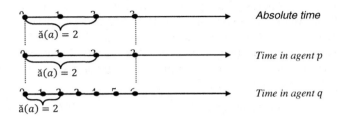

Fig. 1. The action a of global duration 2, is achieved two times faster by the agent q than by agent p

The elementary expression stop specifies a plan behavior without possible evolution and exit represents the successful termination of some plan. In the syntax, any operator $\sim$ as in standard LOTOS: $E_q[]E_r$ specifes a non-deterministic choice, $E_q \gg E_r$ a sequential composition and $E_q[> E_r$ the interruption of the left hand side part by the right one. The LOTOS parallel composition, denoted by $E_q|[L]|E_r$, can model both synchronous composition when (L = Act), denoted by $E_q||E_r$, and asynchronous composition, $E_q|||E_r$ when (L = $\emptyset$). In fact, the LOTOS language exhibits a rich expressivity such that the sequential executions of plans appear to be only a particular case.

Our running example. The example concerns two trucks A and B such that A initially placed in the location l_1 must pick up the load in the location l_2 and delivers it to the location l_4. As the load is initially placed in l_3, B initially placed in the location l_2, proposes to get the load from l_3 in such a way that A can meet it in l_2 and take the load. The problem for A and B is to meet them in minimum time, in case they start at the same time. In order to coordinate, each truck is equipped with a software agent able to discuss and synchronize with the other agents in the system. Both agents A and B refer to the following coordinated plan:

$P ::= E_A|[meet]|E_B$; with $E_A ::= move_A(l_2)$; meet; $move_A(l_4)$; exit and
$E_B ::= move_B(l_3)$; get_load$_B$; $move_B(l_2)$; meet; exit.

Moreover, duration of actions are given by the respective learnt experiences of A and B about transportations. For the simplicity of the example, all durations of actions are assumed equal to 1 time unit.

3   Timed Automata with Action Durations and Relative Time Rates for Coordination Plans

To model duration of actions, every edge of the automaton is annotated by constraints on clocks which implicitly enclose them, of course those that are already started. A single clock is reset on every edge. When clock is reset it corresponds to the beginning of event. The termination of action will be captured by information (temporal formulas) on locations of the automaton, precisely on the destination location. In fact, the duration of an action is either in the constraint of the following edge, if there is dependence between the successive actions, otherwise it is in the next locations and that means: action is not over yet. This elegant way to capture the durations is the effect of the maximality semantics. An example of a daTA A is shown in Fig. 2. The automaton consists of three localities l_0, l_1, l_2 and two clocks x, y. A transition from l_0 to l_1 represents the start of action a (indicating the beginning of its execution), the transition from l_1 to l_2 is labeled by b.

Assuming a time granularity of seconds, the automaton A starts in locality l_0. As soon as the value of y is less than or equal to 4, the automaton can make an a transition to l_1 and reset the clock x to 0. On the locality l_1 the temporal formula $\{x \geq 2\}$ represents information about the duration of the action a (it is important to differentiate it from invariant in timed automata). When x is at most 2 and is at least 5, transition to l_2 can be started (b executed) and y is reset. In the same logic the temporal formula $\{y \geq 7\}$ represents duration of the action b.

Preliminary. In the following we consider $R_{\geq 0}$ a set of nonnegative real numbers. Clocks are real variables take values from $R_{\geq 0}$. Let H be a set of clocks, a clock valuation over H is a function that assigns a nonnegative real number to every clock. V_H is the set of total valuation functions from H to $R_{\geq 0}$. A valuation is noted $v \in V_H$, and for $d \in R_{\geq 0}$, $v + d$ maps every clock x to $v(x) + d$. For $\lambda \subseteq H$, the valuation $v[\lambda := 0]$ is defined by: $(v[\lambda := 0])(x) = 0$ if $x \in \lambda$, $v(x)$ otherwise.

The set $C(X)$ of clock constraints C is defined by the grammar:

$C ::= $ true $|$ false $| x \sim c | C \wedge C$, where $x \in X$, $c \in \mathbb{N}$ and $\sim \in \{<, >, =, \leq, \geq\}$. We write $v \vDash C$ when the valuation v satisfies a clock constraint C over X iff C evaluates to true according to the values given by v.

We also use a subset of constraints where only the atomic form of clocks comparison is allowed. This set is defined by $C_d(H)$ by the grammar: $C ::= x \geq c$, where $x \in X$ and $c \in \mathbb{N}$. This subset represents condition duration over the set of actions noted by Act.

Definition 1 (daTA). A Durational Actions Timed Automaton daTA $\mathcal{A}$ is a tuple (S, s_0, H, T, L_S) over Act, where: S is a finite set of locations. $s_0 \in S$ is an initial location. H is a finite set of clocks. $T \subseteq S \times C(H) \times Act \times H \times S$ is a finite set of edges. An edge $e = (s, g, a, x, s') \in T$ ($s \xrightarrow{G,a,x} s'$) represents an edge from location s to s' that launches the execution of action a whenever guard g becomes true.

$L_S: S \to 2^{C_d(H)}$ is a maximality function which decorates each location by a set of timed formulas named action durations. These formulas indicate the status of action execution at the corresponding state. $L_S(s_0) = \emptyset$ means that no action is yet started.

3.1   Timed Automata with Action Durations and Relative Speed Clocks Model

In this section we define a daTA with relative speed of clocks for modeling MAS; this is what we designate as the relative time rates in the global system.

Definition 2 (daTA with relative time rates). A daTA with relative time rates (daTA-RT) over the set of agents Ag is a structure $A = (\mathcal{A}, \pi)$ where $\mathcal{A} = (S, s_0, H, T, L_S)$ is a daTA and π is a mapping from H to Ag such that, for each $p \in Ag$, we have $\pi^{-1}(p) \subseteq H$.

Note that each clock evolves at the same rate in a particular agent (as the time evolves). This clock is then said to belong to that agent, and the mapping π (owner map) describes this in the above definition. We suppose that, in daTA with relative time rates, all clocks in H evolve at relative rates. Each rate characterizes the speed of an agent p. It depends on some absolute time given by the function $\tau_p: \mathbb{R}_{\geq 0} \to \mathbb{R}_{\geq 0}$ with $\tau_p(0) = 0$ and $\tau_p(t)$ returns the local time in each agent $p \in Ag$ for the instant t of absolute time. Moreover, τ is a tuple of local time rate functions such that $\tau = (\tau_p)_{p \in Ag}$. The function τ_p is the p local time rate. For a time value t, the mapping function $\tau: \mathbb{R}_{\geq 0} \to \mathbb{R}_{\geq 0}^{Ag}$ assigns the tuple $(\tau_p(t))_{p \in Ag}$ to $\tau(t)$.

3.2   From Basic LOTOS with Action Durations to daTA with Relative Time Rates

In this section, we informally present the manner of generating in an operational way a daTA-RT starting from a Basic LOTOS specification with action durations. The approach is very close with the one of [4] for the generation of MLTS (Maximality based labeled transition system). In our context it's viewed as an unfolding operation of the behavior expression to state transition structure. Take again the behavior of the

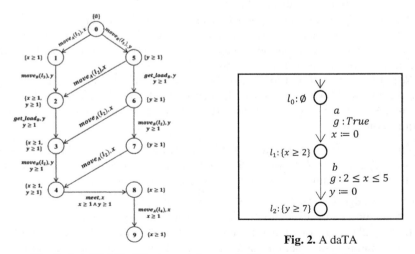

Fig. 2. A daTA

Fig. 3. A daTA-RT of the transport example (Our running example)

system described in the example of transport which is expressed as the parallel composition of two subsystems with synchronization on the action *meet*.

Recall that the behavior of system is specified by the following Basic LOTOS with action durations expression: $E_A|[meet]|E_B$. As already presented (in section 3.2), all states of the daTA-RT encapsulate a timed formula representing duration conditions of actions.

The generation of the daTA-RT's structure starts from the initial expressions, as a form of unfolding structure. To each configuration is associated a daTA-RT state as well as a behavior of sub-expression; (i.e. configurations corresponding daTA-RT's states) combines the expression to developed and duration conditions inherited from the previous step of unfolding, in the form $_F[E]$ where $F \in 2^{Cd(H)}$. In the initial state of the coordinated plan $P ::= E_A|[meet]|E_B$, no action is running, which explains why the duration conditions set is empty in the initial configuration. The initial configuration (State) of daTA-RT is $s_0 = {}_\emptyset[E_A|[meet]|E_B]$ where no action was launched yet. From this configuration, action $move_A(l_2)$ can be allowed. A clock x, is assigned to this occurrence of $move_A(l_2)$, it will be initialized to zero. Action $move_A(l_2)$ does not await the end of any other action to be able to comply, from where the guard of the transition is true.

$$\underbrace{{}_\emptyset[E_A]|[meet]|\,{}_\emptyset[E_B]}_{config_0} \xrightarrow{true,\ move_A(l_2),\ x} \underbrace{{}_{x\geq1}[meet, move_A(l_4), exit]|[meet]|\,{}_\emptyset[E_B]}_{config_1}$$

The duration condition of the configuration $config_1$ corresponding to state s_1 is $\{x \geq 1\}$, which means that action $move_A(l_2)$ is running at this step of execution. From the configuration $config_1$ corresponding to state s_1, the only possible transition to construct is that corresponding to the launching of the action $move_B(l_3)$, from where the derivation

$config_1$
$$\xrightarrow{\emptyset,\ move_B(l_3),\ y} \underbrace{{}_{x\geq1}[meet, move_A(l_4), exit]|[meet]|_{y\geq1}[get\_load_B; move_B(l_2); meet; exit]}_{config_2}$$

With the same reasoning, we obtain $config_3$ and $config_4$, note the guard in this step is $\{y \geq 1\}$, this expresses dependence of loading B and the termination of moving B.

$$config_2 \xrightarrow{\{y\geq1\},\ get_{loadB},\ y} \underbrace{{}_{x\geq1}[meet, move_A(l_4), exit]|[meet]|_{y\geq1}[move_B(l_2); meet; exit]}_{config_3}$$

The clock y is assigned to the action get_load_B because of its discharge at the time of get_load_B.

$$config_3 \xrightarrow{\{y\geq1\},\ move_B(l_2),\ y} \underbrace{{}_{x\geq1}[meet, move_A(l_4), exit]|[meet]|_{y\geq1}[meet; exit]}_{config_4}$$

From the configuration $config_4$, action meet can comply only if the two actions $move_A(l_2)$ and $move_B(l_2)$ finished their execution, in other words, only if duration conditions belonging to the set $\{x \geq 1, y \geq 1\}$ are all satisfied, from where the set

$\{x \geq 1, y \geq 1\}$ corresponding to the condition $x \geq 1 \wedge y \geq 1$. The following transition becomes possible:

$$config_4 \xrightarrow{\{x \geq 1 \wedge y \geq 1\}, \; meet, \; x} \underbrace{x_{\geq 1}[move_A(l_4), exit]|[meet]|_{x \geq 1}[exit]}_{config_8}$$

For any action of synchronization, the assigned clock must evolve according to the slowest agent speed. In this example a clock x, which evolves according to the rate of truck A (τ_A), is assigned to the action meet. Thus, the truck B, which is the faster, must wait that truck A finished the synchronization action before going on. This mechanism ensures the synchronization on the end of each synchronized action. The configurations $config_9$ and $config_{10}$ are obtained as follows:

$$config_8 \xrightarrow{\{x \geq 1\}, \; move_A(l_4), \; x} \underbrace{x_{\geq 1}[exit]|[meet]|_{\emptyset}[exit]}_{config_9} \quad \text{and}$$

$$config_9 \xrightarrow{\{x \geq 1\}, \; \delta, \; x} \underbrace{x_{\geq 0}[stop]|[meet]|_{x \geq 0}[stop]}_{config_{10}}$$

The same reasoning is applied in the following way to the other branch of the transition system where the action $move_B(l_3)$ begins its execution before the action $move_A(l_2)$:

$$config_0 \xrightarrow{\emptyset, move_B(l_3), y} \underbrace{{}_{\emptyset}[E_A]|[meet]|_{y \geq 1}[get\_load_B; move_B(l_2); meet; exit]}_{config_5}$$

The system cannot execute any action starting from configuration $config_{10}$, end of the unfolding operation of $E_A|[meet]|E_B$. The abstraction of this unfolding (transformation) is depicted by the daTA-RT structure in Fig. 3.

4   The Semantics of daTA-RT model

In the literature [1], an equivalence relation is proposed to aggregate states of the timed transition system (configurations) such that an equivalence class represents a configurations set. The equivalence classes of clock valuations are named clock regions. The design of Multi agents system becomes coherent if the components share a conjoint perception of time [5]. Therefore, it is important that the general perception is consistent. This perception takes its full dimension when calculating the semantics graph of the model. This motivates the redefinition of concepts like clock regions and region automaton. We will hereafter focus on the effect of the relative clock speeds.

4.1   Equivalence Classes of Clock Valuations

Let $A = ((S, L_S, s_0, H, T), \pi)$ be a daTA-RT over Act and a set of agents Ag.

Definition 3 (slope$_{xy}$). Let x (resp. y) be a clock that belongs to the agent p (resp. q) and evolves according to the rate function τ_p (resp. τ_q). We define slope$_{xy}$ as the ratio of local-time rate functions τ_q and τ_p, noted $\text{slope}_{xy} = \frac{\tau_q}{\tau_p}$. (see Fig. 4).

Given a pair of clocks, x and y (within respectively agent p and q), their owner speeds will make them diverging from time reference at a certain speed. That is equal to the ratio between their owner rates. It represents the slope of the straight line in Fig. 4. As there are only finitely many clock constraints on clock x, we can determine the largest integer $c_x \in \mathbb{N}$ with which x is compared in some clock constraint (guard) of the daTA-RT A. In the remainder and for every pair of clocks x and y, the parameter slope$_{xy}$ is assumed be an integer constant whatever the value of time t.

Definition 4 (equivalence relation $\sim$). We define the equivalence relation $\sim$ over the set of all clock valuations, $v \sim v'$ iff all the following conditions hold:

1.   For all $x \in H$, either $\lfloor v(x) \rfloor$ and $\lfloor v'(x) \rfloor$ are the same, or both $v(x)$ and $v'(x)$ are greater than c_x.
2.   For all $x, y \in H$ with $v(x) \leq c_x$, $v(y) \leq c_y$ and x (resp. y) evolves according to τ_p (resp. τ_q):

$$c. \frac{1}{\text{slope}_{xy}} \leq v(x) \leq (c + 1). \frac{1}{\text{slope}_{xy}} \text{ iff } c. \frac{1}{\text{slope}_{xy}} \leq v'(x) \leq (c + 1). \frac{1}{\text{slope}_{xy}} \text{ for } c \in \mathbb{N} \text{ and}$$

$$\text{fract}\Big(\text{slope}_{xy}v(x)\Big) \leq \text{fract}\big(v(y)\big) \text{ iff fract}\Big(\text{slope}_{xy}v'(x)\Big) \leq \text{fract}\big(v'(y)\big)$$

An equivalence class of clock valuations induced by $\sim$ is a clock region of A.

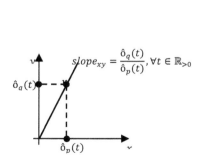

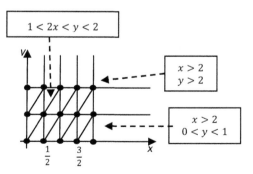

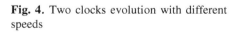

Fig. 4. Two clocks evolution with different speeds   **Fig. 5.** Clock Regions Deducted by the Relation $\sim$

4.2   The Representation of Clock Regions

Each equivalence class of clock valuations can be specified by a finite set of clock constraints it satisfies. The notation [v] represents the clock region to which v belongs.

Example. we consider two clocks x and y which evolve at different rates such that $slope_{xy} = 2$, $c_x = 2$ and $c_y = 2$. The clock regions obtained by the Definition 4 (equivalence relation) are depicted in Fig. 5. Thus, we have 15 corner points (e.g. $[x = 0.5 \wedge y = 2]$), 38 open line segments (e.g. $[0 < 2x = y < 1]$) and 23 open regions (e.g. $[0 < 2x < y < 1]$).

Definition 5 ($slope_{max}$). For each clock $x \in H$, we define $slope_{max(x)}$ as the largest value of $slope_{xy}$ for all $y \in H$.

Reconsider the example above: $slope_{max(x)} = max(slope_{xy}, slope_{xx}) = max\left(\frac{2}{1}, 1\right) = 2$, $slope_{max(y)} = max(slope_{yx}, slope_{yy}) = max\left(\frac{1}{2}, 1\right) = 1$. Note that if x is the fastest clock in H then $slope_{max(x)} = slope_{xx} = 1$. $\frac{1}{slope_{max(x)}}$ is the smallest amount of time in which x cannot stay in the same region.

In the example, the clock x changes the region each half unit of time corresponding to $\frac{1}{slope_{max(x)}} = \frac{1}{2}$, when y do this change each one unit of time (except for regions represented by points). The representation of a clock region accords with the two following points:

For each clock x which evolves according to τ_p, there is one clock constraint taken from the set:

$$\{x = c \mid c = 0, \frac{1}{slope_{xy}}, 2\frac{1}{slope_{xy}}, \dots, 1, 1 + \frac{1}{slope_{xy}}, 1 + 2\frac{1}{slope_{xy}}, \dots, c_x \text{ for all } y \in H\}$$

$$\cup \left\{\wedge_{y \in H} \left(c - \frac{1}{slope_{xy}} < x < c\right) \mid c = \frac{1}{slope_{xy}}, 2\frac{1}{slope_{xy}}, \dots, 1, 1 + \frac{1}{slope_{xy}}, 1 + 2\frac{1}{slope_{xy}}, \dots, c_x. \forall y\right\}$$

$$\cup \{x > c_x\}. \tag{1}$$

for each pair of clocks x and y which evolve respectively according to τ_p and τ_q such that $c < x < c + \frac{1}{slope_{max(x)}}$ and $d < y < d + \frac{1}{slope_{max(y)}}$ appear in (1) for some c and d, whether $slope_{xy}(x - c)$ is less than, equal to or greater than $y - d$.

4.3   The Time-Successors of Clock Regions

In the following, we introduce the time-successor relation over clock regions. When time advances from any clock valuation v in the region α, we will reach all its time-successors α'. Formally, we say that α' is a time-successor of the region α if there are v in α, v' in α', $t \in \mathbb{R}_{>0}$ such that $v' = v \oplus \tau(t)$, with $v \oplus \tau(t) = (v(x) + \tau_p(t))_{\pi^{-1}(x)=p}$.

For example, in Fig. 5 the five time-successors of the region $\alpha = [(1.5 < x < 2), (1 < y < 2x - 2)]$ are: itself, $[(x = 2), (1 < y < 2)]$, $[(x > 2), (1 < y < 2)]$, $[(x > 2), (y = 2)]$ and $[(x > 2), (y > 2)]$. These regions are those covered by a line drawn from any point in α parallel to the line $y = slope_{xy}x = 2x$ (in the upwards direction). To compute each time-successor of a region α, we must give : (i). for every clock x, a constraint of the form $(x = c)$ or $\left(c < x < c + \dfrac{1}{slope_{max(x)}}\right)$ or $(x > c_x)$ and (ii). for every pair x and y such that $(c < x < c + \dfrac{1}{slope_{max\ (x)}})$ and $(d < y < d + \dfrac{1}{slope_{max\ (y)}})$ appear in (i), the ordering relationship between $slope_{xy}(x - c)$ and $y - d$.

To compute the possible time-successors, three cases are distinguished: **First case:** Each clock x in the region α satisfies the constraint $(x > c_x)$, so α has only one time-successor, itself. This is the case of region $[(x > 2), (y > 2)]$ in Fig.5.

Second case: This case is considered when there is at least, in the region α, one clock x which satisfies the constraint $x = c$ for some $c \le c_x$. The set H_0 contains all clocks appearing in similar constraint form as x. The clock region α will be changed immediately when the time advances, because the fractional part of each clock in H_0 becomes different from 0. The clock regions α and β have the same time-successors where β is specified by: A set of clock constraints which can be given as follows: For each clock $x \in H_0$: (i). If α satisfies $(x = c_x)$ then β satisfies $(x > c_x)$; (ii). If α satisfies $(x = c)$ then β satisfies $(c < x < c + \dfrac{1}{slope_{max(x)}})$. For each clock $x \notin H_0$, the clock constraint in α remains the same in β. The ordering relationship between $slope_{xy}(x - c)$ and $y - d$ of each pair of clocks x, y in α is the same as that in β, such that $x < c_x$ and $y < c_y$ hold in the region α.

For example, in Fig. 5 the time-successors of the region $[(x = 0), (0 < y < 1)]$ are the same as the time-successors of the region $[0 < 2x < y < 1]$.

Final case: If the first and the second case do not apply, then let H_0 be the set of clocks x for which the region α satisfies two constraints: $c < x < c + \dfrac{1}{slope_{max(x)}}$ $and\ slope_{xy}(x - c) \ge y - d.$

For all clocks y for which the region α satisfies $d < y < d + \dfrac{1}{slope_{max(y)}}$ Thus, when time advances, clocks in H_0 take the values $c + \dfrac{1}{slope_{max\ (x)}}$. Therefore, the time-successors of the region α are α, β and all the time-successors of β which is specified by :

1- A set of clock constraints which can be given as follows: (a) For each clock $x \in H_0$, if α satisfies $(c < x < c + \dfrac{1}{slope_{max(x)}})$ then β satisfies $(x = c + \dfrac{1}{slope_{max(x)}})$; (b) For each clock $x \notin H_0$, the clock constraint in α remains the same in β.

2- For each pair of clocks x and y such that $(c < x < c + \dfrac{1}{slope_{max(x)}})$ and $(d < y < d + \dfrac{1}{slope_{max(y)}})$ appear in (1.b), the ordering relationship between $slope_{xy}(x - c)$ and $y - d$ in α remains the same in β.

For example, in Fig. 5 the time-successors of the region $[0 < 2x < y < 1]$ include itself, $[(0 < x < 0,5), (y = 1)]$ and all time-successors of $[(0 < x < 0,5), (y = 1)]$.

Algorithm (region automaton). Let $A = ((S, s_0, H, L_S, T), \pi)$ be a daTA-RT over the set of agents Ag. The region automaton $R(A)$ is an automaton over the alphabet Act such that: - The configurations of $R(A)$ are of the form $< s|\alpha >$ where s is a state of A and α is a clock region. The initial configuration is of the form $< s_0|[v_0] >$ where $v_0(x) = 0$ for every $x \in H$. - A transition of $R(A)$, from the configuration $< s|\alpha >$ to $< s'|\alpha' >$, is labeled by $a \in Act$ iff there is a transition (s, G, a, x, s') in T and a clock region α'' which satisfies, α'' is a time-successor of the region α, and $\alpha'' \vDash g$ and $\alpha' = [\{x\} \mapsto 0]\alpha''$.

5   Conclusion

In this paper we have proposed an extension of the timed automata with action durations model, it has a capacity of describing timed plans with action durations that can be shared in between coordinated agents. We claim that also agents can be heterogeneous, they can reasonably be (re)synchronized to start the execution of any coordinated plan and that they can behave under relative time rates. Taking benefit from the semantics of such model, we demonstrated how to build a finite (time) region graph. The model is illustrated by a simple but realistic use case, wherein the coordination of truck is required. Agents are currently reduced to having one clock; however, the extension to several is immediate. *The implementability investigation*: In its current version our proposal is able to handle timed maximality bisimulation of behaviors; however region graph is not used for implementing practical tools because of the complexity of size and algorithms. A zone graph (based on convex polyhedra called zones) was proposed as an alternative for efficient implementations [10]; we intend to complete this work in this direction particularly in the sense of the scalability domain. As perspectives we intend to explore the ways of   real applications and the formal comparison with other famous specification models such as petri net and its various extensions.

References

1. Alur, R., Dill, D.: A theory of timed automata. Theoretical Computer Science, 183–235 (1994)
2. Kitouni, I., Hachichi, H., Bouaroudj, K., Saidouni, D.E.: Durational Actions Timed Automata: Determinization and Expressiveness. International Journal of Applied Information Systems (IJAIS) 4(2), 1–11 (2012); Published by Foundation of Computer Science, New York, USA
3. Bolognesi, T., Brinksma, E.: Introduction to the ISO specification language LOTOS. Computer Networks and ISDN Systems 14, 25–59 (1987)
4. Courtiat, J.P., Saidouni, D.E.: Relating Maximality-based Semantics to Action Refinement in Process Algebras. In: Proceedings of FORTE 1994, pp. 293–308. Chapman and Hall (1995)
5. Lenzen, C., Locher, T., Wattenhofer, R.: Tight bounds for clock synchronization. In: Proceedings of the 28th ACM Symposium on Principles of Distributed Computing, pp. 46–55 (2009)

6. Pereverzeva, I., Troubitsyna, E., Laibinis, L.: Formal Development of Critical Multi-Agent Systems: A Refinement Approach. In: IEEE European Dependable Computing Conference (EDCC), pp. 156–161 (2012)
7. Guellati, S., Kitouni, I., Matmat, R., Saidouni, D.-E.: Timed Automata with Action Durations - From Theory to Implementation. In: Dregvaite, G., Damasevicius, R. (eds.) ICIST 2014. CCIS, vol. 465, pp. 94–109. Springer, Heidelberg (2014)
8. Corchuelo, R., Arjona, J.L.: A top down approach for MAS protocol descriptions. In: Proceedings of the 2003 ACM Symposium on Applied Computing, pp. 45–49 (2003)
9. Graja, Z., Migeon, F., Maurel, C., Gleizes, M.-P., Kacem, A.H.: A Stepwise Refinement based Development of Self-Organizing Multi-Agent Systems. In: Dalpiaz, F., Dix, J., van Riemsdijk, M.B. (eds.) EMAS 2014. LNCS, vol. 8758, pp. 40–57. Springer, Heidelberg (2014)
10. Bouyer, P., Laroussinie, F.: Model Checking Timed Automata. In: Modeling and Verification of Real-Time Systems, pp. 111–140. ISTE Ltd. John Wiley & Sons, Ltd. (2008)
11. Chaouche, A.-C., El Fallah Seghrouchni, A., Ilié, J.-M., Saïdouni, D.E.: A Higher-Order Agent Model with Contextual Planning Management for Ambient Systems. In: Kowalczyk, R., Nguyen, N.T. (eds.) TCCI XVI. LNCS, vol. 8780, pp. 146–169. Springer, Heidelberg (2014)
12. Layadi, S., Kitouni, I., Belala, N., Saidouni, D.E.: About Decidability of Dynamic Timed Automata with Relative Time Rates. Submitted in: IGI-Global International Journal of Embedded and Real-Time Communication Systems, IJERTCS (2014)
13. Dima, C., Lanotte, R.: Distributed time-asynchronous automata. In: Jones, C.B., Liu, Z., Woodcock, J. (eds.) ICTAC 2007. LNCS, vol. 4711, pp. 185–200. Springer, Heidelberg (2007)
14. Akshay, S., Bollig, B., Gastin, P., Mukund, M., Kumar, K.N.: Distributed Timed Automata with Independently Evolving Clocks. Fundamenta Informaticae 130(4), 377–407 (2014)

Computational Intelligence:
Object Recognition
and Authentification

A Novel Technique For Human Face Recognition Using Fractal Code and Bi-dimensional Subspace

Benouis Mohamed[1], Benkkadour Mohamed Kamel[2],
Tlmesani Redwan[2], and Senouci Mohamed[1]

[1] Computer Science Department, University Of Oran, Algeria
mhbenouis@yahoo.com, msenouci@yahoo.fr
[2] Computer Science Department, UniversitySidi Bel Abbes, Sidi Bel Abbes, Algeria
[2] INTTIC, Oran, Algeria
kamel.live@com, rtlemsani@ito.dz

Abstract. Face recognition is considered as one of the best biometric methods used for human identification and verification; this is because of its unique features that differ from one person to another, and its importance in the security field. This paper proposes an algorithm for face recognition and classification using a system based on WPD, fractal codes and two-dimensional subspace for feature extraction, and Combined Learning Vector Quantization and PNN Classifier as Neural Network approach for classification. This paper presents a new approach for extracted features and face recognition .Fractal codes which are determined by a fractal encoding method are used as feature in this system. Fractal image compression is a relatively recent technique based on the representation of an image by a contractive transform for which the fixed point is close to the original image. Each fractal code consists of five parameters such as corresponding domain coordinates for each range block. Brightness offset and an affine transformation. The proposed approach is tested on ORL and FEI face databases. Experimental results on this database demonstrated the effectiveness of the proposed approach for face recognition with high accuracy compared with previous methods.

Keywords: Biometric · Face recognition · 2DPCA · 2DLDA · DWT · PNN · WPD · IFS · Fractal codes · LVQ

1 Introduction

The security of persons, goods or information is one of the major concerns of the modern societies. Face recognition is one of the most commonly used solutions to perform automatic identification of persons. However, automatic face recognition should consider several factors that contribute to the complexity of this task such as the occultation, changes in lighting, pose, expression and structural components (hair, beard, glasses, etc.)[1]. several techniques have been proposed in the past in order to solve face recognition problems. Each of them evidently has their strengths and weaknesses, which, in most of the cases, depend on the conditions of acquiring

© IFIP International Federation for Information Processing 2015
A. Amine et al. (Eds.): CIIA 2015, IFIP AICT 456, pp. 31–42, 2015.
DOI: 10.1007/978-3-319-19578-0_3

information. Recently, several efforts and research in this domain have been done in order to increase the performance of the recognition, such as support vector machine (SVM),Markov hidden model (HMM), probabilistic methods (Bayesian networks) and artificial neural networks. This latter has attracted researchers because of its effectiveness in detection and classification of shapes, which has been adopted in new face recognition systems [2].

2   Face Recognition System

A face recognition system is a system used for the identification and verification of individuals, which checks if a person belongs to the system's database, and identifies him/her if this is the case.

The methods used in face recognition based on 2D images are divided into three categories: global, local and hybrid methods.

- Local or analytical facial features approaches. This type consists on applying transformations in specific locations of the image, most frequently around the features points (corners of the eyes, mouth, nose,). They therefore require a prior knowledge of the images...
- Global approaches use the entire surface of the face as a source of information without considering the local characteristics such as eyes, mouth, etc.
- Hybrid methods associate the advantages of global and local methods by combining the detection of geometrical characteristics (or structural) with the extraction of local appearance characteristics.

This article is organized as follows: Basic notions concerning Two-dimensional subspace, wavelet transform theory are provided in Section 2. Fractal codes features are presented in section 3. Feature vectors results from two-dimensional subspaces is applied to a Combined LVQ and PNN classifier are described in Section 4. Section 5 provides face recognition system based on PNN, LVQ, the experimental results and Comparison between the serval's types of features obtained using WPD, DWT, IFS, 2DPCA and 2DLDA. A comparison with other approaches is also done in section 6. Conclusion and future works are presented in Section 7.

2.1   Two-Dimensional Principal Component Approach Analysis (2DPCA)

Proposed by Yang in 2004 [4], 2DPCA is a method of feature extraction and dimensionality reduction based on Principal Component Analysis (PCA) that deals directly with face images as matrices without having to turn them into vectors like as the traditional global approach.

2.2   The Steps of Face Recognition by 2DPCA

Considering training set S of N face images, the idea of this technique is to project a matrix X of size (n×m) via a linear transformation like that:

$$Y_i = X . R_i \tag{1}$$

Where Y_i is the principal component vector of size (n 1), and R_i is the base projection vector of size (m 1). The optimal vector R_i of the projection is obtained by maximizing the total generalized variance criterion

$$J(R) = R^T . G_t . R \tag{2}$$

Where G_t is the covariance matrix of size (m m) given by:

$$G_t = \frac{1}{M} \sum_{j=1}^{M} (X_j - \overline{X})^T (X_j - \overline{X}) \tag{3}$$

With X_j: The jth image of the training set
$\overline{X}$: The average image of all the images in the training set.

$$\overline{X} = \frac{1}{M} \sum_{j=1}^{M} X_j \tag{4}$$

In general, one optimal projection axis is not enough. We must select a set of projection axes like:

$$\{R_1, R_2, \ldots, R_d\} = arg\ max\ J(R) \qquad (5)$$

$R_i^T . R_j = 0, i \neq j, i, j = 1, \ldots, d$
These axes are the eigenvectors of the covariance matrix corresponding to the largest "d" Eigenvalues. The extraction of characteristics of an image using 2DPCA is as follows

$$Y_k = X . R_k \quad ; k=1 \ldots d \tag{6}$$

Where $[R_1, R_2, \ldots, R_d]$ is the projection matrix and $[Y_1, Y_2, \ldots, Y_d]$ is the features matrix of the image X.

2.3   The 2DLDA Approach

In 2004, Li and Yuan [5] have proposed a new two-dimensional LDA approach. The main difference between 2DLDA and the classic LDA is in the data representation model. Classic LDA is based on the analysis of vectors, while the 2DLDA algorithm is based on the analysis of matrices.

2.4   Face Recognition Using 2D LDA

Let X is a vector of the n-dimensional unitary columns. The main idea of this approach is to project the random image matrix of size $(m \times n)$ on X by the following linear transformation:

$$Y_i = A_j X \tag{7}$$

Y: the m-dimensional feature vector of the projected image A.

Let us suppose L: class numbers.

M: The total number of training images

The training image is represented by a matrix $m \times nA_j (j = 1, \ldots \ldots M)$

$\bar{A}_i$ (i=1 …L): The mean of all classes

N_i: Number of samples in each class

The optimal vector projection is selected as a matrix with orthonormal columns that maximizes the ratio of the determinant of the dispersion matrix of the projected inter-class images to the determinant of the dispersion matrix of the projected intra-class images;

$$J_{FLD}(X_{opt}) = \arg\max_W \frac{|X^T S_b X|}{|X^T S_w X|} \tag{8}$$

$$P_b = \text{trace } (S_b)$$

$$P_W = \text{trace } (S_W)$$

The unitary vector X maximizing J(X) is called the optimal projection axis. The optimal projection is chosen when X_{OPT} maximizes the criterion, as the following equation:

$$X_{OPT} = argmax_X J(X) \tag{9}$$

If S_W is invertible, the solution of optimization is to solve the generalized eigenvalue problem.

$$S_b X_{opt} = \lambda S_W X_{opt} \tag{10}$$

Like that λ is the maximum Eigenvalues of $S_W^{-1} S_b$

In general, it is not enough to have only one optimal projection axis. We need to select a set of projection axes,$x_1, x_2, \ldots x_d$ under the following constraints:

$$\{x_1, x_2, \ldots x_d\} = argmax_X J(X) \tag{11}$$

Indeed, the optimal projection axes$x_1, x_2, \ldots x_d$ are orthonormal eigenvectors of $S_W^{-1} S_b$ corresponding to the best first "d" eigenvalues permitting to create a new projection matrix X, which is a matrix of size n × d :$X = [x_1, x_2, \ldots x_d]$

We will use the 2DLDA optimal projection vectors $x_1, x_2, \ldots x_d$ to extract the image features; we use the equation (08).

3   Discrete Wavelet Transform

Discrete wavelet transform (DWT) is a well-known signal processing field tool; it is widely used in feature extraction and compression and de-noising applications. The discrete wavelet transform has been used in various face recognition studies. The main advantage of the wavelet transform over the Fourier transform is the time-scale location. Mallat [8] shows that the DWT may be implemented using a filters bank including a low-pass filter (PB) and a high-pass filter (PH).

Discrete Wavelet Package Decomposition (D-WPD) is a wavelet transform where signal is passed through more filters that the Discrete Wavelet Transform (DWT). In the DWT, each level is calculated by passing only the previous approximation coefficients through low and high pass filters. However in the D-WPD, both the detail and approximation coefficients are decomposed [7] [8].

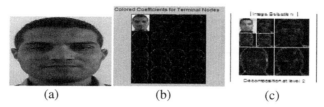

(a)   (b)   (c)

Fig. 1. Wavelet decomposition at different levels
(a) Original image
(b) 2-level wavelet decomposition using WPD
(c) 2-levels wavelet decomposition using DWT

4   Fractal Theory Codes

Fractal theory of iterated contractive transformation has been used in several areas of image processing and computer vision. In this method, similarity between different parts of an image is used for representing of an image by a set of contractive transforms on the space of images, for which the fixed point is close to the original image. This concept was first proposed by Barnsley [9], [10]. Jacquin was the first to publish an implementation of fractal image coding in [11]. Despite the number of researchers and the proposed methods, several factors can significantly affect face recognition performances, such as the pose, the presence/absence of structural components, facial expressions, occlusion, and illumination variations. Different image compression methods have been focused for a long time to reduce this massive information, but fractal image compression is a relatively recent technique based on representation of an image by contractive transforms, for which the fixed point is close to original image.

Suppose we are dealing with a 64*64 binary image in which each pixel can have on of 256 levels (ranging from black to white). Let R_1, R2,....., R_{256} be 4*4 non-overlapping sub-squares of the image (range blocks); and let D be the collection of all 8*8 pixel overlapping sub-squares of the image (Domain blocks) as depicted in Fig .2 The collection D contains 57*57=3249 squares. For each R block, search through all of D blocks a $D_i \in D$ which minimizes equation (12) .There 8 ways to map one square onto another. Each square can be rotated to 4 orientations or flipped and rotated into 4 other orientations as shown in Fig.2 having 8 different affine transformations means comparing 8*3249=25992 domain squares with each of the 256 range squares.

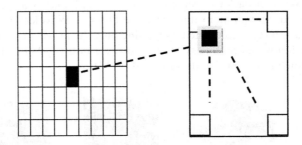

Fig. 2. One of the block mapping in partitioned function systems representation (IFS)

1	2
3	4

4	3
2	1

3	4
1	2

2	1
4	3

4	2
3	1

2	4
1	3

3	1
4	2

1	3
2	4

Fig. 3. Eight different affine transformations

$$collage\ Error = min\|R_i - w(D_i)\|^2 \tag{12}$$

As mentioned before ,a D_i block has 4 times as many pixels as an R_i ,so we must either sub-sample (choose 1 from each 2*2 sub-square of D_i) or average the 2*2 sub-squares corresponding to each pixel of R when we minimize equation (12) .minimizing equation means two things .First it means finding a good choice for Di second, it means finding a good contrast and brightness setting S_i and O_i for W_i. In equation (13)

$$w_i \begin{bmatrix} x \\ y \\ z \end{bmatrix} = \begin{bmatrix} a_i & b_i & 0 \\ c_i & d_i & 0 \\ 0 & 0 & s_i \end{bmatrix} \begin{bmatrix} x \\ y \\ z \end{bmatrix} + \begin{bmatrix} c_i \\ f_i \\ o_i \end{bmatrix} \tag{13}$$

A choice of D_i , along with a corresponding S_i and O_i determines a map W_i. The type of image partitioning used for the range blocks can be so different. A wide variety of partitions have been investigated, the majority being composed of rectangular blocks. Different types of range block partitioning were described in[12].In this research we used the simplest possible range partition consists of the size square blocks, that is called fixed size square blocks (FSSB) partitioning. The procedure for finding a fractal model for a given image is called encoding; compression; or searching for a fractal image representation. After finding the best match ,fractal elements which of 6 real numbers (a, b, c, d, e, f) are selected as follows . (a, b, c, d) are (x, y) coordinates of the D block and its corresponding R block respectively .(e) is the index of affine transformation that makes the best match.(it is a number between 1 and 8) ,(f) is the intensity is a number between 0 and 256.

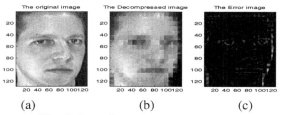

(a)   (b)   (c)

Fig. 4. Decoding algorithm results (IFS)
(a) Original image
(b) Decoded image after 8 iteration for N=8
(c) The error image

In this paper, fractal code is introduced in order to extract the face features from the normalized face image based WPD. After fractal coding, where each domain is compared with all regions of the image, we obtain a set of transformations which can approximate the face image. Each transformation is represented by parameters of contrastS_i, brightness O_i, spatial coordinates of Range/Domain, and rotation W_i.The output of fractal code is the feature matrix with 2D-dimension used as a database of face which is applied two-dimensional subspace for reduction, discrimination and speed time.

5   Face Classification Using Neural Networks

Several studies have shown improved face recognition systems using a neural classification compared to classification based on Euclidean distance measure [14].

5.1   Probabilistic Neural Networks

The probability neural network is proposed by D. F. Specht for solving the problem of classification in 1988 [15]. The theoretical foundation is developed based on Bayes decision theory, and implemented in feed-forward network architecture.
PNN represent mathematically by the following expression

$$a = radbas(\|IW - x\|b) \tag{14}$$

$$y = compet(LW\alpha) \tag{15}$$

The structure PNN: The PNN architecture consists of two layers [15] [16]:

The first layer computes distances from input vector to the input weights (IW) and produces a vector whose elements indicate how close the input is to the IW.

The second layer sums these contributions for each class of inputs to produce as its net output a vector of probabilities .Finally a compete transfer function on the output of the second layer picks up the maximum of these probabilities and produces a 1 for that class and a 0 for the other classes. The architecture for this system is shown above.

The probability of neural network with backs propagation networks in each hidden unit can approximate any continuous non linear function. In this paper, we use the Gaussian function as the activation function:

$$radbas = \exp\left[(-n^2)\right] \tag{16}$$

Finally, one or many larger values are chosen as the output unit that indicates these data points are in the same class via a competition transfer function from the output of summation unit [11], i.e.

$$compet(n) = e_i = [000\ 0_1 0\ .....\ 0_i], n(I) = MAX(n)$$

5.2   Linear Vector Quantization (LVQ)

The vector quantization technique was originally evoked by Tuevo Kohonen in the mid 80's [15] [17]. Both Vector quantization network and self organizing maps are based on the Kohonen layer, which is capable of sorting items into appropriate categories of similar objects. Such kinds of networks find their application in classification and segmentation problems.

LVQ network comprises of three layers: Input layer, Competitive layer and Output layer [17]. The number of neurons in each layer depends on the input data and the class of the system. The input neurons are as many as the input matrix features of the training pattern, and the number of the output neurons is equal to the number of person's to which face patterns are classified. The number of hidden neurons is heuristic .In order to implement a face recognition system by our approach, we follow this methodology:

- stage pre-processing using technique WPD
- coding image using fractal code
- feature extraction using 2DPCA/2DLDA
- classification using LVQ and PNN network

6   Results and Discussion

In order to evaluate and test our approach described for face recognition system, we chose three databases: ORL, FEI [18] [19] and our database of our laboratory. All experiences were performed in Matlab installed on a laptop with a dual core processor T5870 with 2.03 GHz and 2 GB of RAM.

To evaluate the performance of our proposed approach, we chose two test databases: ORL and FEI. The global performance of algorithms tested on the FEI database is not as better as that of the ORL database. There are two main reasons:

- The image quality of the ORL database is better than that of the FEI database.

- The FEI database is more complex due to variations in the face details and head orientations.
- After a series of experiences, we chose the best values of parameters in order to fix the choice of Eigenvalues, which give a better recognition rate.

Adding Some Effects: It is wanted to test our system with and without added noisy in the two data base in order to evaluate robustness of these approaches namely 2DPCA, 2DLDA, DWT,WPD ,fractal codes combined by using two classifier LVQ and PNN.

Noise: Two types of noise are used in this simulation: the Saltand Pepper type noise with a noise density a=0.06 (Figure 5 (a)) and Gaussian noise with mean m=0, variance v=0.04 .Figure 5 illustrates these effects which are obtained as follows.

(**a**)Salt&pepper Noise (**b**) Gaussian Noise (**c**) Gaussian Noise m=0, v=0.01 m=0, v=0.04

(**a**)Salt&pepper Noise (**b**) Gaussian Noise (**c**) Gaussian Noise m=0, v=0.01 m=0, v=0.04

Fig. 5. Adding Noise (database face ORL &FEI)

The Pre-processing Stage: We proposed to add a preprocessing stage in order to improve our system's performance in speed by reducing the size and eliminating redundant information from the face images by the means of the DWT and WPD technique, and in other hand reduce the memory and compute of our neural network-training algorithm (PNN) and LVQ.

We performed face recognition analysis through WPD and DWT with various wavelet series: Daubechies, Gabor, Coiflets, Symlets and Gauss. In order to select a best wavelet to enhance a rate recognition.

The fractal code is used on WPD and DWT coefficients, derived from WPD to generate detailed high frequency features of animation which forms Feature set one. In order to have fractal feature vectors with the same length, the size of the face must be normalized (32 × 32). The normalized image is coded by 64 transformations using fractal code. Consequently, we obtained 320 fractal features as each transformation is coded on 5 parameters, as already explained in Section 3. Table 2 shows the performance of our system using fractal features for the two databases.

Feature Extraction Using 2DPCA/2DLDA: After reducing the dimensional of the face images using IFS. We used the 2DPCA and 2DLDA feature extraction approaches in order to extract the weight images (Features images in the new space) which must be converted into vectors before implementing the classifier network (LVQ and PNN).

Choice of the Number of Eigenvalues: Two dimensional methods do not escape this problem, and the choice of the appropriate number depends on the used method and faces database. In our experiences, we have selected the best eigenvalues corresponding to the best variance values (eigenvectors)

Selection Parameters and Architecture System Classifier
PNN :our neural network training algorithm used in system face recognition is not require many parameters compared other neural networks (MLP,BP,LVQ.etc),that only parameter that is needed for performance of the network is the smoothing parameter σ .Usually, the researchers need to try different σ in a certain range to obtain one that can reach the optimum accuracy[16][17]. To get a higher recognition rate, we have made a series of experiments to choose the best smoothing parameter σ used in PNN. The probabilistic Neural Network used in our system is composed of two layers

Input Layer: The first layer is the input layer and the number of hidden unit is the number of independent variables and receives the input data (number of feature extraction for each approach used in this paper)

Output Layer: gives the number of faces used in the Database training (ex: ORL 200 person's).

LVQ: The changes of LVQ classifier parameters have a high effect on the classification results. In this paper, we found that the best learning rate increases the recognition rate of the system whereas the learning rate is a critical parameter that affected in the recognition process. We use a different number of learning rate (0.1, 0.2, 0.3, and 0.6) with 500 epochs and 80 hidden Neurons experiments.

Table 1. The recognition rate obtained by different methods on the database ORL with added noisy

Type of classifier	DWT-2DPCA	DWT-2DLDA	WPD-2DPCA	WPD-2DLDA
LVQ	93%	94%	**94%**	**96%**
PNN	94.8%	95%	**96%**	**98%**

Table 2. The recognition rate obtained by different methods on the database FEI with added noisy

Type of classifier	WPD-2DPCA	WPD-2DLDA	WPD/IFS-2DPCA	WPD/IFS-2DLDA
LVQ	90%	92 .8%	**95%**	**96%**
PNN	95%	96%	**99%**	**99%**

Table 3. The running time (s) obtained by different methods on the database FEI with added noisy

	DWT-2DPCA	WPD-2DLDA	WPD&IFS-2DPCA	WPD&IFS-2DLDA
PNN	1.20	1.25	**2.10**	**2.05**
LVQ	1.25	1.45	**2.08**	**1.98**

Discussion

After these series of experiments, we clearly see the superiority of the two-dimensional methods combined with a probabilistic neural classifier combining those of a LVQ classifier (table.1).

In table 2 ,we present the recognition rate obtained when using all fractal features ,and those reduced by the bi-dimensional subspace analysis .There is trade -off between encoding time and average of recognition rate because when N(domain range decreases ,size of features vector will increase so LVQ and PNN learns more details and its generalization ability become weak. As feature extraction is faster for N=8 and average of recognition rate is also fair so we encoded input faces with this R blocks size. The classification results for face is shown in table .2 for N=8.

We also note that the choice of optimal component and the choice smoothing parameter, which represents a better recognition, rate for methods, 2DPCA and 2DLDA and accuracy of classification PNN and LVQ.

In table 3, we present the running time obtained when using fractal codes .computational complexity of fractal encoding is the disadvantage of fractal features in our system which can be improving by adaptive search to speed-up fractal image compression.

7 Conclusion

In this paper, we propose an approach for face recognition based on the combination of two approaches, one used for the reduction of space and feature extractions in two dimensions and the other for classification and decision.

A hybrid approach is introduced in which, through the bi-dimensional subspace analysis, the most discriminating wavelet fractal features are extracted and used as the input of a neural network (LVQ, PNN). The performance of our method is both due to the fidelity of fractal coding for representing images, the WPD algorithm to speed up the features extraction step, and the 2DPCA and 2DLDA which highlights all discriminating features.

As a perspective, we propose to use this approach in an uncontrolled environment (video surveillance) based on video sequences (dynamic images) in order to make the task of face recognition more robust.

References

1. Jain, A.K. (ed.).: Handbook of Biometrics. Michigan State University, USA Patrick Flynn University of Notre Dame, USA Arun A. Ross West Virginia University, USA © Springer Science+Business Media, LLC (2008)
2. Pato, J.N., Millett, L.I. (eds.).: Biometric recognition challenges and opportunities Whither Biometrics Committee Computer Science and Telecommunications Board Division on Engineering and Physical Sciences Copyright by the National Academy of Sciences (2010)
3. Zhang, D., Zhou, Z.-H. (2D) 2PCA: Two-directional two-dimensional PCA for efficient face representation and recognition. Neuro Computing 69, 224–231 (2005)
4. Nguyen, N., Liu, W., Venkatesh, S.: Random Subspace Two-Dimensional PCA for Face Recognition. Department of Computing, Curtin University of Technology, WA 6845, Australia
5. Yang, J., Zhang, D.: Two-Dimensional PCA: A New Approach to Appearance-Based Face Representation and Recognition 26(1) (January 2004)
6. Noushath, S., Kumar, G.H., Shivakumara, P. (2D)LDA: An efficient approach for face recognition. Pattern Recognition 39(7), 1396–1400 (2006)
7. Mallat, S.: A theory of multiresolution signal decomposition: the wavelet representation. IEEE Transactions on Pattern Analysis and Machine Intelligence 11(7), 674–693 (1989)
8. Feng, G.C., Yuen, P.C., Dai, D.Q.: Human face recognition using PCA on wavelet subband. SPIE Journal of Electronic Imaging 9(2), 226–233 (2000)
9. Barnsley, M.: Fractals Everywhere. Academic Press, San Diego (1988)
10. Jacquin, A.E.: Fractal image coding: A review. Proc. of the IEEE 81, 1451–1465 (1993)
11. Jacquin, A.E.: A Fractal Theory of Iterated Markov Operators with Applications to Digital
12. Image Coding, PhD thesis, Georgia Tech, 1989. Y. Fisher, Fractal Image Compression: Theory and Application, Springer-Verlag Inc. (1995)
13. Ebrahimpour-Komleh, H.: Face recognition using fractal codes. In: Proceedings of International Conference on Image Processing 2001. IEEE, Thessaloniki (2001)
14. Nazish.: Face recognition using neural networks. Proc. IEEE INMIC 2001, 277–281 (2007)
15. Specht, D.F.: Probabilistic neural network and the polynomial adaline as complementary techniques for classification. IEEE Trans. Neural Networks 1(1), 111–121 (1990)
16. Neural network toolbox matlabUser's Guide COPYRIGHT 1992 - 2002 by The MathWorks, Inc.
17. Computational intelligence paradigms: theory & applications using MATLAB / S. Sumathi and Surekha Paneerselvam. 2010 by Taylor and Francis Group
18. ORL. The ORL face database at the AT&T (Olivetti) Research Laboratory (1992)
19. FEI. The FEI face database at the Artificial Intelligence Laboratory of FEI in São Bernardo do Campo, São Paulo, Brazil (June 2005/March 2006)

Computational Intelligence:
Image Processing

A New Rotation-Invariant Approach
for Texture Analysis

Izem Hamouchene[✉] and Saliha Aouat

Artificial Intelligence Laboratory (LRIA), Computer science Department,
University of sciences and technology (USTHB), Algiers, Algeria
{ihamouchene,saouat}@usthb.dz

Abstract. Image processing and pattern recognition are one of the most important area of research in computer science. Recently, several studies have been made and efficient approaches have been proposed to provide efficient solutions to many real and industrial problems. Texture analysis is a fundamental field of image processing because all surfaces of objects are textured in nature. Thus, we proposed a new texture analysis method. In this paper, we proposed a novel texture analysis approach based on a recent feature extraction method called neighbor based binary pattern (NBP). The NBP method extract the local micro texture and is robust against rotation, which is a key problem in image processing. The proposed system extract two-reference NBP histograms from the texture in order to calculate a model of the texture. Finally, several models have been constructed to be able to recognize textures even after rotation. Textured images from Brodatz album database were used in the evaluation. Experimental studies have illustrated that the proposed system obtain very encouraging results robust to rotation compared to classical method.

Keywords: Rotation invariance · Texture analysis · Feature extraction · Neighbor based binary pattern

1   Introduction

Texture analysis is one of fundamental domain in image processing and computer vision. In today's world, automatic image processing without human intervention has become an active research area. In fact, there is not a strict definition of the texture, but the texture can be defined as a visual pattern composed of entities that have characteristic such as brightness, color, shape, size, etc. Texture is present in most of real life objects in nature. This makes it fundamental and essential to analyze images. Texture can be subdivided into coarse, micro, macro, regular, periodic, aperiodic, random and stochastic type [1].

Texture analysis has been presented by Haralick [5]. Different approaches have been developed structural, statistical and transformed based approach. These approaches have been applied in different, various and recent applications such as face recognition [2], Fingerprint matching [3] and image segmentation [4]. Textured images are analyzed by identifying the local and global properties of the images.

© IFIP International Federation for Information Processing 2015
A. Amine et al. (Eds.): CIIA 2015, IFIP AICT 456, pp. 45–53, 2015.
DOI: 10.1007/978-3-319-19578-0_4

One of the key problem of image analysis is rotation. Indeed, how recognize a researched texture even after rotation. The rotation invariant problem remains unsolved today. In this study, we proposed a new system robust against rotation and extract pertinent patterns of the texture.

This paper is organized as follows: The next section we explain the recent feature extraction method applied on the proposed system, the neighbor based binary pattern (NBP). In section 3 we present the architecture of our proposed system. Section 4 illustrates experimental results using the proposed system and the last section conclude the paper.

2   Neighbor Based Binary Pattern

The neighbor based binary pattern (NBP) is a very simple and efficient method to describe the texture. The NBP method was proposed for the first time by Izem et al. [6] [7]. This method was inspired by a famous feature extraction operator called Local Binary Pattern (LBP) [8] [9]. The important advantage of the LBP operator is its monotonic gray-scale transformation invariance [10] [11] [12] and its computational simplicity which makes it able to analyze an image in a very short time.

The idea of the NBP method is to consider one analysis window of 3x3 pixels. Each neighbor of the central pixel is thresholded by the next neighbor. Thus, if the central pixel is a noise it is not a problem because the value of the central pixel is not considered. In the other hand, if one neighbor is a noise, not all the pattern will be wrong but only 1 bit. . This minimizes the error rate of the recognition. So, each neighbor is encoded by the value 1 if its value is greater than the next neighbor is and 0 otherwise. The binary code is interpreted as a decimal number and represent the value of the central pixel in the NBP number. This process is illustrated in Fig. 1

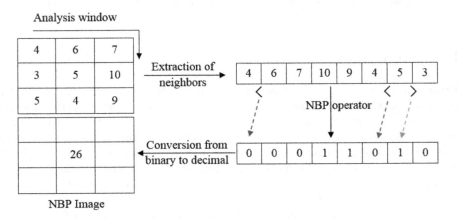

Fig. 1. Neighbor based Binary Pattern

Fig. 1. Illustrates the obtained NBP value using the NBP method. The first neighbor (value 4) is less than the second (value 6). Thus, the first neighbor is encoded by the value 0. After that, the obtained binary code is converted into a decimal number.

Because it is difficult to find a general parametric model for this distribution, the features of the obtained NBP image are approximated by a two dimensional discrete patterns histogram. This histogram is created to collect up the occurrences of each pattern. The obtained histogram is used to describe the texture as show in Fig. 2. Usually, the histograms are normalized.

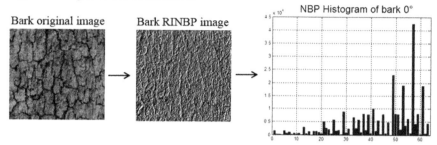

Fig. 2. Extraction of the NBP histogram

Fig. 2. Illustrates the extraction of the NBP histogram. We can notice from the Fig. 2 that a small rotation in the input image would cause a change in the output NBP code. Thus, if the patterns are extracted from the input image and this image is rotated by an angel θ, the extracted patterns will be different because the extraction starts always from the same point. That is the weakness of the classical LBP operator. In this work, we proposed a new system robust against the rotation problem.

3   Proposed system

In this section, we will explain the architecture of the proposed system. This system is robust against rotation and solve the rotation invariant problem. Some applications example will be illustrated and one illustration, which summarizes the proposed system, will be given.

The idea of the proposed system is to construct a model histogram of each texture. After that, compare the histogram of the researched texture with all model histograms to classify the texture. In order to solve the rotation problem, which is a fundamental problem on image processing and pattern recognition, we proposed to create a model histogram from each texture. First, two NBP histogram are extracted from two textured images, which have the same texture but different orientation. After that, a threshold histogram ($Hist_{th}$) is calculated based on the two NBP histograms. The threshold histogram contains the minimum and the maximum value of each bin of the two histograms. Indeed, the $Hist_{th}$ is the union of the two NBP histograms. This process is illustrated in Fig. 3.

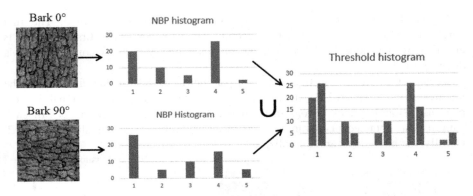

Fig. 3. Construction of the model histogram

Fig. 3. Illustrates the construction of the model histogram of the Bark texture. The threshold histogram of the Bark texture is constructed using the angles 0 and 90. Each bin of the threshold histogram, called model histogram, is an interval between the minimum and the maximum of the two NBP histogram of the two references images. Thus, a double threshold histogram is obtained and considered as a model of the texture.

In order to classify one query texture, a similarity distance is calculated between the NBP histogram of the query texture and the model histogram. The similarity vector is calculated following the formula 1.

$$- \ \vdots \ \vdots \ \vdots \vdots \ . \qquad = \ - \ \vdots \ \vdots \ \vdots \qquad \vdots \ \vdots \ \vdots \qquad (1)$$

Where his_{tq} is the NBP histogram of the researched texture. $Hist_{th}$ is the model histogram. Finally, a binary vector v is extracted where 1 means that the bin belongs to the interval of the model and 0 otherwise. The extraction of the similarity vector v is illustrated in Fig. 4.

Figure 4 illustrates the extraction of the similarity vector v. First, the NBP histogram is extracted from the query texture. After that, the intersection between the NBP histogram and the model histogram is encoded by 1, if the bin is in the double threshold, and 0 otherwise. The number of occurrence of the value 1 represents the similarity measure.

Query texture NBP histogram

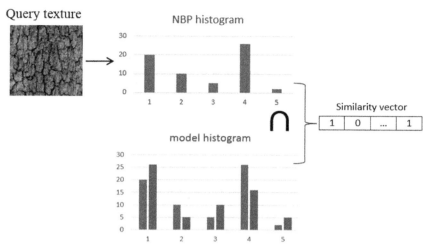

Fig. 4. Extraction of the similarity vector

4 Experimental results

In this section, the evaluation of the proposed system will be illustrated. In order to evaluate the performances of our proposed system, we used textured images from Brodatz album database [13]. Brodatz album is a famous benchmark for textured images. In the experimentation, we used twelve textured images (bark, brick, bubbles, grass, leather, pigskin, raffia, sand, straw, water, weave and wood) illustrated in Fig. 5.

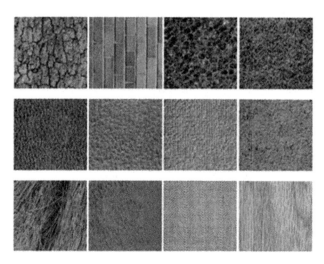

Fig. 5. Textured images from Brodatz album

Each image is digitized at seven different rotation angles: 0, 30, 60, 90, 120, 150, and 200 degree. The size of the images are 512x512 pixels with 256 gray levels as illustrated in Fig. 6, which contains a total of 84 images (12 different images with their 7 rotations).

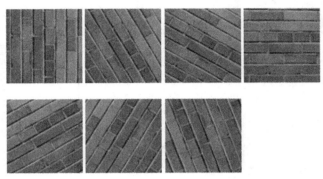

Fig. 6. Brick texture on seven orientation

In order to construct the model database of the system, model histograms are extracted from each texture. Thus, we obtain twelve model histograms. A classification process is applied to classify the query textures. First, the NBP histogram of the query texture is extracted. After that, the similarity measure is calculated between the NBP histogram of the researched texture and all model histograms of the system. Finally, the query texture is classified according to the most similar model.

In the evaluation part, all textured images of the database are considered as query texture. So, 84 test images (twenty images and its seven different orientation).

In order to compare the proposed system and the traditional system; the recognition averages of each texture are compared. The traditional texture classification system consider one textured image of each texture as reference. After that, the NBP histogram of the query texture is compared with all NBP histograms of the reference images and classified according to the most similar texture. The average recognition rate of each texture of the database (texture1 to texture 12) using the two recognition systems are illustrated in Table 1.

Table 1 illustrates the average of the recognition rate of each texture. We can notice that few textures are better recognized using the traditional method. However, most of all textures are well recognized using the proposed system and better classified. The traditional system consider only one orientation as reference. In fact, the weaknesses of the traditional system (rotation) are improved in our method with the model histogram (Double threshold histogram). This allows us to analyze the image with different orientations. This represents the strength of our method. The obtained comparison results are also illustrated in Fig. 7.

Table 1. Recognition rate of each texture

System	Traditional	Proposed
Bark	100,00	100,00
Brick	85,71	81,23
Bubbles	100,00	95,91
Grass	71,42	100,00
Leather	55,10	85,71
Pigskin	73,46	100,00
Raffia	51,02	100,00
Sand	100,00	100,00
Straw	42,85	95,26
Water	46,93	100,00
Weave	100,00	100,00
Wood	46,93	100,00
Recognition Rate	**67,19**	**89,09**

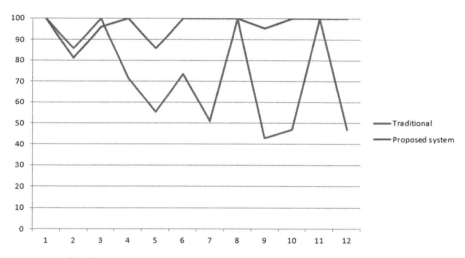

Fig. 7. Recognition rate using the traditional and proposed system

We can notice in the Fig. 7 that the traditional system (blue histogram) gives a lower performance compared to the proposed method (red histogram). Thus, we can see that the results given by our method are better than the classical method.

From the experiments and based on these obtained results, the global rate of the classical method is 67,19% and the proposed method is 89,09%. We can draw a conclusion that the proposed method, which is based on double threshold model histogram, is robust against rotation. Thus, the proposed system extract a robust model from the texture.

5   Conclusion

In this paper, we proposed a new rotation invariant system using the NBP method to extract models that describe the texture. First, the NBP method is applied on two textured images, which are in different orientation. After that, a double threshold histogram is calculated based on the two NBP histograms extracted from the two images and considered as model of the input texture. The model histogram is the union of the two NBP histograms. Finally, this process is applied on all textures of the database to extract models from each texture.

A similarity measure is calculated between the query texture and the model histograms. This measure is the intersection between the NBP histogram of the query texture and all model histograms. Each bin of the query texture histogram is encoded by 1 if its value is between the double threshold model histogram and 0 otherwise. Finally, a binary vector is extracted, which is the similarity vector. The query texture is classified according to the most similar vector. The obtained results show the efficiency of the proposed method compared to the traditional system. The robustness against rotation of the model histogram and the applied feature extraction method are the advantages of the proposed system.

In future works, we will combine other approaches to get more information from the texture like multi resolution methods. We will also improve the classification and the similarity measure to improve the recognition rate. We will also study the behavior and the robustness of our approach applied on real textured images.

References

1. Richards, W., Polit, A.: Texture matching. Kybernatic 16, 155–162 (1974)
2. Baohua, Y., Yuan, H., Jiuliang, C.: Combining Local Binary Pattern and Local Phase Quantization for Face Recognition. In: Biometrics and Security Technologies (ISBAST), pp. 51–53 (March 2012)
3. Jain, A.K., Ross, A., Prabhakar, S.: Fingerprint matching using minutiae and texture features. In: International Conference on Image Processing, vol. 3, pp. 282–285 (2001)
4. Hamouchene, I., Aouat, S., Lacheheb, H.: Texture Segmentation and Matching Using LBP Operator and GLCM Matrix. In: Chen, L., Kapoor, S., Bhatia, R. (eds.) Intelligent Systems for Science and Information. SCI, vol. 542, pp. 389–407. Springer, Heidelberg (2014)
5. Harlick, R.: Statistical and structural approaches to texture. Proc. of IEEE 67(5), 786–804 (1979)
6. Hamouchene, I., Aouat, S.: A New Texture Analysis Approach for Iris Recognition. In: AASRI Conference on Circuit and Signal Processing (CSP 2014), vol. 9, pp. 2–7 (2014)
7. Hamouchene, I., Aouat, S.: A cognitive approach for texture analysis using neighbors-based binary patterns. In: IEEE 13th International Conference on Cognitive Informatics & Cognitive Computing (ICCI*CC), August 18-20, pp. 94–99 (2014)
8. Ojala, T., Pietikäinen, M., Harwood, D.: A Comparative Study of Texture Measures with Classification Based on Feature Distributions. Pattern Recognition 29, 51–59 (1996)
9. Ojala, T., Pietikäinen, M.: Unsupervised Texture Segmentation Using Feature Distributions. Pattern Recognition 32, 477–486 (1999)

10. Guo, Z., Zhang, L., Zhang, D.: A Completed Modeling of Local Binary Pattern Operator for Texture Classification. IEEE Transactions on Image Processing 19(6), 1657–1663 (2010)
11. Xueming, Q., Xian-Sheng, H., Ping, C., Liangjun, K.: An effective local binary patterns texture descriptor with pyramid representation. Pattern Recognition 44(10-11), 2502–2515 (2011)
12. Baohua, Y., Yuan, H., Jiuliang, C.: Combining Local Binary Pattern and Local Phase Quantization for Face Recognition. In: Biometrics and Security Technologies (ISBAST), pp. 51–53 (March 2012)
13. Brodatz, P.: Textures: A Photographic Album for Artists and Designers. Dover Publications, New York (1966)

Multi-CPU/Multi-GPU Based Framework for Multimedia Processing

Sidi Ahmed Mahmoudi[✉] and Pierre Manneback

University of Mons, Faculty of Engineering, Computer science department
20, Place du Parc. Mons, Belgium
{Sidi.Mahmoudi,Pierre.Manneback}@umons.ac.be

Abstract. Image and video processing algorithms present a necessary tool for various domains related to computer vision such as medical applications, pattern recognition and real time video processing methods. The performance of these algorithms have been severely hampered by their high intensive computation since the new video standards, especially those in high definitions require more resources and memory to achieve their computations. In this paper, we propose a new framework for multimedia (single image, multiple images, multiple videos, video in real time) processing that exploits the full computing power of heterogeneous machines. This framework enables to select firstly the computing units (CPU or/and GPU) for processing, and secondly the methods to be applied depending on the type of media to process and the algorithm complexity. The framework exploits efficient scheduling strategies, and allows to reduce significantly data transfer times thanks to an efficient management of GPU memories and to the overlapping of data copies by kernels executions. Otherwise, the framework includes several GPU-based image and video primitive functions, such as silhouette extraction, corners detection, contours extraction, sparse and dense optical flow estimation. These primitives are exploited in different applications such as vertebra segmentation in X-ray and MR images, videos indexation, event detection and localization in multi-user scenarios. Experimental results have been obtained by applying the framework on different computer vision methods showing a global speedup ranging from 5 to 100, by comparison with sequential CPU implementations.

Keywords: GPU · Heterogeneous architectures · Image and video processing · Medical imaging · Motion tracking

1 Introduction

During the last years, the architecture of central processing units (CPUs) has so evolved that the number of integrated computing units has been multiplied. This evolution is reflected in both general (CPU) and graphic (GPU) processors which present a large number of computing units, their power has far exceeded the CPUs ones. In this context, image and video processing algorithms are well adapted for acceleration on the GPU by exploiting its processing units in parallel,

© IFIP International Federation for Information Processing 2015
A. Amine et al. (Eds.): CIIA 2015, IFIP AICT 456, pp. 54–65, 2015.
DOI: 10.1007/978-3-319-19578-0_5

since they consist mainly of a common computation over many pixels. Several GPU computing approaches have recently been proposed. Although they present a great potential of GPU platform, hardly any is able to process high definition image and video efficiently and accordingly to the type of Medias (single image, multiple image, multiple videos and video in real time). Thus, there was a need to develop a framework capable of addressing the outlined problem.

In literature, one can categorize two types of related works based on the exploitation of parallel and heterogeneous platforms for multimedia processing: one related to image processing on GPU such as presented in [19], [12] which proposed CUDA[1] implementations of classic image processing and medical imaging algorithms. A performance evaluation of GPU-based image processing algorithms is presented in [15]. These implementations offered high improvement of performance thanks to the exploitation of the GPU's computing units in parallel. However, these accelerations are so reduced when processing image databases with different resolutions. Indeed, an efficient exploitation of parallel and heterogeneous (Multi-CPU/Multi-GPU) platforms is required with an effective management of both CPU and GPU memories. Moreover, the treatment of low-resolution images cannot exploit effectively the high power of GPUs since few computations will be launched. This implies an analysis of the spatial and temporal complexities of algorithms before their parallelization.

On the other hand, video processing algorithms require generally a real-time treatment. We may find several methods in this category, such as understanding human behavior, event detection, camera motion estimation, etc. These methods are generally based on motion tracking algorithms that can exploit several techniques such as optical flow estimation [6], block matching technique [20], and scale-invariant feature transform (SIFT) [9] descriptors. In this case also, several GPU implementations have been proposed for sparse [11] and dense [14] optical flow, Kanade-Lucas-Tomasi (KLT) feature tracker and SIFT feature extraction algorithm [17]. Despite their high speedups, none of the above-mentioned implementations can provide real-time processing of high definition videos. Our contribution consists on proposing a new framework that allows an effective and adapted processing of different type of Medias (single image, multiple images, multiple videos, video in real time) exploiting parallel and heterogeneous platforms. This framework offers:

1. Smart selection of resources (CPU or/and GPU) based on the estimated complexity and the type of media to process. In fact, additional computing units are exploited only in case of intensive and parallelizable tasks.
2. Several GPU-based image and video primitive functions ;
3. Efficient scheduling of tasks and management of GPU memories in case of Multi-CPU/Multi-GPU computations ;
4. Acceleration of several real-time image and video processing applications.

The remainder of the paper is organized as follows: section 2 presents our GPU-based image and video processing functions. The third section is devoted

---

[1] CUDA. https://developer.nvidia.com/cuda-zone

to describe the proposed framework for multimedia processing on parallel and heterogeneous platforms. Experimental results are given in section 4. Finally, conclusions and future works are discussed in the last section.

2   GPU-Based Primitive Functions

This section presents our image and video primitive functions that could be exploited by our framework for accelerating several computer vision methods.

2.1   Image Processing Primitive Functions

2.1.1   Noise Elimination we proposed the GPU implementation of noise elimination methods using the smoothing (or blurring) approach. The latter consists on applying a 2-D convolution operator to blur images and remove noise. We developed GPU version of linear, median and Gaussian filtering which represent the most used techniques for noise elimination. This GPU implementation consists of selecting the same number of CUDA threads as the number of image pixels. This allows for each CUDA thread to apply the multiplication of one pixel value with filter values. All the CUDA threads are launched in parallel. More details about this implementation are presented in [12].

2.1.2   Edges detection we proposed a GPU implementation of the recursive contours detection method using Deriche technique [3]. The noise truncature immunity and the reduced number of required operations make this method very efficient. Our GPU implementation of this method is described in [12], based on the parallelization of its four steps on GPU. Fig. 3(c) illustrates an example of edges detection.

2.1.3   Corners detection we developed the GPU implementation of Bouguets corners extraction method [2], based on Harris detector [5]. This method is efficient thanks to its invariance to rotation, scale, brightness, noise, etc. Our GPU implementation of this method is described in [16], based on parallelizing its four steps on GPU. Fig. 3(b) illustrates an example of corners detection.

Moreover, we have integrated the GPU module of the OpenCV [2] library that disposes of many GPU-based image processing algorithms such as FFT, Template Matching, histogram computation and equalization, etc.

2.2   Video Processing Primitive Functions

2.2.1   Silhouette extraction the computation of difference between frames presents a simple and efficient method for detecting the silhouettes of moving objects, we propose a GPU implementation of this method using three steps.

---

[2] OpenCV GPU Module. www.opencv.org

First, we load the two first frames on GPU in order to compute the difference between them within CUDA in parallel. Once the first image displayed, we replace it by the next video frame in order to apply the same treatment. Fig. 1(a) presents the obtained result of silhouette extraction. This figure shows two silhouettes extracted, that present two moving persons. In order to improve the quality of results, a threshold of 200 was used for noise elimination.

2.2.2   Sparse optical flow estimation the sparse optical flow method consists of both features detection and tracking algorithms. The first one enables to detect features that are good to track, i.e. corners. To achieve this, we have exploited our corners extraction method (section 2.1.3). The second step enables to track the features previously detected using the optical flow method, which presents a distribution of apparent velocities of movement of brightness pattern in an image. It enables to compute the spatial displacements of images pixels based on the assumption of constant light hypothesis which supposes that the properties of consecutive images are similar in a small region. Our GPU implementation is detailed in [11]. Fig. 1(b) presents an example of sparse optical flow estimation using a Full HD video frame with characteristic points detected with the Harris corner detector and then tracked with the Lucas-Kanade method. Displacements are marked with arrows. Note that the arrows located on the static objects like trees or a building are there as a result of moving camera.

(a) GPU based silhouette extraction   (b) GPU based sparse optical flow estimation

Fig. 1. GPU based video processing primitive functions

2.2.3   Dense optical flow estimation the GPU implementation of dense optical flow is based on the same process of sparse optical flow estimation. The only difference (compared to sparse) is that the tracking step is applied on all frames pixels. Thus, the number of selected CUDA threads is equal to the number of images pixels which requires more computation.

Notice that the image processing primitive functions have been adapted for treating videos also. Moreover, we have integrated the GPU based video processing algorithms of the OpenCV library such as frames interpolation, MOG (Mixture Of Gaussian) model, morphological operations, etc.

3   The Proposed Framework

The presented results and tests within sections 3 and 4 were run with Linux 64 bits on the following hardware:

 - CPU: Intel Core (TM) i7, 980 3.33GHz, RAM : 8GB;
 - GPU: 4 x NVIDIA GeForce GTX 580, RAM : 1.5GB.

The GPU-based primitive functions are exploited within our framework for processing different types of Medias: single image, multiple images, multiple videos and video in real time. The framework allows to select in an efficient way the adapted resources (CPU or/and GPU) in order to reduce the computation times with an optimal exploitation of computing units.

3.1   Single Image Processing on GPU

This kind of methods is applied on single images, which are displayed on screen at the end of processing. These algorithms are well adapted for GPU parallelization since they consist on common computations over many pixels. However, the use of graphics processing units offers high acceleration when processing high resolution images only. Indeed, performance can be either reduced with GPUs when treating low resolution images since we cannot benefit enough from the GPU. Therefore, we propose a treatment based on the estimated complexity of algorithms. The proposed treatment for single images is summarized in three steps: complexity estimation, resources selection, adapted processing.

3.1.1   Complexity estimation we propose to estimate the algorithm complexity f_c using the equation 1.

$$f_c = f \; \times \; comp\_pix \; \times \; size \qquad (1)$$

where :

1. **f (Parallel fraction)** : Amdahl's law [4] proposed an estimation of the theoretical speedup using N processors. This law supposes that f is the part of program that can be parallelized and (1-f) is the part that can't be made in parallel (data transfers, dependent tasks, etc.). Indeed, high values of f can provide better performance and vice versa.

2. **comp_pix (computation per-image):** graphic processors enable to accelerate image processing algorithms thanks to the exploitation of the GPU's computing units in parallel. These accelerations become more significant when we apply intensive treatments since the GPU is specialized for highly parallel computation. The number of operations per pixel presents a relevant factor to estimate the computation intensity.
3. **size :** represents the resolution of input image.

3.1.2   Resources selection based on the estimated complexity f_c, we can have a good guidance for selecting the adapted resource (CPU or GPU) for computation. In fact, we launched for execution several GPU classic image processing (edge detection, corners detection. . .) algorithms using different image resolutions. These experiments allowed to define the value of f_c from which the GPU starts offering better performance than the CPU. This value is called the threshold S. Once the threshold defined, we compare the estimated complexity f_c for each input algorithm with the threshold S.

If $f_c > S$, the treatment is applied on GPU, else the CPU is used for processing. Notice that within our above-mentioned materiel, we have obtained a threshold S of 800000, that correspond to an algorithm with these parameters:

1. parallel fraction: 0.5 ;
2. number of operations per pixel comp_pixel: 10 ;
3. image resolution: 400×400.

We note also that the threshold value can change with other material configurations, since the number of GPUs computing units and the size of memories is not the same. Therefore, we propose to compute the threshold at each changement of material.

3.1.3   Adapted processing after selecting the adapted resource, CPU treatments are launched in case of low intensive algorithms ($fc < S$). The OpenCV library is employed for this aim. Otherwise, in case of high intensive algorithms ($fc > S$), we apply GPU treatment with three steps:

1. **Loading of input images on GPU :** first, the input images are loaded on GPU memory.
2. **CUDA parallel processing :** before launching the parallel processing of the current frame, the number of GPU threads in the so called blocks and grid has to be defined, so that each thread can perform its processing on one or a group of pixels in parallel. This enables the program to process the image pixels in parallel. Note that the number of threads depends on the number of pixels. Once the number and the layout of threads is defined, different CUDA functions (kernels) are executed sequentially, but each of them in parallel using multiple CUDA threads.

3. **OpenGL Visualization :** the output image is directly visualized on screen through the video output of GPU. Therefore, we propose to exploit the graphic library OpenGL enabling fast visualization, since it works with buffers already existing on GPU.

3.2   Multi-CPU/Multi-GPU Based Processing of Multiple Images

In case of multiple images treatment, performance can be less improved for two reasons: the first one is the inability to visualize many output images using only one video output that requires a transfer of results from GPU to CPU memory. The second constraint is the high computation intensity due to treatment of large sets of images. In order to overcome these constraints, we propose an implementation exploiting both CPUs and GPUs that offers a faster solution for multiple images processing. This implementation is based on the executive support StarPU [1] which offers a runtime for heterogeneous multicore platforms. For more detail, we refer authors to [8]. The employed scheduling strategy has been improved by taking into account the complexity factor f_c described in section 3.1.1. Indeed, high intensive tasks have higher priority for GPU computation. The low intensive tasks will be affected with a low priority for GPU. This allows to maximize the exploitation of available resources. As result, the repartition of tasks depends mainly on their computational intensity.

3.3   Multi-CPU/Multi-GPU Based Processing of Multiple Videos

This kind in methods is applied on a group of video sequences in order to extract some significant features. The latter can be exploited in several applications such as similarity computation between videos, videos indexation and classification. The real time processing is not required in this case. The treatment of a set of videos can be presented by the treatment of a set of images since a video is always represented by a succession of frames. Therefore, we propose a Multi-CPU/Multi-GPU treatment for multiple videos as shown in section 3.2.

3.4   Real Time Videos Processing on Multiple GPUs

In this case, we propose to exploit GPUs only since the video frames should be processed in order. This excludes the possibility of using heterogeneous platforms, which defines an order based on the employed scheduling strategy. Our approach of video processing on single or multiple GPUs consists of three steps:

1. **GPUs selection :** the program, once launched, first detects the number of GPUs in the system, and initializes all of them. Then, the input image frame is first uploaded to each GPU. This frame is virtually divided into equally sized subframes along y dimension and once the image data is available, each GPU is responsible for treating its part of the frame (subframe).

2. **Multi-GPU computation :** in this step, each GPU can apply the required GPU treatment (exp. optical flow computation). The related algorithm can be selected from our GPU primitive functions, or introduced by the framework user. We note also that the number of CUDA threads depends on the number of pixels within each subframe.

3. **OpenGL visualization :** at the end of computations for each frame (the subframes). The results can be displayed on screen using the OpenGL graphics library that allows for fast visualization, as it can operate on the already existing buffers on GPU, and thus requires less data transfer between host and device memories. In case of Multi-GPU treatments, each GPU result (subframe) need to be copied to the GPU which is charged of displaying. This, however, is a fast operation since contiguous memory space is always transferred. Once the visualization of the current image is completed, the program goes back to the first step to load and process the next video frames.

Otherwise, the framework can be used for processing multiple videos simultaneously using multiple GPUs. Indeed, each video stream is loaded and processed with one GPU. At the end of computations for each GPU (actual frame), the result is copied to the GPU which is charged for displaying. Each GPU result is visualized in a separated window in the same screen. Fig. 3.4 summarizes our framework showing the selected resources for each type of media. The figure shows also the primitive functions that could be exploited within the framework for accelerating different computer vision examples that require intensive computations.

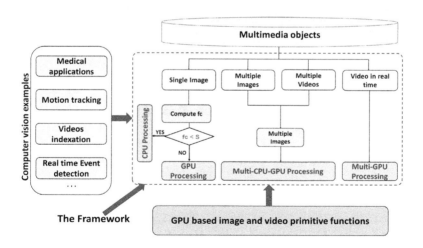

Fig. 2. Multi-CPU/Multi-GPU based Framework for Multimedia Processing

4   Experimental Results

The proposed framework has been exploited in several high intensive applications related to image and video processing such as image pre-processing, vertebra segmentation, videos indexation, event detection and localization.

4.1   CPU/GPU Based Image Pre-processing

Most of image processing methods apply a pre-processing step that allows to prepare the image for treatment. We can cite edges and corners detection methods which are so exploited for this aim. Based on our framework, we propose to accelerate these methods using CPU or GPU since the treatments are applied on single image. As presented in our framework, a complexity estimation is applied to select the convenient resource (CPU or GPU). Table 1 presents the selected resources and performance of corners and edges for different image resolutions. For each one, the complexity is evaluated using the above-mentioned metrics (section 3.1.1). The parallel fraction f presents the percentage of parallelizable computing part relative to total time, while the remaining part (1 - f) is presented by transfer (loading, visualization) operations. The computation per pixel is presented by the average of operations number between the steps of contours and corners detection. As result, the CPU is selected for treating low intensive methods, while the GPU is selected for high intensive ones. This allows to obtain fast results with a reduced energy consumption. In order to validate our results, we have calculated the ratio of acceleration (ACC) with GPU compared to CPU.

(a) Input image   (b) Corners   (c) Edges

Fig. 3. Edges and corners detection within our framework

Table 1. CPU/GPU based processing of single image processing (edges and corners detection), $S = 8.0 * 10^5$

Images	f	$comp_{pix}$	f_c	$f_c > S$	CPU/GPU ?	Acc	
256 × 256	0.55	6.1	$2.2 * 10^5$	No	CPU	00.87	↘
512 × 512	0.81	6.1	$1.3 * 10^6$	Yes	GPU	05.88	↗
1024 × 1024	0.86	6.1	$5.5 * 10^6$	Yes	GPU	12.01	↗
3936 × 3936	0.90	6.1	$8.5 * 10^7$	Yes	GPU	19.85	↗

As shown in Table 1, the GPU is selected only in case of methods that can benefit from the GPU's power. Otherwise, the CPU is selected. Fig. 3 presents an example of edges and corners detection within our framework.

4.2 Multi-CPU/Multi-GPU Based Vertebra Segmentation

The context of this application is the cervical vertebra mobility analysis on X-Ray or MR images. The main objective is to detect vertebra automatically. The computation time presents one of the most important requirements for this application. Based on our framework, we propose a hybrid implementation of the most intensive steps, which have been defined with our complexity factor f_c. Our solution for vertebra detection on Multi-CPU/Multi-GPU platforms is detailed in [8] for X-Ray images, and in [7] for MR images. Fig. 4(a) presents the results of vertebra detection in X-ray images, while Fig. 4(b) is related to present the detected vertebra in MR images. Notice that the use of heterogeneous platforms allowed to improve performance with a speedup of 30 × for vertebra detection within 200 high resolution (1472×1760) X-ray images, and a speedup of 98 × when detecting vertebra in a set of 200 MR images (1024 × 1024).

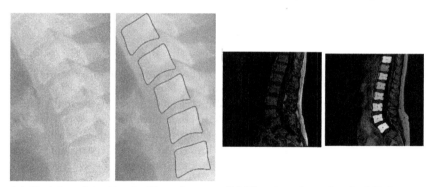

(a) Vertebra detection in X-ray images   (b) Vertebra detection in MR images

Fig. 4. Vertebra detection in X-ray images

4.3 Multi-CPU/Multi-GPU Based Videos Indexation

The aim of this application is to provide a novel browsing environment for multimedia (images, videos) databases. It consists on computing similarities between videos sequences, based on extracting features of images (frames) composing videos [18]. The main disadvantage of this method is the high increase of computing time when enlarging videos sets and resolutions. Based on our framework, we propose a heterogeneous implementation of the most intensive step of features extraction in this application. This step, detected within our complexity estimation equation, is presented by the edge detection algorithm which provides relevant information for detecting motions areas. This implementation is detailed in [13] showing a total gain of 60% (3 min) compared to the total time of the application (about 5 min) treating 800 frames of a video sequence (1080x720).

4.4   Multi-GPU Based Event Detection and Localization in Real Time

This application is used for event detection and localization in real time. It consists of modeling normal behaviors, and then estimating the difference between the normal behavior model and the observed behaviors. These variations can be labeled as emergency events, and the deviations from examples of normal behavior are used to characterize abnormality. Once the event detected, we localize the areas in video frames where motion behavior is surprising compared to the rest of motion in the same frame. Based on our framework, we propose a Multi-GPU implementation of the most intensive steps of the application. The latter are also defined within the above-mentioned complexity factor f_c. This implementation is detailed in [10]. Notice that performed tests show that our application can turn in multi-user scenarios, and in real time even when processing high definition videos such as Full HD or 4K standards. Moreover, the scalability of our results is achieved thanks to the efficient exploitation of multiple graphic cards. A demonstration of GPU based features detection, features tracking, and event detection in crowd video is shown in this video sequence: https://www.youtube.com/watch?v=PwJRUTdQWg8..

5   Conclusion

We proposed in this paper a new framework that allows an adapted and effective exploitation of Multi-CPU/Multi-GPU platforms accordingly to the type of multimedia (single image, multiple images, multiple videos, video in real time) objects. The framework enables to select firstly the computing units (CPU or/and GPU) for processing, and secondly the methods to be applied depending on the type of media to process and the algorithm complexity. Experimental results showed different use case applications that have been improved thanks to our framework. Each application has been integrated in an adapted way for exploiting resources in order to reduce both computing time and energy consumption. As future work, we plan to improve our complexity estimation by taking into account more parameters such as tasks dependency, GPU generation, etc. we plan also to include primitive functions related to 3D image processing within our framework. The latter will be exploited for several medical imaging applications that could be applied larger sets of images and videos.

References

1. Augonnet, C., Thibault, S., Namyst, R., Wacrenier, P.-A.: StarPU: A Unified Platform for Task Scheduling on Heterogeneous Multicore Architectures. In: Sips, H., Epema, D., Lin, H.-X. (eds.) Euro-Par 2009. LNCS, vol. 5704, pp. 863–874. Springer, Heidelberg (2009)
2. Bouguet, J.Y.: Pyramidal Implementation of the Lucas Kanade Feature Tracker, Description of the algorithm. Intel Corporation Microprocessor Research Labs, 851–862 (2000)

3. Deriche, R., Blaszka, T.: Recovering and characterizing im-age features using an efficient model based approach. In: Proceedings of the Conference on Computer Vision and Pattern Recognition, New York, USA, pp. 530–535 (1993)
4. Grama, A., Gupta, A., Karypis, G., Kumar, V.: Introduction to Parallel Computing, 2nd edn. Pearson Education Limited (2003)
5. Harris, C.: A combined corner and edge detector. In: Alvey Vision Conference, pp. 147–152 (1988)
6. Horn, B.K.P., Schunk, B.G.: Determining Optical Flow. Artificial Intelligence 2, 185–203 (1981)
7. Larhmam, M.A., et al.: A portable multi-cpu/multi-gpu based vertebra localization in sagittal mr images. In: International Conference on Image Analysis and Recognition, ICIAR 2014, pp. 209–218 (2014)
8. Lecron, F., et al.: Heterogeneous computing for vertebra detection and segmentation in x-ray images. International Journal of Biomedical Imaging: Parallel Computation in Medical Imaging Applications 2011, 1–12 (2011)
9. Lowe, D.G.: Distinctive image features from scale-invariant keypoints. International Journal of Computer Vision (IJCV) 60(2), 91–110 (2004)
10. Mahmoudi, S.A., et al.: Multi-gpu based event detection and localization using high definition videos. In: International Conference on Multimedia Computing and Systems (ICMCS), pp. 81–86 (2014)
11. Mahmoudi, S.A., Kierzynka, M., Manneback, P., Kurowski, K.: Real-time motion tracking using optical flow on multiple gpus. Bulletin of the Polish Academy of Sciences: Technical Sciences 62, 139–150 (2014)
12. Mahmoudi, S.A., Lecron, F., Manneback, P., Benjelloun, M., Mahmoudi, S.: GPU-Based Segmentation of Cervical Vertebra in X-Ray Images. In: IEEE International Conference on Cluster Computing HPCCE Workshop, pp. 1–8 (2010)
13. Mahmoudi, S.A., Manneback, P.: Efficient exploitation of heterogeneous platforms for images features extraction. In: 3rd International Conference on Image Processing Theory, Tools and Applications (IPTA), pp. 91–96 (2012)
14. Marzat, J., Dumortier, Y., Ducrot, A.: Real-time dense and accurate parallel optical flow using CUDA. In: Proceedings of WSCG, pp. 105–111 (2009)
15. Park, K., Nitin, S., Man, H.L.: Design and Performance Evaluation of Image Processing Algorithms on GPUs. IEEE Transactions on Parallel and Distributed Systems 28, 1–14 (2011)
16. Ricardo Possa, P., Mahmoudi, S.A., Harb, N., Valderrama, C., Manneback, P.: A multi-resolution fpga-based architecture for real-time edge and corner detection. IEEE Transactions on Computers 63, 2376–2388 (2014)
17. Sinha, S.N., Fram, J.-M., Pollefeys, M., Genc, Y.: Gpu-based video feature tracking and matching. In: EDGE, Workshop on Edge Computing Using New Commodity Architectures (2006)
18. Tardieu, D., al.: Video navigation tool: Application to browsing a database of dancers' performances. In: QPSR of the numediart research program, vol. 2(3), pp. 85–90 (2009)
19. Yang, Z., Zhu, Y., Pu, Y.: Parallel Image Processing Based on CUDA. In: International Conference on Computer Science and Software Engineering China, pp. 198–201 (2008)
20. Zhu, S., Ma, K.-K.: A new diamond search algorithm for fast block-matching motion estimation. IEEE Transactions on Image Processing 9(2), 287–290 (2000)

Full-Reference Image Quality Assessment Measure Based on Color Distortion

Zianou Ahmed Seghir[1(⊠)] and Fella Hachouf[2]

[1] University Khenchela, Faculty. ST,
ICOSI Lab., BP 1252 El Houria, 40004 Khenchela, Algeria
[2] Laboratoire d'Automatique et de Robotique, Université Constantine1, Algeria
zianou_ahmed_seghir@yahoo.fr

Abstract. The purpose of this paper is to introduce a new method for image quality assessment (IQA). The method adopted here is assumed to be Full-reference measure. Color images that are corrupted with different kinds of distortions are assessed by applying a color distorted algorithm on each color component separately. This approach use especially *YIQ* color space in computation. Gradient operator was successfully introduced to compute gradient image from the luminance channel of images. In this paper, we propose an alternative technique to evaluate image quality. The main difference between the new proposed method and the gradient magnitude similarity deviation (GMSD) method is the usage of color component for the detection of distortion.

Experimental comparisons demonstrate the effectiveness of the proposed method.

Keywords: Gradient similarity · Quality assessment · Test image · Color distortion · Color space

1 Introduction

Over the past decade, image quality assessment methods based objective methods have grown significantly to tackle problems of image assessment. The challenge of these problems is to construct an algorithm that can automatically predict perceived quality of image.

There is no doubt that the subjective test is the most accurate measure for quality assessment because it reflects the true human perception. On the other hand, it is time consuming and expensive. There are three kinds of measures that are used for objective image quality assessment, full-reference (FR), reduced-reference (RR) and no-reference (NR). In this paper, the discussion is confined to FR metrics, where the reference images are available.

There has been extensive work on objective image quality assessment. The most popular method for full reference image quality assessment is the Structural Similarity Index [2] (*SSIM*). It contains three parts: Luminance Comparison, Contrast Comparison and Structure Comparison. However, it fails in measuring the badly blurred

© IFIP International Federation for Information Processing 2015
A. Amine et al. (Eds.): CIIA 2015, IFIP AICT 456, pp. 66–77, 2015.
DOI: 10.1007/978-3-319-19578-0_6

images [3]. In [4], an approach based on edge-region information, distorted and displaced pixels (ERDDM) is developed. Initially, the test and reference images are divided into blocks of 11×11 pixels, and then distorted and displaced pixels are calculated which can be used to compute the global error. In [6], *DTex* metric is proposed with consideration of the texture masking effect and contrast sensitivity function. In [17], it was shown that the masking effect and the visibility threshold can be combined with structure, luminance and contrast comparison to create the image quality measure (gradient similarity measure (GSM)). Most Apparent Distortion (MAD) designed in [23, 24] yields two quality scores, i.e., visibility-weighted error and the differences in log-Gabor subbands statistics. The proposed measure in [13] applies phase congruency [15] to image quality measure. This measure differs in their correlations with the subjective quality and carrying out times. Gradient magnitude similarity deviation (GMSD) is proposed [14], where the pixel-wise gradient magnitude similarity (GMS) is used to capture image local quality, and the standard deviation of the overall GMS map is computed as the final image quality index.

The gradient images are sensitive to image distortions, whereas different local structures in a distorted image suffer different degrees of degradations. This motivates us to investigate the use of global variation of gradient based local quality map for overall image quality prediction. In fact, color deformation cannot be well differentiated by gradient. In addition, the gradient is computed from the luminance channel of images. Therefore, to make the image quality assessment measures own the ability to deal with color distortions, chrominance information should be taken into consideration.

The aim of this paper is to improve the GMSD to take color distortion in consideration. As a result, we use a proposed gradient operator and *YIQ* color space [1] to produce gradient image and color distortion from the reference and test images, respectively.

The rest of the paper is organized as follows. In Section 2, our proposed image quality measure is defined. In section 3, performance of the proposed method is compared with others measures using images with different types of distortion. We finish by the conclusion.

2   Proposed Method

Before introducing the proposed measure notion, some useful concepts must be visited. The reference and test images are represented by $Ref\,(M,N)$ and $Dis\,(M,N)$ respectively.

The proposed method uses gradient similarity and Color distortion to form map.

In addition, all variables used in the proposed method are defined next:

Ref: reference image.
Dis: test image.
$M \times N$: the image size.
G_1: gradient image of   *Ref*.
G_2 : gradient image of   *Dis*.
G_map: Gradient similarity map.

CFI_map and *CFQ_map* : chromatic features.

C_1, C_2:   positive constants.

GSCDM : Gradient similarity based Color distortion measure.

2.1   Gradient Similarity

In order to reflect the differences between *Ref* and *Dis* at the local level, we compute image gradient of the reference and test images. Different operators are used to compute the image gradient, such as the Sobel operator [7], the Prewitt operator [7] and the Scharr operator [8], and in this paper a new gradient operator is proposed, which shows very favorable outcome. It defines as:

Mask	Gx	Gy
	$\begin{pmatrix} 4 & 0 & -4 \\ 3 & 0 & -3 \\ 4 & 0 & -4 \end{pmatrix}/11$	$\begin{pmatrix} 4 & 3 & 4 \\ 0 & 0 & 0 \\ -4 & -3 & -4 \end{pmatrix}/11$

This later consists of a pair of 3×3 convolution kernels and is used for detecting vertical and horizontal edges in images.

The partial derivatives Gx and Gy of an image are computed as:

$$G = \sqrt{Gx^2 + Gy^2} \tag{1}$$

Also, the gradient operators (G) of the reference and test images are computed. As a result, the G_2 and G_1 of the test and reference images are produced, respectively.

The gradient similarity is computed in proposed method and hence the Gradient map (*G_map*) is formed as

$$G\_map = \frac{2G_1 \cdot G_2 + C_1}{G_1{}^2 + G_2{}^2 + C_1} \tag{2}$$

2.2   Color Space Transformation

The color distortion cannot be differentiating by gradient. Hence, to make the image quality assessment measures possess the ability to deal with color distortions, special considerations are given to chrominance information. As a result, these formulas approximate the conversion between the *RGB* color space and *YIQ* [1]

$$\begin{bmatrix} Y \\ I \\ Q \end{bmatrix} = \begin{bmatrix} 0.299 & 0.587 & 0.144 \\ 0.596 & -0.275 & -0.321 \\ 0.212 & -0.528 & 0.311 \end{bmatrix} \begin{bmatrix} R \\ G \\ B \end{bmatrix} \tag{3}$$

Let I_1 (I_2) and Q_1 (Q_2) be the I and Q chromatic channels of the reference and distorted images respectively. Similar to the definitions of *CFI_map* and *CFQ_map*, the similarity between chromatic features is defined as follows:

$$CFI\_map = \frac{2I_1 . I_2 + C_2}{I_1{}^2 + I_2{}^2 + C_2}$$

$$CFQ\_map = \frac{2Q_1 . Q_2 + C_2}{Q_1{}^2 + Q_2{}^2 + C_2} \tag{4}$$

The similarity between the chrominance components (color distortion map) is simply defined as:

$$CD\_map = CFI\_map . CFQ\_map \tag{5}$$

2.3   Global Error

Finally, the gradient similarity based Color distortion map (***GSCD_map***) is expressed as:

$$GSCD\_map = G\_map . CD\_map \tag{6}$$

The total gradient similarity based Color distortion measure (*GSCDM*) is defined as the standard deviation of the ***GSCD* map**:

$$GSCDM = \sqrt{\frac{1}{N.M} \sum_{p=1}^{M} \sum_{q=1}^{N} \left(\overline{GSCD} - GSCD\_map(p,q) \right)^2} \tag{7}$$

Where

$$\overline{GSCD} = \frac{1}{N.M} \sum_{p=1}^{M} \sum_{q=1}^{N} GSCD\_map(p,q) \tag{8}$$

Flowchart depicting computation of the proposed measure is shown in Fig. 1.

3   Results

In order to evaluate the accuracy of the proposed method; we follow the standard performance assessment procedures utilized in the video quality expert's group (VQEG) FR-TV Phase II test [5]. The objective and subjective scores [5], are fitted with the logistic function. Five parameters non-linear mapping (θ_1, θ_2, θ_3, θ_4 and θ_5) are utilized to change the set of quality ratings by the objective quality measures to a set of the predicted Difference Mean Opinion Score (*DMOS/MOS*) values denoted *DMOS*p/*MOS*p.

In equation (9), the logistic regression function is introduced which is employed for the nonlinear regression.

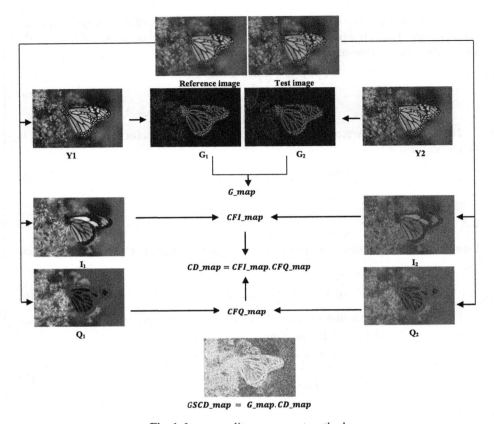

Fig. 1. Image quality assessment method

$$f(VQR) = \theta_1 \left(\frac{1}{2} - \frac{1}{\exp(\theta_2(VQR - \theta_3))} \right) + \theta_4 VQR + \theta_5 \qquad (9)$$

Where VQR is the value of the objective method and θ_1, θ_2, θ_3, θ_4, θ_5 are selected for the most excellent fit.

In this test, four metrics are used [26]: the Root mean square prediction error ($RMSE$), the Spearman rank-order correlations coefficient ($ROCC$), Kendall rank-order correlation coefficient ($KROCC$) and The Pearson linear correlation coefficient (CC). $ROCC$ and $KROCC$ evaluate the prediction monotonicity. CC and $RMSE$ assess the prediction accuracy. $ROCC$, $KROCC$ and CC are better with values closer to 1 or -1. Thus, $RMSE$ is better when its values are small.

The first index CC (Pearson linear correlation coefficient) is defined by:

$$CC = \frac{\sum_{i=1}^{n}(DMOS(i) - \overline{DMOS})(DMOS_p(i) - \overline{DMOS_p})}{\sqrt{\sum (DMOS(i) - \overline{DMOS})^2}\sqrt{\sum (DMOS_p(i) - \overline{DMOS_p})^2}}$$ (10)

Where the index i denotes the image sample and n denotes the number of samples.

The second index is the Spearman rank-order correlations coefficient (*ROCC*); it is defined by:

$$ROCC = 1 - \frac{6 \sum (DMOS(i) - DMOS_p(i))^2}{n(n^2 - 1)}$$ (11)

The third index is Kendall rank-order correlation coefficient (*KROCC*) [25]. It is designed to capture the association between two ordinal variables. Its estimate can be expressed as follows:

$$KROCC = \frac{\sum_{i=1}^{n}\sum_{j=1}^{n} sgn(DMOS(i) - DMOS(j))sgn(DMOS_p(i) - DMOS_p(j))}{n(n-1)}$$ (12)

where:

$$sgn(DMOS(i) - DMOS(j)) = \begin{cases} 1 \; if \; (DMOS(i) - DMOS(j)) > 0 \\ 0 \; if \; (DMOS(i) - DMOS(j)) = 0 \\ -1 if \; (DMOS(i) - DMOS(j)) < 0 \end{cases}$$

and

$$sgn(DMOS_p(i) - DMOS_p(j)) = \begin{cases} 1 \; if \; (DMOS_p(i) - DMOS_p(j)) > 0 \\ 0 \; if \; (DDMOS_p(i) - DMOS_p(j)) = 0 \\ -1 if \; (DMOS_p(i) - DMOS_p(j)) < 0 \end{cases}$$

The forth one is the Root mean square prediction error (*RMSE*) between subjective (*DMOS*) and objective (*DMOS*P) scores. It is defined by:

$$RMSE = \sqrt{\frac{1}{n}\sum_{i=1}^{n}(DMOS(i) - DMOS_p(i))^2}$$ (13)

To judge the performance of the proposed approach, four kinds of databases are used: TID2008 database [9], CSIQ database [10], LIVE database [11] and TID2013 database [12]. The characteristics of these four databases are summarized in table 3.

The performance of GSCD metric is compared with PSNR, SSIM [2,16], Multiscale-SSIM (MS-SSIM) [18,16], Visual Singal-to-Noise Ratio (VSNR) [19,16], Visual Information Fidelity (VIF) [20,16], Information Fidelity Criterion (IFC) [21,16], Noise Quality Measure (NQM) [22, 16], DTex [6], GSM [17], MAD [23,24], ERDDM [4], GSMD [14] and FSIM [13].

A comparative study of Sobel, Perwitt, Scharr and proposed operator is presented in Table 1 (TID2008 database is used in this experience), from which proposed operator could accomplish better performance than the other three. Furthermore, the choice of *YIQ* color space needs to be proved. To this end, we run the proposed method with different four color spaces. The results are summarized in table 2 (TID2008 database is used in this experience).

Table 1. ROCC and KROCC values using four gradient operators

Gradient operator	Sobel	Perwitt	Scharr	Proposed operator
ROCC	0.8983	0.8996	0.8963	**0.9000**
KROCC	0.7143	0.7171	0.7104	**0.7175**

Table 2. ROCC and KROCC values using four color spaces

Color space	Lab	ycbcr	HSV	YIQ
ROCC	0.7684	0.8937	0.2983	**0.9000**
KROCC	0.5789	0.7110	0.2125	**0.7175**

The classification of the performance of all measures according to their ROCC values is presented in Table 8 reveal the reliability of the GSCD. Tables 4, 5, 6 and 7 show the obtained results. The top three measures for each assessment measure are highlighted in bold. We can see that the top methods are mostly GSCD, GMSD, FSIM and MAD. GSCD correlates much better with the subjective results than the other measures. Looking at the curves (Fig.2), the GSCD values are very close to DMOS and MOS, proving the efficiency of this measure.

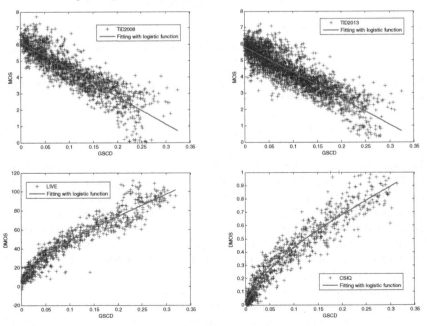

Fig. 2. Scatter plots of subjective scores versus scores from the proposed scheme on IQA databases

Moreover, an interesting result is obtained from the comparison of the GSCD with GMSD, FSIM and MAD in Tables 5 (TID2008 database). The values of ROOC are close to 1; this means that GSCD has a similar performance as the methods or earlier works. Results clearly indicate that our GSCD measure performs quite well and is competitive with other IQA measures.

In addition, to compare the efficiency of different models, the average execution time required an image of size 512×384 is calculated (the image is taken from TID2008 database). All metrics were run on a TOSHIBA Satetillete T130-11U note-book with Intel Core U4100 CPU@1.30 GHz and 3G RAM. The software platform used to run all metrics was MATLAB R2007a (7.4.0). Table 8 shows the required time in seconds per image. It is shown in Table 9 that the proposed measure takes more time than the PSNR, the GMSD, and the SSIM and it is faster than the Fsim.

VIF, VSNR, IFC, MS-SSIM, GSM, MAD, DCTex, NQM and ERDDM also take much longer processing time than the proposed method.

Moreover, we adjusted the parameters based on a dataset of TID2008 database. The adjusting measure was that the parameters values giving to a higher ROCC would be chosen. As a result, the parameters required in the proposed method were set as: C_1= 100, C_2=2050.

Table 3. Four databases and their characteristics

Database	Source Images	Distorted Images	Distortion Types	Image Type	Observers
TID2008	25	1700	17	color	838
CSIQ	30	866	6	color	35
LIVE	29	779	5	color	161
TID2013	25	3000	25	color	971

Table 4. Performance comparison for image quality assessment measures on live database

Method	ROCC	KROCC	CC	RMSE
PSNR	0.8756	0.6865	0.8723	13.3597
SSIM	0.9479	0.7963	0.9449	8.9454
MS-SSIM	0.9513	0.8044	0.9409	9.2593
VSNR	0.9280	0.7625	0.9237	10.4694
VIF	**0.9632**	**0.8270**	**0.9598**	**7.6670**
IFC	0.9259	0.7579	0.9268	10.2643
NQM	0.9086	0.7413	0.9122	11.1926
ERDDM	0.9496	0.8128	0.9619	6.3204
DCTex	0.9483	0.8066	0.9443	8.9897
GSM	0.9554	0.8131	0.9437	9.0376
MAD	**0.9669**	**0.8421**	**0.9674**	**6.9235**
Fsim	**0.9645**	**0.8363**	**0.9613**	**7.5296**
GMSD	0.9603	0.8271	0.9603	7.622
GSCD	0.9596	0.8222	0.9538	8.2074

Table 5. Performance comparison for image quality assessment measures on TID2008 database

Method	ROCC	KROCC	CC	RMSE
PSNR	0.5794	0.4210	0.5726	1.1003
SSIM	0.7749	0.5768	0.7710	0.8546
MS-SSIM	0.8542	0.6568	0.8451	0.7173
VSNR	0.7049	0.5345	0.6823	0.9810
VIF	0.7496	0.5868	0.8090	0.7888
IFC	0.5675	0.4236	0.7340	0.9113
NQM	0.6243	0.4608	0.6142	1.0590
ERDDM	0.5961	0.4411	0.6685	0.998
DCTex	0.4973	0.4095	0.5605	1.1113
GSM	0.8554	0.6651	0.8462	0.7151
MAD	0.8340	0.6445	0.8306	0.7474
Fsim	**0.8840**	**0.6991**	**0.8762**	**0.6468**
GMSD	**0.8907**	**0.7094**	**0.8788**	**0.6404**
GSCD	**0.9000**	**0.7175**	**0.8830**	**0.629**

Table 6. Performance comparison for image quality assessment measures on TID2013 database

Method	ROCC	KROCC	CC	RMSE
PSNR	0.6396	0.4698	0.669	0.9214
SSIM	0.7417	0.5588	0.7895	0.7608
MS-SSIM	0.7859	0.6047	0.8329	0.6861
VSNR	0.6812	0.5084	0.7402	0.8392
VIF	0.6769	0.5147	0.7720	0.7880
IFC	0.5389	0.3939	0.5538	1.0322
NQM	0.6432	0.474	0.6858	0.9023
ERDDM	0.5623	0.4124	0.6352	1.230
DCTex	0.5863	0.4573	0.6495	0.9425
GSM	0.7946	0.6255	0.8464	0.6603
MAD	0.7807	0.6035	0.8267	0.6975
Fsim	**0.8510**	**0.6665**	**0.8769**	**0.5959**
GMSD	**0.8044**	**0.6343**	**0.859**	**0.6346**
GSCD	**0.8681**	**0.6855**	**0.8819**	**0.5844**

Table 7. Performance comparison for image quality assessment measures on CSIQ database

Method	ROCC	KROCC	CC	RMSE
PSNR	0.8005	0.5984	0.7998	0.1576
SSIM	0.8756	0.6907	0.8612	0.1334
MS-SSIM	0.9133	0.7393	0.8990	0.1150
VSNR	0.8104	0.6237	0.7993	0.1578
VIF	0.9195	0.7537	0.9277	0.0980
IFC	0.7671	0.5897	0.8384	0.1431
NQM	0.7402	0.5638	0.7433	0.1756

Table 7. (*Continued*)

ERDDM	0.8626	0.6781	0.8295	0.1466
DCTex	0.8042	0.6420	0.7915	0.1605
GSM	0.9126	0.7403	0.8979	0.1156
MAD	**0.9467**	**0.7970**	**0.9502**	**0.0818**
Fsim	0.9310	0.7690	0.9192	0.1034
GMSD	**0.957**	**0.8133**	**0.9541**	**0.0786**
GSCD	**0.9602**	**0.8194**	**0.9578**	**0.0755**

Table 8. Ranking of IQA metrics' performance on four databases

Method	Live	TID2008	TID2013	CSIQ
PSNR	14	12	11	12
SSIM	10	7	7	8
MS-SSIM	7	5	5	6
VSNR	11	9	8	10
VIF	**2**	8	9	5
IFC	12	13	14	13
NQM	13	10	10	14
ERDDM	8	11	13	9
DCTex	9	14	12	11
GSM	6	4	4	7
MAD	**1**	6	6	**3**
Fsim	**3**	**3**	**2**	4
GMSD	4	**2**	**3**	**2**
GSCD	**5**	**1**	**1**	**1**

Table 9. Running time of the competing IQA models

Method	Time (second)	Method	Time (second)
PSNR	0.0493	ERDDM	9.6089
SSIM	0.1917	DCTex	0.5327
MS-SSIM	1.1304	GSM	1.4003
VSNR	1.5018	MAD	15.6235
VIF	5.1429	Fsim	2.4990
IFC	4.6738	GMSD	0.1602
NQM	1.8846	GSCD	0.4361

4   Conclusion

This paper describes an efficient method for image quality assessment. Its main feature is that this new method uses the gradient similarity and color distorted measure. The reference and test images are transformed respectively using color distorted and gradient mask. The difference between the reference and test images is computed using simple function. A comparative study has been carried in this work.

The obtained results are competitive with the previous works.

Future works following this study will include the use of others characteristics to assess image quality.

References

1. Yang, C., Kwok, S.H.: Efficient gamut clipping for color image processing using LHS and YIQ. Opt. Eng. 42(3), 701–711 (2003)
2. Wang, Z., Bovik, A.C., Sheikh, H.R., Simocelli, E.P.: Image quality assessment: From error measurement to structural similarity. IEEE Trans. Image Processing 13(4), 600–612 (2004)
3. Guan-Hao, C., Chun-Ling, Y., Sheng-Li, X.: Gradient-based structural similarity for image quality assessment. In: Proc. ICIP 2006, pp. 2929–2932 (2006)
4. Ahmed Seghir, Z., Hachouf, F.: Edge-region information measure based on deformed and displaced pixel for Image Quality Assessment. Signal Processing: Image Communication 26(8-9), 534–549 (2011)
5. Final VQEG report on the validation of objective quality metrics for video quality assessment: http://www.its.bldrdoc.gov/vqeg/projects/frtv_phaseI/
6. Zhang, F., Ma, L., Li, S.: Practical image quality metric applied to image coding. IEEE Trans. Multimedia 13, 615–624 (2011)
7. Jain, R., Kasturi, R., Schunck, B.G.: Machine Vision. McGraw-Hill, NewYork (1995)
8. Jähne, B., Haubecker, H., Geibler, P.: Handbook of Computer Vision and Applications. Academic, New York (1999)
9. Ponomarenko, N., Egiazarian, K.: Tampere Image Database, TID 2008, http://www.ponomarenko.info/tid2008.htm
10. Larson, C., Chandler, D.M.: Categorical Image Quality (CSIQ) Database 2009, http://vision.okstate.edu/csiq
11. Sheikh, H.R., Seshadrinathan, K., Moorthy, A.K., Wang, Z., Bovik, A.C., Cormack, L.K.: Image and Video Quality Assessment Research at LIVE 2004 (2004), http://live.ece.utexas.edu/research/quality
12. Ponomarenko, N., et al.: Color image database TID2013: Peculiarities and preliminary results. In: Proc. 4th Eur. Workshop Vis. Inf. Process., pp. 106–111 (June 2013)
13. Zhang, L., Zhang, L., Mou, X., Zhang, D.: FSIM: A feature similarity index for image quality assessment. IEEE Transactions on Image Processing 20(8), 1–26 (2011)
14. Xue, W., Zhang, L., Mou, X., Bovik, A.C.: Gradient Magnitude Similarity Deviation: A Highly Efficient Perceptual Image Quality Index. Presented at IEEE Transactions on Image Processing, 684–695 (2014)
15. Kovesi, P.: Image features from phase congruency. Videre: Journal of Computer Vision Research 1(3), 1–26 (1999)
16. Gaubatz, M.: Metrix MUX Visual Quality Assessment Package: MSE, PSNR, SSIM, MSSIM, VSNR, VIF, VIFP, UQI, IFC, NQM, WSNR, SNR
17. http://foulard.ece.cornell.edu/gaubatz/metrix_mux/
18. Liu, A., Lin, W., Narwaria, M.: Image quality assessment based on gradient similarity. IEEE Transactions on Image Processing 21(4), 1500–1512 (2012)

19. Wang, Z., Simoncelli, E.P., Bovik, A.C.: Multi-scale structural similarity for image quality assessment. In: Proc. IEEE Asilomar Conf. Signals, Syst., Comput., Pacific Grove, CA, pp. 1398–1402 (November 2003)
20. Chandler, D.M., Hemami, S.S.: VSNR: A wavelet-based visual signal-to-noise-ratio for natural images. IEEE Trans. Image Process. 16(9), 2284–2298 (2007)
21. Sheikh, H.R., Bovik, A.C.: Image information and visual quality. IEEE Trans. Image Process. 15(2), 430–444 (2006)
22. Sheikh, H.R., Bovik, A.C., de Veciana, G.: An information fidelity criterion for image quality assessment using natural scene statistics. IEEE Trans. on Image Processing 14(12), 2117–2128 (2005)
23. Damera-Venkata, N., Kite, T.D., Geisler, W.S., Evans, B.L., Bovik, A.C.: Image quality assessment based on degradation model. IEEE Trans. on Image Processing 9(4), 636–650 (2000)
24. Larson, E.C., Chandler, D.M.: Most apparent distortion: Full-reference image quality assessment and the role of strategy. J. Electron. Imaging 19(1), 011006:1–011006:21 (2010)
25. Larson, E., Chandler, D.: Full-Reference Image Quality Assessment and the Role of Strategy: The Most Apparent Distortion, http://vision.okstate.edu/mad/
26. Chok, N.S.: Pearson's Versus Spearman's and Kendall's Correlation Coefficients for Continuous Data. Master's Thesis, University of Pittsburgh (2010)
27. Wang, Z., Li, Q.: Information content weighting for perceptual image quality assessment. IEEE Trans. Image Process. 20(5), 1185–1198 (2011)

Computational Intelligence:
Machine Learning

Biomarker Discovery Based on Large-Scale Feature Selection and MapReduce

Ahlam Kourid[(⊠)] and Mohamed Batouche

Computer Science Department, College of NTIC, Constantine 2 University – A. Mehri, 25000, Constantine, Algeria
ahlem.kou@gmail.com, mohamed.batouche@univ-constantine2.dz

Abstract. Large-scale feature selection is one of the most important fields in the big data domain that can solve real data problems, such as bioinformatics, where it is necessary to process huge amount of data. The efficiency of existing feature selection algorithms significantly downgrades, if not totally inapplicable, when data size exceeds hundreds of gigabytes, because most feature selection algorithms are designed for centralized computing architecture. For that, distributed computing techniques, such as MapReduce can be applied to handle very large data. Our approach is to scale the existing method for feature selection, Kmeans clustering and Signal to Noise Ratio (SNR) combined with optimization technique as Binary Particle Swarm Optimization (BPSO). The proposed method is divided into two stages. In the first stage, we have used parallel Kmeans on MapReduce for clustering features, and then we have applied iterative MapReduce that implement parallel SNR ranking for each cluster. After, we have selected the top ranked feature from each cluster. The top scored features from each cluster are gathered and a new feature subset is generated. In the second stage, the new feature subset is used as input to the proposed BPSO based on MapReduce which provides an optimized feature subset. The proposed method is implemented in a distributed environment, and its efficiency is illustrated through analyzing practical problems such as biomarker discovery.

Keywords: Feature selection · Large-scale machine learning · Big data analytics · Bioinformatics · Biomarker discovery

1   Introduction

With the progress of high technology in several fields that produce an important volume of data such as Microarray and Next generation sequencing in bioinformatics [1], deal with high dimensional data becomes a challenge for several tasks in machine learning. Feature selection is one of the techniques of reduction dimensionality [2] that is effective in removing irrelevant data; increasing learning accuracy, therefore becomes very necessary for machine learning tasks. Scalability can become a problem for even simple and centralized approaches, for that feature selection methods based on parallel algorithm will be the mainly choice for dealing with large-scale data. Many parallel algorithms are implemented using different parallelization techniques

© IFIP International Federation for Information Processing 2015
A. Amine et al. (Eds.): CIIA 2015, IFIP AICT 456, pp. 81–92, 2015.
DOI: 10.1007/978-3-319-19578-0_7

such as MPI (The Message Passing Interface), and MapReduce. MapReduce is a programming model for distributed computation, derived from the functional programming concepts, and is proposed by Google for large-scale data processing in a distributed computing environment [3].

Recent comparisons studies of feature selection methods in high-dimensional data have shown that the combination of K-means clustering and filter method based SNR (Signal to Noise Ratio) score combined with binary PSO is a graceful method for classification problem [4]. The method is applied for classification of DNA microarray data. To resolve redundancy in gene expression values one approach i.e. sample based clustering by using k-means clustering algorithm is used and the genes (features) are being grouped into number of clusters. After clustering SNR ranking is being used to rank each gene (feature) in every cluster. The gene subset selected by taking the top scored gene (feature) from each cluster is validated with an SVM classifier, and will be taken as the initial search space to find the optimized subset by applying PSO and the optimized subset is used to train different classifier such as SVM [4]. However, the existing method is limited over large scale datasets. In order to overcome that problem we present our method that is suitable for very large data and that has the potential for parallel implementation, based on parallel Kmeans on MapReduce for clustering a huge amount of features, so similar features having the same characteristics will be grouped in the same cluster, and on an iterative MapReduce that implement parallel SNR ranking for each cluster. Finally, the top non-redundant ranked features selected are input to BPSO on MapReduce to select the relevant features.

2   Parallel Programming Paradigm and Framework

In order to implement our approach to cope with large scale data sets, we are using Hadoop platform and MapReduce as parallel programming paradigm .

2.1   MAPREDUCE

MapReduce is a functional programming model that is well suited to parallel computation. The model is divided into two functions which are map and reduce .In MapReduce; all data are in the form of keys with associated values. The following notation and example are based on the original presentation [3]:

A. **Map Function**
A map function is defined as a function that takes a single key-value pair and outputs a list of new key-value pairs. The input key may be of a different type than the output keys, and the input value may be of a different type than the output values:

$$\text{Map :}(K1, V1) \rightarrow \text{list} ((K2, V2)) \tag{1}$$

B. Reduce Function

A reduce function is a function that reads a key and a corresponding list of values and outputs a new list of values for that key. The input and output values are of the same type.

$$\text{Reduce} :(K2, \text{list } (V2)) \rightarrow \text{list } (V2) \tag{2}$$

2.2   HADOOP Platform

Hadoop is an open source Java based framework to store and process large amounts of data. It allows distributed processing of data which is present over clusters using functional programming model.   MapReduce is the most important algorithm implemented in Hadoop. Each Map and Reduce is independent of other Maps and Reduces. Processing of data is executed in parallel to other processes. A job scheduler or job tracker tracks MapReduce jobs which are being executed. Tasks like Map, Reduce and Shuffle are accepted from Job Tracker by a node called Task Tracker. Hadoop architecture is defined as follows: Hadoop consists of two components, the Hadoop Distributed File System (HDFS) and MapReduce, performing distributed processing by single-master and multiple-slave servers. There are two elements of MapReduce, namely JobTracker and TaskTracker, and two elements of HDFS, namely DataNode and NameNode. [5].

3   Scaling Up Feature Selection Algorithm

For scaling up the existing method for feature selection, we propose an approach based on MapReduce which is composed of two stages. The first stage consists in filtering the set of features by selecting the top scored features whereas the second stage optimizes the obtained subset of selected features.

3.1   Filtering the Set of Features

This stage is scalable and implements K-means clustering on MapReduce and SNR ranking on MapReduce for each cluster. It is designed for the purpose of eliminating redundancy in features and selecting the top scored features [6]. And it is composed of the following steps:

Step1: clustering features (genes) with parallel K-means on MapReduce. As by applying clustering technique we can group similar type of features in the same cluster, so that best features from each cluster can be selected.
Step2: mappers read lines (features) and compute SNR score for each feature.
Step3: according to the paradigm shuffle and sort in MapReduce, the final output file contains ranked SNR values. Top ranked features are selected in two cases:

- One output file: the top ranked features are selected from this file.
- Multiple output files: each file is ranked by SNR value, for that Terasort can be used to rank all SNR values from these files. Terasort is a standard map/reduce sort, and it is implemented as benchmark in hadoop [7].

Step4: After that the best scored feature in a cluster is selected, and go to step 2 for the next cluster. We can assure that applying SNR and selecting the best scored feature from each cluster the resultant feature gene subset have no redundancy.

Step5: top features (genes) ranked from each cluster are aggregated and validated with SVM classifier using the evaluation method 10 foldCV.

The system architecture for the proposed method in stage-I- is illustrated in **Fig.1**.

3.2   Optimizing the Subset of Selected Features

This stage aims to select an optimized subset of features from the subset selected in the previous stage. It is parallel, and can provide scalability to a certain degree because of the SVM classifier which is sequential. In this stage; we have used four MapReduce jobs described by the following steps:

Step1: the subset of features selected and validated in the previous stage, is the input to the novel BPSO proposed based on MapReduce, we have divided the particles of swarm into groups, so that the input file contains particles defined by their groups, in the first MapReduce job, mappers evaluate fitness (accuracy of SVM) of particles in parallel.

Step2: in the second MapReduce job, mappers read output file from the first job and emit the group identifier as key in order to group particles. Reducers evaluate Gbestg of each group in parallel, and emit "one" as key and the Gbestg of the group with fitness of Gbestg of the group as value.

Step3: the third MapReduce job evaluates the Gbestglobal, which is the maximum of all Gbestg of each Group. The output file of this job contains the Gbestglobal and its fitness.

Step4: the file output of the first job in HDFS is the input of the fourth job, in this job mappers read the output file of the third job that contains Gbestglobal and its fitness from HDFS, in order to evaluate the new positions and the new velocities in parallel. The output of this job is the new swarm for the next iteration.

The system architecture for the proposed method in stage-II- is illustrated in **Fig.2**.

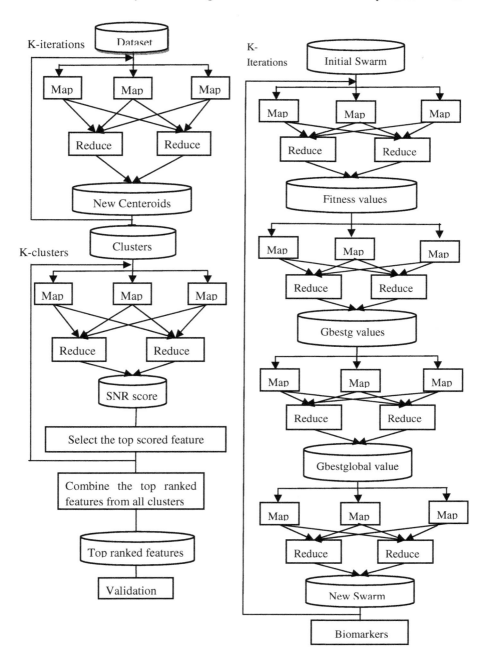

Fig. 1. System architecture of the proposed method stage-I-

Fig. 2. System architecture of the proposed method stage-II-

4   Implementation of the Proposed Approach

In order to implement the proposed approach for scaling up the existing method for feature selection, we describe in the following the algorithms and map/reduce functions.

4.1   The First Stage

In this stage, we are using K-means along with SNR ranking on MapReduce which are defined as follows:

Algorithm 1. Kmeans on MapReduce.

Input : Training data (features) .
Output: Clusters.

Algorithm 1.1. k-means::Map

Input: Training data $x \in D$, number of clusters k, distance measure d
1: If first Map iteration **then**
2:   Initialize the k cluster centroids C randomly
3: Else
4: Get the k cluster centroids C from the previous Reduce
step.
5: Set $S_j = 0$ and $n_j = 0$ for j = $\{1, \dots, k\}$
6: For each $x_i \in D$ do
7:$y_i = $ arg $\min_j d(x_i, c_j)$
8:$S_{y_i} = S_{y_i} + x_i$
9:$n_{y_i} = n_{y_i} + 1$
10:For each j $\in \{1, \dots, k\}$ **do**
11:   Output(j, $<S_j, n_j>$)

Algorithm 1.2. k-means::Reduce

Input : List of centroid statistics – partial sums and counts $[<S_j^l, n_j^l>]$ – for each
centroid j $\in \{1, ..., k\}$
1:For each j $\in \{1, ..., k\}$ **do**
2:   Let λ be the length of the list of centroid statistics
3 :$n_j = 0$, $S_j = 0$
4 :   For each l $\in \{1, ..., k\}$ **do**
5 :$n_j = n_j + n_j^l$

6 :S_j= S_j + S_j^l

7 :c_j = $\frac{S_j}{n_j}$

8 :Output (j, c_j)

The whole clustering is run by a Master, which is responsible for running the Map (cluster assignment) and Reduce (centroid re-estimation) steps iteratively until k-means converges [8].

Algorithm 2. SNR on MapReduce

Input :Clusters .
Output: Feature subset of top scored features from clusters.

— List: contains target classes of samples in order.
— Record: contains values of samples for feature$_i$.
— DFS: is a distributed directory system for storage of output and input files of MapReduce.
— ID_feature: is an identifier characterizes each feature.
— file_cluster$_i$:contains features of cluster i.

Clustering features withAlgorithm 1.
For each cluster i do
DFS.put (file_cluster$_i$)

Map function (parallel over features) (key: ID_feature, value: record)
List= [class1, class2, class2.......................]
Iterate over record and list
compute $\mu 1$, $\mu 2$
compute $\sigma 1$, $\sigma 2$
compute SNR
Output (SNR, (ID_feature, record))

Reduce Function (key: SNR, value :(ID_feature,   record)
Output (SNR, (ID_feature, record))
Select top scored feature.
DFS.delete (file_cluster$_i$).

Aggregation and validation of the top scored features selected.

4.2   The Second Stage:

In this stage, we are using Binary PSO on MapReduce which is composed of four MapReduce jobs. In Hadoop, a mechanism of JobControl classes is provided to execute the four jobs sequentially.

Algorithm 3. PSO on MapReduce

Input : Initial swarm of particles and the subset of top features selected and validated .
Output: Best solution Gbest.

-    GroupP: we have defined at the beginning several groups of particles, GroupP is the identifier of each group.
-    P: position of a particle, Pbest: best position of a particle, FitPbest: fitness of Pbest, Gbest: global position of particles, FitGbest: fitness of Gbest, V: velocity of a particle.

First job
Mapper (key: ID_particle, value: (P, Pbest, FitPbest, Gbest, FitGbest, V, GroupP) (parallel mappers)
Initial Pbest, FitPbest, Gbest, FitGbest are empty.
fitness (): function of evaluation of the fitness of the designed particle (accuracy SVM) and take as input P and features selected.
If fitness (P) >FitPbest
Pbest=P.
FitPbest= fitness (P).
Emit(ID_particle, (P, Pbest, FitPbest, Gbest, FitGbest, V, GroupP))
Reducer (key: ID_particle, value: (P, Pbest, FitPbest, Gbest, FitGbest, V,GroupP) (parallel reducers)
Emit(ID_particle, (P, Pbest, FitPbest, Gbest, FitGbest, V,GroupP)) (file-output1 in HDFS)

Second job
Mapper (key: ID_particle, value: (P, Pbest, FitPbest, Gbest, FitGbest, V, GroupP) (parallel mappers)
Emit(GroupP, (ID_particle ,P, Pbest, FitPbest, Gbest, FitGbest, V))
Reducer (key: GroupP, value: (ID_particle, P, Pbest, Gbest, FitGbest, V) (parallel reducers)
Initial Gbestg is empty.
Cpt: number of 1 in Gbest, initialized to 0.
For all values
Gbestg = maximum of all Gbest with minimum number of Cpt (in case of equality between Gbest).
FitGbestg= FitGbest of Gbestg.
Emit (ONE, (Gbestg, FitGbestg)) (file-output2 in HDFS)

Third job

Mapper (key: ONE, value: (Gbestg, FitGbestg) (parallel reducers)
Emit (ONE, (Gbestg, FitGbestg))
Reducer (key: ONE, value: (Gbestg, FitGbest) (parallel reducers)
Initial Gbestglobal is empty. Cpt1: number of 1 in Gbestg, initialized to 0.
For all values
Gbestglobal = maximum of Gbestg with minimum number of Cpt1 (in case o equality between Gbestg)
FitGbestglobal= FitGbest of Gbestglobal.
Emit (Gbestglobal, (FitGbestglobal)) (file-output3 in HDFS)

Fourth job

Mapper (key: ID_particle, value: (P, Pbest, FitPbest, Gbest, FitGbest, V, GroupP) (parallel mappers)
Read file-output3 from HDFS
Gbest = Gbestglobal
FitGbest = FitGbestglobal
V'= New_Velocity (V, P, Pbest, Gbest) /* New_Velocity is a function for the   evaluation of the new velocity*/
P'= New_Position (P, V') /* New_Position is a function for the evaluation of the new position*/
P=P', V=V'
Emit(ID_particle, (P, Pbest, FitPbest, Gbest, FitGbest V, GroupP))
reducer (key: ID_particle, value: (P, Pbest, FitPbest, Gbest, FitGbest, V, GroupP) (parallel reducers)
Emit(ID_particle, (P, Pbest, FitPbest, Gbest, FitGbest, V, GroupP))

Repeat the execution of jobs K-iterations.

5   Results and Experiments

We have used tow datasets of cancer RNA-seq gene expression data (gastric cancer, ESCA (esophageal carcinoma)): gastric dataset derived from the main source of gene expression data Omnibus. The last, ESCA derived from TCGA (Cancer Genome Atlas), and four gene expression microarray datasets (tow ovarian cancer datasets, gastric cancer dataset, ESCC dataset (esophageal squamous cell carcinoma)) derived from Omnibus. Our approach is implemented on two-node cluster (master and slave), both master machine and slave machine are equipped with dual core processor and 4GB RAM memory for master node, and 2 GB for slave node. The operating system installed on the two nodes is Linux Ubuntu 13.10. The experiment is done using hadoop-1.2.1 and mahout 0.9 [9]. The cluster is configured in fully-distributed mode [10]. We have used support vector machine (SVM) to obtain classification accuracy, and the cross validation method 10 foldCV for performance evaluation of the classifier SVM. In order to improve the scalability of our method we have used a synthetic dataset (duplicate genes of each dataset), the size of data increased reaches 5GB for each dataset. Experiment is done with 5 clusters and 10 clusters. The performance of our method is compared to other approaches in the literature: an approach Based on Neighborhood Rough Set and Probabilistic Neural Networks Ensemble is proposed for the classification of Gene Expression Profiles [11], in [12] authors proposed a new selection method of interdependent genes via dynamic relevance analysis for cancer diagnosis. However, in the work presented in [13] a sequential forward feature selection algorithm to design decision tree models is suggested for the identification of biomarkers for Esophageal Squamous Cell Carcinoma. The obtained results are shown on Table 1, Table 2 and Table 3.

Table 1. Accuracy of SVM and number of genes selected in our method with normal datasets and comparison with other approaches

dataset	Ng	BPSO on MapReduce				[11]		[12]		[13]	
		Se	Sp	Acc	#	Acc	#	Acc	#	Acc	#
Ovrian [11]	15154	1	0,98	99	3	96	9	-	-	-	-
Gastric [12]	4522	1	1	100	2	-	-	96	14	-	-
ESCC [13]	22477	0,96	0,96	96	2	-	-	-	-	97	2
Ovrian	54675	1	1	100	2	/		/		/	
Gastric	21475	1	1	100	1						
ESCA	26540	1	1	100	2						

Ng: number of genes, **Se:** sensibility, **Sp:** specificity, **Acc:** accuracy (%), **#:** number of genes selected.

Table 2. Accuracy of SVM and number of genes selected in our method with large-scale datasets and comparison with other approaches

dataset	Size dataset	BPSO on MapReduce				[11]		[12]		[13]	
		Se	Sp	Acc	#	Acc	#	Acc	#	Acc	#
Ovarian [11]	5GB	1	0,98	99	3	96	9	-	-	-	-
Gastric [12]	5GB	1	1	100	2	-	-	96	14	-	-
ESCC [13]	5GB	0,96	0,96	96	2	-	-	-	-	97	2
Ovarian	5GB	1	1	100	2	/		/		/	
Gastric	5GB	1	1	100	1						
ESCA	5GB	1	1	100	2						

Table 3. List of biomarkers discovered

Type of cancer	Biomarkers	Related to cancer
Gastric cancer	**VSIG2** (V-set and immunoglobulin domain containing 2)	Selected from 22 gastric cancer biomarkers [14].
	D26129_at (RNS1 Ribonuclease A (pancreatic))	Considered among the non-regulated genes in gastric cancer [15].
	M62628_s_at (Alpha-1 Ig germline C-region membrane-coding region)	
Ovarian cancer	**METTL7A** (methyltransferaselike 7A)	Selected among the 28 genes markers linked to cancer [16].
	GALC (galactosylceramidase)	Selected Among the new differentially expressed genes in cell lines MKN45 gastric cancer [17].
Esophageal cancer	**ADAM12** (ADAM Metallopeptidase Domain 12)	Biomarkers of two types of cancer, breast cancer and bladder cancer [18].
	GPR155 (G protein-coupled receptor 155)	Melanomabiomarker for mouse [19].
	SH3BGRL (SH3 domain binding glutamate-rich protein)	Selected from 20 potential biomarkers of breast cancer [20]

6   Conclusion and Future Work

In this paper, we presented a large-scale feature selection based on MapReduce for biomarker discovery. From the obtained results and comparative analysis we can conclude that our method performs well, and gives better performance than centralized approaches. For that, our method can be applied to handle large-scale datasets and to overcome the challenge of feature selection in Big Data, especially for biomarker discovery in bioinformatics. Our method is auto-scalable and can be executed in a distributed environment with any number of nodes. Our future work is to implement our approach on Spark for better performance in time execution.

References

1. Jay, S., Hanlee, J.: Next-generation DNA sequencing. Nature Biotechnology 26(10), 1135–1145 (2008)
2. Yvan, S., Inaki, I., Larranaga, P.: A review of feature selection techniques in bioinformatics. Bioinformatics 23(19), 2507–2517 (2007)
3. Dean, J., Ghemawat, S.: MapReduce: Simplified Data Processing on Large Clusters. In: OSDI 2004: Sixth Symposium on Operating System Design and Implementation, Sponsored by USENIX, in Cooperation with ACM SIGOPS, pp. 137–150 (2004)
4. Barnali, S., Debahuti, M.: A Novel Feature Selection Algorithm using Particle Swarm Optimization for Cancer Microarray Data. Procedia Engineering 38, 27–31 (2012)
5. Azli, A., et al.: Distributed visual enhancement on surveillance video with Hadoop Mapreduce and performance evaluation in pseudo distributed mode. Australian Journal of Basic and Applied Sciences 8(9), 38 (2014)
6. Kourid, A.: Iterative MapReduce for Feature Selection. International Journal of Engineering Research & Technology 3(7) (2014)
7. White, T.: Hadoop the definitive guide. O'Reilly Media (2012)
8. Bekkerman, R., Bilenko, M., Langford, J.: Scaling up Machine learning. Cambridge University Press (2011)
9. Sean, O., et al.: Mahout in action. Manning Publications (2011)
10. Gaizhen, Y.: The Application of MapReduce in the Cloud Computing. In: Intelligence Information Processing and Trusted Computing (IPTC), pp. 154–156. IEEE (2011)
11. Yun, J., Guocheng, X., Na, C., Shan, C.: A New Gene Expression Profiles Classifying Approach Based on Neighborhood Rough Set and Probabilistic Neural Networks Ensembl. In: Lee, M., Hirose, A., Hou, Z.-G., Kil, R.M. (eds.) ICONIP 2013, Part II. LNCS, vol. 8227, pp. 484–489. Springer, Heidelberg (2013)
12. Sun, X., et al.: Selection of interdependent genes via dynamic relevance analysis for cancer diagnosis. Journal of Biomedical Informatics 46(2), 252–258 (2013)
13. Tung, C.W., et al.: Identification of Biomarkers for Esophageal Squamous Cell Carcinoma Using Feature Selection and Decision Tree Methods. The ScientificWorld Journal (2013)
14. Yang, S., Chung, H.C., et al.: Novel biomarker candidates for gastric cancer. Oncology Reports 19(3), 675–680 (2008)
15. Geetha Ramani, R., Gracia Jacob, S.: Benchmarking Classification Models for Cancer Prediction from Gene Expression Data: A Novel Approach and New Findings. Studies in Informatics and Control 22(2), 133–142 (2013)
16. Li, X., et al.: SSiCP: a new SVM based Recursive Feature Elimination Algorithm for Multiclass Cancer Classification. Bio-Medical Materials and Engineering 23, S1027–S1038 (2014)
17. Tuan, T.F., et al.: Putative tumor metastasis-associated genes in human gastric cancer. International Journal of Oncology 41(3), 1068–1084 (2012)
18. Fröhlich, C., et al.: Molecular Profiling of ADAM12 in Human Bladder Cancer. Clinical Cancer Research 12(24), 7359–7368 (2006)
19. Hacker, E., et al.: Reduced expression of IL-18 is a marker of ultraviolet radiation-induced melanomas. Int. J. Cancer 123(1), 227–231 (2008)
20. Mayer, M.: Breast Cancer Prognostic Biomarkers. Accelerating science (2014)

Social Validation of Solutions in the Context of Online Communities

An Expertise-Based Learning Approach

Lydia Nahla Driff[✉], Lamia Berkani, Ahmed Guessoum, and Abdellah Bendjahel

Artificial Intelligence Laboratory (LRIA), Department of Computer Science, USTHB,
Bab Ezzouar, Algeria
driff.nahla@gmail.com, l_berkani@hotmail.com,
{lberkani,aguessoum}@usthb.dz

Abstract. Online Communities are considered as a new organizational structure that allows individuals and groups of persons to collaborate and share their knowledge and experiences. These members need technological support in order to facilitate their learning activities (e.g. during a problem solving process).We address in this paper the problem of social validation, our aim being to support members of Online Communities of Learners to validate the proposed solutions. Our approach is based on the members' evaluations: we apply three machine learning techniques, namely a Genetic Algorithm, Artificial Neural Networks and the Naïve Bayes approach. The main objective is to determine a validity rating of a given solution. A preliminary experimentation of our approach within a Community of Learners whose main objective is to collaboratively learn the Java language shows that Neural Networks represent the most suitable approach in this context.

Keywords: Learning Community · Social Validation · Expertise-Based Learning · Machine Learning

1 Introduction

Today, with the great development of Information and Communication Technologies, a wide diversity of social learning frameworks have been promoted, including Online Learning Communities (OLCs) and social networks. The notion of OLC has been defined in different ways, exploring mainly the social aspects of collaborative learning (Laister and Kober, 2013) and the research and theory concerned with social support for learning (Swan and Shea, 2005).

One of the most important challenges of such communities is to enhance the knowledge exchange and sharing among the different members. With the increasing number of interactions, members collectively produce new knowledge in various formats (documents, solutions to problems, etc.) that will subsequently be published to the whole community (Le Boulch, 2009).The production of this knowledge is increasingly developed by members of the community who have different levels of expertise (experts,

© IFIP International Federation for Information Processing 2015
A. Amine et al. (Eds.): CIIA 2015, IFIP AICT 456, pp. 93–104, 2015.
DOI: 10.1007/978-3-319-19578-0_8

novices, etc.) and this highlights the need for validation of the new knowledge before it is stored and published to the rest of the community so as to ensure its reliability.

Validation is the expression of a judgment on a concept or whatever needs to be assessed after study/observation. This judgment can be favorable or not. Social validation of a concept is a collective action that aims at the evaluation of this concept based on various judgments and opinions expressed by different people from the field (Herr and Anderson, 2008), on the basis of statistical analysis, or approved opinions, experiences, etc. Its main objective is the assessment whether the concept is good or not and this can be represented by a degree of validity which is the percentage of conformity of the concept.

We focus in this work on the social validation of the proposed solutions within an OLC. We aim to support members in this process, providing them with a tool that will help them to "automatically" validate newly proposed solutions. We address the need to ensure the credibility of the validation process and we propose an expertise-based learning approach, by reusing past experiences (i.e. previous validations made by supervisors).

The review of the literature about social validation shows that little work has focused on this aspect in an educational setting. We especially mention the work proposed by Cabana et al. (2010) about the social validation on collective annotations where the authors addressed the problem of scalability (i.e. a resource which is more and more annotated is less and less exploitable by individuals). The authors proposed a way to socially validate collective annotations with respect to the social theory of information. Berkani et al. (2013) proposed a social validation of learning objects based on two features: (1) the members' assessments, formalized semantically, and (2) an expertise-based learning approach, applying a machine learning technique. The authors used neural networks because of their proven efficiency in many domains such as complex problem solving.

The remainder of this paper is structured as follows. In Section 2, we present the context of the study. Our contribution is presented in Section 3, where we give a detailed description of the parameters that are related to the evaluation of a solution. Then, we present the application of the aforementioned Machine Learning techniques to any given solution using the defined parameters. The experimental results are presented in Section 4 where a discussion of the strengths and weaknesses of each technique is presented. The conclusion and perspectives are stated in Section 5.

2   Context of the Study

In our study, we consider a learning community related to the domain of higher education. The members of this community target the learning of the JAVA programming language and its different concepts. The main objective of this community is to improve the learners' skills and his acquisition of new knowledge.

We assume that the community includes members with different skill levels (beginners, advanced, experts, etc.) and the Java language includes various concepts (classes, abstraction, and so on), including the handling of tools (Java web GUI, JVM, etc.).

We have found out that the discussion forum and/or the Frequently Asked Questions are services that can be considered as the most used by the community members. Indeed, these often use these services in their interactions and information exchange.

However, one of the problems encountered by the community members is the validation of the proposed solutions; several questions can be asked at this point: Is a given solution correct? If yes, to what extent is it accurate? And, more importantly, who has validated it? Was it validated by a set of members, by a single expert, or within some other setting? This is why we focus in this work on the social validation of a solution, and we try to automate this process in order to support community members in their learning activities.

Automation is very cost-effective when it comes to time saving. It helps avoid several phases and replaces the manual work done by the supervisor (or teacher) whose role is to validate the solutions that are proposed by the community members (or learners). On the other hand, the social validation can give some precision about the obtained results by considering distinct opinions that are based on different criteria.

In the next section, we present our approach for automating the process of social validation, bearing in mind that we consider the validation of one solution at a time.

3   Contribution

In our work, we have tried to automate the validation process using Machine Learning (ML) techniques. The choice for these techniques has been dictated by the fact that they allow to take into account the rich experience (knowledge repository) in terms of validations of solutions throughout the lifetime of a community. As such, they directly take into account the existing experience, which makes them very different from conventional algorithmic methods where an exact and accurate understanding of the factors that are taken into account in any validation of a solution is required.

We start by the modelling of the solution validation problem in terms of some specific parameters that need to be represented. Our goal is to define an evaluation in a unique way so as to be able to manipulate it in the (automatic) training phase.

In this section, we present these parameters as well as the process followed by each of the considered ML techniques.

3.1   Parameters of an Evaluation

As explained above, the prediction of a degree of validity for a given solution is collective, based on the various members' assessments of the solution. To this end, we have defined the parameters that we consider as being the most important and significant ones to identify, characterize, and implement each assessment (see Fig. 1). Thus we believe that the evaluation by a given member M_i concerns the level of the evaluator, the assigned score, the confidence, the evaluation context, the skill level and the success. We now explain each of these parameters.

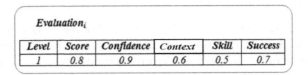

Fig. 1. Parameters of an evaluation

1. ***Level of the evaluator:*** Each assessment corresponds to a single member. This member has a certain amount of knowledge and expertise which are measured by the parameter "Level". In our case, a member is either a Professor, a PhD student, a Master's student, a student preparing a Bachelor's degree or a member with basic knowledge.

   The evaluator's Level is predefined in this user's profile at the time of his registration into the community. The value of this "level" is a coefficient that depends on the significance of the evaluator's level with respect to all the existing levels in the community.

$$Coefficient(Level) = Score/N \tag{1}$$

where: N is the number of levels

Table 1. Computation of the level of the evaluator

Level	Coefficient
Professor	5/5=1
PhD	4/5=0.8
Master's	3/5=0.6
Bachelor's	2/5=0.4
Basic	1/5=0.2

2. ***Score:*** For each evaluation, a score will be given by the evaluating member. This score represents the member's opinion of the solution being evaluated: the evaluator may assign a high score if the solution is good or very good, and an average score if the solution is not quite correct, or even a low score if the solution is judged incorrect.

3. ***Confidence:*** The score given by an evaluating member reflects his opinion. A percentage of confidence is assigned by the evaluator himself to each score he gives: if he is sure of his score, he will give a high degree of confidence; otherwise, the degree of confidence will be lower.

4. ***Evaluation context:*** In evaluating a solution, the member does his assessment of the solution based on a given source. This source could be a book, a document, an article, etc. The importance of the sources is different based on each one's credibility. We thus assign a weight to each source to indicate its reliability. The evaluation context can take several formats: tested results, research outcome, a similar problem, an approved opinion, or a new problem.

5. *Skill level:* A profile is associated with each member of the community. This profile is mainly used to retrieve information about the expertise of a member according to what he/she described as areas of expertise with respect to all the areas identified in the community by the input parameter "degree of expertise". As such, for a given problem in a specific domain, a member will have a certain level of expertise that we call "skill level". More precisely, this level represents the quality of a member in relation to his expertise in a specific area. This will allow us to get an idea about the credibility of his evaluation.

Three cases can be distinguished:

- Either the domain belongs to the member's skills set (high rate)
- Or the domain belongs to the member's centre of interest (average rate)
- Or the member has no knowledge at all about the domain (low rate)

In order to calculate the skills level of a member with respect to the domain of the solution under evaluation, we need to calculate the similarity between all of the member's areas of expertise and the domain of this solution. To this end, we have defined a taxonomy that encompasses the existing domains in a given community and have added rules that cover all the possible cases for the relative positions of two domains in the taxonomy. We summarize these rules in the following table:

Table 2. Similarity rules

	Description	Similarity
Rule 1	D is the same as D'	$\text{Sim} = 1$
Rule 2	D (direct or indirect) parent of D'	$\text{Sim} = 1$
Rule 3	D (direct/indirect) son of D'	$\text{Sim} = \dfrac{|\text{weight}(D) - \text{weight}(D')|}{\Delta\text{Lev}}$
Rule 4	D and D' are independent	$\text{Sim} = \begin{cases} \text{weight}(D_c) \text{ if D and D' at the same level} \\ \dfrac{\text{weight}(D_c)}{\Delta\text{Lev}} \quad \text{otherwise} \end{cases}$

where:

D is the problem domain;
D' is one of the member's domains of expertise
Dc is the closest (parent) domain common to D and D'
ΔLev is the difference between the levels of D and D'

The skill level of a member is calculated in relation to all his areas of expertise using an ontology that uses the mentioned degrees of expertise (see Fig.2). These degrees reflect the coverage of subdomains (son nodes) from the related domain (parent node) in terms of knowledge. For example, a member who has knowledge in the field IGraphic, *a-fortiori* covers the subdomains Swing and AWT.

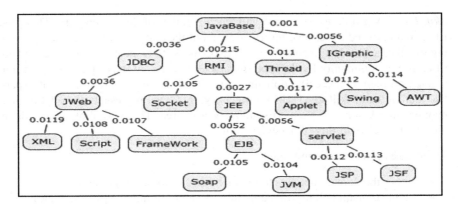

Fig. 2. Example of a taxonomy for the Java domain

This skill level is calculated according to the following steps:
Calculate the similarity between each domain of expertise D_i and the desired/searched-for domain D:

$$Similarity(D, Di) \tag{2}$$

Associate the similarity of each domain with the member's degree of expertise on D_i

$$Similarity(D, Di) * Expertise(M, Di) \tag{3}$$

Find the domain that corresponds to the value that maximizes the obtained values using the expression:

$$k = argmax_i(Similarity(D, Di) * Expertise(M, Di)) \tag{4}$$

Calculate the *quantum* which represents the amount of acquired skills in other domains to be added to the global competence of the member. The aim is not to neglect this additional skill.

$$Quantum= \{\{i = 1 - N\} \text{ and } i \neq k, (Similarity(D, Di) *Expertise(M, Di) / 10*(N - 1) \} \tag{5}$$

We point out that the number 10 is a factor that we can manipulate to increase or decrease the quantum with which we will adjust the additional competency provided by other domains rather than that giving the maximum of similarity.
Calculate the final competency of M with respect to D given that this value must be at least equal to a maximum value and does not exceed the value 1.

$$Competency (M, D) = min[1, ((S_k* P_k) * (1 + quantum))] \tag{6}$$

where:

S_k is the similarity between the domain D_k which maximizes the competence
of M and the domain of the solution
P_K is the member's expertise
D is the domain of the solution

6. The degree of success: An active member may be considered as a trusted source
   because of his correct assessments in two cases: (1) he generally evaluates positively solutions that at the end of the validation process obtain a high degree of validity; and (2) he generally evaluates negatively solutions that at the end of the validation process are assigned a low degree of validity.

   Accordingly, we assign to him a degree of success which represents the distance of
   one of his evaluations to the final validity of the solution according to the score he
   gave it. The following is the formula we propose to calculate the degree of success:

$$Success(Si) = 1 - |Score - validity(Si)| \tag{7}$$

A member's success score is calculated with respect to the relative success of all
the solutions he has evaluated:

$$Success = \frac{1}{N}\sum_{i=1}^{N}(Success(Si)) \tag{8}$$

3.2   Use of Machine Learning Techniques

Machine Learning (ML) techniques are powerful in terms of their flexibility and ease
of extraction of hidden relations that exist within data of the various applications they
could be used for. We have decided to use ML in our problem of social validation of
solutions; the intuition is to have automated learning from past experience of users'
evaluations and the experts' assessments of the quality of these evaluations. We use
the representation of an evaluation as presented above and apply different ML techniques on data given in this representation.

3.2.1   Modelling of Machine Learning Methods

We are mainly interested in three methods: Genetic Algorithms (GA) (See (Goldberg,
1989), (Holland, 1992) and (Mitchell, 1996)); Neural Networks (NN) (See (Muller
and Reinhardt, 1994) and (Fausett, 1994)); and the Naïve Bayes Approach (Mitchell,
1997), as presented in the following sub-sections:

3.2.1.1 Genetic Algorithms: Genetic algorithms (GA) are often used for optimization.
In our case, we have used a similar approach to Data Mining guided by the GA to
highlight useful information for solving our problem. The approach proceeds as follows in the learning phase:

- Consider an initial population as a set of evaluations, carried out on different solutions, and represented using the six aforementioned parameters.

- Conduct a series of crossings and mutations by randomly changing the parameter values.
- Keep the final population which corresponds to the final validity predicted by a supervisor. The fitness function used is the following:

$$Fitness = \frac{1}{N+1}\sum_{i=1}^{N}(c_i * x_i)\qquad(9)$$

where x_i is the value of the attribute and c_i its coefficient.

- Encode the population obtained after the previous step using a binary encoding.
- Apply an algorithm for mining association rules such as the Close algorithm (Pasquier et al., 1999; Pei et al, 2000).

Gradually enrich the rule base with new rules. These new rules will be added to cater for newly encountered cases that are not covered by the already generated rule base.

In our context, an Association Rule (Han et al., 2006; Sarawagi et al, 2000) is an implication of the form $X \rightarrow Y$ where X is a conjunction of Attribute-Value pairs of the form "$Attribute_i = Value_j$" and Y is a pair Attribute-Value of the same form which represents the degree of validity of an evaluation. Example:

$$If \left((Score = 0,8) \text{ and } (Confidence = 0,6) \text{and} (Success = 0,9) \right) \text{ then } Validity$$
$$= 0,8\qquad(10)$$

The CLOSE algorithm is used for the extraction of informative association rules based on the informative content of the database (Pasquier et al., 1999; Pei et al, 2000).

3.2.1.2 Neural Networks: Artificial Neural Networks (ANNs) have been designed to mimic information flow in the human brain. Neural networks are efficient for complex problem solving, especially for pattern matching, classification, and optimization problems. In our case, we have used this method to predict a degree of validity of a given evaluation.

After designing several models of ANNs, we have tried various learning and activation functions, varying the number of neurons in each case. We have selected the NN architecture as follows for as good a learning phase as possible:

- Design a multilayer perceptron containing: six inputs, twenty neurons on the hidden layer and one neuron on the output layer.
- Feed in input into the network each 6-value input describing an evaluation of a solution.
- Give as output the validity score given by the supervisor for the given input.
- Train the network until the best learning is obtained (trying various architectures).
- Once a good learning has been achieved, simulate the network.

3.2.1.3 Naive Bayes Approach: The Naive Bayes Approach is a probabilistic approach based on conditional probability calculations. It is called Naïve due to the assumption it makes of independence of the various events (attributes) it considers. In spite of this, this assumption has not prevented them from providing an efficient and often good approach. In our case, we have considered a set of evaluations on various solutions, represented using the six parameters. We present below the steps followed for the calculation of the probabilities:

- Calculate the probability of the validity value Vi :

$$P(V_i) = \frac{Frequency(value_i)}{N} \tag{11}$$

where N is the number of evaluations considered for the learning.

- Calculate the conditional probability that an attribute takes a value $value_i$, given that V_i is the value of the validity:

$$P(value_i/V_i) = \frac{Frequency(value_i)}{P(V_i)} \tag{12}$$

- Calculate the conditional probabilities that the validity takes different possible values V_i bearing in mind that the attributes have some given values.

$$P(Vi/attribute_i = value_1, attribute_j = value_2, \ldots, attribute_n = value_m) \tag{13}$$

- Consider the validity V_i corresponding to the maximal probability of the set obtained as the validity of the evaluation.

3.2.2 Application of the Machine Learning Techniques

In the case of a new solution to be validated, the steps to be followed are as follows:

- Represent all the evaluations of the solution using the six attributes.
- Predict a degree of validity for each one of the evaluations for the three methods.
- In the case of the GA: associate with each evaluation the most suitable rule, and then generate rules based on the validity rates for each evaluation.
- In the case of the ANN approach: simulate each evaluation by the ANN assigning a validity rate for each evaluation.
- In the case of the Naïve Bayes approach: calculate the probabilities of the evaluations and associate each evaluation with a validity rate.
- Remove the incorrect values from the set of validity rates.
- Apply a credibility formula to calculate the final validity:

$$FinalValidity = \sum_{i=1}^{N}(Credibility_i * Validity_i) \tag{14}$$

4   Implementation and Tests

4.1   Description of the Testing Phase

In order to test our approach, we have developed an online community platform for Java learning, including the different functionalities related to our approach. Furthermore, we have developed a prototype to automatically generate a large number of solutions and their evaluations. This has allowed us to create the database and hence to carry out our learning process. In addition, we have used the community platform, where members can add new problems, propose new solutions or evaluate some existing ones. Then we have represented all the obtained evaluations according to the six parameters, as proposed in section III. Finally, we have applied the selected ML techniques.

4.2   Discussion of the Findings

We have implemented the three ML techniques to predict the degree of validity of a given solution. After some tests and experimentations, we obtained the results shown in the following figures:

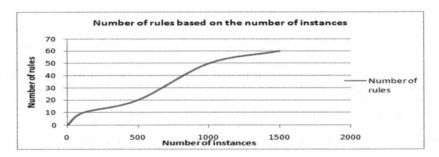

Fig. 3. Increasing number of the association rules (GA approach)

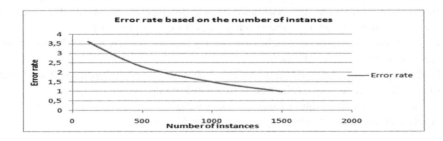

Fig. 4. Error rate of the ANN method

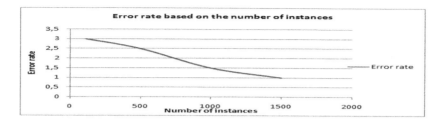

Fig. 5. Error rate of the Naïve Bayes approach

- We can deduce from the application of the GA approach that more and more new solutions are validated, more rules can be generated and the accuracy of the rules application increases improving the degree of validity (see Fig. 3).
- The application of ANNs allows us to conclude that the error rate decreases with the increasing number of examples that are used as input during the ANN learning phase (see Fig. 4).
- Finally, the application of the Naïve Bayes approach allows us to deduce that with the increasing number of examples, the error rate decreases, which implies that the number of correct predictions increases, and hence the results become more accurate (see Fig. 5).

On the other hand, an analysis of the results we have obtained has allowed us to compare the three ML methods on the basis of four criteria (see Table 3).

- *Criterion 1 – Data redundancy:* if data appears frequently, then the learning outcomes are improved.
- *Criterion 2 – Number of instances:* when the number of data instances used in the learning increases, the learning is better guided and gives more accurate results.
- *Criterion 3 – Appropriateness of results:* the learning is considered good if it frequently gives accurate results with low error rates.
- *Criterion 4 –New cases: l*earning is considered good if it can handle well and robustly a situation where a new case arises (a case which was not seen during the learning phase).

Table 3. Comparison of the three ML methods

	GA	ANN	NBA
Criterion 1	Yes	No	Yes
Criterion 2	Yes	Yes	Yes
Criterion 3	Somewhat	Strongly	Always
Criterion 4	Frequently	Somewhat	Never

According to these results and analysis, we conclude that the neural networks have given the best performance compared to the two other approaches. In order to improve the obtained results, it would be very interesting to combine these approaches in different ways and to compare the performance of the different algorithms.

5   Conclusion and Perspectives

We are interested in this work in the problem of social validation of solutions proposed in the context of a learning community. We have considered the evaluations carried out on already proposed solutions and modeled the problem according to several criteria. An automatic validation process was proposed using three machine learning techniques: genetic algorithms, neural networks and the Naive Bayes Approach. An experimental study of the developed prototype has been conducted. The results show that neural networks have given the best performance.

As future work we envisage to make further tests on a real community of learners and collect as much data as possible to enrich the learning. We envisage also to check the possibility of combining some of the different learning techniques and to generalize the process of social validation of more than one proposed solutions to the same problem.

References

1. Berkani, L., Driff, L.N., Guessoum, A.: Social Validation of Learning Objects in Online Communities of Practice Using Semantic and Machine Learning Techniques. In: Amine, A., Mohamed, O.A., Bellatreche, L. (eds.) Modeling Approaches and Algorithms. SCI, vol. 488, pp. 237–247. Springer, Heidelberg (2013)
2. Cabanac, G., Chevalier, M., Chrisment, C., Julien, C.: Social validation of collective annotations: Definition and experiment. Journal of the American Society for Information Science and Technology 61(2), 271–287 (2010)
3. Fausett, L.: Fundamentals of Neural Networks: Architectures, Algorithms, and Applications. Prentice Hall (1994) ISBN: 0133341860
4. Goldberg, D.: Genetic Algorithms in Search, Optimization and Machine Learning. Addison-Wesley Professional, Reading (1989), ISBN 978-0201157673
5. Herr, K., Anderson, L.G.: The Action Research Dissertation: A Guide for Students and Faculty. Thousand Oaks (2008) ISBN 0-7619-2991-6
6. Holland, J.: Adaptation in Natural and Artificial Systems. MIT Press, MA (1992)
7. Laister, J., Kober, S.: Technikum Joanneum Social Aspects of Collaborative Learning in Virtual Learning Environments,
   http://comma.doc.ic.ac.uk/inverse/papers/patras/
8. Le Boulch, D., Bouyssou, D., Grundstein, M.: Towards a redefinition of the relationships between information systems development and individual cognition. In: Information Technologies in Environmental Engineering, Springer, Heidelberg (2009)
9. Mitchell, T.: Machine Learnin. McGraw Hill (1997) ISBN 007042807
10. Mitchell, M.: An Introduction to Genetic Algorithms. MIT Press, MA (1996)
11. Muller, B., Reinhardt, J.: Neural Networks. Springer (1991)
12. Pasquier, N., Bastide, Y., Taouil, R., Lakhal, L.: Discovering frequent closed itemsets for association rules. In: 7th International Conference on Database Theory (January 1999)
13. Pei, J., Han, J., Mao, R.: Closet: An effcient algorithm for mining frequent closed itemsets. In: SIGMOD Int. Workshop on Data Mining and Knowledge Discovery (2000)
14. Swan, K., Shea, P.: The development of virtual learning communities. In: Hiltz, S.R., Goldman, R. (eds.) Asynchronous Learning Networks: The Research Frontier, pp. 239–260. Hampton Press, New York (2005)
15. Han, J., Kamber, M.: Data Mining: Concepts and Techniques, 2nd edn. Morgan Kaufmann Publishers (March 2006) ISBN 1-55860-901-6
16. Sarawagi, S., Thomas, S., Agrawal, R.: Integrating Association Rule Mining with Databases: Alternatives and Implications. Data Mining and Knowledge Discovery Journal 4(2/3) (2000)

Remotely Sensed Data Clustering Using K-Harmonic Means Algorithm and Cluster Validity Index

Habib Mahi[1(✉)], Nezha Farhi[1], and Kaouter Labed[2]

[1] Earth Observation Division, Centre of Space Techniques, Arzew, Algeria
[2] Kaouter LABED, Faculty of Mathematics and Computer Science Mohamed Boudiaf,
University – USTOMB, Oran, Algeria
{hmahi,nfarhi}@cts.asal.dz,
kaouther.labed@univ-usto.dz

Abstract. In this paper, we propose a new clustering method based on the combination of K-harmonic means (KHM) clustering algorithm and cluster validity index for remotely sensed data clustering. The KHM is essentially insensitive to the initialization of the centers. In addition, cluster validity index is introduced to determine the optimal number of clusters in the data studied. Four cluster validity indices were compared in this work namely, DB index, XB index, PBMF index, WB-index and a new index has been deduced namely, WXI. The Experimental results and comparison with both K-means (KM) and fuzzy C-means (FCM) algorithms confirm the effectiveness of the proposed methodology.

Keywords: Clustering · KHM · Cluster validity indices · Remotely sensed data · K-means · FCM

1 Introduction

Clustering is an exploratory data analysis tool that reveals associations, patterns, relationships, and structures in masses of data [1] [2]. Two approaches of clustering algorithms exist in the literature: fuzzy (or soft) and crisp (or hard) clustering. In the first approach, clusters are overlapping and each object belongs to each cluster to a certain degree (or with a certain fuzzy membership level) [3]. The fuzzy c-means (FCM) [4] seems to be the most widely used algorithm in the field of fuzzy clustering. It appears to be an appropriate choice in multiple domains as remote sensing satellite images and pattern recognition [5] [6]. In crisp clustering, clusters are disjoint: each objet belongs to exactly one cluster as example we cite the K-Means (KM) [7] and ISODATA (Iterative Self-Organizing Data Analysis Technique) algorithms [8]. These latter are widely used clustering methods for multispectral image analysis [9]. Also, these algorithms have been successfully used in various topics, including computer vision and astronomy. Their popularity is mainly due to their scalability and simplicity. However, they suffer from a number of limitations. Firstly, the requirement to define a priori the number of K clusters is considered as a handicap and consequently an inappropriate choice of initial clusters may generate poor clustering results [10]. Secondly,

© IFIP International Federation for Information Processing 2015
A. Amine et al. (Eds.): CIIA 2015, IFIP AICT 456, pp. 105–116, 2015.
DOI: 10.1007/978-3-319-19578-0_9

the   KM algorithm and similarly the ISODATA algorithm work best for images with clusters which are spherical and that have the same variance. This is often not true for remotely sensed data with clusters which are more or less elongated with a much larger variability, such as forest for example [11]. Also, convergence to local optimum is always observed in this kind of algorithms [1].

To deal with these drawbacks, considerable efforts have been made to mainly create variants from the original methods. As examples we cite KM and its alternatives K-Harmonic Means, Trimmed k-means and k-modes algorithm [1]. At the same time some works have focused on the developing of measures to find the optimal number of clusters using cluster validity indices [3]. We distinguish fuzzy indices (used with fuzzy clustering) and crisp indices (used with hard clustering). As examples of fuzzy indices we can mention XB index [12] as well as Bezdek's PE and PC indices [13] [14]. DB-index [15], Dunn's index [16] and Calinski-Harabasz index [17] are some of the popular indices used in crisp clustering. [3] [18] [19] give a very important review of different CVIs present in the literature.

In this study we investigate the ability of the K-Harmonic Means clustering algorithm combined with validity indices, especially in unsupervised classification of remote sensing data. The rest of paper is organized as follows. Methodology will be firstly presented in Section 2; the experimentation and the results obtained will be tackled in Section 3. Section 4 concludes the paper.

2   Methodology

In this section we give a brief description of the K-Harmonic Means and four clustering validity indices. Then we present the proposed method in details. In the next sections, the following notation will be adopted:

N: The number of objects in the data set.
x_i: The ith object in the data set.
K: The number of clusters.
c_j: The center of cluster j.
d: The number of dataset dimensions.

2.1   K-Harmonic Means Algorithm

The initialization of centers influence on the K-Means (KM) performance and it is considered as the main drawback of this algorithm. To improve KM, Zhang [20] proposes to use the harmonic mean instead of standard mean in the objective function and has named the new algorithm K-Harmonic Means (KHM).

$$KHM = \sum_{i=1}^{N} \frac{K}{\sum_{j=1}^{K} \frac{1}{\|x_i - c_j\|^q}} \tag{1}$$

New centers clusters are calculated as following [21][22]:

$$c_k = \frac{\sum_{i=1}^{N}\frac{1}{\left[\sum_{l=1}^{K}\frac{\|x_i-c_j\|^q}{\|x_i-c_l\|^q}\right]^2}zx_i}{\sum_{i=1}^{N}\frac{1}{\left[\sum_{l=1}^{K}\frac{\|x_i-c_j\|^q}{\|x_i-c_l\|^q}\right]^2}} \tag{2}$$

2.2 Clustering Validity Indices

In this sub-section, we introduce the clustering validity indices used in this work, namely Davies-Bouldin (DB), Xie-Benie (XB), Pakhira-Bandyopadhyay-Maulik Fuzzy (PBMF), WB index (WB) and WB-XB index (WXI).

- Davies-Bouldin index (DB $\downarrow$) [15]: It is a very popular and used crisp index in clustering algorithms. It requires only two parameters to be defined by the user, the distance measure noted p and the dispersion measure noted q. The DB is defined as follows:

$$DB = \frac{1}{K}\sum_{i=1}^{K}R_i \tag{3}$$

With

$$R_i = max_{i,i \neq j}\left\{\frac{S_i+S_j}{M_{ij}}\right\} \tag{4}$$

Where

$$S_i = \left\{\frac{1}{T_i}\sum_{j=1}^{T_i}\|x_j - c_i\|^q\right\}^{\frac{1}{q}} \tag{5}$$

And

$$M_{ij} = \left\{\sum_{k=1}^{K}\|c_{ki} - c_{kj}\|^p\right\}^{\frac{1}{p}} \tag{6}$$

With

c_{ki}: k^{th} Component of the n-dimensional vector c_i.
c_i: The center of cluster i.
M_{ij}: The Minkowski metric.
T_i: The number of vectors (pixels) in cluster i.

- Xie-Benie index (XB $\downarrow$) [12]: Also called function S, is defined as a ratio of the total variation to the minimum separation of clusters. Its definition is:

$$XB = \frac{1}{N}\frac{\sum_{i=1}^{K}\sum_{j=1}^{N}(\mu_{ij})^m\|x_j-c_i\|^2}{min_{l \neq i}\|c_l-c_i\|^2} \tag{7}$$

- Pakhira-Bandyopadhyay-Maulik Fuzzy index (PBMF ↑) [3]: It is considered as validity index measure for fuzzy clusters. It is formulated as follows:

$$PBMF = \frac{1}{K} \times \frac{E_1}{\sum_{i=1}^{N}\sum_{j=1}^{K}(\mu_{ij})^m\|x_i-c_j\|^2} \times max_{l\neq i}\|c_l - c_i\|^2 \qquad (8)$$

With E_1 is constant for a given dataset.

- WB index (WB ↓) [23]: It is defined as a ration of the measure of cluster compactness to its measure of separation. It is given by:

$$WB = K \frac{\sum_{i=1}^{N}\|x_i-c_{pi}\|^2}{\sum_{i=1}^{K} n_i\|c_i-\bar{X}\|^2} \qquad (9)$$

- WB-XB index (WXI ↓): It is defined as the average between WB and XB indices and is formulated as follows:

$$WXI = (WB\_index + XB\_index) /2 \qquad (10)$$

2.3   Mean Square Error (MSE)

It is a measure of error which is often used in clustering problems. It represents the mean distance of objects in the dataset from the nearest centers [24]. It is formulated as follows:

$$MSE = \frac{\sum_{j=1}^{K}\sum_{X_i \in C_j}\|x_i - c_j\|}{N * d} \qquad (11)$$

2.4   Proposed Method

In this subsection, we present the proposed method which combines the KHM algorithm, the mean square error (MSE) and WXI cluster validity index. This new method is called Growing KHM (GKHM).

For a given data distribution two centers are chosen randomly (Fig. 1. a), the KHM clustering algorithm is then applied to obtain the two initial clusters (Fig. 1. b). Also, the mean square error (MSE) is computed in this stage for each cluster to select the heterogeneous one (MSE is maximal) to be divided. Therefore, two new centers are computed (Fig. 1. c) and the old one is removed. The process is repeated until a number of epochs are satisfied. The complete algorithm for the proposed method is given by the following:

1. Choose two centers randomly from the dataset.
2. Run the KHM algorithm with these two centers
3. **Repeat**

4. epoch =1
5. Compute MSE for each cluster
6. Select the cluster with the maximum MSE value
    - Insert two new centers halfway between the old center and the two extremes of the cluster in order two have two new clusters.
    - Remove the old center
    - Run the KHM algorithm with the new centers (K = 2).
7. Compute the WXI^{epoch} of all the clusters and save it in the vector V with the related centers
8. **Until** (epoch number's reached)
9. Select the minimum value of WXI in V i.e. The final number of clusters
10. Clustering dataset with the appropriate centers.

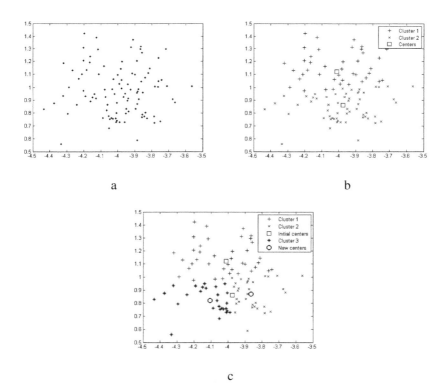

a

b

c

Fig. 1. Process of new centers: a) Data Initialization, b) Data Sampling, c) New Centers Generation

3   Experimental Results

This section is devoted to experiments that ensure the validity and effectiveness of the proposed method. It is divided into three subsections. In the first subsection, an experiment is conducted by using synthetic datasets to select the most suitable cluster validity index for our work. In the second subsection, a comparison of our approach with both KM and FCM algorithms is drawn. The last subsection concerns the clustering of real satellite images using the proposed method and its results. All the experiments results have been obtained using the MATLAB software package.

3.1   Comparison between the Four Cluster Validity Indices

In order to select the best clustering validity index, we experimentally evaluated their performance on four different synthetic datasets using the basic KHM. Some of the datasets namely S1 and S4 are plotted in Fig. 2 respectively. Each dataset consists of 5000 points representing 15 clusters. All the datasets can be found in the SIPU web page http://cs.uef.fi/sipu/datasets.

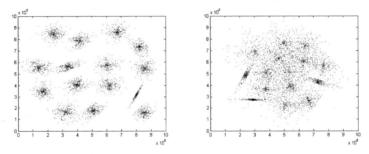

Fig. 2. Synthetic data S1 and S4

In this paper, we have used four synthetic datasets S1-S4 which have the same number of clusters (K=15) and the same Gaussian distribution with increasing overlap between the clusters. The overlapping is an additional criterion which allows us to select the optimal cluster validity index between indices used in this work. For this end, we have applied the KHM algorithm as mentioned before for each dataset by varying the number of clusters from 2 to 20; and, the values of the four CVI's are computed for different K. The results reported in Tables 1 and 2 show only the best values obtained by the four CVI's and their corresponding number of clusters K.

From Table 1, we can see that WB and XB cluster validity indices give the best values for the KHM algorithm and reach their minimum respectively at the optimal

Table 1. Comparison between DB, WB, PBMF and XB indices for S1 dataset

	Cluster Validity Indices			
K	DB	WB	PBMF	XB
13	**0.40**	0,49	$2,99 \times 10^{10}$	0,08
14	0.42	0,36	**$9,69 \times 10^{10}$**	0,06
15	0.44	**0,24**	$4,26 \times 10^{10}$	**0,04**

Table 2. Comparison between DB, WB, PBMF and XB indices for S4 dataset

	Cluster Validity Indices			
K	**DB**	**WB**	**PBMF**	**XB**
4	0.84	1.89	**2.32 x 10^{10}**	0.16
11	**0.64**	1.17	1.18 x 10^{10}	0.11
14	0.65	0.96	1.25 x 10^{10}	**0.09**
15	0.72	**0.90**	0.77 x 10^{10}	0.14

number of clusters (K=15). On the other hand, the DB and PBMF cluster validity indices approximate the number of clusters (K=13 and K=14).

From Table 2, we notice that WB index still offers the best values for the KHM algorithm and reaches its minimum for the optimal clusters number (K=15). The XB index approximate the solution and has its optimum value nearly to the solution (K=14). However, DB and PBMF fail to find a near best solution by returning a completely wrong number of clusters (K=11 and K=4) and having an unstable minimum.

In Summary, the results show that all the cluster validity indices provide an accurate estimation of the clusters number when the clusters in dataset present a small distortion. However, several knee points are detected with exception of the WB index. For clusters with a largest distortion, case of the S3 and S4 datasets, the DB and PBMF indices fail to find the optimal number of clusters. These conclusions lead us to say that only the WB and the XB indices can be used for this kind of datasets. According to the obtained results; the combination of WB and XB indices seems interesting and the new index called WXI (Equation 9) was deduced and tested.

Table 3. Comparison of the minimal values of the WXI for S1,S2,S3 and S4

	S1	S2	S3	S4
OVI	0.13	0.23	0.45	0.49
K	15	15	14	15

The results of WXI are very promising since the error margin reported in Table 3 is acceptable. Indeed, the combination of WB and XB indices has maximized the performances of both of them and erased the deficiency of each one.

3.2 Comparison with KM and FCM Algorithm

In this section, different tests have been performed using GKHM, KM and FCM over 50 iterations. The WXI has been computed in each test and used to compare between their results.

In order to compare between the GKHM and the two other algorithms using the WXI, we have computed up each of them to 50 iterations with a static number of clusters (K=15) for the KM and the FCM. The results appear in Figures 3 and 4.

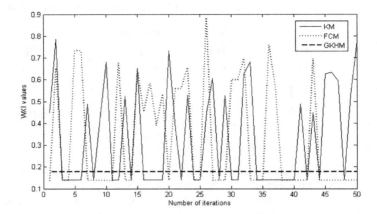

Fig. 3. Comparison between the GKHM, the KM and the FCM for S1 using the WXI

Form Fig. 3, we notice that the KM and the FCM reach inferior minimums than the GKHM but the results are very fluctuant and change constantly; it brutally increases after reaching the minimum which indicates unstable algorithms unlike the GKHM which is totally stable and remains on its minimum value.

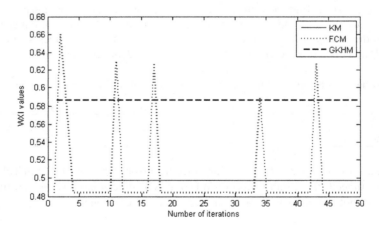

Fig. 4. Comparison between the GKHM, the KM and the FCM for S4 using the WXI

The results in Fig. 5 represent the WXI values for the high overlap data synthetic S4. The curves shape shows that the KM and GKHM are stable; however, only the first algorithm gives the best results. In contrast, the shape of the FCM curve stays very fluctuant and unstable.

Table 4. The average results of the WXI at 50 iterations for all synthetic datasets

	Aver- age_WXI_KM	Average_ WXI _FCM	Average_ WXI _GKHM
S1	0.45	0.43	**0.17**
S2	0.32	0.30	**0.29**
S3	**0.42**	0.45	0.53
S4	**0.49**	0.50	0.64
Average	0.42	0.42	**0.40**

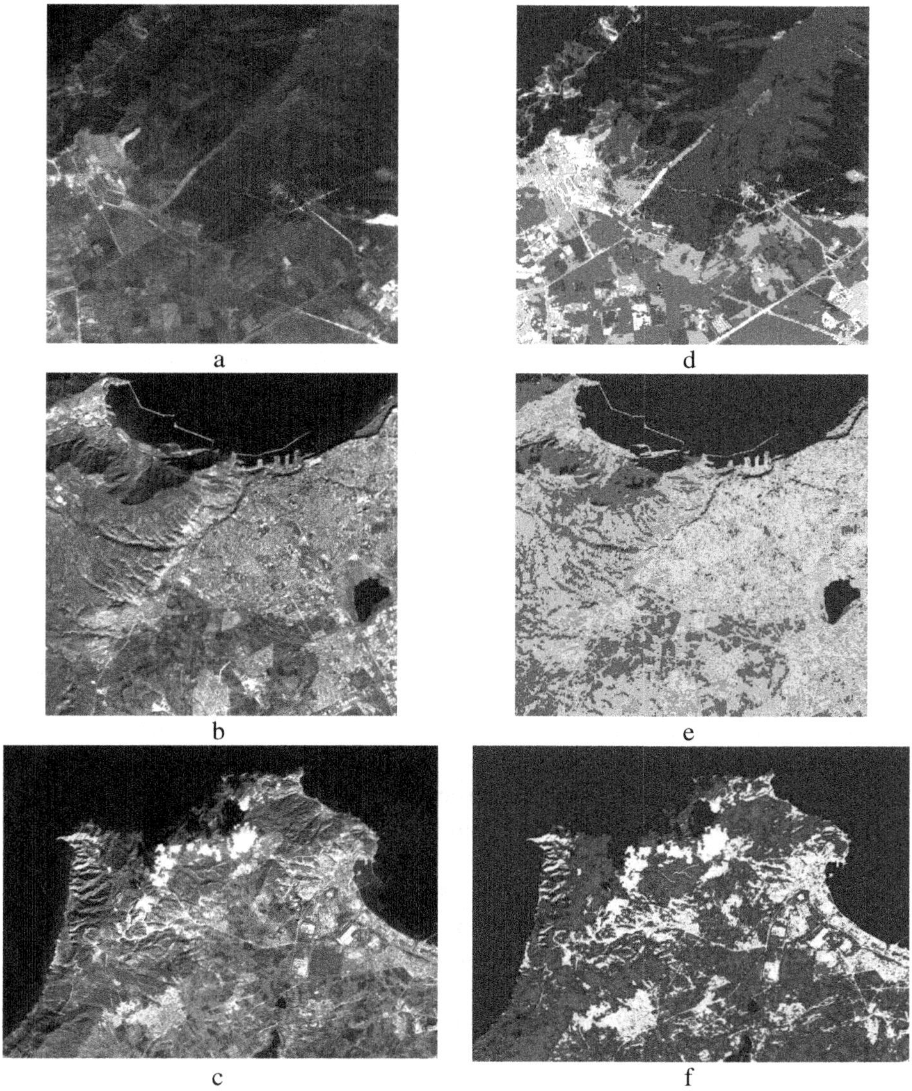

Fig. 5. Clustering using the GKHM on remote sensed data sets

From Table 4, we notice that the GKHM is a totally stable algorithm and tends to minimize the WXI values more than the KM and FCM, especially when data are well-separated. However, the GKHM responds less well when dealing with high over-lapped datasets. In the case of FCM and KM, the results are unstable due to their high dependency on their centers number initialization. The three algorithms have approximately the same results with better global issues for GKHM concerning datasets tested in this paper.

3.3   Experiment on Remotely Sensed Data

In the last experiment, the clustering has been performed on three multispectral remotely sensed data; the details of the image sets are as follows:
- A Landsat 8 sub-scene of Oran the image has three spectral data channels and size of 400 x 400. The spatial resolution is 30 meters (Fig. 6.a).
- A Spot 5 sub-scene of Oran the image has three spectral data channels and size of 400 x 400. The spatial resolution is 20 meters (Fig. 6.b).
- A Landsat 8 sub-scene of Arzew the image has three spectral data channels and size of 600 x 800. The spatial resolution is 30 meters (Fig. 6.c).

The clustering results of the three remotely sensed data by the proposed method are shown in Fig. 6.d with eight clusters, Fig. 6.e with five clusters and Fig. 6.f with six clusters, respectively. The visual comparison with the corresponding original images shows that the obtained results appear generally satisfying even if we notice some confusion between water pixels and shadow ones, case of the second image.

4   Conclusion

A new clustering method for multispectral remotely sensed data has been proposed in this paper. The method combines both the K-Harmonic means algorithm and the clustering validity index in order to find the optimal number of clusters and perform the classification task. Note that the K-harmonic means has been used with only two clusters and the increasing of the centers number has been provided by an automatic insertion of the new clusters. However, some improvements can be made, especially by reducing the time processing cycle. Also, the developed algorithm uses internally a combination of validity indices in order to return an optimal number of clusters.

Other improvements could be done by testing the GKHM on large datasets including high-dimensional datasets and shape sets.

A further research will involve the application of new validity indices such as DB* index [25], the comparison with both the enhanced differential evolution KHM [26] and the modified version of k-means algorithm proposed by Celebi and al. [27] and finally the use of the ensemble clustering technique.

References

1. Gan, G., Ma, C., Wu, J.: Data Clustering: Theory, Algorithms, and Applications. ASA-SIAM Serieson Statistics and Applied Probability. SIAM, Philadelphia (2007)
2. Jain, A.K., Dubes, R.C.: Algorithms for Clustering Data. Prentice-Hall, Englewood (1988)
3. Pakhira, M.K., Bandyopadhyay, S., Maulik, U.: A Study of Some Fuzzy Cluster Validity Indices, Genetic Clustering and Application to Pixel Classification. Fuzzy Sets and Systems 155, 191–214 (2005)
4. Bezdeck, J.C.: FCM: Fuzzy C-Means algorithm. Computers and Geoscience 10, 191–203 (1984)
5. Gong, X.-J., Ci, L.-L., Yao, K.-Z.: A FCM algorithm for remote-sensing image classification considering spatial relationship and its parallel implementation. In: International Conference on Wavelet Analysis and Pattern Recognition, ICWAPR 2007, November 2-4, vol. 3, pp. 994–998 (2007)
6. Gao, Y., Wang, S., Liu, S.: Automatic Clustering Based on GA-FCM for Pattern Recognition. In: Second International Symposium on Computational Intelligence and Design, ISCID 2009, December 12-14, vol. 2, pp. 146–149 (2009)
7. McQueen, J.: Some methods for classification and analysis of multivariate observations. In: Proc. 5th Berkeley Symp. Mathematics, Statistics and Probability, pp. 281–296 (1967)
8. Ball, G., Hall, D.: ISODATA: A novel method of data analysis and pattern classification. In Technical report, Stanford Research Institute, Menlo Park, CA, USA (1965)
9. Huang, K.: A Synergistic Automatic Clustering Technique (Syneract) for Multispectral Image Analysis. Photogrammetric Engineering and Remote Sensing 1(1), 33–40 (2002)
10. Zhao, Q.: Cluster validity in clustering methods. Ph.D. dissertation. University of Eastern Finland (2012)
11. Korgaonkar, G.S., Sedamkar, R.R., KiranBhandari.: Hyperspectral Image Classification on Decision level fusion. In: IJCA Proceedings on International Conference and Workshop on Emerging Trends in Technology, vol. 7, pp. 1–9 (2012)
12. Xie, X.L., Beni, A.: Validity measure for fuzzy clustering. IEEE Trans. Pattern Anal. Mach. Intell. 3, 841–846 (1991)
13. Bezdek, J.C.: Cluster validity with fuzzy sets. J. Cybernet. 3, 58–73 (1974)
14. Bezdek, J.C.: Mathematical models for systematics and taxonomy. In: Eighth International Conference on Numerical Taxonomy, San Francisco, CA, pp. 143–165 (1975)
15. Davies, D., Bouldin, D.: A cluster separation measure. IEEE PAMI 1(2), 224–227 (1979)
16. Dunn, J.C.: A fuzzy relative of the isodata process and its use in detecting compact well separated clusters. J. Cybernet. 3, 32–57 (1973)
17. Calinski, R.B., Harabasz, J.: Adendrite method for cluster analysis. Commun. Statist. 1–27 (1974)
18. Arbelaitz, O., Gurrutxaga, I., Muguerza, J., Prez, J.M., Perona, I.: An extensive comparative study of cluster validity indices. Pattern Recognition 46(1), 243–256 (2013)
19. Halkidi, M., Batistakis, Y., Vazirgiannis, M.: Clustering validity checking methods: Part II. SIGMOD Record 31(3), 19–27 (2002)
20. Zhang, B.: Generalized K-Harmonic Means Boosting in Unsupervised Learning. Technical Reports, Hewllet Laborotories, HPL-2000-137 (2000)
21. Zhang, L., Mao, L., Gong, H., Yang, H.: A K-harmonic Means Clustering Algorithm Based on Enhanced Differential Evolution. In: 2013 Fifth International Conference on Measuring Technology and Mechatronics Automation, 2014 Sixth International Conference on Measuring Technology and Mechatronics Automation, pp. 13–16 (2013)

22. Thangavel, K., Karthikeyani Visalakshi, K.: Ensemble based Distributed K- Harmonic Means Clustering. International Journal of Recent Trends in Engineering 2(1), 125–129 (2009)
23. Zhao, Q., Fränti, P.: WB-index: a sum-of-squares based index for cluster validity. Knowledge and Data Engineering 92, 77–89 (2014)
24. Malinen, M.I., Mariescu-Istodor, R., Fränti K-means*, P.: Clustering by gradual data transformation. Pattern Recognition 47(10), 3376–3386 (2014)
25. Thomas, J.C.R.: New Version of Davies-Bouldin Index for Clustering Validation Based on Cylindrical Distance. In: V Chilean Workshop on Pattern Recognition, November 11-15 (2013)
26. Zhang, L., Mao, L., Gong, H., Yang, H.: A K-harmonic Means Clustering Algorithm Based on Enhanced Differential Evolution. In: 2013 Fifth International Conference on Measuring Technology and Mechatronics Automation (ICMTMA), January 16-17, pp. 13–16 (2013), doi:10.1109/ICMTMA.2013.1
27. Emre, C.M., Kingravi, H.A., Vela, P.A.: A comparative study of efficient initialization methods for the k-means clustering algorithm. Expert Systems with Applications (2013)

Computational Intelligence: BioInformatics

Comparison of Automatic Seed Generation Methods for Breast Tumor Detection Using Region Growing Technique

Ahlem Melouah[✉]

Department of Informatics, Labo LRI, Badji-Mokhtar Annaba University,
P.O.Box 12, 23000, Annaba, Algeria
ahlem.melouah@univ-annaba.dz

Abstract. Seeded Region Growing algorithm is observed to be successfully implemented as a segmentation technique of medical images. This algorithm starts by selecting a seed point and, growing seed area through the exploitation of the fact that pixels which are close to each other have similar features. To improve the accuracy and effectiveness of region growing segmentation, some works tend to automate seed selection step. In this paper, we present a comparative study of two automatic seed selection methods for breast tumor detection using seeded region growing segmentation. The first method is based on thresholding technique and the second method is based on features similarity. Each method is applied on two modalities of breast digital images. Our results show that seed selection method based on thresholding technique is better than seed selection method based on features similarity.

Keywords: Medical image segmentation · Medical informatics · Automatic seed selection · Region growing · Tumor detection

1 Introduction

The basic segmentation aim is to divide an image into different regions based on certain criteria. The regions with connected pixels of similar values can provide important cues for extracting semantic objects. Since, image segmentation is mainly used to locate an objects or an object boundary in an image thus it can be used in applications which involve a particular kind of object recognition such as breast tumor.

Though researchers introduced several images segmentation methods but, most of these methods are not suitable for medical images. Image segmentation using seeded region growing (SRG) technique has increasingly become a popular method because of its ability to involve a high-level knowledge of anatomical structures in seed selection process [Jianping et al. 2005]. In most of the region growing algorithms, all the neighbors need to be evaluated for the region to be grown. The region growing starts with a seed pixel and repeatedly adds new pixels as long as the segmentation criterion is satisfied [Deboeverie et al. 2013].

© IFIP International Federation for Information Processing 2015
A. Amine et al. (Eds.): CIIA 2015, IFIP AICT 456, pp. 119–128, 2015.
DOI: 10.1007/978-3-319-19578-0_10

One of the most important factors in region growing process is seed pixel selection. Seed pixel is often chosen close to the center of the region of interest (ROI). For example, if we are to segment a tumor from the background, it is always advisable to select the seed point for the tumor in the middle of the tumor [Najarian and Splinter 2012]. If seeds are not properly selected, the final segmentation results would be definitely incorrect [Massich et al. 2011]. Despite the existence of many automatic seed selection methods, SRG algorithm still suffers from the problems of automatic seed generation [Mehnert and Jackway1997; Jianping et al. 2001].

In this paper, two automatic seed point selection methods are compared. The first method based on thresholding technique is proposed by Al-Faris et al. [Al-Faris et al. 2014]. The second method based on features similarity is proposed by Yuvaria and Ragupathy [Yuvarai and Ragupathy 2013]. The same data and the same criteria have been used in this comparison.

The rest of the paper is organized as follows: Section 2 describes experimental automatic seed selection methods. Section 3 gives a view on experimentation. Section 4 presents some results with discussion. Section 5 draws our conclusion.

2   Automatic Seed Selection Methods

For the region growing to be effectively achieved, the crucial part is the position of the seed pixel which must be selected from where the region growing may start [Mesanovic et al. 2013]. Up to now, some works use a semi-automatic region growing algorithm and still need user interaction for seed selection. Other works are fully automatic and the user has only a verification role. Among these later works those proposed by Al-Faris et al. [Al-Faris et al. 2014] and Yuvarai et al. [Yuvarai and Ragupathy 2013]. Al-Faris et al. exposed an automatic seed selection method based on the thresholding technique. Yuvaria et al. developed an automatic seed selection method based on features similarity. The description of these two methods is detailed in the following.

2.1   Seed Selection Method Based on Features Similarity (SSFS)

In order to detect a mass in a mammogram using SRG segmentation, Yuvarai and Ragupathy proposed a new seed point selection method based on features similarity. Statistical features like mean, dissimilarity, sum average, sum variance and auto correlation are considered as significant features able to identify a mass. These features are computed and fixed for masses which have been previously identified by an expert. Seed selection process starts by initializing a mask, and then calculates its features from the regions within the mask. If the mask features do not match with the mass predefined features, the mask is therefore shift. Otherwise, the initial pixel of the mask is taken as seed point.

2.2   Seed Selection Method Based on Thresholding Technique (SSTT)

Al-Faris et al. [Al-Faris et al. 2014] used SRG for breast MRI tumor segmentation with seed point selection based on the thresholding technique. A new algorithm is developed for automatic evaluation of the suitable threshold value. This algorithm searches for the maximum value in each row in the image and saves it temporarily. This process is repeated for all the rows until the last. Then, a summation of the temporarily stored values is calculated. The mean maximum raw is then calculated by dividing the summation value by the number of rows in the image. The resultant mean value will be considered as the threshold value for the binarization process. In order to remove the unwanted small white speckles in the image which do not belong to the ROI and enhance the boundary of the suspected regions, the morphological open operation (erosion followed by dilation operations) has been applied. To extract ROI, all the regions are ranked in an ascending order according to their density values. After, the highest region will be chosen as the main suspected region. The seed is the pixel of this main suspected region with maximum intensity value.

3   Experiments

3.1   Dataset

In this study, two databases with different modalities of breast digital images are considered:

1. RIDER breast MRI dataset downloaded from the National Biomedical Imaging Archive [10].   The dataset includes more than 1000 breast MRI images for five patients. All the images are axial 288 X 288 pixels. The dataset also includes Ground Truth (GT) segmentation which has been manually identified by a radiologist.

2. MiniMIAS database provided by the Mammographic Image Analysis Society (MIAS) [11].   MiniMIAS consists of a variety of normal mammograms as well as mammograms with different characteristics and several abnormalities. The mammograms are digitized at a resolution of 1024x1024 pixels and at 8-bit grey scale level. All the images include the locations of all the abnormalities that may be present.

3.2   Seed Point Selection Criterion

Region growing is one of the most popular techniques for medical images segmentation due to its simplicity and good performance [Saad et al. 2012]. But, this performance is deeply influenced by seed point position. Therefore, selecting a good set of initial seeds is very important. To determine the good seed position, Massich [Massich et al. 2011] tested 10 areas-of-interest selected at different distances and orientations from the lesion center. The 10 tested areas are: The area 1 is the zone located outside the lesion; the areas from 2 to 5 are the zones situated on the boundaries of the lesion; the areas from 6 to 9 are the zones placed near the lesion center and, the area 10 is the lesion center.   The best segmentation results are obtained by using the seed points located in area 10. The segmentation performance decrease when the seed position moves away from the lesion center. Consequently, a seed point can be placed in three different areas:

1. Inside the ROI; in this situation, segmentation result is more and more accurate if seed position approximates the ROI center.
2. On the border of the ROI; in this situation, there are two possibilities, either the segmentation fails or success.
3. Outside the ROI; in this situation, the segmentation fails.

Figure 1 gives an example of these three situations. If the seed is centered in the ROI (figure 1.a), therefore the SRG segmentation well extracts the lesion (figure 1.e). If the seed is placed on the border of the ROI (Figure 1.b and Figure 1.c), therefore the SRG segmentation can success (figure 1.f) or can fail (figure 1.g). The SRG segmentation fails (figure 1.h) if the seed is placed outside the ROI (figure 1.d).

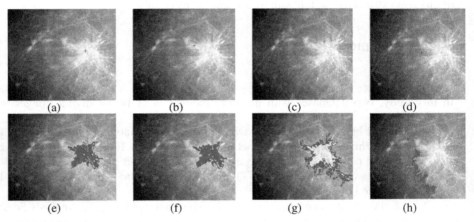

Fig. 1. Examples of different seed placement (left column) and correspondent segmentation results (right column)

To sum it up, the seed position can be considered as a good criterion in the comparison between automatic seed generation methods. The seed position is adequate if and only if the seed is placed inside the ROI. In addition, the best method is the method which generates seeds close the lesion center.

4   Results and Discussion

Considering the fact that the initial seed selection has a great influence on the final segmentation accuracy, we propose a comparative study of two automatic seed selection methods: SSFS and SSTT. The behavior of the two methods was examined using a randomly selected dataset from MiniMIAS database and Rider database. We notify that, in region growing segmentation process, the same similarity measure and the same threshold value have been used for the two methods.

4.1   Mammograms dataset

To evaluate the performance of the experimental methods, 28 mammograms with tumors are taken from MiniMIAS database. The two methods are applied on each tested image.

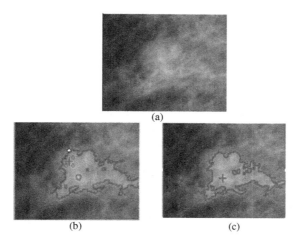

Fig. 2. Seed point generation example on mammogram. (a) Original image. (b) Seed generation result and segmentation result using SSFS. (c) Seed generation result and segmentation result using SSTT.

Figure 2 presents the results of the experimental methods on a mammogram test example. The original image is illustrated in Figure 2(a). Figure 2(b) shows seed generation result and segmentation result using SSFS method.   Figure 2(c) shows seed generation result and segmentation result using SSTT method.   We can see clearly that the two methods place correctly the seed inside the ROI, but at different positions.

According to the obtained results from all the tested mammograms, the seeds repartition area of each method is surrounded in figure 3. On a prototype image we have delimited separately the zones covered by SSFS and SSTT methods. The blue line delimits the SSFS zone and the red line delimits the SSTT zone. From this illustration three observations can be made:

1. The two methods SSFS and SSTT succeed in placing some seeds inside and close to the center of the ROI.
2. The SSTT method fails in some cases because it places a number of seeds outside the ROI.
3. The SSFS method gives better results than the SSTT method because in the worst case, the seed point is placed on the ROI boundary.

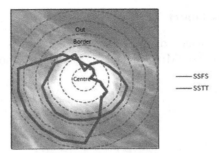

Fig. 3. Seeds repartition areas illustration for mammograms dataset

A priori, we can suppose that the SSFS method is more powerful than the SSTT method. But, when we look to the plot of the figure 4, this supposition becomes weak. The plot shows that the SSTT method places most seeds inside the ROI while the SSFS method places the majority of seeds on the ROI boundary.

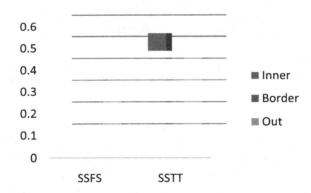

Fig. 4. Static results of the SSFS method and the SSTT method on the mammograms dataset

From the results above, we conclude that the SSFS method can easily find the ROI but, has some difficulties to point their centre. On the contrary, the SSTT method is more powerful in locating the centre area if it success in detecting the ROI.

4.2   Rider Dataset

To evaluate the performance of the experimental methods on another dataset, 20 breast IRM images with tumors were taken from Rider database. Seed point generation example by the two considered methods is shown in the following:

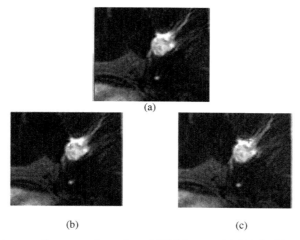

(a)

(b)   (c)

Fig. 5. Seed point generation example on breast IRM image   (a) Original image (b) Seed generation result and segmentation result using SSFS. (c) Seed generation result and segmentation result using SSTT.

Figure 5 illustrates seed generation results and segmentation results using the two methods (SSFS and SSTT) on breast IRM example. The original image is illustrated in Figure 5(a).   Figure 5(b) shows seed generation result and segmentation result using the SSFS method.   Figure 5(c) exhibits seed generation result and segmentation result using the SSTT method.   This example shows that the SSTT method places its seed farther from the centre of ROI than the SSFS method. This fact is not correct for all the seeds generated by the SSTT method. As it is presented in figure 6, the SSTT method places all its seeds in an area (represented by red line) included in the repartition area (represented by blue line) of the SSFS method. So, the SSFS method gives better results than the SSFS method in most cases.

Fig. 6. Seeds repartition areas illustration for IRM dataset

The statistical data presented by the plot of the figure 7 confirms the efficiently of SSTT method in comparison with the SSFS method.

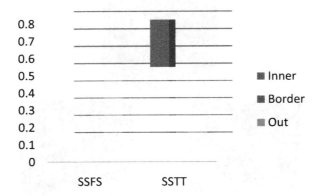

Fig. 7. Static results of the SSFS method and the SSTT method on the   breast IRM dataset

4.3   Discussion

In this work, two automatic seed selection methods have been studied and evaluated. The SSFS method and the SSTT method are tested using mammograms and breast IRM images. From the obtained results some conclusions can be drawn:

1. It is possible to apply the SSFS method and the SSTT method for both modalities. The SSTT method introduced for the IRM breast images gives good results for the mammograms as well. Despite the SSFS method had been developed, originally, for mammograms it gave also acceptable results for IRM breast images.
2. The SSTT method performs well if there are no undesirable regions. Undesirable regions are the regions with high intensity like labels, artifacts ...etc. So, if these undesirable regions are removed by using pre-processing stage, the performance of the SSTT method will certainly increase.
3. Masses predefined features values were carefully studied by the authors of the SSFS method. These references values which allow good tumors detection in mammograms can be inappropriate for IRM images. Hence, references values must be modified for each new used database this repeated modification will be an obstacle for the SSFS method adaptability. However, if references values are carefully selected, the SSFS performance will consequently augment. Unfortunately, it is very hard to fix the best references values for each used database.
4. The SSTT method has proved to be more efficient in matter of spotting the ROI centre compared to the SSFS method. The SSTT method selects the high intensity pixel as a seed, while the SSFS method selects the first pixel of the mask as a seed. The SSTT method seed selection criterion makes it possible to place the seed close to the ROI centre. On the other hand, the SSFS method seed selection criterion favours the seed placement on the ROI boundary.

5   Conclusion

Since region growing technique often gives good segmentation results that correspond well to the observed edges, it is widely used in medical images. Typically, a seeded region growing algorithm includes two major steps. The first step is seed point generation by selecting an initial seed point somewhere inside the suspected lesion. The second step is region formation which starts from the seed point and grows progressively to fill a coherent region. As, region growing results are sensitive to the initial seeds, the accurate seed selection is very important for image segmentation. In this work, we have implemented, tested and evaluated two automatic seed selection methods. The SSTT method proposed by Al-Faris et al. is based on the thresholding technique. The SSFS method proposed by Yuvaria et al. is based on features similarity. The tests were elaborated on two different kinds of breast images modalities: mammograms and IRM. Both the SSTT and the SSFS methods deal well with mammograms. But, as far as IRM is concerned, the SSTT method performs better than SSFS method.

References

1. Jianping, F., Guihua, Z., Body, M., Hacid, M.S.: Seeded region growing: an extensive and comparative study. Pattern Recognition Letters 26(8), 1139–1156 (2005)
2. Deboeverie, F., Veelaert, P., Philips, W.: Image segmentation with adaptive region growing based on a polynomial surface model. Journal of Electronic Imaging 22(4), 1–13 (2013)
3. Najarian, K., Splinter, R.: Biomedical signal and image processing, 2nd edn. CRC Press, Taylor & Francis Group, United States of America (2012)
4. Massich, J., Meriaudeau, F., Pérez, E., Marti, R., Oliver, A., Marti, J.: Seed selection criteria for breast lesion segmentation in Ultra-Sound images. In: Workshop on Breast Image Analysis in Conjunction with MICCAI, pp. 57–64 (2011)
5. Mehnert, A., Jackway, P.: An improved seeded region growing algorithm. Pattern Recognition Letters 18(10), 1065–1071 (1997)
6. Jianping, F., Yau, D.K.Y., Elmagarmid, A.K., Aref, W.G.: Automatic image segmentation by integrating color-based extraction and seeded region growing. IEEE Trans. Image Process. 10(10), 1454–1466 (2001)
7. Al-Faris, A.Q., Umi Kalthum, N., MatIsa, N.A., Shuaib, I.L.: Computer-Aided Segmentation System for Breast MRI Tumour using Modified Automatic Seeded Region Growing (BMRI-MASRG). J. Digit. Imaging 27, 133–144 (2014)
8. Yuvarai, K., Ragupathy, U.S.: Automatic Mammographic Mass Segmentation based on Region Growing Technique. In: 3rd International Conference on Electronics, Biomedical Engineering and its Applications (ICEBEA 2013), Singapore, pp. 29–30 (April 1, 2013)
9. Mesanovic, N., Huseinagic, H., Kamenjakovic, S.: Automatic Region Based Segmentation and Analysis of Lung Volumes from CT Images. International Journal of Computer Science and Technology 4(2), 48–51 (2013)

10. US National Cancer Institute: reference image database to evaluate therapy response (RIDER) MRI breast, 2007 The Cancer Imaging Archive (TCIA), http://cancerimagingarchive.net./about-archive.html
11. http://peipa.essex.ac.uk/info/mias.html
12. Mohd Saad, N., Abu-Bakar, S.A.R., Muda, S., Mokji, M., Abdullah. A.R.: Automated Region Growing for Segmentation of Brain Lesion in Diffusion-weighted MRI. In: Proceeding of the International MultiConference of Enginneers and Computer Scientists, Hong Kong, vol. 1, pp. 14–16 (March 2012)

IHBA: An Improved Homogeneity-Based Algorithm for Data Classification

Fatima Bekaddour$^{(\boxtimes)}$ and Chikh Mohammed Amine

Abou Bekr Belkaid University, Tlemcen , Algeria
fatima.bekaddour@gmail.com,
am_chikh@yahoo.fr

Abstract. The standard Homogeneity-Based (SHB) optimization algorithm is a metaheuristic which is proposed based on a simultaneously balance between fitting and generalization of a given classification system. However, the SHB algorithm does not penalize the structure of a classification model. This is due to the way SHB's objective function is defined. Also, SHB algorithm uses only genetic algorithm to tune its parameters. This may reduce SHB's freedom degree. In this paper we have proposed an Improved Homogeneity-Based Algorithm (IHBA) which adopts computational complexity of the used data mining approach. Additionally, we employs several metaheuristics to optimally find SHB's parameters values. In order to prove the feasibility of the proposed approach, we conducted a computational study on some benchmarks datasets obtained from UCI repository. Experimental results confirm the theoretical analysis and show the effectiveness of the proposed IHBA method.

Keywords: Metaheuristics · HBA · Improvement · Machine Learning · Medical Informatics

1 Introduction

Nowadays, metaheuristics approaches represent a well-established method toward solving complex and challenging optimization problems. Offering suboptimal (optimal) quality solutions in a reasonable time, they may be considered as complement to exact optimization methods. Among popular metaheuristics, there are: Genetic Algorithm [1] emulates Darwinian evolution theory; Simulated Annealing imitates annealing process of melts [2] and Particle swarm optimization stems from biology where a swarm coordinates itself in order to achieve a goal [3].

Recently, Pham and Triantaphyllou [4][5][6]developed a new metaheuristic called HBA: Homogeneity-Based Algorithm. The Standard HBA metaheuristic (SHB) is used in conjunction with traditional data mining approaches (such as: ANN: Artificial Neural Network, DT: Decision Tree...) .The main idea of SHB algorithm is to simultaneously balance both fitting and generalization [5] by adjusting classification model through the use of the concept of Homogenous Set and Homogeneity Degree [4].This is done in order to reduce the total misclassification cost of the inferred models. However, a problem with SHB algorithm is that may not adopt computational complexity

© IFIP International Federation for Information Processing 2015
A. Amine et al. (Eds.): CIIA 2015, IFIP AICT 456, pp. 129–140, 2015.
DOI: 10.1007/978-3-319-19578-0_11

of the used classification model. This is due to the way objective function is defined. For the SHB metaheuristic, the total misclassification cost is described by computing only the three type of errors (false positive, false negative and the unclassifiable cases) with their penalty costs. Additionally, for this metaheuristic, only Genetic Algorithm (GA) is adopted to find optimally thresholds values, used to control the balance between the fitting and the generalization. This may reduce SHB's freedom degree.

In this article, we extend works in [4][5][6]. New contributions lies in (1) modifying the SHB's objective function to support structural complexity of the used classifier model (2) Proposing a meta-optimization based solution to the problem of tuning SHB's parameters. The IHBA (Improved Homogeneity-Based) algorithm enhances average results obtained in comparison to the standalone algorithms. Rest of this paper is organized as follows:

The standard HBA metaheuristic (SHB) is presented in the following section, before the proposed approach IHBA is elaborated. Section 3 describes some famous benchmark datasets used to test the proposed approach and explains respective results. Last section concludes the paper.

2   Methodology

2.1   Standard Homogeneity Based-Algorithm (SHB)

SHB is a recent metaheuristic, developed by Pham and Triantaphyllou in [4][5][6]. The main idea of SHB algorithm is to adopt a simultaneously balance between generalization in order to minimize total misclassification cost (TC) [4][5][6]. Let C_{FP}, C_{FN}, C_{Uc} be the penalty costs for the false positive, false negative and unclassifiable cases respectively. Also, let us denote RateFP, RateFN, RateUc as the false positive, false negative, unclassifiable rates, respectively. Then TC is defined as follow:

$$TC=\min \ (C_{FP}*Rate_{FP}+C_{FN}*Rate_{FN}+C_{UC}*Rate_{UC}) \tag{1}$$

SHB algorithm is used in conjunction with data mining techniques to create classification system that would be optimal in term of TC value. There is a fundamental key issue regarding the SHB algorithm [4][5][6]:

- The more compact and homogenous decision regions are, the more accurate the inferred models are. In addition, the denser the decision regions are, the more accurate the inferred models are.

The density measurement for a homogenous set is called Homogeneity Degree (HD) [4]. In [4][5][6] ,the authors   proposed a way to compute HD as follow:

$$HD= \ln \ (nc) \ / \ h \tag{2}$$

Where nc is the number of points in a given set **C**, and h is defined in **Heuristic rule.**

The SHB algorithm stops when all of the homogenous sets have been treated. Note that SHB metaheuristic utilize GA (Genetic Algorithm) to find optimal values of the controlling threshold: β^-, β^+, α^-, α^+.

Heuristic Rule: if *h* is set equal to the minimum value in set *C* and this value is used to compute the density *d(x)* using equation 3, then *d(x)* approaches to a true density.

$$d(x) \approx \frac{1}{n * h^D} \sum_{i=1}^{n} \prod_{m=1}^{D} \varphi\left(\frac{x^m - x_i^m}{h}\right) \qquad (3)$$

Where φ is the kernel function, defined in D-dimensional space and *n* is the number of points in a given set **C**.

The following pseudo-code describes the SHB algorithm:

```
Start
Initial parameters setting (α⁺, α⁻, β⁺, β⁻).
1. Apply a Data Mining approach on a training dataset T1
to infer positive and negative classification models.
2. Break the inferred models into hyper spheres.
3. For each hyper sphere C do:
   Determine whether C is homogenous or not.
       If so, computer HD using formula 2.
       Else fragment C into smaller hyper spheres.
4. Sort HD in decreasing order.
5. For each homogenous set C do:
   If [(HD ≥ β⁺(β⁻)] then
       Expand C using HD and α⁺(α⁻).
   Else
       Break C into smaller homogenous sets.
end
```

2.2   A Modified SHB Objective Function

As presented above, SHB algorithm modifies an existing classification pattern such that the total misclassification cost TC (formula 1), will be optimized or significantly reduced. Nevertheless, SHB metaheuristic objective function neglects the structural complexity of a given classification model. For example, The ANN (Artificial Neural Network) structural complexity is defined as the total number of weights and bias, figured in its architecture and the time needed for network learning. It is proved by choosing theses parameters effectively minimize the network error and perform better results.

In this regards, we have proposed a modified objective function, adopting the computational complexity design function [7] to compute the penalty of a given pattern classification architecture as follow:

$$fobj = Penality * \frac{\alpha 1 * TC_{Training} + \alpha 2 * TC_{Generalization}}{\alpha 1 + \alpha 2} \qquad (4)$$

Where $(\alpha 1, \alpha 2) > 0 \in \Re$ (usually $\alpha 1 \leq \alpha 2$), are factors indicating importance degree of the learning and the generalization errors respectively. Penalty presents the model architecture influence of the objective function value as follow [7]:

$$Penality = 5 * 10^{-8} * e^{f(x)} + 5 * 10^{-5} * y + 1 \tag{5}$$

Where: y is the number of epochs necessary in the model training; f(x) is the Structural complexity of a classification model.

Using different values of C_{FP}, C_{FN}, C_{Uc} in objective function formula (4) , we design others objective functions formula (6-7-8) as follows:

$$fobj = Penality * \frac{\alpha1*(RateFP_{Train}+RateFN_{Train})+\alpha2*(RateFP_{Gener}+Ra \text{ 刚e} FN_{Gener})}{\alpha1+\alpha2} \tag{6}$$

$$fobj = Penality * \frac{\text{州}1*TC1_{Train}+\alpha2*TC1_{Gener}}{\alpha1+\alpha2} \tag{7}$$

Where: $TC1_{Train} = 3RateFP_{Train} + 3RateFN_{Train} + 3RateUc_{Train}$

$TC1_{Gener} = 3RateFP_{Gener} + 3RateFN_{Gener} + 3RateUc_{Gener}$

$$fobj = Penality * \frac{\alpha1*TC2_{Train}+\alpha2*TC2_{Gener}}{\alpha1+\alpha2} \tag{8}$$

Where: $TC2_{Train} = RateFP_{Train} + 20RateFN_{Train} + 3RateUc_{Tr\text{援}in}$

$TC2_{Gener} = RateFP_{Gener} + 20RateFN_{Gener} + 3RateUc_{Gener}$

Note that, (RateFP$_{Train}$, RateFN$_{Train}$, RateUc$_{Train}$) represent FP, FN and Uc rates during the training phase and   (RateFP$_{Gener}$, RateFN$_{Gener}$, RateUc $_{Gener}$) represent   FP, FN and UC rates during the test phase.

- **In Formula 6:** we do not penalize Uc, but penalize the same cost for FP, FN.
- **In Formula 7:** we penalize all three error types by unit equal to three.
- **In Formula 8:** we penalize more FN than the other type of errors.

2.3   Tuning SHB Parameters by Means of Metaheuristics

Within the scope of SHB algorithm, there are four parameters which are used to control the balance of fitting and generalization that would minimize (or significantly reduce) the total misclassification cost (TC):

- Two expansion factors α^-, α^+, to be used for expanding the negative and the positive homogenous sets.
- Two breaking factors β^-, β^+, to be used for breaking the negative and the positive homogenous sets.

Note that, if the expansion parameters values (α^-, α^+) are too high, then this would result in the oversimplification problem. On the contrary, too low expansion parameters values may not be sufficient to overcome the overfitting problem. The opposite situation is true with the breaking factors values (β^-, β^+). Authors in [4][5][6] propose to only use genetic algorithm(GA) to find optimal threshold values for α^-, α^+, β^-, β^+. This may reduce the freedom degree of the SHB algorithm .

This article employs several metaheuristics approaches to formally test the existence of a relationship between performance and effective parameters values. In particular, (PSO: Particle Swarm Optimization, SA: Simulated Annealing and GA: Genetic Algorithm) metaheuristics are used for the SHB algorithm parameters α-, α+, β -, β+. That is these parameters represents individual variables and *fobj* described in formula 4 is taken as objective function. Since PSO, SA and GA metaheuristics approaches are tested using a dataset to find optimal values for (α-, α+, β -, β+), a calibration dataset is needed. This requirement can be fulfilled in the following way: the original training dataset T is divided into two datasets: T1 (for example: 90%) for training data mining models to infer positive and negative classification models, and T2 as a calibration dataset.

In the first phase, hyperspheres that cover decision regions are employed to obtain homogenous set (using step 3to 5 described in the pseudo-code of SHB algorithm) . Then, classification models (homogenous sets) are evaluated by using the calibration dataset T2 to compute *fobj*. Next, metaheuristic bloc could replace the default tuning parameters GA (Genetic Algorithm) and determine the new threshold values (α-, α^+, β-, β^+).

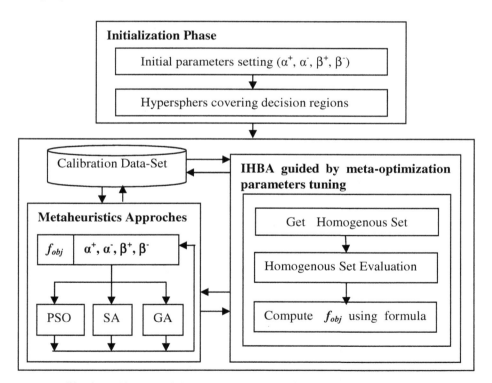

Fig. 1. Architecture of the proposed system to determine IHBA parameters

In fact, this leads to a meta-optimization approach, which means that any metaheuristic is used to search for the best tuning of parameters of metaheuristic in solving a given optimization problem [3]. After a number of iterations, the proposed approach returns the optimal threshold values of (α-, α^+, β -, β^+). It is to be emphasized that by employing metaheuristics bloc during SHB algorithm iterations , permit to estimate effective parameters setting for SHB metaheuristic and therefore, allow to approximate a functional relationship between classifier's performance and effective parameters . The architecture of the overall system is depicted in figure 1.

3   Some Computational Results

3.1   Benchmark Data Sets

This paper studies two medical data sets: Appendicitis (AP), and Thyroid (TR). **Table 1** shows a summary of the main characteristics of these datasets. The benchmark chosen present a variety of descriptions (including number and type of attributes, number of instances…). The first dataset is Appendicitis, created by Kapouleas and Weiss (1989) [8] from Rutgers university. The features were obtained from laboratory tests as follow: WBC1, MNEP, MNEA, MBAP, HNEP and HNEA. The second medical dataset is thyroid disease, obtained from UCI repository [9]. It consists of five continuous attributes. The task is to identify whether a patient is normal or suffers from   hyper (hypo) -thyroidism.

Table 1. Medical datasets characteristics

Datasets	No. Instances	No. Features	Training Dataset	Testing Dataset
Appendicitis	106	7	79	27
Thyroid	215	5	143	72

3.2   Results and Discussion

The following are some computational results obtained from several experiments performed for each data mining approaches used in such work. Experiments were conducted with two datasets obtained from UCI repository [9]. As discussed before, we considered three scenarios for the IHBA objective function. Also, we choose different setting for $(\alpha_1, \alpha2)$ factors that are used to weigh the importance degree attributed to the learning and the generalization errors respectively.

Initially, we assigned an equal weight $(\alpha_1=\alpha_2=1)$ to the learning and the generalization errors for ANFIS (Adaptative Neuro-Fuzzy Inference System) [10], LVQ (Learning Vector Quantization) [11] and PMC (Perception Multi-layers). Then, we chose a larger weight to the generalization than the training error $(\alpha_1=0.5; \alpha_2=1)$. Finally, we attributed more importance to the ability of learning than the ability of finding correct output value for an unknown data sample $(\alpha_1=1; \alpha_2=0.5)$.The results of these simulations are shown in Table 2, 3 and 4. According to those tables, it appears that α_1 and $\alpha2$ factors have influence on the final results. Those Tables show the misclassification testing error rate (TC_{Test}) and f_{eval} (the objective function evaluation) obtained for original algorithms (ANFIS, LVQ, PMC) and the proposed IHBA approach. The colon improvement presents any improvement rate achieved by the IHBA when compared with that of the standalone algorithm.

Table 2. Results in minimizing ($f_{eval}=FP+ FN$)

Datasets	Alg	$\alpha 1$ $\alpha 2$	Original-Alg TC_{Test} f_{eval}		IHBA TC_{Test} f_{eval}		Improv (%)
AP	ANFIS	1 1	3	26.9	11.1	30.9	No.impr
		0.5 1	3	19.3	3.7	19.8	No.impr
		1 0.5	3	38.2	0.00	37.1	2.87
	LVQ	1 1	11	14.4	3.7	10.7	25.69
		0.5 1	3	7.08	3.7	7.55	No.impr
		1 0.5	11	13.8	3.7	11.3	18.11
	PMC	1 1	7	16.3	7.4	16.5	No.impr
		0.5 1	3	7.86	7.4	10.9	No.impr
		1 0.5	14	18.2	7.4	15.8	13.18
TR	ANFIS	1 1	69	40.8	30.5	21.5	47.30
		0.5 1	69	51.1	27.7	23.6	53.81
		1 0.5	69	35.1	27.7	21.3	39.31
	LVQ	1 1	25	23.4	26.3	24.0	No.impr
		0.5 1	69	69.6	26.3	41.0	41.09
		1 0.5	25	22.8	26.3	23.2	No.impr
	PMC	1 1	4	2.78	5.5	3.6	No.impr
		0.5 1	2	2.1	1.3	1.61	23.33
		1 0.5	2	2.6	5.5	3.81	No.impr

In a first scenario (formula 6), we did not penalize for the unclassifiable cases (Uc), and penalized by one unit the FP (False Positive) and the FN (False Negative) errors. The results of this scenario are shown in Table 2. This table shows that the average values of f_{eval} obtained from the IHBA on the AP and TR datasets were 17.83, 18.18 respectively. Furthermore, theses values of f_{eval} were optimal than the average values of f_{eval} achieved by the stand-alone algorithms on AP and TR datasets by about 6.65, 22.76 respectively.

In the second scenario (formula 7), we assumed that all three error types would be penalized by an identical value, equal to three units. The results are presented in Table 3. The average values for f_{eval} obtained from IHBA on AP, TR datasets were 147.55, 75.75 respectively. These values for f_{eval} were less than the average values of f_{eval}

Table 3. Results in minimizing $(f_{eval}= 3FP+ 3FN+3Uc)$

Datasets	Alg	$\alpha1$	$\alpha2$	Original-Alg TC_{Test}	f_{eval}	IHBA TC_{Test}	f_{eval}	Improv (%)
	ANFIS	1	1	233.33	193.1	288.9	221.0	No.impro
		0.5	1	233.33	208.0	300.0	252.6	No.impro
		1	0.5	233.33	189.6	300.0	211.9	No.impro
AP	LVQ	1	1	233.33	144.2	166.6	110.6	23.3
		0.5	1	233.33	171.8	144.4	112.1	34.7
		1	0.5	233.33	108.7	144.4	78.88	27.4
	PMC	1	1	233.33	160.9	155.5	119.9	25.5
		0.5	1	233.33	181.2	155.5	126.5	30.2
		1	0.5	233.33	121.8	155.5	94.47	22.4
	ANFIS	1	1	220.8	129.3	91.66	64.64	50.0
		0.5	1	220.8	162.6	95.83	79.26	51.5
		1	0.5	220.8	109.9	95.83	68.21	37.9
TR	LVQ	1	1	283.3	174.9	83.33	74.43	57.4
		0.5	1	220.8	218.2	83.33	126.0	No.impro
		1	0.5	283.3	138.3	83.33	71.33	48.4
	PMC	1	1	212.5	113.6	108.3	58.90	48.1
		0.5	1	216.7	153.8	133.3	95.41	37.9
		1	0.5	212.5	80.04	108.3	43.57	45.5

achieved by original algorithms by about 18.16 and 41.8 on the AP, and TR datasets respectively. In the last scenario (formula 8), we assumed that the FN would be more penalized than the other two types of errors (FP, FN). In particular, table 4 shows that the average values for f_{eval} obtained from IHBA on the AP and TR datasets were 236.63, 94.29 respectively .This table, shows that the f_{eval} were less than the original algorithms (ANFIS, LVQ, PMC) by about 0.43, 63.23 when applied on the   AP and TR datasets respectively.

When comparing the tables 2, 3, 4, it appears that PMC and ANFIS models, usually obtain better results. However, ANFIS is more practical due to its transparency. Additionally, in some cases, the f_{eval} value of a standalone approach yielded better values than the one achieved by the IHBA metaheuristic. A reason for that is that the standalone algorithm may have reached the global optimal value (or close to that) for f_{eval} .Note that the number of membership functions and hidden layers affect the structural complexity of the neuro-fuzzy system and the artificial neural network models respectively, in this work, we proposed to use two membership function for ANFIS system and one hidden layer for LVQ and PMC classification models .

The best architecture model found for ANFIS, LVQ and PMC models were (128,20,20) for AP and (32,20,20) for TR dataset respectively.

Table 4. Results in minimizing $(f_{eval}=FP+ 20FN+3Uc)$

Datasets	Alg	α1 α2	Original-Alg TC_{Test} f_{eval}		IHBA TC_{Test} f_{eval}		Improv (%)
	ANFIS	1 1	296.29	174.0	300.00	175.9	No.impr
		0.5 1	296.29	215.5	292.59	213.0	1.16
		1 0.5	296.29	136.3	288.88	133.9	1.76
AP	LVQ	1 1	211.11	187.8	281.48	223.3	No.impr
		0.5 1	225.92	229.4	281.48	266.7	No.impr
		1 0.5	211.11	194.0	281.48	217.7	No.impr
	PMC	1 1	288.88	367.6	281.48	363.8	1.03
		0.5 1	225.92	265.9	281.48	304.9	No.impr
		1 0.5	203.7	203.2	281.48	230.5	No.impr
	ANFIS	1 1	1327.6	670.8	30.55	21.6	96.8
		0.5 1	1327.6	891.0	30.55	25.52	97.1
		1 0.5	1327.6	455.1	40.27	25.56	94.4
TR	LVQ	1 1	221.05	121.9	30.55	26.24	78.4
		0.5 1	1327.6	1358	30.55	488.9	63.9
		1 0.5	221.05	88.57	30.55	24.8	71.9
	PMC	1 1	222.36	12.47	97.22	51.8	No.impr
		0.5 1	225.00	158.2	155.5	109.6	30.7
		1 0.5	221.05	116.5	101.3	74.64	35.9

In order to shed some light upon the second contribution, Table 5 provides an overview of the results obtained throughout the empirical comparison of different meta-optimization based solution (PSO, SA and GA) to the problem of tuning SHB's parameters. The colon improvement 1 shows any improvement of f_{eval} achieved by IHBA enhanced by means of metaheuristics approaches to find optimal thresholds values $(\alpha^+, \alpha^-, \beta^+, \beta^-)$, when compared with the standalone algorithms under the first consideration (where $\alpha_1=0.5$, $\alpha_2=1$) and by using ANFIS model. The colon improvement 2 shows any improvement of f_{eval} achieved by IHBA enhanced by means of meta-optimization parameters tuning, when compared with best results obtained with IHBA under the first consideration, where $\alpha_1=0.5$; $\alpha_2=1$. We have simulated this scenario ($\alpha_1=0.5$, $\alpha_2=1$), because it seems to be more realistic that the ability to learn the model is less relevant than the ability to generalize (i.e. find a correct output value for an unknown data sample).

The colon parameters setting specify different parameters configuration for considered metaheuristics (PSO, SA and GA). In particular, PSO algorithm has been applied with different values of number of iterations (50, 100), population size (20, 40), social attraction and cognitive attraction(0.25, 0.7). In case of SA metaheuristic, we optimized SHB's factors $(\alpha^+, \alpha^-, \beta^+, \beta^-)$ by setting different values of iteration number (500, 1000) and the perturbation function. The initial temperature was set either to 50 or 100. In the GA, each chromosome encodes the two expansion thresholds values (α^+, α^-) and the two breaking thresholds values (β^+, β^-). The population evolves in search for the optimal values of these parameters. We have applied the GA with different values of: number of generation (200, 1000), population size (15, 35) and crossover fraction (0.5, 0.7). Mutation fraction equaled 0.01.

Table 5. Results of IHBA   improved by means of   parametes tuning $(f_{eval}=FP+FN)$

Data sets	Meta-Heuristic	Parameters Setting	Results TC_{Test} f_{eval}		Improv1 Rate	Improv2 Rate
AP	PSO	100 ; 20 ; 0.7 ; 0.25	3.7	37.1	No.impr	No.impro
		50 ; 20 ; 0.25 ; 0.7	7.4	39.6	No.impr	No.impro
		50 ; 40 ; 0.7 ; 0.25	3.7	37.1	No.Impr	No.Impr
		100 ; 40 ; 0.25 ; 0.7	0.00	34.6	No.impr	No.impro
	SA	500;50 ;Fast	3.7	37.1	No.impr	No.impro
		1000;100. Fast	3.7	37.1	No.impr	No.impro
		1000 ;50 ; Bolz	14.8	44.5	No.impr	No.impro
		500 ;100 ;Bolz	3.7	37.1	No.impr	No.impro
	GA	15; 200; 0.5; 0.01	0.00	34.6	No.impr	No.impro
		35;1000; 0.7 ;0.01	0.00	34.6	No.impr	No.impro
		35; 200; 0.5; 0.01	3.7	37.1	No.impr	No.impro
		15;1000; 0.7 ;0.01	0.00	34.6	No.impr	No.impro
TR	PSO	100 ; 20 ; 0.7 ; 0.25	2.77	12.0	76.4	48.9
		50 ; 20 ; 0.25 ; 0.7	26.4	27.8	45.6	No.impro
		50 ; 40 ; 0.7 ; 0.25	9.60	16.7	67.3	29.23
		100 ; 40 ; 0.25 ; 0.7	25.0	26.9	51.0	No.impro
	SA	500;50 ;Fast	2.77	12.0	76.4	48.9
		1000;100. Fast	2.77	12.0	76.4	48.9
		1000 ;50 ; Bolz	2.77	12.0	76.4	48.9
		500 ;100 ;Bolz	2.77	12.0	76.4	48.9
	GA	15; 200; 0.5; 0.01	12.5	18.5	63.7	21.4
		35;1000; 0.7 ;0.01	11.1	17.6	65.5	25.4
		35; 200; 0.5; 0.01	2.77	12.0	76.4	48.9
		15;1000; 0.7 ;0.01	11.1	17.6	65.5	25.4

It is clearly visible, that the PSO metaheuristic achieved better results (in minimizing f_{eval}), for big number of iterations, population size and cognitive attraction. Simulated annealing algorithm was slightly worse than GA metaheuristic.

Table 5 shows that the average values of f_{eval} obtained from IHBA approach improved by means of meta-optimization approaches on AP and TR datasets were 37.09 and 16.45 respectively. In addition, these values of f_{eval} were less than those achieved by standalone methods and IHBA approach depicted in Table 2 on TR dataset by about 68.08 and 32.9 respectively. Note that, The proposed IHBA approach improved by means of parameters tuning based on (PSO, SA and GA) metaheuristics, when applied on AP dataset, found no improvement of f_{eval} , compared to original results depicted in Table 2. A reason for that, is that the standalone approaches or IHBA may have achieved optimal (or near-optimal) values of f_{eval} .

4   Conclusion

Considering importance of parameters tuning of a given metaheuristic algorithm, in this paper, we proposed an Improved Homogeneity Based-Algorithm which uses computational complexity of a classifier model as a modified objective function. Additionally, we employed several metaheuristics approaches (Simulated annealing, Genetic Algorithm and Particle Swarm Optimization) to find optimally thresholds values, used to refine the inferred models regions obtained by applying a classification method. The proposed method IHBA (Improved Homogeneity-Based Algorithm) tested on some benchmarks data sets from the UCI repository indicated the increased performance of the proposed algorithm in comparison with the standalone algorithms (ANFIS, LVQ and PMC). Future works will extend the SHB metaheuristic with feature subset selection aiming to reduce classification time and making HBA applicable to higher data dimensionality.

References

1. Holland, J.H.: Adaptation in Natural and Artificial Systems. University of Michigan Press, Ann Arbor (1992, 1975) (re-issued by MIT Press)
2. Kirkpatrick, S., Gelatt Jr., C.D., Vecchi, M.P.: Optimization by simulated annealing. Science 220, 671–680 (1983)
3. Talbi, E.-G.: Metaheuristics: From Design to Implementation. Wiley (June 2009)
4. Pham, H.N.A., Triantaphyllou, E.: The impact of overfitting and overgeneralization on the classification accuracy in data mining. In: Maimon, O., Rokach, L. (eds.) Soft Computing for Knowledge Discovery and Data Mining, part 4, ch. 5, pp. 391–431. Springer, New York (2007)
5. Pham, H.N.A., Triantaphyllou, E.: Prediction of diabetes by employing a new data mining approach which balances fitting and generalization. In: Lee, R., Kim, H.-K. (eds.) Computer and Information Science. SCI, vol. 131, pp. 11–26. Springer, Heidelberg (2008)
6. Pham, H.N.A., Triantaphyllou, E.: An application of a new meta-heuristic for optimizing the classification accuracy when analyzing some medical datasets. Expert Systems with Applications 36(5), 9240–9249 (2009)
7. Carvalho, A.R., Ramos, F.M., Chaves, A.A.: Metaheuristics for the feedforward artificial neural network (ANN) architecture optimization problem. Neural Computing and Applications 20(8), 1273–1284 (2011)
8. Weiss, S.M., Kapouleas, I.: An empirical comparison of pattern recognition, neural nets and machine learning classification methods. In: Shavlik, J.W., Dietterich, T.G. (eds.) Readings in Machine Learning. Morgan Kauffman Publ., CA (1990)

9. UCI repository of machine learning databases, University of California at Irvine, Department of Computer Science, http://archive.ics.uci.edu/ml/datasets/Thyroid+Disease (last accessed 2015)

10. Jang, J.S.R.: Anfis: adaptative network-based fuzzy inference système. IEEE Trans. on Systems, Man and Cybernetics (1993)

11. Kohonen, T.: The Self-Organizing Map. Proceedings of the IEEE 78(9), 1464–1480 (1990)

Multiple Guide Trees in a Tabu Search Algorithm for the Multiple Sequence Alignment Problem

Tahar Mehenni[✉]

Computer Science Department,
University Mohamed Boudiaf of M'sila, 28000 M'sila, Algeria
tmehenni@univ-msila.dz

Abstract. Nowadays, Multiple Sequence Alignment (MSA) approaches do not always provide consistent solutions. In fact, alignments become increasingly difficult when treating low similarity sequences. Tabu Search is a very useful meta-heuristic approach in solving optimization problems. For the alignment of multiple sequences, which is a NP-hard problem, we apply a tabu search algorithm improved by several neighborhood generation techniques using guide trees. The algorithm is tested with the BAliBASE benchmarking database, and experiments showed encouraging results compared to the algorithms studied in this paper.

Keywords: Multiple sequence alignment · Tabu search · Neighborhood · Guide tree

1 Introduction

Multiple sequence alignment (MSA) is a very interesting problem in molecular biology and bioinformatics. Although the most important regions of DNA are usually conserved to ensure survival, slight changes or mutations (indels) do occur as sequences evolve. Methods such as sequence alignment are used to detect and quantify similarities between different DNA and protein sequences that may have evolved from a common ancestor.

Sequence alignment is the way of inserting dashes into sequences in order to minimize (or maximize) a specified scoring function [1,26]. There are two classes of sequencing; pairwise sequence alignment (PwSA) and multiple sequence alignment (MSA). The latter is simply an extension of pairwise alignments that align 3 or more sequences. Both MSA and PwSA can further be categorized as global or local methods. As global methods attempt to align entire sequences, local methods only align certain regions of similarity.

The majority of multiple sequence alignment heuristics is now handled using progressive approach [13]. Progressive also known as hierarchical or tree methods, generate a multiple sequence alignment by first aligning the most similar sequences and then adding successively less related sequences or groups to the alignment until the entire query set has been incorporated into the solution. Sequence relatedness is described by the initial tree that is based on Pair

© IFIP International Federation for Information Processing 2015
A. Amine et al. (Eds.): CIIA 2015, IFIP AICT 456, pp. 141–152, 2015.
DOI: 10.1007/978-3-319-19578-0_12

wise alignments which may include heuristic Pair wise alignment methods. Some well-known programs using progressive strategies are ClustalW [28], Muscle [6], MULTAL [12] and T-COFFEE [20]. This approach has the advantages of speed and simplicity. However, its main disadvantage is the local minimum problem, which comes from the greedy nature of the approach.

Another approach is to prune the search space of the Dynamic Programming (DP) algorithm for simultaneously aligning multiple sequences, e.g., MSA [11, 18], OMA [23] etc. Algorithms of this approach often find better quality solutions than those of the progressive approach. However, they have the drawbacks of complexity, running time and memory requirement, so they can only be applied to problems with a limited number of sequences (about 10).

The iteration-based approach is also applied to the multiple sequence alignment. Iterative alignment methods produce alignment and refine it through a series of cycles (iterations) until no further improvements can be made. It is deterministic or stochastic depending on the strategy used to improve the alignment. This approach includes iterative refinement algorithms, e.g,. PRRP [10], simulated annealing [14], genetic algorithms (SAGA [19], MAGA [29]), Ant Colony [3] and Swarm Intelligence [15]. Therefore, they can evade being trapped in local minima.

In this paper, we present an iteration-based approach using tabu search features to find the global alignment of multiple sequences, where the neighbors are generated using a set of operations on the guide tree of the initial solution.

The remaining of the paper is organized as follows. In section 2, we present the related work in MSA using tabu search. Section 3, describes our algorithm. Experimental results are presented in section 4 and the study is concluded in section 5.

2   Related Work

Tabu Search (TS) [8, 9] was developed by Fred Glover in 1988. It was initiated as an alternative local search algorithm addressing combinatorial optimization problems in many fields like scheduling, computer channel balancing, cluster analysis, space planning etc. Tabu search is an iterative heuristic approach that uses adaptive memory features to align multiple sequences. The adaptive memory feature, a tabu list, helps the search process to avoid local optimal solutions and explores the solution space in an efficient manner.

In [24], authors propose a tabu search algorithm for multiple sequence alignment. The algorithm implements the adaptive memory features typical of tabu searches to align multiple sequences. Both aligned and unaligned initial solutions are used as starting points for this algorithm. Aligned initial solutions are generated using Feng and Doolittles progressive alignment algorithm [7]. Unaligned initial solutions are formed by inserting a fixed number of gaps into sequences at regular intervals. The quality of an alignment is measured by the COFFEE objective function [21]. In order to move from one solution to another, the algorithm moves gaps around within a single sequence and performs block moves.

This tabu search uses a recency-based memory structure. Thus, after gaps are moved, the tabu list is updated to avoid cycling and getting trapped in a local solution.

[17] develops in his thesis several tabu searches that progressively align sequences. He begins by a simple tabu, called Tabu A, using Dynamic Programming (DP). Then, he proposes other modified versions of tabu search, using at each time a new feature for the previous algorithm, like subgroups alignment, intensification and diversification.

In this paper, we develop a novel tabu search algorithm, by adapting similar procedures of Tabu search developed by [17], and adding a new and efficient technique for generating neighbors using guide trees.

3   Algorithm Overview

We first give a general description of the tabu search components of our method (initial solution, neighborhood generation and intensification method), and then provide a summarizing pseudo-code description of the main algorithm.

Tabu search works by starting from an initial solution, and iteratively explores the neighborhood of current solution by generating the moves called neighbors. In each iteration, the neighbors are evaluated through the alignment score and the best neighbor, provided it is not in the tabu list, is selected and applied to the current solution. This produces a new current solution for the next iteration. The applied neighbor is added to the tabu list and it is not allowed for a specified number of iteration called tabu tenure.

3.1   Initial Solution

The generation of an initial solution is an important step towards getting a final improved alignment. A good initial solution can effectively converge faster and hence cut the computational cost. The initial solution of the tabu search is represented by a tree that is generated using the neighbor-joining guide tree (NJ) [25], which fixes the order of the partial alignments in the progressive alignment.

The NJ method constructs guide trees by clustering the nearby sequences in a stepwise manner. In each step of the sequence clustering, it minimizes the sum of branch lengths, selecting the two nearest sequences/nodes and joining them. Next, the distance between the new node and the remaining ones is recalculated. This process is repeated until all sequences are joined to the root of the guide tree. Figure 1 gives an example of a guide tree produced by 5 sequences.

The MSA is obtained from the tree as follows: the pair of sequences on the lowest level are aligned first. Then, the entire branch containing these two sequences is aligned starting from the lowest level and progressing upward to sequences on higher levels. After the MSA is determined, the alignment is scored.

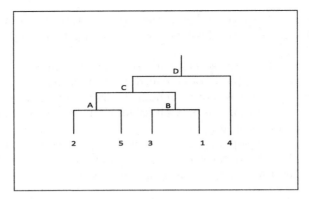

Fig. 1. An example of a guide tree generated by NJ Clustering Algorithm as Initial solution for the Tabu Search

The most popular scoring scheme is the sum of all pairwise alignments score: Sum-of-Pairs Score (SP).

$$SP = \sum_{i=1}^{n-1} \sum_{j=i}^{n} Score(S_i, S_j) \tag{1}$$

where

$$Score(S_i, S_j) = \max \begin{cases} (S_{i-1}, S_{j-1}) + s(x_i, y_j) \\ (S_{i-1}, S_j) - d \\ (S_{i-1}, S_j) + d \end{cases}$$

where $s(x_i, y_j)$ is the score for matching symbols x_i and y_j and d is the penalty for introducing a gap.

3.2   Neighborhood Generation

The neighborhood of the current solution may be generated by one of the four ways: swapping, node insertion, branch insertion or distance variation.

Generation by Swapping. The simplest way of generating a neighborhood is swapping the order of the sequences (i.e. leaves) while maintaining the same guide tree topology. the number of guide trees generated by swapping is $n(n-1)/2$, where n is the number of sequences to be aligned. Figure 2 shows two guide trees (b and c) generated from the initial guide tree a by swapping the order of the sequences.

Generation by Node Insertion. Neighbors can be generated from the current solution (i.e. the current guide tree) by performing certain insertions of nodes. The node insertion makes it possible to move a sequence node to another location

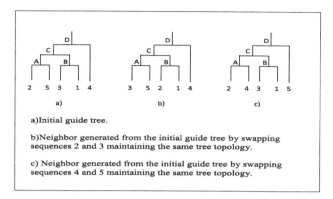

a)Initial guide tree.

b)Neighbor generated from the initial guide tree by swapping sequences 2 and 3 maintaining the same tree topology.

c) Neighbor generated from the initial guide tree by swapping sequences 4 and 5 maintaining the same tree topology.

Fig. 2. Two examples of neighbors generated by swapping technique from the initial solution

of the guide tree. This will change the topology of the initial guide tree, and the new guide tree can be considered as a neighbor of the original one.

The neighborhood can be generated randomly by this technique, since the topology of the initial guide tree is not predetermined. However, we can make only n node insertions to obtain exactly n neighbors, by selecting randomly a node to share one of the sequences (leaves) of the guide tree. More precisely, for each sequence, we choose randomly a node and move it to share this sequence, and so on. Figure 3 shows two guide trees (b and c) obtained by inserting nodes to share predetermined sequences of the initial guide tree a.

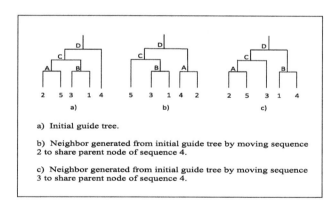

a) Initial guide tree.

b) Neighbor generated from initial guide tree by moving sequence 2 to share parent node of sequence 4.

c) Neighbor generated from initial guide tree by moving sequence 3 to share parent node of sequence 4.

Fig. 3. Two examples of neighbors generated by node insertion technique from the initial solution

Generation by Branch Insertion. Another way to generate neighbors from the current guide tree is the branch insertion, which is moving a branch of the guide tree (or a sub-tree) to another location. The new guide tree resulting of this move is considered as a neighbor of the current guide tree. This will change the topology of the initial guide tree.

Neighbors are generated randomly by branch insertion move. However, we can make only n branch insertions to generate exactly n neighbors for the current guide tree. For each sequence, we choose randomly a branch (or sub-tree) and move it to share this sequence, and so on. Figure 4 shows two guide trees (b and c) obtained by inserting branches to share predetermined sequences of the initial guide tree a.

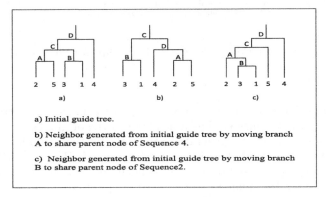

a) Initial guide tree.

b) Neighbor generated from initial guide tree by moving branch A to share parent node of Sequence 4.

c) Neighbor generated from initial guide tree by moving branch B to share parent node of Sequence2.

Fig. 4. Two examples of neighbors generated by branch insertion technique from the initial solution

Generation by Distance Variation. The last technique used to generate a neighborhood is the distance variation. Since the initial guide tree is obtained using NJ clustering algorithm, we can produce N different guide trees based on the NJ clustering algorithm, N being defined by the user. Each tree corresponds to a variation of the original obtained by NJ but adding some random noise into the distances in order to introduce some variability. The variation introduced in the guide tree is low enough to keep the distance criteria but significant enough to provide the necessary flexibility to generate multiple alternative trees [22]. Figure 5 shows two guide trees (b and c) produced by adding variation to distances in the NJ clustering algorithm used to obtain the initial guide tree a.

3.3   Intensification Method

Generally, an intensification procedure revisits and examines good solutions. It maintains the good portions of this solution and searches to find a better neighboring solution.

When a single MSA continues to have the highest score for many iterations, the intensification phase aims to escape the local minima by taking out a solution from the tabu list and restart another search process.

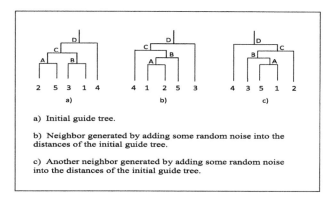

a) Initial guide tree.

b) Neighbor generated by adding some random noise into the distances of the initial guide tree.

c) Another neighbor generated by adding some random noise into the distances of the initial guide tree.

Fig. 5. Examples of neighbors generated by distance variation technique from the initial solution

3.4   Tabu Search Algorithm

Our Tabu Search algorithm consists of generating a neighborhood of a multiple sequence σ using the techniques cited above, i.e. Swapping (SWP), Node insertion (NI), Branch insertion (BI) and Distance variation (DV). The best MSA σ' having the higher score S_{max} is selected for the next iteration and put in the tabu list $TabuList$. This process is iterated until a T_{max} global running time is met . The pseudo-code of our tabu search algorithm is given in Algorithm 1. The details of this algorithm are explained below.

Algorithm 1. Tabu Search Algorithm for MSA

1: **procedure** GTREETABU
2:     Generate σ an initial MSA using NJ algorithm;
3:     S_{max}:=Score(σ); $\sigma_{max} := \sigma$; TabuList:=[];
4:     **while** not T_{max} **do**
5:         Generate a neighborhood $N(\sigma)$ using: SWP, NI, BI or DV.
6:         set σ' such that
7:         $S_{\sigma'}$:=$\max_{\eta \in N(\sigma)}$Score($\eta$) and $\sigma' \notin$ TabuList
8:         **if** $S_{\sigma'} > S_{max}$ **then**
9:             $S_{max} := S_{\sigma'}$; $\sigma_{max} := \sigma'$
10:             Insert σ' in TabuList
11:        **end if**
12:        set σ:=σ'
13:    **end while**
14: **end procedure**

After generating an initial solution using NJ clustering algorithm, its score is computed. While a time execution T_{max} is not reached, the tabu search is iteratively executed. Each iteration begins by generating the neighborhood of the current solution by one of the techniques among: Swapping, Node insertion, Branch insertion, Distance variation. For each neighbor, we compute its score in order to set the best neighbor having the highest score as the new current solution. This new solution is inserted in the tabu list which has a variable length depending on the number of iterations with or without improvement. If there is improvement in a certain number of continuously iterations, the length is increased in order to insert other possible solutions. The length of tabu list is decreased if within many iterations there is no improvement. In this case, a solution will be get out from the tabu list in order to restart another search process in the intensification mode.

4   Experimental Results and Discussion

The proposed approach is implemented in MATLAB and tested on Intel Core i3-380M Laptop with 2 GB. To demonstrate the effectiveness of our approach, we have evaluated it on BAliBASE 2 benchmark base [2]. BAliBASE is a database of manually refined multiple sequence alignments. It can be viewed at http://www-igbmc.u-strasbg.fr/BioInfo/BAliBASE2/index.html or can be downloaded from ftp://ftp-igbmc.u-strasbg.fr/pub/BAliBASE2/.

BAliBASE database is divided into five reference sets. Reference 1 contains alignments of equidistant sequences of similar length, with no large insertions or extensions. Reference 2 aligns up to three "orphan" sequences (less than 25% identical) from reference 1 with a family of at least 15 closely related sequences. Reference 3 consists of up to 4 sub-groups, with less than 25% residue identity between sequences from different groups. The alignments are constructed by adding homologous family members to the more distantly related sequences in reference 1. Reference 4 contains alignments of up to 20 sequences including N/C-terminal extensions (up to 400 residues), and Reference 5 consists of alignments including internal insertions (up to 100 residues) [2].

We analyzed the tabu search results from two aspects. The very first set of tests was aimed at to verify the efficiency of our techniques of generating the neighborhood. The techniques are: Swapping (SWP), Node Insertion (NI), Branch Insertion (BI) and Distance Variation (DV). For each neighborhood technique, we ran an extensive set of tests on all the datasets provided by BAliBASE, and computed the scores. The scores using tabu search with each neighborhood generation technique are shown in Table 1. The Number of Test Cases in Reference 1, Reference 2, Reference 3, Reference 4 and Reference 5 are respectively 82, 23, 12, 12 and 12.

One can see in Table 1 that all the neighborhood generation techniques perform well in average for all the reference sets. However, it seems that Branch Insertion and Distance Variation give the best results for all the sequences of Reference 2, Reference 3, Reference 4 and Reference 5. Node insertion gives best results for sequences of Reference 1. We can see that, for all the datasets provided by BAliBASE, Swapping is not the adequate neighborhood technique. This can be explained by the nature of the neighbors generated by a certain technique.

Table 1. Results given by tabu search using four neighborhood generation techniques on the BAliBASE benchmark database

Neighbor-hood	Reference 1	Reference 2	Reference 3	Reference 4	Reference 5	Average
SWP	90.0	93.0	76.3	87.4	85.1	86.36
NI	**90.1**	90.0	78.5	85.6	93.3	87.50
BI	90.05	**93.8**	80.7	**93.7**	**97.9**	**91.23**
DV	90.0	93.5	**82.0**	91.8	95.1	90.48

For the Swapping technique, the neighbors have the same topology, so they are not very different and this will not give more amelioration of the alignment score. For the rest of techniques, the neighbors have not the same topology, but Branch insertion and Distance variation techniques seem to generate more complex guide trees, and this will give more chances to explore different solution spaces and thus, ameliorate the alignment score.

In order to verify the efficiency of our algorithm, we performed another set of tests where the results of our tabu search algorithm using a certain neighborhood technique is compared to other MSA tools. For each references set, we use the adequate neighborhood generation technique which gives the best results, and compare it to the most competitive MSA tools in the literature, such as CLUSTALW 1.83 [28], SAGA [19], MUSCLE [6], ProbCons [5], T-Coffee [20], SPEM [30], PRALINE [27], IMSA ([4] and Tabu Search developed by [24] (called in this paper TS-Riaz) . Except for SAGA and TS-Riaz, which are taken from [24], the results of the other programs are taken from the work of Layeb et al. [16].

The results of our method illustrate clearly the effectiveness of using Tabu Search to perform the multiple sequence alignment. As it can be seen in Table 2, our algorithm performs well in all the references sets. Our method gives good results compared to the other MSA tools. In fact, it gives the second best score for the sequences set Reference 4, the third best score for Reference 3 and Reference 5, and it is in the fourth place for the remaining sets, i.e. Reference 1 and Reference 2. We can see in Table 2 that our Tabu search using Branch Insertion neighborhood technique has a good place for three sequences sets over five, i.e. Reference 2, Reference 4 and Reference 5. Using the Distance Variation neighborhood technique gives the third best score for Reference 3 set, and Node Insertion gives the fourth best score for Reference 1. It can be seen overall, that our tabu search method using Branch Insertion neighborhood technique gives in average the second best score compared to the other algorithms studied in the paper.

Table 2. Results given by Tabu Search using neighborhood techniques compared with other methods on the BAliBASE benchmark database.

Method	Reference 1	Reference 2	Reference 3	Reference 4	Reference 5	Average
CLUSTALW	85.8	93.3	72.3	83.4	85.8	84.12
SAGA	82.5	**95.4**	77.7	78.0	86.8	84.08
MUSCLE	**90.3**	64.4	**82.2**	91.8	**98.1**	85.36
ProbCons	90.0	**94.0**	**82.3**	90.9	**98.1**	91.06
T-Coffee	86.8	**93.9**	76.7	92.1	94.6	88.82
SPEM	**90.8**	93.4	81.4	**97.4**	97.4	**92.08**
PRALINE	**90.4**	94.0	76.4	79.9	81.8	84.5
IMSA	83.4	92.1	78.6	73.0	83.6	82.14
TS-Riaz	76.0	88.9	71.5	77.3	90.5	80.84
TS-SWP	90.0	93.0	76.3	87.4	85.1	86.36
TS-NI	**90.1**	90.0	78.5	85.6	93.3	87.50
TS-BI	90.05	**93.8**	80.7	**93.7**	**97.9**	**91.23**
TS-DV	90.0	93.5	**82.0**	91.8	95.1	90.48

5   Conclusion

In this paper we have demonstrated the efficiency of using tabu search to align multiple sequences. Our algorithm uses several neighborhood generation techniques. To evaluate our approach, we have used BAliBASE benchmark. Firstly, we studied different techniques to produce the neighborhood, then we compared our algorithm to the most recent and competitive MSA tools. We have observed through experiments on BAliBASE that for Reference 1 and Reference 2, the alignments generated by our method are encouraged. For the remaining references, tabu search performs better than most of the other methods studied in this paper.

There are several issues for future work. First, tabu search comes with a number of parameters that can be experimented with to observe the respective effect on the search process. The parameters like tabu list size, tabu tenure, termination criteria, and neighborhood size can have a direct influence on the quality of the final alignment. Further studies are needed to test different scoring schemes and tabu search features.

References

1. Abbas, A., Holmes, S.: Bioinformatics and management science: some common tools and techniques. Operations Research 52(2), 165–190 (2004)
2. Bahr, A., Thompson, J.D., Thierry, J.C., Poch, O.: BAliBASE (benchmark alignment database): enhancements for repeats, transmembrane sequences and circular permutations. Nucleic Acids Res. 29(1), 323–326 (2001)
3. Blum, C., Valles, M.Y., Blesa, M.J.: An ant colony optimization algorithm for DNA sequencing by hybridization. Computers and Operations Research 38, 3620–3635 (2008)
4. Cutello, V., Nicosia, G., Pavone, M., Prizzi, I.: Protein multiple sequence alignment by hybrid bio-inspired algorithms. Nucleic Acids Research 39(6), 1980–1990 (2010)
5. Do, C., Mahabhashyam, M., Brudno, M., Batzoglou, S.: ProbCons: Probabilistic consistency-based multiple sequence alignment. Genome Res. 15(2), 330–340 (2005)
6. Edgar, R.: MUSCLE: Multiple sequence alignment with high accuracy and high throughput. Nucleic Acids Res. 32, 1792–1797 (2004)
7. Feng, D., Doolittle, R.: Progressive sequence alignment as a prerequisite to correct phylogenetic trees. Journal of Molecular Evolution 24(4), 351–360 (1987)
8. Glover, F., Laguna, M.: Tabu Search. Kluwer Academic Publishers, Boston (1997)
9. Glover, F., Taillard, E., de Werra, D.: A user's guide to tabu search. Ann. Oper. Res. 41, 3–28 (1993)
10. Gotoh, O.: Significant improvement in accuracy of multiple protein sequence alignments by iterative refinement as assessed by reference to structural alignments. J. Mol. Biol. 264, 823–838 (1996)
11. Gupta, S.K., Kececioglu, J.D., Schaffer, A.A.: Improving the practical space and time efficiency of the shortest-paths approach to sum-of-pairs multiple sequence alignment. J. Comp. Biol. 2(3), 459–472 (1995)
12. Higgins, D.G., Taylor, W.R.: Multiple sequence alignment, Protein Structure Prediction -Methods and Protocols. Humana Press (2000)
13. Kemena, C., Notredame, C.: Upcoming challenges for multiple sequence alignment methods in the high-throughput era. Bioinformatics 25, 2455–2465 (2009)
14. Kim, J., Pramanik, S., Chung, M.J.: Multiple sequence alignment using simulated annealing. Comp. Applic. Biosci. 10(4), 419–472 (1994)
15. Lalwani, S., Kumar, R., Gupta, N.: A review on particle swarm optimization variants and their applications to multiple sequence alignments. Journal of Applied Mathematics and Bioinformatics 3(2), 87–124 (2013)
16. Layeb, A., Selmane, M., Bencheikh ELhoucine, M.: A new greedy randomized adaptive search procedure for multiple sequence alignment. International Journal of Bioinformatics Research and Applications (2011)
17. Lightner, C.: A Tabu Search Approach to Multiple Sequence Alignment. Ph.D. thesis, North Carolina State University, Raleigh, North Carolina (2008)

18. Lipman, D., Altschul, S., Kececioglu, J.: A tool for multiple sequence alignment. Proc. Natl. Acad. Sci. 86, 4412–4415 (1989)
19. Notredame, C., Higgins, D.G.: SAGA: Sequence alignment by genetic algorithm. Nucl. Acids Res. 24, 1515–1524 (1996)
20. Notredame, C., Higgins, D., Heringa, J.: T-Coffee: a novel method for fast and accurate multiple sequence alignment. J. Mol. Biol. 302, 205–217 (2000)
21. Notredame, C., Holmes, L., Higgins, D.: COFFEE: an objective function for multiple sequence alignments. Bioinformatics 14(5), 407–422 (1998)
22. Orobitg, M., Guitaro, F., Cores, F., Llados, J., Notredame, C.: High performance computing improvements on bioinformatics consistency-based multiple sequence alignment tools (2014), http://dx.doi.org/10.1016/j.parco.2014.09.010
23. Reinert, K., Stoye, J., Will, T.: An iterative method for faster sum-of-pairs multiple sequence alignment. Bioinformatics 16, 808–814 (2000)
24. Riaz, T., Wang, Y., Li, K.: Multiple sequence alignment using tabu search. In: Proceeding of Asia-Pacific Bioinformatics Conference (APBC 2004), pp. 1–10 (2004)
25. Saitou, N., Nei, M.: The neighbor-joining method: a new method for reconstructing phylogenetic trees. Mol. Biol. Evol. 4(4), 406–425 (1987)
26. Shyu, C., Sheneman, L., Foster, J.: Multiple sequence alignment with evolutionary computation. Genetic Programming and Evolvable Machines 5, 121–144 (2004)
27. Simossis, V., Heringa, J.: PRALINE: a multiple sequence alignment toolbox that integrates homology-extended and secondary structure information. Nucleic Acids Res. 33, 289–294 (2005)
28. Thompson, J., Higgins, D., Gibson, T.: ClustalW: improving the sensitivity of progressive multiple sequence weighting, position-specific gap penalties and weight matrix choice. Nucleic Acids Res. 22, 4673–4680 (1994)
29. Yokoyama, T., Watanabe, T., Taneda, A., Shimizu, T.: A web server for multiple sequence alignment using genetic algorithm. Genome Informatics, 12, 382–383 (2001)
30. Zhou, H., Zhou, Y.: SPEM: improving multiple sequence alignment with sequence profiles and predicted secondary structures. Bioinformatics 21, 3615–3621 (2005)

Information Technology:
Text and Speech Processing

Noise Robust Features Based on MVA Post-processing

Mohamed Cherif Amara Korba[1,2]([✉]), Djemil Messadeg[3],
Houcine Bourouba[2], and Rafik Djemili[4]

[1] Mohammed Cherif Messaadia University, Souk-Ahras, Algeria
[2] PI:MIS Laboratory, May 8, 1945 University, Guelma, Algeria
[3] LASA Laboratory, Badji Mokhtar University, Annaba, Algeria
[4] August 20, 1955 University, Skikda, Algeria
{amara_korba_cherif,messadeg,bourouba2004
rafik_djemili}@yahoo.fr

Abstract. In this paper we present effective technique to improve the performance of the automatic speech recognition (ASR) system. This technique consisting mean subtraction, variance normalization and application of temporal auto regression moving average (ARMA) filtering. This technique is called MVA. We applied MVA as post-processing stage to Mel frequency cespstral coefficients (MFCC) features and Perceptual Linear Prediction (RASTA-PLP) features, to improve automatic speech recognition (ASR) system.

We evaluate MVA post-processing scheme with aurora 2 database, in presence of various additive noise (subway, babble because, exhibition hall, restaurant, street, airport, train station). Experimental results demonstrate that our method provides substantial improvements in recognition accuracy for speech in the clean training case. We have completed study by comparing MFCC and RSTA-PLP After MVA post processing.

1 Introduction

Most speech recognition systems are sensitive to the nature of the acoustical environments within which they are deployed. The performance of ASR systems decreased dramatically when the input speech is corrupted by various kinds of noise sources. It is quite significant when the test environment is different from the training environment.

In the last two decades, substantial efforts have been made and also number of techniques have been presented to cope with this issue improve the ASR performance. Unfortunately these same algorithms frequently do not provide significant improvements in more difficult environments.

MFCC and RASTA-PLP have served as very successful front-ends for the Hidden Markov Model (HMM) based speech recognition. Many speech recognition systems based on these front-ends have achieved a very high level of accuracy in clean speech environment [14], [15]. However, it is well-known that MFCC is not robust enough in noisy environments, which suggests that the MFCC still has insufficient sound representation capability, especially at low signal-to-noise-ratio (SNR).

© IFIP International Federation for Information Processing 2015
A. Amine et al. (Eds.): CIIA 2015, IFIP AICT 456, pp. 155–166, 2015.
DOI: 10.1007/978-3-319-19578-0_13

This paper presents noise-robust technique that is simple and effective. The technique post-processing speech features using MVA [10],[11],[12]. The advantage of this technique, it makes no change to the recognition system, it does not change the size of the space, it can be applied on any acoustic feature. it has been shown in [10] and [11] the efficacy of this technique on the database Aurora 2.0 and Aurora 3.0.

This paper is organized as follows: in section 2, we describe MVA post-processing technique, in section3, we show a graphical comparison between different features, in section 4, we present experimental result and in section 5 the work is concluded.

2   Definition and Analyze of MVA Post-Processing Technique

2.1   Definition of MVA Post-Processing Technique

In this part, we describe different steps of development of MVA post-processing technique, Figure 1 provided a block diagram.

For a given utterance, we represent the data by matrix C whose element $C_d(t)$ is the dth component of the feature vector at time t, $t = 1 \ldots T$, the number of frames in the utterence and $d = 1 \ldots D$, the dimension of the feature space, in other words, each column of C represents a time sequence.

$$\begin{bmatrix} C_1(1) & \cdots & C_1(T) \\ \vdots & \ddots & \vdots \\ C_d(1) & \cdots & C_d(T) \end{bmatrix} \tag{1}$$

The first step we application mean subtraction (MS) [6], [7] defined by:

$$\bar{C}_d = C_d(t) - \mu_d \tag{2}$$

Where μ_d is mean vector estimated from data and $\bar{C}_d$ is the subtracted feature.

$$\mu_d = \frac{1}{T}\sum_{t=1}^{T} C_d(t) \tag{3}$$

MS is an alternate way to high-pass filter cepstral coefficients, it force the average values of cepstral coefficients to be zero in both the training and testing domains. it also removes time-invariant distortions introduced by the transmission channel and recording device.

The second step is Variance normalization (VN) [8], [9] defined by:

$$\tilde{C}_d = \frac{\bar{C}_d(t)}{\sqrt{\sigma_d}} \tag{4}$$

Where σ_d is variance vector estimated from data.

$$\sigma_d = \frac{1}{T}\sum_{t=1}^{T}(C_d(t) - \mu_d)^2 \tag{5}$$

The third step is processing by a mixed auto-regression moving average (ARMA) filtering. In this study we have used two types of ARMA filters: Non Causal ARMA Filter defined by

$$\check{C}_d(t) = \begin{cases} \frac{\sum_{i=1}^{M} \check{C}_d(t-i) + \sum_{j=0}^{M} \tilde{C}_d(t+j)}{2M+1} & if \ M < t \leq T - M \\ \tilde{C}_d(t) & Otherwise \end{cases} \tag{6}$$

and Causal ARMA Filter defined by :

$$\check{C}_d(t) = \begin{cases} \dfrac{\sum_{i=1}^{M} \check{C}_d(t-i) + \sum_{j=0}^{M} \tilde{C}_d(t+j)}{2M+1} & if \ M < t \leq T \\ \tilde{C}_d(t) & Otherwise \end{cases} \qquad (7)$$

where M is the order of ARMA filter.

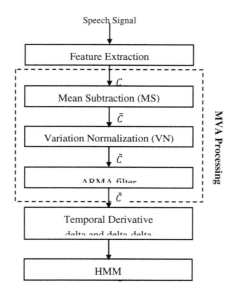

Fig. 1. Block diagram of MVA post-processing technique

In all our experiments, the performances of ASR system are enhanced by adding time derivatives to the basic static parameters for different features. The delta coefficients are computed using the following regression formula:

$$\Delta(t) = \frac{\sum_{b=1}^{B} d\left(\check{C}_d(b+1) - \check{C}_d(b-1)\right)}{2\sum_{b=1}^{B} b^2} \qquad (8)$$

Where $\Delta(t)$ is the delta coefficient computed in terms of the corresponding static coefficients $\tilde{C}_d(t-B)$ to $\tilde{C}_d(t+B)$. The same formula is applied to the delta to obtain acceleration coefficients.

2.2   Effect of Normalization and ARMA Filter on Acoustic Features

In Fig. 2 and fig. 3 the time sequences of C0 and C1 are plotted for both features RASTA-PLP and MFCC of the utterance of digit string "98Z7437" corrupted by different levels of additive subway noise from the Aurora 2.0 database. For both RASTA-PLP and MFCC features, we see enormous differences between the plots of the clean case and the more noisy case. In particular, the clean and noisy plots have quite a different average value and dynamic range.

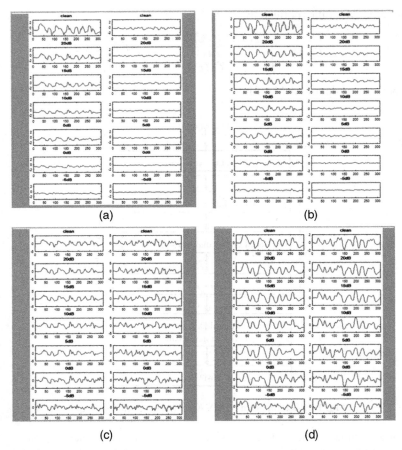

(a)   (b)

(c)   (d)

Fig. 2. The time sequence of C0 and C1 coefficients of RASTA-PLP features for the digit string "98Z7437" corrupted by additive subway noise, (a) RASTA-PLP features, (b) time sequence of RASTA-PLP + MS, (c) time sequence of RASTA-PLP + MS + VN, (d) time sequence of RASTA-PLP + MVA.

After MS and VN is applied, the difference between the clean and noisy cases are made much less severe After MS and VN is applied, the differences between the clean and noisy cases are made much less severe. Still, however, some differences remain between the clean and noisy cases. We notice in particular the case of C1, that after the application of MS and VN, the time sequences in noisy speech show spurious spikes relative to the clean case. In order to further reduce differences, we apply ARMA filtering which smoothes out the sequences thus making them more similar to each other. We remark that, the effects of noise on the MVA features are less severe for both MFCC and RASTA-PLP features.

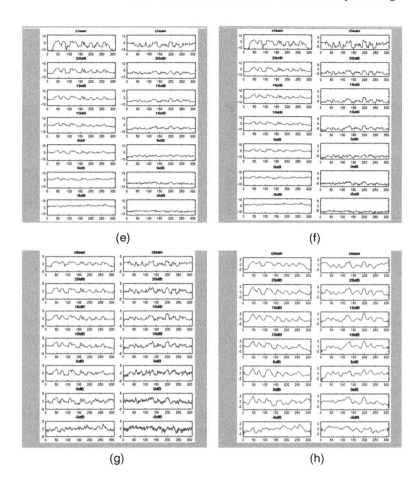

Fig. 3. The time sequence of C0 and C1 coefficients of MFCC features for the digit string "98Z7437" corrupted by additive subway noise, (e) MFCC features, (f)   time sequence of MFCC + MS, (g) time sequence of MFCC + MS + VN, (h) time sequence of MFCC + MVA

3   Graphical Comparison between the Different Features

Fig. 4 shows a sample comparison between baseline MFCC features and corresponding MFCC MVA post-processing features for the digit string "98Z7437" corrupted with Subway noise at different levels of noise (clean, 20dB, 15dB, 10dB, 5dB, 0dB, -5dB). As standard in MFCC, a window size of 25 ms with an overlap of 10 ms was chosen, and Cepstral features were obtained from DCT of log-energy over 23 Mel-scale filter banks.

The degradation of spectral features for baseline MFCC features in the presence of noise is evident; whereas MFCC with MVA post-processing features obtained with No Causal ARMA filter prevail at elevated noise levels. For SNR $\leq$ 0dB we can see clearly that MFCC with MVA is better noise robustness than MFCC baseline features.

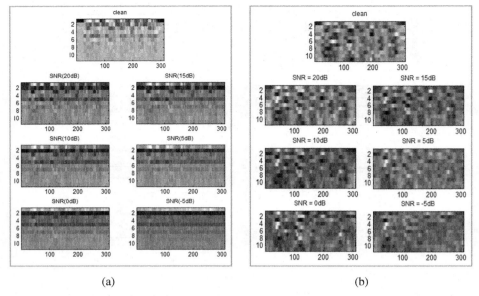

(a)   (b)

Fig. 4. (a) Baseline MFCC features for the digit string "98Z7437" corrupted by subway noise, (b) MFCC with MVA post-processing features for the digit string "98Z7437" corrupted by subway noise. (No causal ARMA filter used, filter order = 5)

3.1   Speech Features Description

This part contains a short description of the most widely used acoustic features in automatic speech recognition. Many of current ASRs are based on Mel frequency cepstral coefficients MFCC [5] or RASTA-PLP coefficients [3],[4]. They operate efficiently in the clean environment, by against the performances of ASR decreases dramatically in presence of noise. To remedy this problem, we introduced a post-processing stage to improve their performances without bringing changes in their structures. Table 1 shows the configuration of MFCC and RASTA-PLP features used for experiences.

4   Experiments

We first describe in detail the Aurora 2 database, then, we present experimental results that are intended to show the contribution of MVA post-processing technique for both acoustic features MFCC and RASTA-PLP in the presence of large variety of additive noise. We determine type and order of ARMA filter that gives the best speech accuracy for acoustic features used (MFCC and RASTA-PLP).

4.1   Description of Aurora 2 Database

Our speech recognition experiments were conducted using the Aurora 2 database and task [2]. The Aurora task [2] has been defined by the European Telecommunications Standards (ETSI) to standardize a robust feature extraction technique for a distributed speech recognition framework.

The Aurora 2 database is a subset of the TIDigits, which contains a set of connected digit utterances spoken in English; while the task consists of the recognition of the connected digit utterances interfered with real noise artificially added in a wide range of SNRs (-5dB, 0dB, 5dB, 10dB, 15dB, 20dB and Clean) and the channel distortion is additionally included in Set C. Noise signals are recorded at different places including suburban train, babble, car, exhibition hall, restaurant, street, airport and train station.

Two training modes are defined, training on clean data only and training on clean as well as noisy data (multi-condition). For the first mode, training data contain 8440 clean utterances produced by 55 male and 55 female adults. For the multi-condition training, 8440 utterances from TIDigits training parts are equally split into 20 subsets with 422 utterances in each subset. Four types of noise, Suburban train, babble, car, and exhibition hall noises are added to 20 subsets at 5 different SNRs (5dB, 10dB, 15dB, 20 dB and Clean).

The testing data consist of 4004 utterances from 52 male and 52 female speakers in the TIDigits test part are divided into four subsets with 1001 utterances in each. One noise is added to each subset at SNRs of 20 to -5 dB in decreasing steps of 5 dB after speech and noise are being filtered with the G. 712. Three test sets are defined as below:

Test Set A: four types of noise, babble, car, suburban train, and exhibition hall are added to the four subsets of utterances to produce 28028 utterances (4x7x1001 utterances). This set leads to a high match of training and test data as it contains the same noises as used for the multi-condition training mode.

Test Set B: the other type of noise, street, restaurant, airport and train station, are added to the four subsets of utterances to produce 28028 utterances (4x7x1001 utterances), similar to test A.

Test Set C: two types of noise, suburban train and street, are individually added to two of the four subsets of utterances to produce 14014 utterances (2x7x1001 utterances). Speech and noise are filtered with the MIRS frequency characteristic before adding.

In this study we used two sets of tests, Test Set A and Test Set B. for all experiments HMM baseline system is trained in clean condition.

4.2   The HTK Recognizer

For the baseline system, the training and recognition tests used the HTK recognition toolkit [1], which followed the setup originally defined for the ETSI Aurora evaluations.

Each digit was modeled as a left to right continuous density HMM with 16 states with each state having 3 mixtures. Two pause models, silence "sil" and short pause "sp", were defined. The "sil" model had three states with six Gaussian mixtures per state. The "sp" model had one state with six Gaussian mixtures.

Script files provided with the Aurora 2 database for the purpose of training and testing a HTK based recognizer were used in the evaluation of the front-ends. The version of HTK used was HTK 3.3. We used the RASTA-PLP implementation that is valuable at [13], we used the version of conventional MFCC processing implemented as part of HTK platform. Configurations of RASTA-PLP and MFCC features used in our experiments are given by the table 1.

Table 1. features parameters used for experimental analysis

Configuration features	MFCC	RASTA-PLP
Frame length (ms)	25	25
Frame shift (ms)	10	10
Pre-emphasis coefficient	0.97	NO
Analyses window	Hamming	NO
frequency range	64 – 4000 Hz	0 – 4000 Hz
No. Mel filterbanks	23	/
LPC Model order	/	11
Rasta filter	/	do
Appended log frame energy	yes	yes
Appended features	$\Delta + \Delta \Delta$	
Δ window (frames)	±4	±4
$\Delta\Delta$ window (frames)	±1	±1
Feature dimension	39	39

4.3   Analyses

The tables below were done to determine type and order of ARMA filter that gives the best recognition accuracy for each acoustic feature. Tables show the contribution importance of order of filter on the performances of ASR system.

For all our experiments, best results have been obtained with the non-causal ARMA filter for both acoustic features. We varied the order of the filter until 9, the best performances of the system have been obtained with order $M = 6$.

Table 2. Comparison of different type and order ARMA filters, word accuracy Rasta-PLP, Test speech average over SNR (clean, 20, 15, 10, 5, 0, -5dB)

	Filter Order				
Filter Type	2	3	4	5	6
Causal ARMA filter	67.52	69.09	69.06	68.94	**68.98**
Non Causal ARMA filter	68.33	68.63	69.74	69.66	**70.46**

Table 3. Comparison of different type and order ARMA filters, word accuracy MFCC, Test speech average over SNR (clean, 20, 15, 10, 5, 0 -5dB)

	Filter Order				
Filter Type	2	3	4	5	6
Causal ARMA filter	67.57	66.84	67.74	69.35	**70.55**
Non Causal ARMA filter	67.67	69.10	69.53	70.05	**71.40**

4.4   Performance of MVA pPost-processing

In this section we describe the recognition accuracy obtained using MVA post-processing for MFCC and RASTA-PLP features, under various noise conditions at different SNR levels (Clean, 20, 15, 10, 5, 0, -5dB).

In figure 5, remarkably improvements have been achieved up to 20% compared to RASTA-PLP features without any normalization, up to 10% to features with MSVN normalization and up to 5% to features with MS normalization.

In figure 6, Substantial improvements have been achieved up to 25% compared to MFCC features without any normalization, up to 15% to features with MS + VN normalization and up to 8% to features with MS normalization.

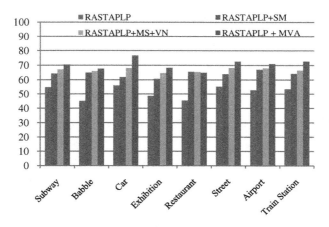

Fig. 5. Comparison of recognition accuracy for different RASTA-PLP features configuration (MVA: use non causal ARMA filter, M = 6), the recognition accuracy is calculated on an average of 7 SNR levels. (Clean, 20dB, 15dB, 10dB, 5dB, 10dB, 5dB, 0dB, -5dB).

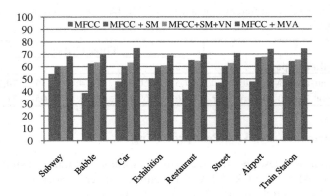

Fig. 6. Comparison of recognition accuracy for different MFCC features configuration (MVA: use non causal ARMA filter, M = 6), the recognition accuracy is calculated on an average of 7 SNR levels. (Clean, 20dB, 15dB, 10dB, 5dB, 10dB, 5dB, 0dB, -5dB).

Figure 7 shows a comparison between MFCC features and Rasta-PLP features, in the presence of stationary noise subway, street and car the RASTA-PLP features are more efficient compared to MFCC features, but in the presence of noises majority babble, suburban train, exhibition hall, restaurant, airport and the train station the MFCC coefficients provide best performance to ASR system.

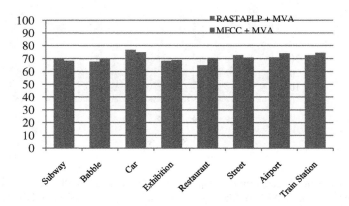

Fig. 7. Comparison of recognition accuracy for MFCC + MVA features with RASTA-PLP + MVA features (MVA: use non causal ARMA filter, M = 6 for both types of features), the recognition accuracy is calculated on an average of 7 SNR levels. (Clean, 20dB, 15dB, 10dB, 5dB, 10dB, 5dB, 0dB, -5dB).

5   Conclusions

In this paper, we introduce MVA technique to MFCC and RASTA-PLP features to improve the noise robustness of speech features. We have shown that normalization techniques followed by ARMA filter are vital for conditions with major mismatch between training and test condition.

The experimental results show that application of MVA to the Aurora 2 database can provide further robustness to noise for various types of features, and higher accuracy rates can be thereby achieved.

Acknowledgment. This work was supported by PI:MIS laboratory of Guelma University. The authors would like to thank Professor A. Boukrouche and H. Doghmane for Helpful discussion.

References

1. Young, S., et al.: The HTK Book Version 3.3 (2005)
2. Hirsch, H.G., Pearce, D.: The AURORA Experimental Framework for the Performance Evaluations of Speech Recognition Systems under Noisy Conditions. In: Proc. ISCA ITRW ASR (2000)
3. Hermansky, H.: Perceptual linear prediction analysis of speech. J. Acoust. Soc. Am. 87(4), 1738–1752 (1990)
4. Hermansky, H., Morgan, N.: RASTA processing of speech. IEEE. Trans. Speech Audio Process. 2(4), 578–589 (1994)
5. Davis, S.B., Mermelstein, P.: Comparison of parametric representations for monosyllabic word recognition in continuously spoken sentences. IEEE Trans. Acoust., Speech, and Signal Processing 28(4), 357–366 (1980)
6. Atal, B.: Effectiveness of linear prediction characteristics of the speech wave for automatic speaker identification and verification. Journal of the Acoustical Society of America 55, 1304–1312 (1974)
7. Furui, S.: Cepstral analysis technique for automatic speaker verification. IEEE Trans. Acoust., Speech, Signal Process. 29(2), 254–272 (1981)
8. Jain, P., Hermansky, H.: Improved mean and variance normalization for robust speech recognition. In: IEEE Int. Conf. Acoust., Speech and Signal Processing (May 2001)
9. Cook, G.D., Kershaw, D.J., Christie, J.D.M., Seymour, C.W., Waterhouse, S.R.: Transcription of broadcast television and radio news: the 1996 abbot system. In: Proc. IEEE Int. Conf. Acoust., Speech, Signal Process. (ICASSP), Munich, Germany (1997)
10. Chen, C.-P., Bilmes, J., Kirchhoff, K.: Low-resource noise-robust feature post-processing on Aurora 2.0. In: Proc. Int. Conf. Spoken Lang. Process. (ICSLP), pp. 2445–2448 (2002)
11. Chen, C.-P., Filali, K., Bilmes, J.: Frontend post-processing and backend model enhancement on the Aurora 2.0/3.0 databases. In: Proc. Int. Conf. Spoken Lang. Process. (ICSLP), pp. 241–244 (2002)
12. Chen, C.-P., Bilmes, J.: MVA processing of speech features Dept. Elect. Eng., Univ. Washington, Seattle, WA, Tech. Rep. UWEETR- 2003-0024 (2003), http://www.ee.washington.edu/techsite/papers

13. Ellis, D.: PLP and RASTA (and MFCC, and inversion) in MATLAB using melfcc.m and invmelfcc.m (2006),
    http://labrosa.ee.columbia.edu/matlab/rastamat/
14. Stuttle, M.N., Gales, M.J.F.: A Mixture of Gaussians Front End for Speech Recognition. In: Eurospeech 2001, Scandinavia, pp. 675–678 (2001)
15. Potamifis, J., Fakotakis, N., Kokkinakis, G.: Improving the robustness of noisy MFCC features using minimal recurrent neural networks. In: Proceedings of the IEEE-INNS-ENNS International Joint Conference on Neural Networks, IJCNN 2000, vol. 5, pp. 271–276 (2000)

Arabic Texts Categorization: Features Selection Based on the Extraction of Words' Roots

Said Gadri[1(✉)] and Abdelouahab Moussaoui[2]

[1] Department of ICST, University of M'sila, 28000, Algeria
kadri.said28@yahoo.fr
[2] Department of Computer Sciences, University Farhat Abbes of Setif,
Setif, 19000, Algeria
moussaoui.abdel@gmail.com

Abstract. One of methods used to reduce the size of terms vocabulary in Arabic text categorization is to replace the different variants (forms) of words by their common root. The search of root in Arabic or Arabic word root extraction is more difficult than other languages since Arabic language has a very different and difficult structure, that is because it is a very rich language with complex morphology. Many algorithms are proposed in this field. Some of them are based on morphological rules and grammatical patterns, thus they are quite difficult and require deep linguistic knowledge. Others are statistical, so they are less difficult and based only on some calculations. In this paper we propose a new statistical algorithm which permits to extract roots of Arabic words using the technique of n-grams of characters without using any morphological rule or grammatical patterns.

Keywords: Root extraction · Information retrieval · Bigrams technique · Arabic morphological rules · Feature selection

1 Introduction

Arabic is one of the oldest and the most used language in the world, it is spoken by over 300 million people in Arabic world, and used by more than 1.7 billion Muslims over the world because it is the language of the Holy Quran, here we can distinguish two types of Arabic; a more classical language, as found in the Holy Quran or poetry, a standardized modern language, and regional dialects [1]. We note also that Arabic language is a semitic language [2, 3] based on 28 cursives letters written from right to left.

The word in Arabic is formed of the root part and some affixes (antefixes, prefixes, infixes, suffixes) that form the word (سألتمونيها Saaltmwnyha). The Arabic root extraction is a very difficult task which is not the case for other languages as English or French, because Arabic is a very rich language with a very difficult structure and complex morphology. Arabian linguists show that all nouns and verbs of Arabic language are derived from a set of roots containing about 11347 roots; more than 75 % of them are trilateral roots [4].

© IFIP International Federation for Information Processing 2015
A. Amine et al. (Eds.): CIIA 2015, IFIP AICT 456, pp. 167–180, 2015.
DOI: 10.1007/978-3-319-19578-0_14

There are many applications based on the roots of words in Arabic processing such as: text's classification, text summarizing, information retrieval, data and text mining. [5,6].

The Arabic words ' roots can be classified according to the vowels letters (أ ، و ، ي a, w, y) into two types [7], strong roots that do not contain any vowel (ذهب ، خرج ، فتح go, come out, open), vocalic roots that contain at least one vowel (أوى ، وعد shelter, promise). Arabic roots can be further classified according to the number of their characters into four types: Trilateral roots which form most words in Arabic language [4] (e.g., علم ، كتب ، خرج know, write, come out), Quadrilateral roots (e.g., دحرج ، طمأن roll, assure), Quinquelateral roots (e.g., انكسر، اقتصد ، انطلق ، broken, economize, start) and Hexalateral roots (استعمل ، استحسن اقشعّر use, enjoy, tremble).

There are two classes of methods used to extract the roots of Arabic words, the first class is based on morphological rules, so its methods simulate the same process of an expert linguist during his analysis of a given Arabic word [1], [8,9,10,11], which make the process of extracting root difficult and complex because of the diversity of morphological formulas and the multiplicity of words forms for the same root when changing the original characters position in the word (e.g., علم ، عالم ، علوم ، عوالم ، معالم know, scientist, sciences, worlds, landmarks) [12,13]. The second class is formed of statistical methods which are simple, fast, and do not require any morphological rules but some calculations [14,15, 16,17, 18,19,20].

In this paper, we propose a new statistical method which permits to extract roots of Arabic words using the approach of n-grams of characters without using any morphological rule. The paper is organized as follows: the first section is a general introduction to the field of study. The second section presents some related works, so we review some papers that treat the problem of extraction of Arabic word's roots. In the third section we introduce our new algorithm. The fourth section presents the experiments that we have done to test our new method and also presents the obtained results. In the last section we conclude our work by summarizing our realized work and giving some ideas to improve it in the future.

2   Related Works

Many researchers proposed some algorithms to extract Arabic words roots, some of these algorithms are based on morphological rules. Thus, they are called morphological methods. Others do not use any morphological rule but some statistical calculations, so they are called statistical algorithms.

In the first class of algorithms, we can note the following: [9], [21] Khoja's roots extractor removes the longest suffix and prefix. It then matches the remaining word with verbal and noun patterns, to extract the root. The roots extractor makes use of several linguistic data files such as a list of all diacritics, punctuation characters, definite articles, and stop words [22,23,24,25]. [13] Propose a linguistic approach for root extraction as a preprocessing step for Arabic text mining. The proposed approach is composed of a rule-based light stemmer and a pattern-based infix remover. They propose an algorithm to handle weak, eliminated-long vowel, hamzated and geminated words. The accuracy of the extracted roots is determined by comparing them with a predefined list of 5,405 trilateral and quadrilateral roots. The linguistic approach performance was tested on texts' collection consists of eight categories, the author achieved a success ratio about 73.74%. [26] Presents a new Arabic root extractor that tries to assign a unique root for each Arabic word without having an Arabic roots list, a word patterns list, or the list of Arabic prefixes and suffixes. The algorithm predict the letters positions that may form the word root one by one, using rules based on the relations between the Arabic word letters and their placement in the word. This algorithm consists of two parts, the first part gives the rules that distinguish between the Arabic definite letter "ال AL, La" and the original word letters "ال". The second part segments each word into three parts and classifies its letters according to their positions. The author tested her proposed algorithm using the Holy Quran words and obtained an accuracy of 93.7% in root extracting process.

In the second class of algorithms we can note the following: [14] Developed a root extraction algorithm which does not use any dictionary, their algorithm categorizes all Arabic letters according to six integer weights, ranging from 0 to 5, as well as the rank of the letter which is determined by the position this letter holds in a word. The weight and rank are multiplied together, and the three letters with the smallest product constitute the root of the word. We note that [14] did not explain on what basis did it use such ranking or weighting. [10] Proposes an algorithm to extract tri-literal Arabic roots, this algorithm consists of two steps; in the first step they eliminate stop words as well prefixes and suffixes. In the next step, they remove the repeated word's letters until only three letters are remained, and then they arrange these remaining letters according to their order in the original word, which form the root of the original word. The obtained results were very promising and give an accuracy of root's extraction over than 73%. [27] Propose a new way to extract the roots of Arabic words using n-grams technique. They used two similarity measures; the "Manhattan distance measurement" and the "Dice's measurement". They tested their algorithm on the Holy Quran and on a corpus of 242 abstracts from the Proceedings of the Saudi Arabian National Computer Conferences. They concluded from their study that combining the n-grams with the Dice's measurement gives better results than using the Manhattan distance measurement. [28] propose a new algorithm to find a system that assigns, for every non vowel word a unique root. The proposed system consists of two modules; the first one consists of analyzing the context by segmenting the words of the sentence into its elementary morphological units in order to extract its possible roots. So, each word is segmented into three parts (prefix, stem and suffix). In the second module, they based on the context to extract the correct root among all possible roots of the word. They validate their algorithm using NEMLAR Arabic writing corpus that consists of 500,000 words, and their proposed algorithm gives the correct root in more than 98% of the training set and 94% of the testing set. [29] Propose a new algorithm which use the n-grams technique. In this technique, both the word and its assumed root are divided into pairs called bi-grams, then the similarity between the word and the root is calculated using equation (1) [30]. This process is repeated for each root in the roots list:

$$S = 2 \times C/(A + B) \tag{1}$$

Where:

A = Number of unique bi-grams in the word (A)

B = Number of unique bi-grams in the root (B)

C = Number of similar unique pairs between the word (A) and the root (B)

To use equation (1) for extracting the word's root, we must have: the word (A) and the potential roots (B) to compare with, then the similarity measuring is conducted by computing the value of (S) between the word (A) and each potential roots (B).

3   The Proposed Algorithm

In our new algorithm, we use also the n-grams technique to extract Arabic words roots, for this purpose, we proceed according to the following steps:

Step 1: we segment the word for which we want to find the root, and all the roots of the list into bigrams (2-grams).

For example if we have the word "يذهبون" and a list of six (06) roots (فتح ، خرج ، ذهب ، وجد ، وهب ، نهب), we proceed the segmentation step as follows:

W = "يذهبون" ➔ (يذ، يه ، يب ، يو ، ين ، ذه ، ذب ، ذو ، ذن ، هب ، هو ، هن ، بو ، بن ، ون)

R_1 = "فتح" ➔ (فت ،فح ، تح)

R_2 = "خرج" ➔ (خر ، خج ، رج)

R_3 = "ذهب" ➔ (ذه ، ذب ، هب)

R_4 = "وجد" ➔ (وج ، ود ، جد)

R_5 = "وهب" ➔ (وه ، وب ، هب)

R_6 = "نهب" ➔ (نه ، نب ، هب)

Step 2: we calculate the following parameters:

N_W : The number of unique bigrams in the word w

N_{R_i} : The number of unique bigrams in the root Ri

N_{WR_i} : The number of common unique bigrams between the word W and the root Ri

$N_{W\bar{R_i}}$: The number of bigrams belonging to the word w and do not belong to the root Ri

$$(N_{W\bar{R_i}} = N_W - N_{WR_i})$$

$N_{R_i\bar{W}}$: The number of bigrams belonging to the root Ri and do not belong to the word w

$$(N_{R_i\bar{W}} = N_{R_i} - N_{WR_i})$$

For the previous example we have:

N_W=18, N_{R_1}=3, N_{R_2}=3, N_{R_3}=3, N_{R_4}=3, N_{R_5}=3, N_{R_6}=3, N_{WR_1}=0, N_{WR_2}=0, N_{WR_3}=3, N_{WR_4}=0, N_{WR_5}=1, N_{WR_6}=1, $N_{W\bar{R_1}}$ = 18, $N_{W\bar{R_2}}$ = 18, $N_{W\bar{R_3}}$ = 15, $N_{W\bar{R_4}}$ = 18, $N_{W\bar{R_5}}$ = 17, $N_{W\bar{R_6}}$ = 17, $N_{R_1\bar{W}}$ = 3, $N_{R_2\bar{W}}$ = 3, $N_{R_3\bar{W}}$ = 0, $N_{R_4\bar{W}}$ = 3, $N_{R_5\bar{W}}$ = 2, $N_{R_6\bar{W}}$ = 2 .

Step3: we take only the roots having at least one common bigram with the word w ($N_{WR_i} \geq 1$) as candidate roots among the list of all roots in order to reduce the calculation time.

In our previous example, we can take only the roots: $R_3 =$ "ذهب", $R_5 =$ "وهب", $R_6 =$ "نهب" with $N_{WR_i} = 3, 1, 1$ respectively.

Step4: we calculate the distance $D(w, R_i)$ between the word W and each candidate root R_i (R_3, R_5, R_6) according to the following equation :

$$D(w, R_i) = 2 * N_{wR_i} + k * N_{w\bar{R}_i} + k * N_{R_i\bar{w}} \qquad (2)$$

Where: k is a constant which must take a high value (we put here $k=100$)
For the previous example we obtain:
D(w, R$_3$) = 2*3+15*100+0*100 = 1506
D(w, R$_5$) = 2*1+17*100+2*100 = 1902
D(w, R$_6$) = 2*1+17*100+2*100 = 1902

Step5: in the last step, we assign the root that has the lowest value of distance $D(w, R_i)$ among the candidate roots to the word W. it is the required root.

In our example, the root of the word "يذهبون" is "ذهب"
Finally, we note that our new algorithm has the following advantages:

1. Does not require the removal of affixes whose distinction from the native letters of the word is quite difficult.
2. Works for any word whatever the length of the root.
3. Valid for strong roots and vocalic roots which generally pose problems in Arabic during their derivation, because of the complete change of their forms.
4. Does not use any morphological rule nor patterns but simple calculations of distances.
5. Very practical algorithm and easy to implement on machine.

4   Experimentations and Obtained Results

To validate our proposed algorithm, we used three corpus which can be classified according their sizes into: small corpus, middle corpus, and large corpus.
Each one is constituted of many files as indicated below:

1. The file of derived forms (gross words) which contains morphological forms of words derived from many Arabic roots.
2. The file of roots which contains many Arabic roots, we note that these roots are trilateral, quadrilateral, quinquelateral, and hexalateral. We note also that many of them are vocalic roots which contain at least one vowel.

3. The file of golden roots which contain the correct roots of all words present in our corpus (the file in (1)), this golden list was prepared by an expert linguist and used as reference list, i.e., by comparison between the list of obtained roots (extracted by the system) and the reference list (established by the expert), we can calculate the roots extraction accuracy (success ratio).

Table 1. Corpus used in experiments

Corpus	Size of derived words' file	Size of the roots' file	Size of the golden roots' file
Small corpus	50	25	50
Middle corpus	270	135	270
Large corpus	1500	450	1500

Table 2. An example of morphological forms (gross words)

Word	Word	Word	Word	Word
مأخذ	أوامر	باحث	اجتماعات	مأخذ
مؤاخذة	مؤتمر	بحوث	اجتماعيات	مؤاخذة
مؤاخذون	مؤامرة	أبحاث	جموع	مؤاخذون
مؤاخذات	متأمرون	باحثون	جوامع	مؤاخذات
مؤازرة	يأتمرون	باحثات	يجمعون	مؤازرة
مأكل	يأتمرن	ابتهال	يجمعن	مأكل
أكلات	أمرهم	مبتهل	اجتهاد	أكلات

Table 3. An example of trilateral, quadrilateral, quinquelateral, hexalateral roots

Trilateral roots	Quadrilateral roots	Quinquelateral roots	Hexalateral roots
زرع	أكرم	انطلق	استعمل
صنع	أعان	انكسر	استحسن
تجر	أعطى	احتوى	استعان
جمع	حطّم	اقتصد	اخشوشن
نفر	ربّى	اخضرّ	ادهامّ
طار	حاسب	تحدّى	احرنجم
سعل	طمأن	تنازل	اقشعرّ
صدع	زلزل	تدحرج	اطمأنّ

Table 4. Examples of obtained results when segmenting words into bi-grams

Word	N-grams	Nb.Ng
	Ng.Frequencies	(N_W)
يتعلمون	يت يع يل يم يو ين تع تل تم تو تن عل عم عو عن لم لو لن مو من ون	28
	1 1 1 1 1 1 1 1 1 1 1 1 1 1 1 1 1 1 1 1 1 1 1 1 1 1 1 1	
عالم	عا عل عم ال ام لم	6
	1 1 1 1 1 1	
كاتب	كا كت كب ات اب تب	6
	1 1 1 1 1 1	
كتاتيب	كت كا كت كي كب تا تت تي تب ات اي اب تي تب يب	12
	2 1 1 1 1 1 2 2 1 1 1 1	
اقتصاد	اق ات اص اا قت قص قا قد تص تا تد صا صد اد	14
	1 1 1 1 2 1 1 1 1 1 1 1 1 1	
يقصدون	يق يص يد يو ين قص قد قو قن صد صو صن دو دن ون	15
	1 1 1 1 1 1 1 1 1 1 1 1 1 1 1	
استخدم	اس ات اخ اد ام ست سخ سد سم تخ تد تم خد خم دم	15
	1 1 1 1 1 1 1 1 1 1 1 1 1 1 1	
سنستدرجهم	سن سس ست سد سر سج سه سم نس نت ند نر نج نه نم ست سد سر سج سه سم تد تر تج ته تم در دج ده دم رج ره رم جه جم هم	30
	1 1 1 1 1 1 1 1 1 1 1 1 1 1 1 1 1 1 1 1 1 1 2 2 2 2 2 1 1 1 1 1	
متذبذب	مت مذ مب مذ مب تذ تب تذ تب ذب ذذ ذب بذ بب ذب	9
	1 2 2 2 3 1 1 1	
متلألئ	مت مل مأ مل مئ تل تأ تل تئ لأ لل لئ أل أئ لئ	12
	1 2 1 1 2 1 1 1 2 1 1	
يهزمونهم	يه يز يم يو ين يه هز هم هو هن هه هم زم زو زن زه زم مو من مه مم ون وه وم نه نم هم	23
	1 1 1 1 1 1 1 1 1 1 1 1 2 1 1 1 3 1 1 1 2 1 2	
المتربّي	ال ام ات ار اب آ اي لم لت لر لب لّ لي مت مر مب مّ مي تر تب تّ تي رب رّ ري بّ بي يّ	28
	1 1 1 1 1 1 1 1 1 1 1 1 1 1 1 1 1 1 1 1 1 1 1 1 1 1 1 1	
المربّون	ال ام ار اب آ او ان لم لر لب لّ لو لن مر مب مّ مو من رب رّ رو رن بّ بو بن وّ وّن ون	28
	1 1 1 1 1 1 1 1 1 1 1 1 1 1 1 1 1 1 1 1 1 1 1 1 1 1 1 1	
طائرات	طا طئ طر طا طت ائ ار اا ات ئر ئا ئت را رت ات	13
	1 1 1 1 1 2 1 1 1 1 1 1 2	

Table 5. Examples of obtained results when segmenting roots into bi-grams

Root	N-grams	Nb.Ng
	Ng.Frequencies	(N_{R_i})
كلم	كل كّ كم لّ لمّ م	6
	1 1 1 1 1 1	
عالج	عا عل عج ال اج لج	6
	1 1 1 1 1 1	
قصد	قص قد صد	3
	1 1 1	
اقتصد	اق ات اص اد قت قص قد تص تد صد	10
	1 1 1 1 1 1 1 1 1 1	
كتب	كت كب تب	3
	1 1 1	
علم	عل عم لم	3
	1 1 1	
عمل	عم عل مل	3
	1 1 1	
خدم	خد خم دم	3
	1 1 1	
كمل	كم كل مل	3
	1 1 1	
كمن	كم كن من	3
	1 1 1	
خمد	خم خد مد	3
	1 1 1	
درج	در دج رج	3
	1 1 1	
ذبذب	ذب ذذ ذب بذ بب ذب	4
	1 1 1 3	
لألأ	لأ لل لأ ال اأ لأ	4
	1 1 1 3	
هزم	هز هم زم	3
	1 1 1	
طار	طا طر ار	3
	1 1 1	
ربّى	رب رّ ري بّ بيّ يّ	6
	1 1 1 1 1 1	
عقد	عق عد قد	3
	1 1 1	
تأتأ	تأ تت تأ أت اأ تأ	4
	1 1 1 3	

Table 6. Extraction of some Arabic words roots using our new algorithm

Word	Nearest roots	Nb.Common bi-grams	Distance values	Extract ed root	Correct root
يتعلمون	كلم ، عالج ، علم ، عمل ، كمن	2 ، 3 ، 1 ، 3 ، 1	2806 ، 3202 ، **2506** ، 2704 ، 2902	علم	علم
عالم	كلم ، عالج ، علم ، عمل	2 ، 3 ، 3 ، 1	1002 ، 606 ، **306** ، 504	علم	علم
كاتب	اقتصد ، كتب	3 ، 1	1402 ، **306**	كتب	كتب
كتاتيب	اقتصد ، كتب ، تأتأ	1 ، 3 ، 1	2002 ، **906** ، 1402	كتب	كتب
اقتصاد	قصد ، اقتصد ، عقد	1 ، 10 ، 3	1106 ، **420** ، 1502	اقتصد	اقتصد
يقصدون	قصد ، اقتصد ، عقد	1 ، 3 ، 3	**1206** ، 1906 ، 1602	قصد	قصد
استخدم	اقتصد ، خمد ، خدم	3 ، 2 ، 3	1906 ، 1404 ، **1206**	خدم	خدم
سنستدرجهم	اقتصد ، خدم ، درج ، هزم	1 ، 3 ، 1 ، 1	3802 ، 3102 ، **2706** ، 3102	درج	درج
متذبذب	كتب ، ذبذب	4 ، 1	1002 ، **508**	ذبذب	ذبذب
متلألئ	عمل ، كمل ، تأتأ ، لألأ	3 ، 1 ، 1 ، 1	1302 ، 1302 ، 1402 ، 1006	لألأ	لألأ
يهزمونهم	كمن ، هزم	3 ، 1	**2402** ، 2006	هزم	هزم
المتربّي	كلم ، عالج ، اقتصد ، كتب ، علم ، ربّى ، طار	1 ، 1 ، 1 ، 1 ، 1 ، 6 ، 1	2902 ، 3202 ، 3602 ، 2902 ، **2212** ، 2902 ، 2902	ربّى	ربّى
المربّون	كلم ، عالج ، علم ، كمن ، ربّى ، طار	1 ، 1 ، 1 ، 1 ، 3 ، 1	2902 ، 3202 ، 2902 ، 2902 ، **2806** ، 2902	ربّى	ربّى
طائرات	اقتصد ، طار	3 ، 1	2102 ، **1006**	طار	طار

Table 7. Obtained results when extracting the words roots

Corpus	Nb.Roots	Nb.Words	Cor. Results	Wr.Results	Suc.Rate	Err.Rate
Small	25	50	49	1	98,00	2,00
Middle	135	270	253	17	94,07	5,93
Large	450	1500	1358	142	90,53	9,47

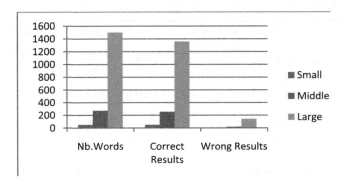

Fig. 1. Correct and wrong results in number of words

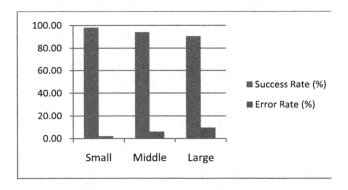

Fig. 2. Calculation of success rate and error rate

5   Comparison with Other Algorithms

To show the effectiveness of our proposed algorithm, we concluded our work by establishing a comparison against other known algorithms. For this purpose, we took a sample words list and tried to extract the root of each word using three very known algorithms which are: khodja stemmer, Nidal et al stemmer, and our proposed stemmer, the obtained results are shown in table 8.

In the other hand, we illustrated the obtained results when applying the three above algorithms on the three corpus used in the experimentation, namely: the small corpus, the middle corpus, and the large corpus, and then we summarized the obtained accuracy for each algorithm in table 9.

Table 8. Extraction of some words roots using the three algorithms

Word	Extracted root			
	Khodja algorithm	Nidal et al algorithm	Our proposed algorithm	Correct root
يتعلّمون	علم	علم	علم	علم
كاتب	كتب	كتب	كتب	كتب
كتاتيب	Not stemmed	كتب	كتب	كتب
اقتصاد	قصد	اقتصد	اقتصد	اقتصد
سنستدرجهم	Not stemmed	درج	درج	درج
متلألئ	Not stemmed	لألأ	لألأ	لألأ
المربّي	ربأ	ربّى	ربّى	ربّى
المربّون	ربن	ربّى	ربّى	ربّى
طائرات	طور	طار	طار	طار
ولولة	ليل	ولول	ولول	ولول
وقيعة	قوع	وقع	وقع	وقع
يزنونهم	زنن	نهب	وزن	وزن
زلازل	Not stemmed	تنازل	زلزل	زلزل
حواسيب	Not stemmed	نسي	حسب	حسب
نوازل	نزل	تنازل	نزل	نزل

Table 9. Illustration of obtained accuracy for the three algorithms

Corpus	Size		The obtained accuracy (suc_ rate, err_ rate)%					
	Nb.roots	Nb.words	Khodja algorithm		Nidal et al algorithm		Our proposed algorithm	
Small	25	50	68,00	32,00	92,00	8,00	98,00	2,00
Middle	135	270	83,70	16,30	63,33	36,66	94,07	5,93
Large	450	1500	73,26	26,74	57,79	42,21	90,53	9,47

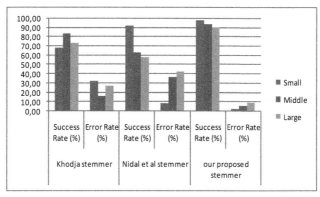

Fig. 3. Comparison between three algorithms

6   Discussion

From table 8, we see that khodja stemmer algorithm fails sometimes in getting the correct root of the given word and for many words it produced one of two results: (1) not stemmed (i.e., حواسيب , متلألئ , سنستدرجهم) completely a new word and sometimes a wrong word that does not exist in Arabic language (i.e.,(ربن ، المربّون) (طور ، طائرات) , (قوع ، وقيعة)). The same thing can be said for Nidal et al algorithm although it's gives best results than khodja algorithm, but it fails for many words like : (سجد، ناسج), ، زنن) (نسي، حواسيب), (يزنونهم), (سجد، ناسج). For the same cases, our algorithm gives always the correct root and the failure in our algorithm is very limited.

From Table 9 and figure 3, we can deduce that our proposed algorithm gives the best results for the three used corpus with a very high accuracy. We note here the value 98 % for the small corpus, 94,07 % for the middle corpus, and 90,53 % for the large corpus

7   Conclusion and Perspectives

In this paper we have studied how we can reduce the size of terms in Arabic text categorization by replacing many words by their common root. In this purpose, we exposed the most known algorithms and techniques in the field, Including morphological algorithms mainly based on the use of morphological rules and grammatical patterns of Arabic, and statistical algorithms which are the newest in the field, and require only simple calculations of distances. We also proposed a new statistical algorithm based on bigrams technique. This algorithm is fast and easy to implement on machine, does not require the removal of affixes nor the use of any morphological rules and grammatical patterns, capable to find all types of roots, i.e., trilateral, quadrilateral, quinquelateral, and hexalateral roots. There is no difference between strong roots and vocalic roots in our new algorithm. We also established a comparison between our proposed algorithm and two other algorithms which are very known in the field, namely: Khodja algorithm, Nidal et al algorithm. The first one fails sometimes in getting the correct root of the given word and for many words it produced one of two results: (1) not stemmed word (2) completely a new word and sometimes a wrong word that does not exist in Arabic. The same thing can be said for second one, although it gives best results than the first, but it fails for many words. For the same cases, our new algorithm gives always the correct root, the failure is very limited, and the obtained success ratio of root extraction is very promising.

In our future work, we plan to apply our new algorithm on corpus of Arabic words with big sizes, to improve the obtained success rate, and to apply it in extracting the root of words in other languages such as English and French.

References

1. Fatma, A.H., Keith, E.: Rule-based Approach for Arabic Root Extraction: New Rules to Directly Extract Roots of Arabic Words. Journal of Computing and Information Technology CIT Journal, 57–68 (2014)
2. Ghazzawi, S.: The Arabic Language in the Class Room, 2nd edn. Georgetown University, Washington DC (1992)
3. ETHNOLOGUE, http://www.ethnologue.com/statistics/size (accessed January 16, 2014)
4. Al-Kamar, R.: Computer and arabic language computerizing. Dar Al Kotob Al-Ilmiya, Cairo (2006)
5. Ghwanmeh, S., Kanaan, G., Al-Shalabi, R., Rabab'ah, S.: Enhanced algorithm for extracting the root of Arabic words. In: Proceeding of the 6th International Conference on Computer Graphics, Imaging and Visualization, August 11-14, pp. 388–391. IEEE Xplore Press, Tianjin (2009)
6. Yousef, N., Al-Bidewi, I., Fayoumi, M.: Evaluation of different query expansion techniques and using different similarity measures in Arabic documents. Eur. J. Sci. Res. 43, 156–166 (2010)
7. Wightwick, J., Gaafar, M.: Arabic Verbs and Essentials of Grammar, 2E (Verbs and Essentials of Grammar Series), 2nd edn., p. 160. McGraw-Hill Companies, Inc. (2007) ISBN-10: 0071498052
8. Al-omari, A., Abuata, B., Al-kabi, M.: Building and Benchmarking New Heavy/Light Arabic Stemmer. In: The 4th International conference on Information and Communication systems (ICICS 2013) (2013)
9. Shereen, K., Garside, R.: Stemming Arabic text. Technical report, Computing Department, Lancaster University (1999),
http://www.comp.lancs.ac.uk/computing/users/khoja/stemmer.ps (last visited 1999)
10. Momani, M., Faraj, J.: A novel algorithm to extract tri-literal Arabic roots. In: Proceedings of the IEEE/ACS International Conference on Computer Systems and Applications, May 13-16, pp. 309–315. IEEE Xplore Press, Amman (2007)
11. Al shalabi, R.: Pattern-based stemmer for finding Arabic roots. Information Technology Journal 4(1), 38–43 (2005)
12. Hajjar, A.E.S.A., Hajjar, M.: Zreik, K.: A system for evaluation of Arabic root extraction methods. In: Proceeding of 5th International Conference on Internet and Web Applications and Services (ICIW), May 9-15, pp. 506–512. IEEE Xplore Press, Barcelona (2010)
13. Al-Nashashibi, M.Y., Neagu, D., Yaghi, A.A.: An improved root extraction technique for Arabic words. In: Proceeding of 2nd International Conference on Computer Technology and Development (ICCTD), November 2-4, pp. 264–269. IEEE Xplore Press, Cairo (2010)
14. Al-shalabi, R., Kanaan, G., Al-Serhan, H.: New Approach for Extracting Arabic Roots. In: Proceedings of the International ArabConference on Information Technology (ACIT 20003), Alexandria, Egypt, pp. 42–59 (2003)
15. Rehab, D.: Arabic Text Categorization. The International Arab Journal of Information Technology 4(2), 125–131 (2007)
16. Al-Nashashibi, M.Y., Neagu, D.: Ali. A. Y.: Stemming Techniques for Arabic Words: A Comparative Study. In: 2nd International Conference on Computer Technology and development (lCCTD 2010), pp. 270–276 (2010)

17. Kanaan, G., Al-Shalabi, R., Al-Kabi, M.: New Approach for Extracting Quadrilateral Arabic Roots. Abhath Al-Yarmouk, Basic Science and Engineering 14(1), 51–66 (2005)
18. Ghwanmeh, S., Al-Shalabi, R., Kanaan, G., Khanfar, K., Rabab'ah, S.: An Algorithm for extracting the Root of Arabic Words. In: Proceedings of the 5th International Business Information Management Conference (IBIMA), Cairo, Egypt (2005)
19. Mohamad, A., Al-Shalabi, R., Kanaan, G., Al-Nobani, A: Building an Effective Rule-Based Light Stemmer for Arabic Language to Improve Search Effectiveness. The International Arab Journal of Information Technology, 9(4) (July 2012), (received February 22, 2010) (accepted May 20, 2010)
20. Al-Shalabi, R., Kanaan, G., Ghwanmeh, S.: Stemmer Algorithm for Arabic Words Based on Excessive Letter Locations. In: IEEE Conference (2008)
21. Shereen, K.: Stemming Arabic Text, http://zeus.cs.pacificu.edu/shereen/research.htm
22. Larkey, L., Connell, M.E.: Arabic information retrieval at UMass in TREC 2010. In: Proceedings of TREC 2001, NIST, Gaithersburg (2001)
23. Larkey, S., Ballesteros, L., Margaret, E.: Improving Stemming for Arabic Information Retrieval: Light Stemming and Occurrence Analysis. In: Proc. of the 25th ACM International Conference on Research and Development in Information Retrieval (SIGIR 2002), Tampere, Finland, pp. 275–282 (2002)
24. Larkey, S., Ballesteros, L., Margaret, C.E.: Light Stemming for Arabic Information Retrieval. In: Arabic Computational Morphology. Text, Speech and Language Technology, vol. 38, pp. 221–243 (2007)
25. Sawalha, M., Atwell, E.: Comparative Evaluation of Arabic Language Morphological Analyzers and Stemmers. In: Proceedings of COLING-ACL (2008)
26. Hawas, F.A.: Exploit relations between the word letters and their placement in the word for Arabic root extraction. Comput. Sci. 14, 27–431
27. Hmeidi, I.I., Al-Shalabi, R., Al-Taani, A.T., Najadat, H., Al-Hazaimeh, S.A.: A novel approach to the extraction of roots from Arabic words using bigrams. J. Am. Soc. Inform. Sci. Technol. 61, 583–591 (2010)
28. Boudlal, A., Belahbib, R., Belahbib, A., Mazroui, A.: A markovian approach for Arabic root extraction. Int. Arab J. Inform. Technol. 8, 91–98 (2011)
29. Yousef, N., Aymen, A.E., Ashraf, O., Hayel, K.: An Improved Arabic Word's Roots Extraction Method Using N-gram Technique. Journal of Computer science JSC 10(4) (2014), Published Online http://www.thescipub.com/jcs.toc
30. Frakes, W.B.: Stemming Algorithms. In: Frakes, W.B., Baeza-Yates, R. (eds.) Information Retrieval: Data Structures and Algorithms, pp. 131–160. Prentice-Hall India (1992) ISBN-10: 8131716929

Restoration of Arabic Diacritics Using a Multilevel Statistical Model

Mohamed Seghir Hadj Ameur[✉], Youcef Moulahoum, and Ahmed Guessoum

NLP, Machine Learning and Applications (TALAA) Group
Laboratory for Research in Artificial Intelligence(LRIA)
Department of Computer Science, University of Science and Technology Houari
Boumediene (USTHB)
Bab-Ezzouar, Algiers, Algeria
{mohamedhadjameur,moulahoum.youcef}@gmail.com, aguessoum@usthb.dz

Abstract. Arabic texts are generally written without diacritics. This is the case for instance in newspapers, contemporary books, etc., which makes automatic processing of Arabic texts more difficult. When diacritical signs are present, Arabic script provides more information about the meanings of words and their pronunciation. Vocalization of Arabic texts is a complex task which may involve morphological, syntactic and semantic text processing.

In this paper, we present a new approach to restore Arabic diacritics using a statistical language model and dynamic programming. Our system is based on two models: a bi-gram-based model which is first used for vocalization and a 4-gram character-based model which is then used to handle the words that remain non vocalized (OOV words). Moreover, smoothing methods are used in order to handle the problem of unseen words. The optimal vocalized word sequence is selected using the Viterbi algorithm from Dynamic Programming.

Our approach represents an important contribution to the improvement of the performance of automatic Arabic vocalization. We have compared our results with some of the most efficient up-to-date vocalization systems; the experimental results show the high quality of our approach.

Keywords: Statistical language model · Arabic language · Hidden markov model · Automatic vocalization · Dynamic programming · Smoothing · Corpus · Viterbi algorithm.

1 Introduction

Arabic texts are generally written without diacritical signs (newspapers, books, etc.) this does not pose a problem for people who have a certain mastery of Arabic since they can easily infer the diacritical signs from the context of the words. However, this can be problematical for non-native Arabic speakers. As a matter of fact, the absence of diacritical signs in words also makes their automatic processing more difficult. Indeed, when diacritics are present, the Arabic

© IFIP International Federation for Information Processing 2015
A. Amine et al. (Eds.): CIIA 2015, IFIP AICT 456, pp. 181–192, 2015.
DOI: 10.1007/978-3-319-19578-0_15

script provides more information about words meanings and their pronunciations. As such, Arabic vocalization is used in order to increase the performance of many applications such as Arabic text-to-speech (TTS) [1,10] and speech recognition [16].

Arabic diacritics restoration (text vocalization) is the process of assigning Arabic diacritics such as fatha ("a" sound as in "apple"), damma ("oo" sound as in "book") and kasra ("i" sound as in "in") to a given text (or script). Arabic diacritical signs are represented in Table 1.

Table 1. Arabic diacritical signs

Diacritic	Example	Pronunciation
Fatha	ذَهَبَ	/t//a/
Damma	الطفلُ	/t//u/
Kasra	البيتِ	/t//i/
Tanween Damma	كِتَابٌ	/t//un/
Tanween Kasra	كِتَابٍ	/t//in/
Tanween Fatha	كِتَابًا	/t//an/
Sukuun	الوقْت	/t/
Shadda	مُدَرِّسَة	/t//t/

During the last few years, the statistical approaches have been proven to be more efficient in the tackling of different problems of natural language processing. For the vocalization problem more specifically, most of the recent work was based on statistical approaches which can be either purely statistical ones or hybrid methods that combine a statistical language model and some other treatments.

Hybrid methods, such as [7] which uses a morphological tagger or [4] which uses *AlKhalil Morpho Sys* [4], depend on the effectiveness (accuracy) of these morphological analysers and taggers. Purely statistical methods however do not have such a dependence. Recent works based on purely statistical methods have reported very interesting results. This is the case for [9] which uses only a word-based bigram language model and the work of [2] which uses a character-based 4-gram model.

In this paper, we aim to further improve the previous statistical Arabic text vocalization approaches used in [9] and [2] by proposing a new simple but efficient system that relies on a purely statistical language model coupled with dynamic programming which combines these two approaches; thus our vocalization system is based on two models: the first one is a bi-gram word-based model [9] which is first used for vocalization and the second one is a 4-gram character-based model [2] which is used to handle the words that remain non-vocalized (OOV words). Smoothing methods are used in order to handle the problem of unseen words; the optimal vocalized word sequence is selected using the Viterbi algorithm [12].

This paper is organized as follows: Section 2 gives an overview of the state of the art vocalization systems. Section 3 explains our approach to restoring Arabic diacritics using a statistical language model and dynamic programming. Section 4 presents our tests and experimental results. A conclusion of our work is given in Section 5.

2   Related Work

Vocalization approaches can be divided into two main categories: Rule-based and Statistical Approaches. During the last decade, the statistical approaches have widely been used in a variety of natural language processing applications which have proven their efficiency. For the vocalization problem, most of the recent work was based on statistical approaches. These statistical approaches can be classified into two categories: purely statistical methods, or hybrid methods that combine a statistical language model and some other treatments.

In terms of purely statistical methods, one may cite [6] where the authors presented a vocalization approach based on Hidden Markov Models (HMMs). The hidden states correspond to the vocalized words and each one of them has a single emission leading to a non vocalized word (an observed state). In [2], a similar approach was used but with a character-based 4-gram model (a sequence of 4 consecutive vocalized letters) instead of a word-based model. The most recent work based on purely statistical methods is [9] where its authors used a statistical bigram language model coupled with dynamic programming to choose the most likely sequence of diacrtics. They improved their own work in [8] by using a higher order n-gram statistical language model.

For the methods which use a hybrid approach, we can mention [7] whose authors developed a hybrid system which combines a statistical n-gram language model (where n equals 1, 2 or 3) combined with a morphological tagger. In a similar way, in [3] a statistical n-gram language model is also used along with morphological analysis using *AlKhalil Morpho Sys* [4]. In [15], an approach was proposed which combines lexical retrieval, bigram-based and SVM-statistical prioritized techniques. In [14], the authors proposed two methods: the first uses an n-gram statistical language model along with A^* lattice search while the second method attempts to segment each Arabic word into all its possible morphological constituents then proceed in a similar way as the first one. The authors reported that their second approach gives better results. Finally, in [17], a statistical classifier was proposed which is based on the maximum entropy principle, which uses the combination of a wide array of lexical, segment-based and part-of-speech tag features in order to select the best classification.

It turns out that Arabic text vocalization is not yet optimal as will be shown in Section 4.4. No system is currently good enough to restore diacritics with high enough a quality as to be able to build solid applications on it. For this reason, we have decided to dig deeper into this problem. This has led us to building a system which has given very encouraging results as will be shown in the sequel.

3   Arabic Text Vocalization Approach

In this section we will formally introduce the problem of Arabic text vocalization and present the different models generated in our system.

3.1   Formalizing the Problem

Vocalization of Arabic text (or Restoration of Arabic Diacritics) is the process of assigning diacritical signs to each word in a given text or script.

This problem can be formalized as follows: given a sequence of non-vocalized words (or script) $W = w_1, w_2, ..., w_n$, the vocalization task is to find the best sequence of vocalized words $V = v_1, v_2, ..., v_n$ from all the possible vocalization sequences of W.

Assigning a score to each possible vocalized word sequence can be used to select the best vocalization from all the possible ones. This score can be calculated using the Chain rule:

$$P(W) = \Pi_{k=1}^{n} P(W_k | W_1^{k-1}) \tag{1}$$

By making the independence assumption (Markov assumption) for the n-grams model, instead of using the whole history (chain-rule) the n-gram model can approximate the history of a given word using just the last k words. The probability will thus be estimated as follows:

$$P(W_n | W_1^{n-1}) = P(W_n | W_{k-(n-1)}^{n-1}) \tag{2}$$

Using the Markov assumption in the case of a bi-gram language model, we will have:

$$P(W_n | W_1^{n-1}) = P(W_n | W_{n-1}) \tag{3}$$

$P(W_n | W_{n-1})$ is computed using the Maximum Likelihood Estimation (MLE):

$$P(W_n | W_{n-1}) = \frac{C(W_{i-1}, W_i)}{C(W_{i-1})} \tag{4}$$

where $C(W_{i-1}, W_i)$ and $C(W_{i-1})$ are the counts of the bi-gram $W_{i-1} W_i$ and the uni-gram W_{i-1} respectively.

3.2   Presentation of the Vocalization System

This section presents the global structure of our vocalization system. The automatic vocalization of Arabic texts consists of two main phases: vocalization using a bi-gram word-based model followed, for the unresolved cases, by vocalization using a 4-gram character-based model. This is illustrated in Figure 1 and explained in more details in the following two subsections. We should point out that we have decided for our word-based model to restrict ourselves to bi-grams for computational efficiency reasons. Going for higher-order n-Gram models would indeed be costly in execution time in an application which should be as fast as possible to be integrate into larger, possibly online, applications. As to the 4-gram character-based model, this is due to the fact that we have analyzed that 4 letters are can be quite rich a background to allow for reasonably good diacritization, especially that this second model is used as a complement to the word-based one.

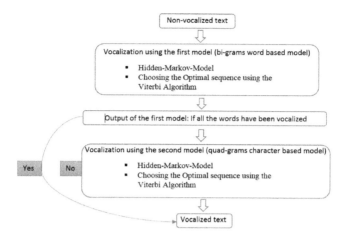

Fig. 1. The Vocalization System

3.3   The First Model

Our first model is a bi-gram-based language model. To illustrate it, let us consider the following non-vocalized sentence:

خلق الإنسان علمه البيان

The functioning of the first model can be summarized in the following steps:

The first step is to build a dictionary which associates for each non vocalized word all its possible vocalizations.

In the second step, a lattice is created for the non-vocalized sequence $W = w_1, w_2, ..., w_n$ which gives, for each non-vocalized word w_i, all its possible vocalizations from the dictionary. In order to simplify the explanation, our example considers only a subset of the possible vocalizations of each word (as shown in Figure 2). Given the assumption, the size of the subset of possible vocalizations would be $8 * 4 * 8 * 2 = 512$.

The third step consists in associating to each possible vocalization (e.g. in Figure 2, each sentence among the 512 possible ones) a probability using the bi-gram language model:

$$P(W_n|W_1^{n-1}) = P(W_n|W_{n-1}) \tag{5}$$

For example one of the possible vocalizations is:

خَلَقَ الْإِنْسَانَ عَلَّمَهُ الْبَيَانَ

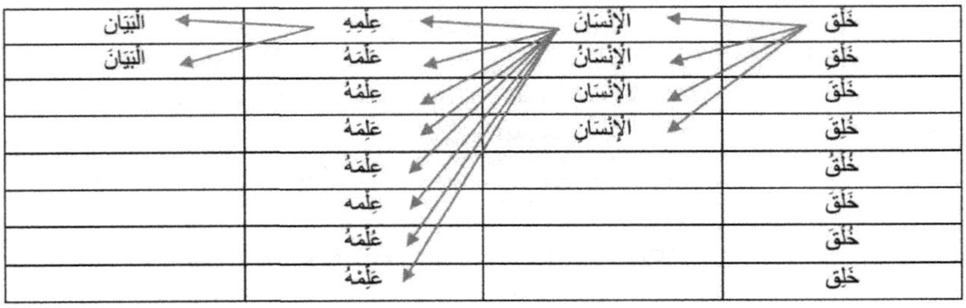

خَلَق	الْإِنْسَانَ	عِلْمِهِ	الْبَيَانَ
خَلَق	الْإِنْسَانُ	عَلَّمَهُ	الْبَيَانَ
خَلَق	الْإِنْسَانَ	عِلْمَهُ	
خَلَق	الْإِنْسَان	عَلَّمَهُ	
خَلَق		عِلْمِهِ	
خَلَق		مِلْمِهِ	
خَلَق		عَلَّمَهُ	
خَلَق		عَلَّمَهُ	

Fig. 2. Some of the possible vocalizations for a non-vocalized sentence

The probability of the above sentence is calculated as follows:

$$P \text{ (خَلَقَ الْإِنْسَانَ عَلَّمَهُ الْبَيَانَ)} =$$

$$P \text{ (خَلَقَ)} * P \text{ (الْإِنْسَانَ | خَلَقَ)} * P \text{ (عَلَّمَهُ | الْإِنْسَانَ)} * P \text{ (الْبَيَانَ | عَلَّمَهُ)}$$

Similarly, probabilities are assigned to all the possible vocalized word sequences.

The forth and final step is to find among all the possible vocalizations the one that has the highest probability.

$$v_1, \widehat{v_2, ...,} v_n = argmax(\Pi_{k=1}^{n} P(v_k|v_{k-1})) \tag{6}$$

The number of all possible vocalizations is very large as mentioned in Figure 2. Let N be the average number of all the possible vocalizations for each word and L the length of the non vocalized sequence (i.e. the number of words in it). The number of all possible vocalizations will then be N^L. Trying to find the best vocalization by a brute-force approach would have an exponential complexity $(O(N^L))$ and is clearly not efficient. An alternative is to use , the Viterbi algorithm, a Dynamic programming approach. To this end, let us present our Hidden Markov Model (HMM) which will be used as an input to the Viterbi algorithm to get the best vocalization.

Hidden Markov Model Our Hidden Markov Model (HMM) is defined by:

- A set of states which represent the vocalized words $v_1, v_2, ..., v_n$.
- A set of observations which represent the non-vocalized words $w_1, w_2, ..., w_n$.
- The transition matrix which contains the transition probabilities $P(v_i|v_{i-1})$

Generally each sequence in the HMM depends on two probabilities (transitions and emissions). In our model however, only the transition probabilities are considered.

The Viterbi Algorithm. The best vocalized sequence is chosen from the HMM using the Viterbi algorithm which is a very efficient algorithm for selecting the best vocalization sequence [12]. The latter uses a recursive relation in which the probability of each node at a given level i is calculated according to its preceding level $i - 1$ (see Figure 3).

Fig. 3. Finding the optimal vocalized sequence using the Viterbi algorithm

As shown in Figure 3, the weight of each node of index (i, j) of level i is calculated from all the nodes of its preceding level $i - 1$, using the following formula:

$$P(i, j) = max_{k=1, v_{i-1}}(P(i, j|i - 1, k) * p(i - 1, k)) \qquad (7)$$

where i and j are the indexes of the line and colon, respectively, in the transition matrix.

v_{i-1} is the number of all possible vocalization for word $i - 1$.

After calculating the weights of all nodes (in this forward-moving computation), while keeping track of the best nodes on this path, back-tracing is done in order to find the optimal path.

The Viterbi algorithm allows to efficiently solve the problem of selecting the best vocalization sequence.

In the next section, we introduce the smoothing method we use in order to handle the problem of unseen bigrams.

Handling the Problem of Unseen bi-grams. The maximum likelihood estimation (MLE) is calculated using Equation 4. This equation assigns a null probability to any bi-gram that does not belong to the training corpus. According to Jurafsky and Martin ([11]), almost 99% of all the possible combinations of bi-grams may be missing from any given corpus. This is why the use of smoothing methods are necessary in order to avoid having null probabilities (as a result of the products of probabilities). This problem is handled by taking some of the probability mass from the existing n-grams and distributing it to the non-found n-grams.

Additive Smoothing: One of the simplest smoothing methods is Additive Smoothing [5] which assumes that each of the n-grams occurs one more time than its actual occurrence count. Thus we add one to all the n-grams. This yields in the case of bi-grams:

$$P_{add}(w_i|w_j) = \frac{K + c(w_i, w_j)}{(K * V) + c(w_i)} \tag{8}$$

where K is a constant between 0 and 1 and V is the size of the vocabulary.

Absolute Discounting: Absolute discounting [11] is an interpolated smoothing method [13] which is obtained by discounting a constant D between 0 and 1 from each non-null probability mass. This yields in the case of bi-grams:

$$P_{abs}(w_i|w_j) = \frac{max(c(w_i, w_j) - D, 0)}{c(w_i)} + \frac{D}{c(w_i)} N_{1+}(w_i{}^*) P_{abs}(w_j) \tag{9}$$

where $P_{abs}(w_j) = \frac{1}{V}$, V is the vocabulary size.
$N_{1+}(w_i{}^*)$ is the number of all the words without repetition that follow w_i in the training corpus. In the next section we explain our second model.

3.4   Letter-Based Model

The second model is a 4-gram character-based model which is used to handle the words that remain non-vocalized (out of vocabulary words, OOV). The HMM used in this model is now introduced.

Letter-Based Hidden Markov Model Our HMM is defined by states that represent the vocalized letters and observations that represent the non-vocalized letters. It consists of:

- A set of states which represent the vocalized letters $q_1, q_2, ..., q_n$.
- A set of observations which represent the non-vocalized letters $l_1, l_2, ..., l_n$.
- The transition matrix which contains the transitions $P(q_i|q_{i-1}, q_{i-2}, q_{i-3})$.
- The emission matrix which contains $P(l_i|q_i)$.

This model is used in a similar way to the previous model. The same smoothing methods are used and the optimal path is selected using the Viterbi algorithm. This model has the capacity to vocalize any Arabic word; this is why it is used as a final step to ensure the complete vocalization of the non-vocalized script.

4   Implementation and Tests

In this section, we start by presenting the corpus we have used and some statistics relating to it. We then move to presenting the results of testing our implementation.

The source code of our vocalization system is available at https://github.com/Ycfx/Arabic-Diacritizer under the GNU General Public License (*GPL*).

4.1 Corpus Construction

The largest part of our corpus is automatically retrieved from the site http://www.al-islam.com/ using a URL-rule-based crawler. This site is an Islamic religious site that contains vocalized text about a number of subjects (Hadith, Commentaries of the Quran, etc.). A vocalized *Holy Quran* was also downloaded from http://tanzil.net/ and added to the corpus. Each downloaded vocalized text goes through cleaning, tokenisation, and normalisation steps to finally yield a properly vocalized corpus. On the other hand, its non-vocalized version is obtained by simply deleting the diacritical signs from the vocalized corpus.

4.2 Corpus Statistics

We have created a large Arabic corpus which contains more than 10 million words (tokens) 2. We have used 90% of the total words of the corpus for the training phase and the remaining 10% for the testing phase.

Table 2. Corpus statistics

	Corpus
Sentences	799 470
Tokens	10 634 921
Types	379 429

4.3 Evaluation Measures

To measure the performance of the different vocalization systems we have used the Word Error Rate (*WER*) and the Diacritic Error Rate (*DER*) measures:

- *WER1*: the number of words vocalized wrongly by the system (taking into account the diacritic of the last letter of the word).
- *WER2*: the number of words vocalized wrongly by the system (not taking into account the diacritic of the last letter of the word).
- *DER1*: the number of characters vocalized wrongly by the system (taking into account the diacritic of the last letter).
- *DER2*: the number of characters vocalized wrongly by the system (not taking into account the diacritic of the last letter).

4.4 Results

In this section we will start by presenting the results obtained by changing the smoothing parameters, then we give a detailed comparison of our system with the state of the art vocalization systems.

Table 3. The impact of the smoothing parameters on the vocalization system

Smoothing methods	WER1	WER2	DER1	DER2
Absolute discounting (K=1)	11.85	6.67	4.63	3.49
Absolute discounting (K=0.5)	11.57	6.30	4.34	3.23
Absolute discounting (K=0.1)	**11.53**	**6.28**	**4.30**	**3.18**
Additive smoothing (D=1)	16.87	9.49	8.10	6.86
Additive smoothing (D=0.5)	15.75	9.16	7.85	6.83
Additive smoothing (D=0.1)	15.41	9.05	7.77	6.83

Impact of the Smoothing Parameters on the Vocalization System. Table 3 shows the impact of changing the smoothing parameters on the vocalization system. The K and D smoothing parameters were investigated for additive and absolute discounting methods respectively.

The experimental results prove that the use of smoothing methods has a noticeable influence on the overall performance of the vocalization system. The best performance of our system was achieved using absolute discounting with $D = 0.1$, where the results we obtained were 11.53% in terms of Word Error Rate *(WER1)* and 6.28% when the case ending was ignored (*WER2*), and in terms of Diacritic Error Rate the results were 4.30% for *DER1* and 3.18% when ignoring the last diacritical mark (*DER2*). These results show that the Absolute Discounting method gives a better practical performance in comparison to Additive Smoothing.

Comparison of our System with the Different Vocalization Systems. In order to evaluate the overall performance of our vocalization system, we have compared its performance to some of the most efficient implementations available today. However since these systems have not been tested on the same corpus, the conclusions should be taken with some caution. The results of the comparison are summarized in Table 4.

When case ending (the last diacritical sign) is ignored *(WER2,DER2)*, the results were clearly better for all the compared systems, which is explained by the added difficulty when attempting to vocalize the last letter *(WER1,DER1)*.

Table 4. Comparing the performance of our system to those of some other vocalization systems

Vocalization Systems	WER1	WER2	DER1	DER2
Zitouni et al (2006) [17]	37	15	23	10
Habash et al (2007) [7]	14.9	4.8	5.5	2.2
Shaalan et al (2009) [15]	12.16	**3.78**	-	-
Rashwan et al (2011) [14]	12.5	3.8	**3.1**	**1.2**
Hifny et al 2013) [9]	12.5	7.4	-	-
Bebah et al (2014) [3]	21.11	9.93	7.37	3.75
Our system	**11.53**	6.28	4.30	3.18

Our system gives the best result in terms of *WER1*, next to best on *DER1*, and its performance on the other measures is very close to the best results reported in the literature. That our system performs extremely well on *WER1* and *DER1* is indeed what we want; it shows that other systems have problems handling the last letter diacritic which is very crucial in Arabic.

Our system performance has thus been proven to be very competitive; It shows the effectiveness of the multilevel approach we have adopted for the vocalization problem.

5   Conclusion

We have presented in this paper a multilevel statistical vocalization model. Our system is based on two models: the first one is a bi-gram word-based model which is used first for vocalization and the second one is a 4-gram letter-based model which is used as a back-off, i.e. to handle the words that remain non-vocalized after the application of the first model. We have used smoothing methods to handle the problem of unseen words and the Viterbi algorithm to select the optimal path, i.e. best vocalization sequence, in the HMM. The results shows the efficiency of our vocalization system in comparison to other state-of-the-art systems.

Our system can be improved in several ways which we intend to explore:

– Our first model is based on bi-gram probabilities only; the use of n-gram models with $n > 2$ should yield better results.
– We can enrich the corpus by adding many more modern Arabic texts to it.
– In this work, only two smoothing methods have been used; using other smoothing methods could give better results.

References

1. Ahmed, M.E.: Toward an arabic text to speech system. The Arabian Journal of Science and Engineering 16(4B) (1991)
2. Alghamdi, M., Muzaffar, Z.: Kacst arabic diacritizer. In: The First International Symposium on Computers and Arabic Language, pp. 25–28 (2007)
3. Bebah, M., Amine, C., Azzeddine, M., Abdelhak, L.: Hybrid approaches for automatic vowelization of arabic texts. arXiv preprint arXiv:1410.2646 (2014)
4. Boudlal, A., Lakhouaja, A., Mazroui, A., Meziane, A., Bebah, M., Shoul, M.: Alkhalil morpho sys1: A morphosyntactic analysis system for arabic texts. In: International Arab Conference on Information Technology (2010)
5. Chen, S.F., Goodman, J.: An empirical study of smoothing techniques for language modeling. In: Proceedings of the 34th Annual Meeting on Association for Computational Linguistics, pp. 310–318. Association for Computational Linguistics (1996)
6. Gal, Y.: An hmm approach to vowel restoration in arabic and hebrew. In: Proceedings of the ACL 2002 Workshop on Computational Approaches to Semitic Languages, pp. 1–7. Association for Computational Linguistics (2002)

7. Habash, N., Rambow, O.: Arabic diacritization through full morphological tagging. In: Human Language Technologies 2007: The Conference of the North American Chapter of the Association for Computational Linguistics; Companion Volume, Short Papers, pp. 53–56. Association for Computational Linguistics (2007)
8. Hifny, Y.: Higher order n gram language models for arabic diacritics restoration. In: Proceedings of the 12th Conference on Language Engineering, Cairo, Egypt (2012)
9. Hifny, Y.: Restoration of arabic diacritics using dynamic programming. In: 2013 8th International Conference on Computer Engineering & Systems (ICCES), pp. 3–8. IEEE (2013)
10. Hifny, Y., Qurany, S., Hamid, S., Rashwan, M., Atiyya, M., Ragheb, A., Khallaaf, G.: An implementation for arabic text to speech system. In: The Proceedings of the 4th Conference on Language Engineering (2004)
11. Jurafsky, D., Martin, J.H.: Speech and language processing. Pearson Education India (2000)
12. Neuhoff, D.L.: The viterbi algorithm as an aid in text recognition. IEEE Transactions on Information Theory 21(2), 222–226 (1975)
13. Ney, H., Essen, U., Kneser, R.: On structuring probabilistic dependences in stochastic language modelling. Computer Speech & Language 8(1), 1–38 (1994)
14. Rashwan, M.A., Al-Badrashiny, M.A.S., Attia, M., Abdou, S.M., Rafea, A.: A stochastic arabic diacritizer based on a hybrid of factorized and unfactorized textual features. IEEE Transactions on Audio, Speech, and Language Processing 19(1), 166–175 (2011)
15. Shaalan, K., Abo Bakr, H.M., Ziedan, I.: A hybrid approach for building arabic diacritizer. In: Proceedings of the EACL 2009 Workshop on Computational Approaches to Semitic Languages, pp. 27–35. Association for Computational Linguistics (2009)
16. Vergyri, D., Kirchhoff, K.: Automatic diacritization of arabic for acoustic modeling in speech recognition. In: Proceedings of the Workshop on Computational Approaches to Arabic Script-based Languages, pp. 66–73. Association for Computational Linguistics (2004)
17. Zitouni, I., Sorensen, J.S., Sarikaya, R.: Maximum entropy based restoration of arabic diacritics. In: Proceedings of the 21st International Conference on Computational Linguistics and the 44th Annual Meeting of the Association for Computational Linguistics, pp. 577–584. Association for Computational Linguistics (2006)

A New Multi-layered Approach for Automatic Text Summaries Mono-Document Based on Social Spiders

Mohamed Amine Boudia[1(✉)], Reda Mohamed Hamou[2], Abdelmalek Amine[3],
Mohamed Elhadi Rahmani[4], and Amine Rahmani[5]

Dr. Moulay Tahar University SAÏDA
Department of Computer Saida, Laboratory Knowledge Management
and Complex Data (GeCoDe Lab), Dr. Moulay Tahar University SAÏDA, Saida, Algeria
{mamiamounti,hamoureda,abd_amine1}@yahoo.fr,
r_m_elhadi@yahoo.fr, aminerahmani2091@gmail.com

Abstract. In this paper, we propose a new multi layer approach for automatic text summarization by extraction where the first layer constitute to use two techniques of extraction: scoring of phrases, and similarity that aims to eliminate redundant phrases without losing the theme of the text. While the second layer aims to optimize the results of the previous layer by the metaheuristic based on social spiders. the objective function of the optimization is to maximize the sum of similarity between phrases of the candidate summary in order to keep the theme of the text, minimize the sum of scores in order to increase the summarization rate, this optimization also will give a candidate's summary where the order of the phrases changes compared to the original text. The third and final layer aims to choose the best summary from the candidate summaries generated by layer optimization, we opted for the technique of voting with a simple majority.

Keywords: Automatic summary extraction · Data mining · Social spider · Optimization · Scoring similarity

1   Introduction and Problematic

Every day, the mass of electronic textual information is increasing, making it more and more difficult access to relevant information without using specific tools. In other words access to the content of the texts by rapid and effective ways is becoming a necessity.

A summary of a text is an effective way to represent its contents, and allow quick access to their semantic content. The purpose of a summarization is to produce an abridged text covering most of the content from the source text.

« We can not imagine our daily life, one day without summaries », underline Inderjeet Mani. Newspaper headlines, the first paragraph of a newspaper article, newsletters, weather, tables of results of sports competitions and library catalogs are all summarized. Even in the research, the authors of scientific articles must accompany their scientific articles by a summary written by themselves.

© IFIP International Federation for Information Processing 2015
A. Amine et al. (Eds.): CIIA 2015, IFIP AICT 456, pp. 193–204, 2015.
DOI: 10.1007/978-3-319-19578-0_16

Automatic summary can be used to reduce the search time to find the relevant documents or to reduce the treatment of long texts by identifying the key information.

Our work uses automatic summarization by extraction, because it is a simple method to implement and gives good results; only in the previous works, produce the automatic summary by extraction consists to use only one technique at a time (Score, Similarity sentence or prototype) and respects the order of the sentences in the original document, our work answers the following questions:

- What is the contribution of the use of two methods of summarization at the same time on the quality of summary?
- Can the bio-inspired method based on the social spiders brings more for the automatic summary and increase the quality of the summary?

2   Our Proposed Approach

To create a summary by extraction, it is necessary to identify textual units (phrases, clauses, sentences, paragraphs) considered salient (relevant), then the select the textual units that hold the main ideas of the text with a certain order, in order to build a summary.

The approach presented in this article obeys the following steps:

2.1   Pretreatment

Simple cleaning: a stop words will not be removed, because the method of automatic summarization by extraction aims to extract the most informative sentences without modifying them: if we remove the empty words without information on their morphosyntactic impact in sentences, we risk having an inconsistent summary of a morphological point of view.

Then cleaning is to remove emoticons, to replace spaces with "_" and remove special characters (#, \, [,] ....).

— Choice of term: for automatic summarization by extraction we will need two representations:

-     Bag of words representation   • Bag of sentence representation.

Both representations are introduced in the vector model.

The first representation is to transform the text into a vector v_i (w_1, w_2, ..., $w_{|T|}$) where T is the number of all the words that appear at least once in the text. The weight w_k indicates the occurrence of t_k word in the document.

The second representation is to transform the text into a V'I vector (q_1, q_2, ..., $q_{|R|}$) where R is the number of all the phrases that appear at least once in the text. The q_k weight indicates the occurrence of t_k sentence in the document.

And finally a word phrases- occurrence matrix will be generated after the two previous representation, the size of this matrix is equal to (the number of words in the text) X (the number of words in the text); p_{ik} weight is the number occurrence of the word i in the sentence j;

2.2   Layer 1 : Pre-summary

Weighting and Pre-summary.

Weighting.
Once the "Word-Phrase" matrix is ready, we calculate a weighting of "Word-Phrase" matrix using a known encodings (tf-idf or tfc) with a small modification to the adapted the concept of a mono-document summarization.

The weight of a term in a sentence t_k p_i is calculated as:

- *TF-IDF.*

$$tf - idf(t_k, p_i) = tf(t_k, p_i) * \log(\frac{A}{B})$$ (1)

$tf(t_k, p_i)$: the number of occurrences of the term tk in the phrase pi;
A : the total number of sentences in the text;
B : the number of sentences in which the tk term appears at least once.

- *TFC.*

$$\text{tfc}(t_k, p_i) = \frac{tf-idf\,(t_k,p_i)}{\sqrt{\sum_{i=1}^{|p|} tf-idf\,(t_k,p_i)^2}}$$ (2)

After calculating the weighting of each word, a weight is assigned to each sentence. The generated summary is then generated by displaying the highest score of the source document sentences.

This score of a sentence is equal to the sum of the words in this sentence:

$$\text{SCORE}\,(p_i) = \sum_{k=0}^{nbr\_word} Mik$$ (3)

Primitive summary
"Suggested process claims on the principle that high-frequency words in a document are important words" [Luhn 1958]

The final step is to select the N first sentences that have the highest weight and which are considered the most relevant. The process of extracting the first N sentences intended to build the summary is defined either by a threshold, in this case, the score of the sentence must be greater than or equal to the threshold in order that this sentence will be extracted the second method is to fix a number N of phrase to be extracted, all phases will be ranked in descending order according of their score, and we take only the first N phrases.

Elimination of Rehearsals and Theme Detection: Using SIMILARITY Method Summarization by Extraction
The result of the previous step is a set of phrases which is a high score. Just we have a possibility that two or more sentences have a high score but they are similar, so we proceed to the elimination of phrases that resembling. The similarity between the

sentences that have been selected at the end of the previous step with known metrics (Euclidean ......).

Two parameters are used to adjust the elimination of repetitions: similarity threshold and reduction rate, the first parameter defined the point that we can consider two sentences as similar, and the second parameter indicates the number of resemblance to eliminate, to decrease the entropy information. When the similarity between two sentences is greater: they the phrase that has the highest score stay and we remove the other sentence.

The similarity is also used to detect the sentence that has more relation with the them of the text. According to the domain experts, it is the sentence which is most similar to the other sentences holds the theme text.

2.3   Layer 2: Optimization Using Social Spiders

Optimization Using Social Spiders

Natural Model

— **Environment**: a set of pickets which serve weaving wire brackets, this pickets have different sizes.
— **Weaving**: weaving is to create a link between the current and the last visited pick
— **Movement**: movement allows the spider to move in the environment on the wire woven by her or by others spider in the same canvas. The selection of the new position dependent upon a finite number of criteria. The wire has a flexibility F which is one of the major criteria of movement of the spider, the flexibility F represents the maximum weight with a correction relative to its diameter that can be held by the wire.
— **Communication**: social spiders communicate with the others in the weaving task, movement or capture prey; communication can be done by two different methods; by vibration on the wire or by the concentration of hormonal substances that spider left on a wire. Each vibration intensity and each concentration of substances has a specific meaning to others spiders, and this means that each spider must have two receivers (vibration and concentration).
— **System dynamics**: It is built on the principle of stigmergy: the behavior of agents have effects on the environment (wire-laying) in return behavior is influenced by the context of the agent (environment).

Artificial Model

— **Environment** : a picket grid (N * N). N is the square root of the number of phrases after layer 1 (pre-summary and the elimination of similar phrases) where each pickets is representing a sentence, the pickets have different sizes that representing the score of the phrase. Initially, all the wires are woven so as to have a complete graph;
    The number of spiders is equal to or less than the number of phrases, each spider is placed on a pole (phrase) randomly.

— **Weaving :** the wires are woven in the beginning of each iteration in order to have a complete graph. The similarity s_{xy} between two phrases ph_x ph_y represents the diameter of wire woven between the two picket x and y associate to phrases ph_x to and p_{hy}, as given the similarity is commutative (s (x, y) = s (y, x)): the diameter of wire woven between the two picket x and y will be a uniform.

— **Movement:** movement of the spider is incremental and random; Every spider save in its memory every way which she followed. To save result, a weight of path should be: Superior to the "lower threshold of the summary rate" and Less the "upper threshold of the summary of rates."

    We associated to the social spider i in iteration j a P_{ij} weight initialized to zero and it equal to the sum of the weights of k SCORE sentences   whose social spider i have visited during the iteration j.

    The wire has a flexibility that F depends on its diameter is constant and represents the maximum weight that can load on itself, with artificial model F Is defined as follows.

$$Flexible\left(fil_{ij}\right) = Seuil\ supérieur\ de\ taux\ de\ résumé\ *\ diametre\left(fil_{ij}\right) \quad (4)$$

$$diametre\left(fil_{ij}\right) = similarité\left(phrase_i, phrase_j\right) \quad (5)$$

Noting that:

- Abstract rate threshold is constant.

If i social spider during operation j with Pij weight passes through the wire (x, y), it will execute this pseudo-algorithm:

```
If P   is lower than F(x,y) then
    ij
    the spider will go to the wire (x,y)
    updating the current path
    Update the weight P   ,
                       ij
If the wire is torn
```

Social spider i will go into pause waiting for the end of the iteration j.

    We will give these two observations:

(a) F(x,y) is higher than F(w,z) is equivalent to say that the similarity between the sentence x and the sentence y is greater than the similarity between the sentence w and the sentence z because "upper threshold of the summary of rates" is constant.

(b) The interpretation of F(x,y) is higher than F(w,z), is that by optimizing with social spider: if choice between wire (x,y) and the wire (w,z) the spider will choose the first wire because it safe for her . If his current weight Pij is high; the second wire risk to tear.

From observations A and B, we can deduce that the optimization is to minimize the weight of the summary, to maximize the similarity to preserve the theme of the candidate summary, while respecting the dice constrained utility and semantics represented by the interval [lower threshold summary of rates, upper rates higher threshold] noting that the lower and upper thresholds are summarized determined and fixed as language experts.

- **The utility constraint:** Automatically produce a summary with higher summary score "upper threshold of the summary of rates," is not helpful.
- **The semantic constraint:** Automatically produce a summary with lower summary score "lower threshold of the summary of rates," losing a lot of semantics.

— **End of iteration :** when all the spider will be in pause state, the iteration j will be declared finished, the spider will rewoven the spiders randomly choose their new start position and start the iteration j + 1.

— **Communication :** Each spider leaves a trace on hormonal stakes visited so that other spiders will not take this part of the way. First it ensures diversity between different summaries candidate that is greater coverage suspected combination spiders consider this shift pickets the number they share with each spider that operates on the canvas, and moves with the constraint of not exceeding M common stake in the same order with another spider .

Secondly, communication is used to avoid the repetition of sentences in the summary. In cases where social spider returns while moving on a picket that it been already have been visited by itself in current iteration it makes a flashback and continues his trip without considering this visit.

The duration of evaporation of communication hormone spider is equal to an iteration, it should be noted that the hormone density can not be cumulative.

— **System dynamics:** It is built on the principle of stigmergy: the behavior of agents have effects on the environment, in return behavior is influenced by the context of the agent.

Each spider keeps in mind, the best visited paths, after a number of spider iterations, every spider returns the best paths.

— **Path :** is a series of picket visited in chronological order, and is a summarization. Recall that each picket is a phrases (see the initial state).

— **End of the optimisation of the social spiders:** when the number of iterations performed reached the maximum number of iterations, each spider returns all paths (where each path, is a candidate summary). Was associated with each path or summarization ie a set of candidate evaluations indices. And launching a voting algorithm compared these evaluation indices to choose the best candidate summary to remember.

2.4   Layer 3: Evaluation and Vote

Candidates generated by the previous layer abstracts will be evaluated by several evaluations metric, and then we will classify pairs. R1 and R2 are two abstracts candidate rate by N metric evaluation, the number of associated point R1 represents the number of evaluation indicating that the quality of R1 is greater than or equal to R2 and aims to it. The summary with most points will win the duel and will face another until there will be more challenger. Summary will be declared the winner as the best back to resume.

3   Experimentation

Under the assumption that the weight of a sentence indicates its importance in the document and under assumption that two similar sentences have the same meaning; we applied the algorithms summarized by extracting in occurrence Scoring and similarity phrases. Our method is oriented for the moment to the generation of a mono-document summary using a biomimetic approach (Social Spider).

3.1   Used Corpus

Was used as the text corpus "Hurricane" in French, which contains a title and 20 sentences and 313 words, after the pretreatment process and vectorization bag of words, we get 171 different token. And we have took three references summaries produced successively by Summarizer CORTEX, Essential Summarizer, and a summary produced by a human expert.

3.2   Validation

We evaluated the summaries produced by this algorithm with the metric ROUGE (Lin 2004) which compares a candidate summary (automatically produced) and Summary Reference (created by human experts or other automatic summarization systems known).

The Evaluation Measure Recall - Oriented Understudy for Gisting Evaluation
We evaluate the results of this work by the measure called Recall - Oriented Understudy for Gisting Evaluation (ROUGE) proposed by (Lin, 2004) involving the differences between distributions of words.

$$ROUGE\ (N) = \frac{\sum_{s \in R_{ref}} \sum_{s \in R_{can}} Co - occurences\ (R_{ref}, R_{can}, N)}{Nbr - NGramme\ (N)_{R_{ref}}} \qquad (6)$$

F-Measure for the Evaluation of Automatic Extraction Summaries
We have proposed in our work before an adaptation of the F-measure for the validation of automatic summarization by extraction, as this technique is based on phrases to keep and delete

Confusion matrix	Candidate sumarry

Word K : number of words to keep
Word R: number of words to remove

Automatic summary		word K	word R
Reference	Word K	X	Y
summary	Word R	Z	W

Table 1. Adaptation of the F-measure for the validation of automatic summarization

From the confusion matrix, we can calculate: the recall, precision than we combined the two measures to calculate the F-Measure like that:

$$F - Mesure = \frac{2 * (Précision * Rappel)}{(Précision + Rappel)} \qquad (7)$$

3.3   Result

Results of Layer 1 : Before Optimisation with Social Spiders

Phrases score threshold / Similarity threshold similarity	Metric evaluation	0,60						0,65					
		REG	Cortex	Humain	Nbr word	Nbr Phrase	Reduced rates	REG	Cortex	Humain	Nbr word	Nbr Phrase	Reduced rates
0,60	ROUGE	0,67	0.71	0.55	245	15	21,72%	0,67	0,68	0,52	224	13	28,43%
	F-Mesure	0,49	0,46	0.32				0.55	0.50	0.47			
0,65	ROUGE	0,65	0,69	0.55	232	14	25,87%	0,72	0,68	0,53	221	12	29,39%
	F-Mesure	0.51	0.49	0.37				0.58	0.54	0.52			
0,70	ROUGE	0,61	0,68	0.51	230	14	26,51%	0,71	0,69	0,56	208	10	33,54%
	F-Mesure	0.57	0.51	0.44				0.64	0.62	0.55			
Phrases score threshold / Similarity threshold similarity	Metric evaluation	0,70						0,75					
		REG	Cortex	Humain	Nbr word	Nbr Phrase	Reduced rates	REG	Cortex	Humain	Nbr word	Nbr Phrase	Reduced rates
0,60	ROUGE	0,73	0,74	0,55	193	10	38,33%	0,67	0,67	0,58	123	6	60,70%
	F-Mesure	0.61	0.64	0.59				0.43	0.47	0.45			
0,65	ROUGE	0,67	0,70	0,57	180	8	42,49%	0,68	0,68	0,58	113	5	63,89%
	F-Mesure	0.58	0.59	0.56				0.42	0.45	0.41			
0,70	ROUGE	0,71	0,68	0,54	143	7	54,31%	0,71	0,74	0,64	110	4	64,85%
	F-Mesure	0.57	0.55	0.55				0.39	0.45	0.38			

Fig. 1. Result of Layer 1: Before optimization with Social Spider

— In Yellow: the local optimal candidate summary before optimization, quoted just for illustration, but will not be used for optimization with social spiders.

— In the Green: abstract global optimal candidate before optimization, which will be used for optimization with social spiders,

Results of Layer 3 : After Optimization with the Social Spider and VOTE.
We used two social spiders parameter combined with Number of iterations = 500

	Combine1	Combine 2
Threshold higher discount rate	55% =0,55	50%= 0,50
Threshold lower discount rate	27,5%=0.275	30%=0,30
Number of spiders	3	3
Maximum number of common stake in the same order	5	5

	Metric evaluation	REG	Cortex	Humain	Nbr word	Nbr Phrase	Reduced rates	Execution time
Before Optimization	ROUGE	0,71	0,69	0,56	208	10	33,54%	819 ms
	F-Mesure	0.64	0.62	0.55				
Optimizing social spider (Combine 1)	ROUGE	0.72	0.73	0.60	205	9	34,50%	3602 ms
	F-Mesure	0.66	0.67	0.57				
Optimizing social spider (Combine 2)	ROUGE	0.72	0.75	0.61	195	9	37,69%	2762 ms
	F-Mesure	0.68	0.72	0.66				

Fig. 2. Optimization *of 1st summary candidate score threshold=0.65*, threshold of similarity=0.70

	Metric evaluation	REG	Cortex	Humain	Nbr word	Nbr Phrase	Reduced rates	Execution time
Before Optimization	ROUGE	0,73	0,74	0,55	193	10	38,33%	833 ms
	F-Mesure	0.61	0.64	0.59				
Optimizing social spider (Combine 1)	ROUGE	0.68	0.66	0.47	187	9	40,25%	3859 ms
	F-Mesure	0.64	0.62	0.55				
Optimizing social spider (Combine 2)	ROUGE	0.75	0.78	0.62	190	9	39,29%	2591 ms
	F-Mesure	0.65	0.66	0.6				

Fig. 3. Optimization *of 2nd summary candidate score threshold=0.70*, threshold of similarity=0.60

We conducted a series of experiments to find and fix the most optimal parameters of social spiders.

3.4 Interpetation

We experimented document "Hurricane" using the coding TFC for the first stage (scoring) and several similarity distances (second stage) to try to detect theUSER sensitive about the best results we summarized validated by the metric RED by comparing the summary reference from REG system COTREX and a human expert who summed us the text "Hurricaine". All tests on data representation parameters were performed to éviterde misjudge our new approach based on a biomimetic approach in this case social spiders.

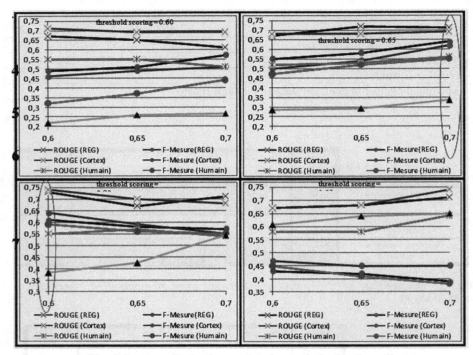

Fig. 4. Summary Evaluation graph before optimization (layer 1)

The first sub-graph (top left corner) indicates incoérence between the two F-evaluation metric measurement and ROUGE incoérence this is resulting from a false assessment of ROUGE summary. This is explained by the weak against the ROUGE summary negligible rate reduction: in fact a summary has low reduction rate will have the lesco-occurrences of N-grams number between him and a set of reference summaries Rref larger than a summary has greatly reduced rates.

The second sub-graph (top right corner) and the third sub-graph (bottom left) sub-graph shows complete coherence between the three evaluation indexes: reduction rate, F-Measure and ROUGE. While the fourth sub.

According to the experimental set of results when we set the target parameter values, it has turn out that:

(a) Increasing number of iterations and the increase in social spiders influences the execution time, the candidate summary quality is not reached by the change of these two parameters

(b) Maximum number of common stake in the same order minimizes the number of abstracts same candidate before the vote and can cover the maximum possible case

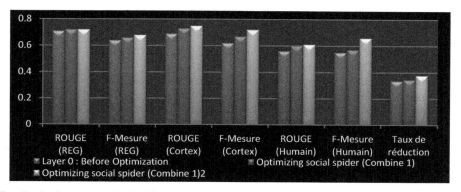

Fig. 5. Optimization of the first summary candidate score threshold=0.65, threshold of similarity= 0.70

The graph below shows explicitly that the second parameter optimization combined with social spiders return results better compared to the first combination, this is explained by the given interval of utility and semantics represented by two thresholds: upper and lower discount rate is reduced, which allows well-directed social spider. While the first combined with a wider interval, that channels less the optimization work.

We note that the execution time optimization combined with the first is greater than the second combines this means that the search field combines 1 is greater than the second combination.

8   Conclusion and Perspective

In this article, we presented new ideas: the first is to have used two techniques of extraction summary after another to improve the rate of reduction without loss of semantics.

The second idea is the use of a biomimetic approach that has the representation of strength graph, social spiders can almost total coverage on a graph using the communication module.

Given the results obtained, our approach based on a biomimetic approach (social spiders) can help solve one of the problems of textual data exploration and visualization will.

Prospects we will try to improve this approach using the WordNet thesaurus, and use a summary based on feelings using the SentiWordNet. We'll also try to explore other biomimetic methods. For nature still has not revealed all the secrets.

Reference

1. Luhn, H.P.: The automatic creation of literature abstracts. IBM Journal of Research and Development 2(2), 159–165 (1958)
2. Edmundson, H.P.: Automatic Abstracting, TRW Computer Division. Thompson Ram Wooldridge. Inc., Canoga Park (1963)
3. DeJong, G.: An overview of the FRUMP system. In: Strategies for Natural Language Processing 113 (1982)
4. Fum, D., Guida, G., Tasso, C.: Forward and backward reasoning in automatic abstracting. In: Proceedings of the 9th Conference on Computational Linguistics, vol. 1, pp. 83–88. AcademiaPraha (July 1982)
5. Salton, G., Singhal, A., Mitra, M., Buckley, C.: Automatic text structuring and summarization. Information Processing& Management 33(2), 193–207 (1997)
6. Mitra, M., Buckley, C., Singhal, A., Cardie, C.: An Analysis of Statistical and Syntactic Phrases. In: RIAO, vol. 97, pp. 200–214 (June 1997)
7. Teufel, S., Moens, M.: Argumentative classification of extracted sentences as a first step towards flexible abstracting. In: Advances in Automatic Text Summarization, pp. 155–171 (1999)
8. Mani, I., House, D., Klein, G., Hirschman, L., Firmin, T., Sundheim, B.: The TIPSTER SUMMAC text summarization evaluation. In: Proceedings of the Ninth Conference on European Chapter of the Association for Computational Linguistics, pp. 77–85. Association for ComputationalLinguistics (June 1999)
9. Kim, S.N., Medelyan, O., Kan, M.Y., Baldwin, T.: Semeval-2010 task 5: Automatic keyphrase extraction from scientific articles. In: Proceedings of the 5th International Workshop on Semantic Evaluation, pp. 21–26. Association for Computational Linguistics (July 2010)
10. Boudin, F., Morin, E.: Keyphrase Extraction for N-best reranking in multi-sentence compression. In: North American Chapter of the Association for Computational Linguistics (NAACL) (June 2013)
11. Hovy, E., Lin, C.Y., Zhou, L., Fukumoto, J.: Automated summarization evaluation with basic elements. In: Proceedings of the Fifth Conference on Language Resources and Evaluation (LREC 2006), pp. 604–611 (May 2006)
12. Donaway, R.L., Drummey, K.W., Mather, L.A.: A comparison of rankings produced by summarization evaluation measures. In: Proceedings of the 2000 NAACL-ANLPWorkshop on Automatic Summarization, vol. 4, pp. 69–78. Association for Computational Linguistics (April 2000)
13. Cuevas, E., Cienfuegos, M., Zaldívar, D., Pérez-Cisneros, M.: A swarm optimization algorithm inspired in the behavior of the social-spider. Expert Systemswith Applications 40(16), 6374–6384 (2013)
14. Hamou, R.M., Amine, A., Rahmani, M.: A new biomimetic approach based on social spiders for clustering of text. In: Lee, R. (ed.) Software Engineering Research, Management and Appl. 2012. SCI, vol. 430, pp. 17–30. Springer, Heidelberg (2012)
15. Hamou, R.M., Amine, A., Lokbani, A.C.: The Social Spiders in the Clustering of Texts: Towards an Aspect of Visual Classification. International Journal of Artificial Life Research (IJALR) 3(3), 1–14 (2012)

Building Domain Specific Sentiment Lexicons Combining Information from Many Sentiment Lexicons and a Domain Specific Corpus

Hugo Hammer[✉], Anis Yazidi, Aleksander Bai, and Paal Engelstad

Department of Computer Science, Oslo and Akershus University College of Applied Sciences, Oslo, Norway
{hugo.hammer,anis.yazidi,aleksander.bai,paal.engelstad}@hioa.no

Abstract. Most approaches to sentiment analysis requires a sentiment lexicon in order to automatically predict sentiment or opinion in a text. The lexicon is generated by selecting words and assigning scores to the words, and the performance the sentiment analysis depends on the quality of the assigned scores. This paper addresses an aspect of sentiment lexicon generation that has been overlooked so far; namely that the most appropriate score assigned to a word in the lexicon is dependent on the domain. The common practice, on the contrary, is that the same lexicon is used *without adjustments* across different domains ignoring the fact that the scores are normally highly sensitive to the domain. Consequently, the same lexicon might perform well on a single domain while performing poorly on another domain, unless some score adjustment is performed. In this paper, we advocate that a sentiment lexicon needs some further adjustments in order to perform well in a specific domain. In order to cope with these domain specific adjustments, we adopt a stochastic formulation of the sentiment score assignment problem instead of the classical deterministic formulation. Thus, viewing a sentiment score as a stochastic variable permits us to accommodate to the domain specific adjustments. Experimental results demonstrate the feasibility of our approach and its superiority to generic lexicons without domain adjustments.

Keywords: Bayesian decision theory · Cross-domain · Sentiment classification · Sentiment lexicon

1 Introduction

With the increasing amount of unstructured textual information available on the Internet, sentiment analysis and opinion mining have recently gained a groundswell of interest from the research community as well as among practitioners. In general terms, sentiment analysis attempts to automate the classification of text materials as either expressing positive sentiment or negative sentiment. Such classification is particularity interesting for making sense of huge amount of text information and extracting the "word of mouth" from different domains like product reviews, movie reviews, political discussions etc.

© IFIP International Federation for Information Processing 2015
A. Amine et al. (Eds.): CIIA 2015, IFIP AICT 456, pp. 205–216, 2015.
DOI: 10.1007/978-3-319-19578-0_17

There are two main approaches to sentiment classification

- *Sentiment lexicon:* A sentiment lexicon is merely composed of sentiment words and sentiment phrases (idioms) characterized by sentiment polarity, positive or negative, and by sentimental strength. For example, the word 'excellent' has positive polarity and high strength whereas the word 'good' is also positive but has a lower strength. Once a lexicon is built and in place, a range of different approaches can be deployed to classify the sentiment in a text as positive or negative. These approaches range from simply computing the difference between the sum of the scores for the positive lexicon and the sum of the scores for the negative lexicon, and subsequently classifying the sentiment in the text according to the sign of the difference.
- *Supervised learning:* Given a set of documents with known sentiment class, the material can be used to train a model to classify the sentiment class of new documents.

A major challenge in sentiment classification is that the classification method normally is highly sensitive to the domain. A method that performs well in one domain, may not perform well in a different domain. It is worth mentioning that the later problem is common and well studied in the field of Machine Learning, since supervised learning is especially sensitive to the domain, and typically it performs well only in the domain of the annotated documents. The later problem is referred to in the literature as cross-domain classification.

Several methods have been suggested to overcome this challenge in the field of sentiment analysis. However, they are merely inspired by the legacy research on cross-domain classification in the field of machine learning. These methods are often referred to as cross-domain sentiment classification [1]. The premises of these methods is to adjust a supervised classifier to the domain of interest. The approaches consist of either using a small annotated corpus or, alternatively, a large non-annotated corpus from the domain of interest [2,3,4].

In this paper we study another problem, which is very common in practice, but to the best of our knowledge has not been studied in the literature. For many languages several different sentiment lexicons are available, and it is often difficult to know which sentiment lexicon is preferable. Ideally one would like to use the information from all the lexicons, but this is often challenging since the scores of a sentiment word varies between the lexicons and may also be contradictory. In addition there is usually also a large amount of text from the domain of interest, e.g. a large set of product reviews that we want to classify with respect to sentiment. We present a method that builds domain specific sentiment lexicons using information from the sentiment lexicons and the corpus from the domain of interest in an advantageous way. The suggested method is based on Bayesian decision theory.

Before, we proceed to presenting our solution and our experimental results, we shall present a brief review of the related work. Most of the research within cross domain sentiment classification focuses on devising approaches to join information from labelled and/or unlabelled corpuses from different domains and the domain of interest to improve sentiment classification.

Bollegale et al. [5] argue that a major challenge of applying a classifier trained on one domain to another is that features may be quite different in different domains. The authors suggest to develop a sentiment sensitive thesaurus to expand the number of features in both the training and test sets.

Pan et al. [6] consider the case with unlabelled data in the domain of interest and labelled data from an other domain. To bridge the gap between the domains, the authors propose a spectral feature alignment algorithm to align domain-specific words from different domains into unified clusters, with the help of domain independent words as bridges.

Chetviorkin and Loukachevitch [7] propose a statistical features based approach in order to discriminate sentiment words in different domains do develop domain specific sentiment lexicons. The method requires labeled corpuses from both the domain of interest and the other domains.

Contextual sentiment lexicons takes the context of the sentiment words into account. Such lexicons are usually even more sensitive to the domain than ordinary sentiment lexicons are. Gindl et al. [8] suggest a method that identifies unstable contextualizations and refines the contextualized sentiment dictionaries accordingly, eliminating the need for specific training data for each individual domain.

In [9], the authors identified words that exhibit dis-ambiguity based on cross-domain evaluations. In simple terms, if a word gets a positive score in a domain with high confidence and a negative score in another domains, then this terms is considered dis-ambiguous. The next step was to create a domain-independent lexicon by simply excluding the words which are dis-ambiguous across domains. In [10], a taxonomy is used to determine the domain such as movies, politics, sports, then the different lexicons are learned on a domain basis. However, the authors did not discuss adjusting the scores across domains.

2 Joining Information from Sentiment Lexicons and Domain Specific Corpus

Our method consists of two parts. First we join the information from the sentiment lexicons, and second we adjust this information using the domain specific corpus.

2.1 Posterior Expected Sentiment Score

We assume that we have a total of n_L sentiment lexicons consisting of a total of n_W sentiment words occurring in at least one of the sentiment lexicons. We denote the sentiment words $w_1, w_2, \ldots, w_{n_W}$. Let $s_{i,i(j)}$, $i = 1, \ldots, n_W$, $j = 1, \ldots, |s_i|$ denote the sentiment score for sentiment word w_i in sentiment lexicon $i(j) \in \{1, 2, \ldots n_L\}$. $|s_i|$ denotes the number of lexicons that word i occurs in, while $i(1), i(2), \ldots, i(|s_i|)$ are references to these lexicons. Naturally $|s_i| \leq n_L$, $i = 1, 2, \ldots, n_W$. We assume that $s_{i,i(j)}, j \in 1, \ldots, |s_i|$ are independent outcomes from $N(\mu_i, \sigma)$ denoting a normal distribution with expectation μ_i and standard deviation σ. Further we assume that outcomes from different sentiment words are independent. We associate prior distributions to the unknown parameters $\mu_i \sim N(0, \tau)$ and $\sigma^2 \sim \text{InvGamma}(\alpha, \beta)$. From the regression model we can estimate the posterior distributions $P(\mu_i | s_{i,i(1)}, \ldots, s_{i,i(|s_i|)}), i = 1, \ldots, n_W$ which will be used in the next Section.

2.2 Bayesian Decision Theory

In the traditional decision theory we assume that we have a set of stochastic variables $X_1, X_2, \ldots, X_n$ where $X_i \sim f(x|\theta)$ and in the Bayesian framework we assume a prior distribution $\theta \sim p(\theta)$. We want to decide a value for the unknown parameter θ and denote this decision (action) a. In Bayesian decision theory we chose a value a minimizing the posterior expected loss

$$\widehat{a} = \operatorname*{argmin}_a \left\{ E_\theta(L(a; \theta) | x_1, x_2, \ldots, x_n) \right\}$$

$$= \operatorname*{argmin}_a \left\{ \int_\theta L(a; \theta) \, p(\theta | x_1, x_2, \ldots, x_n) \, d\theta \right\}$$

where $p(\theta | x_1, x_2, \ldots, x_n)$ is the posterior distribution and $L(a; \theta)$ the loss function that returns the loss of the decision $\theta = a$. The most common loss function is the quadratic loss $L(a; \theta) = (a - \theta)^2$ which results in the action $\widehat{a} = E_\theta(\theta | x_1, x_2, \ldots, x_n)$, the posterior expectation.

2.3 Corpus Loss Function

In this section we join the information from the sentiment lexicons and the domain corpus minimizing the posterior expected loss. Our loss function consists of two parts. The first part is the quadratic loss function based on the sentiment lexicons

$$L_1(a_i; \mu_i) = (a_i - \mu_i)^2$$

The second part of the loss function incorporates information from a corpus from the domain of interest. We assume that the corpus consist of D document and could for example be a large set of product reviews, movie reviews or news articles that we need to classify with respect to sentiment. We assume that the true sentiment classes of these documents are unknown, but still these documents contain valuable sentiment information by the fact that sentiment words in the same document tend to have similar values [11]. For example a positive review typically consists of more positive than negative sentiment words. In traditional sentiment lexicon based classification this valuable information is not used. In the second part of the loss function we incorporate this information setting that the loss increases if a_i differs more from the expected sentiment value of the neighboring sentiment words in the same document

$$L_2(a_i; \mu_1, \mu_2, \ldots, \mu_{n_W}) = \sum_{d=1}^{D} \sum_{k=1}^{N_{id}} \sum_{p=1}^{P_{id}} \frac{1}{\delta(w_{ikd}, \widetilde{w}_{kdp}) + 1} [a_i - \psi(w_{ikd}, \widetilde{w}_{dp}) \widetilde{\mu}_{dp}]^2$$

where N_{id} is the number of times w_i occurs in document d, w_{ikd} occurrence number k of sentiment word w_i in document d. Further, $\widetilde{w}_{d1}, \ldots, \widetilde{w}_{dP_{id}}$ denote the other occurrences of sentiment words in document d except w_{ikd} and $\widetilde{\mu}_{d1}, \ldots, \widetilde{\mu}_{dP_{id}}$ is the expected sentiment value of these sentiment words according to the model in Section 2.1.

The word 'good' has a positive sentiment while the phrase 'not good' has a negative sentiment. Thus the word 'not' results in a shift in sentiment. Words like 'not', 'never', 'none', 'nobody' are referred to as sentiment shifters [1] and it is natural to change the sentiment of a sentiment word if it is close to a sentiment shifter. The function $\psi(w_{ikd}, \widetilde{w}_{dp})$ includes the sentiment shift in the comparison of w_{ikd} and $\widetilde{w}_{dp}$. If there are no shifters close to either w_{ikd} or $\widetilde{w}_{dp}$ no shift is necessary, and $\psi(w_{ikd}, \widetilde{w}_{dp}) = 1$. If there is a sentiment shifter close to w_{ikd} or close to $\widetilde{w}_{dp}$ the sentiment of one of them is shifting, and thus $\psi(w_{ikd}, \widetilde{w}_{dp})$ is equal to -1. In some rare cases there is more than one sentiment shifter close to w_{ikd} and $\widetilde{w}_{dp}$. We than use the rule that two shifters outweigh each other. Thus, more generally, we use the rule that if in total there is an odd number of sentiment shifters close to w_{ikd} and $\widetilde{w}_{dp}$, then $\psi(w_{ikd}, \widetilde{w}_{dp})$ is equal to -1, or else it is equal to 1.

Finally, the function $\delta(w_{ikd}, \widetilde{w}_{dp})$ returns the number of words between w_{ikd} and $\widetilde{w}_{dp}$. The shorter the distance $\delta(w_{ikd}, \widetilde{w}_{dp})$, the more likely the sentiment values are expected to be similar [12,13]. Thus, we set the loss inversely proportional to the distances $\delta(w_{ikd}, \widetilde{w}_{dp}) + 1$.

The overall loss function is a weighted sum of the two loss functions presented above.

$$L(a_i) = \alpha N_i L_1(a_i) + (1 - \alpha) L_2(a_i), \ \alpha \in [0, 1]$$

where $N_i = \sum_{d=1}^{D} N_{id}$, the number of times w_i occurs in the corpus. With $\alpha = 1$, the loss function only depends on the sentiment lexicons and not on the corpus. The lower the value α, the more the loss function depends on information from corpus $(L_2(a_i))$.

Let $\widehat{a}_i$ denote that value of a_i that minimizes the posterior expected loss

$$\widehat{a}_i = \underset{a_i}{\operatorname{argmin}} E\left[L\left(a_i\right)\right]$$

with respect to the posterior distributions of $\mu_i, i = 1, 2, \ldots, n_w$. Straight forward computations gives

$$\widehat{a}_i = \frac{\alpha N_i E_i + (1 - \alpha) \sum_{d=1}^{D} \sum_{k=1}^{N_{id}} \sum_{p=1}^{P_{id}} \frac{\psi(w_{ikd}, \widetilde{w}_{dp})}{\delta(w_{ikd}, \widetilde{w}_{dp}) + 1} \widetilde{E}_{dp}}{\alpha N_i + (1 - \alpha) \sum_{d=1}^{D} \sum_{k=1}^{N_{id}} \sum_{p=1}^{P_{id}} \frac{1}{\delta(w_{ikd}, \widetilde{w}_{dp}) + 1}}$$

where E_i denote the posterior expectation $E(\mu_i | s_{i,i(1)}, \ldots, s_{i,i(|s_i|)})$ and similarly $\widetilde{E}_{dp}$ is the posterior expectation of $\widetilde{\mu}_{dp}$. In accordance with Section 2.2, with $\alpha = 1$ the sentiment value $\widehat{a}_i$ becomes equal to the posterior expectation, E_i.

3   Preexisting Sentiment Lexicons

For the method in Section 2 we use three different sentiment lexicons developed for the Norwegian language.

Translation. The first sentiment lexicon was generated by translating the well-known English sentiment lexicon AFINN [14] to Norwegian using machine translation (Google translate) and doing further manual improvements. We denote this lexicon AFINN in the rest of the paper.

Synonym Antonym Word Graph. To create the second sentiment lexicon we first built a large undirected graph of synonym and antonym relations between words from three Norwegian thesauruses. The words were nodes in the graph and synonym and antonym relations were edges. The full graph consists of a total of 6036 nodes (words), where 109 of the nodes represent the seed words (51 positive and 57 negative), and there are 16475 edges (synonyms and antonyms) in the graph. The seed words were manually selected, picking words that are used frequently in the Norwegian language and that span different dimensions of both positive sentiment ('happy', 'clever', 'intelligent', 'love' etc.) and negative sentiment ('lazy', 'aggressive', 'hopeless', 'chaotic' etc.). The sentiment lexicon was generated using the Label Propagation algorithm [15], which is the most common algorithm for this task. The initial phase of the Label Propagation algorithm consists of giving each positive and negative seed a word score 1 and -1, respectively. All other nodes in the graph are given score 0. The algorithm propagates through each non-seed words updating the score using a weighted average of the scores of all neighbouring nodes (connected with an edge). When computing the weighted average, synonym and antonym edges are given weights 1 and -1, respectively. The algorithm is iterated until changes in scores are below some threshold for all nodes. The resulting score for each node becomes our derived sentiment lexicon. For more details, we refer the reader to our previous work [16]. We denote this sentiment lexicon LABEL in the rest of the paper.

From Corpus. The third sentiment lexicon was constructed using the corpus based approach [17] on a large Norwegian corpus consisting of about one billion words. We started with 14 seed words, seven with positive and seven with negative sentiment and computed the Pointwise mutual information (PMI) between the seed words and the 5000 most frequent words in the corpus and 8340 adjectives not being part of the 5000 most frequent words. The computed PMI scores lay the foundation for the sentiment lexicon. For more details, see [18]. We denote this lexicon PMI in the rest of the paper.

Based on the sentiment lexicons described above, we generated three sentiment lexicons using the method in Section 2 with $\alpha = 0, \alpha = 0.5$ and $\alpha = 1$. In the rest of the paper we denote these sentiment lexicons W0, W0.5 and W1, respectively. We adjusted the sentiment lexicons towards the domain of product reviews using the text from 15118 product reviews from the Norwegian online shopping sites www.komplett.no, mpx.no. For the sentiment shifter function $\psi(w_{ikd}, \widetilde{w}_{dp})$ in the loss function L_2 in Section 2.3 recall that the sentiment of a sentiment word is shifted if a sentiment shifter is close to the sentiment word. In the computations in this paper we decided to shift sentiment if the sentiment shifter was one or two words in front of the sentiment word. We only used the sentiment shifter 'not' ('ikke'), but also considered other sentiment shifters, such as 'never' ('aldri'), and other distances between the sentiment word and the shifter. However, the selected approach presented in this paper seems to be the best for such lexicon approaches in Norwegian [19].

4   Evaluating Classification Performance

For each of the product reviews from `www.komplett.no` and `mpx.no` a rating from 1 to 5 is known and is used to evaluate the classification performance of each of the sentiment lexicon described above.

For each lexicon, we computed the sentiment score of a review by simply adding the score of each sentiment word in a sentiment lexicon together, which is the most common way to do it [20]. Similar as for the sentiment shifter function $\psi(w_{ikd}, \widetilde{w}_{dp})$ in L_2 we shifted the sentiment of a sentiment word if the sentiment shifter 'not' ('ikke') was one or two words in front of the sentiment word. Finally the sum is divided by the number of words in the review, giving us the final sentiment score for the review.

Classification Method. We divided the reviews in two equal parts, one half being training data and the other half used for testing. We used the training data to estimate the average sentiment score of all reviews related to the different ratings. The computed scores could look like Table 1. We classified a review from

Table 1. Average computed sentiment score for reviews with different ratings

Rating	1	2	3	4	5
Average sentiment score	−0.23	−0.06	0.04	0.13	0.24

the test set using the sentiment lexicon to compute a sentiment score for the test review and classify to the closest average sentiment score from the training set. E.g. if the computed sentiment score for the test review was −0.05 and estimated averages were as given in Table 1, the review was classified to rating 2. In some rare cases the estimated average sentiment score was not monotonically increasing with the rating. Table 2 shows an example where the average for rating 3, is higher than for the rating 4. For such cases, the average of the two

Table 2. Example were sentiment score were not monotonically increasing with rating

Rating	1	2	3	4	5
Average sentiment score	−0.23	−0.06	0.18	0.10	0.24

sentiment scores were computed, $(0.10 + 0.18)/2 = 0.14$, and classified to 3 or 4 if the computed sentiment score of the test review was below or above 0.14, respectively.

Classification Performance. We evaluated the classification performance using average difference in absolute value between the true and predicted rating for each review in the test set

$$\text{Average abs. error} = \frac{1}{n} \sum_{i=1}^{n} |p_i - r_i|$$

where n is the number off reviews in the test set and p_i and r_i is the predicted and true rating of review i in the test set. Naturally, a small average absolute error would mean that the sentiment lexicon performs well.

Note that the focus in this paper is not to do a best possible classification performance based on the training material. If that was our goal, other more advanced and sophisticated techniques would be used, such as machine learning based techniques. Our goal is rather to evaluate and compare the performance of sentiment lexicons, and the framework described above is chosen with respect to that.

5   Results

This section presents the results of classification performance on product reviews for the different sentiment lexicons. The results are shown in Table 3. Training

Table 3. Classification performance for sentiment lexicons on `komplett.no` and `mpx.no` product reviews. The columns from left to right show the sentiment lexicon names, the number of words in the sentiment lexicons, mean absolute error with standard deviation and 95% confidence intervals for mean absolute error.

	N	Mean (Stdev)	95% conf.int.
AFINN	2260	1.17 (1.11)	(1.14, 1.19)
W0.5	14987	1.24 (1.17)	(1.22, 1.27)
W1	14987	1.29 (1.17)	(1.26, 1.31)
LABEL	6036	1.38 (1.27)	(1.36, 1.41)
W0	14987	1.52 (1.37)	(1.49, 1.55)
PMI	13340	1.53 (1.34)	(1.50, 1.56)

and test sets were created by randomly adding an equal amount of reviews to both sets. All sentiment lexicons were trained and tested on the same training and test sets, making comparisons easier. This procedure was also repeated several times, and every time the results were in practice identical to the results in Tables 3, documenting that the results are independent of which reviews that were added to the training and test sets.

Recall that we constructed W0, W0.5 and W1 based on the lists AFINN, LABEL and PMI which we call the source lexicons in the rest of this paper. We see that the source lexicons varies quite much in performance, ranging from 1.17 to 1.53, with the AFINN lexicon being the best. This indicates that translation of sentiment lexicons from one language to another can be an efficient way to construct viable sentiment lexicons (at least when the languages are related, such as the two Germanic, Indo-European languages, English and Norwegian.) Both of the sentiment lexicons that solely rely on corpus (PMI and W0) perform poorer than the other sentiment lexicons. Even though the performance of the source lexicons varies quite much, the performance of W0.5 and W1 is very good and almost as well as the best of the source lexicons (AFINN) and much better than the two other source lexicons (LABEL and PMI). Interestingly W0.5 performs significantly better than both W1 (paired T-test p-value $= 0.022$) and W0 (p-value $= 2.3 \cdot 10^{-7}$) showing that the best sentiment lexicon is the one that is constructed by combining the information from both the source sentiment lexicons and the product review corpus.

Tables 4 and 5 show sentiment words that have the largest difference in sentiment score between the two sentiment lexicons W0 and W1 and that occur at least 50 times in the product review corpus. These were the sentiment words that were adjusted the most when the information from the product review corpus were included. Similar to other corpus based methods, noise is introduced, and we observe examples of this noise in the tables. E.g. we see that words like 'fabulous' and 'awesome' have been changes from a positive score to negative/neutral and that words like 'jerk', 'dirty' and 'damn' have been changed from a negative score to positive/neutral. On the other hand, we also see several words that

Table 4. Sentiment words where the sentiment scores are decreased the most when the information from the corpus is included. Columns from left to right: Sentiment words in Norwegian, in English, sentiment scores in the sentiment lexicons W0 and W1 and the difference between these sentiment scores.

Norwegian	English	Lexicon W1	Lexicon W0	Difference
skada	damaged	−0.35	1.78	−2.13
gult	yellow	0.19	2.26	−2.07
forklarer	explains	−0.33	1.68	−2.01
rikelig	plenty	−0.45	1.53	−1.98
fabelaktige	fabulous	−0.33	1.61	−1.93
knotete	tricky	0.14	2.07	−1.93
fantastisk	awesome	0.20	2.11	−1.91
dårligt	bad	−0.09	1.82	−1.91
søt	sweet	−0.43	1.31	−1.74
forholdet	relationship	−0.07	1.66	−1.73
jublet	cheered	−0.47	1.26	−1.73
finale	finale	−0.07	1.65	−1.73
anvendelig	applicable	0.29	2.00	−1.71
kontakter	contacts	0.01	1.66	−1.65

Table 5. Sentiment words where the sentiment scores are increased the most when the information from the corpus is included. Columns from left to right: Sentiment words in Norwegian, in English, sentiment scores in the sentiment lexicons W0 and W1 and the difference between these sentiment scores.

Norwegian	English	Lexicon W1	Lexicon W0	Difference
vinne	win	1.19	−1.20	2.39
nedsatt	reduced	0.37	−1.84	2.22
angitt	specified	0.37	−1.81	2.19
vunnet	won	0.79	−1.37	2.15
sjokkerende	shocking	0.85	−1.29	2.14
reklamerte	advertised	0.18	−1.91	2.09
dust	jerk	0.74	−1.29	2.03
skittent	dirty	0.23	−1.75	1.99
akseptabel	acceptable	0.34	−1.48	1.81
jævlig	damn	0.06	−1.75	1.81
misvisende	misleading	0.22	−1.55	1.76
sensitiv	sensitive	0.05	−1.68	1.73
jenter	girls	0.27	−1.43	1.70
uregelmessig	irregular	0.03	−1.67	1.70
alminnelige	general	0.37	−1.30	1.68

seem to have been changed to a more reasonable score. E.g. we see that words like 'damaged', 'tricky', 'bad', and 'contacts' are changed from a positive score to a negative/neutral value. There are also examples of words that seem to be changed in a reasonable way with respect to the domain of product reviews. E.g. the word 'reduced' is in many contexts a word with negative sentiment, but with respect to product reviews the word is mostly used to state that prices are reduced, which is a positive statement. In Table 5, we see that the word is changed from a negative to a positive sentiment score when the corpus is included.

6   Conclusions

In this paper, we have developed a method to construct domain specific sentiment lexicons by combining the information from many pre-existing sentiment lexicons with an unanotated corpus from the domain of interest. Trying to combine this sources of information has not been investigated in the literature earlier.

In order to cope with these domain specific adjustments, we adopt a stochastic formulation of the sentiment score assignment problem instead of the classical deterministic formulation. Our approach is based on minimizing the expected loss of a loss function that punishes deviations from the scores of the source sentiment lexicons and inhomogeneity in sentiment scores for the same review.

Our results show that a lexicon that combines information from both the source sentiment lexicons and the domain specific corpus performs better than a lexicon that only rely on information from the source lexicons. This lexicon shows an impressive performance that is almost as good as the best of the source lexicons.

References

1. Liu, B.: Sentiment Analysis and Opinion Mining. Synthesis Lectures on Human Language Technologies. Morgan & Claypool Publishers, Toronto (2012)
2. Aue, A., Gamon, M.: Customizing sentiment classifiers to new domains: A case study. In: Proceedings of Recent Advances in Natural Language Processing (RANLP) (2005)
3. Blitzer, J., Dredze, M., Pereira, F.: Biographies, Bollywood, boom-boxes and blenders: Domain adaptation for sentiment classification. In: Proceedings of the Association for Computational Linguistics (ACL) (2007)
4. Tan, S., Wu, G., Tang, H., Cheng, X.: A novel scheme for domain-transfer problem in the context of sentiment analysis. In: Proceedings of the Sixteenth ACM Conference on Conference on Information and Knowledge Management, CIKM 2007, pp. 979–982. ACM, New York (2007), http://doi.acm.org/10.1145/1321440.1321590, doi:10.1145/1321440.1321590
5. Bollegala, D., Weir, D., Carroll, J.: Cross-Domain Sentiment Classification Using a Sentiment Sensitive Thesaurus. IEEE Transactions on Knowledge and Data Engineering 25(8), 1719–1731 (2013)
6. Pan, S.J., Ni, X., Sun, J.T., Yang, Q., Chen, Z.: Cross-domain Sentiment Classification via Spectral Feature Alignment. In: Proceedings of the 19th International Conference on World Wide Web, WWW 2010, pp. 751–760. ACM, New York (2010)
7. Chetviorkin, I., Loukachevitch, N.V.: Extraction of Russian Sentiment Lexicon for Product Meta-Domain. In: COLING, pp. 593–610 (2012)
8. Gindl, S., Weichselbraun, A., Scharl, A.: Cross-Domain Contextualization of Sentiment Lexicons. In: Coelho, H., Studer, R., Wooldridge, M. (eds.) ECAI. Frontiers in Artificial Intelligence and Applications, vol. 215, pp. 771–776. IOS Press (2010)
9. Weichselbraun, A., Gindl, S., Scharl, A.: Extracting and grounding context-aware sentiment lexicons. IEEE Intelligent Systems 28(2), 39–46 (2013)
10. Owsley, S., Sood, S., Hammond, K.J.: Domain specific affective classification of documents. In: AAAI Spring Symposium: Computational Approaches to Analyzing Weblogs, pp. 181–183 (2006)
11. Turney, P.: Thumbs up or thumbs down? Semantic orientation applied to unsupervised classification of reviews. In: Proceedings of the Association for Computational Linguistics (ACL), pp. 417–424 (2002)
12. Ding, X., Liu, B., Yu, P.S.: A Holistic Lexicon-based Approach to Opinion Mining. In: Proceedings of the 2008 International Conference on Web Search and Data Mining, WSDM 2008, pp. 231–240. ACM, New York (2008)
13. Chetviorkin, I., Loukachevitch, N.: Two-Step Model for Sentiment Lexicon Extraction from Twitter Streams. In: Proceedings of the 5th Workshop on Computational Approaches to Subjectivity, Sentiment and Social Media Analysis, pp. 90–96. Association for Computational Linguistics (2014)
14. Nielsen, F.Å.: A new ANEW: Evaluation of a word list for sentiment analysis in microblogs. CoRR abs/1103.2903 (2011)
15. Zhu, X., Ghahramani, Z.: Learning from labeled and unlabeled data with label propagation. Technical report, Technical Report CMU-CALD-02-107, Carnegie Mellon University (2002)
16. Hammer, H., Bai, A., Yazidi, A., Engelstad, P.: Building sentiment lexicons applying graph theory on information from three Norwegian thesauruses. In: Norweian Informatics Conference (2014)

17. Turney, P.D., Littman, M.L.: Measuring praise and criticism: Inference of semantic orientation from association. ACM Transactions on Information Systems (TOIS) 21(4), 315–346 (2003)
18. Bai, A., Hammer, H.L., Yazidi, A., Engelstad, P.: Constructing sentiment lexicons in Norwegian from a large text corpus. In: The 17th IEEE International conference on Computational science and Engineering (CSE), pp. 231–237 (2014)
19. Hammer, H.L., Solberg, P.E.: vrelid, L.O.: Sentiment classification of online political discussions: A comparison of a word-based and dependency-based method. In: Proceedings of the 5th Workshop on Computational Approaches to Subjectivity, Sentiment and Social Media Analysis. Association for Computational Linguistics, pp. 90–96 (2014)
20. Bing, L.: Web Data Mining. Exploring Hyperlinks, Contents, and Usage Data. Springer (2011)

Improved Cuckoo Search Algorithm
for Document Clustering

Saida Ishak Boushaki[1(✉)], Nadjet Kamel[2], and Omar Bendjeghaba[3]

[1] LRIA (USTHB) and University of Boumerdes, Boumerdes, Algeria
saida_2005_compte@yahoo.fr
[2] LRIA (USTHB) and University of Ferhat Abas Setif, Sétif, Algeria
nkamel@usthb.dz
[3] LREEI (UMBB) and University of Boumerdes, Boumerdes, Algeria
benomar75@yahoo.fr

Abstract. Efficient document clustering plays an important role in organizing and browsing the information in the World Wide Web. K-means is the most popular clustering algorithms, due to its simplicity and efficiency. However, it may be trapped in local minimum which leads to poor results. Recently, cuckoo search based clustering has proved to reach interesting results. By against, the number of iterations can increase dramatically due to its slowness convergence. In this paper, we propose an improved cuckoo search clustering algorithm in order to overcome the weakness of the conventional cuckoo search clustering. In this algorithm, the global search procedure is enhanced by a local search method. The experiments tests on four text document datasets and one standard dataset extracted from well known collections show the effectiveness and the robustness of the proposed algorithm to improve significantly the clustering quality in term of fitness function, f-measure and purity.

Keywords: Document clustering · Vector space model · Cuckoo search · Cosine similarity · F-measure · Purity · Metaheuristic · Optimization

1   Introduction

The high advance of the internet has led to exponential growth of the amount of information available in the World Wide Web (WWW). Consequently, exploring the data and finding the relevant information on the web became hard tasks. Over the past decades, many approaches have been developed in order to manage and organize efficiently this large set of documents. For this purpose, clustering is the well known method used by the scientific community dealing by the datamining. It is unsupervised technique [1] [2], that extract hidden structural characteristics in the data and gathering the highly similar objects in the same group, whereas segregates dissimilar objects in different ones. Due to the importance task of the clustering technique, it has been applied in variety engineering and field like image segmentation, pattern recognition and gene-expression. The algorithms of clustering are divided into different categories: hierarchical clustering algorithms, nominal data

© IFIP International Federation for Information Processing 2015
A. Amine et al. (Eds.): CIIA 2015, IFIP AICT 456, pp. 217–228, 2015.
DOI: 10.1007/978-3-319-19578-0_18

clustering, density based clustering, cohonen networks and partitioning relocation clustering. The last category of clustering contains algorithms with linear time complexity. This makes the partitional algorithms more suitable for web clustering. One of the most famous partitional algorithms is the K-means [3] due to its simplicity and efficiency. However, this algorithm may give a poor results this is due to its random initialization and local exploration, which leads to a local minimum. Actually, nature inspired algorithms cope the shortcoming of a local solution by a global one [4]. One of the most recent metaheuristic algorithms is cuckoo search (CS) optimization [5] [6]. It is based on the interesting breeding behaviour such as brood parasitism of certain species of cuckoos and typical characteristics of Lévy flights. The results of experiment comparison show that the cuckoo search algorithm outperform the most famous metaheuristics [7] [8] [9].

In order to improve the clustering result, and inspired from the hybrid algorithm proposed in [10], we propose in this paper a new algorithm for document clustering, based on CS. In this algorithm, CS is enhanced by additional functions. Which make it superior to conventional CS in term of fitness, convergence speed and external quality.

The remaining of this paper is organized as follows: in section 2, we present most recent metaheuristics algorithms proposed for web document clustering. In section 3, the formal definitions of document clustering are presented. In section 4, we present the fundamental steps of a cuckoo search algorithm for the clustering problem. The improved cuckoo search adapted for document clustering is presented in section 5. Numerical experimentation and results are provided in Section 6. Finally, the conclusion and future work are drawn in Section 7.

2   Related Works

Document clustering based on nature inspired algorithms is an active research field. In 2013, Kamel et al. [11] overcome the weakness of K-means in the initial seed by a hybrid algorithm based on K-means, PSO and Sampling algorithms for document clustering. Leticia Cagnina et al. [12] have presented an improved version of the discrete particle swarm optimization (PSO) algorithm. This version includes a different representation of particles, a more efficient evaluation of the function to be optimized and some modifications in the mutation operator. In 2014, Wei Song et al. proposed a fuzzy control genetic algorithm (GA) in conjunction with a novel hybrid semantic similarity measure for document clustering. It outperforms the conventional GA [13]. In 2013, A novel document clustering algorithm based on ant colony optimization algorithm was proposed by Kayvan Azaryuon and Babak Fakhar. It improves the standard ants clustering algorithm efficiency by making ant movements purposeful, and on the other hand, by changing the rules of ant movement [14]. S. Siamala Devi et al. have used the hybrid K-means with harmony search (HS) to do the comparison between the concept called coverage factor and the concept factorization method for document clustering problem [15]. The experimental results show that factorization produces better results. Recently, the experimental results of

[7] shown that the cuckoo search (CS) clustering achieves best results compared to the well known and recent algorithms: K-means, particle swarm optimization, gravitational search algorithm, the big bang–big crunch algorithm and the black hole algorithm. More recently, in our previous work, we have proposed a new hybrid algorithm for document clustering based on CS and K-means [10]. This new hybrid algorithm outperforms the CS and K-means in term of fitness and external quality.

3   Formal Definitions

Let S be a set of n objects O_1, $O_2,...,O_n$, each object is defined in multi dimensional space. Clustering S into k clusters means dividing it into k groups or clusters C_1, $C_2,...,C_k$, such that:

$$\begin{cases} C_i \neq \{ \ \} & \text{for i} = 1,..,\text{k} \\ C_i \cap C_j = \{ \ \} & \text{for i} = 1,..,\text{k, j} = 1,..,\text{k and i} \neq \text{j} \\ C_1 \cup C_2 \cup .. \cup C_K = S \end{cases} \quad (1)$$

In addition, the objects in the same cluster are similar and the objects in different clusters are dissimilar. This property is proportional to the quality of the clustering.

In our case, data are documents. They are represented by using the vector space model (VSM) [10] [16].

The cosine distance is the most used and the best one for document clustering [17]. Given two documents d_i and d_j represented by two vectors v_i and v_j, respectively, the cosine distance is given by the following formula:

$$\cos(d_i, d_j) = \frac{v_i^t v_j}{|v_i| |v_j|} \quad (2)$$

Where $|v_i|$ is the norm of the vector v_i

To evaluate the quality of clustering results, we have used two external quality indexes: the famous F-measure and Purity [2] [10].

4   Cuckoo Search Clustering Algorithm

For solving the clustering problem, the standard cuckoo search algorithm is adapted to reach the centroids of the clusters that optimize predefined fitness function. We have used the fitness function presented in [18]. The goal of this function is to find the solution that maximizes the similarity between each document and the centroid of the cluster that is assigned to. This objective function is given by the following formula:

$$\text{Fitness} \quad \text{Maximize} \quad \sum_{i=1}^{k} \sum_{d_l \in C_i} \cos(d_l, c_i) \qquad (3)$$

Where: k is the number of clusters and $\cos(d_l, c_i)$ is the cosine distance between the document d_l and the nearest centroid c_i of the cluster C_i.

The cuckoo search clustering algorithm (CSCA) is given by the following steps [7] [10]:

1. Generate randomly the initial population of *nb_nest* host nests;
2. Calculate the fitness of these solutions and find the best solution;
   3. While (t < *Max_Iter*) or (stop criterion);
   (a) Generate *nb_nest* new solutions with the cuckoo search;
   (b) Calculate the fitness of the new solutions;
   (c) Compare the new solutions with the old solutions, if the new solution is better than the old one, replace the old solution by the new one ;
   (d) Generate a fraction (p_a) of new solutions to replace the worse nests;
   (e) Compare these solutions with the old solutions. If the new solution is better than the old solution, replace the old solution by the new one;
   (f) Find the best solution;
   4. End while;
5. Print the best nest and fitness;

5   Improved Cuckoo Search Clustering Algorithm

Cuckoo search clustering algorithm can achieve the best global solution compared to most other metaheuristics. Usually, this global solution is obtained after huge number of iterations due to the slow convergence of the algorithm. It is obvious that in CSCA, the research area is explored using the standard cuckoo function [19]. In the present work, we propose to perform after each new solution generated by the standard cuckoo function an auxiliary local research in the research area in order to improve the solution. If this local search finds a solution that is better than the existing one, then it will be replaced by the new reached one.

For each current solution (host nest), the local search procedure exploits this one by calculating the gravity center of each cluster using the equation (4). Thus, the solutions are replaced only if their new fitness is better. The pseudo code of the new improved cuckoo search clustering algorithm (ICSCA) is presented in Fig. 1.

$$gc_i = \frac{1}{n_i} \sum_{\forall d_l \in C_i} d_l \qquad (4)$$

Where gc_i is the gravity center of the cluster C_i, d_l denotes the document that belong to the cluster C_i and n_i is the number of documents in cluster C_i.

```
Begin
1. Set the initial parameters:
 - p_a (the probability of worse nests)
 - nb_nest (the number of host nest is the population size)
 - k (number of clusters)
 - Max_Iter (the maximum number of iterations)
2. Generate randomly the initial population of nb_nest host
   nests;
3. For each solution change the empty clusters
4. Calculate the fitness of each solution using the
   equation(3)and find the best nest;
5. While (t < Max_Iter) or (stop criterion)
  5.1 Generate nb_nest new solutions using the standard
      cuckoo search function;
  5.2 For each new solution change the empty clusters;
  5.3 Calculate the fitness of each new solution using the
      equation (3);
  5.4 For each solution compare the new solutions with the
      old solutions, if the new solution is better than the
      old one, replace the old solution by the new one ;
  5.5 Generate nb_nest new solutions by calculating the
      gravity center of each cluster using equation (4)
  5.6 For each new solution change the empty clusters;
  5.7 Calculate the fitness of each new solution using the
      equation (3);
  5.8 For each solution compare the new solutions with the
      old solutions, if the new solution is better than the
      old one, replace the old solution by the new one;
  5.9 Generate a fraction (p_a) of new solutions to replace
      the worse nests;
  5.10 For each new solution change the empty clusters;
  5.11 Calculate the fitness of each new generated solution
       using the equation (3);
  5.12 Compare the new solutions with the old solutions, if
       the new solution is better than the old one, replace
       the old solution by the new one ;
  5.13 Find the best solution;
End while;
6. Print the best nest and fitness;
End
```

Fig. 1. ICSCA procedure

To illustrate this idea, we give an example. In Fig. 2, we have three clusters and we can see that the objects are more similar to their gravity center than to the centroid generated by the standard cuckoo function.

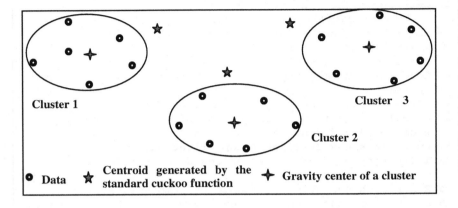

Fig. 2. Example of local search

To illustrate this idea, we give an example. In Fig. 2, we have three clusters and we can see that the objects are more similar to their gravity center than to the centroid generated by the standard cuckoo function.

We should notice that another primary function must be performed after each new generated solution. The main goal of this function is to ensure that there is no empty cluster. The simple way for doing this is to replace the empty cluster by a random one.

6   Experiments and Results

In order to test the efficiency of each auxiliary function added to the standard cuckoo search clustering algorithm, we compare between three algorithms: standard cuckoo search clustering algorithm (CSCA), standard cuckoo search algorithm augmented by the change empty cluster function (CSDC+CEC) and the improved cuckoo search document clustering (ICSCA) enhanced by the local search procedure and the change empty cluster function.

6.1   Datasets

Two kinds of datasets are used in the whole of experiments: four text document datasets and one standard dataset. The text document datasets are extracted from two well known collections: Classic3 [20] and Text REtrieval Conference (TREC) collections [21]. The description detail of text document datasets is given in Table 1, where the standard dataset is obtained from the famous UCI Machine Learning Repository. The description detail of standard dataset is given in Table 2.

Table 1. Summary of text document datasets

datasets	Number of documents	Number of terms	Classes description	Number of groups
Classic300	300	5471	100, 100, 100	3
Classic400	400	6205	100, 100, 200	3
Tr23	204	5833	6, 11, 15, 36, 45, 91	6
Tr12	313	5805	9, 29, 29, 30, 34, 35, 54, 93	8

Table 2. Description of standard dataset

datasets	Number of instances	Number of attributes	Classes description	Number of groups
Iris	150	4	50, 50, 50	3

6.2   Related Parameters

For the purpose of comparison, the number of iterations is fixed to 100 iterations for the text datasets and only 20 iterations for the Iris standard dataset. We note that for all runs, the probability of worse nests was set to 0.25, while the population size was set to 10. The cosine distance is used as similarity measure for all experiment tests.

6.3   Results and Comparisons

The three algorithms: (CSCA), (CSDC+CEC) and (ICSCA) are compared for the different datasets in term of best fitness value and two external validity indexes (F-measure and purity). In Table 3 we present the best fitness value of the three algorithms for each datasets.

As we can see from this table, the ICSCA can reach the best results in comparison with the CSCA and CSCA+CEC. In addition, the CSCA+CEC is better than CSCA and the gap between them is proportional to the number of clusters. As the number of cluster increases, more than the gap increases.

Table 3. Best fitness value

Datasets	CSCA	CSCA+CEC	ICSCA
Classic300	28.0540	28.3145	56.3282
Classic400	36.7592	36.8108	70.5629
Tr23	29.1706	59.4068	88.5799
Tr12	35.7372	41.5007	93.4783
Iris	149.6669	149.7503	149.8383

For each datasets, the convergence behaviors in term of fitness function obtained by the different algorithms are illustrated in Fig. 3, Fig. 4, Fig. 5, Fig. 6 and Fig. 7.

From these figures, it is clear that the ICSCA can reach the best results in a few iterations number for all datasets. Also, we should notice that the gap between graph variation obtained by the CSCA, and CSCA+CEC algorithms is proportional to the number of cluster. In fact, they are close to each other for Classic300 dataset and Classic400. This is due to the small probability of empty cluster. However, for the Tr12 dataset the gap is more significant due to the big number of clusters.

From Fig. 7, it is obvious that the proposed algorithm speed up the convergence behavior of fitness function. Thus, the cosine distance is accurate for the clustering of the standard dataset.

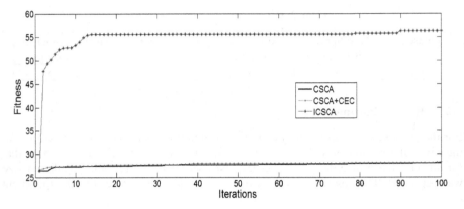

Fig. 3. Graph variation of fitness function of Classic300

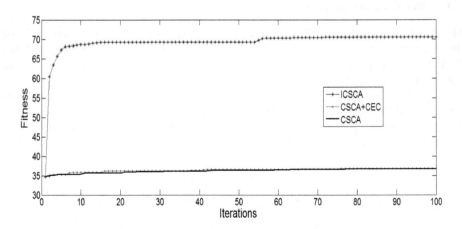

Fig. 4. Graph variation of fitness function of Classic400

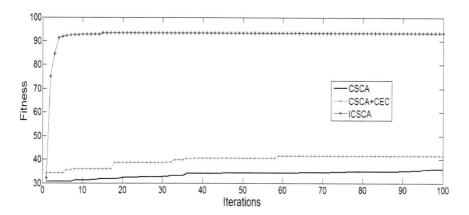

Fig. 5. Graph variation of fitness function of Tr12

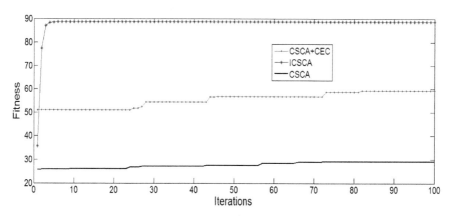

Fig. 6. Graph variation of fitness function of Tr23

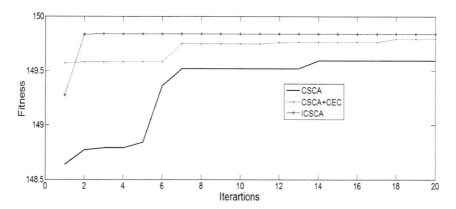

Fig. 7. Graph variation of fitness function of Iris

The recorded F-measure and purity by the different algorithms for each dataset is given in Table 4. and Table 5. From these tables, it is clear that the proposed algorithm can improve significantly the quality of the clustering results.

Table 4. F-measure comparison of CSCA, CSCA+CEC and ICSCA on the differents datasets

Datasets	CSCA	CSCA+CEC	ICSCA
Clasic300	0.3800	0.4160	0.7728
Classic400	0.4109	0.4308	0.6878
Tr23	0.3997	0.4636	0.5476
Tr12	0.2851	0.4187	0.6017
Iris	0.7778	0.9131	0.9666

Table 5. Purity comparison of CSCA, CSCA+CEC and ICSCA on the differents datasets

Datasets	CSDC	CSDC+CCN	ICSDC
Classic300	0.3854	0.3895	0.7863
Classic400	0.3933	0.4071	0.6468
Tr23	0.3138	0.4672	0.4710
Tr12	0.3923	0.4865	0.6532
Iris	0.6667	0.9158	0.9697

The calculated percents that ICSCA improve upon the CSCA+CEC, in terms of fitness function (CPF), f-measure (CPFM) and purity (CPP) is presented in Table 6. It can be stated from this table that the proposed ICSCA is more effective than the CSCA+CEC.

Table 6. Percents improvements of ICSCA improve upon the CSCA+CEC

Datasets	CPF(%)	CPFM(%)	CPP (%)
Classic300	0.4973	0.4616	0.5046
Classic400	0.4783	0.3736	0.3705
Tr23	0.3293	0.1533	0.0080
Tr12	0.2552	0.3041	0.2552
Iris	0,0022	0,0553	0,0555

7   Conclusion

The paper presents an improved cuckoo search clustering algorithm (ICSCA). The novelty of the proposed algorithm is to enhance the conventional cuckoo search clustering by a local search procedure. The experiment results show that the proposed ICSCA is more robust than the CSCA+CEC and CSCA, in term of fitness value, f-measure and purity, when applied on four well known text document dataset and Iris standard dataset. Furthermore, the percent improvement of ICSCA upon the CSCA+CEC is significant.

The proposed ICSCA can also speed up significantly the convergence behavior when applied on Iris standard dataset. Therefore, the cosine distance is accurate for the clustering of the standard dataset. Finally, as future work, we plan to extend the proposed approach for the incremental document clustering.

References

1. Jain, A.K., Murty, M.N., Flynn, P.J.: Data clustering: a review. ACM Computing Surveys (CSUR) 31(3), 264–323 (1999)
2. Patel, D., Zaveri, M.: A Review on Web Pages Clustering Techniques. In: Wyld, D.C., Wozniak, M., Chaki, N., Meghanathan, N., Nagamalai, D. (eds.) NeCoM/WeST/WiMoN 2011. CCI, vol. 197, pp. 700–710. Springer, Heidelberg (2011), doi: 10.1007/978-3-642-22543-7_72.
3. Huang, X., Su, W.: An Improved K-means Clustering Algorithm. Journal of Networks 9(1), 161–167 (2014), doi:10.4304/jnw.9.01.161-167.
4. Hruschka, E.R., Campello, R.J.G.B., Freitas, A., et al.: A Survey of Evolutionary Algorithms for Clustering. IEEE Transactions on Systems, Man, and Cybernetics, Part C: Applications and Reviews 39(2), 133–155 (2009), doi:10.1109/TSMCC.2008.2007252
5. Yang, X.-S., Deb, S.: Cuckoo Search via Levy Flights. In: World Congress on Proceedings of World Congress on Nature & Biologically Inspired Computing, NaBIC 2009, December 9-11, pp. 210–214. IEEE Publications, Coimbatore (2009), doi:10.1109/NABIC.2009.5393690
6. Yang, X.-S., Deb, S.: Engineering Optimisation by Cuckoo Search. International Journal of Mathematical Modelling and Numerical Optimisation 1(4/2010), 330–343 (2010), doi:10.1504/IJMMNO.2010.03543
7. Saida, I.B., Nadjet, K., Omar, B.: A New Algorithm for Data Clustering Based on Cuckoo Search Optimization. In: Pan, J.-S., Krömer, P., Snášel, V. (eds.) Genetic and Evolutionary Computing. AISC, vol. 238, pp. 55–64. Springer, Heidelberg (2014), doi:10.1007/978-3-319-01796-9_6.
8. Civicioglu, P., Besdok, E.: A Conceptual Comparison of the Cuckoo-search, Particle Swarm Optimization, Differential Evolution and Artificial Bee Colony Algorithms. Artificial Intelligence Review 39(4), 315–346 (2013), doi:10.1007/s10462-011-9276-0
9. Civicioglu, P., Besdok, E.: Comparative Analysis of the Cuckoo Search Algorithm. In: Yang, X.-S. (ed.) Cuckoo Search and Firefly Algorithm. SCI, vol. 516, pp. 85–113. Springer, Heidelberg (2014), doi:10.1007/978-3-319-02141-6_5.
10. Saida, I.B., Kamel, N., Omar, B.: A New Hybrid Algorithm for Document Clustering Based on Cuckoo Search and K-means. In: Herawan, T., Ghazali, R., Deris, M.M. (eds.) Recent Advances on Soft Computing and Data Mining SCDM 2014. AISC, vol. 287, pp. 59–68. Springer, Heidelberg (2014), doi:10.1007/978-3-319-07692-8_6.
11. Kamel, N., Ouchen, I., Baali, K.: A Sampling-PSO-K-means Algorithm for Document Clustering. In: Pan, J.-S., Krömer, P., Snášel, V. (eds.) Genetic and Evolutionary Computing. AISC, vol. 238, pp. 45–54. Springer, Heidelberg (2014), doi:10.1007/978-3-319-01796-9_5
12. Cagnina, L., Errecalde, I.M.: An Efficient Particle Swarm Optimization Approach to Cluster Short Texts. Information Sciences 265, 36–49 (2014), doi:10.1016/j.ins.2013.12.010

13. Song, W., Zhen Liang, J., Cheol Park, S.: Fuzzy Control GA with a Novel Hybrid Semantic Similarity Strategy for Text Clustering. Information Sciences 273, 156–170 (2014), doi:10.1016/j.ins.2014.03.024
14. Azaryuon, K., Fakhar, B.: A Novel Document Clustering Algorithm Based on Ant Colony Optimization Algorithm. Journal of Mathematics and Computer Science 7, 171–180 (2013)
15. Devi, S.S., Shanmugam, A.: Hybridization of K-means and Harmony Search Method for Text Clustering Using Concept Factorization. International Journal of Advanced Research in Computer Engineering & Technology (IJARCET) 3(8) (August 2014)
16. Salton, G., Wong, A., Yang, C.S.: A Vector Space Model for Automatic Indexing. Communications of the ACM 18(11), 613–620 (1975), doi:10.1145/361219.361220.
17. Huang, A.: Similarity Measures for Text Document Clustering. In: NZCSRSC 2008, Christchurch, New Zealand (April 2008)
18. Zhao, Y., Karypis, G.: Empirical and Theoretical Comparisons of Selected Criterion Functions for Document Clustering. Machine Learning 55, 311–331 (2004), Kluwer Academic Publishers. Manufactured in The Netherlands
19. Xing, B., Gao, W.-J.: Cuckoo Inspired Algorithms. In: Innovative Computational Intelligence: A Rough Guide to 134 Clever Algorithms. ISRL, vol. 62, Part II, Ch. 7, pp. 105–121. Springer International Publishing, Switzerland (2014), doi:10.1007/978-3-319-03404-1_7
20. Classic3 and Classic4 DataSets, Tunali, Volkan, http://www.dataminingresearch.com/index.php/2010/09/classic3-classic4-datasets/
21. Text retrival conference TREC, http://trec.nist.gov/

Information Technology: Requirement Engineering

Supporting Legal Requirements in the Design of Public Processes

Amina Cherouana[✉] and Latifa Mahdaoui

University of Sciences and Technology Houari Boumediene (USTHB), Algiers, Algeria
{acherouana,lmahdaoui}@usthb.dz

Abstract. Nowadays, business processes have become an ubiquitous part in public institutions, and the success of an e-government system depends largely on their effectiveness. However, despite the large number of techniques and technologies that are successfully used in the private sector, these cannot be transferred directly to public institutions without taking into account the strongly hierarchical nature and the rigorous legal basis on which public processes are based. This work presents an approach allowing the consideration of the legal requirements during the public processes design. Its main particularity is that these requirements are encapsulated using a legal features model supporting a formal semantic. This one prevents the violation of legal requirements and ensures that the processes evolution will in compliance with them.

Keywords: E-government · Information and Communication Technologies (ICT) · Business Process Management (BPM) · Public Process Design · Legal Requirements

1 Introduction

E-government is a phenomenon of an era in which e-business is becoming vital in both the private and the public sector. It is composed of a set of administrative processes (considered as business processes) whose mission is to serve citizens or businesses.

Indeed, the concept of business process has become an ubiquitous part in public institutions, and the success of an e-government system depends largely on their effectiveness. Consequently, the enormous and the spectacular benefits achieved in the industry and the private sector through the adoption of Business Process Management (BPM) haven't been without impact on public institutions. Let's note that the BPM is a process-centric approach which includes concepts, methods and technologies to support the design, administration, configuration, enactment, and analysis of business processes.

However, despite the large number of techniques and technologies that are successfully used in the private sector, these cannot be transferred directly to public institutions without taking into account the strongly hierarchical nature and the rigorous legal basis

© IFIP International Federation for Information Processing 2015
A. Amine et al. (Eds.): CIIA 2015, IFIP AICT 456, pp. 231–242, 2015.
DOI: 10.1007/978-3-319-19578-0_19

on which public processes are based. The Government Process Management (GPM) is the thinking that derives from the application of BPM for public processes [18][19][20]. The process models in a such context are characterized by a set of rules, principles and specific models, collectively here referred to as legal requirements.

This work focuses on the design of public processes. Hence, the main problem in this context is to say: 'how to ensure that the designed public process models are on conformity with the legal framework governing public institutions?'. Under this issue, this paper proposes an approach allowing the consideration of the legal requirements during the public processes design. Let's specify that the legal requirements are mentioned in the law and the set of legal texts which constitute a source of valuable and incontrovertible knowledge.

The main particularity of this approach is that the legal requirements are encapsulated using a legal features model supporting a formal semantic. This semantic prevents the violation of legal requirements and ensures that the processes evolution is in compliance with them. In addition, the legal features model constitutes the core from which the first global models of public processes will be derived. These ones are, then, enriched with organizational aspects undescribed in the law and specific to each institution. Let's note that the legal features model is implemented using the Ontology Web Language (OWL) based on the Description Logics (DL) and the first, as well as the final, models of public processes are generated using the Workflow Nets formalism (WfN).

The remaining of this paper is structured as follow:

- Several research works can be inscribed in the same category as this work and try to propose solutions for the consideration of the legal requirements. A classification of these works and our positioning regarding these ones are made in the second section.
- The presentations of the proposed approach, as well as the description of its component intentions and strategies are made in the third section.
- This approach was tested and validated with the cooperation of an annex of Algerian Fiscal Administration. An overview of the results is presented in the fourth section.

2   Related Works

The legal requirements are mentioned in the law which includes the set of decrees and legal texts that are associated to each public institution. These contain the set of components, management rules and instructions regarding a public administrative procedure [5][6][20]. They also regulate strictly how to create a certain output [4].

Consequently, the consideration of legal requirements characterizing public institutions has become a major preoccupation in several research works. A thorough study of these has allowed us to classify them into three different orientations as shown below:

Table 1. Related Works Classification

Orientation	Description	Examples of related works
Normative Studies	Refers to the works that focus on the description of legal requirements as a distinctive aspect of public institutions, and the demonstration of the importance of their consideration in the proposal of any IT solution	Ximeng & al., 2009 [1] Saarenpaa & al.,2003 [2] Lenk, 1997 [3]
Methodologies and tools	Refers to the works that attempt to develop appropriate methodologies, tools and techniques to the support of legal requirements. They also covers the works that propose specific conceptual and methodological frameworks	Ciaghi & al., 2011 [4] Schumacher & al., 2013 [5] Alpar & al., 2005 [6]
Compliance assessment and verification	Refers to the works whose purpose is the assessment of implementation results and the verification of the compliance degree with the legal aspect	Amboala & al., 2010 [7] Wastell & al., 2001 [8] Zuo & al., 2010 [9]

This work belongs to the second category. Among works explored in this category are that of [4] who combine the principle of Business Process Reengineering (BPR) with a goal-oriented framework in order to analyze and to model the law. The emerged processes are then visualized using a subset of UML diagrams. In the same sense, there exists the works of [5] which propose framework for extraction and feeding processes from legal texts. The framework applies pipes and filters architecture and uses NLP tools to perform information extraction steps. A third example is that of [6] who focus on the problem of legal requirements modeling using the EPC language (Event-Driven Process Chain). They propose, then, an extension of the graphical notations of this language very responded in the business field.

The main particularity of the solution developed comes to the use of a formal semantic for a legal requirements support. In the following, a detailed description of the proposed solution and its intentions is made.

3   Approach Description

As mentioned above, the main concern of this work is the consideration of the legal requirements during the design of public processes. Therefore, the proposed solution consists, firstly, to encapsulate them into a legal features model supporting a formal semantic. This latter is represented using an ontological framework devoted to the semantic conception and implementation of public processes. It allows preventing the violation of legal requirements and ensuring that the processes evolution will in compliance with them.

The resulting legal features model constitutes the core from which the first global models of public processes must be derived. At this level, passage rules have been defined and implemented to ensure the automatic passage. These models are, then, enriched with organizational aspects undescribed in the law and specific to each institution in order to generate public process models. The figure.1 shows in detail the different intentions and strategies of the proposed approach.

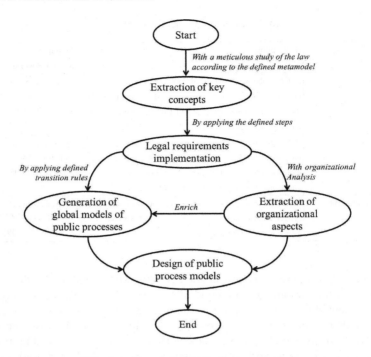

Fig. 1. Approach for Public Process Design

We use the MAP model [25] in order to represent clearly the approach phases, as well as the interrelations between them. The map is represented using an oriented and a labeled graph. The nodes represent intentions and the links represent strategies.

3.1 Extraction of Key Concepts

The first intention to achieve is the extraction of the key concepts which will be used in the legal requirements implementation intention. Hence, the starting point of this approach is a "*meticulous study of the law*" governing the targeted institution.

Several types of law exist, therefore it is important to operate a selection procedure and keep only those which provide information and knowledge that can be instantiated in the process (e.g. executive decrees and procedural decrees).

We have developed a law meta-model below (Figure 2) to describe the main concepts to be extracted. It covers all components that must be addressed in public processes design. Let's note that a key concept must not be questioned during the design process: it is necessary but not sufficient. A law is structured as several articles. It represents the primordial source providing the key concepts grouped in the following dimensions:

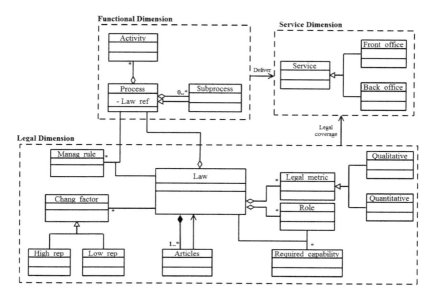

Fig. 2. Law Meta-Model for Public Process Design

3.2 Legal Requirements Implementation

Once the key concepts extraction was established, we pass to the implementation of the legal requirements governing the public processes. The main objective is to encapsulate the legal requirements through assets serving as the basis for the prevention of their violation. This one includes the definition of process parts, the structural relationships, as well as the description of dependencies between processes. The three "*defined steps*" to achieve this intention are shown in the figure 3:

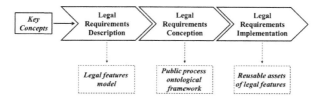

Fig. 3. Defined Steps for Legal Requirements Implementation

Legal Requirements Description
The objective of this phase is the generation of legal features model encapsulating the legal requirements. This phase uses as input the key concepts derived from the previous intention.

We adopt the feature model of Feature-Oriented Domain Analysis method [10]. This model is an explicit representation as a tree where nodes constitute the set of characteristics and the arcs specify the relationship between them. Let's specify that some features may have variations to choose and which will be resolved using the description logic (DL) during the implementation of legal requirements.

Legal Requirements Conception

It essentially comprises the construction of public processes ontology through a specific ontological framework. Indeed, we have defined a specific ontological framework for the semantic representation of public processes based on the legal features model. It is composed of two levels: (1) ontological framework associated to a public process, and (2) ontological framework associated to a public activity.

We have used the method of Uschold and King [12] who propose a method for enterprise's ontology construction. This latter is a two-level ontology, where the high-level is used to describe the domain concepts which, for their part, are placed in the second level [13][14]. We have selected the following corpus to describe the high-level

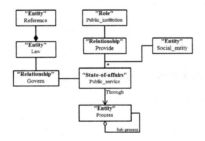

Fig. 4. Ontological Framework for a Public Process

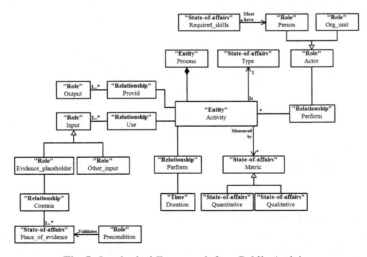

Fig. 5. Ontological Framework for a Public Activity

of our ontology: Entity, Relationship, Role, State-of-affairs and Time. These concepts are required to model any public process.

Legal Requirements Implementation

Legal requirements implementation is made with Ontology Web Language (OWL) based on the Description Logics (DL). Its main objective is the creation of assets that provide a basis from which the public process models will be derived.

This step includes also the configuration of the processes from the static variations points using a set of description logic axioms. This one favors the reuse of assets [15][16], prevent the violation of dependencies between variants of the features model by treating characteristics as components and dependencies as constraints [17].

3.3 Generation of Global Models of Public Processes

The purpose of this intention is the generation of the first global models as a Workflow Nets. Thus, a transformation rules allowing the passage from legal features model to Workflow Nets has been defined. For space reasons, these rules can't be presented in this paper. However, an example of the resulting global model will be presented in the relevant section in the case study.

This phase includes also the definition of execution order and the configuration of dynamic variations points. At this level, it is not possible to add behavior that has not been modeled beforehand and therefore not described in the law. Thus, all possible behaviors described in the law must appear in the resulting model. To solve this problem, we have done recourse to the approach proposed by Gottschalk & al. These authors have developed a configuration approach which is based on the restriction of the behavior for the Workflow Nets [22][23].

3.4 Extraction of Organizational Aspects

This intention covers mainly the: (1) identification of quick gains by identifying the flow in accordance with law, (2) collecting metrics of the current processes which allows, on one hand, to enrich those described in the law and produce an analytical view of the organization, and on the other hand, to establish a baseline for measurement and improvement of future processes, (3) extraction of actors with their appropriate skills in order to identify those able to occupy the roles extracted from the law, and to identify the need to improve capacity or to define new roles [20][21].

3.5 Design of Public Process Models

This is the intention where the public process models conform to the law are delivered. It comprises the necessary steps to transform the global dynamic models to the implementable models. It is during this phase where the integration of the organizational aspect is made. This last consists to define new activities/additional processes, new options and alternatives for processes within the project. It also includes the description of created or redefined jobs, the assignments of roles according to their capacity, as well as defining of business and managerial personnel with their job objectives. The manner in which their performance will be measured and managed is also changed or developed.

4   Case Study: Algerian Fiscal Administration

The Algerian fiscal administration is a public institution responsible for establishing the tax base, its perception and its control. It belongs to the category G2B (Government to Business), which imposed the study of the different stakeholders, as well as their rights and obligations towards the fiscal administration. Three categories of taxpayers are distinguished: (1) physical person, (2) capital company, and (3) foreign company which is divided to those installed and others not installed. For the test and the validation of this approach we have cooperate with the local Annex of Algiers.

4.1   Extraction of Key Concepts

A set of decrees (between executive and procedural) were selected to analyze and to extract legal requirements related to the tax regime on which taxpayers are subject (ex. Decree N°. 96-31, Decree N°. 08-98, Decree N°. 01-353, etc) [26]. The analysis of these documents has allowed identifying more than twenty processes each having a set of associated key concepts. These are conforming to the key concepts described in the law meta-model (Figure 2).

4.2   Legal Requirements Implementation

Legal Requirements Description

A fragment of the resulting legal features model related to the Algerian Fiscal Administration is shown in the following figure:

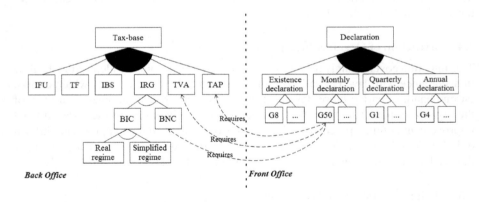

Fig. 6. Fragment of Legal Features Model of the Algerian Fiscal Administration

The back office represents the set of internal processes of the fiscal administration. For example, the global process "Tax-base", is composed of all taxable procedures described in the law (IFU, TF...). The front office represents the set of provided services to the different taxpayers. For example, "Declaration" is composed of all statements that the concerned must declare (Existence declaration, Monthly declaration...).

Legal Requirements Conception

The purpose of this phase is to build public processes ontology. It is made from the high-level ontology (Figure 4 and Figure 5). Let's note that each public process and its component activities must be designed and then implemented. An example of public process ontology (the Monthly declaration process) is shown in the figure7.

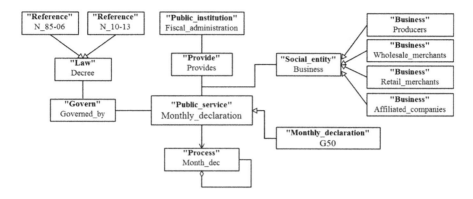

Fig. 7. Ontology Overview of the "Monthly_declaration" Process

Legal Requirements Implementation

The implementation of the legal requirements starts with the implementation of the high-level ontology with its components concepts and dependencies between them. The latter is, subsequently, imported to create the assets of different legal features. Remember that a set of axioms is also implemented in this phase. In addition, the assets consistency and the concepts classification and positioning have been checked using a specific reasoner, before their use in the next intention.

4.3   Generation of Global Models of Public Processes

This phase must be initiated by the generation of the first global models of public processes by applying defined rules, and defining the execution order of the extracted components. As example, the application of the defined rules on the back-office gives the following model:

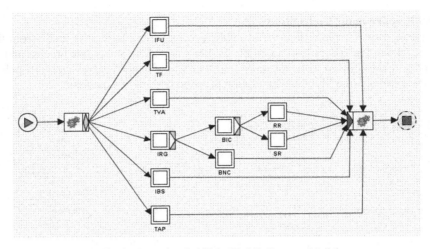

Fig. 8. Example of a Global Public Process Model

Let's recall that the resolution from the dynamic variation points was also made according to the mentioned approach [22][23].

4.4   Extraction of Organizational Aspects

This phase begins with the representation of current operational processes with BPMN notation. BPMN is located at the analysis level. It was introduced to provide a graphical notation easy to understand. These current models are, subsequently, analyzed and confronted with implemented assets.

This analysis allowed extracting several flows, activities, qualitative/ quantitative operational metrics and identifying needs to define new alternatives in the next phase. For extracted roles, establishing the matrix of capabilities [24] has provided useful information on current and future skills needs.

4.5   Design of Public Process Models

An overview of public process model "IFU" is shown in Figure 9. The development of this model is made by integrating the organizational aspect delimited by the constraints

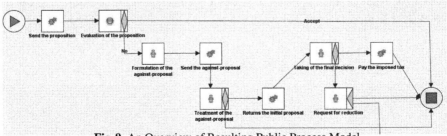

Fig. 9. An Overview of Resulting Public Process Model

of the implemented assets (ex. the sub-processes must be triggered by the tax administration, the taxpayer has 30 days to express its decision, etc.) and other issues from the previous phase (ex. time allowed for the tax inspector in order to treat against-proposal).

5   Conclusion

The objective of efficiency and effectiveness improvement of the e-government is a primordial problem. The processes of such system must obey to certain requirements of process models described in the law and the set of legal texts. For this fact, the internal processes are partially ruled and governed by a legal framework.

We have focused in this work to propose a design approach allowing the consideration and the support of the legal requirements governing a given public institution. The main particularity of this approach is that the legal requirements are encapsulated using a features model supporting a formal semantic. This last is represented using an ontological framework devoted to the semantic conception and implementation of public processes.

Several aspects can also be developed in order to evolve this approach. We focus now on the first intention and we try to develop a cooperative platform for the meticulous study of the law strategy in accordance with the law meta-model presented previously.

References

1. Ximeng, L.: Research on E-government Initiatives and Enabling IT, PhD thesis, University of Hong Kong (2009)
2. Saarenpää, A.: A Legal Framework for *E*-Government. In: Traunmüller, R. (ed.) EGOV 2003. LNCS, vol. 2739, pp. 377–384. Springer, Heidelberg (2003)
3. Lenk, K.: Business process reengineering in the public sector: opportunities and risks. In: Beyond BPR in Public Administration: An Institutional Transformation in an Information Age, pp. 151–165. IOS Press (1997)
4. Ciaghi, A., et al.: Villa_orita, Improving Public Administrations via Law Modeling and BPR. In: AFRICOM (2011)
5. Schumacher, P., Minor, M., Schulte-Zurhausen, E.: Extracting and enriching workflows from text. In: 14th International Conference on Information Reuse and Integration (IRI). IEEE (August 2013)
6. Alpar, P., Olbrich, S.: Legal requirements and modelling of processes in e-government. Electronic Journal of e-Government 3(3), 107–116 (2005)
7. Amboala, T., Japang, M., Likoh, J., Yuszreen, M.: Business Process Reengineering In Labuan Fire Services Operations: A Case Study. Labuan e-Journal of Muamalat and Society LJMS – Special Issue 4(2010), 14–25 (2010)
8. Graham Wastell, D., Kawalek, P., Willetts, M.: Designing alignment and improvising change: Experiences in the public sector using the SPRINT methodology. In: ECIS 2001, pp. 1125–1136 (2001)
9. Zuo, L., Liu, Y.: Notice of Retraction Organizational Change Pattern Based on Business Process Reengineering. In: International Conference on E-Business and E-Government (2010)
10. Kang, K., Cohen, S., Hess, J., Novak, W., Peterson, A.: Feature-Oriented Domain Analysis (FODA) Feasibility Study, Technical Report CMU/SEI-90-TR-21, SEI. Carnegie Mellon University, Pittsburgh, Pennsylvania (1990)

11. Thum, T., Kastnery, K., Erdwegy, S., Siegmund, N.: Abstract Features in Feature Modeling. In: 15th International Software Product Line Conference (2011)
12. Uschold, M., King, M., Moralee, S., Zorgios, Y.: The enterprise ontology. Knowledge Engineering Review 13(1), 31–90 (1996)
13. Penicina, L.: Choosing a BPMN 2.0 Compatible Upper Ontology. In: eKNOW 2013: The Fifth International Conference on Information, Process, and Knowledge Management (2013)
14. Semy, S.K., Pulvermacher, M.K., Obrst, L.J.: Toward the Use of an Upper Ontology for U. S. Government and U. S. Military Domains: An Evaluation, Corporate Head-quarters Bedford, Massachusetts (2004)
15. Huang, Y., Key, S.: Ontology-Based Configuration for Service-Based Business Process Model. In: IEEE International Conference on Services Computing (SCC) (2013)
16. Döhring, M., Reijers, A., Smirnov, S.: Configuration vs. adaptation for business process variant maintenance: An empirical study. Information System Journal 39, 108–133 (2013)
17. Mafazi, S., Mayer, W., Grossmann, G., Stumptner, M.: A Knowledge-based Approach to the Configuration of Business Process Model Abstractions. Journal of Knowledge-Based Configuration- Survey and Future Directions 15, 47–66 (2012)
18. Zhang, N., Hou, X.: Government Process Management under electronic government and its application. In: International Conference on E-Business and E-Government (ICEE), pp. 1–4 (2011)
19. Xuefang, X.: Study of government information construction based on BPR. In: International Colloquium on Computing, Communication, Control, and Management, CCCM 2009, vol. 1, pp. 318–320 (2009)
20. Cherouana, A., Mahdaoui, L.: Towards a methodological framework for the Government Process Management. In: International Conference on Research Challenges in Information Science (RCIS), Valencia, Spain (2012)
21. Cherouana, A., Mahdaoui, L.: Study of OSSAD applicability in a GPM framework. In: International Conference on Electronic Governance (ICEGOV), Seoul, Republic of Korea (2013)
22. Gottschalk, F., Van der Aalst, W., Jansen-Vullers, M., Marcello, L.R.: Configurable Workflow Models. Int. J. Cooperative Inf. Syst. 17(2), 177–221 (2008)
23. Gottschalk, F., Wagemakers, T.A.C., Jansen-Vullers, M.H., van der Aalst, W.M.P., La Rosa, M.: Configurable Process Models: Experiences from a Municipality Case Study. In: van Eck, P., Gordijn, J., Wieringa, R. (eds.) CAiSE 2009. LNCS, vol. 5565, pp. 486–500. Springer, Heidelberg (2009)
24. Jeston, J., Nelis, J.: Manage by Process - A Roadmap to Sustainable Business Process Management. Published by Elsevier Ltd., (2008)
25. Rolland, C., Prakash, N., Benjamin, A.: A Multi-Model view of Process Modelling. Requirement Engineering 4, 169–187 (1999)
26. Algerian Official Journal – JORA, www.joradp.dz/

Requirement Analysis in Data Warehouses to Support External Information

Mohamed Lamine Chouder[(✉)], Rachid Chalal, and Waffa Setra

LMCS (Laboratoire de Methodes de Conception de Systemes),
ESI (Ecole nationale Superieure d'Informatique), Algiers, Algeria
{m_chouder,r_chalal,w_setra}@esi.dz

Abstract. In strategic decision-making, the decision maker needs to exploit the strategic information provided by decision support systems (DSS) and the strategic external information emanating from the enterprise business environment. The data warehouse (DW) is the main component of a data-driven DSS. In the field of DW design, many approaches exist but ignore external information and focus only on internal information coming from the operational sources. The existing approaches do not provide any instrument to take into account external information. In this paper, our objective is to introduce two models that will be employed in our approach: the requirement model and the environment model. These models are the basis of our DW design approach that supports external information. To evaluate the requirement model, we will illustrate with an example how to obtain external information useful for decision-making.

Keywords: Data warehouse · Design · Requirement analysis · External information · Business environment

1 Introduction

A data warehouse (DW) that supports external information is a knowledge source for strategic decision-making. It provides historical information about the enterprise business environment. External information is the strategic information useful for decision-making, about competitors, customers, markets, suppliers, products. Unfortunately, this type of information is informal, heterogeneous and unstructured, which makes the process of developing a DW that satisfies decision-makers needs a difficult and a complex task. For many years, it is widely accepted that the basis for designing a DW is multidimensional (MD) modeling [1, 2]. Today, the MD form is natural to decision makers, by means of its structure composed of analysis measures and dimensions that represent the context for analysis.

In the literature, two different categories of DW design approaches exist: data-driven and requirement-driven. The former starts from operational sources to define the MD model of the DW [3, 4]. The latter tries to identify the requirements to build the DW and define its contents [5]. These approaches collect requirements through different orientations: users, processes, and goals and using different techniques

(See section 2). In this work, our interest is concentrated on requirement-driven, mostly goal-oriented, DW design approaches for two reasons: (i) the strategic goals of the organization in the business environment are considered the main resource to identify external information requirements; (ii) the structure of the external information source, which will aliment the DW, is not defined, unlike in operational sources, so it must be defined. We argue that in the field of DW design, the existing approaches focus only on internal information coming from operational sources. These approaches raise the importance of external information, but ignore it and do not provide any instrument to support it.

To answer this, we propose a goal-oriented requirement analysis approach in DWs to support external information. This approach can be used to build a DW that contains strategic information useful for decision-making. In this paper, the models that will be employed in our approach are detailed: the requirement model and the environment model. The former is an improved requirement model from the model proposed in [6]. This model aims to identify the strategic decision-making needs for external information. The latter represents useful information for strategic decision-making about some environment elements (competitor, customer, market, product, and supplier). In a future work, a set of processes will be defined to show how to use the models described in this paper for defining external information requirements and the underlying MD model. To evaluate our proposal, the requirement model will be illustrated using an example: the strategic goal "Increase market share". To do this, a set of guidelines are defined to show how to obtain external information useful for decision-making.

The remainder of this paper is organized as follows. Section 2 discusses related work. In Section 3, the models employed in our approach are described. Section 4 represents the illustration of the requirement model with an example. Finally, Section 5 points out the conclusion and future work.

2   Related Work

In the last decade, various DW design approaches were proposed to define requirements using different techniques. For example: Business process models in [7], Goal-Question-Metric approach in [8], use cases in [9], best practices in [10], traditional requirements engineering (RE) process in [11], Decision processes analysis in [5], Map goal model in [12], GDI model in [13], extended Tropos in [14], extended i* framework in [15], etc... Due to lack of space, in this section we give a brief description of the most relevant requirement-driven, mostly goal-oriented, DW design approaches.

Starting with [13], DW requirements are determined in the broader context of the goals and objectives of an organization. At first, in an organizational perspective, requirements are grouped into several levels of abstraction using the Goal-Decision-Information (GDI) model. It starts by determining goals, then the decisions that influence the satisfaction of these goals. Finally, the information needed to make decisions is identified. At second in a technical point of view, information scenarios are applied for each decision, to define DW contents and their proprieties. This approach shares similarities with ours in abstraction levels and because it deals with decisional goals, however, it does not consider external information.

[14] presented GRAND, a goal-oriented approach, which has extended the early phase of Tropos [16] to the requirements engineering of DWs. Tropos is an agent-oriented method, which is a variant of i* [17]. In requirement analysis, the stakeholder's dependencies are represented in an actor diagram. Then, two perspectives are adopted, organizational and decisional. In the former, facts and attributes are identified and associated with goals of different actors. In the latter, each fact is related to their dimensions and a set of measures is found out and associated with facts. In conceptual modeling, this approach can be either employed, within requirement-driven or mixed requirement/data-driven, to specify the conceptual MD model. This approach share similarities with ours in goal reasoning. However, it does not consider decisional goals unlike [13] and does not provide any instrument to take into account external information.

In [15] another goal-oriented approach is proposed based on the i* framework [17]. At first, the strategic, decisional and informational goals are identified through interviews. The information requirements (tasks and resources) are obtained from the informational goals of different actors using two i* models: Strategic Dependency (SD) model and Strategic Rational (SR) model. This latter is applied for the DW actor to define the rational model, which will give rise to the design of a conceptual MD model using a UML profile [18]. In this approach, organizational modeling unlike [14] and external information are not supported.

In recent years, many researchers focus on understanding the business context in which the DW will be implemented. In [19] an extended version of the work in [15] was proposed to align DW requirements with the business strategy. This approach considered the business strategy using VMOST (vision, mission, objective, strategy, and tactics) and the business motivation model (BMM) to align DW goals and the organization strategy. In the same direction, another effort has been made by [20] to align the i* concepts for requirement analysis in DWs with the business strategy model proposed in the business intelligence model (BIM) [21].

BIM is a business modeling language that offers many diagrams to help business users make sense of data manipulated in business intelligence systems. Different reasoning techniques about goals, goal influences, situations and indicators are used to define a complete business strategy plan [22]. The interesting thing for us in this model is that external and internal situations, that influence the fulfillment of a goal, are identified. Then, one or many external indicators are associated with an external situation (e.g. number of competitors). However, the authors do not indicate how to identify these indicators and how to represent them in a data perspective (dimensions and measures). In addition, this model is used to shape the organizational strategy, not to build a DW.

Although, the formalisms used in the presented approaches for requirement analysis step are different, their expressivity is very close, and show that a core of common information has been identified [23]. In the next section, we will present an outline of our approach for requirement analysis in DWs to support external information, which is not supported in the above-presented approaches.

3   Requirement Analysis in DWs to Support External Information

In strategic decision-making, the decision maker needs to exploit mainly the information emanating from the enterprise business environment. This information is qualified as external information. Since DW design approaches try to provide organizations with information to support decision-making. A DW design approach should be defined to support external information useful for decision-making. Therefore, better decisions will be taken and strategic goals are achieved.

In our work, the strategic objectives that the organization must achieve are considered the strategic goals to identify external information. This latter is the information required to support decision-making that must be provided by the DW. A number of proposals for requirement analysis in DWs have been made as seen in section 2 with focus on information coming from operational sources. Many efforts also have been made to define the system development lifecycle (SDLC) for DW development. Some approaches take the ER diagram or the database scheme of operational sources as an input to their DW requirement analysis stage [4]. In [13], the authors argue that DW development must be rooted by the set of goals and decisions interesting the organization rather than the schema of operational sources.

In our approach, we propose a hybrid SDLC (See table 1) where the DW schema and the source schema[1] are defined at the same time. In requirement analysis, two models are adopted: a requirement model and an environment model. The former is used to identify external information required for decision-making. The latter is a UML class diagram, which will be used in requirement analysis to derive information that must be provided by the DW represented in the form of dimensions and measures. In addition, in conceptual design, this model will give rise to the design of the DW multidimensional schema and the schema of the data source that will aliment the DW.

Table 1. The proposed SDLC

Stage	Output
Requirement analysis	Requirement diagram,
	Specific environment model
Conceptual design	DW multidimensional schema, Source conceptual schema
Logical design	DW logical schema, Source logical schema
Physical design	DW physical schema, Source physical schema

In the following subsections, the models that will be employed in our approach are described in detail. The manner of using the described models together in requirement analysis is not addressed in this paper. This aspect will be extended in a future work.

---

[1] The source schema is the structure of the data source that will aliment the DW in contrast with operational sources

3.1   The Requirement Model

The requirement   model is an improvement to the strategic goal model proposed in a previous work [6]. In our model, a strategic goal is considered as an objective that is to be met by the organization at the strategic level. From the implementation process of a strategic goal, a set of goals are derived [6]. Once a goal is defined, it either needs means to concretize it or decisions to realize it.

As shown in Fig.1 a strategic goal consists of a set of goals, which makes a goal hierarchy. A goal can be either qualified as an operational goal or a decisional goal. The latter is a long-term goal in the strategic/tactical level of the organization that needs decisions to realize it. Whereas an operational goal is an objective that can be met by a transactional information system, which is concretized by realization and control means.

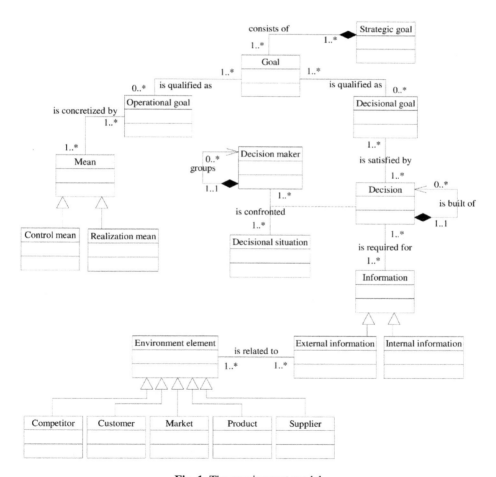

Fig. 1. The requirement model

A decision is the intention to perform the actions that cause its implementation to fulfill decisional goals [13]. Decision-making is an activity that results in the selection of the decision to be implemented. While performing this activity, the decision maker is in a decisional situation where he/she requires the appropriate information to select the right decision among alternative decisions. As shown in Fig.1, a decision can be built out of other decisions as in [13]. A decision maker, which can be an individual or a group, is confronted to a decisional situation where decisions have to be taken. The association 'is satisfied by' between decisional goal and decision identifies the decisions which, when taken can lead to decisional goals satisfaction.

Knowledge necessary to take decisions is represented by the form of information. Fig.1 shows that there is an association 'is required for' between information and decision. This association identifies the information required to take a decision. The information can be external or internal. The internal information branch is out the scope of our interest. External information is the specification of data that will be stored in the DW. It is the information about environment elements (competitor, customer, market, product, and supplier). As shown in Fig.1, the association 'is related to' between external information and environment element identifies the information about the environment.

To offer a graphical support for requirement modeling, the notation of some elements from the i* framework [17] will be used. The graphical extended notation is summarized in Fig.2.

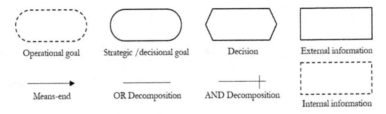

Fig. 2. The notation used in requirement modeling

3.2   The Environment Model

As seen in the previous subsection, information about the environment is necessary in strategic decision-making, which has an impact on the enterprise competitiveness. The business environment can be defined as the external factors that influence directly or immediately the enterprise. It is composed of two categories: (i) the macro-environment, which is the general environment that integrates political, economic, social, technological, legal... aspects; (ii) the micro-environment, that is our concern, is the close environment constituted with factors like customers, competitors, markets, products, and suppliers...

One of the largest used models in analyzing the environment is the Porter's five forces model [24]. It identifies five forces influencing the enterprise in a competitive environment: rivalry between competitors, threat of potential entrants, bargaining power of suppliers, bargaining power of customers, and threat of substitute products/services. Taking into account these forces, we can assume that the five major elements of the enterprise environment are: competitor, customer, market, product, and supplier. The literature on environment analysis only proposes outlines and does not provide any structuration of information about the enterprise business environment [25]. Therefore, the proposal of an environment model, which will offer a generic view of this environment.

The first model produced by our research team is the competitor model [25] (See Fig.3). In this paper, only this model will be described in detail. Nevertheless, the other parts of the environment model have the same definition, as the competitor model, described in the next paragraph. The competitor model assembles informational bricks serving for the acquisition of information about the competitor. This model has been modeled based on the UML class diagram for many reasons: (i) it is largely used today, so it is familiar to designers; (ii) it permits to represent different points of view. In addition, to facilitate its navigation and use, the model has been conducted using the meta-modeling principle. Thus, it consists of two levels of modeling: meta-class level and class level.

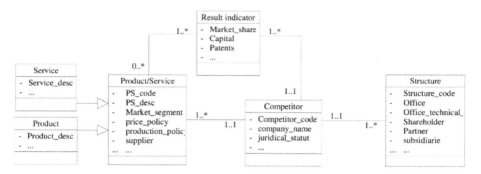

Fig. 3. Competitor meta-model [25]

As illustrated in Fig.3, the competitor meta-model regroups different meta-classes that are related to the competitor:

- Result indicator meta-class regroups financial, statistical, and commercial results about the competitor like capital, market share, patents…
- Structure meta-class represents: (i) information about the competitor identity, structural and organizational aspects, shareholders, partners…; (ii) information about the competitor-implemented strategies, techniques used for each enterprise domain: commercialization, distribution, projects funding, provision, research and development…
- Product meta-class is the main component in this model. It describes information about the competitor activity (products and services) and policies applied to products.

Fig.4 shows the product meta-model where the product class has many associations with other classes: campaign, customer opinion, market, supplier, price-policy, production-policy, promotion.

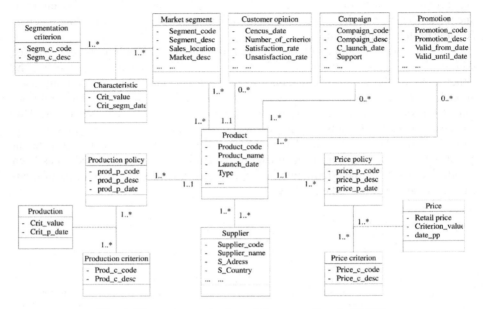

Fig. 4. The product meta-class of the competitor model [25]

In a future work, the environment model will be used in requirement analysis with the requirement model to shape the external information required in the form of dimensions and measures. In addition, it will be used in conceptual design to define the MD model and the schema of the data source that will aliment the DW. In the next section, the requirement model will be illustrated with an example and a set of guidelines are defined to show how to use it.

4   Sample Application of the Requirement Model

In this section, we propose a set of guidelines to show how to use the requirement model. These guidelines are used to demonstrate how to derive external information useful for decision-making from the strategic goal "Increase market share". The outcome of requirement modeling is a requirement diagram.

Guideline 1. The process of implementing a strategic goal must be described. It will be analyzed to identify a set of goals relative to a strategic goal. See [6] for more details on how to do this task semi-automatically.

Guideline 2. The goals identified in the previous step are qualified as decisional goals or operational goals. Operational goals are excluded. The resulted hierarchy is modeled as a goal hierarchy using the goal notation and decomposition links.

Guideline 3. A set of decisions is identified for each decisional goal and linked to their respective goals with a means-end link. After that, complex decisions are decomposed. The decision hierarchy is modeled using the decision notation and decomposition links.

Guideline 4. For each decision, a decisional situation is identified. A decisional situation is the description of the decisional problem, which identifies the internal and external variables that influence the decision-maker when taking a decision. Therefore, it could define the nature of the information needed.

Guideline 5. From the decisions and decisional situations identified in the previous step, environment elements are identified. The external information needed to take a decision is defined in the form "information about environment elements". This external information is associated with a means-end link to each decision in the requirement diagram.

Example. Fig.5 shows the resulted requirement diagram of requirement modeling, after analyzing the strategic goal "Increase market share". This goal is built out of two decisional goals: "Increase sales" and "Retain customer loyalty". For the goal "Increase sales", two decisions are identified "Launch a new product" and "Open new sales channels". Moreover, for the goal "Retain customer loyalty", the decision "Improve quality of existing products" is identified.

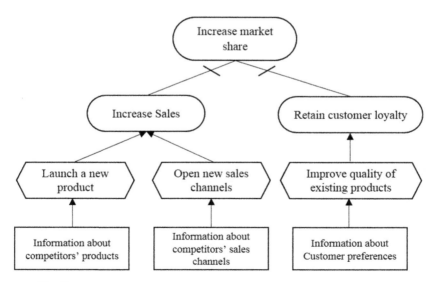

Fig. 5. Requirement diagram for the strategic goal "Increase market share"

For the decision "launch a new product", two environment elements are identified product and competitor. Therefore, the external information "information about competitors' products" is associated to the decision "launch a new product". Identically "information about competitors' sales channels" is associated with the decision "open new sales channels". Furthermore, "information about customer preferences" is associated to the decision "improve quality of existing products".

5   Conclusion

In this paper, we have presented the first step of a goal-oriented approach for requirement analysis in DWs to support external information. As existing approaches mainly focus on internal information coming from operational sources, our approach provides the means to build a DW that contains strategic information about the enterprise business environment. We were limited to the description of the models that will be employed in our approach: the requirement model and the environment model. The former is used to identify external information required for strategic decision-making. The latter represents information useful for decision-making about the enterprise business environment. Immediate planned future work involves defining a set of processes to show how to use these models to shape the external information required in the form of dimensions and measures. Then to obtain the underlying MD model and the structure of the data source that will aliment the DW.

References

1. Kimball, R., Ross, M.: The data warehouse lifecycle toolkit. John Wiley & Sons (2002)
2. Inmon, W.H.: Building the data warehouse. John wiley & sons (1996)
3. Golfarelli, M., Maio, D., Rizzi, S.: The dimensional fact model: a conceptual model for data warehouses. International Journal of Cooperative Information Systems 7, 215–247 (1998)
4. Hüsemann, B., Lechtenbörger, J., Vossen, G.: Conceptual data warehouse design. Universität Münster. Angewandte Mathematik und Informatik (2000)
5. Winter, R., Strauch, B.: A method for demand-driven information requirements analysis in data warehousing projects. In: Proceedings of the 36th Annual Hawaii International Conference on System Sciences, p. 9. IEEE (2003)
6. Boukrara, A., Chalal, R.: Specification of useful information for the strategic decision support: risks-based approach. International Journal of Decision Sciences, Risk and Management 4, 276–293 (2012)
7. Böhnlein, M., Ulbrich-vom Ende, A.: Business process oriented development of data warehouse structures. In: Data Warehousing, pp. 3–21. Springer (2000)
8. Bonifati, A., Cattaneo, F., Ceri, S., Fuggetta, A., Paraboschi, S.: Designing data marts for data warehouses. ACM Transactions on Software Engineering and Methodology 10, 452–483 (2001)
9. Bruckner, R., List, B., Scheifer, J.: Developing requirements for data warehouse systems with use cases. In: AMCIS Proceedings, p. 66 (2001)

10. Schiefer, J., List, B., Bruckner, R.: A holistic approach for managing requirements of data warehouse systems. In: AMCIS Proceedings, p. 13 (2002)
11. Paim, F.R.S., de Castro, J.F.B.: DWARF: An approach for requirements definition and management of data warehouse systems. In: Proceedings of 11th IEEE International Requirements Engineering Conference, pp. 75–84. IEEE (2003)
12. Gam, I., Salinesi, C.: A requirement-driven approach for designing data warehouses. In: Proceedings of Requirements Engineering: Foundation for Software Quality (REFSQ) (2006)
13. Prakash, N., Gosain, A.: An approach to engineering the requirements of data warehouses. Requirements Engineering 13, 49–72 (2008)
14. Giorgini, P., Rizzi, S., Garzetti, M.: GRAnD: A goal-oriented approach to requirement analysis in data warehouses. Decision Support Systems 45, 4–21 (2008)
15. Mazón, J.-N., Pardillo, J., Trujillo, J.: A model-driven goal-oriented requirement engineering approach for data warehouses. In: Hainaut, J.-L., et al. (eds.) ER Workshops 2007. LNCS, vol. 4802, pp. 255–264. Springer, Heidelberg (2007)
16. Bresciani, P., Perini, A., Giorgini, P., Giunchiglia, F., Mylopoulos, J.: Tropos: An agent-oriented software development methodology. Autonomous Agents and Multi-Agent Systems 8, 203–236 (2004)
17. Yu, E.S.-K.: Modelling strategic relationships for process reengineering. University of Toronto (1995)
18. Luján-Mora, S., Trujillo, J., Song, I.-Y.: A UML profile for multidimensional modeling in data warehouses. Data & Knowledge Engineering 59, 725–769 (2006)
19. Cravero Leal, A., Mazón, J.N., Trujillo, J.: A business-oriented approach to data warehouse development. Ingeniería e Investigación 33, 59–65 (2013)
20. Maté, A., Trujillo, J., Eric, S.: Aligning Data Warehouse Requirements with Business Goals. In: iStar, pp. 67–72 (2013)
21. Barone, D., Yu, E., Won, J., Jiang, L., Mylopoulos, J.: Enterprise modeling for business intelligence. In: van Bommel, P., Hoppenbrouwers, S., Overbeek, S., Proper, E., Barjis, J. (eds.) PoEM 2010. LNBIP, vol. 68, pp. 31–45. Springer, Heidelberg (2010)
22. Horkoff, J., Barone, D., Jiang, L., Yu, E., Amyot, D., Borgida, A., Mylopoulos, J.: Strategic business modeling: representation and reasoning. Softw. Syst. Model. 13, 1015–1041 (2014)
23. Golfarelli, M.: From User Requirements to Conceptual Design in Data Warehouse Design. In: Data Warehousing Design and Advanced Engineering Applications: Methods for Complex Construction (2010)
24. Porter, M.E.: Competitive Strategy: Techniques for Analyzing Industries and Companies. Free Press (1980)
25. Chalal, R., Boukrara, A., Saddok, M., Guiri, S.: A model for the aquisition of competitor information for strategic decision support. In: ISKO-France (2013)

Engineering the Requirements of Data Warehouses: A Comparative Study of Goal-Oriented Approaches

Waffa Setra[✉], Rachid Chalal, and Mohamed Lamine Chouder

LMCS (Laboratoire de Methodes de Conception des Systemes)
ESI (Ecole nationale Superieure d'Informatique), Algiers, Algeria
{W_setra,r_chalal,m_chouder}@esi.dz

Abstract. There is a consensus that the requirements analysis phase in the development project of a data warehouse (DW) is of critical importance. It is equivalent to application of requirements engineering (RE) activities, to identify the useful information for decision-making, to be met by the DW. Many approaches has been proposed in this field. Our focus is on goal-oriented approaches which are requirement-driven DW design approaches. We are interested in investigating to what extent these approaches went well with respect to the RE process. Thus, theoretical foundations about RE are presented, including the classical RE process. After that, goal-oriented DW design approaches are described briefly; and evaluation criteria, supporting a comparative study of these approaches, are provided.

Keywords: Data warehouse · Goal-oriented approach · Requirements engineering process · Comparative study · Evaluation criteria

1   Introduction

In the last years, great interest has been shown in the field of Data warehouse (DW) design [1]. Indeed, many design approaches has been proposed in this field. These approaches are usually classified into two categories: data-driven and requirement-driven. The former also called supply-driven designs the DW starting from a detailed analysis of the data sources [1,2,3,4]. The user is not much involved in this category of approaches [5]. The latter also called demand-driven, attempts to identify the information requirements from business users [6,7,8,9]. We focus on the requirement-driven approaches.

Requirements analysis is the initial phase of DW design cycle [10]. It is equivalent to application of requirements engineering (RE) activities, to identify the useful information for decision-making, to be met by the DW. Requirement-driven DW design approaches define requirements through different orientations: process, user and goal. Process-oriented approaches   [5], [11,12,13] analyze requirements by identifying the business processes of the organization. User-oriented approaches identify the target users and specify their individual needs to integrate them into a unified requirement model [14,13]. Goal-oriented approaches [8], [15,16,17,18,19]

© IFIP International Federation for Information Processing 2015
A. Amine et al. (Eds.): CIIA 2015, IFIP AICT 456, pp. 254–265, 2015.
DOI: 10.1007/978-3-319-19578-0_21

identify goals and objectives of users that guide decisions at various levels of the organization. Most of requirement-driven DW design approaches are goal-oriented. Many authors recognize that these approaches provide a better definition of user requirements [15], [20], for two reasons: (i) the gathered requirements are validated by identifying conflicting goals; (ii) the different modelling alternatives to achieve a goal are provided [21]. However, in the beginning of a DW development project, identifying users' objectives and goals is a crucial step, where achieving the goals is an important indicator of the organization's activity [22].

RE is an important field dedicated to requirements definition. It is concerned by transforming users' expectations into agreed requirements through a well-defined process, called RE process. RE applied in the field of DW allows determining users' requirements. In this paper, our interest is on goal-oriented DW design approaches. Many approaches have been proposed in this field. As yet, there is no common strategy for these approaches [23]. Furthermore, we argue that the process of RE is not completely applied in this field. Besides, there is no common RE process for DWs. Indeed, if we consider that a structure of an approach is the set of its activities; the proposed approaches does not share the same structure. The purpose of this paper, is to extract the invariant steps from the classical RE process, in order to identify a set of criteria (see section 3.1), to allow evaluating the goal-oriented DW design approaches; in other words, to see what does each approach provide to support those criteria.

In this work, a general overview is shown, as well as a comparative study, of six famous goal-oriented approaches for DW design. The comparison highlights the evaluation criteria based on the classical RE process. The remainder of this paper is structured as follows: section 2 gives theoretical foundation of RE. In section 3, a brief description of goal-oriented approaches is given as well as the criteria to evaluate these approaches are defined in order to make a comparative analysis. Finally, Section 4 summarizes our work and presents our conclusions.

2   RE: Theoretical Foundation

2.1   What Is RE

The first definition of RE was given in the software engineering area [22]. It was qualified as visionary, referenced by many authors[24],[25] and specifies that: "requirements definition is a careful assessment of the needs that a system is to fulfil. It must say why a system is needed, based on current or foreseen conditions, which may be internal operations or an external market. It must say what system features will serve and satisfy this context. And it must say how the system is to be constructed" [26]. [26] stated that "requirements definition must encompass everything necessary to lay the groundwork for subsequent stages in system development".

Thus, RE must address firstly the 'why' dimension, justifying the existence of the system, which many authors translate to 'goal' or 'objective' [19], [27,28,29]. Then it addresses the 'what' dimension, specifying the system's functions to fulfil the goals

[27,28,29]. Besides, RE must take into account the 'how' dimension, by specifying the constraints to be applied on the system under consideration. Lamsweerde [27] has added the 'who' dimension, to address assigning responsibilities to humans, devices or softwares. While Zave [29] claimed that RE deals also with the evolution of the software's specifications over time. In RE, two types of requirements exist: Functional and non-functional. The former describes the functions to be performed by the system. The latter defines constraints on the way the functional requirement should be satisfied. A taxonomy of non-functional requirements can be found in [27].

The above-presented definition is taken from the software engineering field. In the literature, the aspects of RE engineering highlighted by the authors above were taken back in other fields: information systems [20], [30,31,32], DWs [17], [19], [33]. Since our interest is in the field of DWs, RE for DWs is detailed in section 3.

2.2   The RE Process

The RE process is composed of several activities highly intertwined. This property is observed at the different RE process models proposed [27], [34,35,36], while other authors [27], [34] , [36] affirm that the RE process is iterative and incremental. Two common concepts frequently used in RE : system-as-is and system-to-be [27]. The former means the system as it exists now while the latter means the system as we want it to be. The role of RE is to identify requirements that will change the system from the as-is state to the to-be state. We consider that a system is a set of components (human, software, hardware…) interacting with each other to satisfy a purpose.

Nuseibeh and Easterbrook [37] proposed a RE process that consists of six activities: elicitation, modelling, analysis, specification, validation and management of requirements. Other authors, in particular Kotonya and Sommerville [34] have highlighted all the above activities except modelling activity which was included in the elicitation activity. The standard (ISO/IEC/IEEE/29148:2011) [38], proposed four activities for the RE process which are: defining the requirements of the stakeholders, requirements analysis, verification and validation, and finally the requirements management.

These differences are not necessarily justified by an omission or addition of activities, but can be considered as different ways of seeing the process. In the following, the activities of the RE process are described based on [27], [36] and [38].

Domain Understanding and Requirements Elicitation. Domain understanding consists of studying the system-as-is within its organizational and technical context. It leads to understand the domain in which the problems are rooted and identify the roots of the problems [27]. As a result:

- Stakeholders involved in the RE process must be identified;
- A comprehensive picture, of the organization's objectives, actors, roles and dependencies among them , in which the system-as-is takes place, is formed;

- The scope of the system-as-is is defined (objectives, components, information flowing through it and constraints);
- Strengths and weaknesses of the system-as-is, as perceived by the identified stakeholders are determined;
- A glossary of terms should be established to provide definitions of key concepts on which everyone should agree.

This result will be utilized for the rest of RE activities. Once the requirements engineer acquires some knowledge about the domain, he starts eliciting requirements. Elicitation is "a cooperative learning process in which the requirement engineer and the system stakeholders work in close collaboration to acquire the right requirements. This activity is obviously critical. If done wrong, it will result in poor requirements and, consequently in poor software" [27]. In this activity, the requirement engineer aims to collect, capture, explore and model the requirements of the system-to-be from a multitude of sources. Modelling is important in this activity because the system needs to be represented faithfully, so that this representation can be understandable by users.

To perform the elicitation activity, a variety of techniques exists: interviews, questionnaires, surveys, prototyping, observation... These techniques has been classified in [27], [37].

Evaluation and Agreement. This activity aims to examine and interpret the elicitation phase results, in order to:

- Clarify the requirements, remove inconsistencies and ensure completeness and non-redundancy;
- Identify and resolve conflicting concerns;
- Assess and resolve risks associated with the system that is being shaped;
- Compare the alternative options identified during elicitation with regard to quality objectives and risks, and select best options on that basis;
- Prioritize requirements in order to resolve conflicts or avoid exceeding budget and deadlines etc...

To support the evaluation activity, a variety of qualitative and quantitative techniques is presented in [27].

Specification and Documentation. The agreed requirements emerging from the evaluation activity must be detailed, structured and documented in the specification document. So that they can be understood by all users involved in the RE process. Specification can be formal, semi-formal or informal, see [27] for more details. The specification document is the main product of RE [36], [38]. It traces the process and includes descriptions of various elements, techniques and tools that have led to the result. Requirements must be classified by users to prepare the validation step [38].

Requirements Consolidation. Also called validation activity, as referred by [37,38]. Requirements engineer detects and corrects errors. He certifies that the requirements meet the expectations of users, and define the expected functionality of the system. A variety of verification method is proposed by the standard (ISO/IEC/IEEE 29148: 2011) [38]. Among the products of this step: a corrected version of the requirements produced by the previous activity; a set of acceptance test sets produced from the requirements specification; and an eventual prototype of the system-to-be.

Requirements Evolution. This activity considers the different versions of requirements. Indeed, Requirements may change due to different causes. Thus requirements before change and after change as well as the causes of change have to be noted in the specification document. Therefore a new version of this document is produced at each change. In [30], [38], a whole process for change management is proposed. Requirements change is inevitable, it should be anticipated from the beginning as well as requirements traceability should be maintained. The former is guaranteed by assigning an attribute to each requirement, in order to specify whether it is stable or may change. The latter, has to be planned from the beginning of the project for two reasons: (i) trace the evolution of requirement and justify any change and (ii) track back the requirement into the initial objectives so that one can argue that they are satisfied.

These activities compose the classical RE process, which emanate from the software engineering field. A DW can be seen as a software system having the specificity of supporting decision making. Engineering the requirements of DWs is a step of DW design known as requirement analysis for DW design. In the next section, this step is discussed through goal-oriented approaches. A set of criteria to evaluate these approaches are described, and comparative analysis is made among six famous goal-oriented approaches.

3   RE for DWs

In this section, a link is made between RE process seen above (section 2), and requirement analysis for DW design. First of all, it is clear that the system-as-is, is represented by the organization before building the DW, while the system-to-be is the DW within the organization. Second, talking about the RE dimensions mentioned above "why, what, who and how" (subsection 2.1); the "why" dimension concerns identifying the high-level objectives and goals of the stakeholders and decision makers involved in the DW development project [16]. While the "what" dimension, is concerned by identifying what information is relevant for decision making [18]. We call that "useful information" for decision making, which should be stored in the DW. The "who" dimension, cares about identifying the stakeholders and decision makers involved in the DW development project. Finally the "how" dimension is not introduced in DWs. We assume that it is concerned about implementation constraints to be applied on the DW. The concept requirement introduced above (section 2) represent, for DW, information requirements that supports decision-making [19], [33],

[39]. In the following, we use the term requirement to refer to information requirement.

Despite the large number of goal-oriented DW design approaches proposed, as yet, there is no common strategy of requirement analysis in DW design [23]. Besides, we argue that there is no common RE process for DW. [40] Proposed a set of activities for goal-oriented approaches, with various models for each activity. This work was exploited by [41] in a comparative study of goal-oriented DW design approaches. The authors evaluated these approaches according to the models used in each step of requirements analysis. Our purpose, is to extract the invariant steps from the classical RE process to be applied in DW requirement analysis, in order to identify a set of criteria to evaluate goal-oriented DW design approaches. In the following subsections, those criteria will be described, and will be used to compare the goal-oriented DW design approaches. Then we give a brief description of the compared approaches, and discuss the result.

3.1   Evaluation Criteria

The context of RE for DW is specific, since DW is dedicated to decision making [33]. We assume that the classical RE process is not completely applied in DW requirement analysis. Thus, in order to see what are the current practices in this field, we studied this classical RE process in the context of DW, and extracted a set of evaluation criteria, then assigned for each criterion a coefficient that reflects its weight in the process of requirements analysis for DWs. The assigned weights are of three types:

- Elementary: criterion qualifies an elementary activity of the RE process. (weight 1)
- Important: Elementary and requires great importance. (weight 2)
- Mandatory: Important and must qualify each approach. (weight 3)

The criteria we suggest, include the following:

Elicitation: In goal-oriented DW design approaches, requirement elicitation is the most complex activity [41] for the following reasons: in one hand DWs are used exclusively for decision making [15], [19], [42]. In the other hand, goal-oriented DW design approaches are based on the analysis of high-level goals [27]. The problem, at this level, is in extracting the goals from decision makers. If in case a decision maker knows how to express his goals, which is not often the case, in some other cases, decision makers poorly express their goals, or less, they are not able to formulate them. The requirement elicitation is the first activity of the RE process, the remaining steps depend on it. If the goals are poorly defined, the DW may not meet the needs of decision makers. Considering the importance of this phase it will have weight (2).

Specification: this criterion qualifies the specification activity, where the elicited goals are analyzed (conflict detection, errors, redundancy) and modelled. The concerns of the requirements engineer is to find, according to the decision makers, which models may be used to specify their needs so that they can be able to understand. It is about mapping the real-world needs into a requirements model [40]. It is a core activity for the RE process and prepares for validation step, therefore it bear the weight (2).

Validation: A consensus on the elicited goals, between the requirement engineer and decision makers must be established through validation. Validation of requirements is paramount for further stages of DW design. If requirements are not validated by decision makers, the risk that the DW will not address their needs increases, which will bring the project to failure. Therefore, validation is mandatory and deserve the weight (3).

Requirements' evolution management: One will not flee the fact that requirements evolve throughout the requirement analysis in DW design. Besides, it's not impossible that they evolve even after validation. A DW not taking into account the evolving requirements is certainly not at the same effectiveness as another one supporting it. Furthermore, a decision maker, always, seeks to meet its objectives in one way or another. Elsewhere, it does not include the fact that he succeeds to express all his needs. It is important to plan, from the beginning of requirement analysis, for alternatives to the defined requirements [27], [42]. Also, anticipate requirements subject to change or evolution. This criterion represent the requirement evolution activity in the classical RE process. Besides, regarding its contribution to the effectiveness of DW, this criterion deserves the weight (2).

Traceability: How will it be possible to affirm that a goal is satisfied? How to define to which goal is associated a given requirement? To answer this, traceability is introduced. It consists on tracing the path from the goal to the relevant information in DW [43]. Traceability helps assessing the impact of changes and rationale comprehension, by identifying which parts of the implementation belong to which requirement [44]. It also supports the reusability and maintainability of DW, since the scope of each part of the project is known and defined thanks to the traces. In turn, these benefits help lowering the costs associated with the project [45,46]. Distinction is made between post-traceability and pre-traceability [47]. The former is about the traceability of the requirement, its deployment, and its use. Whereas the latter is the traceability of a requirement back to its origin which is goal in our context. Thus, since the first RE's task, it is essential to think about keeping trace of everything. This is necessary to justify delays and possibly identify the cause of failures. For all these reasons, the weight (3) is the most suitable for this criterion.

Reusability: DW implementation is a complex and costly activity in resources and time [48]. It also requires specific developments to the characteristics and needs of the organization. However, decision-making projects for the same field of activity or even different business areas have similarities [49]. It is certainly possible to find situations which we have already faced; avoid falling in unrealistic requirements on the basis of earlier experiences; or even propose to decision makers new requirements through anticipation [8]. Reusing requirements, or reusing existing Data marts [8] or even DWs, promote saving time and reliability in future projects. Therefore, this is elementary for each approach and carries the weight (1).

3.2   Comparative Analysis

Six famous goal-oriented DW design approaches have been studied. The study consists of capturing the satisfied criteria for each approach. In the following, these approaches are briefly described.

1. (Bonifati & al 2001) [15]: the approach starts by gathering information from business analysts and/or managers about the company goals and needs [15]. This is accomplished through the Goal/Question/ Metrics paradigm. The goals obtained are aggregated and refined, until a small number of goals subsume all the collected information. Each aggregated goal is specified by an abstraction sheet, which expresses its characteristics in great detail. From abstraction sheets, it is possible to extract the specifications of ideal star schemas which represent users' information requirements for the DW.
2. (Paim & al 2003) [42]: The approach is named DWARF. The authors adopted the classical RE process for DW, adding traceability and compliance of requirements. DWARF is divided into a series of well-defined stages. Each stage presented in a development cycle, applies different levels of abstraction that detail the application more deeply each time, with the goal of creating a baseline for requirements. The latter are specified for data marts and grouped to specify the DW .The authors insisted on the documentation activity of each step of the approach.
3. (Gam & Salinesi 2006) [8]: the approach is called CADWA. In CADWA, the information requirement are extracted from (i) the goals presented by the strategic plan of the organization, (ii) decision makers business plans, (iii) transactional systems, and (iv) the existing DW or data marts models that can be reused. In the next stage the authors create a model using the MAP goal model, to represent the current and future information requirements of decision makers.
4. (Mazon & al 2007) [33]: This approach starts by identifying a hierarchy of goals with tree levels of abstraction: Strategic goals which are fulfilled by decisional goals which are in turn fulfilled by information goals. From information goals, the information required for decision making is directly derived. The authors adapted the strategic rational (SR) model of the i* modelling framework [50] and used it to specify goals and information requirements of decision makers. Traceability does not appear explicitly in the approach. However, the models used allowed pre-traceability of requirement from goals to information requirements.
5. (Giorgini & al 2007) [17]: the approach is called GRanD. It adopts two perspectives for DW requirement analysis. The former is organizational modeling centered on stakeholders and aims to shape the organization. The latter is decisional modeling which is directly related to the information needs of decision makers [17]. Traceability is not made explicit by the approach. However, GRanD is based on an adapted i* modelling framework [50]. Therefore, pre-traceability of requirements can be guaranteed through the proposed models.
6. (Prakash & Gosain 2008) [19]: The authors focus first on the context of the organizational goals. Thus, A GDI (Goal Decision Information) model was proposed with three levels of abstraction. It starts by identifying organizational goals. A goal enables to identify the set of decisions that are relevant. For each

decision, a set of required information to make it, is determined. This organizational view is translated into a technical view by the use of the informational scenario. The latter is written for each decision available in the GDI organization scheme, to capture the required information for decision making.

Table 1. A comparative study of the goal-oriented DW design approaches

The approach	Elicitation (2)	Specification (2)	Validation (3)	evolution management (2)	Traceability (3)	Reusability (1)	weight
Bonifati & al 2001	X	X					4/13
Paim & Castro 2003	X	X	X	X	X		12/13
Gam & Salinesi 2006	X	X				X	5/13
Mazon & al 2007	X	X			X		7/13
Giorgini & al 2007	X	X			X		7/13
Prakash & Gosain 2008	X	X			X		7/13

A set of conclusions is made on basis of table 1. First, all the approaches focus on the elicitation and specification activities of the RE process. These two activities are basic for the RE process. Second, validation criterion which represents validation activity, has not shown great importance from the approaches. It is mentioned above that it is of great importance (section 3.1). Besides, it refers to a basic activity of the classical RE process. Consequently this criterion needs more importance for next approaches. Third, traceability is not well addressed. It is made implicit by the models proposed. More efforts has to be made to satisfy that criterion, due to its contribution to the proper conduct of the RE process. Forth, requirement evolution management criterion is only satisfied by the DWARF approach. It was addressed by a horizontal activity since the beginning of the approach until the end. Finally, concerning reusability criterion, only CADWA [8] applied it by reusing existing structures of DWs or data marts.

DWARF [42] has encompassed the large number of criteria since it applied the classical RE process. Consequently, it has the highest weight among the approaches. [17], [19] and [33] has well addressed the elicitation and specification criteria. This what made of them powerful approaches, but still, they have to incorporate validation activity in the process of the approach, and plan for a better traceability.

4   Conclusion

In this paper, a comparative study was made among goal-oriented DW design approaches. We have investigated to what extent these approaches went well with respect to the classical RE process. Our study was based on six evaluation criteria, which were defined directly from the RE process for many reasons. We argue that a DW is more than a software system, it has the specificity of providing useful information to support decision-making. Thus, RE process for DWs has to be applied carefully. In addition, there is no standard approaches for DW design despite the considerable efforts made in the field. The main motivation of this work is to serve as a starting point for researchers to think at developing a standard RE process for DW design. Consequently, this comparative study can be useful for researchers in achieving a common understanding in the field and providing a solid foundation for the research community.

References

1. Inmon, W.H.: Building the data warehouse, 2nd edn. (1996)
2. Golfarelli, M., Maio, D., Rizzi, S.: The dimensional fact model: a conceptual model for data warehouses. International Journal of Cooperative Information Systems 7, 215–247 (1998)
3. Hüsemann, B., Lechtenbörger, J., Vossen, G.: Conceptual data warehouse design. In: Proceedings DMDW, Stockholm, Sweden, pp. 3–9 (2000)
4. Moody, D., Kortink, M.: From enterprise models to dimensionalmodels: a methodology for data warehouse and data mart design. In: Proceedings DMDW, Stockholm, Sweden (2000)
5. List, B., Bruckner, R.M., Machaczek, K., Schiefer, J.: A Comparison of Data Warehouse Development Methodologies Case Study of the Process Warehouse. In: Hameurlain, A., Cicchetti, R., Traunmüller, R. (eds.) DEXA 2002. LNCS, vol. 2453, pp. 203–215. Springer, Heidelberg (2002)
6. Bruckner, R., List, B., Scheifer, J.: Developing Requirements for Data Warehouse Systems with Use Cases. In: AMCIS 2001 Proceedings, pp. 329–335 (2001)
7. Winter, R., Strauch, B.: A Method for Demand-driven Information Requirements Analysis in Data Warehousing Projects. In: The Hawai'i International Conference on Systems Sciences, January 6-9 (2003)

8. Gam, I., Salinesi, C.: A Requirement-driven Approach for Designing Data Warehouses. In: Foundations for Software Quality, Luxembourg, pp. 1–15 (June 2006)
9. Prakash, N., Gosain, A.: Requirements Driven Data Warehouse Development. In: 1st JIIT A10, Sector 62 NOIDA 201307, India (2003)
10. Golfarelli, M.: Data warehouse life-cycle and design. In: Encyclopedia of Database Systems, pp. 658–664. Springer (2009)
11. List, B., Schiefer, J., Tjoa, A.M.: Process-Oriented Requirement Analysis Supporting the Data Warehouse Design Process A Use Case Driven Approach (2000)
12. Schiefer, J., List, B., Bruckner, R.: A holistic approach for managing requirements of data warehouse systems. In: AMCIS 2002 Proceedings, vol. 13 (2002)
13. Kimball, R., Ross, M.: The data warehouse toolkit: the complete guide to dimensional modeling. John Wiley & Sons (2011)
14. 24765:2010, ISO\IEC\IEEE: Systems and software engineering Vocabulary (2010)
15. Bonifati, A., Cattaneo, F., Ceri, S., Fuggetta, A., Paraboschi, S.: Designing Data Marts for Data Warehouses. ACM Transactions on Software Engineering and Methodology 10(4), 452–483 (2001)
16. Giorgini, P., Rizzi, S., Garzetti, M.: Goal-Oriented Requirement Analysis for Data Warehouse Design (2005)
17. Giorgini, P., Rizzi, S., Garzetti, M.: GRAnD: A goal-oriented approach to requirement analysis in data warehouses. Decision Support Systems 45, 4–21 (2007)
18. Mazón, J.-N., Trujillo, J.: An MDA approach for the development of data warehouses. Decision Support Systems 45, 41–58 (2008)
19. Prakash, N., Gosain, A.: An approach to engineering the requirements of data warehouses. Requirements Eng. 13, 49–72 (2008)
20. Rolland, C.: Reasoning with goals to engineer requirements. In: Enterprise Information Systems V, pp. 12–20. Springer (2005)
21. Giorgini, P., Mylopoulos, J., Nicchiarelli, E., Sebastiani, R.: Formal reasoning techniques for goal models. Journal on Data Semantics I, 1–20 (2003)
22. Stefanov, V., List, B.: Business Metadata for the DataWarehouse. In: 10th IEEE International Enterprise Distributed Object Computing Conference Workshops, 2006, p. 20. IEEE (2006)
23. Cravero Leal, A., Mazón, J.N., Trujillo, J.: A business-oriented approach to data warehouse development. Ingeniería e Investigación 33, 59–65 (2013)
24. Lamsweerde, A.V.: Requirements engineering in the year 2000: A research perspective. In: 22nd International Conference on Software Engineering, Invited Paper. ACM Press (2000)
25. Mylopoulos, J., Borgida, A., Yu, E.S.K.: Representing Software Engineering Knowledge. Automated Software Engineering 4, 291–317 (1997)
26. Ross, D.T., Schoman, K.E.: Structured Analysis for Requirements Definition. IEEE Transactions on Software Engineering 3, 10 (1977)
27. Van Lamsweerde, A.: Requirements engineering: from system goals to UML models to software specifications (2009)
28. Rolland, C., Prakash, N.: From Conceptual Modelling to Requirements Engineering. Annals of Software Engineering on Comparative Studies of Engineering Approaches for Software Engineering (2001)
29. Zave, P., Jackson, M.: Classification of Research Efforts in Requirements Engineering. ACM Computing Surveys 29, 7 (1997)
30. Dardenne, A., Lamsweerde, A.V., Fickas, S.: Goal-directed requirements acquisition. Science of Computer Programming 20, 3–50 (1993)

31. Rolland, C., Grosz, G., Kla, R.: Experience With Goal-Scenario Coupling in Requirements Engineering. In: Fourth IEEE International Symposium on Requirements Engineering (RE 1999), June 7-11 (1999)
32. Si-Saïd, S., Rolland, C.: Formalising guidance for the crews goal-scenario approach to requirements engineering. In: The 8th European - Japanese Conference on Information Modelling and Knowledge Bases, May 25-29, p. 20 (1998)
33. Mazón, J.-N., Pardillo, J., Trujillo, J.: A model-driven goal-oriented requirement engineering approach for data warehouses. In: Hainaut, J.-L., et al. (eds.) ER Workshops 2007. LNCS, vol. 4802, pp. 255–264. Springer, Heidelberg (2007)
34. Kotonya, G., Sommerville, I.: Requirements Engineering: Process and Techniques (1998)
35. Loucopoulos, P., Karakostas, V.: System Requirements Engineering. McGraw-Hill Book Company Europe (1995)
36. Rolland, C.: De la modélisation conceptuelle à l'ingénierie des exigences. Journal Techniques de l'Ingénieur, 23 (2011)
37. Nuseibeh, B., Easterbrook, S.: Requirements Engineering: A Roadmap. In: International Conference on Software Engineering, pp. 4–11. ACM Press (juin 2000)
38. 29148:2011, ISO\IEC\IEEE: Systems and software engineering — Life cycle processes — Requirements engineering, pp. 95 (2011)
39. Winter, R., Strauch, B.: Information Requirements Engineering for Data Warehouse Systems. In: ACM Symposium on Applied Computing, SAC 2004, Nicosia, Cyprus, March 14-17, pp. 1359–1365 (2004)
40. Kavakli, E., Loucopoulos, P.: Goal driven requirements engineering: evaluation of current methods. In: Proceedings of the 8th CAiSE/IFIP8, pp. 16–17 (2003)
41. Leal, A.C., Sepúlveda, S., Mate, A., Mazón, J.-N., Trujillo, J.: Goal oriented requirements engineering in data warehouses: A comparative study. Ingeniería E Investigación 34, 66–70 (2014)
42. Paim, F.R.S., de Castro, J.F.B.: DWARF: An approch for requirement definition and management of DW systems. In: 11th IEEE International Requirement Engeneering Confrence (2003)
43. Hull, E., Jackson, K., Dick, J.: Requirements Engineering, 2nd edn., p. 201. Springer (2005)
44. Antoniol, G., Canfora, G., Casazza, G., De Lucia, A., Merlo, E.: Recovering traceability links between code and documentation. IEEE Transactions on Software Engineering 28, 970–983 (2002)
45. Ramesh, B., Stubbs, C., Powers, T., Edwards, M.: Requirements traceability: Theory and practice. Annals of Software Engineering 3, 397–415 (1997)
46. Ramesh, B., Jarke, M.: Toward reference models for requirements traceability. IEEE Transactions on Software Engineering 27, 58–93 (2001)
47. Pohl, K.: PRO-ART: Enabling requirements pre-traceability. In: Proceedings of the Second International Conference on Requirements Engineering, pp. 76–84 (1996)
48. Carneiro, L., Brayner, A.: X-META: A Methodology for Data Warehouse Design with Metadata Management. In: Design and Management of Data Warehouses (DMDW), pp. 13–22 (2002)
49. Annoni, E., Ravat, F., Teste, O., Zurfluh, G.: Les systèmes d'informations décisionnels : une approche d'analyse et de conception à base de patrons. Revue des Sciences et Technologies de l'Information, série ISI, «Méthodes Avancées de Développement des SI » 10, 81–106 (2005)
50. Yu, E.S.: Towards modelling and reasoning support for early-phase requirements engineering. In: Proceedings of the Third IEEE International Symposium on Requirements Engineering, pp. 226–235. IEEE (1997)

Information Technology:
OLAP and Web Services

Research and Analysis of the Stream Materialized Aggregate List

Marcin Gorawski[✉] and Krzysztof Pasterak

Silesian University of Technology,
Institute of Computer Science,
Akademicka 16, 44-100 Gliwice Poland
{Marcin.Gorawski,Krzysztof.Pasterak}@polsl.pl

Abstract. The problem of low-latency processing of large amounts of data acquired in continuously changing environment has led to the genesis of Stream Processing Systems (SPS). However, sometimes it is crucial to process both historical (archived) and current data, in order to obtain full knowledge about various phenomena. This is achieved in a Stream Data Warehouse (StrDW), where analytical operations on both historical and current data streams are performed. In this paper we focus on Stream Materialized Aggregate List (StrMAL) – a stream repository tier of StrDW. As a motivating example, the liquefied petrol storage and distribution system, containing continuous telemetric data acquisition, transmission and storage, will be presented as possible application for Stream Materialized Aggregate List.

Keywords: Materialized aggregate list · Stream data warehouse · Stream processing

1 Introduction

Nowadays, the necessity of processing, storing and analyzing of very large data volumes (considered also as *BigData*) is constantly growing. This implies development of newer and more advanced systems, that are able to satisfy this need. Moreover, from the perspective of various enterprises, organizations and other data producers and consumers, the outcome information is expected to be reliable, most up-to-date and obtained in the shortest time possible. These requirements determine the attractiveness of solutions already present on market, as well as constitute new objectives for developers [22].

In the following paper we focus on Stream Data Processing Systems (SPS). They are designed to process current and continuously generated data with relatively high frequency. When non-stream solutions (i.e. those relying on persistent data) are concerned, processing unit enforces collecting data from sources. Stream oriented systems have to process incoming data almost instantly as they arrive, since data are produced and actively delivered by sources. There are representative examples of Stream Processing Systems [1–6, 26, 27], however they are relatively not as popular as classic, traditional data storage systems.

© IFIP International Federation for Information Processing 2015
A. Amine et al. (Eds.): CIIA 2015, IFIP AICT 456, pp. 269–278, 2015.
DOI: 10.1007/978-3-319-19578-0_22

The example of application involving instant and immediate analysis of data delivered continuously is a liquefied petrol storage and distribution system. Such an installation consists of multiple petrol stations, where various measurements are gathered and transmitted to the centralized or distributed analysis platform.

Each petrol station is equipped with fuel tanks where liquefied fuel is stored and dispensing devices which act as sale endpoints. These appliances generate two streams of data supplemented with delivery records entered by station workers or detected automatically. Usually fuel volume and temperature is measured in tanks, whereas the amount of sold fuel is returned from meters installed in dispensers.

The common analysis performed upon the aforementioned values aims to detect various anomalies and other adverse phenomena that can occur at petrol stations. The most dangerous example is fuel leak [15, 24], which introduces very serious consequences to the environment. In order to prevent such a threat, it is crucial to detect any volume of fuel leaked from tank and piping as fast as possible.

This paper is organized as follows. Section 2 contains information concerning data stream storage problems with theoretical base of a Stream Materialized Aggregate List (StrMAL) described. In Section 3 the architecture of StrMAL is presented along with examples of its most important features. Section 4 contains test results performed over a StrMAL engine, whereas Section 5 summarizes the paper.

2   Data Stream Storage

A Data stream [8, 12–14] can be defined as an infinite sequence of tuples with unique timestamps and attributes carrying information describing various phenomena at subsequent moments of time. Stream Processing Systems usually do not provide any storage operation in their work flow, since they are designed to produce answers immediately as new data arrive. Optional data storage is sometimes used to provide static data as an extension to stream data.

Under certain circumstances an instant access to historical data stored in a database, as well as efficient processing performed on current data is required. Analyzing the history is necessary in learning process, where different trends, dependencies, and rules are discovered and remembered [21]. Later, gathered knowledge is used to filter current stream in order to detect any desired events. This process frequently involves browsing data on a certain level of detail – in other words – on different aggregation levels. Moreover, data retrieval and aggregation operations should not interfere with insertion of newly arrived data, which often cannot be completely eliminated.

The problem of processing both stored and current data has lead to the idea of the Stream Data Warehouse [7, 9, 19, 20, 23, 25]. It is an unified processing platform capable to produce immediate answers to complex queries concerning current and archived data. In current mode, data can be processed before they are persisted in any data structure, as in Stream Processing Systems.

2.1   Problems and Issues

As a consequence of data stream nature, it is virtually not possible to store a whole stream in a memory. In addition, at a given moment of time, the stream contains only the most current tuples, since all read before have been already removed and archived, which forces searching the history (database).

Moreover, data in a stream are produced relatively frequently and in a unpredictable manner, which causes database to be updated very often and irregularly. High intensity of modifying transactions, being made in parallel with queries consisting of large range data retrieval, can lead to serious decrease in overall performance.

Relative database systems are designed to execute versatile CRUD (Create, Read, Update and Delete) operations on the whole dataset stored inside their internal memory. However, in stream appliances, updates take place only at the end of a time frame, i.e. tuples arrive and are organized ascending by timestamps. In this cause, it is not possible that once stored piece of data is updated.

Repetitive execution of the same or similar operations (e.g. aggregation) of the same datasets is usually time consuming and thus leading to unnecessary delays. In order to prevent these adverse situations, results of time costing operations can be stored along with query parameters to provide access to once computed values. As mentioned before, there are no updates on historical data causing the materialized data to be immutable.

2.2   Stream Materialized Aggregate List

Many items that are sequentially arranged (as tuples in a data stream) can be stored in a list data structure. In such a form, it is easy to view all subsequent elements in proper order. When browsing tuples from a stream, consecutive retrieving is the only operation considered here, which can be described as forward iterating over list.

An aggregate list [16–18] can be defined as a sequential data structure, containing a subset of an aggregated stream (stream of aggregated tuples). It is stored in memory and acts as a physical representation of stream, beginning from certain moment of time. Because of the limited capacity of list, it is assumed that all aggregates already read can be replaced with more fresh data.

When considering various data collections, extracting data access operations into a separate interface is a common practice. Such an interface is called an *iterator* and is used to traverse any data structure (as aggregate list for example). Thus, an iterator can be used for retrieving tuples from a stream.

The aforementioned issues became a motivation for designing a solution which is capable to provide an uniform access to any data stream, efficiently manage available memory, and avoid redundant operations. It is done by using aggregate list, iterator interface, and aggregate materialization techniques. The solution has been named a Stream Materialized Aggregate List [11] and is designed to act as a data storage tier of a Stream Data Warehouse [10].

It is possible to create several iterators attached to a single list and pointing to different elements. In such a situation, the distance (measured in time units) between them is unconstrained and can be arbitrary long, causing the whole list to occupy very large amount of memory. In order to prevent this situation, the following solution is used: the aggregate list itself is not located in memory, instead its active fragments (tuples being currently in use) are stored inside each iterator.

Moreover, in order to increase memory management efficiency, the following solution is used [17, 18]: each iterator contains a static array which corresponds to an iterator-specific aggregate list fragment. As far as successive aggregates are retrieved from an iterator and become outdated, they are replaced by newer ones. Each array is logically divided into pages (basic units). Due to that, certain number of ready-to-read aggregates is always available. When the need of new aggregates creation occurs, a whole page at once is produced and replaces the old one.

3 Architecture of StrMAL

The Stream Materialized Aggregate List was implemented using multilayer concept. Each of them is realizing separate functionalities and is responsible for another stage of aggregates production. Figure 1 presents the overall architecture of StrMAL. Four layers have been denoted by the following acronyms: SDL, APL, DML, and CL – they are described later in the text.

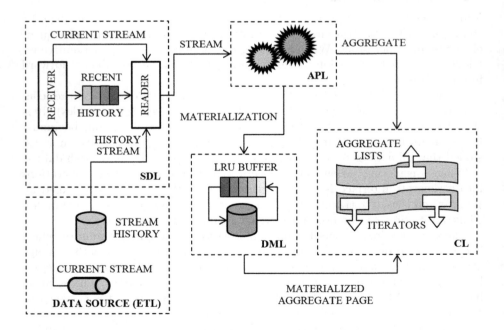

Fig. 1. Architecture of the StrMAL engine

In the Stream Distribution Layer (SDL) the process of aggregate list production begins with collecting data required for aggregation. It is done, depending on start time specified in query, by using current or historical stream. This layer provides a uniform access to data streams, irrespective of their origin (source) and start time.

The Aggregate Production Layer (APL) retrieves desired streams from the SDL and, basing on parameters obtained from client, performs aggregation. Outcome aggregates are delivered to clients and materialized (persisted for future use).

The Data Materialization Layer (DML) involves persisting aggregates in database, along with query parameters. Besides storing, this layer also provides searching and retrieving mechanisms. Cache memory (LRU buffer) is used to achieve better performance of I/O operations.

The Client Layer (CL) is responsible for communication with clients and providing them aggregates produced in the APL with data retrieved from the SDL or materialized aggregates read from the DML. It integrates all mentioned layers and uses them to prepare, produce, and serve results.

3.1   Current and Historical Stream Support

One of the major tasks of the Stream Distribution Layer is to collect tuples from current stream and store them temporally in a buffer called History Table (HT). It is performed in order to provide a flexible bridge between current and historical data. When the SDL is queried for a data stream beginning from a certain timestamp, first it performs a lookup over the HT to determine whether the desired data have been already produced – and when it is true – if they are still in the HT or have been persisted in a database.

The Stream Distribution Layer can operate in four states, depending on the distance between current and searched time. Each state determines the source from which data are retrieved and other working principles, such as next state reached under state-specific circumstances. These states are named as follows:

1. TAB – tuples are read from the History Table,
2. DB – tuples are read from a database,
3. SYNC – synchronization with the current stream,
4. CUR – tuples are read from the current stream.

The TAB is the starting state, when the SDL is queried with a specific timestamp and the History Table is searched to find whether the desired tuple is present in it. When the tuple is not found in the HT, it either has not been generated and acquired by the system or it has been archived and stored in a database. In the former case the SDL remains in the TAB state waiting for tuple to appear in the HT, whereas in latter cause, the SDL switches into the DB state and reads tuples from a database until the end of batch (certain number of tuples) is reached. After that, the SDL switches back into the TAB state.

In the other situation, after successful lookup, SDL remains in TAB state until the end of HT is reached (there are no more tuples to read). Such a circumstance denotes that next tuple ought to be retrieved from the current stream. However this process cannot simply be performed by switching into CUR state (when subsequent tuples are read from the current stream). SDL needs to synchronize with the current stream – it is done by entering SYNC state. In that state the SDL assures that no tuples will be omitted during switching – i.e. tuples being removed from the current stream and not yet written into the HT. Figure 2 presents state diagram of the Stream Distribution Layer.

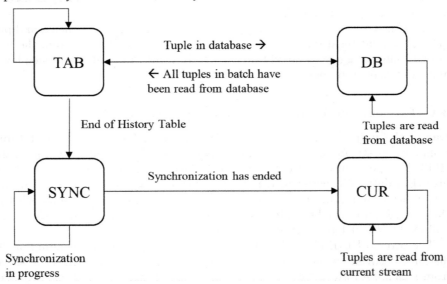

Fig. 2. State diagram of the SDL

4   Test Results

First test was conducted in order to verify the impact of History Table on archived tuple read time. The objective to that study was to simulate the situation involving reading subsequent tuples from current stream with variable time gap (delay) between each read operation. In such a case client reading tuples desynchronizes with stream and is obliged to perform a lookup in database containing archived data. When HT is used, it stores recent history of stream and allows the client of SDL to retrieve desired data from buffer instead of database.

Figure 3 presents tuple read time (in microseconds) with buffering in HT applied depending on HT size (in number of tuples). Three different delays were used: 1 s, 2 s, and 5 s. The starting size of HT was set to 8 and it was doubled respectively when there were any calls to database. The test was finished when all tuples were read from the buffer allowing client not to operate on persistent storage at all. Results show that tuple read time when using HT in 100% is about 6 times shorter than in the 5 s delay example (where almost 100% of read operations were made on a database).

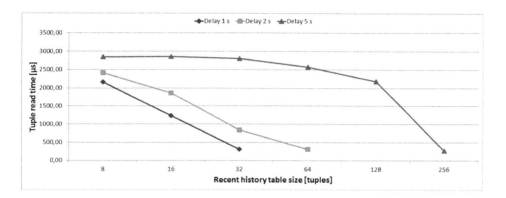

Fig. 3. Tuple read time depending on HT size

Next test was conducted to verify the percentage of HT calls in historical data retrieval depending on aggregate consumption time. Aggregates were read from CL and the following delays were introduced: 300 ms, 400 ms, 500 ms, 550 ms, 600 ms, 750 ms, and 1000 ms. Such values have been selected after preliminary tests which showed that below 300 ms there are no calls to any historical data because every tuple is read directly from the current stream. Between 500 ms and 600 ms an additional measure was performed (at 550 ms) due to high variability in that range. Four different sizes of History Table were used: 8, 16, 64, and 256 (measured in number of tuples).

Figure 4 shows that for two first examples (HT sizes: 8 and 16) the percentage of calls to HT suddenly dropped from 100% to about 10% at delay set to about 600 ms. It means that 90% of calls to historical data sources were made to database causing the overall aggregate production time to be longer. When HT size was set to 256 tuples about 40% of calls were still made to HT, even when aggregate consumption time was equal to 1 s.

Results of performed tests showed that using the History Table as buffering mechanism, while performing seamless switching between historical and current data sources, is legitimate. Tuple read time is noticeably shorter and database system is less loaded causing the whole process of aggregate production more efficient.

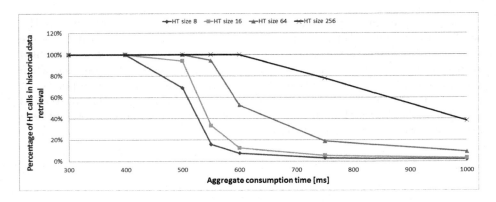

Fig. 4. Percentage of HT calls depending on aggregate consumption time

5 Summary

In this paper we have described the architecture of the Stream Materialized Aggregate List engine, which is a component of Stream Data Warehouse, responsible for storing and serving data streams on various levels of aggregation. The StrDW itself is still at the planning stage, while its components, such as described StrMAL engine, are being intensively developed and tested.

In the nearest future we intend to design all concepts and modules of the StrDW, with spatial indexing, distributed architecture and low-latency query processing issues included. The target system is expected to process data streams in OLAP manner, allowing the analysis on currently changing multidimensional aggregated data to be performed in decision supporting applications with critical time requirements with distributed environment and concurrency issues involved, such as the aforementioned liquefied petrol storage and distribution system.

References

1. Abadi, D.J., Ahmad, Y., Balazinska, M., Çetintemel, U., Cherniack, M., Hwang, J.-H., Lindner, W., Maskey, A., Rasin, A., Ryvkina, E., Tatbul, N., Xing, Y., Zdonik, S.B.: The design of the borealis stream processing engine. In: CIDR, pp. 277–289 (2005)
2. Abadi, D.J., Carney, D., Çetintemel, U., Cherniack, M., Convey, C., Lee, S., Stonebraker, M., Tatbul, N., Zdonik, S.: Aurora: A new model and architecture for data stream management. The VLDB Journal 12(2), 120–139 (2003)
3. Arasu, A., Babcock, B., Babu, S., Cieslewicz, J., Datar, M., Ito, K., Motwani, R., Srivastava, U., Widom, J.: Stream: The stanford stream data manager. Technical Report 2003-21, Stanford InfoLab (2003)
4. Arasu, A., Widom, J.: A denotational semantics for continuous queries over streams and relations. SIGMOD Rec. 33(3), 6–11 (2004)

5. Babcock, B., Babu, S., Datar, M., Motwani, R., Widom, J.: Models and issues in data stream systems. In: Proceedings of the Twenty-first ACM SIGMOD-SIGACT-SIGART Symposium on Principles of Database Systems, PODS 2002, pp. 1–16. ACM, New York (2002)
6. Barga, R.S., Goldstein, J., Ali, M.H., Hong, M.: Consistent streaming through time: A vision for event stream processing. In: CIDR, pp. 363–374, http://www.cidrdb.org
7. Bateni, M., Golab, L., Hajiaghayi, M., Karloff, H.: Scheduling to minimize staleness and stretch in real-time data warehouses. Theory of Computing Systems 49(4), 757–780 (2011)
8. Gilbert, A.C., Kotidis, Y., Muthukrishnan, S., Strauss, M.: Surfing wavelets on streams: One-pass summaries for approximate aggregate queries. In: Proceedings of the 27th International Conference on Very Large Data Bases, VLDB 2001, pp. 79–88. Morgan Kaufmann Publishers Inc., San Francisco (2001)
9. Golab, L., Johnson, T., Shkapenyuk, V.: Scheduling updates in a real-time stream warehouse. In: IEEE 25th International Conference on Data Engineering, ICDE 2009, pp. 1207–1210 (2009)
10. Gorawski, M.: Advanced data warehouses. Habilitation. Studia Informatica 30(3B), 386 (2009)
11. Gorawski, M.: Time complexity of page filling algorithms in materialized aggregate list (mal) and mal/trigg materialization cost. Control and Cybernetics 38(1), 153–172 (2009)
12. Gorawski, M., Chrószcz, A.: The design of stream database engine in concurrent environment. In: OTM Conferences (2), pp. 1033–1049 (2009)
13. Gorawski, M., Gorawska, A., Pasterak, K.: Evaluation and development perspectives of stream data processing systems. In: Kwiecień, A., Gaj, P., Stera, P. (eds.) CN 2013. CCIS, vol. 370, pp. 300–311. Springer, Heidelberg (2013)
14. Gorawski, M., Gorawska, A., Pasterak, K.: A survey of data stream processing tools. In: Information Sciences and Systems, pp. 295–303. Springer International Publishing (2014)
15. Gorawski, M., Gorawska, A., Pasterak, K.: Liquefied petroleum storage and distribution problems and research thesis. In: Kozielski, S., Mrozek, D., Kasprowski, P., Malysiak-Mrozek, B., Kostrzewa, D. (eds.) BDAS 2015. CCIS, vol. 521, pp. 540–550. Springer, Heidelberg (2015)
16. Gorawski, M., Malczok, R.: Multi-thread processing of long aggregates lists. In: PPAM, pp. 59–66 (2005)
17. Gorawski, M., Malczok, R.: On efficient storing and processing of long aggregate lists. In: Tjoa, A.M., Trujillo, J. (eds.) DaWaK 2005. LNCS, vol. 3589, pp. 190–199. Springer, Heidelberg (2005)
18. Gorawski, M., Malczok, R.: Towards storing and processing of long aggregates lists in spatial data warehouses. In: XXI Autumn Meeting of Polish Information Processing Society Conference Proceedings, pp. 95–103 (2005)
19. Kakish, K., Kraft, T.A.: Etl evolution for real-time data warehousing. In: 2012 Proceedings of the Conference onInformation Systems Applied Research New Orleans Louisiana (2012)
20. Polyzotis, N., Skiadopoulos, S., Vassiliadis, P., Simitsis, A., Frantzell, N.: Meshing streaming updates with persistent data in an active data warehouse. IEEE Transactions on Knowledge and Data Engineering 20(7), 976–991 (2008)
21. Sigut, M., Alayón, S., Hernández, E.: Applying pattern classification techniques to the early detection of fuel leaks in petrol stations. Journal of Cleaner Production 80, 262–270 (2014)

22. Stonebraker, M., Çetintemel, U., Zdonik, S.: The 8 requirements of real-time stream processing. SIGMOD Rec. 34(4), 42–47 (2005)
23. Thiele, M., Bader, A., Lehner, W.: Multi-objective scheduling for real-time data warehouses. Computer Science - Research and Development 24(3), 137–151 (2009)
24. United States Environmental Protection Agency. Preventing Leaks and Spills at Service Stations. A Guide for Facilities (2003),
    http://www.epa.gov/region9/waste/ust/pdf/servicebooklet.pdf
25. Vassiliadis, P., Simitsis, A.: Near real time etl. In: New Trends in Data Warehousing and Data Analysis. Springer US (2009)
26. Wu, E., Diao, Y., Rizvi, S.: High-performance complex event processing over streams. In: Proceedings of the 2006 ACM SIGMOD International Conference on Management of Data, SIGMOD 2006, pp. 407–418. ACM, New York (2006)
27. Zdonik, S.B., Stonebraker, M., Cherniack, M., Çetintemel, U., Balazinska, M., Balakrishnan, H.: The Aurora and Medusa projects. IEEE Data Eng. Bull. 26(1), 3–10 (2003)

SOLAP On-the-Fly Generalization Approach Based on Spatial Hierarchical Structures

Tahar Ziouel$^{(\boxtimes)}$, Khalissa Amieur-Derbal$^{(\boxtimes)}$, and Kamel Boukhalfa$^{(\boxtimes)}$

High School of Computer Sciences, Algiers
t_ziouel@esi.dz
USTHB University, Algiers
{kderbal,kboukhalfa}@usthb.dz

Abstract. On-the-fly generalization, denotes the use of automated generalization techniques in real-time. This process creates a temporary, generalized dataset exclusively for visualization, not for storage or other purposes. This makes the process well suited to highly interactive applications such as online mapping, mobile mapping and SOLAP. BLG tree is a spatial hierarchical structure widely used in cartographic map generalization and particularly in the context of web mapping. However, this structure is insufficient in the context of SOLAP applications, because it is mainly dedicated to the geographic information processing (geometric features), while SOLAP applications manage a very important decision information that is the measure. In this paper, we propose a new structure, SOLAP BLG Tree, adapted to the generalizaion process in the SOLAP context. Our generalization approach is based on this structure and uses the simplification operator. Combining the topological aspect of geographical objects and the decisional aspect (the measure).

Our experiments were performed on a set of vector data related to the phenomenon of road risk.

Keywords: On-the-fly map generalization · Hierarchical spatial structures · Spatial data warehouses · SOLAP

1 Introduction

Business intelligence is a major decision-making tool for strategic and daily management of data in the enterprise. It provides essential information in several forms to users (decision makers) so that they can analyze and manage their business by taking effectives decisions. Data warehousing and On Line Analytical Processing (OLAP) are technologies intended to support business intelligence. Indeed, Analysts and decision makers in the enterprise can thus analyze interactively and iteratively multidimensional data at a detailed or aggregated level of granularity through online Analytical Processing tools, OLAP, [1] [2] [3]. Nevertheless, these data may have a geographic component that OLAP systems cannot process due their lack of tools for managing spatial data. A new technology has so, emerged, Spatial OLAP (SOLAP), resulting from integrating GIS technology (Geographic Information System) and OLAP [4] [5].

© IFIP International Federation for Information Processing 2015
A. Amine et al. (Eds.): CIIA 2015, IFIP AICT 456, pp. 279–290, 2015.
DOI: 10.1007/978-3-319-19578-0_23

SOLAP has been defined by [6] *as a visual platform built especially to support rapid and easy spatio-temporal analysis and exploration of data following a multidimensional approach comprised of aggregation levels available in cartographic displays as well as in tabular and diagram displays.*

SOLAP enriches the analysis of classical OLAP systems capabilities in many ways. For instance, providing visual information through maps and interacting with them by formulating queries directly on the cartographic display. Thus, the cartographic component in OLAP systems represents a graphic interface to spatial data warehouses (SDW) which introduce spatial data as subject or analysis axes.

In this context, the analysis of multi-dimensional spatial data often requires navigating through different levels of detail, in order to study the evolution of a phenomenon (fact), and thus allows an effective decision-making. On-the-fly generalization process is therefore well suited to this context, because it can interactively adapt the visualized geographic information to decision-makers needs [7]. However it only addresses the cartographic aspect, at the expense of the decisional one, which is important in multidimensional analysis.

Widely addressed in cartography, on-the-fly generalization, well suited to highly interactive applications such as SOLAP, consists in generating temporary data at different levels of detail from the most detailed level. Different on-the-fly generalization approaches have been developed [8] and classified in two main groups. The first group relies on fast map generalization algorithms that generate coarser levels-of-detail in real-time. [9]. The second group utilizes hierarchical spatial data structures [10] [11]. To the best of our knowledge, no work has proposed a generalization approach for SOLAP, nor the consideration of the decision making aspect (measure) in the generalization process.

In this paper, we propose an on-the-fly generalization approach for SOLAP systems. The approach we propose integrates topographic appearance (distance) and decision-making aspects (measure) for an on-the-fly generalization suited to cartographic experts and decision makers.

The present paper is organized as follows; the next section introduces some research work related to the addressed issue. Section 3 presents a detailed description of the proposed approach. The different steps of our experiments and some results are described in section 4. Section 5 concludes the paper and presents some perspectives.

2   Related Work

Several research work have addressed the generalization for more than three decades [12] [13] [14]. On-the-fly generalization has emerged with the development of highly interactive applications of cartography such as web mapping. The main used operators are selection and simplification [8]. Among research work that have adressed on-the-fly generalization, we can cite [15] [16] carried in the contexte of the European project GiMoDig [17]. The objective of this project is to develop and test methods for providing spatial data to mobile users through real-time generalization. The work presented in [18], combines multiple representation and cartographic generalization and uses an implementation of multi-agent system where each agent was equipped with a genetic patrimony.

Since cartographic generalization creates a hierarchy of levels of detail, it is natural to use hierarchical structures such as tree structures for storage of the geometry (point, line, polygon) of an object in the highest level of detail. This structure is enriched with information that reflect the importance of a hierarchical level, from which, requested levels of detail may be generated. The generalization process is therefore, speeded up with rapid access to the elaborate structures. For each type of spatial data, corresponds an appropriate hierarchical structure that enables interactive and rapid generalization of geographic objects. BLG tree (Binary Line Generalization tree) has been proposed for linear objects [19] [20], it applies the simplication generalization operator that uses a variant of the Douglas-Peucker algorithm [21]; instead of deleting the less important vertices, it stores them in the structure. The GAP tree (Generalized Area partitionning) has been proposed for the selection and fusion of polygons [20] [10] [11]. The Quadtrees have been proposed for point objects point objects, they allow applying the selection, simplification, aggregation and displacement operators [8] [22].

Furthermore, as we have already mentioned in Section 1, and to the best of our knowledge, there are no research work that have addressed integration of generalization in SOLAP. Nevertheless, some work focused on integration of spatial data as dimension or fact in SDW [4] [7].

In this paper, we propose to integrate on-the-fly generalization process in SOLAP, to adapt the level of detail that meets the decision-makers needs. The approach we propose focuses on linear objects that represent rivers, roads, etc. These latters constitute a geographical dimension linked to the phenomenon of road risk that we consider as use case study. BLG tree structure is dedicated to cartographic generalization of linear objects (roads in our case study). However, this structure cannot be efficiently used in decision-making process, because they don't consider the main decisional information in SOLAP, that is *the measure*.

To better understand this problem, we propose the example illustrated in Figure 1. The analyzed map contains six objects with associated measures. As presented in this example, among the objects at the most detailed level , the object C possesses the greatest measure (30), despite its geometric size is not indicative (see figure 1.a). When reducing the scale, the classical generalization process is triggered, considering only the topographic aspect, the object C is imperceptible (see figure 1.b) despite its decision relevance (the greatest measure) compared to the objective of the analysis performed by the decision-makers.

We propose a generalization approach based on a new version of BLG tree adapted to SOLAP called SOLAP BLG tree.

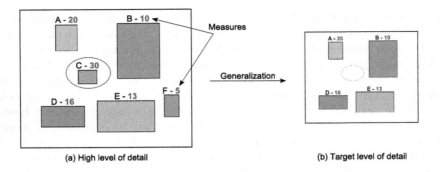

(a) High level of detail   (b) Target level of detail

Fig. 1. Traditional generalization results

3   Proposed Approach

The main objective of our approach is to develop an on-the-fly generalization system adapted to SOLAP applications. This system must be able to combine the decision and cartographic aspects to produce maps adapted to the needs of decision makers. Figure 2 shows the overall architecture of our approach. The spatial data warehouse stores decision data (measures, fact, dimensions, etc.) and cartographic data. The latter represented in a single level of detail (the highest one). When the user sends his request, the result is extracted from the stored data. It does not necessarily reflect the level of detail requested by the decision maker, therefore an on-the-fly generalization process is necessary to adapt this result to the expressed need.

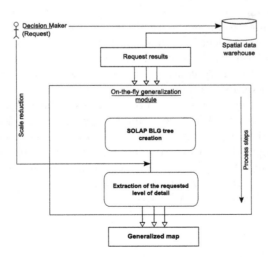

Fig. 2. Global architecture of our approach

The generalization process that we propose is based on SOLAP BLG tree structure. A set of parameters related to the decision aspect is integrated to the structures including the importance function, aggregation etc. All these concepts are described as in the following sections.

3.1   SOLAP BLG Tree

The creation of the SOLAP BLG tree revolves around two main steps: (1) the attribution of an importance value to each point of the polyline and (2) Creating the Hierarchy considering the importance of the points. Indeed, a polyline object (road, river, etc.) consists of a set of points (vertices). SOLAP BLG tree stores these points in a hierarchical structure. Each node of the structure consists of a point of the polyline along with its importance value elaborated by the following function: the importance $I(p)$ for each point p will be determined according to its distance $D(p)$ and its associated measure $M(p)$ as follows: $I(p) = f(D(p), M(p))$. This function can be described by the sum of its cartographic importance (distance) and its decisional importance (measure):

$$I(p) = D(p) + M(p) \tag{1}$$

The distance $D(p)$ is the orthogonal distance between the segment connecting the two end points and the point p of the polyline. $M(p)$ represents the measure at the point p. A node in the structure is created to represent a point p_i, which importance value is $M(p_i)$.

The polyline (p_1, p_n) will be processed as follows: If the node root is represented by p_k (a point on the polyline) having the highest importance value, the creation of other nodes follows an iterative process addressing all the points of the segments $[p_1, p_k]$ and $[p_k, p_n]$. To illustrate this process, we propose the following example on road risk analysis; we focus on the number of accidents recorded on road segments connecting ten cities represented by c_1 to c_{10} points (see Figure 3). Each segment carries a measure that represents the number of accidents reported on the segment connecting city c_i to city c_{i+1}.

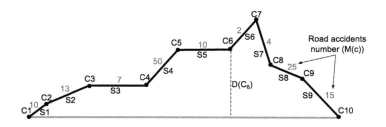

Fig. 3. Polyline (road) representation in SOLAP

We emphasize that in this case, the measures are associated with road segments, or the process requires their transposition to the endpoints constituting these segments. To do this we propose that the measure of each point p_i is determined by the maximum value of the measure of the segments to which the point pi belongs: Let $M(p_i)$ be the measure at point p_i.

$$M(p_i) = Max(M([p_{i-1}, p_i]), M([p_i, p_{i+1}])$$

Furthermore, the values of the measures and distances such as identified have different domains. Indeed there is a significant difference between these two parameters. A normalization step is thus necessary, in order to make the values comparable to each other. To do this we will restrict values between 0 and 1. For each value V of a measure or a distance, its normalized value V' is calculated as follows:

$$V' = \frac{V - V_{min}}{V_{max} - V_{min}} \tag{2}$$

Thus, the BLG structure of the original polyline depicted in figure 3 is as shown in figure 4.

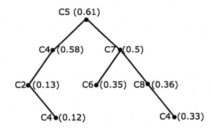

Fig. 4. The built SOLAP BLG tree structure

3.2   Proposed Generalization Process

The on-the-fly generalization process adapted to SOLAP context is guided by the SOLAP BLG tree structure according to the method described below.

Once these structures built, they are saved in a session work. When navigating between the different levels of detail, the on-the-fly generalization process is triggered to retrieve only the visible points in the required level of detail. The selection of these points is performed by comparing the importance values previously stored with a threshold value. The latter is determined by the visualization scale and other cartographic parameters that require the intervention of an expert cartographer. In the context of this work we used experimentally determined thresholds. Indeed, the threshold determines the tree traversal depth, by selecting only the nodes whose relevance value is greater than the threshold.

Measures Aggregation. The measures associated with the different objects are subject to an aggregate function that determines the measures of the resulting objects. This maintains the importance of the decision-making aspect of the different requested levels of detail. This aggregation function is developed according to the analyzed fact. For example for the analysis of the road risk phenomenon, the proposed aggregation function is the sum function, to preserve the information on the total number of accidents on the generalized object.

To aggregate polylines measures, we propose the creation of a data structure, containing the values of the measures associated with the different segments constituting the initial polyline depicted in Figure 3 as shown in the example of table 1.

Table 1. Data structure dedicated to measures storage

Segment	S1	S2	S3	S4	S5	S6	S7	S8	S9
Measure	10	13	7	50	10	2	4	25	15

During the generalization with the BLG tree, we obtain a new polyline where the segments S_i to S_k are removed and replaced by a new segment formed by the first point of S_i and the last point of S_k, to evaluate the measure associated with this new segment, one can read the above table and sum the measures corresponding to the segments from S_i to S_k.

To illustrate this process we will use the polyline shown in Figure 5, in each segment we took the values of measures in accordance with the table above. After simplification of the polyline we get two segments formed by the points C_1, C_5 and C_{10}, the points C_2 through $C4$ are deleted along with the points C_6 through C_9. The measure associated with the new segment $[C_1, C_5]$ represents the sum of the measures contained in the table (measure of the segments S_1 through S_4).

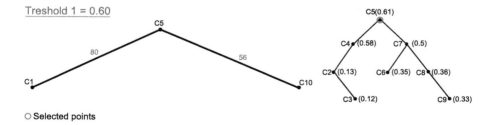

Fig. 5. SOLAP BLG tree generalization results

It is therefore clear that the displayed map will be simplified in order to highlight the information requested by the query.

4   Experimentation

The validation of our approach involves the construction of the proposed spatial structure SOLAP BLG tree used in in the implemented generalization process. We choose the road risk as a case study given its socio-economic impact worldwide. According to statistics from the World Health Organization [23], the road causes each year more than 1.2 million deaths and between 20 to 50 million wounded. In a previous work, we addressed this phenomenon by incorporating spatial information [24] [25].

Our tests are performed on vector spatial data. We used multiple softwares and hardawre ressources to implement our generalization prototype : (1) Oracle 11g Enterprise Edition as DBMS (Management System Database) via its component Oracle Spatial. (2) Oracle MapViewer for viewing the map of the analyzed area. (3) Oracle Weblogic Server on which MapViewers components are deployed. (4) Oracle Map Builder was used to load the geographical data in the DBMS and the construction of the map. (5) Oracle JDeveloper tool as a code editor.

Our experiments were performed on a data set that represents the road theme of Dar El Beida municipality in Algiers enriched by different measures representing the number of accidents recorded on the considered roads (Figure 6).

4.1   SOLAP BLG tree Test

To test the SOLAP BLG tree, we selected a road in Dar El Beida municipality. This road is shown in red in Figure 6. It includes 28 segments each one having a measure. Our generalization system simplifies this road at smaller scales, taking into account the decision aspect (measures).

Fig. 6. Road network of Dar El Beida and the selected road

Figure 7 illustrates a detailed representation of the selected route; segments with the highest number of accidents are highlighted.

The SOLAP BLG tree corresponding to the selected route is shown in Figure 8. The root node contains the point p_{14}, which has the highest importance value. Points stored in the top levels are the points having the highest importance values.

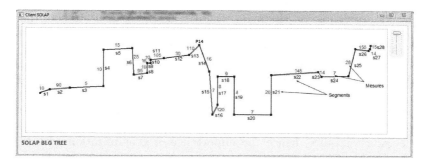

Fig. 7. Detailed description of the selected raod

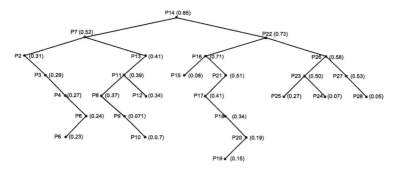

Fig. 8. SOLAP BLG tree corresponding to the selected road

Following the proposed approach, the generalization of the selected road allows to restore only the segments points visible at the required scale. From a more detailed scale, we can analyze the results obtained at different scales (see Figure 5). For example in scale 1: 5000 all relevant segments road except the

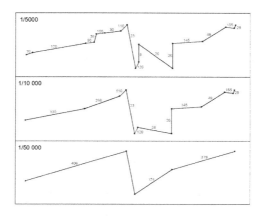

Fig. 9. Generalization results guided by SOLAP BLG tree

segment $S2$ are visible on the map, whereas, at the scale 1: 10,000, there are only four relevant segments and at the scale 1: 50,000 relevant segments are no longer visible.

Figure 10 shows a comparison between the results of the generalization with SOLAP BLG as part of this work and the results of the generalization with the classic BLG tree. We can see that at the same scale 1: 10 000, relevant road segments are visible in the case of SOLAP BLG tree (segments S13, S16, S22 and S26), while they are no longer in the case of classical BLG tree, despite their decision relevance, hence the importance of generalization with SOLAP BLG tree in the SOLAP context.

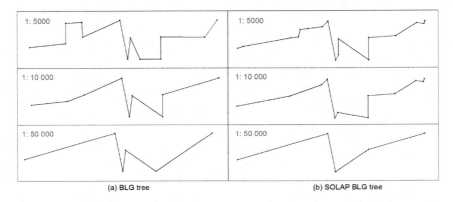

(a) BLG tree   (b) SOLAP BLG tree

Fig. 10. Comparaison between the results of generalization by the SOLAP BLG tree and the BLG tree

5   Conclusions and Future Issues

This paper presented an on-the-fly generalization approach adapted to SOLAP applications. This process is intimately linked to the highly interactive applications in cartography such as web mapping, mobile mapping and SOLAP applications. But this latters, require the simultaneous consideration of cartographic and decisional aspects by integrating the measure in the process.

Our proposed approach is based on SOLAP BLG tree, it consists on adapting BLG tree structure, initially dedicated to cartographic generalization, to SOLAP. It focuses on linear objects (roads in our case study) and integrates the measure in order to adapt the level of detail that meets the decision-makers needs.

To validate our approach, we chose the road risk phenomenon as analysis subject, this is particularly due to its worldwide socio-economic impact. In addition, the use of map in the analysis of such phenomenon is of major interest for decision-makers because it is closely related to geographic information represented by the road object and the locality to which it belongs. In our experiments, we have highlighted the contribution of the proposed structure in the context of SOLAP through the various implemented functions such as importance function, and whose application has allowed preserving measures while providing cartographic perceptibility.

As future issues, we suggest : (1) improving the current solution by adapting the other generalization operators (as is smoothing, displacement, typification, exaggeration, etc.) to SOLAP applications. This will allow generating a better quality of maps and hence, improve the decision making process. (2) Adapt the generalization process to SDW by using another generalization approach, for example, the one, based on rapid generalization algorithms and (3) elaborate a comparative study between the implemented approaches according to some defined criteria in order to assess their effectiveness in a given context of use.

References

1. Chaudhuri, S., Dayal, U.: An overview of data warehousing and olap technology. ACM Sigmod Record 26(1), 65–74 (1997)
2. Kimball, R., Ross, M., et al.: The data warehouse toolkit: the complete guide to dimensional modelling. Wiley, New York (2002)
3. Thomsen, E.: OLAP solutions: building multidimensional information systems. John Wiley & Sons (2002)
4. Rivest, S., Bédard, Y., Proulx, M.J., Nadeau, M., Hubert, F., Pastor, J.: Solap technology: Merging business intelligence with geospatial technology for interactive spatio-temporal exploration and analysis of data. ISPRS Journal of Photogrammetry and Remote Sensing 60(1), 17–33 (2005)
5. Malinowski, E., Zimányi, E.: Advanced data warehouse design: from conventional to spatial and temporal applications. Springer Science & Business Media (2008)
6. Bédard, Y.: Spatial olap. In: Forum Annuel sur la RD, Géomatique VI: Un Monde Accessible, pp. 13–14 (1997)
7. Bimonte, S., Bertolotto, M., Gensel, J., Boussaid, O.: Spatial olap and map generalization: Model and algebra. International Journal of Data Warehousing and Mining (IJDWM) 8(1), 24–51 (2012)
8. Bereuter, P., Weibel, R.: Algorithms for on-the-fly generalization of point data using quadtrees. In: Proceedings AutoCarto 2012 (2012)
9. Weibel, R., Burghardt, D.: Generalization, on-the-fly. In: Encyclopedia of GIS, pp. 339–344. Springer (2008)
10. van Oosterom, P., Meijers, M.: Towards a true vario-scale structure supporting smooth-zoom. In: Proceedings of the 14th ICA/ISPRS Workshop on Generalisation and Multiple Representation, Paris, vol. 48 (2011)
11. van Oosterom, P., Meijers, M., Stoter, J., Šuba, R.: Data structures for continuous generalisation: tgap and ssc. In: Abstracting Geographic Information in a Data Rich World, pp. 83–117. Springer (2014)
12. Sarjakoski, L.: Conceptual models of generalisation and multiple representation. In: Generalisation of Geographic Information: Cartographic Modelling and Applications. Elsevier, Amsterdam (2007)
13. Gaffuri, J.: Généralisation automatique pour la prise en compte de thèmes champ: le modèle GAEL. PhD thesis, Université Paris-Est (2008)
14. Stanislawski, L.V., Buttenfield, B.P., Bereuter, P., Savino, S., Brewer, C.A.: Generalisation operators. In: Abstracting Geographic Information in a Data Rich World, pp. 157–195. Springer (2014)

15. Lehto, L., Sarjakoski, L.T.: Real-time generalization of xml-encoded spatial data for the web and mobile devices. International Journal of Geographical Information Science 19(8-9), 957–973 (2005)
16. Foerster, T., Lehto, L., Sarjakoski, T., Sarjakoski, L.T., Stoter, J.: Map generalization and schema transformation of geospatial data combined in a web service context. Computers, Environment and Urban Systems 34(1), 79–88 (2010)
17. GiMoDig: Geospatial info-mobility service by real-time data-integration and generalisation (2001)
18. Lejdel, B., Kazar, O.: Genetic agent approach for improving on-the-fly web map generalization. CoRR (2012)
19. Van Oosterom, P.: The reactive-tree: A storage structure for a seamless, scaleless geographic database. In: Autocarto-Conference. ASPRS American Society for Photogrammetry and Remote Sensing, vol. 6, pp. 393–393 (1991)
20. Van Oosterom, P.: Variable-scale topological data structures suitable for progressive data transfer: The gap-face tree and gap-edge forest. Cartography and Geographic Information Science 32(4), 331–346 (2005)
21. Douglas, D.H., Peucker, T.K.: Algorithms for the reduction of the number of points required to represent a digitized line or its caricature. Cartographica: The International Journal for Geographic Information and Geovisualization 10(2), 112–122 (1973)
22. Bereuter, P., Weibel, R.: Real-time generalization of point data in mobile and web mapping using quadtrees. Cartography and Geographic Information Science 40(4), 271–281 (2013)
23. Bencherif, H., Boubakour, F., Belkacem, N.: Les accidents de la route dans les médias de masse en algérie. du traitement de l'information à sa diffusion. Communication Information Médias Théories Pratiques 30(1) (2012)
24. Amieur, K.D., Frihi, I., Boukhalfa, K., Alimazighi, Z.: De la conception d'un entrepôt de données spatiales à un outil géo-décisionnel pour une meilleure analyse du risque routier (2013)
25. Derbal, K., Ibtissem, F., Boukhalfa, K., Alimazighi, Z.: Spatial data warehouse and geospatial decision making tool for efficient road risk analysis. In: 2014 1st International Conference on Information and Communication Technologies for Disaster Management (ICT-DM), pp. 1–7. IEEE (2014)

QoS-Aware Web Services Selection Based on Fuzzy Dominance

Amal Halfaoui$^{(\boxtimes)}$, Fethallah Hadjila, and Fedoua Didi

Computer Science Departement,
Tlemcen University, Algeria
{a_halfaoui,f_hadjila,f_didi}@mail.univ-tlemcen.dz
http://www.univ-tlemcen.dz/

Abstract. The selection of an appropriate web service for a particular task has become a difficult challenge due to the increasing number of web services offering similar functionalities. Quality of web services (QoS) becomes crucial for selecting web services among functionally similar components. However, it remains difficult to select an interesting Web services from a large number of candidates with a good compromise between multiples QoS aspect. In this paper, we propose a novel concept based on dominance degree to rank functionally similar services. We rank Web services by using a fuzzification of Pareto dominance called Average-Fuzzy-Dominated-Score($AFDetS()$). We demonstrate the effectiveness of the $AFDetS$ through a set of simulations by using a real Dataset.

Keywords: Web service selection · dominance · Skyline · Ranking · QoS

1   Introduction

Nowadays, an increasing number of Web services is published and accessible over the web, they are designed to perform a specific task, which essentially consists of either altering the word state (e.g.,an on line shopping service) or returning some information to the user (e.g.,news Web service).

As the Web is populated with a considerable number of Web services, there exists a large number of service providers competing to offer the same functionality, but with different Quality Of Service(QoS) such as response time, price, etc. Consequently, QoS is thus a crucial criterion to select among functionally similar Web services.

Example. Consider a Web service for sending SMS, there are many Web services providing this functionality (e.g., Click Send, Inteltech, Etc.), but with different QoS. Table1 provides such functionality along with real QoS parameters taken from the publicly available Quality of Web services data.[1] Web services were obtained by using the keyword SMS which represents the tag associated to the functionality of the desired Web services. Each Web service has four *QoS* parameters q_1, q_2, q_3 and q_4, says respectively Response Time, Throughput (i.e.,Total

---

[1] http://www.uoguelph.ca/~qmahmoud/qws

© IFIP International Federation for Information Processing 2015
A. Amine et al. (Eds.): CIIA 2015, IFIP AICT 456, pp. 291–300, 2015.
DOI: 10.1007/978-3-319-19578-0_24

Table 1. A set of Sending SMS Web Services

Service provider		operation	$q1(ms)$	$q2$(hits/sec)	$q3(\%)$	$q4(\%)$
S_1	acrosscommunications.com	SMS	113.8	5.2	81	84
S_2	sjmillerconsultants.com	SMS	179.2	0.7	65	69
S_3	webservicex.net	SendSMS	1308	6.3	67	84
S_4	webservicex.net	SendSMSWorld	3103	5.3	79.3	91
S_5	smsinter.sina.com.cn	SMSWS	751	6.8	64.3	87
S_6	sms.mio.it	SendMessages	291.07	5.2	53.6	84
S_7	www.barnaland.is	SMS	436.5	4.5	43.2	84
S_8	emsoap.net	emSoapService	424.54	4.3	11.9	80

Number of invocations/period of time) Reliability(Ratio: number of error messages/total messages) and Best Practices (the respect of the specifications). To select an adequate Web service, users need to examine all of them manually. The user may also face difficulties in balancing between different quality metrics. The skyline presents a good solution for reducing the number of candidate Web services [1],[2] and simplifying the process of selection as it overcomes the major limitation of the current approaches that require users to assign weights over different QoS attributes. The skyline is a subset of Web services that are not(Pareto) dominated by any other Web service. A Web service S_i is said to Pareto domine another Web service S_k if and only if S_i is better than or equal to S_k in all QoS parameters and better than S_k in at least on one QoS parameter.

According to our example (Table1), the service S_1 dominates S_6,S_7,S_8. Services S_1,S_3,S_4,S_5 belong to the skyline and they are no comparable between them. We can remark that computing skyline reduce the candidates services, in our example we eliminates 50% of the candidate services. However, it remains a challenge to compute skylines in high dimensional data [3],[4]. In addition to that, on the report of [5] the authors show that the skyline may lose some interesting Web services like S_6 which is dominated by S_4 while S_4 is the worst service in term of response time, however S_6 has a good response time and is closer to S_4 on the other QoS parameters.

Motivated by this, we propose an extension of Pareto dominance relationship called Averaged-Fuzzy-Dominated-score $AFDetS()$ to associate a score to each service and rank them, We also propose a comparison between the dominated-score $AFDetS$ and Dominating score used in [5] and confirm that the use of the Dominated score is more interesting than the Dominating score in Ranking service, this fact is also confirmed in [19]. The rest of the paper is organized as follows. In the next section, we discuss related work. In Section 3, we provide the formal definition of $AFDetS$ and show it application on our example Table1. Section 4 presents the results of our experimentation. Finally, section 5 gives conclusions and an outlook on possible continuations of our work.

2   Related Work

A lot of efforts have been devoted to the problem of QoS-aware Web service selection. Some of them use the linear programming technique [7], [8]. Linear programming techniques are used in [7] to find the optimal selection of component services and gives an extensible model to evaluate the QoS parameters, Linear programming techniques are extended in [8] to include local constraints. Others work use combinatorial model and graph model [9] where the authors use heuristic algorithm to solve the problem of service selection with multiple QoS constraints. In [10] the authors present a selection algorithm to evaluates multiples QoS based on an ontology. Nevertheless, the majority of these approaches are more suitable for limited number of Services(the selection process has an exponential space complexity) and limited number of QoS, especially when the users has to assign weights on QoS attributes.

In recent research, the skyline paradigm is introduced as a good and efficient mechanism to reduce the number of service candidates and simplify the process of selection. The idea of skyline comes from the old research like contour problem, maximum vector and convex hull and was introduced into databases by Borzsonyi [11] who develops three algorithms: BNL, DC and B-tree, this leads to develop and ameliorate several other algorithms like SFS [12], SaLSa [13], Zorder, [14] and NN[3]. Some of these algorithms exploit index structures like [14],[3] to enhance the skyline computation process. However, the size of skyline increases under a high number of QoS and sometimes privileges Web services with bad compromise between QoS.

To handle the problem of large skyline, some works combine the advantage of the skyline and ranking and define variants of skyline like [1],[15],[16] and [17]. In [15] the authors present skyline frequency concept which is the number of subspaces where a point p is skyine, however this lead to calculate skyline of all subspaces and results in a hight computational time, further more authors introduce an approximate algorithm to reduce the computation space. In [1] Chan et al. present the notion of k-dominance which relax the pareto dominance to a subset of k parameters, however There exists cyclic dominance relationship (CDR) which leads to the loss of skylines in addition k-dominance often returns an empty set. In [17] lin et al. propose top-*krepresentative* skyline but this method is more suitable for anti-correlated data [18] in addition to that, k-representative skyline is considered as NP-hard for more than three dimensional dataset. In [16] the authors present the skyline graph which maps the dominance of different skyline subspaces into a weighted directed graph and use link-based techniques to rank skyline, however, the problem of dominance on a large space is still solved. These approaches rely on Pareto dominance relationship thus, they don't consider or privilege services with a good compromise between parameters, this drawback can be solved by the fuzzification of Pareto dominance in order to rank incomparable services.

The Fuzzy dominance was used in databases community like [20] the authors show the goal of fuzzification of the concept of Pareto dominance and it application in Evolutionary Multiobjectif Optimization. Other works use this principle and applied it in Genetic or particle Swarm Algorithm. In service computing community, [5] use the fuzzy-dominance and propose the α-dominance to rank Web service based on QoS parameters and associates the fuzzy-dominating score to Web services.

Like mentioned in [20] the measures between two vectors a, b "a dominates b by degree α" and "a is dominated by b to degree α" is not symmetric, In addition to that, in [19] the authors demonstrates that the use of the dominated measure is more efficient in selecting the top-k services than the dominating measure. Our work is close to [5]. However, [5] use fuzzy-dominating relationship to compare the services instead of use fuzzy-dominated measure in ranking services. According to these observations, we define the Fuzzy Dominated relationship $Fdet$ and the Average Fuzzy dominated Score $AFDetS()$. The next section presents the definition of this concept and it utilization in our context.

3   Problem Formalization

In this section, we are going to study the fuzzification of the Pareto dominance relation , and show it application on our example (Table1). To allow for a uniform measurement of Web Services, we first normalize the different QoS value in the range [0,1].

3.1   Normalization of QoS Parameters

let be S a set of similar functionally services $S = S_1, .., S_n$. Suppose that we have R quantitative Q_oS values for a service S_i. we use the vector $Q(S_i) = \{Nq_1(S_i), .., Nq_r(Si)\}$ to represent the Q_oS attributes of a service S_i where the function $Nq_k(S_{ij})$ represent the k-th Normalized quality attribute of S_i. We convert the negative attributes(time, cost) into positive attributes by multiplying their values by -1 so that the higher value is the higher quality. We normalize the different QoS values in the range $[0, 1]$, as follow :

$$Nq_k(S_i) = \frac{q_k(S_i) - Qmin(q_k)}{Qmax(q_k) - Qmin(q_k)} \tag{1}$$

Where $Nq_k(S_{ij})$ is the normalized QoS value of the Web service S_{ij} on the QoS parameter q_k and $Qmin(q_k)$ (resp.$Qmax(q_k)$) is the minimum (resp. maximum) value of the QoS parameter q_k. Table2 shows the QoS values of Web services example of Table 1 after normalization.

3.2   Fuzzification of Pareto Dominance Relation

Services of the same functionality differ only in term of Qos. Like mentioned above, the skyline consists of the set of points which are not pareto dominated by any other.

Table 2. Web Services with Normalized QoS

Web service	$Nq1$	$Nq2$	$Nq3$	$Nq4$
s1	1	0.74	1	0.68
s2	0.98	0	0.77	0
s3	0.60	0.92	0.80	0.68
s4	0	0.75	0.98	1
s5	0.79	1	0.76	0.82
s6	0.94	0.74	0.60	0.68
s7	0.89	0.62	0.45	0.68
s8	0.90	0.59	0	0.50

Definition 1 (*Pareto Dominance.*) *Let S_i and S_j be two Web services, Given a set of d QOS parameters $Q = \{q_1, ..., q_d\}$, We say that S_i dominates S_j denoted by $S_i \succ S_j$, iff $\forall q_k \in Q$, $q_k(S_i) \geq q_k(S_j)$ and $\exists q_t \in Q$, $q_t(S_i) > q_t(S_j)$.*

Pareto dominance does not differentiate between Web services with good compromise and those with bad compromise, to clarify this, let us return to our example (Table2) and consider S_4 and S_5, in fact neither S_4 dominates S_5 nor S_5 dominates S_4, the two services are incomparable and belong to the skyline because S_4 is better than S_5 in q_3 and q_4, and S_5 is better than S_4 in q_1 and q_2. However we can consider that S_5 is better than S_4 since $q_1(S_5) = 0.79$ is much higher than $q_1(S_0) = 0$. In addition to that, $q_3(S_5) = 0.76$ and $q_4(S_5) = 0.82$ are almost close to (respectively) $q_3(S_4) = 0.98$ and $q_4(S_4) = 1$. For this reason, it is interesting to fuzzify the Pareto dominance. The goal of the fuzzification of Pareto dominance is to allow a practically usable numerical comparison between two service and express the extent to which a Web service (more or less) is dominated by another one.

To compute the Fuzzy dominance degrees it's important to distinguish between the measure of two concepts : the dominating score and the dominated Score between two service S_i and S_j. The first one express the degree to which S_i dominates S_j and the second express the degree to which S_i is dominated by Sj and the measure of dominance is not symmetric. We will use in our work the concept of dominated relation. We define bellow the fuzzification of the dominated relation.

Definition 2 (*Fuzzy-Dominated Score.*) *let be S a set of functionally similar services, S_i and $S_j \in S$. Let $Q = \{q_1, ..., q_d\}$ be a vector of d QoS parameters. First we define the monotone comparison function $\mu_{\varepsilon,\lambda}$ to express the degree to which u is dominated by v, where u represent $q_k(s_i)$ and v represent $q_k(s_j)$ as follow:*

$$\mu_{\varepsilon,\lambda}(u,v) = \begin{cases} 0 & if\ (u-v) \geq \varepsilon \\ |u-v-\varepsilon|\ /\ |\lambda+\varepsilon| & if\ \lambda+\varepsilon \leq (u-v) < \varepsilon \\ 1 & if\ (u-v) < \lambda+\varepsilon \end{cases} \tag{2}$$

Where $\varepsilon, \lambda \in [-1, 0], \varepsilon + \lambda \geq -1$
Then, we define the Fuzzy-Dominated score $FDet(S_i, S_j)$ *to express the degree to witch* S_i *is dominated by* S_j *as follow:*

$$FDet(s_i, s_j) = \frac{1}{d} \sum_{k=1}^{d} \mu_{\lambda, \varepsilon}(q_k(s_i), q_k(s_j))) \tag{3}$$

Let us reconsider our example and compare Web services S_4 and S_5 by using $FDet()$, with $\varepsilon = -0.1$ and $\lambda = -0.2$ we have $FDet(S_4, S_5) = 0.5$ and $FDet(S_5, S_4) = 0$ this mean that S_5 is not fuzzy dominated by S_4 and is little more better than S_4. This concept gives a good compromise between QoS. In fact, this is more expressing than S_4 and S_5 not comparable by Pareto dominance. In what follows, we use the $FDet()$ to rank Web services

Definition 3 (*Averaged-Fuzzy-Dominated-Score.*) *In order to rank a Web service* S_i *in it class* S, *we first, make pairwise comparison with the other services and associate it a score by:*

$$AFDetS(S_i) = \frac{1}{|S| - 1} \sum_{j=1, i \neq j}^{n} FDet(S_i, S_j) \tag{4}$$

Then, we retain service with lower $AFDetS()$ *on a higher ranking position*

The Table3 show the services of our example (Table 1) after computing $AFDetS$ score and ranking with $\varepsilon = 0$ and $\lambda = -0.2$

Table 3. Services'Rank according to $AFDetS()$

Rank Web service	AFDedS()	Nq1	Nq2	Nq3	Nq4
s1	0,071	1	0,74	1	0,68
s5	0,107	0,79	1	0,76	0.82
s6	0,143	0,94	0,74	0,60	0,68
s3	0,25	0,60	0,92	0,80	0,68
s7	0,286	0,89	0,62	0,45	0,68
s4	0,312	0	0,75	0,98	1
s8	0,393	0,90	0,59	0	0,50
s2	0,571	0,98	0	0,77	0

We can observe that the top service is S_1 which is better than the others in q_1, q_2 and has a good value in the other QoS parameters. We remark that services that have some $QoS = 0$ are at the bottom of the ranking. Let us consider S_6 and S_4, according to the result provided by Pareto dominance S_4 belong to the skyline, but S_6 does not, however S_4 have the worst response time(q_1)) and S_6 has a good compromise between QoS parameters. According to (Table3: Fuzzy-Dominated Score)S_4 was downgraded to the Rank 7, On the other hand, the

Service S_6 which has a good compromise between QoS parameters was set up to the 3rd rank.

From this result, we confirm that the use of $Fed()$ can give more interesting results in term of balanced of QoS than the other approaches.

4   Experimental Evaluation

In order to evaluate and prove the effectiveness of our approach, we compare the result of using Fuzzy-Dominated with the Fuzzy-Dominating score. For this purpose, we implement the function fuzzy-dominating proposed in [6] and termed it $AFDingS$ and compare it to our Approach $AFDetS$. All the experiments are conducted on the same software and hardware, which were Intel i3-2365M CPU @ 1.40GHz 4 processors, 4.0GB of RAM, Ubuntu 13.10, Netbeans 7.4. Several simulations have been made by varying the parameters:

- ε, λ,
- d:number of QoS parameter,
- n:number of services of the same class S.

For each simulation we take the Top-5 services generated by the algorithms $AFDetS$ and $AFDingS$ and compare them. Different Services' subsets were taken from the real QoS dataset provided by [23]. The dataset includes informations about 2507 real-world web services. Each service comprise measurement of nine QoS parameters. The service name and its WSDL address are also included in the dataset. We group functionally similar Services into clusters, for example the cluster "sms" (sending sms) contains 30 real services. The cluster "search"(ie. Search Engine Web services such as Google Search,Amazone, etc.) contain 92 services.

a-Varying ε and λ: We present below two scenarios (Table4) and (Table5) by varying ε and λ on a set of 30 services belonging to the class SMS. Each service has 4 QoS parameters.

Table 4. Top-5 Services Rank according to $AFDingS$,$AFDetS()$ with $\varepsilon = 0, \lambda = -0.2$

Top-5 AFDingS			Top-5 AFDetS		
Si	$AFDingS$	$Qos(q_1, q_2, q_3q_4)$	Si	$AFDetS$	$Qos(q_1, q_2, q_3q_4)$
S5	0.566	[0.787, 1.0, 0.758, 0.818]	S12	0.071	[1.0, 0.738, 1.0, 0.682]
S4	0.551	[0.0, 0.754, 0.975, 1.0]	S5	0.107	[0.787, 1.0, 0.758, 0.818]
S12	0.529	[1.0, 0.738, 1.0, 0.682]	S6	0.143	[0.941, 0.738, 0.603, 0.682]
S30	0.423	[0.6, 0.918, 0.797, 0.682]	S30	0.25	[0.6, 0.918, 0.797, 0.682]
S6	0.329	[0.941, 0.738, 0.603, 0.682]	S7	0.286	[0.0, 0.754, 0.975, 1.0]

Table 5. Top-5 Services according to $AFDingS$, $AFDetS()$ with $\varepsilon = -0.1, \lambda = -0.2$

Top-5 AFDingS			Top-5 AFDetS		
Si	$AFDingS$	$Qos(q_1, q_2, q_3, q_4)$	Si	$AFDetS$	$Qos(q_1, q_2, q_3 q_4)$
S4	0.443	[0.0, 0.754, 0.975, 1.0]	S5	0.0	[0.787, 1.0, 0.758, 0.818]
S5	0.421	[0.787, 1.0, 0.758, 0.818]	S12	0.036	[1.0, 0.738, 1.0, 0.682]
S12	0.036	[1.0, 0.738, 1.0, 0.682]	S6	0.107	[0.941, 0.738, 0.603, 0.682]
S30	0.321	[0.6, 0.918, 0.797, 0.682]	S30	0.143	[0.6, 0.918, 0.797, 0.682]
S6	0.223	[0.941, 0.738, 0.603, 0.682]	S7	0.25	[0.892, 0.623, 0.453, 0.682]

We can observe from the results on (Table 4) and (Table 5) that the ranking given by $AFDetS$ is more interesting than the one given by $AFDingS$ even if we vary ε and λ the top-1 is always better according to $AFDetS$. The service S4 (Table 5)is the top-1 according to $AFDing$ while it does not belong to the top-5 according to $AFDetS$ because of its bad first criterion value. We can say that $AFDetS$ favors services with good value in all parameters and discards services with worst values in some QoS parameters even if the others are good.

b-Varying d and n: We present below two scenarios by varying d from 7 to 9 on a set of 92 services belonging to the class search. We fixed $\varepsilon = -0.1$ and $\lambda = -0.2$. The result of the top-5 services provided by $AFDtingS$ and $AFDetS$ approach are shown in (Table6) and (Table7).

Table 6. Top-5 Services($AFDingS()$ Vs. $AFDetS()$) with $d = 7$

	Si	$Score$	$Qos(q_1, q_2, q_3 q_4, q_5, q_6, q_7)$
	S70	0.409	[0.183, 0.904, 0.618, 0.964, 0.767, 1 , 0.815]
	S30	0.388	[0.164, 0.904, 1 , 0.964, 0.767, 1 , 0.815]
AFDingS	S24	0.385	[0.005, 1 , 0.829, 1 , 0.767, 1 , 0.667]
	S72	0.381	[0.474, 0.795, 0.260, 0.807, 0.767, 0.667, 0.815]
	S16	0.365	[0.003, 1 , 0.419, 1 , 1 , 0.667, 0.111]
	S30	0.005	[0.164, 0.904, 1 , 0.964, 0.767, 1 , 0.815]
	S52	0.006	[0.016, 0.819, 0.955, 0.94, 0.767, 1 , 0.667]
AFDetS	S24	0.006	[0.005, 1 , 0.829, 1 , 0.767, 1 , 0.667]
	S70	0.008	[0.183, 0.904, 0.618, 0.964, 0.767, 1 , 0.815]
	S45	0.022	[0.042, 0.831, 0.382, 0.940, 0.767, 1 , 0.667]

From (Table6), we can observe that the ranking given by $AFDetS$ is more interesting than the one given by $AFDingS$. The top-1($AFDetS$) is the service S30. This latter has better value than the top-1($AFDingS$) on q_3. Moreover, service S30 is close to service S7 on q_1 parameter. We can remark that the service S16 is included into top-5($AFDingS$) while it does not belong to the top-5($AFDetS$) because of its bad values on q_3 and q_7. In fact,it is replaced by service S45 witch has a good compromise between its QoS parameters.

Table 7. Top-5 Services(*AFDingS*() Vs. *AFDetS*()) with $d = 9$

	Si $Score$	$Qos(q_1, q_2, q_3 q_4, q_5, q_6, q_7, q_8, q_9)$
AFDingS	S24 0.397	[0.050, 1 , 0.829, 1 , 0.767, 1 , 0.667, 0.004, 0.958]
	S16 0.366	[0.003, 1 , 0.419, 1 , 1 , 0.667, 0.111, 0.030, 0.358]
	S60 0.344	[0.016, 0.988, 0.955, 1 , 0.333, 1 , 0.259, 0.008, 0.337]
	S55 0.328	[0.179, 0.916, 0.244, 0.976, 0.767, 1 , 0.815, 0.066, 0.800]
	S70 0.318	[0.183, 0.904, 0.618, 0.964, 0.767, 1 , 0.815, 0 , 0.021]
AFDetS	S24 0.006	[0.050, 1 , 0.829, 1 , 0.767, 1 , 0.667, 0.004, 0.958]
	S45 0.018	[0.042, 0.831, 0.382, 0.940, 0.767, 1 , 0.667, 0.030, 0.937]
	S55 0.018	[0.179, 0.916, 0.244, 0.976, 0.767, 1 , 0.815, 0.066, 0.800]
	S52 0.024	[0.016, 0.819, 0.955, 0.940, 0.767, 1 , 0.667, 0.017, 0.105]
	S30 0.027	[0.064, 0.904, 1 , 0.964, 0.767, 1 , 0.815, 0.092, 0.053]

Let us consider now the ranking with $d = 9$ (Table7). The two ranking methods have the same top-1 (service S24). However, the other services given by *AFDetS* are different from those provided by *AFDingS*. The service S16 and the service S70 witch belong to (top-5(*AFDingS*)) are discarded by *AFDetS* from the top-5 because they contains some bad values (close /or equal to 0) on some *Qos* criteria. This two services are replaced by respectively the service S45 and the service S30 by the *AFDetS* approach, we can remark that these two services present a good compromise between their *QoS* parameters.

5 Conclusion

In this paper, we have presented an approach for ranking QoS-based-Web services. We have presented a fuzzification of the Pareto-dominance and introduced the concept *AFDetS* which associates a score to a service according to the Fuzzy dominated relation. We demonstrate that the fuzzy dominated concept can offer an alternative to compare services when they are non comparable with pareto dominance. Experimental results show that the proposed approach is effective in comparison with the Fuzzy Dominating ranking. For future work, we can use this concept for the web service composition.

References

1. Chan, C.-Y., Jagadish, H.V., Tan, K.-L., Tung, A.K.H., Zhang, Z.: On high dimensional skylines. In: Ioannidis, Y., et al. (eds.) EDBT 2006. LNCS, vol. 3896, pp. 478–495. Springer, Heidelberg (2006)
2. Lee, J., You, G., Hwang, S.: Personalized top-k skyline queries in high-dimensional space. Information Systems 34(1), 45–61 (2009)
3. Kossmann, D., Ramsak, F., Rost, S.: Shooting stars in the sky: an online algorithm for skyline queries. In: Proceedings of the 28th International Conference on Very Large Data Bases 2002, pp. 275–286. VLDB Endowment, Hong Kong (2002)

4. Papadias, D., et al.: Progressive skyline computation in database systems. ACM Transactions on Database Systems (TODS) 30(1), 41–82 (2005)
5. Benouaret, K., Benslimane, D., HadjAli, A.: On the use of fuzzy dominance for computing service skyline based on qos. In: ICWS 2011, pp. 540–547 (2011)
6. Benouaret, K., Benslimane, D., Hadjali, A.: A fuzzy framework for selecting top-k Web services compositions. Applied Computing Review (2011)
7. Zeng, L., Benatallah, B., Ngu, A.H.H., Dumas, M., Kalagnanam, J., Chang, H.: Qos-aware middleware for web services composition. IEEE Trans. Software Eng. 30(5), 311–327 (2004)
8. Ardagna, D., Pernici, B.: Adaptive service composition in flexible processes. IEEE Trans. Software Eng. 33(6), 369–384 (2007)
9. Yu, T., Zhang, Y., Lin, K.-J.: Efficient algorithms for web services selection with end-to-end qos constraints. TWEB 1(1) (2007)
10. Wang, X., Vitvar, T., Kerrigan, M., Toma, I.: A qos-aware selection model for semantic web services. In: Dan, A., Lamersdorf, W. (eds.) ICSOC 2006. LNCS, vol. 4294, pp. 390–401. Springer, Heidelberg (2006)
11. Borzsonyi, S., Kossmann, D., Stocker, K.: The Skyline Operator. In: Proceedings of the 17th International Conference on Data Engineering 2001, pp. 421–430. IEEE Computer Society (2001)
12. Chomicki, J., Godfrey, P., Gryz, J., Liang, D.: Skyline with Presorting. In: Proc. 19th IEEE Intl Conf. Data Eng. (ICDE), pp. 717–816 (2003)
13. Bartolini, I., Ciaccia, P., Patella, M.: Efficient Sort-Based Skyline Evaluation. ACM Trans. Database Systems 33(4), 1–45 (2008)
14. Lee, K.C.K., Zheng, B., Li, H., Lee, W.-C.: Approaching the skyline in z order. In: VLDB, pp. 279–290 (2007)
15. Chan, C.Y., et al.: Finding k-dominant skylines in high dimensional space, pp. 503–514 (2006)
16. Vlachou, A., Vazirgiannis, M.: Ranking the sky: Discovering the importance of skyline points through subspace dominance relationships. Data and Knowledge Engineering 69(9), 943–964 (2010)
17. Lin, X., et al.: Selecting stars: The k most representative skyline operator, pp. 86–95 (2007)
18. Alrifai, M., Skoutas, D., Risse, T.: Selecting skyline services for qos-based web service composition. In: WWW, pp. 11–20 (2010)
19. Skoutas, D., Sacharidis, D., Simitsis, A., Sellis, T.: Ranking and clustering web services using multi-criteria dominance relationships. IEEE Trans. on Services Computing (2010)
20. Koppen, M., Vicente Garcia, R.: A fuzzy scheme for the ranking of multivariate data and its application. In: Proceedings of the 2004 Annual Meeting of the NAFIPS (CD-ROM), Banff, Alberta, Canada, pp. 140–145 (2004)
21. Köppen, M., Vicente-Garcia, R., Nickolay, B.: Fuzzy-pareto-dominance and its application in evolutionary multi-objective optimization. In: Coello Coello, C.A., Hernández Aguirre, A., Zitzler, E. (eds.) EMO 2005. LNCS, vol. 3410, pp. 399–412. Springer, Heidelberg (2005)
22. Köppen, M., Veenhuis, C.: Multi-objective particle swarm optimization by fuzzy-Pareto-dominance meta-heuristic. Int. J. Hybrid Intell. Syst. 3(4), 179–186 (2006)
23. Al-Masri, E., Mahmoud, Q.H.: Investigating web services on the world wide web. In: WWW, pp. 795–804 (2008)

Information Technology:
Recommender Systems
and Web Services

A Hybrid Model to Improve Filtering Systems

Kharroubi Sahraoui[1](✉), Dahmani Youcef[2], and Nouali Omar[3]

[1] National High School of Computer Science E.S.I, and Ibn Khaldoun University
Tiaret, Tiaret, Algeria s_kharroubi@esi.dz
[2] Department of Computer Science, Ibn Khaldoun University, Tiaret, Algeria
[3]
dahmani_y@yahoo.fr
[4] Basic Software Laboratory, C.E.R.I.S.T, Ben Aknoun, Algeria
o_nouali@cerist.dz

Abstract. There is a continuous information overload on the Web. The problem treated is how to have relevant information (documents, products, services etc.) at time and without difficulty. Filtering system also called recommender systems have widely used to recommend relevant resources to users by similarity process such as Amazon, MovieLens, Cdnow etc. The trend is to improve the information filtering approaches to better answer the users expectations. In this work, we model a collaborative filtering system by using Friend Of A Friend (FOAF) formalism to represent the users and the Dublin Core (DC) vocabulary to represent the resources "items". In addition, to ensure the interoperability and openness of this model, we adopt the Resource Description Framework (RDF) syntax to describe the various modules of the system. A hybrid function is introduced for the calculation of prediction. Empirical tests on various real data sets (Book-Crossing, FoafPub) showed satisfactory performances in terms of relevance and precision.

Keywords: Recommender systems · Resource description framework · Dublin core · FOAF · Semantic

1 Introduction

The multiplicity of the services offered via the Web excites the Net surfers to expose and communicate an enormous traffic of data of various formats. The gigantic mass of existing information and the speed of its instantaneous production triggers the problem of informational overload. This phenomenon known under the name big data imposes multiple difficulties such as management, storage, the control and the security of circulated data. On the other hand, the access to relevant information in time is a major occupation of the developers and users, in spite of his availability it is lost in the mass. The performances of the existing tools degrade when we handle large volume of data, more precisely the search engines are involved by this phenomenon in terms of recall and precision as well as the process of the indexing. Our work is more particularly listed under filtering information tab, specifically custom filtering in order to submit

© IFIP International Federation for Information Processing 2015
A. Amine et al. (Eds.): CIIA 2015, IFIP AICT 456, pp. 303–314, 2015.
DOI: 10.1007/978-3-319-19578-0_25

the useful information to the users. Many commercial and educational sites are based on the filtering algorithms to recommend their products such as the Amazon, Movielens, Netflix, EducationWorld etc [5]. Filtering systems (FS), known as "recommender systems", have become essential with the increasing variety of web resources such as news, games, videos, documents or others [10]. The majority of the recent FS explores semantic information and share the metadata of the resources in order to improve the relevance factor[8]. Additionally, another type of these systems is based on ontology for conceptualizing and valorising the application domain, which makes it possible to increase their performances [1]. However, FS suffer from some common weaknesses, such as cold start, sparsity and scalability. In our study, we adopted the RDF model to represent all elements of the system with an open and interoperable manner. With the formalism Friend Of A Friend (FOAF), we weighted the attributes of the user profiles in order to gather them by degree of similarity. In addition, the items of system are represented by the Dublin Core vocabulary (DC) in RDF model to describe the web resources formally. These two formalisms that are recommended by W3C ensure interoperability and easy integration of the data. This approach allowed us to avoid focusing the approaches on a specific and closed field, and treats all kinds of resource using the URI and namespace clauses. The rest of the paper is organized as follows, we will briefly review the various forms of FS in section 2. The section 3 presents the details of our proposal. The results of experiments followed by discussions were exposed in section 4. In the end, we conclude our work with a conclusion and perspective.

2   State of the Art

The number of Internet users has now reached 38.8% of the world population in 2013 against 0.4% in 1995 according to statistics provided by ITU (http://www.itu.int/en/ITU-D/Statistics/Pages/stat/default.aspx). On the other hand, resources called commonly items occur at an incredible speed either by users or companies. Current tools are not consistent with this huge volume of data in order to analyze, control or have relevant information at time. The birth of FS is used to manage information overload by filtering [3,8]. Items can be extremely varied DVDs, books, images, web pages, restaurants ... etc. These systems are now increasingly present on the web and certainly will become essential in the future with the continuous increase of data [12]. According to how to estimate the relevance, researchers classify recommendation algorithms into three main approaches: content-based, collaborative and hybrid [4]. In the first approach, the system will support the content of the thematic items "documents" to compare them with a user profile, itself consists of topics explaining his interests, that is to say, the system compares the document themes with those of the profile and decides if the document is recommended or rejected according to the threshold of satisfaction function [17]. In the second approach, also known as social, the system uses the ratings of certain items or users and in order to recommend them to other users through the application of similarity process and without it being necessary to analyze the content of items [2], in this approach, there are two main techniques which builds on memory-based algorithms, that operates a portion or all of the ratings to generate a new prediction [12] and which is founded on the model-based algorithms to create a descriptive model of the user so, estimate the prediction. The collaborative approaches are widely adopted in recommender systems such as Tapestry [4] GroupeLens [15], Amazon, Netflix ... etc. The hybrid methods operate to attenuate the insufficiencies of each of the two previous approaches by combining them in various manners. Recently, a new generation of FS boosted by semantic web formalisms or adaptable to contexts that uses a taxonomies or ontologies [13]. Commonly, these systems have shortcomings that prevent the recommendation process and degrade their performances, like the effect of the funnel where the user does not profited from the innovation and diversity of the items recommended in content-based filtering; the scalability where the system handles a large number of users and items online what makes difficult to predict in time; the sparsity problem, where there's a lack of sufficient evaluations to estimate the prediction well as the problem of the cold start to a user and/or item lately integrated into the system [11]. In this paper, we will extend the filtering systems in an open and interoperable specification, each component of the system is formalized by an appropriate RDF vocabulary. The following section explains the basic concepts of this specification.

3   Proposed Approach

Our study focuses on reducing the sparsity problem through the similarity of items via the values of DC properties, as well as the similarity of users through the values of FOAF properties. The values of properties are heterogeneous type nominal, ordinal, qualitative, etc ., so we have defined several functions of encoding and normalization to convert these properties in a numeric scale. i.e. quantitative values in the range [0-1].

3.1   RDF Specification

Resource Description Framework RDF (http://www.w3.org/TR/2004/REC-rdf-syntax-grammar-20040210/) is a data model for the description of various types of resources (person, web page, movie, service, book etc.). It treats the data and its properties and the relationship between them, in other words it is a formal specification by meta-data, originally designed by W3C, whose purpose is to allow a com-munity of users to share the same meta-data for shared resources. However, an RDF document is a set of triplet ¡subject, predicate, object¿ where the subject is the resource to be described, the predicate is the property of this resource and the object it is the value of this property or another resource. One of the great advantages of RDF is its extensibility through the use of RDF schemas that can be integrated and not mutually exclusive with the use of namespace and URI (Uniform Resource Identifier) concepts [7]. It is always possible to present a RDF document by a labelled directed graph. For example, "the book Semantic

Web for the Working Ontologist written by Dean Allemang on July 5, 2011", in
RDF/XML Syntax: < ?xml version="1.0"? >

```
<rdf:RDF xmlns:ss="http://workingontologist.org/"
xmlns:rdf="http://www.w3.org/1999/02/22-rdf-syntax-ns#"
xmlns:xsd="http://www.w3.org/2001/XMLSchema#"
xmlns:rdfs="http://www.w3.org/2000/01/rdf-schema#">
<rdf:Description rdf:about="http://www.amazon.fr/
Semantic-Web-Working-Ontologist-Effective/dp/0123859654/">
<ss:written_by rdf:resource="http://www.cs.bu.edu/fac/
allemang/"/> </rdf:Description>
<rdf:Description rdf:about="http://www.amazon.fr/
Semantic-Web-Working-Ontologist-Effective/dp/0123859654/">
<ss:hasTitle>SemanticWeb for the WorkingOntologist</ss:hasTitle>
</rdf:Description>
<rdf:Description rdf:about="http://www.amazon.fr/
Semantic-Web-Working-Ontologist-Effective/dp/0123859654/">
<ss:hasDate >July 5, 2011 </ss:hasDate >
</rdf:Description>
</rdf:RDF>
```

Our solution (figure1) based on a modelling in RDF through FOAF and Dublin
core standards,describing the set of the users and items.

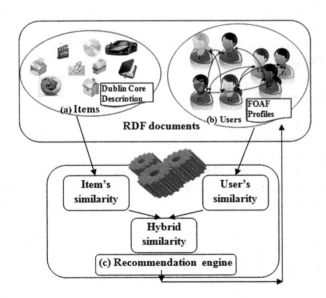

Fig. 1. Overall scheme of the proposal

Thus, in order to keep the collaborative filtering approach we took into account the feedback of the users in the process of computing similarity, moreover we used a hybrid function to define the prediction value. To facilitate the integrity and interoperability, all the documents are represented in RDF/XML notation.

3.2 Item's Representation

A social FS consists of resources items, the users profiles and the histories which memorizes the interactions of the users (ratings) about items recommended. We exploited the meta-data of the Dublin core vocabulary as being a standardization description of items, the attributes values of the vocabulary allowed us to calculate the degree of similarity between items and group them into communities.

Dublin Core vocabulary. Dublin Core DC (*http://dublincore.org*) is a set of simple and effective elements to describe a wide variety of web resources, the standard version of this format includes 15 elements of which semantics has been established by an international consensus coming from various disciplines recommended by W3C. These elements are gathered in three categories those which describe the contents (*Cover, Description, Type, Relation, Source, Subject*) and those which describe the individual properties (*Collaborator, Creator, Editor, Rights*) and others for instantiations (*Date, Format, Identifier, Language*), the current version is known as 1.1, validated in 2007 and revised in 2012 by DCMI (Dublin Core Metadata Initiative, (*http://dublincore.org/documents/dces/*).

Description of items. The core of FS is to form properly the communities, according to well determined criteria, in our research we propose to form the items by taking of account the qualifier DC meta-data QDCMI. We define the set of items as follows:
$I = \{(i_1^1, i_1^2, ...i_1^p), (i_2^1, i_2^2, ...i_2^p), ...(i_m^1, i_m^2, ...i_m^p)\}$ where i_k^j represent the jth property for item k which is identified by its URI and is specified by its qualifiers. We group items by degree of similarity, so I_1 the set of properties assigned to the i_k item and I_2 is the set of properties assigned to the i_l item, then the degree of similarity between i_k and i_l by cosine measurement is given by:

$$sim(i_k, i_l) = \frac{\sum_{j \in I_1 \cap I_2} i_k^j \cdot i_l^j}{\sqrt{\sum_{j \in I_1} \left(i_k^j\right)^2} \cdot \sqrt{\sum_{j \in I_2} \left(i_l^j\right)^2}} \quad (1)$$

This similarity value, allows to group items based on their associated DC properties.

3.3 User's Representation

The objective of FS is to deliver the relevant items to the user, because the formation of the communities depends on the attributes values defined in the user profile. Among the most common current practices we adopted the FOAF vocabulary to represent our profiles.

FOAF vocabulary. FOAF (Friend Of A Friend), is an RDF vocabulary for describing in structured manner a person and his relationships (*http://www.foaf-project.org*). However, it can be used to search for individuals and communities: CV, social networks and management of the online communities, online identification and management of participation in projects etc. A file FOAF can contain various information (*name, family_name, dateOfBirth, gender, mbox, Home Page, weblog, interest, accountName, Knows,etc.*). The major advantage of this representation is the ability to integrate other vocabularies as *DC* (describing a resource), *BIO* (to reveal biographical information), *MeNow* (describing the current status of a person), relationship (to see the type of relation maintained with a person).

Modelling of the user profile. Following the very high number of the users in interaction, it is very important to well form the community as a building block in the FS and assuming one for all and all for one. In order to formulate knowledge, we organized the user profile with categories of FOAF properties and each category c_i associated with a weight w_i, thus we defined the FOAF similarity according to n categories registered in profile by:

$$sim_f = w_1 sim_{c1} + w_2 sim_{c2} + ... w_n sim_{cn} \quad \begin{cases} \sum_i w_i = 1 \\ 0 \le w_i \le 1 \end{cases} \quad (2)$$

For our study, we retained three principal categories according to the evolution on the time axis, the first category $c1$, as no evolutionary, includes the non-changeable foaf properties such as: *name, birth_day, gender, mbox,etc.*, the second category in the medium and long term $c2$ contains the foaf changeable properties such as: *account, focus, homepage, phone, skypeID, status, depiction* etc., and the third category $c3$ is defined as category of the preferences includes the foaf properties which interest and preferred by the user like *know, interest, logo, topic_interest, weblog, workplace, based_near, membership* etc. so each class is properly associated with a weight w_i . However, the similarity by foaf properties based on the three categories mentioned above becomes:

$$sim_f = w_1 sim_{c1} + w_2 sim_{c2} + w_3 sim_{c3} \quad (3)$$

Let $u_{f1} = f_1^1, f_1^2, ..., f_1^k$ and $u_{f2} = f_2^1, f_2^2, ..., f_2^k$ the set of the foaf properties of the user u_{f1} and u_{f2} user in a given c_i class, then the value of similarity between these two users by the measurement of cosine that given by the following relation:

$$sim_{ci}(u_{f1}, u_{f2}) = \frac{\sum_{j=1}^{k} f_1^j \cdot f_2^j}{\sqrt{\sum_{j=1}^{k} (f_1^j)^2} \cdot \sqrt{\sum_{j=1}^{k} (f_2^j)^2}} \quad (4)$$

If the value of similarity of two users is close to 1 meant that they belong to the same community.

3.4   Recommendation Engine

The purpose of a FS is to distribute relevant items to users, and avoid a hard task of search in a "big data", the current recommender systems lean on the hybrid approaches which our research is belongs. We have proposed a hybrid similarity based on three types of relationships.

Hybrid similarity. In order to adjust the values of predictions, we conceived a formula to calculate the hybrid similarity, definite as follows:

$$sim_h = \alpha sim_{dc} + \beta sim_f + \gamma sim_r \tag{5}$$

The parameters $\alpha, \beta, \gamma \in [0, 1]$ adjusted by the system administrator according to the efficiency and availability of data.

- sim_{dc}, similarity that using the Dublin Core vocabulary for describing items. By the use of the URI, while identifying item and by exploiting its own metadata allowing reduce the sparsity problem.
- sim_f, similarity which depends on the representation of the profiles by the means of FOAF formalism, in favour of the variety of the fields and the availability of the data in profile, thus, we can overcome the problem of cold start of a new user and to still better forming the communities.
- sim_r, concretize the principal of collaboration through the ratings histories of users to estimate the prediction and to establish the recommendation, so consider their implicit tastes that are often difficult to value by attributes depicted in profile.

Prediction function. Before proceeding to the recommendation task, the system calculates the predicted value of an i item for the active user a, for that, we must select the S most similar items to i_l, then we retain the rating feedback of this user for these S similar items according to the relation:

$$p_{a,l} = \frac{\sum_{m=1}^{s} r_{a,m} \cdot sim_h(i_l, i_m)}{\sum_{m=1}^{s} sim(i_l, i_m)} \tag{6}$$

Where $r_(a, m)$: is the rating value of the current user on the mth similar item. S: size of the most similar items.

Recommendation process . The recommendation process is purely automatic and directly related to the prediction value, so a given item is deemed relevant and deserves to be sent to the user if and only if its predictive value is greater than a given threshold.

$$R_{a,l} = \begin{cases} i_l & recommended \ to \ u_a & if \ p_{a,l} \geq \rho \\ i_l & not \ recommended \ to \ u_a & otherwise \end{cases} \tag{7}$$

4   Experimentation

This section is devoted to the experimental results of our hybrid solution on real data sets. For evaluation and comparison, we implemented item-CF (item based collaborative filtering) approach widely referenced in Collaborative filtering search [6].

4.1   Datasets

For experimental tests we exploited two sets of data:

- $Book - Crossing$ dataset (http://www.informatik.unifreiburg.de/ cziegler/ BX/), a free download dataset for ends of research collected by Cai-Nicolas Zeigler in 2004 from the famous Amazone.com site. The dataset constitutes of 278858 users producing 1149780 votes for 271379 books.
- $foafPub$ dataset (http://ebiquity.umbc.edu/resource/), is a set of data extracted from FOAF files collected during the year 2004, includes 7118 FOAF documents collected from 2044 sites and distributed under the Creative Commons license (v2.0). This set has allowed us to import FOAF properties by SPARQL queries to determine the similarity sim_f.

Our empirical tests require the deployment of a parser to extract FOAF and DC properties through the SPARQL engine of the framework jena 2-6-4 ($https://jena.apache.org/$). Several functions have been defined to aggregate and standardize heterogeneous properties. 80% of the data sets allocated to the training phase and 20% for testing phase.

4.2   Relevance Metrics

To evaluate the method presented in this article, we held a special metric and widely used in the FS, it is MAE, and two other metrics, recall and precision of information retrieval field [16,9].

- MAE: Mean Absolute Error, calculating the mean absolute difference between predictions p_i retained by the system and the real evaluations e_i given by users. This measure is simple to implement and directly interpretable.

$$MAE = \frac{\sum_{i=1}^{N} |p_i - e_i|}{N}$$

- $Precision$: it is the ratio between the number of relevant items returned by the system and the total number of items returned.

$$P = \frac{N_{pr}}{N_r}$$

- $Recall$: it is the ratio between the number of relevant items returned by the system and the total number of existing relevant items in the database.

$$R = \frac{N_{pr}}{N_p}$$

These metrics respectively measures the error, the effectiveness and the quality of FS.

4.3   Results and Discussion

In this section, we discuss the experimental results obtained, for that, we divide the dataset size in two parts, one having a proportion of 80% has dedicated for training phase and the other of proportion of a 20% has dedicated for test phase. From Figure 2, the curves show that the MAE error is minimal in the neigh-

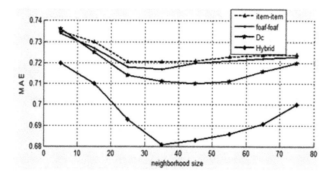

Fig. 2. Comparison of MAE

bourhood range [25-45] and important in outside of this range, it means that as the number of neighbours is less than 25 so there are not enough neighbours to calculate the similarity which lowers the prediction quality, unlike the other side, or the number of neighbours exceeds 45, there are sufficient neighbours, but less similar which degrades prediction quality , this explains that between 25 and 45 there are enough better similar neighbours. Also we observe that the DC curve illustrates a slightly favourable result compared to the FOAF curve, as the items are identified and enriched by descriptions and meta-data with certain stability better than valorising links and subjective opinions between a user's networks. The best result is obtained in Hybrid curve, or the error is reduced to 0.68 for a neighbourhood size of 35, this favourable result is argued by exploiting items implicit information's and estimating attributes of user profiles and links between them such as *see also* or *know* properties, which form a social network on the web and therefore a rich database that reduces the MAE, in addition, taking into account the opinions of users through their notes with respect to the items recommended what leads to a profitable collaboration. Two conclusions can be drawn the benefit of this additional data mass reduces the effect of sparsity as a problem moderating filtering systems, and adequately addresses the cold start problem for a new item. Moreover, the URI clause for the unique resource identification in rdf documents lowers the effect of scalability. In the experiment below, we study the behaviour of our algorithms via the precision and recall metrics. Figure 3 shows a better accuracy rate (up to 73%) for the Hybrid solution, indicates the ability of the system to reject irrelevant items with minimal attribute values.

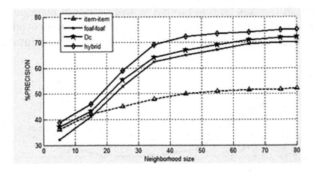

Fig. 3. Precision rate

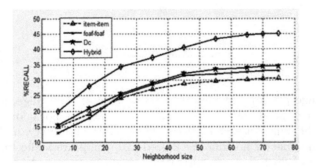

Fig. 4. Recall rate

We also observe that the recall rate (figure 4) which reaches a maximum rate of 45% for the optimal Hybrid solution involves the role of property values of adopted vocabularies to filter only the relevant items.

5   Conclusion and Future Work

Filtering systems are powerful and widely used systems on the web, especially for e-commerce or custom search. Our idea is not to hold closed applications that hide behind a particular data warehouse, but go further, and exploit all kinds of information and to highlight it for integrity, dissemination and interoperability. In order to alleviate the limitations of collaborative filtering systems, we have presented in this paper, a hybrid model based on the FOAF formalism to better appreciate and enrich user profiles via social networks and information networks. The weighted classification that we have defined for the representation yield more adaptable and flexible profiles and still better adjustable, which alleviate the sparsity problem. On the other hand, the use of DC elements to describe items in a standard way leads to the good development of communities and overcome the problem of cold start for a new resource. The notable progress in the results founded by the formal use of meta-data to describe the valued resources and links with a standard and unified structure. Moreover, the union of similarities adopted for the recommendation is considered a balance between using different data sources and therefore increased the quality of prediction. In our opinion, the system model seems to a network of resources in collaboration with a network of properties describing these resources. The adoption of RDF syntax to the representation and implementation ensures openness, sharing and interoperability of all kind of data on the web, thus allows concretizing and developing semantics via these new practices, we think it is important to study the problem of scalability and reduce the computation time through the reduction techniques of the vector space, thus we also plan to still improve the rate of recall by the semantic disambiguation techniques of the users profiles.

References

1. Sieg, A., Moba, B., Burke, R.: Improving the effectiveness of collaborative recommendation with ontology-based user profiles. In: Proceedings of the 1st Interna Workshop on Information Heterogeneity and Fusion in Recommender Systems, HetRec 2010 (2010)
2. Sarwar, B.M., Karypis, G., Konstan, J.A., Riedl, J.: Item based collaborative filtering recommendation algorithms. In: Proceedings of the 10th International Conference on World Wide Web (WWW 2001), pp. 285–295 (May 2001)
3. Goldberg, D., Nichols, D., Oki, B.M., Terry, D.: Using collaborative filtering to weave an information tapestry. Communications of ACM 35(12), 61–70 (1992)
4. Adomavicius, G., Tuzhilin, A.: Toward the next generation of recommender systems: a survey of the state-of-theart and possible extensions. IEEE Transactions on Knowledge and Data Engineering 17(6), 734–749 (2005)
5. Adomavicius, G., Jingjing, Z.: Stability of Collaborative Filtering Recommendation Algorithms. Citeseer (2012), doi:10.1.1.221.7584
6. Hassanzadeh, H., Keyvanpour, M.R.: Semantic Web Requirements through Web Mining Techniques. International Journal of Computer Theory and Engineering 4(4) (August 2012)
7. Konstan, J.A., Riedl, J., Borchers, A., Herlocker, J.L.: Recommender systems: a GroupLens perspective. In: Recommender Systems, Papers from 1998 Workshop. Technical Report WS98-08. AAAI Press (1998)
8. Herlocker, J.L., Konstan, J.A., Terveen, L.G., Riedl, J.: Evaluating collaborative filtering recommender systems. ACM Transactions on Information Systems 22(1) (2004)

9. Abrouk, L., Gross-Amblard, D., Cullot, N.: Community Detection In The Collaborative Web. International Journal of Managing Information Technology 2(4) (2010)
10. Albanese, M., dAcierno, A., Moscato, V.F., Persia, A.: A multimedia recommender system. ACM Transactions on Internet Technology (TOIT) 13(1) (2013)
11. Cuong Pham, M., Cao, Y., Klamma, R., Jarke, M.: A Clustering Approach for Collaborative Filtering Recommendation Using Social Network Analysis. Journal of Universal Computer Science 17(4) (2011)
12. Beam, M.A., Michael, A., Kosicki, G.M.: Personalized News Portals: Filtering Systems and Increased News Exposure. Journalism & Mass Communication Quarterly 91(1), 59–77 (2014)
13. Mohammadnezhad, N., Mahdavi, M.: An effective model for improving the quality of recommender systems in mobile e-tourism. International Journal of Computer Science & Information Technology 4(1) (February 2012)
14. Resnick, P., Iacovou, N., Suchak, M., Bergstrom, P., Riedl, J.: Grouplens: an open architecture for collaborative filtering of netnews. Proceedings ACM (1994)
15. Bahrehmand, A., Rafeh, R.: Proposing a New Metric for Collaborative Filtering. Journal of Software Engineering and Applications 4, 411–416 (2011)
16. Burke, R.: Hybrid recommender systems: survey and experiments. UserModelling and User-Adapted Interaction 12(4), 331–370 (2002)
17. Meyffret, S., Médini, L., Laforest, F.: Confidence on Collaborative Filtering and Trust-Based Recommendations. In: Huemer, C., Lops, P. (eds.) EC-Web 2013. LNBIP, vol. 152, pp. 162–173. Springer, Heidelberg (2013)

Towards a Recommendation System for the Learner from a Semantic Model of Knowledge in a Collaborative Environment

Chahrazed Mediani[1(✉)], Marie-Hélène Abel[2], and Mahieddine Djoudi[3]

[1] Laboratoire des réseaux et des système distribués, Département d'Informatique, Faculté des sciences, Université Ferhat Abbas de Sétif -1-, Sétif, Algérie
`chahrazed_mediani@yahoo.fr`
[2] Sorbonne universités, Université de technologie de Compiègne, Compiègne, France
`marie-helene.abel@utc.fr`
[3] Laboratoire XLIM-SIC et équipe TechNE, UFR Sciences SP2MI, Université de Poitiers, Poitiers, France
`mahieddine.djoudi@univ-poitiers.fr`

Abstract. Collaboration is a common work between many people which generates the creation of a common task. A computing environment can foster collaboration among peers to exchange and share knowledge or skills for succeeding a common project. Therefore, when users interact among themselves and with an environment, they provide a lot of information. This information is recorded and classified in a model of traces to be used to enhance collaborative learning. In this paper, we propose (1) the refinement of a semantic model of traces with indicators calculated according to Bayes formulas and (2) the exploitation of these indicators to provide recommendations to the learner to reinforce learning points with learners, of his/her community of collaboration, identified as "experts".

Keywords: Collaboration · Trace · Indicator · Recommendation system

1 Introduction

The advent of Information and Communication Technologies and particularly Web 2.0 technologies have facilitated learning based primarily on exchanges and resource sharing between learners of the same community (Abel, 2008). On its side, collaborative learning is a process leading to the progressive construction of knowledge. This learning derived from the current of constructivism allows a person to build knowledge from interaction with his surroundings. When these interactions are performed using digital technology, they leave traces. These traces are usually saved in a model of traces (Settouti et al., 2006) and thus made usable for various purposes such as updating a learner model. Taking account the learner activities within a Computing Environment for Human Learning (CEHL) to guide him in his learning is complex. The learner model allows to consider knowledge of all kinds (preferences, motivations, acquired

© IFIP International Federation for Information Processing 2015
A. Amine et al. (Eds.): CIIA 2015, IFIP AICT 456, pp. 315–327, 2015.
DOI: 10.1007/978-3-319-19578-0_26

knowledge or not, mistakes, etc.). As part of our work, we focus on the interactions between learners via a CEHL and with a CEHL to make recommendations to guide learner in their learning. To this end, we have chosen to characterize a number of actions that a learner can perform in a CEHL to define learning indicators to establish recommendations. Learning is the result of personal and collaborative actions. We therefore consider the traces resulting of these two axes.

To do this, we have chosen to refine the collaboration model of traces proposed by (Wang et al, 2014) and illustrated in the environment E-MEMORAe 2.0 (Abel, 2009). So we have introduced measures to estimate some parameters, unmeasurable and unobservable by observable indicators describing the state of the learner activities and the progression of his knowledge when interacting within a community of learners.

In the following, we state our problem before presenting the limitations of existing work related to measures established to make recommendations to learners. We then detail our approach based on a model of traces increased by indicators and its exploitation through a case study before concluding and advancing the prospects for this work.

2   Motivation

The Information and Communication Technologies and the emergence of collaborative learning platforms have enabled the implementation of collaborative CEHL and related issues such as the lack of information on the learner evolution within the community and the state of his knowledge and his activities in his group. This information is needed to measure the contribution of each member in the community and may be useful in defining the responsibilities of each member of the group. This information is also useful for the learner himself; this allows him to have a state of his learning and to allow him to prepare himself for a more relevant evaluation. To remedy these problems, the analysis of the leaner interaction traces with a learning environment has become a research topic that is rapidly evolving.

3   Related Work

In the context of CEHL, trace-based study is not just about how to analyze the traces but also how to complete them and exploit them to improve learning (Ollagnier-Belbame et al., 2007). Among the works that have been done in the context of CEHL to support observation, we can mention the work treating the analyzing of the learner behavior and the characterization of his activities (Georgeon et al., 2006), and those that treat the interpretation of learner interactions with computing environments and with other users (Siebra et al., 2005), (George, 2004). There are several learning environments where interactions between the system and users are traced, we mention, for example: the collaborative learning environment Drew (Dialogical Reasoning Educational Web tool) (Corbel and al., 2002). COLAT tool (Collaboration Analysis Tool) (Avouris et al., 2004) is an independent tool for any learning system for the analysis of collaborative activities from the log files and video recordings. Recently, much work has been done to automate, acquire and distribute knowledge. For example, AdaLearn (Alian Al-Akhras and 2010) is an adaptive learning environment that saves learner responses in his profile to latter allow to direct him through recommendations. (Sani et al., 2012) propose an ontology-based architecture to model the learner and adapt learning styles to learners' profiles. (Li et al., 2012) define an original traces model that distinguishes private actions, individual, collective and collaborative. (Wang et al. 2014) define a method to exploit this model based on TF-IDF method to calculate the index of competence of each learner on a given knowledge. This calculation takes into account the activities of the learner about the knowledge in question, but it does not take into account the acquisition of the knowledge. Under this model, a learner can be proficient in knowledge without being proficient in the knowledge that characterizes it.

4 Our Approach

Our approach is to refine the collaborative model of traces of (Li et al., 2012), and taken up by (Wang et al, 2014), by a number of measures to build indicators on the state of the learner knowledge and the progression of his knowledge within a group in a learning session. Among These parameters: we retain the mastery degree of knowledge represented by a concept. To achieve these goals, we have adopted the following approach: (i) propose a semantic model to measure indicators of the contribution of each student in the group, (ii) estimate the contribution of indicators using Bayesian formulas (Triola 2010), this contribution should take into account the knowledge of the learner and his activities, (iii) propose a set of recommendations to assist the learner in his learning and prepare him for a more appropriate evaluation.

As shown in Figure 1, the architecture of the recommendation system that we propose is composed of two modules operating three models: a trace collection module, a pedagogical content model, a learner model, a collaboration model and a recommendation module. This system is used to collect traces of users and store them in a database of traces. A trace is a time sequence of observed containing all user actions to perform a given task.

The first module of our system treats the collecting primary traces in native format. The second module classifies the primary traces coming from the first module as high-level traces along the trace model (Li, 2013). Depending on the content of traces model and pedagogical content model, algorithms for learning indicators calculations of the learner are applied in the recommendation module. For that, the recommendation system must select good recommendations that guide the user in achieving his learning task. We will illustrate this system of recommendations within the collaborative learning platform E-MEMORAe 2.0 (Abel and Leblanc, 2009).

In the next subsections, we present the principle of the main components of the recommendation system, namely the pedagogical content model, collaborative model, collection of traces and the learner model. The calculation of learning indicators and the recommendation module will be presented in the following sections.

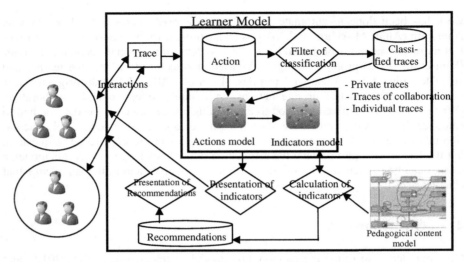

Fig. 1. Architecture of the recommendation system

4.1   Pedagogical Content Model

The content model of learning environments usually consists of a set of elements representing elementary fragments of domain knowledge studied. These elements, often organized in a hierarchy, are named (concepts, notions, knowledge elements, subjects) and they can be of different types. Our content model consists of application ontologies. The application ontology specifies the concepts of a particular application. These concepts represent concepts to be learned of a training unit. A concept is therefore a particular concept that needs to be assimilated by the learner during learning. The concepts are used to index the pedagogical resources treating them. This provides a way to reuse these resources. These concepts are organized in a hierarchy that also represents several types of relationships (specialization and others). Among the ontologies of applications built as part of the E-MEMORAe 2.0 environment: Ontology for the teaching unit "Information Technology". For these applications ontologies, we propose to add the attribute "weight" to the relationship of type "is a" between each concept and its sub concepts (0<= weight<= 1) with the sum of the weights of sub-concepts equal to 1. This value is determined by the responsible of training and represents the degree of contribution of this concept in the acquisition of the father concept (Figure 2).

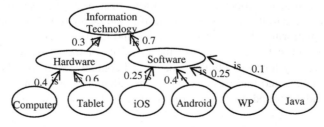

Fig. 2. Part of the application ontology "Information Technology"

4.2   Collaboration Model

Our model allows organizing collaborative spaces for students working in groups on the same problem. Thus forming a work site and exchange for the group and allowing, on the one hand, to each member of the group to access resources (documents and other) for the group and, on the other hand, to memorize his work (documents, ideas, knowledge, solutions, etc.) on the Treaty problem. The MEMORAe 2.0 environment allows each user to choose to access a private space or spaces of groups to which he belongs.
• The private space: space where each user can set his own resources. The content of this space is accessible only by that user.
• Space group: space is only accessible by members of the group and in which they share and exchange resources.

4.3   Collect of Traces

The traces collection is to observe the student in a learning situation and memorize his activities traces to infer the learner model. This collection mode is interesting because it captures the learner interaction the learner without distracting him from his main task. In E-Memorae2.0, these actions are stored in the database traces and classified according to the actions model of the E-MEMORAe 2.0 platform. According to this model, we have three types of traces: Private traces belonging to the private space, traces of collaboration that belong to the space of collaboration and individual traces that are private traces and traces of collaboration. For each type of traces, we have three types of activities that can be conducted by the learner: learning resources consultations (documents), resources creation (conversations, meetings, questions, answers, notes and wikis) and resources additions (documents and annotations).

Example: Figure 3 shows an example of interaction on different concepts, of a group of users using a histogram. Each line represents the collaboration traces of a user for each concept.

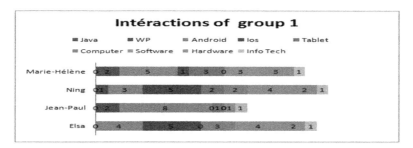

Fig. 3. Example of collaborative interactions in a group

The following table summarizes the actions, of figure 2, performed by members of the group 1. For a given concept, each cell of the table represents the number of actions performed by the learner for each type of activity (C: Consultation, R: Creation,

A: Addition). The number before the parenthesis is the sum of the learner actions for the concept.

Table 1. Summary of users' actions of group 1

	Elsa	Jean-Paul	Ning	Marie-Hélène	Total
Java	0(0C,0R,0A)	0(0C,0R,0A)	0(0C,0R,0A)	0(0C,0R,0A)	**0(0C,0R,0A)**
WP	0(0C,0R,0A)	2(1C,1R,0A)	1(0C,0R,1A)	2(0C,1R,1A)	**5(1C,2R,2A)**
Android	4(1C,3R,0A)	8(4C,3R,1A)	3(1C,1R,1A)	5(4C,1R,0AS)	**20(10C,8R,2A)**
Ios	5(2C,1R,2A)	0(0C,0R,0A)	5(2C,2R,1A)	1(0C,0R,1A)	**11(4C,3R,4A)**
Tablet	0(0C,0R,0A)	1(0C,1R,0A)	2(1C,0R,1A)	3(0C,2R,1A)	**6(1C,3R,2A)**
Computer	3(2C,0R,1A)	0(0C,0R,0A)	2(0C,0R,2A)	0(0C,0R,0A)	**5(2C,0R,3A)**
Software	4(2C,1R,1A)	0(0C,0R,0A)	4(1C,2R,1A)	3(1C,1R,1A)	**11(4C,4R,3A)**
Hardware	2(1C,1R,0A)	1(0C,1R,0A)	2(1C,0R,1A)	3(0C,2R,1A)	**8(2C,4R,2A)**
Info_Tech	1(1C,0R,0A)	1(1C,0R,0A)	1(1C,0R,0A)	1(1C,0R,0A)	**4(4C,0R,0A)**
Total	**19(9C,6R,4A)**	**13(6C,6R,1A)**	**20(7C,5R,8A)**	**18(6C,7R,5A)**	**60(28C,24R,18A)**

C : Consultation, **R** : Creation, **A** : Addition.

4.4   Learner Model

Our learner model is a subset of the pedagogical content model. The pedagogical content is decomposed into a set of elements and the learner model is represented by a set of measurable values associated to these elements. These values vary between 0 (not mastered) and 1 (mastered). The structure of the learner model is the same as the Bayesian network (Figure 4). The elements (concepts and activities) of the learner model become nodes in the Bayesian network. The weight of each element is replaced, for each variable, by a probability to estimate the mastery degree of the learner knowledge. These probabilities vary between 0 (not mastered) and 1 (mastered). The relationship of type "is-a" in the learner model become conditional dependencies between variables forming arcs of the Bayesian network. The elements of knowledge or concepts represent unobservable variables while other elements which are the learning activities used to measure the mastery degree of the learner knowledge (tests, exercises, forums, etc.), represent the observable variables which are added to the Bayesian network.

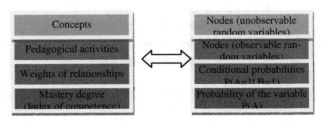

Fig. 4. Relationship between our learner model and a Bayesian network

5   Construction of the Learner Model from Indicators

For a given concept, we aim to measure the degree of mastery of this concept by the learner from the activities related to the concept which he conducted in his group space (contribution by activities) and also from the knowledge acquired by navigating the sub concepts and implementation of activities related to his sub-concepts (contribution by the sub-knowledge). For each concept, we assign a weight P1 to the contribution activities and a weight P2 to the contribution by the sub-concepts. The sum of these weights must be equal to one.

Example: P1 = 0.6, P2 = 0.4.
Each concept is linked to a set of activities, so we can estimate the degree of the learner contribution based on the number of the learner activities carried out in his group. We assign to each type of activity a weight (parameter) which represents the degree of contribution of his activities in the calculation of the mastery degree of this concept by the learner. This setting can distinguish concepts that require a more theoretical activity (consultation) from practical (realization of an exercise, creating a resource). The sum of the weights of the types of activities should be equal to one.

Example: For a given concept, Poids_consultation = 0.2, Poids_création = 0.5 and Poids_addition = 0.3. (These weights can vary from one concept to another).

To realize our contribution model, we use the format of Resource Description Framework (RDF). RDF graph is a model that is used to formally describe Web resources and metadata. Figure 5 shows the RDFS graph of our knowledge model. An ellipse is a class resources and a rectangle represents a property.

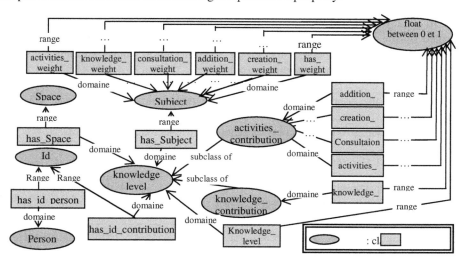

Fig. 5. The knowledge model in the platform E-MEMORAe 2.0

5.1   Indicators Calculation

To measure learning indicators (mastery degree of a concept, degree of contribution by activities, degree of contribution by the sub concepts), of the learner in his space group, we apply Bayesian formula. The Bayesian network is a probabilistic technique that has been developed in the research context to describe the uncertainty of facts in artificial intelligence. Bayesian networks allow easy representation of causal relationships in the learner model. Generally, the learner model information is related to each other. In other words, the learner's knowledge affects each other, for example, motivation to learn, has a direct influence on the ability to perform the task. And as the student model has an hypothetical character, using probabilities, uncertainty is processed. The calculation we retain is based on the following formula:

Consider a partition $A_1, A_2, ..., A_n$ of the set E of events: $A_1 \cup A_2 \cup ... \cup A_n = E$, $A_i \cap A_j = \emptyset$ for $i \neq j$, $P(E) = 1$. For any event B:

$$P(B) = P(A_1) \cdot P(B \mid A_1) + P(A_2) \cdot P(B \mid A_2) + ... + P(A_n) \cdot P(B \mid A_n). \quad (1)$$

$P(B \mid A)$: the conditional probability that event B is true given that the event A is already true. We apply equation (1) to calculate the previous indicators.

The Contribution by the Activities
For a learner i in a space S, the index of the contribution by activities AC(i, j) for a concept j is calculated as follows:

$$AC(i, j) = \sum_{k=1}^{n} P(k) * contribution\_value(k) \quad (2)$$

With n: the number of types of activities, in our case n = 3. $P(k)$: the weight of the type of activity k (consultation, creation or addition), contribution_value(k) : is relative frequency estimated by the ratio between the number of activities of type k performed by the learner in the group and the number of all activities of type k performed by all the members of the group S. contribution_value is either consultation_value, creation_value or addition_value.

Example: for the concept "Android", suppose that: Poids_consultation = 0.2, Poids_création = 0.5 and Poids_addition = 0.3. Using table1, we calculate the contribution by the activities of the members of group 1 for this concept (Table 2).

Table 2. Contributions by the activities of the users of group1 for "Android"

	Consultation_value	Creation_value	Addition_value	Activities_value
Elsa	1/10=0.1	3/8 = 0.375	0/2 = 0	0.1*0.2+0.375*0.5+0*0.3 = 0.1975
Jean-Paul	4/10= 0.4	3/8 = 0.375	1/2 = 0.5	0.4*0.2+0.375*0.5+0.5*0.3 = 0.4175
Ning	1/10 = 0.1	1/8 = 0.125	1/2 =0.5	0.1*0.2+0.125*0.5+0.5*0.3 = 0.2325
Marie-Hélène	4/10 = 0.4	1/8 = 0.125	0/2 =0	0.4*0.2+0.125*0.5+0*0.3 = 0.1425

We calculate the contribution by activities of Marie-Hélène for all the concepts.

Table 3. Contributions by the activities of "Marie-Hélène" for all the concepts

	Java	WP	Android	Ios	Tablet	Computer	Software	Hardware	Info_Tech
Marie-Hélène	0	0.4	0.142	0.075	0.483	0	0.274	0.4	0.05

The Contribution by sub-knowledge .

For a learner i, the index of contribution by sub-knowledge for a concept j KC(i, j) is equal to:

$$KC(i, j) = \sum_{k=1}^{n} P(k) * knowledge\_level(k) \tag{3}$$

n is the number k of the sub-concepts related to the father concept j. P (k): the weight attached to each sub-concept k. (These weights are defined in the ontology of application).

Example: The concept "Android" has no sub concepts thus:

$$KC(Marie\text{-}Hélène, Android) = 0$$

The Global Contribution (Mastery Degree)

Now, the mastery degree or the knowledge level of the learner i on the concept j KL(i, j) is equal to:

$$KL(i, j) = P1 * AC(i, j) + P2 * KC(i, j) \tag{4}$$

P1 and P2 are the weights connected to both contributions (activities_contribution and knowledge_contribution respectively).

Example: The concept "Android" has no sub-concept. So the only contribution for this concept is the contribution by activities (P1 = 1, P2 = 0).

KL(Marie-Hélène, Android) = P1 * AC (Marie-Hélène, Android) + P2 * KC (Marie-Hélène, Android)

$KL_{(Marie\text{-}Hélène, Android)} = 1*0.1425 + 0*0 = 0.1425$

Table 5 summarizes Marie-Hélène mastery levels for high-level concepts.

Table 4. Knowledge levels of "Marie-Hélène" for the sub-concepts

	Java	**WP**	**Android**	**Ios**	**Tablet**	**Computer**
Marie-Hélène	0	0.4	0.142	0.075	0.483	0

Now, we will infer the mastery degree of Marie-Hélène for the concepts Software, Hardware and Information Technology. Suppose, for these concepts, the weight attached to activities P1 = 0.6 and the weight attached to the sub-concepts P2 = 0.4.

$KL_{(Marie\text{-}Hélène, Software)} = P1 * AC_{(Marie\text{-}Hélène, Software)} + P2 * KC_{(Marie\text{-}Hélène, Software)}$

By applying equation (3):

$KC_{(Marie\text{-}Hélène, Software)} = 0.25*0.075 + 0.4*0.142 + 0.25*0.4 + 0.1*0 = 0.159$

Applying equation (4) :

$$KL_{(\text{Marie-Hélène,Software})}=0.6*0.274+0.4*0.159= 0.228$$

Table 5 summarizes Marie-Hélène mastery levels for high-level concepts.

Table 5. Knowledge levels of "Marie-Hélène" for high-level concepts

	Software	Hardware	Information Technology
Marie-Hélène	0.228	0.356	0.119

6   The Recommendation Module

The objective is to generate recommendation knowledge to the learner about his learning path from learning indicators stored in the indicators model. A recommendation R consists of an action proposal to achieve.

$$R = <u, s, c, task, (o_1, o_2, \ldots, o_n)>$$

• u: the traced user.
• s: the workspace.
• c: the concept concerned by the recommendation.
• task: the task we have to recommend the user to do it. It is either consult resources, add resources, create resources or consult other concepts.
• (o1, o2, ..., on): all users of the space s that can help the user u in achieving the task task.

Recommendation Algorithm
    Input: Indicators model, P: Person, S: Space, C: Concept, ε : threshold between 0 and 1/n (n: number of members of the group). RB : Recommandations Base.
    Output: Recommendations Knowledge.

```
Indicators := Search_indicators(A,C,S) in the indicators model.
if AC(P, C) < ε then
  if consultation_value < ε then
    U:= search_all_users(S, 'consultation_value> ε')
    Add(<P,S,C,'consult_resources',U>, RB).
  endif
  if addition_value < ε then
    U := search_all_users(S, 'addition_value > ε')
    Add(<P,S,C,'add_resources',U>, RB).
  endif
  if creation_value < ε then
    U := search_all_users(S, 'creation_value > ε')
    Add(<P,S,C,'create_resources',U>, RB).
  endif
endif
if  KC(C) < ε then
```

```
CO := search_all_sub_concepts(C, 'knowledge_level < ε')
U := search_all_users(S, 'knowledge_level > ε')
    For all sub-concept Cj of CO do
    Add(<P,S,Cj,'consult_concept',U>, RB).
    endfor
endif
end.
```

According to our model, if the mastery degree of a concept is below a certain threshold. Our algorithm can determine if this is due to the fact that the student has not achieved enough of activities in his workspace. If this is the case, the algorithm also determines if it is consultation, addition or creation activities. And in this case, he recommends the learner to perform more activities and provides a list of students in his group identified as "experts" that can assist him in the implementation of these activities. The algorithm can also determine if the problem is due to the lack of mastery of one or more sub-concepts and in this case, the algorithm recommends the learner to work more on these sub-concepts with learners who have already acquired skills for these sub-concepts.

7   Discussion

Our approach allows measuring some learning indicators such as the mastery level, of a concept by a learner, which is calculated according to the different activities that he has carried out within a group (collaboration space) on the concept and its sub concepts.

Returning to the previous example, we calculated the learning indicators of Marie-Hélène, within the group1 composed of four members, for each concept of the application ontology that contains the concepts to be learned of a training unit. If we apply the recommendation algorithm to Marie-Hélène on the concept "Information Technology" with a threshold of 0.25 (1/4), we obtain:

$KL_{(Marie-Hélène\ InfTech)} = 0.119 < 0.25$

We have: $AC_{(Marie-Hélène,\ InfTech)} = 0.05$ (consultation_value = 0.25, creation_value = 0, addition_value = 0). Marie-Hélène will be recommended to work on creating and adding resources with members of his group productive on these actions.

$KC_{(Marie-Hélène\ InfTech)} = 0.3 * 0,356 + 0.7 * 0,228 = 0,227 < 0.25$

The recommendation also focuses on sub concepts.

$KL_{(Marie-Hélène\ Software)} = 0.228 < 0.25$ and $KL_{(Marie-Hélène,\ Hardware)} = 0.356 > 0.25$

The work should be done especially on the sub-concept Software.

Let us now apply the recommendation algorithm to Marie-Hélène on the concept Software with the same threshold, we get:

$AC_{(Marie-Hélène,\ Software)} = 0.274 > 0.25$ and $KC_{(Marie-Hélène\ Software)} = 0.159 < 0.25$

Marie-Hélène must therefore be recommended to work on the sub-concepts of Software with learners who have already had expertise on these sub concepts.

We have: $KL_{(Marie-Hélène,\ Java)} = 0 < 0.25$, $KL_{(Marie-Hélène,\ WP)} = 0.4 > 0.25$, $KL_{(Marie-Hélène,\ Android)} = 0.1425 < 0.25$, $KL_{(Marie-Hélène,\ Ios)} = 0.075 < 0.25$.

These sub-concepts are: Java, Android and Ios.

8　Conclusion

The traces are very important elements in collaborative environments. Their analysis aims to understand and follow the learning of a learner or group of learners and qualify the use, usability and acceptability of collaborative environment to make it more adaptive. In this paper, we proposed an architecture for a recommendation system for the learner. This architecture is based on an original model of the learner taking into account the definition of data (learning indicators). A knowledge base containing this information was constructed. Interaction data recorded were used to construct indicators of learners' state, group state and the progression of the training session. The absence of such indicators in current learning and teaching environments has allowed us to justify our work. We have chosen to use a Bayesian formula to calculate the knowledge level of a learner on a concept of the application ontology describing the pedagogical content of training.

We are currently working to deploy the recommendation module within the environment E-MEMORAe2.0 in order to test it with students from the University of Setif.

References

1. Abel, M.H.: Apport des Mémoires Organisationnelles dans un contexte d'apprentissage. mémoire d'habilitation à diriger des recherches, université de technologie de Compiègne (2008)
2. Abel, M.H., Leblanc, A.: Knowledge Proc of sharing via the E-EMORAe2.0 platform. In: The International Conference on Intellectual Capital, Knowledge Management & Organizational Learning, pp. 10–19 (2009)
3. Avouris, N., Komis, V., Margaritis, M., Fiotakis, G.: An environment for studying collaborative learning Activities. Educational Technology & Society 7(2), 34–41 (2004)
4. Corbel, A., Girardot, J.J., Jaillon, P.: DREW: A Dialogical Reasoning Web tool. In: The International Conference on Information and Communication Techonologies in Education (ICTE), Badajoz, Spain, November 20-23 (2002)
5. George, S.: Analyse automatique de conversations textuelles synchrones d'apprenants pour la détermination de comportements sociaux. Revue Sciences et technologies de l'information et de la communication pour l'éducation et la formation (STICEF) Numéro spécial: technologies et formation à distance, 165-193 (2004)
6. Georgeon, O., Mille, A., Bellet, T.: Abstract: un outil et une méthodologie pour analyser une activité humaine médiée par un artefact technique complexe. Ingénierie des Connaissances IC 2006, Nantes (2006)
7. Li, Q., Abel, M.H., Barthès, J.P.: Facilitating Experience Groups Sharing Collaborative Trace. In: Proceeding of Reuse Exploitation. and In International Conference on Knowledge Management and Information Sharing, pp. 21–30 (2012)
8. Ollagnier-Beldame, M.: A.: Faciliter l'appropriation des EIAH par les apprenants via les traces informatiques d'interactions. Sticef spécial traces (2007)
9. Sani, M.R.F., Mohammadian, N., Hoseini, M.: Ontological learner modeling. Procedia - Social and Behavioral Sciences 46, 5238–5243 (2012)

10. Settouti, L., Prié, Y., Mille, A., Marty, J.-C.: Système à base de traces pour l'apprentissage humain. Colloque international TICE 2006, Technologies de l'Information et de la Communication dans l'Enseignement Supérieur et l'Entreprise (2006)
11. Siebra, S., Salgado, A.C., Brézillon, P., Tedesco, P.: A learning interaction memory using contextual information. The CONTEXT 2005 Workshop on Context and Groupware, Paris, France (2005)
12. Triola, M. F.: Baye's Theorem. Pearson education (2010)
13. Wang, N., Abel, M.H., Barthès, J.P., Negre, E.: Towards a Recommender System from Semantic Traces for Decision Aid. KMIS, Rome (October 2014)

Toward a New Recommender System Based on Multi-criteria Hybrid Information Filtering

Hanane Zitouni[1(✉)], Omar Nouali[2], and Souham Meshoul[1]

[1] Department of Computer Science, University Abdelhamid Mehri, Constantine, Algeria
h_zitouni@esi.dz, smeshoul@gmail.com
[2] Department of Research Computing, CERIST, Algiers, Algeria
onouali@cerist.dz

Abstract. The Communities of Practice of E-learning (CoPEs) are virtual spaces that facilitate learning and acquisition of new knowledge for its members. To achieve these objectives CoPE members exchange and share learning resources that can be (online courses, URLs, articles, theses, etc ...). The growing number of adherents to the CoPE increases the number of learning resources inserted into the memory of this learning space. As consequence, access to relevant learning resource and collaboration between members who have similar needs become even more difficult. Therefore, recommender systems are required to facilitate such tasks. In this paper we propose a personalized recommendation approach dedicated to CoPE that we call Three Dimensions Hybrid Recommender System (3DHRS). The approach is hybrid as it uses collaborative filtering supported by content based filtering to eliminate the problems of cold start and new item. Furthermore, it considers three criteria namely role, interest and evaluation to efficiently solve the new user, and sparsity issues. A prototype of the proposed system has been implemented and evaluated through the use of Moodle platform as it hosts many communities of practice. Very promising results in terms of mean absolute error have been obtained.

Keywords: Information filtering · Multi-criteria · Role · Interest · CoPE · Personalized recommendation

1 Introduction

The Communities of Practice of E-learning (CoPEs) allow their members with different roles namely teachers, tutors, learners...etc, among others to collaborate and share their experiences [1]. So they constitute an environment of sharing of learning resources, problems already solved, learned lessons in practice and any other learning option. When conducting learning activities, the members of the CoPE may need to find members who have a similar profile to share knowledge or experts in the field to get advising. They may also need to get easy access to educational resources related to their field of interest and to be constantly informed about new relevant learning resources. In order to fulfil these needs recommender systems are required (RS).

© IFIP International Federation for Information Processing 2015
A. Amine et al. (Eds.): CIIA 2015, IFIP AICT 456, pp. 328–339, 2015.
DOI: 10.1007/978-3-319-19578-0_27

Recommender Systems (RS) can be defined [2] as system that allows guiding the user in a personalized way to interesting or useful objects in a large space of possible options. RS are a specific type of information filtering (IF) devoted to present information items (movies, music, books, news, images, web pages, etc ...) that are likely to interest the user. Typically, a RS compares the profile of a user to some reference characteristics, and seeks to predict the "opinion" that he would give. These characteristics may come from either the item itself or from the social environment. The first case refers to content-based filtering while the second case refers to collaborative filtering. When both cases are considered hybrid filtering is achieved [3], [4].

Content Based Filtering (CBF) or cognitive filtering [5], [6], [7] is an important topic in information filtering. It is mainly based on comparing contents of documents (topics) to profiles consisting of themes. Each system user has a profile that describes its own interests. On arrival of a new document, the system compares the representation of the document with the profile to predict user satisfaction on this document. Although CBF is an important technique for information filtering, it suffers from Over-specialization: content-based method provides a limit degree of novelty, since it has to match up the features of profile and items. A totally perfect content-based filtering may suggest nothing "surprising".

Collaborative Filtering (CF) is considered as one of the most successful approaches for building recommender systems. It uses behaviours, activities and known preferences of a group of users to predict and make recommendations of the unknown preferences for other users [8].Typically this technique mainly based on an evaluation criterion is known as Classic Collaborative Filtering (CCF).

Unlike CBF, a CCF approach ignores the form and the content of items. Therefore, does not require any kind of document analysis and complex recommendations could be made. However, CCF raises some issues that should be properly addressed [9], [10] namely:

−*First-Rater problem*: also known as new item problem or clod start item. This problem concerns new items with no ratings. It is impossible for the system to recommend such items to someone because they can't be compared to the other products due to the missing ratings.

−*Sparsity problem*: A similar problem occurs if there is a big amount of products in the system and users don't rate too many products. Thus, it is difficult to find sufficiently correlated users.

−*No preferences*: also known new user problem or cold start user. At the beginning, a new user does not have any preference values; this makes impossible to give any recommendations to him, because he cannot be compared to other users.

−*Cold start problem*: This problem occurs at the beginning of use of the system in critical cases where the system lacks data to make personalized filter of good quality.

In order to reap advantage from both information filtering approaches and to deal with their issues as well, we propose architecture of a three dimensions hybrid recommender system (3DHRS) that includes three layers namely a CF layer, a CBF layer and a user layer. The main contribution consists in fostering the CCF within the CF layer by considering two other dimensions besides evaluation dimension namely role and interest, supported by domain ontology.

Following this introduction, we present in section 2 some related work that propose recommender systems in context of e-learning. In section 3, we describe the proposed approach 3DHRS.In section 4, the developed prototype along with the obtained experimental results are described. Finally, conclusion and future work are given.

2 Related Work

In the e-learning domain, several number of recommender systems have been developed. Such systems play an important educational role. The following table 1 reviews some recent approaches.

Table 1. E-learning recommender systems

Systems	Technique	Object(s) recommended	Dedicated to CoPE	Short description
Alterred Vista system [11].	CF	-Learning resources -People (with similar tastes)	No	Clusters users based on the evaluations of learning resources
RACOFI ([12], [13]).	Hybrid recommendation	-Learning resources	No	Combines two recommendation approaches CF and association rules
QSIA ([14], [15])	CF	-Learning resources	Yes	Used in the context of online communities
CYCLADES [16].	CF	-Learning resources	No	Proposed an environment where users search, access, and evaluate (rate) digital resources
A similar sequencing system [17].	Markov chain model	-Learning paths	No	Calculate transition probabilities of possible learning objects in a sequenced course of study
an evolving e-learning system [18].	Hybrid recommendation	-Learning resources	No	Recommendation takes place both by engaging a Clustering Module and a CF module
ReMashed [19].	Hybrid recommendation	-Services	No	Recommendations based on CF combined with Web2.0 sources

The following observations can be made based on features reported on table 1 and a thorough investigation of most developed RS that we conducted in our study:

–A lot of recommender systems are based on CF only or CF combined with another technique;

–Many of these systems recommend only learning resources while a few others recommend other objects like learning paths, services, people with similar tastes, etc ;

–Most of the systems based on CF create the communities of actors on use only the criterion of evaluation (mono-criterion);

–Almost all the systems proposed are not designed for CoPE.

These facts have motivated our work in proposing a new recommendation approach of users and learning resources, based on content based filtering and multi-criteria collaborative filtering. In the following, a detailed description is given.

3   Proposed Approach

Our study on recommender systems focuses on CoPE which is considered as virtual space for exchanging and sharing: problem solutions; of learning resources; services, etc, by the actors of e-learning during their learning process.

In this paper we propose to use personalized recommendation based on information filtering, in order to guide users to valuable resources, and actors in a wide space of options. Indeed, our recommender system will: Recommend valuable resources that can meet the needs of actors, and recommend also expert members who will validate certain knowledge, do suggestion of members who have a similar profile to improve the collaboration and knowledge exchange between different CoPE actors.

3.1   The Basic Concepts

Following are some basic concepts of our approach to recommendation:

- *User*: Users are the actors of the CoPE. Each user is characterized by: a role, a field of expertise and interests.
- *Items:* are learning resources exchanged and shared among different users.
- *Evaluation* is a measure of satisfaction about a specific item it can be:
    -*Explicit*: It's a given user rating on a scale of 1 to 5.
    -*Implicit*: The system induces user satisfaction through his actions.
- *Profile* is a description for each user. It contains a static part where personal data about the user (name, surname, age, address,…etc.) are saved and a dynamic part that contains dynamic data that like interests, ratings, interactions etc. On arrival of a new document, the system compares the representation of the document with the profile to predict user satisfaction on this document.
- *Community:* It is a set of users gather based on a specific criterion.
- *Recommendation:* A list of Top-K elements where the target user will like his majority. These elements can be either users or items.
- *Similarity:* The similarity is a numerical value that measures the similarity between items or users based on predefined criteria.
- *Prediction:* it is a numeric value that estimates whether the user likes or dislikes the recommended item or the user.
- *Metadata of learning resources*: is data used to define or describe other data. Metadata is used to describe and index the content of the learning resources.

3.2   General Architecture

The general architecture of our 3DHRS encompasses three main layers, as shown on Figure 1, namely: the layer of Collaborative Filtering (CF), Layer of Content Based Filtering (CBF), and the user layer.

The features of these different layers can be described as follows starting from the lowest layer to the highest one.

- **Collaborative Filtering layer (CF)**

CF layer is the deepest layer. It is considered as the core of 3DHRS. It consists of two sub-layers, one based mainly on technical Classic Collaborative Filtering and the other sub-layer called Multidimensional/Semantic (M/S). Figure 2 shows the general architecture of this layer.

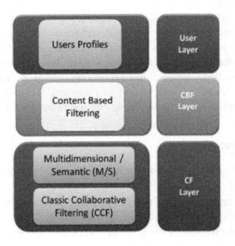

Fig. 1. General Architeture of 3DHRS

✓ *Sub layer Classic Collaborative Filtering (CCF)*

CCF sub-layer relies on a memory based and user centered technique of classic collaborative filtering. It processes the ratings that users have made on certain documents in order to recommend the same documents. Documents should be interesting and of good quality with varied themes. However it requires proper handling of new user and sparsity problems. In our work, we propose a solution to these problems by adding the multidimensional/Semantic (M /S) sub-layer.

✓ *Sub layer Multidimensional / Semantic (M/S)*

According to our study we find that CoPEs members, who have a common role and/or common interest(s), are very often interested by the same resources. Therefore, we suggest to add two dimensions role and interest to the evaluation dimension to foster the CCF sub-layer and eliminate or even minimize the problems of *new user*, and *sparsity*. User' s interests are handled using a domain ontology, (in order to discover semantically similar interests with different syntax).

- ***Content Based Filtering layer (CBF)***

At boot a recommender system based on CF suffers from the problem of *cold start*. In fact, the system has no information on users and items. Collaborative filtering methods cannot operate on an empty matrix of ratings. Another instance of this problem is when a *new item* is added and no pre-rating on this item is provided. This causes the system to ignore the item and as a consequence, the item cannot be recommended. The solution that we propose in this context is to use a layer of content-based filtering (CBF) which allows the system to propose items that are close to the best profile by comparing the content of the analyzed resource to interests of users. However, this technique is much more used on text-based resources (where content analysis is not expensive), while in the field of CoPE, resources are of various types (text, multimedia, PDF files, etc). As a consequence, we propose to use metadata [20] describing learning resources; we support the view of [21] and [22] who proposed to support the standard metadata describing the domain ontology. Figure 3 shows the basic principle of this layer.

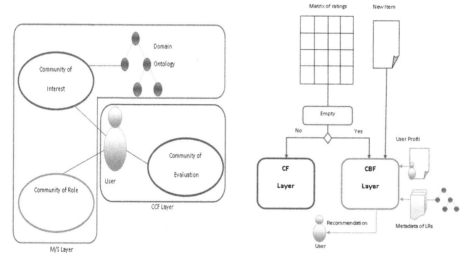

Fig. 2. Collaborative Filtering layer   **Fig. 3.** Content Based Filtering layer

- ***User layer***

This is the only explicit layer for users; his main role is to create user profiles based on the collected data. Figure 4 presents the basic principle of this layer.

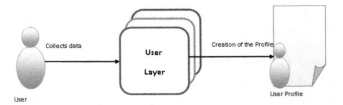

Fig. 3. User layer

3.3   Recommendation Engine

The recommendation engine allows 3DHRS to recommend: *Learning Resources* and *users*. There are four main engine processes of 3DHRS designed to perform the following tasks: pre-evaluation, evaluation of recommendations, creation of communities and finally production of recommendations.

1) Pre- evaluation
Given an empty matrix of ratings or a recently new added item, it is essential to go through a pre-evaluation step. It is mainly based on the CBF.

The basic principle of this step is to compare the interests of the user extracted from his profile to key words describing the items represented in metadata. The comparison between the user preferences and keywords that describe the item is done using the similarity calculation. For this, we adopted the formula of *Jaccard coefficient* defined as:

$$\text{Sim}(i,u) = \frac{|K_i \cap I_u|}{|K_i \cup I_u|} \tag{1}$$

Where: *Sim(i,u)* is a measure of similarity between the user *u* and the item *i*, *u* is the target user, K_i isa set of key-words that describe an item *i*, I_u is a set of interests of the user *u*.

2) Evaluation of recommendations
The next step is the evaluation, which provides the ability for users to know the existing items and evaluate them in an explicit way (which is to give a rating on a scale of 1 to 5) or implicitly where the system induces user satisfaction through his actions.

3) Formation of communities
In 3DHRS, communities are formed based on three criteria: roles, interests and user's evaluations.

✓ *Communities of Role/Interest*
The communities of role/interest are communities formed by users who have the same role and/or the same interest based on the matrix of roles and vector of interests.

The matrix of roles is a binary matrix. In order to fill the matrix of roles, it is necessary to calculate the similarity of role based on the following formula:

$$\text{Sim}_R(u,x)=\begin{cases} 0 \text{ if } u,x \text{ have not the same role} \\ 1 \text{ if } u,x \text{ have the same role} \end{cases} \tag{2}$$

Where: u is Target user, x is Any user, $Sim_R(u,x)$ is the measure of similarity of roles between u and x.

To know if two users have one or more common interests, it is necessary to calculate a similarity of interests between them based on their vectors of interests. To measure the degree of similarity of interests between different users, we suggest using the following formula:

$$\text{Sim}_I(u,x)=\frac{|I_u \cap I_x|}{|I_u \cup I_x|} \tag{3}$$

Where: u is Target user, x is Any user, $Sim(u,x)$ is the measure of interest similarity between u and x, Iu is the vector of interests of the user u, Ix is the vector of interests of the user x.

To assign two users to the same community of role/ interest, we measure the degree of similarity of role / interest $(Sim_{R/I})$, which is calculated by the following formula:

$$\text{Sim}_{R/I}(u,x)=\frac{\text{Sim}_R(u,x)+\text{Sim}_I(u,x)}{2} \tag{4}$$

✓ *Community of evaluation*

The creation of evaluation community is based mainly on similarity of evaluation. There are three main methods to calculate this similarity: *cosine similarity, the modified cosine similarity* and *Pearson correlation coefficient similarity (PCC)*. Many experiments show that the last one can represent the similarity of users or items better than the other methods ([23], [24], [25]). So, we adopted it in order to create the community of evaluation, the formula of PCC is defined below:

$$\text{Sim}_E(u,x)=\frac{\sum_{i \in I_{ux}}\left(R_{u,i}-\bar{R}_u\right)\left(R_{x,i}-\bar{R}_x\right)}{\sqrt{\sum_{i \in I_{ux}}\left(R_{u,i}-\bar{R}_u\right)^2}\sqrt{\sum_{i \in I_{ux}}\left(R_{x,i}-\bar{R}_x\right)^2}} \tag{5}$$

Where: u is Target user, x is Any user, $Sim_E(u,x)$ is the measure of evaluation similarity between u and x, $I_{ux}(I_{ux} = I(u) \cap I(x))$ is the set of evaluated item by u and x, $R_{u,i}, R_{x,i}$ represent evaluations of the user u and x for the item I, $\bar{R}_u, \bar{R}_x$ are respectively the average evaluations from user u and x for all items.

4) Production of recommendations

To produce recommendations of items and users, it is necessary to calculate a prediction of users and items. For this, we propose the following formulas:

$$\text{Pred}_U(u,x) = \frac{\beta_1 \text{Sim}_R(u,x) + \beta_2 \text{Sim}_I(u,x) + \beta_3 \text{Sim}_E(u,x)}{\beta_1 + \beta_2 + \beta_3} \tag{6}$$

Where: u is target user, x is any user, $\beta_1, \beta_2, \beta_3$ are coefficients where $\beta_1 = \beta_2 = \beta_3 = 1$ except if $Sim_R(u,x) = 0$, $Sim_I(u,x) \neq 0$, $Sim_E(u,x) \geq 0$ and the role of x is « expert » in this case $\beta_1 = 0$, $\beta_2 = \beta_3 = 3$.

The main objective behind using coefficients $\beta_1, \beta_2, \beta_3$ is to promote the recommendation of users who have role as "expert" and share at least one common interest with the target user.

$$\text{Pred}_I(u,i) = \frac{\alpha_1 (\overline{R}_{R/I,i}) + \alpha_2 (\overline{R}_{E,i})}{\alpha_1 + \alpha_2} \tag{7}$$

Where: u is the target user, i is an item, α_1, α_2 are coefficients where : $\alpha_1 = \alpha_2 = 1$, R/I is the community of Role/Interest, E is the community of evaluation , $\overline{R}_{R,i}, \overline{R}_{E,i}$ are respectively the average evaluations of role community and evaluation community: with respect to the item i where: $(R/I) \cap E = \emptyset$.

If u is a new user, $\text{Sim}_E(u,x) = 0$ .So, he will not be assigned to a community of evaluation but he may benefit from the recommendations coming from his community of role/ interest This is what we call *initial recommendation*.

After calculating the predictions, we can make a recommendation of a list of Top-K users, and Top-K most predicted items.

4   Implementation and Experimentation

To test the proposed approach it was necessary to find a CoPE. For that we propose to use the plat form moodle[1] that hosts many communities of practice involved in the development of the platform. Among these communities we have: "Moodle Exchange" (ME) offers a virtual place where we can share learning resources in a free community perspective. The figure 5 represents a screenshot of the home interface of Moodle Exchange. Just after the creation of the CoPE: ME we will enhance their environment by the integration of 3DHRS that will provide actors of CoPE: ME a recommendation of resources and users. Figure 6 presents screenshot of this integration. In order to test our prototype, we used as performance measure the *Mean Absolute Error* (MAE) which is computed by the following formula:

$$\text{MAE} = \frac{\sum_{u,i} |p_{u,i} - n_{u,i}|}{n} \tag{8}$$

---

[1] https://moodle.org/

Where: $n_{u,i}$ is the score given by the user u on item i, $p_{u,i}$ Predicted note, n is the total number of predicted scores.

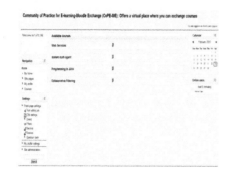

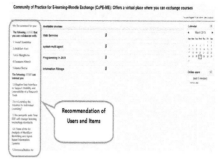

Fig. 5. Home Interface of Moodle Exchange

Fig. 6. The Integration of 3DHRS in CoPE: ME

The obtained results are described in Figures 7 and 8 where K refers to the number of recommended users and items respectively.

As can be observed on these plots, the values of MAE lie within the range [0.04, 0.37] in the case of users recommendation and [0.06, 0.36] in the case of items recommendations. It is clear that the achieved values are very low which indicate that good quality recommendations have been provided.

In order to show the advantage of the proposed 3DHRS over a CCF approach, a comparative study has been performed. Figures 9 and 10 show the achieved MAE values using both approaches for a list of top-k users (respectively top-k items), where k = 10. We can see that 3DHRS outperforms CCF in case of recommendation of users where 3DHRS MAE values are smaller than those of CCF. In case of recommendation of items, competitive results have been obtained.

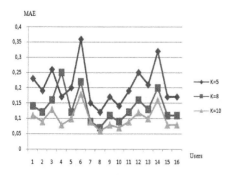

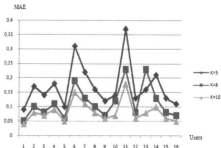

Fig. 7. MAE of Recommendation of top-k Users

Fig. 8. MAE of Recommendation of top-k Items

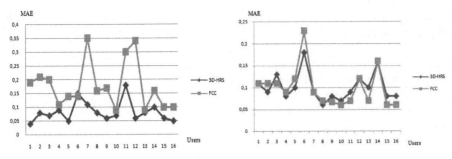

Fig. 4. MAE of 3DHRS VS MAE of CCF in case of users recommendation

Fig. 10. MAE of 3DHRS VS MAE of CCF. in case of items recommendation.

5   Conclusion

In this paper, we described a new approach to personalized recommendation dedicated for the CoPE, which is mainly based on collaborative filtering supported by the notion of multi-criteria, and combined with content based filtering. Actually we were faced with a challenge to use the technique of information filtering while reducing the impact of the related cold start issues. The proposed approach was implemented using a prototype on which we applied some experiments, the results were very promising.

As future work, it would be interesting to further improve the recommendation of users by adding other mechanisms such as RDF vocabulary (Resource description Framework) and activity concept.

References

1. Hamburg, I.: eLearning 2.0 and Social, Practice-oriented Communities to Improve Knowledge in Companies. In: Fifth International Conference on Internet and Web Applications and Services 2010 (2010)
2. Burke, R.: Hybrid Recommender Systems: Survey and Experiments. User Modeling and User-Adapted Interaction 12(4), 331–370 (2002); ISSN 0924-1868
3. Ansari, A., Essegaier, S., Kohli, R.: Internet recommendation systems. Journal of Marketing Research 37, 363–375 (2000)
4. Shahabi, C., Banaei-Kashani, F., Chen, Y.-S., McLeod, D.: Yoda: An Accurate and Scalable Web-Based Recommendation System. In: Batini, C., Giunchiglia, F., Giorgini, P., Mecella, M. (eds.) CoopIS 2001. LNCS, vol. 2172, pp. 418–432. Springer, Heidelberg (2001)
5. Lang, K.: NewsWeeder: Learning to Filter Netnews. In: Proceedings of the 12th International Conference on Machine Learning (ICML1995), CA, USA, pp. 331–339 (1995)
6. Lieberman, H.: Letizia: An agent that assists web browsing. In: Proceedings of the14th International Joint Conference on Artificial Intelligence, IJCAI 1995, Canada, pp. 924–929 (1995)
7. Pazzani, M., Billsus, D.: Learning and Revising User Profiles: The Identification ofInteresting Web Sites, Machine Learning, vol. 27, pp. 313–331. Kluwer Academic Publisher (1997)

8. Su, X., Khoshgoftaar, M.T.: A Survey of Collaborative Filtering Techniques. Advances in Artificial Intelligence, Article ID 421425, 19 pages (2009)
9. Melville, P., Mooney, R.J., Nagarajan, R.: Content-Boosted Collaborative Filtering for Improved Recommendations. In: Proceedings of the 18th National Conference on Arti. (2002)
10. Meier. Community Building Processes Using Collaborative Filtering Information. Thesis on System Research Group University of Fribourg (2008)
11. Recker, M.M., Wiley, D.A.: An interface for collaborative filtering of educational resources. In: Proc. of the 2000 International Conference on Artificial Intelligence, Las Vegas, USA, pp. 26–29 (2000)
12. Anderson, M., Ball, M., Boley, H., Greene, S., Howse, N., Lemire, D., McGrath, S.: RACOFI: A Rule-Applying Collaborative Filtering System. In: Paper presented at the conference IEEE/WIC COLA 2003, Halifax, Canada (October 2003)
13. Lemire, D., Boley, H., McGrath, S., Ball, M.: Collaborative Filtering and Inference Rules for Context-Aware Learning Object Recommendation. International Journal of Interactive Technology and Smart Education 2(3) (2005)
14. Rafaeli, S., Barak, M., Dan-Gur, Y., Toch, E.: QSIA a web-based environment for learning, assessing and knowledge sharing in communities. Computers & Education 43(3), 273–289 (2004)
15. Rafaeli, S., Dan-Gur, Y., Barak, M.: Social Recommender Systems: Recommendations in Support of E-Learning. International Journal of Distance Education Technologies 3(2), 29–45 (2005)
16. Avancini, H., Straccia, U.: User recommendation for collaborative and personalised digital archives. International Journal of Web Based Communities 1(2), 163–175 (2005)
17. Huang, Y.M., Huang, T.C., Wang, K.T., Hwang, W.Y.: A Markov-based Recommendation Model for Exploring the Transfer of Learning on the Web. Educational Technology & So-ciety 12(2), 144–162 (2009)
18. Tang, T.Y., McCalla, G.I.: Smart Recommendation for an Evolving E-Learning System: Architecture and Experiment. International Journal on E-Learning 4(1), 105–129 (2005)
19. Drachsler, H., Pecceu, D., Arts, T., Hutten, E., Rutledge, L., van Rosmalen, P., Hummel, H., Koper, R.: ReMashed - Recommendations for Mash-Up Personal Learning Environments. In: Cress, U., Dimitrova, V., Specht, M. (eds.) EC-TEL 2009. LNCS, vol. 5794, pp. 788–793. Springer, Heidelberg (2009)
20. Zitouni, H., Berkani, L., Nouali, O.: Recommendation of Learning Resources and Users Using an Aggregation-Based Approach. In: Publié au 2ième IEEE Workshop sur les Systèmes d'informations Avancés Pour les Enterprises (IWAISE 2012), Algérie (2012)
21. Bouzeghoub, A., Defude, B., Duitama, J.-F., Lecocq, C.: Un modèle de description sémantique de ressources pédagogiques basé sur une ontologie de domaine, vol. 12 (2005)
22. Abdelwahed, E.H., Lazrek, A.: Des ontologies pour la description des ressources pédagogiques et des profils des apprenants dans l'elearning (2006)
23. Breese, J., Hecherman, D., Kadie, C.: Empirical analysis of predictive algorithms for collaborative filtering. In: Proceedings of the 14th Conference on Uncertainty in Artificial Intelligence, UAI 1998, pp. 43–52 (1998)
24. Billsus, D., Pazzani, M.J.: Learning Collaborative Information Filters. In: Proceedings of ICML 1998, pp. 46–53 (1998)
25. Jun Feng, Z., Xian, T., Jing Feng, G.: An Optimized Collaborative Filtering Recommendation Algorithm. Journal of Computer Research and Development 14(10), 1842–1847 (2004)

Information Technology:
Ontologies

A New Approach for Combining the Similarity Values in Ontology Alignment

Moussa Benaissa[(⊠)] and Abderrahmane Khiat

LITIO Laboratory, University of Oran1 Ahmed Ben Bella,
B.P 1524 El M'Naouar, 31000, Oran, Algeria
moussabenaissa@yahoo.fr,
abderrahmane_khiat@yahoo.com

Abstract. Ontology Alignment is the process of identifying semantic correspondences between their entities. It is proposed to enable semantic interoperability between various knowledge sources that are distributed and heterogeneous. Most existing ontology alignment systems are based on the calculation of similarities and often proceed by their combination. The work presented in this paper consists of an approach denoted PBW (Precision Based Weighting) which estimates the weights to assign to matchers for aggregation. This approach proposes to measure the confidence accorded to a matcher by estimating its precision. The experimental study that we have carried out has been conducted on the Conference[1] track of the evaluation campaign OAEI[2] 2012. We have compared our approach with two methods considered as the most performed in recent years, namely those based on the concepts harmony and local confidence trust respectively. The results show the good performance of our approach. Indeed, it is better in terms of precision, than existing methods with which it has been compared.

Keywords: Ontologies · Ontology alignment · Ontology matching · Semantic correspondences · Similarity · Aggregation of the similarities · Combination of the similarities

1   Introduction

The Semantic Web Community, defined as a futuristic extension of the current web, has adopted ontologies as the cornerstone for its achieving in order to overcome the crucial problem of semantic heterogeneity that is inherent to its distributed and open nature. However, these ontologies are themselves heterogeneous. This heterogeneity may occur at syntactic, terminological, conceptual or semiotic levels [5].

Ontology alignment, defined as the process of identification of semantic correspondences between entities of different ontologies to be aligned [5], is proposed

---

[1] http://oaei.ontologymatching.org/2012/conference

[2] OAEI (Ontology Alignment Evaluation Initiative) organizes evaluation campaigns aiming at evaluating ontology matching technologies. http://oaei.ontologymatching.org/

© IFIP International Federation for Information Processing 2015
A. Amine et al. (Eds.): CIIA 2015, IFIP AICT 456, pp. 343–354, 2015.
DOI: 10.1007/978-3-319-19578-0_28

as a solution to the problem of semantic heterogeneity by enabling the semantic interoperability between various sources of information.

We globally distinguish two approaches to identify the alignment between ontologies: reasoning-based approaches and those based on the calculation of similarities [12].

Most of the existing ontology alignment systems are based on the calculation of similarities between entities to align. In this category, we distinguish two types of systems: (1) systems which implement one single technique and (2) systems which combine several techniques, in order to estimate the similarity between two entities. The latter systems have become more frequent due to their flexibility and their easy extension [7]. Moreover, with the increasing complexity of ontologies on the Web (number and volume), the alignment cannot be performed reasonably in a purely manually way. Therefore it is imperative to develop automatic or at least semi-automatic systems to identify the alignment [11]. This situation is dictated by the lack of human expert especially in dynamic systems and by the concern to accelerate the alignment process [1].

Precisely, we propose in this paper an ontology alignment approach based on the calculation of similarities and which fits into the category of methods that combine several matchers. It is a statistical approach based on two heuristics to aggregate similarity values calculated by different matchers. The first estimates the candidate final alignment from the alignments identified by matchers, considering their intersection. The second provides an estimate of the weight to be assigned to the matchers with a view of their combination using a weighted summation strategy.

The rest of the paper is organized as follows. In the Section 2, we present some preliminary notions on ontology alignment in order to facilitate the reading of the paper content. The Section 3 contains the description of some related work to our approach. In the Section 4, we present an example in order to illustrate our approach. The Section 5 is dedicated to the presentation of the proposed approach. The Section 6 contains the experimental results obtained during the evaluation of our approach. Finally we give a conclusion and some future perspectives.

2   Preliminaries

In this section we present some preliminary notions of ontology alignment in order to facilitate the reading of the paper content. We outline the notions of ontology, similarity calculation techniques and alignment, respectively. We refer the reader, for more details, to the following references [5] [4].

2.1   Notion of Ontology

Definition: Ontology is a six tuple [2]: $O = <C, R, I, H^C, H^R, X>$ where:

- C: set of concepts.
- R: set of relations.
- I: set of instances of C and R.
- H^C: denotes a partial order relation on C, called hierarchy or taxonomy of concepts. It associates to each concept its super or sub-concepts.

- H^R: denotes a partial order relation on R, called hierarchy or taxonomy of relations. It associates to each relation its super or sub-relations.
- X: set of axioms.

2.2   Techniques of the Similarities Calculation

There are basically five types of methods to calculate similarities [1]:

1. *Terminological Methods.* These methods are based on string matching and can be applied to the names, labels and descriptions of the entities. We cite as an example of matcher of this category: the edit distance.
2. *Linguistic Methods.* These methods are based on external resources as dictionary and thesaurus in order to calculate the similarities between the names, labels and descriptions of the entities. We cite as an example of a matcher of this category: similarity based on WordNet (Wu-Palmer).
3. *Structure-based Methods.* These methods exploit the internal structure (domain, range, properties and cardinality, etc.) and the external structure (hierarchy and the relation-ship between other entities) of the entities in order to calculate their similarities. We cite as an example of a matcher of this category: Resnik similarity.
4. *Semantic-based Methods.* These methods are essentially deductive and inferential and are based on formal semantic of generic or specific domains. We cite as an example of a matcher of this category: SAT solvers.
5. *Instance-based Methods.* These methods exploit the instances associated to the concepts (extensions) to calculate the similarities between them. We cite as an example of a matcher of this category: Jaccard similarity.

2.3   Notion of Ontology Alignment

The alignment of two ontologies is the process of identification of semantic correspondences between their entities. In this section, we briefly introduce the basic necessary concepts on the alignment in order to facilitate the reading of the paper content.

2.3.1. Notion of Correspondence

Let O and O' two ontologies. A Correspondence M between O and O' is quintuple < Id, e, é, r, n > where:

- Id: is a unique identifier of the correspondence M;
- e and e' are the entities of O and O' respectively (concepts, relations or instances);
- r: is the semantic relation between e and e' (equivalence ($\equiv$), more specific ($\subseteq$), more general ($\supseteq$), disjunction ($\perp$));
- n: is a measure of confidence, typically a value within [0, 1].

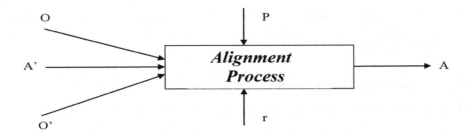

Fig. 1. Alignment Process

2.3.2. Notion of Alignment
The alignment can be defined as a set of correspondences. The alignment process (Fig. 1) receives as input two ontologies O and O' and produces as output an alignment A between entities of O and O'. Other elements complete this definition, namely:

- An initial alignment A' to be completed or refined by the process.
- The external resources r such as a thesaurus or a dictionary.
- The parameters P such as thresholds or weights.

The alignment process consists generally of the following steps:

1. *Analysis*: This step consists of extracting both the entities (concepts, relations, instances) of the two ontologies O and O ' and their characteristics which will be used to identify the alignment.
2. *Calculation of Similarities*: this step consists to execute the different matchers in order to calculate the similarities between entities to align.
3. *Similarity Values Aggregation*: This step consists to combine the similarity values calculated by the matchers in the previous step, into one value.
4. *Selection*: This step consists of applying a strategy, for example a threshold strategy in order to filter the alignment defined in the previous step. Other optimization techniques can also be applied at this level to optimize the extraction of the final alignment.
5. *Improvement of the Alignment*: descriptive logic techniques can be applied at this level to improve the final alignment by diagnosing and repairing any inconsistencies identified in the final alignment.

3   Related Works

The aggregation of similarity values calculated by different matchers consists to combine them into one single value. There are basically three types of approaches to achieve this aggregation: the **weighting**, the **vote** and the **argumentation** [5]. In the vote strategy, the matchers are considered as independent sources of information and the decision to include a correspondence in the alignment is taken on the basis of a simple majority vote by the matchers for this correspondence. The argument strategy allows negotiating an alignment by exchanging arguments between agents. In the weighting strategy several techniques are proposed to combine the similarity values.

In [3], the authors quote the following strategies to combine similarity values calculated by different matchers: (1) Max: this strategy selects the maximum similarity value among the values calculated by different matchers); (2) Min: this strategy selects the minimum similarity value among the values calculated by different matchers); (3) Average (this strategy calculates the average value of the similarities calculated by different matchers); and (4) Weighting (this strategy calculates the weighted sum of the similarities calculated by different matchers). The latter, which is more frequent in ontology alignment systems [7], requires an estimate of the weights that reflect the importance of each matcher. In some systems this weights approximation is done manually by a human expert. This approach is difficult to implement given the enormous number of possible configurations [11] and has the major drawback to run correctly on a specific alignment task and not on another. It is therefore suitable that the weights estimation be specific to the current alignment task [8].

Several studies have addressed the problem of the weights estimation of different matchers. In [14], the authors propose an approach based on information theory and estimate the weight of each matcher based on the calculation of entropy (uncertainty of information) from the similarity values calculated by this matcher.

The works described in [9] and [13] present an approach based on genetic algorithms to give an estimate of weights assigned to different strategies used.

In [8] the authors propose the harmony concept for weighting the different matchers. The harmony **h** of a similarity matrix **sim** of **n** rows and **m** columns is defined by: « *the number of pairs of entities (e_i, e'_j) for which the similarity **sim** (e_i, e'_j) is the maximum at the same time on the row i and column j, divided by the maximum number of concepts of ontologies to align O and O'* ". This value **h** is assigned as weight to the matcher associated to the matrix **sim**. In [2] the authors propose a local confidence measure for a pair of entities unlike that proposed in [8], which is global to the entire similarity values matrix. This measure, denoted m, is defined for an entity e of the ontology O, by: $m = m_r - m_{nr}$ where m_r is the average of similarity values of entities that are associated to e and m_{nr} is the average of similarity values of entities that are not associated to e.

Other works such as [6] and [10] use machine learning techniques for automatic configuration of weights to be assigned to the matchers.

* The approach proposed in this paper is situated in the category of weighting techniques that combine the similarity values calculated by different matchers. It consists of a heuristic that estimates the weights to assign to the matchers. Contrary to the techniques mentioned above, this approach is of statistical nature and estimates the weights by an estimation of the precision standard metric.

4   Illustrative Example of the Approach

Let two ontologies O and O' which contain the concepts O: {Product, Provider, Creator} and O': {Book, Translator, Publisher, Writer} respectively.

The application of the edit distance metric and that based on WordNet between concepts of O and O' has generated the following two matrices of similarities.

1) If we filter out the matrix of similarities (Table 1) calculated with the edit distance, with a threshold s = 0.15 we obtain the following alignment:
A1= {(Product, Translator), (Provider, Translator), (Provider, Publisher), (Provider, Writer), (Creator, Translator), (Creator, Writer)}.

Table 1. The Similarity Values Calculated by Edit Distance

O /O'	Book	Translator	Publisher	Writer
Product	0.14	0.20	0.11	0.14
Provider	0.12	0.20	0.44	0.50
Creator	0.14	0.50	0.11	0.43

2) If we filter out the second matrix of similarities (Table 2) calculated using WordNet, with a threshold s = 0.15 we obtain the following alignment:
A2= {(Product, Book), (Product, Writer), (Provider, Writer), (Provider, Book), (Creator, Book), (creator, Translator), (Creator, Writer)}.

Table 2. The Similarity Values Calculated Using WordNet

O /O'	Book	Translator	Publisher	Writer
Product	0.18	0.12	0.12	0.15
Provider	0.17	0.11	0.14	0.29
Creator	0.18	0.47	0.12	0.15

The alignment A which consists of the semantic correspondences identified by the two matchers simultaneously is as follows: A = A1 ∩ A2 = {(Creator, Translator), (Provider, Writer), (Creator, Writer)}. A represents the estimator of final candidate alignment.

The estimator of the precision of the matcher edit distance is: $P_1 = 3/6 = 0.50$.
The estimator of the precision of the matcher based on WordNet is: $P_2 = 3/7 = 0.43$.
The weights to be assigned to matchers are: $w_1 = 0.50$ and $w_2 = 0.43$.
The matrix of the combined similarities is as follows:

Table 3. The Combined Similarity Values

O /O'	Book	Translator	Publisher	Writer
Product	0.16	0.16	0.11	0.14
Provider	0.14	0.16	0.30	0.40
Creator	0.16	0.49	0.11	0.30

If we filter out the matrix of combined similarities (Table 3), with a threshold s = 0.30 we obtain the following alignment, (Provider, Publisher), (Provider, Writer), (Creator, Translator), (Creator, Writer)}. For more details about the approach see section 5.

5   The Proposed Approach

The architecture of our approach denoted PBW (Precision Based Weighting) is illustrated in Fig. 2. We have in input two ontologies O_1 and O_2 to be aligned. The *Analysis Module* performs the entities extraction from O_1 and O_2 using API Jena. Then, the *Similarities Generation Module* calculates for each pair of concepts (C, C') ∈ $O_1 \times O_2$ three similarity values using three techniques namely: the edit distance [5], the Jaro metric [5] and the similarity metric based on WordNet (Wu-Palmer algorithm) [5]. It should be noted at this level that the parameter object of the comparison is primarily the *aggregation method of similarity values* (the estimation of the weights to be assigned to matchers).

For that reason, we have set the same matchers for all three compared methods H, LCD (see the section 3 for the definition of these methods) and PBW in order to not have the results skewed by the choice of matchers. Therefore, the selection of the matchers has not been the subject of special attention. We have limited to the linguistic-based and string-based matchers. These similarity values are used by the *Weights Estimation Module* in order to calculate the confidence to be associated to the matchers mentioned above. The *Similarities Combination Module* generates then the combined similarity values using a weighting summation strategy. Finally, the *Alignment Extraction Module* selects the final alignment. This selection is simply performed by filtering the combined similarity values on a given threshold.

The contribution of the paper lies in the combination of similarity values. We detail below the principle of the proposed approach.

The approach proposed in this paper is an aggregation approach of similarity values calculated by several matchers. It fits into the category of automatic techniques for assigning weights to matchers which estimates their importance. We give in this section its principle.

Let O and O' be two ontologies to be aligned and let $M_1, \ldots, M_k$ k matchers which execute in parallel and calculate the similarity values between entities $e_1, \ldots, e_n$ for O and $e'_1, \ldots, e'_m$ for O' respectively. Let us note $S_1, \ldots, S_k$ the similarities matrices generated by matchers $M_1, \ldots, M_k$ respectively. The problem here is to assign to each matcher M_i a weight w_i which expresses its importance in a given alignment task.

The intuition behind this approach consists to assign to the matcher M_i the weight w_i which is equal to an estimation of the precision of M_i. Indeed, as the precision metric is a good estimation of the matcher quality; we propose to use it as an estimator of the weight that will be assigned to the matcher.

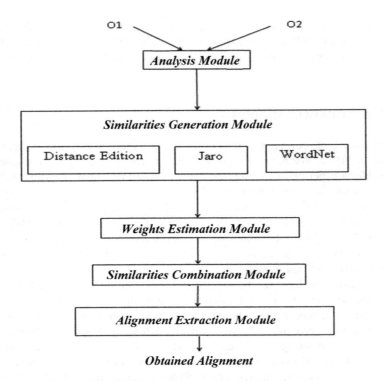

Fig. 2. The Architecture of the Application

We distinguish for the matcher M_i two subsets among the set of semantic correspondences between entities of ontologies O and O' to be aligned. On one hand we have the set P_i of the correspondences qualified positively and which belong to candidate alignment and On the other hand, we have the set N_i of those, negatively qualified and which do not belong to candidate alignment. The set P_i is defined as follows:

$$P_i = \{(e_i, e'_j) \in O \times O' / (S_i(i, j) \geq s \text{ where } s \text{ is a given threshold}\}.$$

Since to estimate the precision of a matcher, we need a reference alignment and in the absence of such alignment we propose to estimate it (the reference alignment) by the set P which denotes the set of positive correspondences identified simultaneously by all matchers. In other words: $P = \cap_{i=1,\ldots,k} P_i$. We therefore propose for the matcher M_i the following estimator for the precision: $w_i = |P_i \cap P|/|P_i|$

Where |E| denotes the number of all elements of the set E. This estimator represents the weight to be assigned to M_i.

The approach can be made operational by the following process:

–   Calculate, for each matcher M_i, the set P_i defined above.

- Calculate the set P. In some alignment tasks, the case where P is empty can occur. The weights assigned to the matchers are therefore is null. To overcome this situation, we have estimated P, for each matcher M_i, as follows: P = {(e_i, e'_j) ∈ O x O' / $(S_i (i, j) \geq s$ where s is a threshold relatively high}. We have retained the following formula to specify the threshold: s = the highest similarity value calculated by the matcher M_i from which a particular constant value n is subtracted. For example, if the maximum similarity value is equal to 0.80 and n=0.25 then s = 0.8*0.25=0.40.
- Assign to each matcher M_i the weight w_i.
- Calculate the matrix of combined similarity values M. the matrix M is calculated by the following formula: M $(i, j) = (\sum_k w_k * S_k (i, j)) / (\sum_k w_k)$.
- Filter M according to the threshold s.

6 The Experimental Study

In order to evaluate our approach, we have used the conference track of OAEI 2012 evaluation campaign. This track consists of a collection of 16 ontologies describing the field of the conferences organization. It is constituted of 21 tests for which reference alignments are available, from a total of 120 possible tests resulting from the pairwise combination of 16 ontologies. Each test consists of two ontologies and a reference alignment.

The tests have been carried as follows: we have implemented the three methods (H, PBW and LCD), then we have executed these methods on ontologies tests of the conference track.

As evaluation criteria we have used the standard metrics that are precision, recall and F-measure to evaluate our approach. These metrics are defined as follows:

$$\text{Precision} = P(A, R) = \frac{|R \cap A|}{|A|} \quad \text{Recall} = R(A, R) = \frac{|R \cap A|}{|R|} \quad \text{F-measure} = \frac{2 * \text{Recall} * \text{Precision}}{\text{Recall} + \text{Precision}}$$

Where |R| denotes the number of the reference alignment mappings and |A| denotes the number of matches found by our approach.

We envision in this experimental analysis to compare our precision based weighting approach of the similarity values aggregation (Noted PBW-method in the graphs) with the two most efficient aggregation methods [10] [15] namely the method based on the harmony concept [8] (Noted H-method in the graphs) and the method based on the concept of local confidence [2] (Noted LCD-method in the graphs).

It should be noted at this level that our approach as well as those with which it has been compared belong to the same category of methods based on the weighting.

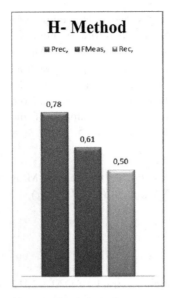
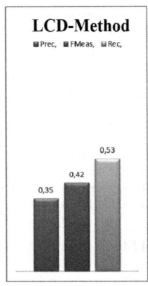
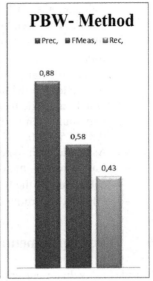

Fig. 3. The Global Results (All Tests of Conference Track) of the Three Methods

We have adopted the following methodology in order to conceive the experimental protocol. For each of the 21 tests of the conference track, we have calculated three matrices of similarities by the matchers edit distance, Jaro and WordNet, respectively. Subsequently, from these matrices we calculated the weights to assign to the matchers by the three compared methods (harmony, local confidence and our method). Then we have calculated the matrices of the combined similarities and we have selected the alignments by filtering using a given threshold s for each of the three methods. Finally, for each test we have calculated precision, recall and F-measure for each method. To conclude, we have calculated the average precision, recall and F-measure for all tests of the conference track.

The results are shown in Fig. 3 and Fig. 4.

The experimental results obtained (Fig. 3) show that globally i.e. for all tests:

1. Our approach PBW is significantly more efficient than the H and LCD methods in terms of precision.
2. Our approach PBW is more efficient than the LCD method and slightly less efficient than the H method in terms of F-measure.
3. Our approach PBW is less efficient than the H and LCD methods in terms of recall.

The analysis of the detailed results on all tests of the conference track (Fig. 4) show that our approach is more efficient than H and LCD methods in terms of precision for all tests of the conference track of OAEI 2012 evaluation campaign, considered individually.

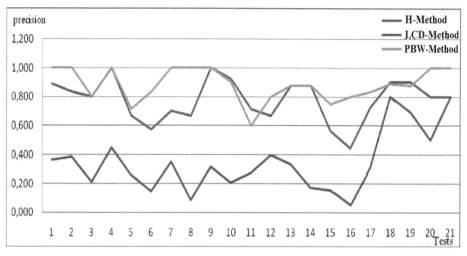

Fig. 4. The Detailed Results of the Three Methods in Terms of Precision

7   Conclusion and Perspectives

We have presented in this paper a dynamic approach to estimate automatically the weights to be assigned to different matchers in a given alignment task, in order to combine the similarity values calculated by the matchers in a context of ontology alignment.

The experimental results show the good performance of our proposed approach. Indeed, it is better in terms of precision than other methods, local and global, deemed among the most efficient ones in recent years. In addition, it shows a good F-measure relative compared to the local method.

As future perspective we envision to intensify the experiments by considering other tests and combining other similarities calculation techniques.

References

1. Bellahsene, Z., Duchateau, F.: Tuning for Schema Matching Schema Matching and Mapping. In: Bellahsene, Z., Bonifati, A., Rahm, E. (eds.) Data-Centric Systems and Applications. Springer (2011)
2. Cruz, I., Antonelli, F.P., Stroe, C.: Efficient selection of mappings and automatic quality-driven combination of matching methods. In: International Workshop on Ontology Matching (2009)
3. Do, H., Rahm, E.: COMA - A system for flexible combination of schema matching approaches. In: Proceedings of the 28th VLDB Conference, Hong Kong, China (2002)
4. Ehrig, M.: Ontology Alignment: Bridging the Semantic Gap. Springer (2007)
5. Euzénat, J., Shvaiko, P.: Ontology Matching. Springer (2013)
6. Ichise, R.: Machine learning approach for ontology mapping using multiple concept similarity measures. In: ACIS-ICIS. IEEE Computer Society (2008)

7. Li, J., Tang, J., Li, Y., Luo, Q.: RiMOM: A Dynamic Multistrategy Ontology Alignment Framework. IEEE Transactions on Knowledge and Data Engineering 21 (2009)

8. Mao, M., Peng, Y., Spring, M.: A harmony based adaptive ontology mapping approach. In: Proceedings of International Conference on Semantic Web and Web Services, SWWS (2008)

9. Martinez-Gil, J., Alba, E., Aldana-Montes, J.: Optimizing Ontology Alignments by Using Genetic Algorithms. In: Gueret, C., Hitzler, P., Schlobach, S. (eds.) Nature Inspired Reasoning for the Semantic Web, CEUR Workshop Proceedings (2008)

10. Ngo, D.: Enhancing Ontology Matching by Using Machine Learning, Graph Matching and Information Retrieval Techniques. Thèse de doctorat de l'université de Grenoble (2012)

11. Rahm, E.: Towards Large-Scale Schema and Ontology Matching. Schema Matching and Mapping. In: Bellahsene, Z., Bonifati, A., Rahm, E. (eds.) Data-Centric Systems and Applications. Springer (2011)

12. Silvana, C., Ferrara, A., Montannelli, S., Varese, G.: Ontology and Instance Matching. In: Paliouras, G., Spyropoulos, C.D., Tsatsaronis, G. (eds.) Multimedia Information Extraction. LNCS (LNAI), vol. 6050, pp. 167–195. Springer, Heidelberg (2011)

13. Wang, J., Ding, Z., Jiang, C.: GAOM: Genetic Algorithm based Ontology Matching. In: Proceedings of IEEE Asia-Pacific Conference on Services Computing (2006)

14. Wang, R., Wu, J., Liu, L.: Strategies Prediction and Combination of Multi-strategy Ontology Mapping. In: Zhu, R., Zhang, Y., Liu, B., Liu, C. (eds.) ICICA 2010. CCIS, vol. 106, pp. 220–227. Springer, Heidelberg (2010)

15. (Site 1), http://oaei.ontologymatching.org/2011/results/oaei2011.pdf (accessed January 2015)

Exact Reasoning over Imprecise Ontologies

Mustapha Bourahla[✉]

Computer Science Department, University of M'sila,
Laboratory of Pure and Applied Mathematics (LMPA),
BP 166 Ichebilia, M'sila 28000, Algeria
mbourahla@hotmail.com

Abstract. A real world of objects (individuals) is represented by a set
of assertions written with respect to defined syntax and semantics of
description logic (formal language). These assertions should be consistent
with the ontology axioms described as terminology of knowledge. The
axioms and the assertions represent ontology about a particular domain.
A real world is a possible world if all the assertions and the axioms
over its set of individuals, are consistent. It is possible then to query the
possible world by specific assertions (as instance checking) to determine
if they are consistent with it or not. However, ontology can contain vague
concepts which means the knowledge about them is imprecise and then
query answering will not possible due to the open world assumption if the
necessary information is incomplete (it is currently absent). A concept
description can be very exact (crisp concept) or exact (fuzzy concept) if
its knowledge is complete, otherwise it is inexact (vague concept) if its
knowledge is incomplete. In this paper we propose a vagueness theory
based on the definition of truth gaps as ontology assertions to express
the vague concepts in Ontology Web Language (OWL2) (which is based
on the description logic SROIQ(D)) and an extension of the Tableau
algorithm for reasoning over imprecise ontologies.

Keywords: Vagueness · Ontology · OWL · Description logics · Automatic reasoning

1 Introduction

Formalisms for dealing with vagueness have started to play an important role in
research related to the Web and the Semantic Web [7,13]. Ontologies are the definition of domain concepts (extensions) and the relations between them. Formal
ontologies are expressed in well-defined formal languages (for example, OWL2)
[3,6] that are based on expressive description logics (for example, SROIQ(D))
[1,14,4]. We say ontology is vague if it has at least a vague definition of a concept. A concept (an extension) is vague if it defines a meaning gap with which
we cannot decide the membership of certain objects (vague intension).

We state the problem with the following example. Assume an ontology defining a concept called *Expensive* in a domain about cars. The meaning of the
concept is vague. This vagueness is pervasive in natural language, but until now

© IFIP International Federation for Information Processing 2015
A. Amine et al. (Eds.): CIIA 2015, IFIP AICT 456, pp. 355–366, 2015.
DOI: 10.1007/978-3-319-19578-0_29

is avoided in ontologies definitions. For the concept *Expensive*, we can define three sub-extensions, definitely expensive extension (there are some car prices that we regard as definitely expensive), definitely cheap extension (others we regard as definitely cheap cars) and a vagueness extension, average car prices are neither expensive nor cheap. The source of this indecision is the imprecise definition of concepts that is caused by lack of rigorous knowledge.

Related Works: Almost all concepts we are using in natural language are vague (imprecise). Therefore common sense reasoning based on natural language must be based on vague concepts and not on classical logic. The rising popularity of description logics and their use, and the need to deal with vagueness, especially in the Semantic Web, is increasingly attracting the attention of many researchers and practitioners towards description logics able to cope with vagueness. There are many works in literature for dealing with vagueness and most of them express it as a concept property as those based on fuzzy logics.

The notion of a fuzzy set proposed by Lotfi Zadeh [15] is the first very successful approach to vagueness. Fuzzy description logics (FDLs) are the logics underlying modes of reasoning which are approximate rather than exact, assertions are true to some degree [13,2,8,12]. In this case, any concept instance will have a degree of membership that is determined by a defined fuzzy function. The vagueness under fuzzy theory is treated by extended fuzzy description logics that are supported by fuzzy semantics and fuzzy reasoning. The fuzzy description logics are applied in many domains. The fuzzy knowledge base is interpreted as a collection of constraints on assertions. Thus, the inference is viewed as a process of propagation of these constraints.

Assertions in fuzzy description logics, rather being satisfied (true) or unsatisfied (false) in an interpretation, are associated with a degree of truth using semantic operators, where the membership of an individual to the union and intersection of concepts is uniquely determined by its membership to constituent concepts. This is a very nice property and allows very simple operations on fuzzy concepts. In addition to the standard problems of deciding the satisfiability of fuzzy ontologies and logical consequences of fuzzy assertions from fuzzy ontologies, two other important reasoning problems are the best truth value bound problem and the best satisfiability bound problem.

In our work, the concepts are treated as having a fixed meaning (not a balanced meaning), shared by all users of the ontology; we propose instead that the meaning of a vague concept evolves during the ontology evolution, from more vague meaning to less vague meaning until it reaches if possible, a situation where it becomes non-vague concept. This meaning instability is the base of our vagueness theory that is used for reasoning over vague ontologies. Both theories represent two different approaches to vagueness. Fuzzy theory addresses gradualness of knowledge, expressed by the fuzzy membership, whereas truth gap theory addresses granularity of knowledge, expressed by the indiscernibility relation. The result of reasoning over vague ontology using truth gap theory is the posterior description that represents a revision of the prior description on the light of the evidence provided by acquired information. This property can be used to draw conclusions from prior knowledge and its revision if new evidence is available.

The other closest work to ours is the work in [10] which presents a framework for adjusting numerical restrictions defining vague concepts. An inconsistency problem can happen when aligning the original ontology to another source of ontological information or when ontology evolves by adding learned axioms. This adjustment is used to repair the original ontology for avoiding the inconsistency problem by modifying restrictions parameters called adaptors specified as concept annotations. The idea of this work is close to ours in the sense that we reduce the truth gaps when adding new assertions as learned knowledge to the ontology to guide the reasoning process which will play the same role as adjusting the vague concept restrictions. However, this work differs from our approach by the repair (modification) process applied on the original ontology to avoid introduced inconsistency. In our approach, we define the vague concepts as super concepts over restriction definitions. So, we don't have the problem of inconsistency to repair the ontology.

This paper is organized as follows. We begin in Section 2, by presenting Ontology Web Language (OWL2) and its correspondent description logic (SROIQ(D)). In Section 3, a vagueness theory is proposed to show how to express vague concepts and to describe the characteristics of vague ontologies. Section 4 presents the extended version of Tableau algorithm, to reason over imprecise ontologies. At the end, we conclude this paper by conclusions and perspectives.

2   Description Logics and Ontology Web Language

Ontologies are definitions of concepts and the relationships between them. They can be represented formally using formal languages. These formal description languages are based on well-defined Description Logics (DLs) [1], a family of knowledge representation formalisms. OWL2 DL is a variant of SROIQ(D) [4], which consists of an alphabet composed of three sets of names. The set $\mathcal{C}$ of atomic concepts corresponding to classes interpreted as sets of objects, the set $\mathcal{R}$ of atomic roles corresponding to relationships interpreted as binary relations on objects and the set $\mathcal{I}$ of individuals (objects). It consists also of a set of constructors used to build complex concepts and complex roles from the atomic ones. The roles (object or concrete) are called properties; if their range values are individuals (relation between individuals) then they are called object (abstract) properties. If their range values are concrete data (relation between individual and a concrete data) then they are called data (concrete) properties. The set of SROIQ(D) complex concepts can be expressed using the following grammar:

$$C ::= \top \mid \bot \mid A \mid \{a\} \mid \neg C \mid C \sqcap D \mid C \sqcup D \mid \exists o.Self \mid \forall o.Self \mid \quad (1)$$
$$\exists o.C \mid \forall o.C \mid \exists c.P \mid \forall c.P \mid \geq n\ s.C \mid \leq n\ s.C$$

Where $\top$ is the universal concept, $\bot$ is the empty concept, A is an atomic concept, a an individual, C and D are concepts, o an object role, c a concrete role, s a simple role w.r.t. $\mathcal{R}$, and n a non-negative integer. P is a predicate over a concrete domain that can have the form

$$P ::= DataType\,[\sim value] \mid P \sqcap P \mid P \sqcup P, \quad \sim \in \{<, \leq, >, \geq\} \qquad (2)$$

The data type can be any recognized data type as integer, real, etc. This syntax allows expressing concepts and roles with a complex structure. However, in order to represent real world domains, one needs the ability to assert properties of concepts and relationships between them. The assertion of properties is done in DLs by means of an ontology (or knowledge base). A SROIQ(D) ontology is a pair $\mathcal{O} = \langle \mathcal{T}, \mathcal{A} \rangle$, where $\mathcal{T}$ is called a terminological box and $\mathcal{A}$ is called an assertional box. The terminological box consists of a finite set of axioms on concepts and roles. There are inclusion axioms on concepts, object and concrete roles to define a hierarchy (taxonomy) on the names of concepts and roles, (we write $C \sqsubseteq D$ to denote inclusion axioms on concepts, where C and D are concepts, $C \equiv D$ as an abbreviation for $C \sqsubseteq D \wedge D \sqsubseteq C$ and $r_1 \sqsubseteq r_2$ for role inclusion, where r_1 and r_2 are object (concrete) roles, the same equivalence abbreviation can be applied on roles). The assertional box consists of a finite set of assertions on individuals. There are membership assertions for concepts ($C(a)$ means the object (individual) a is member of C), membership assertions for roles ($o(a, b)$ means the objects a and b are related by the object property o and $c(a, d)$ means the object a has the data property (concrete role) c with a value equals d).

Thus, the assertional box $\mathcal{A}$ of a knowledge base, provides a description of a world. It introduces individuals by specifying their names, the concepts to which they belong, and their relations with other individuals. The semantics of the language uses either the closed world assumption or the open world assumption. With the closed world assumption, we consider that the world is limited to what is stated. It is this assumption that is normally adopted in databases. In description logics, it is rather the assumption of the open world which prevails. This open world assumption has an impact in the way of making inferences in description logics. The inference is more complex with the assumption of the open world; it is often called to consider several alternative situations for the proof. Another important aspect of description logic is that it does not presuppose the uniqueness of names (the standard names). That is, two different names do not necessarily mean that there is case to two separate entities in the described world. To be sure that two different entities a and b are represented, should be added the assertion $a \neq b$ to the assertional box $\mathcal{A}$.

3   Vagueness Theory for Imprecise Ontologies

We define a concept C as vague if it has a deficiency of meaning. Thus, the source of vagueness is the capability of meaning (it has borderline cases). For example, the concept *Expensive* is extensionally vague and it remains intentionally vague in a world of expensive and non-expensive cars. This means that there are truth-value gaps where a vague concept is extensionally (intensionally) definitely true

(tt), definitely false (ff) and true or false (tf). Let us consider the following ontology.

$$\mathcal{O} = \left\langle \begin{array}{l} \mathcal{T} = \left\{ \begin{array}{l} Dom(price) \equiv \top, Rge(price) \equiv (int[\geq 0]) \sqcap (int[\leq 100]), \\ Dom(speed) \equiv \top, Rge(speed) \equiv (int[\geq 100]) \sqcap (int[\leq 300]), \\ ExpensiveCar \equiv Car \sqcap \exists price.(int\,[\geq 50]), \\ NonExpensiveCar \equiv Car \sqcap \exists price.(int\,[\leq 30]), \\ SportsCar \equiv Car \sqcap \exists speed.(int\,[\geq 200]), \\ NonSportsCar \equiv Car \sqcap \exists price.(int\,[\leq 150]), \\ ExpensiveCar \sqsubseteq Expensive, \\ NonExpensiveCar \sqsubseteq \neg Expensive, \\ SportsCar \sqsubseteq Sports, \\ NonSportsCar \sqsubseteq \neg Sports, \\ ExpensiveSportsCar \equiv Car \sqcap Expensive \sqcap Sports \end{array} \right\}, \\[4pt] \mathcal{A} = \left\{ \begin{array}{l} Car(a), Car(b), Car(c), Car(d), ExpensiveSportsCar(c), \\ price(a, 25), price(b, 55), price(c, 40), price(d, 45), \\ speed(a, 220), speed(b, 250), speed(c, 160), speed(d, 180) \end{array} \right\} \end{array} \right\rangle \quad (3)$$

Where *price* and *speed* are two concrete roles with the universal concept as their domains and their ranges Rge are defined by two integer intervals. In this knowledge base (ontology), we assume the price of a definitely expensive car ($ExpensiveCar$) is greater than or equal to fifty units and it is less than or equal to one hundred units, and a definitely no-expensive car ($NonExpensiveCar$) has a price between zero and thirty units. The concept $Expensive$ and its complement are subsuming two complex concept expressions ($ExpensiveCar$ and $NonExpensiveCar$). Each concept expression contains a sub-expression that is defined as quantified (universal or existential) restriction on a concrete role (for example, the concrete role is *price* and the restricted sub-expressions are $\exists price.(int\,[\geq 50])$ for the concept $ExpensiveCar$ and $\exists price.(int\,[\leq 30])$ for the concept $NonExpensiveCar$). By the same way, we define the vague concept $Sports$ and the concept $ExpensiveSportsCar$ as a conjunction of the concepts Car, $Expensive$ and $Sports$.

We have taken advantage of the open world assumption in description logics to define vague concepts. This ontology satisfies the assertions $Expensive(b)$ and $\neg Expensive(a)$ but the assertions $Expensive(d)$ and $(\neg Expensive)(d)$ are both not satisfied. With this knowledge base (ontology), we will assign tt to $Expensive(b)$, ff to $Expensive(a)$, and tf to $Expensive(d)$. This means, there is a deficiency of meaning (truth value gaps) between $Expensive$ and $\neg Expensive$. Consequently, the concept $Expensive$ is considered vague and the same thing for the vague concept $Sports$. The assertion $ExpensiveSportsCar(c)$ is considered as acquired information to state that c is an expensive sports car in spite of the fact that the terminology does not imply this assertion from information of the object c. We will see how this acquired (learned) information will be used to decide on other instances.

Thus, the satisfaction of a membership assertion to a vague concept depends on the concrete property value and the truth gaps. The vagueness definition of a concept will create one or more truth gaps. These are convex intervals (or ordered sequences) of values from a concrete domain with which the satisfaction of a membership assertion to the vague concept cannot be decided. There are two borderline values for each interval (or sequence). They are the lower (l) and the upper (u) bounds of a truth gap. Thus, we associate with each vague concept C a set of truth gap assertions according to a concrete role r (or to different concrete roles) used by its description.

These truth gaps assertions can be formulated using the description logic SROIQ(D) as a result of ontology description pre-processing. This will augment the ontology $\mathcal{O} = \langle \mathcal{T}, \mathcal{A} \rangle$ by the membership and property assertions to be $\mathcal{O} = \langle \mathcal{T}, \mathcal{A} \cup \{ C(\mathit{tt}), (\neg C)(\mathit{ff}), r(x_i, l_i), r(y_i, u_i) \} \rangle$ if C is checked to be a vague concept according to a concrete role r, tt and ff are considered as two additional dummy individuals. The individuals x_i, y_i are either tt or ff with the conditions $x_i \neq y_i \wedge x_{i+1} = y_i$, l_i and u_i are numerical values from the range of the concrete role r with $l_i < u_i < l_{i+1}$ for $1 \leq i < n$, where n is the number of the truth gaps. This description should verify the following vagueness consistency.

Lemma 1. *(vagueness consistency). The truth gaps set defined of any vague concept C associated with a role r (or a set of roles) should verify the condition of acceptability (vagueness consistency), this means $\forall i = 1, \cdots, n-1 : x_i \neq y_i \wedge y_i = x_{i+1} \wedge l_i < u_i < l_{i+1} < u_{i+1}$. This vagueness consistency condition can be formulated using the assertions on the dummy individuals tt and ff as*

$$(\{ C(\mathit{tt}), r(\mathit{tt}, d_1), r(\mathit{tt}, d_2), (\neg C)(\mathit{ff}), r(\mathit{ff}, d) \} \subseteq \mathcal{A} \Rightarrow d \notin [d_1, d_2]) \wedge$$
$$(\{ (\neg C)(\mathit{ff}), r(\mathit{ff}, d_1), r(\mathit{ff}, d_2), C(\mathit{tt}), r(\mathit{tt}, d) \} \subseteq \mathcal{A} \Rightarrow d \notin [d_1, d_2]) \tag{4}$$

A non-vague (crisp) concept C will have an empty set of truth gaps according to any concrete role r.

The intuition for this vagueness theory is as follows. An ontology is considered the knowledge base of an intelligent agent; if the ontology (knowledge base) $\mathcal{O}$ contains a vague concept C with respect to a concrete role r and one of its truth gaps has the smallest interval $[l, u]$, where the assertions $r(\mathit{tt}, u), r(\mathit{ff}, l)$ are in $\mathcal{O}$. The agent cannot decide if an individual (object) a with r-property value within the interval $[l, u]$ if it belongs to C or to its complement (we say that the knowledge base is incomplete). We assume that at a moment, assertions like $C(a), r(a, d)$ are added to the ontology $\mathcal{O}$, where $l < d < u$. This new information will change the ontology agent beliefs by reducing the truth gap interval to be $[l, d]$. We call that the individual a is similar to the dummy individual tt because they belong to the same concept C. Then, the individual tt will inherit the property of a. Now, if we add the assertions $(\neg C)(b), r(b, d')$ with $u > d' > d$, this will produce a vagueness inconsistency according to this vagueness theory because the agent has already changed its beliefs so that every property assertion of an individual with respect to the concrete role r where its range is greater than d should be member of the concept C. This vagueness theory is used to adjust the truth intervals (or the truth gaps) described in the original ontology by acquired new information.

3.1   Semantics for Vagueness Theory

The formal semantics of DLs is given in terms of interpretations. A SROIQ(D) interpretation is a pair $I = (\Delta^I, (.)^I)$ where Δ^I is a non-empty set called the domain of I, and $(.)^I$ is the interpretation function which assigns for every $A \in \mathcal{C}$ a subset $(A)^I \subseteq \Delta^I$, for every $o \in \mathcal{R}$ a relation $(o)^I \subseteq \Delta^I \times \Delta^I$, called object role, for every $c \in \mathcal{R}$ a relation $(c)^I \subseteq \Delta^I \times \mathcal{D}$, called concrete role ($\mathcal{D}$ is a data type as integer and string) and for every $a \in \mathcal{I}$, an element $(a)^I \in \Delta^I$. We say the interpretation I is a model of a SROIQ(D) ontology $\mathcal{O} = \langle \mathcal{T}, \mathcal{A} \rangle$, if it satisfies all the assertions in $\mathcal{T}$ and $\mathcal{A}$. In addition, it is a model of any satisfied assertion by the ontology $\mathcal{O}$. If C_r is a vague concept with respect to the concrete role r and $x_i, y_i \in \{t\!\!t, f\!\!f\}$, then the interpretation function is extended to complex concepts and roles according to their syntactic structure.

$$(\top)^I = \Delta^I$$
$$(\bot)^I = \emptyset$$
$$(\{a\})^I = (a)^I$$
$$(r)^I = (r)^I \cup \{(x_i, l_i), (y_i, u_i) \wedge x_i \neq y_i = x_{i+1} \wedge l_i < u_i, \ i = 1, \cdots, n\}$$
$$(C_r)^I = (C)^I \cup \{t\!\!t\}$$
$$(\neg C_r)^I = (\neg C)^I \cup \{f\!\!f\}$$
$$(C_r \sqcap D_r)^I = (C_r)^I \cap (D_r)^I$$
$$(C_r \sqcup D_r)^I = (C_r)^I \cup (D_r)^I$$
$$(\exists o.Self)^I = \{a \in \Delta^I | \exists(a, b) \in (o)^I \wedge a = b\}$$
$$(\forall o.Self)^I = \{a \in \Delta^I | \forall(a, b) \in (o)^I \Rightarrow a = b\}$$
$$(\exists o.C_r)^I = \{a \in \Delta^I | \exists(a, b) \in (o)^I \wedge b \in (C_r)^I\}$$
$$(\forall o.C_r)^I = \{a \in \Delta^I | \forall(a, b) \in (o)^I \Rightarrow b \in (C_r)^I\}$$
$$(\exists c.P)^I = \{a \in \Delta^I | \exists(a, d) \in (c)^I \wedge P(d)\}$$
$$(\forall c.P)^I = \{a \in \Delta^I | \forall(a, d) \in (c)^I \Rightarrow P(d)\}$$
$$(\geq n\ s.C_r)^I = \{a \in \Delta^I | \ |\{b|(a, b) \in (s)^I \wedge b \in (C_r)^I\}| \geq n\}$$
$$(\leq n\ s.C_r)^I = \{a \in \Delta^I | \ |\{b|(a, b) \in (s)^I \wedge b \in (C_r)^I\}| \leq n\}$$

Where n is the number of truth gaps for the vague concept C, $P(d)$ means the value d verifies the predicate P and $|S|$ is the cardinality of the set S. The predefined concepts like the universal concept $\top$, the empty concept $\bot$, the atomic concepts A and the nominative concepts $\{a_1, a_2, \cdots, a_n\}$ are defined as crisp concepts and then they will not be considered as vague concepts.

Example 1. The new ontology after generation of truth gap assertions on the original ontology $\mathcal{O} = \langle \mathcal{T}, \mathcal{A} \rangle$ described in (3), is $\mathcal{O}^{new} = \langle \mathcal{T}^{new}, \mathcal{A}^{new} \rangle$ where, $\mathcal{T}^{new} = \mathcal{T}$ and using the syntax of SROIQ(D), $\mathcal{A}^{new} = \mathcal{A} \cup \{Expensive(t\!\!t),$ $(\neg Expensive)(f\!\!f), Sports(t\!\!t), (\neg Sports)(f\!\!f), price(f\!\!f, 0), price(f\!\!f, 30), price(t\!\!t,$ $50), price(t\!\!t, 100), speed(t\!\!t, 200), speed(t\!\!t, 300), speed(f\!\!f, 100)\}, speed(f\!\!f, 150)\}$. The new interpretations with these introduced assertions are as follows. The

interpretation for the concrete role *price* is $(price)^I = \{(a, 25), (b, 55), (c, 40),$
$(d, 45), (\mathit{ff}, 0), (\mathit{ff}, 30), (\mathit{tt}, 50), (\mathit{tt}, 100)\}$ and for the concrete role *speed*, the interpretation is $(speed)^I = \{(a, 220), (b, 250), (c, 160), (d, 180), (\mathit{ff}, 100), (\mathit{ff}, 150),$
$(\mathit{tt}, 200), (\mathit{tt}, 300)\}$. The interpretation of the vague concept $Expensive_{price}$ is
$\{b, c, \mathit{tt}\}$.

This new ontology containing concept truth gaps is considered vague and then it is incomplete for reasoning. An ontology is complete if we can assign only the definite truth values (tt and ff) to assertions. A vague (incomplete) ontology is an ontology that has at least one vague concept and then it is possible to assign the value ff to certain assertions. In addition, a vague ontology should be acceptable (Lemma 1), which means all the truth gap sets should be acceptable. We define a partial order between ontologies that is noted by $\langle \mathfrak{O}, \leq \rangle$, where $\mathfrak{O}$ is a non-empty set of ontologies describing a domain. If $\mathcal{O}_1$ and $\mathcal{O}_2$ are two ontologies from $\mathfrak{O}$ we write $\mathcal{O}_1 \leq \mathcal{O}_2$, if $\mathcal{O}_1$ is less complete than $\mathcal{O}_2$ (we say also that $\mathcal{O}_2$ extends $\mathcal{O}_1$). The relation $\leq$ (we call it also the extension relation) is based on comparison of truth gaps and it is transitive and antisymmetric. By this partial order definition, there is a canonical normal ontology $\mathcal{O}_n$ that is the least complete ontology, which can be extended by other complete ontologies.

The set $\mathfrak{O}$ has a base ontology that corresponds to description of which all other descriptions are extensions. This base ontology is composed of the terminological assertions and eventually some membership assertions. A condition that can be imposed on domain ontology is its completeability. It states that any intermediate ontology can be extended to a complete ontology. We suppose that ontology $\mathcal{O}$ has a vague concept C, with an acceptable set of truth gaps defined by the assertions set $\{C(\mathit{tt}), (\neg C)(\mathit{ff}), r(x_1, l_1), r(y_1, u_1), r(x_2, l_2), r(y_2, u_2), \cdots, r(x_n, l_n), r(y_n, u_n)\}$, then we define the ontology extension ($\oplus$) by the assertions $\{C(a), r(a, d)\}$ as follows.

$$\langle \mathcal{T}, \mathcal{A}\,[C(\mathit{tt}), (\neg C)(\mathit{ff}), \cdots, r(x_i, l_i), r(y_i, u_i), \cdots]\rangle \oplus \langle \mathcal{T}, \{C(a), r(a, d)\}\rangle =$$
$$\left\langle \mathcal{T}, \mathcal{A} \cup \{C(a), r(a, d)\} \cup \left\{ \begin{array}{l} r(x_i, d) \ if \ x_i = \mathit{tt} \wedge l_i < d < u_i \\ r(y_i, d) \ if \ y_i = \mathit{tt} \wedge l_i < d < u_i \end{array} \right\} \right\rangle$$

$$\langle \mathcal{T}, \mathcal{A}\,[C(\mathit{tt}), (\neg C)(\mathit{ff}), \cdots, r(x_i, l_i), r(y_i, u_i), \cdots]\rangle \oplus \langle \mathcal{T}, \{(\neg C)(a), r(a, d)\}\rangle =$$
$$\left\langle \mathcal{T}, \mathcal{A} \cup \{(\neg C(a)), r(a, d)\} \cup \left\{ \begin{array}{l} (x_i, d) \ if \ x_i = \mathit{ff} \wedge l_i < d < u_i \\ r(y_i, d) \ if \ y_i = \mathit{ff} \wedge l_i < d < u_i \end{array} \right\} \right\rangle$$

This extension guarantees the ontology stability if the acquired informations are satisfied by the ontology description to be extended.

Lemma 2. *(stability property of $\langle \mathfrak{O}, \leq \rangle$). Let α be an assertion, we say $\langle \mathfrak{O}, \leq \rangle$ is stable if*

$$\forall \mathcal{O}_1, \mathcal{O}_2 \in \mathfrak{O}, \mathcal{O}_1 \leq \mathcal{O}_2 : \mathcal{O}_1 \models \alpha \Rightarrow \mathcal{O}_2 \models \alpha \ and \ \mathcal{O}_2 \not\models \alpha \Rightarrow \mathcal{O}_1 \not\models \alpha$$

The complete ontology may not be available to remove completely the vagueness, thus it is necessary to work with the most extended ontology. This means, the truth-valuation is based upon the most extended ontology. Ontology can be extended to complete ontology by learned assertions as a process of ontology evolution when using an intelligent agent or inferred assertions. The learned assertions can be imported from other domain ontologies, RDF databases or simply added by the user. In the following, we propose an extension of reasoning that can take into account the proposed vagueness theory.

4   Reasoning over Imprecise Ontologies

An interpretation I is a model of an ontology $\mathcal{O} = \langle \mathcal{T}, \mathcal{A} \rangle$ denoted by $I \models \mathcal{O}$ if I satisfies all the axioms in $\mathcal{T}$ and all the assertions in $\mathcal{A}$. The reasoning is for checking concept and role instances and for query answering over a satisfiable ontology [9,11]. Ontology satisfiability is to verify whether ontology $\mathcal{O}$ admits at least one model where consistency properties should be verified. Concept instance checking is to verify whether an individual a is an instance of a concept C in every model of $\mathcal{O}$, i.e., whether $\mathcal{O} \models C(a)$. Role instance checking is to verify whether a pair (a, b) of individuals is an instance of a role r in every model of $\mathcal{O}$, i.e., whether $\mathcal{O} \models r(a, b)$.

The satisfaction properties will be extended to deal with the vagueness in ontologies. A vague (imprecise) ontology is satisfiable if it generates acceptable truth gaps for all its concepts (note that an empty set of truth gaps is acceptable). For example, if we modify the concept $ExpensiveCar$ in the vague ontology of the previous example to be $Car \sqcap \exists price. (int [\geq 55]) \sqsubseteq \neg Expensive$, this will change the set of truth gaps assertions associated with the vague concept $Expensive$ to be $\{Expensive(tt), (\neg Expensive)(ff), price(tt, 50), price(tt, 100), price(ff, 0), price(ff, 55)\}$. This set of truth gaps is not acceptable because it is a false set of assertions according to the vagueness consistency stated in (4). Nevertheless, the vague ontology is satisfiable by using the traditional reasoning techniques. However, if we add the assertions $\{Car(d), price(d, 52)\}$ to the assertional box, the vague ontology becomes inconsistent because d is now at the same time expensive car and no-expensive car, although the ontology was initially satisfiable. In the following, we will extend the reasoning Tableau algorithm to cope with the problem of vague ontologies using this proposed vagueness theory.

The principle of this reasoning algorithm is the expansion of a finite configuration $T = \{A_1, \cdots, A_n\}$ of assertions that is represented as a set of subsets, each subset is composed of assertions on individuals, using well defined rules until no rule can be applied on at least one subset (satisfaction) or contradictions (clashes) are observed within all subsets (unsatisfaction). We will have a clash in a subset A_i when a contradiction happens in it. There are three types of contradictions: $\perp(a) \in A_i$, $C(a) \in A_i \wedge (\neg C)(a) \in A_i$, or unacceptable truth gaps assertions. If no expansion rule can be applied in A_i we say that A_i is open. The terminological box should be normalized to apply the expansion rules. It is necessary to begin the inference with formulas that are independent from any terminology. This means elimination of the definitions (equivalence axioms) and subsumptions (inclusion axioms) in the terminological box. If it contains no cycle in the definitions (which will be the case most of the time), it will happen simply by replacing all the terms in the formula by their definitions in the terminology. Obviously, if a term of formula has no definition in terminology, it remains unchanged. We repeat this process until the resulting formula contains no term which has a definition in the terminology.

For reasoning over vague ontologies using the proposed vagueness theory, we have added the following two expansion rules that should be applied after every expansion by a classical Tableau rule (the reader can be referred to [4,5,9] for the classical Tableau rules). We will get a clash (contradiction) if any new set of truth gaps assertions is not acceptable (Lemma 1 and Equation 4). The configuration length depends on ontology description and property being checked. Using the DL syntax of SROIQ(D), these two rules can be formulated as

$$V - Rule^+(DL) : \frac{A_i \in T \land \{C(a), r(a,d), C(\mathit{t\!t})\} \subseteq A_i}{(T \setminus A_i) \cup (A_i \cup \{r(\mathit{t\!t}, d)\})} r(\mathit{t\!t}, d) \notin A_i$$

$$V - Rule^-(DL) : \frac{A_i \in T \land \{(\neg C)(a), r(a,d), (\neg C)(\mathit{f\!f})\} \subseteq A_i}{(T \setminus A_i) \cup (A_i \cup \{r(\mathit{f\!f}, d)\})} r(\mathit{f\!f}, d) \notin A_i$$

These two rules will augment the assertions subset A_i by the property assertion $r(\mathit{t\!t}, d)$ if A_i contains the assertion $C(a) \land r(a,d) \land C(\mathit{t\!t})$ (the rule $V - Rule^+(DL)$) or by the property assertion $r(\mathit{f\!f}, d)$ if A_i contains the assertion $(\neg C)(a) \land r(a,d) \land (\neg C)(\mathit{f\!f})$ (the rule $V - Rule^-(DL)$). We explain this algorithm extension on a simple example of an instance checking using the ontology described in (3). We want to check the membership of the individual d (instance checking) to the class $ExpensiveSportsCar$ ($\mathcal{O} \models ExpensiveSportsCar(d)$). This means that we want to prove that $(\neg ExpensiveSportsCar)(d)$ is inconsistent with the ontology description. After elimination of terminological axioms and normalization as preliminary steps before applying Tableau Rules, we have:

$$T^0 = \left\{ A_0^0 = \left\{ \begin{array}{l} ((\neg Car) \sqcup (\neg Expensive) \sqcup (\neg Sports))(d), Car(a), Car(b), \\ Car(c), Car(d), price(a, 25), price(b, 55), price(c, 40), price(d, 45), \\ speed(a, 220), speed(b, 120), speed(c, 160), speed(d, 180), \\ (\neg Expensive)(a), Expensive(b), Expensive(c), Sports(a), \\ (\neg Sports)(b), Sports(c), Expensive(\mathit{t\!t}), price(\mathit{t\!t}, 50), price(\mathit{t\!t}, 100), \\ (\neg Expensive)(\mathit{f\!f}), price(\mathit{f\!f}, 0), price(\mathit{f\!f}, 30), Sports(\mathit{t\!t}), \\ speed(\mathit{t\!t}, 200), speed(\mathit{t\!t}, 300), (\neg Sports)(\mathit{f\!f}), \\ speed(\mathit{f\!f}, 100), speed(\mathit{f\!f}, 150) \end{array} \right\} \right\}$$

Using the classical expansion rule of the disjunction, we obtain the configuration:

$$T^1 = \left\{ \begin{array}{l} A_0^1 = A_0^0 \cup \{(\neg Car)(d)\}, \\ A_1^1 = A_0^0 \cup \{(\neg Expensive)(d)\}, \\ A_2^1 = A_0^0 \cup \{(\neg Sports)(d)\} \end{array} \right\}$$

We observe a clash in the subset A_0^1 (it contains $Car(d)$ and $(\neg Car)(d)$). By applying the rules $V - Rule^+(DL)$ and $V - Rule^-(DL)$, we get:

$$T^2 = \left\{ \begin{array}{l} A_0^2 = A_0^1 = \Box, \\ A_1^2 = A_1^1 \cup \left\{ \begin{array}{l} price(t\!t, 55), price(t\!t, 40), price(f\!f, 25), price(f\!f, 45), \\ speed(t\!t, 220), speed(f\!f, 120), speed(t\!t, 160) \end{array} \right\}, \\ A_2^2 = A_2^1 \cup \left\{ \begin{array}{l} price(t\!t, 55), price(t\!t, 40), price(f\!f, 25), \\ speed(t\!t, 220), speed(f\!f, 120), speed(t\!t, 160), speed(f\!f, 180) \end{array} \right\} \end{array} \right\}$$

It is clear that the subset A_1^2 of assertions contains unacceptable truth gaps assertions (the following implication $\{Expensive(t\!t), price(t\!t, 40), price(t\!t, 50), (\neg Expensive)(f\!f), price(f\!f, 45)\} \in A_1^2 \Rightarrow 45 \notin [40, 50]$ is false). The same thing for the subset A_2^2, where the implication $\{Sports(t\!t), speed(t\!t, 160), speed(t\!t, 200), (\neg Sports)(f\!f), speed(f\!f, 180)\} \in A_2^2 \Rightarrow 180 \notin [160, 200]$ is also false. Thus a clash is observed in the two subsets which makes d a member of $ExpensiveSportsCar$. The principle of this approach is as follows. Without this vagueness theory, d which has the price of 45 (greater than 30 and less than 50) and the speed of 180 (greater than 150 and less than 200) cannot be decided by the classical reasoners, as $Expensive$, $Sports$, $\neg Expensive$ and $\neg Sports$ because the definitions of $Expensive$ and $Sports$ are vague. However, the ontology contains an assertion indicating that the price 40 of c is an expensive price ($Expensive(c)$) and its speed 160 makes it a sports car; this information can help the reasoner to decide that the car d of price 45 and of speed 180 is also an expensive sports car.

5   Conclusion

In this paper, we have presented a vagueness theory to deal with the problem of ontologies containing vague concepts. The vague property (characteristic) of a concept is based in general, on certain concept data properties that may generate truth gaps. With the traditional reasoning methods, it is not possible to decide the membership of an individual (object) to a vague concept (class) if its data property is in the truth gap. Ontologies could have extension (evolution), where assertions may be added, intentionally or as result of inferences. This ontology evolution can reduce the truth gaps and then logically it will be possible to infer on previously undecided assertions. This proposed vagueness theory is used to extend the current reasoning method to take into account this vagueness notion. Implementation of this approach is one of our perspectives.

References

1. Baader, F.: What's new in description logics. Informatik-Spektrum 34(5), 434–442 (2011)
2. Bobillo, F., Delgado, M., Gomez-Romero, J., Straccia, U.: Joining gödel and zadeh fuzzy logics in fuzzy description logics. International Journal of Uncertainty, Fuzziness and Knowledge-Based Systems 20(4), 475–508 (2012)

3. Hitzler, P., Krötzsch, M., Parsia, B., Patel-Schneider, P.F., Rudolph, S. (eds.): OWL 2 Web Ontology Language: Primer. W3C (2009)
4. Horrocks, I., Kutz, O., Sattler, U.: The even more irresistible SROIQ. In: Proc. of the 10th Int. Conf. on Principles of Knowledge Representation and Reasoning, KR 2006, pp. 57–67. AAAI Press (2006)
5. Horrocks, I., Sattler, U.: A tableau decision procedure for SHOIQ. Journal of Automated Reasoning 39(39–3), 249–276 (2007)
6. Krötzsch, M.: OWL 2 profiles: An introduction to lightweight ontology languages. In: Eiter, T., Krennwallner, T. (eds.) Reasoning Web 2012. LNCS, vol. 7487, pp. 112–183. Springer, Heidelberg (2012)
7. Lukasiewicz, T., Straccia, U.: Managing uncertainty and vagueness in description logics for the semantic web. J. Web Sem. 6(4), 291–308 (2007)
8. Lukasiewicz, T., Straccia, U.: Description logic programs under probabilistic uncertainty and fuzzy vagueness. Int. J. Approx. Reasoning 50(6), 837–853 (2009)
9. Lutz, C., Milicic, M.: A tableau algorithm for DLs with concrete domains and GCIs. Journal of Automated Reasoning 38(1–3), 227–259 (2007)
10. Pareti, P., Klein, E.: Learning vague concepts for the semantic web. In: Porc. Joint WS on Knowledge Evolution and Ontology Dynamics. In Conj. with ISWC 2011, vol. 784, CEUR workshop proceedings (2011)
11. Pérez-Urbina, H., Horrocks, I., Motik, B.: Efficient query answering for owl 2. In: Bernstein, A., Karger, D.R., Heath, T., Feigenbaum, L., Maynard, D., Motta, E., Thirunarayan, K. (eds.) ISWC 2009. LNCS, vol. 5823, pp. 489–504. Springer, Heidelberg (2009)
12. Stefan, B., Peñaloza, R.: Consistency reasoning in lattice-based fuzzy description logics. Int. J. Approx. Reason (2013)
13. Straccia, U.: Foundations of Fuzzy Logic and Semantic Web Languages. CRC Studies in Informatics Series. Chapman & Hall (2013)
14. Turhan, A.-Y.: Introductions to description logics – A guided tour. In: Rudolph, S., Gottlob, G., Horrocks, I., van Harmelen, F. (eds.) Reasoning Weg 2013. LNCS, vol. 8067, pp. 150–161. Springer, Heidelberg (2013)
15. Zadeh, L.A.: Knowledge representation in fuzzy logic. IEEE Transactions on Knowledge and Data Engineering 1(1), 89–100 (1989)

Defining Semantic Relationships to Capitalize Content of Multimedia Resources

Mohamed Kharrat[✉], Anis Jedidi, and Faiez Gargouri

MIRACL - Multimedia, InfoRmation systems and Advanced Computing Laboratory,
University of Sfax, Sfax, Tunisia
med_khr@yahoo.fr, anis.jedidi@isimsf.rnu.tn,
faiez.gargouri@isimsf.rnu.tn

Abstract. Existing systems or architectures hardly provide any way to localize sub-parts of multimedia objects (e.g. sub regions of images, persons, events…), which represents hidden semantics of resources. To simplify and automate discovering hidden connections between such resources, we describe and evaluate in this paper, an algorithm for creating semantic relationships between multimedia news resources, giving a contextual schema (represented in RDF) as a result. This latter, which could eventually be used under any retrieval system, is integrated in our main multimodal retrieval system.

We have also proposed and introduced a special measure of accuracy since evaluation relies on users' intentions. An experimental evaluation of our algorithm is presented, showing encouraging results.

Keywords: Semantic · Multimedia · Relationships

1   Introduction

Semantic web is one of the most important challenges in web realm which has been subject of many researches in recent years.

One of the main elements for processing semantic web is to go further knowledge and annotation. In fact, developing semantic retrieval systems, needs information extraction, harvesting knowledge and various methods of data.

Advances in multimedia technologies have made possible the storage of huge multimedia documents collections on computer systems. But the lack of efficiency is perceived as the main obstacle for a large-scale deployment of semantic technologies. In order to allow an efficient exploitation of these collections, designing tools for accessing data resources is required.

One of the biggest challenges is the exploitation of these collections, particularly hidden or non-exploitable relations as well as search and querying. To address this problem, we propose a mechanism to generate a new defined set of hidden semantic relationships between multimedia documents.

Within the same framework, our main system [5] proposes to retrieve multimedia documents using a multimodal approach. The main characteristic of our system is the

© IFIP International Federation for Information Processing 2015
A. Amine et al. (Eds.): CIIA 2015, IFIP AICT 456, pp. 367–378, 2015.
DOI: 10.1007/978-3-319-19578-0_30

use of two languages, XQuery and SPARQL to query the description of multimedia resources. Performance of our system can be significantly increased by using a semantic relationship contextual schema (see Figure1) for semantic relationships, by applying rules through an algorithm described in this paper.

The importance of discovering such links is essentially for retrieving relevant hidden resources in results.

The algorithm which is exposed here, allows the generation and publication of linked data from metadata. Any resource which is composed of many parts could or could not have many relationships with other resources.

In addition, we introduce a special measure that allows a user to rate the correctness of each relationship and penalize irrelevant ones based on its own perception.

The aim of this paper is to present how to implement semantic relationships between data along with multimedia news resources to enhance our ability to "understand" those latter ones. In fact, news descriptive meta-data available for users, are difficult to learn about their content and capabilities, this is why we are seeking for strengthening by establishing this feature to our main system.

The next step will be the integration of this mechanism over XQuery language, which gives the possibility to add new relationships through queries. This means, we will create new relationships based on the resources which are the results of queries. In fact, XQuery will be first used to build semantic relationships over queries based on functions, and secondly, it will be used to harness them .

The last part of the paper is structured as follows. Section 2 provides an overview of closely related work. We present proposed semantic relationships and a complementary inference reasoning to build these relationships in section 3. We evaluate our approach in section 4 and finally we conclude in section5.

2   Related Work

As far as we know, there are no other works reported addressing the task of creating semantic relationships from XML content of multimedia resources. Then, we are going to briefly present here some previous studies which are quite close to our work, consisting mainly on automatic identification of relationships from unstructured documents or the use of lexical patterns for relations discovery between concepts. These have the advantage of the simplicity of collecting training corpora automatically.

While authors use a graph in [6] to model relationships between phrases inside semantic corpus Wordnet using numbers, our method does not use a graph.

Authors in [7] Establish missing semantic relations between Wikipedia entities by discovering automatically the missing entity links in Wikipedia infoboxes, which are important for creating RDF links between DBpedia instances.

Several other approaches have been proposed having various methods and techniques. Solution proposed in [3], identify semantic links between persons, products, events and other entities from Twitter based on entities topics and their types according to time axis.

In [2], authors compute concept-concept relatedness and concept-category relatedness based on heuristics by Category links and related links in Wikipedia.

In [4], author proposes RelFinder: an interactive discovery of relationships between DBpedia objects which is controlled by users, combined with the automatic mechanisms according to topological and semantic dimensions.

Our problem shares some resemblance with works in[1], where author creates new links in precise region on images. This region represents the most relevant part in XML document of each image using hierarchical structure and adds weights for every link. The goal is to ameliorate the image retrieval in the semi-structured documents.

In contrast to our approach, all these works treat mono-media documents. They propose descriptions which allow establishing relations between annotated concepts, resources and parts of resources. These works do not take into account multimedia resources and the set of sturdy relations which are between resources or between parts of a same resource. In addition, most of them, do not consider the semantic side.

In the following section, we introduce relations and rules which allow us to extract semantics from multimedia resources.

3   Semantic Relationships

We introduce here, a contextual schema which constitutes formalism for semantic relationships representation. It expresses meaning in a form that is both logically precise and humanly readable. This schema is implemented to be used in our multimodal system and represented using RDF.

The basic assumption underlying our approach is textual descriptions of resources always hide semantics that cannot always be discovered notably between concepts. Besides, meaning of some data is sometimes either unknown, ambiguous or implicit.

However, not all semantically related concepts are interesting for end users. In this paper, we have identified a number of semantic relations.

Media fragments are really parts of a parent resource. The use of identifiers seems therefore appropriate to specify these media fragments. As for any identifier, access to the parent identifier shall be possible in order to inspect its context. Providing a way being used as agreed to localize sub-parts of multimedia objects (e.g. sub regions of images, temporal sequences of videos etc.) is fundamental.

All resources in our collection are described with NewsML annotation standard for news documents. In this standard, metadata itself comes in bewildering variety. There are specific terms to describe every type of media. We harness them to extract contextual relations to be used in semantic and contextual recognition. Most visual and audio features (motion, speech, text) will be used to describe each part. For example, in order to describe the content of video news, we apply concepts to describe scenes like meeting, speech, interview, live reporting or events/topics like sports, politics and commercials. Notably, we also apply the identities of persons that can be recovered from the visual flow (person who appears on the screen), from audio or from textual information.

Our goal is to make a semantic search based on both content and structure at the same time. We do not propose to use existing links between resources, but we create our own links.

Our algorithm takes as input a resource and generates a new relationship if links exit with some other resources.

```
<?xml version="1.0"?>
<resources><resource  id="IMAGE01" type="image">
<link name= "AI">
<resource  id="IMAGE02" type="image"></resource>
<resource  id="VIDEO01" type="video"></resource>
</link>
</resource>
<resource id="VIDEO07" type="video"> <link name="SH"><resource
id="IMAGE03" type="image"></resource>
...
</link>
```

Fig. 1. Sample of Contextual Schema

3.1   Relationships Mechanism

The task of relationships building is a crossing problem between textual relations and semantic relations.

For instance, the textual expression "P talks in R" indicates a semantic relation Talk between entity "P" which is represented by a resource and another resource "R".

This semantic relationship can be expressed textually in several ways: for example "P, said something about X" or "a quotation of P in R".

There are several components to make a coherent relationship, including specific textual expressions as well as constraints on the entities involved in the relation. For instance, in the Talk relation, "P" must be a Person and "R" a Resource. The details of every relationship are given below.

T: Talk
This type of relationships describes links between resource R which contains {person, organization, team…} talking. This relation must be between an image and another type of document.

TA: Talk About
This type of relationships describes links between resource R which represents {document, report, documentary…} and another resource R'.

S: Speak
This type of relationships describes links between resource R which contains only a person and another resource R'.

SA: Speak About
This type of relationships describes links between resource R which contains only a person speaking, and another resource R'.

SH: Show
This type of relationships describes links between a resource R {documentary, event, interview…} which shows {person, organization, team, place…} and another resource R'.

AI: Appear In

This type of relationships describes links between a resource R which represents {person, organization, team, place…} and appears in another resource R' which represents {event, scene, sequence…}.

In the following, we briefly explain the mechanism via rules that must be used to create these relationships.

Algorithm

```
Input: Xml resource r
Output: relation between two or more resources in contex-
tual schema CS
For all r   {R} do
{Extract  metadata from r and r'
If any verified module
{ If   in CS
Add new relation to CS
End If}
Else
Execute module inference
End If
End For
Return  r ↔ r'
```

Rule 1:

$$Talk(\exists R \supset \{image\} \land R' \supset \{video, audio, text\}$$
$$\land \exists a \langle objet \rangle, \langle person \rangle, or \langle ganization \rangle \supset R \supset R' \land \exists \{\langle interview \rangle, \langle report \rangle\} \supset R \qquad (1)$$

To add the new relationship Talk, the resource origin R must be an image and the destination R' could be any type (video, audio, text). Secondly metadata like ‹object›, ‹person› or ‹organization› must exist in the two resources. In addition, ‹interview› or ‹report› must be present in the destination resource.

Rule 2:

$$Speak(\exists$$
$$R \supset \{image\} \land R' \supset \{video, audio\} \land \exists \{\langle person \rangle\} \supset R \supset R' \land \exists \{\langle interview \rangle \lor \langle speech \rangle\} \supset R' \qquad (2)$$

To add the new relationship Speak, the resource origin R must be an image and the destination R' could be (video or audio). Secondly, the metadata only ‹person› must exist in the two resources. In addition, ‹interview› or ‹speech› must be present in the destination resource.

Rule 3:

$$TalkAbout(\exists R, R' \supset \{image, video, audio, text\} \land R \equiv R' \land type(R) \neq type(R') \qquad (3)$$

To add the new relationship TalkAbout, the resource origin R and the destination R' could be of any type of media (image, video, audio, text). Secondly, we fix a similarity threshold between metadata of both resources using TFIDF measure between XML's tags of these resources. The type of related resources must be different, (e.g. we could not relate two images or two videos).

Rule 4:

$$\text{SpeakAbout}(\exists\\ R \supset \{\text{video,audio}\} \land R' \supset \{\text{image,video,audio,text}\} \land \exists \{\langle\text{person}\rangle\} \supset R \land R \equiv R' \quad (4)$$

To add the new relationship SpeakAbout, the resource origin R must be a video or an audio resource and the destination R' could be of any type (image, video, audio, text). Secondly, metadata ‹person› must exist in the original resource. Finally, we fix a similarity threshold between metadata of both resources using TFIDF measure between XML tags of resources.

Rule 5:

$$\text{Show}(\exists R \supset \{\text{video,image}\} \land R' \supset \{\text{image,video,audio,text}\} \land$$
$$\exists\{\langle\text{documentary}\rangle, \langle\text{event}\rangle, \langle\text{interview}\rangle\} \supset R \land\ R \equiv R' \quad (5)$$

To add the new relationship Show, the resource origin R could be only a video or an image and the destination R' could be any type (image, video, audio, and text). Secondly metadata {documentary, event, interview…} must exist in the original resource. Finally, we fix a similarity threshold between metadata of both resources using TFIDF measure between XML tags of resources.

Rule 6:

$$\text{AppearIn}(\exists R \supset \{\text{image}\} \land R' \supset \{\text{video,image}\} \land$$
$$\exists\{\langle\text{objet}\rangle, \langle\text{person}\rangle, \langle\text{organization}\rangle\} \supset R \supset R' \quad (6)$$

To add the new relationship AppearIn, the resource origin R must be only an image and the destination R' could be (image or video). Secondly metadata like ‹object›, ‹person› or ‹organization› must exist in the two resources.

3.2   Inference reasoning

Since XML does not support or suggest reasoning mechanisms, we have to rely on an underlying logical formalism.

We define here some inductive rules to deduce new relationships from existing relationships.

Case 1: $\exists\ \text{link}(R1,R2) \land \text{proximity}(R3,R2) \Rightarrow \text{link}(R1,R3)$ (7)

R1→R2 are two related resources, so if the new resource R3 has proximity with R2 then R1→R3

Case 2: $\exists(\text{link}(R1,\{R\}) \equiv \text{link}(R2,\{R\})\ ) \Rightarrow R1 = R2$ (8)

Case 3: $\exists(\ \text{link}(R1,R2) \land \text{link}(R1,R2) \land \text{link}(R1,R3)) \Rightarrow R2 \equiv R3 \equiv R4$ (9)

If there is semantic relationship between resource R1 and other resources as follow:

R1→R2 ; R1→R3 ; R1→R4

Then, there will be similarities between R2, R3 and R4.

We define link (R,R') as an existing semantic relation between R and R' and Proximity (R,R') as the similarity between R and R' calculated by the measure below.

3.3   Similarity Measure

We use this computation whenever a similarity measure is needed. It is composed of three steps.

First step:

Pre-processing: this module is concerned with pre-processing operations preparing the input resource to be linked. It checks if a resource R is typed.

Second step:

- Comparing ‹keyword› of R and R' for equality or similarity
- Comparing ‹title› of R and R' for equality or similarity

Third step:

Similarity is defined by some functions:

The Jaccard coefficient measures similarity between sample sets, and is defined as the size of the intersection divided by the size of the union of the sample sets:

$$J(A, B) = \frac{|A \cap B|}{|A \cup B|} \qquad (10)$$

In addition, we use term frequency. This count is usually normalized to prevent a bias towards longer documents (which may have a higher term count regardless of the actual importance of that term in the document) to give a measure of the importance of the term t_i within the particular document d_j. Thus we have the term frequency, defined as follows:

$$tf_{i,j} = \frac{n_{i,j}}{\sum_k n_{k,j}} \qquad (11)$$

where $n_{i,j}$ is the number of occurrences of the considered term (t_i) in document d_j, and the denominator is the sum of number of occurrences of all terms in document d_j, that is, the size of the document $| d_j |$.

A threshold parameter is used   here and changes during evaluation.

In the main system, queries attempt to find semantic contents such as specific people, objects and events in a broadcast news collection. We define the following classes: Named person, Named object and General object.

Our retrieval system needs to go through the following steps to find relevant multimedia resources for content-based queries without any user feedback or manual query expansion.

4   Evaluation

In this section we present the results of the experimental evaluation that we have conducted on the semantic relationships extraction using real datasets. The objective is to evaluate the efficiency of the schema transformation. We have used several resources sets attempting to cover many domain variations, features and special cases.
The algorithm has been implemented using PHP language on the top of the open source, native XML database.

4.1   Accuracy Evaluation

We present the performance of the schema transformation generation processes of previous sections, then we examine the efficiency of the said processes.

The experiments were conducted on a 2.53GHz Intel Core I5 machine with 4GB of RAM, running MS 8. All results are averaged over three runs.

The basic characteristics (e.g., number of elements, attributes, etc.) of the XML resources are not shown in the evaluation. In this experiment, we have chosen a context about international politics and United States politics mainly but not exclusively. We have also used various contexts, as sports, terrorism, or Internet privacy.

Annotation has an important role here, there is a consequence and a difference between, for example, the keyword "Angela Merkel" appearing or not in "keyword" tag, and/or in "subject" tag too. Besides, taking for example, the keyword Hillary Clinton which could exist in other forms like Hillary Rodham Clinton or even Hillary Diane Rodham Clinton, has a real impact on results. This depends on news agencies, but actually, we did not deal with this point.

Table 1 shows results by number of used resources. Even a small number of resources is used, we believe that the use of a huge database could not have an impact on the results or on the performances. The result of the variation of used thresholds is presented in table 2. We can observe that by increasing it, redundancy decreases but the total number found decreases too.

Finally, as expected, the XML Schema file size slightly affects the time consumed by this transformation, e.g. a single iteration for a result set size of 20 resources takes about 3 seconds.

Table 1. Results values by modifying the number of resources

Resources	Total	Erroneous	Valid	Not detected
5	5	2	3	2
20	8	2	6	3
30	11	3	8	5

Table 2. Results values using variable thresholds

	Total	Not found	Redundancy
Similarity thre-shold >1	8	3	1
Similarity thre-shold >1.5	7	3	0

Table 3. Sample of the results values by relationship types

Relationship	Detected	Erroneous	Not detected
Show	1		1
Appear In	2	1	1
Talk	0		
Talk About	1		
Speak	1	1	
Speak About	3		1

In table 3, we present the results by relationship types. We assume and believe that the contents are the primary determinants of these results.

In fact, there is a lot of data which are made by humans, so the same content could be written in many ways hence influencing the interpretation even if made by humans. Consequently, this can result in weak structures. The fact of omitting Named Entity or describing differently a situation could change retrieval results.

Also the fact of using resources with the same context is very important, because otherwise, we could have zero relationships. Finally, the rank of metadata in XML resources is also computed and has an effect on results too.

e.g.:

<genre qcode="genre:WarConflict"></genre>

   <genre qcode="genre:Politics"></genre>

These two tags do not have the same impact if the creator of the metadata considers the importance of the rank of those genres or chooses to put the inverse.

We note that we have more relationships between the same type of resources than between different types even those between videos and texts. We have an interesting number of relations. We can note that the factor "type" is important.

Notice that the poor descriptions of images has impacts on the results because usually images are not well annotated, seeing their nature. In addition, images have no <title> tag. Besides, the image sometimes describes a general context and does not specify persons or known entities, e.g. a picture containing scenes of injury or dead bodies.

Furthermore, we would measure the Recall as the fraction of the relations that are relevant and successfully retrieved, and the Precision as the fraction of retrieved documents that are relevant to the result obtained according to our perception.

$$Precision = \frac{|Correct\ detected\ relations|}{|Total\ retrieved\ relations|} \qquad (12)$$

Precision: a fraction of documents that are relevant among the entire retrieved document. Practically it gives accuracy of the results.

$$Recall = \frac{|Correct\ detected\ relations|}{|Total\ correct\ relations\ |} \tag{13}$$

Recall: a fraction of the documents   that is retrieved and relevant among all relevant documents. Practically it gives coverage of the results.

Precision is more important than Recall in our case, because the irrelevant/wrong relationships has   negative repercussions on the results in our retrieval system. Figure 2 shows that the overall precision of our system is 0.69 indeed.

Consider also that normally, the number of used resources do not affects results. Performance will be quite close to this limit even if we increase this number. In some cases, for example, in the absence of connexion between resources, we could get 0 relationships which does not imply irrelevance of the algorithm.

In the next section, we introduce a new measure more meaningful than Recall and Precision.

4.2   Accuracy Metrics

It is well known, that the policy of the user providing relevance feedback can have a strong impact on the evaluation results. Since the user's views differ, judging the correctness of the retrieved relationships is a challenging task besides the distinction between relevant combination of relationships which is related to different interpretations.

In fact, the correctness of a detected relation is not a bivalent value as it is based on the user's perception. A relation could be irrelevant or missed. In essence, for an evaluation, a missed relation is better than an irrelevant one because this latter could have repercussions on the research results.

We employ and invite three testers to evaluate how closely the results satisfied their intentions.

For every user, we compare its interpretation with the original one. To assess the correctness of the algorithm, the results were manually examined by domain experts, and for this reason, we introduced a special measure that is Alg_i.

This measure allows a user to rate the correctness of each relationship and penalize the irrelevant ones, depending on its own perception.

Let us consider the following:

i, j : indexes of documents and k: number of relationships where:

$$\begin{matrix} i,j \\ i \neq j \end{matrix} \in\ ]0,1[^2 \qquad k \in \{1 \rightarrow 6\}$$

M : number of users
I : {indexes of all documents}
S: relations between I & j and

$$Alg_i\{L_{ij}^k\}$$

For every Alg$_i$ we associate a subset E_{ij} (indexes of relations between fixed i and j)

$$Alg_{X1}: \{L_{ij}^s\}$$

Alg(x1) =C1=C1*+C1**

To compute C1, we fixe X* and X** which are penalties

To penalize (-) $\leftrightarrow$ X*

To penalize (+)$\leftrightarrow$X**

Where: X** « X*

```
01.    In case of irrelevant relationship
02.    Initializing  C1*←0
03.    For i,j ∈ I  /i≠j
04.    For k ∈ E_ij
05.    For s∈ X_ij and s≠k :C1*←C1*+X*
06.    Return C1*
07.    In case of missed relationship
08.    Initializing C1**←0
09.    For i,j ∈ I  /i≠j
10.    For s ∈ X_ij
11.    For k ∈ E_ij and s≠k :C1**←C1**+X**
12.    Return C1**
```

0<=C1<=6X*

X*∈]0,1[

$0<=G=\frac{C1+C2+\cdots+CM}{M}<=6X*$

0 <= G <=1

We simply have to set X as a scalar to get results. According to our metric, the more the number tends towards zero, the more this number is relevant. In our case, X is set to 1/3. We perceive through figure 3, that all obtained results are close and good. This has an important impact on ambitious efforts to detect relationships with more efficiency.

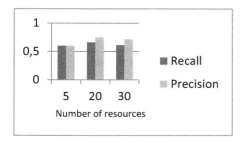

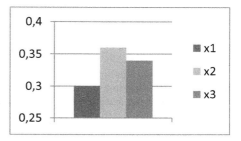

Fig. 2. Accuracy Recall & Precision   **Fig. 3.** Accuracy of Alg$_i$

5   Conclusion

Metadata provides rich semantic relationships that can be used for retrieval purposes. In order to capitalize hidden connexions and relationships between resources, we have presented in this paper a proposition for interlinking multimedia resources semantically through defined rules, and then, results are supplied as a contextual schema of RDF triples. The goal of this schema is primarily refining querying, and adding more semantics to our retrieval system.

The experimental results show that our approach can accurately find hidden relations between resources, and thus our main retrieval system will perform in a better way.

Actually, among obtained relations, there are some wrongly detected relations and some correct ones which are not detected. The next step is to continue exploring ways to improve the Precision of the construction of the relationships with poorer performance. In particular, the use of inference that may express ambiguous relationships, depending on the context, needs to be further enhanced. We also plan to try this algorithm with yet newer relationships based on resulting resources, we could build new relationships that will be used in second time.

We will continue investigating on the best combination of annotation and recommendation for using keywords to get better result.

References

1. Aouadi, H., Torjmen, M.: Exploitation des liens pour la recherche d'images dans des documents XML. In: Conférence Francophone en Recherche d'Information et Applications – CORIA (2010)
2. Bu, F., Hao, Y., Zhu, X.: Semantic Relationship Discovery with Wikipedia Structure. In: 22nd International Joint Conference on Artificial Intelligence IJCAI 2011, Barcelona, pp. 1770–1777 (2011)
3. Celik, I., Abel, F., Houben, G.-J.: Learning Semantic Relationships between Entities in Twitter. In: Auer, S., Díaz, O., Papadopoulos, G.A. (eds.) ICWE 2011. LNCS, vol. 6757, pp. 167–181. Springer, Heidelberg (2011)
4. Heim, P., Lohmann, S., Stegemann, T.: Interactive Relationship Discovery via the Semantic Web. In: Aroyo, L., Antoniou, G., Hyvönen, E., ten Teije, A., Stuckenschmidt, H., Cabral, L., Tudorache, T. (eds.) ESWC 2010, Part I. LNCS, vol. 6088, pp. 303–317. Springer, Heidelberg (2010)
5. Kharrat, M., Jedidi, A., Gargouri, F.: A system proposal for multimodal retrieval of multimedia documents. In: 9th IEEE International Symposium on Parallel and Distributed Processing with Applications. ISPA, Busan-Korea (2011)
6. Stanchev, L.: Building Semantic Corpus from WordNet. In: IEEE International Conference on Bioinformatics and Biomedicine Workshops, Philadelphia (2012)
7. Xu, M., Wang, Z., Bie, R., Li, J., Zheng, C., Ke, W., Zhou, M.: Discovering Missing Semantic Relations between Entities. In: Alani, H., et al. (eds.) ISWC 2013, Part I. LNCS, vol. 8218, pp. 673–686. Springer, Heidelberg (2013)

Security and Network Technologies:
Security

A Multi-agents Intrusion Detection System Using Ontology and Clustering Techniques

Imen Brahmi[1]([✉]), Hanen Brahmi[1], and Sadok Ben Yahia[2]

[1] Faculty of Sciences of Tunis, Computer Science Department,
Campus University, 1060 Tunis, Tunisia
imen.brahmi@gmail.com
[2] Institut Mines-TELECOM, TELECOM SudParis,
UMR CNRS Samovar, 91011 Evry Cedex, France
sadok.benyahia@fst.rnu.tn

Abstract. Nowadays, the increase in technology has brought more sophisticated intrusions. Consequently, Intrusion Detection Systems (IDS) are quickly becoming a popular requirement in building a network security infrastructure. Most existing IDS are generally centralized and suffer from a number of drawbacks, *e.g.*, high rates of false positives, low efficiency, etc, especially when they face distributed attacks. This paper introduces a novel hybrid multi-agents IDS based on the intelligent combination of a clustering technique and an ontology model, called OCMAS-IDS. The latter integrates the desirable features provided by the multi-agents methodology with the benefits of semantic relations as well as the high accuracy of the data mining technique. Carried out experiments showed the efficiency of our distributed IDS, that sharply outperforms other systems over real traffic and a set of simulated attacks.

Keywords: Intrusion detection system · Multi-agents · Clustering · Ontology

1 Introduction

As far the cost of information processing and Internet accessibility is dropping, more and more organizations are becoming vulnerable to a wide variety of cyber threats. Therefore, network security is becoming a major challenge. Consequently, software tools, that can automatically detect a variety of intrusions, are of a compelling need. An *Intrusion Detection Systems* (IDS) has been of use to detect and defend intrusions more proactively in short period.

Even that IDSs have become a standard component in security infrastructures, they still have a number of signicant drawbacks [14]. Indeed, they suffer from problems of reliability, relevance, disparity and/or incompleteness in the presentation and manipulation of knowledge as well as the complexity of attacks. This fact hampers the detection ability of IDS, since it causes the generation excessive of false alarms and decreases the detection of real intrusions. In addition, most of the IDSs use centralized architectures. Unfortunately this strategy has

© IFIP International Federation for Information Processing 2015
A. Amine et al. (Eds.): CIIA 2015, IFIP AICT 456, pp. 381–393, 2015.
DOI: 10.1007/978-3-319-19578-0_31

several drawbacks [4]. Indeed, the central processing node can lead to a single point of failure. Clearly, whenever the central processing node is attacked, then the whole IDS has been damaged. Besides, the transfer of all the information at a central processing unit implies a great need on network resources and leads to much network load on the system. Consequently, the centralized IDS suffers from scalability problems [4]. Moreover, the communication and cooperation between a centralized IDS components are badly missing. To palliate these problems, the integration of a multi-agents technology within the IDS seemed to be an appropriate solution. In fact, the use of multi-agents system for intrusion detection offers a new alternative to the IDS with several advantages listed in literature, *e.g.*, independently and continuous running, minimal overhead, scalability, *etc.*, [4]. Therefore, multi-agent technology makes the resilience of the system strong and thus ensures its safety [6]

Alongside, the concept of ontology has emerged as a powerful method for domain knowledge representation and sharing. It can improve the intrusion detection features giving the ability to share a common conceptual understanding threats and design the signature rules [1,7,10,13,20]. In fact, the use of the ontologies and OWL (*Ontology Web Language*) within the intrusion detection context has different advantages: (*i*) Grasping the semantic knowledge about the intrusion detection subject; (*ii*) Expressing the IDS much more by building better rules of signatures using the SWRL (*Semantic Web Rule Language*) [9]; and (*iii*) Making intelligent reasoning [6,10]. In this respect, it is possible to design a multi-agents architecture based on a knowledge basis represented as an ontology. The use of such architecture reveals conducive to the development of IDSs [6].

In this paper, we investigate another way of tackling the aforementioned problems. Thus, we introduce a new distributed IDS, called OCMAS-IDS (*Ontology and Clustering based Multi-AgentS Intrusion Detection System*). OCMAS-IDS is based on the integration of the multi-agents technology, the ontology and the clustering technique. In this respect, our proposed system uses a set of agents that can be applied to a number of tasks, namely: data capturing, detecting the known and unknown attack categories and ultimately alerting the administrator. Through extensive carried out experiments on a real-life network traffic and a set of simulated attacks, we show the effectiveness of our proposal in terms of (*i*) the scalability and (*ii*) the detection ability of our system.

The remaining of the paper is organized as follows. Section 2 sheds light on the related work. We introduce our new distributed intrusion detection system based on the multi-agents technology in Section 3. We then relate the encouraging results of the carried out experiments in Section 4. Finally, Section 5 concludes and points out avenues of future work.

2   Scrutiny of the Related Work

Recently, few approaches, within the intrusion detection field, are dedicated to the integration of multi-agents technology and ontology model. Approaches fitting in the distributed IDS trend using ontological structure attempt to enhance the IDS accuracy and performing intelligent reasoning.

Worth of mention that the first research of applying ontology within intrusion detection context was done by Undercoffer et al. [20] in 2003. In this respect, the authors developed an ontology focused on the target (*centric*) and supply it within the format of the logical description language DARPA *DARPA Agent Markup Language + Ontology Inference Layer* (DAML + OIL). This ontology allows modeling the domain of computer attacks and facilitates the process of reasoning to detect and overcomes the malicious intrusions.

Mandujano [13] proposed a detection tool composed of a multi-agents architecture and an ontology focused on attacker, called FROID (*First Resource for Outbound Intrusion Detection*). FROID attempts to protect a set of nodes in a network using the ontology OID (*Outbound Intrusion Detection*). The proposed system is characterized by its intention to detect known attacks based on signatures. Thus, the main drawback of FORID system is that in case of an emerging attack, it will ignore it since this new attack has not yet been listed in the base of signatures.

In addition, Abdoli and Kahani [1] proposed a system, called ODIDS. The system includes two types of agents: IDSAGENT and MASTERAGENT. Based on the techniques of the semantic web, they have built an ontology for extracting semantic relationships between intrusions. The main moan that can be addressed to the ODIDS system stands in the fact that the MASTERAGENT is a central point of failure. Hence, if an intruder can prevent it from working (*e.g.*, blocking or slowing the host where it is running), the entire system will be damaged. Another criticism of the ODIDS system is time wasting, since the system needs more time to make a connection between the MASTERAGENT and the IDSAGENTS on the network and to send and receive messages between them.

Azevedoln et al. [3] proposed an autonomic model, called AUTOCORE, which includes a set of intelligent agents as well as a domain ontology CORESEC, in order to perform intrusion detection independently. The system makes use of CORESEC as an ontology knowledge base with high-level concepts for information [3]. The agents are then responsible for enabling the analysis of network traffic and the detection of malicious activities. However, the approach does not consider the secure state which is important to judge false positive alerts and successful possibility of attacks [12].

In [7], Djotio et al. proposed a MONI system based on an ontology model, called NIM-COM. The MONI system includes a multi-agents IDS to achieve a distribution of the detection activities. In addition, MONI is endowed with a *Case Based Reasoning* (CBR) mechanism to learn new attacks. Even though CBR is considered as a powerful reasoning paradigm and easy to set up, it suffers from re-engineering problems [14]. This lack of flexibility of the knowledge representation is with no doubt an inherent CBR limitation.

With the same preoccupation, Isaza et al. [10] developed a multi-agents architecture for the detection and prevention of intrusions, called OntoIDPSMA. The representation of known attacks has been designed using a semantic model based on ontology specifying signatures and reaction rules. The authors integrated an Artificial Neural Network (ANN) technique and the clustering algorithm

K-MEANS for the identification of new attacks. However, the most significant disadvantage of ANN relies on the fact that its ability to identify an intrusion is completely dependent on the accurate training of the system, data and the methods that are used. Moreover, the configuration of an ANN is delicate and can significantly affect the results [18]. In addition, the performance of K-MEANS and its effectiveness as a method for detecting new attacks depends on the random selection of the number of initial groups. Therefore, a "bad choice" of this number will decrease the detection of actual intrusions and increase the generation of false alarms [4].

Due to its usability and importance, detecting the distributed intrusions still be a thriving and a compelling issue. In this respect, the main thrust of this paper is to propose a hybrid distributed IDS, called OCMAS-IDS, which integrates : (i) a multi-agents technology; (ii) an ontology; and (iii) an unsupervised clustering technique. The main idea behind our approach is to address limitations of centralized IDSs by taking advantage of the multi-agents paradigm as well as the ontological representation.

3   The OCMAS-IDS System

Agents and multi-agents systems are one of the paradigms that best fit the intrusion detection in distributed networks [4]. In fact, the multi-agents technology distributes the resources and tasks and hence each agent has its own independent functionality, so it makes the system perform work faster [6].

The distributed structure of OCMAS-IDS is composed of different cooperative, communicant and collaborative agents for collecting and analyzing massive amounts of network traffic, called respectively: SNIFFERAGENT, MISUSEAGENT, ANOMALYAGENT and REPORTERAGENT. Figure 1 sketches at a glance the overall architecture of OCMAS-IDS.

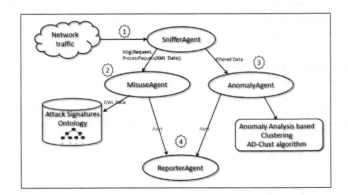

Fig. 1. The architecture of OCMAS-IDS at a glance

Worth of mention that the combination of the detection known attacks as well as the unknown ones can lead to improve the performance of the IDS and enhances its detection ability [11]. Consequently, OCMAS-IDS efficiently merges the detection of both types of attacks. It incorporates a MISUSEAGENT specialized on known attacks detection, as well as an ANOMALYAGENT competent on unknown attacks detection. The processing steps of OCMAS-IDS can be summarized as follows:

1. The SNIFFERAGENT captures packets from the network. Indeed, a distributed IDS must undertake to analyze a huge volumes of events collected from different sources around the network. Consequently, the SNIFFERAGENT permits to filter the packets already captured. Besides, it converts them to XML, using the XSTREAM library[1]. Finally, the pre-processed packets will be sent to others agents to be analysed;

2. The MISUSEAGENT receives the packets converted to XML from the SNIFFERAGENT. It transforms these packets to OWL format in order to be compatible with the SWRL rules stored in the ontology. Now, it is ready to analyze the OWL packets to detect those that correspond to known attacks. Indeed, the MISUSEAGENT searches for attack signatures[2] in these packets, by consulting the ontology ASO (*Attack Signatures Ontology*). Consequently, if there is a similarity between the OWL packets and the SWRL rules that define the attack's signatures, then the agent raises an alert to the REPORTERAGENT;

3. The filtered network packets are fed into an ANOMALYAGENT, which uses the clustering algorithm $\mathcal{AD}$-$\mathcal{C}$LUST to detect the unknown attacks. Likewise, the agent sends an alert to the REPORTERAGENT, if an attack is identified;

4. Finally, the REPORTERAGENT generates reports and logs.

OCMAS-IDS detects the known attacks through the intelligent agent MISUSEAGENT, which uses an ontology to enrich data intrusions and attack signatures by semantic relationships. In what follows, we present the proposed ontology used within our system OCMAS-IDS.

3.1   The Attack Signatures Ontology (ASO)

Since last few decades, Raskin et *al.* [16] opened a new field, that focuses on using *Ontology* within information security and its advantages. In fact, ontologies present an extremely promising new paradigm in computer security domain. They can be used as basic components to perform automatic and continuous analysis based on *high-level* policy defined to detect threats and attacks [10]. Moreover, they enable the IDS with improved capacity to reason over and analyze instances of data representing an intrusion [7,20]. Furthermore, the interoperability property of the ontologies is essential to adapt to the problems of the systems distribution, since the cooperation between various information systems is supported [3,7].

---

[1] Available at: http://xstream.codehaus.org/ .

[2] An attack signature is a known attack method that exploits the system vulnerabilities and causes security problem [4].

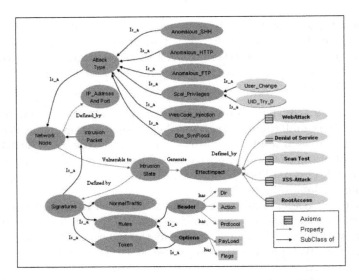

Fig. 2. The Attack Signatures based Ontology ASO

Within the OCMAS-IDS system, an ontology, called ASO (*Attack Signatures based Ontology*), is implemented, in order to optimize the knowledge representation and to incorporate more intelligence in the information analysis. Moreover, OCMAS-IDS integrates into its internal structure the interoperability between agents since they use the same model of ontology. The ASO ontology is characterized by network components, intrusion elements, classification defining traffic signatures and rules classes and instances. Figure 2 depicts a fragment of the ontology ASO, which implements the intrusion detection knowledge. The ASO ontology allows the representation of the signatures basis for known attacks, used with the agent MISUSEAGENT. The power and usefulness of ontology, applied to the signature basis issue, provide a simple representation of the attacks expressed by the semantic relationships between intrusion data. We can also infer additional knowledge about intrusion due to the ability of the ontology to infer new behavior by reasoning about data. Therefore, this fact improves the process of decision support for an IDS [1,6,20].

The signature basis incorporates rules provided by the ASO ontology, that allows a semantic mean for reasoning and inferences. In fact, the rules are extracted using the SWRL language (*Semantic Web Rule Language*). The latter extend the ontology and enriches its semantics by the deductive reasoning capabilities [9]. It allows to handle instances with variables (?x, ?y, ?z). Thus, the SWRL rules are developed according to the scheme: *Antecedent → Consequent*, where both antecedent and consequent are conjunctions of atoms written $a_1 \wedge ... \wedge a_n$. Variables are indicated using the standard convention of prefixing them with a question mark (*e.i.*, "?x"). The following example shows a rule represented with SWRL.

Example 1. NetworkHost(?z) ∧ IntrusionState(?p) ∧ GeneratedBY(?p,?z) ∧ SQLInjection(?p) ∧ Directd_To(?p,?z) → SystemSQLInjectionState(?p,?z)

Using this syntax, a rule asserting that the composition of the network host(z) and an intrusion state(p) properties implies the attack *"SQL Injection"* property.

When constructing our ontology, we designed and implemented multiple rules to define various attacks and signatures. The defined rules allow properties inferences and reasoning process. The attack properties, *e.g.*, *WebAttack, SQLInjection, DoS, dDoS*, and so on, are defined as ontology' attributes identifying the type of an intrusion.

Even thought, the known attacks are detected, it remains nevertheless the problem of the new attacks detection. In this respect, additionally to the MISUSEAGENT, based on the ontology, OCMAS-IDS uses an ANOMALYAGENT based on the clustering analysis. The algorithm is described in the following subsection.

3.2   The Clustering Algorithm AD-Clust

Needless to remind that the application of the data mining techniques within the intrusion detection context can effectively improve the detection accuracy, the detection speed, and enhance the system's own security [2]. Thus, as an intelligent analysis task, the ANOMALYAGENT provides the crossroads of multi-agents systems with the clustering technique, in particular the *AD-CLUST* algorithm. The idea behind this technique is that the amount of normal connection data is usually overwhelmingly larger than that of intrusions [5]. Whenever this assumption holds, the anomalies and attacks can be detected based on cluster sizes, *i.e*, large clusters correspond to normal data, and the rest of the data points, which are outliers, correspond to attacks [19].

AD-CLUST, (*Anomaly Detection-based Clustering*), is an unsupervised clustering algorithm introduced by Brahmi et al. in [4,5], to improve the quality of the K-MEANS algorithm applied within the intrusion detection context. Indeed, the latter suffers from a greater time complexity, which becomes an extremely important factor within intrusion detection due to the very large packets sizes [15]. Moreover, the *number of clusters dependency* and the *degeneracy* constitute the drawbacks that hamper the use of K-MEANS for anomaly detection [15]. In this respect, the *AD-CLUST* algorithm combines two prominent categories of clustering, namely: distance-based [19] as well as density-based [8]. It exploits the advantages of the one to palliate the limitations of the other and vice versa.

The processing steps of our algorithm *AD-CLUST* can be summarized as follows [4]:

1. Extraction of the density-based clusters that are considered as candidate initial cluster centers. The density-based clustering is used as a preprocessing step for the *AD-CLUST* algorithm;

2. Compute the Euclidean distance between the candidate cluster center and the instance that will be assigned to the closest cluster. For an instance x_i and a cluster center z_i, the Euclidean distance is defined as:

$$distance(x_i, z_i) = \sqrt{\sum_{i=1}^{n} (x_i - z_i)^2} \qquad (1)$$

3. The size of a neighborhood of instances is specified by an input parameter. We use the k' parameter to distinguish it from the k parameter used by the K-MEANS algorithm. Hence, k' specifies the minimal number of instances in a neighborhood and controls the granularity of the final clusters of the clustering-based density. If k' is set to a large value, then a few large clusters are found. To reduce the number of candidate clusters k' to the expected number k, we can iteratively merge the two most similar clusters. Otherwise, if k' is set too small, then many small clusters will be generated. The clusters will be split, new clusters will be created to replace the empty ones and the instances will be re-assigned to existing centers. This iteration will continue until there is no empty cluster. Consequently, the outliers of clusters will be removed to form new clusters, in which instances are more similar to each other. In this way, the value of initial cluster centers k will be determined automatically by splitting or merging clusters;

4. Within the detecting phase, the $\mathcal{AD}$-$\mathcal{C}$LUST algorithm performs the detection of intrusions. Thus, for each novel instance I the algorithm proceeds as follows:

   (a) Compute the Euclidean distance and find the cluster that presents the shortest distance with respect to I.
   (b) Classify I by the category of the closest cluster. Clearly, if the distance between I and the cluster of "normal" instances is the shortest one, then I will be a normal instance. Otherwise, I is an intrusion.

4   Experimental Results

In order to assess the overall performance of OCMAS-IDS in a realistic scenario, a prototype of the proposed architecture was implemented using Sun's Java Development Kit 1.4.1, the well known platform JADE[3] 3.7, the Eclipse and the JPCAP[4] 0.7. The ontology ASO is designed using PROTÉGÉ[5].

Through the carried out experiments, we have to stress on evaluating the performance of our system in terms of (i) the scalability-related criteria such as network bandwidth, detection delay and system response time; and (ii) the detection ability. During the evaluations, we compare the results of the OCMAS-IDS system $vs.$ that of the centralized IDS SNORT [17] and the multi-agents

---

[3] Available at: http://jade.tilab.com
[4] Available at: http://netresearch.ics.uci.edu/kfujii/jpcap/doc/
[5] Available at: http://protege.stanford.edu/download/download.html

based ontology one MONI[6] [7]. All experiments were carried out on equivalent machines equipped with a 3GHz Pentium IV and 8GB of main memory. We used machines that were connected via a switch, thus forming a switched network. Moreover, we simulated attacks using the well known tool *Metasploit*[7] version 3.5.1. The simulated eight different attack types are:

- **attack1**: DoS Smurf;
- **attack2**: Backdoor Back Office;
- **attack3**: SPYWARE-PUT Hijacker;
- **attack4**: Nmap TCP Scan;
- **attack5**: Finger User;
- **attack6**: RPC Linux Statd Overflow;
- **attack7**: DNS Zone Transfer; and
- **attack8**: HTTP IIS Unicode.

4.1 The Scalability Evaluation

In order to test the scalability of OCMAS-IDS, we study the relationship between the bandwidth consumption and a number of attack types. Moreover, the variation of the detection delay according to the number of packets is evaluated. Additionally, we assess how the response time varies with respect to eight attack types.

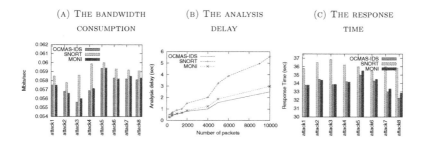

Fig. 3. The bandwidth consumption, the analysis delay and the response time of OCMAS-IDS *vs.* SNORT and MONI

As depicted in Figure 3 (a), the maximum bandwidth consumed by OCMAS-IDS and MONI is lower compared to that of SNORT. For example, the maximum bandwidth consumed by OCMAS-IDS is 0.06 Mbits/sec, which is very low as well. The reduction of the network bandwidth consumption is owe to the use of

---

[6] We thank Mrs. Djotio et *al.* [7] for providing us with the implementation of MONI system.

[7] Available at: http://www.metasploit.com/

the multi-agents system. Thus, the OCMAS-IDS system is not greedy in bandwidth consumption, which is definitely a desirable feature for any distributed system [4].

Besides, Figure 3(b) plots the detection delay against the number of packets, using the OCMAS-IDS, MONI and SNORT systems. According to this figure, we can answer the question: why the realization of the multi-agents IDS is advantageous? Clearly, the results show that the detection delay of both systems linearly increases with the number of packets. Moreover, the gap between both curves related to the detection delay of OCMAS-IDS and MONI is small, since both systems are based on multi-agents technology. In addition, Figure 3(b) highlights that our proposed system OCMAS-IDS is faster than the system SNORT. This can be explained by the fact that agents operate directly on the host whenever an action has to be taken, their response is faster than systems where actions were taken by the central controller, i.e., SNORT.

Figure 3 (c) illustrates the response time required by OCMAS-IDS with respect to the attack types. On the one hand, we remark that the detection of all attack types, on average, result in lower response time compared to that of SNORT, due to its centralized detection engine. In addition, this figure proved how fast our system respond. For example, the response time of OCMAS-IDS was 35 seconds for attack5, which is absolutely negligible.

On the other hand, within MONI, the ontology model is developed under JADE. Differently, the ontology ASO of our system OCMAS-IDS is designed under PROTÉGÉ and queried with SWRL. The response time of OCMAS-IDS is better than that of MONI. The main reason is that in the case of OCMAS-IDS, the inferred model is computed only once before the matching starts and used throughout all the queries. Thus, the figure indicates that OCMAS-IDS outperforms MONI and permits the exploitation of the semantics of ASO.

To sum up, it is clear from the obtained results that the performance of the OCMAS-IDS will not deteriorate too much with the increase in the number of attacks, which is justified by its low bandwidth consumption, reduced detection delay and quick response time. Likewise, in case of more machines are connected to the network, the OCMAS-IDS system still withstand the load and swiftly deliver the results.

4.2   The Detection Ability

In order to evaluate the detection ability of an IDS, two interesting metrics are usually of use [4]: the *Detection Rate* (DR) and the *False Positive Rate* (FPR). Indeed, the DR is the number of correctly detected intrusions. On the contrary, the FPR is the total number of normal instances that were "incorrectly" considered as attacks. In this respect, the value of the DR is expected to be as large as possible, while the value of the FPR is expected to be as small as possible.

With respect to Figure 4 (a), we can remark that the FPR of OCMAS-IDS and MONI is significantly lower compared to that of SNORT. This fact is due to the adaptive mechanisms used by the agents, enabling both systems,

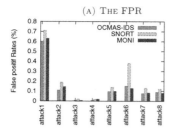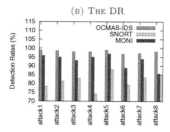

Fig. 4. The FPR and the DR of OCMAS-IDS *vs.* SNORT and MONI

i.e., OCMAS-IDS and MONI, to better suit the environment. Consequently, the false alarms can be reduced correspondingly. For example, for attack3 the FPR of SNORT can reach values as high as 0.019% compared to 0.007% of MONI and 0.005% of OCMAS-IDS.

Moreover, Figure 4 (b) shows that the DR of OCMAS-IDS is higher than that of MONI. Moreover, among the three investigated IDS, SNORT has the lowest DR. For instance, for attack3, whenever OCMAS-IDS and MONI have the DR 97.9% and 94.9%, respectively, SNORT has 74.1% DR. This is due to his centralized architecture.

Knowing that a main challenge of existing IDSs is to decrease the false alarm rates [4], the main benefit of our system is to lower the false alarm rate, while maintaining a good detection rate.

5 Conclusion

In this paper, we focused on a distributed architecture and multi-agents analysis of intrusions detection system to tackle the mentioned above challenges, *i.e.*, the high detection delay, the high bandwidth consumption as well as the low detection ability. Thus, we introduced a multi-agents intrusions detection system called *OCMAS-IDS* based on an efficient ontology model, called ASO, as well as a clustering algorithm called *AD-CLUST*. The carried out experimental results showed the effectiveness of the OCMAS-IDS system and highlighted that our system outperforms the pioneering systems fitting in the same trend.

Future issues for the present work mainly concern: (*i*) the alert correlation techniques by using the multi-agents system and ontology [12].

References

1. Abdoli, F., Kahani, M.: Ontology-based Distributed Intrusion Detection System. In: Proceedings of the 14th International CSI Computer Conference CSICC 2009, Tehran, Iran, pp. 65–70 (2009)
2. Azad, C., Jha, V.K.: Data Mining in Intrusion Detection: A Comparative Study of Methods, Types and Data Sets. International Journal of Information Technology and Computer Science (IJITCS) 5(8), 75–90 (2013)

3. Azevedoln, R.R., Dantas, E.R.G., Santos, R.C., Rodrigues, C., Almeida, M.J.S.C., Freitas, F., Veras, W.C.: An Autonomic Ontology-Based Multiagent System for Intrusion Detection in Computing Environments. The International Journal for Infonomics 3(1), 1–7 (2010)
4. Brahmi, I., Ben Yahia, S., Aouadi, H., Poncelet, P.: Towards a Multiagent-Based Distributed Intrusion Detection System Using Data Mining Approaches. In: Cao, L., Bazzan, A.L.C., Symeonidis, A.L., Gorodetsky, V.I., Weiss, G., Yu, P.S. (eds.) ADMI 2011. LNCS, vol. 7103, pp. 173–194. Springer, Heidelberg (2012)
5. Brahmi, I., Ben Yahia, S., Poncelet, P.: $\mathcal{AD}$-$\mathcal{C}$LUST: Détection des anomalies basée sur le Clustering. In: Atelier Clustering Incrémental et Méthodes de Détection de Nouveauté en conjonction avec 11ème Conférence Francophone d'Extraction et de Gestion de Connaissances EGC 2011, Brest, France, pp. 27–41 (2011)
6. Brahmkstri, K., Thomas, D., Sawant, S.T., Jadhav, A., Kshirsagar, D.D.: Ontology Based Multi-Agent Intrusion Detection System for Web Service Attacks Using Self Learning. In: Meghanathan, N., Nagamalai, D., Rajasekaran, S. (eds.) Networks and Communications (NetCom2013). LNEE, vol. 284, pp. 265–274. Springer, Heidelberg (2014)
7. Djotio, T.N., Tangha, C., Tchangoue, F.N., Batchakui, B.: MONI: Mobile Agents Ontology based for Network Intrusions Management. International Journal of Advanced Media and Communication 2(3), 288–307 (2008)
8. Duan, L.: Density-Based Clustering and Anomaly Detection. In: Mircea, M. (ed.) Business Intelligence - Solution for Business Development, pp. 79–96 (2012)
9. Horrocks, I., Patel-Schneider, P.F., Boley, H., Tabet, S., Grosof, B., Dean, M.: SWRL: A Semantic Web Rule Language Combining OWL and RuleML (2004), http://www.w3.org/Submission/SWRL/
10. Isaza, G.A., Castillo, A.G., López, M., Castillo, L.F.: Towards Ontology-Based Intelligent Model for Intrusion Detection and Prevention. Journal of Information Assurance and Security 5, 376–383 (2010)
11. Kim, G., Lee, S., Kim, S.: A Novel Hybrid Intrusion Detection Method Integrating Anomaly Detection With Misuse Detection. Expert Systems with Applications, 41(4, pt. 2), 1690–1700 (2014)
12. Li, W., Tian, S.: An Ontology-Based Intrusion Alerts Correlation System. Expert Systems with Applications 37(2010), 7138–7146 (2010)
13. Mandujano, S., Galvan, A., Nolazco, J.A.: An Ontology-Based Multiagent Approach to Outbound Intrusion Detection. In: Proceedings of the International Conference on Computer Systems and Applications, AICCSA 2005, Cairo, Egypt, pp. 94–I (2005)
14. PinzóN, C.I., De Paz, J.F., Herrero, Á., Corchado, E., Bajo, J., Corchado, J.M.: idMAS-SQL: Intrusion Detection Based on MAS to Detect and Block SQL Injection Through Data Mining. Information Sciences 231, 15–31 (2013)
15. Ranjan, R., Sahoo, G.: A New Clustering Approach For Anomaly Intrusion Detection. International Journal of Data Mining and Knowledge Management Process (IJDKP) 4(2), 29–38 (2014)
16. Raskin, V., Hempelmann, C.F., Triezenberg, K.E., Nirenburg, S.: Ontology in Information Security: A Useful Theoretical Foundation and Methodological Tool. In: Proceedings of the 2001 Workshop on New Security Paradigms, NSPW 2001, Cloudcroft, New Mexico, pp. 53–59 (2001)
17. Roesch, M.: Snort - Lightweight Intrusion Detection System for Networks. In: Proceedings of of the 13th USENIX Conference on System Administration (LISA 1999), Seattle, Washington, pp. 229–238 (1999)

18. Sodiya, A., Ojesanmi, O., Akinola, O.C., Aborisade, O.: Neural Network based Intrusion Detection Systems. International Journal of Computer Applications 106(18), 19–24 (2014)
19. Syarif, I., Prugel-Bennett, A., Wills, G.: Unsupervised Clustering Approach for Network Anomaly Detection. In: Proceedings of the 4th International Conference on Networked Digital Technologies (NDT 2012), Dubai, AE, pp. 135–145 (2012)
20. Undercoffer, J., Joshi, A., Pinkston, J.: Modeling Computer Attacks: An Ontology for Intrusion Detection. In: Proceedings of the 6th International Workshop on the Recent Advances in Intrusion Detection, Pittsburgh, PA, USA, pp. 113–135 (2003)

On Copulas-Based Classification Method for Intrusion Detection

Abdelkader Khobzaoui$^{1(\boxtimes)}$, Mhamed Mesfioui^2, Abderrahmane Yousfate^3, and Boucif Amar Bensaber^2

^{1} Computer sciences Department, University of Saida
^{2} Département de mathématiques et informatique, Université du Québec, Trois-Rivières, C.P, 500, Québec, Canada, G9A 5H7
^{3} Laboratoire de mathématiques (LDM), University of Sidi Bel Abbès

Abstract. The intent of this paper is to develop a nonparametric classification method using copulas to estimate the conditional probability for an element to be a member of a connected class while taking into account the dependence of the attributes of this element. This technique is suitable for different types of data, even those whose probability distribution is not Gaussian. To improve the effectiveness of the method, we apply it to a problem of network intrusion detection where prior classes are topologically connected.

Keywords: Intrusion detection · Classification · Copula function · Copula density estimator · Empirical copula

1 Introduction

Let a set of d attributes $(a_1, a_2, \ldots, a_d)$ characterizing a vectorial space E. Let also $(x_1, x_2, \ldots, x_n)$ a set of E used as a learning set over m classes denoted $(\omega_1, \omega_2, \ldots, \omega_m)$ which are actually some disjoint subsets of E. To avoid the use of some predetermined probability laws of the attributes systematically, we intent to build a copulas-based classification model that estimates the true attributes laws and their dependency. Then one assigns each entity of E to its most likely class ω_i; $i \in \{1, \ldots, m\}$. This entity must be well-assigned when it verifies an optimal probabilistic criterion.

In deterministic classification, this model builds, over the set E, an equivalence relation $\mathcal{R} \subset E \times E$ where $E/\mathcal{R}$ is a partition of E. In nondeterministic classification, for some adapted risks, classes are built using probability distributions. Each realization of the observed phenomenon distributes all elements over the different classes which yields to a partition of E. Partition changes with realizations (samples). To assign k elements o7ver m classes, in the deterministic case, one has only k steps to carry out all the affectations; each step requires m simplified tests. However, in the nondeterministic case, if one enumerates all possibilities for distributing k entities over m classes, then one finds m^k possibilities; each possibility requires k assigning steps. Each element is assigned to

Funded in part by DGRSDT, Algiers (PNR : Data mining and applications)

© IFIP International Federation for Information Processing 2015
A. Amine et al. (Eds.): CIIA 2015, IFIP AICT 456, pp. 394–405, 2015.
DOI: 10.1007/978-3-319-19578-0_32

the class ω_j via a conditional probability $f(x \mid j)$ which can be estimated using the training data. Actually, we seek the most likely class k (maximum likelihood estimation) solution of : $k = \arg\max_j (f(x \mid j))$ where $f(x \mid j)$ denotes the conditional probability density function for x being a member of group ω_j.

To reduce the complexity of the problem, one assigns elements to their respective classes as in deterministic affectation. Elements whose ranges are near apexes are the most likely affected. In this case, each step requires m complicated tests; that means $k.m$ complicated tests.

In the following we'll denote $f^j(x)$ instead $f(x \mid j)$.

Many applications algorithms and models have been proposed to estimate this conditional probability density function : kernel-density estimator [32], k-nearest-neighbours (KNN) method [19], Learning Vector Quantisation (LVQ) [12], Support Vector Machines (SVM)[20] ...

In this work we present the use of the empirical copula function as an alternative for modeling dependence structure in a supervised probabilistic classifier. The set E is identified to a vector space $\mathbf{R}^d$ over the field $\mathbf{R}$ and we use the law of the considered phenomenon over E which can be well estimated if learning sample is sizable. So, the conditional probability density function $f^j(x)$ is estimated according the following algorithm:

Algorithm 1. Conditional probability density estimation

Require: :

- $\{X_i\}_{i=1}^n$ an iid random sample from a $d-$dimensional distribution F with density f.
- $\Omega = \{\omega_1, \cdots, \omega_m\}$ m learning classes.

1. **for** each $j \in \{1, \cdots, m\}$ **do**
2.   Transform the observations X_i^j to $U_i^j = F_{ni}^j(X_i)$ where F_{ni}^j estimates the ith marginal distribution restricted to a class ω_j and X_i^j denotes observation from the class ω_j
3.   Estimate the marginal densities f_i^j for class ω_j.
4.   Estimate the joint density of the transformed data restricted to the class ω_j. this density w'il be noted c^j and it is equivalent to the copula density.
5.   Estimate the joint density of the original data restricted to a class ω_j by:

$$f^j(x) = c^j \left(F_1(x_1), \ldots, F_d(x_d)\right) \prod_{i=1}^d f_i^j(x_i)$$

6. **end for**

This approach allows to mitigate the curse of dimensionality and to treat the data in all situations even if the variance does not exist. It considers also the non-linear relationships between attributes.

New observation x will be affected to the class ω_r such that

$$r = \arg\max_j f^j(\mathbf{x})$$

The content of the paper is the following: The second section of the paper gives a short mathematical background of copula functions, Section 3 presents a copula based probabilistic model for classification. Section 4 presents the experimental setting to detect and identify intrusion in computer network and Section 5 summarizes the conclusions

2   Copulas Theory

Copulas play an important role in several areas of statistics and in Machine Learning as a tool of studying scale-free measures of dependence and as starting point for constructing families of bivariate distribution especially in applications where nonlinear dependencies are common and need to be represented.

The best definition of a copula is that given by referring to well know Sklar's theorem [28], [18], which states how a copula function is related to joint distribution functions.

Theorem 1 (Sklar's Theorem). *Let F be any d-dimensional distribution function over real-valued random variables with marginals $f_1, f_2, ..., f_d$, then there exists a copula function C such that for all $x \in \bar{\mathbf{R}}^d$*

$$F(x_1, \ldots, x_d) = C(f_1(x_1), \ldots, f_d(x_d)) \tag{1}$$

where $\bar{\mathbf{R}}$ denotes the extended real line $[-\infty, \infty]$ and $C : [0,1]^p \to [0,1]$.

The copula distribution can also be stated as joint distribution function of standard uniform random variables:

$$C(u_1, \ldots, u_p) = P(U_1 \leq u_1, \ldots, U_p \leq u_p) \tag{2}$$

where $U_i \sim U(0,1)$ for $i = 1, \ldots, p$.

Note that if $f_1(x_1), \ldots, f_d(x_d)$ in (1) are all continuous, then C is unique. Otherwise, C is uniquely determined on $Ran(f_1) \times Ran(f_2) \times \cdots \times Ran(f_d)$, where Ran stands for the range.

Conversely, if C is an d-copula and $f_1, \ldots, f_d$ are distribution functions, then the function F defined above is an d-dimensional distribution function with margins $f_1, \ldots, f_d$. For the proof, see [28].

From Sklar's theorem we see that for continuous multivariate distribution functions, the univariate margins and the multivariate dependence structure can be separated, and the dependence structure can be represented by a copula.

An important consequence of theorem 1 is that the d-dimensional joint density F and the marginal densities $f_1, f_2, \ldots, f_d$ are also related:

$$f(x_1, \ldots, x_d) = c(F_1(x_1), \ldots, F_d(x_d)) \prod_{i=1}^{d} f_i(x_i) \tag{3}$$

where c denotes the density of the copula C. The equation (3) shows that the product of marginal densities and a copula density builds a d-dimensional joint density.

The unique copula function related to the multivariate distributions F with continues margins $f_i; 1 \leq i \leq d$ is determined by

$$C(u_1, \ldots, u_d) = F(F_i^{-1}(u_1), \ldots, F_i^{-1}(u_d)) \tag{4}$$

where

$$F_i^{-1}(s) = \{t \mid F_i(t) \geq s\} \tag{5}$$

denote the pseudo-inverse of the univariate margins $F_1, \cdots, F_d$.
Copulas are essentially a way of transforming the random variable $(X_1, \cdots, X_d)$ into another random variable $(U_1, \cdots, U_d) = (F_1(X_1), \cdots, F_d(X_d))$ having the margins uniform on $[0, 1]$ and preserving the dependence among the components. Without the continuity assumption, care must be taken to use equation (4); see [21] or [17].

3   Copula Function Estimation

To estimate copula functions, the first issue consists in specifying how to estimate separately the margins and the joint law. Moreover, some of these functions can be fully known. Depending on the assumptions made, some quantities have to be estimated parametrically, or semi or even non-parametrically. In the latter case, we have to choose between the usual methodology of using "empirical counterparts" and invoking smoothing methods well-known in statistics: kernels, wavelets, orthogonal polynomials, nearest neighbors,... A non-parametric estimation of copula treats both the copula and the marginals parameter-free and thus offers the greatest generality.

Unlike the marginal and the joint distributions which are directly observable, a copula is a hidden dependence structure. This makes the task of proposing a suitable parametric copula model non-trivial and is where a non-parametric estimator can play a significant role.

Indeed, a non-parametric copula estimator can provide initial information needed in revealing and subsequent formulation of an underlying parametric copula model[3].

Non-parametric estimation of copulas dates back to Deheuvels [6], who proposed the so-called empirical copula defined by

$$C_n(\mathbf{u}) = \frac{1}{n} \sum_{i=1}^{n} \mathbb{I}\left(F_{n,1}(X_{i1}) \leq u_1, \ldots, F_{n,d}(X_{i,d}) \leq u_d\right) \tag{6}$$

where $F_{n,i}$ are the empirical distribution function given by

$$F_{n,j}(x) = \frac{1}{n} \sum_{i=1}^{n} \mathbb{I}(X_{i,j} \leq x) \tag{7}$$

with j=1,...,d and $\mathbf{u} \in [0, 1]^d$.

Let R_i be the rank of X_i among the sample $X_1, \ldots, X_n$. Observe that C_n is a function of ranks $R_1, R_2, \ldots, R_n$, because $F_{n,j}(X_i) = \dfrac{R_{i,j}}{n}$ $i = 1, \ldots, n$, namely;

$$C_n(\mathbf{u}) = \frac{1}{n} \sum_{i=1}^{n} \mathbb{I} \left(\frac{R_{i,1}}{n} \leq u_1, \ldots, \frac{R_{i,d}}{n} \leq u_d \right). \tag{8}$$

From this representation, one can consider $C_n(\mathbf{u})$ as discrete multivariate distribution with uniform marginals takings values in the set $\left[\dfrac{1}{n}, \dfrac{2}{n}, \ldots, 1 \right]$. and so his density:

$$c_n(\mathbf{u}) = \frac{\partial C(u_1, \ldots, u_d)}{\partial u_1, \cdots, \partial u_d} \tag{9}$$

can be estimated by a standard kernel function:

$$\hat{c}_n(\mathbf{u}) = \frac{1}{n} \sum_{j=1}^{n} \prod_{i=1}^{d} h_i^{-1} K \left(\frac{u_i - U_{ji}}{h_i^{-1}} \right) \tag{10}$$

where U_i is the transformed of the original data given by $U_i = F_{n,i}^j(X_i)$ as described above. And a uni-variate kernel function $K(u)$ is any functions satisfying the following conditions:

(a) $K(x) \geq 0$ and $\int_{\mathbf{R}} K(x)dx = 1$
(b) $\int_{\mathbf{R}} xK(x)dx = 0$ (Symmetric about the origin)
(c) Has finite second moment e.g. $\int_{\mathbf{R}} x^2 K(x)dx < \infty$

So, we have to choice both kernel function K and their smoothing parameter or bandwidth h. Actually, selection of K is a problem of less importance, and different functions that produce good results can be used (see table 1 for some examples).

In this paper, we use the Gaussian one given by:

$$K(v) = \frac{1}{\sqrt{2\pi}} \exp(-\frac{v}{2}).$$

In practice, the choice of an efficient method for the calculation of h; for an observed data sample is a more complex problem, because of the effect of the bandwidth on the shape of the corresponding estimator. If the bandwidth is small, we will obtain an under-smoothed estimator, with high variability. On the contrary, if the value of h is big, the resulting estimator will be very smooth and farther from the function that we are trying to estimate[23](see figure 1).

For evaluating the tradeoff between bias and variance. Silverman[31] has suggested a frequently used rule-of-thumb bandwidth

$$h_n = 0.9(min(\hat{\sigma}, \frac{IQR}{1.34})n^{\frac{1}{5}},$$

Table 1. some kernel functions

	Kernel	K(x)
1	uniform	$\frac{1}{2}\mathbf{1}_{(\lvert x\rvert\leq1)}$
2	Epanechnikov	$\frac{3}{4}(1-x^2)\mathbf{1}_{(\lvert x\rvert\leq1)}$
3	Gaussian	$\frac{1}{\sqrt{2\pi}}\exp\left(-\frac{x}{2}\right)$
4	triangular	$(1-\lvert x\rvert)\mathbf{1}_{(\lvert x\rvert\leq1)}$
5	Triweight	$\frac{35}{32}(1-x^2)^3\mathbf{1}_{(\lvert x\rvert\leq1)}$
6	Tricube	$\frac{70}{81}(1-x^3)^3\mathbf{1}_{(\lvert x\rvert\leq1)}$
7	Biweight(Quartic)	$\frac{15}{16}(1-x^2)^2\mathbf{1}_{(\lvert x\rvert\leq1)}$
8	Cosine	$\frac{\pi}{4}cos(\frac{\pi}{2}x)\mathbf{1}_{(\lvert x\rvert\leq1)}$

where IQR is the interquartile range (the difference between the 75th and 25th percentile) and $\hat{\sigma}$ is the sample standard deviation. Like all desirable bandwidth selection procedures, this bandwidth gets smaller as the number of observations n increases, but does not go to zero "too fast"[8].

4   The Probabilistic Classifier

As noted, the aim of this work is to develop a non-parametric classification method using a copula functions to estimate the conditional probability density $f^j(x)$ for one element x being a member of class ω_j. Actually, we use the empirical copula function estimator as tool to estimating $f^j(x)$ given by the equation 3.

Consider a set of m class $\omega_1, \ldots, \omega_m$. Each class ω_j is characterized by a d-random vector $\mathbf{X}^j = (X_1^j, \ldots, X_d^j)$. Let $(X_{11}^j, \ldots, X_{1d}^j), \ldots, (X_{n1}^j, \ldots, X_{nd}^j)$ be a random sample arises from the class ω_j. The distribution of component $\mathbf{X}_i^j$ of the random vector $\mathbf{X}^j$ may be estimated by

$$F_{n,i}^j(x_i) = \frac{1}{n}\sum_{k=1}^{n}\mathbb{I}\left(X_{ki}^j \leq x_i\right).$$

The density function of this component is also estimated by

$$\hat{f}_i^j(x_i) = \frac{1}{n}\sum_{j=1}^{n}K(x_i - X_{ji})$$

where

$$K(x) = \frac{1}{\sqrt{2\pi}}\exp(-\frac{x^2}{2})$$

The density function of the random vector $\mathbf{X}_j$ can be estimated by

$$\hat{f}^j(\mathbf{x}) = \hat{c}^j\left(F_{n,1}^j(x_1), \ldots, F_{n,d}^j(x_d)\right)\prod_{i=1}^{d}\hat{f}_i^j(x_i) \tag{11}$$

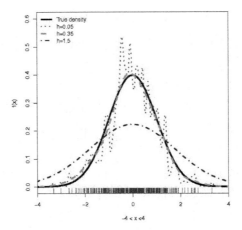

Fig. 1. Standard normal distribution density and its kernel density estimate (KDE) with different bandwidths obtained from a random sample of size 500. Solid line : True density (standard normal). Dotted line : KDE with h=0.05. Dashed line : KDE with h=0.35. Dot-dash line : KDE with h=1.5

where $\hat{c}^j$ denotes the estimator of the copula density associated to a random vector $\mathbf{X}^j$ estimated by a standard kernel function as described in equation 10.

So, all elements of our classifier are constructed, namely: $\hat{c}$ the copula density estimators, $\hat{f}_i^j$ the marginal density estimators, and $\hat{f}^j$ the joint density estimators.

The goal of the classifier is to determine, given a new observation x, its most likely corresponding class ω_r which is chosen as follow:

$$r = \arg\max_j \hat{f}^j(\mathbf{x})$$

Finally, we will describe the main steps of our classifier:

Algorithm 2. The probabilistic classifier algorithm

---

1. Let $\mathbf{x} = (x_1, \dots, x_d)$ a new observation.
2. For each $j \in \{1, \cdots, m\}$ Do
3. For each $i \in \{1, \cdots, d\}$ Do

   - $u_i^j \leftarrow F_{n,i}^j(x_i)$
   - Compute $\hat{f}_i^j(x_i)$

4. EndFor
5. Compute $\hat{c}^j\left(F_{n,1}^j(x_1), \dots, F_{n,d}^j(x_d)\right)$ as described above
6. Compute $\hat{f}^j(\mathbf{x})$ from equation(11)
7. EndFor
8. affect the observation x to the class ω_r such that

$$r = \arg\max_j \hat{f}^j(\mathbf{x})$$

---

5   Application

To verify the effectiveness and the feasibility of the proposed algorithm, we use the KDD'99 dataset ([5]), was originally provided by MIT Lincoln, Labs which contains a standard set of data to be audited, which includes a wide variety of intrusions simulated in a real-world military network environment.

The KDD'99 dataset includes a set of 41 features, gathered in 7 symbolic ones and 34 numeric. A complete description of all 41 features is available in [5]. These features are divided into four categories:

1. The intrinsic features of a connection, which includes the basic features of individual TCP connections. For example, duration of the connection, the type of the protocol (tcp, udp, etc), network service (http, telnet, etc), etc.
2. The content feature within a connection suggested by domain knowledge is used to assess the payload of the original TCP packets, such as number of failed login attempts.
3. The same host features examine established connections in the past two seconds that have the same destination host as the current connection, and calculate statistics related to the protocol behavior, service, etc.
4. The similar same service features examine the connections in the past two seconds that have the same service as the current connection.

These features describe 23 behaviors of which one corresponds to a normal traffic and the 22 others correspond to attacks which are gathered in four categories as summarized in table 2 :

1. DOS (Denial of service): making some computing or memory resources too busy so that they deny legitimate users access to these resources.
2. R2L (Root to local): unauthorized access from a remote machine according to exploit machine's vulnerabilities.
3. U2R (User to root): unauthorized access to local super user (root) privileges using system's susceptibility.
4. PROBE: host and port scans as precursors to other attacks. An attacker scans a network to gather information or find known vulnerabilities.

We used the train data-set which is about 494 020 connection record and test data-set is about 4 898 431. First, the symbolic variables are converted to numeric ones, the zero colones and repeated rows are removed we obtained 145 586 rows for training and 1 074 992 for test.

Calculations are performed under the R Environment for Statistical Computing [24] [25] using the parallel packages snow[29] and snowfall[30] under Linux RedHat enterprise 6 workstation on Intel Core I7 with 16 Go of Ram and 4 physical cores.

As confusion matrix between all behaviors is too big, we present in Table 3 table a summarized confusion matrix between the five categories of behaviors(described above). This condensed representation allows us to compare our results with those presented by other authors which have used the same data set.

Table 2. Class label in KDD '99 Dataset

Id-Attack	Attack	Category
1	back	dos
2	buffer_overflow	u2r
3	ftp_write	r2l
4	guess_passwd	r2l
5	imap	r2l
6	ipsweep	probe
7	land	dos
8	loadmodule	u2r
9	multihop	r2l
10	neptune	dos
11	nmap	probe
12	normal	normal
13	perl	u2r
14	phf	r2l
15	pod	dos
16	portsweep	probe
17	rootkit	u2r
18	satan	probe
19	smurf	dos
20	spy	r2l
21	teardrop	dos
22	warezclient	r2l
23	warezmaster	r2l

Conditional distributions are on rows. For example the first row means that normal behavior is identified as normal with estimate probability 97.375% (True Negative Attacks). It is identified as DOS behavior with estimate probability 0.406%, as PROB behavior with estimate probability 2.038% as as R2L behavior with estimate probability 0.175% and U2R behavior with estimate probability 0.006%. These four last identifications are said "False Positive Attacks". From second to fifth rows when behavior is identified as Normal, this identification is said "False Negative Attacks" else it is said "True Positive Attacks".

In order to evaluate the performances of our method, we compare the our results with those obtained by other authors which have used the same data set.

Table 3. Results by Attacks categories

	Normal	Dos	Probe	R2L	U2R
Normal	97.375	0.406	2.038	0.175	0.006
Dos	0.068	97.357	2.563	0.010	0.002
Probe	4.928	4.199	90.548	0.094	0.231
R2L	0.000	0.000	0.000	100.000	0.000
U2R	0.000	0.000	0.000	0.000	100.000

Table 4. Performance comparison of proposed Algorithm

Method	Normal	Dos	Probe	U2R	R2L
MCAD[26]	95.20	99.20	97.0	72.80	69.20
KDD cup 99 Winer [22]	99.50	97.10	83.30	13.20	08.40
GP Multi- Transformation[10]	99.93	98.81	97.29	45.20	80.22
C.N.B.D.[11]	99.72	99.75	99.25	99.20	99.26
PNRule[1]	99.50	96.9	73.20	06.60	10.70
ESC-IDS-1[33]	98.20	99.5	84.10	14.10	31.50
Prazen-window N.I.D.[34]	97.38	96.71	99.17	93.57	31.17
Model 1(a)[13]		97.40	83.80	32.80	10.70
SVM-IDS [9]	99.80	92.5	98.30	05.10	70.20
NN Classifier wiht GDA[27]	98.95	98.63	96.50	24.12	12.08
SVM+DGSOT[14]	95.00	97.00	91.00	23.00	43.00
I.C.A.[7]	69.60	98.00	100.00	71.40	99.20
C.L.C. [15]	73.95	99.88	87.83	61.36	98.50
Multi- PD[16]		97.30	88.70	29.80	09.60
ADWICE[4]		98.30	96.00	81.10	70.80
Our method	**97.375**	**97.357**	**90.548**	**100.00**	**100.00**

6 Conclusion

The method proposed, in this paper, presents many interesting advantages with respect to previous proposals in the field of intrusion detection, when applied to KDDCup'99 data set.

The obtained results, confirm the fact that copulas are flexible and powerful tool of studying scale-free measures of dependence and as starting point for constructing families of multivariate distribution especially in applications where nonlinear dependencies involved in the study and need to be represented. That occurs essentially when attributes probability laws are non-gaussian.

References

1. Agarwal, R., Joshi, M.V.: PNrule: A New Framework for Learning Classifier Models in Data Mining. In: Proceedings of the First SIAM International Conference on Data Mining, Chicago, IL, USA, April 5-7 (2001)
2. Chao, M., Xin, S.Z., Min, L.S.: Neural network ensembles based on copula methods and Distributed Multiobjective Central Force Optimization algorithm. Engineering Applications of Artificial Intelligence 32, 203–212 (2014)
3. Chen, S.X., Huang, T.-M.: Nonparametric estimation of copula functions for dependence modelling. The Canadian Journal of Statistics 35(2) (2007)
4. Burbeck, K., Nadjm-Tehrani, S.: ADWICE – anomaly detection with real-time incremental clustering. In: Park, C.-S., Chee, S. (eds.) ICISC 2004. LNCS, vol. 3506, pp. 407–424. Springer, Heidelberg (2005)
5. DARPA Intrusion Detection Data set, http://www.ll.mit.edu/mission/communications/ist/corpora/ideval/data/index.html

6. Deheuvels, P.: La fonction de dépendance empirique et ses propriétés. Un test non paramétrique díndépendance. Bulletin de la classe des sciences. Acadimie Royale de Belgique 65, 274–292 (1979)

7. Dayu, Y., Qi, H.: A Network Intrusion Detection Method using Independent Component Analysis. In: International Conference on Pattern Recognition (ICPR), Tampa, FL, pp. 8–11 (2008)

8. DiNardo, J., Tobias, J.L.: Nonparametric Density and Regression Estimation. Journal of Economic Perspectives 15(4), 11–28 (2001)

9. Eid, H.F., Darwish, A., Hassanien, A.E., Ajith, A.: Principle Components Analysis and Support Vector Machine based Intrusion Detection System. In: 10th International Conference on Intelligent Systems Design and Applications (2010)

10. Faraoun, K.M., Boukelif, A.: Securing network trafic using geneticaly evolved transformations. Malaysian Journal of Computer Science 19(1) (2006)

11. Farid, D.M., Harbi, N., Rahma, Z.M.: Combining naive bayes and decision tree for adaptive intrusion detection. International Journal of Network Security & Its Applications (IJNSA) 2(2) (2010)

12. Kohonen, T.: Self-Organizing Maps, 3rd edn. Springer (2000)

13. Nguyen, H.A., Choi, D.: Application of Data Mining to Network Intrusion Detection: Classifier Selection Model. In: Ma, Y., Choi, D., Ata, S. (eds.) APNOMS 2008. LNCS, vol. 5297, pp. 399–408. Springer, Heidelberg (2008)

14. Khan, L., Awad, M., Thuraisingham, B.: A new intrusion detection system using support vector machines and hierarchical clustering. The International Journal on Very Large Data Bases 16(4), 507–521 (2007)

15. Levin, I.: KDD-99 Classifier Learning Contest LLSoft's Results Overview. ACM SIGKDD Explorations Newsletter 1(2), 67–75 (2000)

16. Maheshkumar, S., Gursel, S.: Application of Machine Learning Algorithms to KDD Intrusion Detection Dataset within Misuse Detection Context. In: Proceedings of the International Conference on Machine Learning, Models, Technologies and Applications, Las Vegas (MLMTA 2003), vol. 1, pp. 209–215 (2003)

17. Marshall, A.: Copulas, marginals and joint distributions. In: Rüschendorff, L., Schweizer, B., Taylor, M. (eds.) Distributions with Fixed Marginals and Related Topics, pp. 213–222. Institute of Mathematical Statistics, Hayward (1996)

18. Mayor, G., Suñer, J., Torrens, J.: Sklar's theorem in finite settings. IEEE Transactions on Fuzzy Systems 15(3), 410–416 (2007)

19. Michie, D., Spiegelhalter, D.J., Tayler, C.C.: Machine Learning, Neural and Statistical Classification. Ellis Horwood Series in Artificial Intelligence. Prentice Hall, Upper Saddle River (1994)

20. Müller, K.R., Mika, S., Rätsch, G., Tsuda, K., Schölkopf, B.: An Introduction to Kernel-Based Learning Algorithms. IEEE Transactions on Neural Networks 12, 181–201 (2001)

21. Nelsen, R.: An Introduction to Copulas, 2nd edn. Springer, New York (2006)

22. Pfahringer, B.: Winning the KDD99 classification cup: bagged boosting. ACM SIGKDD Explorations Newsletter 1(2), 65-66 (2000)

23. Quintela-del-Río, A., Estévez-Pérez, G.: Nonparametric Kernel Distribution Function Estimator with kerdiest: An R Package for Bandwidth Choice and Applications. Journal of Statistical Software 50(8) (2012)

24. The Comprehensive R Archive Network, http://cran.r-project.org/

25. Rossiter, D.G.: Tutorial: Using the R Environment for Statistical Computing: An example with the Mercer & Hall wheat yield dataset. University of Twente, Faculty of Geo-Information Science & Earth Observation (ITC) Enschede, NL (2014)

26. Santosh, K., Sumit, K., Sukumar, N.: Multidensity Clustering Algorithm for Anomaly Detection Using KDD'99 Dataset. Advances in Computing and Communications 190(pt.8), 619–630 (2011)
27. Singh, S., Silakari, S.: Generalized Discriminant Analysis algorithm for feature reduction in Cyber Attack Detection System. International Journal of Computer Science and Information Security 6(1) (2009)
28. Sklar, A.: Fonction de répartition á n dimensions et leurs marges. Publ. Inst. Statist. Univ. Paris 8, 229–231 (1959)
29. snow: Simple Network of Workstations,
    http://cran.r-project.org/web/packages/snow/index.html
30. snowfall: Easier cluster computing (based on snow),
    http://cran.r-project.org/web/packages/snowfall/index.html
31. Silverman, B.W.: Density Estimation for Statistics and Data Analysis. Monographs on Statistics and Applied Probability. Chapman and Hall, London (1986)
32. Terrell, D.G., Scott, D.W.: Variable kernel density estimation. Annals of Statistics 20(3), 1236–1265 (1992)
33. Toosi, A.N., Kahani, M.: A new approach to intrusion detection based on an evolutionary soft computing model using neuro-fuzzy classifiers. Computer Communications 30, 2201–2212 (2007)
34. Yeung, D.Y., Chow, C.: Parzen-window Network Intrusion Detectors. In: 16th International Conference on Pattern Recognition, Quebec, Canada, pp. 11–15 (2002)

On-Off Attacks Mitigation against Trust Systems in Wireless Sensor Networks

Nabila Labraoui [1(✉)], Mourad Gueroui [2], and Larbi Sekhri[3]

[1] STIC Laboratory, University of Tlemcen, Tlemcen, Algeria
`nabila.labraoui@mail.univ-tlemcen.dz`
[2] PRISM Laboratory, University of Versailles Saint-Quentin en Yvelines, Versailles, France
`mourad.guerroui@prism.uvsq.fr`
[3] ICN Laboratory, University of Oran, Es Senia, Algeria
`larbi.sekhri@univ-oran.dz`

Abstract. Trust and reputation systems have been regarded as a powerful tool to defend against insider attacks caused by the captured nodes in wireless sensor networks (WSNs). However, trust systems are vulnerable to on-off attacks, in which malicious nodes can opportunistically behave good or bad, compromising the network with the hope that bad behavior will be undetected. Thus, malicious nodes can remain trusted while behaving badly. In this paper, we propose O^2Trust, On-Off attack mitigation for Trust systems in wireless sensor networks. O^2Trust adopts the penalty policy against the misbehavior history of each node in the network as a reliable factor that should influence on the calculation of the trust value. This punishment future helps to perceive malicious node that aim to launch intelligent attacks against trust-establishment and consequently on-off attack is mitigated efficiently.

1 Introduction

Wireless sensor networks (WSNs) [1] provide a technological basis for many different security critical applications such as critical infrastructure monitoring, healthcare and battlefield. However, WSNs are often deployed in unattended, harsh and hostile environment that makes them under the threat of various types of attacks, including node compromise. In a node capture attack, an adversary tries to physically tamper with a node in order to extract the cryptographic secrets. Hence, the compromised node can participate in the network as a legitimate node and cannot be identified whether it is genuine or not. This attack can give rise to many subsequent powerful insider attacks [2]. Unfortunately, traditional safety mechanisms based on cryptography, cannot adequately defend against network insider attacks, although they are effective to outsider attacks [3].

Trust and reputation systems have been regarded as a powerful tool to defend against insider attacks caused by the captured nodes in WSNs [4]. Generally, trust establishment is used to record feedback about the security evaluations of other nodes. Thus, efficient trust management systems can help well-behaved nodes to avoid working with misbehaving nodes, as well as to detect these malicious ones [5]. How-

© IFIP International Federation for Information Processing 2015
A. Amine et al. (Eds.): CIIA 2015, IFIP AICT 456, pp. 406–415, 2015.
DOI: 10.1007/978-3-319-19578-0_33

ever, building a robust trust and reputation system presents several important challenges on its own [6], because it is susceptible to attacks such as bad-mouthing and on-off attacks [7, 8]. In this work we consider the on-off attack in which malicious nodes can opportunistically behave good or bad, compromising the network with the hope that bad behavior will be undetected. Malicious nodes can remain trusted while behaving badly. As it is mentioned in [8], almost all reputation-based trust models are vulnerable to on-off attack, because they focus more on recent behavior of the node rather than comprehensively combining the nodes' past behavior with its instantaneous behavior. As a consequence, a malicious node can easily dissimulate any misbehavior history by either displaying good behavior or waiting during later time periods to increase its trust value. By this way, it continues its attack.

To address the above problem, we present in this paper O^2Trust: On-Off attack mitigation for Trust systems in wireless sensor networks. O^2Trust adopts the *Penalty Policy* against the misbehavior history of each node in the network. Unlike previous trust models that focus on recent behavior and thus are not sensitive enough to perceive contradictory behavior, in our proposal, we focus on frequency misbehavior history as a reliable factor that should influence on the calculation of the trust value for a node. This punishment future helps to perceive malicious node that aim to launch intelligent attacks against trust-establishment and consequently on-off attack is mitigated.

The rest of this paper is organized as follows. In Section 2, we present an overview of related works. Section 3 describes the proposed trust model. Evaluation results and theoretical analyses of the proposed model are provided in Section 4 and Section 5. Section 6 concludes the paper.

2 Related Works

Ganeriwal and Srivastava [9] proposed the first reputation and trust based model designed and developed exclusively for sensor networks; the RFSN (Reputation-based Framework for high integrity Sensor Networks) model uses the Beta distribution as a mathematical tool to represent and continuously update trust and reputation. To differently weight the old and new interactions, an aging factor is introduced for trust updating; more weight is given to recent interactions. Chen proposed in [10], a Task-based Trust framework for Sensor Networks (TTSN), where sensor nodes maintain reputation for neighbor nodes of several different tasks and use the reputation to evaluate their trustworthiness. The method for trust calculation and trust updating is almost the same as described in RSFN [9]. Sheikh et al. [11] proposed GTMS a Group-based Trust Management Scheme, in which the whole group will get a single trust value. He et al. [12] proposed attack-resistant and lightweight trust management scheme (ReTrust) for medical sensor network followed a hierarchical architecture, comprised of master nodes and sensor nodes. The authors use the window mechanism to forget previous actions. Moreover, they introduce an aging-factor parameter, which is different for each time unit m in the window.

3   The Proposed Trust Model: O^2Trust

In this section, we will present a novel trust model for wireless sensor networks named on-off attack mitigation for trust systems in WSNs (O^2Trust).

3.1   Overview

The design of O^2Trust is based on *penalty policy* that is based on misbehavior history. In O^2Trust, the evaluation model reflects nodes' real-time trust state accurately and is very sensitive to past malicious actions. This policy deals efficiency with the dynamic and contradictory misbehavior of malicious nodes. Dynamicity of the misbehavior is not considered under traditional trust estimation models because trust values are obtained based on current behavior, which does not indicate continuity of misbehavior. In other terms, only weight of measured misbehavior is considered rather than periodicity of the misbehavior along with weight of measured misbehavior.

Unlike the previous trust models, the trust value computation in our scheme is based on two components: reputation evaluation and penalty check (see Fig.1). Reputation evaluation is based on direct and/or indirect observations, and represents the accumulative assessment of the long-term behavior, while the penalty check is based on misbehavior history that represents how much a node has misbehaved in the past.

3.2   Trust Value Computation

The calculation of a trust value needs two parts of information: direct trust value and indirect trust value. Direct trust value can be obtained when a node has direct transactions with a node.   Let $T_{i,j}$ denotes the trust value from node i to node j. It is defined in (1).

$$T_{i,} = \alpha \, DT_{i,j} + (1-\alpha) \, IT_{i,j} \quad (1)$$

where $DT_{i,j}$ is the direct trust value from node i to node j, $IT_{i,j}$ represents the indirect trust value of node j, α is the confidence factor   and $0 \le \alpha \le 1$.

A) Direct Trust Evaluation

To calculate the direct trust value, we consider two factors: the reputation rating and the penalty factor. Let $DT_{i,j}^t$ denotes the current direct trust value of node j from the view point of node i and $DT_{i,j}^{t-1}$ denotes the past direct trust value. $Rep_{i,j}^t$ and $PF_{i,j}^t$ denote the current reputation rating and the penalty factor respectively. Therefore the trust value for node j at node i is:

$$DT_{i,j}^t = \begin{cases} \frac{DT_{i,j}^{t-1}+(1-PF_{i,j}^t)}{2+PF_{i,j}^t} & if \ Rep_{i,j}^t = 0 \\ \frac{DT_{i,j}^{t-1}+(1-Rep_{i,j}^t)}{2+PF_{i,j}^t} & otherwise \end{cases} \quad (2)$$

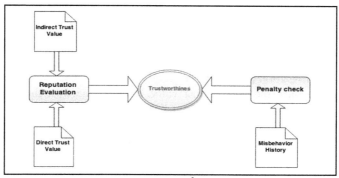

Fig. 1. Components of O²Trust

If current reputation rating $Rep_{i,j}^t$ is equal to zero that means that the node j well-behaves at this moment, but there is no evidence that it is honest. To protect our trust model from on-off attacks, penalty factor that represents the misbehavior history, is used to calculate the current trust value.

In this paper, we can use one of the trust factors depending on the interactions between two neighbor nodes such as packet receive, send, delivery and consistency, to measure a node's reputation According to the quality of services provided by cooperating nodes, we classify interaction quality into two categories: successful (S) and unsuccessful (U).

In O²Trust each sensor calculates individual trust values for only one-hop neighbors, contrary to GTMS [11] in which each sensor calculates individual trust values for all the cluster members. As a result, nodes do not keep trust information about every node in the network. Keeping neighborhood information implies significant lower energy consumption, less processing for trust computation, and less memory space.

Let $Rep_{i,j}^t$ denotes the current reputation rating which represents the current misbehavior of node j from the view point of node i at time t. It is defined in (3).

$$Rep_{i,j}^t = \frac{U_{i,j}}{U_{i,j} + S_{i,j}} \qquad (3)$$

$S_{i,j}$ denotes the total number of successful interactions of node i with j during a time period t and $U_{i,j}$ denotes the total number of unsuccessful interactions of node i with j during a time period t.

Due to the uncertainty of current reputation rating value based on recent interactions experience, we introduce the penalty factor to compute the trust value and to enhance the flexibility of our trust model. Penalty factor, accumulates measured misbehavior over time. It detects the dissimulated misbehavior. So, according to our proposed method if measured misbehavior is consistent, it is always greater than pre-defined threshold, and each time penalty factor will be increased until it reaches to maximum value (that is one). We define the penalty factor of node j estimated by node i as follow:

$$PF_{i,j}^t = \begin{cases} Min\{[Rep_{i,j}^t + (1-\theta) \times PF_{i,j}^{t-1}], 1\ \}, & if\ DT_{i,j}^t \geq THR1 \\ Min\{[Rep_{i,j}^t + \theta \times PF_{i,j}^{t-1}], 1\ \}, & otherwise \end{cases} \qquad (4)$$

where θ is the forgetting factor for accumulated misbehavior, which ranges from [0.5, 1] and $THR1$ is a threshold that can be tuned according to the system and security requirements.

Contrary to previous trust models, in which recent rating will carry more weight and therefore past misbehavior can be completely dissimulated, in our trust model we use an adaptive forgetting factor to improve on-off attack detection. According to Equation (4) once the node's trust value is under the trust threshold $THR1$, aging factors for previous accumulative misbehavior (penalty factor) will be different. In this case, we will weigh more on the penalty factor in order to more decrease the trust value. It means the malicious node that launches on-off attack, requires a longer time to recover its trust value once it has been defined as a malicious node.

B) Indirect Trust Value

The indirect trust value is computed based on the recommendations given by neighbors when it is often not possible for a node to directly assess the trust value of another node. However, the reliability of trust and reputation models could be easily compromised by various dishonest recommendation attacks, i.e., self-promoting, bad-mouthing and collusion.

To deal with the bad-mouthing attack and collusion attack, we use a lightweight averaging function to aggregate the indirect values. So, if node i needs a recommendation about node j, it will ask only trustworthy nodes (only one-hop neighbors) in unicast mode because it is more energy efficient than broadcast mode [13]. If the direct trust of a neighbor node is larger than the trust threshold value (for example 0.6), it is declared as trustworthy neighbor.

Let us assume that be the set of the trustworthy recommenders of the node j defined as:

$$\psi = \{DT_{k,j}, 0 \leq k \leq M - 1 \} \tag{5}$$

were M is the total number of recommenders and $DT_{k,j}$ is the direct trust from recommender k to node j. Then the indirect trust value of node j $IT_{i,j}$ can be defined as:

$$IT_{i,j} = \frac{1}{M} \sum_{\substack{k=0 \\ k \neq j}}^{M-1} DT_{k,j} \tag{6}$$

In [13], Liang and Shi found that the lightweight average aggregation algorithm performs better than complex algorithms.

C) Decision making

After calculating the global trust value $T_{i,j}$ that relies on [-1, 1], each node i will classify trust into three states as follows:

$$Mp(T_{i,j}) = \begin{cases} T: trusted, & if \quad 1 \geq T_{i,j} \geq THR1 \\ U: uncertain, & if \quad THR1 \geq T_{i,j} \geq THR2 \\ M: malicious, & if \quad THR2 \geq T_{i,j} \geq -1 \end{cases} \tag{7}$$

where $THR2 < THR1 < 1$ and $THR1$, $THR2$ are a threshold that can be tuned according to the system and security requirements to determine the node's status. Since these values depend on network and security requirements, it will be set accordingly.

According to the trust state, each node can make a decision to cooperate or non-cooperate with the interacted node in the considered operation.

4   Performance Evaluation

In this section, we present results of our simulations showing the effectiveness of our trust model. MATLAB software is used as simulation tool to assess the performance of our model. A comparative study between O^2Trust, *RFSN* [9] and *Retrust* [12] is given.

Concrete simulation scene is a square area of 100 m x 100 m, with 100 randomly deployed nodes. The communication radius is 25 m. An optimistic initialization strategy of trust value is adopted. So, the initial trust state of nodes is set as trusted (i.e., with initial trust value equal to 0.8).

Simulation is set up as follows. Each sensor node SN randomly selects one of its one-hop neighbors to transmit packets. Suppose that SN i ask SN j to forward packets, SN i can observe how many packets j has forwarded, i.e number of successful transactions. Next, SN i compute its direct trust value $DT_{i,j}^t$ according to equation (2). We can summarize the simulation parameters in Table 1.

Table 1. Simulation parameters

Parameter	Value	Description
$\alpha, (1 - \alpha)$	(0.8, 0.2)	Weight ratio of direct and indirect value
θ	0.6	Forgetting factor
THR1	0.6 or 0.7	Trust threshold (for trusted nodes)
THR2	0,4	Trust threshold (for malicious nodes)
Initial trust value	0.8	The value assigned to a new node.

In on-off attack, strategic malicious nodes behave well and badly alternatively with the aim of remaining undetected while causing damage. Unfortunately, these malicious nodes may suddenly conduct attacks as they accumulate higher trust value. Thus, the attack cycle consists of two periods: on period and off period. When the attack is on, malicious node launches attacks; i.e. drops the received packets, and during the off period, performs well, i.e forwards received packets. Since the on period has an implication on the trust value of the malicious node, it will try to increase its trustworthiness during the off period.

4.1   Analysis of Penalty Factor Impact

In this section, we analyze the property of our trust model that combines penalty factor with reputation evaluation to derive trust value. We must demonstrate that the penalty factor helps to perceive the dissimulated misbehavior in on-off attack.

Our scheme has a feature whereby it continuously decreases the trust value of a malfunctioning or malicious node when it misbehaves in a repetitive manner. In order to validate the effectiveness of penalty factor and its influence on trust computation, we consider the actions of two types of nodes in the network: the benevolent nodes and the malicious ones. The benevolent nodes are the nodes that always behave well. While the malicious nodes are nodes that persistently misbehave.

The trust value's evolution of benevolent nodes and malicious nodes in O^2Trust is shown in fig. 2. In this experience, we calculate the average of trust values of fifty nodes of each type (benevolent and malicious). We can see that the trust value of the benevolent nodes in O^2Trust increases constantly. The factor penalty has no effect on the trust value since the behavior of trusted node is always good. However, the trust value's evolution of the malicious nodes decreases constantly as long as the malicious node persists in its misbehavior. We can see in the Fig.2, that in the first off period of attack (between 0 and 15 time units), the malicious node behaves well and its trust value follows the same evolution of the benevolent trust value. However, in the first on period (between 15 and 20 time units), it triggers the attack and its trust value falls off sharply. Consequently, its trust status changes from trusted to malicious in three time units. Since our proposed model always decreases the trust value of malicious node, the recovery rate in the off period is slower when the trust value is under the trust threshold. On the other hand, in the second on period (between 40 and 45 time units), the trust status changes from trusted to malicious in two time units. This can be explained by the fact that its last misbehavior is taken into account and as long as the malicious nodes repeat the on period, the penalty factor influences the trust value by checking the accumulated misbehavior in the past. So, it is difficult to the malicious node to recover its trust value in the off period, because the frequency of its past misbehavior is not discarded like in the previous trust models.

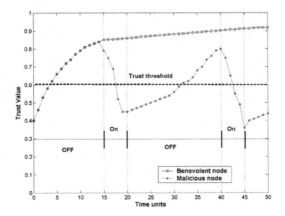

Fig. 2. Influence of penalty factor on trust computation

Consequently, considering the penalty factor in trust computation can effectively make the trust model more sensitive to on-off attack.

4.2   On-off Attack Resilience

To evaluate how our trust model can mitigate on-off attack, we introduce the malicious detection rate metric called MDN that is defined as equation (8):

$$MDN = \frac{|D|}{|M|} \tag{8}$$

Where $|D|$ denotes the number of detected malicious nodes and $|M|$ denotes the number of total malicious nodes. It is typically used to evaluate the efficiency of a trust model.

Values of the system parameters such as trust threshold and forgetting factor, are selected based on heuristic and previously defined values in the literature [11, 14, 15, 16].

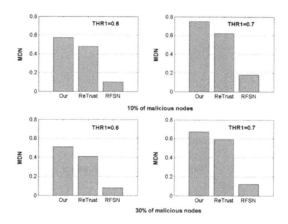

Fig. 3. Detection rate of on-off attack

Fig. 3 depicts the detection rate of on-off attack under two trust threshold values: THR1=0.6 and THR1=0.7. For each trust threshold, we consider 10% and 30% of on-off attacker nodes among 100 nodes in the network. We can clearly see that our trust model outperforms ReTrust and RFSN. While considering 10% of malicious nodes, the detection rate in O^2Trust remains 57% and 75% with the trust threshold equal to 0.6 and 0.7 respectively. However, when the proportion of malicious nodes is equal to 30%, the detection rate of O^2Trust decreases quietly and remains 51% and 67% with the trust threshold equal to 0.6 and 0.7 respectively. This is a satisfactory detection rate in trust management. On the other hand, MDN of RFSN is very lower because it cannot efficiently deal with this kind of attack and cannot recognize malicious nodes sensitively since it focus on recent behavior. Therefore, the past misbehavior is discarded. We can also notice that when trust threshold is high, the on-off attack detection rate is also high. However, nodes might be assessed as untrustworthy even though they might not actually be malicious nodes.

We can conclude that O^2Trust is a fine-grained trust model that can portray unpredictable behaviors from malicious nodes and outperforms RFSN and ReTrust scheme. Consequently, on-off attack can be mitigated efficiently.

5   Conclusion

Trust systems are very useful mechanisms to thwart insider attacks. However, building a robust trust model is very challenging, because malicious nodes participate in the behavior rating process and can distort the trust value by cheating. In this paper, we proposed O^2Trust, a trust model to mitigate on-off attack. O^2Trust adopts the Penalty Policy against the misbehavior history of each node in the network. By considering misbehavior history, it is difficult to a malicious node to recover its trust value as long as it persists in its misbehavior. Simulation results show that O^2Trust is an efficient and on-off attack-resistant trust model. However, how to select the proper value of the weight and the defined threshold is still a challenge problem, which we plan to address in our future research endeavors.

References

1. Akyildiz, I.F., Weilian, S., Sankarasubramaniam, Y., Cayirci, E.: A survey on sensor networks. IEEE Communications Magazine 40(8), 102–114 (2002)
2. Krau, C., Schneider, M., Eckert, C.: On handling insider attacks in wireless sensor networks. Information Security Technical Report 13(3), 165–172 (2008)
3. Han, G., Jiang, J., Shu, L., Niu, J., Chao, H.C.: Management and applications of trust in Wireless Sensor Networks: A survey. Journal of Computer and System Sciences 80(3), 602–617 (2014)
4. Labraoui, N., Gueroui, M., Aliouat, M., Petit, J.: Reactive and adaptive monitoring to secure aggregation in wireless sensor networks. Telecommunication Systems 54(1), 3–17 (2013)
5. Boukerche, A., Ren, Y.: A trust-based security system for ubiquitous and pervasive computing environments. Computer Communications 31, 4343–4351 (2008)
6. Mármol, F.G., Pérez, G.M.: Providing trust in wireless sensor networks using a bio-inspired technique. Telecommunication Systems 46(2), 163–180 (2010)
7. Lopez, J., Roman, R., Agudo, I., Fernandez-Gago, C.: Trust management systems for wireless sensor networks: Best Practices. Computer Communications 33(9), 1086–1093 (2010)
8. Alzaid, H., Alfaraj, M., Ries, S., Jøsang, A., Albabtain, M., Abuhaimed, A.: Reputation-based trust systems for wireless sensor networks: A comprehensive review. In: Fernández-Gago, C., Martinelli, F., Pearson, S., Agudo, I. (eds.) Trust Management VII. IFIP AICT, vol. 401, pp. 66–82. Springer, Heidelberg (2013)
9. Ganeriwal, S., Srivastava, M.: Reputation-based framework for high integrity sensor networks. ACM Transactions on Sensor Networks (TOSN) 4(3) (2008)
10. Chen, H.: Task-based trust management for wireless sensor networks. International Journal of Security and Its Applications 3(2), 21–26 (2009)

11. Shaikh, R.A., Jameel, H., d'Auriol, B.J., Lee, H., Lee, S., Song, Y.J.: Group-based trust management scheme for clustered wireless sensor networks. IEEE Transactions on Parallel and Distributed Systems 20(11), 1698–1712 (2009)
12. Daojing, H., Chun, C., Chan, S., Bu, J., Vasilakos, A.V.: ReTrust: attack-resistant and lightweight trust management for medical sensor networks. IEEE Transactions on Information Technology in Biomedecine 16(4), 623–632 (2012)
13. Liang, Z., Shi, W.: Analysis of recommendations on trust inference in open environment. Performance Evaluation 65(2), 99–128 (2008)
14. Yu, H., Shen, Z., Miao, C., Leung, C., Niyato, D.: Survey of trust and reputation management systems in wireless communications. Proceeding of IEEE 98(10), 1755–1772 (2010)
15. Bao, F., Chen, I.R., Chang, M.J., Cho, J.: Trust-Based Intrusion Detection in Wireless Sensor Networks. In: Proceedings of IEEE International Conference on Communications (ICC), pp. 1–6 (2011)
16. Sun, Y.L., Zhu, H., Liu, K.J.R.: Defense of Trust management vulnerabilities in distributed networks. IEEE Communication Magazine 46, 112–119 (2008)

A Real-Time PE-Malware Detection System
Based on CHI-Square Test and PE-File Features

Mohamed Belaoued$^{(\boxtimes)}$ and Smaine Mazouzi

Department of Computer Science
Université 20 août 1955-Skikda, Algeria
{m.belaoued,s.mazouzi}@univ-skikda.dz

Abstract. Constructing an efficient malware detection system requires taking into consideration two important aspects, which are the accuracy and the detection time. However, finding an appropriate balance between these two characteristics remains at this time a very challenging problem. In this paper, we present a real-time PE (Portable Executable) malware detection system, which is based on the analysis of the information stored in the PE-Optional Header fields (PEF). Our system used a combination of the Chi-square (KHI²) score and the Phi (φ) coefficient as feature selection method. We have evaluated our system using Rotation Forest classifier implemented in WEKA and we reached more than 97% of accuracy. Our system is able to categorize a file in 0.077 seconds, which makes it adequate for real-time detection of malware.

Keywords: Malware · Malware analysis · Chi-square test (KHI²) · PE-optional header

1   Introduction

Malware, abbreviation for 'malicious software', is a term used to designate any computer program that is designed to accomplish unauthorized actions without the user's consent. The number of new discovered malware has grown steadily over the past ten years. Therefore, it is crucial to have an efficient protection against this kind of malicious programs. The existing anti-malware techniques can be broadly classified in three classes, which are signature-based, behavioral-based and heuristic-based techniques [1]. Signature-based techniques are widely used by most of commercial antivirus software (AV). These techniques are very accurate for detecting known malware that exist in the signatures' database [1]. However, they are not able to deal with unknown malware or newly launched ones, often developed after discovering a zero-day exploit [2]. Even if the recent AV have become more accurate, they are still very slow to take countermeasures when a new threat is discovered [3, 4].

The behavioral analysis also known as dynamic analysis consists of monitoring the execution of the analyzed program in an isolated environment (i.e. Sandbox or virtual machine) [5]. During the monitoring process, the actions that the program accomplishes (such as API calls, Systems calls, network traffic, etc.) are recorded and used

© IFIP International Federation for Information Processing 2015
A. Amine et al. (Eds.): CIIA 2015, IFIP AICT 456, pp. 416–425, 2015.
DOI: 10.1007/978-3-319-19578-0_34

to generate behavior features for categorizing the program (malware or benign). Such techniques are very accurate and they are able to detect unknown malware [5]. However, their main drawback is that the monitoring process is run for a couple of minutes at most, therefore it can't observe the entire capabilities of the program [4]. Moreover, the time required for the monitoring process makes such techniques not suitable for real-time detection.

The heuristic-based analyses investigate different file features such as Opcode instructions, structural information (Such as header information), and API (Application Programming interface) calls [1],[5]. These sets of information are used as features for the classification process, which is generally done using machine learning-based classifiers such as decision trees and Bayes Algorithm [1],[6]. The Heuristic based Anti-malware systems are very accurate and are able to deal with unknown malware [1],[5, 6]. They are also easy to implement compared to the behavioral ones. However, the existing systems suffer from the inconvenient of their high processing overhead, since most of them use a large number of features, which yields to intensive computations. Due to that, most of the existing heuristic techniques are inadequate for real-time detection, which is a very suitable characteristic especially in such sensitive systems.

In this paper, we introduce a real-time PE (Portable Executable, See section 2) malware detection system, which consists of three different components, which are the PE-parser, feature selection module and a decision module. The PE parser was developed using Python language, and it statically (i.e. without executing the analyzed program) extracts the information contained in the PE-Optional header fields (PEF, see Section 2). PE header information (including Optional header ones) are very quick to extract, which is convenient for our real-time purposes. For the same purposes, our analysis was restricted on the Optional header only. We believe that using other types of features such as File-header fields or other structural information will considerably increase the number of features, which will have a direct impact on the detection time. The feature selection module was also developed using Python, and it is based on the KHI² test, which is a statistical method used for hypothesis testing [7]. The decision module is based on Rotation Forest classifier [8] that is available in Waikato Environment for Knowledge Analysis (WEKA) [9].

This paper is organized as fellows: Section 2 introduces the PE file format in order to facilitate the comprehension of the rest of the sections. Section 3 is devoted to most known related works, published in the literature. In section 4, we present our proposed system's architecture. In section 5, we present our experimental results. Section 6 concludes our work and underlines its perspectives.

2   PE File Format

PE is an abbreviation for Portable Executable[10], and it represents the common file format for binary executables and DLLs under Windows operating systems. A PE file is structured in layers and it is mainly composed of a DOS Header, PE Header, Section Headers (Section table), and a number of sections, as shown in "figure 1".

| MS-DOS Header |
| MS-DOS Header |
| Unused |
| MS-DOS2.0 Stub |
| Unused |
| PE Header |
| Section Headers |
| Section 1 |
| Section 2 |
| ... |
| Section n |

Fig. 1. PE file format

- The DOS Header is used if the file is run from the DOS. So it can then check whether it is a valid executable or not.
- The PE header is an IMAGE_NT_HEADERS data structure, which contains three members: PE-Signature, File Header, and the Optional Header. This latter is the subject of our work and is composed of several fields [10] as illustrated in figure 2. The values of the latter fields will be used as discriminators for the benign-malware categorization process.

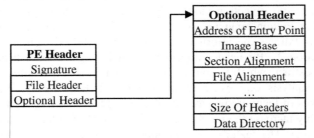

Fig. 2. Members of the PE-Optional Header

3   Related Work

In the last decade, security researchers have introduced new malware detection methods, in order to overcome the limitations of the standard signature-based ones. Schultz et al. [11] were the first authors to introduce a machine learning based malware detection system. The proposed system is based on the analysis of different information contained in the PE file such as strings and API calls. They used a classification method based on Naïve Bayes, and they achieved 97.11% of accuracy.

The method presented in [12] is based on API calls and Naïve Bayes classifier. The extracted APIs were used to construct models of suspicious behaviors, by grouping some APIs according to scenarios that a malware can accomplish, such as obtaining the system's directory, writing malicious data into files, and registry updates. They achieved an overall accuracy of 93.7%.

Ye et al. [2] have introduced a malware detection system that is based on the analysis of the set of APIs called by PE programs. The authors proposed a feature selection method based on the KHI² test. They used an Object Oriented Association (OOA) mining based classification method. Their system achieved an overall accuracy of 67.5% and a detection time of 0.09s.

The system proposed by Salehi et al. [4] is based on analyzing API calls and their arguments. They trained their system using different classifiers and they have obtained an overall accuracy of 98.1%. Extracting APIs arguments requires executing the program; therefore, this method has the inconvenient of dynamic approaches mentioned previously.

4   Proposed Method

Our proposed malware detection system categorizes a file in three different phases, which are the feature extraction, the feature selection, and the decision (classification).

4.1   Feature Extraction

As mentioned previously, our system relies on the analysis of the PE Optional Header fields (PEFs) and in order to extract these features from the analyzed file we developed a module written in Python by using a third party Python module called pefile [13]. PEFs are generated by concatenating the field's name and value (ex. CheckSum0 designates that the feature CheckSum has a value equal to 0).

4.2   Feature Selection

In order to reduce the number of obtained PEFs and keep only the most relevant ones, we developed a feature selection method, which is based on the chi-square (KHI²) test. The KHI² is a statistical method, which is used to determine whether there is a significant association between two qualitative variables. This association is expressed by the distance D between an observed frequency O and an expected one E (which represents the case of independence between the variables) and the greater is that distance stronger is the correlation between the variables. In our case, we will study that association between the variable 'PEF' that has two modalities: "present" and "absent". This variable represents the presence or not of a specific PEF in a PE file. The second variable is "PE" that has also two modalities: "Malware" and "Benign" that corresponds to the two categories of PE files that we used.

The first step to do when conducting a KHI² test, is to define the two hypotheses H_0 and H_1 that one will be accepted, and the other rejected. H_0 and H_1 represent respectively the case of independency and the case of dependency between the two variables. Note that accepting H_0 for a PEF means that it is not specific to any category of PE-files. Therefore, it will be considered as irrelevant and will be removed. In our case, H_0 and H_1 are defined as follows:

- H_0: The presence or absence of a PEF is independent of the PE file's type (malware or benign).
- H_1: The presence or absence of PEF is related to the PE file's type (malware or benign).

For every PEF, we have a contingency table as shown in table 1.

Table 1. Contingency Table of a PEF.

	PEF: Present	**PEF: Absent**	**Row Total**
PE: Malware	N1	N2	N
PE: Benign	M1	M2	M
Column total	N1+M1	N2+M2	T

N, M, and *T* are respectively the total number of malware PE, the total number of benign PE, and the total number of all PE files (*T=N+M*). *N1* and *N2* are respectively the number of malware PE that have a **PEF** and the number of malware PE that do not have the **PEF**, such as *N = N1 +N2*. *M1* and *M2* are respectively the number of benign PE that have a **PEF** and the number of benign PE that do not have the **PEF**, such as *M = M1 + M2*. The KHI² score (*D²*) is calculated using the formula (1):

$$D^2 = \sum \frac{(O_{r,c} - E_{r,c})^2}{E_{r,c}} \tag{1}$$

Where $O_{r,c}$ is the observed frequency count at level *r* of row variable and level *c* of column variable. And $E_{r,c}$ is the expected frequency. $E_{r,c}$ is defined by equation (2).

$$E_{r,c} = \frac{n_r \times n_c}{T} \tag{2}$$

Where n_r, and n_c represent respectively the sum on row *r* and the sum on column *c*. After calculating the KHI² values for the obtained PEFs, we have to determine which of two hypotheses are accepted or rejected for every PEF. To do that, we have to compare the obtained KHI² scores of every PEF to a threshold, which represents the theoretical KHI² value (χ^2). That value is obtained by first calculating the degree of freedom (**DF**), and choosing a signification level α that represents the error probability when accepting or rejecting an hypothesis. Considering **DF** and α, the χ^2 value is obtained from the KHI² distribution table [14]. **DF** is calculated using the following equation:

$$DF = (R-1) \times (C-1) \tag{3}$$

Where *R*, and *C* are respectively the number of modalities of the first and the second variables. After rejecting all the PEFs that are not correlated ($D^2 \leq \chi^2$), we will calculate the φ coefficient using the formula (4) for the remaining ones. The φ coefficient is a normalization of the KHI² score (*D²*), which is used to measure the strength of the dependency between the two variables [15]. In our work, that coefficient will be used to generate the different PEFs' subsets, which are grouped according to their correlation's strength (relevance).

$$\varphi = \sqrt{\frac{D^2}{T}} \tag{4}$$

The value of φ ranges between 0 and 1, therefore, the strength of the relationship can be divided in 4 different classes:

- $\varphi \approx 0.25$: Weak correlation.

- $\varphi \approx 0.50$: Medium correlation.

- $\varphi \approx 0.75$: Strong correlation.

- $\varphi \approx 1$: Very strong correlation.

Our obtained PEFs will be divided into non-disjoints subsets according to the φ values mentioned previously.

4.3   Classification

In order to evaluate our malware detection system we have used Rotation Forest classifier [8] that is implemented in WEKA [9]. Therefore, our classification module takes as an input the PEFs subsets represented as an .arff file. The .arff file is the data file format supported by WEKA, and it is automatically generated using a python script. The classifier is then trained and models are generated for each feature subset of the training set. The obtained models are then tested on previously unseen PE-files contained in our test set.

5   Experimentation

5.1   Dataset

We collected a dataset composed of 552 PE files (338 malware and 214 benign programs). This dataset will be split into 80% training set and 20% test set. The infected PE dataset was downloaded from Vxheavens.com and contains 12 different malware categories as shown in table 2.

Table 2. Used malware dataset

N°	Malware Type	Counts	N°	Malware Type	Counts
1	Backdoor	27	7	Trojan	59
2	Email-Worm	19	8	Trojan-Downloader	24
3	Exploit	28	9	Trojan-Dropper	32
4	Hacktool	22	10	Trojan-Spy	18
5	Net-Worm	16	11	Virus	42
6	P2P-Worm	17	12	Worm	34
TOTAL = 338					

The benign PE files include some utility software downloaded from Softpedia.com and some Windows system files collected from a clean installation of windows XP. We scanned the whole dataset by more than 40 AV available on the website Virus-Total.com, in order to make sure that they are correctly labeled (malware, benign).

5.2   Results and Evaluation

In this subsection, we will present the obtained experimental results from the feature extraction phase until the decision phase. We first start by the obtained PEFs after the feature extraction phase. As presented in Table 3, we have obtained 590 PEFs with their corresponding frequencies in malware and benign PE (observed frequencies).

Table 3. Overview of the obtained PEFs list and their corresponding frequencies

N°	Optional Header field	Value	Frequency	
			Malware (271)	Benign(172)
1	BaseOfCode	4096	271 (100%)	172 (100%)
2	BaseOfData	102400	4 (1%)	1 (1%)
...	...	...	...	...
86	CheckSum	0	259 (96%)	5 (3%)
87	CheckSum	102910	1 (1%)	0 (0%)
...	...	...	...	...
589	Subsystem	2	226 (83%)	106 (62%)
590	Subsystem	3	45 (17%)	66 (38%)

We will calculate the KHI² and φ values (as presented in the subsection 4.2) for the obtained PEFs and remove the non-relevant ones that have KHI² < 3.84 (3.84 is the X² value for DF=1 and alpha =0.05). The obtained results are presented in table 4.

Table 4. KHI² scores and φ values of the selected PEFs

N°	PEF	KHI²	φ
1	CheckSum0	375.21	0.92
2	MajorImageVersion0	370.57	0.91
3	DllCharacteristics0	355.91	0.9
4	MajorOperatingSystemVersion5	346.02	0.88
5	MinorOperatingSystemVersion0	341.92	0.88
...	...	...	...
50	SizeOfInitializedData28672	3.86	0.09

As presented in Table 4, we have obtained a final list of 50 PEFs with their corresponding KHI² scores and φ values. We will divide these features into different groups (subsets) according to their φ values. At the end of the feature selection phase, we have obtained three different subsets: G1, G2, and G3 that contain PEFs that have respectively $\varphi \geq 0.75$, $\varphi \geq 0.5$, and $\varphi \geq 0.25$. We have respectively 11, 14, and 22 PEFs in G1, G2, and G3. We have used a forth subset G4 that contains the complete 590 extracted PEFs, the aim from that is to see whether our feature selection method have improved the obtained results or not.

Next, we will evaluate our system's performance by training the Rotation Forest classifier using different features subsets and see which subset will generate the best results. The performance of a classifier is generally evaluated by calculating three different metrics which are Detection rate (DR), False Alarm rate (FA), and Accuracy (AC) and they are calculated using the equations 5, 6 and 7 respectively:

$$DR = \frac{TP}{TP + FN} \times 100\% \tag{5}$$

Where TP (true positive) and FN (false negative) represent respectively malware that were correctly classified as malware and malware that were wrongly classified as benign.

$$FA = \frac{FP}{FP + TN} \times 100\% \tag{6}$$

TN (true negative) and FP (false positive) represent respectively benign programs that were correctly classified as benign, benign program that were wrongly classified as malware. The accuracy (AC) represents the rate of files that were correctly classified in their class.

$$AC = \frac{TP + TN}{TP + TN + FP + FN} \times 100\% \tag{7}$$

The fourth metric that we will use to evaluate our system's performance is the detection time (DT), which represents the average time required for categorizing a file and it is expressed in seconds per file. DT includes the feature extraction time, .arff file generation time, and the classification time. The obtained results are presented in table 5.

Table 5. Experimental results

Group	φ	PEF Counts	DR	FA	AC	DT
G1	≥ 0.75	11	98.51%	7.14%	96.33%	0.075
G2	**≥ 0.50**	**14**	**100.00%**	**7.14%**	**97.25%**	**0.077**
G3	≥ 0.25	22	98.51%	9.52%	95.41%	0.079
G4	-	590	97.01%	7.14%	95.41%	0.116

From the results presented in the above table, we can see that our proposed feature selection method was able to increase the accuracy of our system by +1.84% (from 95.41% with G4 to 97.25% with G2) and that using only 14 PEFs. It was also able to reduce the categorization time by 33% (from 0.116s with G4 to 0.077s with G2). Note that the feature extraction phase took 0.037s, the .arff file generation also required 0.037s, and the classification phase took 0.003s.

5.3   Comparison

In this subsection, we will evaluate our system's performance by comparing it with the previously cited methods. The results are presented in table 6.

Table 6. Results of the comparison with the previously cited methods for malware detection

Method	Feature Type	DR	AC
Our method	**PEFs**	**100%**	**97.25%**
Schultz et al. [11]	Strings	97.43%	97.11%
Salehi et al. [4]	APIs+Args	99.2%	98.4%
Wang et al. [12]	APIs	94.4%	93.71%
Ye et al. [2]	APIs	88.16%	67.5%

From the results presented in Table 6, we can see that our system outperforms three of the four presented systems with an improvement in accuracy that varies from 0.14 % to 30%. The system proposed by Salehi et al. [4] is more accurate than our system (+1.15%). However, our system has a better detection rate.

If we consider the detection time (categorization time), we can conclude that our system is adequate for real-time detection. The proposed system is able to categorize a file in 0.077s, which is a very satisfying performance, compared with the system proposed by Ye et al. [2] which categorizes a file in 0.09s. The system proposed by Salehi et al. [4] needs to monitor the analyzed program during 2 minutes in order to extract API calls and their arguments, that represents almost 3000 times the required time by our proposed features extraction method.

6   Conclusion and Future Works

In this paper, we have presented a real-time PE-malware detection system that is based on the analysis of the PE-optional Header information. The proposed system uses an efficient feature selection method, which is based on the KHI² test. This latter allowed us to achieve a high accuracy and a low detection time, using only 2% of the initially extracted features. As future works, we project to combine different types of features such as APIs calls, and Opcode, in order to increase the accuracy of our system.

References

1. Bazrafshan, Z., Hashemi, H., Fard, S.M.H., Hamzeh, A.: A survey on heuristic malware detection techniques. In: Proceedings 2013 5th Conference on Information and Knowledge Technology (IKT), Shiraz, pp. 113–120 (2013)
2. Ye, Y., Li, T., Jiang, Q., Wang, Y.: CIMDS: Adapting postprocessing techniques of associative classification for malware detection. IEEE Transactions on Systems, Man and Cybernetics Part C: Applications and Reviews 40, 298–307 (2010)
3. June, I.: Anti-malware vendors slow to respond. Computer Fraud & Security, 1–2 (2010)

4. Salehi, Z., Sami, A., Ghiasi, M.: Using feature generation from API calls for malware detection. Computer Fraud & Security Bulletin, 9–18 (2014)
5. Aycock, J.D.: Computer viruses and malware. Springer, Heidelberg (2006)
6. Shabtai, A., Moskovitch, R., Elovici, Y., Glezer, C.: Detection of malicious code by applying machine learning classifiers on static features: A state-of-the-art survey. Information Security Technical Report 14, 16–29 (2009)
7. Fornasini, P.: The Chi Square test. The Uncertainty in Physical Measurements:An Introduction to Data Analysis in the Physics Laboratory, pp. 187–198. Springer Science & Business Media (2009)
8. Rodríguez, J.J., Kuncheva, L.I., Alonso, C.J.: Rotation forest: A New classifier ensemble method. IEEE Transactions on Pattern Analysis and Machine Intelligence 28, 1619–1630 (2006)
9. Witten, I.H., Frank, E.: Data Mining: Practical machine learning tools and techniques. Morgan Kaufmann, San Francisco (2005)
10. Pietrek, M.: Peering Inside the PE: A Tour of the Win32 Portable Executable File Format. Microsoft Systems Journal-US Edition 9, 15–38 (1994)
11. Schultz, M.G., Eskin, E., Zadok, E., Stolfo, S.J.: Data mining methods for detection of new malicious executables. Proceedings. In: 2001 IEEE Symposium on Security and Privacy, S&P 2001, Oakland, CA, pp. 38–49 (2001)
12. Wang, C., Pang, J., Zhao, R., Liu, X.: Using API sequence and bayes algorithm to detect suspicious behavior. In: Proceedings of the 2009 International Conference on Communication Software and Networks, ICCSN 2009, Macau, pp. 544–548 (2009)
13. https://code.google.com/p/pefile/
14. Koskska, S., Nevison, C.: Statistical tables and formulae. Springer, New York (1989)
15. Farrington, D.P., Loeber, R.: Relative improvement over chance (RIOC) and phi as measures of predictive efficiency and strength of association in 2x2 tables. Journal of Quantitative Criminology 5, 201–213 (1989)

Security and Network Technologies:
Wireless Sensor Networks

Balanced and Safe Weighted Clustering Algorithm for Mobile Wireless Sensor Networks

Amine Dahane$^{(\boxtimes)}$, Nasr-Eddine Berrached, and Abdelhamid Loukil

Intelligent Systems Research Laboratory (LARESI)
University of Sciences and Technology of Oran
P.O. Box 1505, Oran, Algeria
amineusto.laresi@gmail.com

Abstract. The main concern of clustering approaches for mobile wireless sensor networks (WSNs) is to prolong the battery life of the individual sensors and the network lifetime. In this paper, we propose a balanced and safe weighted clustering algorithm which is an extended version of our previous algorithm (ES-WCA) for mobile WSNs using a combination of five metrics. Among these metrics lie the behavioral level metric which promotes a safe choice of a cluster head in the sense where this last one will never be a malicious node. The goals of the proposed algorithm are: offer better performance in terms of the number of re-affiliations which enables to generate a reduced number of balanced and homogeneous clusters, this algorithm, coupled with suitable routing protocols, aims to maintain stable clustering structure. We implemented and tested a simulation of the proposed algorithm to demonstrate its performance.

Keywords: WSNs · Clustering · Homogenous Clusters · Energy Efficiency · Security

1   Introduction

After the success of theoretical research contributions in previous decade, wireless sensor networks (WSNs) [1,2] have become now a reality. Their deployment in many societal, environmental and industrial applications makes them very useful in practice. These networks consist of a large number of small size nodes which sense ubiquitously some physical phenomenon (temperature, humidity, acceleration, noise, light intensity, wind speed, etc.) and report the collected data to the sink station by using multi-hop wireless communications. The clustering concept, that means grouping nodes which are close to each other, has been studied largely in ad-hoc networks [2,3,4,5,6,7,8] and recently in WSNs [9,10,11,12,13] where the purpose in general is to reduce useful energy consumption and routing overhead, however, cluster-heads must be selected carefully and diligently. Recent research studies recognize that organizing mobile WSNs, in the sense defined above, into clusters by using a clustering mechanism is a challenging task [9,10]. This is due to the fact that cluster heads (CHs) carry out extra work, and consequently consume more energy compared with cluster members (CMs) during the network operations and this will lead to untimely death causing network partition and therefore failure in communication link. For this reason, one of the frequently encountered problems in this mechanism is to search for the best way to elect CH for each

© IFIP International Federation for Information Processing 2015
A. Amine et al. (Eds.): CIIA 2015, IFIP AICT 456, pp. 429–441, 2015.
DOI: 10.1007/978-3-319-19578-0_35

cluster. Indeed, a CH can be selected by computing quality of nodes, which may depend on several metrics: connectivity degree, mobility, residual energy and distance of a node from its neighbors. Significant improvement in performance of this quality can be achieved by combining these metrics [2,3,8,9,13,14].

In this paper, we propose balanced and safe weighed clustering algorithm for mobile WSNs (BS-WCA) using a combination of the above metrics with the behavioral level metric which we have added. Our approach enables to generate a reduced number of balanced and homogeneous clusters in order to minimize the energy consumption of the entire network and prolong sensors lifetime. In the other sense, the behavioral level is decisive and allows the proposed clustering algorithm to avoid any malicious node in the neighborhood to become a CH, even if the remaining metrics are in its favor. The election of CHs is carrying out using weights of neighboring nodes which are computed based on selected metrics. So, this strategy ensures the election of legitimate and trustworthy CHs with high weights. The Node-Weight heuristic assigns node-weights based on the suitability of nodes acting as cluster heads and the election of the cluster head is done on the basis of the largest weight among its neighbors. This means that a node decides to become a cluster head or stay as an ordinary node depending on the weights of its one hop neighbors [2].

The preliminary results obtained through simulation study demonstrate the effectiveness of our algorithm in terms of number of equilibrate clusters, number of re-affiliations, by comparing it with WCA [2], DWCA [14] and SDCA [11].

These results also reveal that our approach is very suitable if we plan to use in network layer reactive routing protocols instead of proactive ones after the clustering mechanism was launched. The contribution of our paper is as follows:

-   Maintaining stable clustering structure and offering better performance in terms of the number of re-affiliations using the proposed algorithm BS-WCA.

The remaining part of this paper is organized as follows: We first, in Section 2, discuss the existing studies. The details of our approach are described in section 3. Section 4 introduces and explains the selected metrics for the proposed approach of clustering. A special attention was reserved for this last aspect in this research. More details on the proposed algorithm are provided in section 5. Section 6 presents the simulation tool developed for the evaluation and provides simulation results to show the effectiveness of the proposed algorithm. Section 7 concludes the paper.

2   Related Works

In this section, we outline some approaches of clustering used in Ad-hoc networks and WSNs. Abbasi *et al.* [15] presented taxonomy and classification of typical clustering schemes, and then summarized different clustering algorithms for WSNs based on classification of variable convergence and constant convergence time protocols. They also highlighted objectives, features, and algorithms complexity. Research studies on clustering in Ad-hoc networks evolve surveyed works on clustering algorithms [16] and cluster head election algorithms [3,10]. For the single metric based on clustering, as in paper [17], the node with the least stability value is elected as CH among its neighbors, however the choice of CH which has a lower energy level, could quickly become a bottleneck of its cluster. Safa *et al.* [4] designed and implemented a dynamic energy efficient clustering algorithm (DEECA) for mobile Ad-hoc networks (MANETs) that increases the network lifetime, however, the cluster formation in this scheme is not based on connectivity so the formed clusters are not well connected; this induces an increase of re-affiliation rate and re-clustering situations. Other proposals use strategy based on weights computing in order to elect CHs [2,3,8,14].The main strategy of these algorithms is based mainly on adding more metrics such as connectivity degree, mobility, residual energy and distance of a node from its neighbors, corresponding to some performance in the process of electing CHs. Although, the algorithms using this strategy allow to ensure the election of a better CHs based only on their high weights computed from the considered metrics, but unfortunately they does not ensure that the elected CHs are legitimated nodes, which is to say if the election process of CHs is safe or not. Safa *et al.* [5] propose a novel cluster-based trust-aware routing protocol (CBTRP) for MANETs to protect forwarded packets from intermediary malicious nodes. The proposed protocol ensures the passage of packets through trusted routes only by making nodes monitor the behavior of each other and update their trust tables accordingly. However, in CBTRP all nodes monitor the network which lead rapid drainage of node energy and therefore minimize the lifetime of the network. Khalil *et al.* [18] proposed a protocol called DICAS, which uses local monitoring and mitigates the attacks against control traffic by detecting, diagnosing and isolating the malicious nodes. Hsin *et al.* [19] proposed a self-monitoring mechanism that pays more attention to the system-level fault diagnosis of the network, especially for detecting node failures. However, they did not deal with malicious behaviors. Little effort has been made in introducing security aspect in clustering mechanism. Yu *et al.*[7] tried to secure clustering mechanism against wormhole attack in ad-hoc networks (communication between CHs) but after forming clusters, not during the election procedure of CHs. Hai *et al.*[21] propose a lightweight intrusion detection framework integrated for clustered sensor networks by using an over-hearing mechanism to reduce the sending alert packets. Elhdhili *et al.* [6] propose a reputation based clustering algorithm (RECA) that aims to elect trustworthy, stable and high energy cluster heads but during the election procedure, not after forming clusters. Benahmed *et al.* [11] used clustering mechanism based on weighted computing as an efficient solution to detect misbehavior nodes during distributed monitoring process in WSNs. However, they focused only on the misbehavior of malicious nodes and not on the nature of attacks, the formed clusters are not homogeneous, the proposed secured distributed clustering algorithm (SDCA) is not coupled with routing protocols and doesn't give much importance to energy consumption.

In the context of these surveyed research works about clustering in both ad-hoc networks and WSNs, we classified our contribution among approaches based on the computing of the weight of each node in the network, this approach focuses around strategy of distributed resolution which enables to generate a reduced number of balanced and homogeneous clusters in order to minimize the energy consumption of the entire network and prolong sensors lifetime. Moreover, we introduced a new metric (the behavioral level metric) which promotes a safe choice of a cluster head in the sense where this last one will never be a malicious node.

3   Our Approach

In the literature, no research has thought to use energy efficiency and monitoring mechanism using the same cluster-based architecture. Our first objective is to make the network able to self-organize in order to achieve its tasks with a least cost. In this context, we must determine the parameters for generating a reduced number of stable and balanced clusters. Our second objective is to propose a mechanism that assures the distributed monitoring of WSNs security reasons. This mechanism uses a cluster-based architecture, as well as new set of metrics and rules for diagnosing the state of the sensors. The advantages of this solution are that it reduces the flow of communication and provides stable surveillance environment. This approach gives more importance to the election criteria of nodes responsible for monitoring the network. The details of this approach are illustrated in our proposed algorithm BS-WCA.

4   .Metrics for CHs Election

This section introduces the different metrics used for cluster-head election. In our earlier work [9], we insisted in Mobility (Mi), connectivity (Ci), residual energy (Eri) and distance of node ni (Di) to its neighbors. In this paper, we focus our study on behavior level metric.

- **The Behavior Level of a Node n_i (BLi)**

The behavioral level of a node n_i is a key metric in our contribution. Initially, each node is assigned an equal static behavior level "$BL_i=1$".
However, this level can be decreased by the anomaly detection algorithm if a node is misbehavior as illustrated by Fig 1.

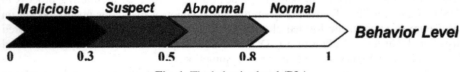

Fig. 1. The behavior level (BL$_i$)

For computing the behavior level of each node, nodes with a behavior level less than threshold behavior will not be accepted as CH candidates even if they have the other interesting characteristics such as high energy, high degree of connectivity or low mobility. Nevertheless, abnormal node and suspect node can always belong to a cluster as a CM but never as a CH. So, we define the behavior level of each sensor node n_i, noted BL_i, in any neighborhood of the network as presented in Fig.1. BL_i is classified by the following mapping function $(Mp(BL_i))$:

$$Mp(BL_i) = \begin{cases} Normal\ node: & 0.8 \leq BL_i \leq 1 \\ Abnormal\ node: & 0.5 \leq BL_i < 0.8 \\ Suspect\ node: & 0.3 \leq BL_i < 0.5 \\ Malicious\ node: & 0 \leq BL_i < 0.3 \end{cases} \tag{1}$$

The values in the formula (1) are chosen on the basis of several reputed models of WSNs adopted by numerous researchers like Shaikh et al. [20] and Hai et al. [21]. For each node, we must calculate its weight P_i, according to the equation:

$$P_i = w_1 * BL_i + w_2 * Er_i + w_3 * M_i + w_4 * C_i + w_5 * D_i \tag{2}$$

Where w_1, w_2, w_3, w_4, and w_5 are the coefficients corresponding to the system criteria, so that:

$$w_1 + w_2 + w_3 + w_4 + w_5 = 1 \tag{3}$$

We propose to generate homogeneous clusters whose size lies between two thresholds: $Thresh_{Upper}$ and $Thresh_{Lower}$. These thresholds are arbitrarily selected or depend on the topology of the network. Thus, if their values depend on the topology of the network, they are calculated as follows according to [12]:

$$Thresh_{Upper} = \frac{1}{2}(\delta_{12}(u) + AVG) \tag{4}$$

$$Thresh_{Lower} = \frac{1}{2}(\delta_{12}(v) + AVG) \tag{5}$$

With:

$$\delta_{12}(u) = \max(\delta_{12}(u_i): u_i \in U) \tag{6}$$

$$\delta_{12}(v) = \min(\delta_{12}(v_i): v_i \in U) \tag{7}$$

$$AVG = \frac{\sum_{i=1}^{n} \delta_{12}(u_i)}{N} \tag{8}$$

Where:
-   u represents the node that has the maximum number of neighbors with one jump;
-   v represents the node that has the minimum number of neighbors with one jump;
-    AVG denotes the average cardinal of the groups with one jump of all the nodes of the network;
-   N is the number of nodes in the network.

The weight P_i calculated for each sensor is based on the above parameters $(BL_i, M_i, D_i, Er_i$ and $C_i)$. It means for our case the trust level of each node in the network. The values of coefficients w_i should be chosen depending on the importance of each metric in considered WSNs applications. For instance, we can assign a greater value to the metric BL_i compared to other metrics if we promote the safety aspect in the clustering mechanism. We can also assign a same value for each coefficient w_i in case when all metrics are considered having the same importance. An approach based on these weights will enable us to build a self-organizing algorithm able to form small number of homogenous clusters in size and radius by grouping geographically close nodes. The resulting weighted clustering algorithm reduces energy consumption and guaranty the choice of legitimate CHs.

5   Weighted Clustering Algorithm (BS-WCA)

In this section, we first give assumptions of the proposed algorithm: Balanced and Safe Weighted Clustering Algorithm (BS-WCA).

Then we present, in detail, an extended version of ES-WCA [9] followed by an illustrative example.

5.1   Assumptions

Before heading into the technical details of our algorithm, this paper is based on the same assumptions as in [9]. We add the fact that a malicious node can use its own ability to move freely in the space area. The behavior of the malicious node by moving frequently inside a same cluster or from a cluster to another is a normal behavior to not attract attention of the neighborhood and therefore to be detected .

5.2   Re-affiliation Phase

During the first phase, it may not be possible for all clusters to reach the $Thresh_{Upper}$ threshold. Moreover, it is possible that clusters whose size is lower than $Thresh_{Lower}$ may be created, since there is no constraint relating to the generation of these types of clusters. BS-WCA uses four types of messages in the Re-affiliation phase. The message RE_AFF_CH, that is sent in the network by the CH which the cluster size is less than $Thresh_{Upper}$. The second one is the REQ_RE_AFF message that is sent by the neighbors of CH if it wants to join this cluster. Finally a CH must send a response ACCEPT_RE_AFF message or DROP_AFF message as illustrated by Fig. 2. Hence, in this second phase, we tried to reduce the number of clusters formed and reorganize them in order to obtain balanced and homogeneous clusters. For that, we propose to re-affiliate the sensor nodes belonging to clusters that have not attained the cluster size$Thresh_{Lower}$to those that did not reach $Thresh_{Upper}$.

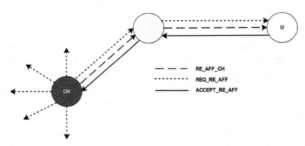

Fig. 2. Procedure of Re-affiliation of node 'U' to a cluster

We demonstrate our set up phase algorithm and re-affiliation phase with the help of four figures (Fig. 3, Fig. 4, Fig. 5 and Fig. 6).

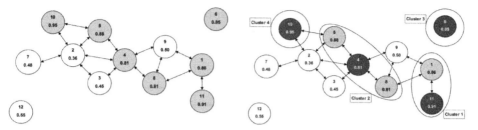

Fig. 3 Topology of the network   **Fig. 4.** Identification of clusters nodes

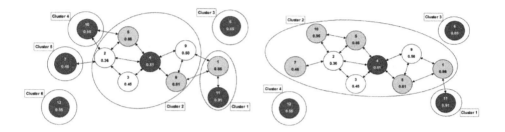

Fig. 5. The final identification of clusters   **Fig. 6.** The final identification of clusters

---

Algorithm: Re-affiliation Phase Algorithm

Inputs: $Thresh_{Upper}$, $Thresh_{Lower}$;
Outputs: set of clusters
Begin
1: **For** num_cl = 1 to Count (Cluster) **Do**
2:      **If** (Size (Cluster [num_cl]) < $Thresh_{Upper}$)
          Then
3:          CH sends a message "RE_AFF_CH" to its neighbours
            (N(CH));
4:          J = Count (N(CH));
          EndIf
5:   **For** I = 1 to J **Do**
6:      **If** ($n_i \in N$(CH) receives the message)
            && ($n_i \in$ (Size(Cluster[num_cl]) <$Thresh_{Lower}$)
            Then
7:          n_i sends a Select message "REQ_RE_AFF" to the CH;
8:      **If** (Size (Cluster [num_cl]) < $Thresh_{Upper}$)
            Then
9:          CH sends a message "ACCEPT_RE_AFF" to n_i ;
10:         CH updates its state vector;
11:         CH → CH → Size = Size + 1;
12:         n_i updates its state vector;
13:         n_i → CH → ID = ID;
14:         **Else** CH sends a "FIN_ AFF" message to n_i ;
15:         Go to 2;
          EndIF
16:     **Else** n_i sends a "DROP_AFF" message to CH;
        EndIf
      End For
    End For
End.

Table I shows the values of the different criteria for the nodes that have behavior level $BL_i > 0.8$ (Normal nodes). Table II shows the weights P_i of neighbors for each node that have behavior level $BL_i > 0.8$.

Table 1. Values of the various criteria of normal nodes

Ids	BL_i	En	C_i	D_i	M_i	P_i
1	0.86	3842.12	3	1.15	1.20	769.632
4	0.81	4832.54	5	2.30	0.30	968.133
5	0.88	4053.25	3	1.30	0.55	811.829
6	0.85	4620.43	0	0.00	0.20	924.361
8	0.81	4816.80	4	1.05	1.40	964.753
10	0.95	3650.25	2	0.55	0.10	730.805
11	0.91	4819.60	1	0.70	2.20	964.753

Table 2. Weight P_i of neighbors

Ids	1	4	5	6	8	10	11
1	769.632	-	-	-	964.753	-	964.753
4	-	968.133	811.829	-	964.753	-	-
5	-	968.133	811.829	-	-	730.805	-
6	-		-	924.361	-	-	-
8	769.632		-	-	964.753	-	-
10	-	968.133	811.829	-	-	730.805	-
11	769.632		-	-	-	-	964.753

Nodes in Fig.3 are presented by circles containing their identity Ids at the top and the levels of behavior at the bottom. According to table 2, node 1 has a choice between CH11 and CH8 (they have the same weight), but the behavior level of node 11 is greater than the node 8 ($BL_{11}>BL_8$), so node 1 will be attached to CH11. For the other nodes, we have various conditions. Node 4 declares itself as a CH. Node 5 will be attached to CH4. Node 6 declares itself as a CH, because it is an isolated node. Node 8 will be attached to CH4. Node 10 is connected with CH5, but node 5 is attached to CH4; thus, node 10 declares itself as a CH. Node 11 declares itself as a CH. These results give us the representation shown in Fig.4. Node 2 is connected with CH4 and CH10. Node 2 will be attached to CH4, because CH4 has the maximum weight (968.133). Node 3 is connected with CH4, which implies that node 3 will be attached to CH4. Node 7 is not connected with any CH, so node 7 declares itself as CH. Node 9 is connected with CH4, and then node 9 will be attached to CH4. Node 12 is not connected with any CH, which implies that node 12 declares itself as a CH. These results give us the representation shown in Fig.5. We propose to generate homogeneous clusters whose size lies between two thresholds: $Thresh_{Upper}= 9$ and $Thresh_{Lower}= 6$. For that, we suggest to re-affiliate the sensor nodes belonging to the clusters that have not attained the cluster size $Thresh_{Lower}$ to those that did not reach $Thresh_{Upper}$. Node 4 have the highest weight and his size is less than $Thresh_{Upper}$. Nodes 1, 7 and 10 are neighbors of the node 4 with 2 hops and belong to the clusters that have not attained the cluster size $Thresh_{Lower}$, so these nodes get merged to cluster 2. Clusters 1, 3, and 4 will be homogeneous with cluster 1 when the network becomes densely. At the end of this example, we obtain a network of four clusters (as shown in Fig. 6).

There are five situations that require the maintenance of clusters:

- Battery depletion of a node.
- Behavior level of a node less than or equal 0.3.
- Adding, moving or deleting a node.

In all of these cases, if a node n_i is CH then the set-up phase will be repeated.

6 Implementation Results

In this section, we present our simulator 'Mercury' and the results of our work. To determine and evaluate the results of the execution of algorithms that are introduced previously, the number of sensors (N) to deploy must be less than or equal to 1000. There are two types of sensor node deployment on the sensing field: random and manual. "Mercury" offers users the ability to select a sensor type from 5 predefined types. Each one has its characteristics (radius, energy, etc.). The user can also introduce his own characteristics. The unity of the used energy is the nano joules (1 Joule = 10^9 NJ).

6.1 Discussion and Results

In all experiments, N varies between 10 and 100 sensor nodes, the transmission range (R) varies between 10 and 70 meters (m) and the used energy (E) equal to 50000 NJ. By default, for each set of simulation, we conduct 100 runs with different node generations and report the average. The sensor nodes are randomly distributed in a "570m × 555m" space area by the following function:

$for\ (int\ n = 0;\ n\ <\ node\_tobe\_deployed;\ n + +)$
{
    $X\_ = rand(\ )\quad \%\quad image\_Field\_Of\_Collecting\ - > width;$
    $Y\_ = rand(\ )\quad \%\quad image\_Field\_Of\_Collecting\ -> Height;$
}

To measure the performance of BS-WCA algorithm, we considered the following four metrics:

a. The number of clusters;
b. The number of re-affiliations;

The values of weighting factors used for simulation were:

$$w_1 = 0.3,\ w_2 = 0.2,\ w_3 = 0.2,\ w_4 = 0.2\ and\ w_5 = 0.1.$$

Note that these values are arbitrary at this time and should be adjusted according to the system requirements. To evaluate the performance of the BS-WCA algorithm with other algorithms, we studied the effect of the density of the networks (number of sensor nodes in a given area) and the transmission range on the average number of formed clusters. Then we compare it with a DWCA (Distributed Weighted Clustering Algorithm) proposed in [14], WCA (A weighted Clustering Algorithm for Mobile Ad-hoc Networks) proposed in [2] and SDCA (secured distributed clustering algorithm) proposed in [11]. We omit presenting all results and the monitoring phase due to the space limitation. The highlight of our work is summarized in a comprehensive strategy for monitoring the network that will be presented in our future works. The goal is to detect and remove the malicious nodes

Fig.7 depicts the average number of clusters that are formed with respect to the total number of nodes in the network. The communication range used in this experience is 200m. As we can see in Fig. 7, the proposed algorithm produced the same number of clusters than DWCA when the node number is equal to 20 nodes. If the node density has increased, BS-WCA would have produced constantly less clusters than SDCA and DWCA regardless of node number. The result of BS-WCA is so unstable between 60 and 90 because we use a random deployment so if the distance between the nodes increases, the number of clusters increases too. When there were 100 nodes in the network, the proposed algorithm produced about 61.91% fewer clusters than DWCA [14] and about 38.46% than SDCA [11]. As a result, our algorithm gave better performance in terms of the number of clusters when the node density in the network is high, because BS-WCA generates a reduced number of balanced and homogeneous clusters, whose size lies between two thresholds: $Thresh_{Upper}$ and $Thresh_{Lower}$ (Re-affiliation Phase) in order to minimize the energy consumption of the entire network and prolong sensors lifetime.

Fig.8 shows the variation of the average number of clusters with respect to the transmission range. The results are shown for varying N. We observe that the average number of clusters decreases with the increase in the transmission range. As we can see in Fig.10, the proposed algorithm produced 16% to 35% fewer clusters than WCA when the transmission range of nodes was 10m. If the node density increased, BS-WCA produced constantly fewer clusters than WCA regardless of node number. When there were 70 nodes in the network, the proposed algorithm produced about 47% to 73% fewer clusters than WCA. According to the result, our algorithm gave better performance in terms of the number of clusters when the node density and transmission range in the network are high.

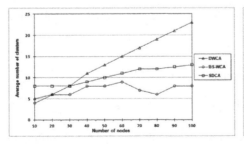
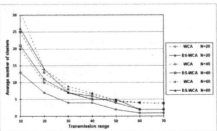

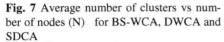

Fig. 7 Average number of clusters vs number of nodes (N) for BS-WCA, DWCA and SDCA

Fig. 8. Average number of clusters vs transmission range BS-WCA and WCA

Fig.9 depicts the average number of re-affiliations that are formed with respect to the total number of nodes in the network. We propose to generate homogeneous clusters whose size lies between two thresholds: $Thresh_{Upper} = 18$ and $Thresh_{Lower} = 9$. The number of re-affiliations increased linearly if there were 30 or more nodes in the network for both WCA and DWCA, but for our algorithm the number of re-affiliations increased starting from 50 nodes. According to the results, our algorithm gave better performance in terms of number of re-affiliations. The main reason is that the frequency of invoking the clustering algorithm is lower in BS-WCA, thus resulting in longer duration of stability of the topology. The benefit of decreasing the number of re-affiliations mainly comes from the localized re-affiliation phase in our algorithm. From Figure 10 it is observed that the sensor nodes 3 and 19 are malicious and have a behavior level less than 0.3. We also note that the sensor 11 is suspicious so if it continues to move frequently it's behavior will gradually be decreased until it reaches the malicious state in this case this node will be deleted from the neighborhood and finally it will be added to the black list. The behavior level of these nodes decreased by 0.001 units when it moves one meter away from its original location but this malicious node does nothing just mobility so in our future works, we will detect the internal misbehavior nodes during distributed monitoring process in WSNs by the follow-up of the messages exchanged between the nodes.

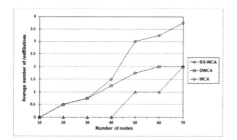

Fig. 9. Average number of re-affiliations

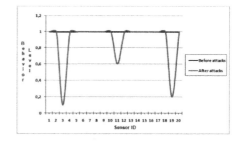

Fig. 10. Behavior level of some sensors before and after attacks

7   Conclusions

In this paper, we have presented a new algorithm called "BS-WCA" for the self-organization of mobile sensor networks. Obtained results from simulations prove that our algorithm outperforms WCA, DWCA and SDCA. It yields a low number of clusters and preserves network structure better than WCA and DWCA by reducing the number of re-affiliations. The proposed algorithm chooses the most robust and safe CHs with the responsibility of monitoring the nodes in their clusters and maintaining clusters locally. As a result of this work, we plan to add a monitoring phase which analyses and detects specific misbehavior in the WSNs by the follow-up of the messages exchanged between the nodes.

Acknowledgements. The authors are grateful to the anonymous referees and Professor Bouhadiba F. for their insightful comments and valuable suggestions, which greatly improved the quality of the paper.

References

1. Akyildiz, I.F., Su, W., Sankarasubramaniam, Y., Cayirci, E.: Wireless sensor networks: A Survey. Computer Networks 38(2), 393–422 (2002)
2. Chatterjee, M., Das, S., Turgut, D.: WCA: a weighted clustering algorithm for mobile ad hoc networks. Journal of Cluster Computing (Special Issue on Mobile Ad-hoc Networks) 5, 193–204 (2002)
3. Zabian, A., Ibrahim, A., Al-Kalani, F.: Dynamic Head Cluster Election Algorithm for clustered Ad-hoc Networks. Journal of Computer Science 4(1) (2008)
4. Safa, H., Artail, H., Tabet, D.: A cluster-based trust-aware routing protocol for mobile ad-hoc net-works. Wireless Networks 16(4), 969–984 (2010)
5. Safa, H., Mirza, O., Artail, H.: A Dynamic Energy Efficient Clustering Algorithm for MANETs. In: IEEE International Conference on Wireless & Mobile Computing, Networking & Communication, pp. 51–56 (2008)
6. Elhdhili, M., Azzouz, L., Kamoun, F.: Reputation based clustering algorithm for security management in ad hoc networks with liars. International Journal of Information and Computer Security 3(3), 228–244 (2009)
7. Yu, Y., Zhang, L.: A Secure Clustering Algorithm in Mobile Ad-hoc Networks. In: 2012 IACSIT Hong Kong Conferences, vol. 29, pp. 73–77 (2012)
8. Agarwal, R., Gupta, R., Motwani, M.: Review of Weighted Clustering Algorithms for Mobile Ad-hoc Networks. Computer Science and Telecommunications 33(1), 71–78 (2012)
9. Dahane, A., Berrached, N., Kechar, B.: Energy Efficient and Safe Weighted Clustering Algorithm for Mobile Wireless Sensor Networks. In: The 9th International Conference on Future Networks and Communications, Procedia Computer Science, Niagara Falls, Ontario, Canada, August 17 -20, vol. 34, pp. 63–70 (2014)
10. Soro, S., Heinzelman, W.B.: Cluster head election techniques for coverage preservation in wire-less sensor networks. Ad-Hoc Networks Journal 7(5), 955–972 (2009)
11. Benahmed, K., Merabti, M., Haffaf, H.: Distributed monitoring for misbehavior detection in wireless sensor networks. Security and Communication Networks 6(4), 388–400 (2013)
12. Lehsaini, M., Guyennet, H., Feham, M.: An efficient cluster-based self-organization algorithm for wireless sensor networks. Int. Journal. Sensor Networks 7(1-2), 85–94 (2010)
13. Darabkh, K.A., Ismail, S., Al-Shurman, M.: Performance evaluation of selective and adaptive heads clustering algorithms over wireless sensor networks. Journal of Network and Computer Appli-cations 35(6), 2068–2080 (2012)
14. Choi, W., Woo, M.: A Distributed Weighted Clustering Algorithm for Mobile Ad Hoc Net-works. In: Proc. of the IEEE Advanced International Conference on Telecommunications and Interna-tional Conference on Internet and Web Applications and Services (AICT/ICIW 2006), p. 73 (2006)
15. Abbassi, A., Younis, M.: A Survey on Clustering Algorithms for Wireless Sensor Networks. Computer Communications Journal 30(14-15), 2826–2841 (2007)
16. Chawla, M., Singhai, J., Rana, J.L.: Clustering in Mobile Ad- hoc Networks: A Review. International Journal of Computer Science and Information Security (IJCSIS) 8(2), 293–301 (2010)

17. Er, I.I., Seah, W.K.G.: Mobility-based d-Hop Clustering Algorithm for Mobile Ad Hoc Networks. In: IEEE Wireless Communications and Networking Conference (WCNC 2004), pp. 2359–2364 (2004)
18. Khalil, I., Bagchi, S., Shroff, N.B.: LITEWORP: a lightweight Counter measure for the wormhole attack in multihop wireless networks. In: International Conference on Dependable Systems and Networks, pp. 612–621 (2005)
19. Hsin, M.L.: Self-monitoring of wireless sensor networks. Computer Communications 29(4), 462–476 (2006)
20. Shaikh, R.A., Jameel, H., Lee, S., Y.J., et al.: Trust management problem in distributed wireless sensor networks. In: Proceedings of the 12th IEEE International Conference on Embedded and Real-Time Computing Systems and Applications (RTCSA), pp. 411–414 (2006)
21. Hai, T.H., Huhi, E.N., Jo, M.: A lightweight intrusion detection framework for wireless sensor net-works. Wireless Communications and Mobile Computing (Wiley) 10(4), 559–572 (2010)

Distributed Algorithm for Coverage and Connectivity in Wireless Sensor Networks

Abdelkader Khelil and Rachid Beghdad[✉]

Faculty of Sciences, University Abderrahmane Mira of Béjaïa 06000, Béjaia, Algeria
{khalilabdelkader,rachid.beghdad}@gmail.com

Abstract. Even if several algorithms were proposed in the literature to solve the coverage problem in Wireless Sensor Networks (WSNs), they still suffer from some weaknesses. This is the reason why we suggest in this paper, a distributed protocol, called Single Phase Multiple Initiator (SPMI). Its aim is to find Connect Cover Set (CCS) for assuring the coverage and connectivity in WSN. Our idea is based on determining a Connected Dominating Set (CDS) which has a minimum number of necessary and sufficient nodes to guarantee coverage of the area of interested (AI), when WSN model is considered as a graph. The suggested protocol only requires a single phase to construct a CDS in distributed manner without using sensors' location information. Simulation results show that SPMI assures better coverage and connectivity of AI by using fewer active nodes and by inducing very low message overhead, and low energy consumption, when compared with some existing protocols.

Keywords: Wireless Sensor Network (WSN) · Coverage · Connectivity · Distributed Algorithm · Connected Dominating Set (CDS)

1   Introduction

With the recent advances in micro-electronics technologies and wireless communications, a new type of networks has emerged: Wireless Sensor Networks (WSNs). This type of networks includes a large number of devices called sensors deployed over a geographical area to be monitored. A sensor is able to sense, process and transmit data over a wireless communication channel. The applications of WSNs include battlefield surveillance, healthcare, environmental and home monitoring, industrial diagnosis and so on [1].

A fundamental issue in WSNs is the coverage problem [2, 3] that mainly consists in ensuring continuous and effective observation of geographical area while taking into account some constraints, in particular the connectivity of active sensors. The coverage can be considered as a measure of the monitoring quality produced by a sensor network [4].

WSNs are usually dense and redundant (more than 20 nodes/m³ [5]). So, the coverage of AI can be done, but it is not optimal if all nodes contribute for observing this AI. So, this drawback motivates a connected cover set (CCS) to be employed in a WSN. Conceptually, a CCS is a set of active nodes, which can ensure coverage and connectivity. So, it provides many advantages to QoS of network.

© IFIP International Federation for Information Processing 2015
A. Amine et al. (Eds.): CIIA 2015, IFIP AICT 456, pp. 442–453, 2015.
DOI: 10.1007/978-3-319-19578-0_36

The WSN use the Connected Dominating Set Algorithm to construct a temporary CCS. Only the dominating nodes are responsible for sensing area, and other nodes (dominated nodes) can close the communication modules to save energy, in order to make the network life maximum. Various CDS algorithms [6-12] have been developed but they still suffer from some weaknesses, this is the reason why we focused on the solution of such a problem.

In this paper, we present a novel energy-efficient CDS algorithm for WSN called a Single Phase Multiple Initiator (SPMI). The main contributions of our solution are: (1) high coverage ratio, (2) small number of active nodes, (3) connectivity guaranteed and (4) very low communication overhead, which reduces energy consumption

The rest of this paper is organized as follows. Section 2 presents related work; Section 3 presents concepts relative to graph theory, a set of notations, assumptions of our work and the problem definition. Our solution will be described in Section 4. In Section 5, simulation results will be presented and finally, Section 6 concludes this paper.

2   Related Work

Numerous algorithms for constructing a *CDS* have been surveyed in literature. We cite some of them as follow:

A simple distributed and localized algorithm is proposed in [8] called *CDS-Rule-K* algorithm. It constructs a *CDS* in two phases. The first phase uses marked method to generate a non-optimal *CDS*. Initially all nodes broadcast hello message to receive neighbor tables, and exchange their neighbor tables. If a neighbor node is not covered by other nodes, then it is marked as a node of *CDS*. The second phase uses pruning rules to cut redundant leaf nodes. The pruning rule specifies that if all adjacent nodes are covered by marked brother nodes, then the node is a redundant leaf node, so it is pruned and broadcasts an updates message.

In [9], Yuanyuan and al. present an energy-efficient *CDS* algorithm (*EECDS*), it is based on two phases. In first phase solves a maximal independent set (*MIS*). Initially, all nodes are dyed white. The algorithm started from a white node, while it is dyed black and broadcasts a black message. When receiving a black message, a white neighbor node was stained gray and broadcasts a gray message. When receiving a gray message, a white neighbor node broadcasts query messages to get the states and priorities of nodes around, and sets a timer. If the timer times out ago, it did not receive any black message from its adjacent nodes, then it is dyed black and broadcasts a black message, or remain white until all the nodes in the network were stained gray or black. All the black nodes form a *MIS*. The algorithm in the second phase selects a number of connection nodes to connect the *MIS*. It starts from a non-independent node, while it is dyed blue and broadcast a blue message. When receiving a blue message, an independent node is dyed blue and broadcasts invitation messages. When receiving the invitation message, non-independent nodes compute the priority and broadcast update messages. A non-independent node with the greatest priority is stained blue and broadcasts a blue message until all the black nodes were stained blue. All the blue nodes form a *CDS*.

In [10], Wightman and Labrador have proposed a *CDS* algorithm called *A3*. It uses four forms of messages: Hello message, Children recognition message, Parent recognition message and sleeping message. The sink node starts the protocol by transmitting an initial hello message to their neighboring nodes. Nodes which are not in the range of sink node then this node accepts the message has not been covered by another node; it sets its state as covered, selects the transmitter as its parent node and answers back with a Parent recognition message. If a parent node does not accept any Parent recognition messages from its neighbors, it also turns off. The parent node sets a certain amount of time to accept the answers from its neighboring node. Once this time out, the parent node sorts the list in decreasing order according to the selection metric. Then, parent node broadcasts a children recognition message that includes the complete sorted list to all its candidates. Once the candidate nodes accept the list, they set a timeout period proportional to their position on the candidate list. During that timeout nodes wait for sleeping message from their brothers. If a node accepts a sleeping message during the time out period, it turns itself off.

In [11], Sajjad Rizvi and al. have proposed a *CDS* algorithm called *TC1* for improving the algorithm in [10]. It uses only one type of message: Hello message contains the parent *ID* of the Sender. The initiator node (sink) starts the protocol by transmitting hello message to their neighboring nodes. The neighbor nodes which received a hello message record their parent *ID* and calculate a timeout period according to their residual energy and distance from the sender. The child node which expires its timeout sends a hello message to its neighboring nodes too. So if the parent node receives this message, it will be a dominator node. This process continues until the complete topology is formed with nodes acting as *CDS* for rest of the nodes in the network.

In [12], ShiTing-jun and al. have proposed a *CDS* algorithm called *IPCDS*. It uses the staining and markers methods to solve the *MIS* and *CDS*, and uses the pruning rule to further reduce the *CDS*. Initially, all nodes are dyed white and have been marked. The initiator node (white node) starts the protocol; it is dyed black and broadcasts a black message. When at first receiving black, a white neighbor node is marked as the child of nodes broadcasting message. Upon receiving a black message, if the white neighbor node is not marked, it is dyed gray and broadcasts gray messages. Upon receiving a gray message, if the white neighbor node is not marked, then according the residual energy and *RSSI* (Received Signal Strength Indicator) sets the timer value. If the timer times out ago, it received a black message by broadcasted the brother node, it is dyed gray and broadcasts gray messages, or it is dyed black and broadcasts black messages. Upon receiving a black message broadcasted by the child node, the gray node was stained black and broadcasts black messages. Upon the black node is in line with the pruning rule, it is dyed gray and broadcasts gray messages. This process continues until all nodes in the network are stained gray or black. At the end of algorithm, all the black nodes form a *CDS*.

3   Preliminaries

A.   WSN Model

The network is modeled by a graph $G = (S, E)$, where S represents the vertices set and E the set of edges. An edge between two vertices u and v exists if u can communicate *v*. For a sensor *u*, it characterizes by alone identity denoted *ID(u)* and we distinguish two different ranges: communication range, denoted *CR*, and sensing range, denoted by *SR*. Two sensors are communicated if and only if the distance between them is at most equal to *CR*. The covered area from a node u (also called monitored or sensed area) is the surface within which if an event occurs it will be sensed by the sensor u. This area is modeled as a disk of radius *SR* centered at *u*. Similarly, the communication area, inside which the sensor u can send and receive messages, is modeled by a circle of radius *CR* centered at *u*. In this work, we consider $CR \leq 2*SR$.

B.   Definitions

In this subsection we define the concept on which our work is based, i.e. Connected Dominating Set (*CDS*).
    - Connected Dominating Set:

Given an undirected graph *G=(S,E)*, a Dominating Set (*DS*) of *G* is a subset of vertices $D \subseteq S$, such that any vertex *u* of the graph is either in *D* or has a neighbor $v \in D$ [18]. A graph has more than one dominating set. When a *DS* is connected, it is denoted as a *CDS*; that is, any two nodes in the *DS* can be connected through intermediate nodes from the *DS*.

C.   Solution Assumptions

In this work, we assume a randomly deployed network. Once disseminated, sensors are assumed to be static. The network consists of nodes deployed in high density in order to ensure initial connectivity. Furthermore, the network is homogeneous, that is all sensors have the same sensing radius and the same communication ranges. We also assume that sensors have a unique identifier (*ID*). Finally, we assume that each sensor knows its degree.

D.   Problem Definition

The random deployment of sensors is the most used for a broad range of applications in inaccessible environments. Due to the unplanned nature of this deployment type, a *WSN* could lead to sensing holes which decrease drastically the reliability of the network. In order to overcome this shortcoming, sensor nodes are disseminated in high density. Although, dense deployment minimizes the sensing holes, allows fault tolerance and increases the reliability of applications, it has its own drawbacks; maximizes the redundancy which decreases energy efficiency. Monitoring the same region of the interest area by several sensors involves a waste of energy. This behavior is in conflict with the most critical constraint of a *WSN* (energy efficient). Thus, it is crucial to have a solution that reduces redundancy in order to assure a good coverage ratio and connectivity.

4   SPMI Solution

A.   *SPMI Overview*

The *SPMI* requires a single phase to generate a *CDS*. Nodes in the *CDS* are called dominators while the *nonCDS* nodes are referred to dominated. The aim of the *SPMI* is to generate a small set of dominators while keeping the message overhead and energy consumption low. The suggested algorithm allows the construction of *CDS* which has a minimum number of necessary and sufficient nodes in a distributed manner. In fact, each sensor performs the algorithm independently from the others in order to determine its status: *Dominator* (active) or *Dominated* (passive). Initially, all sensors are in uncovered state for a timeout and make their decision to be in active or in passive state. The active nodes form a *CDS* of the network, they provide coverage (monitoring) of the interest area.

The nodes having a higher level energy than their one hop neighbors, they will be the parents of their neighbors and they form *DS*. To make this set connected, we activate the child nodes that have a higher degree and further away from their parents. So the brothers of active child node will be in passive state.

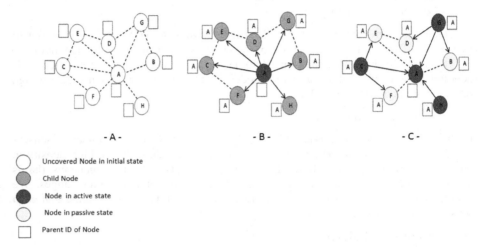

- A -   - B -   - C -

○ Uncovered Node in initial state

◉ Child Node

● Node in active state

○ Node in passive state

▭ Parent ID of Node

Fig. 1. An illustrative example

Figure 1.A represents a simple topology of 08 nodes which are uncovered in initial state; each node computes a timeout based on its level energy. In the figure 1.B, the node *A* will be in active state because it has a higher level energy than its neighbors, and it broadcasts a message which is received by nodes (*B, C, D, E, F, G* and *H*) under its communication area. After receiving, they will be children of node *A* and they recalculate (update) their timeout based on the degree and further away from their parents.

In the figure 1.C; When the timeout of nodes *C, G* and *H* expire without receiving any message from other nodes, they turn themselves in active state and broadcast a message (including their *ID* and parents *ID*) to their neighbors. The children nodes *E* and *F* are turned themselves in passive state after receiving a message which has the same parent *ID* from the node *C*. Also; the children nodes *B* and *D* are turned themselves in passive state after receiving a message from the node *G*.

So our algorithm maintains the node *A* is in active state, and in its communication range, it actives only three nodes (*C, G and H*) to assure more the coverage and connectivity; and put the other nodes in passive state which never send message to keep their energy.

B.   SPMI Description

Each sensor i is characterized by variables:

E_{ini}: initial energy (assumed to be the same for all nodes).

RE_i: residual energy.

$REP_i=E_{ini}/RE_i$: residual energy percentage.

T_{cons}: time constant.

T_i: waiting time or timeout.

ID_i: identifier of the node i.

$Parent_iID$: parent identifier of the node i.

$State_i$: indicates the sensor state, it may take one of values: *Uncovered, Dominator or Dominated.*

$Degree_i$: the one-hop neighbors number of node i.

$RSSI_j$: the signal strength of parent node j received by the child node i. It uses for estimation the distance between the nodes [16] [17].

$RSSI_c$: the minimum required signal strength to ensure connectivity.

The functions used by a node i are:

receive msg (ID_j, $parent_jID$): that is the node i which has received a domination message from an active neighbor j.

send msg (ID_i, $parent_iID$): that is the node i which has sent a domination message.

calculate (T_i): the node i computes a timeout T_i according to the formula (1). A timeout is inversely proportional to the remaining energy level.

$$T_i = T_{cons} /REP_i \qquad (1)$$

Recalculate (T_i): when the node i receives a message from its parent node j, then the node i recalculates the timeout according to the formula (2). A timeout inversely proportional to the remaining energy level, Degree and distance between the node i and node j.

$$T_i = T_{cons} / (REP_i + Degree_i +(RSSI_c /RSSI_j)) \qquad (2)$$

So, at first each node i computes a timeout Ti according to the formula (1) *(line1)*. Sensors with a higher residual energy percentage have a shorter timeout that expires earlier. Therefore, these sensors have more chance to be in active state. Sensors with a lower residual energy percentage have a longer timeout that expires later.

During this time, the sensor listens to messages sent by neighbors (*lines 2&4*): When the first receiving the message (*line7*), then the node will be the child of node broadcasting message and it recalculates its timeout according to the formula (2) (*line8*) (sensors with a higher residual energy percentage, higher degree and farther from parent node have a shorter timeout that expires earlier). If the node receives another message and its parent *ID* is the same of the parent *ID* in the message received (*line11*), then the node decides directly to change its state to a *Dominated* without sending any message (*line16*). If the timeout expires without receiving any message or receiving massages having parent *ID* different from the node's parent *ID*, the node then concludes that it is *Dominator* node (*line19*) and broadcasts a message announcing domination to its one-hop neighbors (*line20*). At the end of the algorithm, all *Dominator* nodes are members of the *CDS*.

SPMI algorithm is formally as follows:

For all Sensor *i*

BEGIN
1. *Calculate(T_i); parent$_i$ID=void; State$_i$=Uncovered; Verf=true*;
2. While ($T_i <> 0$) do
3. Begin
4.   Listen;
5.   If *receive msg (ID$_j$, parent$_j$ID)* then
6.   Begin
7.   If *(parent$_i$ID is void)* then
8.   *parent$_i$ID =ID$_j$; recalculate(T_i)* ;
9.   Else
10.   Begin
11.   If *(parent$_i$ID == parent$_j$ID)* then
12.   *Verf=false*; Break;
13.   End if;
14.   End if;
15. End While;
16. If (*Verf == false*) then State$_i$ = *passif (dominated)*
17. Else
18. Begin
19.   State$_i$ = *active ; (dominator)*
20.   Send msg *(ID$_i$, parent$_i$ ID)* ;
21. End if ;
END.

Figure 2 will illustrate the state diagram of the *SPMI* algorithm

Case1: *if the parent ID of node is different from the parent ID in any received message or the node never receives any message.*

Case2: *if the parent ID in the received message is the same of the node's parent ID.*

Fig. 2. The state diagram of the *SPMI* algorithm

5   Simulation

We simulate our solution by using Java language to evaluate *SPMI* Algorithm and compare its performance to other Algorithms.

A.   Simulation Parameters

Experimental results were obtained from randomly generated networks in which nodes are deployed over a square sensing field. The initial graph, the one formed right after the deployment, is connected. Simulations were carried over densities varying from 10 to 100 nodes. The results presented hereafter are the average of 100 iterations for each simulated scenario. The performance metrics include: 1- number of active nodes; 2- number of messages used in the CDS building process; 3- amount of energy used in the process; and 4- coverage ratio. Table 1 lists all the parameters used in simulation.

Table 1. Simulation parameters

Parameter	Value	Parameter	Value
Range	200mx200m	SR	50 m
Nodes	10,20,40,60,80,100	$RSSI_c$	80
CR	63m	T_{cons}	100 ms

B.   Performance Evaluation

In this subsection, we compare the performances of *SPMI* with other solutions: *A3* algorithm [10]; *EECDS* [9]; *CDS-Rule-K* algorithm [8]; *TC1* algorithm [11] and the *IPCDS* algorithm [12].

1- CDS Size :

Figure 3 shows that when the network density increases, the numbers of nodes generated by the six kinds of algorithm are increased. It is clear that *SPMI* generated less *CDS* size compared to *EECDS* and *CDS-Rule-k*; and it is nearly similar to *IPCDS*. But it is more than *TC1* and *A3*. This difference of active nodes size is exploited by *SPMI* for assuring more connectivity and coverage in *WSN*, such that only 6 to 17 nodes are active for different sensors populations.

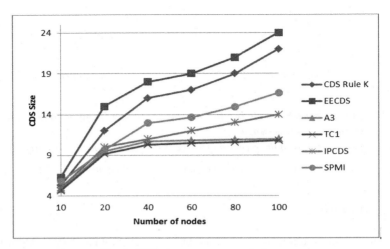

Fig. 3. CDS size versus network size

2- *Message Overhead:*

Figure 4 shows the message overhead of the six kinds of algorithm with respect to network size. The message overhead was evaluated based on the number of messages sent by nodes during the *CDS* construction. *SPMI* requires significantly lower message overhead compared to all five algorithms when the network density increases.

The efficiency of *SPMI* algorithm in terms of the number of message sent is due to it requires a single phase and one message at most for each node. Contrary to *EECDS*, CDS- *Rule-k* and *IPCDS* which require two phases and high amount of exchanges of messages, the *A3* and *TC1* need a single phase but the number of message is high than *SPMI*, they require three messages and one message respectively for each node.

3- *Energy Consumption:*

In order to evaluate the energy efficiency, we used a discrete energy model. Every node has an initial energy equal to 100 units. An active node consumes 1 unit of energy during 1 unit of time and 0 if it is passive. The energy required to transmit a message is 1 unit and the one spent for its reception is 0.2; the consumption in listening state is the same one as at the reception of a message. Notice that these energy consumptions are in correspondence with the reality. Indeed, for a Mica2 sensor [14], the energy spent in listening state is equal to that required for the reception of a message and energy used to transmit a message is equal to five times the energy of its reception [13, 15].

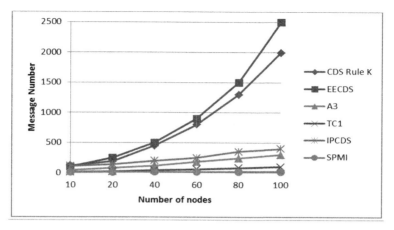

Fig. 4. Message overhead versus network size

Figure 5 represents the total energy consumption by the all six algorithms while varying the deployed nodes number.it is clear that *EECDS* and *CDS-Rule-k* algorithms consume a high significant amount of energy and their energy increases linearly with the number of neighbors. The other algorithms consume less amount of energy; they are similar and their energies are nearly constant with the size of network; but the *SPMI* consumes the lowest energy for constructing the *CDS*. This can be explained by the low number of messages exchanged between nodes. This shows that our algorithm is scalable and can be used for a large network deployment.

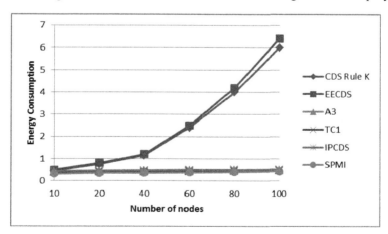

Fig. 5. Total energy consumption versus network size

4- Coverage Ratio:

The coverage ratio is evaluated by dividing the deployment area to cells. A cell is considered covered if its center is covered.

Figure 6 represents the average coverage ratio which is defined as the percentage of interest area covered by active nodes of the four algorithms.

We can say that although the two algorithms (*EECDS* and *CDS-Rule-k*) produce an almost similar coverage with the selected active nodes. The *A3* algorithm covers the same or more area compared to *EECDS* and *CDS-Rule-k*.

SPMI is still better; it covers more area than other algorithms. Such as it provides a better coverage ratio with 86.29% for the lowest density, this ratio increases gradually until it exceeds 99.66% for the highest density. For 100 deployed nodes, it is shown in Figure.5 that *SPMI* provides an improvement of coverage ratio equal to 3.96%, 2% and 1.96% compared to *CDS-Rule-k*, *EECDS* and *A3* respectively. This is due to select far nodes from the parent node according to formula (2).

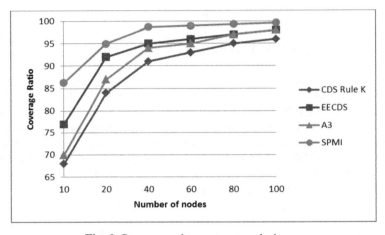

Fig. 6. Coverage ratio versus network size

6   Conclusion

In this paper, we have proposed a distributed algorithm called *SPMI* that can construct a *CDS* in a single phase to maintain the coverage and connectivity in Wireless Sensor Networks. The *SPMI* limits the number of exchanged messages among nodes and keeps the number of active nodes low. Simulation has been done to validate the effectiveness of the suggested algorithm. The results show that, *SPMI* outperforms the other algorithms [8-12] in terms of coverage ratio which is the most important metric. It also competes perfectly in terms of selected active nodes while reducing the communication overhead significantly, what decreases the energy consumption.

Our future work will focus the coverage and connectivity problem in case of mobile nodes and with the presence of obstacles.

References

1. Akyildiz, I.F., Su, W., Sankarasubramaniam, Y., Cayirci, E.: Wireless sensor networks: a survey. Computer Networks Journal 38(4), 393–422 (2002)
2. Huang, C.F., Tseng, Y.C.: A survey of solutions to the coverage problems in wireless sensor networks. Journal of Internet Technology 6(1), 1–8 (2005)
3. Cardei, M., Wu, J.: Energy-efficient coverage problems in wireless ad hoc sensor networks. Computer Communications Journal 29(4), 413–420 (2006)
4. Meguerdichian, S., Koushanfar, F., Potkonjak, M., Srivastava, M.B.: Coverage problems in wireless ad-hoc sensor networks. In: 20th Annual Joint Conference of the IEEE Computer and Communications Societies, vol. 3, pp. 1380–1387 (2001)
5. Rajavavivarme, V., Yang, Y., Yang, T.: An overview of wireless sensor network and applications. In: Proceedings of the 35th Southeastern Symposium on System Theory, pp. 432–436 (March 2003)
6. Khelil, A., Beghdad, R.: Coverage and Connectivity Protocol for Wireless Sensor Networks. In: Proceedings of The 24th International Conference of Microelectronics ICM 2012, Algeria, December 17-20 (2012)
7. Pazand, B., Datta, A.: Minimum dominating sets for solving the coverage problem in wireless sensor networks. In: Youn, H.Y., Kim, M., Morikawa, H. (eds.) UCS 2006. LNCS, vol. 4239, pp. 454–466. Springer, Heidelberg (2006)
8. Wu, J., Cardei, M., Dai, F., Yang, S.: Extended dominating set and its applications in ad hoc networks using cooperative communication. IEEE Trans.on Parallel and Distributed Systems 17(8), 851–864 (2006)
9. Yuanyuan, Z., Jia, X., Yanxiang, H.: Energy efficient distributed connected dominating sets construction in wireless sensor networks. In: Proceedings of the ACM International Conference on Communications and Mobile Computing, pp. 797–802 (2006)
10. Wightman, P.M., Labrador, M.A.: A3: A Topology Construction Algorithm for Wireless Sensor Network. In: Proc. IEEE Globecom (2008)
11. Karthikeyan, A., et al.: Topology Control Algorithm for Better Sensing Coverage with Connectivity in WSN. Journal of Theoretical and Applied Information Technology JATIT (June 2013)
12. Shi, T., Shi, X., Fang, X.: A Virtual Backbone Construction Algorithm Based on Connected Dominating Set in Wireless Sensor Networks. In: Proceedings of the 2014 International Conference on Computer, Communications and Information Technology (CCIT) (2014)
13. Ye, F., Zhang, H., Lu, S., Zhang, L., Hou, J.: A randomized energy-conservation protocol for resilient sensor networks. Wireless Networks 12(5), 637–652 (2006)
14. MICA2 Mote Datasheet. Available from Crossbow Technology Inc. (2009), http://www.xbow.com/
15. Anastasi, G., Falchi, A., Passarella, A., Conti, M., Gregori, E.: Performance measurements of motes sensor networks. In: Proceedings of the 7th ACM International Symposium on Modeling, Analysis and Simulation of Wireless and Mobile Systems, pp. 174–181 (2004)
16. Pu, C.-C., Chung, W.-Y.: Mitigation of Multipath Fading Effects to Improve Indoor RSSI Performance. IEEE Sensors Journal 8(11), 1884–1886 (2008)
17. Hood, B., Barooah, P.: Estimating DoA From Radio-Frequency RSSI Measurements Using an Actuated Reflector. IEEE Sensors Journal 11(2), 413–417 (2011)

Optimizing Deployment Cost in Camera-Based Wireless Sensor Networks

Mehdi Rouan Serik[✉] and Mejdi Kaddour

LITIO Laboratory, University of Oran 1, BP 1524, El-M'Naouer, 31000 Oran, Algeria
{rouan.mehdi,kaddour.mejdi}@univ-oran.dz

Abstract. We discuss in this paper a deployment optimization problem in camera-based wireless sensor networks. In particular, we propose a mathematical model to solve the problem of minimizing the number of cameras required to cover a set of targets with a given level of quality. Since solving this kind of problems with exact methods is computationally expensive, we rather rely on an adapted version of *Binary Particle Swarm Optimization* (BPSO). Our preliminary results are motivating since we obtain near-optimal solutions in few iterations of the algorithm. We discuss also the relevance of hybrid meta-heuristics and parallel algorithms in this context.

Keywords: Camera-based wireless sensor networks · Minimum cost deployment · Coverage quality · Binary particle swarm optimization

1 Introduction

Wireless Sensor Networks (WSN) are particular ad-hoc networks defined as a set of cooperating nodes disseminated in a given geographic area in order to collect its data about some phenomenon autonomously. Specifically, Camera-based wireless sensor networks (WSN) form an emerging research area with many promising applications. Potential applications include remote video surveillance, monitoring and assisting elderly and health patients, and habitat monitoring.

We study in this paper the cost deployment of camera-based WSNs, where the main concern is to determine the optimal minimum number of cameras, along with their positions and their orientations to track a given set of targets with a prescribed level of quality. This problem can be solved with various exact mathematical programming tools such as Branch and Bound. However, as the problem size increases, solving such problems using these exact methods becomes computationally intractable. In fact, Ai and Abouzeid [1] have demonstrated that this problem is NP-hard. A traditional way to deal with such difficult problems is to rely upon meta-heuristic methods. In particular, we adapt the generic procedure of *Particle Swarm Optimization* (PSO) to solve this deployment problem. We also introduce a quality coverage parameter which serves to ensure that each target in the solution is covered with a sufficient level of quality. Indeed, as the targeting objects move away from the sensing camera, the level of details falls off. Our preliminary results show that the proposed method behaves well both in computational performances and solution quality.

© IFIP International Federation for Information Processing 2015
A. Amine et al. (Eds.): CIIA 2015, IFIP AICT 456, pp. 454–464, 2015.
DOI: 10.1007/978-3-319-19578-0_37

The rest of paper is organized as follows. Section 2 reviews the relevant literature on this topic. Section 3 formulates the problem and describes the proposed
coverage model. The detailed mathematical model is given in Section 4, while
the proposed PSO-based algorithm is described in Section 5. Section 6 assesses
and discusses the obtained results. Finally, The last section concludes the paper
and suggests some future research directions.

2   Related Works

Existing literature in the field distinguishes typically two important kinds of
deployment problems: target coverage and area coverage. We focus here on the
first one. One version of the problem consists on covering a maximum number
of targets with a minimum number of sensors. In [1], authors proposed an exact
integer linear program (ILP) and a Centralized Greedy Algorithm (CGA) for
the maximum coverage with minimum sensors (MCMS) problem. Then, they
provided a Distributed Greedy Algorithm (DGA) solution. They showed that
DGA does better than the two other methods (ILP and CGA) by incorporating a
measure of the sensors' residual energy into DGA. Aziz *et. al.* [2] proposed a new
algorithm to optimize sensor coverage using PSO and Voronoi diagrams. PSO is
used to find the optimal deployment of sensors providing the best coverage, while
Voronoi diagram is used to evaluate the fitness of the solution. They showed that
the proposed algorithm achieves a good coverage with a better time efficiency
than existing approaches.

Authors in [12] improved the field of view (FOV) coverage of a camera network. They considered randomly scattered cameras in a wide area, where each
camera may adjust only its orientation and not its localisation. They also implemented a PSO algorithm and efficiently found an optimal orientation for each
camera. They considered also region of interest in the search space (ROI) and
occlusions. In [6], authors considered the area coverage problem in a 2D/3D-grid
space. The solution process was based on Particle Swarm Optimization Inspired
Probability (PSO-IP). For comparison purposes, they also implemented alternative methods based on Tabu Search, genetic algorithms and simulated annealing.
Results showed that the proposed PSO-IP overcomes the three other methods
especially with large instances. Unlike these two works, we deal with targets
coverage not area coverage. We give also a mathematical model to the coverage
problem. Note that our solution approach is partly inspired by this last work.
But as far as we know, no existing work has formulated a problem similar to
ours, in particular by considering a continuous measure of sensing quality.

3   Problem Definition

We assume that a set of N camera sensors $\{S_i : i = 1, \ldots, n\}$ are deployed on
the euclidean space A. For each camera S_i, we are given its Cartesian coordinates
(X_{S_i}, Y_{S_i}) and its orientation φ in A. The field of vision of each camera is modeled

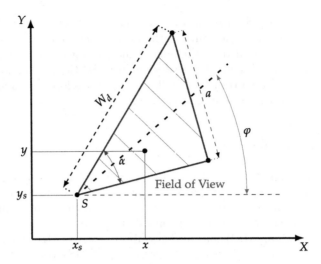

Fig. 1. Camera's field of view

as in [8] by isosceles triangle as depicted in Fig. 1, where α represents the aperture of the camera and W_d its working distance.

A target located on the coordinates (x, y) is assumed to be covered by a given camera with coordinates (x_s, y_s) if the three following constraints are satisfied:

$$cos(\varphi) \cdot (x - x_s) + sin(\varphi) \cdot (y - y_s) \leq W_d \tag{1a}$$

$$-sin(\varphi) \cdot (x - x_s) + cos(\varphi) \cdot (y - y_s) \leq$$
$$\frac{a}{2W_d} \cdot (cos(\varphi) \cdot (x - x_s) + sin(\varphi) \cdot (y - y_s)) \tag{1b}$$

$$-sin(\varphi) \cdot (x - x_s) + cos(\varphi) \cdot (y - y_s) \geq$$
$$-\frac{a}{2W_d} \cdot (cos(\varphi) \cdot (x - x_s) + sin(\varphi) \cdot (y - y_s)) \tag{1c}$$

3.1   Coverage Model

Coverage models determine first if a given target can be covered or not by some sensor, but can also measure a corresponding quality parameter [11]. This is accomplished by calculating the geometric relation between sensors and targets. In most cases, it consists in calculating the euclidean distance and angles, but some research works assume also that the sensing quality of a sensor is reduced with the increase of the distance away from the sensor [5], [10]. In our case, we make a similar assumption by adopting a directional disk model where the coverage parameter for a given sensor/target pair is represented by a non negative real number calculated as follows:

$$f(d(s,z)) = \frac{C}{d^\alpha(s,z)} \tag{2}$$

where $d(s,z)$ is the distance separating camera s from target z, α is the exponent attenuation and C is a constant. In particular, we assume that quality decreases quadratically as a function of the distance ($\alpha = 2$).

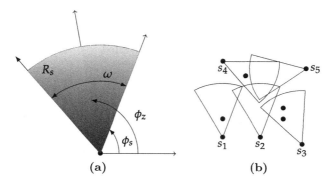

Fig. 2. Illustrations of : 2a Directional Model ; 2b Three active cameras covering 4 targets

4   Mathematical Model

The adopted model assumes a known number of targets, in a given space, where the objective is to cover these targets optimally. Table 1 define the formal notations used in our model.

Table 1. Problem's formal notations

Variables	Designation
n	number of possible camera locations
m	number of possible angles
t	number of targets
δ	quality parameter
d_{ij}	distance between camera i and target j
(x_i, y_i)	Cartesian coordinate of the camera i
(x_j^t, y_j^t)	Cartesian coordinates of the target j
φ_k	angle k

let b_{ij} and O_{ik} binary variables defined as follows:

$$b_{ij} = \begin{cases} 1 & \text{if camera at position } i \text{ covers target } j \\ 0 & \text{otherwise} \end{cases}$$

$$O_{ik} = \begin{cases} 1 & \text{if camera at position } i \text{ has active angle } k \\ 0 & \text{otherwise} \end{cases}$$

The objective of our optimization problem is defined as follows:

$$\min \sum_{i=1}^{n} \sum_{k=1}^{m} O_{ik} \tag{3}$$

This objective implies the minimization of the number of deployed cameras, provided that the following constraints are satisfied.

$$\sum_{k=1}^{m} O_{ik} \leq 1, \quad \forall i = 1, \dots, n. \tag{4}$$

The above constraint ensures that at most one angle is active per each camera. $\sum_{k=1}^{m} O_{ik} = 0$, corresponds to the situation where no camera is deployed at location i.

$$\sum_{i=1}^{n} b_{ij} \geq 1, \quad \forall j = 1, \dots, t. \tag{5}$$

This constraints ensures that each target is covered by at least one camera.

Now, the minimum coverage quality for each target is satisfied through the following constraint:

$$\sum_{i=1}^{n} b_{ij} \frac{C}{d_{ij}^{\alpha}} \geq \delta, \quad \forall j = 1, \dots, t. \tag{6}$$

where C is a constant and α is the attenuation exponent.

Given some locations of a camera i oriented with angle k, the following three constraints enforce, as described above in (1a),(1b) and (1c), that some target j is covered properly if $b_{ij} = 1$.

$$\sum_{k=1}^{m} O_{ik} \left[cos(\varphi_k) \cdot (x_j^t - x_i) + sin(\varphi_k) \cdot (y_j^t - y_i) \right] \leq d + L_1(1 - b_{ij}),$$

$$\forall i = 1, \dots, n, \quad \forall j = 1, \dots, t. \tag{7}$$

$$\sum_{k=1}^{m} O_{ik} \left[-\left(sin(\varphi_k) + \frac{a}{2d} cos(\varphi_k) \right) (x_j^t - x_i) + \left(cos(\varphi_k) - \frac{a}{2d} sin(\varphi_k) \right) (y_j^t - y_i) \right]$$

$$\leq L_2(1 - b_{ij}) \quad \forall i = 1, \dots, n, \quad \forall j = 1, \dots, t. \tag{8}$$

$$\sum_{k=1}^{m} O_{ik} \left[\left(sin(\varphi_k) - \frac{a}{2d} cos(\varphi_k) \right) (x_j^t - x_i) - \left(cos(\varphi_k) - \frac{a}{2d} sin(\varphi_k) \right) (y_j^t - y_i) \right]$$

$$\leq L_3(1 - b_{ij}) \quad \forall i = 1, \ldots, n, \quad \forall j = 1, \ldots, t. \tag{9}$$

where L_1, L_2, L_3 are large constants, which are introduced to make theses constraints meaningless when $b_{ij} = 1$.

The above objective with the introduced constraints define a mixed-integer problem which is hard to solve in general. In particular, it is not easy to move from one solution to another when applying some meta-heuristic algorithm for example. Hence, we relax this model by moving the coverage constraints (5)-(6) into the objective, as follows.

$$\min \left\{ \sum_{i=1}^{n} \sum_{j=1}^{m} O_{ij} - \sum_{i=1}^{n} \sum_{j=1}^{t} b_{ij} \left(1 + \frac{C}{d_{ij}^{\alpha}} \right) \right\} \tag{10}$$

Subject to (4),(7)-(9).

5 Particle Swarm Optimization

Particle swarm optimization (PSO) is a meta-heuristic method invented by *Russel Eberhart* (Electrical Engineer) and *James Kennedy* (socio-psychologist) in 1995. This algorithm, inspired by social behaviour, has been introduced as an optimization tool dealing with real numbers initially and with integers lately [7]. It is mostly inspired from the manner in which a flock of birds moves with various individuals leading the flock during the travel at different periods of time. The PSO algorithm consists of a group of individuals named particles. Each particle $p < $ `Swarm_size` is a potential solution to an optimization problem, having its own position in the space search. After each iteration, it moves in function of one of its components:

- Actual velocity V ;
- Best solution L_b ;
- Actual position X ;
- Best neighbourhood solution G_{best} ;

The movement of each particle obeys to the equations:

$$V_{k+1} = \omega.V_k + C_1 r_1 (P_b - X_k) + C_2 r_2 (P_g - X_k) \tag{11}$$

$$X_{k+1} = X_k + V_{k+1} \tag{12}$$

where $X = (x_{ik}), V = (v_{ik}), i = 1, 2, \ldots, n, k = 1, 2, \ldots m$, denote the distance/angle and the velocity vectors, respectively. ω is the inertia weight, r_1 and r_2 are two random numbers uniformly chosen in $[0, 1]$, and C_1, C_2 are constant values. Finally k is the iteration index.

A given solution for the deployment problem is a number of cameras with corresponding positions and active angles (see Fig. 3a). We adopt a binary representation of the position vector X. Besides, since PSOs require movements, we define two different types of moves:

1. Rotation: selecting a different camera for an active camera.
2. Displacement: moving one camera from position i to position i'.

These movements are guided by the velocity parameter. Thus, we redefine (11) as follows:

$$V = (v_{ik}, \forall k = 1, 2, \ldots, m) = \begin{cases} 1 & \text{if } alea > \frac{1}{1+(G_{best}-L_b)} \\ 0 & \text{otherwise} \end{cases} \tag{13}$$

Where **alea** is a random number from $[0, 1]$, then Eq. (12) become:

$$X_{k+1} = X_k \oplus V_{k+1} \tag{14}$$

A camera rotation is defined through the logical operator "exclusive OR", i.e., to invert a zero bit to one in the X vector, while a camera displacement is defined through a binary shift, and this will be a position swap. As a stopping criteria, we define a maximum number of iterations. Algorithm 1 gives an overview of our implemented PSO.

Algorithm 1. Proposed PSO algorithm

---

1. **for all** $(p < $ Swarm_size$)$ **do**
2.   Random_init(p);
3. $L_b(p) = $ Fitness(p);
4. **end for**
5. $G_{best} = \min\limits_{p} \{L_b(p)\}$;
6. **repeat**
7.   alea=rand();
8.   **for all** $(p < $ Swarm_size$)$ **do**
9.   Calculate $V(p)$ using (13);
10.   move(p);
11.   **if** Fitness(p) $< L_b(p)$ **then**
12. $L_b(p) = $ Fitness(p);
13.   **end if**
14.   **end for**
15. $G_{best} = \min\limits_{p} \{L_b(p)\}$;
16.   Update positions with (14);
17. **until** Stop criteria satisfied

For comparison purposes, we implemented a standard *Simulated Annealing Algorithm* (SA) [9]. The basic idea behind comes from the principles of statistical mechanics whereby the annealing process requires heating and then slowly cooling a substance to obtain a strong crystalline structure. At each iteration, a random neighbour is generated. Movements that improve the cost function are always accepted. Otherwise, the neighbour is selected with a given probability that depends on the current temperature and the amount of degradation ΔE of the objective function. This probability is calculated as follows:

$$P(\Delta E, T) = e^{\frac{-\Delta E}{T}}$$

where ΔE represents the fitness difference. This is algorithm is used in large-scale optimization problems in wireless sensors networks as in [6], [4].

6   Experiments and Results

We discuss in this section various experiments related to our approach. First, the most important parameter to be defined in order to implement a PSO algorithm is the solution coding or representation. Each solution is encoded in binary where the vector X represents camera positions and angles (Fig 3a) and (Fig 3b). The experiments were executed on a computer with Intel © Core ^{TM} i3-2350 M CPU @ 2.30 GHz CPU and 4.0 GB of RAM.

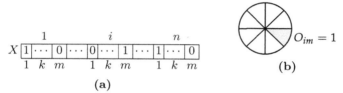

(a)

(b)

Fig. 3. PSO solution: 3a X Position vector; 3b Active angle

Table 2a gives parameters used to implement the method. `Swarm_size` and `Steps` represent the number of particles (potential solutions) involved in PSO and iteration's number, respectively. C_1 and C_2 represent learning factors of the algorithm, most often set to 2.0 [3]. W_d represents the working distance of a camera (extrinsic parameter), X_{max} and Y_{max} are the grid dimensions. Q_{max} and Q_{min} are, respectively, the maximum and the minimum quality coverage of a camera. Here we require a certain level of quality in target covering. C is a constant which specifies how the quality coverage decreases when moving away from the sensor.

In Fig 4, we give an initial solution then a final one found by PSO algorithm. The figures show that we can easily find a good solution consisting of two cameras covering nine targets. As shown in Tab 2b, finding such a solution does not require more than a hundred of iterations in a very brief time for a small number of targets (less than a half of a second). We observe also the high success rate over all executions.

As shown in (Fig 4d) we clearly obtanin better average fitness by the proposed PSO than the one obtained by the SA for fifty executions of the two methods.

Table 2. PSO and SA parameters and executions

(a)

Parameters	Values
Swarm_size	30
Steps	300
C_1, C_2	1.4
n	10
m	8
t	10
L_1, L_2, L_3	Max_DBL
C	10.0
Q_{max}	0.4
Q_{min}	0.05
W_d	10
X_{max}, Y_{max}	100
T	1000.0

(b)

Exec	Fit.	n_s	n_t	Steps	time (s)
1	−7.018	2	9	200	0.706
2	−7.050	3	10	167	0.566
3	−8.057	2	10	85	0.109
4	−7.033	2	9	52	0.041
5	−7.048	3	10	1	0.003
6	−7.036	2	9	269	0.78
7	−7.032	2	9	61	0.052
8	−7.035	2	9	170	0.12
9	−7.058	3	10	131	0.509
10	−7.058	3	10	61	0.05

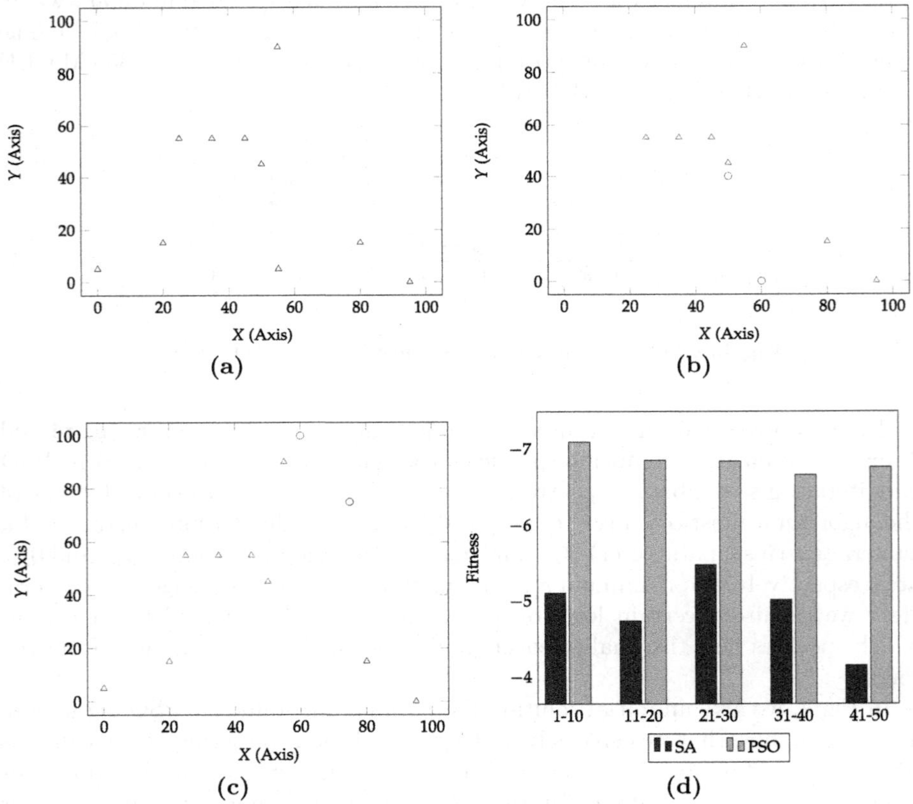

(a)

(b)

(c)

(d)

Fig. 4. Illustrations of: 4a Initial target positions; 4b Random initial solution; 4c Final solution found by PSO; 4d PSO vs SA

Finally, note that compared to *Y. Morsly et. al.* approach in [6] and *Yi-Chun Xu et al.* in [12], we consider a coverage quality parameter and deal with targets instead of area coverage. Here we must determine camera's positions and orientation, while coverage quality can be specified by the user. Even if we assume mobile targets, the proposed method can easily re-adapt the solution to the new scenario; this is guaranteed by the camera's movement (displacement and rotation).

7   Conclusion

We have proposed a mathematical mixed-integer model for the deployment of camera-based wireless sensor networks. Solving such models with exact is only feasible with small problem instances, beyond which, the use of approximative method such as meta-heuristics is required. In literature, only a few papers treat the target-based coverage model along with a coverage quality parameter. Hence, we have introduced an additional problem parameter to account for coverage quality. We have adapted a PSO algorithm to minimize the number of active cameras used to cover targets with certain quality. The proposed method gives easily a significant improvement of the initial random solution in few steps. Compared to SA, our PSO returns better solutions. We envisage later to calculate exact solutions by a ILP solver and then compare the results with ours. Moreover, we are working to introduce connectivity and energy-efficiency criteria to our problem. Finally, we are considering to use parallel versions of PSO and evaluate their performance over multiple platforms.

References

1. Ai, J., Abouzeid, A.A.: Coverage by directional sensors in randomly deployed wireless sensor networks. Journal of Combinatorial Optimization 11(1), 21–41 (2006)
2. Aziz, N.A.B.A., Mohemmed, A.W., Alias, M.Y.: A wireless sensor network coverage optimization algorithm based on particle swarm optimization and voronoi diagram. In: International Conference on Networking, Sensing and Control, ICNSC 2009, pp. 602–607. IEEE (2009)
3. Gorse, D.: Binary particle swarm optimisation with improved scaling behaviour. In: European Symposium on Artificial Neural Networks, Computational Intelligence and Machine Learning (2013)
4. Kannan, A.A., Mao, G., Vucetic, B.: Simulated annealing based wireless sensor network localization with flip ambiguity mitigation. In: IEEE 63rd Vehicular Technology Conference, VTC 2006-Spring, vol. 2, pp. 1022–1026. IEEE (2006)
5. Megerian, S., Koushanfar, F., Qu, G., Veltri, G., Potkonjak, M.: Exposure in wireless sensor networks: theory and practical solutions. Wireless Networks 8(5), 443–454 (2002)
6. Morsly, Y., Aouf, N., Djouadi, M.S., Richardson, M.: Particle swarm optimization inspired probability algorithm for optimal camera network placement. IEEE Sensors Journal 12(5), 1402–1412 (2012)
7. Poli, R., Kennedy, J., Blackwell, T.: Particle swarm optimization. Swarm Intelligence 1(1), 33–57 (2007)

8. Trucco, E., Umasuthan, M., Wallace, A.M., Roberto, V.: Model-based planning of optimal sensor placements for inspection. IEEE Transactions on Robotics and Automation 13(2), 182–194 (1997)
9. Van Laarhoven, P.J., Aarts, E.H.: Simulated annealing. Springer (1987)
10. Veltri, G., Huang, Q., Qu, G., Potkonjak, M.: Minimal and maximal exposure path algorithms for wireless embedded sensor networks. In: Proceedings of the 1st International Conference on Embedded Networked Sensor Systems, pp. 40–50. ACM (2003)
11. Wang, B.: Coverage problems in sensor networks: A survey. ACM Computing Surveys (CSUR) 43(4), 32 (2011)
12. Xu, Y.C., Lei, B., Hendriks, E.A.: Camera network coverage improving by particle swarm optimization. Journal on Image and Video Processing 3 (2011)

A version of LEACH Adapted to the Lognormal Shadowing Model

Chifaa Tabet Hellel[1], Mohamed Lehsaini [1(✉)], and Hervé Guyennet [2]

[1] STIC Laboratory, University of Tlemcen, Tlemcen, Algeria
[2] FEMTO-ST/DISC UFR ST, University of Franche-Comte, Besançon, France
tabetchifaa@gmail.com, m_lehsaini@mail.univ-tlemcen.dz,
herve.guyennet@femto-st.fr

Abstract. The most protocols designed for wireless sensor networks (WSNs) have been developed for an ideal environment represented by unit disc graph model (UDG) in which the data is considered as successfully received if the communicating nodes are within the transmission range of each other. However, these protocols do not take into account the fluctuations of radio signal that can happen in realistic environment. This paper aims to adapt LEACH protocol for realistic environment since LEACH is considered as the best cluster-based routing protocol in terms of energy consumption for WSNs. We have carried out an evaluation of LEACH based on two models; lognormal shadowing model (LNS) in which the probability of reception without error is calculated according to the Euclidian distance separating the communicating nodes and probabilistic model in which the probability of reception is generated randomly. In both models, if the probability of successful reception is lower than a predefined threshold, a multi-hop communication is incorporated for forwarding data between cluster-heads (CHs) towards the base station instead of direct communication as in original version of LEACH. The main aims of this contribution are minimizing energy consumption and guaranteeing reliable data delivery to the base station. The simulation results show that our proposed algorithm outperforms the original LEACH for both models in terms of energy consumption and ratio of successful received packets.

Keywords: LEACH · Lognormal shadowing model · Multi-hop scheme · Probabilistic model · Unit Disc Graph model · WSNs

1 Introduction

WSNs are composed of hundreds and thousands of small devices called "sensor nodes" distributed over a monitoring area for sensing data and sending it to a remote base station directly or via a multi-hop communication scheme depending on the application designed [1]. This novel technology has allowed the appearance of many applications such as; military, security, medical, environment monitoring, etc, due to the low cost of sensor nodes. Moreover, with this technology our way of life has been revolutionized since it allowed us to interact with the surrounded environment.

© IFIP International Federation for Information Processing 2015
A. Amine et al. (Eds.): CIIA 2015, IFIP AICT 456, pp. 465–475, 2015.
DOI: 10.1007/978-3-319-19578-0_38

Routing process is a fundamental operation in wireless sensor networks. It consists in establishing path to transmit a message from a source node to a remote base station according to the main routing schemes: hierarchical, location-based, data-centric and QoS-aware [2]. However, cluster-based routing in wireless sensor network is considered as the perfect solutions for minimizing energy consumption [3,4]. In this scheme, the network is divided into clusters wherein each cluster contains a number of members which sense data from its environment and send it to its corresponding cluster-head (CH). The latter is responsible for gathering data received from its members. If the distance between the source node and the destination node will increase, the energy consumption also increases, thereby a cluster-based routing scheme is recommended. Among the protocols proposed, LEACH (Low Energy Adaptive Clustering Hierarchy) [5] is considered as the best cluster-based protocol for saving energy. Nevertheless, the performance of these protocols may degrade in non-ideal environments.

In this paper, we used the lognormal shadowing model [6] and the probabilistic model to simulate a non-ideal environment, and we evaluated the performance of LEACH with these both models. Then, we proposed an improved version of LEACH to overcome the limitations of the original version. The proposed version involves a CH-to-CH routing scheme to guarantee reliable delivery. This routing scheme is used if the probability of reception of packets without error between cluster-heads and the base station is lower than a predefined threshold. Moreover, this scheme also permits to minimize energy consumption.

The rest of paper is organized as follow; in section 2, we give an overview on LEACH protocol and discuss some works that improve LEACH related to our requirements. Section 3 presents our improved version of LEACH to be adapted in realistic environment, and in section 4, we illustrate performance of LEACH and the proposed contribution in non-ideal environment. Finally, in section 5, we conclude our paper.

2   Related Work

Since LEACH protocol is considered among the best cluster-based routing protocols in terms of energy efficiency, a lot of researches have been enhancing this protocol to reduce its limitations. In the following, we present briefly LEACH protocol and some variants of it.

LEACH [5] is a cluster-based routing protocol that aims to minimize energy consumption and thereby increasing network lifetime. In LEACH, the network is divided into clusters and each cluster is headed by a cluster-head which is elected by itself by generating a random number between 0 and 1. If the number generated is lower than a predefined threshold, the concerned node becomes a CH for the current round. The threshold is computed by each sensor node according to the equation (1).

$$T(i) = \begin{cases} \frac{p}{1-p*\left(r \bmod \frac{1}{p}\right)} & if \ i \in G \\ 0 & otherwise \end{cases} \tag{1}$$

where p is the percentage of cluster-heads, r is the current round, G is the set of nodes that have not been selected as cluster-heads in the last $(1/p)$ rounds.

LEACH is performed in two phases: setup phase and steady phase. In setup phase, each CH broadcasts an advertisement message to construct its cluster, and each non-CH that receives this message joins the adequate cluster based on the RSSI (Received Signal Strength Indication) of the message received. Once the clusters are formed, a TDMA (Time Division Multiple Access) schedules are assigned to member nodes in each cluster. In steady phase, each member transmits its sensed data to its corresponding CH in its scheduled time-slot, and then the CH aggregates all data received from its members and sends it to the remote base station directly. To avoid interference between cluster-heads, each CH chooses a CDMA (Coding Division Multiple Access) code that is different from other clusters to communicate with the base station.

In [7], the authors have proposed a multihop routing scheme with lower energy adaptive clustering hierarchy called MR-LEACH. In this scheme, the CHs are responsible to aggregate data sensed by their members and act as relay nodes for remote CHs from the base station. MR-LEACH increases network lifetime since it uses a multihop routing scheme. This protocol is performed in three phases: cluster formation at lowest level, cluster discovery at different levels and scheduling. At the beginning of each round, cluster formation phase is lunched to construct a table in which each node maintains the information about its neighbors (node identifier, residual energy and node status) by using a 'Hello' message. Then, CHs broadcast a HEAD-MSG message in its vicinity and each non-CH chooses its respective CH among those in its neighborhood based on the strength of RSSI. In cluster discovery, the base station broadcasts its identifier (ID). Each CH that receives this broadcasted message records the identifier of the base station and replies by a beacon signal with its ID. CHs that are closest to the base station are in level one i.e. they could reach the base station by single hop. Then, BS broadcasts again a control message, the CHs that are at level two reply to this message forwarded by CHs of level one and the BS would record cluster-head's ID and its level. Similarly, this process is repeated until no new CH is discovered. After that, the BS will form a cluster of CHs. In scheduling phase; after cluster formation, a TDMA scheduling is used for communication between CHs at different levels.

In [8], the authors proposed MH-LEACH which uses a new scheme for multihop communication to minimize energy consumption. MH-LEACH is carried out in two phases to establish paths towards the base station. In the first phase, the cluster-heads are selected as in the original version of LEACH protocol, and then each CH broadcasts an announcement message within its vicinity. Each non-CH that receives this message chooses the closest one based on the RSSI of the message received. Moreover, the base station performs the same process. In the second phase; each CH sends its initial route to reach the base station and the latter send back the route to the CH to confirm that there is a route between the considered CH and the base station. Therefore, a routing table is created by each CH that contains a list of available routes to the base station and the shortest one is used.

In [9], the authors proposed an improved version of LEACH in which a multihop scheme is used and the election of the cluster-heads is done according to its residual energy. In this protocol, a multihop routing scheme for intra-cluster communication and a chain structure routing scheme for inter-cluster communication. The proposed protocol is performed in three phases: cluster formation, data delivery and update of clusters. At the beginning of the first phase, each node generates a random number between 0 and 1 and compares it with a predefined threshold to which the energy factor is added as illustrated by the equation (2).

$$T(n) = \begin{cases} \frac{p}{1-p*\left(r \bmod \frac{1}{p}\right)} \cdot \frac{E_n}{E_{Average}} & if \ n \in G \\ 0 & otherwise \end{cases} \quad (2)$$

where E_n is the residual energy and $E_{Average}$ is the average residual energy of all nodes.

Each CH sets H to 0, where H is the number of hops from CH, and broadcasts a message containing (H=0, ID) in its vicinity. Each non-CH that receives this message joins the cluster to which it belongs the transmitter CH and sets its own CH to the CH of the message received and H to H+1, and PID with the ID of its parent. Then, this node also broadcasts a message containing (H_j,ID). If a node receives more than one message it compares its own H with H of the sending nodes and it updates its H with the lowest one among those received. For intra-cluster communication, each node sends its packet to its parent and this latter sends it to its parent until reach the CH, and in inter-cluster communication, CH transmits data in chain structure. The concerned CH chooses the closest CH from it as the next hop and this process is repeated until reach the base station. In update of clusters, at the end of a round the remaining energy of CH may not be sufficient for the next round so the CH must be replaced by the node with the greatest residual energy.

In [10], an enhanced version of LEACH is proposed whose aims are saving energy by using a CH-to-CH multihop scheme and creating a backup path between clusterheads to achieve fault-tolerance in the presence of failures. At the beginning, the base station broadcasts a HELLO message and each CH that receives this message calculates the RSSI. If RSSI is higher than a predefined threshold, this CH is closest to the base station and if not the CH is away from it and therefore it needs a relay node to reach the base station. The relay node is one of the CHs that are closest to the base station and it is selected based on the RSSI of a message exchanged between CHs and a variable called C_{red} which is a random number comprised between 0 and 1. If each of these parameters is higher than a threshold, this CH is considered as perfect relay node. However, the failure of one CH on the multihop path can affect the entire path and then the information cannot reach the base station, in this case a backup path is incorporated to this multihop path to ensure fault-tolerance and reliable delivery.

3   Contribution

Before presenting our contribution, we give a brief description of the lognormal model and probabilistic model. Then, we evaluate the performance of LEACH protocol with the both models to point out its weaknesses over an ideal environment.

3.1   Lognormal Shadowing Model

The lognormal shadowing model [6] is considered as a realistic model. It takes into account the fluctuations of radio signal caused by several factors such as noise, the presence of obstacles, weather conditions, etc... to evaluate the link quality between communicating nodes. The link quality is used to determine the probability of successful reception between communicating nodes in order to know if the message is received or it is corrupted by the destination node. Since this probability implied several factors, it may be difficult to obtain an accurate evaluation for all these factors which are themselves prone to errors. Therefore, we assume that signal strength gradually decreases according to the distance; thereby the probability of reception without errors can be computed according to the distance separating two nodes. We used the fluctuation of the signal model described in [11] as presented by the equation (3).

$$F(x) = \begin{cases} 1 - \dfrac{\left(\frac{x}{R_c}\right)^{2\alpha}}{2} & if \ 0 < x \leq R_c \\ \dfrac{\left(\frac{2R_c - x}{R_c}\right)^{2\alpha}}{2} & if \ R_c < x \leq 2R_c \\ 0 & otherwise \end{cases} \tag{3}$$

where α is the attenuation factor that depends on the environment and x is the distance separating the two communicating nodes. R_c is the transmission range and if the distance between two nodes is equal to R_c, the probability of successful reception is 0.5.

3.2   Probabilistic Model

In this model, the probability of reception without errors is generated randomly between each two communicating nodes. This model is used to illustrate the link quality. Moreover, the probability of successful reception is independent of the distance separating the communicating nodes but it depends on the factors which exist in the environment such as the presence or the absence of obstacles. Fig. 1 shows that node A can communicate with the node B but it cannot communicate with the node C although the distance that separates it with the node C is lower than that of the node B.

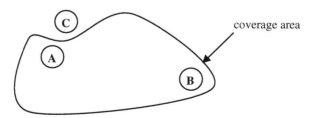

Fig. 1. Communication in probabilistic model

3.3   Proposed Scheme

In WSNs, LEACH is considered one of the best protocols in terms of energy efficiency. Several proposed protocols compare its effectiveness to LEACH and a lot of improved versions of LEACH have been proposed to reduce its limitations but they cannot guarantee its functionalities in a realistic environment. Our proposed algorithm aims to minimize energy consumption and ensures reliable delivery to the base station in a realistic environment based on lognormal shadowing model and probabilistic model.

We have proposed a multihop scheme instead of direct communication scheme between clusterheads and the base station to overcome the limitations of LEACH, such as when a CH aggregates data received from its members it computes the probability of reception without error of its packet to the base station. If this probability is higher than a predefined threshold, the packet is received correctly via direct communication by the base station and if not it means that the communication link is unreliable and in this case a multihop communication scheme will be incorporated to ensure the successful reception of packets by the base station. The proposed routing schemes are performed according to the following algorithms:

Algorithm 1: Routing scheme based on LNS model
- CH_s: Set of clusterheads
- BS: Base station whose coordinates (x_b, y_b)
- d: Euclidean distance between CH(x,y) and BS
- CH_D: Set of clusterheads that can send data directly to the BS
- CH_R: Set of clusterheads that use relay nodes to reach the BS

Begin
$CH_D = \varnothing$
$CH_R = \varnothing$
For (CH $\in CH_s$) **do**
- CH(x,y) calculates the Euclidean distance that separates it from the BS

$$d = \sqrt{(x - x_b)^2 + (y - y_b)^2}$$

- CH computes the probability of reception without error

$$Pr(d) = 1 - \frac{\left(\frac{d}{R_c}\right)^{2\alpha}}{2}$$

    if (Pr(d) > Threshold) **then**

        $CH_D = CH_D \cup \{CH\}$

    else

$$CH_R = CH_R \cup \{CH\}$$

    end if

end For

- Let CH a clusterhead

if (CH ∈ CH$_D$) **then**

   - CH sends directly aggregated data to BS

else

   - CH selects a (CH$_r$ ∈ CH$_D$) as relay node with minimum distance to BS

   Min = ∞

   For (CH$_i$ ∈ CH$_D$) **do**

   - Computes the distance between CH(x,y) and CH$_i$(x$_i$,y$_i$)

$$dd = \sqrt{(x - x_i)^2 + (y - y_i)^2}$$

     if dd < Min **then**

       Min = dd

       CH$_r$ = CH$_i$

     end if

     end for

   - CHr is selected as relay node by CH

end if

End

Algorithm 2: Routing scheme based on probabilistic model

- CH$_s$: Set of clusterheads
- BS: Base station
- CH$_D$: Set of clusterheads that can send data directly to the BS
- CH$_R$: Set of clusterheads that use relay nodes to reach the BS

Begin

CH$_D$ = ∅

CH$_R$ = ∅

For (CH ∈ CH$_s$) **do**

  - CH generates a random number (rd_number) comprise between 0 and 1

  if (rd_number ≥ 0.5) **then**

$$CH_D = CH_D \cup \{CH\}$$

else

$$CH_R = CH_R \cup \{CH\}$$

end if

end For

- Let CH a clusterhead

if (CH ∈ CH$_D$) **then**

-   CH sends directly aggregated data to BS

else

-   CH selects a (CH$_r$ ∈ CH$_D$) as relay node such as CH and CH$_r$ have a maximum probability.

    pr = 0

    For (CH$_i$ ∈ CH$_D$) **do**

    - CH generates a random number (rd_number) between CH and CH$_i$

        if (rd_number > pr) **then**

            pr = rd_number

            CH$_r$ = CH$_i$

        end if
    end for

-   CH$_r$ is selected as relay node by CH

end if

End

4   Simulation Results

Several simulations have been carried out to illustrate the performance of our contribution using TOSSIM simulator [12], and compared them with the original version of LEACH in terms of energy consumption and the ratio of successful received packets at the base station. For that, we used a network that contains respectively 20, 40, 60, 80 and 100 stationary nodes, which are randomly deployed on a 100m x 100m square area and the initial energy of each node is equal to 2 joules. The simulations were performed in 600 seconds, and we used a threshold p= 0.7 for probability of reception without error in LNS model. We used this threshold to avoid on the one hand the ideal model whose threshold is 0.5 and the other to avoid a highly disturbed environment. Moreover, for probabilistic model, we used a threshold of p=0.5 i.e. a clusterhead generates a random number comprise between 0 and 1 and if this number is higher than 0.5 we assume that this clusterhead can communicate directly with the base station. Table I summarize simulation parameters.

Table 1. Simulation Parameters

Parameter	Value
Deployment Area	100m x 100m
Simulation Time	600 sec
Number of nodes	20, 40, 60, 80, 100
Packet size	29 bytes
Initial node energy	2 Joules
Threshold for LNS model	p = 0.7
Threshold for probabilistic model	p = 0.5

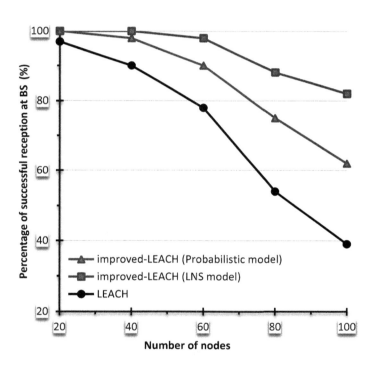

Fig. 2. Evaluation of ratio of successful received packets at BS with p=0.7

Fig. 2 shows that the ratio of successful packets received at base station with a probability of p=0.7 in improved LEACH is higher than in original LEACH and also the ratio is higher with probabilistic model compared with LEACH. In improved LEACH the unreliability of links between a clusterhead and the base station can be treated by a multihop communication by against, in original LEACH the packet will be lost due to the unreliable links.

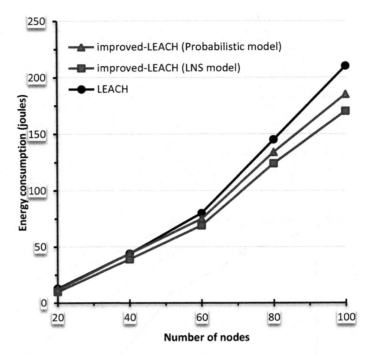

Fig. 3. Energy consumption in LEACH and Improved-LEACH

Fig.3 illustrates that energy consumption in improved LEACH based on LNS model or Probabilistic model is lower than in LEACH because in the improved version, the multihop transmission scheme minimizes energy consumption but the direct communication in LEACH consumes more energy.

5   Conclusion

In this paper, we have evaluated LEACH protocol in a realistic environment represented by lognormal shadowing model and a probabilistic model. However, results obtained illustrated that the performance of LEACH degrades in this kind of environment. Therefore, we have proposed an improved version of LEACH to overcome its weaknesses with realistic environment. The proposed scheme aims to find an optimal multihop path over links error which is modeled by LNS model and probabilistic model.

The simulation results showed that our contribution outperforms the original version of LEACH in terms of energy consumption and ratio of successful packets received at the base station. Moreover, our contribution deals with fault tolerance in LEACH, ensures reliable delivery and minimizes energy consumption.

References

1. Chanak, P., Banerjee, I.: Energy efficient fault-tolerant multipath routing scheme for wireless sensor networks. The Journal of China Universities of Posts and Telecommunications 20(6), 42–61 (2013)
2. Akkaya, K., Younis, M.A.: Survey on routing protocols for wireless sensor networks. Ad Hoc Networks 3(3), 325–349 (2005)
3. Tyagi, S., Kumar, N.: A systematic review on clustering and routing techniques based upon LEACH protocol for wireless sensor networks. Journal of Network and Computer Applications 36(2), 623–645 (2013)
4. Vlajic, N., Xia, D.: Wireless sensor networks: to cluster or not to cluster? In: International Symposium on World of Wireless, Mobile and Multimedia Networks, pp. 260–268 (2006)
5. Heinzelman, W.R., Chandrakasan, A., Balakrishnan, H.: Energy-efficient communication protocol for wireless microsensor networks. In: Proceedings of the 33rd IEEE Annual Hawaii International Conference on System Sciences, Hawaii, pp. 1–10 (2000)
6. Rappaport, T.S.: Wireless Communications Principles and Practice, 2nd edn. Prentice Hall Release (2001)
7. Farooq, M.O., Dogar, A.B., Shah, G.A.: MR-LEACH: Multi-hop Routing with Low Energy Adaptive Clustering Hierarchy. In: Proceeding of Fourth IEEE International Conference on Sensor Technologies and Applications (IEEE), Venice, Italy, pp. 262–268 (2010)
8. Neto, J., Antoniel Rego, A., Andr-Cardoso, A., Jnior, J.: MH-LEACH: A Distributed Algorithm for Multi-Hop Communication in Wireless Sensor Networks. In: Proceeding of The Thirteenth International Conference on Networks (ICN), Nice, France, pp. 55–61 (2014)
9. Yang, H., Xu, J., Wang, R., Qian, L.: Energy-Efficient Multi-hop Routing Algorithm Based on LEACH. In: Wang, R., Xiao, F. (eds.) CWSN 2012. CCIS, vol. 334, pp. 578–587. Springer, Heidelberg (2013)
10. Tabet Hellel, C., Lehsaini, M., Guyennet, H.: An Enhanced Fault-tolerant Version of LEACH for Wireless Sensor Networks. International Journal of Advancements in Computing Technology(IJACT) 6(6), 50–57 (2014)
11. Kurvilla, J., Nayak, A., Stojmenoviç, I.: Hop count optimal position based packet routing algorithms for ad hoc wireless networks with a realistic physical layer. IEEE Journal on Selected Areas in Communications 23(6), 1267–1275 (2005)
12. Levis, P., Lee, N., Welsh, M., Culler, D.: TOSSIM: accurate and scalable simulation of entire TinyOS applications. In: The First ACM International conference on Embedded networked sensor systems (SenSys 2003), New York, USA, pp. 126–137 (2003)

Security and Network Technologies: Energy and Synchronisation

High Velocity Aware Clocks Synchronization Approach in Vehicular Ad Hoc Networks

Khedidja Medani[✉], Makhlouf Aliouat, and Zibouda Aliouat

Faculty of sciences, Ferhat Abbas University Sétif 1 Algeria
Khadidja-medani@hotmail.fr,
{aliouat_m,aliouat_zi}@yahoo.fr

Abstract. Clock synchronization plays an important role in communications organization between applications in Vehicular Ad hoc NETworks (VANETs) requiring a strong need for coordination. Having a global time reference or knowing the value of a physical clock (indeed with an acceptable approximation) of cooperative process involved in the provision of a service by distributed applications, takes on a fundamental importance in decentralized systems, particularly in VANETs. The intrinsic and constraining features of VANETs, especially the high mobility of vehicles make the clock synchronization mechanisms more complex and require a concise and a specific adequacy. The aim of the work reported in this paper is to propose a new protocol for clocks synchronization for VANETs, sufficiently robust, with a good precision, and convenient to the main constraint such high nodes mobility. Our proposed protocol, named Time Table Diffusion (TTD), was simulated using a combination of two simulators: VanetMobiSim and NS2 to evaluate its performance in terms of convergence time and number of messages generated. The obtained results were conclusive.

Keywords: VANETs · Clocks synchronization · Intelligent Transportation System · Worthwhile Road Traffic · Time Table Diffusion · TTD

1   Introduction

Over the last decade, the use of wireless ad hoc network in transportation domain has drawn particular researchers' attention in order to promote them to a satisfactory rank regarding to the numerous advantages they may provide. So, communications between vehicles (IVC: Inter Vehicular Communications) have becoming one of the most active researching area. This applicative aspect has given a new communication paradigm that ensures to the classical transportation systems more efficiency, security, conviviality, and performances. So this gives rise to the so-called intelligent transportation systems (ITS). Although vehicular ad hoc networks (VANETs) as well as Wireless Sensor Networks (WSNs) are derived from the same source namely Mobile Ad hoc NETwoks (MANETs), the satisfying results obtained from researches and works done in these fields cannot be directly applied in the context of VANETs, because the specificities of the latter are more stringent in one side and plentiful in the

© IFIP International Federation for Information Processing 2015
A. Amine et al. (Eds.): CIIA 2015, IFIP AICT 456, pp. 479–490, 2015.
DOI: 10.1007/978-3-319-19578-0_39

other. For example, the velocity of nodes in VANETs may reaches extreme values while energy is abundant and does not represent any constraint. So, the high mobility environments related to road infrastructure imposes new constraints like radio obstacles, the effects of multipath and fading.

Various common services such as communication, coordination, security, and time distribution channel access method for time slot (TDMA: Time Division Multiple Access) depend strongly on the existence of synchronized clocks of different nodes (vehicles) of a considered VANET network. Thus, clock synchronization requires the availability of a common time reference for all vehicles, and since these clocks drifted naturally, it is crucial to realize synchronization with an appropriate period and accuracy.

In contrast to other dynamic networks, high mobility of VANETs imposes new requirements in terms of immediate reactivity and high dynamic connectivity. Consequently, the clock synchronization methods used in Ad Hoc networks (MANETs and WSNs) are not suitable, it is therefore important to adapt them specifically to the context of VANET or proposing new well suited. Few works devoted to the problematic of clocks synchronization in VANETs were reported in the literature, such as: RBS [1] CTS [2], TTT [3] and HCS [4].

The aim of the work reported in this paper is to propose a new protocol, for synchronizing node's clocks in VANETs, independently of the network topology, based on a decentralized approach, and requiring no use of a Global Positioning System (GPS) component or an existing infrastructure. The proposed protocol should be able of providing debrided synchronization where each node moves freely with the time of its local clock, but stores the needed data to synchronize other nodes. It should also provide a good precision (of the order of micro seconds), robustness against failure of nodes, and a low cost in terms of convergence time and number of messages generated.

This paper is organized as follows: After an introduction of the problematic in Section 1, Section 2 presents previous work related to clock synchronization in VANETs. Section 3 is devoted to the presentation of our proposition (TTD: Time Table Diffusion), while Section 4 is dedicated to the exhibition of simulation results of TTD. We conclude our work with a conclusion and future perspectives.

2   Related Work

Several protocols for clock synchronization in VANETs have been proposed. These protocols are classified into two approaches (Fig. 1):

2.1   Centralized Approach

Among the proposed algorithms in centralized approach include GNSS: Global Synchronization for Satellite Navigation System [5] and Synchronization in ad hoc networks based on UTRA TDD [6]. These algorithms have the advantage of implementation simplicity, but however require the use of a GPS component, which may raise the problem of transmission signals power which may interfere with communications in progress within nodes.

2.2   Decentralized Approach

Decentralized synchronization algorithms are sufficient for inter vehicular communications and better than the centralized ones in terms of fault tolerance. These algorithms are classified into three categories according to the time information exchange mode between vehicles [7] and are as follows:

- Burst position measurement: Each node programs the periodic transmission of a pulse and corrects its own local after receiving the new burst.
- Continuous correlation of timing signals: Each node continuously transmits a signal sequence and calculates the phase offset using the received sequence. Examples of synchronization protocols based on this method are presented in [8] [9].
- Clock-sampling methods: Each node reads its clock time and transmits it explicitly to other neighboring nodes. At each reception, the offsets are calculated as the difference between the local time and the time clocks of neighboring nodes. This method is superior to the other two methods in terms of simplicity, because it directly exchanges time information, without regard to phase. Among the protocols based on this method include those described in [1] [2] [3].

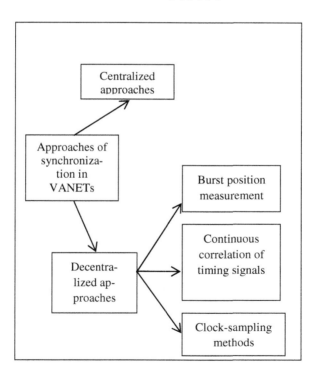

Fig. 1. Clock synchronization protocols classification in VANETs

3   Clock Synchronization with Time Table Diffusion Protocol

Our proposition named Time Table Diffusion (TTD) exploits the idea of transferring a time table implemented by the TTT protocol [3] for clock synchronization in mobile sensor networks. The basic idea is to choose a transporter node (T) to transfer a time table containing the offsets related to different nodes. These offsets are calculated by the offset delay estimation method [10]. Transferring time table by the transporter node makes nodes able to calculate their relative clock offsets with the nodes in the time table without even having any message exchanges. Thus, this will offers a great advantage since it contributes to avoid network congestion.

TTD provides synchronization in vehicular environments independent of the network topology in which each node has a unique identity in the network.

TTT protocol uses nodes mobility to transfer time table. The clock offset associated to each node will be kept in the memory of node in a time table, and upon communicating with a new node, the time table would be transferred to the other node. This process provides a long convergence time (in order of seconds) which make a conflict with the real time applications of VANETs (alert messages ...).

To explain the functioning of TTD, synchronization steps are illustrated in Fig. 2.

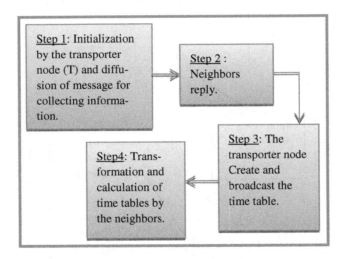

Fig. 2. Synchronization steps in TTD

The synchronization process begins with broadcasting of a message by the transporter node for collecting information. Neighboring nodes respond to transporter node to construct the time table (Time_table). Once the latter one is built, it should be broadcasted later by the transporter node. We describe these steps in the sequel:

3.1   Step 1

In this step, the transporter node broadcasts an advertisement message to initiate the synchronization process and to collect information needed to build the time table. The broadcasting message contains the identity of the transporter node T and t_0, the timestamp indicating the sending instant of this message.

Each node begins this step with sending CTS (Clear to Send) messages. The first node sending its CTS becomes the transporter node in its neighborhood.

3.2   Step 2

A node i that receiving the advertisement message of the transporter node T marks it at the receiving instant of t_{1i}, and then sends a response message to the transporter node T. The response message contains the identity i of the node, and the timestamps t_0, t_{1i}, and t_{2i} where t_{2i} represent the instant of sending response message. One node i may join more than one transporter node at the same time.

3.3   Step 3

When T receives the reply from node i at the instant t_{3i}, using timestamps t_0, t_{1i}, t_{2i}, and t_{3i}, T can calculate the offset relative to node i (Δ_{iT}) according to the equation (1) below and saves the result in the time table where the index access is the identity of node i.

$$\Delta_{iT} = ((t_{1i} - t_0) - (t_{3i} - t_{2i}))/2. \tag{1}$$

Fig. 3 hereafter illustrates the messages exchange between the transporter node T and a node i:

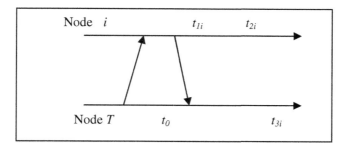

Fig. 3. Messages exchange between the transporter node T and a node i

After T has completed the construction of the time table, it has to broadcast it to all its neighbors' node allowing them to build their own time tables.

3.4   Step 4

When a node i receives the time table from a transporter node T, it can build its own table as follows:

Node i will search in the received table the corresponding value to its identity (Δ_{iT}), and stores the inverse of this value in its own table in the location corresponding to the identity of the node T (*time_table(T)*=-Δ_{iT}). The principle is the following:

$$\Delta_{iT} = C_i - C_T. \tag{2}$$

Multiplying both sides of (2) by (-1), we obtain:

$$\Delta_{Ti} = C_T - C_i. \tag{3}$$

Where, C_T is the clock value of node T at the instant t, and C_i is the clock value of node i in the same instant t.

To synchronize itself with the rest of the nodes table, node i will add Δ_{Ti} value to all values in the table according to the following principle:

$$\Delta_{jT} = C_j - C_T. \tag{4}$$

$$\Delta_{Ti} = C_T - C_i. \tag{5}$$

By adding the two parts of (4) and (5) we obtain:

$$\Delta_{jT} + \Delta_{Ti} = (C_j - C_T) + (C_T - C_i) = \Delta_{ji}. \tag{6}$$

As shown in Fig. 4, depending on the transporter node (that depend on the random number generated by each node), we can find two neighbors not synchronized (node 2 and node 4 participate to the synchronization process under different transporter nodes, that make nodes 2 and 4 two neighbors not synchronized).

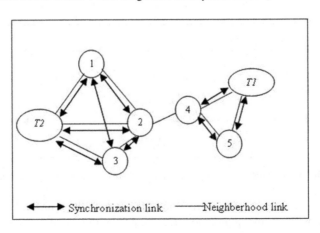

Fig. 4. Problem posed by the random time

A solution to this problem is that inspired from [8] which consist to larger the range of synchronization packet transmission to be equal double that of data packet transmission. In this way, a transporter node T ensures the synchronization of the nodes joining with all its neighbors (one hop) and in most cases, the synchronization on multi-hop paths.

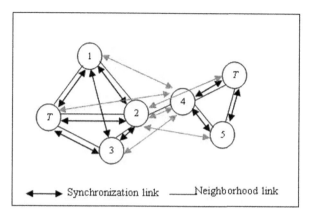

Fig. 5. Improved initial model of the synchronization by TTD

For mobility management, and since the clocks drifted naturally (the live duration of synchronization is an important evaluation criteria of synchronization's algorithms), it is crucial to achieve often synchronization process cycles as shown in Fig. 6.

Table 1. Exchange message type and their content

Message	Number	Content
The avertissement message sent by the transporter node (ADV_T).	n_t, where n_t is the number of transporter nodes in the current cycle.	Transporetr node identity and the timestamp t_0.
Neighbords reply (JOIN_RESPONSE).	$\sum_{0}^{n_t-1} N_i$	Neignbord i identity and timestamps t_0, t_{1i}, t_{2i}.
Time table (TIME_TABLE).	n_t	Time table built by the transporter node

The number of messages necessary to accomplish the synchronization is calculated as follows: Assuming there are Ni nodes within the synchronization scope of a transporter node Ti, where Ti $\in$ T (where T is the set of transporter nodes in the current cycle). We can summarize the number and content of messages required for synchronization, as shown in Table I.

According to this table, the number of messages (nbMsg) necessary to accomplish the synchronization can be estimated as follows:

$$nbMsg = \sum_{i=0}^{n_t-1} (N_i+2) \tag{7}$$

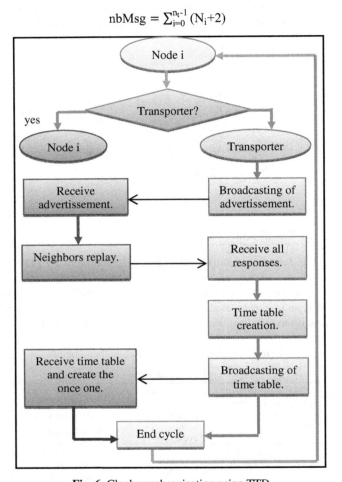

Fig. 6. Clock synchronization using TTD

4   Simulation Results

We simulated the proposed protocol using the combination of the simulator NS2 and the mobility generator VanetMobiSim. Clocks values used in simulation are randomly generated according to the law of GAUSS (0 average, $\delta = 10$ ppm) [11].

We tested a number of scenarios by changing essential parameters to evaluate the performances of our proposed protocol where nodes are initially placed in random positions and their movement direction follows the mobility model implemented by VanetMobiSim in Intelligent Driver Model with Lane Changing (IDM_LC: It regulates vehicle speed based on movements of neighboring vehicles (e.g., if a car in front brakes, the succeeding vehicles also slows down). The implementation reflects restrictions of the spatial environment. Vehicles moving according to the IDM_LC model support smart intersection management: they slow down and stop at intersections, or act according to traffic lights, if present. The implementation reflects restrictions of the spatial environment. Also, vehicles are able to change lane and perform overtaking in presence of multi-lane roads).

Table 2. Simulation Parameters

Topologie (m2)	1000*1000
Nodes number	30/50/100/200/300
Speed (m/s)	7/10/15/20/25/30/35
Trafic light	6
Mobility model	Randomly according to IDM_LC with 2 obstacles every 100 m²
Range data transmission (m)	250/500/1000
Simulation time (s)	1000

The metrics used to analyze the simulation results are the number of messages generated and the time of convergence (convergence time is the time required to accomplish the synchronization process).

Fig. 7 shows that the convergence time in TTD increases with increasing of nodes number, this is due to the large number of neighbors reply messages. In contrast, nodes speed has no influence on the convergence time because TTD solution uses broadcast (Fig.8). This property is an advantage for the proposed algorithm and makes it usable in different vehicles mobility environments (urban, suburban, and highway).

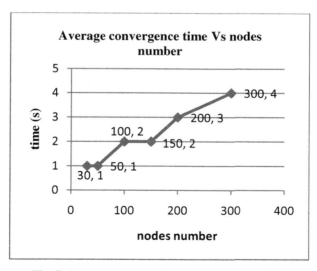

Fig. 7. Convergence time Vs nodes number   in TTD

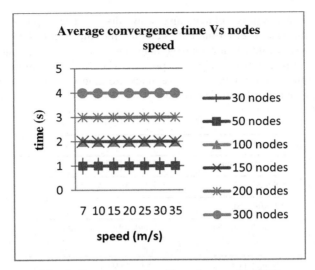

Fig. 8. Convergence time Vs nodes speed in TTD

However, convergence time in TTT [3] increases in urban environments characterized by a minimal speed compared to other vehicles mobility environments. This is because the TTT protocol uses node mobility as an essential factor for time table transfer. Thus, the convergence time shown by our protocol is less than that shown by the reference protocol TTT under the same conditions, as shown in Fig. 9.

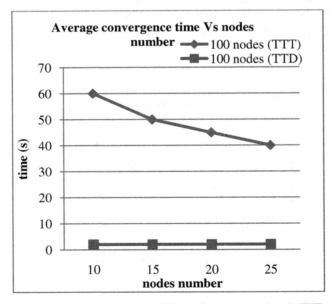

Fig. 9. Convergence time in TTD Vs Convergence time in TTT

The number of messages required to accomplish the synchronization process is not fixed and depends on two essentials factors; nodes number and transporter nodes number (that depends on the transmission range). On one hand, the number of messages increases with a large number of nodes (as shown in Fig. 10); logically this is due to the phase of neighborhood replays, the most consuming phase in the synchronization process in term of messages number.

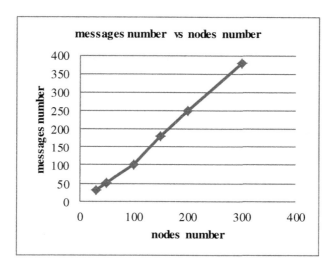

Fig. 10. Messages number Vs nodes number

On the other hand, depending on the transmission range, that affects the transporter nodes number, the number of messages increases with a the increasing of the number of transporter nodes. For example, in a topology 1000 * 1000 (m^2) with a number of nodes equal to 30 (low density network), we can achieve a data transmission range up to 1000 m, in this case, only one transporter node is sufficient to achieve the synchronization process, **so we** can reach a minimum number of messages that is equal to the nodes number in the network plus one.

5   Conclusion

Although clock synchronization in VANETs is a very important research area, few works have been reported so far in the specialized literature. In this paper, we propose a new efficient synchronization protocol taking into account the specific constraints imposed by VANET environments. The proposed solution called TTD (Time Table Diffusion) provides released clock synchronization in a vehicular environment independently of the network topology. TTD achieves synchronization with a good accuracy of the order of a microsecond, and in most cases, synchronization of multi-hop paths. The proposed solution is simulated with the combination of VanetMobiSim-NS2 to evaluate its performance in terms of number of messages generated and convergence time. The simulation results showed that TTD provides a best convergence time compared to its homologues TTT (TTT provide best result than RBS in term of convergence time).

References

1. Elson, J., Girod, L., Estrin, D.: Fine-Grained Network Time Synchronization using Referece Broadcasts, vol. 36, pp. 147–163. ACM (2002)
2. Shizhun, W., Anjum, P., Maziar, N.: Converging Time Synchronization Algorithm for Highly Dynamic Vehicular Ad Hoc Networks (VANETs), vol. 6, pp. 443–448. IEEE (2010)
3. Reza, K., Lim, M., Sim, H., Tat Ewe, A.T., Wei, S.: Time Table Transfer Time Synchronization. In: Mobile Wireless Sensor Networks, vol. 5. PIERS Proceedings, Beijing (2009)
4. Sam, D., Cyril Raj, V.: A Time Synchronized Hybrid Vehicular Ad Hoc Network of Roadside Sensors and Vehicles for Safe Driving. Journal of Computer Science 11, 1617–1627 (2014)
5. Scopigno, R., Cozzetti, H.: GNSS synchronization in Vanets. In: 2009 3rd International Conference on IEEE New Technologies, Mobility and Security (NTMS), vol. 5(11), pp. 1–5 (2009)
6. Ebner, A., Rohling, H., Halfmann, R., Lott, M.: Synchronization in ad hoc networks based on UTRA TDD. In: The 13th IEEE International Symposium on Personal, Indoor and Mobile Radio Communications, vol. 4 (2002)
7. Rentel, C.H.: Network Time Synchronization and Code-based Scheduling for Wireless Ad Hoc Networks. Carleton University, Ottawa (2006)
8. André, E., Hermann, R., Matthias, L., Rüdiger, H.: Decentralized Slot Synchronizatio. In: Highly Dynamic Ad Hoc Networks, vol. 2, pp. 494 – 498. IEEE (2002)
9. Nakagawa, E., Sourour, M.: Mutual Decentralized Synchronization for Intervehicule Communications, vol. 48(16). IEEE (1999)
10. Mills, D.L.: Internet Time Synchronisation: The Network Time Protocol, vol. 39. IEEE (1991)
11. Lombardi, M.A.: Frequency Measurement. The Measurement, Instrumentation and Sensors Handbook. CRC Press (1999)
12. André, E., Lars, W., Hermann, R.: Aspects of Decentralized Time Synchronization in Vehicular Ad hoc Networks. In: 1st International Workshop on Intelligent Transportation, Humburg (2004)

An Energy-Efficient Fault-Tolerant Scheduling Algorithm Based on Variable Data Fragmentation

Chafik Arar[✉], Mohamed Salah Khireddine, Abdelouahab Belazoui, and Randa Megulati

Department of Computer Science, University of Banta
BATNA 05000, Algeria
chafik.arar@gmail.com,
{mkhireddine,belazoui}@yahoo.fr,
randa_meguellati@hotmail.fr
http://www.univ-batna.dz

Abstract. In this article, we propose an approach to build fault-tolerant distributed real-time embedded systems. From a given system description and a given fault hypothesis, we generate automatically a fault tolerant distributed schedule that achieves low energy consumption and high reliability efficiency. Our scheduling algorithm is dedicated to multi-bus heterogeneous architectures with multiple processors linked by several shared buses, which take as input a given system description and a given fault hypothesis. It is based on active redundancy to mask a fixed number L of processor failures supported in the system, and passive redundancy based on variable data fragmentation to tolerate N buses failures. In order to maximize the systems reliability, the replicas of each operation are scheduled on different reliable processors and the size of each fragmented data depends on GSFR and the bus failure rates. Finally, we show with an example that our approach can maximize reliability and reduce energy consumption when using active redundancy.

Keywords: Energy consumption · Scheduling · Embedded systems · Real time systems · Reliability · Active redundancy · Multi-bus architecture · variable data fragmentation

1 Introduction

Nowadays, heterogeneous systems are being used in many sectors of human activity, such as transportation, robotics, and telecommunication. These systems are increasingly small and fast, but also more complex and critical, and thus more sensitive to faults. Due to catastrophic consequences (human, ecological, and/or financial disasters) that could result from a fault, these systems must be fault-tolerant. This is why fault tolerant techniques are necessary to make sure that the system continues to deliver a correct service in spite of faults Jalote [1], [2],

A fault can affect either the hardware or the software of the system; we chose to concentrate on hardware faults. More particularly, we consider processors

© IFIP International Federation for Information Processing 2015
A. Amine et al. (Eds.): CIIA 2015, IFIP AICT 456, pp. 491–502, 2015.
DOI: 10.1007/978-3-319-19578-0_40

and communication faults [3], [4]. In the literature, we can identify several fault-buses tolerance approaches for distributed embedded real-time systems, which we classify into two categories: proactive or reactive schemes.

In the proactive scheme [5], [6], multiple redundant copies of a message are sent along distinct buses. In contrast, in the reactive scheme only one copy of the message, called primary, is sent; if it fails, another copy of the message, called backup, will be transmitted. In [7], an original off-line fault tolerant scheduling algorithm which uses the active replication of tasks and communications to tolerate a set of failure patterns is proposed; each failure pattern is a set of processor and/or communications media that can fail simultaneously, and each failure pattern corresponds to a reduced architecture. The proposed algorithm starts by building a basic schedule for each reduced architecture plus the nominal architecture, and then merges these basic schedules to obtain a distributed fault tolerant schedule. It has been implemented in [8].

In [9], a method of identifying bus faults based on a support vector machine is proposed. In [2], faults of buses are tolerated using a TDMA (Time Division Multiple Access) communication protocol and an active redundancy approach. In [10] authors propose a fine grained transparent recovery, where the property of transparency can be selectively applied to processes and messages. In [11] authors survey the problem of how to schedule tasks in such a way that deadlines continue to be met despite processor and communication media (permanent or transient) or software failure.

In this paper, we are interested in approaches based on scheduling algorithms that maximize reliability and reduce energy consumption [12], [13], [14] when using active redundancy to tolerate processors faults and passive redundancy based on variable data fragmentation to tolerate buses faults.

The remaining of this paper is structured as follows: In section 2, we give detailed description of our system models. In section 3, we present our solution and we give detailed description of our scheduling algorithm. Section 4 shows with an example how our approach can maximize reliability and reduce energy consumption when using active redundancy. We finally conclude this work in section 5.

2   System Description

Distributed real-time embedded systems are composed of two principal parts, which are the algorithm (software part) and the distributed architecture (hardware part). The specification of these systems involve describing the algorithm (algorithm model), the architecture (architecture model), and the execution characteristics of the algorithm onto the architecture (execution model).

The algorithm is modeled as a data-flow graph noted ALG. Each vertex of ALG is an operation (task) and each edge is a data-dependence. A data-dependence, noted by $\rightarrow$, corresponds to a data transfer between a producer operation and a consumer operation. $t_1 \rightarrow t_2$ means that t_1 is a predecessor of t_2 and t_2 is a successor of t_1. Operations with no predecessor (resp. no successor) are the input interfaces (resp. output).

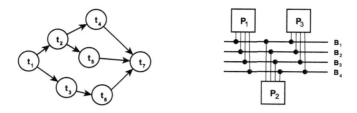

Fig. 1. ALG and ARC graphs

The architecture is modeled by a non-directed graph, noted ARC, where each node is a processor, and each edge is a bus. Classically, a processor is made of one computation unit, one local memory, and one or more communication units, each connected to one communication link. Communication units execute data transfers. We assume that the architecture is heterogeneous and fully connected. Figure 1 presents an example of ALG with seven operations t_1, t_2, t_3, t_4, t_5, t_6 and t_7 and ARC, with three processors P_1, P_2, P_3 and four buses B_1, B_2, B_3 and B_4.

Our real-time system is based on cyclic executive; this means that a fixed schedule of the operations of ALG is executed cyclically on ARC at a fixed rate. This schedule must satisfy one real-time constraint which is the length of the schedule. As we target heterogeneous architecture, we associate to each operation t_i a worst case execution time (WCET) on each processor P_j of ARC, noted $Exe(t_i, P_j)$. Also, we associate to each data dependency $data_i$ a worst case transmission time (WCTT) on each bus B_j of the architecture, noted $Exe(data_i, B_j)$.

We assume only processors and buses failures. We consider only transient bus faults, which persist for a short duration. We assume that at most L processors faults and N bus faults can arise in the system, and that the architecture includes more than L processors and N buses.

3 The Proposed Approach

In this section, we first discuss the basic principles used in our solution, based on scheduling algorithms. Then, we describe in details our scheduling algorithm. The aims of this algorithm are twofold, first, maximize the reliability of the system and minimize the length of the whole generated schedule in both presence and absence of failures; Secondly, reduce energy consumption. In our approach. we achieve high reliability, reducing consuption and fault tolerance in tow ways:

3.1 Active Redundancy with Changing Frequency

In order to tolerate up to L arbitrary processors faults, our solution is based on active redundancy approach. The advantage of the active redundancy of operations is that the obtained schedule is static; in particular, there is no need for complex on-line re-scheduling of the operations that were executed on a processor when the latter fails; also, it can be proved that the schedule meets a required real-time constraint, both in the absence and in the presence of faults. In many embedded systems, this is mandatory. To tolerate up to L processors faults, each operation t of Alg is actively replicated on $L+1$ processors of Arc (see Figure 2). We assume that all values returned by the $L+1$ replicas of any operation t of Alg are identical.

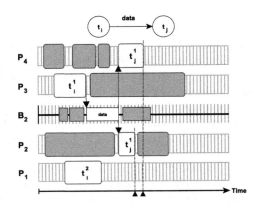

Fig. 2. Active redundancy

Voltage, Frequency and Energy Consumption: the maximum supply voltage is noted V_{max} and the corresponding highest operating frequency is noted F_{max}. For each operation, its WCET assumes that the processor operates at F_{max} and V_{max} (and similarly for the WCCT of the data-dependencies). Because the circuit delay is almost linearly related to $1/V$, there is a linear relationship between the supply voltage V and the operating frequency F. In the sequel, we will assume that the operating frequencies are normalized, that is, $F_{max} = 1$ and any other frequency F is in the interval $[0, 1]$. Accordingly, the execution time of the operation or data-dependency M placed onto the hardware component C (be it a processor or a communication link) running at frequency F (taken as a scaling factor) is :

$$Exe(M, C, F) = \frac{Exe(M, C)}{F} \tag{1}$$

To calculate the power consumption, we follow the model presented in [15]. For a single operation placed onto a single processor, the power consumption P is :

$$P = P_s + h(P_{ind} + P_d) \tag{2}$$

Where P_s is the static power (power to maintain basic circuits and to keep the clock running), h is equal to 1 when the circuit is active and 0 when it is inactive, P_{ind} is the frequency independent active power (the power portion that is independent of the voltage and the frequency; it becomes 0 when the system is put to sleep, but the cost of doing so is very expensive),

$$P_d = C_{ef} * V^2 * F \tag{3}$$

P_d is the frequency dependent active power (the processor dynamic power and any power that depends on the voltage or the frequency), C_{ef} is the switch capacitance, V is the supply voltage, and F is the operating frequency.

For processors, this model is widely accepted for average size applications, where C_{ef} can be assumed to be constant for the whole application. For a multiprocessor schedule S, we cannot apply directly the previous equation. Instead, we must compute the total energy $E(S)$ consumed by S, and then divide by the schedule length $L(S)$:

$$P(S) = \frac{E(S)}{L(S)} \tag{4}$$

We compute $E(S)$ by summing the contribution of each processor, depending on the voltage and frequency of each operation placed onto it. On the processor P_i, the energy consumed by each operation is the product of the active power $P_{ind}^i + P_d^i$ by its execution time.

In our approach, as $L+1$ replicas of each operation are scheduled actively on $L+1$ distinct processors, the energy consumed by the system is maximal. In order to reduce energy consumption, we propose to execute the $L+1$ replicas of an operation with different frequencies F. As all the $L+1$ replicas of an operation may have different end execution time (see Figure 2 for the replicas t_j^1 and t_j^2), we choose to align the execution time of all the replica by changing the frequency F of each replica (As shown in Figure 3).

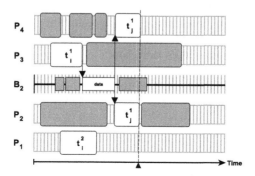

Fig. 3. Changing the frequency of t_j^1

3.2   Passive Redundancy with Variable Data Fragmentation

In order to use efficiently the bus redundancy of the architecture, we propose to use a mechanism of communication, based on variable data fragmentation. Variable data fragmentation allows the fast recovering from buses errors, and it may also reduce the error detection latency. (the time it takes to detect the error). The communication of each data dependency $t_i \to t_j$ is fragmented into $N+1$ fragments $data = data_1 \bullet \cdots \bullet data_{N+1}$, sent by t_i to t_j via $N+1$ distinct buses (see Figure 4); The associative operation ($\bullet$) is used to concatenate two data packets. As our approach uses variable data fragmentation, the size of each fragmented data depends on $GSFR$ and the bus failure rates λ_B.

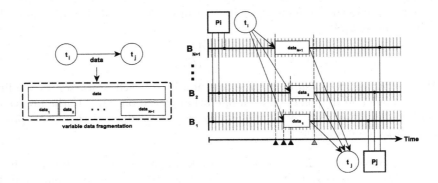

Fig. 4. Variable data fragmentation

GSFR is the failure rate per time unit of the obtained multiprocessor schedule. Using the GSFR is very satisfactory in the area of periodically executed schedules. In such cases, applying brutally the exponential reliability model yields very low reliabilities due to very long execution times (the same remark applies also to very long schedules). Hence, one has to compute beforehand the desired reliability of a single iteration from the global reliability of the system during its full mission; but this computation depends on the total duration of the mission and on the duration of one single iteration.

Our fault tolerance heuristic is GSFR-based to control precisely the scheduling of each fragmented data from the beginning to the end of the schedule. In [16], The GSFR of scheduling an operation t_i, noted $\Lambda(S_n)$, by the following equation:

$$\Lambda(S_n) = \frac{-\log(\prod_i e^{-\lambda_k exe(t_i, P_j) + \sum_k \sum_j \lambda_c exe(dpd_j^k, b_c)})}{\sum_i^j exe(t_i, p_j) + \sum_k^m exe(dpd_k, b_m)} \tag{5}$$

Variable data fragmentation operates in three phases :

1. First, in order to tolerate at most N communication bus errors, each data dependency is fragmented into $N+1$ fragments of equal size. The initial size of each fragment is calculated by:

$$Size(data_i) = \frac{Size(data)}{N+1} \tag{6}$$

The main problem with the equal size data fragmentation comes from the difference between ending time of different fragments (Figure 5(a)) because the destination operation must wait to getting all the fragments of the data dependency to start execution.

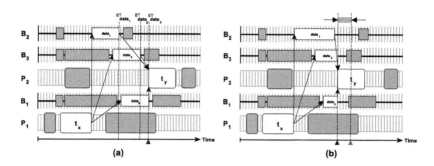

Fig. 5. Ending time : (a) ET in equal size data fragmentation, (b) Minimize difference between ending time

2. Second, the goal of passing from equal size data fragmentation to variable data fragmentation (Figure 5(a)) is to minimize the difference between ending time ET of different fragments (Figure 5(b)).

$$ET_{data_1} \leq ET_{data_2} \leq \cdots \leq ET_{data_{N+1}}$$
$$Minimize(ET_{data_{i+1}} - ET_{data_i})_{i \in \{1,\cdots,N+1\}} \tag{7}$$

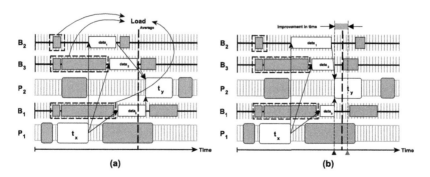

Fig. 6. (a) the Average Load $Load_{Average}$, (b) and the improvement in time of the scheduling

With variable data fragmentation based on minimizing the difference between ending time, another problem can occur and grows extremely the execution time. The bus over which accumulates data may also fail, therefore the quantity of data to be retransmitted is more important.

3. Third, the definition of a compromise between the load of each communication bus and the maximum data to be transmitted on this bus, as illustrated in Figure 6(a). Variable data fragmentation must not exceed this value when defining the new fragments size. The improvement in time of the scheduling is shown in Figure 6(b).

The algorithm that enable variable data fragmentation is show in figure 7.

Algorithm VDF
Input: data-dependence $(data = t_i \rightarrow t_j)$, N.
Output: the set of $N + 1$ affectation $(data_i(B_x))$.

1. Each data dependency $(data = t_i \rightarrow t_j)$ is fragmented into $N + 1$ fragments of equal size:

$$Size(data_1) = \cdots Size(data_{N+1}) = \frac{Size(data)}{N + 1}$$

2. Compute the loading sill of buses.

$$Load_{Average} = \frac{\sum \lambda_{B_i} * Load(B_i)}{N + 1}$$

3. Schedule the $N + 1$ fragments of data-dependence on $N + 1$ bus.
4. Order the data fragments according to their ending Time.

$$ET_1 \leq ET_2 \leq \cdots \leq ET_{N+1}$$

5. Compute the sum of the shift of Ending Time.

$$Sum^{new}_{shift-time} := 0; Sum_{shift-time} = \sum ET_{i+1} - ET_i;$$

6. **While** $(Sum^{new}_{shift-time} \leq Sum_{shift-time})$ **do**
   (a) $Sum_{shift-time} := Sum^{new}_{shift-time}.$

   (b) Fragment the data Fragment with the last end time on tow fragments $(data(ET_{N+1}) = data_A \bullet data_B)$, respecting the following three conditions:

       i. $Size(data_A) \geq Siz_{min}(data_{ET_1})$
       ii. $Siz(data_{ET_1} + Size(data_B) \leq Load_{Average}$
       iii. $ET_1 + Size(data_B)B_{data_1} \leq ET_{N+1}$

   (c) Order the data fragments according to their new ending time ET_i.

   (d) Compute the new value of $Sum^{new}_{shift-time}$

$$Sum^{new}_{shift-time} = \sum ET_{i+1} - ET_i;$$

   End While.

End

Fig. 7. VDF : The variable data fragmentation algorithm

3.3 Scheduling Algorithm

The principles of our approach are implemented by a scheduling algorithm, called Energy Fault Tolerant Heuristic *(EFTH-VDF)*. It is a greedy list scheduling heuristic, which schedules one operation at each step (n). It generates a distributed static schedule of a given algorithm Alg onto a given architecture Arc, which minimizes the system's run-time, and tolerates upto L processors and N buses faults, with respect to the real-time and the distribution constraints. At each step of the greedy list scheduling heuristic, the pressure schedule function (noted by $\sigma(n)(t_i, P_j)$) is used as a cost function to select the best operation to be scheduled.

$$\sigma^{(n)}(t_i, P_j) = S_{t_i,P_j}^{(n)} + \overline{S}_{t_i}^{(n)} - R^{(n-1)} \tag{8}$$

The *EFTH-VDF* algorithm (show in figure 8) is divided into seven steps.

Algorithm EFTH-VDF
Input: *ALG, ARC, N*;
Output: a reliable fault-tolerant schedule;

Initialize the lists of candidate and scheduled operations:
n := 0;
$T_{cand}^{(0)} := \{t \in T \mid pred(t) = \emptyset\}$;
$T_{sched}^{(0)} := \emptyset$;

While $(T_{cand}^{(n)} \neq \emptyset)$ **do**

1. For each candidate operation t_{cand}, compute $\sigma^{(n)}$ and GSFR on each processor P_k.

2. For each candidate operation t_{cand}, select the best processor $p_{best}^{t_{cand}}$ which minimizes $\sigma^{(n)}$ and GSFR.

3. Select the most urgent candidate operation t_{urgent} between all t_{cand}^i of $T_{cand}^{(n)}$.

4. For each data dependencies whose t_{urgent} is the producer operation: Fragment the data communication on N fragments using the variable data fragmentation algorithm;

5. Schedule t_{urgent} and its fragmented data;

6. Update the lists of candidate and scheduled operations:
   $T_{sched}^{(n)} := T_{sched}^{(n-1)} \cup \{t_{urgent}\}$;
   $T_{cand}^{(n+1)} := T_{cand}^{(n)} - \{t_{urgent}\} \cup \{t' \in succ(t_{urgent}) \mid pred(t') \subseteq T_{sched}^{(n)}\}$;
7. n := n + 1;

End while
End

Fig. 8. The EFTH-VDF algorithm

4   Simulations, Results and Discussion

We have applied the *EFTH-VDF* heuristic to an example of an algorithm graph and an architecture graph composed of four processors and four buses. The algorithm graph is show in Figure 9. The failure rates of the processors are respectively 10^{-5}, 10^{-5}, 10^{-6} and 10^{-6}, and the failure rate of the Buses SAM_{MP1}, SAM_{MP2}, SAM_{MP3} and SAM_{MP4} are respectively 10^{-6}, 10^{-6}, 10^{-5} and 10^{-4}.

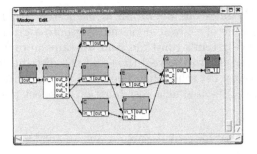

Fig. 9. Algorithm graph

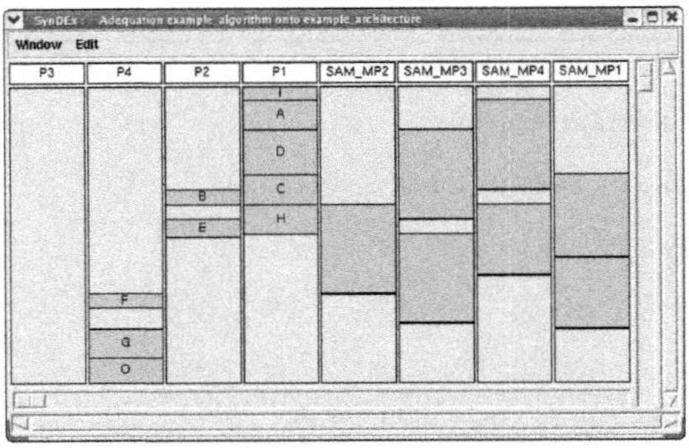

Fig. 10. Schedule generated by SynDEx

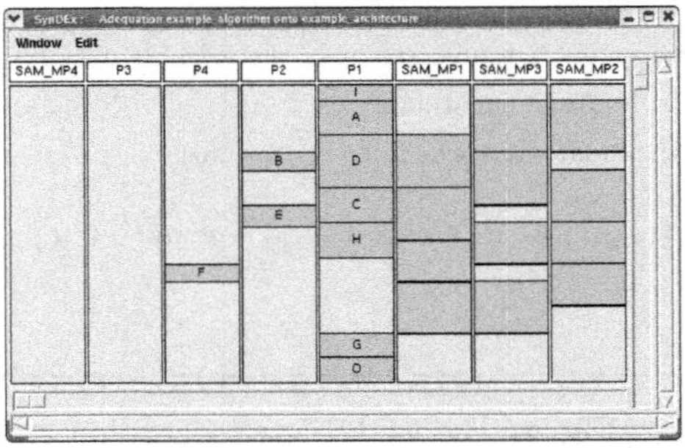

Fig. 11. $EFTH - VDF$ without changing frequencies

Figure 10 shows the non-fault-tolerant schedule produced for our example with a basic scheduling heuristic. (for instance the one of SynDEx). SynDEx [17] is a tool for optimizing the implementation of real-time embedded applications on multi-component architecture.

Figure 11 shows the fault-tolerant schedule produced for our example with a *EFTH-VDF* scheduling heuristic without changing frequencies. The schedule length generated by this heuristic is 21.6. The GSFR of the non-reliable schedule is equal to 0.0000287. The energy E is equal to 36.7.

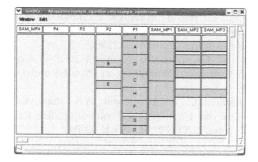

Fig. 12. A schedule generated by $EFTH - VDF$

Figure 12 shows the fault-tolerant schedule produced for our example with a *EFTH-VDF* scheduling heuristic. The schedule length generated by this heuristic is 27.3. The GSFR of the non-reliable schedule is equal to 0.0000276. The energy E is equal to 23.21.

5 Conclusion

We have proposed in this paper a solution to tolerate both processors and communication media faults in distributed heterogeneous architectures with multiple-bus topology. The proposed solution, based on active redundancy, is a list scheduling heuristic called *EFTH-VDF*. It generates automatically distributed static schedule of a given algorithm onto a given architecture, which minimizes the system's run-time, and tolerates upto L processors and N buses faults, with respect to real-time and distribution constraints. The scheduling strategy based on variable frequency and variable data fragmentation minimizes energy consumption and take communication failures into account.

References

1. Jalote, P.: Fault-Tolerance in Distributed Systems. Prentice Hall, Englewood Cliffs (1994)
2. Kopetz, H.: Real-time systems: design principles for distributed embedded applications. Springer Science & Business Media (2011)
3. Grünsteidl, G., Kantz, H., Kopetz, H.: Communication reliability in distributed real-time systems. In: Distributed Computer Control Systems 1991: Towards Distributed Real-Time Systems with Predictable Timing Properties, p. 123 (2014)
4. Jun, Z., Sha, E.H., Zhuge, Q., Yi, J., Wu, K.: Efficient fault-tolerant scheduling on multiprocessor systems via replication and deallocation. International Journal of Embedded Systems 6(2), 216–224 (2014)
5. Kandasamy, N., Hayes, J.P., Murray, B.T.: Dependable communication synthesis for distributed embedded systems. Reliability Engineering & System Safety 89(1), 81–92 (2005)

6. Dulman, S., Nieberg, T., Wu, J., Havinga, P.: Trade-off between traffic overhead and reliability in multipath routing for wireless sensor networks. In: Wireless Communications and Networking Conference (2003)
7. Dima, C., Girault, A., Lavarenne, C., Sorel, Y.: Off-line real-time fault-tolerant scheduling. In: 9th Euromicro Workshop on Parallel and Distributed Processing, pp. 410–417 (2001)
8. Pinello, C., Vincentelli, L.C., Fault-tolerant, A.S.: deployment of embedded software for cost-sensitive real-time feedback-control applications design. In: Automation and Test in Europe, DATE 2004. IEEE (2004)
9. Song, H., Wu, H.: The applied research of support vector machine in bus fault identification. In: 2010 Sixth International Conference on Natural Computation (ICNC), vol. 3, pp. 1326–1329. IEEE (2010)
10. Izosimov, V., Pop, P., Eles, P., Peng, Z.: Scheduling and optimization of fault-tolerant embedded systems with transparency/performance trade-offs. ACM Transactions on Embedded Computing Systems (TECS) 11(3), 61 (2012)
11. Krishna, C.: Fault-tolerant scheduling in homogeneous real-time systems. ACM Computing Surveys (CSUR) 46(4), 48 (2014)
12. Huang, J., Buckl, C., Raabe, A., Knoll, A.: Energy-aware task allocation for network-on-chip based heterogeneous multiprocessor systems. In: 2011 19th Euromicro International Conference on Parallel, Distributed and Network-Based Processing (PDP), pp. 447–454. IEEE (2011)
13. Agrawal, P., Rao, S.: Energy-aware scheduling of distributed systems using cellular automata. In: 2012 IEEE International Systems Conference (SysCon), pp. 1–6. IEEE (2012)
14. Agrawal, P., Rao, S.: Energy-aware scheduling of distributed systems. IEEE (2014)
15. Zhu, D., Melhem, R., Mosse, D., Elnozahy, E.: Analysis of an energy efficient optimistic tmr scheme. In: Proceedings of the Tenth International Conference on Parallel and Distributed Systems, ICPADS 2004, pp. 559–568. IEEE (2004)
16. Girault, A., Kalla, H.: A novel bicriteria scheduling heuristics providing a guaranteed global system failure rate. IEEE Transactions on Dependable and Secure Computing 6(4), 241–254 (2009)
17. Forget, J., Gensoul, C., Guesdon, M., Lavarenne, C., Macabiau, C., Sorel, Y., Stentzel, C.: Syndex v7 user manual (2013)

Genetic Centralized Dynamic Clustering in Wireless Sensor Networks

Mekkaoui Kheireddine[1](✉), Rahmoun Abdellatif[2], and Gianluigi Ferrari[3]

[1] GeCoDe Laoratory, University of Dr Tahar Moulay, Saida, Algeria
[2] EEDIS Laboratoty, University of Djilllai Liabes, SBA, Algeria
[3] WASNLab Laboratory, University of Parma, Parma, Italy
mekdar@hotmail.com

Abstract. In order to overcome the energy loss involved by commu- nications in wireless sensor networks (WSN), the use of clustering has proven to be effective. In this paper, we proposed a dynamic centralized genetic algorithm (GA)-based clustering approach to optimize the clus- tering configuration (cluster heads and cluster members) to limit node energy consumption. The obtained simulation results show that the pro- posed technique overcomes the LEACH clustering algorithm.

1 Introduction

Wireless sensor networks (WSNs) are used in many domains, such as mili- tary surveillance, disaster management, forest fire detection, seismic detection, habitat monitoring, biomedical health monitoring, inventory tracking, animal tracking, hazardous environment sensing and smart spaces, general engineering, commercial applications, home applications, underwater applications, etc [1]. In- deed, according to [2], WSNs are considered to be one of the new technologies that will change our life, they are listed, also in [3], as one of the key technologies of the internet of things.

The sensor nodes (or motes) are physical entities characterized by: (i) a bat- tery with a limited energy; (ii) a processor with limited processing capabilities; (iii) and a transceiver [4]. The nodes can be deployed in monitoring areas in order to gather multiple types of information (e.g., humidity, light, temperature, wind,...) and then transmit the gathered information to the gateway sensor node (Access Point or Sink), possibly using multi-hop routing strategy [5]. In turn, the sink transmits the collected information to the end users.

Since it might often be difficult to replace exhausted batteries (e.g., WSNs may be deployed in inaccessible areas) [6], extending the lifetime of the WSN is crucial. In the literature, many papers show that the source of highest energy consumption in the sensor node is the transceiver [7], making strategies which minimize the use of the transceiver very attractive. Several techniques can be used to save energy, among which clustering consists in grouping sensors in several clusters, so that each cluster has a single cluster-head and several cluster- members. In each cluster, the cluster-members gather information on the sensed area and send it to the cluster-head. In turns, the cluster-head processes the data

© IFIP International Federation for Information Processing 2015
A. Amine et al. (Eds.): CIIA 2015, IFIP AICT 456, pp. 503–511, 2015.
DOI: 10.1007/978-3-319-19578-0_41

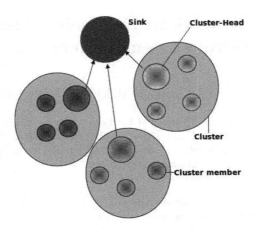

Fig. 1. Clustered WSN

received from its members and sends it to the sink. A graphical representation of a clustered WSN is shown in Fig. 1.

In a clustered WSN, data collected by the sensors is communicated to its cluster-head, for data processing and redundancy elimination. Therefore, sensors communicate data over short distances in each cluster (to cluster-heads), so that the energy spent in communication will be lower than that spent with sensors communicating directly to the sink [8].

Clustering can be static or dynamic. In a *static* scenario, the cluster-heads are fixed and tend to exhaust their energies rapidly, making this clustering unsuitable for WSNs [9]. In fact, the network becomes nonfunctional in the absence of cluster-heads. In the presence of *dynamic* clustering, the clusters change over the time, equalizing the energy consumption across all nodes and, thus, extending the network lifetime.

In this paper, our goal is to maximize network lifetime (defined as the time interval from the nodes' deployment to the instant at which a given percentage of deployed nodes die [6]) by minimizing the average energy consumption of all nodes. In order to do this, all nodes can be promoted to the role of cluster-heads. In order to reach this goal and guarantee full coverage (i.e., the clusters are spread over the entire network), we rely of on the use of a genetic algorithm (GA), which determines, in each cycle, wether or not a node can be chosen to play the role of a cluster-head.

2   Related Work

The idea of using clustering has been adopted by many authors. The linked clustering algorithm (LCA) was one of the first approaches [10]. In the LCA algorithm, each node has a unique ID. In this algorithm a node play the role of cluster-head if its ID is the highest one in its neighboring.

LEACH is the most popular clustering algorithm for WSNs [9]. LEACH allows a fixed percentage of nodes to become cluster-heads (namely, 5% of the nodes) and leads to the creation of clusters in a distributed way, with the nodes taking autonomous decisions. Each node decides to become a cluster-head with probability p. A node which does not become cluster-heads determines its cluster by choosing the nearest cluster-head. On average, LEACH provides low energy consumption and a uniform energy distribution among the nodes. However LEACH has also some drawbacks. Because of the probabilistic selection of the cluster-heads, a node with a very low energy can be selected as cluster-head. Moreover, since the selection of cluster-heads is probabilistic, the chosen cluster-heads may be placed in the same area, so that a good coverage can not be guaranteed: in fact, some nodes will be disconnected from the network (i.e., they will not attach to any cluster-head). Moreover, the use of a fixed percentage of cluster-heads may lead (network-wide) to higher energy consumption, as the number of cluster-heads depend on several factors, such as node spatial density [11].

EEHC is a randomized and distributed clustering algorithm, whose goal is to maximize the network lifetime [12]. This algorithm is executed in two levels. In the first level, denoted as "initial," volunteer nodes, which do not belong to any cluster, may decide to be cluster-heads with probability p and they announce their decisions to their neighbors. The nodes that do not receive an announcement, within a specified time interval t, become forced cluster-heads. In the second level, denoted as "extended," the clustering algorithm is recursively repeated to form hierarchical clustering, where new cluster-heads are selected from the already formed cluster-heads, until a final base station is reached.

In [13], the authors consider a GA and adapt, on the basis of software services, its parameters to determine the energy consumption and, therefore, extend the network lifetime. In [6], the authors proposed a GA-inspired routing protocol (GROUP): in particular, they use GA and simulated annealing (instead of the greedy chain) to select routing paths efficiently.

3   System Model

The conditions and assumptions behind the considered network model are compliant with those considered in [9] for LEACH. More precisely, they can be summarized as follows.

1. The base station is fixed, is not energy-constrained, and has a high computing capacity.
2. All the nodes deployed are energy/power-constrained and homogeneous.
3. The data processing power is very low with respect to the power required to transmit and receive data.

The nodes' radio communication specifications are set as in [9,4,6]. In particular, we assume that the radio module dissipates: $E_{elec} = 50$ nj/bit in transmission/receiver circuitry; and $\epsilon_{amp} = 100$ pJ/bit/m^2 in the transmitter amplifier.

Considering free space communications, in order to transmit a k-bit message over a distance d (dimension: [m]) a node consumes the following amount of energy:

$$E_{Tx}(k, d) = E_{elec} \times k + \epsilon_{amp} \times k \times d^2. \tag{1}$$

When receiving a k-bit message a node consumes the following amount of energy:

$$E_{Rx}(k) = E_{elec} \times k. \tag{2}$$

4   The Proposed Approach

4.1   The Problem

In a clustered WSN, if a few cluster-heads are used, then most of the nodes are likely to have a long transmit radio range to send the collected data to their cluster-heads and this tends to quickly deplete their batteries' energies. If a large number of cluster-heads is used, this leads mostly to a one-hop network (most nodes are cluster-heads and must reach the base station in one hop): this consumes also quickly the battery energy [4,8].

The best clustering strategy consists in optimizing (i) the number of cluster-heads and (ii) their positions. In particular, a node can be promoted to cluster-head according to several parameters: its residual energy, its distance to the sink, and the sum of the distances to its cluster-members. This suggests the use of GAs to find the optimal combination of these parameters.

4.2   The Proposed Algorithm

In this paper, we consider *dynamic* clustering, i.e., re-clustering is considered to avoid early death of cluster-heads. The proposed GA is executed at the sink (i.e., it is *centralized*), due to the needed computing capacity, and the obtained results (in terms of clustering configuration) are communicated to the nodes. At each re-clustering round, each node can then be either a cluster-head or a cluster-member. This centralized approach is expected to overcome the main limitations of LEACH, where the number of cluster-heads is fixed and their spatial distribution is arbitrary, i.e,, there is no coordination [9].

In order to use a GA, a WSN needs to be "codified." In particular, we use a binary representation, in which each node is represented either by 0 (if it is a cluster-member) or by 1 (if it is a cluster-head). Each codified network is called a "chromosome." A set of chromosomes is called a "generation."

The used GA is based on exploration and exploitation of the entire research space using an evolutionary strategy, it helps us to find an optimal combination of cluster-heads, cluster-members and their distributions in the monitoring area, among many combinations existing in the research space, making the energy consumption and the network coverage, optimal. Each potential solution is characterized by a value called fitness, which determines the optimality of solutions. In correspondence to a generation, the GA keeps the best chromosomes and drops others according to their fitness function. Each chromosome, in fact, represents a potential solution. The GA then applies the following genetic operators to generate new offsprings [14].

- *Selection.* The selection process is used to choose the best chromosomes from a generation. In our simulation, the roulette wheel algorithm is used to perform the selection.
- *Crossover.* To apply crossover, we choose arbitrary two chromosomes from a generation, we choose, also, two random positions in the chosen chromosomes and we used the two point crossover, to generate two new offsprings, that will belong to the next generation.
- *Mutation.* The mutation is used to avoid the super chromosome problem. It means if one chromosome is selected many times in the same generation, the crossover will not produce new chromosomes, since the parents are the same chromosome. Hence, the mutation is used to change, in each chromosome, an arbitrary bit. Several tentatives have been performed so to come up with the best-run GA parameters in terms of runtime and convergence. The best crossover and mutation probabilities are 0.75 and 0.2, respectively.

As mentioned above, each chromosome is then evaluated with a fitness function which attributes a higher chance to the best solutions to survive. The fitness of a candidate chromosome can be expressed as follows:

$$\text{Fitness} = f(NNN, NCH, DNCH, RECH) \tag{3}$$

where:

- NNN is the number of networked nodes;
- NCH is the number of cluster-heads;
- $DNCH$ is the sum of the distances between the cluster-members (CMs) and their cluster-heads (CHs), i.e.,

$$DNCH = \sum_{i \in \{\text{CHs}\}} \sum_{j \in \{\text{CMs}\}} \text{Distance}(\text{CH}_i, \text{CM}_j);$$

- $RECH$ is the sum of residual (cumulative) energy at the cluster-heads (dimension: [mW]), i.e.,

$$RECH = \sum_{i \in \{\text{CHs}\}} \text{Residual energy at the CH}_i.$$

In order to optimize the proposed clustering mechanism, we consider the following (heuristic) fitness function:

$$\text{Fitness} = (NNN)^{\alpha_1} + \left(\frac{NNN}{NCH}\right)^{\alpha_2}$$
$$+ (10^3 \cdot RECH)^{\alpha_3} + DNCH^{\alpha_4}$$

where: the exponential parameters $\{\alpha_i\}_{i=1}^4$ need to be properly optimized; the fraction NNN/NCH represents the average cluster dimension; the multiplicative term 10^3 used for $RECH$ properly weighs the energy dimension. By trial and error, the best fitness function (i.e., the best configuration of the exponents $\{\alpha_i\}_{i=1}^4$) turns out to be

$$\text{Fitness} = (NNN)^6 + \left(\frac{NNN}{NCH}\right)^5$$
$$+ (10^3 \cdot RECH)^2 + DNCH.$$

5   Performance Analysis

In order to validate the proposed clustering approach, we carry out a simulation-based performance analysis, considering different scenarios, by varying the node spatial density, the number of nodes, and the sink position. In each scenario, a given number of sensors is randomly deployed in a square monitored area, with side length 800×600. The sink, placed within the region, runs the GCDC algorithm (for Genetic Centralized Dynamic Clustering) and informs the sensors of the decided clustered configuration. After receiving the decision, each node knows if it is a CH or a cluster member. The GCDC algorithm is periodically run by the sink in order to avoid that a node death compromises network connectivity. We assume that all nodes have batteries with initial energy equal to 0.25 J. The dimension k of the messages to be transmitted is set to 100 bits. We assume that random "events" (e.g., acoustic signal detection, motion detection, etc.) happen in the monitored area: in particular, each random event is detected by its nearest neighbor, which needs to report this observation to the sink. In all considered scenarios, the performance of the GDC algorithm is compared with that of LEACH. Two values of the initial number of nodes in the WSN are considered: 100 (low node spatial density) and 1000 (high node spatial density).

In Figure 2, the residual network energy is shown as a function of the simulation time (expressed in event number), considering two values for the initial number of nodes: (a) 100 and (b) 1000. It can be observed that GCDC algorithm allows to save more energy than LEACH. The energy saving is not relevant at the beginning, whereas it becomes more significant as the time passes by. This is due to the fact that the GCDC algorithm updates the network clustered topology very efficiently. This behaviour is more pronounced in the scenario with 100 nodes (low node spatial density).

In Figure 3, we investigate the network connectivity evolution, considering (a) NNN (i.e., the network coverage) and (b) the number of dead nodes, as a function of the simulation time (in terms of event number). In both cases, the initial number of nodes in the WSN is set to 100 (low node spatial density). From the results in Figure 3 (a), it can be observed that the number of nodes connected (i.e., becoming cluster members or heads) by the GCDC algorithm is larger than that guaranteed by LEACH. This is more evident at the beginning of the simulation, when all nodes (having full battery energies) could be

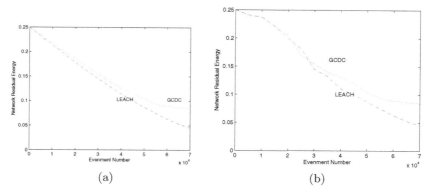

(a)   (b)

Fig. 2. Network residual energy as a function of the simulation time (in terms of event number). The initial number of nodes in the network is set to: (a) 100 or (b) 1000.

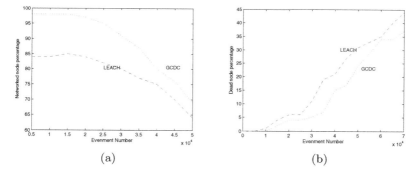

(a)   (b)

Fig. 3. Network connectivity evolution, in terms of (a) NNN and (b) number of dead nodes, as a function of the simulation time (in terms of event number). The initial number of nodes in the WSN is 100.

connected, whereas the improvement brought by GCDC reduces for advancing simulation time, as a larger and larger number of nodes die. The performance difference is due to the fact that LEACH *a priori* sets the number of CHs to 5% of the total number of nodes without identifying their positions: this likely leads to overlapped clusters (i.e., two CHs may be close to each other), leaving other nodes (without a sufficiently close CH) disconnected. The GCDC algorithm does not determine a priori the number of CHs but, rather, the GA determines the optimized number of CHs, along with their positions, to cover the entire monitored area efficiently. In Figure 3 (b), the number of dead nodes (after energy depletion) is shown: as expected from Figure 3 (a), the death rate with GCDC is lower than that with LEACH, owing to the clustering procedure which takes into account the nodes' residual energies.

In Figure 4, the network connectivity evolution, considering (a) NNN (i.e., the network coverage) and (b) the number of dead nodes as functions of the

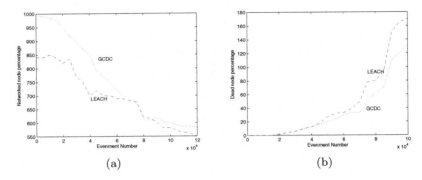

Fig. 4. Network connectivity evolution, in terms of (a) NNN and (b) number of dead nodes, as a function of the simulation time (in terms of event number). The initial number of nodes in the WSN is 1000.

simulation time (in terms of event number), is investigated in a scenario with 1000 initial nodes (high node spatial density). By comparing the results in Figure 4 (a) with those in Figure 3 (a), it can be concluded that the performance improvement, in terms of NNN, brought by GCDC is more pronounced in dense network. In particular, since, according to the results in Figure 4 (b), the death rates of GCDC and LEACH are approximately the same, it means that the GCDC is very efficient in reclustering the topology in order to guarantee a high level of connectivity to the surviving nodes.

6   Conclusion

In this paper, we have presented a novel clustering algorithm, denoted as GCDC, which uses a GA to optimize the number and the corresponding locations of CHs. The performance of our algorithm has been compared with that of LEACH. The obtained results show that the proposed clustering algorithm reduces the (network-wide) energy depletion rate and guarantees a better network coverage. An interesting research direction consists in applying the proposed GA-based clustering algorithm to duty-cycled WSNs.

References

1. Huafeng, W., et al.: An acoa-afsa fusion routing algorithm for underwater wireless sensor network. International Journal of Distributed Sensor Networks, 4110–4118 (2012)
2. Ilyas, M., Mahgoub, I.: Handbook of Sensor Networks: Compact Wireless and Wired Sensing Systems. CRC Press LCC (2012)
3. Jianbin, X., Ting, Z., Yan, Y., Wenhua, W., Songbai, L.: Cooperation-based ant-colony algorithm in wsn. Journal of Networks 8(4) (2013)

4. Mekkaoui, K., Rahmoun, A.: Short-hops vs. long-hops - energy efficiency analysis in wireless sensor networks. In: CIIA 2011:Proceedings of the Third International Conference on Computer Science and its Applications (CIIA11), University of Saida, Algeria, pp. 13–15 (2011)
5. Akyildiz, I.F., Vuran, M.C.: Wireless Sensor Networks, Jon S.Wilson
6. Chakraborty, A., Mitra, S.K., Naskar, M.K.: A genetic algorithm inspired routing protocol for wireless sensor networks. International Journal of Computational Intelligence Theory and Practice 6(1) (2011)
7. Odey, A.J., Li, D.: Low power transceiver design parameters for wireless sensor networks. Wireless Sensor Network 4(10), 243–249 (2012)
8. Abbasi, A.A., Younis, M.: A survey on clustering algorithms for wireless sensor networks. Computer Communications 30(14), 2826–2841 (2007)
9. Heinzelman, W.R., Chandrakasan, A., Balakrishnan, H.: Energy efficient communication protocol for wireless microsensor networks. In: Proceedings of the 33rd Hawaii International Conference on System Sciences, HICSS 2000, p. 8020. IEEE Computer Society, Washington, DC (2000)
10. Dechene, D.J., Jardali, A.E., Luccini, M., Sauer, A.: Wireless sensor networks a survey of clustering algorithms for wireless sensor networks, Department of Electrical and Computer Engineering, The University of Western Ontario, Canada, Tech. Rep (2006)
11. Jin, S., Zhou, M., Wu, A.S.: Sensor network optimization using agenetic algorithm. In: Proceedings of the 7th World Multiconference on Systemics, Cybernetics, and Informatics, Orlando, FL, pp. 109–116 (2003)
12. Bandyopadhyay, S., Coyle, E.J.: An energy efficient hierarchical clustering algorithm for wireless sensor networks. In: Twenty-Second Annual Joint Conference of the IEEE Computer and Communications, INFOCOM 2003, pp. 1713–1723 (2003)
13. Norouzi, A., Babamir, F.S., Zaim, A.H.: 'A New Clustering Protocol for Wireless Sensor Networks Using Genetic Algorithm Approach. Wireless Sensor Network 3(11), 362–370 (2011)
14. Holland, J.H.: Genetic algorithms. Scientific American 267(1), 66–72 (1992)

Security and Network Technologies: Potpourri

Region-Edge Cooperation for Image Segmentation Using Game Theory

Omar Boudraa$^{(\boxtimes)}$ and Karima Benatchba

Doctoral School (STIC), High School of Computer Sciences (ESI),
Oued Smar, Algiers, Algeria
{o_boudraa,k_benatchba}@esi.dz

Abstract. Image segmentation is a central problem in image analysis. It consists of extracting objects from an image and separating between the background and the regions of interest. In the literature, there are mainly two dual approaches, namely the region-based segmentation and the edge-based segmentation. In this article, we propose to take advantage of Game theory in image segmentation by results fusion. Thus, the presented game is cooperative in a way that both players represented by the two segmentation modules (region-based and edge-based) try coalitionary to enhance the value of a common characteristic function. This is a variant of the parallel decision-making procedure based on Game theory proposed by Chakraborty and Duncan [1]. The involved pixels are those generated from the cooperation by results fusion between the edge detector (Active contour) and the region detector (Region growing) posing a decision-making problem. Adding or removing a pixel (to/from) the region of interest depends strongly on the value of the characteristic function. Then, and to study the effectiveness and noise robustness of our approach we proposed to generalize our experimentations, by applying this technique on a variety of images of different types taken mainly from two known test databases.

Keywords: Region-based segmentation · Edge-based segmentation · Region-edge cooperation · Game theory · Nash equilibrium

1 Introduction

Image segmentation plays a key role in image analysis. In addition, it determines the quality of characteristics measures calculated later in image understanding process. However, there are mainly two dual approaches of segmentation. The edge-based segmentation approach that locates the boundaries of objects; and the region-based segmentation approach which partitions the image into a set of regions. Each region defines one or more connected objects.

In order to improve the results of each approach by trying to combine their own advantages, researchers have created what is called cooperative segmentation [2].

Game theory is a strong tool for analyzing situations, modeling and determining the best strategy(ies), often used in Economics and in a variety of domains. This theory proves interesting in this case given the principle of duality region-edge and the problem of antagonism between the two image segmentation approaches.

© IFIP International Federation for Information Processing 2015
A. Amine et al. (Eds.): CIIA 2015, IFIP AICT 456, pp. 515–526, 2015.
DOI: 10.1007/978-3-319-19578-0_42

In our contribution, we propose to take advantage of Game theory in image segmentation by results fusion. It is to treat both types of segmentation, in a coalitionary way as two players exchanging information in *"Game Theory Integrator"* module to simultaneously improve their individual results.

This article consists of three sections. The first section presents general information on individual and cooperative techniques of image segmentation, its different forms and a bibliographical study on the integration of Game theory in image segmentation and its contribution. The second section details our contribution. While, the last section is devoted to experimentations, results and evaluation of the performance of our approach and its robustness to noise.

2   Around Image Segmentation and Game Theory

2.1   Image Segmentation

Segmentation is the partition of an image into a set of distinct regions (which do not overlap) and whose union is the whole image [3].

2.2   Image Segmentation Approaches

Image segmentation methods can be divided essentially into two categories which are based on two properties between neighboring pixels: *discontinuity* and *similarity*. The *discontinuity* is used by edge-based segmentation approach (boundary), while the *similarity* of pixels is used by region-based segmentation approach.

Edge Approach
The edge approach tries to identify changes between regions. In general, an edge element is a point of the image belonging to the boundary between two or more objects having different grayscale levels.

Derivate methods
The derivate methods are most used to detect the pixels intensity transitions [4]. Overall, they can be classified into two big categories: *Gradient* approach that uses the first derivative and *Laplacian* approach that uses the second derivative.

Deformable models
Segmentation algorithms based on deformable models have the advantage, compared to derivate methods that provide closed edges or surfaces [5]. These methods include: *Active contours* and *Level sets*.

Limitations of the edge-based segmentation
Edge-based segmentation has some limitations and drawbacks such as the difficulty of identification and classification of parasite edges. In addition, the detected edges are not always closed. Nevertheless, the major weakness is that the edge-based segmentation does not give comprehensive information on the content of the image [6].

Region Approach

This approach consists in dividing the image into distinct regions [7]. In contrast to the edge approach, there methods are interested in the region content. The most common techniques for region-based segmentation are shown in the following.

Region growing

Region growing technique is based primarily on the notion of seed. A seed is one pixel or set of pixels (region). From it, regions are constructed by aggregation of adjacent and homogeneous pixels (grayscale, color similarity...etc.) [7]. The Region growing process stops when all pixels have been processed (assigned to a region).

This technique is simple and quick to perform. In addition, it allows the object segmentation in complex topology [8]. Whereas, the choice of initial germs and homogeneity criterion is critical.

Region Splitting

Region splitting technique involves image partitioning into homogeneous regions according to a given criterion. Its principle is to consider the image as the initial region, which then is divided into regions. The splitting process is repeated for each new region until homogeneous regions [9]. Its drawback is the *over-segmentation*.

Region Merging

Region merging technique is a bottom-up method. Initially, each image pixel is considered as an elementary region. The method tents gradually to merge the related regions that satisfy a given predicate P [9].The process is repeated until the satisfaction of a stopping criterion (usually the visiting of the entire image) [10]. However, this method can introduce the *sub-segmentation* effect.

Region Splitting and Merging

It is a hybrid method, in which, a splitting step is performed first. Its result is injected to the second process (merging similar regions) that corrects the possible effect of over-segmentation introduced by the splitting process.

Limitation of region-based segmentation

Region-based segmentation has some disadvantages that we present below:

- The obtained regions do not always correspond to the objects in the image.
- The limits of the obtained regions are generally imprecise.
- The difficulty of identifying criteria for pixels aggregation or regions division.

Cooperative Approach

As we have seen previously, the region and the edge approaches have both advantages and disadvantages. Researchers have tried to take benefits from the strengths of both approaches and duality concepts between them and gave rise to what is called the cooperative segmentation. It combines the advantages of both solutions: *precision* and *speed* of edge-based segmentation, *boundary closures* and *density* of the extracted information of region-based segmentation [2].

Depending how to cooperate the both processes, the researchers proposed three different approaches: *Sequential cooperation, fusion results cooperation* and *mutual cooperation*.

Sequential cooperation
The general principle of the sequential cooperation is one of the individual techniques is executed first. Its result is then exploited by the second technique [11].

Fusion results cooperation
In fusion results cooperation, region-based and edge-based segmentation are executed in parallel and independently. Cooperation takes place at their respective results.

Mutual cooperation
In mutual cooperation approach, different segmentation techniques are executed in parallel while mutually exchanging information.

2.3   About Game Theory

Game theory is a formalism that aims to study the *planned, real* or *posteriori* justified behavior of agents deal with situations of *antagonism* (opposition), and seek to highlight *optimal* strategies [12]. It is based on the concept of game defined by a set of players (considered as rational agents), all the possible strategies for each player, and the gains specification of players for each combination of strategies [13].

Types of Games
The most popular types of games are:

- *Cooperative and non-cooperative games.*
- *Finite and infinite games.*
- *Synchronous and asynchronous games.*
- *Zero-sum games and non-zero-sum games.*
- *Complete information games and perfect information games.*

Nash Equilibrium
In 1950, *John Nash* has defined a stable interaction situation if no player has interest to change its strategy knowing strategies of others. The game becomes stable that no player can only change its strategy without weakening his own position [14].

Theoretically, it is said that a combination of strategies $s*$ is a Nash equilibrium if the following inequality is satisfied for each player i [14].

$$u_i(s_i^*, s_{-i}^*) \geq u_i(s_i, s_{-i}^*). \forall\, s_i \in S_i \tag{1}$$

More Clearly, if player i anticipates that the other players will choose the strategies associated with the combination of strategies s_{-i}^*, it can only maximize its gain u by choosing the strategy s_i^*.

2.4   Image Segmentation and Game Theory

Works on the matching between Game theory and image segmentation are not numerous. One possible reason is that Game theory is based primarily to satisfy economic needs. Whereas, the first published work is that of A. CHAKRABORTY et al. in 1999 [15, 1]. In this section, we will quote it with other work in this domain.

- Work of (A. CHAKRABORTY et al. in 1999) is an original and outstanding work that is based on a solid mathematical model integrating Game theory in image segmentation by mutual cooperation between the edge detector (Active contour) and the region detector (Markov Random Fields). It represents a reference work.
- (E. Cassel et al. in 2007) proposed a modified and simplified implementation of Chakraborty and Duncan approach [1]. This simplification involves removing the "Prior information about the form to segment" in the equation of the edge detector. The authors in [16] opted for the "Region growing" as region detector and the morphological operation "closure" for the edge detector.
- Even, (K. ROY et al. in 2010) have proposed an approach to iris and pupil segmentation based on Chakraborty and Duncan work [1]. However, this approach is suitable particularly on this special field of application. For this, they integrated pre-treatments and post-treatments phases in their procedure. In this work, the "Region growing" and "Level sets" methods were used. [17]
- The last two works consist of two individual segmentation approaches (edge-based segmentation only). (B. IBRAGIMOV et al. in 2011) proposed a supervised algorithm based on Game theory and dynamic programming for the segmentation of lung fields [18], while (M. KALLEL et al. in 2013) proposed an approach based on Game theory to restore and segment simultaneously noisy images [19].

3   Cooperative Segmentation Approach Using Game Theory

Now, we present our approach. We propose segmentation by results fusion, suggesting a cooperative game where both players, represented by the two segmentation modules, try coalitionary to improve the value of a common characteristic function. This is mainly based on the work done by Chakraborty and Duncan [1]. This choice is based on the fact that their procedure is original, robust and has been proven mathematically. Indeed, Cassel et al [16] and Roy et al [17] works gives us the opportunity to suggest improvements and changes in the cost functions of this procedure.

3.1   Game Formulation

Now, we define our game and detail its constituting elements, its type and nature.

Game Components
Following Chakraborty and Duncan procedure [1], the objective functions are:
For the *region-based segmentation module* (player 1),

$$F^1(p^1, p^2) = min_x \left[\Sigma_{i,j}[y_{i,j} - x_{i,j}]^2 + \lambda^2 \left(\Sigma_{i,j}(x_{i,j} - x_{i-1,j})^2 + \Sigma_{i,j}(x_{i,j} - x_{i,j+1})^2 \right) \right] + á \left[\Sigma_{(i,j) \in A_p}(x_{i,j} - u)^2 + \Sigma_{(i,j) \in \overline{A_p}}(x_{i,j} - v)^2 \right].$$
(2)

Where:

— $A_{\vec{p}}$ Corresponds to the set of points which lie inside the contour vector $\vec{p}$, while $\overline{A_{\vec{p}}}$ correspond to the points that lie outside it. Thus, $A_{\vec{p}} \cup \overline{A_{\vec{p}}} = \{(i,j) ; 1 \leq i \leq M, 1 \leq j \leq N\}$ = Whole image.

— $u_{i,j}$ represents the information concerning the intensities of points inside the contour and $v_{i,j}$ for points outside.

Also, y is the intensity of the original image, x is the segmented image provided by p^1, u and v corresponds to the intensity mean value of the image on the inside (outside respectively) of the contour given by p^2. The first term attempts to minimize the difference between the values of the pixels intensities found in the region and to strengthen continuity. Whereas, the second term is trying to match between the region and the detected contour.

Whereas, the objective function of player 2 (*edge-based segmentation module*) is:

$$F^2(p^1, p^2) = arg \; max_{\vec{p}}[M_{gradient}(I_g, \vec{p}) + \hat{a}M_{region}(I_r, \vec{p})]$$
(3)

Where $\vec{p}$ denotes the contour parameterization proposed by p^2, I_g is the gradient image, and I_r is the segmented region obtained by p^1. $M_{gradient}$ represents a correspondence measure (matching) between the gradient image I_g and the detected contour. While, M_{region} is a matching measure between the segmented region image I_r and the contour vector $\vec{p}$, β is its weight.

In our approach, we propose a new formula simplifying function F^2 by replacing:

• $M_{gradient}$ and M_{region} by Abdou and Pratt measure [4].
• Contour parameterization $\vec{p}$ by the constituent pixels of the Active contour.
• The gradient image I_g by *Canny* detector.
• The image of the segmented region I_r only by its boundary.

Finally, we proposed to unify the two cost functions above in one function F:

$$F = \frac{F_{i-1}^1(p^1,p^2) - F_i^1(p^1,p^2)}{F_{i-1}^1(p^1,p^2)} + \frac{F_i^2(p^1,p^2) - F_{i-1}^2(p^1,p^2)}{F_{i-1}^2(p^1,p^2)}$$
(4)

Adding or removing a pixel (to/from) the region of interest depends strongly on the improvement or deterioration of this function value. F_i^1 and F_i^2 represent the cost functions of the two segmentation modules, the index i determines whether the pixel i is taken into account or not (i-1 for no and i for yes).

Not only it takes into account the two cost functions, it also helps to normalize the rate of improvement or deterioration of each function because the variation of the function F^1 is almost always greater than those of F^2 as both are not commensurable.

Game Type

By inference, the proposed game is a: *Finite*, *Cooperative* and *Non-zero-sum* game.

3.2   Architecture of the Adopted Approach

We can summarize the organization of our system through a series of interactive modules for segmentation of an image. Each one is presented in the following:

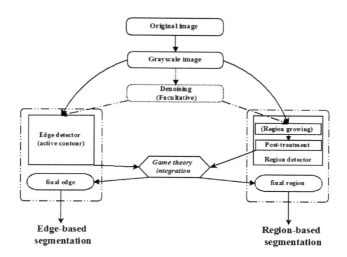

Table 1. Fig. **1.** Overview of the proposed system

Grayscale Conversion
This pretreatment is designed to simplify the image which makes easier the application of our procedures and comparisons; by reducing the amount of information.

Denoising
It consists of an optional treatment, serving to smooth the image (blur effect), reduces noise (unwanted signals) and reduces detail in order to improve the image quality.

Region Detector
As a region detector module, we opted for the Region growing technique. The growing is through the aggregation of candidates' pixels similar to the initial germ of the region, while seeking to minimize the following cost function [16]:

$$E = \sum_{i,j}(y_{i,j} - x_{i,j})^2 + \ddot{e}^2 \left(\sum_{i,j} \sum_{i_s,j_s}(x_{i,j} - x_{i_s,j_s})^2 \right) \tag{5}$$

Where i_s and j_s are the pixel neighborhood of the indices $x_{i,j}$ (in the classification image). The classification image (or segmentation) is initialized by the pixel intensity values in the image processed by the famous Otsu's thresholding technique [20]. That is applied to the grayscale image in order to overcome the problem of non-initialization of neighboring pixels that's not yet been processed.

In our case, and in order to reduce the number of calculations, we proposed at each iteration an estimation of the formula (5). We apply it only on the current pixel and its neighbors while following a *4-connected* neighborhood scheme.

Post-treatment
In order to improve the detected region, any obtained agglomeration (non-significant small regions, holes and parasite pixels) that are located entirely within the region of interest are filled and aggregated to the pixels of the region.

Edge Detector
As edge detector, we have focused our choice on "Active contour" method. This choice is based on the fact that Active contours are closed and one-pixel thickness (i.e., they do not require post-treatments). However, we can remedy it major problem (not detecting of concave shapes) in the phase of Game theory integration.

In our implementation, thresholding image generated by the Otsu method [20] constitutes the input of the edge detector module. This Active contour is designed to fit the region in which the initial seed belongs.

Game Theory Integration
After running the two detectors for a sufficient number of iterations, Game theory can take place in order to improve the results of the two detectors cooperatively.

The involved pixels are those generated through the cooperation by results fusion between the edge and region detectors posing a decision-making problem. Thus, we first address the list of pixels located inside the Active contour and which does not belong to the region of interest (considering first the nearest pixel to the region of interest) (see Fig. 2). At the end of each iteration, an update of the region and the edge configurations is made.

Adding or removing a pixel to the region of interest is highly depending of the improvement or deterioration of the function value defined in formula (4).

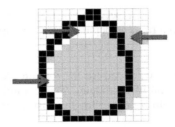

Fig. 1. Preliminary results and places where Game theory will be applied

4   Experimental Results

In this section, a summary of the tests and the obtained results is presented to demonstrate the effectiveness of our region-edge cooperation approach, we test it on a variety of different-kinds images (synthetic, real and medical: sane and added noise) from two known images databases ([21], [22] and a set of MRI-type medical images found on the Internet). Also, we compare the individual approach results (Region growing only) to those of the proposed cooperative approach.

To evaluate the segmentation results, We will use the following methodology. First, we start our tests on the proposed approach by fixing a few parameters and varying the other, in a guided and judicious manner. This allows us to adjust the parameters of the various modules and study their impact on segmentation quality. Then, we test our cooperative approach to all the images of the three benchmarks, while determining for each image the region of interest to extract.

Obtained results are therefor compared and evaluated using the following criterion:

— **Borsotti criterion:** Uniformity and contrast. 0 nearest value represents best result.
— **Zeboudj criterion:** Contrast intra-inter region. 1 nearest value represents best result.

The comparison is done using the criteria mean values.

After testing our cooperative approach to sane images (net), and to discuss its robustness to noise, we propose to evaluate the same image after adding artificial noise.

Fig. 3 shows the results of the individual methods implementation (Active contour and Region growing) and the proposed cooperative approach on a real image from the BCU database [22]. Visual analysis of this figure shows that the cooperative segmentation using Game theory improves in parallel manner the results therefor obtained by correcting lacunas generated by the individual methods, namely the poor detection of concave regions in the Active contours and excess pixels presented in the result of segmentation by Region growing technique.

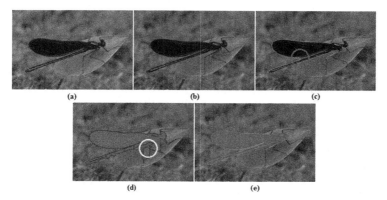

Fig. 2. Segmentation results of individual and cooperative approaches applied to a real image issued from the BCU database [22] (a) Original image (b) Grayscale image (c) Active Contour (d) Region growing (e) Image segmentation by region-edge cooperation using Game theory

4.1 Tests Results on Sane Images

The analysis of the registered segmentations results in terms of *Borsotti* and *Zeboudj* global mean values, allows us to go out with the following consequences:

1. As shown in the histogram of Fig. 4, the mean value of *Borsotti* criterion remains good and more or less stable for the set of all images used in the tests in the case of individual segmentation (Region growing) and the case of the integration of Game theory in the image cooperative segmentation.
2. Whereas, we observe an improvement in *Zeboudj* criterion in the second compared to the first which shows the effectiveness of the approach and the contribution of Game theory in image segmentation field.

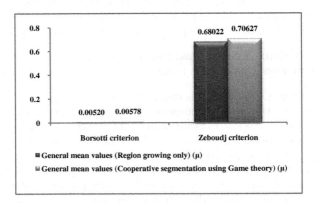

Fig. 3. General means values of Borsotti and Zeboudj criteria (without and with) integration of Game theory

4.2   Tests Results on Noisy Images

In this section we perform the operation of adding noise to three test images of different natures (Image (a) (synthetic), Image (b) (real) and Image (c) (medical)) while varying the percentage of added noise from 5% to 25%, which is randomly distributed over the whole of each of these images. Knowing that a percentage of 25% means that half of the image corresponds to noise (25% of pepper type and 25% of salt type); this represents a high rate of parasites pixels. The results obtained are illustrated in Fig.5.

Qualitative visual comparison between the original image and the segmented images produced by this technique shows that:

1. The degree of robustness to noise differs from one image to another; the synthetic and medical images have both a good robustness against noise varying from 5% to 25%, in which the quality of regions of interest segmentation is inversely proportional to the percentage of noise.
2. The real image segmentation result is good for percentages of 5% and 10% of added noise. However, it becomes very bad (invalid) from 15% of added noise.
3. Areas affected by the deterioration are often the borders rather than the interior of the region of interest (it is clearly visualized in the images (b) and (c)).
4. Generally, the qualities of the segmentation results provided by our approach applied to all three test images are reliable for a percentage of noise strictly less to 15%. This proves the robustness of the implemented procedure to the added noise.

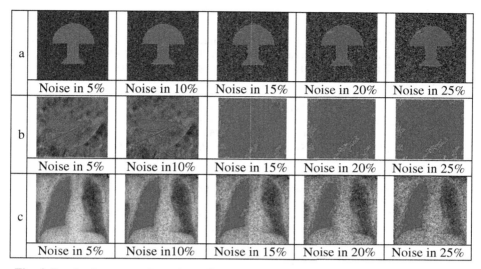

Fig. 4. Result of segmentation using a Game theory-based approach applied to different images after adding the salt and pepper noise (a) Synthetic image, (b) Real image, (c) Medical image

5   Conclusion and Discussions

In this article, we studied the possibility of Game theory integrating in image segmentation by region-edge cooperation. Indeed, we proposed a modified and simplified version of the parallel decision-making procedure as described in the work of Chacraborty and Duncan [1]. Whereas, the proposed modification helps to make the game cooperative, so that both players try coalitionary to improve the value of a common characteristic function within a framework of segmentation by results fusion.

Provided performance indices either digital or visual showed its effectiveness and its robustness to poor conditions of the input image (specifically image noise problem). Nevertheless, our method has had some inconveniences to running as:

- Results are depending on optimizing of parameters number, which is relatively big.
- Calculation time is sometimes very high estimated at a few hours.
- Procedure and by its nature can detect a single region of interest at a time.

Many prospects may be cited, for any enrichment of our study. Among them:
- Improvements of the detection procedure for all the regions of the image.
- Proposing of other gaming models, such as the players are pixels or image objects.
- Proposing image segmentation by mutual cooperation.
- Find an automatic parameters adjustment to the input image characteristics.

References

1. Chakraborty, A., Duncan, J.S.: Game-theoretic integration for image segmentation. IEEE Transaction on Pattern Analysis and Machine Intelligence, 12–30 (1999)
2. Bonnin, P., Zavidovique, B.: La segmentation coopérative: comment combiner détection de contours et croissance de régions? In: 14th Symposium Gresti Juan Les Pins (1993)
3. Haralick, R.M., Shapiro, L.G.: Image Segmentation techniques. Computer Vision Graphics Image Processing 29, 100–132 (1985)
4. Abdou, I.E., Pratt, W.K.: Quantitative design and evaluation of enhancement/thresholding edge detectors. Proceedings of the IEEE 67(5), 753–763 (1979)
5. Semchedine, M., Toumi, L.: Système Coopératif de Classification Floue Possibiliste avec Rejet d'Ambiguïté: Application à la segmentation d'images IRM. In: International Conference on Computer Integrated Manufacturing CIP (2007)
6. Acharya, T.A.: Image Processing, Principles and Applications: chapitre 7. A Wiley-Interscience Publication (2005)
7. Kornpobst, P.: Segmentation de régions, Odyssée Project. INRIA (1996)
8. Meliani, M.: Segmentation d'Image par Coopération Régions-Contours. Schoolmaster memory at National School of Computer Sciences, Algiers (2012)
9. Baillie, J.C.: Cours de Segmentation Module D9: traitement d'images et vision artificielle. ENSA (2003)
10. Maître, H.: Le traitement des images. Hermès, Traité IC2, Paris, France (2003)
11. Sebari, I., Dong-Chen, H.: Les approches de segmentation d'image par coopération région-contour. Revue Télédétection 7(1-2-3-4), 499–506 (2007)
12. Techno-Science.net.: Théorie des jeux : définition et explications, http://www.techno-science.net/?onglet=glossaire&definition=6426 (consulted on July 28, 2012)
13. Chaib-draa, B.: Chapitre 1 : Introduction à la Théorie des Jeux. Laval University, Computer Science & Software Engineering (CSSE) Department, Canada (2008), http://www.damas.ift.ulaval.ca/~coursMAS/ComplementsH10/Intro-TJ.pdf
14. Techno-Science.net.: Équilibre de Nash: définition et explications , http://www.techno-science.net/?onglet=glossaire&definition=6491
15. (consulted on July 28, 2012)
16. Chakraborty, A., Duncan, J.S.: Integration of boundary finding and region-based segmentation using game theory. In: XIVth International Conference on Information Processing in Medical Imaging, pp. 189–200 (1995)
17. Cassell, E., Kolar, S., Yakushev, A.: Using Game Theory for Image Segmentation (2007), http://www.angelfire.com/electronic2/cacho/machine-vision/ImSeg.pdf
18. Roy, K., Suen Ching, Y., Bhattacharya, P.: Segmentation of Unideal Iris Images Using Game Theory. In: ICPR 2010, pp. 2844-2847 (2010)
19. Ibragimov, B., Vrtovec, T., Likar, B., Pernus, F.: Segmentation of lung fields by game theory and dynamic programming. In: 4th International Workshop on Pulmonary Image Analysis - PIA 2011, Toronto, ON, Canada, September 18, pp. 101–111 (2011)
20. Kallel, M., Aboulaich, R., Habbal, A., Moakher, M.: A Nash-game approach to joint image restoration and segmentation. Applied Mathematical Modelling (2013), http://hal.inria.fr/hal-00648708
21. Otsu, N.: A threshold selection method from grey-level histograms. IEEE Transactions on Systems, Man, and Cybernetics SMC-9(1), 62–66 (1979)
22. BSDS500. Real images database found in, http://www.eecs.berkeley.edu/Research/Projects/CS/vision/grouping/BSR/BSR_bsds500.tgz (consulted on May 26, 2014)
23. Synthetic, B.: images database found in, http://pages.upf.pf/Sebastien.Chabrier/download/ImSynth.zip (consulted on May 27, 2014)

Improved Parameters Updating Algorithm for the Detection of Moving Objects

Brahim Farou[1,2(✉)], Hamid Seridi[2], and Herman Akdag[3]

[1] Computer Science Department, Badji Mokhtar-Annaba University, P.O.B 12, 23000 Annaba, Algeria
farou@ymail.com
[2] LabSTIC, Guelma University, POB 401, 24000 Guelma, Algeria
seridihamid@yahoo.fr
[3] LIASD, Paris 8 University, 93526 Saint-Denis, France
Herman.akdag@ai.univ-paris8.fr

Abstract. The presence of dynamic scene is a challenging problem in video surveillance systems tasks. Mixture of Gaussian (MOG) is the most appropriate method to model dynamic background. However, local variations and the instant variations in the brightness decrease the performance of the later. We present in this paper a novel and efficient method that will significantly reduce MOG drawbacks by an improved parameters updating algorithm. Starting from a normalization step, we divide each extracted frame into several blocks. Then, we apply an improved updating algorithm for each block to control local variation. When a significant environment changes are detected in one or more blocs, the parameters of MOG assigned to these blocks are updated and the parameters of the rest remain the same. Experimental results demonstrate that the proposed approach is effective and efficient compared with state-of-the-art background subtraction methods.

Keywords: Background subtraction · Motion detection · MOG · Machine vision · Videosurveillance

1 Introduction

The detection of moving object is the key step in many computer vision applications such as video surveillance, control applications, human machine interaction, and motion analysis. The challenge in such systems is to achieve high sensitivity in the detection of moving objects while maintaining a good discrimination rates and low processing time. The intrinsic nature of environment with illumination changes, shadows, waving flags, dust, bootstrapping and ghosts make tasks even more difficult. Recently, important efforts in this field have been focused on developing theories, methods and systems to deal with this problems and the most widely adopted techniques for handling these issues are optical flow, frame differencing and background subtraction. Background subtraction process is usually used with the assumption that the im-ages extracted form

© IFIP International Federation for Information Processing 2015
A. Amine et al. (Eds.): CIIA 2015, IFIP AICT 456, pp. 527–537, 2015.
DOI: 10.1007/978-3-319-19578-0_43

video without any additional objects follow a fixed behavior and can be well described by a statistical model. In this case, the appearance of a new object in background will make this part inappropriate with the building model. The main idea in such approach is to model each pixel separately by a probability density function. Works done in [31] showed that GMM provides a good compromise between quality and execution time compared to other methods. The first use of GMM for modeling the background was proposed by Friedman and Russell [11].However Stauffer and Grimson [26] proposed the standard algorithm with an efficient update equations. Some extensions are given by [20,12,14] to improve the model adaptation speed. Other GMM algorithms were also proposed [27,34] to remove GMM drawback. Unfortunately, local variations and instant changes in brightness remains the major problem of GMM [33,13]. In the last decade, several studies have attempted to improve the performance of GMM in environments with multiple dimming and high condensation background. Initial ideas focused on substitution of using color characteristics [2] Setiawan et al. [24]or infrared camera [23]. Hybrid models such as GMM and K-means [3], GMM and fuzzy logic [1], Markov Random Fields [22],GMM and adaptive background [9,25], have been proposed to overcome GMM drawbacks. Other works have focused on improving the learning speed [15,28] through an adaptive learning rate [29], Better settings White and Shah [32] and the execution time [17] by using real parallel operations on multi-processor machines. Other systems use two backgrounds [4] to solve the problem of change in brightness between day and night or use Multi-level approaches [5,6,7]. Despite many algorithms have been pro-posed in the literature, the detection of moving objects in complex and dynamic environments is still far from being completely solved. In this paper, we will focus on the detection of moving objects in video surveillance through a fixed camera. To overcome the problems mentioned before, we propose a new and efficient background subtraction method based on GMM and local background monitoring. To cover all sections, the rest of the paper is organized as follows. The Preprocessing task is presented in Section 2. Section 3 is devoted to the similarity measurement. The background subtraction method and the proposed algorithm is presented in section 4 and section 6. We present in section 5 a local monitoring method used to update the MOG parameters. Results and discussion are presented in Section 6. Section 7 concludes the paper.

2 Preprocessing

The objective of the preprocessing task is to make the images more appropriate to apply algorithms in any system component allowing improvement in the success rates. In this phase, we start by transforming the captured video into a set of images. Then, we apply median filter to remove noise from the image. The extracted images from the video is done in the RGB color space, but this representation is not adequate because of the influence of light on the description of objects [28]. For this reason, we made a transfer to HSL model recognized to be one of the closest model of human perception and it provides a direct control of chromaticity. The following are supplementary preprocessing techniques applied in our system.

2.1 Histogram Equalization

Histogram Equalization is an illumination normalization technique that uses the distribution of the original image to generate an image with uniform histogram. The objective of histogram equalization is to minimize the contrast in areas that are too light or too dark for an image.

2.2 Contour Detection

Contour correspond to the local variations in the intensity of the image pixel values. It is applied to preserve local features despite the influence of brightness. There are numerous contour detection techniques, but the context of real time processing lead to use a fast contour detection algorithm with inherent smoothing properties that can be adapted to different conditions of noise and artifacts. We used Soblel filter reported to be the best filter under real time consideration.

2.3 Splitting

This operation is only used in the initialization step. We divide the first frame into N equal size blocks to minimize local variations and to simplify the monitoring task. We noticed that the number of areas greatly influences on system quality. A large number of areas lead us to the starting point (pixel-based approach). In case where the number of areas is small (the size of the area is large), local variations accumulated in the same area force the system to consider the latter as an intense variation. In this way, all pixels belonging to the area will be updated. However, the number of blocks may change in processing time to improve system performance.

3   Similarity Measurement

The similarity between two sequences of measurement is a measure that quantifies the dependency between them. The use of similarity measure requires solving three major problems. The first one is to find the saved image that best matches the observed image. The second problem involves locating an object of interest in an observed image. The last one is the presence of rotational and scaling differences between the stored and observed image. In our case, the two first problems are similar and resolved by using contour detection algorithm. Indeed, the original image is divided into a set of blocks and the similarity is applied, not to detect any type of object, but to measure the blocks dependence at the same position between the reference image and the observed image. The use of a binary image containing only contours, reduces the brightness change effect since the contours are invariant to the latter. The third problem is not probable since the camera is static and it has no zoom effect. Various similarity measures have been proposed in the literature. However, each measure has its own strengths and weaknesses and a measure that performs well on one type of images may not work on another types. In this paper we use Pearsons correlation coefficient which is reported in the literature as the best similarity measure on various image types.

4   Mixture of Gaussians

MoG is a statistical model that assumes the data where originates from a weighted sum of several Gaussian distributions. Stauffer and Grimson [26] presented an adaptive GMM method to model a dynamic background in image sequences. If K Gaussian distributions are used to describe the history of a pixel, the observation of the given pixel will be in one of the K states at one time [3]. K determines the multimodality of the background and the selection of K is generally based on the available memory and computing power. Stauffer and Grimson [26] proposed to set K from 3 to 5. First, each pixel is characterized by its intensity in the HSL color space. Then, the probability of observing the current pixel value is given by the following equation in the multidimensional case:

$$P(P_t) = \sum_{i=1}^{k} w_{i,t} \cdot \eta(P_t, \mu_{i,t}, \Sigma_{i,t}) \tag{1}$$

Where: k is the number of associated Gaussians to each pixel, $w_{i,t}$ is the calculated weight, $\mu_{i,t}$ is the mean and $\Sigma_{i,t}$ is the covariance matrix that are respectively evaluated for the ith Gaussian at time t. η is a Gaussian probability density function:

$$\eta(P_t, \mu, \Sigma) = \frac{1}{2\pi^{\frac{n}{2}} |\Sigma|^{\frac{1}{2}}} \exp^{\frac{1}{2}(P_t - \mu)\Sigma^{-1}(P_t - \mu)} \tag{2}$$

For real time consideration, the update of the model is carried out by using an online K-Means approximation algorithm [3], [8]. After the parameters initialization, a first foreground detection can be made and the parameters are updated. When the new frame incomes, each pixel value is checked through the existing k Gaussian distributions, until a match is found. A pixel matched a Gaussian distribution if the pixel value is within 2.5 standard deviations of distribution according to Eq. 3.

$$\frac{|P_t - \mu_i|}{\sigma_i} < 2.5 \tag{3}$$

When a match is found with one of the k Gaussian, we look for the Gaussian distribution classification. If the Gaussian distribution is identified as a background, the pixel is classified as background. Otherwise, the pixel is classified as foreground. The prior weights of the K distributions are updated according to Eq. 4:

$$W_{k,t} = (1 - \alpha) \cdot W_{k,t-1} + \alpha M_{k,t} \tag{4}$$

Where: α is the learning coefficient which determines the model adaptation speed and $M_{k,t}$ is equal to 1 for the distribution which satisfy 3and 0 for others. After updating weights, a normalization step is carried out to ensure that the sum of the weights is always equal to 1. For the unmatched components, μ and σ parameters remain unchanged. The parameters of the distribution which matches the new observation are updated using the following equations:

$$\mu_{k,t} = (1 - \varphi_k) \cdot \mu_{k,t-1} + \varphi_k \cdot P_t \tag{5}$$

$$\sigma_{k,t}^2 = (1 - \varphi_k) \cdot \varphi_{k,t-1}^2 + \varphi_k (P_t - \mu_{k,t})^T (P_t - \mu_{k,t}) \tag{6}$$

With

$$\varphi_t = \alpha \eta (P_t / \mu_k \sigma_k) \tag{7}$$

If none of the distributions satisfy the Eq. 3, then the pixel is associated with first plan and the parameters of the least probable distribution is replaced by a new Gaussian with the current value as its mean value, an initially high variance, and a low prior weight parameter according to Eq. 8,Eq. 9 and Eq. 10 described below:

$$\sigma_{k,t}^2 = Large \quad Initial \quad Variance \tag{8}$$

$$W_{k,t} = Low \quad Prior \quad Weight \tag{9}$$

$$\mu_{k,t} = P_t \tag{10}$$

W is the initial weight value for the new Gaussian. If w is higher, the distribution is chosen as the background model for a long time. To decide if P_t is included in the background distributions, the distributions are ordered according to the value of $W_{k,t}/\sigma_{k,t}$. This ordering use the assumption that a background pixel corresponds to a high weight with a weak variance for the reason that the background is practically constant and it is more present than moving objects. The first β distributions that verify the Eq. 11 are selected to represent the background.

$$\beta = \arg \min \left(\Sigma_{k=1}^b W_{k,t} > B \right) \tag{11}$$

The threshold B represents the minimum portion of the total weight given to background model. If a small value for B is chosen, then the background becomes unimodal. If B is higher, a multi-modal distribution caused by a repetitive background motion could result from a variety of background component that allows the background to accept more than one Gaussian distribution. The use of unique threshold B for GMM implies a miss classification especially when scene contains both dynamic and static area. A higher threshold can achieve correct classifications in a dynamic background but makes incorrect detection of moving objects in stationary background.

5   Adaptive Local Monitoring

Methods based on MOG use the pixel value for detecting a probable change in the background based on the assumption that a moving object is a set of pixels in movement. This vision is very useful because it requires no a priori knowledge of objects and their trajectories. However, the natural environment is far from perfect. The presence of dust, the change in brightness, rain, wind,etc. influence on pixel value making unwanted local variation and leading to a misdetection of motion. The false pixel detection induces the system to make errors in the following steps, either by the deformation of the moving objects or by signaling a false movement. To overcome these problems, we proposed an adaptive local monitoring algorithm for each block to control local variation. From the start of the process of detecting moving objects, the monitoring task is enabled by assigning an observer to each block. The role of the latter is to monitor and report the presence of any activity that may be a movement. The decision of the presence or absence of movement is ensured by calculating the similarity between two states of the same block. Indeed, after assigning a block for each monitor, it stores the initial state which contains only contour. The first state is taken without the presence of moving objects. The second state represents the image in process. For the convenience of the update algorithm, each pixel has been labeled with the block number to which it belongs. It is used to provide updates to the concerned pixels only. So if a significant activity in a block of the image is detected, the parameters of the Gaussian assigned to all pixels of this block decide whether there has been any motion, and will be updated according to the proposed model. The parameters of the Gaussian assigned to other blocks will not undergo any change. This process will eliminate local variation, because only blocks with significant change will be considered by the system.

6   Results and interpretation

The system presented in this paper is implemented in Java on a computer with an Intel Core i5 2.67 GHz and a 4GB memory capacity. In this section, we shall present results of our method while challenging real-world situations. We take in addition to our database, three publicly available Benchmark Dataset Collection. The first one (BDC1) has six sequences in the Dataset (campus, highway I, highway I2, highway II intelligent room and laboratory) [21]. The second (BDC2) has nine sequences (bootstrap, a campus, a curtain, an escalator, a fountain, a hall, a lobby, a shopping mall and a water surface) [18].The last one (BDC3) has two sequences (highway and hallway) [16]. Our database (BDC4) has four sequences (campus, a hallway, a highway and a public park). In BDC4, The outdoor videos are recorded in a random situation and without any assumption on the observed scene where a group of clouds is passing in the sky, causing sudden illumination changes. For measuring accuracy we used different metrics, namely Precision and Recall.

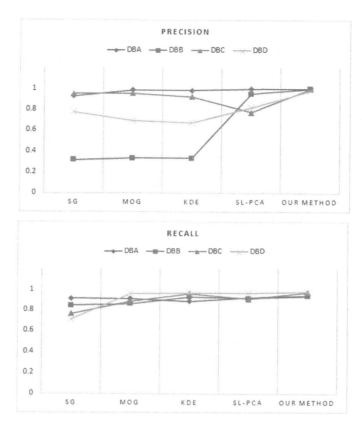

Fig. 1. Precision and recall results for MOG [26], SL-PCA [19], SG [30], KDE [10], and our method

Fig. 2. Background subtraction results in personnel video database in both indoor and outdoor environments

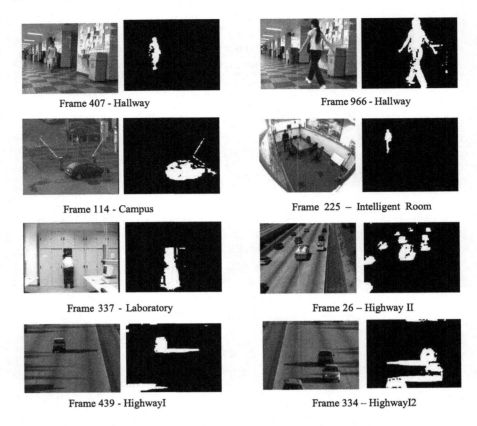

Frame 407 - Hallway

Frame 966 - Hallway

Frame 114 - Campus

Frame 225 – Intelligent Room

Frame 337 - Laboratory

Frame 26 – Highway II

Frame 439 - HighwayI

Frame 334 – HighwayI2

Fig. 3. Background subtraction results in public video database

Recall gives the percentage of corrected pixels classified as background when compared with the total number of background pixels in the ground truth. Precision gives the percentage of corrected pixels classified as background as compared at the total pixels classified as background by the method.

$$Recall = \frac{TP}{TP + FN} \tag{12}$$

$$Precision = \frac{TP}{TP + FP} \tag{13}$$

FP and FN refer to pixels misclassified as foreground (FP) or background (FN) while TP account for accurately classified pixels respectively as foreground. A good performance is obtained when the detection rate is high without altering the precision.

Figure.1 clearly shows that our method outperform the well-known background subtraction methods in term of precision and recall. Figure.2 and Figure.3 show some qualitative results on both public and personal databases. They show that our system is able to give a very good subtraction in environment without any assumption on lighting condition. They also show the effectiveness of the proposed system in outdoor and indoor environment.

7 Conclusion

In this paper, we proposed a background subtraction system for image sequences extracted from fixed camera using an improved parameters updating algorithm for mixture of Gaussians. To overcome the brightness and local variation we first made a transition from RGB to HSL color space. Then we divided the image into N areas and assigned to each one a local monitoring algorithm that allows selecting regions with a very large change using Pearsons Correlation Coefficient. Transfer to HSL color space has significantly decreased light effect on the system behavior through accumulating all brightness variations in a single component (L). While segmenting the image into regions have eliminated local variations caused mainly by the presence of dust. Tests conducted on databases show that our system has a good sensitivity, more accuracy compared with well-known methods. In future work, our algorithm will be adjusted by dividing the image into homogenous regions and solving the problem of shadow and color similarity between moving objects and background.

References

1. Baf, F.E., Bouwmans, T., Vachon, B.: Fuzzy statistical modeling of dynamic backgrounds for moving object detection in infrared videos. In: Computer Vision and Pattern Recognition (2009)
2. Caseiro, R., Henriques, J.F., Batista, J.: Foreground Segmentation via Background Modeling on Riemannian Manifolds. In: International Conference on Pattern Recognition, pp. 3570–3574 (2010)
3. Charoenpong, T., Supasuteekul, A., Nuthong, C.: Adaptive background modeling from an image sequence by using K-Means clustering (2010)
4. Cheng, F.C., Huang, S.C., Ruan, S.J.: Illumination-Sensitive Background Modeling Approach for Accurate Moving Object Detection. IEEE Transactions on Broadcasting 57, 794–801 (2011)
5. Cristani, M., Bicegi, M., Murino, V.: Integrated Region-and Pixel-based Approach to Background Modeling (2002)
6. Cristani, M., Murino, V.: A spatial sampling mechanism for effective background subtraction. In: Computer Vision Theory and Applications, pp. 403–412 (2007)
7. Cristani, M., Murino, V.: Background Subtraction with Adaptive Spatio-Temporal Neighborhood Analysis. In: Computer Vision Theory and Applications, pp. 484–489 (2008)
8. Djouadi, A., Snorrason, G.F.D.: The Quality of Training Sample Estimates of the Bhattacharyya Coefficient. IEEE Transactions on Pattern Analysis and Machine Intelligence 12, 92–97 (1990)
9. Doulamis, A., Kalisperakis, I., Stentoumis, C., Matsatsinis, N.: Self Adaptive background modeling for identifying persons' falls. In: International Workshop on Semantic Media Adaptation and Personalization (2010)

10. Elgammal, A.M., Harwood, D., Davis, L.S.: Non-parametric Model for Background Subtraction (2000)
11. Friedman, N., Russell, S.J.: Image Segmentation in Video Sequences: A Probabilistic Approach. In: Uncertainty in Artificial Intelligence, pp. 175–181 (1997)
12. Hayman, E., Olof Eklundh, J.: Statistical Background Subtraction for a Mobile Observer. In: International Conference on Computer Vision, pp. 67–74 (2003)
13. Hedayati, M., Zaki, W.M.D.W., Hussain, A.: Real-time background subtraction for video surveillance: From research to reality. In: International Colloquium on Signal Processing & Its Applications (2010)
14. Kaewtrakulpong, P., Bowden, R.: An improved adaptive background mixture model for real time tracking with shadow dectection (2001)
15. Kan, J., Li, K., Tang, J., Du, X.: Background modeling method based on improved multi-Gaussian distribution. In: International Conference on Computer Application and System Modeling (2010)
16. Li, L., Huang, W., Gu, I.Y.H., Tian, Q.: Statistical modeling of complex backgrounds for foreground object detection. IEEE Transactions on Image Processing 13, 1459–1472 (2004)
17. Li, X., Jing, X.: FPGA based mixture Gaussian background modeling and motion detection 4, 2078–2081 (2011)
18. Martel-brisson, N., Zaccarin, A.: Learning and Removing Cast Shadows through a Multidistribution Approach. IEEE Transactions on Pattern Analysis and Machine Intelligence 29, 1133–1146 (2007)
19. Oliver, N.M., Rosario, B., Pentland, A.P.: A Bayesian Computer Vision System for Modeling Human Interactions. IEEE Transactions on Pattern Analysis and Machine Intelligence 22, 831–843 (2000)
20. Power, P.W., Schoonees, J.A.: Understanding Background Mixture Models for Foreground Segmentation (2002)
21. Prati, A.: c, I.M., Trivedi, M.M., Cucchiara, R.: Detecting Moving Shadows: Formulation, Algorithms and Evaluation
22. Schindler, K., Wang, H.: Smooth Foreground-Background Segmentation for Video Processing (2006)
23. Seki, M., Okuda, H., Hashimoto, M., Hirata, N.: Object modeling using gaussian mixture model for infrared image and its application to vehicle detection. Journal of Robotics and Mechatronics 18(6), 738 (2006)
24. Setiawan, N.A., Ju Hong, S., Woon Kim, J., Woo Lee, C.: Gaussian Mixture Model in Improved HLS Color Space for Human Silhouette Extraction (2006)
25. Sheng, Z.B., Cui, X.Y.: An adaptive learning rate GMM for background extraction. Optoelectronics Letters 4, 460–463 (2008)
26. Stauffer, C., Grimson, W.E.L.: Adaptive Background Mixture Models for Real-Time Tracking. Computer Vision and Pattern Recognition 2, 2246–2252 (1999)
27. Stenger, B., Ramesh, V., Paragios, N., Coetzee, F., Buhmann, J.M.: Topology Free Hidden Markov Models: Application to Background Modeling. In: International Conference on Computer Vision, pp. 294–301 (2001)
28. Suo, P., Wang, Y.: An improved adaptive background modeling algorithm based on Gaussian Mixture Model. In: International Conference on Signal Processing Proceedings (2008)
29. Wang, H., Suter, D.: A re-evaluation of mixture of Gaussian background modeling [video signal processing applications]. In: International Conference on Acoustics, Speech, and Signal Processing, vol. 2 (2005)

30. Wren, C.R., Azarbayejani, A., Darrell, T., Pentland, A.: Pfinder: Real-Time Tracking of the Human Body. IEEE Transactions on Pattern Analysis and Machine Intelligence 19, 780–785 (1997)
31. Yu, J., Zhou, X., Qian, F.: Object kinematic model: A novel approach of adaptive background mixture models for video segmentation (2010)
32. Zang, Q., Klette, R.: Evaluation of an Adaptive Composite Gaussian Model in Video Surveillance (2003)
33. Zhang, L., Liang, Y.: Motion Human Detection Based on Background Subtraction. In: International Workshop on Education Technology and Computer Science (2010)
34. Zivkovic, Z., Heijden, F.V.D.: Recursive Unsupervised Learning of Finite Mixture Models. IEEE Transactions on Pattern Analysis and Machine Intelligence 26, 651–656 (2004)

Towards Real-Time Co-authoring of Linked-Data on the Web

Moulay Driss Mechaoui[(✉)], Nadir Guetmi, and Abdessamad Imine

[1] University of Sciences and Technology Oran 'Mohamed Boudiaf' USTO-MB
Mathematics and Computer Science Faculty
Oran, Algeria
[2] LIAS/ISAE-ENSMA, Poitiers University
Chasseneuil, France
[3] Université de Lorraine and INRIA-LORIA Grand Est
Nancy, France
moulaydriss.mechaoui@univ-usto.dz,
nadir.guetmi@ensma.fr,
abdessamad.imine@loria.fr

Abstract. Real-time co-authoring of Linked-Data (LD) on the Web is becoming a challenging problem in the Semantic Web area. LD consists of RDF (Resource Description Framework) graphs. We propose to apply state-of-the art collaborative editing techniques to manage shared RDF graphs and to control the concurrent modifications. In this paper, we present two concurrency control techniques. The first one is based on client-server architecture. The second one is more flexible as it enables the collaborative co-authoring to be deployed in mobile and P2P architecture and it supports dynamic groups where users can leave and join at any time.

Keywords: Linked-Data · Collaborative editing systems · Optimistic replication

1 Introduction

Recently, providing collaborative co-authoring tools in the Web Semantic is becoming more attractive as they enable semantic web data to be produced in online mode and to be available to a large public. Linked Data (LD) is recently used to replace collections of offline RDF data [3]. The goal of LD is to enable people to share structured data on the web as easily as they can share documents today. It uses RDF technology that (i) relies on HTTP URIs to denote things; (ii) provides useful information about a thing at that thing's URI; and (iii) includes in that information other URIs of LD. Tabulator [2] is a LD browser, designed to provide the ability to navigate the web of linked things. In [3], Berners-Lee et al. raise some interesting challenges when adding collaborative co-authoring mode in Tabulator. This mode consists in collaboratively editing the LD which is represented by a RDF graph.

In this paper, we sketch two solutions that may meet to some extent the read-write requirement in LD browser. We consider a RDF graph as a shared data

© IFIP International Federation for Information Processing 2015
A. Amine et al. (Eds.): CIIA 2015, IFIP AICT 456, pp. 538–548, 2015.
DOI: 10.1007/978-3-319-19578-0_44

which can be edited and updated by several users. To control the concurrent access to this shared data, we propose to apply state-of-the art collaborative editing techniques [9,6]. The CRDT (Commutative Replicated Data Type) is a class of algorithms that is emerging for ensuring consistency of highly dynamic content on P2P networks. However, this approach incurs some overhead they do not consider directly a set as a list (or a sequence) [1]. Also, with the continuously growing amount of structured data available on the Semantic Web there is an increasing desire to replicate such data to mobile devices. This enables services and applications to operate independently of the network [18,11]. Classical replication techniques cannot be properly applied to mobile systems because they do not adopt to changing user information needs, and they do not consider the technical, environmental, and infrastructural restrictions of mobile devices. We think that Operational Transformation (OT) approach [4,14] may be a good candidate as it supports unconstrained interaction. Indeed, it allows any user to modify any shared data consistently at any time without any restrictions on users's actions.

The rest of the paper is organized as follows. Section 2 presents the ingredients of OT approach. In Section 3, we suggest two concurrency control procedures for managing the collaborative edition of RDF graphs. Section 4 discusses performance evaluation, and concludes.

2 Transformational Approach

Principle. Operational Transformation (OT) is an optimistic replication technique which allows many users (or sites) to concurrently update the shared data and next to synchronize their divergent replicas in order to obtain the same data [17]. The updates of each site are executed on the local replica immediately without being blocked or delayed, and then are propagated to other sites to be executed again. Accordingly, every update is processed in four steps: (i) *generation* on one site; (ii) *broadcast* to other sites; (iii) *reception* on one site; (iv) *execution* on one site.

A crucial issue when designing shared data with a replicated architecture and arbitrary messages communication between sites is the *consistency maintenance* (or *convergence*) of all replicas. To illustrate this problem, consider the following example:

Example 1. Consider the following group text editor scenario (see Figure 1.(a)): there are two users (on two sites) working on a shared document represented by a sequence of characters. These characters are addressed from 0 to the end of the document. Initially, both copies hold the string "*efecte*". User 1 executes operation $op_1 = Ins(1, f)$ to insert the character f at position 1. Concurrently, user 2 performs $op_2 = Del(5)$ to delete the character e at position 5. When op_1 is received and executed on site 2, it produces the expected string "*effect*". But, when op_2 is received on site 1, it does not take into account that op_1 has been executed before it and it produces the string "*effece*". The result at site 1 is different from the result of site 2 and it apparently violates the intention of

op_2 since the last character e, which was intended to be deleted, is still present in the final string. Consequently, we obtain a *divergence* between sites 1 and 2. It should be pointed out that even if a serialization protocol [4] was used to require that all sites execute op_1 and op_2 in the same order (*i.e.* a global order on concurrent operations) to obtain an identical result *effece*, this identical result is still inconsistent with the original intention of op_2.

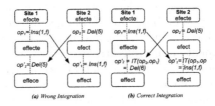

(a) *Wrong Integration*   (b) *Correct Integration*

Fig. 1. Serialization of concurrent updates

To maintain convergence, the OT approach has been proposed by [4]. When User X gets an operation op that was previously executed by User Y on his replica of the shared object User X does not necessarily integrate op by executing it "as is" on his replica. He will rather execute a variant of op, denoted by op' (called a *transformation* of op) that *intuitively intends to achieve the same effect as op*. This approach is based on a transformation function (or algorithm) IT that apply to couples of concurrent operations defined on the same state.

Example 2. In Figure 1.(b), we illustrate the effect of IT on the previous example. When op_2 is received on site 1, op_2 needs to be transformed according to op_1 as follows: $op'_2 = IT((Del(5), Ins(1, f)) = Del(6)$. The deletion position of op_2 is incremented because op_1 has inserted a character at position 1, which is before the character deleted by op_2. Next, op'_2 is executed on site 1. In the same way, when op_1 is received on site 2, it is transformed as follows: $IT(Ins(1, f), Del(5)) = Ins(1, f)$; op_1 remains the same because f is inserted before the deletion position of op_2.

Intuitively we can write the transformation IT as follows:

```
IT(Ins(p1,c1),Ins(p2,c2)) =
        if (p1 < p2) return Ins(p1,c1)
        else return Ins(p1+1,c1)
        endif;
```

OT Model. Using the OT approach, each site is equipped by two main components [4,10]: the *integration component* and the *transformation component*. The integration component determines how an operation is transformed against a given operation sequence (*e.g.*, the log buffer). It is also responsible for receiving, broadcasting and executing operations. It is rather *independent* of the type of the shared data. The transformation component is a set of IT algorithms which is responsible for merging two concurrent operations defined on the same state. Every IT algorithm is *specific* to the semantics of a given shared data.

The most known OT-based theoretical framework is established by Ressel et al. [10]. They define two consistency criteria:

- **Causality.** If one operation op_1 causally precedes another operation op_2, then op_1 must be executed before op_2 at all sites.
- **Convergence.** When all sites have performed the same set of operations, the copies of the shared data must be identical.

It has been proved that any integration component can achieve convergence in the presence of arbitrary transformation paths if its IT algorithm satisfies two properties $TP1$ and $TP2$ [10]. For all op, op_1 and op_2 pairwise concurrent operations with $op_1' = IT(op_1, op_2)$ and $op_2' = IT(op_2, op_1)$:

- **TP1**: $[op_1 ; op_2'] \equiv [op_2 ; op_1']$.
- **TP2**: $IT(IT(op, op_1), op_2') = IT(IT(op, op_2), op_1')$.

Property $TP1$ defines a *state identity* and ensures that if op_1 and op_2 are concurrent, the effect of executing op_1 before op_2 is the same as executing op_2 before op_1. This property is necessary but not sufficient when the number of sites is greater than two. Property $TP2$ defines an *update identity* and ensures that transforming op along equivalent and different operation sequences will give the same operation.

Properties $TP1$ and $TP2$ are sufficient to ensure the convergence for *any number* of concurrent operations which can be executed in *arbitrary order* [10]. Accordingly, by these properties, it is not necessary to enforce a global total order between concurrent operations because data divergence can always be repaired by operational transformation. However, finding an IT algorithm that satisfies $TP1$ and $TP2$ is considered as a hard task, because this proof is often unmanageably complicated [13]. To overcome this difficulty, we proposed in [6] a formal methodology for designing and analyzing IT algorithms by using a theorem prover.

Several OT-based integration components have been proposed in the groupware research area. These components may be categorized in two categories. The first one does not require $TP2$ property: it relies on client-server architecture for enforcing a unique transformation order. We can cite in this category algorithms like SOCT4 [16] and TIBOT [7]. As for the second category, it requires $TP2$ property. This constraint enables the concurrent operations to be synchronized in a decentralized way. Algorithms such as adOPTed [10] SOCT2,4 [15,16] and GOTO [14] belong to this category.

3   Our Proposals

To manage all concurrent access for editing collaboratively a shared RDF graph, we need a concurrency control procedure. In this section, we first argue how to map a RDF graph into a sequence data structure. According to centralized and decentralized architectures, we suggest two concurrency control procedures.

3.1   RDF Graph as a Sequence

When publishing LD on web, information about resources is represented using the RDF. Any expression in RDF is a collection of *triples*, each consisting of a *subject*, a *predicate* (also called property) and an *object*. The subject of a triple is the URI describing resource. The object can either be a simple literal value (*e.g.*, a string, a number) or the URI of another resource. The predicate indicates what kind of relation exists between subject and object. The predicate is a URI too. A set of such triples is called an RDF graph. This can be illustrated by a node and directed-arc diagram, in which each triple is represented as a node-arc-node link.

Usually a set is implemented by means of a list. It means we can use operations, such as insert and delete, to edit a shared list. Thus, we can reuse the state-of-the-art of collaborative editing systems.

For instance, the following three english statements (this example is taken from [8]):

- <http://www.example.org/index.html>has a creator whose value is John Smith
- <http://www.example.org/index.html>has a creation-date whose value is August 16, 1999
- <http://www.example.org/index.html>has a language whose value is English

could be represented by the RDF graph shown in Figure 2.

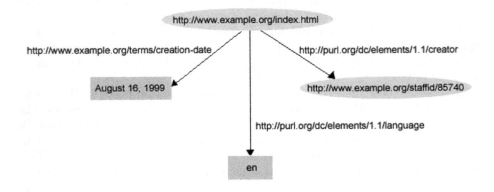

Fig. 2. An RDF Graph

An RDF graph can be serialized into a sequence of triples and considered as a text where each line corresponds to a simple triple of subject, predicate and object. For example, the third statement shown in Figure 2 would be written as a text line:

```
<http://www.example.org/index.html>
                <http://purl.org/dc/elements/1.1/language> "en" .
```

By considering an RDF graph as a sequence, each triple is addressed simply by a position within the sequence. Therefore, we assume that the sequence of triples can be modified by the following primitive operations:
- $Ins(p, t)$ which adds triple t at position p;
- $Del(p, t)$ which deletes triple t at position p.

Updating a triple (*e.g.*, by modifying the predicate URI) can be expressed by a sequence of delete (by removing the old triple) and insert (by adding the new one) operations.

3.2   Ingredients of Collaboration

Each user's site has a local copy of RDF graph and a unique identity. We assume that the RDF graph is serialized in the same way on every site.

Every site generates operations sequentially and stores these operations in a stack also called a *log*. When a site receives a remote operation op, the integration component executes the following steps:

1. from the local log it determines the sequence seq of operations that are concurrent to op;
2. it calls the transformation component in order to get operation op' that is the transformation of op according to seq;
3. it executes op' on the current state;
4. it adds op' to the local log.

3.3   Centralized Solution

In this section, we propose a real-time co-authoring based on client-server architecture. Indeed, users can edit collaboratively a shared RDF graph by reconciliating their divergent copies via a particular site called *server*. We think that SOCT4 [16] is most appropriate to this kind of architecture.

In SOCT4, the operations are ordered globally by using a timestamp given by the server. When an operation is generated on site s, it is immediately executed (to satisfy real-time constraint), but it is not propagated until it gets a timestamp from the server and all the operations which precede it according to the timestamp order have been received and executed on s. Moreover, this operation is transformed against all concurrent operations (operations received after its generation and preceding it in the global order) before to be propagated. To ensure convergence, SOCT4 requires only the property $TP1$ to be satisfied by the IT algorithm.

Example 3. Consider two users editing a shared RDF graph as described in Figure 3. Initially, each site has an empty copy. The index of each operation represents the timestamp given by the server. Two local insertion operations op_1 and op_2 have been executed by user 1 (at site 1). Concurrently, user 2 has executed another insertion operation op_3. The added triples t_1, t_2 and t_3 are

$site\,1$	$site\,2$
$op_1 = Ins(0, t_1)$	$op_3 = Ins(0, t_3)$
$op_2 = Ins(1, t_2)$	
$s_1 = synchronize$	
	$s_2 = synchronize$
$s_3 = synchronize$	

Fig. 3. Scenario of collaboration

respectively as follows (where UR1 is `http://www.example.org/index.html` and UR2 is `http://www.example.org/staffid/85740`):

```
<UR1> <http://www.example.org/terms/creation-date> "August 16, 1999" .

<UR1> <http://purl.org/dc/elements/1.1/language> "en" .

<UR1> <http://purl.org/dc/elements/1.1/creator> <UR2> .
```

1. At point s_1, site 1 decides to synchronize with other sites. As there is no concurrent operation available, op_1, op_2 are sent to site 2 (via the server) in their original forms.

2. At point s_2, site 2 cannot send op_3 as long as it did not receive the precedent operations (according to the timestamp order). Thus the synchronization calls IT algorithm to produce the following transformations:

$$op'_1 = IT(op_1, op_3) = Ins(0, t_1)$$
$$op'_3 = IT(op_3, op_1) = Ins(1, t_3)$$
$$op'_2 = IT(op_2, op'_3) = Ins(1, t_2)$$
$$op''_3 = T(op'_3, op_2) = Ins(2, t_3)$$

op'_1, op'_2 are executed on site 2, and op''_3 is broadcast to other sites.

3. At point s_3, site 1 decides again to synchronize. The remote operation op''_3 is executed directly (without transformation) after op_1 and op_2.

4. Note that, after point s_3, sites 1 and 2 have the same log, namely op_1, op_2 and op''_3. However, site 1 has performed the following sequence:

$$op_1$$
$$op_2$$
$$op''_3 = IT(IT(op_3, op_1), op_2)$$

while site 2 has executed the following sequence:

$$op_3$$
$$op''_1 = IT(op_1, op_3)$$
$$op''_2 = IT(op_2, op'_3)$$

As SOCT4 requires only $TP1$ property, the above sequences are equivalent in the sense that they produce the same RDF graph. The operations are stored in the log according to the timestamp order but they may be executed in different orders at different sites.

It should be noted that SOCT4 has been used successfully in the development of a File Synchronizer [9] distributed with the industrial collaborative development environment, LibreSource Community[1], proposed by ARTENUM Company. LibreSource is a platform for hosting virtual teams. Users can register and create channels for synchronizing shared data. On a single server, LibreSource can host several projects, several groups of users, and grant fine grain access to the resources.

Although SOCT4 ensures causality and convergence properties, it degrades the responsiveness of the system as all messages are exchanged via a server. Moreover, it does not scale because it is based on a single point of failure.

3.4   Decentralized Solution

Integration algorithms based on $TP2$ property enable concurrent operations to be synchronized in a decentralized way. Thus, they avoid a single point of failure. Nevertheless, these algorithms have limited scalability with the number of users. Indeed, all proposed OT frameworks rely on a fixed number of users during collaboration sessions. This is due in the fact that they use vector timestamps to enforce causality dependency. The vector timestamps do not scale well, since each timestamp is a vector of integers with a number of entries equal to the number of users.

In [5], we proposed a new framework for collaborative editing to address the weakness of previous OT works. The features of our framework are as follows:

1. It supports an unconstrained collaborative editing work (without the necessity of central coordination). Using optimistic replication scheme, it provides simultaneous access to shared data.
2. Instead of vector timestamps, we use a simple technique to preserve causality dependency. Our technique is minimal because only direct dependency information between operations is used. It is independent on the number of users and it provides high concurrency in comparison with vector timestamps.
3. Using OT approach, reconciliation of divergent copies is done automatically in decentralized fashion.
4. Our framework can scale naturally thanks to our minimal causality dependency relation. In other words, it may be deployed easily in Peer-to-Peer (P2P) networks.

Example 4. Consider the scenario given in Example 3. In our framework, operations op_1 and op_2 will be related by a dependency. This is due in the fact that their added triples are adjacent (positions 0 and 1) and created by the same user. Thus, op_1 must be executed before op_2 at all sites. This dependency relation is minimal in the sense that when op_2 is broadcast to all sites it holds only the identity of op_1 as it depends on directly.

1. At site 1, op_3 is considered as concurrent. It is then transformed against op_1 and op_2. The following sequence is executed and logged in site 1:

---

[1] http://dev.libresource.org

$op_1 = Ins(0, t_1)$
$op_2 = Ins(1, t_2)$
$op_3'' = IT(IT(op_3, op_1), op_2) = Ins(2, t_3)$

2. At site 2, op_1 and op_2 are concurrent with respect to op_3. They must be transformed before to be executed after op_3 according to their dependency relation. Thus, the following sequence is executed and logged in site 2:

$op_3 = Ins(0, t_3)$
$op_1' = IT(op_1, op_3) = op_1$
$op_2' = op_2$

Unlike the others OT-based integration algorithms, we minimize the transformation steps when integrating a remote operation depending on another operation. Indeed, at site 2, the new form of op_2 is deduced from the executed form of op_1 (without transformation as in Example 3). On the other hand, the sequences of sites 1 and 2 are not identical but equivalent.

4   Performance Evaluation

Our experimentation consists to compare the response time of generating and integrating a sequence of remote triples over a local ones. We use two sites (Site1 and Site2), initially the log of each sites is empty. Each site generates locally a sequence of operations; the sites communicate the generated operations to be integrated. The sizes of the sequence are varied from 50 000 to 1 000 000 triples. The percentage of insertions in the sequence and the log are variants from 50%, 80% to 100%.

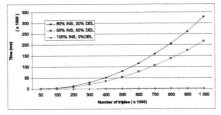
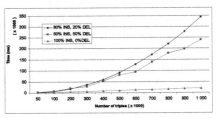

(a) Generation + Integration time of a sequence of triples over an empty RDF document

(b) Generation + Integration time of a sequence of triples over a RDF document containing 10 000 triples

Fig. 4. Updating RDF document

We implement a prototype of Optic [5] in java, compiled by NetBeans 6.8 with JVM heap size 1GB, and executed on a computer running Windows XP SP2 with an Intel (R) Core (TM) 2 CPU E7400 @ 2.80 GHz and 2 GB RAM. We calculate the sum of the generation time of the sequence in the Site1 with the time of integration of the same sequence in the Site2. For every generation and integrating sequence three times are executed and the average time is recorded.

The Figure 4(a) present the time of generation and integration of a varied sequences of triples over an empty RDF document. When the percentage of insertions in the sequence is 100% the performance of our algorithm increases. This is due to the minimal causality dependency between insertions operations computed during the local generation of triples. The Figure 4(b) illustrate the time of generation and integration of a varied sequences of triples over a RDF document containing 10 000 triples. The performance decreases when the percentage of deletion increases. This degradation of performance is caused by the canonizing of the log [5] (tidy insertion operation before deletion operations). The rate of deletion operations in the log has a direct impact on the performance of the Optic algorithm.

5   Conclusion

In this paper, we have dealt with the problem of the real-time co-authoring of LDW. In this respect, we have suggested two solutions based on OT approach.

In centralized and decentralized solutions we propose in this paper, the shared RDF graph is serialized into a sequence of triples that can be altered by simple operations: insertion and deletion of triples. Mapping RDF graph into sequence of triples is given in order to reuse state-of-the art collaborative editing techniques including some systems in which we participated [9,6]. This mapping is simple. But, if the RDF graph must satisfy some requirements based on semantic aspects (*e.g.*, graph connectiveness), preconditions must be added to operations. For example, we can state that the delete operation $Del(p, t)$ is enabled iff the p exits and the object of t is not a subject of another triple. It is not sure that this delete operation will be still enabled when it is integrated in another site which has added concurrently triple t' whose the subject is the object of t. Two solutions are possible: either writing another IT algorithm based on new constraints, or tolerating the violation of some requirements during some periods with the possibility to stabilize in correct state (by undoing some operations).

The question of adapting these solutions in existing semantic web browsers remains open in this paper. It will be interesting to plug these solutions in a given browser in order to evaluate the cost of mapping a RDF graph into a sequence. Using this implementation, we can also make measurements to experimentally validate the impact of OT approach on real-timeliness and scalability. On the other hand, designing a new IT algorithm for shared RDF graphs based on updates proposed in the recent version of SPARQL/Update [12] is an exciting and challenging problem.

References

1. Aslan, K., Molli, P., Skaf-Molli, H., Weiss, S.: C-set: a commutative replicated data type for semantic stores. In: Fourth International Workshop on REsource, RED (2011)

2. Berners-Lee, T., Chen, Y., Chilton, L., Connolly, D., Dhanaraj, J., Hollenbach, R., Lerer, A., Sheets, D.: Tabulator: Exploring and analyzing linked data on the semantic web. In: SWUI06 Workshop at ISWC 2006, Athens, Georgia, USA (2006)
3. Berners-Lee, T., Hollenbach, J., Kanghao, L., Presbery, E., Pru d'ommeaux, J., Schraefel, M.: Tabulator redux: Writing into the semantic web (2008), http://eprints.ecs.soton.ac.uk
4. Ellis, C.A., Gibbs, S.J.: Concurrency Control in Groupware Systems. In: SIGMOD Conference, vol. 18, pp. 399–407 (1989)
5. Imine, A.: Conception Formelle d'Algorithmes de Réplication Optimiste. Vers l'Edition Collaborative dans les Réseaux Pair-à-Pair. Phd thesis, University of Henri Poincaré, Nancy, France (December 2006)
6. Imine, A., Rusinowitch, M., Oster, G., Molli, P.: Formal design and verification of operational transformation algorithms for copies convergence. Theoretical Computer Science 351(2), 167–183 (2006)
7. Li, R., Li, D., Sun, C.: A time interval based consistency control algorithm for interactive groupware applications. In: IEEE ICPADS 2004, Los Alamitos, CA, USA, pp. 420–429 (2004)
8. Manola, F., Miller, E.: Rdf primer (2004), http://www.w3.org/TR/rdf-primer/
9. Molli, P., Oster, G., Skaf-Molli, H., Imine, A.: Using the transformational approach to build a safe and generic data synchronizer. In: Proceedings of the 2003 International ACM SIGGROUP Conference on Supporting Group Work, pp. 212–220. ACM Press (2003)
10. Ressel, M., Nitsche-Ruhland, D., Gunzenhauser, R.: An Integrating, Transformation-Oriented Approach to Concurrency Control and Undo in Group Editors. In: ACM CSCW 1996, Boston, USA, pp. 288–297 (November 1996)
11. Sacco, O., Collina, M., Schiele, G., Corazza, G.E., Breslin, J.G., Hauswirth, M.: Fine-grained access control for RDF data on mobile devices. In: Lin, X., Manolopoulos, Y., Srivastava, D., Huang, G. (eds.) WISE 2013, Part I. LNCS, vol. 8180, pp. 478–487. Springer, Heidelberg (2013)
12. Seaborne, A., Manjunath, G.: Sparql/update: A language for updating rdf graphs (2008), http://jena.hpl.hp.com/~afs/SPARQL-Update.html
13. Sun, C., Agustina.: Exhaustive search of puzzles in operational transformation. In: CSCW 2014, pp. 519–529 (2014)
14. Sun, C., Ellis, C.: Operational transformation in real-time group editors: issues, algorithms, and achievements. In: ACM CSCW 1998, Seattle, Washington, United States, pp. 59–68 (1998)
15. Sun, C., Jia, X., Zhang, Y., Yang, Y., Chen, D.: Achieving Convergence, Causality-preservation and Intention-preservation in real-time Cooperative Editing Systems. ACM Trans. Comput.-Hum. Interact. 5(1), 63–108 (1998)
16. Vidot, N., Cart, M., Ferrié, J., Suleiman, M.: Copies convergence in a distributed real-time collaborative environment. In: ACM CSCW 2000, Philadelphia, USA (December 2000)
17. Yi, X., Chengzheng, S., Mo, L.: Achieving convergence in operational transformation: Conditions, mechanisms and systems. In: CSCW 2014, pp. 505–518 (2014)
18. Zander, S., Schandl, B.: Context-driven RDF data replication on mobile devices. Semantic Web 3(2) (2012)

Software Engineering:
Modeling and Meta Modeling

A High Level Net for Modeling and Analysis Reconfigurable Discrete Event Control Systems

Ahmed Kheldoun[1,4(✉)], Kamel Barkaoui[2], JiaFeng Zhang[3], and Malika Ioualalen[1]

[1] MOVEP, Computer Science Department, USTHB, Algiers, Algeria
ahmedkheldoun@yahoo.fr, mioualalen@usthb.dz
[2] CEDRIC-CNAM, 292 Rue Saint-Martin 75141, Cedex 03, Paris, France
kamel.barkaoui@cnam.fr
[3] School of Electro-Mechanical Engineering, Xidian University, Xi'an, 710071, China
zhangjiafeng628@gmail.com
[4] Sciences and Technology Faculty, Yahia Fares University, Medea, Algeria

Abstract. This paper deals with automatic reconfiguration of discrete event control systems. We propose to enrich the formalism of recursive Petri nets by the concept of *feature* from which runtime reconfigurations are facilitated. This new formalism is applied in the context of automated production system. Furthermore, the enhanced recursive Petri net is translated into rewriting logic, and by using Maude LTL model-checker one can verify several behavioural properties related to reconfiguration.

Keywords: Reconfigurable control systems · Feature · Recursive Petri nets · Rewriting logic · Maude

1 Introduction

The new generation of discrete event control models is adressing new creteria as flexibility and agility. The need of flexibility and adaptability leads to integrate reconfigurability features in these models, but it makes the system more complex and its development a hard task. Therefore, an approach for the design safe and reconfigurable systems is a crucial need. The Petri net formalism is one of the most used tools to model and analyse discrete event systems [2].

Recently, recursive Petri nets (RPNs) [3] are proposed to specify flexible concurrent systems where functionalities of discrete event systems such as abstraction, dynamicity, preemption, recursion are preponderant. In fact, RPNs have ability to model dynamic creation of threads which behave concurrently.

In this paper, we introduce the concept of *feature* proposed in [13] to deal with reconfiguration at runtime. More precisely, the reconfiguration is modelled by combining the interruption and the activation/deactivation of transitions which is ensured by : *application condition* and *update expression*.

The remainder of this paper is organized as follows. Section 2 gives a brief overview of related work. Section 3 recalls the syntax and semantic of the formalism RPNs. The formalism which enrich RPN by the concept of *feature*, named reconfigurable RPN and denoted by R^2PN, is presented in Section 4. Section 5 presents a case study of a

© IFIP International Federation for Information Processing 2015
A. Amine et al. (Eds.): CIIA 2015, IFIP AICT 456, pp. 551–562, 2015.
DOI: 10.1007/978-3-319-19578-0_45

reconfigurable automated production system, and we present in Section 6 its modelling in terms of R^2PN. The verification of the obtained model is done by using the LTL model-checker of Maude [6] [11] and is described in Section 7. Section 8 concludes this paper and depicts further research work.

2   Related Work

Many researchers have tried to deal with formal modeling of control systems with potential reconfigurations. The author of [1] proposed self-modifying nets that can modify their own firing rules at runtime, however, most of the net basic properties such as reachability, boundedness and liveness become indecidable on these nets. In [4], the authors developped a Reconfigurable Petri Nets (RPN) for modeling adaptable multimedia and protocols that can self-modify during execution. They modelled the reconfiguration by introducing the concept of *modifier* places. The authors of [5] presented net rewriting systems (NRS) where a reconfiguration of the net is obtained by a rewriting rules execution. The rewriting rules are similar to production of graph grammars. However, the formalism of NRS is Turing powerful and, thus, automatic verification is no longer possible in that case. Recently, in [7], the authors proposed Reconfigurable timed net condition/event systems (R-TNCES) for modeling reconfigurable discrete event control systems. In this formalism, the system is represented by a set of control componnents and a reconfiguration is modelled by enabling/disabling some control components modules by changing condition/event signals among them.

In this paper, we present a new formalism named Reconfigurable RPN (R^2PN) enriches RPN by the concept of feature selection introduced in [13]. Indeed, in R^2PN, the reconfiguration is modelled by combining the interruption and refinement with the activation/deactivation of transitions which is ensured by : *application condition* and *update expression*. Moreover R^2PN captures the behaviour of entire reconfigurable discrete event control system in a concise modular model, opening the way for efficient analysis and verification.

3   Recursive Petri Nets

The formalism of RPN [3] consider two types of transitions : elementary and abstract. Moreover a starting marking is associated to each abstract transition and a semi-linear set of final markings is defined.

Definition 1. *(Recursive Petri Nets). A Recursive Petri Net [3] is defined by a tuple* $N = \langle P, T, Pre, Post, \Omega, I, \Upsilon, K \rangle$ *where:*

- *P is a finite set of places.*
- *T is a finite set of transitions where* $T = T_{el} \uplus T_{abs}$ *named respectively, the set of elementary and abstract transitions,*
- *I is a finite set of indices called termination indices,*
- *Pre is a mapping defined as :* $Pre : T \rightarrow P^{\oplus}$, *where* $P^{\oplus}$ *is the set of finite multi-sets over the set P,*

- *Post is a mapping defined as : Post : $T_{el} \cup (T_{abs} \times I) \to P^{\oplus}$,*
- *Ω is a mapping $T_{abs} \to P^{\oplus}$ associating to each abstract transition an ordinary marking,*
- *Υ is a family indexed by I of termination sets, where each set represents a set of final markings (i.e. un element of $P^{\oplus}$),*
- *$K : T_{el} \to T_{abs} \times I$, maps a set of interrupted abstract trasitions, and their associated termination indexes, for every elementary transition.*

Example 1. Let's use the net presented in Fig.1(a) to highlight RPN's graphical symbols and associated notations. (i) An elementary transition is represented by a filled rectangle; its name is possibly followed by a set of terms $(t', i) \in T_{abs} \times I$. Each term specifies an abstract transition t', which is under the control of t, associated with a termination index to be used when aborting t' consequently to a firing of t. For instance, t_0 is an elementary transition where its firing preempts threads started by the firing of t_1 and the associate index is 1. (ii) An abstract transition t is represented by a double border rectangle; its name is followed by the starting marking $\Omega(t)$. For instance, t_1 is an abstract transition and $\Omega(t_1) = p_5$ means that any thread, named refinement net, created by firing of t_1 starts with one token in place p_5. (iii) Any termination set can be defined concisely based on place marking. For instance, Υ_0 specifies the final marking of threads such that the place p_6 is marked at least by one token. (iv) The set I of termination indices is deduced from the indices used to subscript the termination sets and from the indices bound to elementary transitions i.e. interruption. In this example, $I = \{0, 1\}$.

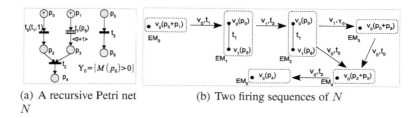

(a) A recursive Petri net
N

(b) Two firing sequences of N

Fig. 1. A recursive Petri net and Two possible firing sequences

Informally, a RPN generates during its execution a dynamical tree of marked threads called an extended marking, which reflects the global state of a such net. This latter denotes the fatherhood relation between the generated threads (describing the inter-threads calls). Each of these threads has its own execution context.

Definition 2. *(Extended Marking). An extended marking [3] of a recursive Petri net is a labelled tree*
$$EM = \langle V, M, E, A \rangle \text{ where:}$$

- *V is the (possibly empty) finite set of nodes. When it is non empty, v_0 denotes the root of the tree,*

- M is a mapping $V \rightarrow P^{\oplus}$ associating an ordinary marking for each node,
- $E \in V \times V$ is the set of edges,
- A is a mapping $E \rightarrow T_{abs}$ associating an abstract transition for each edge.

Any ordinary marking can be seen as an extended marking composed by a unique node. The empty tree is denoted by $\perp$. Note contrary to ordinary nets, RPNs are often disconnected since each connected component may be activated by the firing of abstract transitions. In a RPN, we have two kinds of markings: extended markings and ordinary markings. An extended marking represents the state of the RPN. An ordinary marking represents an execution context of the thread as in Petri nets.

Definition 3. *(Enabled transition or cut step [3]).*

- *A transition is enabled in a node v of an extended marking $EM \neq \perp$ denoted by $EM \xrightarrow{v,t}$ if $\forall p \in P : M(v)(p) \geq Pre(p,t)$,*
- *A cut step τ_i is enabled in a node v if $M(v) \in \Upsilon_i$.*

The firing of an elementary transition updates the current marking using ordinary firing rule like in Petri nets. The firing of an abstract transition refines it by a new sub-net (i.e. creation of new thread, named its child) which starts its own token game, from a starting marking whose value is attached to the abstract transition. Once a final marking is reached, a cut step closes the corresponding sub net, kills its children and produces tokens, indicated by the $Post$ function, in the appropriate output places of the abstract transition. Formal definitions of firing rules are defined in [3]. Due to lack of space, we explain their principls through our illustrated example of Fig.1(a).

Example 2. Fig.1(b) highlights a firing sequences of RPN represented in Fig.1(a). The graphical representation of any extended marking EM is a tree where an arc $v_i(m_i) \xrightarrow{t_{abs}} v_j(m_j)$ means that v_j is a child of v_i created by firing the abstract transition t_{abs} and m_i (reps. m_j) is the marking of v_i (reps. v_j). Note that the initial extended marking EM_0 is reduced to a single node v_0 whose marking is $p_0 + p_1$. From the intial extended marking EM_0, the abstract transition t_1 is enabled; its firing leads to the extended marking EM_1 which contains a fresh node v_1 marked by the starting marking $\Omega(t_1)$. Then, the firing of the elementary transition t_3 from node v_1 of EM_1 leads to an extended marking EM_2, having the same structure as EM_1 but only the marking of node v_1 is changed. From node v_1 in EM_2, the cut step τ_0 is enabled; its firing leads to an extended marking EM_3 by removing the node v_1 and change the marking on its node predecessor i.e. v_0 by adding $Post(p_3, t_1, 0)$. Also, another way to remove nodes in extended marking is using the concept of preemption associated to the elementary transitions. For instance, from node v_0 in EM_2, the elementary transition t_0 with associated preemption $(t_1, 1)$ is enabled; its firing leads to an extended marking EM_4 by removing the node v_1.

4   Reconfigurable Recursive Petri Nets

Reconfigurable Recursive Petri nets (R^2PNs) enriches RPN by the concept of feature selection introduced in [13]. In fact, R^2PNs extend RPN by associating transitions and cut steps with application conditions and update expressions. An application condition is a logical formula over a set of features, describing the feature combinations to which the transition applies. It consitutes a necessary (although not sufficient) condition for the transition to fire. In fact, if the application condition is false, means that the transition is desactivated. An update expression, describes the feature selection evolves after firing a transition.

A feature is defined as a prominent or distinctive user-visible aspect, quality or characteristic of a system. A feature is defined in [13] as follows :

Definition 4. *(Feature [13]). A feature is an end-user visible characteristic of a system.*

The concept of feature has been introduced by the software design community to specify and distinguish products in product lines [9][13]. Now, let's define the set of application conditions over a set of features.

Definition 5. *(Application condition). An application condition φ [9] is a logical (boolean) contraint over a set of features F, defined by the following grammar: $\varphi ::= true \mid a \mid \varphi \wedge \varphi \mid \neg\varphi$, where $a \in F$. The remaining logical connectives can be encoded as usual. We write Φ_F to denote the set of all application conditions over F.*

Definition 6. *(Satisfaction of application conditions [9]). Given an application condition φ and a sub set of features FS, called a feature selection, we say that FS satisfies φ, written as $FS \models \varphi$, iff: (1) $FS \models true$ always; (2) $FS \models a$ iff $a \in FS$; (3) $FS \models \neg\varphi$ iff $FS \not\models \varphi$; (4) $FS \models \varphi_1 \wedge \varphi_2$ iff $FS \models \varphi_1$ and $FS \models \varphi_2$*

Definition 7. *(Update). An update[9] is defined by the following grammar: $u ::= noop \mid a\ on \mid a\ off \mid u; u$, where $a \in F$ and F is a set of features. We write U_F to denote the set of all updates over F. Given a feature selection $FS \subseteq F$, an update expression modifies FS according to the following rules:* r1: $FS \xrightarrow{noop} FS$; r2: $FS \xrightarrow{a\ on} FS \cup \{a\}$; r3: $FS \xrightarrow{a\ off} FS \setminus \{a\}$; r4: $\dfrac{FS \xrightarrow{u_0} FS' \quad FS' \xrightarrow{u_1} FS''}{FS \xrightarrow{u_0;u_1} FS''}$.

We are now in position to introduce R^2PNs.

Definition 8. *(Reconfigurable Recursive Petri nets). A R^2PNs is a tuple $EN = \langle N, F, f, u \rangle$, where :*

- $N = \langle P, T, Pre, Post, \Omega, I, \Upsilon, K \rangle$ *is RPN,*
- F *is a set of features,*
- $f : T \cup \{\tau_i\} \to \Phi_F$ *is a function associating to each transition and cut step with an application condition from Φ_F where $i \in I$,*
- $u : T \cup \{\tau_i\} \to U_F$ *is a function associating to each transition and cut step with an update from U_F where $i \in I$.*
  We write u_t resp. u_{τ_i} to denote the update expression $u(t)$ resp. $u(\tau_i)$ associated to a transition t resp. a cut step τ_i.

we write $FS \models f(t)$ if the feature selection FS satisfies the application condition associated with transition t. In the following, graphically, each transition of R^2PN is annotated by an application condition and an update expression in the following way:

$$\frac{application\ condition}{update\ expression}$$

Definition 9. *(A state of Reconfigurable RPN). A state of a Reconfigurable RPN $EN = \langle N, F, f, u \rangle$ is a tuple $S = (EM, FS)$ where $EM = \langle V, M, E, A \rangle$ is an extended marking and $FS \subseteq F$ is a feature selection.*

Definition 10. *(Enabled transition or cut step). Let $S = (\langle V, M, E, A \rangle, FS)$ be a state of R^2PN $EN = \langle N, F, f, u \rangle$ where $N = \langle P, T, Pre, Post, \Omega, I, \Upsilon, K \rangle$. Let a node $v \in V$.*

- *A transition t is enabled in a node v, if $\forall p \in P : M(v)(p) \geq Pre(p, t)$ and $FS \models f(t)$,*
- *A cut step τ_i is enabled in a node v, if $M(v) \in \Upsilon_i$ and $FS \models f(\tau_i)$.*

Definition 11. *(Firing rules of Reconfigurable RPN). Let $S = (EM, FS)$ be a state of R^2PN $EN = \langle N, F, f, u \rangle$ where $N = \langle P, T, Pre, Post, \Omega, I, \Upsilon, K \rangle$. Let a node $v \in V$.*

- *The firing of an elementary transition t from a node v leads to a state $S' = (EM', FS')$ where $EM \xrightarrow{v,t} EM'$ as Definition12. in [3]. and $FS \xrightarrow{u(t)} FS'$,*
- *The firing of an abstract transition t from a node v leads to a state $S' = (EM', FS')$ where $EM \xrightarrow{v,t} EM'$ as Definition13. in [3]. and $FS \xrightarrow{u(t)} FS'$,*
- *The firing of a cut step τ_i from a node v leads to a state $S' = (EM', FS')$ where $EM \xrightarrow{v,\tau_i} EM'$ as Definition14. in [3]. and $FS \xrightarrow{u(\tau_i)} FS'$.*

Therefore, the analysis of R^2PN is based on constructing its extended reachability graph, which is used for checking properties such as reachability, deadlock and liveness.

5   Case Study : Automated Production Systems

In this research work, we use a reconfigurable production devices called, FESTO[7] as a running example. We assume that the device may perform some particular reconfiguration scenarios according to well-defined conditions. FESTO is composed of three units: distribution, test and processing units. The distribution unit is composed of a pneumatic feeder and a converter to forward cylindrical work pieces from a stack to the testing unit which is composed of the detector, the tester and the elevator. The testing unit checks of work pieces for height, material type and color. Work pieces that successfully pass this check are forwarded to the rotating disk of the processing unit, where the drilling of the work piece is performed. We assume in this work two drilling machines $Dr1$ and $Dr2$ to drill pieces. The result of the drilling operation is next checked by a checking machine and the work piece is forwarded to another mechanical unit. Three production modes (called local configurations) can be performed by $FESTO$.

- $Light1$: For this production mode, only the drilling machine $Dr1$ is used;
- $Light2$: To drill work pieces for this production mode, only the drilling machine $Dr2$ is used;
- $High$: For this production mode, where $Dr1$ and $Dr2$ are used at the same time in order to accelerate the production.

$Ligth1$ is the default production mode of $FESTO$ and the system completely stops in the worst case if the two drilling machines are broken. We assume that $FESTO$ may perform four reconfiguration scenarios as shown in Fig.2.

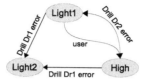

Fig. 2. Reconfiguration scenarios of $FESTO$

6 Modeling $FESTO$ Using Reconfigurable RPN

The automated production system $FESTO$ is modelled as follows: $EN_{FESTO} = \langle EN_{Beh}, EN_{Adapt} \rangle$ where EN_{Beh} represents the behaviour module of $FESTO$ and EN_{Adapt} is the adaptor which represents possible reconfiguration scenarios may be applied by the reconfigurable control system $FESTO$.

The adaptor EN_{Adapt} of $FESTO$ is shown in Fig.3. It is represented by ERPN where each place specifies one beahviour. As shown in Fig.3, we have three places p_{L1}, p_{L2} and p_{Hi} which specify the three production modes $Light1$, $Light2$ and $High$. Each one of these places may contain at most one token and the marking of such place means that its associated production mode is currently applied by the production system $FESTO$. For instance, the place p_{L1} is marked, which means the current production mode applied by $FESTO$ is $Light1$ i.e.the initial production mode. The set of elemenatry transitions represent the set of reconfiguration scenarios of $FESTO$. For instance, the elementary transition t_{L1ToL2} models the reconfiguration scenario that allows the production system $FESTO$ to transform from the first production mode $Light1$ to the second production mode $Light2$ when drilling machine $Dr1$ is broken. In fact, the firing of this transition will interrupt the abstract transition $Drill_{L1}$, which models the first production mode $Light1$, and update the current feature selection FS by applying its associated update expression $Dr1\ off;Dr2\ on$ as shown in Fig.3.

The behaviour EN_{Beh} of $FESTO$ which is a union of multiple R^2PNs is formalised as follows: $EN_{Beh} = \bigcup_{i \in \overline{1..3}} EN_{Beh_i}$, with $EN_{Beh_i} = \langle P_i, T_i, Pre_i, Post_i, \Omega_i, I_i, \Upsilon_i, K_i, F_i, f_i, u_i \rangle$ is a R^2PN models one possible behaviour of reconfigurable control system of $FESTO$. Fig.4 models the behaviour of $FESTO$ using ERPN. All the transitions shown in Fig.4, where their *application condition* and *update expression* are omitted, are annotated by the term : $\frac{true}{noop}$. This means that this set of transitions are common to all behaviours of $FESTO$. The set of features F contains the set of drilling machines which may be used to select the proper behaviour of $FESTO$ i.e. $F = \{Dr1, Dr2\}$. As noted in Fig.4, the abstract transitions $Distribute$, $Test$ and $Process$ models the distribution, tester and processing unit. The firing of one of these transitions will create a thread representing the behaviour of associating unit.

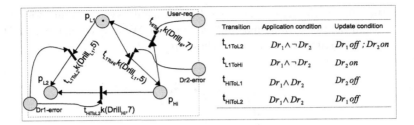

Transition	Application condition	Update condition
t_{L1ToL2}	$Dr_1 \wedge \neg Dr_2$	$Dr_1\,off$; $Dr_2\,on$
t_{L1ToHi}	$Dr_1 \wedge \neg Dr_2$	$Dr_2\,on$
t_{HiToL1}	$Dr_1 \wedge Dr_2$	$Dr_2\,off$
t_{HiToL2}	$Dr_1 \wedge Dr_2$	$Dr_1\,off$

Fig. 3. R^2PN represents FESTO's adaptor

For instance, the firing of the abstract transition $Process$ creates a thread, models the behaviour of processing unit, which starts by one token i.e. workpiece in place p_{12}. The workpiece is then forwarded to the drilling machines by firing the elementary transition $Rotate$. After, three abstract transitions $Drill_{L1}$, $Drill_{L2}$ and $Drill_{Hi}$ may be enabled; they model the drilling's step according to the three production modes $Light1$, $Light2$ and $High$. But each one of these abstract transitions is associated an application condition which restricts its activation (firing) to the set of bound features F. As described above, the default production mode of $FESTO$ is $Light1$, where only the drilling machine $Dr1$ is used, so the initial feature selection $FS_0 = \{Dr1\}$. In this case, only the abstract transition $Drill_{L1}$ is enabled. The firing of this abstract transition will create a thread, models the drilling's step, which starts by one token in place p_{17}. Note that the created thread can use only the drilling machine $Dr1$ represented by the elementary transition $Dr1\text{-}L1$. Moreover, this thread presents two types of termination :

- $Properly\ termination$: it means that the workpiece is well drilled and the place p_{18} is marked. So, a final marking belongs to termination's set Υ_4 is reached, then the cut step τ_4 may be enabled. The firing of τ_4 terminates the current thread and puts a workpiece in the place p_{14} in order to perform the remains operations such as $Checker$ and $Evacuate$.
- $Termination\ by\ interruption$: this termination occured when the production system $FESTO$ applies a reconfiguration as described above for adaptor module. For instance, from Fig.3, firing the elementary transition t_{L1ToL2} will interrupt the thread created by the abstract transition $Drill_{L1}$ with termination index 5 and update the feature selection FS_0. The new obtained feature selection $FS_1 = \{Dr2\}$. In fact, the workpiece is put it in the place p_{13} and only the abstract transition $Drill_{L2}$ may be enabled, which specify the drilling's step according to the second production mode $Light2$.

7   Verification of Reconfigurable Control Systems

In this section, we outline the conversion from R^2PNs to a Maude specification [6] and the use of its Linear Temporal Logic (LTL) model checker [11].

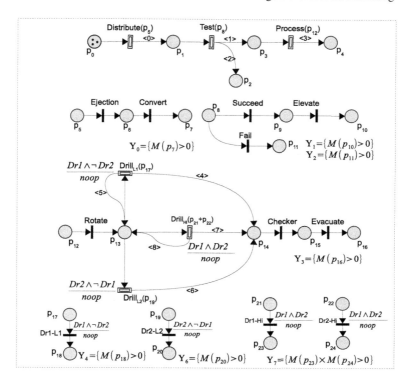

Fig. 4. R^2PN represents FESTO's behaviour

7.1 Maude and Its Model-Checker

Maude is a high-performance reflective language and system supporting rewriting logic specification [12]. It has been developed at SRI (URL: http://maude.cs.uiuc.edu/) International for over two decades. A system, under Maude, is represented using membership equational logic describing its set of states and a set of rewrite rules representing its state transitions. Maude is stricly typed, where the types are called *sorts* and can be built hierarchically using *subsorts*. Maude's basic programming statements are equations and rules, and have in both cases a simple rewriting semantics in which instances of the left-hand side pattern are replaced by corresponding instances of the right-hand side. One aim using Maude is its LTL model-checker which can be used to verify properties as reachability, deadlock or liveness for a specified model. Model checking can be used to prove properties, specified in LTL when the set of states reachable from an initial state in a system module is finite. In [11], the author presents more details about syntax and semantic of LTL.

7.2 Conversion of R^2PN to a Maude specification

Like in [8], the state of a R^2PN is described by a term $State(EM, fs)$ of sort $STATE$ where:

– EM is an extended marking represented, in a recursive way, as a dynamical tree by the term $[M_{Th}, tabs, ThreadChilds]$ of sort $Thread$ where M, of sort $Marking$, represents the internal marking of Th. The term $tabs$ represents the name of the abstract transition whose firing (in its thread father) gave birth to the thread Th. Note that the root thread is not generated by any abstract transition, so the abstract transition which gave birth to it, is represented by the constant $nullTrans$. The term $ThreadChilds$ represents a finite multiset of threads generated by the firing of abstract transitions in the thread Th. We denote by the constant $nullThread$, the empty thread.

– fs is a feature selection, of sort FS, represented by a list of terms of sort $Term$. We denote by the constant $empty$, the empty list of feature selection.

We have also impleneted two functions in the module $FeatureSel$ needed by our formalism R^2PN. The first function is $SATAC(ac : AC, fs : FS) : Bool$ which checks the truth value of an application condition ac, of sort AC, for a given feature selection fs. The second function is $UPDATE(u : UE, fs : FS) : FS$ which returns the new feature selection after applying the update expression u, of sort UE, for a given feature selection fs.

Moreover, each transition firing and cut step execution is formally specified in Maude by a labelled rewrite rule as follows :

– Rule associated to an elemetary transition t with $K(t) = \phi$, application condition $ac(t)$ and update expression $ue(t)$

```
crl[t]: State(<p; N+Pre(p,t)> (*) <p'; M> , fs) =>State(<p; N
    )> (*) <p'; M + Post(p',t)> , UPDATE(ue(t), fs) if SATAC(
    ac(t), fs) .
```

– Rule associated to an elemetary transition t with $K(t) = \{(t_{absi}, k), (t_{absj}, m), ..\}$, application condition $ac(t)$ and update expression $ue(t)$

```
crl[t]: State([<p;N+Pre(p,t)>(*)<p';M>(*)<p'_i;A>(*)<p'_j;B>,
    absTrans,Thread],fs) => State([<p; N>(*)<p'; M+Post(p',t)
    >(*)<p'_i; A+Post(p'_i, t_{absi},k)>(*)<p'_j; B+Post(p'_j,t_{absj},m)>,
    absTrans, DeleteThread(t_{absi},t_{absj},...,Thread)], UPDATE(ue(t
    ), fs) if SATAC(ac(t), fs) .
```

– Rule associated to an abstract transition t with starting marking $\Omega(t)$, application condition $ac(t)$ and update expression $ue(t)$

```
crl[t]: State([<p;N+Pre(p,t)>, absTrans, Thread] , fs) =>
    State([<p; N)>, absTrans, Thread[<p'; Ω(t)>, t, nullThread
    ]] , UPDATE(ue(t), fs) if SATAC(ac(t), fs) .
```

– Rule associated to a cut step τ_i with application condition $ac(\tau_i)$ and update expression $ue(\tau_i)$

```
crl[τ_i]: State([<p;N>, absTrans, Thread[<p';N'> , tabs,
    Thread1]] , fs) => State([<p; N+Post(p, tabs, i)>,
    absTrans, Thread, UPDATE(ue(τ_i), fs) if (Υ_i and SATAC(ac(τ_i
    ), fs)) .
```

7.3   Implementation Using the Maude Tool

Since we give a Maude specification for the formalism R^2PN, we can benefit from the use of the LTL model-checker of the Maude system for verification purpose where the generated state space must be finite. For instance, one can check the liveness property over EN_{FESTO} for its initial behaviour $Ligth1$. We suppose that the system starts by 100 tokens i.e. workpieces, this is specified in Maude by : $eqinitialState = State(< p0; 100 > (*) < pL1; 1 >, Dr1)$. A liveness condition is : *each workpiece must reach (from all reachable markings) the final state where the place p_4 is marked*. This can be phrased as "*For all paths and from all states, $State(< p4; 100 > (*) < pL1; 1 >, Dr1)$ can finally be reached*". In Maude, this is stated by $[] <> State([< p4; 100 > (*) < pL1; 1 >, nullTrans, nullThread], Dr1)$., and proven to be *valid* by its model checker in Fig.5(a). We suppose in this case that there is no *fail* during the workpieces's test process.

Let take another example and we focus on the case, when an error occurs, whether the control module can respond and select a proper behaviour. We define the following LTL formula : $\alpha : [](Behaviour(Light1)/ Drill - Down(Dr1) => <> Behaviour(Light2)))$, where, the predicate $Behaviour$ allows to know the current behaviour applied by the production system $FESTO$. The predicate $Drill-Down$ indicates which among drilling machines $Dr1$ ord $Dr2$ is break-down.

This LTL formula means that, always, if the current production mode of $FESTO$ is $Light1$, drill machine $Dr1$ is broken, the production system $FESTO$ will eventually select the production mode $Light2$. This LTL formula is proved to be *valid* in Fig.5(b).

Now, let's define a LTL proprty β by replacing in the formula α the production mode $Light2$ by $High$. In Fig.5(c), this formula is proved to be *not valid* and the model-checker returns the expected *counterexample*.

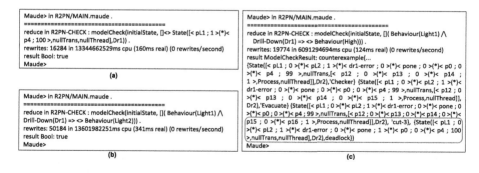

Fig. 5. (a) Model checking of the liveness condition for first production mode of $FESTO$, (b) Model checking of the LTL property α and (c) *Counterexample* generated by model checking of the LTL property β

8 Conclusion and Future Work

This research work copes with the reconfiguration issue of discrete control systems. We have proposed Renconfigurable RPN (R^2PN) which enriches RPN by the concept of *feature* to deal with reconfigurations at runtime. R^2PN allows instance of threads in RPN to be renconfigurable. We have shown the efficiency of R^2PN through a case study represented by a reconfigurable production system. A verification method for R^2PN has also been presented by using the LTL model-cheker of Maude.

In the future, we will plan to extend our formalism in order to model time constraints which are of great importance in real-time systems. Therefore, one can verify some properties with respect to time constraints using Real-Time Maude model-checker [10].

References

1. Valk, R.: Self-modifying nets, a natural extension of petri nets. In: Proceedings of the Fifth Colloquium on Automata, Languages and Programming, pp. 464–476 (1978)
2. Murata, T.: Petri nets: Properties, analysis and applications. Proceedings of the IEEE 77(4), 541–580 (1989)
3. Haddad, S., Poitrenaud, D.: Recursive Petri nets – Theory and application to discretee event systems. Acta Informatica 44(7-8), 463–508 (2007)
4. Guan, S.-U., Lim, S.-S.: Modeling adaptable multimedia and self-modifying protocol execution. Future Gener. Comput. Syst. 20(1), 123–143 (2004)
5. Badouel, M.L.E., Oliver, J.: Modeling concurrent systems: Reconfigurable nets. In: Proc. Int. Conf. on Parallel and Distributed Processing Techniques and Applications (PDPTA 2003), pp. 1568–1574. CSREA Press (2003)
6. Clavel, M., Duran, F., Eker, S., Lincoln, P., Marti-Oliet, N., Meseguer, J., Quesada, J.: Maude: specification and programming in rewriting logic. Theoretical Computer Science 285(2), 187–243 (2002), rewriting Logic and its Applications
7. Zhang, J., Khalgui, M., Li, Z., Mosbahi, O., Al-Ahmari, A.: R-tnces: A novel formalism for reconfigurable discretee event control systems. IEEE Transactions on Systems, Man, and Cybernetics: Systems 43(4), 757–772 (2013)
8. Barkaoui, K., Hicheur, A.: Towards analysis of flexible and collaborative workflow using recursive eCATNets. In: ter Hofstede, A.H.M., Benatallah, B., Paik, H.-Y. (eds.) BPM Workshops 2007. LNCS, vol. 4928, pp. 232–244. Springer, Heidelberg (2008)
9. Muschevici, R.: Modelling Diversity in Software Product Lines. PhD thesis, KU Leuven university, Belgium (December 2013)
10. Ölveczky, P.C., Meseguer, J.: Real-Time Maude: A tool for simulating and analyzing realtime and hybrid systems. In: 3rd International Workshop on Rewriting Logic and its Applications (WRLA 2000). Electronic Notes in Theoretical Computer Science, vol. 36 (2000)
11. Eker, S., Meseguer, J., Sridharanarayanan, A.: The maude LTL model checker. Electronic Notes in Theoretical Computer Science 71, 162–187 (2004)
12. Meseguer, J.: Conditioned rewriting logic as a united model of concurrency. Theor. Comput. Sci. 96, 73–155 (1992)
13. Kang, K., Cohen, S., Hess, J., Novak, W., Peterson, A.: Feature-oriented domain analysis (foda) feasibility study. Software Engineering Institute, Carnegie Mellon University, Tech. Rep. CMU/SEI-90-TR-021 (1990)

Hybrid Approach for Metamodel and Model Co-evolution

Fouzia Anguel[1,3(✉)], Abdelkrim Amirat[2], and Nora Bounour[3]

[1] Chadli Bendjedid University, El Tarf, Algeria.
fanguel@yahoo.fr
[2] LiM Laboratory, Mohammed Chérif Messaadia University, Souk-Ahras, Algeria
abdelkrim.amirat@yahoo.com
[1,3] LISCO Laboratory. Badji Mokhtar University.Annaba, Algeria
nora_bounour@yahoo.fr

Abstract. Evolution is an inevitable aspect which affects metamodels. When metamodels evolve, model conformity may be broken. Model co-evolution is critical in model driven engineering to automatically adapt models to the newer versions of their metamodels. In this paper we discuss what can be done to transfer models between versions of a metamodel. For this purpose we introduce hybrid approach for model and metamodel co-evolution, that first uses matching between two metamodels to discover changes and then applied evolution operators to migrate models. In this proposal, migration of models is done automatically; except, for non resolvable changes, where assistance is proposed to the users in order to co-evolve their models to regain conformity.

Keywords: Metamodel evolution · Model migration · Co-evolution · Matching · Evolution operator

1 Introduction

In Model-Driven Engineering (MDE)[1], metamodels and domain-specific languages are key artifacts as they are used to define syntax and semantics of domain models [1]. Since in MDE metamodels are not created once and never changed again, but are in continuous evolution, different versions of the same metamodel are created and must be managed [2]. The evolution of metamodels is a considerable challenge of modern software development as changes may require the migration of their instances. Works in this direction exist already. Several manual and semi-automatic approaches for realizing model migration have been proposed. Each approach aims to reduce the effort required to perform this process. Unfortunately, in several cases it is not possible to automatically modify the models to make them conform to the updated metamodels. This is so because certain changes over metamodels require introducing additional information into the conformant model. In the literature, three general approaches to the migration of models exist: manual, state-based, operator- based [3]. Manual approaches are tedious and error prone. State-based approaches also called difference-based approaches allow synthesizing a model migration based on the

A. Amine et al. (Eds.): CIIA 2015, IFIP AICT 456, pp. 563–573, 2015.
DOI: 10.1007/978-3-319-19578-0_46

difference between two metamodel versions. In contrast, operator-based approaches allow to incrementally transforming the metamodel by means of coupled operations which also encapsulate the corresponding model migration. They allow capturing the intended model migration already when adapting the metamodel. A major drawback of the later approach has been overly tight coupling between the tool performing the migration, and the recorder tracking the changes made to the models.

Usually, existing approaches try to find how to best accomplish model co-evolution. Essentially, we can define two main requirements: the correctness of migration and minimizing the effort of migration by automating as far as possible the process.

In this paper, we propose an alternative solution to model migration which combines state-based and operator based principles to co-evolve models and metamodels. Our vision to resolve this problem is to generate evolution strategies with their corresponding model migration strategies. We focus on including users decisions during metamodel and model co-evolution process to ensure semantic correctness of evolved models.

The rest of the paper is structured as follows. Section 2 gives an overview of basic concepts and describes the metamodel and model co-evolution problem Section 3 presents our proposed approach for solving the model co-evolution problem. In section 4, we present some proposed approaches in the past and situates our solution. Section 5 presents some guidelines to implement proposed framework. Finally, section 6 concludes and gives some future works.

2   Background

2.1   Models and Metamodels

In this section we present the central MDE definitions used in this paper. The basic assumption in MDE is to consider models as first-class entities. An MDE system basically consists of metamodels, models, and transformations. A model represents a view of a system and is defined in the language of its metamodel [1]. In other words, a model contains elements conforming to concepts and relationships expressed in its metamodel [4]. A metamodel can be given to define correct models. In the same way a model is described by a metamodel, a metamodel in turn has to be specified in a rigorous manner; this is done by means of meta-metamodels [5]. This may be seen as a minimal definition in support of the basic MDE principle "Everything is considered as a model" [1]. The two core relations associated to this principle are called representation "Represented by" and conformance "Conform To". A model conforms to a metamodel, when the metamodel specifies every concept used in the model definition, and the models uses the metamodel concepts according to the rules specified by the metamodel [1].

In this respect, the object management group (OMG) [6] has introduced the four level architecture which organizes artifacts in a hierarchy of model layers (M0, M1, M2, and M3). Models at every level conform to a model belonging to the upper level. M0 is not part of the modeling world as depicted in Fig.1, so the four level architecture should more precisely be named (3+1) architecture [1]. One of the best known metamodels in the MDE is the UML (Unified Modeling Language) metamodel; MOF (Meta-Object Facility) is the metametamodel of OMG that supports rigorous definition of modeling languages as UML [6].

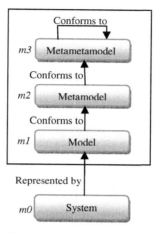

Fig. 1. The 3+1 MDA organisation [2]

2.2   Metamodel Evolution and Model Co-evolution

Metamodels may evolve in different ways, due to several reasons [2]: during design, alternative metamodel versions are developed and well-known solutions are customized for new applications. During implementation, metamodels are adapted to a concrete metamodel formalism supported by a tool. During maintenance, errors in a metamodel are corrected. Furthermore, parts of the metamodel are redesigned due to a better understanding or to facilitate reuse. The addition of new features and/or the resolution of bugs may change metamodels, thus causing possible problems of inconsistency to existing models which conform to the old version of the metamodel and may become not conform to the new version. Therefore to maintain consistency, metamodel evolution requires model adaptation, i.e., model migration; so these two steps are referred as model and metamodel co-evolution [7]. Metamodel and model co-evolution is a term that denotes a coupled evolution of metamodels and models [7], which consists to adapt (co-evolve) the models conforming to the initial version of the metamodel, such that they conform to the target (evolved) version, preserving the intended meaning of the initial model if possible [7], as illustrated in Fig.2. Furthermore, model adaptations should be done by means of model transformations [8]. A model transformation takes as input a model conforming to a given metamodel and produces as output another model conforming to the evolved version of the given metamodel [4].

A number of works proposed the classification of metamodel changes according to their corrupting effects. Metamodel changes are grouped on three categories [9]:

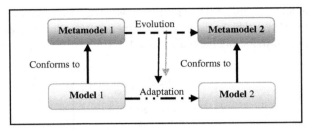

Fig. 2. Model Co-evolution [7]

- Not breaking changes, changes occurring in the metamodel don't break the models conformance to the metamodel.
- Breaking and resolvable changes, changes occurring in the metamodel do break the models, which can be automatically resolved.
- Breaking and non-resolvable changes, changes do break the models and cannot be automatically resolved and user intervention is required.

However, a uniform formalization of metamodel evolution is still lacking. The relation between metamodel and model changes should be formalized in order to allow reasoning about the correctness of migration definitions.

2.3   Logic Programming

Logic programming is a programming paradigm based on formal logic [10]. A program written in a logic programming language is a set of sentences in logical form, expressing facts and rules about some problem domain. Major logic programming language families include Prolog, Answer Set Programming (ASP) and Datalog. In all of these languages, rules are written in the form of clauses (H :- B1, ..., Bn). These clauses are called definite clauses or Horn clauses and are read declaratively as logical implications (H if B1 and ... and Bn). Logic programming is used in artificial Intelligence knowledge representation and reasoning.

We have find this formalism very powerful to represent relationships between changes and consequently, from an initial set of changes inferring all possible evolution strategies. Currently, to our best knowledge, there is no approach that uses an intelligent reasoning for defining model migrations. Therefore, we have integrated logic programming in our proposal to resolve model co-evolution problem.

3   Proposed Approach

In this section we describe our proposal to ensure the co-evolution of model with their metamodels. The overall evolution and co-evolution process is presented in Fig.3.

Our approach is hybrid because it exports techniques from state-based and operator based approaches and uses also a reasoning mechanism from artificial intelligence. It contains four phases: changes detection, generation and validation of evolution strategies, determination of migration strategies and migration of models.

In the first step; differences between two metamodel versions need to be determined by using matching technique. In the second step we use an inference engine to generate different evolution strategies by assembling atomic changes in possible compound ones; in the third step we explore a library of operators to obtain different migration procedures, which will be assembled to constitute migration strategies. In the last step users employ a selected evolution strategy and consequently, the migration strategy will be applied over a specific model conforming to the old version in order to obtain a new model conforming to the newer metamodel version.

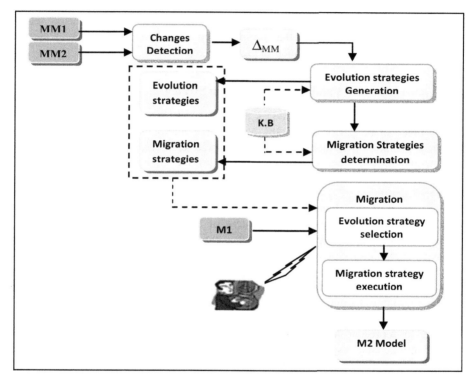

Fig. 3. An overview of metamodel and model co-evolution process

3.1   Detection of Changes

The detection of differences between models is essential to model development and management practices. Thus evolution from one metamodel version to the next can be described by a sequence of changes. Understanding how metamodels evolve or discovering changes that have been performed on a metamodel is a key requirement before undertaking any migration operation on models to co-evolve them. In fact, we distinguish two ways for discovering changes: matching approaches and recording approaches [11]. In Our approach, for detecting the set of changes performed to the older version of the metamodel in order to produce the new one, we use generic algorithm. Whereas current generic approaches only support detecting atomic changes, some language-specific approaches also allow detecting composite changes; but only for one specific modeling language.   Primitive differences between metamodels versions are classified in three basic categories: additions, deletions, and updates of metamodel elements. These differences represent elementary changes (i.e. atomic).

In fact, composite or compound changes have been already considered in previous works like [12,13]. But, we envision tackle the problem differently. We call evolution strategy a possible sequence of changes; here changes are either elementary or composite. Thus, a set of composite changes is inferred from the detected set of atomic changes, by using rules that define composite changes in terms of atomic changes. This mechanism is detailed in the following section.

3.2   Generation and Validation of Evolution Strategies

Detected differences are represented as elementary changes specifying fine-grained changes that can be performed in the course of metamodel evolution. There are a number of primitive metamodel changes like create element, rename element, delete element, and so on. One or more of such primitive changes compose a specific metamodel adaptation However, this granularity of metamodel evolution changes is not always appropriate.

Often, intent of the changes may be expressed on a higher level. Thus, a set of atomic changes can have together the intent of a composite change. For example, generation of a common superclass sc of two classes c1 and c2 can be done through successive applications of a list of elementary changes, such as 'Add_class   sc', 'Add_reference   from c1 to sc', and 'Add_reference' from c2 to sc. One way to resolve the problem of identifying composite changes is to use operation recording. But, this solution has some drawbacks.

In our proposal, we use logical predicate with the language Prolog. Horn clauses are used to represent knowledge. Therefore, we formally characterize changes. Detected atomic changes are represented as positive clauses (i.e. facts) and composite changes are specified by rules such as Left hand side contains the composite change and the Right hand side contains a set of associated atomic changes. Thus, the applicability of a compound change can be restricted by conditions in the form of rules. According to this principle, we have formalized a knowledge base. The definition of changes is inspired from the literature [7, 14]. The knowledge base is used by the inference engine to generate possible evolution strategies. Finally, evolution strategies must be validated. This step consists of applying each evolution scenario defined by the strategy on the old input version of the metamodel. If it results the newer input version then the tested strategy is valid and it is retained else the strategy in test is rejected. The final output is a set of valid evolution strategies.

C : set of classes
A : set of attributes
Auxiliary predicates

subclasse(s : C, c:C) : s is subclass of c
added_class(c:C) : c is added to the metamodel
added_attribute(a:A,c:C) : a is added to the class c of the metamodel.
deleted_attribute(a:A,c:C) : a is deleted from the class c of the metamodel.
Is_attribute_of(a:A,c:C) : a is an attribute of the class c.
added_supertype ((s : C, c:C) .   specialization/generalization reference is added
                                                between s and c.
deleted _supertype ((s : C, c:C) : specialization/generalization reference between
                                                s and c is removed.
added-reference (r :R, s: C, d:C) : r is an added reference having as source s class
                                                and d as target class.
Extract-superclass(sc ,c1,c2 :C) :- added_class(sc: C),
                                                added_supertype ((sc : C, c1:C),
                                                added_supertype ((sc : C, c2:C).

Complex changes are specified through rules. As an instance, we consider extract super class operation where a class is generalized in a hierarchy by adding a new general class and two references to their subclasses.

3.3   Determination of Migration Strategies

In this step we import techniques of operator based-approaches. We use in this phase a library of operators. Thus, we specify a change as an evolution operation. An operation evolution can be either simple or composite and every operation is defined through a set of parameters. We associate to it information about how to migrate corresponding models in response to a metamodel evolution forming a migration procedure. Migration procedure is encoded as a model transformation that transforms a model such that the new model conforms the metamodel undergoing the change. Furthermore, we explicitly specify in migration procedures some assistance specifications for each change requiring additional information from user to solve it. This makes our library different of that used in previous works [13]. The library does not contain evolution steps but only the migration procedure referenced with evolution operation. In our proposal we take from the library migration procedures corresponding to changes in the evolution strategy; after their instantiation, we assemble them to constitute the complete migration strategy which will be associated to the evolution strategy. The final result in this step is a set of couples (evolution strategy, migration strategy) specified to co-evolve input models conforming to the specified metamodel.

3.4   Migration

This phase takes as input an instance model conforming to the initial metamodel. This model is also called user model. To transform the model to newer version of the metamodel, firstly one of available evolution strategies previously inferred is considered. According to the taken evolution strategy associated migration strategy will be automatically generated and then applied to the input model. For breaking and irresolvable changes, the system assists establish adequate migration procedure by presenting alternative solutions. Additionally, users can provide additional information to complete the change on the model if necessary. For instance, if the new attribute must be initialized, the user must also be requested for the initial value. If the user is satisfied by the resulted model the process is achieved, otherwise he can try again by selecting other proposed evolution strategy and the process continues so that, until user satisfaction or no choice is available.

3.5   Implementation

In this section, we give details and technical choices made to implement a prototype of the proposed framework. As meta-metamodel, we use Ecore from the Eclipse Modeling Framework (EMF) [16]. However, our approach is not restricted to Ecore, as it can be transferred to all object-oriented metamodeling formalisms.

For the definition of rules specifying knowledge base used to infer evolution strategies, we have adopted an adequate formalism for logic programming Prolog [10]. Prolog is chosen because in one hand it is a language of knowledge representation [17] and in the other hand using inference rules eliminates programming to get eventual compound changes, the task is performed by the inference engine of Prolog. Furthermore, Prolog interpreters are developed in several languages, which facilitates the use of the prolog formalism.

The computation of the differences between metamodel versions is performed with The Eclipse plug-in EMF Compare [18]. This tool provides algorithms to calculate the delta between two versions of a model and visualizes them using tree representations. EMF Compare is capable of detecting the following types of atomic operations:

- Add: A model element only exists in the revised version.
- Delete: A model element only exists in the origin version.
- Update: A feature of a model element has a different value in the revised version than in the origin version.
- Move: A model element has a different container in the revised version than in the origin version.

4   Related Works

In this section we will give an overview of current metamodel and model co-evolution approaches and already implemented systems. Over the last few years, the problem of metamodel evolution and model co-evolution has been investigated by several works like [4], [7-9], [12-13], [19-21]. Currently, there are several approaches that focus on resolving inconsistencies occurring in models after metamodel evolution [3], a classification of these model migration approaches is proposed in [3]. This classification highlights three ways to identify needed model updates: manually, based on operators, and by using metamodel matching. When manually approaches like in [19-21], updates are defined by hand. In operators based approaches, like [7],[13], metamodels changes are defined in terms of co-evolutionary operators [14]. Those operators define conjointly the evolution on the metamodel and its repercussion on the models. Finally, in metamodel matching, like [4], [9], [12], versions of metamodels are compared and differences between them are used to semi-automatically infer a transformation that expresses models updates. Manual specification approach like Flock [21] is very expressive, concise, and correctness is also assured but finds difficulties with large metamodels since there is no tool support for analyzing the changes between original and evolved metamodels [22]. Operator based approaches like [13] ensure expressiveness, automaticity, and reuse [23], it was been perceived as strong in correctness, conciseness and understandability [22] but its lack is in determining which sequence of operations will produce a correct migration. Analysis of existing model co-evolution approaches, and comparison results of some works [3], [24-25] has yielded guidance for defining some requirements to our approach. To take advantage of state-based and operator-based approaches, previously discussed. We have proposed an alternative solution where we applied a hybrid approach to define model migration. The solution presented in this paper has a number of similarities with the techniques illustrated in [13], but it differs from this approach because it takes as input results of a matching process. Therefore, it permits evolving models with different tools. Another, strength of our solution is the proposed reasoning mechanism, which allows finding different evolution strategies and consequently different migration strategies. Proposed solution minimizes as far as possible the user effort to migrate models. Thus user intervention is limited to a control task in the end of the process to validate results which permits to increase expressivity and correctness.

5   Conclusion

In this paper we have proposed an alternative solution to automate the co-evolution of models and metamodels. In our proposal we use a hybrid approach. It takes advantages from state-based and operator based approaches. This solution consists of using a library of coupled operation and also a knowledge base of changes definition

The benefits of this approach are numerous, notably automaticity of the co-evolution is augmented compared with other techniques because even for changes requiring specific information, we have predict automatic model migration with user assistance. Moreover, our solution is independent from any modeling environment. It is easily adapted to various modeling environment. Using an intelligent logic mechanism to infer compound changes and evolution strategies increase effectiveness of our proposal. This makes our solution distinguishable from existing works.

However, currently the evaluation of the proposed framework is not performed. For a complete validation, we will conduct case studies with industrial models. In the long term, we want to study the possibilities to extend our solution to support representation of semantic in models and preserving semantics within the migration process as introduced in [26].

References

1. Bézivin, J.: On the Unification Power of Models. Software and systems Modeling (So-SyM.) 4(2), 171–188 (2005)
2. Favre, J.M.: Meta-model and model co-evolution within the 3D software space. In: International Workshop on Evolution of Large-scale Industrial Software Applications ELISA 2003, Amsterdam, pp. 98–109 (2003)
3. Rose, L.M., Kolovos, D.S., Paige, R.F., Polack, F.A.C.: An analysis of approaches to model migration. In: Joint MoDSE-MCCM Workshop (2009)
4. Garcés, K., Jouault, F., Cointe, P., Bézivin, J.: Managing Model Adaptation by Precise Detection of Metamodel Changes. In: Paige, R.F., Hartman, A., Rensink, A. (eds.) ECMDA-FA 2009. LNCS, vol. 5562, pp. 34–49. Springer, Heidelberg (2009)
5. Amirat, A.: Contribution à l'élaboration d'architectures logicielles à hiérarchies multiples, Thèse de Doctorat en Informatique, Université de Nantes, France (2010)
6. OMG: MOF QVT Final Adopted Specification (2005), http://www.omg.org/docs/ptc/05-11-01.pdf
7. Wachsmuth, G.: Metamodel adaptation and model co-adaptation. In: Ernst, E. (ed.) ECOOP 2007. LNCS, vol. 4609, pp. 600–624. Springer, Heidelberg (2007)
8. Amirat, A., Menasria, A.: ne Gasmallah:Evolution Framework for Software Architecture using Graph Transformation Approach. In: The 12th International Arab Conference on Information Technology (ACIT'2011), Riyadh, Saudi Arabia, December 11-14, pp. 75–82 (2011)
9. Gruschko, B., Kolovos, D.S., Paige, R.F.: Towards synchronizing models with evolving metamodels. In: International Workshop on Model-Driven Software Evolution (2007)
10. Savoy, J.: Introduction à la programmation logique Prolog (2006), http://members.unine.ch/jacques.savoy/lectures/SemCL/Prolog.pdf
11. Didonet Del Fabro, M., Bézivin, J., Jouault, F., Breton, E., Gueltas, G.: AMW: A Generic Model Weaver. In: IDM 2005 Premières Journées sur l'Ingénierie Dirigée par les Modèles, Paris (2005)
12. Cicchetti, A.: Difference Representation and Conflict Management in Model-Driven Engineering, Phd thesis (2008)
13. Herrmannsdoerfer, M., Benz, S., Juergens, E.: Automatability of Coupled Evolution of Metamodels and Models in Practice. In: Czarnecki, K., Ober, I., Bruel, J.-M., Uhl, A., Völter, M. (eds.) MODELS 2008. LNCS, vol. 5301, pp. 645–659. Springer, Heidelberg (2008)
14. Herrmannsdoerfer, M., Vermolen, S.D., Wachsmuth, G.: An Extensive Catalog of Operators for the Coupled Evolution of Metamodels and Models. In: Malloy, B., Staab, S., van den Brand, M. (eds.) SLE 2010. LNCS, vol. 6563, pp. 163–182. Springer, Heidelberg (2011)
15. Jouault, F., Kurtev, I.: Transforming models with ATL. In: Model Transformations in Practice Workshop at MoDELS Montego Bay, Jamaica, pp. 128–138 (2005)
16. EMF Eclipse Modeling Framework, http://www.eclipse.org/emf
17. Gaizauskas, R., Humphreys, K.: XI A Simple Prolog-based Language for Cross-Classification and Inheritance. In: Proceedings of the 7th International Conference on Artifi-cial Intelligence: Methodology, Systems, Applications (AIMSA 1996), Sozopol, Bulgaria, pp. 86–95 (1996)
18. EMFCompare, Eclipse modeling Project, http://www.eclipse.org/emf/compare/

19. Sprinkle, J., Karsai, G.: A domain-specific visual language for domain model evolution. Journal of Visual Languages and Computing 15, 291–307 (2004)
20. Narayanan, A., Levendovszky, T., Balasubramanian, D., Karsai, G.: Automatic Domain Model Migration to Manage Metamodel Evolution. In: Schürr, A., Selic, B. (eds.) MODELS 2009. LNCS, vol. 5795, pp. 706–711. Springer, Heidelberg (2009)
21. Rose, L.M., Kolovos, D.S., Paige, R.F., Polack, F.A.C.: Model Migration with Epsilon Flock. In: Tratt, L., Gogolla, M. (eds.) ICMT 2010. LNCS, vol. 6142, pp. 184–198. Springer, Heidelberg (2010)
22. Rose, L.M., Herrmannsdoerfer, M., Mazanek, S., Gorp, P.V., Buchwald, S., Horn, T., Kalnina, E., Koch, A., Lano, K., Schätz, B., Wimmer, M.: Graph and model transformation tools for model migration. Software and System Modelling Journal (2012)
23. Herrmannsdoerfer, M.: COPE – A Workbench for the coupled evolution of metamodels and models. In: Malloy, B., Staab, S., van den Brand, M. (eds.) SLE 2010. LNCS, vol. 6563, pp. 286–295. Springer, Heidelberg (2011)
24. Iovino, L., Pierantonio, A., Malavolta, I.: On the Impact Significance of Metamodel Evolu-tion in MDE. Journal of Object Technology 11(3), 1–33 (2012)
25. Herrmannsdörfer, M., Wachsmuth, G.: Coupled Evolution of Software Metamodels and Models. In: Mens, T., Alexander, S., Cleve, A. (eds.) Evolving Software Systems, p. 404. Springer (2014)
26. Cicchetti, A., Ciccozzi, F.: Towards a Novel Model Versioning Approach based on the Sep-aration between Linguistic and Ontological Aspects. In: ME 2013 Models and Evolution Workshop, pp. 58–65 (2013)

Extracting and Modeling Design Defects Using Gradual Rules and UML Profile

Mohamed Maddeh[1(✉)] and Sarra Ayouni[2]

[1] SOIE, ISG Tunis, Le Bardo, Tunis, Tunisia
maddeh_mohamed@yahoo.com
[2] Faculty of Sciences of Tunis, Tunis, Tunisia
s_ayouni@yahoo.fr

Abstract. There is no general consensus on how to decide if a particular design violates a model quality. In fact, we find in literature some defects described textually, detecting these design defects is usually a difficult problem. Deciding which object suffer from one defect depends heavily on the interpretation of each analyst. Experts often need to minimize design defects in software systems to improve the design quality. In this paper we propose a design defect detection approach based on object oriented metrics. We generate, using gradual rules, detection rules for each design defect at model level. We aim to extract, for each design defects, the correlation of co-variation of object oriented metrics. They are then modeled in a standard way, using the proposed UML profile for design defect modeling. We experiment our approach on 16 design defects using 32 object oriented metrics.

Keywords: Object oriented metrics · Data Mining · Gradual rules · Design defects detection · UML profile

1 Introduction

Design defects which are also called design anomalies, refer to design situations that adversely affect the development of software like bad smells [9] and antipatterns [2]. The first one (i.e., bad smells) was proposed by Beck [9]. In fact, the author defines 22 sets of symptoms of common defects. The second one (i.e., anti-patterns) was introduced by Brown et al. [2]. A set of refactoring suggestions are associate for each defect type. Detecting these defects at the model level is a promising way to improve software maintenance process [4][6][21]. In addition, it is difficult to identify and express these anomalies as rules [17], since they are not formalized and based on a simple textual description.

In general, design defects are evaluated using rules in the form of metric/threshold combinations. Some works propose rules manually identified [1][17], other propose algorithms that generate these rules[5][11][14]. Both approaches are suffering from two major difficulties. The first one is due to the large number of possible metrics combinations, in fact, it is difficult to find the best suitable rule. The second problem is to find the best threshold for each metric. In this paper, we propose a predictive

© IFIP International Federation for Information Processing 2015
A. Amine et al. (Eds.): CIIA 2015, IFIP AICT 456, pp. 574–583, 2015.
DOI: 10.1007/978-3-319-19578-0_47

design defects detection that focuses on model level in order to correct them before there propagation to the code. Also, instead of affecting a threshold for metrics, we generate, using gradual rules a correlation of co-variation of metrics characterizing the object oriented design defects. We model each defect using UML profile, defect are then represented as an UML class diagram summarizing the relevant information from the most significant textual descriptions in literature.

The remainder of the paper is structured as follows. In section 2, we present the related works. In section 3, we give the problem statement. In Section 4, we introduce the general process of the approach. In sections 5, we validate the proposed approach and section 6 is reserved for conclusion.

2   Related Works

Several studies have recently focused on detecting design defects in software using different techniques. In [14] authors propose a new framework M-RAFACTOR for the detection and correction of design defects based on object oriented metrics. Marinescu [9] defined a list of rules relying on metrics to detect what he calls design flaws of OO design at method, class and subsystem levels. Erni et al. [18] use metrics to evaluate frameworks with the goal of improving them. Another model refactoring is presented by Marc Van Kempen et al. [13], based on SAAT (Software Architecture Analysis Tool). It allows calculating metrics about UML models the metrics are then used to identify the flaws or anti-patterns. Authors represent the structure using class diagrams, and the behaviour of each class using statecharts. After that they examine the metrics for refactoring a centralized control structure into one that employs more delegation. For the four previous contributions it is difficult to manually define threshold values for metrics in the rules.Moha et al. [15], in their DÉCOR approach, they start by describing defect symptoms using an abstract rule language. These descriptions involve different notions, such as class roles and structures. In [11] defect detection is considered as an optimization problem. They propose an approach for the automatic detection of potential design defects in code. The detection is based on the notion that the more code deviates from good practices, the more likely it is bad.

3   Problem Statement

There are many open issues that need to be addressed when detecting design defects. In this paper, we first focus on how to define detection rules when dealing with quantitative information and then how to give a unified representation of defects specifications.

In fact, we notice that the textual description of design defects presented by authors depend on a subjective interpretations of analysts. As fact, for a same design we can find variable set of defects depending on the criteria's used by designer team. To bridge the gap between the description and the detection process, each design defect must be formalized for the standardization of the definition of symptoms detection. In this paper we intend to use gradual rules to formalize design defects. In the context of our research the generated gradual rules are represented as a correlation of co-variation of object oriented metrics. Once, gradual rules identified each design defect is then modeled using the UML profile for design defects. We have proposed an UML profile for design defect modeling. It summarizes the most relevant information and replaces all textual descriptions existing in literature by one class diagram for each design defect.

4   The General Process

As presented in figure 1, we start with the domain analysis of the knowledge extracted from the textual description of design defects. In fact, domain analysis is a process in which information used in developing software systems is identified, captured, and organized to be reusable when creating new systems [8]. In our context, information about design defects must be well structured and reusable for the automated detection process. Thus, we have studied the textual descriptions of design defects. We present an antipattern example named the Blob.

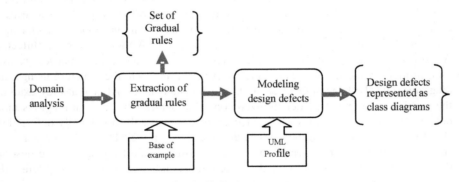

Fig. 1. General process

The Blob (called also God class [16]) corresponds to a large controller class that depends on data stored in surrounded data classes. A large class declares many fields and methods with a low cohesion. After the domain analysis for the Blob antipattern, we extract the relevant information. Indeed the blob is an interclass and behavioral defect, related to static and behavioral diagrams. The detection of the blob is based on the analysis of the class diagram and the sequence diagrams. As presented in table1, this research is based on 16 design defects.

These design defects are evaluated using object oriented metrics that are also identified at this step. Metrics must be measurable at model level, and useful for detection process. In our work we have identified 32 metrics. In what follows, we present some of these metrics:

Access To Foreign Data (ATFD) [12] represents the number of external classes from which a given class accesses attributes, directly or via accessor-methods.

Table 1. Classification of design defects

	Blob	SwissArmyKnife	Lava Flow	Poltergeists	FunctionalDecomposition	God Package	God Classes	Long Parameter List	Data Clumps	Divergent Change	ShotgunSurgery	Lazy Classes	FeatureEnvy	Comments	Data Classes	RefusedBequest
Structural					*			*	*							
Semantic														*		
Behavioral	*	*	*	*		*	*				*	*	*		*	*

Weighted Method Count (WMC) [3] is the sum of the complexity of all methods in a class.

Attribute Per method (APM) is defined as the ratio of the metrics Number of attributes (NOA) and (NOM).

After the metrics identification step we extract for each defect the most significant gradual rules that express the correlation of co-variation of the object oriented metrics. We propose an approach that uses knowledge from previously manually inspected projects, called defects examples.

4.1   Mining Gradual Rules

In our research, gradual rules are used to evaluate poor design by detecting bad smells and antipatterns. Mining gradual rule has been extensively used in fuzzy command systems. However, in last decade, the data mining community has been interested in extracting such kind of rules [7] [10] [19] [20]. Gradual rule convey knowledge of the form « the more/the less A, the more/the less B ». In our context, A and B are object oriented metric. We thus propose to extract rules such as « the more/the less Metrique1, the more/the less Metrique2..., the more/the less Metrique n », such that these metrics characterize a defect X. To the best of our knowledge, no previous study in the literature has paid attention to apply the extraction of gradual rules to the design defects detection. In the following section, we recall the key concepts of gradual rules mining.

Gradual Rules

We consider a data base defined on a schema containing m attributes $(X1, ...,Xm)$ defined on domains dom(Xi) provided with a total order. A data set D is a set of m-tuples of dom(X1),...,dom(Xm). In this scope, a gradual item is defined as a pair of an attribute and a variation {+,-}.The gradual item $Xn+$, means that the attribute Xn is increasing. It can be interpreted by the more A. A gradual itemset, or gradual tendency, is then defined as a non-empty set list of several gradual items.

For instance, the gradual itemset M =A+ B− is interpreted as, the more A and the less B. For example, the relation from Table 2 shows various items about disease symptoms.

Table 2. Disease symptoms

	Patients	Temperature	Lymphocyte	Hemoglobin
T1	P1	37.8	32	14
T2	P2	38.2	17	10
T3	P3	38.1	15	16

This table contains three tuples : {T1,T2,T3}, we study co-variations from one item to another one, as for example the variation of the temperature and hemoglobin. Too kinds of variations are considered: increasing variation and decreasing variation. Each item will hereafter be considered twice: once to evaluate its increasing strength, and once to evaluate its decreasing strength, using the + and - operators.

For example, let us consider the rule "The higher temperature and the higher hemoglobin then lower the lymphocyte" formalized by : R1= (Temperature + Hemoglobin + Lymphocyte -).

4.2   Mining Gradual Design Defect Rules

In this section, we present the extraction of gradual design defects rules. It is based on the GRITE algorithm [10], for GRadualITemset Extraction. For each design flaw, we identify the metric-based heuristics. The majority of works assign a threshold to each metric. The quality of the solution depends on the number of detected defects in comparison to the expected ones in the base of examples. The main limitation of this approach is that it is difficult to find the best threshold.

To overcome this problem, we present another type of correlation between object oriented metrics. To do so, we associate for each defect a metrics table; it represents the different metrics values for each occurrence (Oi) of all defects extracted manually from various projects (Pi). As example, we present in table 3 a part of the metrics table for the defect Data Class. The Data class defect creates classes that passively store data. Classes should contain data and methods to operate on that data.
Where, for a given class C we have:

PS: Package Size, NC: Number of Classes in the model, NOPM: Number Of Packages in the Model, NOC: Number Of Communications, is the number of messages sent by the class C, NMSC: Number Of Messages for the Same Class, is the number of internal messages from C to C, NCC: Number of Connected Classes, is the number of classes that communicates with the class C and NCM: Number of connected messages, is the number of messages sent to the class C.

The GRITE algorithm gives the most frequent sequences of metrics using the minsupport threshold. Where, the minsupport threshold aims at discovering subsets of items that occurs together at least a minsupport time in a database. If minsupport

Table 3. Data Class metrics

		ATFD	NOM	NOA	PS	NC	NOPM	NOC	NMSC	NCC	NCM
P1	O1	03	15	08	22	57	02	05	03	02	01
	O2	02	10	05	28	57	02	04	02	01	00
P2	O3	04	08	10	33	113	04	06	09	00	01
	O4	02	13	07	33	113	04	04	07	04	02
	O5	05	14	08	25	113	04	07	08	04	06
	O6	06	09	11	24	113	04	08	04	06	05
	O7	04	16	13	21	113	04	04	07	09	08
P3	O8	05	17	12	52	368	11	06	06	03	04
	O9	02	13	12	46	368	11	04	05	05	02

is set to be too large, no itemsets will be generated, if minsupport is set to be too small, huge number of itemsets will be generated. Fixing the minsupport threshold depend on the specificities of the problem.

In the context on design defect detection, almost we don't have a very large database comparing to other domains, that's why we set a minsupport value to be more than 0.5. It means that we will extract the gradual rules that occur at least in 50% of the transactions. We can decrease the minsupport thresholds if the program generates no rule, until having at least one rule.

4.3   Modeling Design Defects

Based on UML profile capabilities, we extend the UML metamodel to support and model all key concepts used for the specifications of design defects. We model each defect to create a catalogue of design flaws. We formalize a set of textual and informal design flaws description (avoiding any subjective interpretation) in a well-structured model enclosing all necessary information to deal with design defect detection.

Defined Stereotypes

In this section, we detail the defined stereotypes illustrated in figure 2: RefactoringIndicator is a super-class modeling all possible refactoring indicators. The design flows can be specialized as Antipattern, DesignPatternDefect, BadSmells.

Description contains a textual description of the design flaws. It represents the semantic aspect. The description stereotype is very helpful to understand the meaning of the design defect and the context in which it can be identified.

Metric represents the set of metrics useful forsoftware measurement and design flows detection. The measure of metrics is done over the static and/or dynamic UML diagrams. The UMLDiagram stereotype represents the UML diagrams attached to the metric concept. Each Design pattern defect is attached to a design pattern represented by the stereotype DesignPattern. RefactoringRepository indicates the name of the refactoring primitive, using the attribute PrimitiveName (For the design defects correction).

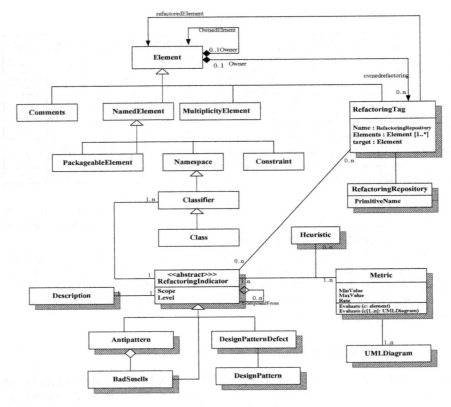

Fig. 2. The UML profile

Figure 3 in the next section presents the UML class diagram of the Data Class defect.

5   Experiments

The experimentations concern the defects Blob, Lazy class, Data class, Feature Envy and Lava flow, using three minsupport thresholds 0.5, 0.8 and 0.9. The Lazy class defect occurs when class isn't doing enough to pay for itself. Every additional class increases the complexity of a project. The Feature Envy defect occurs for methods that make extensive use of another class and may belong in another class. And the Lava flow defect represents the model elements that are not really used in the project due to an overestimation of needs.

The Table 4 presents our results. We choose to select gradual design defect rules that contain more than four metrics to guaranty significant results avoiding an overwhelming rule set. These results indicate the common conditions for the occurrence of a design defect. We have better rules for high minsupport value 0.8, because the

Table 4. Results

		Minsupport	
		0.5	**0.8**
Blob	**R1**	(ATFD+ PS+ NC+ NOPM-)	No Rule
	R2	(ATFD+ NOM+ NOA- NCM+)	
	R3	(ATFD+ NC+ NCM+ NCC+ NOM+)	
	R4	(ATFD+ NMSC+ NOA- PS+ NC+)	
Lazy class	**R1**	(NC+ NCC- ATFD- NCM- PS+)	(NCM- NOM – NC+ NCC- ATFD-)
	R2	(NCM- NOM – NC+ NCC- ATFD-)	(NC+ NCC- ATFD- NCM- PS+)
	R3	(ATFD- NC+ NCM- NOPM- NOM-)	
Data class	**R1**	(APM- ATFD- NC+ PS+ NCC-)	(NOM- PS+ NCC- NC+ NCM+)
	R2	(NOM- PS+ NCC- NC+ NCM+)	
FeatureEnvy	**R1**	(NIC+ NMSMC- NC+ PS+ NOPM-)	No Rule
Lava flow	**R1**	(NC+ NCC- ATFD- NCM- PS+)	(NCM- NOM – NC+ NCC- ATFD-)
	R2	(NCM- NOM – NC+ NCC- ATFD-)	(NC+ NCC- ATFD- NCM- PS+)
	R3	(ATFD- NC+ NCM- NOPM- NOM-)	
	R4	(NIC- NMSMC- CM- NOM+)	(NIC- CM- APM- NC+ NOPM+)
	R5	(NIC- CM- APM- NC+ NOPM+)	

rule is repeated at the majority of the defect occurrence (80%). We have lowest min-support threshold 0.5 guaranty that the extracted rules occurs in at least 50% of the detected defects.

In our case, for a minsupport threshold equal to 0.9 we have no rules for all defects. We notice that the activity of design defects detection depends on the subjectivity of the designer. In fact, our research intends to help designer to improve the quality of models by offering a set of gradual rules characterizing the context in which could occur a design defect. All important information related to defects is now represented using the UML profile. In figure 3 we present an example for the Data Class defect.

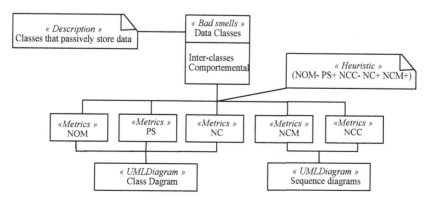

Fig. 3. Data Classes

6   Conclusion

Several design defect detection techniques have been proposed. Most of existing works relies on metrics rule-based detection, applied for the code level. However, it is difficult to identify and express these symptoms as rules [17], since they are not formalized. It is also difficult to find the best threshold for metrics. This work raised some interesting perspectives in order to detect design defects for model level based on the evaluation of correlation of metrics co-variation instead of threshold. We have also proposed an UML profile for design defect modeling. It fully supports design defects modeling needs. It allows antipatterns and bad smells modeling with one unified language. Using the UML profile for design defects, we unify software designer teams with a single and shared design defects specification.

References

1. Brito e Abreu, F., Melo, W.: Evaluating the impact of object-oriented design on software quality. In: The 3rd International SoftwareMetrics Symposium, pp. 90–99 (1996)
2. Brown, W.J., Malveau, R.C., McCormick, H.W.S., Mowbray, T.J.: AntiPatterns: Refactoring Software, Architectures, and Projects in Crisis: Refactoring Software, Architecture and Projects in Crisis. John Wiley & Sons (1998b)
3. Chidamber, S., Kemerer, C.: A metrics suite for object oriented design. IEEE Transactions on Software Engineering 20(6), 476–493 (1994)
4. Corradini, A., Ehrig, H., Kreowski, H.-J., Rozenberg, G. (eds.): ICGT 2002. LNCS, vol. 2505. Springer, Heidelberg (2002)
5. Erni, K.: C, Applying design metrics to object-oriented frameworks. In: IEEE METRICS, pp. 64–74 (1996)
6. Hadar, E., Hadar, I.: The Composition Refactoring Triangle (CRT) Practical Toolkit: From Spaghetti to Lasagna. In: OOPSLA 2006, Portland, Oregon, USA. ACM (2006), 1-9593-491-X/06/0010
7. Hüllermeier, E.: Association rules for expressing gradual dependencies. In: Elomaa, T., Mannila, H., Toivonen, H. (eds.) PKDD 2002. LNCS (LNAI), vol. 2431, pp. 200–211. Springer, Heidelberg (2002)
8. Frakes, W., Prieto-Diaz, R., Fox, C.: DARE: Domain Analysis and Reuse Environment. Annals of Software Engineering (5), 125–141 (1998)
9. Fowler, M., Beck, K., Brant, J., Opdyke, W., Roberts, D.: Refactoring: Improving the Design of Existing Code (1999)
10. Di-Jorio, L., Laurent, A., Teisseire, M.: Mining frequent gradual itemsets from large databases. In: Adams, N.M., Robardet, C., Siebes, A., Boulicaut, J.-F. (eds.) IDA 2009. LNCS, vol. 5772, pp. 297–308. Springer, Heidelberg (2009)
11. Kessentini, M., Kessentini, W., Sahraoui, H., Boukadoum, M., Ouni, A.: Design Defects Detection and Correction by Example. In: 19th IEEE International Conference on Program Comprehension (2011)
12. Marinescu: Detecting Design Flaws via Metrics in Object-Oriented Systems. In: Proceedings of TOOLS USA 2001, pp. 103–116. IEEE Computer Society (2001)
13. Van Kempen, M., Chaudron, M., Kourie, D., Boake, A.: Towards Proving Preservation of Behaviour of Refactoring of UML Models. In: Proceedings of SAICSIT 2005, p. 252 (2005)

14. Mohamed, M., Romdhani, M., Ghedira, K.: M-REFACTOR: A New Approach and Tool for Model Refactoring. ARPN Journal of Systems and Software (July 2011)
15. Moha, N., Guéhéneuc, Y.-G., Duchien, L., Meur, A.-F.L.: DECOR: A method for the specification and detection of code and design smells. Transactions on Software Engineering (TSE), 16 pages (2009)
16. Riel, A.J.: Object-Oriented Design Heuristics. Addison-Wesley (1996)
17. Marinescu, R.: Detection strategies: Metrics-based rules for detecting design flaws. In: Proceedings of the 20th International Conference on Software Maintenance, pp. 350–359. IEEE Computer Society Press (2004)
18. Marticorena, R., Crespo, Y.: Refactorizaciones de especializacion sobre el lenguaje modelo MOON. Technical Report DI-2003-02, Departamento de Informatica. Universidad de Valladolid (septiembre 2003)
19. Yahia, S.A.S.B.: Fuzzy set-based formalization of gradual patterns. In: SoCPaR, 2014, Tunis, Tunisia, pp. 434–439 (2014)
20. Ayouni, S., Laurent, A., Ben Yahia, S., Poncelet, P.: Fuzzy gradual patterns: What fuzzy modality for what result? In: Proceedings of the International Conference on Soft Computing and Pattern Recognition (SoCPaR 2010), Cergy, France (2010)
21. Zhang, J., Lin, Y., Gray, J.: Generic and Domain-Specific Model Refactoring using a Model Transformation Engine. In: Model-driven Software Development – Research and Practice in Software (2004, 2005)

An Approach to Integrating Aspects in Agile Development

Tadjer Houda[1,2(✉)] and Meslati Djamel[3]

[1] Computer Science Department
Badji Mokhtar University, Annaba, Algeria
[2] LabSTIC, Guelma University, POB 401
24000 Guelma, Algeria
tadjerh@yahoo.fr
[3] Computer Science Department, LISCO Laboratory,
Badji Mokhtar-Annaba University, Annaba, Algeria
meslati_djamel@yahoo.com

Abstract. Separation of concerns is an important principle that helps to improve reusability and simplify evolution. The crosscutting concerns like security, and many others, often exist before implementation, in both the analysis and design phases, it is therefore worthwhile to develop aspects oriented software development approaches to handle properly the concerns and ensure their separation.

Moreover agile methods attempt to reduce risk and maximize productivity by carrying out software development with short iterations while limiting the importance of secondary or temporary artifacts, however these approaches have problems dealing with the crosscutting nature of some stakeholders' requirements. The work presented in this paper aims at enriching the agile development using aspect oriented approaches. By taking into account the crosscutting nature of some stakeholders' requirements, the combination of the two approaches improves the software changeability during the repeated agile iterations.

Keywords: Aspect oriented · Constraints · Extreme programming · Separation of concerns · User stories

1 Introduction

Taking into account the concerns in the analysis phase is currently regarded as an important step that could have a positive impact on subsequent development phases and, consequently, there are several Aspect Oriented Requirement Engineering models (AORE models) such as MC AORE model [13], Quality AORE model [10], Vgraph model [16] and Theme/doc model [2].

Moreover agile methods have become, due to their pragmatism, favoured approaches for complex systems development. The use of the early separation of concerns in agile approaches is an important issue which can cause considerable fallout in terms of software development management and clear architectural structuring. We found in literature several agile approaches: Extreme Programming [8], Scrum [14], Feature-Driven

© IFIP International Federation for Information Processing 2015
A. Amine et al. (Eds.): CIIA 2015, IFIP AICT 456, pp. 584–595, 2015.
DOI: 10.1007/978-3-319-19578-0_48

Development (FDD) [11], and Dynamic Systems Development Method (DSDM) [15], Crystal Methodologies [4], Adaptive Software Development (ASD) [5]. Combining aspects oriented approaches with these agile approaches, eliminates the tangling and the scattering of the code they produce and consequently reduces the effort of understanding and changing this code during the repeated agile iterations.

In this paper, we present a work which aims at combining the separation of concerns, requirements' engineering and the well known Extreme Programming approach (Xp), in order to achieve a synergy that enhances the Xp approach of development by a convenient handling of concerns. This work focuses on how aspect concepts can be integrated within the requirement level of the agile development context and particularly in the Xp approach.

In the rest of this paper, we present, briefly, the Xp approach, the aspect oriented requirements engineering. Thereafter, we explain the proposed combination. Then we describe some related work and, finally, we give a conclusion.

2   Agile Approaches

The agile approaches are a family of pragmatic development approaches built to deliver products on time, budget and with high quality. These approaches focus on strong customers' involvement and guarantee that they will be satisfied by their project. The Xp approach is one of the most commonly used among agile approaches [7]. The Xp approach provides a life cycle model of software which is used as a guide for organizing the development team. This model is presented in Figure1. User stories are an important concept in the Xp development and are usually the starting point of all the Xp processes. By choosing them, the customer kick starts the iteration process. They represent what the customer wants the system to do [8]. The system development is a succession of such iterations where the requirements are continuously being defined by means of user stories. These user stories should feed into the release-planning meeting and to the creation of the user acceptance tests.

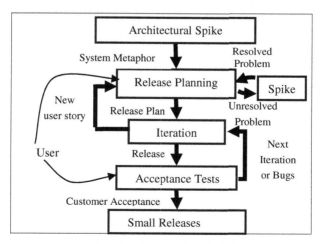

Fig. 1. Lifecycle of project Xp [7]

A release-planning meeting is used to create the release plan, which lays out the overall project. That is, the release plan indicates which user stories will be implemented and in which release this will happen. It also indicates how many iterations are planned and when each iteration will be delivered.

At the beginning of each iteration, an Iteration Planning meeting is held to determine exactly what will happen within that iteration. Such just-in-time planning is considered an easy way to stay on top of changing user requirements.

The acceptance tests are created from the user stories, written at the start of the project. Each iteration implements one or more user stories; these stories will be translated into a series of acceptance tests during the iteration.

3   Aspect Oriented Software Development (AOSD)

In object orientation, applications are modeled and implemented by decomposition of both the problem and solution space into objects, where each object embodies a single concern. However, some concerns still remain scattered throughout many different objects because they don't naturally fit within object boundaries. Such concerns (such as security, mobility, distribution, and logging) crosscut the other concerns. Aspect-oriented programming provides an elegant solution to this problem. Initially, the concept of aspect has been introduced in the context of programming. However, its use has become widespread to cover, among other things, analysis, design and evolution of applications.

To improve the software development, we need fully aspect oriented approaches that support aspects ranging from the analysis phase till implementation and testing. These approaches are often described as Aspect Oriented Software Development (AOSD) and encompass a range of techniques to achieve a better modularity.

Aspect-Oriented Software Development (AOSD) is regarded as a promising method that allows systematic identification, modularization, representation, and composition of such crosscutting concerns. Currently, it is commonly accepted that a good separation of concerns improves system modularity, reduces the complexity of software systems and the tangle of their code, facilitates reuse, improves comprehension, simplifies the integration of components and decreases the change, reducing the cost of adaptation, evolution and maintenance.

The requirement engineering is of vital importance because of its influence on the rest of the development. This is a starting point for many researches that aim at improving the separation of concerns at the requirements' level.

The motivation of these researches lies in reducing the cost of adaptation, evolution and maintenance. According to [3] the main activities in the requirements are: identification, capture, composition and analysis. Currently, several AORE models have been proposed and used as mentioned previously.

4   The Proposed Approach

Our work consists of integrating the aspect oriented approach in the Extreme programming approach and focuses particularly on the analysis phase. Our goal is to incorporate the concepts of AORE in the Xp process to make it more efficient and improve the productivity of the development team.

AORE's goal is the separation of concerns at the level of requirements, which may influence the way of using Xp in a project development. The agile development in general and Xp in particular can benefit from the AORE. In the Xp approach, the user stories represent the requirements of a system in the sense that the requirements are informally described by these stories from the customers. That is why our approach is mainly based on the user stories.

4.1   Steps of the Proposed Approach

Figure 2 summarizes the main steps we propose in our approach. We describe them shortly in the following.

Step 1: Identify User Stories and Constraints. In this stage customers and the development team meet to discuss the main functionalities to be achieved by the system. These functionalities are written by customers in the form of user stories on indexed cards. Each story has a short name that describes the functionality. Other details are added such as the risk to improve planning and performance of iteration. At the end of this stage, the customer must choose the stories to implement in the current iteration. Non functional requirements can address a variety of system needs and they can be considered as constraints on the system's behavior. Thus the customer must identify these constraints.

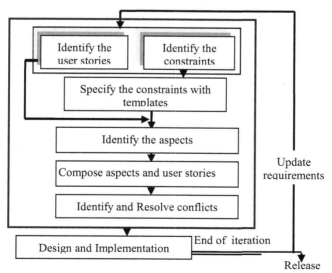

Fig. 2. Steps of the proposed approach

Step 2: Specify the Constraints. Based on the approach described in [10] the constraints are specified using templates as shown in table1.

Each constraint is defined as follows:

Table 1. Template for constraint

Constraint	Description
Name	Name of constraint.
Description	Description of constraint.
Influence	Lists of user stories affected by this constraint.
Priority	Priority assigned for this constraint.
Contribution	Represents how a constraint can be affected by other constraint. This contribution can be negative (-) or positive (+).

Step 3: Identify Aspects. If a constraint affects several user stories then this constraint is an aspect (taking in to account the information in row influence). In other words, if a constraint is triggered from several other user stories so it is considered as an aspect.

Step 4: Compose Aspects and User Stories. In this stage we try to compose crosscutting constraints and user stories in order to find the impact of an aspect on the requirements. We must define composition rules showing how an aspect influences behavior of a set of user stories.

Step 5: Identify and Resolve Conflicts. Identification of conflicts is based on the MCAORE technique [13] which uses a contribution matrix where each aspect may contribute negatively (-) or positively (+) to the others. If aspects have the same priority and contribute negatively then these aspects are in conflicts.

The conflicts in our approach are resolved through effective negotiation with customer who is part of the development team (on site customer).

Step 6: Design and Implementation. Xp like the other agile processes prioritizes pragmatic design for long-team change. The final set of user stories and aspects plus composition rules are used in the implementation, so an aspect oriented programming language could be used.

At the end of an iteration, the customer can check the product by the acceptance tests to detect errors or add other features. Following the change requirements, it is necessary to repeat the separation of concerns again.

4.2   Example

In this section we apply the previous steps to the creation of a website for the company SOUTH COAST NAUTICAL SUPPLIES to augment their print catalog. This example is taken from [5].

Step 1. Identify user stories and constraints. These are the user stories and constraints which are written by the stakeholders:

- User story 1: A user can do a basic simple search that searches for a word or phrase in both the author and title fields.
- User story 2: A user can put books into a "shopping cart" and buy them when he is done shopping.
- User story 3: To buy a book the user enters her billing address, the shipping address and credit card information.
- User story 4: A user can establish an account that remembers shipping and billing information.
- User story 5: A user must be properly authenticated before viewing reports.
- User story 6: An administrator can add new books to the site.
- User story 7: An administrator can delete a book.
- User story 8: An administrator can edit the information about an existing book.

Constraint C1: The system must support peak usage of up to 50 concurrent users.
Constraint C2: For audit purposes, all transactions in the system have to be kept.

In this iteration the first constraint shows that the system must support concurrent manipulation by at least 50 users which implies that there is a *multiple access* system. The second constraint is *audit* means that the action at each step is recorded.

By analysis of the stories identified for this iteration we can extract other constraints which are not written by the stakeholders. For example: User story 5, in this case the security must be guaranteed as the information provided by the user is personal data. The constraint identified here is *security*.

In the same way developers can also identify another constraint is the *login*.

Step 2. Specify the constraints.

Specification is as follows:

Table 2. Template for C1

Name	Multiple access
Description	Multiple users can use the system simultaneously.
Influence	multiple user stories
Priority	must have
Contribution	(+) Audit, (+) login

Table 3. Template for C2

Name	Audit
Description	The action at each step is captured and kept
Influence	multiple user stories
Priority	must have
Contribution	(+) Security, (+) multiple Access, (+) login

Table 4. Template for C3

Name	Security
Description	Only authorized users can access information.
Influence	multiple user stories
Priority	must have
Contribution	(+) Audit, (+) login

Table 5. Template for C4

Name	Login
Description	Provides the ability to connect and disconnect.
Influence	multiple user stories
Priority	must have
Contribution	(+) Audit, (+) Security, (+) multiple Access

Step 3. Identify aspects. From the table 2 to table 5, we deduce the following constraints:

Multiple access, Audit, security and login affect multiple user stories. So, these constraints are crosscutting and therefore represent aspects.

- Aspect1: *Multiple access*
- Aspect2: *Audit*
- Aspect3: *Security*
- Aspect4: *Login*

Step 4. Compose aspects and user stories. To combine aspects with the basic user stories we will first define composition rules indicating how these aspects influence the behavior of a set of basic user stories.

An example of composition rules in the case presented above is:

For safety, there is a recovery situation "Overlap", represented by the qualifiers before or after. Security for User story 5 is applied before viewing the report because we are in front of a protection in this case the composition rule will as follows:

- Security. Overlap. Before user story 5.

For the audit, there is also a situation of "Overlap", represented by before or after. The audit here is applied after each story affected recorded for each action, in this case the composition rule is as follows:
- Audit. Overlap. After all history

Step 5. Identify and Resolve conflicts. The contribution matrix which is symmetrical indicates whether aspects contribute positively or negatively. In our example aspects contribute positively and in this case no conflict appears in this iteration.

Table 6. The contribution matrix

Aspects Aspects	Audit	Security	Multiple Access	Login
Audit		+	+	+
Security				+
Multiple Access				+
Login				

Step 6. Design and Implementation.

At the end of this iteration, suppose that the customer wants to add other constraints.
A second iteration is then necessary. We describe it in what follows.

Step 1. Identify new user stories and constraints. These are user stories and constraints which are written by the customers:

• User story 9: A user can search for books by entering values in any combination of author, title and ISBN.
• User story 10: A user can view detailed information on a book. For example, number of pages, publication date and a brief description.
• User story 11: A user can put books into a "wish list" that is visible to other site visitors.
• User story 12: A user, especially a Non-Sailing Gift Buyer, can search for a wish list based on its owner's name and state.
• User story 13: A user can check the status of her recent orders.
• User story 14: If an order hasn't shipped, a user can add or remove books, change the shipping method, the delivery address and the credit card.
• User story 15: A user can view a history of all of his past orders.
• User story 16: A user can easily re-purchase items when viewing past orders.
• User story 17: A user can see what books we recommend on a variety of topics.
• User story 18: A user can remove books from her cart before completing an order.

Constraint C5: A customer must be able to find one book and complete an order in less than 90 seconds.

Step 2. Specify constraints.

For the next iteration, and due to changes in the requirements, a new specification is necessary (Table 7 to 11).

Table 7. Template for C1

Name	Multiple access
Description	Multiple users can use the system simultaneously.
Influence	multiple user stories
Priority	must have
Contribution	(+) Audit, (+) login, (-)Response time

Specification is as follows:

Table 8. Template for C2

Name	Audit
Description	The action at each step is captured and kept
Influence	multiple user stories
Priority	must have
Contribution	(+) Security, (+) multiple Access, (+) login, (-)Response time

Table 9. Template for C3

Name	Security
Description	Only authorized users can access information.
Influence	multiple user stories
Priority	must have
Contribution	(+) Audit, (+) login, (-)Response time

Table 10. Template for C4

Name	Login
Description	Provides the ability to connect and disconnect.
Influence	multiple user stories
Priority	must have
Contribution	(+)Audit, (+)Security, (+)multiple Access, (-)Response time

Table 11. Template for C5

Name	Response time
Description	Period of time in which the system responds to a service
Influence	multiple user stories
Priority	must have
Contribution	(-) Security, (-)multiple Access, (-) Audit, (-) login

Step 3. Identify aspects. From constraints which affect more than one user story, we deduce the following:

The first four (*Multiple access, Audit, security and login*) are already identified as aspects in the first iteration, the second constraint (response time) is crosscutting as they affect multiple user stories (taking into account the information in row influence) and therefore represent aspect. So for this iteration we add a new aspect:

- Aspect5: Response time

Step 4. Composed aspects and user stories. To combine the new set of aspects with the basic user stories we will define new composition rules indicating how these aspects influence the behavior of a set of user stories.

In this step we try to dial the new aspect 'response time' identified in the previous step with the stories it affects. As this aspect is required in parallel with the stories he forced this leads to use the relation "wrap".

For other aspects just add composition links with the stories of this iteration.

Step 5. Identify and Resolve conflicts. In our example the contributions between aspects are presented in the following table:

Table 12. The contribution matrix

Aspects / Aspects	Audit	Security	Multiple Access	Login	Response time
Audit		+	+	+	-
Security				+	-
Multiple Access				+	-
Login					-
Response time					

This table indicates the presence of conflicts between some aspects, if these aspects apply to the same user stories with the same priority. For example security and response time contribute negatively to each other. They constrain each other's behavior and have the same priority and apply to the the same user story, thus a conflict is arise.

As in this iteration we are faced with a conflict, it is resolved by negotiations between the customer and the development team.

Step 6. Design and Implementation.

The iterations are repeated until there is no need to add or update requirements.

5   Related Work

Several approaches are intended to identify crosscutting concerns during the early stages of development [9]. Aspect Oriented Requirement Engineering (AORE), described in [13], proposes a model for Aspect Oriented Requirement Engineering that supports the separation of crosscutting properties at the requirements level. Concerns and associated requirements are identified from different viewpoints. The rules of composition are defined using XML. In [10], functional requirements are specified using use cases based approach. The quality attributes are detailed extensively in a template, which among other details also lists down the decomposition of the quality attribute, priorities (max, high, low, and min), and influence of the quality attribute. By observing the influence of a quality attribute and associated requirements, crosscutting concerns (quality attributes) are identified. Here, a set of UML models are integrated to the crosscutting quality attributes. Baniassad and Clarke [2] propose the Theme approach that does not identify the crosscutting concerns from traditional requirements engineering approaches. They introduced the concept of action view, clipped action view, base themes, and crosscutting themes to provide support for the aspect orientation in the analysis and design. Theme supports activities of requirements analyses. The results of analyses are mapped to the UML models. Despite the diversity of these approaches, no one among them takes into account the agile development. the FDD approach takes into consideration the integration of aspects in a contextual agile development [12]. In [1], a method is proposed for unifying agile and AO requirements analysis approaches.

6   Conclusion

The Xp approach is a development approach that can produce quickly software of high quality. This development approach may benefit from aspect-oriented requirements engineering approaches in a variety of ways.

The work presented in this article is a proposition of integration between separation of concerns and requirements engineering in an agile development context and particularly in the extreme programming approach. The main contribution of our work is its focus on the user stories and constraints as the starting point of the integration. Our approach is still at its beginning and we are now using it for more complex systems.

References

1. Araujo, J., Ribeiro, J.C.: A scenario and aspect-oriented requirements agile approach. International Journal of Computing Science and Applications 5(3b), 69–92 (2008)
2. Baniassad, E., Clarke, S.: Aspect-oriented analysis and design: Theme Approach. Addison Wesley professional (2005)
3. Baniassad, E., Clements, P.C., Araujo, J., Moreira, A., Rashid, A., Tekierdogan, B.: Discovering Early aspects. IEEE Software (January/February 2006)
4. Cockburn, A.: Crystal methodologies: The Cooperative Game. Addison-Wesley (2006)
5. Cohn.M, User Stories Applied: For Agile Software Development, Addison Wesley (March 2004)
6. Highsmith.J.: Adaptive Software Development. Dorset House, New York (2000)
7. Hunt.J, Agile software construction (2006)
8. Kent, B.: Extreme Programming Explained: Embrace Change. Addison Wesley (2000)
9. Moreira, A., Araújo, J.: The Need for Early Aspects. In: Fernandes, J.M., Lämmel, R., Visser, J., Saraiva, J. (eds.) Generative and Transformational Techniques in Software Engineering III. LNCS, vol. 6491, pp. 386–407. Springer, Heidelberg (2011)

10. Moreria, A., Araújo, J., Brito, I.: Crosscutting quality attributes for requirements engineering. In: SEKE2002: Fourteenth International Conference on Software Engineering and Knowledge Engineering, Ischia, Italy, July 15-19 (2002)
11. Palmer, S.R., Felsing, J.M.: A Practical Guide to Feature-Driven Development. Addison-Wesley (2002)
12. Pang, J., Blair, L.: Refining feature driven development - a methodology for early aspects. In: Early Aspects: Aspect-Oriented Requirements Engineering and Architecture Design (2004)
13. Rashid, A., Moreira, A., Araújo, J.: Modularization and composition of Aspectual Requirements. In: 2nd International Conference on Aspect- Oriented Software Development, Boston, pp. 11–20 (2003)
14. Schwaber, K., Beedle, M.: Scrum: Agile Software Development. Prentice-Hall (2002)
15. Stapleton.J, Dynamic Systems Development Method:The method in practice. Addison-Wesley (1997)
16. Yu, Y., Leite, J.C.S., Mylopoulos, J.: From goals to aspects: discovering Aspects from requirements goal models. In: The 12th IEEE International Requirements Engineering Conference, Kyoto, Japan (2004)

Software Engineering:
Checking and Verification

On the Optimum Checkpointing Interval Selection for Variable Size Checkpoint Dumps

Samy Sadi[✉] and Belabbas Yagoubi

University of Oran1 Ahmed Benbella,
Department of Computer Science
Oran, Algeria
{samy.sadi.contact,byagoubi}@gmail.com

Abstract. Checkpointing is a technique that is often employed for granting fault tolerance for applications executing in failure-prone environments. It consists on regularly saving the application's state in another and fault independent storage such that if the application fails, it can be continued without necessarily restarting it. In this context, fixing the checkpointing frequency is an important topic which we address in this paper. We particularly address this issue considering hybrid fault tolerance and variable size checkpoint dumps. We then evaluate our solution and compare it with state of the art models, and show that our solution brings better results.

Keywords: Optimum Checkpointing Interval · Hybrid Fault Tolerance · Variable Size · Simulation

1 Introduction

Since the accession to information technologies, a lot of efforts have been devoted by the research community in order to make computing systems more fault-tolerant and more reliable. Initially, reliability was chiefly sought to avoid job resubmissions and to lower resource utilization, in a context where the job average length is ever-growing especially after the emergence of computational science and high-performance computing (HPC). Afterwards, and notably due to the advent of Cloud Computing and due to the increasing number of business-sensitive applications, a new practical and financial dimension appeared which drew even more attention to reliability.

The fact is that computing systems are failure-prone and failures are getting more frequent as new systems appear. The reason behind this is not because their components are getting less reliable. Actually, future hardware components and in particular newer generation chips are expected to keep failure rates similar to those of the current generation [14]. However, the number of components per any single system has considerably increased since the last few years and is continually increasing which led to a lower overall system mean time between failures (MTBF). So as to emphasize these lines, a study [2] on large-scale HPC systems has observed an MTBF in the 6.5h–40h range. This value when extrapolated for a peta-scale system, corresponds to a MTBF of only 1.25 hours [11]. Latterly,

© IFIP International Federation for Information Processing 2015
A. Amine et al. (Eds.): CIIA 2015, IFIP AICT 456, pp. 599–610, 2015.
DOI: 10.1007/978-3-319-19578-0_49

another study [16] has observed that in a typical Cloud datacenter, a proportion of 8% of the machines can expect to see at least one failure each year.

In this context, checkpoint-restart or checkpointing has been developed in order to leverage fault tolerance in computing systems. This technique consists on taking frequent snapshots of any job's state, and on saving it on a secondary and fault-independent machine [5]. When the job fails on its primary machine, the saved state on the secondary machine is used to restore the job's state and to continue it. Thus, the job does not need to restart from scratch and a lower execution delay can be expected in failure-prone environments.

A central concern when implementing such fault tolerance technique is about selecting the frequency of checkpointing or the delay between taking two checkpoints. A high checkpointing frequency will ensure to have at any moment a very recent snapshot of the job's state, thus minimizing the potential rework delay after a failure. But in the same time, this will induce a significant overhead to the job execution if the occurrence of failures is very low or nonexistent. In another hand, a too low checkpointing frequency is obviously not a wise choice either, as this will lead to a noteworthy rework delay after failures.

In the present study, the issue under scrutiny is precisely about determining the best checkpointing frequency, also known as the checkpointing interval selection problem. We particularly address this problem considering a variable checkpointing overhead. We assume that the checkpointing overhead, or the time which is necessary to save a job's state into an external device is a function of the previous computing phase's delay. Besides, as new research has been undertaken for hybrid fault tolerance and in particular to predict the occurrence of failures with fair results [7, 12, 13], we also take into consideration this aspect in order to reduce checkpointing frequency.

The organization of this paper is as follows. In the next section, we discuss related work. In section 3, we define and formalize the problem and we present the brought solution. In the penultimate section, we evaluate our solution and we discuss the results. Finally, in section 5 we conclude and we give an overview of our future work.

2   Related Work

Checkpointing and in particular checkpointing interval selection has been extensively studied in the past. In this section, we give a chronological review of most prominent research efforts in the literature.

One of the first contributions was made by Young [17] who managed to give a first order approximation to the optimum checkpointing interval. Young considered that the overhead which is due to checkpointing is (1) constant and independent from the computing phase, and (2) is negligible when compared to the system MTBF. Furthermore, failures occurrence was assumed to be independent and exponentially distributed following a known MTBF. This last assumption, even if adopted in many contributions [4, 6, 8, 15, 17, 18], is only true for the first occurrence of the failures. In fact, failures cluster in time and a failure is more likely to happen after a first failure [16].

In [6], the author showed that the optimum checkpointing interval is deterministic and is a function of the system load. In particular, the author proposed a queuing model where the duration of service interruptions is directly computable knowing the past history of the system.

An $O(n^3)$ algorithm has been proposed in [15] to select the $(n-1)$ potential checkpoint locations which can minimize a given job's execution time. To do so, the authors considered that a job consists of a set of tasks and that checkpoints can only be taken between two consecutive tasks (and not during the task's execution). As opposed to the so far presented contributions, in this contribution authors assumed that checkpointing overhead is not constant and is task-dependant.

An aperiodic checkpointing approach where the checkpointing interval is varying from one checkpoint to another has been proposed in [9]. The authors considered a general failure-rate and no assumption was made regarding the distribution of the failures. Nevertheless, this research specifies that when the distribution of failures is exponential, the optimum placement of checkpoints is equidistant.

A higher order estimate of the optimum checkpointing interval has been provided in [4]. Daly has undertaken to continue the groundwork initiated by Young in [17], and kept most of his assumptions particularly regarding the checkpointing overhead and the failures distribution. However, Daly generalized Young's solution considering the case where the checkpointing overhead is not negligible compared to the system's MTBF.

In [10], the authors proposed an approach for checkpoint placement under incomplete failures information and when the failures distribution is unknown. The min-max principle has been employed to this extent.

An hybrid fault tolerance approach has been proposed in [8]. In this approach, it is assumed that the system has fault-prediction capabilities [7,12,13] which can be used to reduce checkpointing frequency. The authors proposed to partition the job's execution using a preset time interval. At each interval, a decision stage takes place where (1) the job is checkpointed, (2) the job is migrated or (3) no action is taken.

The checkpointing scheduling complexity has been analyzed in [3]. In this research, no assumption was made regarding failures distribution, and checkpointing overhead was assumed to be variable. The authors stated that the checkpointing problem is NP-hard even in the simple case where the failures distribution is uniform. In addition, a dynamic programming algorithm has been proposed to solve the problem.

In [18], the authors exploited failures prediction capabilities in order to define a new formula for computing checkpointing interval. Two main metrics were considered, namely the precision and the recall of failures prediction. These two metrics respectively characterize the capacity of the system to not make false predictions of failures, and the capacity of the system to predict all future failures. We also consider these two metrics in current paper, but we consider variable checkpointing overhead.

3   The Checkpointing Interval Model

In this section, we develop our model for estimating the optimum checkpointing interval considering a variable checkpointing overhead. We draw our inspiration in the model proposed by Young [17] and later used in many other research [4,18].

In the next lines, we first describe the checkpointing process in both the situations where a failures prediction mechanism is employed or not. Then, we give the cost function we want to optimize. Next, and before solving the equation we place some assumptions regarding the failures distribution and the checkpointing overhead function. Once the assumptions placed, we solve the cost function and the optimum checkpointing interval is quantified. Finally, we address a special issue as regards to if the checkpointing overhead function is bounded.

The main symbols used in this paper are described in table 1.

Table 1. Description of used symbols

Symbol	Description
t	Checkpointing interval.
$\delta(t)$	Checkpointing overhead, or the length of the save phase considering t is the length of the compute phase.
δ_{max}	The maximum length of the checkpointing overhead.
α and β	Values characterizing the job's checkpointing overhead.
R	Restart delay before a job can continue on a secondary machine.
C	Total number of real failures during job execution.
C_{tp}	Total number of failures that were predicted (true positives).
C_{fp}	Total number of failures that were predicted but will actually not happen (false positives).
C_{fn}	Total number of failures that were not predicted (false negatives).
p	Precision value in the $[0,1]$ range for failures prediction.
r	Recall value in the $[0,1]$ range for failures prediction.
$n_i(t)$	Number of successful computing phases between the $(i-1)^{th}$ and the ith failure event.
$w_i(t)$	Last computing phase's delay just before the ith failure event happens.
$l_i(t)$	Time lost due to the ith failure event.
$L(t)$	Time lost due to checkpointing and considering all failure events.
S	The submitted job length, or the execution time needed by the job to complete.
M	The mean time between failures (MTBF).
t_{opt}	Optimum Checkpointing interval.

3.1   The Fundamental Checkpointing Process

The checkpointing process consists of multiple sequences of a computing phase where the job is normally executing followed by a save phase where the job's state is written to an external storage. During each save phase the job execution is paused and the job continues in the next computing phase.

The checkpointing interval t represents the length of the computing phase which is also the delay between two consecutive save phases. In this paper, we assume that the save phases are equidistant and that the checkpointing interval stays unchanged during all the job's execution.

During a job's execution one or more failures may happen. After each failure, a restart delay R is necessary for the job to be continued. Moreover, there is an added rework delay $w_i(t)$ corresponding to the not saved job progress due to the ith failure. Refer to Fig.1 for an overview of a job's execution in a context where checkpointing is used.

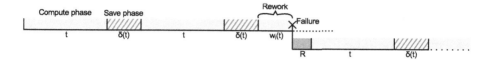

Fig. 1. The Checkpointing Process

3.2   The Hybrid Checkpointing Process

As previously discussed, there is a rapidly growing literature on failures prediction techniques. These techniques can be employed on top of periodic checkpointing in order to trigger additional save phases when a failure is predicted. After the save phase, the job is immediately continued on the secondary machine and no rework delay is necessary as the job state on the secondary machine is up to date. Another important feature of such process, is that checkpointing frequency can be reduced. The hybrid checkpointing process is displayed in Fig.2.

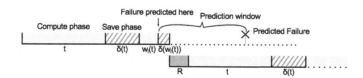

Fig. 2. The Hybrid Checkpointing Process

The level of trust of failures prediction is characterized by three different metrics, namely: the precision(p), the recall(r) and the prediction window.

The precision is the fraction of true positive predictions (C_{tp}) that are made by the system when compared to all the predictions made. In fact, the system might do an erroneous prediction of a future failure. These erroneous predictions are also designated as false positives (C_{fp}).

$$p = \frac{C_{tp}}{C_{tp} + C_{fp}} \tag{1}$$

The recall value represents the ability of the system to predict all future failures. It is the fraction of true positive predictions on the total number of failures. The missed failure predictions are designated as false negatives (C_{fn}) and is used when computing the recall:

$$r = \frac{C_{tp}}{C_{tp} + C_{fn}} \tag{2}$$

The prediction window is the time interval which is left before a predicted failure happens. A good prediction window is big enough so that a save phase can be engaged and completed before the failure happens. If the prediction window is too small, then the failure prediction is pointless as the save phase will not complete. Such predictions are consider to be false negatives in the current paper.

3.3   Cost Function

We define our cost function by considering the time lost due to checkpointing in different scenarios. We start by considering the time lost due to at most one single failure event. After that, we generalize the results to more than one failure event. A failure event is either an actual failure happening, or a failure prediction event.

Single Failure Event Cost Function. We identify four cases as regards to the time lost in the checkpointing process when compared to a job executing in a regular and failure immune system. We present the cost functions for each case. We assume in those that $n_i(t)$ is the number of successful computing phases between the $(i - 1)^{th}$ and the ith failure event.

The first case is when no failure events happen and the job executes normally on the primary machine. In this regard, the time lost is the sum of the delays spent in all the save phases.

$$l_{i,1}(t) = n_i(t) \cdot \delta(t) \tag{3}$$

The second case is when an unpredicted failure happens. Hereof, the time lost consists of all the save phases plus a restart delay (R) and eventually some rework time $(w_i(t))$ which has not yet been saved.

$$l_{i,2}(t) = n_i(t) \cdot \delta(t) + R + w_i(t) \tag{4}$$

The third case is when the system predicts the occurrence of a failure that will really happen (ie: a true positive). In this case, the time lost consists of all the save phases plus a restart delay. The last save phase being the one initiated after the failure prediction. Besides, no rework time is induced in this situation.

$$l_{i,3}(t) = n_i(t) \cdot \delta(t) + R + \delta(w_i(t)) \tag{5}$$

The fourth and final case is when the system predicts a failure which will not happen (ie: a false positive). The time lost is the same as in the third case.

$$l_{i,4}(t) = l_{i,3}(t) = n_i(t) \cdot \delta(t) + R + \delta(w_i(t)) \tag{6}$$

Final Cost Function. We can now express the lost time in the general case and considering multiple failure events. Note that we exclude the special case where $C = 0$, as in this case, the optimum checkpointing interval is obvious and is infinity. Furthermore, we consider that the system where the job runs is failure prone and $C > 0$. The total cost function is thus as follows:

$$L(t) = \sum_{i=1}^{C_{fn}} l_{i,2}(t) + \sum_{i=1}^{C_{tp}} l_{i,3}(t) + \sum_{i=1}^{C_{fp}} l_{i,4}(t) \tag{7}$$

Considering that the job length is S, we can estimate the number of successful computing phases for the job to complete as follows:

$$N(t) = \frac{S}{t} = \sum_{i=1}^{C} n_i(t) \tag{8}$$

The equation 7 can be expanded as follows.

$$L(t) = S \frac{\delta(t)}{t} + (C + C_{fp}) R + C_{fn} w_i(t) +$$
$$(C_{tp} + C_{fp}) \delta(w_i(t)) + \delta(t) \sum_{i=1}^{C_{fp}} n_i(t) \tag{9}$$

The optimum checkpointing interval t_{opt} is the value of t which produces the smallest time lost. In other words, it is the minimum of the function $L(t)$.

3.4   Solving Assumptions

Assumption on the Checkpointing Overhead. We assume that the dump size produced by jobs is linear and is a function of time. Thus, and considering a fixed bandwidth allocation, the checkpointing overhead is function of t and is linear. It can be expressed as follows:

$$\delta(t) = \alpha \cdot t + \beta \tag{10}$$

Of course, this simplistic formulation may not fit for any type of job. One main issue, is that the job's dump size may be bounded with a maximum. Another issue, is that the job's dump size may not be linear.

We will address the first issue in section 3.6. For the second issue, we consider that a fairer approximation can be made using the previous formula as when compared to constant checkpointing overheads. But we do not further address this issue in this paper.

First Assumption on the Failures Distribution. We assume that failures are independent and follow an exponential distribution of mean M. The literature have shown that this is usually only true for the first occurrence of the failure on the machine and tends to be false once the machine have been repaired. Thus this is only pertinent if we did consider repairs.

As the failures distribution is known, we can now estimate the number of failures that will happen for a job of length S. As previously stated, we need $N(t)$ successful computing phases to complete the job. Besides, we know that the probability to complete one computing phase (followed by a save phase) is:

$$Q_1(t) = P(x > t+\delta(t)) = 1-P(x \leq t+\delta(t)) = 1-(1-e^{-(t+\delta(t))/M}) = e^{-(t+\delta(t))/M}$$
(11)

Thus the number of tries to complete $N(t)$ computing phases is:

$$Q_n(t) = \frac{N(t)}{P(x > t + \delta(t))} = N(t) \cdot e^{\frac{t+\delta(t)}{M}}$$
(12)

Finally, the number of failures is:

$$C = Q_n(t) - N(t) = N(t) \cdot (e^{\frac{t+\delta(t)}{M}} - 1)$$
(13)

Second Assumption on the Failures Distribution. We assume that the mean time between failures (M) in the system is big enough such that the checkpointing interval (t) and the restart delay (R) are negligible when compared to it. And as a direct consequence to this assumption, the checkpointing overhead ($\delta(t)$) is also negligible when compared to M.

We know that the first degree Taylor's series expansion is a good approximation for small values. Thus, the equation 13 can be reformulated as follows:

$$C = N(t) \cdot \frac{t + \delta(t)}{M} = S \cdot \frac{t + \delta(t)}{t \cdot M}$$
(14)

Assumption on the Rework Time. We assume that on average, the failure event happens in the middle stage as regards to the computing phase. Because, failures are independent and exponentially distributed, this value is fair enough.

$$w_i(t) = \frac{t}{2}$$
(15)

Assumption on the Moment of Failures Predictions. We need a final assumption as regards to the moment of the failures predictions when those are false predictions (false positives). We assume that those are uniformly distributed as regards to the whole job execution. In other words, we can make the following approximation:

$$\sum_{i=1}^{C_{fp}} n_i(t) = N(t) \cdot \frac{C_{fp}}{C} = \frac{S}{t} \cdot \frac{C_{fp}}{C}$$
(16)

3.5   Solution

Before relaxing the previous assumptions, it is worth to note that C_{tp}, C_{fp} and C_{fn} can be expressed as follows (based on equations 1 and 2):

$$C_{tp} = r \cdot C \tag{17}$$

$$C_{fp} = r \cdot C \cdot \frac{1-p}{p} \tag{18}$$

$$C_{fn} = (1-r) \cdot C \tag{19}$$

Now, after relaxing the assumptions on 9 we obtain (assuming K is a t independent variable):

$$L(t) = \frac{S\,(\alpha+1)(\alpha r - pr + p)}{2\,p\,M} t + \frac{S\,\beta\,(r\,\beta + (r - rp + p)\,(R + M))}{p\,M} t^{-1} + K \tag{20}$$

The optimum checkpointing interval is the minimum of the function $L(t)$. We also know that $L(t)$ attains its minimum when its first derivative function is zero. We thus need to solve:

$$\frac{\mathrm{d}}{\mathrm{d}t} L(t) = 0 \tag{21}$$

From equation 20 we have:

$$\frac{\mathrm{d}}{\mathrm{d}t} L(t) = -\frac{S\,\beta\,(r\,\beta + (r - rp + p)\,(M + R))}{p\,M} t^{-2} + \frac{S\,(\alpha+1)(r\,\alpha - r\,p + p)}{2\,p\,M} \tag{22}$$

We can thus compute optimum checkpointing interval t_{opt} as follows:

$$t_{opt} = \sqrt{\frac{2\,\beta\,((M+R)\,p - (M+R)\,p\,r + (M + R + \beta)\,r)}{(\alpha+1)\,(p - p\,r + \alpha\,r)}} \tag{23}$$

We can get rid of the R and the β terms since we assumed that the restart delay and checkpointing overhead ($\delta(t) \Rightarrow \beta$) are negligible when compared to M. Thus, we obtain after simplification the final formula for the optimum checkpointing interval:

$$t_{opt} = \sqrt{\frac{2\,\beta\,M\,(p - p\,r + r)}{(\alpha+1)\,(p - p\,r + \alpha\,r)}} \tag{24}$$

We can note that the restart delay does not appear in the previous function which agrees with the result brought by Daly [4]. Besides when $r = 0$ and $\alpha = 0$, in other words when no failures predictions are made and when constant checkpointing overhead is assumed, then the optimum checkpointing interval is the same as the one predicted by Young [17]. However, the formula 24 is slightly different from the result brought in [18] when assuming $\alpha = 0$.

3.6   Bounding the Checkpointing Overhead

In the following lines, we address the issue related to when the checkpointing overhead is bounded with a known maximum (δ_{max}). Such use case can be envisioned if the job works on fixed size files. Once a file is totally modified the checkpoint dump size will be the same even if further modifications are made on that file. Thus we can write the following equation:

$$\delta(t) \leq \delta_{max} \tag{25}$$

Replacing $\delta(t)$ using equation 10, t can be bounded and the new optimum checkpointing interval is as follows:

$$t'_{opt} = \min\,(t_{opt}, \frac{\delta_{max} - \beta}{\alpha}) \tag{26}$$

4   Evaluation

We have used the ACS simulator [1] in order to simulate and evaluate our model against state of the art models.

We have run multiple simulations for each tested model using the following simulation input. First, we consider different failure properties. Therefore, different system MTBF values are tested ranging from 1 hour to 10^4 hours. As regards to the precision and recall, we have tested two combinations corresponding to the results reported in the literature [7]. Next, for each simulation, a total of 1000 jobs with a mean length of 500 hours are launched. And finally, for each job, we have considered empirical values for the α, β and R parameters.

Given a simulation input, the simulator computes the finish time for each job and the average job finish time considering all the jobs. This value is used to compare different models including Young's [17], Daly's [4] and Zhu's [18]. We have observed in different simulation scenarios that when using our model, we obtain lower average job finish time when compared to other models. For brevity, we only include the results of the comparison of our model with Zhu's [18] model

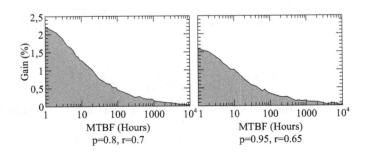

Fig. 3. Time gain percentage of Our Model when compared to Zhu's Model [18] assuming a Constant Checkpointing Overhead ($\alpha = 0$, $\beta = 5min$, $R = 10min$)

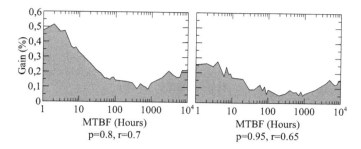

Fig. 4. Time gain percentage of Our Model when compared to Zhu's Model [18] assuming a Variable Checkpointing Overhead ($\alpha = 0.3$, $\beta = 5min$, $R = 10min$)

which is the only model that takes into consideration hybrid fault tolerance among previously compared models. The results are depicted in Fig.3 and Fig.4, and display the gain percentage on the average job finish time when using our model instead of Zhu's model.

5 Conclusion

In this paper, we have brought a new formula for computing the optimum checkpointing interval in systems where hybrid fault tolerance is applied and considering variable size checkpoint dumps. The formula has been compared to state of the art approaches and the results show that our formula brings better results as regards to the job execution time in failure prone environments.

We have considered in this paper that the checkpoint dump size is a function of the execution time and is linear. Therefore, a good direction for future work is considering more general functions for expressing the size of checkpoint dumps.

References

1. Acs - advanced cloud simulator (2014), https://www.github.com/samysadi/acs
2. AReed, D.: High-end computing: The challenge of scale. In: Director's Colloquium, Los Alamos National Laboratory (2004)
3. Bouguerra, M.-S., Trystram, D., Wagner, F.: Complexity analysis of checkpoint scheduling with variable costs. IEEE Transactions on Computers 62(6), 1269–1275 (2013)
4. Daly, J.T.: A higher order estimate of the optimum checkpoint interval for restart dumps. Future Generation Computer Systems 22(3), 303–312 (2006)
5. Egwutuoha, I.P., Levy, D., Selic, B., Chen, S.: A survey of fault tolerance mechanisms and checkpoint/restart implementations for high performance computing systems. The Journal of Supercomputing 65(3), 1302–1326 (2013)
6. Gelenbe, E.: On the optimum checkpoint interval. Journal of the ACM (JACM) 26(2), 259–270 (1979)

7. Gujrati, P., Li, Y., Lan, Z., Thakur, R., White, J.: A meta-learning failure predictor for blue gene/l systems. In: International Conference on Parallel Processing, ICPP 2007, p. 40. IEEE (2007)
8. Li, Y., Lan, Z.: Exploit failure prediction for adaptive fault-tolerance in cluster computing. In: Sixth IEEE International Symposium on Cluster Computing and the Grid, CCGRID 2006, vol. 1, p. 8. IEEE (2006)
9. Ling, Y., Mi, J., Lin, X.: A variational calculus approach to optimal checkpoint placement. IEEE Transactions on Computers 50(7), 699–708 (2001)
10. Ozaki, T., Dohi, T., Okamura, H., Kaio, N.: Distribution-free checkpoint placement algorithms based on min-max principle. IEEE Transactions on Dependable and Secure Computing 3(2), 130–140 (2006)
11. Philp, I.: Software failures and the road to a petaflop machine. In: HPCRI: 1st Workshop on High Performance Computing Reliability Issues. In: Proceedings of the 11th International Symposium on High Performance Computer Architecture, HPCA-11 (2005)
12. Sahoo, R.K., Oliner, A.J., Rish, I., Gupta, M., Moreira, J.E., Ma, S., Vilalta, R., Sivasubramaniam, A.: Critical event prediction for proactive management in large-scale computer clusters. In: Proceedings of the ninth ACM SIGKDD International Conference on Knowledge Discovery and Data Mining, pp. 426–435. ACM (2003)
13. Salfner, F., Lenk, M., Malek, M.: A survey of online failure prediction methods. ACM Computing Surveys (CSUR) 42(3), 10 (2010)
14. Schroeder, B., Pinheiro, E., Weber, W.-D.: Dram errors in the wild: a large-scale field study. In: ACM SIGMETRICS Performance Evaluation Review, vol. 37, pp. 193–204. ACM (2009)
15. Toueg, S., Babaoglu, Ö.: On the optimum checkpoint selection problem. SIAM Journal on Computing 13(3), 630–649 (1984)
16. Vishwanath, K.V., Nagappan, N.: Characterizing cloud computing hardware reliability. In: Proceedings of the 1st ACM Symposium on Cloud Computing, pp. 193–204. ACM (2010)
17. Young, J.W.: A first order approximation to the optimum checkpoint interval. Communications of the ACM 17(9), 530–531 (1974)
18. Zhu, L., Gu, J., Wang, Y., Zhao, T.: Research on optimum checkpoint interval for hybrid fault tolerance. In: Wu, C., Cohen, A. (eds.) APPT 2013. LNCS, vol. 8299, pp. 367–380. Springer, Heidelberg (2013)

Monitoring Checklist for Ceph Object Storage Infrastructure

Pragya Jain[1], Anita Goel[2(⊠)], and S. C. Gupta[3]

[1]Department of Computer Science, University of Delhi, Delhi, India
[2]Department of Computer Science, Dyal Singh College, University of Delhi, India
[3]Department of Computer Science, IIT, Delhi, India
prag_2648@yahoo.co.in,
{goel.anita,gupta.drsc}@gmail.com

Abstract. Object storage cloud is widely used to store unstructured data like photo, emails, video etc. generated from use of digital technologies. The number of object storage services has increased rapidly over the years and so is increased the complexity of the infrastructure behind it. Effective and efficient monitoring is constantly needed to properly operate and manage the complex object storage infrastructure. Ceph is an open source cloud storage platform that provides object storage as a service. Several works have discussed ways to collect the data for monitoring. However, there is little mention of what needs to be monitored. In this paper, we provide an infrastructure monitoring list for Ceph object storage cloud. We analyze the Ceph storage infrastructure and its processes for identifying the proposed lists. The infrastructure monitoring list allows selecting requirements, in contrast to, specifying fresh requirements, for monitoring. The monitoring list helps developer during requirement elicitation of the monitoring functionality when developing a new tool or updating an existing one. The checklist is also useful during monitoring activity for selecting parameters that need to be monitored by the system administrator.

Keywords: Cloud Object Storage · Infrastructure Monitoring · Ceph

1 Introduction

The mass adoption and increasing popularity of digitization technologies has resulted in generation of data in form of videos, photo, blogs, emails, messages, chat data etc. Object storage cloud is a widely adopted paradigm for storing these voluminous data over the Internet. Ceph 0 is open source cloud storage for storing data as object.

The services provided to the subscribers for object storage solutions have rapidly increased and so has complexity of the underlying infrastructure. Monitoring is necessary in cloud to determine health of system and is beneficial for both service provider and consumer 000. There is a need to scale storage nodes, detect and repair failures, manage load surge and improve performance. Due to the elastic nature of cloud, there is a need to constantly monitor the infrastructure at runtime 0 to optimize the use of storage infrastructure with varying demand for storage. Also, disruption in

© IFIP International Federation for Information Processing 2015
A. Amine et al. (Eds.): CIIA 2015, IFIP AICT 456, pp. 611–623, 2015
DOI: 10.1007/978-3-319-19578-0_50

system performance due to reasons like, node failure, system crash, network error, high memory load etc. requires monitoring during runtime. Moreover, processes for storing activity defined in Ceph require monitoring to detect any erroneous action. Furthermore, since Ceph is integrated with many popular clouds, like, Openstack and Eucalyptus for providing storage as a service, defining of monitoring functionality is essential for determining its proper working.

In Ceph, monitoring functionality is incorporated in different ways – (1) Commands are available to monitor storage cluster, (2) Existing freely available infrastructure monitoring tools, like, Nagios are adapted to suit need of Ceph, or (3) New code is written to include infrastructure monitoring functionality. Generally, freely available infrastructure monitoring tools are used for monitoring Ceph.

Several researchers have discussed different architectures 000000 for monitoring cloud for specific purposes. The focus is mainly on efficient ways of collecting and analyzing data. But, none of them address the issue of what needs to be monitored in object storage cloud. Several tools exist that support monitoring of specific features, like, Calamari monitors Ceph cluster, CollectD and Zabbix monitor system performance, Nagios monitors status of resources, Munin monitors storage capacity. Although the tools specify functionality it supports, there is no mention of requirement specification for the monitoring of Ceph.

In this paper, focus is on creation of the requirement specification for infrastructure monitoring of Ceph from the system administrator perspective. It helps during development of tools for the system administrator, in choosing and specifying requirements for the monitoring functionality.

Here, a infrastructure monitoring checklist is presented that facilitates in selecting requirement when developling tools and techniques for monitoring of Ceph. We have classifed the infrastructure monitoring into four components, namely, (1) Background process functionality, (2) Storage infrastructure attributes, (3) Storage usage data, and (4) OS process utilization data. The monitoring checklist is defined for the four identified components of Ceph. The checklist is for both the administrator and the developer, and facilitates during requirement elicitation in identifying the monitoring functionality to be included in a tool. During requirement phase of tool development, functionality needed for monitoring of Ceph can be selected from the checklist.

For understanding requirements of monitoring Ceph and for formulating the checklist, a study of architecture of Ceph, processes in Ceph for storing and managing data, monitoring commands and configurable parameters of Ceph was performed. A study of associated plug-in of some standard open source monitoring software was also performed. This collectively defines understanding storage architecture and available monitoring provisions for Ceph. Using the use-case based approach; the requirements for monitoring have been identified from the system administrator perspective. The components of infrastructure monitoring, based on interaction of system administrator with Ceph infrastructure are defined. The functionality of each identified component of infrastructure monitoring has been identified.

The monitoring checklist allows selecting requirements from the checklist, in contrast to, specifying fresh requirements, when developing new tool for monitoring.

From the checklist, all or part of functionality may be selected. The checklist is for use during requirement elicitation phase, and also for validation and verification of requirements during testing phase of the tool development. The requirement checklist presented here can be easily updated to include any new functionality or feature.

The Ceph infrastructure checklist presented here has been applied to three popular infrastructure monitoring tools of Ceph - Calamari 0, Nagios [18], and CollectD 0 to identify monitoring functionality provided by them. The work is being currently extended to provide generic infrastructure monitoring list for cloud object storage.

In this paper, section 2 gives an overview of Ceph object storage. Section 3 describes Ceph monitoring commands and configurable parameters. Section 4 discusses the components of infrastructure monitoring. Section 5 describes the monitoring checklist in detail. Section 6 illustrates few examples on which the checklist has been applied. Section 7 lists benefits of using the infrastructure monitoring list. Section 8 is a survey of related work. Section 9 states the conclusion.

2   Ceph Object Storage

The Ceph 0 object storage architecture comprises of three main components – Radosgw, Librados and RADOS.

Radosgw is a client interface for object storage that allows end-user to store and retrieve data. It supports Swift and S3 compatible APIs for facilitating end-user to perform various operations, such as, create, read, update and delete data as an object.

Librados is storage cluster protocol that provides native interface to interact with storage cluster and supports different languages, like, C, C++, Java, Ruby and Python. It allows client to interact with Ceph storage cluster, directly, using the defined API.

RADOS 0 is a reliable, autonomous and distributed object store. It consists of two sub-components – Monitor and OSD (Object Storage Device) Daemon. Monitor maintains current status of each component of cluster. Usually, one monitor is sufficient for this purpose, but to ensure high availability, a few monitors are used and a quorum for consensus about current state is established among them. OSD daemon is responsible for reading/writing data to/from storage cluster. OSD daemons communicate with each other to check whether other OSDs are in up and running state and also to replicate data.

3   Ceph Monitoring Commands and Configurable Parameters

In Ceph, several commands 0 exist that provide health of storage cluster and state of individual components, like, their running status and condition. There are also some commands that provide usage statistics of storage cluster.

The component of Ceph storage cluster has some configurable parameters that can be set according to the need of cluster. These parameters can be set at the time of software installation or can be changed dynamically at runtime. Ceph stores its configurable parameters in its configuration file. The configurable parameters 0 are divided into four major sections – global, osd, mon and client.radosgw. Configurable parameters set in 'global' section are applied to all instances of all components. Parameters set in 'osd', 'mon' and 'client.radosgw' is applicable for instances belonging to OSD daemon, monitor and Radosgw, respectively. Configurable parameters define working of different processes running for the component.

4   Components of Infrastructure Monitoring

The classification of Ceph infrastructure into different components provides a framework for categorization of functionality of monitoring, from the administrator perspective. To understand requirements of infrastructure monitoring, a study of the components and processes executing on them has been performed. An in-depth study of different monitoring commands and configurable parameters of Ceph object storage has also been done. The infrastructure monitoring has been divided into four broad components as follows:

- *Background Process* - functionality of processes running in background
- *Storage Infrastructure* - attributes of storage infrastructure
- *Storage Usage* - utilization of storage infrastructure
- *OS Process Utilization* - utilization of OS processes

For Ceph, the authors define infrastructure monitoring as, "Monitoring physical infrastructure, logical infrastructure and associated processes". The components of infrastructure monitoring are briefly described in the following subsections.

4.1   Background Process

During working of the Ceph object storage, several processes run in the background to perform the tasks defined in Ceph. From the different processes present in Ceph software, we identified the processes that are required to be monitored during runtime as shown in Fig. 1. These processes are required to be monitored to check health of system. The background processes that are required to be monitored are - Heartbeat, Authentication, Data scrubbing, Peering, Backfilling, Recovery and Synchronization.

Heartbeat ensures that OSDs responsible for maintaining copies of data are in up and running states. OSDs check heartbeat of other OSDs periodically and report the status to monitor.

Authentication is used to authenticate and authorize the client accessing the storage. Monitor is responsible for authentication process. Client can have different rights for access, like, read-only, write, access to admin commands, etc.

Data scrubbing checks data integrity. The process runs on OSDs and compares objects with their replica stored in another OSD. There are two types of scrubbing– light scrubbing and deep scrubbing. In light scrubbing, metadata of objects is compared to catch bugs. In deep scrubbing, data in objects is compared bit-by-bit. Usually, light and deep scrubbing are performed daily and weekly respectively.

Peering is required for creating an agreement about state of all objects among OSDs that are responsible to keep copy of objects before replication.

Synchronization ensures availability of data in a federated system implemented with multiple regions and multiple zones. A cluster must have a master region and a region must have a master zone. Synchronization process runs on Radosgw. There are two types of synchronization - data synchronization and metadata synchronization. In data synchronization, data of master zone in a region is replicated to a secondary zone of that region. In metadata synchronization, metadata of users and buckets is replicated from master zone in master region to master zone in a secondary region.

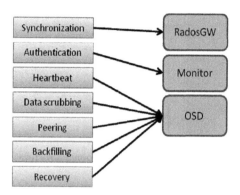

Fig. 1. Background processes for Infrastructure monitoring in Ceph

Backfilling runs when OSD is added or removed to/from Ceph storage cluster. In order to rebalance cluster, objects are moved to or from OSDs. This migration takes place as 'backfilling' at lower priority to maintain operational performance of system.

Recovery runs when OSD crashes and comes back online. In such condition, several objects stored in OSD get outdated and goes in recovery mode, when it restarts. To maintain operational performance of system, recovery process takes place with some limitations.

Several other processes like logging and journaling do not require monitoring during runtime.

4.2   Storage Infrastructure

The storage infrastructure of Ceph is logically divided into clusters which contain few monitors and a large number of OSDs. In a typical scenario, an OSD maps to a storage drive or a RAID group. The storage cluster is divided into pools, which are further divided into Placement Group (PG). Each PG maps to some OSDs.

A pool facilitates segregation of data, logically, based on user's requirement. For providing availability, pool is specified as replicated or erasure-coded. Replicated pool maintains multiple copies of data. In erasure-coded pool, data is divided into number of chunks associated with some code chunks. The data is stored in PGs within a pool. For fault tolerance, each copy of PG is stored in separate OSD. A set of OSDs that are responsible for keeping copy of a PG is called Acting set of that PG and a set of OSDs that are ready to handle incoming client request is Up set of that PG.

Generally, Acting set and Up set of a PG are identical. If they are not found identical, it implies that Ceph is migrating data or an OSD is recovering or there is any problem. One OSD in Acting set is primary OSD. Client communicates with primary OSD to read/write data. Primary OSD interacts with other OSDs to replicate data.

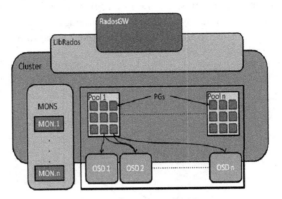

Fig. 2. Ceph Object Storage Structure

Fig. 2 shows object storage infrastructure for Ceph. Monitoring is required at all the different levels of physical and logical infrastructure, for observing existing resources. It helps when there is a need to add or remove resources and to detect failing or failed drives for replacement.

4.3   Storage Usage

The amount of the logical and physical infrastructure that is being consumed is required to be monitored to identify full or near full storage. The logical infrastructure is monitored at different levels - cluster, pool and PG level. This helps in scaling up and scaling down the system resources.

4.4   OS Processes Utilization

The Ceph object storage uses CPU, memory, and network for its own working. Different processes, like, heartbeat, peering etc. run on different components of storage cluster and utilize CPU, memory and network. OS processes utilization is required to be monitored to improve efficiency and performance of system.

5   Infrastructure Monitoring List

For arriving at the monitoring checklist, the Ceph infrastructure was classified under four components - Background process functionality, Storage infrastructure attributes, Storage usage data and OS Process utilization data.

Background process checklist consists of functionality running in background of Ceph. During requirement elicitation, this list helps in deciding process parameters that need to be monitored for Ceph software. The background processes are monitored for three entities – monitor, OSD, and Radosgw.

Heartbeat and peering processes are required to be monitored for finding OSDs in 'Up' and 'Acting' set of a PG, respectively, to check if number of OSDs in Acting set are same as that defined in pool size and OSDs in Up set of a PG are equivalent to OSDs in Acting set of that PG. The users are monitored for authentication to check access permissions according to defined capabilities. Data scrubbing needs to be monitored for type of scrubbing, its frequency, and number of pending scrubs and errors to identify rate of corrupted files found in system so that any abnormality can be identified. Data and metadata synchronization have parameters, such as, errors during sync, wait time, count of shards that are checked or failed, and error listing metadata to determine correct working of system. Backfilling and recovering processes are monitored for their respective status so that impact on system performance can be decreased. Table 1 lists requirement checklist for background process functionality.

Storage Infrastructure checklist defines parameters for logical and physical infrastrcuture that needs to be monitored. During requirement elicitation this list helps in deciding parameters of infrastructure that need to be monitored for Ceph. The storage infrastructure is divided into five levels – cluster, monitor, OSD, pool and PG.

Table 1. Background Process Functionality

Process	Parameters	Monitor	OSD	Radosgw
Heartbeat	OSDs in Up set of a PG	-	✓	-
Authentication	Users with different capabilities	✓	-	-
Data scrubbing	Type – Light/Deep, frequency, scrub pending, no. of errors	-	✓	-
Peering	OSDs in Acting set of PG	-	✓	-
Data synchronization	Sync error, incremental sync error, retry wait time/until next sync, object sync timeout, no. of shards to check/failed, no. of items synced successfully/ processed	-	-	✓
Metadata synchronization	Time to wait for bucket log consistency, Error listing metadata	-	-	✓
Backfilling	Count, frequency, time to wait for retrying	-	✓	-
Recovering	No. of active recovery request/ recovered chunks, time to delay	-	✓	-

At cluster level, parameters are identified as cluster health status, number and list of monitors, OSDs, pools and PGs in cluster. Detail of each OSD, current epoch, and OSD status can be monitored at OSD level. Pool level parameters are number of PGs in pool, pool is replicated or erasure coded etc. At PG level, parameters define state of PG. Table 2 lists requirement checklist for storage infrastructure attributes.

Storage usage checklist consists of parameters that provide data about the usage of storage infrastructure. During requirement elicitation the list helps in deciding parameters for usage of storage infrastructure that need to be monitored. Storage usage data for monitoring is defined at three levels - cluster, pool and PG.

IOPS (Input Output Per Second) measure input/output load to avoid I/O bottleneck in system. Latency provides time taken in data transfer so that in cases of interruption the cause can be found.

Table 2. Storage Infrastructure Attributes

Level	Parameters
Cluster	Cluster ID
	Cluster health status
	Number and list of monitors
	Number and list of OSDs
	Number and list of Pools
	Number and list of PGs
Monitor	Detail – position, name, address, port of monitor
	Current epoch – when map created, last modified
	Status - Running/ not running
	Status of monitor quorum
OSD	Details – id, weight, type, name
	Current epoch – when map created, last modified
	Status - In/out, up/down
Pool	Details - Name, Pool ID
	Number and list of PGs
	Replicated/erasure coded
	Cache tiering status
Placement Group	Detail – PG ID, PG version, timestamp
	PG state (Creating, Peering, Active, Clean, Degraded, Recovering, Backfilling, Remapped, Stale, Unclean, Inactive)

Total storage capacity and free space availble are inspected so that alerts can be raised before system reaches near-full capacity. Amount of data stored and number of objects stored provide estimate of storage capacity. IOPS and latency are monitored at cluster and pool level. Notional value monitored at pool level determines utilized space excluding space used by its replicas. Table 3 lists storage infrastructure usage parameters at different levels.

OS processes checklist contains parameters to determine utilization of operating system processes. During requirement elicitation this list helps in deciding parameters for utilization of OS processes that need to be monitored.

CPU, memory and network utilization data is monitored to determine consumption of OS resources during execution. It helps to identify processes and components that are under utilizing or highly utilizing OS resources so that extra resources can be provisioned based on demand. Table 4 lists parameters for OS process utilization.

Table 3. Storage Usage Data

Level/Parameters	Cluster	Pool	PG
IOPS – read, write	✓	✓	-
Latency – max., avg., min.	✓	✓	-
Overall storage capacity	✓	-	✓
Amount of data stored	Total & Notional	Notional	Total
Number of objects stored	Total	Notional	-
Amount of free space available/ used	Total	Notional	Total

Table 4. OS Process Utilization data

Parameters	Reason
CPU Utilization	Find CPU consumption by processes and system to identify processes and components which have high CPU load and which are under utilized
Memory utilization	Track available memory to determine processes and components that are consuming more memory so that memory can be upgraded
Network utilization	Track network traffic and identify network interfaces that have excessive use

6   Case Study

The infrastructure monitoring functionality lists have been applied for case study to three monitoring software - Calamari 0, Nagios 0, and CollectD 0.

Calamari is management and monitoring service specifically for Ceph. It exposes high level REST APIs and a user interface built on these APIs for monitoring Ceph infrastructure. *Nagios* is open source infrastructure monitoring software that enables organizations to identify and resolve IT infrastructure problems before they have drastic effect on system. Nagios provides some built in plug-ins for monitoring health of cluster and individual components of Ceph object storage, like, check_ceph_health and check_ceph_mon. *CollectD* is daemon that collects system information and helps system administrators to maintain an overview of resources to avoid bottlenecks.

Table 5 displays comparative checklist of the three monitoring software for storage infrastructure, usage and OS process utilization of infrastructure monitoring. In the table, '√' denotes parameter is supported by tool; 'x' not supported. 1st, 2nd and 3rd column for each is for storage infrastructure, usage and OS process, respectively.

Fig. 3 displays percentage of parameters of each monitoring checklist functionality supported by tools in our case study. Some of our key observations are as follows-

- *Calamari* monitors 10% of background processes; 95.65 % of storage infrastructure; 87.5% storage usage; and 33.33% OS processes.
- *Nagios* monitors mainly the status of storage infrastructure (69.56%). It does not monitor background processes, storage usage and OS processes.

- *CollectD* monitors 100% storage usage; 100% OS processes utilization; 38.46% of storage infrastructure. It does not monitor background processes.

Some interesting observations emerging from the case study are as follows-

- Background processes is only monitored 10% by Calamari
- Storage infrastructure is monitored by all three - Calamari, Nagios, CollectD
- Storage usage is monitored by Calamari and CollectD
- OS processes is monitored by Calamari and CollectD

Table 5. Storage infrastructure, Storage usage, and OS processes case study

Level	Parameters–Storage Infrastructure	Parameters–Storage Usage	Parameters–OS Processes	Calamari			Nagios			CollectD	
Cluster	ID	IOPS – read, write	CPU Util.	✓	✓	✓	✓	X	X	X	✓
	Health status	Latency-max/avg/min	Memory Util.	✓	X	X	✓	X	X	X	✓
	No. & list of monitors	Notional data stored	Network Util.	✓	✓	X	✓	X	X	✓	✓
	No. & list of OSD	No. of objects stored	-	✓	✓	-	✓	X	-	✓	✓
	No. & list of Pools	Total data stored	-	✓	✓	-	✓	X	-	✓	✓
	No. &List of PGs	Free space available	-	✓	✓	-	✓	X	-	✓	✓
	-	Used raw storage	-	-	✓	-	-	X	-	-	✓
	-	% of raw storage used	-	-	✓	-	-	X	-	-	✓
	-	Overall storage capacity	-	-	✓	-	-	✓	-	-	✓
Monitor	Detail	-	-	✓	-	-	✓	-	-	X	-
	Current epoch	-	-	✓	-	-	✓	-	-	✓	-
	Status	-	-	✓	-	-	✓	-	-	✓	-
	Monitor quorum status	-	-	✓	-	-	✓	-	-	✓	-
OSD	Detail	-	-	✓	-	-	✓	-	-	X	-
	Current epoch	-	-	✓	-	-	✓	-	-	X	-
	Status- in/out, up/down	-	-	✓	-	-	✓	-	-	✓	-
Pool	Name, ID	IOPS – read, write	CPU Util.	✓	✓	✓	X	X	X	X	✓
	No. & list of PGs	Latency – max/avg/min	Memory Util.	✓	X	X	✓	X	X	✓	✓
	Replicate/Erasure	Notional data stored	Network Util.	✓	✓	X	X	X	X	X	✓
	Cache tiering status	Notional objects stored	-	✓	✓	-	X	X	-	X	✓
PG	Detail	Amount of data used	-	✓	✓	-	X	X	-	X	✓
	-	Free storage capacity	-	-	✓	-	-	X	-	-	✓
	PG state	Total storage capacity	-	✓	✓	-	✓	X	-	✓	✓

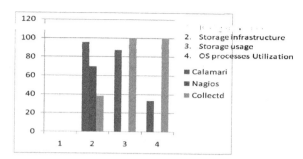

Fig. 3. Graph showing percentage of checklist used by monitoring software

It can be seen that tools offer different coverage for components being monitored and there is no consistency for same. Also background processes are hardly monitored because Ceph does not have commands to provide status of running processes.

7   Benefits of Checklist

The requirement checklist presented here has been derived after performing a detailed study of Ceph storage architecture, processes running in it and exhaustive study of basic monitoring commands and configurable parameters over Ceph.

Usually, infrastructure monitoring software is developed for a specific purpose without planning or preparation of list of possible functionality that can be included. The checklist helps system administrator to choose functionality required to monitor infrastructure of Ceph with minimum effort. The developers use checklist to check functionality required for infrastructure monitoring during development of tool. The checklist allows developer and administrator to include more functionality in monitoring software rather than just basic functionality.

8   Related Work

Cloud monitoring has gathered focus in research. Several researchers discuss about research motivation, approaches used for monitoring cloud and different methodologies applied to monitor a cloud for different purposes. Alhamazani et al. 0 discusses methodology to monitor cloud for facilitating automated QoS management; Adinarayan 0 discuss challenges in monitoring private cloud and describe capabilities of IBM SmartCloud monitoring to tackle these challenges.

Several frameworks are proposed by researchers for different purposes on monitoring the cloud infrastructure 000. Gogouvitis et al. 0 propose an architectural design and implementation of monitoring solution in context of VISION cloud project. Mdhaffar et al. 0 propose dynamic Complex Event Processing architecture for cloud monitoring and analysis; Uriate and Westphall 0 propose monitoring architecture 'Panoptes' for autonomic clouds; Chaves, et al. 0 discuss design and implementation of private cloud monitoring system (PCMONS).

The frameworks and architectures highlight ways of collecting data from system required for monitoring and how to monitor. However, there is no mention of parameters required to be monitored in cloud. Usually, freely available monitoring software, like, Zenoss, Nagios are adapted for incorporating monitoring functionality for Ceph object storage. Our extensive search for work carried out for finding list of parameters required for monitoring Ceph object storage yielded no result.

9   Conclusion and Future Work

In this paper, we have presented infrastructure monitoring list for Ceph object storage. The list eases the task of administrator and developers by providing them a list from where the functionality can be selected. Designers and developers of new monitoring software for Ceph can also use the list as a reference for identifying possible functionality that can be incorporated in monitoring software. The list is extendible and can be updated to add new functionality and features.

Since our functionality checklist is specific for Ceph object storage, other cloud object storage may have some more functionality which does not lie in scope of this paper. In future, the authors aim to develop a generic functionality checklist for cloud object storage system. We also propose to prioritize the proposed list.

References

1. Adinarayan, G.: Monitoring and Capacity Planning of Private Clouds: The Challenges and the Solutions. In: IEEE Int. Conf. on Cloud Computing in Emerging Markets (CCEM), India, pp. 1–3 (2012)
2. Alhamazani, K., et al.: Cloud monitoring for optimizing the QoS of hosted applications. In: IEEE 4th Int. Conf. on Cloud Computing Technology and Science (CloudCom), Taipei, pp. 765–770 (2012)
3. Barbosa de Carvahlo, M., et al.: A cloud monitoring framework for self-configured monitoring slices based on multiple tools. In: 9th Int. Conf. on Network and Service Management (CNSM), Zurich, pp. 180–184 (2013)
4. Chaves, S., et al.: Towards an architecture for monitoring private clouds. IEEE Communications Magazine 49, 130–137 (2011)
5. Gogouvitis, S., et al.: A Monitoring Mechanism for Storage Clouds. In: 2nd Int. Conf. on Cloud and Green Computing, Xiangtan, pp. 153–159 (2012)
6. Grobauer, B., Walloschek, T., Stocker, E.: Understanding cloud-computing vulnerabilities. IEEE Security and Privacy 9, 50–57 (2010)
7. Mdhaffar, A., et al.: A Dynamic Complex Event Processing Architecture for Cloud Monitoring and Analysis. In: IEEE 5th Int. Conf. on Cloud Computing Technology and Science (CloudCom), Bristol, vol. 2, pp. 270–275 (2013)
8. Moses, J., Iyer, R., Illikkal, R., Srinivasan, S., Aisopos, K.: Shared Resource Monitoring and Throughput Optimization in Cloud-Computing Datacenters. In: IEEE Int. Parallel & Distributed Processing Symposium (IPDPS), Anchorage AK, pp. 1024–1033 (2011)
9. Rehman, Z., et al.: A Framework for User Feedback based Cloud Service Monitoring. In: 6th Int. Conf. on Complex, Intelligent and Software Intensive Systems (CISIS), Palermo, pp. 257–262 (2012)

10. Shao, J., Wei, H., Wang, Q., Mei, H.: A Runtime Model Based Monitoring Approach for Cloud. In: IEEE 3rd Int. Conf. on Cloud Computing (CLOUD), Miami, FL, pp. 313–320 (2010)
11. Uriarte, R., Westphall, C.: Panoptes A monitoring architecture and framework for supporting autonomic Clouds. In: IEEE Network Operations and Management Symposium (NOMS), Krakow, pp. 5–9 (2014)
12. Weil, S., et al.: RADOS A Scalable, Reliable Storage Service for Petabyte-scale Storage Clusters. In: 2nd Int. Workshop on Petascale Data Storage, pp. 35–44. ACM, New York (2007)
13. Yongdnog, H., et al.: A Scalable And Integrated Cloud Monitoring Framework Based On Distributed Storage. In: 10th Web Information System and Application Conference, Yangzhou, pp. 318–323 (2013)
14. https://github.com/ceph/calamari
15. http://ceph.com/ceph-storage/object-storage/
16. https://collectd.org/
17. http://ceph.com/docs/v0.78/rados/operations/monitoring/
18. http://www.nagios.org/

Towards a Formalization of Real-Time Patterns-Based Designs

Kamel Boukhelfa[⊠] and Faiza Belala

Department of Software Technologies and Information Systems, Faculty of New Information Technologies and Communication, University of Constantine 2, Ali Mendjeli, Algeria {kamel.boukhelfa,faiza.belala}@univ-constantine2.dz
http://www.univ-constantine2.dz

Abstract. Informal description (UML and text) of design patterns is adopted to facilitate their understanding by software developers. However, these descriptions lead to ambiguities, mainly when we consider Real time Design Patterns that deal with critical problems encountered in the design of real-time systems. Hence, there is a need for formal specification of the DPs and RTDPs to insure their successful application. In this paper, we propose a formalization approach of the system design based on real-time patterns (RTDPs). The processes of instantiation and composition of design patterns, permit us to generate design models (structural and dynamic) of complex systems. The resulting designs are represented in UML-MARTE profile to express the temporal properties and constraints. The algebraic specifications (in Maude language) become more natural and more efficient.

1 Introduction

A design pattern expresses solution of a known and recurrent problem in a particular context [5]. Design patterns are applied in object programming software to improve the quality of the resulting system. The reuse concept is also important in the development of real-time and embedded systems. Thus, design patterns can be used to capture the experience and allow the reuse of the "good" solutions to resolve the problems encountered during the design process of such systems [3]. Intuitively, the term "real-time" refers to design patterns those dealing with the temporal aspects of systems, whereas this is not always the case. Indeed, real-time design patterns deal with the general problems encountered in the design of real-time systems (that may be or not related to the time) such as synchronization or memory allocation. The real-time design patterns vary according to their areas of application and according to the design approaches. Generally, design patterns and also real-time design patterns were described, until now, by using a combination of textual descriptions, object oriented graphical notations such as UML diagrams and sample fragments of code [5], [3]. This informal description of design patterns is adopted to facilitate their understanding by software developers. However, formal specifications provide a precise and rigorous description for better understanding patterns and their instantiation and composition. This

© IFIP International Federation for Information Processing 2015
A. Amine et al. (Eds.): CIIA 2015, IFIP AICT 456, pp. 624–635, 2015.
DOI: 10.1007/978-3-319-19578-0_51

description is then ready for several analysis and verifications upon one or more functional or non-functional properties.

Several research work around design patterns deal with issues related to their representation and specification. We distinguish two points of view adopted for this purpose. The first one concerns all works that adopt the meta-modeling approaches and consequently the definition of patterns modeling languages based on UML. These works aim in general to provide solutions for integrating design patterns in CASE tools. The second kind of research work is characterized by the use of the formal methods to specify the design patterns and then provide suitable models to the analysis and verification stages. However, few studies are particularly interested in RTDPs. In this work, we start from the real-time design patterns as the basic models. Through the instantiation and the composition processes, we conceive design models and represent them in UML-MARTE profile [10]. We use Rewriting Logic [9] as a formal foundation for the specification of the Pattern-Based models and thus, we encode in Maude language [2] the formal specification of both parts of those models, namely the structural and dynamic part.

The rest of this paper is organized as follows: After recalling the used basic concepts of RT Design Patterns, MARTE profile and rewriting logic via its practical language Maude in section 2, we outline in section 3, how it is possible to give a formal base to real-time systems designs thanks to a judicious coupling of UML-MARTE profile and rewriting theories. Then, in section 4, we describe the formalization approach with Maude's object-oriented modules, through a realistic example. Finally, we conclude the paper with constructive remarks and future work.

2 Basic Concepts

2.1 Real-Time Design Patterns

In object oriented programming, design patterns are considered as a mean to encapsulate the knowledge of experienced software designers and represented it in an understandable form in order to permit its reuse. For each design pattern, are defined the roles of classes, relationships between classes and objects, and how this pattern can be applied to resolve a given problem in a specific context. The structure describing a design pattern mainly includes the name, problem, solution and consequence [3]. RT design patterns are a kind of patterns that have evolved specifically for real-time systems, and they provide various approaches to addressing the fundamental real-time scheduling, communications, and synchronization problems [3]. As a GOF design patterns, RTDPs are represented in UML and the most temporal constraints (especially in the interactions) are expressed in the natural language.

2.2   The UML Profile for MARTE

The UML profile for MARTE (Modeling and Analysis of Real-Time and Embedded systems) is an OMG standard. It provides support for specification, design and verification/validation stages. This new profile is intended to replace the existing UML Profile for Schedulability, Performance and Time [10]. Model-based design of RTE systems with MARTE proceeds mostly in a declarative way. The users can annotate their models with real-time or embedded concerns using the extensions defined within the HLAM (High-Level Application Modeling) sub-profile (see the next section). The HLAM package provides possibilities of modeling on one hand quantitative features such as deadline, period and, in the other hand, qualitative features that are related to behavior, communication and concurrency. MARTE provide the NFP package (Non-functional Properties Modeling) in order to specify the NFP of properties in a detailed way [10].

2.3   Rewriting Logic and Maude

Rewriting logic (RL) is known as being the logic of concurrent change, taking into account the state and the concurrent systems calculus. It is shown as a unifying semantic framework of several concurrent systems and models [9]. In RL, a dynamic system is represented by a rewriting theory $\mathcal{R} = (\Sigma, E, R, L)$, describing the complex structure of its states and the various possible transitions between them. The theoretical concepts of the rewriting logic are implemented through the Maude language [9,2] that integrates object oriented programming, used in our formalization to encode the DPs and their meta-models specifications. Maude logical basis gives a clear definition of the object oriented semantics and makes it a good choice for the formal specification of object oriented systems.

3   Formalization Approach Principle

First, we use a given design pattern to generate an UML design (structural and dynamic parts). The resulting design will be enriched by the MARTE notations, namely the concepts defined in HLAM sub-profile, such as RtUnit, PpUnit and Rtfeature, and those defined in the NFP sub-profile, such as NFP_DateTime, NFP_Duration and NFP_Frequency. The second step allows to transcript UML-Marte description to Maude specification. Here, we use Full-Maude, an extension of Maude, that allows us to manipulate the object-oriented concepts, especially objects, classes and attributes. We show in the following sub-sections, how we encode, any system design, described with UML-MARTE and RT Design Patterns coupling, in Maude.

3.1   Static Part

For the structural part, we can note the existence of a correspondence between some concepts of Maude language and UML-MARTE concepts. Unfortunately, this correspondence is not fully established, there are various concepts in UML-MARTE with no direct equivalent in Maude. The structural part of a design pattern is represented as an UML classes diagram and serves as a model to generate, by means of the instantiation mechanism any structural design based on this pattern. The table 1 contains the MARTE concepts and their correspondences in Maude. For some MARTE concepts without direct correspondence, we also propose their definitions in Maude. For the stereotyping, we define a new class for each stereotype and so, the stereotyped class (in MARTE) is represented by a subclass in Maude. While, for the specification of the methods definition within classes, we define a new **sort** called **Method** and we add the declaration of a Maude operation that permits to link each method to its appropriate class (**op Methods : class -> SetMethod**). In addition, we use the predefined concepts in several modules of Maude such as the **SET** module, for defining empty and non-empty set (**Set, NeSet**), and others modules such as **BOOL**, **FLOAT**, **NAT** and **STRING** to express respectively the types Boolean, Float, Natural and string of characters.

Table 1. Correspondence between MARTE and Maude concepts

MARTE Concept	Maude Concept
Class/objet	Class/Oid
Attribute	Attribute
Directed Association	Operation
Non-Directed Association	Two operation (one for each direction)
Association 1..1/1..*/1..n	operation $/op -> $ Set $/$ op $-> $ NeSet (not empty Set)
Composition	Operation
inheritance	Subclass

3.2 Dynamic Part

The dynamic part of a design pattern represents the interaction between different objects instantiated from classes that form a pattern-based design. This part is often represented by a sequence diagram with all the interactions between objects, shown as signals. Firstly, we declare a new sort called **Signal** that expresses the interaction between two objects. Secondly, we define an operation **Instance** that represents the objet creation signal. Thus, we can specify all objects related to a given activity execution (represented as sequence diagram). The objects can be declared at the start of this activity (of **Oid** type) or created during the execution.

3.3 Real-Time Features

MARTE provides Real-time unit concept (*RtUnit*) defined in HLAM package. An *RtUnit* may be seen as an autonomous execution resource, able to handle different messages at the same time. It can manage concurrency and real-time constraints attached to incoming messages [10]. Any real-time unit can invoke services of other real-time units, send signals or data without worrying about concurrency issues. Another important point to consider when modelling concurrency system is to be able to represent shared information. For that purpose, MARTE introduce the concept of protected passive unit (*PpUnit*). PpUnit specify the concurrency policy units either globally for all of their provided services (`concPolicy` attribute), or locally through the `concPolicy` attribute of an `RtService`. We will stereotype the classes as `RtUnit` or `PpUnit` regarding their role in the design model. However, operations can be stereotyped as `RtService` for example. We can add the `rtf` stereotype at the methods dealing with real-time features such as deadline and reference time. The temporal constraints are expressed in OCL (Object Constrained Language) for instance, a maximum time to perform an activity. For the occurrence kind of a signal (`occkind`), we define a Maude operation called `periodic` that permits to identify the nature of this signal appearance (periodically or not). In the case of a periodic signal the `periodVal` operation is defined to get the value of the period. For the simplicity, we consider the default unit of time (ms). The others elements characterizing a signal are represented in Maude language as operations upon this signal. The temporal constraints represent the conditions on the actions that need to be satisfied, they are expressed in the OCL language (Object Constraints Language). In addition, we define two sorts, `Time` and `Value` to specify the temporal variables (eg. triggering instants of signals) and their values. Consequently, it is necessary to have an operation to get the value of an instant t (`Rvalue`) and a conditional equation to check whether the imposed constraints is verified or not (`Satisfy`).

4   Running Example: A "Cruise Control System"

This system controls and regulates the speed of a car according to the encountered situations (obstacle, car ahead too closely, etc.). The controller requires the services of three types of sensors, a Speed Sensor, a Laser device to calculate the distance between the car and obstacles and a radar to detect possible obstacles. For simplicity, only the Speed Sensor is considered.

4.1   System Modelling in MARTE

For modelling the system, we use `Observer` and `Sensor` patterns and we compose their instances to generate the structural design of the system. The composition is achieved in a simple way, namely through the overlapping of common elements in the two instances.

The problem addressed by the `Observer` Pattern is how to notify some number of clients in a timely fashion of a data value according to some abstract policy, such as "when it changes," "every so often," "at most every so often," and "at least every so often" [3]. The basic solution offered by the `Observer` pattern is to have the clients "subscribe" to the server to be notified about the value in question according the defined policy.

A Speed Sensor is defined as a device that measures or detects a physical phenomenon (temperature, pressure, speed, etc.) and transmits the measure values at real-time to the command ends. The RT-Design pattern `Sensor` [1] can be specialized as possible types of sensors : `Active Sensor`, `Passive Sensor`, `Fixed Sensor` and `Mobile Sensor`. We use `Active Sensor` pattern which is able to send signals `Setvalue` to one or more objects for modifying the measured value. The class `measure` stores the data taken by the Sensor, while the attributes (`timestamp`, `validity duration`) are used to represent the characteristics of real-time data supported. The class `Observed element` is used for the physical supervised device description (a wheel for example).

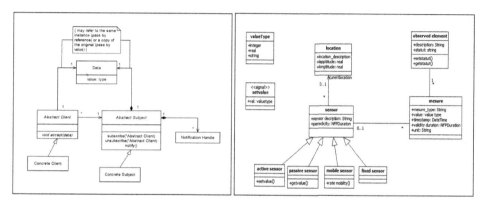

Fig. 1. "Observer" and "Sensor" Real-Time Design patterns Structures

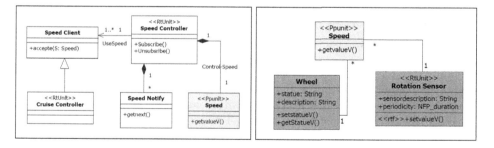

Fig. 2. Instances of the "Observer" and "Sensor"

For the structural design modelling, we use two instances of the pattern `Observer` to model the structure of the sub-systems (*Speed Controller* and *Distance Controller*). For each sub-system, we need to instantiate `Observer` and `Sensor` patterns and so, compose these instances.

We use an instance of `Observer` pattern to model the *Speed Controller* sub-system. The resulting model is represented in MARTE and enriched with temporal and NFP proprieties. In the same way, we proceed for modelling *Distance Controller* sub-system (Fig. 2). Similarly, we use two instances of the `Sensor` RT-Design pattern (Fig. 2) to model the capturing of the speed rotation of a car wheel, the detection of the possible obstacles in front of a car and the distance measure which separate them from the car (Laser device). The composition of the instances of `Observer` and `Sensor` patterns respectively regarding the common elements (the `Speed` class in first case, and `Distance` class in the second one) produces the design model of the complete system. In the dynamic

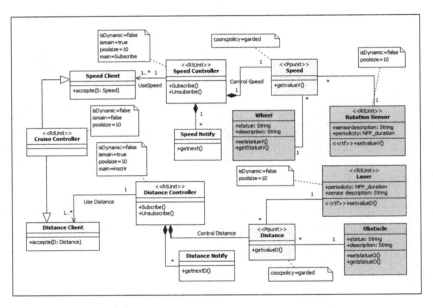

Fig. 3. Structural part of the *"Cruise control system"* in MARTE profile

design modelling, we describe the system by using a sequence diagram. This diagram shows a scenario of data acquisition and how the system will react to synchronous or asynchronous events. The interactions that have temporal properties are stereotyped as `RtFeature`. This allows us to model the temporal behavior of these interactions (occurrence mode, deadline, etc.). MARTE profile also allows us to set time restrictions upon interactions with "time constraint" (eg. `t2-t1<(5ms)`). The figure 4 shows the sequence diagram for the *Cruise Control System* to perform the task of capturing the car speed and the distance in the case of a nearly car. The cruise control object needs two services (internal speed and distance), so it must subscribe into both lists of notification.

At the time t1[i] for example (each action i starts at t1[i] to get a speed value), a message is sent by the speed controller object. This message represents a call to `getvalue` method. The message is stereotyped by `RtFeature` to represent temporal properties such as the period of the occurrence of this message (20 ms). It will be followed by other interactions for notifying the clients. These interactions must be completed at time t2 with a maximum delay of 5 ms.

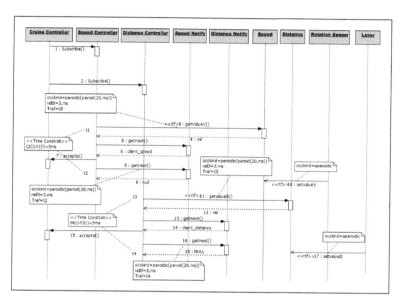

Fig. 4. Dynamic part of the *"Cruise control system"*: Capturing a speed and distance Activity

4.2   Maude Formalization

The major advantage of the rewriting logic and its language Maude is its ability to specify in the same formalism both, the structural and the dynamic aspects of a given system. We start the specification of the structural design part by declaring the several sorts: `Sorts   NFP_duration Method`. Then, we define all classes contained the design, as Real-time units or passive protected units regarding their roles in the design. Stereotyping, inheritance are also defined.

```
class Speed .
class Rotation_Sensor | sensor_description : String ,
                        periodicity : NFP_duration .
class Wheel | statue : String , description : String .
class Speed_Controller . class Speed_Notify .
class Speed_Client . class Cruise_Controller .
class Distance_Client . class Distance .
class Distance_Controller . class Distance_Notify .
class Laser | sensor_description : String , periodicity : NFP_duration  .
class Obstacle | statue : String , description : String .
```

RtUnit and PpUnit stereotypes are considered as inheritance in Maude :

```
class RtUnit | isDymamic : Bool , ismain : Bool ,
                poolsize : Float , main : String .
Subclass Rotation_Sensor Speed_Controller
Distance_Controller Laser < RtUnit .
class PpUnit | concpolicy : String . subclass Speed Distance < PpUnit .
```

The different methods in classes are specified as a Maude operations. Furthermore, we define a `Methods` operation allowing, for each method, to know the class to which it belongs.

```
ops Methods getValue Speed_Subscribe .
Speed_Unsubscribe Distance_Subscribe .
Distance_Unsubscribe getnext  : -> Set{Method} .
```

The specification of the different associations between classes (undirected association is considered as a two associations, one in each direction) is achieved in the following Maude code. Each association is specified as a Maude operation taking as parameter the first class and as result the second one. The multiplicity is also specified by `Set` and `NeSet`sorts for denoting respectively $(1..*)$ and $(0..*)$ multiplicities.

```
--- Associations definition as Maude operation
op Speed_Sensor  : Speed ->    Rotation_Sensor .
op Speed_Measure : Rotation_Sensor  -> Speed .
op Speed_C       : Speed_Controller -> Speed .
op Notified      : Speed_Controller -> Set{Speed_Notify} .
op Use_Speed     : Speed_Controller -> NeSet{Speed_Client} .
--- ...
eq  Methods(Speed) = getValue .
eq  Methods(Speed_Controller) =  Subscribe Unsubscibe .
eq  Methods(NotifieV) = getnext .
```

A dynamic design represented as a sequence diagram and it shows the execution scenario of an activity. In our example, this diagram models the speed/distance capturing activity. The specification of this model is divided in two parts. In the first one, we define all sorts, operations and equations requested for each activity. However, the second is specific for each activity (capturing activity). The important element in this model is the signal. Thus, we define a sort `Signal` and all temporal features are defined as Maude operations upon it.

```
--- General Specification (classes instantiation and temporal features)
sorts Time Signal .
vars  O : Oid  C : class .
op Instance : class -> Oid .
op operation : Signal -> Method .
ops Trigger Targetc : Signal -> Oid .
ceq Target(S : Signal) = < O : C | > if operation(S) in Methods(C) .
op periodic : Signal -> Bool .
op periodVal : Signal -> Float .
ceq periodVal(S : Signal) = v : Float if periodic(S) .
op Time_ref : Signal -> Value .
```

```
op relDl : Signal -> Float .
op Rvalue : Time -> Float .
--- A capturing (Speed and Distance) activity.
Vars  Cruise_C Speed_C Distance_C Notify_Sp Notify_D
      Sp Dis  Rot_Sens Las : Oid .
eq Instance(Cruise_Controller) = < Cruise_C | isDymamic :
   false   ismain : false poolsize : 10 > .
eq Instance(Speed_Client) = < Speed_C | isDymamic : false
   ismain : true  poolsize : 10 main : Speed_Subscribe > .
eq Instance(Distance_Client) =  < Speed_C | isDymamic : false
   ismain : true poolsize : 10  main : Distance_Subscribe >.
eq Instance(Speed_Notify) :   Notify_Sp .
eq Instance(Distance_Notify) : Notify_D  .
eq Instance(Speed) =  < Sp | concpolicy : garded > .
eq Instance(Distance) =  < Dis | concpolicy : garded > .
eq Instance(Rotation_Sensor) = < Rot_Sens |
             isDymamic : false poolsize : 10 > .
eq Instance(Laser) = < Las | isDymamic   false poolsize : 10 > .
```

An algebraic semantic is associated to the Signal term GETVALUE_S through the following equations.

```
var t1 : Time   .
op GETVALUE_S : -> Signal .
eq operation (GETVALUE_S)   = getValue .
eq Trigger (GETVALUE_S)     = Speed_C .
eq Target (GETVALUE_S)      = Sp .
eq Time_ref (GETVALUE_S)    = t1 .
eq periodic (GETVALUE_S)    = TRUE .
eq periodVal(GETVALUE_S)    = 20 .
eq relDl (GETVALUE_S)       = 3.3 .
```

Some rewriting rules are added to Maude specification in order to manage temporal constraints. The following Maude declarations express the essential part.

```
msg Speed_Subscrib_Call : Oid Oid -> Msg [ctor] .
msg Distance_Subscrib_Call : Oid Oid -> Msg [ctor] .
vars C S Not_C : Oid .
op Speed_Subscrib_Signal : -> Signal .
eq operation(Speed_Subscrib_Signal) = Speed_Subscibe .
eq Trigger (Speed_Subscrib_Signal)  = Cruise_C .
eq Target (Speed_Subscrib_Signal)   = Speed_C .
Speed_Subscrib_Call (Cruise_C , Speed_C) .
rl[Speed_Sub] < C : Cuise_Controller > < S : Speed_Controller >
 Speed_Subscrib_Call => < C : Cuise_Controller >
 < S : Speed_Controller > < N : Speed_Notify > .
--- To ensure that a time constraint is verified
msg satisfy : Signal Signal Float -> Bool .
crl [ satisfy ] satisfy ( S1 : Signal , S2 : Signal , T : Flaot)
    if Rvalue( (Time_ref(S2) + reldl(S2)) - Time_ref(S1)) < T .
Satisfy(GETVALUE_S , GETNET_S , 5) .
```

5   Discussion and Conclusion

In the literature, we can find several work on meta-modelling approaches to define languages for design patterns. These works are in general based on UML and they aim to define a common model to all patterns in order to integrate them in CASE tools for assisting the designers (code generation or detection of patterns within a design for example).

Here, we can cite DPML (Design Pattern Modeling Language)[8] which defines a meta-model and a notation for specifying design pattern solutions and solution instances within object models. In the same context, Dae-Kyoo Kim et al. [7] present an UML-based pattern specification language called the role-based meta-modeling language (RBML), allowing to support the development of precise pattern specifications that can be used for the development of pattern tools.

In the context of the formal specification, we can cite two significant works namely, the BPSL (Balanced Pattern Specification Language) [11] and LePUS (LanguagE for Patterns Uniform Specification) [6], they aim to formalize the structural and behavior aspects of design patterns. BPSL uses a subset of first-order logic (FOL) to formalize structural aspect of patterns, while the behavioral aspect is formalized in TLA (Temporal Logic of Actions). LePUS is a fragment of the monadic high-level order logic using a limited vocabulary of entities and relations to describe a design pattern by HOL formulae accompanied by a graphic representation in order to facilitate its understanding.

In a previous work [4], we have proposed a rewriting logic based meta-model approach to formalize design pattern solutions and their instantiations. Our proposed meta-model includes all the common elements of design patterns, so any design pattern can be expressed in terms of this meta-model.

In this work, we are interest to formalize designs based on the real-time design patterns. Thus, we use first patterns instantiation and composition to generate a given design and repent it in UML-MARTE profile. This will permit us to consider the temporal properties and constraints of this RT pattern-based design. In the second time, we embbed in Maude language the representation result of the above design.

Our approach differs in two ways from the above cited works. Firstly, we deal with the real-time design patterns (especially those defined in [3]) and we consider also the temporal properties and constraints. Secondly, we use a common formalism (namely the RL logic) to specify both the structural and behavior aspects of design patterns. The encoding of models in Maude provides executable programs that can be subject to several analysis and verification.

This work is mainly a feasibility study for the proposed approach. We intend to extend the present work in two ways. The first one is to define a profile or a meta-model for real-time patterns to generate all possible patterns. Thus, this will serve to define a pattern instantiation mechanism to generate all possible solutions in conformity with their patterns. The second one is to formalize the defined meta-model and the instantiation mechanism, while ensuring formally the pattern-instance conformity. For this purpose, we plan to explore the RT-Maude (an extension of Maude for specifying and analyzing the real-time and the hybrid systems) to encode the specification that will be more suitable to perform analysis and verification of the system proprieties.

References

1. Rekhis, S., Bouassida, N., Duvallet, C., Bouaziz, R., Sadeg, B.: A process to derive domain-specific patterns: Application to the real time domain. In: Catania, B., Ivanović, M., Thalheim, B. (eds.) ADBIS 2010. LNCS, vol. 6295, pp. 475–489. Springer, Heidelberg (2010)
2. Clavel, M., Durán, F., Eker, S., Lincoln, P., Martí-Oliet, N., Meseguer, J., Talcott, C. (eds.): All About Maude - A High-Performance Logical Framework. LNCS, vol. 4350. Springer, Heidelberg (2007)
3. Douglass, B.P.: Real-time design patterns: robust scalable architecture for real-time systems. The Addison-Wesley object technology series. Addison-Wesley, Boston (2003)
4. Douibi, H., Boukhelfa, K., Belala, F.: A rewriting logic-based meta-model for design patterns formalization. In: PATTERNS 2011: The Third International Conferences on Pervasive Patterns and Applications, pp. 84–89 (2011)
5. Gamma, E., Helm, R., Johnson, R., Vlissides, J.: Design Patterns: Elements of Reusable Object-oriented Software. Addison-Wesley Longman Publishing Co., Inc., Boston (1995)
6. Gasparis, E.: Lepus: A formal language for modeling design patterns. In: Taibi, T. (ed.) Design Pattern Formalization Techniques, pp. 357–372. IGI Global (2007)
7. Kim, D.-k., France, R., Ghosh, S., Song, E.: A uml-based metamodeling language to specify design patterns. In: Patterns, Proc. Workshop Software Model Eng (WiSME) with Unified Modeling Language Conf. (2003)
8. Mapelsden, D., Hosking, J., Grundy, J.: Design pattern modelling and instantiation using dpml. In: CRPIT 2002: Proceedings of the Fortieth International Conference on Tools Pacific, pp. 3–11. Australian Computer Society, Inc., Darlinghurst (2002)
9. Meseguer, J.: Rewriting logic as a semantic framework for concurrency: a progress report. In: Sassone, V., Montanari, U. (eds.) CONCUR 1996. LNCS, vol. 1119, pp. 331–372. Springer, Heidelberg (1996)
10. Omgmarte.org. The uml profile for marte: Modeling and analysis of real-time and embedded systems (2015), http://www.omgwiki.org/marte, http://www.omgwiki.org (Last viewed January 2015)
11. Taibi, T., Ngo, D.C.L.: Formal specification of design patterns - a balanced approach. Journal of Object Technology 2(4), 127–140 (2003)

Author Index

Printed in the United States
By Bookmasters